Your All-in-One Resource

On the CD that accompanies this book, you'll find additional resources to extend your learning.

The reference library includes the following fully searchable titles:

- *Microsoft Computer Dictionary*, 5th ed.
- *First Look 2007 Microsoft Office System* by Katherine Murray
- Windows Vista Product Guide

Also provided are a sample chapter and poster from *Look Both Ways: Help Protect Your Family on the Internet* by Linda Criddle.

The CD interface has a new look. You can use the tabs for an assortment of tasks:

- Check for book updates (if you have Internet access)
- Install the book's sample files
- Find links to helpful tools and resources
- Go online for product support or CD support
- Send us feedback

The following screen shot gives you a glimpse of the new interface.

Microsoft

2007 Microsoft® Office System Inside Out

Jim Boyce
Jeff Conrad
Mark Dodge
Stephanie Krieger
Mary Millhollon
Katherine Murray
S. E. Slack
Beth Sheresh
Doug Sheresh
Craig Stinson
John Viescas

John Pierce,
Contributing Editor

PUBLISHED BY
Microsoft Press
A Division of Microsoft Corporation
One Microsoft Way
Redmond, Washington 98052-6399

Copyright © 2007 by Microsoft Corporation

Library of Congress Control Number: 2006937710

Printed and bound in the United States of America.

3 4 5 6 7 8 9   QWT   2 1 0 9 8

Distributed in Canada by H.B. Fenn and Company Ltd.

A CIP catalogue record for this book is available from the British Library.

Microsoft Press books are available through booksellers and distributors worldwide. For further information about international editions, contact your local Microsoft Corporation office or contact Microsoft Press International directly at fax (425) 936-7329. Visit our Web site at www.microsoft.com/mspress. Send comments to mspinput@microsoft.com.

Microsoft, Microsoft Press, Active Directory, ActiveX, AutoSum, Cambria, DirectX, Excel, FrontPage, Groove, Hotmail, InfoPath, IntelliMouse, Internet Explorer, Jscript, MSDN, MSN, OneNote, Outlook, PivotChart, PivotTable, PowerPoint, Rushmore, Segoe, SharePoint, SmartArt, SQL Server, Visio, Visual Basic, Visual Studio, Windows, Windows Media, Windows Mobile, Windows NT, Windows Server, and Windows Vista are either registered trademarks or trademarks of Microsoft Corporation in the United States and/or other countries. Other product and company names mentioned herein may be the trademarks of their respective owners.

The example companies, organizations, products, domain names, e-mail addresses, logos, people, places, and events depicted herein are fictitious. No association with any real company, organization, product, domain name, e-mail address, logo, person, place, or event is intended or should be inferred.

Acquisitions Editor: Juliana Aldous Atkinson
Developmental Editor: Sandra Haynes
Project Editor: Lisa Culver-Jones
Editorial Production Vendor: Publishing.com

Indexer: Rebecca Plunkett
Technical Reviewer: Rozanne Murphy Whalen
Copy Editor: Kim Wimpsett
Proofreader: Andrea Fox

Body Part No. X12-65176

Contents at a Glance

Table of Contents

What do you think of this book? We want to hear from you!

Microsoft is interested in hearing your feedback so we can continually improve our books and learning resources for you. To participate in a brief online survey, please visit:

www.microsoft.com/learning/booksurvey/

What do you think of this book? We want to hear from you!

Microsoft is interested in hearing your feedback so we can continually improve our books and learning resources for you. To participate in a brief online survey, please visit:

www.microsoft.com/learning/booksurvey/

Acknowledgments

Thanks first and foremost to the authors who contributed their expertise to this book: Jim Boyce, Jeff Conrad, Mark Dodge, Stephanie Krieger, Mary Millhollon, Katherine Murray, Beth Sheresh and Doug Sheresh, Sally Slack, Craig Stinson, and John Viescas. Deep appreciation also goes to Lisa Culver-Jones, the book's project editor, and to Curt Philips and his associates, who gracefully and professionally handled the effort required to edit and produce this book. Thanks finally to friends and colleagues at Microsoft Press, especially Juliana Aldous Atkinson, Sandra Haynes, Lucinda Rowley, and Sally Stickney.

About the CD

The CD-ROM that accompanies this book contains many tools and resources. In the following sections, you can read about what's on the CD, the simple steps required to install it, system requirements, and support information.

What's on the CD

The *2007 Microsoft Office System Inside Out* CD includes the following:

- **Sample files.** Click the Browse Sample Files link on the Welcome page to browse the sample files and resources referenced in the book. These files include Microsoft Office Excel workbooks, sample Microsoft Office Access databases, samples of Microsoft Visual Basic code, and sample XML files.

- **Additional eBooks.** In this section you'll find the following resources:
  - *Microsoft Computer Dictionary*, Fifth Edition
  - *First Look 2007 Microsoft Office System* (Katherine Murray, 2006)
  - Sample chapter and poster from *Look Both Ways: Help Protect Your Family on the Internet* (Linda Criddle, 2007)
  - Windows Vista Product Guide

- **Product Information.** Here you'll find information about additional Microsoft products, including Microsoft Office InfoPath 2007 and Microsoft Office Visio 2007.

- **Resources.** In this section, you'll find links to white papers, Webcasts, user assistance articles, Microsoft Office system business solutions, product support information, online training, insider blogs, tools, and much more.

- **Extending Office.** This section provides links to Microsoft and other third-party tools that will help you get more from your experience with Microsoft Office applications.

- **Bonus Chapters.** Additional chapters from the Microsoft Press *Inside Out* books that are featured in *2007 Microsoft Office 2007 System Inside Out*. These chapters provide additional information about topics such as designing a database, using Outlook to schedule meetings and set up tasks, using Access with Windows SharePoint Services, creating charts, working with external data in Excel 2007, and more.

Using the CD

To use this book's companion CD, insert it in your computer's CD-ROM drive. If Auto-Run is enabled on your computer, you'll see the CD's opening page. If AutoRun is not enabled on your computer, double-click the StartCD.exe file in the root of the companion CD.

System Requirements

The following are the minimum system requirements necessary to run the CD:

- Microsoft Windows Vista, Windows XP with Service Pack (SP) 2, Windows Server 2003 with SP1, or a newer operating system

- 500 megahertz (MHz) or higher processor

- 2 gigabytes (GB) storage space (a portion of this disk space will be freed after installation if the original download package is removed from the hard drive)

- 256 megabytes (MB) RAM

- CD-ROM or DVD-ROM drive

- 1024×768 or higher resolution monitor

- Microsoft Windows or Windows Vista–compatible sound card and speakers

- Microsoft Internet Explorer 6 or later

- Microsoft Mouse or compatible pointing device

> Note
> An Internet connection is necessary to access the some of the hyperlinks. Connect time charges might apply.

Support Information

Every effort has been made to ensure the accuracy of the contents of the book and this CD. As corrections or changes are collected, they will be added to a Microsoft Knowledge Base article. Microsoft Press provides support for books and companion CDs at the following Web site: *www.microsoft.com/learning/support/books/*.

If you have comments, questions, or ideas regarding the book or this CD, or questions that are not answered by visiting the site above, please send them via e-mail to *mspinput@microsoft.com*.

You can also click the Feedback or CD Support links on the Welcome page. Please note that Microsoft software product support is not offered through the preceding addresses.

If your question is about the software, and not about the content of this book, please visit the Microsoft Help and Support page or the Microsoft Knowledge Base at *http://support.microsoft.com*.

In the United States, Microsoft software product support issues not covered by the Microsoft Knowledge Base are addressed by Microsoft Product Support Services. Location specific software support options are available from *http://support.microsoft.com/gp/selfoverview/*.

Microsoft Press provides corrections for books through the World Wide Web at *www.microsoft.com/mspress/support/*. To connect directly to the Microsoft Press Knowledge Base and enter a query regarding a question or issue that you may have, go to *www.microsoft.com/mspress/support/search.htm*.

Note

This companion CD relies on scripting for some interface enhancements. If scripting is disabled or unavailable in your browser, follow these steps to run the CD:

1. From the Computer folder, double-click the drive that contains this companion CD.
2. Open the Webfiles folder.
3. Double-click Welcome.htm to open the CD in your default browser.

Conventions and Features Used in This Book

This book uses special text and design conventions to make it easier for you to find the information you need.

Text Conventions

Convention	Meaning
Abbreviated commands for navigating the Ribbon	For your convenience, this book uses abbreviated commands. For example, "Click Home, Insert, Insert Cells" means that you should click the Home tab on the Ribbon, then click the Insert button, and finally click the Insert Cells command.
Boldface type	**Boldface** type is used to indicate text that you type.
Initial Capital Letters	The first letters of the names of tabs, dialog boxes, dialog box elements, and commands are capitalized. Example: the Save As dialog box.
Italicized type	*Italicized* type is used to indicate new terms.
Plus sign (+) in text	Keyboard shortcuts are indicated by a plus sign (+) separating two key names. For example, Ctrl+Alt+Delete means that you press the Ctrl, Alt, and Delete keys at the same time.

Design Conventions

INSIDE OUT   **This Statement Illustrates an Example of an "Inside Out" Heading**

These are the book's signature tips. In these tips, you'll get the straight scoop on what's going on with the software—inside information about why a feature works the way it does. You'll also find handy workarounds to deal with software problems.

Sidebars

Sidebars provide helpful hints, timesaving tricks, or alternative procedures related to the task being discussed.

TROUBLESHOOTING

This statement illustrates an example of a "Troubleshooting" problem statement.

Look for these sidebars to find solutions to common problems you might encounter. Troubleshooting sidebars appear next to related information in the chapters. You can also use "Index to Troubleshooting Topics" at the back of the book to look up problems by topic.

Cross-references point you to other locations in the book that offer additional information about the topic being discussed.

CAUTION

Cautions identify potential problems that you should look out for when you're completing a task or problems that you must address before you can complete a task.

Note

Notes offer additional information related to the task being discussed.

 When an example has a related file that is included on the companion CD, this icon appears in the margin. You can use these files to follow along with the book's examples.

Introduction

The release of the 2007 Microsoft Office system is another milestone for Microsoft's suite of business productivity software. First, many of the Microsoft Office system programs have a significantly different user interface, which Microsoft has branded the Microsoft Office Fluent interface to denote its ease of use; the manner in which commands and tools you need to accomplish your work flow smoothly into view when you need them (and hide gracefully when you don't); and how it readily presents you with previews and options that make tasks like analysis, editing, and formatting much easier to understand and perform.

The Microsoft Office system continues to grow as well as evolve. The 2007 release consists of several editions (Office Standard 2007 and Office Professional 2007 are two examples) that each comes with a specific mix of desktop programs. The number of desktop programs has grown as well and now includes programs such as Microsoft Office Groove 2007 (a collaboration and information sharing application) and Microsoft Office SharePoint Designer 2007 (a Web site design and solution development tool). The 2007 Office release has updated versions of Microsoft Office InfoPath, Microsoft Office OneNote, and Microsoft Office Visio. It includes real-time communication tools as well as desktop publishing, accounting, and project management programs. And the 2007 Office release features redesigned and newly enriched versions of its most widely used programs—Microsoft Office Access, Microsoft Office Excel, Microsoft Office Outlook, Microsoft Office PowerPoint, and Microsoft Office Word.

The 2007 Microsoft Office system also includes server products, such as Microsoft Office SharePoint Server 2007, that have further transformed the Microsoft Office system into a platform on which software developers and users can build and work with collaboration tools, collect business intelligence, manage business processes and content, and more. But this is just a glimpse of the extent to which the 2007 Microsoft Office system addresses the needs and habits of organizations and individuals that depend on software and information technology for their business and in their personal lives.

Who This Book Is For

The changes and additions to the 2007 Office release may pose a challenge to even skilled users who have worked with programs such as Excel or PowerPoint for years. *2007 Microsoft Office System Inside Out* is intended for people who already have a depth of experience working with Microsoft Windows programs and especially Microsoft Office applications. You might be one of the first people at your company to work with the 2007 Office release, or you may be training others (as you train yourself) how to use it. Software developers and consultants who develop and design solutions with Microsoft Office system programs will find information and insights about how they and other users will work with new features. Anyone who wants a book that features both breadth and depth will find this book to their liking.

A difficult fact to face is that the 2007 Office release is too large to document in a single book. In fact, most of this book was compiled from chapters from books that cover applications such as Access or Excel from top to bottom. Each part of this book, together with the supplementary material you'll find on the book's CD, provides an overview of a program's essential fundamentals as well as chapters that deal with more advanced topics in comprehensive detail.

This book also is written for users who think they've reached the limit of what they can do in Microsoft Office. One of the goals that Microsoft had in designing the 2007 Office release was to make more features—especially more advanced features—easier to find, use, and apply. Menu commands that were tucked away on submenus or on toolbars that weren't always visible are now readily apparent, and what these commands do and the effects they provide are clearly demonstrated to everyone who uses them. Finally, this book is designed for people who want to learn how to make the most of working with Microsoft Office applications together, integrating their features while bringing each application's special purpose to bear on the preparation, analysis, and distribution of documents, presentations, and information.

How This Book Is Organized

2007 Microsoft Office System Inside Out is organized in eight parts. Here's a rundown of what you'll find in each section of the book.

- In Part 1, "Getting Started," you'll be introduced to the 2007 Microsoft Office system, including a full chapter about the Microsoft Office Fluent interface. You'll learn about the security features in the 2007 Office release, including the Trust Center, where you set options for managing your privacy as well as for which macros you will allow to run.

- In Part 2, "Collaboration Essentials," you'll explore several of the 2007 Office release tools and programs that are designed for collaboration and sharing, including Microsoft Office OneNote 2007 and Microsoft Office Groove 2007. You'll also find an overview of how to use Microsoft Office with Windows SharePoint Services.

- Part 3 covers Microsoft Office Word 2007, including formatting and layout techniques, outlining, marking up and revising documents, and page setup. On the book's CD, you'll find additional information about working with new features such as document Themes.

- Part 4 is about Microsoft Office Excel 2007. This part describes techniques for working with worksheets and workbooks, building formulas, using functions, and analyzing data. On the book's CD, you'll find additional information (from the Bonus Chapters tab) about working with charts in Excel and about connecting Excel worksheets to external data.

- Part 5 covers Microsoft Office PowerPoint 2007, including the basics of creating and formatting a presentation; how to work with text; and how to work with objects, diagrams, and charts in a presentation. This section also provides information about collaborating and sharing PowerPoint presentations and explains how to import or export data to and from your PowerPoint slides. In the last chapter in this section, you'll learn how to set up and present a slide show.

- Part 6 brings us to Microsoft Office Outlook, an application in which many information workers spend the better parts of their days—reading e-mail, scheduling meetings, and setting up tasks. To start this section you'll read an overview of Office Outlook 2007, it's new features, and its new user interface. In the chapters that follow you'll read about how to manage e-mail, about security features in Outlook 2007, and how to integrate your use of Outlook with Windows SharePoint Services. The Bonus Chapters area of the book's CD will lead you to chapters in which you can learn about managing tasks, meetings, appointments, and contacts in Outlook 2007.

- In Part 7 of the book, you'll learn about the latest release of Microsoft Office Access. You'll learn in detail about the new Access 2007 user interface, how to create a database and its tables, and how to work with database objects such as queries, forms, and reports. The book's CD includes an additional chapter that teaches you about how to work with Access together with a SharePoint site and an article that covers the fundamentals of database design.

- The final part of the book, "Office Programming Primer," presents an introduction to Visual Basic for Applications, the programming language you use to automate and extend the functionality of Microsoft Office programs, and a primer on working with the Office Open XML Formats, the framework at the heart of the 2007 Office release file formats.

PART 1
Getting Started

John Pierce

Overview of the 2007 Microsoft Office System

Any separation between business information and the software that's used to create and manage it has become harder and harder to see. Although people still conduct business over the phone, in meetings—even at a health club or a restaurant—these kinds of person-to-person encounters lead to electronic documents that detail the products, ideas, and data that companies, their employees, and their customers exchange. And for millions of workers in home offices, small businesses, or large organizations around the globe, with jobs in fields such as administration, architecture, consulting, education, finance, health care, law, marketing, real estate, sales—you name it—this means working with the programs that make up the Microsoft Office system.

The 2007 release of the Microsoft Office system provides many new and updated features: graphics capabilities such as three-dimensional effects for charts and diagrams; the To-Do bar in Microsoft Office Outlook 2007; data visualization capabilities in Microsoft Office Excel 2007 that highlight trends in data series; text building blocks in Microsoft Office Word 2007 that let you identify standard pieces of content, such as the text for a disclaimer or a company description, that can be inserted consistently from document to document whenever they are required. You'll learn about advances such as these and many others throughout the course of this book.

Microsoft has also changed in radical ways the user interface for several of the 2007 Office system programs. These changes may take some getting used to for experienced Microsoft Office users. It's hard to imagine creating or printing a document without opening the File menu or using a toolbar button, but that's what's in store. Of course, the changes to the user interface are intended to make your use of the applications easier, your work with them more effective. Microsoft designed the changes so that you can focus more on the results you want rather than on figuring out how to achieve them. The 2007 Office release programs PowerPoint, Excel, and Word have a new file format as well.

The format is based on the Extensible Markup Language (XML), and although the change in the file format might not affect how you do your work in Microsoft Office, it very likely will affect the kind of work that you and others do and the type of information you work with. XML is often used to transfer data between computer systems and applications, for example. One effect you'll probably see as a result of the wider use of XML in 2007 Office system applications is the ability to work more easily with data stored in back-end systems.

For more information about XML and how it is used in the 2007 Office system, see Chapter 32, "Office Open XML Essentials."

In this overview of the 2007 Office system, you'll see examples of the new user interface. (Chapter 2, "The 2007 Office System User Interface: What's Changed, What's the Same," covers this topic in detail.) This chapter also provides a brief description of the change in file formats and highlights features, applications, and technologies that have been added in this release of the Office system. To start, however, we'll look briefly at some of the context that informed Microsoft's design of the 2007 Office system—context that Microsoft believes also informs your use of the Microsoft Office system programs.

The New World of Work

In May 2005, as part of the groundwork Microsoft laid for building interest and momentum for the 2007 Office system, Bill Gates published a memo titled "The New World of Work." In the memo, which was distributed to corporate executives, business decision makers, and other Microsoft customers (and is available on Microsoft's Web site at *www.microsoft.com/mscorp/execmail/2005/05-19newworldofwork.mspx*), Gates wrote about how software evolved to support the need for information workers to communicate, collaborate, and have access to data. The challenge for the future, Gates said, was "less about getting access to the information people need, and more about making sense of the information they have—giving them the ability to focus, prioritize, and apply their expertise, visualize and understand key data, and reduce the amount of time they spend dealing with the complexity of an information-rich environment."

Okay. If you bought this book, or are right now browsing through it at your local bookstore, the odds are that you're less interested in Bill Gates's theories of the modern workforce than in understanding how you can get your own work done with the various Microsoft Office programs. If that's the case, feel free to skip to the next major section in this chapter, "The New Office User Interface." The focus there is on the software itself. But if you don't mind a little background reading, take about five minutes and see whether you recognize some of the trends that Bill Gates described in his memo. One reason to take the time is to understand why Microsoft and this book emphasize how Microsoft Office system applications work together—the importance of collections of capabilities (sometimes called *solutions*)—and not only how to work with features one at a time.

In many ways, the 2007 Office system is designed to address the ways in which information workers perform their jobs in this day and age. Its capabilities reflect the needs of a mobile and geographically dispersed workforce and the need for rapid and systematic collaboration. Features added in the 2007 Office release also address the fact that information workers are more involved in business processes and formal workflows and that more people throughout an organization make decisions that require the analysis of data. In the next sections, we'll look more closely at two of these areas: how the 2007 Office system supports collaboration and its facilitation of business intelligence.

Collaboration Workspaces and Tools

Where we work and who we work with are more varied and flexible than they once were. Software and computing systems enable many workers to access company networks through wireless connectivity, for example, through mobile devices, or remote connections from home. Project teams and workgroups often consist of people who work in different locations, different companies, even different regions and countries. A mobile and geographically dispersed workforce provides businesses and their employees with a number of opportunities. These characteristics also create specific needs for communication, access to information, clear and efficient processes, a visibility to priorities, and easy-to-use systems and tools.

In Part 2 of this book, "Collaboration Essentials," you can read about Microsoft Windows SharePoint Services. If you're unfamiliar with the SharePoint products and technologies, they're used to build Web sites and to outfit the sites with tools such as document libraries, lists, announcements, and calendars. A SharePoint site can also provide access to information stored in large data systems.

Microsoft Office system applications, such as Excel, Outlook, and Word, work hand-in-hand with SharePoint sites to provide and facilitate collaborative work as well. Microsoft Office SharePoint Server, for example, lets you define a simple workflow that facilitates document reviews. You list the individuals who need to review and approve a document, and each individual is notified in turn when the document becomes available. You can initiate and track document review and approval processes while working within Word 2007. People's familiarity with Word can help accelerate review cycles without requiring people to learn new tools.

You can also connect Outlook 2007 and Windows SharePoint Services to keep calendars, contacts, tasks, and other information in sync in both applications. And you can make Excel 2007 worksheets and workbooks available through SharePoint Server and control who has access to them. Why is this helpful? Think of the problems created when the "final" project budget is distributed to the team through e-mail. Everyone has a separate copy, which means that everyone can make one more change. A worksheet that contains important or confidential information is more secure, and the information in it more reliable, if a single copy is stored in a common workspace where individual access is controlled.

Microsoft Office Groove 2007, an application added to the 2007 Office system, is also designed for team collaboration. Office Groove 2007 is based on the idea of a workspace that invited members can use. Members can have specific roles as participants or workspace managers, for example. Workspace members can use the messaging capabilities of Groove 2007 to stay in touch and to see whether a member is online or offline. They perform work using a number of workspace tools, everything from a discussion tool to an issue tracker to a sketchpad to customized forms. Groove also takes care of keeping data up-to-date and notifies you when a workspace that you're a member of contains information you haven't yet read. Finally, you can set up your Groove account on more than one computer so that you can perform work on your desktop computer when you're in the office and work with the same files on your laptop while on the road.

You can find more information about Groove in Chapter 6, "Working as a Team in a Microsoft Office Groove Workspace," and Chapter 7, "Sharing and Communicating Using Microsoft Office Groove."

Business Intelligence on Your Desktop

To make decisions, you need access to information. You also need the tools to gather and analyze information so that the decisions you make are based on information that's relevant and current. Those might seem like obvious points, but until recently, the integration and distribution of information that's required for people working at their desktops to analyze data thoroughly has been anything but easy. Organizations had to incorporate information from data warehouses, enterprise applications, and other data sources. Sales figures might be stored in one system, for example, and current inventory in another.

New capabilities in Excel 2007, including increased spreadsheet capacity (more columns and rows), more intuitive ways to create formulas, enhanced data visualization tools, plus sorting and filtering advances, provide greater support for business intelligence on the desktop.

Of course, Excel can't provide business intelligence on its own. It needs data to analyze. The new capabilities in Excel are complemented by data connection libraries, a feature in SharePoint Server that simplifies the steps you have to take to find and connect to external data sources. In addition, Excel Services, which helps you create, modify, and share spreadsheets through a Web browser, can provide access to data stored using a product such as Microsoft SQL Server. You can establish a live connection to a data source in Excel 2007 and see metrics and other measures of business performance. The live connection ensures that the data you're reviewing or submitting in a report is accurate and current.

The New Microsoft Office User Interface

In previous versions of Microsoft Office, the commands, buttons, and other controls you used to format text or sort columns of data, for example, were organized on menus and toolbars. The name of a menu provided some sense of the general function of the commands the menu contained, but finding a specific command—especially one for an operation you performed rarely—wasn't always easy. In the 2007 release of Access, Excel, Outlook, PowerPoint, and Word, menu commands and toolbars have been replaced with what Microsoft calls "the Ribbon," a change to the user interface that was designed to make program features easier to find and use. Only time will tell.

For a detailed description of the new user interface, see Chapter 2.

The Ribbon

An example of the Ribbon in Excel 2007 is shown in Figure 1-1. As you can see, the Ribbon organizes commands in a highly graphical way. It uses named tabs along the top of

the window rather than menus. When you click a tab, the Ribbon displays a function-
ally related set of commands. The Page Layout tab, for example, contains commands
related to page orientation, margins, scaling, and the like. The Home tab, rather than
collecting commands related to a specific area, such as page layout, contains a group of
commands that users of an application most often need. For Excel, that includes font
formatting, text alignment, and cell formatting. It's possible that you could create and
format a whole worksheet—a simple one at any rate—and never leave the Home tab.

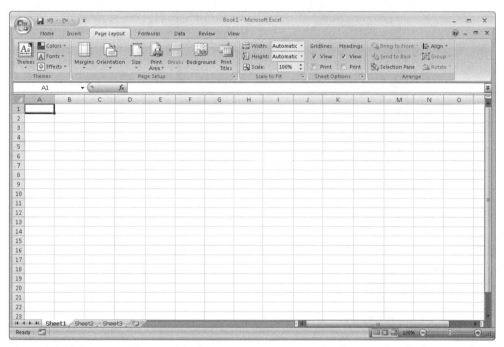

Figure 1-1 In the new Office user interface, commands are organized on a series of tabs. The collection of tabs is known as the Ribbon.

> **Note**
> The Ribbon also provides sets of commands "on demand"—called contextual tabs—when
> you select a particular type of object to work on—for example, a chart, an image, or
> a table.

In Word 2007, shown in Figure 1-2, the tabs on the Ribbon are related to page layout,
working with references, mailings, reviewing documents, and so on. Notice the rem-
nant of a familiar-looking toolbar in the upper-left corner of the window. This part of
the interface is known as the Quick Access Toolbar. It contains buttons for operations
such as saving a file, printing, or undoing and redoing your recent actions.

> **Note**
> You can easily add and remove buttons from the Quick Access Toolbar. You'll learn how to customize the Quick Access Toolbar in Chapter 2.

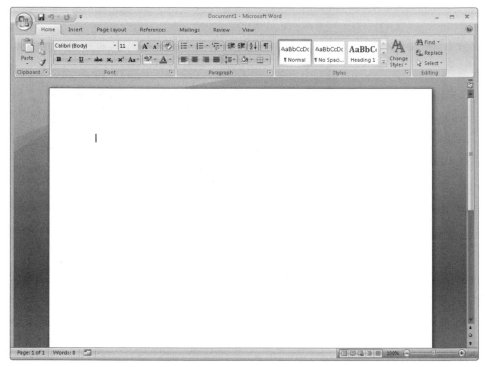

Figure 1-2 In addition to the Ribbon, you can organize commands you use frequently on the Quick Access Toolbar.

Users familiar with Microsoft Office might look at the new interface and wonder how it is that they'll create a new file or open the one they worked on yesterday. In other words, what happened to the File menu? It's gone—at least in name. You get to commands like New, Print, Save, and others that you're used to seeing on the File menu by clicking the Microsoft Office Button in the upper-left corner of the window. Figure 1-3 shows the Office menu open in Excel.

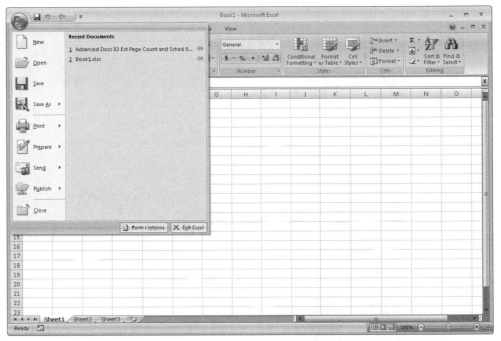

Figure 1-3 Open the Office menu by clicking the Microsoft Office Button. The Office menu contains commands formerly found on the File menu.

> **Note**
>
> The Office menu is also where you'll find your way to the Options dialog box for a specific application. (This command used to be on the Tools menu.) The Options dialog box lets you set preferences for viewing and editing files, security, customization, and other application properties.

Galleries and Live Preview

Galleries are another significant addition to the Microsoft Office user interface. Galleries provide you with examples of text formatting, background colors, and themes. You can choose an item from a gallery when you are working on a document, spreadsheet, presentation, or database. Figure 1-4 shows the built-in Fonts gallery for a presentation in PowerPoint. You can see font styles side by side for comparison and see the results of the choice you make simply by pointing at an item in the gallery—a feature that Microsoft calls Live Preview. Seeing the results of your choice simplifies the processes of laying out, editing, and formatting your work.

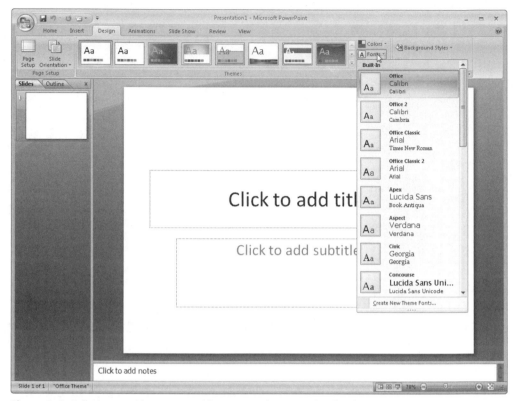

Figure 1-4 Galleries provide an array of formatting choices and styles that you can preview in your document by pointing to a selection in the gallery.

You can learn more about galleries and Live Preview—including how to add your own formatting preferences to a gallery—in Chapter 2.

The New Microsoft Office XML File Formats

In the 2007 Office release, Word, Excel, and PowerPoint now use the Microsoft Office Open XML Formats, which means that their default file formats are based on XML. The XML file format provides a number of benefits: It provides better security for your files, reduces the chance of file corruption, reduces file size, and facilitates data sharing across data storage and retrieval systems.

Network administrators will like the small file size and reduced chance of corruption. Software developers and programmers will take advantage of the XML file format to integrate 2007 Office release applications with other business applications, even applications that aren't published by Microsoft. Any application that supports XML can access and work with data in the new Microsoft Office file format.

If you are interested in reading more about the structure and architecture of the Office Open XML Formats, see the article at *http://msdn2.microsoft.com/en-us/library/ms406049.aspx.*

For most users of Microsoft Office, however, the change in file format will be noticeable mainly in the names of your files. For documents, spreadsheets, and presentations, the default file format now has an "x" on the end of the file name extension (.docx, .xlsx, and .pptx), which indicates XML. If you save a file as a template, the file is saved with the former template extension with an "x" on the end: .xltx in Excel, for example. If a file you are working on contains a macro or Visual Basic code, you have to save it using the new macro-enabled file format. For a Word document, that means you save it as a .docm file (or a .dotm file for a Word template).

If you open a file in Word 2007, for example, that was created in a previous version of Word, you will be asked if you want to convert it to the new format. If you say yes, the document will be saved in the new XML format. If you choose not to convert the file, it will retain its original format. You can open and modify it in the 2007 Office system, but some features of the 2007 Office release won't be available.

If you are using an earlier version of Microsoft Office and you receive a file that was created in the 2007 Office release, you need to download a converter in order to read and edit the 2007 Office system file. You can download a converter at *www.microsoft.com.*

> Note
>
> Another XML-related file format that's part of the 2007 Office system is the XML Paper Specification (XPS) Document format, which is a paginated representation of electronic paper, similar to the widely used Portable Document Format (PDF). The XPS Document format lets you create, share, print, and archive paginated documents without any additional tools. You can open an XPS document in your Web browser.

What Else Is New?

In the following sections, you'll learn about some of the new and updated features in Word, Excel, PowerPoint, Outlook, and Access. This section will also briefly describe Microsoft Office server technologies. Finally, you'll learn about Microsoft Office Online, a Web site that is an essential companion for your work with the Microsoft Office system, and how the 2007 Office release makes more of Office Online's resources available to you.

Microsoft Office Word 2007

One of the features in Word 2007 that users of the application should find particularly helpful is building blocks. Building blocks are frequently-used, standard pieces of content that you include when you're assembling a document such as a sales proposal, a legal pleading, a monthly organizational newsletter, or almost any kind of document for which it's required or helpful to use the same block of text consistently. Let's say each of your company's project proposals is supposed to include a section with brief biographies of your lead engineers. You can save a building block for the bios and then add it to any proposal without retyping it and without hunting down (often by trial and error) an old proposal that includes the text (probably out of date) and copying and pasting it into the document you're now preparing. With a building block (you'll find the built-in building blocks under Quick Parts on the Insert tab), you don't need to re-create content.

Here are a few more new features in Word 2007:

- You can now review a document that's been edited with revision marks side by side with the original document. As you can see in Figure 1-5, the window is divided into three panes—a pane for each version and a third pane that shows which text has been inserted, deleted, or moved.

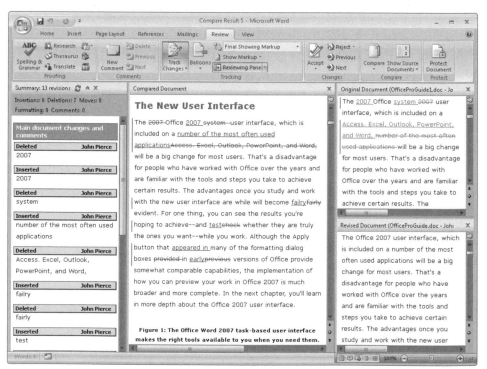

Figure 1-5 You can compare an edited version of a document side by side with the original.

- Word also has a whole host of new formatting features, including charting and diagramming features that include 3-D shapes, transparency, drop shadows, and other effects. Quick Styles and Document Themes are two of the galleries you can choose from when formatting a document.

- You can use the Document Inspector to detect and remove unwanted comments, hidden text, or personally identifiable information. Removing this information, some of which can be sensitive, ensures that it doesn't go out with the document when the document is distributed or published publicly. For more information about using the Document Inspector with Word 2007 and other applications, see Chapter 3, "Managing Security and Privacy in the 2007 Office System."

- If you're a participant in the blogosphere, you'll be happy to know that you can write and submit your blogs right from Word 2007. You can link Word to your blog site, and use it to include elements such as images and tables in your blog.

For detailed chapters about using Word 2007, see Part 3 of this book.

Microsoft Office Excel 2007

The combination of Excel 2007 and Excel Services, mentioned earlier in the chapter, bears some repeating and elaboration. In addition to enabling spreadsheets to be shared more securely among users, Excel Services makes the data you work with in Excel more accessible. Excel Services displays a spreadsheet using HTML, which means that you can review and work with the information contained in the spreadsheet using only a Web browser. You do not need a full version of Excel to do so, although you would need one to create and publish the spreadsheet to begin with. You can navigate, sort, filter, define parameters, and work with PivotTable views in a spreadsheet displayed by Excel Services, and you can do all this work using a Web browser.

Here are a few of the other new and updated features in Excel 2007:

- How much information can you store in a single spreadsheet? Information that fills 1 million rows and 16,000 columns. Not everyone will need a spreadsheet with that level of capacity, but if you're analyzing extremely large data sets, you might.

- Charting capabilities in Excel 2007 have been updated. For one thing, you can build a chart in fewer steps. You also have a wider choice of visual effects for your charts, such as 3-D, soft shadowing, and transparency. The same charting features available to you in Excel are also available in PowerPoint and Word.

- Excel 2007 also provides more tools for spotting trends and variances in your data. You can apply conditional formatting more easily, and then look for patterns and trends using visual tools, such as gradients, thresholds, and performance indicator icons.

For detailed chapters about using Excel 2007, see Part 4 of this book.

Microsoft Office PowerPoint 2007

For PowerPoint, one of the improvements that die-hard and novice users alike will enjoy is slide libraries. You can now store presentations as individual slides on a site supported by Microsoft Office SharePoint Server 2007. Slide libraries are shared sites as well, which means that coworkers and team members can make use of slides from your presentations, and you can see what's available from theirs. Slide libraries also can act as an official repository of sorts. You can use them to store approved slides that must be included in presentations for branding or legal reasons. Slides that you insert from a library into a particular presentation can remain synchronized with the version in the library. You don't have to double-check that the company overview slide is up-to-date.

One other benefit of slide libraries: In PowerPoint 2007, you can define and save your own custom slide layouts. By storing your custom layouts in a slide library, you can share custom slides with other users and also be sure that the next presentation you create is consistent with the layout you saved.

Here are some of the other updates in PowerPoint 2007:

- SmartArt diagrams let you easily create relationship, workflow, or hierarchy diagrams within PowerPoint 2007. You can even convert a bulleted list into a diagram or modify and update existing diagrams.

- With built-in workflow services in Office SharePoint Server 2007, you can initiate, manage, and track review and approval processes from PowerPoint 2007.

- You can uniformly format your presentations with PowerPoint 2007 themes. PowerPoint 2007 themes let you change the look and feel of your entire presentation using a single click. Changing the theme of your presentation not only changes the background color, but also the color of a diagram, table, chart, font, and even the style of any bullet points within a presentation.

- You can now add a digital signature to PowerPoint 2007 presentations to ensure the file's integrity, or mark a presentation as "final" to prevent inadvertent changes. These features ensure that the content of your presentation can be modified or shared only in the way you intended.

For detailed chapters about using PowerPoint 2007, see Part 5 of this book.

Microsoft Office Outlook 2007

Outlook 2007, the 2007 Office system's e-mail client and personal organizer, is used frequently to transmit and store information and documents. Outlook often seems as though it's at the center of the Microsoft Office experience. So much information arrives in, leaves from, and resides in Outlook (for longer than it should, in some cases) that finding information that you have there hasn't always been easy. You can use keywords, dates, or other criteria to search in Outlook 2007 to locate items in your e-mail, calendar, contacts, or tasks. This search feature, called Instant Search, is integrated into the Outlook user interface so that you can conduct searches while working in the program.

Here are a few of the other new features in Outlook 2007:

- Everyone loves a concise to-do list. The new To-Do bar shows the e-mail messages you've flagged and the tasks still to be completed. The To-Do bar also connects to tasks that you may have defined and stored in Windows SharePoint Services or another 2007 Office system program.

- You can more easily share your calendar, even with people working outside your organization. You can create and publish Internet calendars to Office Online, add and share Internet calendar subscriptions, and send calendar snapshots in e-mail.

- Outlook 2007 includes new ways to fend off junk e-mail and malicious sites. To help protect you from divulging personal information to a threatening Web site, Outlook 2007 has an improved junk e-mail filter and has added new features that disable links and warn you about threatening content within an e-mail message.

- You can read and manage Really Simple Syndication (RSS) feeds and blogs in Outlook 2007.

- Attachment Preview lets you preview attachments in the Outlook reading pane.

For detailed chapters about using Outlook 2007, see Part 6 of this book.

Microsoft Office Access 2007

For long-time users of Access, the changes in the 2007 version are pretty dramatic. The user interface has changed, of course, and the trusted database window has been replaced. The good news is that you have an increased number of database templates and applications on which you can base and model your own work. Each of the templates provides tables, forms, reports, queries, and other required database objects. The templates include those for asset tracking, inventory tracking, project management, budgeting, and marketing.

Here are some of the other new features in Access 2007:

- Create multiple reports with different views of the same information. You can modify a report with real-time visual feedback and save various views for different audiences. New grouping, filtering, and sorting capabilities help you display a report's data in informative ways.

- You can link tables to your database from other Access databases, Excel spreadsheets, SharePoint Server sites, Open Database Connectivity (ODBC) data sources, SQL Server databases, and other data sources. You can then use these linked tables to create reports.

- Automatic data-type detection provides a simple, straightforward way to create a table. Access 2007 recognizes whether the data you enter is a date, currency, or other common data type.

- Share information stored in Access 2007 through Windows SharePoint Services. Coworkers can access and edit data and view real-time reports through a Web interface.

- Access 2007 has new field types, such as attachments and a multi-value field. You can attach any document, image, or spreadsheet to a record in your database application. With the multi-value field, you can select more than one value (for example, assign a task to more than one person) in each cell.

For detailed chapters about using Access 2007, see Part 7 of this book.

> ### Rounding Out the Office System Programs
>
> The bulk of this book covers the five main 2007 Office system applications—Access, Excel, Outlook, PowerPoint, and Word. As you've learned in this overview, the 2007 Office system has grown to encompass far more than those five applications. It also includes Microsoft Office Visio, a business drawing application; Groove, the team collaboration tool; Microsoft Office OneNote, an application designed for taking and storing notes; Microsoft Office Publisher, the small-business graphics and design program; and Microsoft Office InfoPath, an electronic forms designer.
>
> Not all of these other applications are covered in this book with as much depth as the "big five." This book does include chapters you can use to learn the basics of working with Groove and OneNote.

2007 Office System Servers

If you don't manage an organization's computers or administer your company's network, you may never install one of the Microsoft Office servers yourself. As you've seen even in this short overview, however, technologies such as Office SharePoint Server and Excel Services are likely to play a significant role in how you use and work with the 2007 Office system. A business that decides to deploy the 2007 Office system will probably not stop with the desktop programs. In this section, you'll learn a little about three other Microsoft Office server technologies—Microsoft Office Forms Server, Groove Server, and Project Server—so that you're familiar with the role they play in the larger 2007 Office system.

Forms Server

Office Forms Server 2007 is similar to Excel Services. Its job is to host and render browser-based InfoPath forms. Electronic forms are elements in any number of business processes, and making them available in a Web browser is an important step in streamlining these processes so that data can be collected, distributed, and integrated more effectively.

Groove Server

You've already learned a bit about Groove 2007. Office Groove Server 2007 is intended to support the deployment of Groove 2007 throughout a single organization.

Project Server

Unless you work with Microsoft Office Project, you probably won't run into Project Server, which is one of the components of what Microsoft dubs its Office Enterprise Project Management (EPM) solution. For most information workers, their experience with the EPM solution will be through Office Project Professional 2007 or a browser-based application known as Project Web Access.

The solution is essentially designed to automate project management functions and to specifically aid in the administration of an entire portfolio of projects—helping you see where resources will be overcommitted or under-used, which tasks are consistently behind, and what percentage of a project you have actually completed.

Templates and Assistance from Microsoft Office Online

An overview of the 2007 Office system would not be complete without some attention to Office Online. This Web site is a source for templates, online assistance, demonstrations, updates to the 2007 Office system, and an assortment of other resources that teach and inform you about the 2007 Office system programs. In the 2007 Office release, Office Online has taken on a larger presence. One of the first places you'll see evidence of this is the links to Office Online that are available when you create a new document, workbook, presentation, or database. Figure 1-6, for example, shows the New Presentation dialog box in PowerPoint 2007. You will see a similar dialog box (or window) in Word, Excel, and Access.

Notice the size and organization of the window, if nothing else. The New dialog box is no longer mostly a list of files at a particular location with some options for applying templates and other themes. Here you can choose to start with a blank presentation, a template you've created, a template that's installed on your computer, or a template from Office Online. The Office Online templates are organized by type: schedules, reports, calendars, and the like. Clicking the link for Schedules, for example, displays previews of the set of templates shown in Figure 1-7. Select the template you want to use, and then click Download to add a copy to your computer.

The Microsoft Office Online links in the New Presentation dialog box (and for the other applications as well) contains links to articles, training, other templates, downloads, and the other resources that Office Online provides.

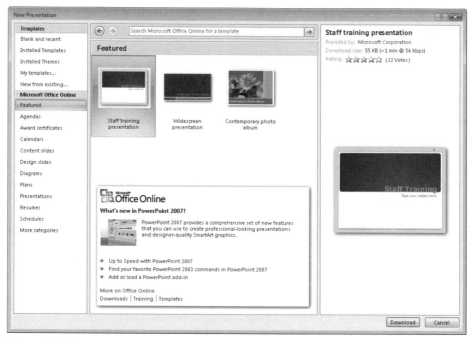

Figure 1-6 The New Presentation dialog box in PowerPoint provides links to templates and other resources on Office Online.

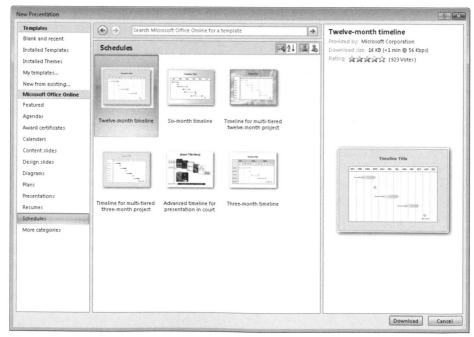

Figure 1-7 Office Online shows groups of templates you can use in a PowerPoint 2007 presentation, for example.

> **Note**
>
> The online Help system in the 2007 Office system is also tied to Office Online. You'll learn more about online Help and the options you have for accessing it in Chapter 2.

That concludes this brief overview of the 2007 Microsoft Office system. Now it's on to the details, starting with the new user interface. In the next chapter, you'll learn more about the Ribbon, galleries, Live Preview, and how to incorporate the new user interface into your day-to-day work with the 2007 Office system programs.

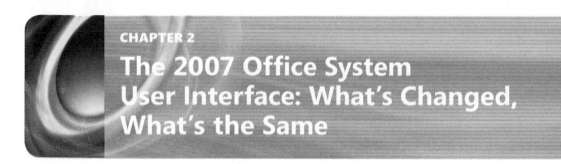

The 2007 Office System User Interface: What's Changed, What's the Same

If you've heard anything about the 2007 Microsoft Office system in advance, chances are that what you've heard about is the Microsoft Office system's new user interface. The changes in the 2007 Office release will surprise many personal computer users who are familiar with the look and feel of the menus, toolbars, dialog boxes, and other controls that have defined the Microsoft Office user interface in previous releases. In the 2007 Office release, you'll work with the Ribbon and tabs instead of menus. Instead of having to select multiple options in a dialog box to combine formatting for text, a background color, and line styles, you can work with new features, such as galleries and Live Preview, to select a set of formats all at once and see how your choice will appear in your document.

Why did Microsoft change the organization and appearance of the user interface that literally millions of people use to work with its software? Research and interviews that Microsoft conducted revealed that many people, including frequent users of Microsoft Office, often had to pause in their work because a menu command or a set of options weren't easy to find or follow. The changes to the user interface are designed in part so that users can find commands they need more quickly. Commands are more visible, more of them are labeled, and their function is often represented more graphically. The second purpose behind the changes was to let users view more easily the results of their actions. You no longer have to open and close a dialog box several times to apply and modify a series of formatting changes. You can now browse through the items displayed in a gallery of styles and see more or less instantly how a particular item will affect your document's appearance.

> **Note**
>
> Lovers of dialog boxes—and the level of detail and control they provide—should not lose heart. You can still get to the dialog boxes you need. For more information about how dialog boxes are used in the 2007 Microsoft Office system, see "Are You Missing Your Favorite Old Dialog Box?" on page 41.

In this chapter, you'll take a look at the 2007 Office release user interface. You'll see examples of the new elements, including the Ribbon, galleries, and the Quick Access Toolbar. And you'll learn more about the 2007 Office online Help, which is integrated into the user interface more thoroughly than in previous releases. We'll start with a quick tour, some descriptions, and a comparison of the new elements with those that may be more familiar. Keep in mind that this chapter is a general orientation to the new user interface. You'll learn more about how to perform specific tasks in the sections of this book that cover individual applications. Later parts of this book also often include more information about how the new user interface is represented in a specific application. For example, the user interface for Microsoft Office Access 2007 will be covered in detail in Chapter 26, "Exploring the New Look of Access 2007."

> **Note**
>
> In the 2007 Office release, the user interface changes affect Microsoft Office Access, Microsoft Office Excel, Microsoft Office Outlook, Microsoft Office PowerPoint, and Microsoft Office Word (the "big five"). (In Office Outlook, only item windows—the windows used for items such as an e-mail message or an appointment—include the user interface that is based on the Ribbon; the Outlook application window displays menus and toolbars.) Programs such as Microsoft Office InfoPath, Microsoft Office OneNote, Microsoft Office Publisher, Microsoft Office Visio, and Microsoft Office Project do not include the new user interface.

A Quick Tour and Comparison

Before you learn in more detail about the main elements of the 2007 Microsoft Office system user interface, in this section you're provided with an orientation to the elements' names, appearance, and general functions. Figure 2-1 shows the application window for Word 2007, with several of the major elements labeled:

- For the most part, menus and toolbars have been replaced by the Ribbon, the strip across the top of the user interface that displays commands. In Figure 2-1, notice that more of the commands are labeled, which helps avoid having to move from control to control scanning ScreenTips to find the command you're looking for.

- The Ribbon is made up of a series of tabs that contain commands, buttons, and galleries. (You'll learn more about galleries shortly.) When you click a tab, the commands shown on the Ribbon change, with each tab representing a functional area of an application. Figure 2-1, for example, shows the Insert tab in Word 2007. You can use this tab to insert pictures, charts, headers and footers, and the like. Figure 2-2 shows the Slide Show tab in PowerPoint 2007.

Microsoft Office Button

Quick Access Toolbar

Ribbon

Figure 2-1 Command tabs, the Ribbon, the Quick Access Toolbar, and the Microsoft Office Button are among the new and updated elements of the 2007 Office release user interface.

- The Quick Access Toolbar sits in the upper-left corner of the window (you can opt to show it below the Ribbon as well) and displays a set of frequently used commands, such as Save, Undo, and Redo. The commands vary from program to program. Later in the chapter, you'll learn how to customize the Quick Access Toolbar to include the set of commands of your choice.

- The Microsoft Office Button reveals a menu that contains the commands you use to work with a document as a whole. It's essentially the old File menu. In many cases, the menu displays a brief description about menu items when you point to a command. Figure 2-3 shows the Microsoft Office Button menu in Excel 2007.

Note

If you find yourself temporarily at sea using the tabs on the Ribbon, the Office online Help includes tables that cross-reference the commands on each tab to the menus on which the commands appeared in previous versions of Microsoft Office. For example, the Options command appeared on the Tools menu in Microsoft Office 2003, but it is now a command on the Office menu.

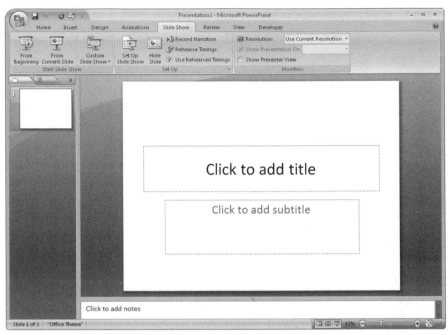

Figure 2-2 Commands on tabs are organized to reflect the main functional areas of a program.

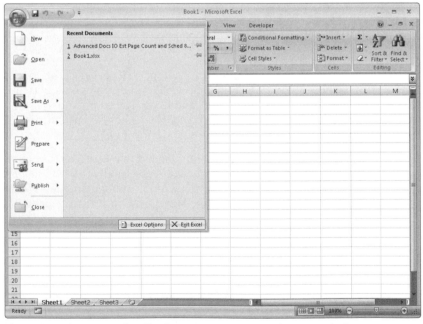

Figure 2-3 The Microsoft Office Button opens a menu of commands that you use to work with a document and its properties.

When you are composing a letter in Word or preparing a presentation in PowerPoint, you'll most often work with the standard tabs and commands on the Ribbon. You'll also use contextual tabs in addition to galleries and Live Preview. Examples of these elements are shown in Figure 2-4.

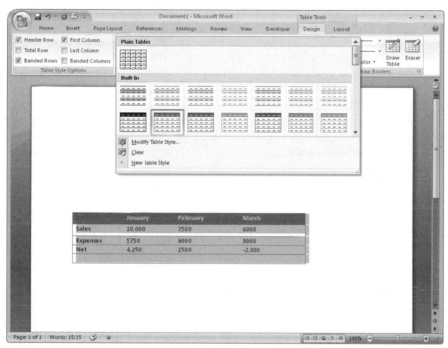

Figure 2-4 Tabs like the Table Tools tab in Word appear in context when you select an object. Many tabs provide galleries of formatting options that you can preview in your document.

- Contextual tabs appear on the Ribbon when you select an object such as a chart, an image, or a table. These tabs contain commands that relate specifically to the type of object.

- Galleries are sets of thumbnail graphics that represent a set of formatting options. You'll see galleries of table styles, backgrounds, and slide layouts, for example.

- Live Preview (which isn't easy to show in a static illustration) is a feature that works together with the styles in a gallery to let you preview the results of formatting choices. To acquaint yourself with Live Preview (and see an example of a gallery as well), create a simple worksheet in Excel. Click the Page Layout tab on the Ribbon, and then click Themes. Move your mouse over the items in the gallery, and watch how the formatting is dynamically updated in the worksheet.

The Ribbon, galleries, and Live Preview introduce fairly dramatic changes, not only with respect to the appearance of the Microsoft Office system user interface, but also in the ways people work with the programs. You'll see a few examples of this later in this chapter and many more examples throughout the rest of this book.

Two elements of the Microsoft Office user interface that many users are familiar with—the status bar and ScreenTips—have been updated as well, with the goals of providing better access to information and assistance with, and more control over, how you view the file you're working with.

- The status bar includes more controls and information, including a Zoom slider that you can use to adjust the magnification of a document. The change in magnification occurs as you move the slider, so you can pick the level you need to view the entire document or just an important section. The status bar also includes buttons for changing how you view your document—from Print Layout to Draft in Word, for example, or from Normal to Slide Show in PowerPoint. These controls appear at the right end of the status bar.

  You can right-click the status bar to reveal the Customize Status Bar menu that lists all the items of information that you can check on the status bar. In Excel 2007, for example, you can select options to show the sum, average, and count of the cells you've selected on a worksheet. You can remove the Zoom slider and the view shortcuts, and you can also see information such as whether a document's permissions have been restricted or whether the Caps Lock key is on.

- ScreenTips still appear when you move the pointer over a command; however, they now provide not only the name of the command, but also a brief description of the command's function. Many also contain a link to topics about the command in the Office online Help. Figure 2-5 shows an example of a new and improved ScreenTip.

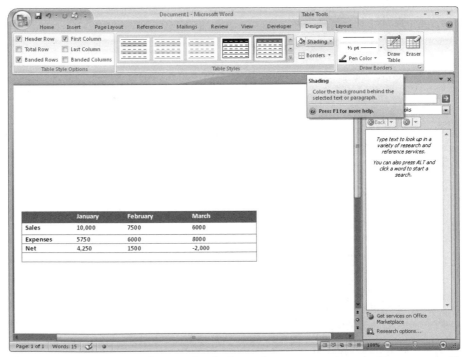

Figure 2-5 ScreenTips provide more details about what a command can do. You can press F1 when you're viewing a ScreenTip to open a Help topic about the command.

To reinforce what's new in the 2007 Office system user interface, Table 2-1 summarizes the elements introduced in this section (as well as a few more) and compares them to the corresponding features in Microsoft Office 2003.

Table 2-1 Comparison of the 2007 Office Release to Microsoft Office 2003

User Interface Elements in the 2007 Office Release	Corresponding Office 2003 User Interface Element
The Ribbon replaces menus and toolbars. The Ribbon is organized into tabs that represent the main functional areas of a program. When you select an object, such as a table or chart, contextual tabs appear on the Ribbon and provide commands relevant for the object.	Menus and toolbars
Most of the task panes you worked with in Office 2003 are replaced by groups of controls in the Ribbon. The few task panes that remain provide additional content to users. In the 2007 Office release, each task pane is its own separate pane. You can display multiple task panes, and you can arrange the position of each independently.	Task panes
Dialog boxes occur in the 2007 Office release, but they are not the main way of working with a program. The settings that users selected in dialog boxes, in many cases, are now assembled in gallery items so that users can see these options and choose the results they want. Dialog boxes can be opened from galleries or from the Ribbon for users who want to use them or when more advanced options are required.	Dialog boxes
Context (or shortcut) menus are still available in the 2007 Office release. Shortcut menus can, like the Ribbon, display galleries to make formatting more efficient.	Context menus
There is no change to keyboard shortcuts that use the Ctrl key in combination with another key, such as Ctrl+S for Save and Ctrl+B for Bold, or a single function key, such as F12 for Save As. The same shortcuts exist and continue to work as they did in Office 2003.	Office 2003 keyboard shortcuts
The 2007 Office release also includes a keyboard shortcut system for the Ribbon using the Alt key. Shortcut keys are displayed on Ribbon controls and tabs. You can also use the Alt key sequences from Office 2003. These work only for features that were in Office 2003; features of the 2007 Office release use only the new keyboard shortcuts.	Office 2003 keyboard shortcuts
In addition to displaying the task status, the status bar in the 2007 Office release displays information such as security warnings. Users can customize the status bar to show additional information about their document.	Status bar

Chapter 2

Let's start looking in more detail at the underlying concepts and how you can use and customize the 2007 Office release user interface. We'll start with the Ribbon and command tabs.

> **Note**
>
> Despite the changes in the appearance and organization of the Microsoft Office user interface, the mechanics of working with your computer are largely unchanged. You still use the mouse, the keyboard, a pen, or some other input device to perform the actions you need to take.

The Ribbon and Command Tabs

Simply put, Microsoft designed the Ribbon so that users could find commands more easily. The Ribbon displays a larger number of commands (fewer are hidden on toolbars that aren't displayed by default or buried in submenus), and the command tabs included on the Ribbon are organized to represent the main functional groups of each program. In Word 2007, for example, the Insert tab features commands that relate to the range of objects you might insert into a document, from graphics and shapes to hyperlinks, headers, and WordArt. The Page Layout tab, next in order on the Ribbon in Word, provides commands for organizing and formatting the page.

The Ribbon also groups commands, which helps show their relationship, and provides visual clues and labels that help users identify features. One visual device the Ribbon uses is button size. The Ribbon displays more frequently used commands in a larger button size and uses groups of smaller buttons to show secondary features that are designed to work together. Figure 2-6 shows the Data tab in Excel. Notice the groups of related commands—Get External Data, for example, or Sort & Filter. Notice, too, the different sizes of the buttons. Compare the size of the Filter button, which you use to perform quick filters, to the Advanced button in that group, which you probably don't use as often.

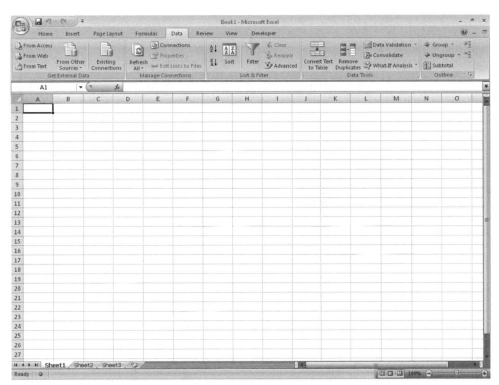

Figure 2-6 On the Ribbon, the size of command buttons calls attention to frequently used commands. Groups of commands show common functions and relationships.

The first tab on the Ribbon is the Home tab. (The Ribbon in Outlook 2007 is an exception in this regard. In Outlook, the first tab in a new message window is named Message; in a new appointment window, the first tab is called Appointment.) Figure 2-7 shows the collection of commands on the Home tab for PowerPoint 2007. The Home tab brings together a set of commands that users tend to work with most often, including the Paste command, for example, together with the Copy and Cut commands. The Home tab generally includes the commands that were part of the Standard and Formatting toolbars in previous releases of Microsoft Office. You can see in Figure 2-7 again how commands are grouped on the Ribbon. The group called Drawing includes a gallery of styles, as well as buttons for controlling a shape's fill, outline, and special effects.

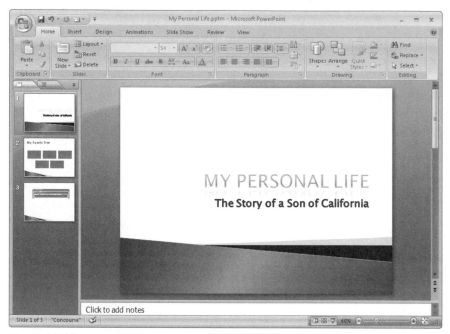

Figure 2-7 The commands on the Home tab are those you will use most often.

In previous releases of Microsoft Office, the whole of the user interface was designed for a base screen resolution of 800 × 600, without much consideration for how its elements would appear on higher or lower screen resolutions. On a lower resolution, say 640 × 480, elements that did not fit in the space available were moved to an overflow menu or required horizontal scrolling. If screen resolution didn't allow a button to appear on a toolbar, it lost its position and relationship to the commands around it.

In the 2007 Office release, the Ribbon's size and display properties adapt to a number of screen resolutions and fit even tablet-size screens. The buttons and other controls maintain their relative position on the Ribbon as well. The groups of controls that make up the Ribbon are designed in several different sizes. As screen resolution decreases, more of the smaller versions of the groups are used. A user with an 800 × 600 screen resolution will need to scroll to see more than 5 table design styles, but a user with a 1400 × 1050 screen resolution might see 15 styles in a single view.

Note

You can minimize the Ribbon to see more of a document by double-clicking the label for the active tab. Click the tab's label again to display the Ribbon.

Keyboard Shortcuts in the 2007 Office Release

Users who like to use keyboard shortcuts to accomplish their work in Office will be pleased to know that the shortcut keys that start with Ctrl have been retained in the 2007 Office release. The function keys have been retained as well. If you want, you can select a program setting to turn on the shortcut keys starting with Alt that are used in Office 2003.

In addition to the keyboard shortcuts from Office 2003, every control displayed in the 2007 Office release user interface includes an associated Key Tip. You can display all available Key Tips by pressing Alt. Press the Key Tip for the tab that includes the control and then the Key Tip for the control itself. The Key Tips for commands on the Insert tab in Word are shown here.

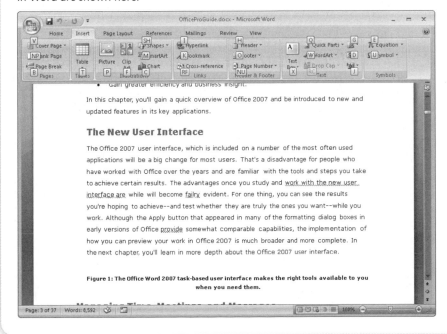

Customizing the Quick Access Toolbar

The 2007 Office release didn't abandon toolbars entirely. In the Quick Tour section earlier in this chapter, you saw the Quick Access Toolbar, which, by default, contains a handful of commands (some vary from program to program). You can also customize the Quick Action Toolbar so that it contains the set of commands you want closest at hand.

Let's say your work often involves designing Excel workbooks that other users fill out to prepare a budget or an expense report. You often apply data validation rules to the workbooks you produce so that you obtain a consistent set of data that can be analyzed more easily. You can add commands for the data validation tools to the Quick Access Toolbar so they are within immediate reach.

You can add as many commands as you want to the Quick Access Toolbar. You can select commands from the standard commands tab on the Ribbon, as well as commands from contextual tabs. Reason would argue, however, that being practical in the number of commands you add to the Quick Access Toolbar maximizes its usefulness. For example, the Standard toolbar in Word 2003 has something like 25 buttons and controls. Adding more than 25 commands to the Quick Access Toolbar might begin to diminish its usefulness because you'll need to take time to find the command you're looking for. You can, however, work with more than one configuration of the Quick Access Toolbar. You can set up the Quick Access Toolbar with a group of commands that you want to use with a specific document and use another group (your default set) for other documents. Customizations that you make to the Quick Access Toolbar are like any other changes you make to that document; you must save the document for the customizations to remain. If you don't save the document, the Quick Access Toolbar will return to the default configuration the next time you open the document.

To customize the Quick Access Toolbar, follow these steps:

1. Click the down arrow at the right end of the toolbar.

2. From the Customize Quick Access Toolbar menu, select a command that you want to add or click More Commands to display the dialog box shown next.

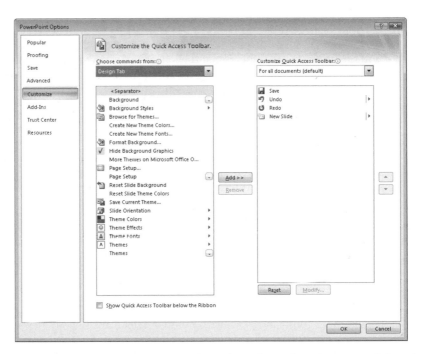

3. In the Choose Commands From drop-down list, select the name of the tab (including standard and contextual tabs) that contains the command you want to add. (You'll learn more about the commands on the Office menu later in this chapter.)

4. In the list of commands, click the name of the command you want to add, and then click Add. (Of course, you can remove commands from the Quick Access Toolbar as well.) After you have assembled the set of commands that you want on the toolbar, use the Move Up and Move Down arrow buttons to reorder the buttons if you want.

5. In the Customize Quick Access Toolbar drop-down list, choose whether to apply this customization to all documents (the default) or to the active document.

> **Note**
>
> You can also right-click a command on the Ribbon to add it to the Quick Access Toolbar.

The Microsoft Office Button and Menu

You no longer see the label *File* at the left side of a Microsoft Office program's application window, but the Microsoft Office applications that display the new user interface still require the familiar File menu commands—New, Open, Save, Save As, Print, and others—that you use to manage documents and other files. You now display these commands by clicking the Microsoft Office Button, which is located in the upper-left corner of the application window (see Figure 2-1 earlier in this chapter).

In addition to finding basic commands such as Save and Print on this menu, you'll notice commands named Prepare, Send, and Publish. The Send command has two subcommands—E-Mail and Internet Fax. You can use these commands to distribute a document, spreadsheet, or presentation using either of these methods.

The Publish command provides options for packaging a PowerPoint presentation on a CD, for example, or saving it to a slide library. In Word, the Publish command includes an option for posting the content of your document as a blog. Other options available through the Publish command let you share a document by using a document management server or through a document workspace that's part of a Microsoft Windows SharePoint Services Web site.

The Prepare command provides a number of features that are new in the 2007 Office release. Several have to do with document permissions and the security of your content—commands such as Inspect Document and Add A Digital Signature. You'll learn more about these commands and other security issues in Chapter 3, "Managing Security and Privacy in the 2007 Office System."

The Run Compatibility Checker command scans a file you've created in one of the 2007 Office release programs to see whether it contains any features that are not supported by earlier versions of the program. Checking compatibility is particularly important in the case of Excel, PowerPoint, and Word, which by default use the Microsoft Office Open XML file formats.

For more information on the Office Open XML file formats, see Chapter 1, "Overview of the 2007 Microsoft Office System." For an introduction to XML, see Chapter 32, "Office Open XML Essentials."

The Microsoft Office Button is also the new entry point to the Options dialog box, where you can select program settings and other options and preferences. Figure 2-8 shows the Popular category in the Options dialog box for Excel.

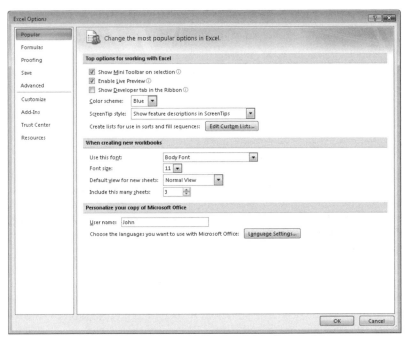

Figure 2-8 The Microsoft Office Button leads to the Options dialog box. You can use this dialog box to customize the Quick Access Toolbar and to set security and other preferences.

The Popular category lets you control several aspects of the 2007 release user interface. As you can see in Figure 2-8, the category includes options such as enabling Live Preview, setting the application's color scheme, and specifying which view should be used by default.

The Advanced category lets you manage specific operations and behaviors of an application. For Excel, this category provides options for how you edit a cell, whether to use AutoComplete, what happens when you press Enter, and similar types of details. In Word the same category controls whether formatting changes are tracked when Track Revisions is enabled, whether text can be dragged and dropped, and other similar behaviors.

You'll learn more about options for the specific applications in Parts 3 through 7 of this book. You'll learn more about the Trust Center in Chapter 3.

The Office menu, as the File menu did, also lists the documents you've worked on most recently. In the 2007 Office release, this list is now able to show 20 or more files. Notice the pushpin icon that appears next to the file names in the list. You can "set" the pushpin for a particular file if you want that file to remain in the Recent Documents list even when the file would otherwise fall off. To set the pushpin, place your pointer over the icon, wait for the message to appear, and then click the pin.

Working in Context: More Tabs, Plus Some Menus and Toolbars

People who have worked regularly with recent versions of Microsoft Office applications have grown used to the features and commands that you can use in context. The best example is the shortcut menu, also called the context or the right-click menu, which provides a set of commands related to an object you've selected—a block of text, a table, or some other type of object—or to your current context (as when you right-click the Windows desktop).

One of the central design principles of the 2007 release user interface is to display commands that relate to the context in which you are working. Shortcut menus are still used for this purpose (even with the improvements and efficiencies that the Ribbon presents, shortcut menus are often a more direct way of working with a feature or a command), as are elements called contextual tabs and the Mini toolbar.

In this section, we'll look in more detail at how the 2007 release user interface supports working in context. You'll learn a little more about contextual tabs, which appear on the Ribbon when you work on a particular type of object, and we'll describe the Mini toolbar, a collection of command buttons that often accompany a shortcut menu and that also appear when you select a block of text such as a paragraph or a heading for a slide in PowerPoint.

> **Note**
>
> Contextual tabs are displayed on the Ribbon not only when you select a specific type of object but also to support specific views. For example, when you view a Word document in Outline view, a tab with outlining commands is displayed.

Contextual Tabs

Some commands and sets of commands aren't needed until a specific type of object is inserted or needs to be edited or formatted. You don't need to wade through the commands required to edit a chart, for example, until you've inserted a chart in your spreadsheet or presentation. In Excel (or other 2007 Office release programs with the new user interface), clicking a chart (or an object such as a table or an image) displays additional tabs on the Ribbon that make available commands used to edit and format the chart. Contextual tabs appear only when they are needed. When a user cancels the selection of the object, the contextual tabs disappear. Having a set of specific commands available on demand, as it were, gives you more room on your screen to work and makes finding commands needed for a specific operation easier. In a more obvious manner than the standard tabs, contextual tabs concentrate the commands related to a particular functional area. Examples of objects that display contextual tabs when you select them are tables, pictures, text boxes, shapes, charts, WordArt, equations, diagrams, PivotTables, headers, and footers. Any item that appears as an object and is capable of being selected displays a contextual tab.

INSIDE OUT   Formatting in Three Stages

In the research and usability studies Microsoft conducted as part of designing the 2007 Office release user interface, they watched users who were formatting various types of documents. Most users applied formatting in three stages: selecting an overall design, modifying visual attributes of the design, and then modifying specific elements, such as a text box or a heading. You can see these principles in play in the way Microsoft designed the user interface for the 2007 release. When a user inserts an object, for example, the Ribbon displays a contextual tab for that object and provides the user with a gallery of styles that can be applied to it. The user can then modify formats such as shadows, fill patterns, or border styles that were defined in the style the user selected from the gallery. As a third step, the user can apply more detailed formatting to a heading, for example, or to the column headings in a table, using other commands on the contextual tab or by opening a formatting dialog box.

The same type of Ribbon layouts and controls are available on a contextual tab as on one of a program's standard tabs. Figure 2-9 shows the commands on the Table Tools tab, the contextual tab that appears when you select a table in Excel.

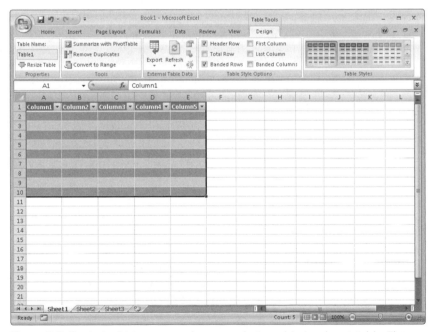

Figure 2-9 Contextual tabs appear when you select an object such as a table. They provide commands for working with the type of object you've selected.

> **Note**
>
> You can also edit and format an object such as a table or chart by using a shortcut menu that is displayed when you right-click the object. The shortcut menu includes commands for the most common tasks related to the type of object. These commands and others are also included on the corresponding contextual tab.

Shortcut Menus and the Mini Toolbar

The type of shortcut menu that many users of Microsoft Office programs (and Windows applications in general) have grown fond of is still an active and integral element in the 2007 release user interface. These menus, which appear when you right-click an object, your desktop, or the background of a document, present a set of commands that apply to the selected object or to the area of a window in which you're working.

In certain situations, shortcut menus have some shortcomings. For example, shortcut menus aren't efficient when you need to apply a command repeatedly or in situations in which you need to work with more than one option at the same time such as changing the font from Arial to Century Gothic (or another font), increasing the font size from 12 to 16, and applying bold to the text of the heading you're changing.

To account for situations such as these, many shortcut menus in the 2007 release have added what Microsoft calls the Mini toolbar, which is shown in Figure 2-10. When you click a command on the Mini toolbar, the shortcut menu vanishes but the toolbar remains visible on the screen. You can use the toolbar to apply several commands without having to right-click a second or third time to display the shortcut menu again.

The Mini toolbar is also displayed when you select text in a document—or at least it begins to show itself. When you select text, the shadowy outline of the Mini toolbar appears near your pointer. If you move the pointer toward the outline of the toolbar, it solidifies its appearance and displays commands such as bold, italic, font color, and bullets. If you move the pointer away from the toolbar, roll the scroll wheel, or press a key or mouse button, the Mini toolbar disappears.

> **Note**
>
> If you'd rather not see the Mini toolbar when you select text, click the Microsoft Office Button, and then click the button for the Options dialog box. In the Popular category, clear the Show Mini Toolbar On Selection check box. This option applies only to the application you are working with—it is not a general setting for the 2007 Office release. The Mini toolbar will still appear as part of a shortcut menu.

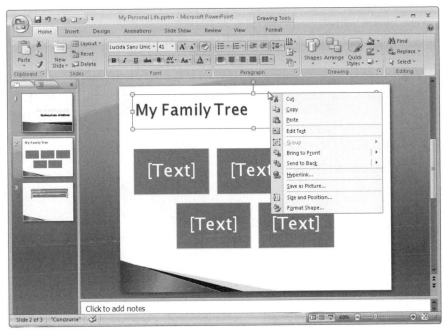

Figure 2-10 The Mini toolbar complements shortcut menus by providing common formatting commands.

Galleries and Live Preview

Microsoft states that the design of the 2007 Office release user interface reflects a results-oriented approach to the work you do with documents, spreadsheets, databases, and the like. You can see how this approach was developed in the way the Ribbon is designed and organized, in the use of contextual tabs, and in tools such as the Mini toolbar. Two other important components of the results-oriented design are galleries and Live Preview. Galleries and Live Preview help users at all skill levels—even those with minimal experience working in a Microsoft Office application—get results that are well coordinated and that have the appearance of being professionally developed. Take a look at Figure 2-11, for example, which shows you a slice of the gallery of themes that you can apply in Excel.

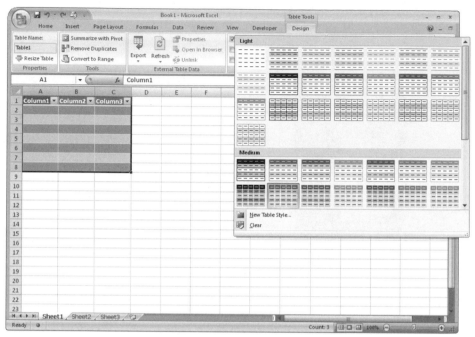

Figure 2-11 Galleries provide collections of styles that you can apply to your document.

The steps required to apply a theme such as these in Office 2003, for example, would have required a user to specify attributes such as font, background fills, borders, and so on. A user would have had to traverse several tabs in a dialog box and then return to make adjustments if the look was not right or needed to be updated. More advanced users can still use the dialog box to apply formatting to specific aspects of a document's appearance, but you are no longer required to learn all the steps involved. For some users, those with more experience, galleries may serve mostly as a timesaving device. For users with less experience, galleries make available many of the advanced features and formatting capabilities in Microsoft Office that until now these users couldn't take advantage of.

Galleries also support Live Preview, a feature you can experience only when you are working in one of the 2007 Office release applications that implement the feature. Live Preview shows you how one of the thumbnail representations or choices in a gallery will appear throughout your document or will affect the appearance of the object you're working with. The document or object's appearance changes as you move the pointer from one item in the gallery to the next. Live Preview, and galleries in general, cuts down on the amount of hands-on experimentation you need to do to get the results you want. Instead, you can see the effects of several alternatives quite rapidly, select the one you want to use, and then fine-tune that style, if necessary, to enhance specific elements.

> **Note**
>
> After you apply a style from a gallery, you can make modifications to that style, but you cannot edit or modify one of the default styles included in a gallery. You can add styles that you define to some galleries. For example, you can modify or define a table style in Word and then save the style with its own name in the Table Style gallery. The items you add to a gallery are listed separately from the gallery's built-in items. For example, a custom table style is listed in the Custom section of the Table Style gallery.

> **Are You Missing Your Favorite Old Dialog Box?**
>
> In previous releases of Microsoft Office, dialog boxes often provided more advanced options for common features. The Font dialog box in Word is an example. It contained font effects well beyond bold, italic, and underline, which could be applied using toolbar buttons. Dialog boxes are still an important part of the 2007 Office release—just not as important or as central as they once were. Dialog boxes continue to be an excellent way to adjust a number of advanced settings at one time, and they also serve as a way to collect input from users. Defining a complicated sort in Excel, for example, is the type of operation that is still best suited for a dialog box in which you enter criteria for each level of the sort. Most command groups on tabs on the Ribbon include a small arrow button in the lower-right corner. You can click this button to open a dialog box related to the group of commands, many of which will be familiar to experienced users of Microsoft Office.

Getting Help

Online help for any software program, whether part of the Microsoft Office system or not, has always been an important element of the interface that the program presents to its users. For many users, it's an essential component of a program, and how it's presented and how you interact with it—not to mention the ease with which you can find information—are important considerations.

In Chapter 1, you learned about Microsoft Office Online, which is itself a key component of the online Help system that Microsoft Office offers. In this chapter, you learned as well how the online Help system has been made more accessible by including links to it in the ScreenTips that the 2007 Office release provides. We'll close this chapter by reviewing in more detail how to use the Microsoft Office online Help system, some alternatives you have for obtaining help, and how you can control and manage the online Help window.

Searching Online Help

Figure 2-12 shows the Help window for Access. Notice the label in the lower-right area of the window that reads Connected To Office Online. This label indicates your connection status. If you're working on a computer that's connected to the Internet, you can search the resources that Office Online provides when you need assistance. If you're not connected to the Internet, you can search the Help files that Microsoft Office installs on your computer. If you don't want to show content from Office Online, click the connection status label, and select Show Content Only From This Computer.

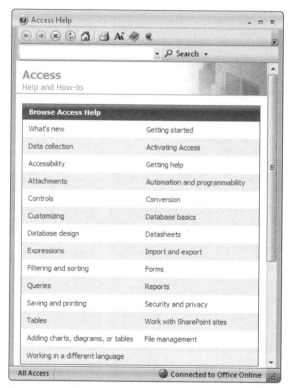

Figure 2-12 Use the connection status label at the bottom of the Help window to control where you search for online Help.

When you are searching Office Online, you also have a choice of what type of help to search for—Help topics, templates, training, or all of these categories together. (You can also include the developer reference for a Microsoft Office program if that information is what you need.) You control the scope and the location of your search by opening the Search menu using the down arrow. The menu is shown in Figure 2-13. Defining the scope and location simply involves selecting an item from the menu. To search for information about a specific term or topic, type the term or topic in the Search box, and then click Search.

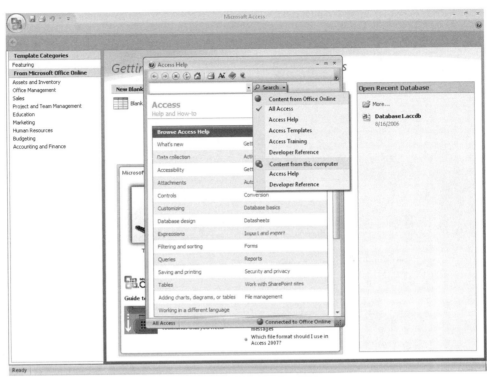

Figure 2-13 The online Help for the 2007 Office release includes materials and resources from Office Online and content that is stored on your computer.

You can adjust the size and position of the Help window, as well as elect to keep the Help window "on top" so that it remains visible and easily accessible even while you are performing work in an application. Other options for viewing the Help window include displaying the table of contents, which will be displayed in a pane to the left of the topic window. The other controls at the top of the Help window resemble those in an Internet browser—a Back and a Forward button, a Stop and a Refresh button, and a Home button.

Managing Security and Privacy in the 2007 Office System

The security of your computer and the privacy of the information you store and transmit using it are of vital concern. How many news stories have you read about computers under attack? Any number of worms, viruses, malware, and the like can do harm to your computer and the data on it. How many stories have you heard about the mistaken disclosure of personal data—or about data not so mistakenly stolen—from large data stores in which confidential and private information of all sorts is stored?

Personal computers, software, and information technology in general have made communications between people much faster, made many workers more productive, and opened opportunities for commerce and leisure in lots of ways. But to offset benefits such as these are problems like spam, identity theft, and information leaks. Computer users and administrators who manage networks and computer systems are more concerned than ever about security and privacy. You may be familiar, for example, with the need to control when a macro can run. Macros are helpful because you can use them to automate repetitive and common tasks, but macros can pose a security risk because the program code they contain can rapidly run through a series of commands and possibly introduce or spread a virus on your computer.

In this chapter, we'll take a look at some of the security and privacy features in the 2007 Microsoft Office release. Many of these features apply to any and all of the 2007 Office release programs that you work with. Others are more specific and relate to one or just a few of the programs. To start, we'll take a look at the Trust Center, which you use to specify how to manage the types of programs and situations that can make your computer and your information more vulnerable.

Working in the Trust Center

In the 2007 Office release, you use the Trust Center to manage security and privacy settings for Microsoft Office applications. The Trust Center provides options related to the specific application you're using—settings for how you want to control connections to external data in Microsoft Office Excel 2007 spreadsheets, for example—as well as settings that apply to how the 2007 Office system in general handles certain security and privacy concerns.

To open the Trust Center in the 2007 Office release programs Word, Excel, PowerPoint, or Access, follow these steps:

1. Click the Microsoft Office Button, and then click Options. (Options will be preceded by the name of the particular program; for example, Access Options.)

2. Click Trust Center.

3. To update and set options in the Trust Center, click Trust Center Settings.

To open the Trust Center in Microsoft Visio, Microsoft Outlook, Microsoft Publisher, or Microsoft InfoPath, follow these steps:

1. On the Tools menu, click Trust Center.

2. Click the security category that you want to work with.

Figure 3-1 shows the Trust Center window for Word 2007. It provides links to privacy options, general security settings for Microsoft Windows, and the Trust Center Settings button.

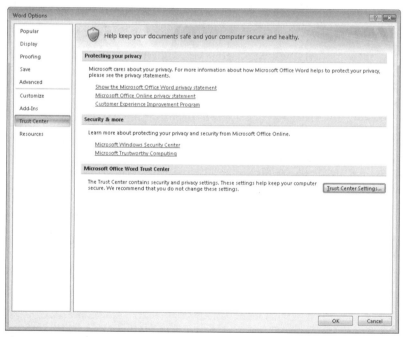

Figure 3-1 The Trust Center provides links to privacy settings and several pages that you use to manage security settings for macros, add-ins, and other potential security threats.

For more information about privacy options, see "Setting Your Privacy Options" later on page 58.

Click Trust Center Settings to display the pages that you use to manage the specific security settings for macros, privacy options, and other security areas. The Macro Settings page for Word 2007 is shown in Figure 3-2. As you can see, the Trust Center is organized into a number of categories—Add-Ins, ActiveX Settings, Privacy Options, and so on. Each category is identified on the left side of the window. Click a label to display the settings and options for that category. The labels and options in other 2007 Office release applications are the same or similar in most cases. We'll look in more detail at a number of the options in these categories later in this section and in the sections ahead.

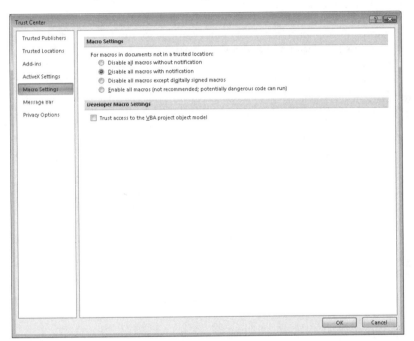

Figure 3-2 The Trust Center includes pages with specific security options for macros, add-ins, ActiveX controls, and other settings.

Note

In Excel 2007, the Trust Center includes an area named External Content. You use this section to specify options for managing connections to external data (a link to a Microsoft Access database or a Microsoft SQL Server database, for example) that are included in an Excel workbook. This area of the Excel Trust Center also lets you specify security settings for links to other Excel workbooks. Three choices are presented in each case—trust all connections or links (which Microsoft doesn't recommend), receive a notification (a prompt) when you're working with a connection or link (the default choice), or to disable all connections or links, which would probably affect the experience of many users who rely on these features.

Chapter 3

Digital Signatures and Trusted Publishers

Many users of the Microsoft Office system rely on macros that they (or possibly a coworker) create to help them perform and complete routine tasks more quickly. Similarly, an add-in can supplement the features and capabilities of a Microsoft Office application. These types of programs, however, can also do a lot of damage to your computer and your data if the program code they contain is designed for malicious purposes. You don't want to run these types of programs without knowing who developed and provided them to you in the first place.

For more information about Trust Center settings for macros and add-ins, see "Setting Security Options for Macros and Add-Ins" on page 54.

Security options for macros and add-ins are related to digital signatures and trusted publishers. A digital signature is used to authenticate documents, e-mail messages, and macros through cryptography. Digital signatures help assure you that whoever signed the program (the publisher) is who they claim to be and that the content included in the program has not been modified or tampered with since it was digitally signed. A digital signature essentially proves the origin of the signed goods.

A publisher is a software developer (Microsoft, an independent software vendor, or someone in your company or department) who has created a macro, add-in, or other type of application extension that you and others will use with Microsoft Office applications. The Trust Center lets you compile a list of publishers that you trust—those publishers whose digital signatures are valid and current and whose code you allow to run.

Here's the information that a publisher has to provide to the security apparatus of Microsoft Office to be considered trustworthy:

- The program (a code project like a macro or an add-in) must include the digital signature of the developer.

- The signature must be valid, current, and issued by a reputable certificate authority.

- The publisher must be included on your list of trusted publishers.

> **Note**
>
> A certificate authority is a commercial entity that issues digital certificates. They know which publishers have been assigned to specific certificates; they sign certificates to attest to their validity; and they keep track of which certificates are current and which have expired. Two of the better known certificate authorities are Certisign and VeriSign.

If a macro or an add-in is digitally signed by one of your trusted publishers in the manner that the Trust Center requires, all goes according to plan. You can run the code without further intervention because you know that it comes from an entity that you trust. But if the Trust Center doesn't detect that all these criteria have been met when you begin to run an add-in or a macro, the program is considered to be potentially unsafe, and you'll see an alert in the Message Bar that notifies you of this fact, as shown in Figure 3-3.

Figure 3-3　You're alerted to a potentially unsafe macro or add-in in the Message Bar.

When you see such an alert, click Options on the Message Bar to display the dialog box shown in Figure 3-4. In the dialog box, you can see an explanation of why the macro was blocked. When a security dialog box such as the one shown in Figure 3-4 appears, you can leave the macro disabled, enable the macro, or choose to trust the publisher by clicking Trust All Documents From This Publisher. You should enable the macro only if you are sure that it comes from a source that you trust. The option to trust the publisher appears only if the digital signature is valid. Clicking this option means that all software that comes from this publisher will be trusted from this point on.

Figure 3-4　The security dialog box provides an option to add a publisher to your trusted publisher's list.

Chapter 3

> **Note**
>
> If you receive a warning indicating that no digital signature is present or that the signature is invalid, you should not enable the content or trust the publisher unless you are sure that the code comes from a trustworthy source. For example, if the document that contains the macro was sent to you in e-mail, be sure you know who the sender is and maybe even check that they sent the message. If not, contact the source of the document for more information.

If you aren't sure which option to choose, you can look at the details of the signature and the certificate that was used to create it to see whether there are any potential problems. Click Show Signature Details in the Security Options dialog box, and you'll see the Digital Signature Details dialog box, shown in Figure 3-5. A valid digital signature is identified by a message at the top of the dialog box, where the digital signature is identified as okay. You should also note the timestamp details in the Countersignatures frame. These details indicate that the certificate authority—in this example, VeriSign—has verified and approved the digital signature. The date for the timestamp (June 24, 2005, in this example) should be a date that falls within the valid date range for the certificate. To see the date range for the certificate, click View Certificate. The publisher should also be a trusted publisher. If the publisher is not trusted by default, you must explicitly trust it. If you don't, the content signed by that publisher does not pass the security checks.

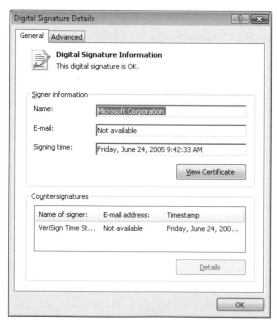

Figure 3-5 Review the details of a digital signature in the Digital Signature Details dialog box.

A digital signature that presents problems will be identified with a red X. The red X can appear for the following reasons:

- The digital signature is invalid. For example, the content has been altered since it was signed.

- This digital signature has expired.

- The certificate associated with the digital signature was not issued by a certificate authority.

- The publisher is not trusted.

When there is a problem with a digital signature, you should contact the source of the signed content or the administrator or department that is responsible for your organization's computer security. If you think that the macro or other program is trustworthy, you can save the document to a trusted location. (You'll learn more about working with trusted locations later in the chapter.) Documents that are stored in a trusted location—like the code that comes from a trusted publisher—are allowed to run without being checked by the Trust Center.

Content from the Outside

External content—content from the outside—is any content that is linked from the Internet or an intranet to an Excel workbook or a PowerPoint presentation. Scam artists can use external content to steal your personal information or to run malicious code on your computer without your knowledge or consent. To help protect your security and privacy, the 2007 Office system blocks external content such as images, linked media, hyperlinks, and data connections in Excel workbooks and PowerPoint presentations. If your workbook or presentation contains external content, when you try to open the file the Message Bar notifies you that the data connection has been disabled.. You will not be able to view or edit the content in your workbook or presentation. If you click Options on the Message Bar, a security dialog box appears, giving you the option to enable the external content. You should only unblock the content if you are sure that it is from a trustworthy source.

Using Trusted Locations

Settings in the Trust Center let you specify to what degree you will trust a file that contains code in a macro, an add-in, or another type of application extension. A *trusted location*, as mentioned earlier, is a folder or document location that Microsoft Office applications such as Word, Excel, PowerPoint, Access, and Visio use to trust documents, allowing the documents to open and run code that they include without notifying you. Figure 3-6 shows the Trusted Locations page of the Trust Center in Excel. You can see that several trusted locations are already defined. These refer to default locations that Microsoft Office creates for storing templates and files that run when you start an application.

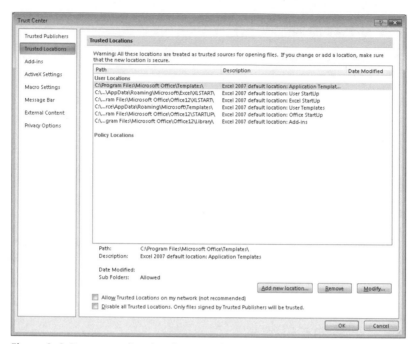

Figure 3-6 Documents listed under Trusted Locations run any code they contain without notification.

Adding a trusted location to the list that the 2007 Office release provides is a decision you should consider carefully, especially if you're thinking of setting up a remote location, such as a server share or a Microsoft Windows SharePoint Services document library or slide library as a trusted location. Notice, for example, that the option Allow Trusted Locations On My Network is not selected by default and is not recommended. You need to be thoughtful because the code included in any document that is stored in a trusted location will run without challenge by Microsoft Office. (Administrators can restrict which locations can be trusted on client computers and what types of locations can be added, so you might not be able to designate every location you want as a trusted location.) Any location that you trust needs to be managed with restricted access so that only those people who are authorized to publish documents and code can use the location.

Trusting all documents that are stored in a particular folder might seem risky, but having the ability to create a single trusted location for all the files you want to work with on a specific project, for example, or simply files that you work with regularly can provide better security. For one thing, it lets you keep security settings that apply to documents not stored in a trusted location at a more restrictive level. In other words, you're not tempted to use less restrictive security settings more widely. Documents stored in a trusted location are trusted for macro code (written in Visual Basic for Applications) and can also update data from remote sources automatically. These documents can initialize ActiveX controls, use add-ins, and so on. Once documents are tucked safely away in a trusted location, they run without displaying security prompts.

> **Note**
>
> Certain folders that are considered high risk, such as the Outlook cache for attachments, the Temp folder, and others in which documents are sometimes stored temporarily, cannot be used as a trusted location.

The steps to add, modify, or remove a trusted location are straightforward in themselves. To create a trusted location, click Add New Location (shown in Figure 3-6), and then fill in the dialog box shown in Figure 3-7. You need to specify the path to the location and select a couple of other options. To modify a location (for example, to specify that subfolders of a location can be trusted along with the parent folder), click Modify. Click Remove to delete a trusted location.

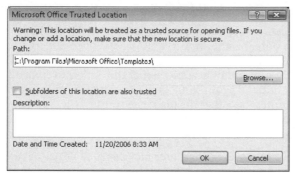

Figure 3-7 You can use this dialog box to add a trusted location or to modify the settings for one that is already set up.

> **Don't Forget Security Updates**
>
> Microsoft Update is a service that delivers updated files and downloads for Windows, Microsoft Office, and other Microsoft programs. Updates often address security vulnerabilities or update features that can help keep your computer secure. In Windows Control Panel, you can choose options for installing updates from Microsoft Update (listed as Automatic Updates). You can choose to install updates automatically or use one of the options that let you decide when to download and install the updates yourself. Of course, you can also choose not to get updates, but that choice means you might miss a critical security patch. (To change your Automatic Updates settings, you must be logged on to Windows with an administrator account.) You can also periodically check for updates for a 2007 Office release program. In Access, Excel, PowerPoint, or Word, click the Microsoft Office Button, and then click Options. Click Resources, and then click Get Updates. If you're working in InfoPath, Microsoft OneNote, Outlook, Publisher, Microsoft Project, SharePoint Designer, or Visio, on the Help menu, click Check For Updates. You can then follow the directions on the Microsoft Update site.

Setting Security Options for Macros and Add-Ins

If you've worked with security settings in Microsoft Office 2003 (using the Security dialog box), you're probably familiar with the settings Very High, High, Medium, and Low. These settings control when macros can run in an Office 2003 application. The Medium setting, for example, lets you choose which macros to run. The High setting allows you to run only those macros that come from trusted sources.

Like the Trust Center in the 2007 Office release, the Office 2003 Security dialog box lets you see your list of trusted publishers. This area of the dialog box includes an option that lets you trust all the add-ins and templates that are installed on your computer.

The Trust Center in the 2007 Office release has replaced these settings with more descriptive ones. In the Trust Center, you can make specific designations for how to handle add-ins, for example, as well as macro settings. As a summary of these settings, and in the event that you want to select security settings to match those you used in Office 2003, Table 3-1 compares the security settings in Office 2003 with those for macros and add-ins in the 2007 Office release. For Office 2003, the table lists the level from the Security dialog box and indicates whether the option to trust all add-ins and templates was selected or not. For the 2007 Office release, the table lists which setting to select in the Trust Center (on either the Macro Settings or the Add-Ins page) and whether you need to select an option regarding trusted locations, which appears on the Trusted Locations page in the Trust Center.

Table 3-1 Comparison of Microsoft Office 2003 and the 2007 Office System Security Settings for Macros and Add-Ins

Microsoft Office 2003		2007 Office System
Level	**Trust all installed add-ins and templates?**	
Very High	Yes	Macro Setting: Disable all macros without notification
Very High	No	Macro Setting: Disable all macros without notification Add-Ins Setting: Disable all application add-ins
High	Yes	Macro Setting: Disable all macros with notification
High	No	Macro Setting: Disable all macros with notification Add-Ins Setting: Require application add-ins to be signed by trusted publisher Disable notification for unsigned add-ins (code will remain disabled) Trusted Locations: Disable all trusted locations; only files signed by trusted publishers will be trusted

Microsoft Office 2003		2007 Office System
Medium	Yes	The default settings in the 2007 Office system match this
		Macro Setting: Disable all macros with notification
Medium	No	Macro Setting: Disable all macros with notification
		Add-Ins Setting: Require application add-ins to be signed by trusted publisher
		Trusted Locations: Disable all trusted locations; only files signed by trusted publishers will be trusted
Low	N/A	Macro Setting: Enable all macros (not recommended; potentially dangerous code can run)

Digitally Signing a Macro Project

To test macro projects on your own computer, you can create a self-signing certificate using a tool called Selfcert.exe. (You can run this tool from the Start menu by selecting Digital Certificate For VBA Projects under Microsoft Office Tools.) Microsoft Office trusts a self-signed certificate only on a computer that has that certificate in the Personal Certificates store. Keep in mind that a digital certificate you create isn't issued by a formal certificate authority. To obtain a digital certificate for signing macros or add-ins you want to share, you need to obtain a digital certificate from a commercial certificate authority. You might also be able to obtain a certificate from your internal security administrator or network administrator.

To create your own digital certificate, click the Start button, point to All Programs, click Microsoft Office, click Microsoft Office Tools, and then click Digital Certificate For VBA Projects. (These steps vary slightly depending on which version of Windows you are using: Windows XP or Windows Vista.) In the Create Digital Certificate dialog box, shown here, enter a name for the certificate, and then click OK. When the certificate confirmation message appears, click OK again.

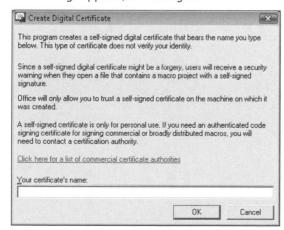

You can then view the certificate in the Personal Certificates store in Microsoft Internet Explorer. (On the Tools menu, click Internet Options, and then click the Content tab. Click Certificates, and then click the Personal tab.)

To digitally sign a macro project, first open the file that contains the project you want to sign. Open the Visual Basic Editor. (You might need to display the Developer tab in Word, Excel, or PowerPoint before you open the Visual Basic Editor.) In the Visual Basic Project pane of the editor, select the project that you want to sign. On the Tools menu, click Digital Signature. If you haven't previously selected a digital certificate or want to use another one, click Choose, select the certificate, and then click OK twice. To use the current certificate, click OK.

You should sign macros only after you have tested your macro or other program because whenever the code in a signed macro project is changed, the digital signature is removed. If you have the valid digital certificate that was used to sign the project on your computer, the macro project is automatically re-signed when you save it. When you digitally sign macros, it is important to obtain a timestamp so that other users can verify your signature even after the certificate used for the signature has expired. If you sign macros without a timestamp, the signature remains valid only for the period of time that your certificate is valid.

Security Settings for ActiveX Controls

An ActiveX control, which might be provided in a text box or on a toolbar, runs in programs such as Internet Explorer and Microsoft Office applications. They can provide additional functions to a program by responding to user input or to changes in the state of a Web page. But because ActiveX controls can access your file system and change settings for the operating system, an ActiveX control can, in effect, take over your computer and damage it.

Figure 3-8 shows the ActiveX Settings page in the Trust Center for PowerPoint. You'll see that the settings here are similar to those for macros and add-ins. You can choose to let these controls run without notification (probably not the wisest choice), disable all controls (which means you have to do without the benefits these controls provide), or impose a level of restriction that helps you weed out the ActiveX controls that could potentially do you harm.

Microsoft has provided developers with guidance for how to make the ActiveX controls they create more secure. The Trust Center also examines an ActiveX control that's part of a document to check whether it contains any well-known indicators that would flag it as potentially unsafe. The Trust Center checks, for example, whether the controls have been marked (digitally signed) as being Safe For Initialization (SFI).

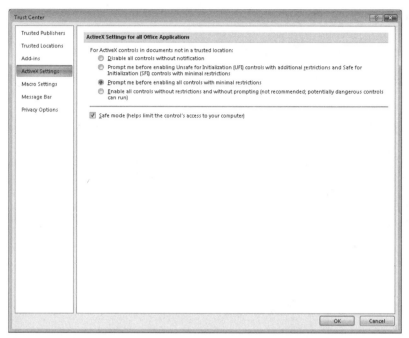

Figure 3-8 The Trust Center provides security settings for ActiveX controls.

The Trust Center also checks the document that contains the ActiveX control. If the document contains a Visual Basic for Applications (VBA) project, the Trust Center is more restrictive because the document contains both macros and ActiveX controls. As it does with a potentially unsafe macro, the Trust Center displays a warning when an ActiveX control is present and lets you choose whether to enable the control or not.

 For the most part, you can probably leave the default setting for ActiveX controls selected. With this setting, you'll receive a prompt asking you to enable any ActiveX control. The first and fourth settings shown in Figure 3-8—that is, disabling or enabling all controls—are either too restrictive or not restrictive enough. The second setting, which refers to SFI controls as well as those considered Unsafe For Initialization (UFI) provides some flexibility in when and how a control is enabled. In a document that contains a VBA project—meaning that a macro project is present—this setting initially prevents all ActiveX controls from running. When you open a document, you're notified about the presence of an ActiveX control. If you choose to enable the control, a UFI ActiveX control is loaded with additional restrictions. An SFI ActiveX control is loaded with minimal restrictions.

In a document that doesn't contain a VBA project, SFI ActiveX controls are enabled with minimal restrictions. The Message Bar doesn't appear, and you won't see any notifications about the presence of ActiveX controls in your documents. However, if there is at least one UFI ActiveX control in the document, you are notified, and any UFI ActiveX controls are disabled.

Setting Your Privacy Options

An important part of privacy is ensuring that your personal information—your e-mail address, a credit card account number, even just your name—is known only to the people you decide to give it to and only in the places where you want it. These days, protecting your privacy can also mean avoiding unwanted advertising or marketing—a lot of which comes across the Internet.

One of the assumptions that underlie the design of the 2007 Office system is that users of the programs are connected to the Internet while they work or have regular access to the Internet. Microsoft has built in certain services that rely on users being connected, services such as displaying updated templates from Microsoft Office Online, up-to-date online Help content, even a product improvement program that you can voluntarily join. To use these services, however, you sometimes need to grant permission to Microsoft to collect data or to maintain the state of the software that you're running. One of the ways that you can control what information Microsoft sends to you and that you send to Microsoft is to review the settings for privacy options in the Trust Center. The Privacy Options page in the Trust Center (as it's displayed in PowerPoint) is shown in Figure 3-9.

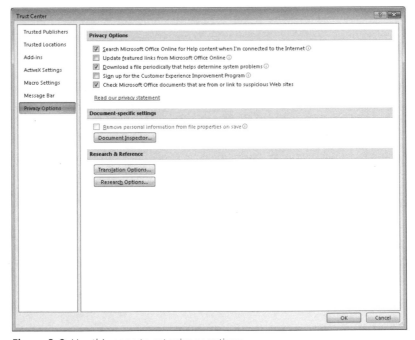

Figure 3-9 Use this page to set privacy options.

For more information about the Document Inspector, see "Removing Hidden and Personal Information from Microsoft Office Documents" on page 61.

> **Note**
>
> In OneNote, Project, and SharePoint Designer, you can view privacy options by clicking Privacy Options on the Help menu.

Some privacy options affect what information and files are downloaded from or sent to Microsoft. Other options, especially those for Word, can help protect your privacy when you share files with other people. Here's a summary of the privacy options you can set. (You can read a little about particular items on the Privacy Options page by clicking the icon at the right of the option's name.)

- **Search Microsoft Office Online For Help Content When I'm Connected To The Internet** Downloads up-to-date online Help from Office Online. You must be connected to the Internet to receive the download. Only the article that you select in the Help system's Search results box is downloaded.

- **Update Featured Links From Microsoft Office Online** (applies to Access, Excel, PowerPoint, Word, and Visio) Downloads headlines and featured templates from Office Online. You must be connected to the Internet to receive the downloads.

- **Download A File Periodically That Helps Determine System Problems** Allows a file to be downloaded from Office Online to your computer so that if your computer becomes unstable or crashes, the Microsoft Office Diagnostics tool runs to help diagnose and repair the problem for you. By selecting this option, you allow Microsoft to ask you to send error reports for certain types of error messages that you might receive. When you send a report, the data can help Microsoft understand and try to fix the problem. You also allow Microsoft to provide you with up-to-date online Help information that helps to troubleshoot the problem on your computer.

- **Sign Up For The Customer Experience Improvement Program** By selecting this option, you allow Microsoft to collect information from your computer, including error messages that are generated by its software, the kind of computer equipment you are using, whether your computer is having any difficulty running Microsoft software, and whether your hardware and software respond well and perform quickly. In general, this information is collected once each day. The information is sent to Microsoft anonymously and is not used in advertising or sales.

Chapter 3

- **Check Microsoft Office Documents That Are From Or Link To Suspicious Web Sites** (applies to Access, Excel, InfoPath, PowerPoint, Visio, and Word) Enables spoofed Web site detection to help protect you from phishing schemes. When Office detects a link to a Web site with a spoofed domain name, you are notified in a security alert. The spoofed Web site detection check is performed locally on your computer. This feature does not send any information to Microsoft.

Additional Privacy Options for Word

Here are some additional privacy options that you can select for your work in Word:

- **Warn Before Printing, Saving, Or Sending A File That Contains Tracked Changes Or Comments** By selecting this option, you see a warning if you try to print, save, or send a document that contains revision marks or comments. Material marked for deletion might be confidential or out of date. Comments might include information that is best kept among the people who reviewed the document.

- **Store Random Number To Improve Merge Accuracy** This option increases your chances of getting good results when you merge tracked changes from multiple reviewers.

- **Make Hidden Markup Visible When Opening Or Saving** Ensures that you see all tracked changes that remain in a document when you open or save it. Seeing the remaining changes lets you remove any unwanted revisions before you send the document out for review.

- **Remove Personal Information From File Properties On Save** This option is available only if you are working with a document that was created in an earlier version of Microsoft Office and you used this option in that version to remove personal information. To remove personal information from this document, click Document Inspector.

INSIDE OUT   The Office 2007 Privacy Statement

Most commercial Web sites post a privacy statement (a link to the statement often appears at the bottom of the page) that describes what personal data is collected by the Web site and how that data is to be used. You can view the privacy statement for the 2007 Office system in several ways. In the Trust Center, you can access the privacy statement by using the link that appears on the Trust Center's home page, shown here. (You can also access the privacy statement by searching in the online Help for *privacy statement*.)

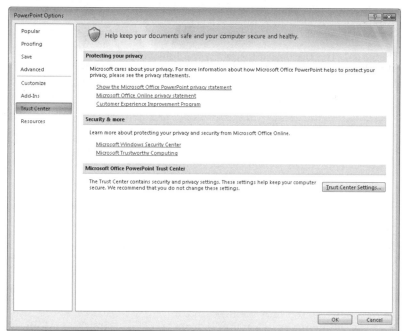

When you click the link in the Trust Center, you'll see a one-page summary of the privacy practices followed by Microsoft in publishing the 2007 Office release. The summary page provides links to the full statement for those interested in reading all the details.

Removing Hidden Data and Personal Information from Microsoft Office Documents

Information that you mean to keep to yourself—or at least within your company's network or among a group reviewing a document—can appear in a file in places that you might not check before you distribute a document, post it on a Web site, or attach it to an e-mail message that you send to a customer, a partner, or your executive team. This information can reveal details about your organization or about the document itself that you might not want to share. So, just as you proofread and review a document for accuracy before you share it, you need to take time to review your documents for hidden data or personal information that might be stored in the document itself or in the document's properties.

This section explains how to use the Document Inspector, a feature in Word, Excel, and PowerPoint that can help you find and remove hidden data and personal information. The Document Inspector uses different modules to let you find and remove hidden data and personal information that might be present in a file you create with one of these programs. When you run the Document Inspector, you can select one or more of the program's modules and check whether any information of that type is hidden or present in the file. Table 3-2 lists the Document Inspector modules for each program.

Table 3-2 The Document Inspector Modules

Word	Excel	PowerPoint
Comments, Revisions, Versions, and Annotations	Comments and Annotations	Comments and Annotations
Document Properties and Personal Information	Document Properties and Personal Information	Document Properties and Personal Information
Custom XML Data	Custom XML Data	Custom XML Data
Headers, Footers, and Watermarks	Headers and Footers	Invisible On-Slide Content
Hidden Text	Hidden Rows and Columns	Off-Slide Content
	Hidden Worksheets	Presentation Notes
	Invisible Content	

The following list describes in more detail the types of hidden data and personal information that the Document Inspector can find and remove:

- **Comments, revision marks from tracked changes, versions, and ink annotations** Items such as revision marks from tracked changes, comments, ink annotations, or document versions can let other people see the names of people who worked on your document, comments from reviewers, and changes that were made to your document. This is the type of information you might not want to circulate beyond the group of people you worked with on a document.

- **Document properties and personal information** Document properties (sometimes known as metadata) provide details about your document. Properties list details such as the document's author, its subject, and its title. Document properties also reveal information such as the name of the person who saved the document most recently, which is information that Microsoft Office maintains about the document. A document might also contain information that can be used to identify you or someone who worked on the document—your name, address, e-mail address, and the like. E-mail messages might include this information in the message header. A program such as Word could include it in a routing slip, a printer location (path), or in the file path used for publishing Web pages.

- **Headers, footers, and watermarks** Word documents and Excel workbooks can contain information in headers and footers. In addition, you might have added a watermark to your Word document.

- **Hidden text** Word documents can contain text that is formatted as hidden text. Hidden text is sometimes used for instructions or other types of comments intended to guide a user in preparing a document. This information should likely be removed before a document is circulated.

- **Hidden rows, columns, and worksheets** In an Excel workbook, rows, columns, and entire worksheets can be hidden. These areas of a worksheet are often used to maintain formulas, for example, some of which might be sensitive and proprietary. A good example would be a discount schedule that your company applies to orders of a certain dollar volume or quantity. If you distribute a copy of a workbook that contains hidden rows, columns, or worksheets, other people might display these rows, columns, or worksheets and view the data that they contain.

- **Invisible content** PowerPoint presentations and Excel workbooks can contain objects that are not visible because they are formatted as such. These objects may have been made invisible for good reason.

- **Off-slide content** PowerPoint presentations can contain objects that are not immediately visible because they were dragged off the slide. This content might include text boxes, clip art, graphics, and tables that were once considered for a presentation but are not part of the finished product.

- **Presentation notes** The Notes section of a PowerPoint presentation can contain text that you might not want to share. Often, these notes are written by or for the individual who is making the presentation and are not considered part of the presentation itself.

- **Document server properties** If your document was saved to a location on a document management server, such as a Document Workspace site or a Windows SharePoint Services document library, the document might contain additional document properties or information related to this server location.

- **Custom XML data** Documents can contain custom XML data that is not visible in the document itself. The Document Inspector can find and remove this XML data.

Note

Developers can create customized Document Inspector modules to check for other hidden information in a document. If your organization has customized the Document Inspector by adding modules, you might be able to check your documents for additional types of information.

Chapter 3

The Document Inspector does its work in three steps. First, you select which modules you want to use. You might want to check for comments and revisions, but you know the document wasn't created with XML, so you don't need to choose that module. After the inspection, you see a report indicating whether and what the Document Inspector found. You then get to choose which information you want to remove from the document. It is a good idea to inspect a copy of the document you're working on rather than the original, because you cannot always restore the information that the Document Inspector removes. After you've made a copy of the document, open the document and follow these steps:

1. Click the Microsoft Office Button, point to Prepare, and then click Inspect Document.

2. In the Document Inspector dialog box, shown here for PowerPoint, select the options for the types of hidden and personal content that you want to check for.

3. Click Inspect.

4. Review the results of the inspection in the Document Inspector dialog box, shown next.

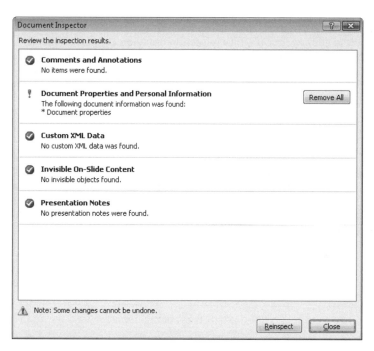

5. Click Remove All next to the items for the types of hidden content that you want to remove from your document.

Applying Information Rights Management

Information rights management. The phrase can sound a little menacing. What information, which rights, and who exactly is doing the managing? In practice, however, some information needs to be treated confidentially and some information needs to be controlled so that it isn't shared more widely than it should be. Information Rights Management, or IRM, provides a tool with which you (and often your network administrators) can specify rights that users have for documents, workbooks, and presentations. These rights can help prevent sensitive information from being printed, forwarded, or copied by someone who doesn't have the responsibility or authority to do so. IRM helps individuals control where their personal or private information goes. It helps organizations manage policies for the use of their confidential and proprietary information. For example, an administrator can configure IRM policies for a company that define who can access content and the level of editing that is permitted for a document, workbook, or presentation. An administrator might define a rights template that specifies that documents, workbooks, or presentations that use that template can be opened only by people inside the company's domain.

> **Note**
>
> In the 2007 Microsoft Office release, Information Rights Management is supported only in Office Professional Plus, Office Enterprise, and Office Ultimate.

The access and usage restrictions that you apply with IRM are enforced no matter where the information goes. In other words, the permission for a file is stored in the file itself; the access rights aren't a matter of where the file is stored. If a document with restricted permission is sent to someone who doesn't have the authority to read or change it, that person sees a message that contains the e-mail address of the document's author (or possibly an address to a Web site), which lets that individual request permission to work with the document. If the document's author chooses not to include an e-mail address, users who aren't authorized to work with the information receive an error message.

Here are some of the ways you can use IRM to protect information:

- Prevent an authorized recipient from forwarding, copying, modifying, printing, faxing, or pasting the information for unauthorized use.

- Prevent restricted content from being copied by using the Print Screen key.

- Set an expiration date so that content in documents can no longer be viewed after a specified period of time.

> **What IRM Won't Do for You**
>
> You should also be mindful of what IRM can't do. For example, IRM doesn't prevent information from being erased, stolen, or captured and transmitted by malicious programs such as Trojan horses, keystroke loggers, and certain types of spyware. IRM doesn't detect and neutralize the actions of computer viruses. It doesn't prevent someone from copying confidential information by hand or from sitting down at the computer of someone who is authorized to view the document and typing the contents of a document into a new document that isn't protected. IRM also doesn't prevent someone from taking a photograph of restricted content while it's displayed on a screen, or prevent restricted content from being copied by third-party screen-capture programs.

Configuring Your Computer to Use Information Rights Management

To use IRM with the 2007 release of Office, you need to install Windows Rights Management Services Client with Service Pack 1. You can install this software yourself from Microsoft's download center, or it might be installed on your computer by an administrator, especially if you work for an organization that's using IRM. If you haven't installed Windows Rights Management Services Client software before you first try to open a file that has been managed with IRM, you'll be prompted by Microsoft Office to download and install it.

The first time you begin to open a document, workbook, or presentation with restricted permission, you must connect to a licensing server to verify your credentials and to download a use license. This process is required for each file with restricted permission. The use license defines the level of access that you have to a file. Content with restricted permission cannot be opened without a use license. Downloading permissions requires that Microsoft Office send your credentials (including your e-mail address) and information about your permission rights to the licensing server. Information contained in the document is not sent to the licensing server.

Restricting Permissions

To restrict access permissions to a document, workbook, or presentation, follow these steps:

1. Save the document, workbook, or presentation.

2. Click the Microsoft Office Button, point to Prepare, point to Restrict Permission, and then click Restricted Access.

3. Select the Restrict Permission To This Document check box.

In the Permission dialog box, shown in Figure 3-10, you can specify users (or groups of users, if your organization's network is set up to use Active Directory) who will have Read access to this document and those users who will have Change access. Users to whom you grant Read permission can read a document, workbook, or presentation, but they don't have permission to edit, print, or copy it. Users granted Change permission can read, edit, and save changes to a document, workbook, or presentation, but they don't have permission to print it. You specify a user by entering the e-mail address for that user. To specify more than one user, separate e-mail addresses with semicolons. You can also click the Read or Change button and select names from your address book or list of contacts.

The More Options button in the Permission dialog box leads you to the Permission dialog box, shown in Figure 3-11, which you can use to specify other types of restrictions, such as an expiration date for a document. For example, you might limit access to this document for five days, after which point permission to the document expires. You can also use this dialog box to allow users to print a document, to let users with Read access copy the content of a document, and to allow the content in a document to be accessed through a macro or another type of program. Notice also that you can enter an e-mail address for the person who unauthorized users can contact to request permissions for the document. By clicking the Insert Hyperlink button at the right of the text box, you can insert the address of a Web site rather than an e-mail address to serve as the point of contact.

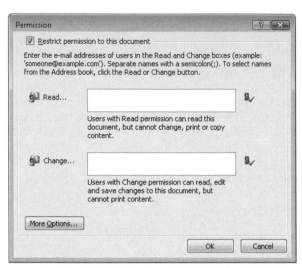

Figure 3-10 The Permission dialog box is used to restrict what a user can do with the content that a document contains.

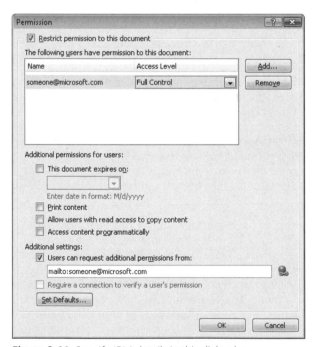

Figure 3-11 Specify IRM details in this dialog box.

The author of a document always has Full Control permission. Other users to whom Full Control is granted can do anything with the document, workbook, or presentation that the document's author can do—and that includes adding or updating IRM restrictions, such as granting permission to other users, specifying whether a document can be printed, and setting or changing an expiration date. After permission for a document has expired for authorized users, the document can be opened only by the document author or by users with Full Control permission to the document. To grant Full Control to a user, use the drop-down list that appears when you move your mouse over the Access Level column.

Your choices for how you can restrict permissions using IRM might be limited if an administrator has set custom permission policies that individuals cannot change.

> **Note**
>
> To view rights-managed content that you have permissions to, open the document, workbook, or presentation. If you want to see the permissions you have, either click View Permission on the Message Bar or click the button on the status bar at the bottom of your screen.
>
> If you want to use a different Windows account to manage files with IRM, open the document, worksheet, or presentation; click the Microsoft Office Button; point to Prepare; point to Restrict Permission; and then click Manage Credentials. In the Select User dialog box, select the e-mail address for the account that you want to use. If you need to add an account, click Add in the Select User dialog box, and then enter your credentials for the new account.

Chapter 3

Assigning a Password to a Document

Another approach to managing the information that's contained in a document, workbook, or presentation is to assign a password that controls who can view the document and who can save changes to it. A password that you assign to control who can open a document uses advanced encryption, which is a standard method for making your file more secure. A password that you assign to control who can modify a document does not use an encryption method. This password is intended as a means to foster collaboration—you provide the password to reviewers who you trust. You can assign one password to control access to the file and a different one to provide trusted reviewers with permission to modify the information in the document. It's important, of course, not to use the same password for both purposes. Use strong passwords that combine uppercase and lowercase letters, numbers, and symbols. Weak passwords don't mix these elements. An example of a strong password is *goTO_55$*. A weak password is something like *Sophie*. Also, you must remember your password. If you forget it, neither you nor Microsoft can retrieve it. Write down the passwords you assign and store them in a secure place, away from the information that they help protect.

> **Note**
>
> Securing an entire Excel workbook with a password is separate from the workbook and worksheet protection that you can set in the Changes group on the Review tab on the Ribbon. For more information about workbook and worksheet protection, see Chapter 12, "How to Work a Worksheet and a Workbook."

To set a password for a document, do the following:

1. Click the Microsoft Office Button, and then click Save As.

2. In the Save As dialog box, click Tools, and then click General Options.

    -   If you want to restrict who can open a document, type a password in the Password To Open text box.

    -   If you want reviewers to enter a password before they can save changes to the document, type a password in the Password To Modify text box.

> **Note**
>
> If you don't want content reviewers to accidentally modify the file, select the Read-Only Recommended check box. When opening the file, reviewers are asked whether they want to open the file as read-only.

3. Click OK, and, when prompted, enter your passwords again to confirm them.

4. Click OK, and then click Save. If prompted, click Yes to replace the existing document.

Changing a Password

To change a password that you've assigned to a document, workbook, or presentation, follow these steps:

1. Open the file using the password to open or the password required for modification. Do not open the file as read-only.

2. Click the Microsoft Office Button, and then click Save As.

3. In the Save As dialog box, click Tools, and then click General Options.

4. Select the current password, and then type a new password.

5. Click OK. When prompted, retype your password to confirm it, and then click OK.

6. Click Save. If prompted, click Yes to replace the existing file.

Removing a Password

When a document is completed—for example, when the document has made its rounds through all its review stages and is ready to be published or distributed—you'll probably want to remove the password. In this case, follow these steps:

1. Open the file using either the password to open or the password required for modification. Do not open the file as read-only.

2. Click the Microsoft Office Button, and then click Save As.

3. In the Save As dialog box, click Tools, and then click General Options.

4. Select the password, and delete it.

5. Click OK.

6. Click Save. If prompted, click Yes to replace the existing file.

Avoiding Phishing Schemes

Chapter 3

Personal information is valuable. Some people want to get yours and other people's through fraudulent means for their own financial gain. They try to trick you into disclosing your information by sending an e-mail message or directing you to a Web site that you think you ought to trust. They disguise their criminal intent by imitating recognizable names and brands. In other words, they go "phishing" with the hope that they'll catch something—your password or PIN, along with your bank account or credit card number, or just your name and phone number, which are all good places to start if you're trying to steal another person's identity. Once criminals have information like this, they might be able to obtain a loan in your name, transfer money from your account to theirs, charge your credit card, and the like.

There are many types of phishing schemes. (For an up-to-date report on phishing schemes that authorities have uncovered, visit the Anti-Phishing Working Group Web site at *www.antiphishing.org/phishing_archive.html*.) Here are some examples of typical schemes and how you can avoid them:

- Never reply to e-mail messages that request your personal information. Most legitimate businesses have a policy whereby they do not ask you for your personal information through e-mail. Don't trust a message that asks for personal information even if it appears legitimate. Wording in phishing e-mail messages is usually polite and accommodating. It encourages you to respond to the message or to click the link that is included in the message, often in language that tries to create a sense of urgency. Usually, spoofed e-mail messages are not personalized, though valid messages from your bank or e-commerce company generally are.

  It's a good rule to never send personal information in regular e-mail messages. Regular e-mail messages are not encrypted. They are plain text that can easily be read. If you have to send an e-mail message that contains information about a personal transaction, use Outlook to digitally sign and encrypt the message. A number of popular e-mail providers and programs support encryption, including MSN, Microsoft Hotmail, Outlook Express, Outlook Web Access, Lotus Notes, Netscape, and Eudora.

- Many phishing schemes ask you to open attachments that can then infect your computer with a virus or spyware. If spyware is downloaded and installed on your computer, it can record the keystrokes that you use to log on to your personal accounts. Any attachment that you want to view should be saved first and then scanned with an up-to-date antivirus program. Outlook blocks attachments of certain file types that can spread viruses. If it detects a suspicious message, attachments of any file type in the message are blocked.

- Do not copy and paste URLs from messages into your browser. It is always best to type a Web address or URL that you know is correct into your browser. Also, you can save the correct URL to your browser's Favorites list. Some of the techniques that criminals have used to forge links are as follows:

  - Link masks, in which the link you see does not take you to the address that you think it will, but somewhere else, usually a spoofed Web site.

  - A homograph, which is a word with the same spelling as another word but with a different meaning. In computers, a homograph attack is a Web address that looks like a familiar Web address but is actually altered. In more sophisticated homograph attacks, the Web address looks exactly like that of a legitimate Web site.

- Do business only with companies that you know and trust. A business Web site should always have a privacy statement that specifically states that the business won't pass on your name and information to other people.

- Review your order confirmations and credit card and bank statements as soon as you receive them to make sure that you are being charged only for transactions you made. Report any irregularities in your accounts.

- Use credit cards for transactions on the Internet. Your personal liability in case someone compromises your credit card is significantly limited. By contrast, if you use direct debit from your bank account or a debit card, your personal liability frequently is the full balance of your bank account. In addition, a credit card with a small credit limit is preferable for use on the Internet because it limits the amount of money that a thief can steal in case the card is compromised. Better yet, several major credit card issuers offer customers the option of shopping online with credit card numbers that expire within one or two months.

By default, the 2007 Office release displays security alerts when you click a link in a document to a Web site with an address that has a potentially spoofed domain name or when you open a file from a Web site with an address that has a potentially spoofed domain name. The option appears on the Privacy Options page of the Trust Center, which is shown in Figure 3-12. When you see an alert, you can then choose whether to continue to visit the Web site. Unless you know the site is for real, it's probably best to click No.

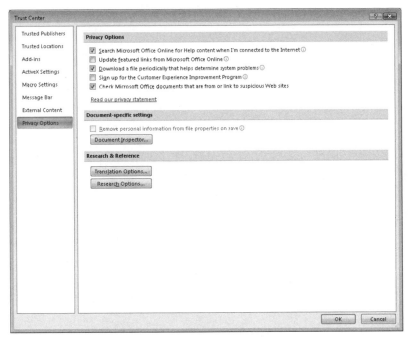

Figure 3-12 By default, Microsoft Office notifies you when it suspects a possible phishing attack. The option is listed at the bottom of the Privacy Options list.

> **Note**
>
> In Outlook 2007, if the Junk E-Mail Filter does not consider a message to be spam but does consider it to be phishing, the message is left in the Inbox, but any links in the message are disabled and you cannot use the Reply and Reply All buttons. If the Junk E-Mail Filter considers the message to be both spam and phishing, the message is automatically sent to the Junk E-Mail folder. Any message sent to the Junk E-Mail folder is converted to plain-text format and all links are disabled. In addition, you cannot use the Reply and Reply All buttons.

Chapter 3

PART 2

Collaboration Essentials

Stephanie Krieger and John Pierce

Collaborating and Sharing with Others

The phrase *effective collaboration* strikes me as one of those corporate-speak terms, like *synergy* or *think outside the box*. They're terms that became popular because they meant something important, but are now used so much for so many different reasons that you might begin to wonder if they really mean anything at all.

So, what does *effective collaboration* mean in the real world in which you live? Literally, of course, it just means working productively with others. But, for this chapter on collaborating and sharing with others, effective collaboration means much more than that. It means:

- Sharing ideas and content more easily.

- Having more dynamic ways to communicate about projects.

- Getting better results with less work.

- Managing and tracking content more easily.

Collaboration in business so often takes the form of documents—from project management to budget planning, business pitches, or legal matters—that not introducing at least some of the improved collaboration solutions in the 2007 Microsoft Office system would be neglectful. This chapter will introduce key solutions for more effective document collaboration and provide a quick reference for getting started with the method of your choice.

Understanding and Using the 2007 Office System Collaboration Environments

Document collaboration tools are evident throughout the 2007 Office release programs. Surely features like enhanced document reviewing tools and content integration between Microsoft Office Word 2007, Microsoft Office Excel 2007, and Microsoft Office PowerPoint 2007 all support collaboration. But, what about dedicated collaboration tools? That is, programs that enable you to share and collaborate on documents across your team—whether that team is within your department, across your company, on a client site, or anywhere at all.

The dedicated collaboration tools in the 2007 Office release are Microsoft Windows SharePoint Services and Microsoft Office Groove 2007. Both of these technologies enable you to share and manage documents across a team and track related tasks, schedules, and resources. Although the capabilities of Windows SharePoint Services and Office Groove 2007 overlap, both have their individual strengths.

- Windows SharePoint Services shared workspaces are where you can share content and information with any size group inside your computer network. This is a powerful and customizable technology that can be used on its own or with other SharePoint Products and Technologies. If your company runs Microsoft Office SharePoint Server 2007, for example, Windows SharePoint Services can integrate even more powerfully with your 2007 Office release programs—such as by managing Office PowerPoint 2007 Slide Libraries where users can efficiently reuse content from decks created across your team or organization.

  Windows SharePoint Services provides productivity tools like task management and discussion boards, but it is also an ideal place to share and manage completed documents because they're stored in a central, secure, and easily accessible location.

- Groove is where you and your team get the work done. Groove workspaces are designed for smaller groups (up to 30) but can be used by any size group. And, they can be automatically accessed by anyone you designate both inside and outside of your computer network, such as consultants with whom you need to collaborate. You can also access your Groove workspace from anywhere, whether or not you are connected to your network. Groove is designed for working together throughout your project, with productivity features such as a Meetings tool that enables you to both plan and hold team meetings, and a Chat tool for instant messaging with members of your workspace.

> **Note**
>
> Although both Windows SharePoint Services and Groove workspaces can be accessed by approved users outside of your network, doing this in Windows SharePoint Services requires additional steps (such as creation of an extranet).

In the 2007 Office release, Groove and Windows SharePoint Services also work effectively together, because you can easily publish completed documents from a Groove workspace to a Windows SharePoint Services shared workspace, where it can be securely stored and indexed for easy access. So, if you have access to both Groove and Windows SharePoint Services, when should you use each? Although your requirements might differ from project to project, here is my recommendation in a nutshell.

- If you need to be able to work on a project easily from anywhere with a team that does not share the same network, you want a Groove workspace.

- If a large number of people on your network or extranet need to easily access a wide range of content, you want a Windows SharePoint Services shared workspace.

Use the overviews that follow to help you determine the best workspace for your work style and your particular project.

Small Business or Individual? Go Live.

If you think you can't use Windows SharePoint Services or Groove because you're not part of a large company, think again. You have a number of options, but one of the best and least expensive ways to go is to subscribe to one of the new Microsoft Office Live services.

Office Live Collaboration and Office Live Essentials are subscription options offering a mix of programs and tools, and both include your own secure, fully hosted SharePoint site.

For home and small business users who buy software through retail outlets rather than through the volume licensing agreements that larger companies use, Groove is available in the new retail suite, Microsoft Office Ultimate 2007. But, if you don't need all the programs in the Ultimate suite, you might want to try the new Office Live Groove subscription service that offers the same functionality as Office Groove 2007.

Creating and Using Shared Workspaces with Windows SharePoint Services

After you sign in to Windows SharePoint Services, you can go in several directions.

- Jump into a document library to grab the content you need
- Add content to an existing library
- Navigate to a project workspace to check task lists, schedules, and agenda items
- Create or edit your own site or workspace

Note

Keep in mind that Windows SharePoint Services provides administrators a great deal of flexibility to assign and limit rights. So, you might have rights to add and edit pages or even create new workspaces on one site, but just read-only access to documents on another.

Understanding the Workspace

A Windows SharePoint Services shared workspace (such as the example shown in Figure 4-1) can consist of any combination of document libraries, lists (such as calendars, links, or tasks), discussion boards, surveys, general Web pages, and additional sites and workspaces (such as a meeting workspace) that reside within the main workspace.

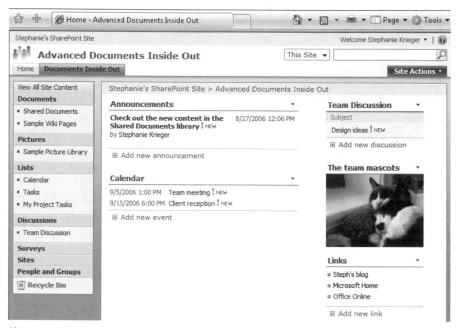

Figure 4-1   The page shown here is a home page for a sample Windows SharePoint Services shared workspace.

Libraries

A Windows SharePoint Services workspace has four types of libraries, including document, form, wiki page, and picture libraries.

- Document, form, and picture library types are similar in structure, and are to some extent interchangeable. For example, you can upload pictures or forms to a document library. In fact, you might encounter some online help content or other sources that refer to all of these as document libraries. However, certain library types also have tools specific to their content types, such as a slide show tool for viewing pictures in a picture library.

- Wiki pages (see Figure 4-2 for an example) are, essentially, collaborative blogs. That is, they are designed for unstructured contributions by multiple authors. Windows SharePoint Services wiki pages support rich text formatting, including tables and pictures, and do not require authors to know any HTML to publish or edit content. Wiki pages automatically create new versions each time someone edits the page, so that you can track changes from one session to the next. To see changes, click History in the bar at the top of a wiki page.

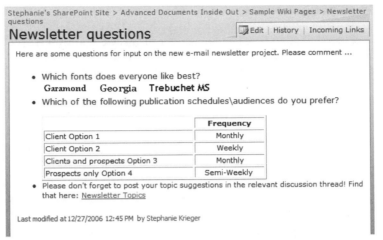

Figure 4-2 The page shown here is a sample wiki page in a Windows SharePoint Services shared workspace.

Lists and Other Communication Tools

A Windows SharePoint Services workspace can include a variety of lists and other tools, depending on the type of workspace. A collaboration workspace typically includes an announcement board, a discussion board (discussions work similarly to newsgroups, where individual users add posts to a given topic), a contact list, and a links list. A meeting workspace might include a project task list, a meeting agenda, a list of objectives, and a list of attendees.

Each of these lists or communication tools includes a link at the bottom of the existing list where you can add new content, such as Add New Link or Add New Announcement. Simply click the option for a step-by-step guide to adding the item you need.

> **Note**
>
> SharePoint sites can include two different types of task lists—a classic task list for managing a group of work items and a project task list that displays your tasks in a Gantt chart, so you can visually track tasks against a project timeline.

Accessing or Adding Content in a SharePoint Document Library

You can access content from a SharePoint library in a few ways. To open an item, you can simply point to the item and click. When you do this, depending on your permissions for the item, it may open automatically in a read-only state within its originating program or give you the option to open it for editing or read-only.

You can also point to an item in a document library and then click the arrow that appears for a list of options including editing the document, checking out the document so that others can't edit it, and viewing the document, as well as options to view file properties and manage permissions to the document. Note that if you do not set specific permissions from this list of options, the individual item will take on the default permissions for the site.

TROUBLESHOOTING

I don't see workspace options when working in a workspace document.

When you open a 2007 Office release document directly from a Windows SharePoint Services workspace, you can access several document management tools directly from the program in which you're editing the document.

In the Document Management task pane, access related documents, tasks, and links from the active workspace, as well as view a list of workspace members along with their online status. You can also click Options at the bottom of this task pane to set Document Management preferences, such as when to automatically show the Document Management task pane.

In programs that use the new Microsoft Office system interface, such as Word, Excel, and PowerPoint, when a workspace document is open, you will see an additional Server option when you click the Microsoft Office Button. Point to Server for several options, including Document Management Information, which opens the task pane.

In the programs that have the new Microsoft Office Button, you can also find Document Management preferences in the Options dialog box. To do this, click the Microsoft Office Button and then click <Program> Options. At the bottom of the Advanced tab, click Service Options.

INSIDE OUT   Review SharePoint Libraries or Lists Using Excel Queries

Under the Actions button on the toolbar at the top of any workspace index page, such as a library or list, try the Export To Spreadsheet option. This option creates a Web query file that you can open in Office Excel 2007.

For libraries, this query provides a list of content along with information about each item from the columns that appear on the library index page (such as date modified or author). For lists such as tasks and calendars, this option can be a great way to get an editable list of upcoming events or tasks (including pertinent information such as due dates) for quick reference. When you open the query file in Excel, you get the option to open it as a table, a PivotTable report, or a PivotChart report.

Adding Content to a Library or List

From the command bar at the top of a document library, you can either create a new document based on templates stored in the workspace, or upload one or more existing documents. Additionally, you can publish existing documents to a shared workspace directly from Word, Excel, or PowerPoint. To do the latter, click the Microsoft Office Button, point to Publish, and then click Document Management Server.

> **Note**
>
> Notice that you can also create a new workspace from the Publish options available through the Microsoft Office Button.

For all other types of workspace content, such as wiki page libraries, calendars, and task lists, just click New in the command bar at the top of the relevant page to add a new item.

Creating or Editing a Windows SharePoint Services Shared Workspace

Provided that you have rights to edit or add to the structure of a Windows SharePoint Services shared workspace, you can do quite a bit with surprisingly little work.

Adding Sites, Pages, or Lists

To add a new page or group of pages to your workspace (such as a document library, task list, survey, or meeting workspace), do the following.

1. At the top right of the active page in your workspace, click Site Actions, as shown here, and then click Create.

2. On the Create Page site, point to a content type to see its description and then click to select the type of content you want to create. Step-by-step instructions and options are provided for every type of space you can create from this location.

Understanding and Using Web Parts

Each visual component on a page in your workspace is a Web Part that you can edit. For example, the announcements, calendar, team discussion, picture, and links are each separate Web Parts in the page image shown earlier in Figure 4-1.

You can edit existing Web Parts (such as changing the title of a Web Part or adding a picture to an image Web Part) or add new Web Parts to an existing page. All existing content types on your site (such as libraries and lists) are automatically available as Web Parts that can be viewed from any site page. Additionally, you can select Web Parts from online services as well as custom Web Parts created for use in your organization.

To edit or add Web Parts for the active page, on the Site Actions menu, click Edit Page. When you do, you will open the shared version of the page for editing.

- To edit an existing Web Part, click the arrow next to Edit on that Web Part and then click Modify Shared Web Part, as shown here.

- To add a Web Part to the page, at the top of the column where you want the new part to appear, click Add A Web Part. Then, to view additional Web Part options beyond the existing site components, in the Add Web Parts dialog box, click Advanced Web Part Gallery And Options.

> **Note**
>
> As an alternative to using the Site Actions menu to enter Edit mode for a given page, you can also click the Web Part menu that appears as an arrow at the top-right corner of any existing Web Part on a page and then click Modify Shared Web Part.

Managing Site Settings and Permissions

To edit settings and user permissions for the active site, on the Site Actions menu, click Site Settings. To edit settings and permissions for all sites within your workspace, from the Site Settings page, under Site Collection Administration, click Go To Top Level Site Settings.

Creating and Using Groove Workspaces

When you start Groove, the Launchbar (shown in the image that follows) opens by default. From the Launchbar, you can access your existing workspaces, create a new workspace, or communicate with other workspace members who are currently online.

If you do not see the Launchbar when you start Groove, you can access your Launchbar, existing workspaces, and a variety of program preferences from the Groove icon in the Windows system tray.

Understanding Your Workspace

A workspace is composed of tools, each managing a different type of content, such as files, discussions, or meetings. Each tool is identified and accessed by a page tab at the bottom of the Groove window, similar to sheets in an Excel workbook, as you see in Figure 4-3.

Figure 4-3 Each tab in a Groove workspace accesses a unique tool, such as the Files, Discussion, and Meetings tools that are shown here.

At the top of the page for any tool is a command bar with options for the actions that you can take within that tool, such as adding new content.

While you're in a workspace, it will update automatically whenever a change occurs, such as when members move between tools, enter or leave a workspace, add or change content in a workspace, or add or modify tools. For example, the number you see beside the Discussion tool in Figure 4-3 indicates how many workspace members are currently in that tool. A number appears on the tab for any tool whenever it is occupied by at least one workspace member.

When a change occurs in a workspace, your screen might simply update to reflect the change, or you might see an alert, depending on your settings. To change your alert level, on the Options menu, click Preferences and then click Alerts. Alerts most often appear as a ScreenTip in the system tray that you can click to perform an action, such as accepting an invitation to join a workspace.

Managing Files in a Workspace

All files for a Groove workspace are stored locally on each workspace member's computer, and they are kept in sync automatically. When you add files or folders to the Files tool in a standard Groove workspace, you are adding copies of those files. Only the copy of a file that is added to your workspace will be affected whenever the file is accessed from the workspace.

When a new member accepts an invitation to join a workspace, the workspace is actually sent to the new member so that copies of all files reside on each member's computer. It is because files reside locally that members can access a workspace from anywhere. However, this is also the reason that Groove recommends not exceeding 2 GB total size for a single workspace. Groove is unable to send workspaces to new members if they exceed this size limit.

Creating a Workspace

To create a new workspace, on the Launchbar, click New Workspace. Then select the type of workspace you need and click OK.

- The workspace type referred to as Standard in the New Workspace dialog box is what most people think of as a Groove workspace, and (except where otherwise specified) it is the workspace type referred to throughout this section. Standard workspaces are created with Files and Discussion tools by default. You can then add additional tools as needed, after the workspace is created.

- A File Sharing workspace is a mechanism for sharing the contents of a folder with other computers or other people. File Sharing workspaces do not appear on the Workspaces menu. You can access File Sharing workspaces from the Launchbar. Or, on the Options menu, click Workspace Manager. When you open a File Sharing workspace, it opens as a folder in Windows Explorer.

- Workspaces based on templates are commonly Standard workspaces to which additional tools and custom settings have already been applied. You can create your own workspace templates or select from templates available online. To select from online templates, in the New Workspace dialog box, click Browse Templates. To create your own workspace template based on an active workspace, on the File menu, click Save Workspace As and then click Template.

> **Note**
>
> When you create a template, it includes all tools in the active workspace on which the template is based (such as Files, Discussion, and Meetings). While saving your template, you get the options to also include existing content in all tools as well as the list of workspace members.

Adding Tools to Your Workspace

Add Tools

To add a tool to the workspace, click the Add Tools icon at the bottom of the workspace window and then select the tool to add. Groove will generate the tool automatically and add the applicable tab to your workspace. In addition to the list of tools you see when you click Add Tools, your company may have custom tools available or you can access additional tools online.

Most tools are designed for multiple pieces of content. So, for example, you can add details for each new meeting to the same Meetings tool. However, you can also add more than one of the same tool type to the workspace when necessary, such as when you want a separate Meetings tool for tracking meetings attended only by managers.

You can rename a tool or customize your alert levels for a particular tool. To take either of these actions, right-click the tab for the applicable tool and then select the command you need.

Inviting Others to Join a Workspace

You can invite anyone to join a Groove workspace. However, those you invite must have Groove 2007 installed on their computer (or have an Office Live Groove account) to access workspaces. Note also that Groove 2007 workspaces are not backward compatible to Groove Virtual Office (the previous version of Groove).

When you invite someone to the workspace, if the recipient has a known Groove account, the invitation will appear in their system tray as a Groove alert. If the recipient does not have a known Groove account, the invitation will be sent by e-mail. If an e-mail recipient has Groove 2007 installed, they can double-click the attached Groove invitation file to open it and respond.

Chapter 4

To send a workspace invitation, at the bottom of the Workspace Members pane, type the name or e-mail address of the recipient and then click Go. Or, click the More option beside the Invite To Workspace heading to list several recipients at once or to search for a recipient in contacts folders as well as the Groove public directory.

Setting Roles and Permissions

Notice that you set the role for recipients (Manager, Participant, or Guest) in the Send Invitation dialog box shown here.

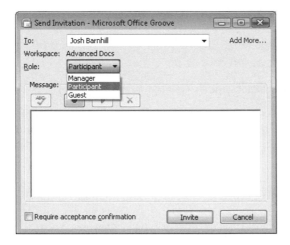

Roles controls a recipient's rights in the workspace. For the easiest workspace management, invite users in the same invitation only when you want to give them the same rights. However, workspace managers can change a member's role at any time through the Workspace Properties dialog box. Find Workspace Properties where you see the Common Tasks list in your workspace or on the Launchbar.

> **Note**
>
> If you send a workspace invitation to someone who is already a member of that workspace, the recipient will see an alert saying that you request them to come to that workspace. You can also send this type of request to members who are online by right-clicking their name in the Workspace Members list and selecting Send Alert To Come Here.

Permissions are controlled by assigned role rather than by individual member. To customize permissions for roles in your workspace, in the Workspace Properties dialog box, click the Permissions tab.

For more information about working with Office Groove 2007, see Chapter 6, "Working as a Team in a Microsoft Office Groove Workspace," and Chapter 7, "Sharing and Communicating Using Microsoft Office Groove."

Using Office OneNote 2007 as a Collaboration Tool

No discussion of document collaboration tools in the 2007 Office release is complete without a mention of Microsoft Office OneNote 2007 shared notebooks and live sharing sessions.

Shared Notebooks and Live Sharing Sessions

In the previous version of Microsoft OneNote, it was possible to create a shared note-taking session, now called a live sharing session. In these sessions, you can invite others on your network or over the Internet to share specified pages of your notebook in real time. During a live sharing session, participants can edit the same pages from their own computers and see notes from all participants as they're taken.

> Note
>
> Any type of note that you can take in Office OneNote 2007 on your computer can be taken during a live sharing session, such as typed notes, handwritten (inked) notes, audio notes, or screen clippings.

In OneNote 2007, it is now also possible to create shared notebooks. You can share a notebook with your other computers as well as with other users, such as when you want to keep a team notebook for a project. Shared notebooks can be accessed and edited by multiple participants simultaneously and automatically remain in sync.

Creating a Live Sharing Session

To create a live sharing session in OneNote, on the Share menu, point to Live Sharing Session and then click Start Sharing Current Session for a task pane that will guide you through the necessary steps. Or, from any open task pane, click the name of the active task pane and then click Start Live Session from the task pane list.

Creating a Shared Notebook

To create a shared notebook, on the Share menu, click Create Shared Notebook. This opens a wizard that walks you through the steps to create and share the notebook. Shared notebooks can use any OneNote template and have all the same capabilities of regular OneNote notebooks.

You can save your shared notebook to a SharePoint site, a network drive, or any shared drive location. Note, however, that to share a notebook, you must have rights to share files and folders on your computer.

For more information about Office OneNote 2007, see Chapter 5, "Organizing and Finding Information in Microsoft Office OneNote."

Chapter 4

Organizing and Finding Information in Microsoft Office OneNote

Collaboration begins with how well you organize yourself. If a coworker or a member of another team you're a part of asks for information or your opinion on an issue, it's helpful if you know right where the information is or have read last week's status report. There's a sense of personal satisfaction that comes with being well organized and well informed—from knowing where to find things. You get more time for yourself if you don't spend more time than is necessary keeping up with your job, your tasks, and your chores. You save not only time but effort when you know about the information you have and what information you need.

This chapter is about Microsoft Office OneNote, a program that was introduced in Microsoft Office 2003. You will often work on your own in Office OneNote 2007—collecting, organizing, and locating information—but OneNote is also designed as a tool that people use to share information.

Office OneNote is essentially an online notebook, a program that you use as you would a three-ring binder. You can divide a OneNote notebook into sections and add pages for notes, drawings, lists, and records. You can also add electronic printouts to a OneNote notebook, audio and video recordings, and copies of and links to Web sites. This chapter describes how to set up and work with OneNote as a step in your collaborative work—organizing yourself so that you can also work effectively as a member of a group.

> **Note**
>
> Office OneNote 2007 is one of the programs in the 2007 Office release that does not have the new user interface, based on the Ribbon and its command tabs. In your work with OneNote, you'll use familiar menus, toolbars, and task panes. For more information about the new user interface, see Chapter 2, "The 2007 Office System User Interface: What's Changed, What's the Same."

Organizing a OneNote Notebook

A OneNote notebook is divided into one or more sections. You can create as many sections as you need, and each section of a notebook can contain as many pages (and subpages) as you require. Each section of a notebook is identified by a tab across the top of the notebook, and each page in a section is identified by a tab that's displayed along the notebook's right side. Figure 5-1 shows a newly created Client notebook, one of the types of notebooks that you can create from a template provided with Office OneNote 2007.

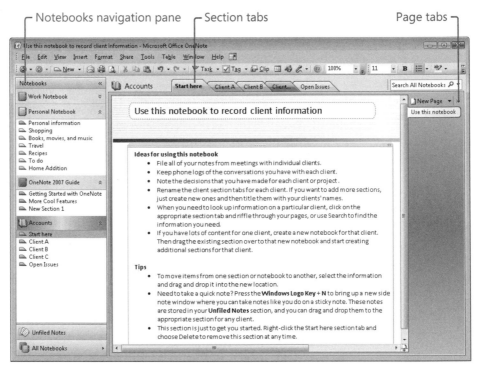

Figure 5-1 A OneNote notebook is made up of sections and pages. Click a section tab to display that section; click a page tab to jump to that page.

Note

When you open Office OneNote 2007, you'll notice that it displays three built-in note-books—a guide to using the program, a sample of a Work notebook, and a sample of a Personal notebook. The pages in these notebooks provide information about how to use OneNote, including tips and tricks and examples of the types of information a specific section or page is designed to contain.

Creating a Notebook

The number of notebooks that you set up in OneNote will be determined by any number of factors. You might find yourself joining a group of coworkers who use OneNote extensively, which means you'll need to do the same because it's the group's common tool. You might set up a notebook for each month of the year, with a series of standard sections in which you record, for example, your progress on work assignments, thoughts about classes and training sessions you want to attend, and the list of tasks you need to complete before you meet with your manager at the end of each week. If you're a project manager, you might create a notebook for each project you're involved with. If you're a sales representative, you could set up a notebook for each account you call on. Attorneys and legal assistants could set up a notebook for each active case.

To start creating a notebook in Office OneNote, follow these steps:

1. On the standard toolbar, click the arrow next to the New button, and then click Notebook. You'll see the dialog box shown here, the first page of the New Notebook Wizard.

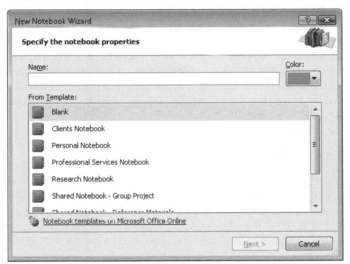

2. In the Name box, type a name for the notebook.

3. From the Color list, select the color you want to apply to this notebook's cover. This color will be displayed on the notebook's icon when the notebook is open and listed in the Notebooks navigation pane.

4. If you want to base this notebook on a template, select the template from the list provided, and then click Next. OneNote provides several built-in templates, and additional templates are available on Microsoft Office Online.

5. Select an option for how you will use the notebook, and then click Next.

You can set up a notebook to be used on a single computer, for use on more than one computer, or as a notebook that you'll share with other users (by locating the notebook on a file server or in a shared folder on the computer on which you create the notebook.) If you initially set up a notebook to use on a single computer, you can share the notebook later so that it is available to you from another computer or can be shared among a group of users.

6. As the final step in creating a notebook, the New Notebook Wizard displays a page on which you can confirm the location where the notebook will be stored.

   If you are creating a shared notebook, verifying this location is particularly important. You need to be sure that you are storing the notebook in a location that other users have access to. By default, notebooks that are set up to be used on a single computer are stored in your default documents folder (My Documents in Microsoft Windows XP; Documents in Microsoft Windows Vista) in a folder named OneNote Notebooks.

   When you click Create to complete the wizard, OneNote opens the notebook you've created. It displays the sections and pages that are defined in a notebook template or, for a blank notebook, a single unnamed section and a blank untitled page, ready for you to start capturing the day's details and thoughts.

The New Notebook Wizard provides links to online Help topics that describe what you need to know about sharing a notebook, either on more than one computer or among a group of users. You'll also learn more about these topics later in the chapter in "Using a Notebook on More Than One Computer" on page 120 and "Working as a Team with Office OneNote 2007" on page 123.

Working in the OneNote Window

In the Notebooks navigation pane along the left side of the OneNote window, each open notebook is listed. In the view shown in Figure 5-2, all but one of the notebooks are shown in expanded view. This view displays the name of the notebook along with the name of each section the notebook contains. The view of the notebook named Work is collapsed so that it shows only the name of the notebook. You can expand or collapse a notebook by clicking the arrow beside the notebook's name.

> **Note**
>
> To open a section of a notebook, click the section's name. To open a specific page, click the page's name. You can also move from section to section by clicking the section tabs or by clicking the Back or Forward button on the toolbar. Click the arrow beside the Back or Forward button to open a list of the pages and sections you've viewed most recently. You can open these lists and then select the page you want to view.

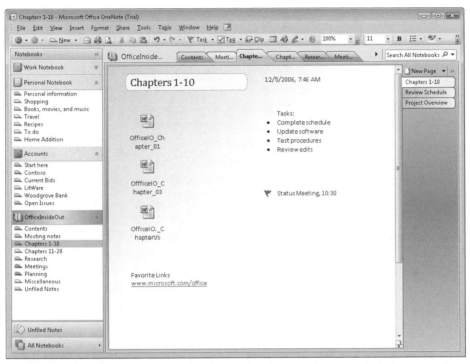

Figure 5-2 Open notebooks are listed in the Notebooks navigation pane. Click the name of a notebook or a notebook section to display it.

You can change the orientation of the navigation pane by clicking the arrow to the right of the Notebooks label at the top of the pane. By clicking the arrow, you collapse the view of each notebook, and OneNote arranges the names of the open notebooks vertically as tabs, as shown in Figure 5-3. This arrangement provides more space on a page you're working with—space for taking notes, making a drawing, and so on. The All Notebooks tab at the bottom of the navigation pane provides another means for displaying a section of an open notebook. By clicking this tab, you see a window, shown in Figure 5-4, that lists each open notebook side by side so that you can scan the list and select the notebook section you need.

You'll learn more about the Unfiled Notes tab later in this chapter, in the sidebar, "OneNote Options," on page 107.

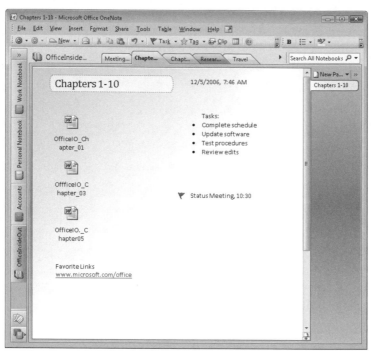

Figure 5-3 The Notebooks navigation pane can be viewed in different ways. Right-click a notebook to rename the notebook, add a section, or change the order of the notebooks.

Organizing Notebook Sections

Nothing prevents you from including only a single section in a notebook. However, if OneNote becomes an application you use regularly to maintain records of your daily work, you'll undoubtedly add another section or two to your notebooks to keep the information you need in order.

You can create a section for a notebook by using the New button on the toolbar, the New command on the File menu, or by right-clicking the tab for a section that's already included in a notebook and then clicking New Section. A section tab is added to the notebook with the temporary name New Section (with the addition of a number, starting with 1, if you've created several sections without naming them.) Enter a name for the section, and then press Enter or click away from the tab.

If a notebook is open and displayed in expanded view in the navigation pane, you need only to click the section name or the section tab to open that section. A notebook doesn't need to be open, however, for you to open a section within it. Also, you can open a specific section of a notebook without opening the complete notebook. (Each section of a notebook is stored as a separate file, with the extension .one, in the OneNote Notebooks folder or in whichever folder you've used to store the notebook.) To open a section that's not already displayed, on the File menu, point to Open, and then click Section. In the File Open dialog box, select the section (the .one file) as you would any other type of file you need to work with.

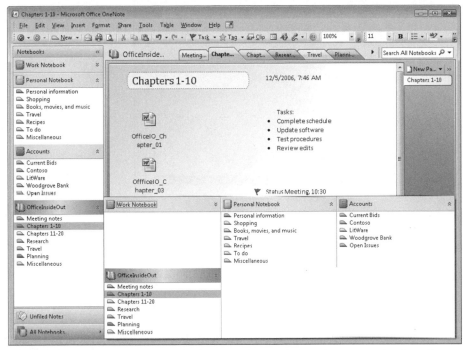

Figure 5-4 The All Notebooks tab displays a window in which each open notebook and its sections are displayed side by side.

Notebook sections can be reordered, renamed, deleted, and grouped. The following list describes these and other ways you can organize the sections in a notebook.

- **Moving and reordering sections** To move a section tab to a new location in the current notebook, drag the section tab to the left or right. A small triangle appears to indicate the new location. When a notebook is expanded in the navigation pane, you can drag any section tab up or down to a new location. When you drag a section in the navigation pane, a horizontal line appears to indicate the new location. You can also right-click a section tab that you want to move, and then click Move. Use the Move Section To dialog box, shown in Figure 5-5, to change the order of the section in the current notebook, to move the section to another notebook or a section group, or to create a section group.

- **Renaming a section** Right-click the tab of the section that you want to rename, and then click Rename. Type a new name for the section, and then press Enter.

- **Deleting a section** Right-click the tab of the section you want to delete, and then click Delete.

Chapter 5

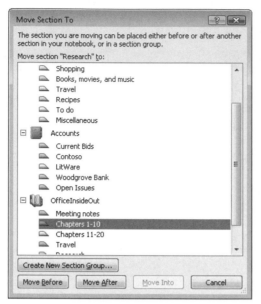

Figure 5-5 You can rearrange notebook sections by using the Move Section To dialog box.

- **Defining a section group** In notebooks that contain a large number of sections, notebooks that you use for multiple purposes, or those to which you want to add another level of organization, you can create and name a section group. To create a section group, on the File menu, point to New, and then click Section Group. You can then add sections to the section group and keep related information together; for example, you could create a section group for each phase of a complex project.

INSIDE OUT   Creating a Table of Contents for a Notebook

On any page in your notebook, you can add a hyperlink that lets you jump to a section in the notebook. Adding hyperlinks to each section of a notebook is useful for cross-referencing notes or for creating a table of contents for a notebook. To add a hyperlink, right-click the tab of the section that the hyperlink should point to, and click Copy Hyperlink To This Section. Click the location on the page where you want the hyperlink to appear, and then paste the hyperlink at that location. OneNote inserts a hyperlink that displays the target section when you click it. You can return to the previous page by clicking the Back button on the OneNote standard toolbar.

Adding and Grouping Notebook Pages

Each page in a notebook includes an area, shown in Figure 5-6, in which you name the page or describe the page's contents. The current date and time are displayed by default below the title area as well. The text you enter for the page's title also appears on the tab that identifies the page. If you leave the title area empty, the first line of your notes becomes the title of the page. To rename a page, double-click its page tab, and then type a different title into the title area.

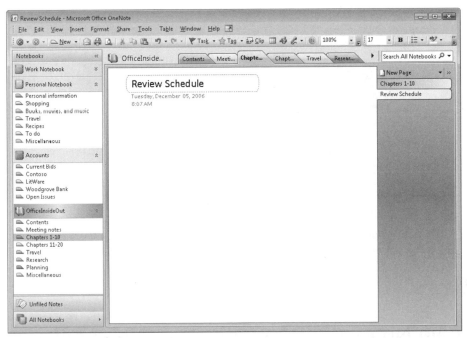

Figure 5-6 Enter a title or description at the top of a page to name the page.

To add a blank page to a section, click New Page, located at the right side of the current page. If you want to add a page that comes from a OneNote template—a page for describing a project overview, for example, or a blank page with college-ruled lines—click the arrow to the right of New Page, and then click More Template Choices And Options. The built-in page templates are displayed in a task pane and are organized in five categories—Academic, Blank, Business, Decorative, and Planners—as shown in Figure 5-7. At the bottom of the task pane, you can click the Save Current Page As Template link to create a page template of your own.

You also have the option of adding a subpage to a page. By using subpages, you can create groups of related pages. Each group has its primary page and as many subpages as you require. You can select a group of pages as a single unit when you need to copy or move the pages or send the pages in an e-mail message. Each subpage can also have a title.

Chapter 5

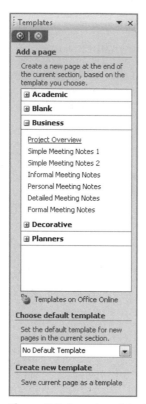

Figure 5-7 Page templates let you build the features of a notebook quickly. You can also save a page that you've designed as a custom template.

Adding Notes and Information to a Notebook

In at least a couple of ways, you work with OneNote differently from how you work with other applications. For example, you can start typing anywhere you want on a OneNote page, not just at the top of the page. Also, you don't have to explicitly save your work in OneNote. The information you add to a notebook is saved automatically.

You can add typed or handwritten notes to a OneNote notebook, and, just as you can with a three-ring binder, you can store printouts in a notebook by printing a file to OneNote. You can add images to a page as well as audio and video recordings, tables, references to files and Web sites, and images of Web sites themselves. In this section, you'll learn how to add content and information to a OneNote notebook.

Adding and Working with Text Notes

You can add a note to a page at any location. In other words, you don't need to start in the upper-left corner of the page, as you generally do when you start working in a new

Microsoft Office Word document, for example. You can arrange notes on a page so that you use one area for phone numbers of people you need to call that day, another for jotting down ideas, and another for your list of tasks—something like the page shown in Figure 5-8.

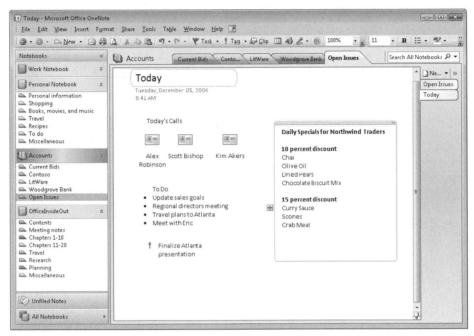

Figure 5-8 You can locate notes on different areas of a page.

> **Note**
>
> The date and timestamp displayed on a page show the date and time when you created the page. As you add information, update the date and the time so that they reflect when you last added a note or other information. To change the date, click the date, and then click the calendar icon that appears. In the calendar, click the date that you want to display on the page. To choose the current date, click Today. When you search notes, the new page date will be used. Change the time by clicking the time and then clicking the clock icon.

To add a note to a page, click on the page where you want the note to appear, and then start typing. If you're using a pen input device (if you're using a Tablet PC, for example) start writing. When you add the note, OneNote frames the text within a container, such as the one shown in Figure 5-9. OneNote wraps the text within the container as the text you enter reaches the border at the container's right side. When you finish the note and move your mouse or pen away from the text, the container disappears.

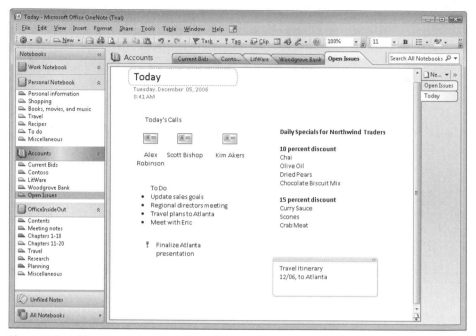

Figure 5-9 Adding a note is as simple as clicking on the page and beginning to type or write.

You can resize a note container by dragging one of its borders. The text will rewrap if you adjust the container's size. You can move a note container from place to place on a page by pointing at the note and dragging it from one of the container's borders. By selecting some of the text in a container and then dragging it away from the container's outline, you split one text container into two. You can also cut or copy a container and paste it on another page.

> **Note**
>
> If you want to work with several note containers at once, use the Lasso Select tool on the Drawing Tools toolbar to draw an outline around text, a drawing, or any other type of content. You can cut, paste, or move that content.

You can add emphasis and organize text in a note in ways that bring attention and order to the notes you add. The text you type on a OneNote page can be formatted in a number of ways by using the Formatting toolbar or commands on the Format menu. Here's a quick rundown of the formatting you can apply to the text of a note:

- Choose a font, size, color, and text effects, such as bold, italic, or underline.

- Create a bulleted or numbered list in a text container. To start a numbered list, type **1** and the first item with the number 1, and then press Enter to automatically number the following items.

- Indent text in the fashion of an outline.

- Highlight text or items of importance.

Tagging Types of Notes

On the Insert menu in OneNote, you can use the Tag command to insert a note with an icon that indicates a specific type of note. The list of note tags that OneNote provides is extensive, including To Do, Idea, Web Site To Visit, Movie To See, and so on. The menu of note tags is shown in Figure 5-10.

Figure 5-10 Tags identify the type of note. You can search for tags and then sort the notes by type.

Let's say you've worked with three notebooks this week and entered a dozen or more notes that you've tagged with the To Do tag, or perhaps the Remember For Later tag. At the end of the week, you want to view all these items, cross off those you've completed, and prioritize those that you haven't for next week. You can do this by pointing to Tag on the Insert menu and then clicking Show All Tagged Notes. Choosing this command displays the Tag Summary task pane and a list of tagged notes similar to the one shown in Figure 5-11.

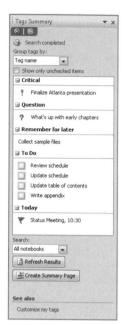

Figure 5-11 All notes that are tagged are listed in this task pane.

With all the note tags listed in one place, you can use the Group Tags By list to sort the notes by tag name, by section, by note text, date, and so on. You can also create a summary page that lists each tagged note for your review. Use the Search list to define the scope of your search for tagged notes, choosing an option such as This Notebook or This Week's Notes.

You can customize built-in note tags (for example, change the name of Books To Read to Books To Buy) and also create tags of your own, which adds a level of personal organization to the work you do in OneNote. Click Customize My Tags (shown near the bottom of Figure 5-11), and the list of current note tags is displayed in a task pane in OneNote, shown in Figure 5-12. To modify the name, image, or another property of a tag, select the tag, and then click Modify in the task pane. To create a tag of your own, click Add, and then complete the Modify Tag dialog box, shown in Figure 5-13.

Figure 5-12 Note tags help you organize notes by type. You can modify tags and create your own as well.

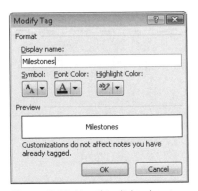

Figure 5-13 Use this dialog box to create your own note tags.

Printing to OneNote

Another way that you can add content to a notebook is to print a file to OneNote. The files you print to OneNote are displayed in color and formatted as they would be if you printed them on paper. In addition, the text the file contains is included in the material that's searched in a OneNote notebook.

For more information about searching in OneNote, see "Finding Your Information" on page 119.

Chapter 5

You can also annotate the files you print to OneNote, adding notes to the author, comments, corrections, and the like. In a OneNote notebook you share with other users, for example, you could print a Microsoft Office PowerPoint 2007 presentation to the notebook, and the team could then review the presentation online, commenting on the text and graphics, the formatting, and other aspects of the PowerPoint file. The appearance of a printed file—the margins, spacing, image placement, and other details—also makes reading more enjoyable. You can also print a file to a notebook as your first printed reference, saving for paper copies only those files that you need to distribute as hard copies.

To insert a file as a printout, on the Insert menu, click Files As Printouts, select the files or files you want to add to your notebook, and then click Insert. OneNote displays a message indicating that the file is being printed, and then a rendering of the file appears, along with a link to the file and a label, as shown in Figure 5-14. To open the file, you can click the link or double-click the label, which reflects the file's name.

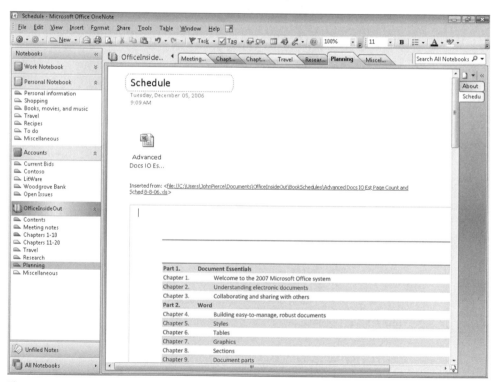

Figure 5-14 A notebook can include a printout of a file. The text of the file is included when you search for information. You can annotate printouts with comments.

OneNote Options

As with other 2007 Office system applications, you can use the Options dialog box in OneNote to change default values, set preferences, and control other aspects of your interaction with the program and how the program behaves. The Options dialog box includes categories for changing display properties, for example, for enabling the search of audio recordings, for managing passwords, and more. A number of specific options are referred to throughout this chapter.

As you assemble the contents of a OneNote notebook—content such as Web sites and printouts of files—you'll want to review the Send To OneNote page in the Options dialog box, shown here.

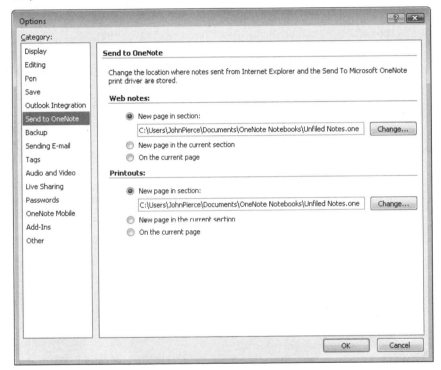

You can use this page to control where file printouts and Web notes appear when you first add them to a notebook. By default, these types of content are sent to a section named Unfiled Notes. That general location is fine for many uses. You can simply move the printout or Web note to the section and page where you want it. But let's say you want to create a notebook section just for Web notes or always send the note to the page you're currently working on. You can change the path that's specified on the Send To OneNote page so that the path points to a different OneNote section (a different .one file), or select one of the other standard options so that the content is added to OneNote in a way you prefer.

Embedding References to Files

You can embed a reference to a file in a OneNote notebook as well. Inserting a link to a file is an efficient way to extend the reach of the information that's available when you're working in OneNote. The link is represented by an icon and a label that you double-click to open the file. It's important to keep in mind that you are opening the file in a writable state—you're not just reviewing the file, in other words. The file can be edited and saved in its originating application.

To insert a file, on the Insert menu, click Files. After the file is inserted on the page, you can right-click the icon to display a context menu that you can use to do a number of things with the file, such as opening it, saving it with another name or at another location, inserting the file as a printout (see the previous section), or creating a hyperlink to the file.

Using Office OneNote and Office Outlook Together

One of the ways to be productive in your work is to lessen the amount of work you do redundantly. If you keep your list of tasks on a legal pad, for example, but also want to record them online in a program such as Microsoft Office Outlook 2007, the transfer takes some extra time. As you build a task list in Office OneNote, however, the tasks you enter can also be set up as tasks in Office Outlook 2007. To do this, on the Insert menu, click Outlook Task. The choices you're provided at that point are shown in Figure 5-15. As you can see in the figure, you can mark a task as complete, delete a task, or open the task in Outlook if you need to record other details about the task in that application.

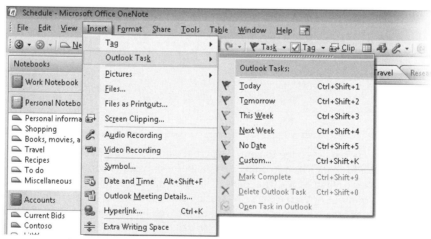

Figure 5-15 You can synchronize the tasks you create in OneNote with your task list in Outlook.

OneNote and Outlook also provide a level of integration with respect to meetings and contacts that you set up and record in Outlook. You can link meeting notes in OneNote to appointments in your calendar in Outlook, and you can link a note related to one of your contacts—a customer or client, for example—to the contact's item in Outlook.

If you need to refer back to a particular meeting or a contact, you can use the link that OneNote creates to jump to the particular item.

To link a meeting item or contact item in Outlook with a note in OneNote, first select the meeting or contact item in Outlook, and then click the Open Or Create Linked Meeting Notes In OneNote button (or the button for linking a contact). A reference to the meeting is created in OneNote, as you can see in Figure 5-16. You can use the note to record attendees, for example, as well as notes about the meeting itself. Click Link To Outlook Item to open the item in Outlook when you need to make reference to it.

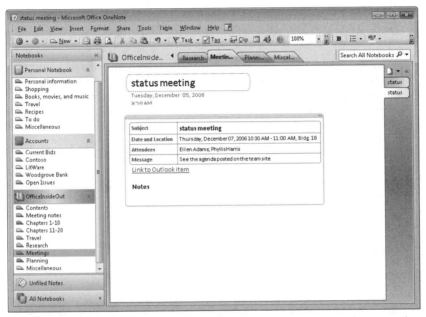

Figure 5-16 Use OneNote to keep additional notes about meetings and contacts that you have set up in Outlook.

> **Note**
> OneNote 2007 lets you move content that you've stored in a notebook to other 2007 Office system applications. For example, you can select a notebook page and then send it to Word 2007 by clicking Send To on the File menu in OneNote.

Inserting Audio or Video Recordings

Usually, someone at a meeting is asked to take notes or minutes so that the business of the meeting and the decisions the participants make are documented and clear. If you're the one assigned to take notes, your attention is split. It's hard to write down a discussion and participate in it at the same time. If your computer is equipped with a microphone (most current laptop computers, including Tablet PCs, have a microphone built in) or a webcam, you can record meetings, lectures, or other presentations and then add the audio and video recordings to a OneNote notebook. After the recordings are part of the notebook, you can share them with others and include the recordings in the information that you search in OneNote.

For more information about searching audio and video recordings, see "Finding Your Information" on page 119.

The sound and video recordings that you make in OneNote are linked to notes you enter when the recording is made. The links between notes and recordings let you search your notes for words or text related to a recording For example, let's say you record the presentation at the quarterly sales meeting and at the point in the presentation when the sales director reveals next quarter's revenue goals, you enter a note with the text "sales goals," also adding a few ideas about how your group will meet its target. When you play back the recording and reach the moment when you entered your note, OneNote highlights the notes you took to accompany the recording, enabling you to return to the note and the ideas you jotted down.

Note

To record audio or video clips in OneNote, Microsoft DirectX 9.0a or later and Microsoft Windows Media Player 9 or later are required.

To record and work with audio and video in OneNote, follow these steps:

1. Click the location on the page where you want to place the recording.

2. On the standard toolbar, click the arrow next to the Record button, and then click either Record Audio Only or Record Video. A timestamp is placed on the page.

3. Start recording your audio notes or video notes.

4. To finish the recording, click Stop on the Audio And Video Recording toolbar, which is shown here.

Note

If you choose Record Audio Only, OneNote records the sound clip as a .wma file. If you choose Record Video, OneNote combines audio and video in a .wmv file, provided that a microphone is connected to your computer or is available as part of the camera you're using. After a video recording has been created in OneNote, you cannot separate the audio portion from the video portion in your notes.

To play an audio or video recording, click the icon next to the notes or click the Play button on the Audio And Video Recording toolbar. You can stop or pause the playback at any time by clicking Stop or Pause on the Audio And Video Recording toolbar.

The See Playback button on the Audio And Video Recording toolbar controls whether OneNote highlights related notes when you play back a specific recording. This button is active by default. If you want to watch or listen without following along in your notes, click the See Playback button to turn this feature off. To play back only the audio portion of a video recording, on the Audio And Video Recording toolbar, click the Hide Video Window button.

Sharing Audio or Video Recordings

You can share the audio and video recordings that you make with people who don't have OneNote installed by sending the recording in an e-mail message. Here are the steps:

1. On the Tools menu, click Options.

2. In the Category list in the Options dialog box, click Sending E-Mail. Select the Attach Embedded Files To The E-Mail Message As Separate Files option, and then click OK.

3. Click the tab of the page that contains the audio or video files you want to send.

4. On the File menu, point to Send To, and then click Mail Recipient (As Attachment). Complete the e-mail message item, and then click Send. In the e-mail message, instruct your recipients to save the .wma or .wmv files to the same location as the OneNote file so that they can play the audio or video right from the page. You can also send just the audio or video recording by sending only the .wma or .wmv file.

You can also simply share pages that include audio and video files by saving the page to a shared location. Save both the OneNote page and the Windows Media Player file (.wma for audio or .wmv for video) to the same location. To listen to the audio recordings or to watch a video recording, users must have Windows Media Player 9 or later installed on their computer. (Windows Media Player is installed with Windows.) To download the latest version of Windows Media Player, visit the following Web site: *www.microsoft.com/ windows/windowsmedia/default.mspx*

Chapter 5

Adding Information to a Notebook from the Web

Information workers, students—almost everyone who uses a personal computer regularly—spend time browsing sites on the Web. People research travel plans, automobile and home purchases, concerts and theatrical events, news, opinion—you name it. Web browsers have a number of tools that you can use to quickly get back to a site you've visited. You can bookmark the site or add it to your Favorites list. You can also refer to your browsing history that Microsoft Internet Explorer or another browser retains to see a list of the sites you've visited recently.

Office OneNote 2007 offers other ways with which you can collect and organize information from the Web. When you install OneNote on your computer, a button or command is added to Internet Explorer that is named Send To OneNote. (The version of Internet Explorer you are using determines whether the Send To OneNote command appears as a toolbar button or on the Tools menu.) The presence of this command, shown in Figure 5-17 in Internet Explorer 7, gives you a broad hint about the compatibility of OneNote and your browser and the ease with which you can add material you find on the Web to the collection of information you compile in a OneNote notebook.

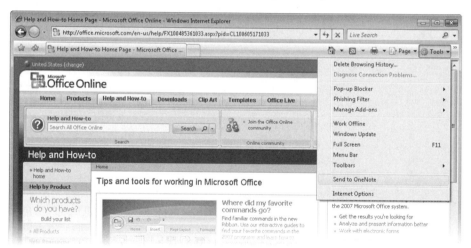

Figure 5-17 You can send a Web page to a notebook from Internet Explorer.

You don't need to have OneNote open to send a Web page to a notebook. Choosing Send To OneNote in Internet Explorer starts OneNote automatically. By default, the Web page you're sending to OneNote is added to the Unfiled Notes area. From there, you can move the page to the section of a notebook where you want it. You can change the default setting so that Web pages are sent to a section in a different notebook, a new page in the current section, or to the current page. These last two settings assume you've got OneNote running at the time. To move an unfiled note to a page in a notebook, right-click the Unfiled Notes tab, and then click Move. In the Move Section To dialog box, you have a couple of options. You can select a notebook, and then click Move Into. Or you can select a section in a notebook, and then click Move Before or Move After. You can also create a new section group into which you can move the note.

> **Note**
>
> A Web page that you send to OneNote may appear in a somewhat altered state. The graphics might not be as crisp, text will probably wrap, and the responsiveness of scrolling from one area of the page to the next can be slow. Still, all the links on the page remain operational. Clicking a link on the Web page you've captured doesn't render the new page in OneNote; instead, it opens the page in your browser.

Sending whole pages isn't the whole story when it comes to the Web and OneNote. You can also define what OneNote describes as a "screen clipping" to add a portion of a Web page to a notebook, and you can simply insert a hyperlink to a Web site as well.

A screen clipping is a device by which you can capture a section of a Web site (or a document, for that matter) and add that clipping to OneNote. You can perform this operation while working in your browser by right-clicking the OneNote icon in the notification area of the taskbar and then clicking Create Screen Clipping. When you choose this command, your screen appears something like a veil, with the page you want to take a clipping from still displayed. In a notification area, you're instructed to drag a rectangle around the area you want to clip. Figure 5-18 shows the result.

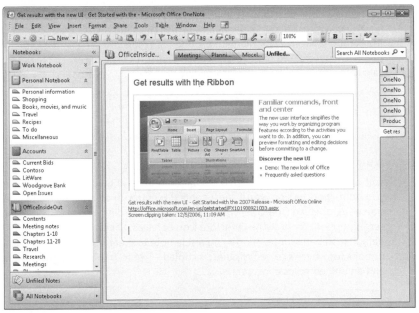

Figure 5-18 You can take a clipping from a Web site (or from a document) and add it to a notebook.

To insert a reference to a Web page in a OneNote notebook, on the Insert menu, click Hyperlink, and then type the site's address and a description in the dialog box shown in Figure 5-19.

Figure 5-19 Adding a hyperlink to a notebook page lets you open a Web site for research or other information when you're working in OneNote

OneNote Calculations

Let's say you've just moved to a new city and are looking for an apartment. Having created a OneNote notebook named Getting Settled, you're checking out rental advertisements online and creating screen clips of the possibilities that interest you. But you also need to know how the rent mounts up and how it will affect your monthly budget. You can make quick calculations such as these in OneNote by typing the numbers you need to crunch, one of the standard numeric operators (+, -, *, or /), and then the equal sign (=). You can also use functions such as *sqrt* to calculate the square root of a number or the caret character (^) to calculate exponents. When you press Enter, OneNote does the math for you—no need to switch to Microsoft Office Excel or take out your pocket calculator.

Note

You can use the OneNote icon in the system tray to initiate a variety of operations. When you right-click the icon, you'll see a context menu with commands for opening a new side note, opening OneNote, starting an audio recording, creating a screen clipping, or setting options for how the OneNote icon behaves. For example, you can change the default icon behavior from opening a side note to creating a screen clipping and also options for where a screen clipping is copied—just to the Clipboard or to the Clipboard and an unfiled notes page.

Capturing Information on Your Windows Mobile–Powered Device

If you have a Microsoft Windows Mobile Smartphone or Pocket PC, you can use the OneNote Mobile program to take notes on your mobile device and then synchronize these notes with a notebook section in OneNote. For example, you can capture pictures of business cards on your phone and add them to OneNote. The text in these images can now be searched. You can also record short text notes or voice recordings on your phone and add these notes to OneNote.

To install OneNote Mobile, on the Tools menu, click Options, and then click OneNote Mobile. On the OneNote Mobile page, click Install OneNote Mobile. Your notes on the device will be synchronized with a notebook named OneNote Mobile Notes whenever you connect your mobile device to your computer.

Inserting an Image in a Notebook

Adding a picture or another graphics file to a notebook page takes only a few steps. On the Insert menu, point to Pictures, and then choose From Files or From Scanner Or Camera. (The latter command is relevant only if you've got a digital camera or a scanner connected to your computer.) Figure 5-20 shows an example of a picture on a page.

Figure 5-20 Images can be inserted in a notebook and the text the images contain included in the information that is searched.

Chapter 5

After you've added an image to a page, you can right-click the image and choose Set Picture As Background. More interestingly, you can add the text that an image file might include to the text that you can search for in OneNote. To do this, right-click the image, and then click Make Text In Image Searchable.

You can annotate pictures that you have inserted into your notes by typing text over them. To add an annotation, click the image you've inserted, and then enter the text of the annotation. If you want to select a picture that you've inserted (to move the image, for example), move the pointer over it. A dashed blue border appears around the picture, and a blue crosshair handle appears next to the picture. Click the border or the handle to select the picture.

Entering Information with a Pen

If you have a Tablet PC or a pen input device, you can use your digital pen to enter handwritten notes or draw pictures and diagrams on a OneNote notebook page. If you are using a Tablet PC, you can convert handwritten notes to text or leave the notes as handwriting. The OneNote search engine treats handwriting entered on a Tablet PC the same as text, so in either format, an entry you search for will be discovered.

You can also mix handwriting and text on the same page. You can change the order of handwritten items in a list by dragging an item, you can add bullets and numbering to your handwritten notes, and you can also mark handwritten notes with a note tag.

If you're using a pen device to work with OneNote, you should become familiar with commands on the Tools menu, which you can use to select a writing tool (together with an ink color and width) and a pen mode. The writing tools include the Text/Selection tool that you'll use when you're working with a keyboard, as well as an assortment of pen colors and widths (thick or thin). You use the Writing Tools command to select an eraser; and use the Lasso Select tool when you need to select more than one item on a page. You can work with these and other writing tools on a toolbar by displaying the My Pens toolbar and the Writing Tools toolbar through the View menu.

Creating a Drawing in OneNote

What good would a notebook be if you weren't given the opportunity to doodle sketches in it—like the home addition you're contemplating or a quick flowchart for the new manufacturing process you've been asked to develop? The drawing tools that OneNote provides include those for basic shapes, an eraser, line tools, fill colors, line weights, rotation, and a tool for duplicating shapes. The Drawing Tools toolbar is shown at the bottom of the window in Figure 5-21.

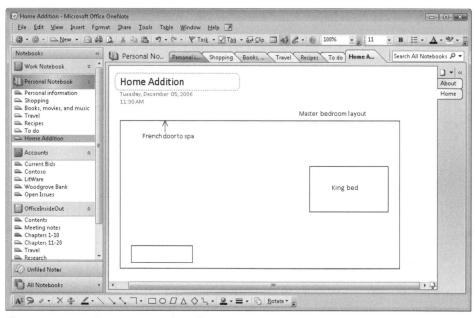

Figure 5-21 Use the Drawing Tools toolbar to sketch in OneNote.

You'll often start a drawing by selecting a basic shape—for example, a rectangle or a diamond, or, for freehand drawing, the Pen tool. You'll also work with the Lasso Select tool, which you use to select a shape or shapes before you copy them, for example, or rotate their orientation. You can use the Lasso Select tool on pages that don't include drawings to select several text containers and copy or delete them as a group.

Creating and Working with Tables in OneNote

Here's how easy it is to create a table on a OneNote page—a table that you might use to quickly plan an itinerary, with cities in one column, dates for your visits in the second, and maybe sites or clients you'll be visiting in a third. Start typing the text you want to use as the heading for the table's first column, just as you would type text for any note you're adding to a notebook. Press Tab, and OneNote formats the text as a column heading and adds a second column ready for input. You can continue to add columns in this manner, and after you've created the number of columns you need, press Enter to begin a new row within the table. A simple table created in OneNote is shown in Figure 5-22.

OneNote 2007 provides a Table menu with commands for working with columns, rows, and the entire table when you need to. OneNote also makes it easy to modify and expand tables through a series of keystrokes. Table 5-1 lists some of the commonly used keystrokes for building a table in OneNote.

Chapter 5

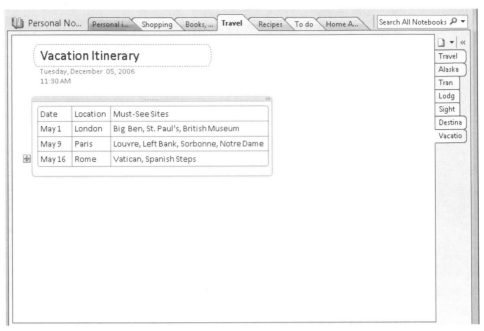

Figure 5-22 OneNote recognizes keystrokes to help you create and build a table.

Table 5-1 Common Keystrokes Used to Build Tables in OneNote

Action	Shortcut
Create more lines inside the last cell of a table	Press Alt+Enter
Insert a row at the end of the table	Press Enter or Tab in the last cell
Insert a row anywhere in the table	Press Ctrl+Enter
Insert a row above the current row	Press Enter at the beginning of the row
Delete a row	Select the row by clicking the row handle, and press Delete or Backspace
Delete a column	Select the column by clicking the arrow that appears at the top of the column, and press Delete or Backspace
Swap rows	Select the row, press Ctrl+C, and then press Ctrl+V at the beginning of the row before which you want to insert the cut row
Split a table	Press Backspace or Delete at the beginning of an empty row
Merge tables	Press Backspace or Delete in the empty space between two tables

Finding Your Information

Being able to find information when you need it is as important as organizing information in the first place. As you assemble information in notebooks, you'll use the search capabilities in OneNote to find and highlight the notes and other nuggets of information that you've compiled.

The search capabilities of OneNote rely on Windows Desktop Search (WDS). This search engine indexes the content of a OneNote notebook automatically in the background. OneNote searches not only the text notes you enter but the text in documents that you've inserted as printouts, text in graphics that you include on a page, and the text in pages from Web sites you send to OneNote.

> **Note**
>
> If you don't have Windows Desktop Search installed when you install OneNote, you're prompted to download and install it. You can also install the search engine through the Options dialog box. On the Tools menu, click Options. In the Options dialog box, click Other, and then click Install Instant Search.

OneNote can also search the content of audio and video recordings, provided that you enable this option in the Options dialog box. (The option is on the Audio And Video page of the Options dialog box in the area labeled Audio Search.) OneNote 2007 uses speech-to-text tools and attempts to analyze audio and video files for recognizable content. For example, if you record a meeting at which you discuss next year's major fundraising event, a search for references to the event would show a link to the audio file in which the event was discussed. If you click the link in the search results window, OneNote opens the page on which the audio file is located and begins playing the recording at the point at which the event began to be discussed. When you select the check box to turn on audio search, OneNote displays a dialog box that provides some information about what you can expect when recordings are included in the content that is searched. For example, the quality of a recording affects whether a search term is found, as do regional accents.

You can conduct a search over all open notebooks, or you can limit the scope of your search, as shown in the list that follows. Keep in mind that if you select a search scope (an item other than All Notebooks, which is the default), the scope you select is used for the next search you conduct (and those that follow that search as well). If you want to switch back to searching all notebooks, for example, you need to select this option the next time you search for information in OneNote.

You can choose one of the following options from the Search In list:

- This Section
- This Section Group

- This Notebook

- All Notebooks

To search in OneNote, type the term or phrase you're searching for in the Search box, select the search scope that you want to use, and then click the Search button. OneNote displays its search results in an area on the right side of the window and highlights each instance of the term you've searched for on the pages where the term appears, as shown in Figure 5-23.

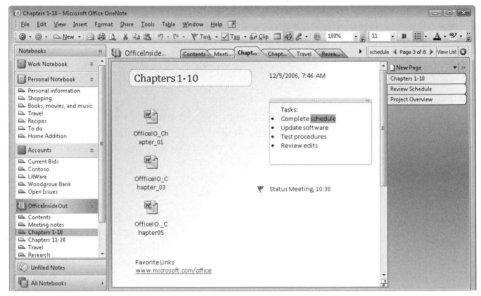

Figure 5-23 Enter the term you want to search, and OneNote highlights instances of the term on notebook pages and lists the pages in a task pane.

Searching through OneNote notebooks helps you find information that might be far afield—for example, a note you remember entering several months ago but don't remember exactly when or in what specific context. You can locate notes that you've taken more recently by sorting pages by date, for example, using a command on the View menu. When you choose this command, notebook pages are listed and grouped in the Page List task pane at the right of the OneNote window. The pages are organized under categories such as Today, Yesterday, Last Week, and even A Long Time Ago. You can then scroll through the list of pages in the task pane to locate a note or other information you're looking for.

Using a Notebook on More Than One Computer

Office OneNote 2007 is all about managing your information, a key aspect of being productive yourself and being an effective member of a team. Managing information on one computer—the computer you use at work, for example—poses enough difficulties, but it's often the case that people use more than one computer—a laptop and a desktop, for example, or a computer at home to complement the computer they use at the office.

If you work on more than one computer, you can set up OneNote notebooks in a shared location, such as a file share on your network. The notebook is available to you from any computer you can use to gain access to that location, provided that the computer has OneNote installed. When you open the notebook from any computer, OneNote creates an offline copy on that computer. Then, whenever OneNote is open on that computer and the computer is connected to the shared location, OneNote synchronizes and merges changes to the notebook from each computer on which the notebook's been used.

Creating a Notebook for Use on More Than One Computer

The New Notebook Wizard in OneNote guides you through the steps for creating a notebook that you can use on multiple computers. The initial steps are the same as those listed in "Creating a Notebook" on page 93. On the New Notebook Wizard's second page, shown in Figure 5-24, you select the option, I Will Use It On Multiple Computers. You should store a notebook that you'll use on more than one computer in one of the following locations:

- A folder or public file share on a home, company, or school network

- A shared folder on a computer on which you have Administrator permissions

- A document library on a Windows SharePoint Services site

- A high-storage-capacity USB (universal serial bus) drive

Figure 5-24 Notebooks that you use on more than one computer should be stored in a location that is available to all of the computers you'll use to work with the notebook.

> **Note**
> The notebook's name that you enter when creating it is added by OneNote to the location's path.

If you want OneNote to create an e-mail message for you that contains a link to the location of the shared notebook, select the option that the wizard provides to send yourself an e-mail message that contains this link. If you choose not to create an e-mail message with a link to the shared notebook when you first set up the notebook, you can do this later by clicking Send Shared Notebook Link To Others on the Share menu and sending a message to yourself.

Share an Existing Notebook Among Your Computers

If you want to set up a notebook that you're already working with so that you can use it on your other computers, you need to move the notebook to a location such as those listed in the previous section. The first step is to close the notebook that you want to share between computers (right-click the title of the notebook in the navigation pane, and then click Close This Notebook). Then follow these steps:

1. On the File menu, click Exit so that OneNote is no longer running.

2. Use the Windows Start menu to open Windows Explorer.

3. Using Windows Explorer, open the folder that contains your OneNote notebooks. By default, your notebooks are stored in the OneNote Notebooks folder in the My Documents folder. (Or the Documents folder in Windows Vista.)

4. Right-click the notebook folder that you want to move to a shared location, and then click Cut.

5. Using Windows Explorer, navigate to a shared location that you can access from your other computers. On the Edit menu in Windows Explorer, click Paste.

6. After Windows Explorer moves the notebook folder to its new location, close Windows Explorer and start OneNote.

7. On the File menu in OneNote, point to Open, and then click Notebook.

8. Browse to the shared location to which you moved your notebook in the previous steps, click the notebook folder, and then click Open.

You can send yourself an e-mail message with a link to the notebook's new location, and then click the link in the message on your other computers to open the notebook quickly. To send the message, on the Share menu, click Send Shared Notebook Link To Others, verify the notebook's new location, and then send the message to an e-mail account that you have access to on your other computers.

Working as a Team with Office OneNote 2007

As a tool for group work, Office OneNote 2007 offers several approaches, some more dynamic than others. You can distribute notebook pages to other people through e-mail, for example, which gets the information into circulation but doesn't provide a vehicle for collecting the opinions and expertise of a team in a single location and doesn't enable more than one team member to work with a notebook at the same time. A shared notebook provides more opportunities for a team to brainstorm together in meetings and provides a tool in which each member of a workgroup can view, add, and edit information.

Working with a Shared Notebook

A OneNote notebook can be shared simply by storing it in a location at which others can also open it, such as a folder share on your own computer, a file server, or a Windows SharePoint Services site (using Windows SharePoint Services 2.0 or later). OneNote guides you through setting up a shared location when you use the Create Shared Notebook command on the Share menu or the shared notebook option in the New Notebook Wizard.

A shared notebook is available for multiple users to work on at the same time or at different times. A workgroup or project team could use a shared notebook to gather and manage information such as the following:

- Meeting or project notes
- Links to department and project budgets
- Brainstorming ideas
- Lists of action items
- Drafts of project reports that team members can annotate
- Project plans

OneNote maintains a copy of a shared notebook on the local computers of the users who work with it. People using the notebook can add and update information while working on their computers, even when they are not connected to the site or server. When a user connects to the network the next time, OneNote reconciles the local copies of the notebook with the version saved on the server, merging changes into each copy of the shared notebook. This ensures that every member of the team has a current copy of the notebook. If two people make a change to the same note at the same time (not a very likely situation), OneNote displays an alert that its effort to merge changes didn't succeed and shows both versions for users to review.

When you select the option to create a shared notebook, shown in Figure 5-25, you need to specify whether you want to locate the notebook on a server or on a shared folder on your computer. As with a notebook that you set up to use yourself on more

Chapter 5

than one computer, you should locate a notebook that you'll share with others in a location such as the following:

- A folder or public file share on a network
- A shared folder on a computer on which you have Administrator permissions
- A document library on a Windows SharePoint Services Web site
- A high-storage-capacity USB drive

Figure 5-25 You can create a shared notebook from the Share menu or by using the New Notebook Wizard.

You also have the option when creating a shared notebook to invite other people to join you in using it. OneNote can create an e-mail message that you send to participants. By clicking the link in the body of the e-mail message, people you invite are directed to the location where you stored the shared notebook.

> **Note**
> To send a link to the shared notebook after it has been created, on the Share menu, click Send Shared Notebook Link To Others.

Protecting a Shared Section

You can choose which notebooks you share and which you keep to yourself. You can also control who has access to specific sections of a shared notebook by assigning a password to a section that you want to protect. A user who wants to work with a notebook section that is protected must enter the password to see the contents of the section's pages.

To assign a password to a notebook section, right-click the section tab, and then click Password Protect This Section. You'll see the Password Protection task pane, shown in Figure 5-26.

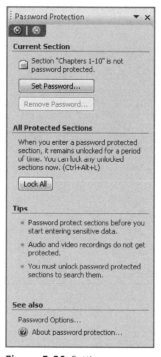

Figure 5-26 Setting up a password lets you control who can see the sections of a shared notebook.

When you click Set Password, you'll be prompted to enter a password and then confirm the password you entered. Passwords you use in OneNote are case-sensitive, so be sure that the Caps Lock key is turned off when you enter a password the first time. You cannot recover a password that you forget, which OneNote reminds you of. Be sure that you have a safe record of the password in the event you forget it.

Office OneNote 2007 saves a password in memory so that you do not have to enter it every time you go back to the section. If you don't work in OneNote for more than a specified period of time (the default period is 10 minutes), OneNote locks protected sections again, and you'll need to enter your password to open the sections. You can change the default time period, which ranges from one minute to one day (and a couple of other options for passwords), by using the Passwords page in the Options dialog box, shown in Figure 5-27.

- To lock notebook sections after a specified amount of time, select Lock Password-Protected Sections After I Have Not Worked In Them For The Following Amount Of Time, and then select the amount of time that you want.

- To lock notebook sections immediately after you've finished working in them, select Lock Password-Protected Sections As Soon As I Navigate Away From Them.

- To make notes in password-protected sections temporarily available to other applications, select Enable Add-In Programs To Access Password-Protected Sections When They Are Unlocked.

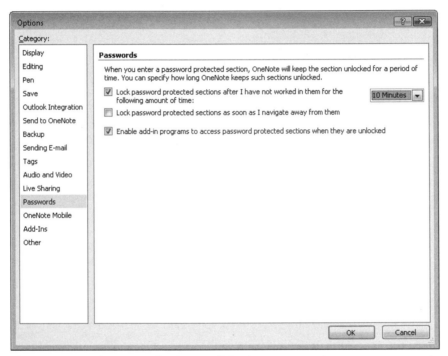

Figure 5-27 Use this page in the Options dialog box to manage how you use passwords in OneNote.

Password-protected sections are not included in notebook searches. To include a protected section in a notebook search, you must unlock the section before you begin to search your notes. Note tags used on the pages within protected sections are not included in the note tag summary unless the sections are first unlocked. Audio and video recordings are stored as separate files in your notebook, and you cannot apply passwords to them.

For more information about using note tags, see "Tagging Types of Notes" on page 103.

Sharing an Existing Notebook

If you have already created a OneNote notebook on your computer and want to give others permission to view and edit it, do the following:

1. In OneNote, close the notebook that you want to share.

2. On the File menu, click Exit to close OneNote.

3. From the Windows Start menu, open Windows Explorer.

4. In your My Documents folder, double-click OneNote Notebooks.

5. Right-click the notebook folder that you want to share, and then click Cut.

6. Using Windows Explorer, open the location where you'll share the notebook with others, and then paste the notebook in that location.

7. Start OneNote again.

8. On the File menu in OneNote, point to Open, and then click Notebook.

9. In the Open Notebook dialog box, browse to the location to which you moved your notebook, click to select the notebook folder, and then click Open.

You can send an e-mail message to other users to let them know where they can find the shared notebook. To send the message, on the Share menu, click Send Shared Notebook Link To Others.

Storing Shared Notebooks on a Windows SharePoint Services Site

As you've read in this chapter, a OneNote notebook can act as a repository for a wide range of information—both formal records, such as meeting transcripts, and brainstorming efforts of individuals and groups. Sharing a OneNote notebook on a SharePoint site provides a way to make this information part of a company's content repository. For example, when a notebook is stored on a SharePoint site, it is protected under the security policy for the site. The content of the notebook also becomes searchable as part of the content repository, making content such as images and audio and video recordings available to an organization.

Sharing a Notebook in a Live Session

Another sharing option in OneNote 2007 is a live sharing session, which enables you to share notebook pages with other users in real time. You can also use OneNote to broadcast note sessions to other OneNote users so that you can share your notes without giving others the ability to edit your notes. At the end of a shared session, each user retains a copy of the shared notes as part of his or her notebook, so there is no need to keep a record of what was discussed.

> **Note**
>
> Password-protected sections cannot be accessed by others during a live sharing session, even if the section is unlocked during the session. To include a protected section in a live sharing session, you must first remove the section's password protection and then start or join the live sharing session.

A live sharing session makes use of peer-to-peer connections—no server infrastructure is required. These sessions are also easy to set up, requiring only a few steps. Here are the steps to follow to initiate a live sharing session:

1.   On the Share menu, point to Live Sharing Session, and then click Start Sharing Current Session. You'll see the Start Live Session task pane, which is shown here:

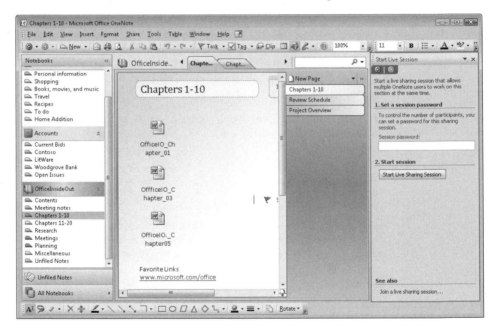

2.   In the task pane, enter a password if you want to control which people can share the session with you.

3.   Click Start Live Sharing Session.

4.   Click OK in the message box that appears, confirming that you want to go ahead and start a shared session. As OneNote initiates the session, you'll see the Current Live Session task pane, shown next.

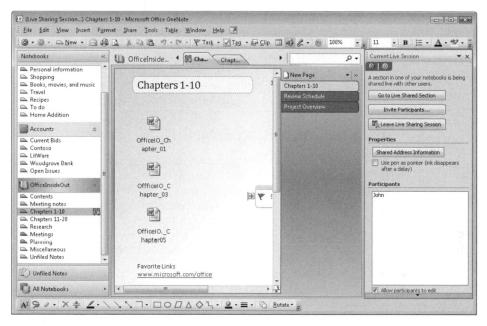

5. To invite other users to join the session, click Invite Participants. In the e-mail message that appears, add the addresses for the people you want to invite, and then send the message. The body of the message will contain the session address, which will appear something like the one shown here. You can also view the session address by clicking Shared Address Information in the task pane.

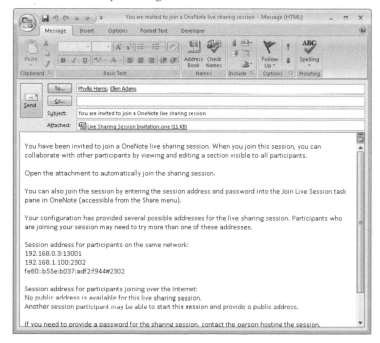

6. When you want to close the shared session, click Leave Live Sharing Session.

To join a live sharing session, you need to know the session address, which you'll receive from the session's originator through e-mail or otherwise. Once you know the address, you can join a session by pointing to Live Sharing Session on the Share menu and then clicking Join Existing Session. In the Join Live Session task pane, enter the shared session address and a password, if one is required, and then click Join Session.

Sharing Notes Using E-Mail

OneNote also lets you share information through e-mail, provided that you are using Outlook 2003 or later. To share information you've collected in OneNote in an e-mail message, click the E-Mail button on the toolbar or use the E-Mail command on the File menu. OneNote creates a file that includes copies of the note pages that you select and attaches the file to the message. The information on the page (including graphics) is formatted in HTML and placed in the body of the e-mail message. Recipients of the message are not required to have OneNote installed to read the information.

If a page has linked audio or video files, OneNote also attaches a copy of these to the message, provided you have selected this option. People receiving the e-mail message who have OneNote installed on their computers can double-click the attachment and add that page to their own notebooks in a special section called Recent Opened Sections.

If you are using an older version of Outlook or are using other e-mail programs, you can still send OneNote notes to others by manually attaching the file containing the selected pages to the message. Neither older versions of Outlook nor other e-mail programs convert the notes to HTML for inclusion in the body of the message, but you can still copy and paste your notes into your e-mail program.

> **Note**
>
> By using the Publish Pages command on the File menu in OneNote, you can create a copy of your OneNote page in a variety of formats, including a single-file Web page, a separate OneNote section, or a Word document. You can post the published file on a file share, Web site, or SharePoint site to share the information with others.

Working as a Team in a Microsoft Office Groove Workspace

Information workers often perform their jobs as part of a group or team—situations in which they need to share information and collaborate to solve problems and reach their goals. A group might consist only of coworkers, or it could be a mix of coworkers, consultants, business partners, and customers. Members of a group like this might work in three or four different locations, which can make it more difficult for them to remain on schedule, establish priorities, and accomplish the work they've initiated or been assigned to do. Often, the tools that groups use to communicate and collaborate support only work that takes place within a single organization, inside the firewall. Costs and security risks increase when these tools need to support the work of a team whose members are in different locations or outside organizational boundaries.

In this chapter and in Chapter 7, "Sharing and Communicating Using Microsoft Office Groove," you'll learn how to use Microsoft Office Groove 2007, an application designed to help teams of workers collaborate, especially on the kind of work that project teams perform. Office Groove 2007 is also designed to work securely over the Internet or a corporate network (based on a user account and data encryption), without requiring a large investment in additional IT resources.

In this chapter, we'll cover the basics of setting up Groove 2007. You'll learn how to create a Groove workspace, set up workspace members, and use workspace tools. In Chapter 7 you'll learn about details such as managing contacts, saving workspace templates, and other tasks that you perform in Groove.

> **Note**
>
> Office Groove 2007 is one of the products included in Microsoft Office Enterprise 2007 and Microsoft Office Ultimate 2007. The Microsoft Office system also includes Microsoft Office Groove Server 2007, which can be deployed in organizations that want more control over the installation and use of Office Groove 2007. With Office Groove Server 2007, organizations can, for example, use their implementation of Active Directory to configure Groove user accounts. They can set up various IT policies that govern the use of Groove, monitor usage, conduct data audits, and centrally back up user accounts. You can find more information about Office Groove Server 2007 on Microsoft Office Online.

Getting Started with Groove

For many users of the Microsoft Office system, Office Groove 2007 is their first experience with the program. Groove is a new addition to the 2007 Office release, but the program has been around for several years. Groove Networks, the company that first published Groove software, was started in 1997. The first version of the program was shipped in 2001. Microsoft acquired Groove Networks in 2005.

Your work in Groove is organized through workspaces that you and other people are members of. You might be the individual who creates a workspace, making you a member by default. You join other workspaces by accepting invitations that people send to you.

In a nutshell, a workspace provides access to information that teams need to share and tools teams need to collaborate on ideas, communicate with each other, and stay organized. You can think of a Groove workspace as a versatile computer application—a program that rolls into one common tools like a text editor, a sketchpad, a discussion board, file shares, and similar sorts of operational and organizational tools that you're used to working with in the Microsoft Office system and Microsoft Windows. Some of the tools that you'll use when you set up or become a member of a workspace in Office Groove 2007 include the following:

- Document collaboration tools used to share files and keep shared files updated. You can also store files on a Windows SharePoint Services Web site through a Groove workspace.

- Discussion tools that let team members conduct online conversations. The Groove workspace Chat tool lets members quickly exchange information as well.

- Meeting and calendar tools that can advise a team of project milestones, meeting times and purposes, and updates.

- Custom forms that teams can use to collect information in a structured format using Microsoft Office InfoPath 2007 or Office Groove 2007 Forms.

- Indicators that tell you who is working in a workspace and whether a team member or contact is online.

- Alerts that tell you when files and information have changed in a workspace and when team members perform important activities.

For more information about workspace tools, see "Outfitting a Groove Workspace with Tools" on page 150.

> **Note**
>
> Groove is integrated with Microsoft Office Communicator 2005 and 2007, so you can initiate a phone call or an instant messaging session with people in your contacts list from Office Groove 2007. For more information, see "Groove Instant Messaging" on page 182.

Setting Up a Groove Account

After installing Groove, you need to set up a Groove account (a user name and password in many cases) by completing the steps in the Account Configuration Wizard, which runs when you first start Groove. The welcome page of the wizard is shown in Figure 6-1.

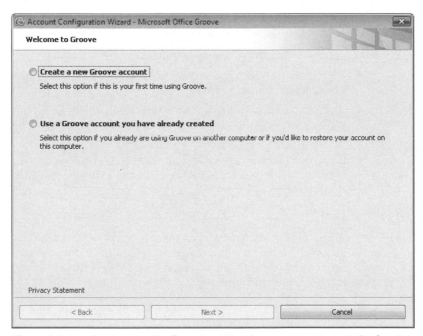

Figure 6-1 Use the Account Configuration Wizard to create an account the first time you use Groove.

Why You Need a Groove Account

You and the people you share files and information with in Office Groove 2007 need to have Groove accounts that are different from, for example, the user account that you use to log on to Windows or your e-mail program. Your Groove account information might be delivered in an e-mail message sent to you by your company's IT department, or you might need to specify the account yourself.

The account is required for security purposes and to control the type of work you and others can perform in a Groove workspace. Your account helps keep shared information synchronized and identifies you to other users of Groove. It also facilitates working with Groove on different computers.

Here are the steps you follow to complete the Account Configuration Wizard:

1. Select Create A New Groove Account, and then click Next. If you want to use a Groove account that you have set up on another computer instead of creating a new account, click Use A Groove Account You Have Already Created.

   If prompted, select a certificate for authenticating your Groove identity. You will see this prompt only if your Groove account is governed by a management policy that requires a signed authentication certificate. Usually, such certificates are used in organizations that use a smart card logon system.

2. Select an option for your Groove account configuration code:

   - If you have a Groove account configuration code, click I Have A Groove Account Configuration Code.

   - If you don't know where to find your Groove account configuration code but you think an administrator has created one for you, click I Need Help Finding My Groove Account Configuration Code.

   - If you don't have a Groove account configuration code and don't believe you require one for this Groove account, click I Don't Have A Groove Account Configuration Code.

3. Click Next.

4. If prompted, enter your Groove account configuration code and Groove account configuration server. Usually, the Groove account configuration server information is filled in for you. If it's not and you're unsure of what to enter in this field, ask your system administrator.

5. Complete the Enter Groove Account Information page with the following information, and then click Next:

   - Enter your account name and e-mail address. The name you enter is the display name by which people will recognize you. Depending on how you obtained Groove, the account name and e-mail address fields may be filled in for you and the fields will not be editable. This is often the case if you obtained Groove at your workplace, either as part of the Microsoft Office system or as a separate application.

   - Enter a password and hint information to keep your account secure.

   - If you selected an authentication certificate on an earlier page in the wizard, you can click the link to use a smart card or certificate to secure your account instead of using a password.

6. Select an option for listing your account identity in the public Groove directory. Listing your account identity lets other Groove users find you and start Groove activities with you.

7. Click Finish.

When you complete the Account Configuration Wizard, Groove creates your account and opens the Launchbar.

About Groove Security

Groove helps keep your data secure in a number of ways. In Groove workspaces, workspace members are assigned roles that grant specific permissions, such as reading or editing. Groove automatically protects your data using random keys stored in your account. Groove also supports two authentication processes for verifying contacts. The first is manual authentication, in which you verify the digital fingerprints of contact identities. The other is certification, in which a digital certificate is assigned to a contact identity by a certificate authority, such as VeriSign. Certification is managed by Groove administrators.

You'll learn more about workspace member roles later in this chapter in "Inviting Workspace Members and Assigning Member Roles" on page 140. For more information about authenticating contacts, see "Verifying Contact Identities" on page 192.

Your memberships in workspaces, as well as messages or invitations you send, are cryptographically "tagged" with your Groove identity. Users who receive your invitations and messages can verify your identity based on this information. All updates you make in a standard workspace are encrypted when you send them and then decrypted when they are received to ensure that only other members of the workspace can read them. Instant messages are also encrypted and then decrypted in the same manner.

The View from the Launchbar

The Launchbar, shown in Figure 6-2, is a cross between a task pane (like those in Microsoft Office 2003 applications) and a window in an instant messaging program. You can use the Launchbar in Groove 2007 to create workspaces, build a contact list, send messages, check on the status of work, and see whether your contacts are online or offline. You can also use the Launchbar to perform administrative tasks related to your work in Groove, such as managing your account and communications.

Note

If you set up Groove to open when you start Windows, you'll log on, and Groove will then display the Launchbar.

Figure 6-2 Use the Launchbar to manage workspaces and contacts.

The Launchbar is organized in two main areas: Workspaces and Contacts. Each area displays status information. The Workspaces area, for example, shows you the status of each workspace you're a member of. The status of a workspace can be Active, Unread, or Read:

- Active simply means the workspace is open and one of its members—you or another member—is doing some work. The number of active members in the workspace is indicated to the right of the workspace's name.

- Unread means that the workspace contains an updated file, new meeting notes, or some other information that you haven't yet reviewed. You need to check out what's new in the workspace.

- Read means that your work in the workspace is current.

Similarly, the Contacts area tells you which of your contacts are online, offline, or actively engaged in a task in a workspace. This information is like the information you might be familiar with seeing about contacts in your instant messaging program.

Both the Workspaces and the Contacts areas are supported by links in a third area, Common Tasks. You can use the View By command in this area, for example, to switch from viewing workspaces by status (the view shown in Figure 6-2) to viewing them in an alphabetical list or by type. You can also use the Common Tasks area to create a folder or turn off alerts that Groove displays to inform you when a certain event has taken place. The list of common tasks changes if you select a specific workspace or a specific contact. When you select a specific workspace, for example, the Common Tasks area provides a link you can use to send someone an invitation to join the workspace and a link for viewing workspace properties. Many of the commands that you can run from the Launchbar are also included among the menu commands that appear in the window in which a workspace is displayed. The advantage of the Launchbar is that you can perform these actions without being active in a workspace.

You can also use the Launchbar to keep in touch with your contacts using Groove's messaging capabilities. The Send Message dialog box, shown in Figure 6-3, includes a text box and tools such as a spelling checker. You can attach files to a message to supplement the information that you provide in the text of the message itself.

For more information about adding and managing contacts in Groove, see Chapter 7.

Figure 6-3 You can use the Send Message dialog box to send messages to your contacts and workspace members.

Here are the steps you follow to send a message to a Groove contact using the Launchbar:

1. In the Launchbar, right-click the name of the contact, and then click Send Message.

2. In the Send Message dialog box, type your message, attach a file if one is required, and then click Send.

> **Note**
>
> Keep in mind that in Groove, a contact and a workspace member are not one and the same. People who are members of the workspaces you belong to might not be listed among your contacts. You can add workspace members to your contact list, however, which makes them part of what is called your list of Known Groove Contacts.

If you are offline when you write a message, Groove 2007 will send the message as soon as you are online again. Groove 2007 alerts, which are displayed above the Windows taskbar, notify you when a message is sent, delivered, opened, and when your contact replies. Figure 6-4 shows an example of an alert that is displayed when you first send a message.

Figure 6-4 Groove displays alerts to inform you when a message has been sent or received.

> **Note**
>
> If you don't want to be alerted each time you send or receive a message, on the Options menu on the Launchbar, click Suppress Alerts.

Groove Workspace Basics

Workspaces are at the center of the capabilities that Groove 2007 provides. Workspaces have members—a virtual team of people involved in a project or members of an organization's finance or marketing department, for example—as well as tools that members use to work together. In this section, you'll learn how to create a standard Groove workspace and how to invite and manage workspace members.

Creating a Workspace

When you need to create and start setting up a workspace in Groove, click the New Workspace link at the top of the Workspaces area on the Launchbar. You then enter a name and specify the type of workspace you're creating. You might also select a workspace template.

For more information about workspace templates, see Chapter 7.

Here are the steps to follow to create a standard workspace in Groove 2007:

1. On the Launchbar, click New Workspace. (You can also use the New command on the File menu on the Launchbar.)

2. In the Create New Workspace dialog box, shown here, select the Standard option.

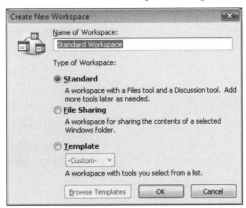

3. Type a name for the workspace, and then click OK.

> **Note**
>
> The descriptions of the standard workspace and the file-sharing workspace provide a sense about the work you can do in Groove. You'll learn more about file-sharing workspaces in Chapter 7.

For a standard workspace, after you click OK in the Create New Workspace dialog box, you'll see the Groove Workspace Explorer, shown in Figure 6-5. The Workspace Explorer provides access to workspace tools (the File tool and the Discussion tool are included by default), as well as to commands you can use to invite people to join the workspace, send messages to other workspace members, manage workspace properties, and change how you view the information that a workspace contains. After reviewing the Workspace Explorer for only a brief period of time, you can begin to see how it ties into and builds on the work that you perform using the Launchbar.

Figure 6-5 The Workspace Explorer for a standard workspace provides access to tools, shared files, and workspace members.

Inviting Workspace Members and Assigning Member Roles

Someone needs to create a workspace, of course, and then invite people (and possibly other computers that the creator of the workspace uses) to become members of that workspace. Each person who becomes a member of a Groove workspace is assigned a role. The individual who creates the workspace has the Manager role by default. Other members of a workspace can be designated workspace managers as well or be assigned the Participant or Guest role.

Each role has standard permissions that affect the type of work a member can do in a workspace. Managers, for example, can do the following:

- Edit files
- Delete files
- Delete the entire workspace
- Invite members
- Remove members
- Add or delete tools
- Cancel outstanding invitations

Members assigned to the Participant role can, by default, add tools to a workspace and invite others to join. Individuals assigned to the Guest role cannot perform any of these functions by default. The Guest role should be assigned to members who need to review the workspace from time to time to check on progress but who are not actively engaged in the proceedings or projects the workspace supports.

Workspace managers can assign a member to a different role after the member has joined the workspace. Managers can also change the permissions associated with a specific role. For more information, see "Setting Roles and Changing Role Permissions" on page 146.

Here are the steps you follow to invite someone who is already a Groove user to join a workspace:

1. In the Workspace Members pane, under Invite To Workspace, enter the name or e-mail address of the person you want to invite to this workspace, as shown here, and then click Go.

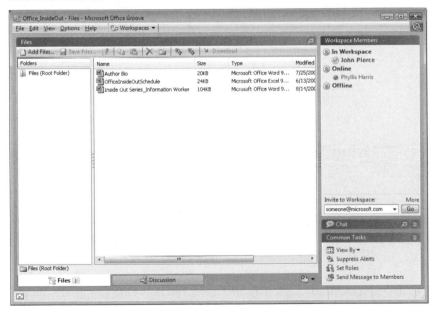

2. To send an invitation to more than one person, click More.

3. In the Add Recipients dialog box, enter the name or e-mail address of the person you want to invite, and then click Add To List. You can repeat this step to include additional people in the invitation.

4. In the Add Recipients dialog box, click OK.

5. In the Send Invitation dialog box, shown next, select a role for the invitee, and type a message if you'd like.

Chapter 6

6. If you want a confirmation that the person has accepted the invitation, select the Require Acceptance Confirmation check box.

7. Click Invite.

You can see whether the person accepts your invitation by monitoring Groove alerts.

Using Your Groove Account on a Second Computer

To use your Groove account on another computer (in other words, to invite the other computer to join the workspace), you need to place a copy of the file that contains your Groove account information on the other computer. After you install Groove on the other computer, all you need to do is double-click your account file, and Groove takes it from there. The information in the workspaces you belong to will be downloaded to the other computer, for example, and you'll see your same list of contacts.

Figure 6-6 shows the dialog box you use to save your Groove account file. You can open this dialog box by clicking Invite My Other Computers on the Options menu on the Launchbar. The dialog box also provides clear instructions for the steps you need to take.

Figure 6-6 You can easily set up your account on another computer using this dialog box.

Knowing When Members Are Present and Accounted For

The Workspace Members pane in the Workspace Explorer lists the names of the members of a workspace and indicates the status of each member. (To show or hide the Workspace Members pane, on the View menu, point to Show/Hide, and then click Members.) The status of a workspace member can be one of the following:

- **In Workspace** Indicates members who currently have the workspace open.

- **Navigating Together** Indicates members who currently have the workspace open and have enabled the Navigate Together feature.

- **Online** Indicates members who are currently online but don't have this workspace open.

- **Idle** Lists members who are currently online but have not performed activities at their computer for at least the past 15 minutes.

- **Offline** Indicates members who are currently offline.

- **Suspended** Indicates members whose workspace data is no longer being synchronized.

Chapter 6

Navigating Together

The Navigate Together option lets workspace members move in unison between work-space tools. When you select Navigate Together, all other members who have the option selected go to the tool that you select. Likewise, you go to the tool another member selects. Use the Navigate Together option on the Options menu to turn this option on or off.

Only members who have Navigate Together selected at the same time navigate together. If other members already have the option selected when you select it, you immediately navigate to their location in the workspace. Navigate Together remains turned on until you turn it off or close the Workspace Explorer.

Navigate Together works with the following actions in a workspace:

- Opening or closing the Chat tool.
- Navigating between tools by clicking tool tabs.
- Navigating between pictures in the Pictures tool and sketches in the Sketchpad tool.
- Navigating in the Calendar tool.
- Opening folders in the Files tool.
- Navigating from page to page in the Notepad tool.

To navigate on your own while Navigate Together is turned on, press Shift and click instead of only clicking. You can do this if you need to work with a different tool on your own.

You can point at a member's name to display a status window with information about the member. In addition, member names appear in different colors, depending on their authentication status.

For more information about authentication status, see "Verifying Contact Identities" on page 192.

You can also organize your view of workspace members in several different ways. Right-click in the Workspace Members pane, and then select the view you want:

- **Alphabetical** Lists all members alphabetically.
- **Status** Categorizes members according to their current status.
- **Verification Status** Categorizes members according to their contact authentication status.

- **Role** Categorizes members according to their role in the workspace.

- **Organization** Categorizes members by the organization listed in their contact properties. If members have no organization listed in contact properties, they are listed under "Unknown Organization."

Regardless of a member's status, you can initiate activities with your coworkers in a workspace. For example, you can right-click a member's name, select Properties, and open the member's Contact card to send a message to that member. You can also select several members, right-click, and select options to send a message or an invitation to a new workspace.

> **Note**
>
> When you are working in the Workspace Members pane, you can click the expand and collapse buttons to open and close member categories, the Chat tool, or the Common Tasks area. If you hide the Workspace Members pane, you also hide the Chat tool and the Common Tasks area.

Chatting with Workspace Members

Each Groove 2007 standard workspace includes a Chat tool. The Chat tool is located near the bottom of the Workspace Members pane.

Workspace members can contribute messages to a discussion in the Chat tool at any time by clicking in the blank box at the bottom of the tool and then clicking the arrow button to send the message. Messages posted in the Chat tool are saved, and the conversation continues for as long as the workspace exists. As with other Groove 2007 tools, the number of users currently involved in a chat is listed. Groove displays an alert to let workspace members know when a message has been posted in the Chat tool. Figure 6-7 shows an example of an active chat in a standard Groove workspace.

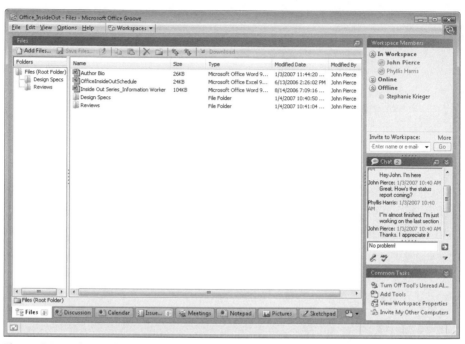

Figure 6-7 A Chat tool is one of the built-in features in a standard Groove workspace.

> **Note**
>
> If you are using Groove 2007 on a Tablet PC, the Chat window may open by default in Ink mode. You will need to click Options, and then click Switch To Text Mode when you want to type in the Groove Chat window.

Setting Roles and Changing Role Permissions

In some workspaces, you might have reason, even temporarily, to change the role of a member after he or she accepts the invitation to the workspace. You might also want to add or remove certain permissions for the Manager, Participant, or Guest roles. For example, you might want to restrict those in the Participant role from adding tools or let them delete tools in a workspace. Only individuals who are workspace managers can make these changes.

To set a workspace member's role, open the workspace, and then follow these steps:

1. On the Options menu, click Set Roles.

2. In the Properties dialog box, select the member whose role you want to set, and then click Change Role.

3. In the Change Role dialog box, shown here, select the new role, and then click OK.

To change the permissions for a workspace role, open the workspace, and then follow these steps:

1. On the Options menu, click Set Roles.

2. In the Properties dialog box, click the Permissions tab, which is shown here.

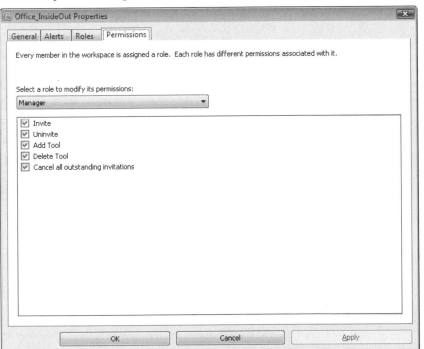

3. On the Permissions tab, select the role whose permissions you want to modify, and then select or clear the check boxes for the privileges you want to grant or deny.

Exploring a Groove Workspace

A standard Groove workspace includes a Files tool and a Discussion tool by default. In the Workspace Explorer, current workspace members are listed in the Workspace Members pane, the Chat tool is at the ready, and you're provided with links to common tasks.

As the number of workspaces you belong to grows, you'll need to switch from one workspace to another from time to time. The Workspace Explorer provides several ways by which you can do this. On the Workspace Explorer toolbar, for example, you can display the Workspaces Selector, shown in Figure 6-8, a drop-down menu that appears in the toolbar. (To hide or display the Workspaces Selector, on the View menu, point to Toolbars, and then click Explorer Toolbar.) You can reposition the Workspaces Selector by dragging it to a different location on the toolbar.

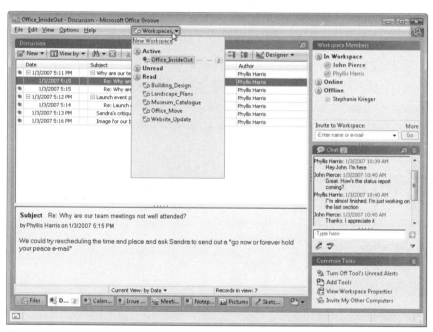

Figure 6-8 The Workspaces Selector lets you to switch between workspaces.

You can also display the Workspace List by clicking Show/Hide, and then Workspace List on the View menu. In the Workspace List, click a workspace's title to open that workspace. By pointing at a workspace, you can display a status window that lists the last modified date and members who are currently in the workspace. The Workspace List is shown in Figure 6-9.

You should become familiar as well with the Workspace Manager, which is shown in Figure 6-10. You open the Workspace Manager by clicking the command of the same name on the Options menu in the Workspace Explorer. The Workspace Manager is another means of viewing your workspaces. You can see the name, status, type, and time when you last had unread information in the workspace. When you select a work-space name in the list, the Workspace Members pane shows which members are active in the workspace and which members are online or offline.

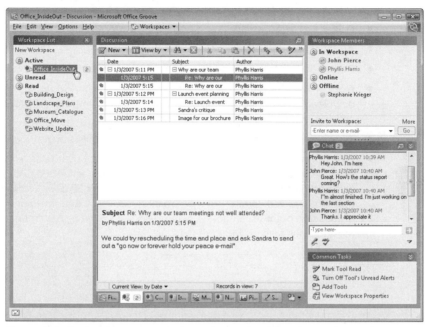

Figure 6-9 The Workspace List, similar to the Workspaces Selector, shows all your available workspaces.

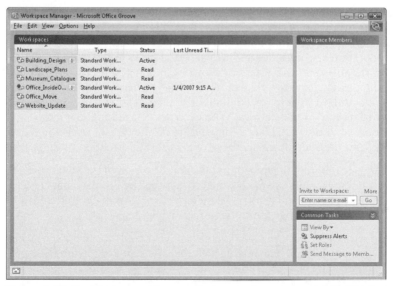

Figure 6-10 The Workspace Manager displays workspaces in a detailed list format.

Ways to List Workspaces in the Workspace List

Groove lets you view workspaces in several different ways. The command you use to select the view you want is View Workspaces By, which is on the View menu. Here's a quick rundown on how you can view a list of your workspaces:

- **Folders** Sorts workspaces by folder.
- **Alphabetical** Lists workspaces in alphabetical order.
- **Status** Sorts workspaces by their status: Active, Unread, or Read.
- **Not On This Computer** Workspaces you have on other computers. You can download the workspace data either from another computer that contains your account or from another workspace member.
- **Type** Sorts workspaces by type, such as standard or file sharing.
- **Last Unread Time** This view organizes workspaces by their relative activity. For example, you can see which of your workspaces were active and updated today, yesterday, within the last seven days, or within the last 30 days. Workspaces that have not received updates for more than 30 days are categorized under Older. Within each of these categories, workspaces are sorted in descending order of most recently read.

Outfitting a Groove Workspace with Tools

A team's manager, as well as each of its participants, needs to keep track of and resolve issues, coordinate tasks, report on their progress, and exchange and evaluate ideas—all while creating and updating documents and related information. Although tools such as e-mail, file shares on servers and shared computers, Web sites, and even specialized collaboration applications support particular tasks and processes, they don't always support consistent data access or provide context and information about the daily activities that a distributed workforce needs. That's where Groove workspace tools come into play. A standard workspace can include tools that support project planning, file sharing, discussions, and meetings. When you set up a standard workspace, you can add the tools you know you'll need (depending on the type of work you'll do in the workspace) and then add others as the activities and information in the workspace develops.

Workspace tools are organized on tabs at the bottom of the Workspace Explorer window. Clicking a tool's tab makes the tool active. The number that appears beside a tool's tab tells you how many workspace members are working with that tool. You can also drag tool tabs to change their position in the workspace.

There are several ways you can add one or more tools to a workspace. You can use the New command on the File menu, click the icon that appears on the right side of the tool tab area, or click Add Tools in the Common Tasks area. One way or the other, you'll select a specific tool (such as the Calendar or the Meetings tool) or arrive at the More

Tools dialog box, shown in Figure 6-11, in which you can select the tool or tools you want to add.

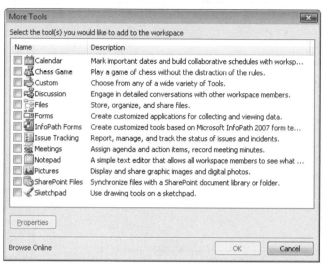

Figure 6-11 The More Tools dialog box gives you access to additional workspace tools.

In the following sections, you'll learn about the basic features and operations of the various tools you can use in a Groove workspace.

For more information about the Groove Forms tool, see Chapter 7.

Keeping a Calendar

The Calendar tool lets you keep track of appointments and meetings, mark due dates for tasks or project milestones, and annotate any of the items you define with details such as a meeting's purpose or what information needs to be refreshed in this week's status report. Figure 6-12 shows the Calendar tool (in monthly view).

Simply click New Appointment (or double-click a date) to add an item to the calendar. In the Add Appointment dialog box, shown in Figure 6-13, you're required to enter a topic in the Subject field and specify the start and end of the appointment or event. In the Details area, you can type a description of the appointment, reminding yourself and informing others what the particular appointment concerns.

Chapter 6

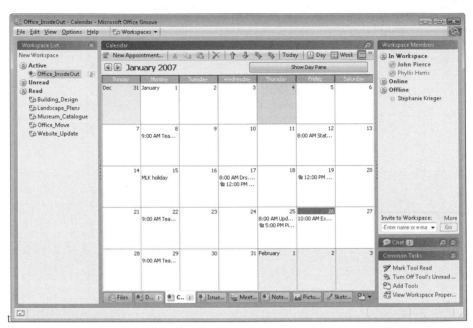

Figure 6-12 The Calendar tool enables you to track important dates and appointments. You can link to appointments from other tools in a workspace.

Figure 6-13 Use the Add Appointment dialog box to enter the specifics of a new appointment or event.

Note

To delete an appointment, right-click the entry for the appointment in the calendar, and then click Delete.

Using the Calendar tool's toolbar, you can adjust how the calendar is displayed, move from appointment to appointment, and perform operations such as exporting, importing, or printing the details of appointments. Here are some of the ways you can work with the Calendar tool:

- You can view appointments for a month, for a specific day, or for a week. You can also show what Groove refers to as the Day Pane (click Show Day Pane), which lists each day's appointments on the right side of the calendar and offers a detailed view beside a week's or month's worth of appointments.

- Move from appointment to appointment by clicking the arrow buttons on the toolbar or by clicking Next Appointment or Previous Appointment on the View menu.

- Create links to specific appointments. To copy a link to an appointment, right-click the appointment and then click Copy Appointment as Link. Open the tool where you want to place the link (for example, in the Details area of a meeting you define in the Meetings tool) and then paste the link there.

> **Note**
>
> You can open a tool in its own window by right-clicking the tool's tab and then clicking Open In New Window.

Topics Under Discussion

You can use the Discussion tool to start or follow an online conversation. It lets you and other workspace members propose and respond to ideas—critiquing, building on, and debating the questions and ideas that affect your work together. The information and opinions recorded in the tool can be archived with a workspace and examined in depth later to extract important details and apply one team's experience to the work of others.

For more information about archiving a workspace, see Chapter 7.

The Discussion tool has two types of entries: topics and responses. In the Discussion tool window, shown in Figure 6-14, you can see a list of subjects (with responses indented) and the content of a posting in a pane below the list. Workspace members add to a conversation by responding to a topic posting. Members can respond to topic postings and to other responses.

When you start a discussion about a topic, you specify a subject. You can also specify a category so that as the number of discussion items increases, items can be organized and grouped. Responses to a specific posting are stored under that category as well, indented under the initial item. A project manager or group leader might want to set up some standard categories at the start of a project to foster discussion on particular areas—schedule, change requests, budget, and the like.

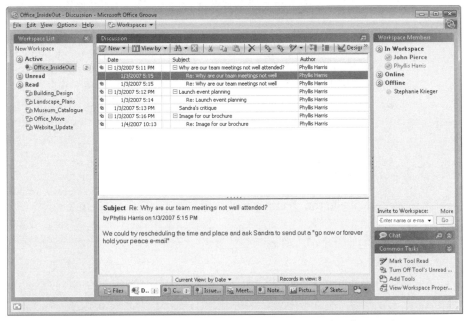

Figure 6-14 Use the Discussion tool to brainstorm, raise issues, and exchange ideas.

Here are the steps you follow to begin a topic of conversation in the Discussion tool:

1. On the Discussion tool's toolbar, click New, and then click Topic.

2. Enter a subject for the topic. If you want to assign the topic to a category, select an item from the Category list, or click the plus (+) sign to set up a new category.

3. Type your thoughts on the topic in the text box below the subject line, and then click Save.

The topic will be displayed in the workspace. Other users can double-click the discussion record to compose a response. Each time you go online, Groove 2007 synchronizes discussion threads so that all workspace members can see the postings and responses other members have contributed.

The Discussion tool's toolbar provides controls for viewing, searching, and navigating through the items. The default views are By Date and By Category. To search for an item in the Discussion tool, click the Search button on the toolbar, and then follow these steps:

1. In the list at the top of the Form Search dialog box, select Topic or Response.

2. In the Subject field, type the subject you're looking for.

3. In the Category list, select a category to search for all the discussion items in a specific category.

4. In the By field, you can enter a workspace member's name. In the On field, enter a date, or choose one from the pop-up calendar.

5. Click Search.

Note

The Discussion tool also provides an advanced search feature that you can use to cull through a long list of discussion items or when you need to apply complex criteria (including logical AND and OR combinations) to your search.

Making Meetings More Effective

It's hard sometimes to get work accomplished at meetings. There's a real art to running and participating in meetings that are effective. Groove's Meetings tool is designed to help members of a workspace prepare for and document meetings and the outcomes of meetings—what decisions were made and who will take what actions. You can use the Meetings tool as a single, centralized location in which to post agendas before the meeting, define guidelines and ground rules for the topics under discussion, and then record meeting minutes. The Meetings tool is shown in Figure 6-15.

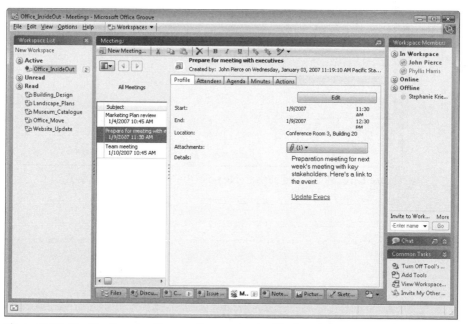

Figure 6-15 The Meetings tool is more than a calendar. Use it to define an agenda, track action items, and record meeting minutes.

To set up a meeting, click New Meeting on the Meetings toolbar. This command starts the Meeting Wizard, shown in Figure 6-16, which you use to enter a profile for the meeting, including the subject of the meeting, the meeting time and location, and other details.

When you click OK in the wizard, the details you've entered appear on the Profile tab in the Meetings tool, which is shown earlier in Figure 6-15. You can then step through each of the other tabs—Attendees, Agenda, Minutes, and Actions—to round out the information about the meeting you've defined. As the names of the tabs indicate, the Meetings tool isn't designed only for setting up meetings. It is designed to capture information at the meeting (you can use the tool to take minutes while the meeting occurs) and to set up a framework for following up on discussions at the meeting—in the form of action items that you assign to meeting attendees and then track their status and rank in priority.

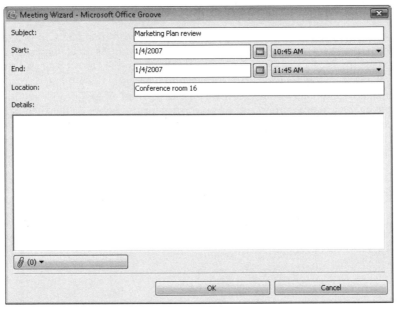

Figure 6-16 Meeting details are entered in the Meeting Wizard.

INSIDE OUT   Linking an Item from One Tool to Another

Let's say you define an action item in the Meetings tool. Now you want to continue discussing this item with other members of the team and also add an appointment to the Calendar tool to mark the date by which the item needs to be resolved. You can link an item, such as a meeting detail or an appointment, from one tool to another. To establish the link, select the item you want to link. Then, on the Edit menu, click Copy As Link. (In some tools, you may be offered a submenu of choices. For example, you can link an entire meeting or just a single action item.) Now switch to the tool you want to link the item to. Create a new appointment, for example, or a new topic in the Discussion tool, and then paste the linked item into the new item. The linked item appears as a hyperlink in blue type and underlined. You can then click the link to see the details of the action item, discussion thread, appointment, or other item. By linking items, you strengthen the network of information that a Groove workspace helps you organize and capitalize on the capabilities of each workspace tool.

Storing, Organizing, and Sharing Files

The Files tool, shown in Figure 6-17, is designed so that workspace members can share and collaborate on many different file types, including files from other Microsoft Office system applications. Any member of a workspace can open any of the files that are available in the Files tool.

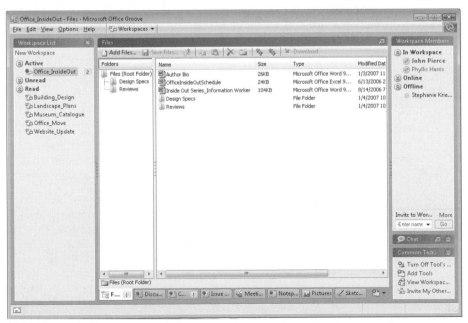

Figure 6-17 The Files tool is a collection of workspace files and folders.

Chapter 6

When a member of a workspace edits or updates a file and saves the changes in Groove 2007, the file is automatically updated for all other workspace members. When several members work on a file at the same time, the first person to save changes will update the original file. If another member saves changes to the original version, a second copy of the file will be created with the editor's name in the title.

You need to follow just two steps to add a file to the Files tool:

1. On the Files toolbar, click Add Files.

2. In the Add Files dialog box, find and select the file(s) you want to add, and then click Open.

You can also save a file that's listed in the Files tool to a folder in Windows. To save a file to a folder in Windows, select the file or files in the Files list, and then click Save Files on the toolbar.

To work with a file from the Files tool, right-click the file, and then use the shortcut menu. The shortcut menu lets you perform operations such as opening and editing a file, printing a file, or sending a file to someone as an attachment in an e-mail message. You can also create new files directly in the Files tool. On the File menu, click New, and then choose the type of file you want to create. The list of file types will be based on the applications that you have installed on your computer.

> **Note**
>
> Groove's SharePoint Files tool builds on the capabilities of the Files tool by linking a Groove workspace to a document library in a Windows SharePoint Services site. The SharePoint site must be built on Windows SharePoint Services (version 3).

Tracking Issues

In collaborative work, when issues are raised, questions often arise as well about who will handle the issue and what kind of progress is being made. Even projects of modest scope can involve a large number of issues, and the effort required to document and track these issues is an area that many groups find to be time-consuming and tedious.

The Issue Tracking tool in Groove consists of two basic forms, plus a group of standard and user-defined views that let you group and organize recorded issues for ease of reference and review. The first form, called the Issue Tracking form, is shown in Figure 6-18. This form includes two tabs—Original Report and Current Status. It is used to identify an issue and includes details such as who entered the issue, which category an issue is assigned to, which workspace member the issue has been assigned to, and the issue's status. The Issue Tracking form also contains a text box you can use to describe the issue and an attachments area so that supporting documents and other files related to the issue can be made part of the record. The issue ID is provided by Groove and identifies the issue and who created the issue record.

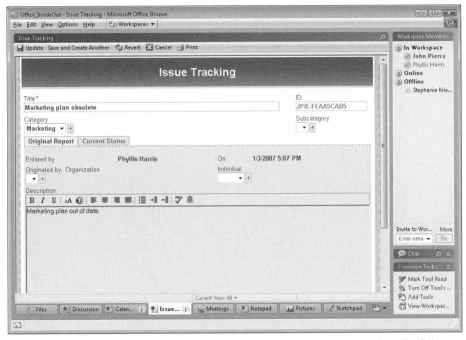

Figure 6-18 The Issue Tracking tool lets you assign issues to workspace members for follow-up and resolution.

The Response form, shown in Figure 6-19, displays the details entered in the Issue Tracking form and provides an area for a member to enter comments in response.

The Issue Tracking tool is designed using the Groove Forms tool. To learn more about the Groove Forms tool, see Chapter 7.

Any workspace member can create an issue record (or respond to an issue). In addition, workspace members who have the necessary permissions can create special keyword records that become part of the lists for fields such as Originated By, Status, Assigned To, and Priority. Permissions are defined as part of the form's design and can be based on member role or given to specific workspace members.

You can create new keywords (assuming that you have the necessary privileges) by choosing one of the keyword record options from the New menu. You might, for example, create new keywords for issue categories and subcategories, or enter the keywords you want to use to classify issues by status and priority. When you or another workspace member records a new issue, these keywords are included in the lists for these fields.

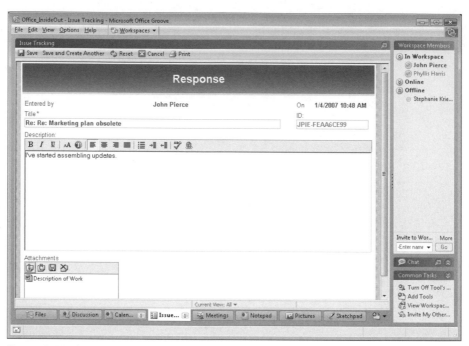

Figure 6-19 The Response form can be used to update workspace members about an issue.

The purpose of defining keywords, of course, is to use them to sort and group the items in a large list of issues. The View By menu on the Issue Tracking toolbar lets you group issues by assignment, priority, and the other fields for which you define keywords. You can also use the Search button in the Issue Tracking tool to locate an issue you're looking for. You can search by title, category, originator, or other fields defined for an issue.

Taking Notes

The Notepad tool is a text editor that workspace members can use to create and save simple documents—meeting agendas or minutes, for example, or lists of specifications, summaries of team decisions, suggestions for process changes, and status reports about project tasks. These possibilities comprise just a few of the possible uses of the Groove Notepad tool, which is shown in Figure 6-20.

The notes you take aren't limited to plain text. The Notepad tool provides formatting features such as bold, italic, and underline, and choices of fonts, font color, and font size. You can also print or export a note, search for text in a note page, and check your spelling. There are quite a few of the familiar word-processing features in this simple notepad. The following list provides more details on several of them:

- **Adding pages to a notepad** You can add pages to a notepad and name each page for reference. For example, think of the context a workspace can provide by keeping the status reports for each week of your project easily accessible in the notepad.

To add a new note page, click New Note, and then add a name for the note in the Title box. Enter content for the note in the editing area. You can right-click to see formatting options, or use the formatting icons on the toolbar. To view note pages, click the Previous or Next buttons to move sequentially among note pages, or select a note in the Note list.

- **Editing notes** To edit a note page in the Notepad tool, go to the page you need to edit, and then click Edit. If another workspace member is already editing the selected note page, Groove prompts you to choose whether you want to edit the note anyway or wait until the other member is finished editing the page. The Edit button in the Notepad tool displays a number if one or more other members are currently editing the selected page. You can point at the Edit button to display a status window that tells you which member is currently editing the page. If you choose to continue and edit the page, Groove saves your changes in a new "conflict" copy of the note page. A conflict page also includes a link back to the original page. Likewise, if you are editing a page and another member begins to edit the same page, Groove briefly displays a message to inform you that another member has started to edit the page. If this occurs, your changes are saved to the original document and the other member's changes are saved in a conflict copy.

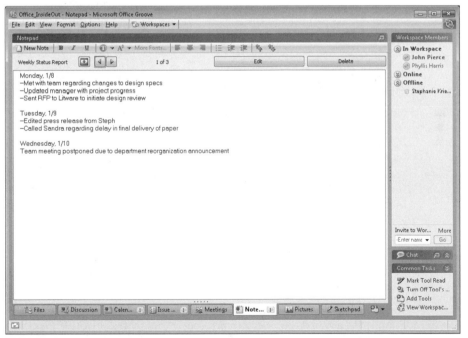

Figure 6-20 The Notepad tool is a text editor, complete with formatting options, that you can use to record information about the activities in a workspace.

- **Exporting notes** You can export a selected note page in a Rich Text Format (RTF) file. You can then open the RTF file in other programs that support this format, such as Microsoft Office Word or WordPad in Windows.

Chapter 6

To export a note, display the page you want to export, and then click Export on the File menu. By default, the notepad uses the title of the note for the file name.

- **Searching for text in a note page** You can search the text in a note page when the note is open for reading or editing. If a note is open for editing, you must click in the text-editing area before you start a search. To search text in a note, on the Edit menu, click the Find command. As you can with similar text-searching features, you can choose options such as case-sensitivity to refine the search.

- **Creating links to note pages** As with other workspace tools, you can create a link that references a specific note page. Open the note page you want to link to. Then, on the Edit menu, click Copy Note As Link. Switch to the tool in which you want to place the link, and then paste the link in the appropriate item—a new appointment or a discussion topic, for example.

- **Printing a note page** To print a note page, on the File menu, click Print.

> **Note**
> You can use familiar keyboard shortcuts when working with the Notepad tool, including Ctrl+C to copy, Ctrl+X to cut, and Ctrl+V to paste.

Adding Pictures to a Workspace

Not every workspace needs to use the Pictures tool, but images are often important to work in architecture, publishing, marketing, and similar business pursuits. The Groove Pictures tool, shown in Figure 6-21, lets you use a workspace to display and share image files in JPEG (.jpg) or bitmap (.bmp) format. Click the Show Picture Details button in the center of the window to see a list of the picture files that have been added to the workspace, as well as information such as file size, type, modified date, and the last person who edited the file.

You add a picture by clicking Add Pictures on the toolbar and then using the Open Picture File dialog box to select the file you want. You can also open a folder on your computer that contains image files, and then drag a file to the Pictures tool and drop it in the picture viewing area or into the list. The Pictures tool automatically scales all pictures you add to the tool to fit the current size of the picture viewer window.

You can edit pictures in the Pictures tool if your computer has a picture-editing program that supports the selected file type. If you open a JPEG file for editing but don't have a program that supports editing this type of file, it will open for display in your Web browser or in a picture viewer. On most computers, bitmap (.bmp) files will open in Microsoft Paint. To open one or more picture files in a graphics-editing program, right-click them in the list, and click Edit. Depending on the graphics program and the operating system, a new window may open for each file. When you edit and save a picture and then return to Groove, you're prompted to save the picture back to Groove. You can export any picture in the Pictures tool to a disk and also copy pictures to another instance of the Pictures tool (in another workspace, for example) or to an image-editing program.

Figure 6-21 The Groove Pictures tool lets you store images related to the topic of a workspace.

Sketching Your Ideas

Sketches that help visualize a business process, a space plan, the relationship between tables in a database—these and many other types of drawings and diagrams—play an important role in business discussions and plans these days. The simple palette and set of tools that the Groove Sketchpad tool (shown in Figure 6-22) provides helps you and other team members brainstorm, draw in the context of a discussion, and just get your ideas down so that you can refine them later.

If you are familiar with a drawing application (Paint, which comes with Windows, for example, or a more sophisticated program, such as Microsoft Office Visio), you'll come up with a number of ways in which you can put the Sketchpad tool to work. Imagine, for example, sketching an organizational chart as you talk through the pros and cons of a small merger, sketching the main stages of a workflow process you want to introduce, or sketching ideas about a room in a house that's under design.

You can add a page to a sketchpad by clicking New Sketch on the File menu or by clicking the button that adds a blank page. (This button sits to the left of the Previous button, just above the drawing page.) To name a sketch, click the label that reads Untitled, and then enter the name you want to use.

Chapter 6

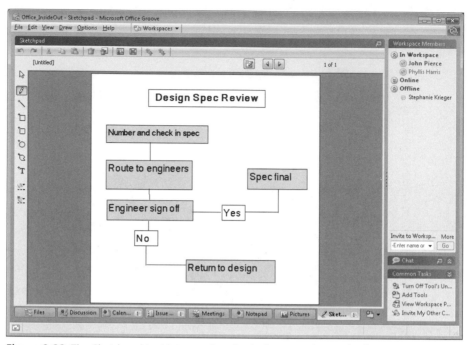

Figure 6-22 The Sketchpad tool lets you draw basic shapes and provides formatting options for fill colors and line colors.

The drawing tools, organized along the left side of the page, include a pointer; a pencil tool for freehand drawings; tools for drawing basic shapes (such as lines, rectangles, and circles); a text box tool for labels; a line color tool; and a fill color tool. These basic drawing features are supplemented by the ability to undo and redo actions as you sketch, add a background image, and navigate from page to page in a sketchbook. You can, of course, add more than one sketchbook to a workspace, keeping one for workflow processes, for example, and a second for organizational charts that you want the team to consider.

INSIDE OUT   More Than Plain Text

In the Sketchpad tool, you don't have to use only plain text. When you add a text box to a sketch, you see the dialog box shown here. Enter the text and then apply the formatting you want, including a choice of fonts and alignment. To edit the text or change the formatting you've applied to a text, double-click the textbox to open this dialog box again.

Sharing and Communicating Using Microsoft Office Groove

Microsoft Office Groove 2007 shows you a lot about how useful well-engineered software can be. For the most part, Office Groove 2007 is straightforward to understand and use. Its basic features—the Discussion tool or Issue Tracking tool that you use in a standard workspace, for example—provide a range of capabilities that facilitate the exchange of ideas and information. Features such as these are some of the reasons that Groove 2007 makes collaborative work go smoothly. Don't be surprised if you come to rely on Groove more and more after you first start working with it.

In this chapter, you'll learn about some of the other features in Groove 2007 that you can use to share information and manage your communications—with other people and between computers. You'll learn how to use Groove to set up a folder on your computer so that you can share and synchronize files in that folder with other people and your other computers. You'll also learn about the communication and messaging tools that Groove provides and about managing the list of Groove contacts. Finally, you'll learn a little something about how to build your own Groove forms that you can add to and use in your workspaces.

> **For more information about the Discussion tool, the Issue Tracking tool, and other features of a standard Groove workspace, see Chapter 6, "Working as a Team in a Microsoft Office Groove Workspace."**

Setting Up and Using a File-Sharing Workspace

Office Groove 2007 provides several different tools for sharing files. As you saw in Chapter 6, one of the tools included in a standard workspace is the Files tool, which workspace members can use to store files that they're working on in common and need to refer to regularly. Groove 2007 also can synchronize files that are stored in a Microsoft Windows SharePoint Services document library.

Another way in which you can share files with coworkers, members of a group, or among different computers that you use is with a file-sharing workspace. A file-sharing workspace lets you specify or create a folder that's part of the Windows file system as a location that you can use on any computer on which you've set up your Groove account.

For example, you can set up a file-sharing workspace on your desktop computer at work and on the notebook computer that you take on the road. When you're online, Groove takes care of updating the files stored in the folder (either automatically or at your request) so that the list of files and their state are in sync.

You can invite other people to share the files stored in the folder as well. Everyone who you invite to use a file-sharing workspace has access to the files and the content that they contain. Figure 7-1 shows a file-sharing workspace along with the Synchronization Tasks and File And Folder Tasks task panes that you use to manage the workspace.

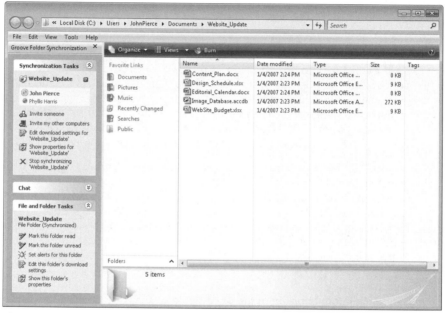

Figure 7-1 You use commands in task panes to manage a file-sharing workspace.

For more information about setting up your Groove account on more than one computer, see "Using Your Groove Account on a Second Computer" on page 142.

You can create a file-sharing workspace while working in an Explorer window in Windows or from Groove by using the New Workspace command. Here are the steps for creating a file-sharing workspace from an Explorer window in Windows Vista:

1. Open the folder you want to use and keep synchronized in a file-sharing workspace.

2. Right-click in the folder list area, point to Groove Folder Synchronization, and then click Start Synchronizing as shown here:

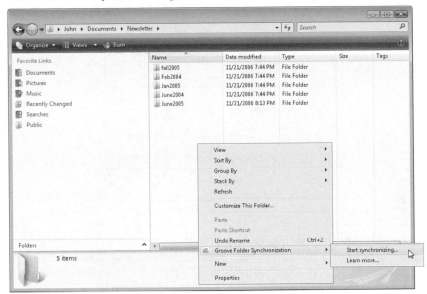

3. Click Yes to confirm the operation, and you'll see the Synchronization Tasks and File And Folders Tasks task panes shown earlier in Figure 7-1.

> **Note**
>
> In Windows XP, the steps for setting up a file-sharing workspace from an Explorer window are essentially the same. In the window, click Folder Sync on the toolbar. In the task pane that appears, click Start Synchronizing. You'll then see the task panes that you use to manage the file-sharing workspace.

Here are the steps you follow to set up a file-sharing workspace from the Groove Launchbar:

1. On the File menu, point to New, and then click Workspace.

2. In the Create New Workspace dialog box, shown next, click File Sharing, and then click OK.

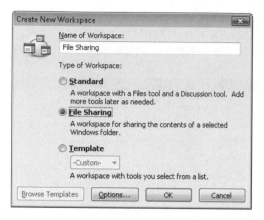

Note

You can enter a name for the file-sharing workspace in step 2, but you don't have to. As you'll see in the next step, Groove presents you with several choices for specifying the folder you want to use. If you pick a folder that is already on your computer, the file-sharing workspace will use the name of that folder.

3. In the dialog box shown here, select an option for creating the folder, and then click OK.

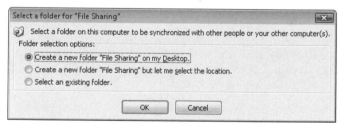

4. If prompted, select a location for creating a folder, or select a current folder, and then click OK.

Using a Subfolder as a File-Sharing Workspace

You can set up a subfolder of a folder that is already defined as a file-sharing workspace as another file-sharing workspace itself. You might want to do this to share the contents of a specific folder in a file-sharing workspace with a different set of people. For example, you might set up a subfolder for project reports that you share with people who aren't a part of the regular project team. Groove displays a message when you start sharing a folder in this way as a reminder that you have selected a folder that is already being synchronized. Keep in mind that members of a file-sharing workspace have access to all the files in the workspace, even if those files are added or updated to a subfolder that's been defined as a file-sharing workspace in which they're not members.

Chapter 7

The Synchronization Tasks task pane (shown earlier in Figure 7-1) provides commands that let you work with and manage a file-sharing workspace. For example, to invite someone to share this folder, click Invite Someone, and then you'll see the dialog box shown in Figure 7-2.

Figure 7-2 File-sharing workspaces can have members with membership roles.

From here, you follow the same steps as those for inviting someone to join a standard workspace. Select or enter the name (or e-mail address) of the person or persons you want to invite, type a message if you want, and then click Invite. Assuming that the people you invite accept your invitation (and you confirm their acceptance), the file-sharing workspace is added to the workspace list in the new member's Launchbar (or your own list of workspaces, if you are the invitee). To start working with the files in the workspace, new members first need to download them.

> **Note**
>
> To remove a member from a file-sharing workspace, right-click the member's name in the Synchronization Tasks task pane, and then click Uninvite. You must be a workspace manager to remove a member from a workspace.

For information about inviting someone to be a member of a standard workspace, see "Inviting Workspace Members and Assigning Member Roles" on page 140.

Downloading Files in a File-Sharing Workspace

The files and data in a file-sharing workspace are not downloaded automatically from the inviter's computer after you accept the invitation. You first need to specify a folder on your computer where the workspace will be located and then specify whether you want to download the data immediately (assuming that another member of the file-sharing workspace is online so that your computer has access to the files) or to download only links. If you choose to download only links, the file-sharing workspace on your computer will list the files in the workspace, and you can download the content of the files later when you need to work with a specific file.

Groove offers a default choice about which option to use, depending on how much data is contained in the file-sharing workspace when you accept the invitation. If the workspace contains 100 files or more, or if any one file is 100 megabytes (MB) or larger, the manual download option is presented as the default option. Otherwise, the option to download the content immediately is suggested as the default. The dialog box that you use is shown in Figure 7-3.

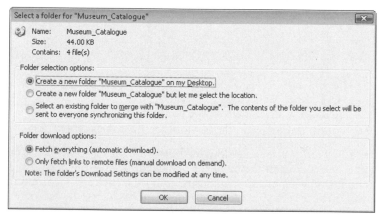

Figure 7-3 After you accept an invitation to a file-sharing workspace, use this dialog box to specify a folder to use on your computer and to download the data that's being shared.

If you download the files immediately (Fetch Everything), Groove goes to work, and copies of the files are created in the location you specified. If you choose the manual option (Only Fetch Links), when you need to work with a file, select it, and then in the File And Folder Tasks task pane, click Download This File. When a file is added to a file-sharing workspace, before it is downloaded it is displayed with a download indicator (a small arrow) and is listed with the file type Microsoft Office Groove Remote File rather than Microsoft Office Excel Worksheet, for example, as you can see in Figure 7-4.

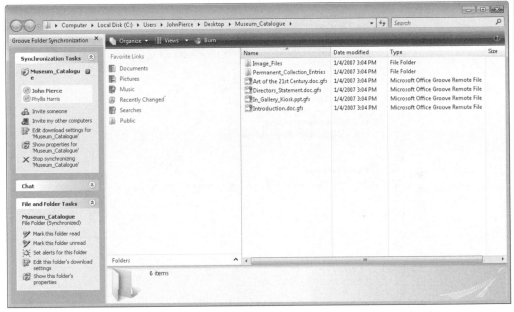

Figure 7-4 You can choose to download files immediately (automatically) or manually when you need to work with them.

INSIDE OUT   File-Sharing Roles and Permissions

In Chapter 6, you can read about workspace roles and permissions for members of a Groove standard workspace. Members of a file-sharing workspace have roles as well—Manager, Participant, or Guest—and each role is granted certain permissions by default. Managers, for example, can invite members, remove a member (by uninviting that member), and cancel outstanding invitations. A Participant can invite others to become members of the file-sharing workspace, but that is the extent of a Participant's privileges. A Guest can look at the files in the file-sharing workspace, but a Guest can't invite, uninvite, or cancel invitations. To change the role of a member, or to change the permissions for a specific role, you need to be someone who is already a workspace manager. If you are, click Show Properties in the Synchronization Tasks task pane. Click the Roles tab to change the role of a member, and click the Permissions tab to change the permissions for a specific role.

Once you're up and running in a file-sharing workspace, you can choose options for how to keep the folder synchronized. For example, you might have elected to download all the data immediately when you first joined. You can maintain that approach for the files that are added to the workspace in the future, or you can switch to downloading files manually. To manage the download settings for the synchronized folder, click Edit This Folder's Download Settings in the File And Folder Tasks task pane. You'll see the dialog box shown in Figure 7-5.

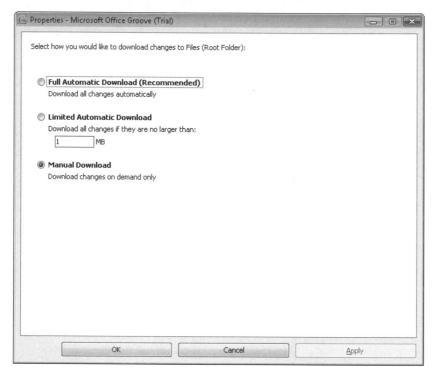

Figure 7-5 Editing the download properties for a folder in a file-sharing workspace lets you choose when to update the folder.

Sadly, the pleasant idea of fetching a file—the word Groove uses when you first join a file-sharing workspace (see Figure 7-3)—is replaced with less lyrical terms. In Figure 7-5, for example, the download settings are set to Manual Download. If you select the Manual Download setting for a file-sharing workspace, you should keep in mind that you'll then need to take care of downloading all the files that other members add to the folder, as well as new files you add to the folder on other computers that you use. You can switch to Full Automatic Download, the recommended approach for keeping up with changes in the files you're sharing between computers and with others, or take the middle road and specify a size limit, in megabytes, for changes that are automatically downloaded. Specifying a size limit might be helpful in cases in which a number of large graphics files are included in a file-sharing workspace or lots of Microsoft PowerPoint slides, which tend to be larger than Microsoft Word, Microsoft Excel, or other types of files.

You can specify that updates for any particular file in the synchronized folder be downloaded automatically so that the file stays current whenever another member saves changes to that file. To select a download option for a file, select the file, click Show This File's Properties in the File And Folder Tasks task pane, and then select the Automatically Keep This File Up To Date option.

The following list summarizes other operations that you'll perform from time to time when you're working with a file-sharing workspace:

- **Managing alerts** By selecting Set Alerts For This Folder, you can control whether Groove alerts you when changes to the folder occur—when a file is added, for example, or a file is updated. Seeing alerts are a yes-or-no proposition here: you either see them or you don't. You can't, for example, see alerts for changes but not see alerts for additions.

  You're given somewhat greater control over the alerts about unread information in a workspace. To set these alerts, click Show Properties For in the Synchronization Tasks task pane, and then click the Alerts tab, shown in Figure 7-6. You can associate a sound with an alert, for example, or set an alert for when a member enters the workspace. You can use the slider to specify whether you receive no alerts, have Groove display an icon to mark unread content, or have Groove display an alert (with a further option for Groove to dismiss alerts if you ignore them.)

For more information about working with Groove alerts, see "Managing Groove Alerts" on page 185.

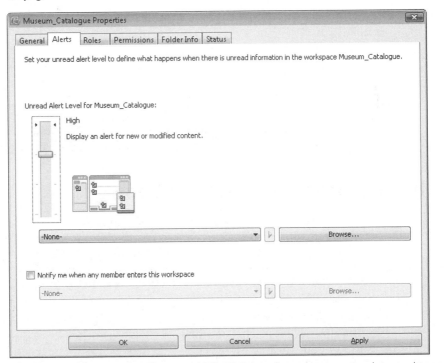

Figure 7-6 Managing alerts for unread information and member presence lets you keep tabs on workspace activities.

- **Folder permissions** Workspace permissions as they relate to a folder (see "File-Sharing Roles and Permissions" on page 173) are managed by clicking Show This Folder's Properties in the File And Folder Tasks task pane and then clicking the Permissions tab. On this tab, you can update the permissions for the three workspace roles—Manager, Participant, and Guest—controlling which roles can and cannot conduct the list of activities shown in Figure 7-7.

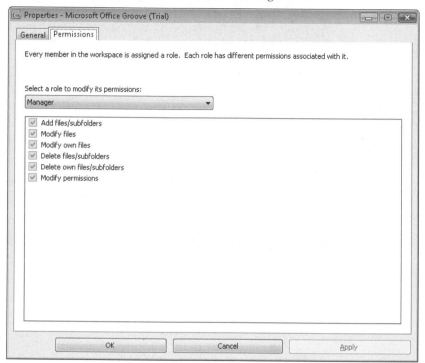

Figure 7-7 Use the Permissions tab to set folder permissions for a file-sharing workspace.

Managing Groove Communications

Communication is a central quality of successful collaboration, and these days that means communication among people who make up a team, as well as the computers they use to keep in touch and to store the files and information they need to work together. The more you read about and work with Groove 2007, you can see that communication of various types occurs frequently within the program, as it synchronizes folders, sends messages, displays alerts, lets you chat, and so on.

In Groove 2007, the Communications Manager reports on the overall status of communications—how much data still needs to be downloaded, for example—as well as the status of individual workspaces and activities such as messages and invitations. Groove 2007 also provides a number of real-time communication tools and options to support team interaction. You saw in Chapter 6, for example, the workspace Chat tool that team

Chapter 7

members can use in the context of a particular workspace. You also saw examples of presence indicators that tell you which of your fellow workspace members are online or away.

In this section, we'll take a look at more of the communication tools that Groove provides, starting with the Communications Manager and then moving on to Groove's instant messaging feature and Groove's use of alerts. You'll learn how Groove helps you keep in touch and keeps you informed. You'll also learn how you can manage communications to your liking when you need some peace and quiet.

Using the Communications Manager

To open the Communications Manager, shown in Figure 7-8, on the Options menu, click Communications Manager. As you can see in the figure, the Communications Manager shows several items in the Activity column: Instant Messages And Invitations, Synchronizing, Receiving Workspace(s), and Miscellaneous Communications (which shows the amount of data being sent or received outside workspaces and messaging activities.) In the Status column, Groove indicates what's going on with each of these activities. For example, to synchronize the data in the file-sharing workspace named Vista_Guide, 466 kilobytes of data still need to be received.

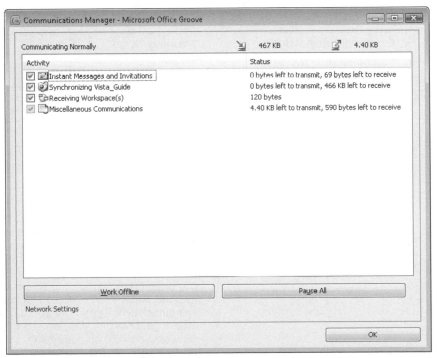

Figure 7-8 Use the Communications Manager to manage the transfer of data, see the status of communication activities, and work offline.

> **Note**
>
> You can also click the status bar on the Workspaces tab of the Launchbar or the Groove Workspace Explorer to open a communications pane that summarizes the status of these activities.

You can also use the Communications Manager for the following tasks, which we'll look at in more detail later in this chapter:

- Pause the transfer of data for a workspace or activity that you select or for all workspaces and activities at the same time.
- Set Groove to work offline.
- View or update network settings.

The data counters at the top of the dialog box, above the Status column, show the amount of data you're currently transmitting and receiving. A status message to the left of the data counters—in Figure 7-8, the message is Communicating Normally—reports on the current state of communication. Table 7-1 lists other status messages you might see and what each one means.

Table 7-1 Communication Status Messages

Communication Status	Meaning
Communicating Normally	You are working online and no communication activities are paused.
Communicating Normally (Some Activities Paused)	You are working online but have paused at least one communication activity.
Working Offline (Since mm/dd/yy, hh:mm)	You are working offline since the time period indicated.
Preparing To Work Offline	You are moving from working online to working offline.
Preparing To Work Online	You are moving from working offline to working online.
Unable To Communicate (Since mm/dd/yy, hh:mm)	Groove cannot detect a local IP address. The time indication lets you know how long communications have been in this state. (Note: An IP—for Internet Protocol—address identifies your computer on the Internet or an intranet. Groove uses this address to create connections to your computer. You'll learn more about how Groove uses IP addresses in "Viewing and Modifying Network Settings" on page 180.)
Not Communicating (Since mm/dd/yy, hh:mm).	All attempts at communicating have failed. The time indicator lets you know how long communications have been in this state

Groove also shows the status of each activity. These activities are summarized in Table 7-2.

Table 7-2 Activity Communication Status Messages

Activity	Status
Synchronizing *workspace name*	Idle: Groove is waiting to send or receive data for the workspace. <Data> Left To Transmit; <Data> Left To Receive: The amount of data Groove is currently sending or receiving for the workspace. Merging Changes: Groove is assimilating data into the workspace. Paused: The workspace is currently paused. Paused: <Data> Left To Transmit; <Data> Left To Receive: You paused the workspace with data left to send or receive. No Longer Being Synchronized: You must be invited to the workspace again. Synchronization Blocked: Groove is downloading a tool to the workspace and cannot synchronize the space until the download is complete.
Sending *workspace name(s)*	<Data> Left To Transmit: Groove is sending the workspace and has data left to transmit. Paused: <Data> Left To Transmit: You paused the workspace as it was sending and it has data left to transmit.
Receiving *workspace name(s)*	<Data> Left To Receive: Groove is installing the workspace and has data left to receive. Paused: <Data> Left To Receive: You paused the workspace as it was installing and it has data left to receive.
Messages and invitations	Idle: Groove is waiting to send or receive messages or invitations. <Data> Left To Transmit; <Data> Left To Receive: The amount of message or invitation data Groove is currently sending or receiving. Paused: The messaging feature is currently paused. Paused: <Data> Left To Transmit; <Data> Left To Receive: You paused the messaging feature with data left to send or receive.
Communications for other accounts	<Data> Left To Transmit; <Data> Left To Receive: The amount of data being sent or received by other accounts on this device.
Miscellaneous communications	<Data> Left To Transmit; <Data> Left To Receive: The amount of data being sent or received outside workspaces and messaging activities.

Pausing Communications

Sometimes you want a pause in the steady exchange of information. You might want to concentrate on the job at hand, for example, or wait until after hours, when the main tasks for the day are done, to download large quantities of data.

In the Communications Manager, you can pause communications for a selected workspace or for messages and invitations. To pause communications for a workspace or activity, clear the check box for the item in the Communications Manager. The status message for the workspace or activity changes to Paused. To begin communications again, select the check box.

You can also click Pause All to pause communications for all workspaces and message activity. Pausing all communications might be useful if you have a large number of workspaces and you want to pause communications for all but one or just a few of them. In that case, you can click Pause All and select only those workspaces for which you want to continue communications.

> **Note**
>
> You can also pause communications for a workspace by selecting it in a workspace list and clicking Pause Communications on the Options menu. You can pause or resume communications for all workspaces by clicking Pause All Communications or Resume All Communications.

Working with Groove Offline

Working offline suspends all Groove communications, which is useful when you want to work only on your local computer or when you prefer that others understand that you are temporarily unavailable by displaying your status as Offline.

To start working offline, click Work Offline in the Communications Manager (or click Work Offline on the Options menu). You'll see a change in the Groove icon in the Windows system tray, as a small *X* is superimposed. To resume working online, click Work Online.

Viewing and Modifying Network Settings

You might never need to check your network settings in Groove. The most likely situation that leads you to view or modify them is when you need technical support and have to provide information about the settings to whomever it is who is helping you.

You can view network settings and diagnostic data for your Groove account by clicking the Network Settings link in Communications Manager. When you click the link, you'll see the dialog box shown in Figure 7-9.

Chapter 7

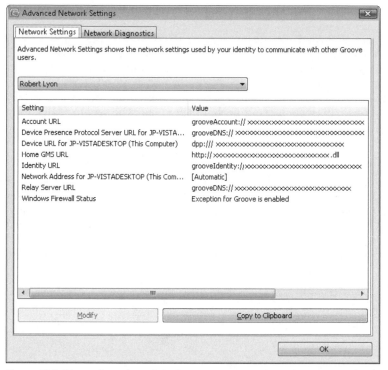

Figure 7-9 Network settings show how your account is set up to receive and send data in Groove.

One of the changes you might be asked to make is to change your network address from Automatic—a setting that means the address is assigned automatically for your computer—to Static—which is an address that you specify. If you select Static, you'll be prompted to enter the address in the dialog box provided. If you select a static address, all the computers you use to work with Groove must also use a static network (or IP) address. Groove validates the static address and warns you if it is invalid. It is always best to check with your network administrator before making changes of this nature. If the address is valid, the list of devices in the Advanced Network Settings dialog box will be refreshed to reflect your change. If you decide to switch to an automatic IP address, Groove removes the static IP address.

> **Note**
> Click Copy To Clipboard to copy the list of network settings so that you can paste it into another application.

Groove Instant Messaging

Groove 2007 includes an instant messaging capability that enables users to send simple text or voice messages to one or more workspace members or contacts. You can send a message to a team member from the Launchbar or right from a workspace. Links to workspace content can be embedded in the text of messages, which can help draw the message recipient's attention to a particular work item. Messages are delivered in real time to recipients who are online, but they can also be sent to offline users, who receive the messages when they return to an online status. New messages appear in your system tray with other Groove alerts.

You can start a message to someone through a number of different routes. Using the Options menu, you can click Send Message to send a message to one of your contacts or to another correspondent. You can click Send Message To Members to send a message to all the members of the workspace that you have open or have selected in the Launchbar. And, when you're viewing your message history (which you'll learn about later in this section), you can use a toolbar button to initiate an exchange of instant messages. Using one or another of these methods, you'll see the Send Message dialog box, shown in Figure 7-10.

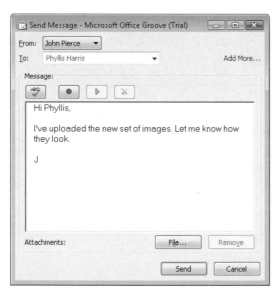

Figure 7-10 Instant messaging is a built-in, real-time communication feature in Groove.

Most of the instant messages you send in Groove will likely be simple text messages, asking someone to update a report, checking to see whether they still plan to come to the 10:00 meeting, and the like. To address the message, select a contact or a workspace member or enter an e-mail address in the To box. Type your message in the Message box, and then click Send. If you have alerts enabled, you'll see one that tells you your message is on the way. On the other end, the recipient of your message will be alerted that the message has arrived (assuming that the recipient is logged on to Groove and is online). If your computer is equipped with a microphone, you can send a voice message through the instant message mechanism. You can also attach files.

> **Note**
>
> Groove's instant messaging and Chat tools are good for basic communication needs. If you need more, you can use Microsoft Office Communicator from Groove. When you are running Groove 2007 and Communicator 2005 or 2007, you can view the awareness states (online, busy, or away, for example) of your Communicator contacts on the Groove Launchbar or in a Groove workspace. When a contact is free, you can right-click to initiate a chat or phone call with that contact in Communicator.

> **Integrating Windows Messenger and Groove**
>
> The first time you start Groove after installing or upgrading the program, you're prompted to add Windows Messenger contacts who also have Groove to your contact list in Groove. If you decide to do this, you can view the Windows Messenger status for the Groove contacts who also run Windows Messenger and start Windows Messenger activities with these contacts, such as chatting or a phone call. You can also address a Groove workspace invitation to any contact in your Windows Messenger contact list even if the contact doesn't have Groove installed at the time. (If you don't add your Windows Messenger contacts the first time you're prompted to do so, you can add them individually at a later time.)

> **Note**
>
> The Integrate Messenger Contacts option is selected by default unless an administrative policy overrides this setting.

On the Groove Launchbar, you see the same contact awareness icons for contacts who only have Groove as you see for contacts who have both Groove and Windows Messenger. To determine which contacts are both Groove and Windows Messenger users, point at the contact. If the contact is in your Windows Messenger contact list, a status window tells you the person's current status in Windows Messenger. If the person is not in your Windows Messenger contact list, you won't see any status information for Windows Messenger. To start Windows Messenger activities with a Windows Messenger contact in Groove, right-click the contact, and select Messenger Actions. If you're not currently signed in to Windows Messenger, you're asked to sign in. After you do this, you can initiate activities.

Managing Groove Messages and Message History

To see a history of the messages you've sent and received from various contacts and workspace members, on the Options menu, click Message History, and you'll see the Message History dialog box, shown in Figure 7-11.

Figure 7-11 Use the Message History dialog box to review past messages, search for information in a message, and to initiate and reply to messages.

The Message History dialog box stores all the messages you've sent or received. You can choose an option in the View list at the top of the dialog box to view all messages, those in your message inbox, or those messages that you've sent. You can sort the list by clicking a column heading to see the messages by date, for example, or grouped by who sent the message to you. You can also preview the text of a message by selecting it in the list. Previewing messages—as you might in your Inbox in Microsoft Outlook—lets you scan your messages.

> **Note**
> You cannot play back audio or open file attachments in your sent messages in the Message History dialog box.

Your message history also includes invitations to workspaces that you've received but have not yet accepted or declined. You can open an invitation from your message history, and after you accept or decline the invitation, it is deleted from the list. If you close the invitation without accepting or declining it, it will continue to be stored in your message history. If an invitee accepts or declines an invitation and includes a response message, this response is included in the message history as an invitation message. You can see the text of invitation responses only in the preview window. The Message History dialog box does not save invitations you send.

You can create new messages, reply to or forward existing messages, change your message list view, and print messages from the Message History dialog box by using the buttons on the toolbar. You can print only one message at a time.

You can also search your message history for messages that include specific text. Select the view in which you want to search for messages, and then click the Search button on the toolbar. In the Find dialog box, enter the text you want to find in a message. Select options if you want to make the search case-sensitive or match only whole words. Click Find Next or Find Previous to find the next or previous message that contains the specified text.

Managing Groove Alerts

As you've seen in many of the examples of Groove features in Chapter 6 and earlier in this chapter, Groove displays alerts to notify you about a number of events and changes to the status of your work. Groove can display or sound an alert to notify you of activities such as the following:

- Information has been added to a workspace.

- Information has been added or updated in a particular workspace tool.

- A specific folder or file has changed.

- A contact has come online or entered a workspace.

- You've received an instant message or invitation.

- To track the status of workspace invitations and messages you have sent or received.

An example of a Groove alert is shown in Figure 7-12.

Figure 7-12 You can turn off alerts and change settings to specify which types of alerts you want to see.

The nice thing about alerts is that many of them do a little more than just let you know that an event has occurred. You can click the alert to open a new workspace, for example, or to open an instant message that someone has sent you. For alerts that only provide status information, click the alert text to close the alert.

You can also right-click an alert to display a context menu that lets you deal with the alert:

- For a message alert, select Open or Delete.

- For an invitation alert, select Open, Delete, or Decline. If you decline an invitation, the sender receives an alert notifying him or her that you've declined the invitation.

- For an unread information alert, select Open to go to the tool that contains the unread information, or select Dismiss to simply close the alert.

- For alerts that track the status of messages or invitations, select Stop Tracking to close these alerts permanently.

Another advantage of Groove alerts is that you can set them according to which contacts, workspaces, tools, and files you work with most frequently. This lets you be sure you keep up with important work. For information about setting alerts for a contact, see the next section, "Working with Groove Contacts." Here are some other ways in which you can work with alerts in Groove:

- To set the alerts for a specific file in a file-sharing workspace, select the file, and then click Set Alerts For This File in the File And Folders Tasks task pane.

- To set alerts for a tool in a standard workspace, on the Options menu, point to Set Alerts, and then click Tool.

- To set alerts for a standard workspace, on the Options menu, point to Set Alerts, and then click Workspace.

In a workspace, for example, you can set alerts for when workspace members enter the workspace, as well as specify options for treating alerts for updates and changes to the information in the workspace—including not showing an alert at all.

Alerts for tools can inherit the settings you apply to the workspace, or you can choose a specific alert setting that you want to apply only to that tool. For example, say you and your coworkers are using the Discussion tool frequently one morning as you figure out how to handle a design change in a specification. You might, even for that day, decide to increase the alert level for the Discussion tool so that you know immediately when someone has added a new item.

When you and others are working with Groove frequently, with several workspaces active, the volume of Groove alerts might be distracting. If that's the case, you can choose options to prevent Groove from showing its alerts. To control the display of alerts, on the Options menu, click Suppress Alerts. The Groove icon in the Windows notification area changes to indicate that alerts are currently turned off.

You'll still receive data (such as new messages and invitations) while alerts are turned off, but the alert indicator will simply blink above the Groove icon in the Windows notification area and no alerts will be displayed. To start showing alerts again, on the Options menu, click Show Alerts.

Working with Groove Contacts

As you use Groove 2007, you build a list of people that you communicate and interact with. The people in this list are referred to as your Known Groove Contacts. Some members of this list will be contacts that you add to the list yourself. The list also includes members of the workspaces that you're a member of. For example, when you join a workspace as an invited member, all other members of that workspace immediately become available to you for starting new activities. Similarly, any person who joins one of your workspaces (either by your invitation or someone else's) immediately becomes available to you.

To see the list of your Known Groove Contacts (shown in Figure 7-13), on the Options menu, click Contact Manager. In the Contact Manager dialog box, you can do such things as the following:

- View contact properties

- Hide or show a contact

- View diagnostic information about a contact

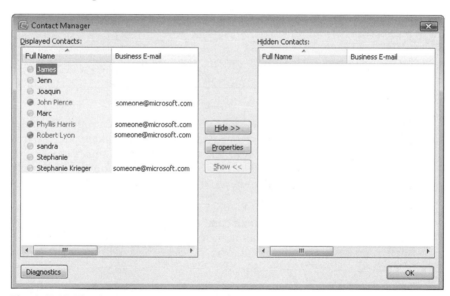

Figure 7-13 The Groove Contact Manager allows you to hide, show, or list a contact's properties.

To work with the properties for a contact, select the contact, and then click Properties. For example, you might want to keep track of the online status of some contacts more than others. To see (or hear) an alert each time a specific contact comes online, click the Alerts tab in the Contact dialog box, and you'll see the page shown in Figure 7-14. You can set the alert level for the contact by moving the slider control.

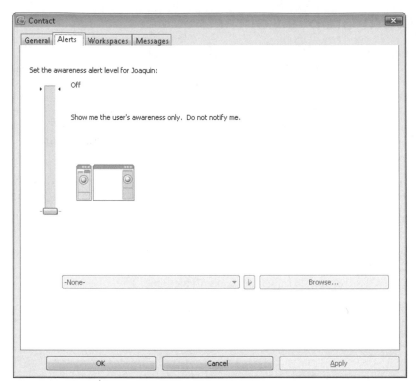

Figure 7-14 You can manage the alert level for a specific contact.

While you're setting alert levels for a contact, you can view options on the other tabs of the Contact dialog box to see which workspaces you share with a particular contact (which may be none), review your message history with this contact, and save the contact as a file so that you can store the contact's information or possibly import the information for your use in a different program.

On the General tab, shown in Figure 7-15, in addition to sending a message or an invitation, you can create an alias for a contact (by clicking More) to specify a different display name. For example, rather than see your coworker's full name—Robert or Victoria, for example—you might use Rob, Bob, or Vicky instead because that's how you know them best.

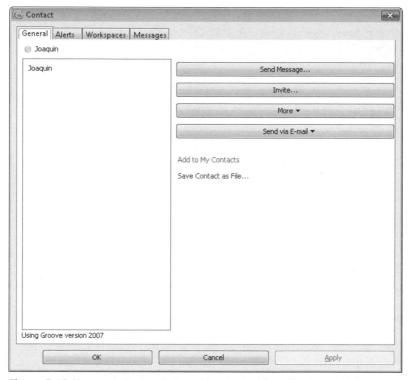

Figure 7-15 You can initiate activities with a contact from the General tab.

Managing Contacts from the Launchbar

Like Groove workspaces, Groove contacts can be managed primarily from the Launch-bar. Use the Contacts tab on the Groove Launchbar, shown in Figure 7-16, to add a contact, set your view of the contact list, send a message to a contact, view a contact's properties, invite a contact to join a workspace, and other tasks, such as these:

- To add a contact to your list of contacts in Groove, click Add Contact on the Launchbar. In the Find User dialog box, type the name of the person you want to add, and then click Find. In the list Groove returns, click the name of the person you want to add, and then click Add.

- To delete a contact from your contact list on the Launchbar, select the contact you want to delete, and press Delete. Contacts that you delete from the contact list on the Launchbar might still appear in lists such as drop-down lists in the Send Message or Send Invitation dialog boxes.

- To send a message to a contact from the Launchbar, select the contact, and then click Send Message in the Common Tasks area. Similarly, you can select a contact and then click Invite To Workspace to send an invitation to that contact to join a workspace that you specify.

Figure 7-16 The Contacts area of the Launchbar contains many commands for working with Groove contacts.

Viewing a Digital Fingerprint

Groove 2007 assigns a digital fingerprint to each identity that you create for your Groove account. The fingerprint—which is something like a digital signature—is represented as a long series of alphanumeric characters. From time to time, you might be asked by another Groove user to tell them your digital fingerprint so that this user can verify your identity before sharing information with you. And, of course, you can ask other Groove users for their digital fingerprints as well.

To see the digital fingerprint associated with any of your Groove identities, on the Options menu, click Preferences, and then click the Security tab. If you have more than one identity for your account, select that identity from the Security Settings For list. (If you have only one identity for your account, which is more often the case, you won't see a drop-down menu.)

Contact-Naming Conflicts

When two or more of your contacts have the same display names, their names are displayed in red in contact lists, workspace member lists, and on their contact information cards. (In Groove, display names are the same if they match exactly after removing leading, trailing, and multiple embedded spaces and converting the name to lowercase text.) You need to know who's who in a situation when contact names are the same so that you don't send a message to the wrong person. To determine whether you're sending a message to Robert Lyon your coworker or Robert Lyon the sales rep who just joined a workspace, Groove provides a dialog box, shown here, that lets you resolve naming conflicts.

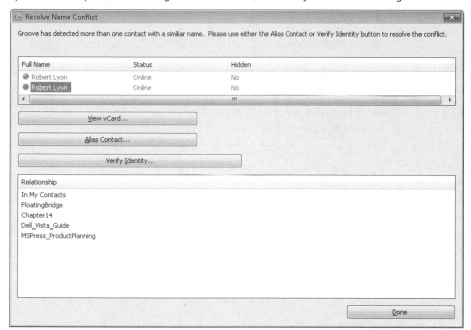

To open this dialog box, right-click a name showing a conflict, and then click Resolve Name Conflict. Now do any of the following:

- Click View vCard to see details for the selected contact. This might help you distinguish between contacts of the same name.

- Click Alias Contact to open the Alias dialog box, where you can enter a unique display name for the contact.

- Click Verify Identity to go through the steps of verifying a contact's identity.

You'll learn more about verifying a contact's identity in the following section.

Verifying Contact Identities

Verifying the identities of the people you work with in Groove is strongly recommended. It lessens the chance that you'll share proprietary or confidential information with people you don't want to. (Depending on your Groove installation, many contact identities may already be verified by an administrator at your organization.) Groove shows the verification status of contacts and workspace members by displaying their names in different colors, as described here:

- Black means you haven't verified the contact or member.

- Green means that the person's identity has been verified by you.

- Teal means that your organization has verified this individual. (Your organization's verification of Groove users may provide you with enough assurance about their identities, but in some cases, you may also want to verify a user's identity yourself.)

- Blue means that your organization has verified the individual but that this person's account is outside your organization's domain.

- Red, as described earlier, means that there's a conflict in names. Groove displays these names in red no matter what their verification status is.

For more information about resolving name conflicts, see "Contact-Naming Conflicts" on the previous page.

Communication policies that your organization might set up for your account can affect whether you can communicate with Groove users who have a specific verification status. For example, you might be able to communicate with any contact without any warning or restriction, but you might not be able to communicate with Groove users who aren't verified by an administrator in your organization.

In other cases, you might receive a warning before you communicate with a user whose identity has not been verified. You'll then be prompted by Groove to verify the user in the Contact Verification Alert dialog box, shown in Figure 7-17.

If you see this dialog box, you can take one of several actions. You can click Properties to see the user's properties, which might provide information you need to be sure the user is valid. You can click Continue to dismiss the alert and send your message or invitation to the user. You can click Cancel to dismiss the dialog box and not send your message.

If you don't take one of these steps and want to verify the identity of the user before you send your message, select the user, and then click Verify Identity. The Verify Identity dialog box, shown in Figure 7-18, displays information about your current relationships with the selected contact, such as workspaces you share, the number of messages you have exchanged, and your organizational relationship. If you do not have any relationships with the selected contact, the Verify Identity dialog box provides instructions for verifying the contact's identity by checking his or her digital fingerprint.

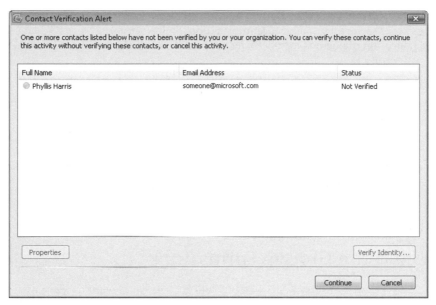

Figure 7-17 The Contact Verification Alert dialog box may appear in cases when you communicate with a contact you have not yet verified.

Figure 7-18 This dialog box shows you information about the relationships you have with a contact, which you can use for reference when you need to verify a contact's identity.

If you are sufficiently assured of the contact's identity based on the information you see, click Verify. In the Verify Identity As dialog box, enter an alternative name for the contact if you think you need one, and then click OK.

If you are not yet sufficiently assured of the contact's identity and want to take more steps to verify it, click More Information. Follow the steps in the Advanced Identity Verification dialog box for checking the contact's digital fingerprint, and then click Verify Identity.

> **Note**
>
> Although rare, you may occasionally have reason to change the verification status of contacts that you have manually verified so that they display as not verified. Right-click a contact (or workspace member) you want to unverify, select Verify Identity, and then click Unverify.

Introducing the Groove Forms Tool

Adventurous users of Groove 2007 will at some point want to work with the Groove Forms tool. With the Forms tool, you can create forms such as the one shown in Figure 7-19, which is the built-in Issue Tracking tool. The forms that you can create can be fairly sophisticated and include form controls such as text boxes, check boxes, drop-down lists, and formatting. You can, of course, also create simpler forms.

To start working with the Forms tool, open a standard workspace, and then, in the Common Tasks area, click Add Tools, select Forms, and click OK. You'll see the welcome page for the Forms tool. When you're ready to start, click Start Here, and you'll see the window shown in Figure 7-20.

> **Note**
>
> If you look closely at the message that Groove displays after you click Start Here, you'll see that it tells you that Groove is preparing the design sandbox. The sandbox is a metaphor, of course, reminiscent of childhood playgrounds, but it is also a term used in software development to specify a locale where you can experiment with designs and approaches before you publish your work. When you get ready to work with a form you've designed, you'll click a button named Publish Sandbox, which will bring your experimentation to light.

Figure 7-19 The built-in Issue Tracking tool is an example of a form created with the Groove Forms tool.

Figure 7-20 To create a Groove form, you need to define a form and its corresponding view.

Designing a Form

For a form that you create with the Forms tool, you need to define both the design of the form—which essentially means the fields and controls that the form contains, the position of the fields, formatting, and any initial values—and a view of the form, which defines which of the fields are displayed when you create a new record using the form. As you can see in Figure 7-20, on the left of the Create Form window is the Design Object pane. This pane provides links for creating a form and a view of the form, as well as a list of system fields and a link to create fields of your own. System fields, such as _Created, _CreatedBy, _ModifedBy, and so on, are used by Groove to keep track of a record. By including these fields on a form, you'll know when a record was created, who created it, and when it was modified, for example.

To start, enter a name for your form (such as Status Report, Proposal, Room Request, or something similar) in the Form Name box. Next, select the check box for each system field that you want to include. Notice that these fields are identified with labels as well as with field names. For example, the label for the system field _CreatedBy is Author. If you want to change a label for a system field (say, change Author to Requestor), click the field name in the Design Object pane, and then change the label in the Modify Field dialog box, shown in Figure 7-21. You can also change the position of the label with respect to the field or change the type of field from a Plain Text control to a Rich Text control (which lets you format the text).

> **Note**
>
> In most cases, keep system fields as plain-text fields. The Rich Text control applies in other cases. For example, a Rich Text control is useful for comments or notes that you want to add text formatting to.

At this point, you can start defining your own fields for the information that you want to collect with the form. For example, a room request form could include a list of room names or numbers, an indication of room capacity, dates when the room is needed, or a calendar showing when the room is available. You might also include check boxes on the form so that whoever is requesting the room can indicate that he or she needs food, audiovisual equipment, a certain arrangement of tables, a speaker's podium, and the like.

To add your own field to a form, click Create New Field in the Design Object pane, and you'll see the Create New Field dialog box. This dialog box lists the types of fields you can add, which is fairly extensive. To see an example and an explanation for a field type, click the field type name. Groove provides a preview, such as the one shown in Figure 7-22, which describes a drop-down list box field.

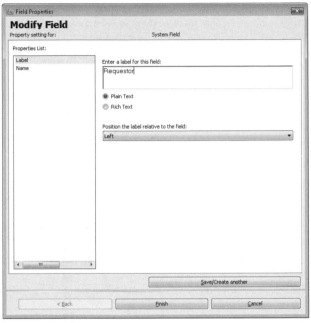

Figure 7-21 You can use this dialog box to change the label for a system field.

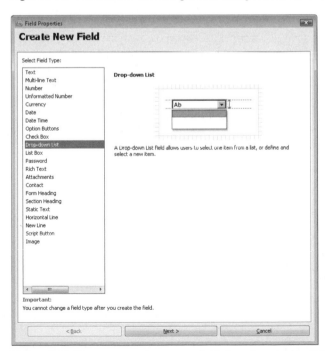

Figure 7-22 You can create your own fields for a form in this dialog box. Different types of fields let you manage user input in a variety of ways.

Each type of field requires information of its own, as well as information that most all types of fields require—a name or label, for instance. As an example, here are the steps you would follow to create a drop-down list field for a form:

1. In the Create New Field dialog box, click Drop-Down List, and then click Next. You'll see the page shown here, where you'll begin to define the properties for the field.

2. Enter a label for the field, such as Room Names.

3. Click Options in the Properties list, and you'll see the page shown next.

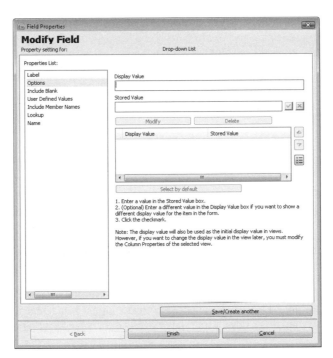

4. In the Display Value box, enter the value for the first item you want to include in the list. (If you want to store this item with a different value—a numerical equivalent, for example—enter that information in the Stored Value list).

5. Click the check mark to add the item to the list, and then repeat steps 4 and 5 to add other items to the list.

6. If you want one of the values to be the default value in the list, select the item, and then click Select By Default. If you want a blank item to appear as the first item in the list, click Include Blank in the Properties list.

7. If you want to let users of your form add their own items to the list you've defined, click User Defined Values in the Properties list, and select that option. Groove also provides you with an option to include workspace member names in the list.

8. If you want to look up values from another tool or control, click Lookup, and fill out that form.

    In text, multi-line text, drop-down lists, list boxes, and static text fields, you can use lookups to obtain values from other fields. A lookup can find field values in the same Forms tool, in a selected Forms tool in the same workspace, or in a selected Forms tool in another workspace. You can also add lookups to macros and form scripts.

9. Click Finish. (Or click Save/Create Another.)

On the Create Form page, the buttons below and to the right of the field list let you manage the appearance and organization of a form's fields. Here are some of the options you have for changing the layout of a form:

- Apply a style to a form, which adds formatting such as a background color, bold fonts, and the like.

- Choose the number of columns in which fields are arranged.

- Change the position of a field.

- Choose the number of columns and rows that a field will span.

- Set field properties; for example, you can specify that a field is hidden or required.

- Select fields and add them to a field group or to a tab group on a form.

Across the top of the form design window, next to the Basics tab, you'll see tabs named Options and Access. On the Options tab, you can choose to use the form you're designing to create responses to a record and to save old versions of the records that are defined in this form. On the Access tab, you can specify which workspace roles and members are allowed to use this form. For example, if you are creating a Status Report form, you probably don't want members with the Guest role to be able to fill out the form because they don't have a role that merits that level of involvement.

Designing a View

In a view of a form, you select which fields will appear as column headings in the list of records that are created using the form. You probably won't want to show all the fields that you've defined for a form in any particular view, which is one reason that Groove lets you define more than one view for a form. For example, in one view you might want to see who created the record, when it was created, who modified it, and when it was modified. In another view, you might include a field called Tasks and another called Status so that you can see a summary of the status of all tasks for a project.

You are asked to define a view of a form when you first save the design. At other times, you can define a view by clicking Create New View in the Design Object pane. In either case, you'll use the window shown in Figure 7-23 to spell out the particulars of a view. Enter a name for a view at the top of the window, and then select the fields that you want the view to contain. Groove shows you a preview of the view at the bottom of the window.

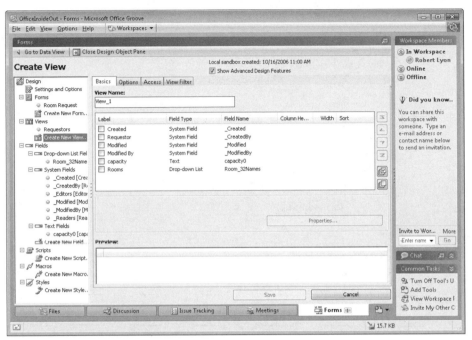

Figure 7-23 You can define more than one view of a form. One view might show record details, and a second view summary information.

For each field that you include in a view, you can set certain properties. For example, you can change the column header, the formatting for the field label, and the order in which records are sorted when you sort by this field. Some of the field properties that you can set depend on which type of field you are working with—a list, a text box, or a check box, for example. To review and change the properties for a field, select the field in the field list, and then click Properties.

The view itself has properties, too. You can set view properties by clicking the Options or Access tab at the top of the window. Figure 7-24 shows the Options tab for a view of a room request form. On the Options tab, you can select the default sorting order— ascending or descending—and display options such as gridlines. You can also select an option that enables the view you're defining to provide data to lookups from other tools, and you can choose not to show this view on the View menu for the form.

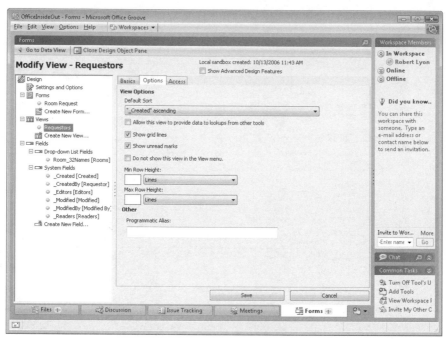

Figure 7-24 Use the Options tab to set properties for a form's view.

On the Access tab, you can select which workspace roles and members can work with this view.

Testing and Publishing Your Form

When you finish defining a view (as well as designing the form itself), click Save, and you'll see the Settings And Options page, shown in Figure 7-25. Here you can make some final adjustments to the features that you'll include with the form. You can select a default form and view (a forms tool can have more than one form and view, remember), select other view options, select features such as whether to allow searches in the form, and so on. The About This Tool tab lets you provide a description and a version number for the form you've designed.

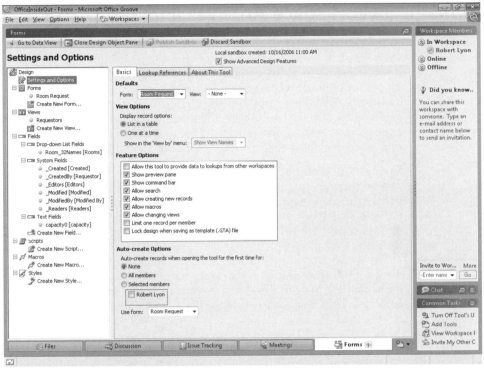

Figure 7-25 You use this page to define the final settings and options for a form.

To make a form available for other workspace members to use, click Publish Sandbox. After Groove does a little processing, you'll see your form as it will appear in a workspace window, available for recording the information it was designed to collect and store. If you want to make changes to the form after you've published it—to either the form's design or to one of its views—point to Designer on the toolbar, and then click the applicable command.

Note

Forms that you create with the Groove Forms tool can be straightforward data-entry forms or more sophisticated forms that include a variety of controls, lookups, and even programming code such as scripts and macros, which can be written in JScript or VBScript. You can also design your own style to add to a form. These design features for a form are displayed in the Design Object pane when you select Show Advanced Design Features at the top of the Form tool's window.

Managing Workspace Archives and Templates

At the end of a project or an event that you've planned and coordinated using Groove, you've probably collected information that will be helpful, if not valuable, some time down the road. In addition, putting together a Groove workspace by arranging a specific set of built-in and custom tools is work that you might want to preserve. You can address both of these cases in Groove by saving a workspace as an archive so that you can refer back to the files, issues, and ideas that inspired you three months ago, or as a template so that you can repeatedly use a certain configuration of tools. (You cannot save a file-sharing workspace as a template or an archive.)

Saving a workspace as an archive preserves the collection of tools and custom tool names, the workspace name, the information collected in the tools, and the list of members in the workspace. To save a workspace as an archive, open or select the workspace, point to Save Workspace As on the File menu, and then click Archive. At that point, you need to confirm or enter the path and file name in the Save As dialog box. If you use the default location, which is a folder named Groove Workspace Archives in your Documents (or My Documents folder), the archived workspace file will be displayed in the file list if you want to import that archive from the Launchbar later. You can also browse for workspace archive files stored in other locations. You can set a password for the archive to help manage access to the data that it contains.

> **Note**
>
> When you restore a workspace from an archive, all members (other than the member restoring the workspace) have a status of Suspended. You can invite these members or other people to join the workspace again.

Saving a Groove workspace as a template follows a similar set of steps. When you save a workspace as a template, you preserve the arrangement of tools and custom tool names (if any), as well as the workspace name. You also have the option to save the contents in the tools and the list of members in the workspace. Follow the same steps to save a workspace as an archive, except click Template. Specify a path and file name in the Save As dialog box, or accept the default location, and then click Save. Groove also provides a default location, Groove Workspace Templates, in your Documents (or My Documents) folder. By using the default location, your template will be listed in the Create New Workspace dialog box, and you can choose the template when you need it. If you choose the option to include the contents of a workspace in a template, you should set a password to protect the template's data. If you include workspace members as an element of the template, these members have a status of Suspended in any workspace you create with the template. You can then invite the members to join the new workspace.

PART 3
Word

Katherine Murray and Mary Millhollon

Mastering Page Setup and Pagination

Documents need some planning. But even after the most thoughtful planning, document designs sometimes travel down unplanned paths, seemingly on their own. Maybe a single-column publication suddenly becomes a multiple-column document, or a piece that wasn't supposed to be a booklet turns out to work perfectly in a booklet format. In these types of cases, everything changes—margins, page orientation, column specifications, headers, and footers. While these kinds of changes might seem daunting—especially when you are working under a tight deadline Microsoft Office Word 2007 can help you efficiently adapt to all sorts of changes with a little know-how.

Whether you successfully plan your work in advance or change strategies midstream, the page setup features of Office Word 2007 help you control page layout. Specifically, when you plan or redesign your pages, you can make choices about page setup specifications and options such as the following:

- Headers, footers, and page number settings

- Top, bottom, left, and right margin sizes

- Document orientation

- Paper size and the tray or cartridge to use when printing

- Whether to print one or two pages per sheet

- Page and text breaks

- Text flow and spacing for languages that use vertical orientation

This chapter covers the preceding topics as well as related page setup features in Word 2007.

INSIDE OUT   Planning Your Page Setup

Although you can select your page settings at any point during the creation or editing of your document, taking time up front to plan basic document settings can save you time, trouble, and corrections later. In addition, if you're creating a standard document for others in your department to use or that you will use repeatedly, getting the basics down early can ensure that you don't have to open multiple documents to readjust margin settings, page size, and other layout options. In those cases, you can use an existing document as a guide or create a template to make the application of current settings and future changes easier.

Planning up front is usually best; however, Word 2007 enables you to change direction whenever you want. Keep in mind that when you make drastic changes to an existing document's setup—such as changing the page from portrait to landscape orientation—the contents of your page will be dramatically affected. For instance, if you switch to landscape orientation after you've entered text and graphics, set headers and footers, and created section divisions in portrait orientation, you'll most likely have to adjust several settings to display your information properly on the shorter, wider page.

Basic Page Setup Options

In many cases, you'll use the page setup options on the Page Layout tab shown in Figure 8-1. Options and commands on the Page Layout tab include Themes, Text Direction (if you have enabled language settings that support Chinese, Japanese, or Korean), Margins, Orientation, Size, Columns, Breaks, Line Numbers, and Hyphenation.

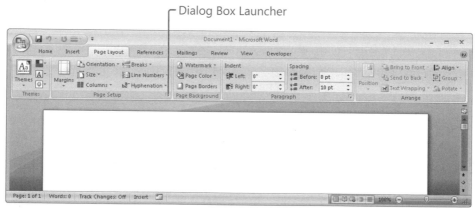

Figure 8-1 The page setup options on the Page Layout tab streamline access to common page layout features, including text direction, margins, page orientation, and breaks.

Changing Margins and Orientation

The page setup items you'll adjust most often are likely to be margins and page orienta-tion. Word 2007 makes accessing these settings a snap by including the Margins and Orientation galleries on the Page Layout tab. The margins of your document control the amount of white space at the top, bottom, right, and left edges of the document. You can also control the amount of space used for the *gutter*, which is the space on the inside edges of facing pages that is reserved for binding. You can customize the gutter setting along the left or top margin of the page.

Changing Margin Settings

When you begin working with a new document, the left, right, top, and bottom margins are set to 1 inch or 2.54 centimeters, depending on your specified unit of measure. Note that this default setting is different from the default margin settings in previous ver-sions of Word. In Word 2007, you can change margin settings in three basic ways.

> **Note**
> To change the default setting for measurement units shown in Word, click the Microsoft Office Button and then click Word Options. In the Advanced category, scroll to the Dis-play area, and then choose a unit of measurement from the Show Measurements In Units Of list box. You can choose to work with inches, centimeters, millimeters, points, or picas.

- Choose a margin setting from the Margins gallery on the Page Layout tab, as shown in Figure 8-2.

- At the bottom of the Margins gallery, click Custom Margins to open the Page Setup dialog box and enter the settings you want in the text boxes provided for the top, bottom, left, and right margins.

> **Note**
> The next time you open the Margins gallery your custom settings will be listed at the top as Last Custom Settings. If you want new documents to default to your custom settings, see "Saving Page Setup Defaults to the Current Template" on page 213.

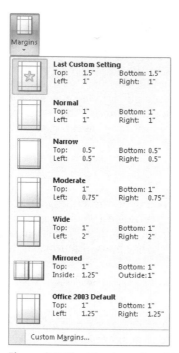

Figure 8-2 The Margins gallery highlights the current margin settings and provides a variety of other common settings, along with the Office 2003 Default margin setting at the bottom of the gallery.

● In Print Layout view, drag the edge of the shaded area on the horizontal or vertical ruler to the margin setting you want as shown here.

Note

Press the Alt key, or hold down both the left and right mouse buttons, while dragging the margin indicators to display exact measurements on the ruler.

Binding Documents

If you'll be binding a document that you create, be sure to specify a gutter margin large enough to accommodate the binding. If your document is printed single-sided, every gutter margin will show the spacing you enter along the left margin. If your document is to be printed double-sided, on the Page Layout tab, click the Page Setup Dialog Box Launcher in the Page Setup group. On the Margins tab, click the Multiple Pages arrow, and then choose Mirror Margins to be sure that the margin settings are applied to the left and right interior margins. If you choose any option other than Normal in the Multiple Pages list in the Pages section of the Page Setup dialog box, Word disables the Gutter Position option and adds the gutter setting to the appropriate margin, such as applying the gutter setting to the inside margins for book fold documents.

Choosing Orientation

A document's orientation affects the way the content is printed on a page. Typically, documents such as letters, invoices, reports, and newsletters use a portrait orientation, and those such as charts, calendars, and brochures use a landscape orientation.

To change the orientation of a document, navigate to the Page Layout tab on the Ribbon, and then click Orientation in the Page Setup group. Click Landscape to orient the document so that it is printed with the long edge of the paper serving as the top of the page. Click Portrait to print the document with the short edge of the paper serving as the top of the page. Note that page orientation options can also be found in the Page Setup dialog box, which can be opened by clicking the Page Setup Dialog Box Launcher.

Selecting a Paper Size and Source

Another page setup task involves preparing your document for final printing. Specifically, you need to specify a paper size and paper source. Word offers a range of paper sizes. The standards are readily available in the Size gallery on the Page Layout tab. You can quickly access paper sizes ranging from letter, legal, and A4 to standard business envelopes. In addition to the usual paper sizes, Word supports numerous envelope, executive, index card, photo, panorama, banner, and custom sizes.

Choosing a Paper Size

To select a standard paper size, click the Size button on the Page Layout tab, and then click a paper size option in the Size gallery, as shown in Figure 8-3.

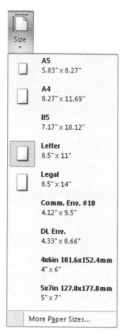

Figure 8-3 Choose a standard paper size from the Size gallery.

Note

To select a paper size other than the standard fare, click More Paper Sizes in the Size gallery to open the Page Setup dialog box. Click the Paper tab to access additional paper sizes in the Paper Size list, or use the Height and Width text boxes to enter custom settings.

Selecting the Paper Source

Paper source refers to the source of the paper, envelopes, or other medium on which you'll print a document. If you're working with a printer that has multiple paper trays, you can select more than one paper source. For example, you can print the first page of a letter on letterhead from one paper source (say Tray 1) and print the pages that follow on blank stock that is contained in a second paper source.

To select a paper source, click the Page Setup Dialog Box Launcher on the Page Layout tab, and then click the Paper tab, shown in Figure 8-4. In the Paper Source area, select the paper source you want to use for your document's first page, and then (if necessary) select the source you want to use for other pages.

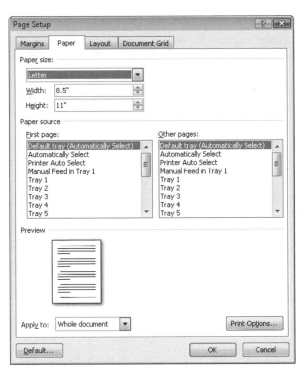

Figure 8-4 Use the Paper Source section in the Page Setup dialog box to select a paper source.

Because so many Page Setup options overlap settings for printing options, Word makes it easy to access printing options from the Paper tab in the Page Setup dialog box. When you're working with Page Setup options, take a moment to check your printing options by clicking the Print Options button in the lower-right corner of the Paper tab. The Print Options button opens the Word Options dialog box, which includes printing options in the Display and the Advanced categories. Coordinating printing and page setup options might come in handy, for instance, if you want to use A4 or legal paper sizes or you plan to use duplex printing. In those cases, you can set your printing and page setup options at the same time, thereby avoiding having to remember to set appropriate printing options when you print the document.

Saving Page Setup Defaults to the Current Template

After you have page settings the way you want them in your document, you can save these specifications as your default settings in the document's template. When you save page setup settings as default settings, Word saves the settings to the current template. If your document isn't based on a custom template, the changes are applied to the Normal template. (By default, all new Word documents use the Normal template if they aren't based on another template.) When you create default page setup settings, they will be applied to all new documents that are created with the template.

> **Note**
>
> Templates can have a .dotx or .dotm file extension, and are equivalent to the .dot extension in previous versions of Word. The main difference between the .dotx and .dotm formats is that the .dotm extension indicates that the template has macro capabilities enabled.

To save page setup settings as the default settings, follow these steps.

1. Place the insertion point where you want to configure the settings to use as the defaults.

> **CAUTION**
>
> If changing the default settings for your Normal template, make those changes sparingly, because your Normal template will take on all settings found in the Page Setup dialog box. Determine which settings the majority of your documents use and set them accordingly. If you need specific settings for certain documents, consider creating a template with those settings rather than modifying your Normal template.

2. Click the Page Layout tab, and then click the Page Setup Dialog Box Launcher in the Page Setup group.

3. Specify the page setup settings you want to apply to the document's template. ("Working with Varying Page Settings" on page 219 describes each available setting in detail.)

4. In the lower-left corner of the Page Setup dialog box, click Default. A message box, shown in Figure 8-5, asks whether you want to change the default settings in the current template and indicates which template you are updating. In Figure 8-5, the Memo.dotm file will be modified. To apply the page settings to the current template, click Yes. If you decide you would rather not alter the template's settings, click No.

Figure 8-5 Making the current page setup settings the new default alters the template attached to the current document.

INSIDE OUT   Backing Up Your Customizations

For best results when backing up templates and restoring the default Normal template, always keep a clean backup copy of your standard templates in a folder other than the Template folder on your hard disk or server. That way, if you need to return to earlier default specifications, you can do so by copying the backup file into the Template folder.

If you are using the Microsoft Windows Vista operating system, you can restore templates to earlier versions by replacing an existing template with a shadow copy. A shadow copy of a file is a backup file that Windows Vista saves when you use the Back Up Files Wizard or have System Protection turned on (which is scheduled to run once a day by default.) To access a list of shadow copies, right-click the template you want to restore and then choose Restore Previous Versions.

To restore your Normal template to its default settings, you can have Word rebuild the Normal template the next time you start the program. To do this, simply exit Word, rename the Normal template file (choose an easy-to-recognize name, such as Normal_old), and then restart Word. Word automatically builds a new Normal template based on the default settings.

Controlling Page and Section Breaks

If you've created any lengthy documents, you know that Word automatically adds page breaks at appropriate points to indicate page divisions and show you how printed pages will appear. Some Word features automatically add sections breaks for you when you insert particular elements, such as Cover Page Building Blocks. In Print Layout and Full Screen Reading views, an automatic page break looks like a space between pages—you can see where one page ends and another begins. In Draft view, page breaks appear as dotted lines. Often, situations arise when you want to add page breaks manually. In Word, you can easily add manual breaks to control pages, sections, and columns.

Note

If you see a solid line instead of the white space allocated to the page margins in Print Layout view, place your mouse pointer on the solid line and double-click the left mouse button to show the white space. You can also set the Show White Space Between Pages In Print Layout View option, which you can find in the Display category in the Word Options dialog box.

Adding Manual Page Breaks

In some cases, you might want to add your own page break to control where content is positioned on the page. For example, you might want to insert a manual page break in the following instances:

- To create a page containing minimal information, such as a cover page or acknowledgments page

- To prevent a paragraph from being divided across two pages

- To ensure that a figure or table and its caption appear on the same page

- To begin a new section with a heading at the top of a page

- To end a section when you don't want anything else printed on the current page

To create a manual page break, place the insertion point where you want to insert the break and then do one of the following:

- Click Breaks in the Page Setup group on the Page Layout tab, and then select Page in the Breaks gallery. (See Figure 8-6.)

- On the Insert tab, click Page Break in the Pages group

- Press Ctrl+Enter

Note

If you want to insert a page break and a blank page simultaneously, on the Insert tab, in the Pages group, click Blank Page.

Creating Additional Sections

Page setup options are applied to a section of a document as opposed to the pages themselves. By default, new documents based on your Normal template contain a single section. If your document requires a change to the page layout, such as varying page margins, orientation, or headers and footers (other than a different first page or a different header or footer for odd and even pages), you need to create additional sections in order to apply these changes.

> **Note**
>
> You can also use styles or text boxes to handle many formatting situations, instead of adding sections within your pages. For more information about text boxes, see Chapter 10, "Advanced Layout and Formatting." For more information about styles, see the Word 2007 online help.

The Breaks gallery, shown in Figure 8-6, provides a much needed visual improvement to the process of creating and modifying section breaks (a task that was often difficult to get right in earlier versions of Word). Now you can clearly see the type of break you want to use *before* you "experiment" with a dialog box option.

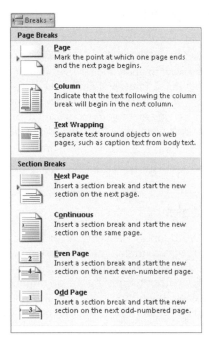

Figure 8-6 The Breaks gallery enables you to view the type of break you are creating before you create it.

> **Note**
>
> To view the section number in the new, customizable status bar, right-click the status bar and then click Section.

To use the Breaks gallery to add a section break, position your cursor where you want to begin a new section and then choose an option in the Breaks gallery. The Breaks gallery includes the following section break options.

Next Page   Ends the current page and starts a new section.

Continuous   Begins the new section at the insertion point.

Even Page   Ends the current page and starts a new section. The new page will always print on an even page.

Odd Page   Ends the current page and starts a new section. The new page will always print on an odd page.

> **Note**
>
> To change page layout settings and insert a section break at the same time, place your insertion point at the location where you want to apply the new settings, or select the portion of the document that will contain the settings, and display the Page Setup dialog box. From the Apply To list at the bottom of any tab in the dialog box, select This Point Forward or Selected Text, respectively. After you make your modifications and click OK, section breaks will be inserted into your document as needed and your page layout settings will be applied to that section.

Inserting Text Wrapping Breaks

When you add a text wrapping break, Word forces a text break for layout reasons without starting a new paragraph. For instance, you might want to break text at a particular position so that the text appears before and after an inline table, graphic, or object, or you might want to present lines of poetry without applying the document's paragraph style (including paragraph spacing) to each line of text. The Text Wrapping break option is similar to inserting a manual line break in your document, which you can add by pressing Shift+Enter. Frequently, text wrapping breaks are used to separate text from Web page objects or other text and are the equivalent of inserting a <br /> tag in XHTML code.

TROUBLESHOOTING

My document includes unwanted breaks.

You finish your document and print a draft or you open a document for editing or review that was created by another individual. What's this? The document is breaking at odd places or including unwanted blank pages?

The underlying problem is that no two printers are the same, and each paginates a document differently. A document that looks perfectly fine on one computer might not look the same if you view it on another or if you print the document using a printer other than the one you normally use. The primary issue is that manual page breaks were used in an effort to control document pagination, such as inserting a manual page break to keep paragraphs together on the same page or to keep a table or figure together with its caption. If you've ever used this method, chances are you've had an ongoing battle of deleting and reinserting manual page breaks. Instead of using manual page breaks, use pagination formatting instead. Pagination formatting allows you to keep paragraphs together on the same page or keep all lines of a paragraph on the same page. By using pagination formatting, you turn the hassle of continuously deleting and reinserting manual page breaks over to Word.

To resolve this problem, first locate and delete the unwanted manual page or section breaks. You may need to display formatting marks to see where these breaks are located. To do so, on the Home tab, in the Paragraph group, click Show/Hide (the button with the paragraph symbol).

Place your insertion point in the paragraph that needs to be formatted with a pagination option. On either the Page Layout tab or the Home tab, in the Paragraph group, click the Dialog Box Launcher to open the Paragraph dialog box. On the Line And Page Breaks tab, use the Keep Lines Together option to keep all lines of a paragraph on the same page and use the Keep With Next option to force a paragraph to stay on the same page as the following paragraph.

Working with Varying Page Settings

Depending on a document's complexity, you might want to vary the margins. For instance, a standard report might have equal margins on the right and left, a format that makes setting margins simple. In contrast, a document you want to bind or fold, or a publication that's designed so that the left and right pages complement each other, might require more finely tuned adjustments to page settings.

When you want to set up a document that requires varying page settings, you can simplify your task by using the Page Setup dialog box to set several options at the same time.

Along with using the Page Setup Dialog Box Launcher and various galleries, you can display the Page Setup dialog box through any of the following techniques:

- Double-click the shaded area of the vertical or horizontal ruler.

> **Note**
>
> To display rulers, click the View Ruler command above the vertical scroll bar, or click Ruler in the Show/Hide group on the View tab.

- Press Alt+P, S, P.

The Page Setup dialog box in Word 2007 (shown in Figure 8-7) looks similar to the Page Setup dialog box in previous versions of Word. If you have support for Chinese, Japanese, or Korean enabled through Microsoft Office language settings, you'll also see the Document Grid tab in the Page Setup dialog box.

Figure 8-7 The Page Setup dialog box enables you to choose settings that affect the margins, paper type, layout, and spacing of your document.

> **Note**
>
> To configure language settings while working in Word, click the Microsoft Office Button and then click Word Options. In the Popular category, click Language Settings, add or remove a language, click OK, and then restart Word if prompted.

To summarize, the tabs in the Page Setup dialog box enable you to enter basic page layout settings as follows:

- **Margins** You can specify settings for the top, bottom, left, right, and gutter margins; choose page orientation; and select formatting for multiple pages. See "Binding Documents" on page 211 for more about using gutter margins.

- **Paper** You can make choices about paper size and the source for the paper and envelopes on which you'll print your information. In addition, you can access printing options in the Word Options dialog box by clicking Print Options.

- **Layout** Enables you to set options for sections, headers and footers, and overall content alignment. In addition, you can open the Line Numbers dialog box by clicking Line Numbers, and the Borders And Shading dialog box by clicking Borders. See "Including Headers and Footers" on page 223 for more information about the Layout tab.

- **Document Grid (available with some Language Settings configurations)** Enables you to control horizontal and vertical text flow as well as line and character spacing in documents that use East Asian languages. Using this tab, you can also specify drawing grid settings (click Drawing Grid), which give you control over the grid display and other grid settings, and you can access the Font dialog box by clicking Set Font.

Multiple Page Settings

The Multiple Pages setting, found on the Margins tab of the Page Setup dialog box, enables you to specify whether your document should include mirror margins, two pages per sheet, book fold, or reverse book fold. To change the page settings for a multiple-page document, follow these steps:

1. Open your document and click the Page Setup Dialog Box Launcher in the Page Setup group on the Page Layout tab.

2. Enter the margins, paper, and layout settings on their respective tabs of the Page Setup dialog box.

3. In the Pages area of the Margins tab, click the Multiple Pages arrow.

4. Click the item you need in the Multiple Pages list (Table 3-1 describes the options), and then specify an option in the Apply To list if you selected Normal, Mirror Margins, or 2 Pages Per Sheet in the Multiple Pages list. If you selected Book Fold or Reverse Book Fold, you can specify how many sheets are in each booklet.

Chapter 8

> **Note**
>
> If your document has more pages than the number of pages you selected for a booklet, Word prints the document as multiple booklets.

Table 3-1 Choosing Page Settings for Multiple Pages

Setting	Preview	Description
Normal		Used for single-sided printing, and each page has a specific left and right margin.
Mirror Margins		Used for duplex printing in which the margins mirror each other and the left and right margins become the inside and outside margins, respectively.
2 Pages Per Sheet		Divides the current page into two pages
Book Fold		Treats each left and right page as a spread, using a gutter and mirror margins as applicable.
Reverse Book Fold		Enables you to create a booklet written in a right-to-left text orientation, such as one written in Arabic or Hebrew, or in an East Asian language that has vertical text (this option is available only when support for a relevant language is enabled.

Aligning Content Vertically Between Margins

Word gives you the option of indicating how you want the content between the top and bottom margins of your page to be aligned. To control vertical alignment, display the Page Setup dialog box, click the Layout tab, click the Vertical Alignment arrow, and then select an alignment option. By default, the vertical alignment is set to Top. You can choose from Top, Center, Justified, or Bottom. Word aligns the page content based on your selection. For example, if you click Center, Word centers the contents of the page between the top and bottom margins. If you choose Bottom, Word aligns the page content with the bottom margin and places any extra space at the top of the page, above the content.

Chapter 8

> ### Creating a Page or Section Border
>
> If you want to set up page and section borders for your document while you're taking care of the rest of your page settings, you can do so by using the Page Setup dialog box or the Page Layout tab. To access border settings, click the Page Borders option in the Page Background group on the Page Layout tab or open the Page Setup dialog box, click the Layout tab, and then click Borders. The Borders And Shading dialog box appears. Similar to the Page Setup dialog box, the Borders And Shading dialog box includes an Apply To list box. Using the Apply To options, you can add borders to selected pages, text and paragraphs, sections, the first page of a section, every page except the first page of a section, and the entire document.
>
> For more information about adding page borders, see Chapter 10, "Advanced Layout and Formatting."

Including Headers and Footers

Adding text to the header (top) and footer (bottom) areas in a Word document serves a number of purposes, but primarily headers and footers are used to repeat information at the top or bottom of each page. You can easily insert page numbers, text, Building Blocks, pictures, and clip art in document headers and footers.

> ### Note
>
> You can see a document's headers and footers only in printed documents, Print Layout view (provided white space between pages is not suppressed), Print Preview, and Full Screen Reading view (if the Show Printed Page option is selected). Headers and footers are hidden in Web Layout, Outline, and Draft view.

Adding Page Numbers

Word enables you to add page numbers in two main ways. You can add basic page numbers by using the Page Number galleries on the Insert tab, or you can add page numbers along with additional content using the built-in or custom Header and Footer galleries. When you use the Page Number galleries on the Insert tab to add a page number, you can select Top Of Page, Bottom Of Page, Page Margins, or Current Position. After you select a position, choose a page numbering design from the gallery of designs, as shown next.

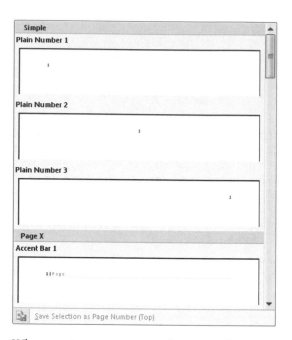

When you insert a page number using the Page Number gallery, Word automatically inserts the selected page number and opens the header and footer layer in your document for additional editing. If you want to add more complex page numbering and additional information, you can add headers and footers, as described in the next section.

Creating Headers and Footers

Headers and footers are special sections of a page that often provide the sort of useful information that many people take for granted—such as page numbers and chapter titles. For example, in a book, the chapter name and book title often appear in the header, while page numbers appear in the footer. You'll often use headers and footers to provide readers with important information about a publication, which could include the title, author, page number, creation date, last modified date, confidentiality statements, graphics, and other items.

You can control whether headers and footers are different for odd and even pages, whether the first page should have a different header or footer, and where headers and footers are placed relative to the edge of a printed page.

To create a header or footer, on the Insert tab, in the Header & Footer group, click Header or click Footer and then select a Building Block from the respective gallery.

Chapter 8

> **Note**
>
> If the header or footer style you select from a the galleries doesn't use your preferred fonts or colors, you can modify or change your document theme (found in the Themes group on the Page Layout tab) before making formatting changes. The fonts and colors shown in the Header and Footer galleries are linked to the document theme and will change if the document theme is changed.

When the header and footer sections are active, you can add text, numbers, field codes, graphics, Building Blocks, and objects to customize your document's headers and footers. This section of the chapter describes how you can edit and customize headers and footers.

When you insert a header or footer, the header and footer areas become accessible, the content area of the document becomes temporarily unavailable, and the Header & Footer Tools tab is displayed along with the Design tab, as shown in Figure 8-8. The Design tab includes the following:

- **Header Gallery** Enables you to edit or remove a header. Also enables you to select a header's contents and save the selection to the Header gallery so that you can use the header in other documents.

- **Footer Gallery** Enables you to edit or remove a footer. Also enables you to select a footer's contents and save the selection to the Footer gallery so that you can use the footer in other documents.

- **Page Number Gallery** Inserts a page number field, such as { PAGE }. You can use this option to add a page number to the top of the page, to bottom of the page, in the page's margins, or at the current position. This gallery also includes the Remove Page Numbers option and the Format Page Numbers option, which opens the Page Number Format dialog box and enables you to apply number formatting, continue numbering from prior pages, or start numbering at a specified page number.

> **Note**
>
> The Header, Footer, and Page Number galleries consist of built-in Building Blocks and those downloaded from Microsoft Office Online. You can add your own custom Building Blocks to the galleries.

Figure 8-8 To create headers and footers in documents, you enter and format numbers, text, Building Blocks, and graphics in the header and footer areas.

- **Date & Time** Opens the Date And Time dialog box, which enables you to insert the current date and time or, if you want the information updated automatically, date fields, such as { DATE \@ "M/d/yyyy" }, and time fields, such as { TIME \@ "h:mm"ss am/pm" }.

- **Picture** Opens the Insert Picture dialog box and displays the images in your Pictures folder by default.

- **Clip Art** Opens and closes the Clip Art task pane and enables you to search for and insert clip art items into your header or footer.

- **Go To Header** Jumps to the header section if you are working in the footer section, thereby enabling you to jump quickly from the footer to the header.

- **Go To Footer** Jumps to the footer section if you are working in the header section, thereby enabling you to jump quickly from the header to the footer.

- **Previous Section** Displays the header or footer used in the previous section, based on the current location of the insertion point. If you click Previous Section while in the footer area, the insertion point jumps to the footer area in the preceding section of your document. Note that you must have section breaks, different first page, or different odd and even headers and footers in your document to use this feature.

- **Next Section** Displays the header or footer used in the next section, based on the current location of the insertion point. If you click Next Section while in the header area, the insertion point jumps to the header area in the next section of your document. Note that you must have section breaks, different first page, or different odd and even headers and footers in your document to use this feature.

- **Link To Previous** Links the headers and footers in the current section to the preceding section. This enables you to create a continuous flow from section to section. You can also click in the header or footer area and click Ctrl+Shift+R to link the header or footer area to the preceding section. Note that you must have more than one section in your document to use this feature.

- **Different First Page** Specifies that you want to format the first page's headers and footers differently. For example, you might prefer to omit the page number on a cover page. This option is also available in the Page Setup dialog box.

- **Different Odd & Even Pages** Enables you to format headers and footers separately for odd and even pages. For example, you might choose to have left page headers display a report's title and right page headers display the title of the current section. This option is also available in the Page Setup dialog box.

- **Show Document Text** Toggles the display of the document's contents. You can hide document text to simplify your view as you create and edit headers and footers.

- **Header From Top** Enables you to control where the header is positioned from the top edge of the page. This option is also available in the Page Setup dialog box.

- **Footer From Bottom** Enables you to control where the footer is positioned from the bottom edge of the page. This option is also available in the Page Setup dialog box.

- **Insert Alignment Tab** Opens the Alignment Tab dialog box to insert a tab relative to the margin or indent. See "Alignment Tabs: The 'Relative' Scoop" on the next page for more information about this new feature.

- **Close Header And Footer** Closes the header and footer areas as well as the Header & Footer Tools tab.

Note

To manually add or edit a document's header and footer, right-click the header or footer area and select Edit Header or Edit Footer, respectively.

Working with Field Codes in Headers and Footers

When you use the Header & Footer Tools and the Design tab to add elements such as page numbers, dates, times, and so forth to headers and footers, Word often accomplishes the task by inserting field codes. You can control field codes in a number of ways, including the following.

- You can edit a field code by right-clicking the field code and then choosing Edit Field. The Field dialog box appears, which enables you to select from various formats that you can use to display the field's data.

- You can toggle the display between field data and field codes by right-clicking a field and choosing Toggle Field Codes.

- To update a field, select the field and press F9. Alternatively, right-click the field and choose Update Field. You can also click a field, such as a date that updates automatically, and click the Update command that appears above the field in a new type of container called a Content Control.

- To control whether fields appear with or without gray backgrounds, click the Microsoft Office Button, click Advanced, scroll to the Show Document Content area, and select an option in the Field Shading list. Available options are: Never, Always, or When Selected.

To create a different header and footer for parts of a document, you must divide the document into sections and then create a header and footer for each section. If you are working in a document divided into sections but you want to continue using the same header and footer from section to section, click in the header or footer for a section and then, on the Design tab, in the Navigation group, click Link To Previous.

INSIDE OUT   Alignment Tabs: The "Relative" Scoop

To align content in a header or footer on the same line, such as a left-aligned company name and a right-aligned date, a common method is to use a manual tab. With a manual tab, however, if the left or right margins change, the alignment of the content will not change and the manual tab needs to be adjusted. More often than not, adjusting a tab is often overlooked, and the header or footer content does not line up with the rest of the document. The solution to this problem is the new Alignment Tab functionality. An alignment tab aligns data relative to the margin or indent, unlike a manual tab, which is set in a fixed position and will not automatically change position if the margins change. To view the Alignment Tab settings, right-click a header or footer in the document and click Edit Header or Edit Footer, respectively, to view Header & Footer Tools. On the Design tab, click Insert Alignment Tab to open the Alignment Tab dialog box, as shown here.

There is a small caveat to using an alignment tab: there is no visual indication that an alignment tab is present; you won't see something like the manual tab indicators you see in the ruler. If you use an alignment tab to align data in a header or footer, it's recommended that any unused manual tabs be removed from the ruler in order to help clarify the formatting. To remove a manual tab, simply drag it off the ruler.

The Alignment Tab dialog box is accessible only when viewing the Header & Footer Tools tab, but these tabs can be inserted anywhere in your document by adding the Insert Alignment Tab command to the Quick Access Toolbar. To do so, right-click Insert Alignment Tab, and then click Add To Quick Access Toolbar.

Deleting Headers and Footers

To delete a header or footer from a document or section, simply open the header and footer areas (double-click in a header or footer area, or right-click a header or footer area and choose Edit Header or Edit Footer) to display the Header & Footer Tools tab and the Design tab. Select Remove Header or Remove Footer, respective, from the Header or Footer gallery. You can also select and delete header and footer content in the same way you select and delete any other content.

CAUTION

If your document contains multiple sections, before you remove or edit headers and footers in your document, remember to turn off the Link To Previous option in following sections to avoid inadvertently changing or deleting headers and footers in those following sections.

Working with the Document Grid

If support for Chinese, Japanese, or Korean is enabled through the 2007 Microsoft Office system language settings, you can use the document grid to help control line and character placement in your documents. To choose grid settings, use the Document Grid tab in the Page Setup dialog box, as shown in Figure 8-9.

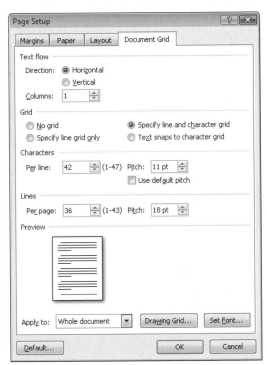

Figure 8-9 The document grid enables you to precisely control line and character spacing in documents that contain East Asian text.

Specifying Document Grid Settings

Using the Document Grid tab, you can control the text flow, number of columns, number of characters per line, character *pitch* (spacing between characters), number of lines per page, and line pitch. To use these features, follow these steps.

1. Click the Page Setup Dialog Box Launcher on the Page Layout tab to open the Page Setup dialog box. Then click the Document Grid tab.

2. If you want text to be displayed vertically, flowing from top to bottom as you type, click Vertical in the Text Flow section. Otherwise, for right-to-left text display, leave Horizontal selected. If you want, specify a number of columns in the Columns box. Notice that the Preview image adjusts to display your page setup settings while you work.

3. To enable the grid feature, select one of the following options.

   - **Specify Line Grid Only** Makes only the settings in the Lines area of the Document Grid tab available. You can choose the amount of space between lines (by selecting the number of lines you want to appear per page) and the pitch, or spacing, between lines.

   - **Specify Line And Character Grid** Makes all settings in both Character and Lines areas available. This setting enables you to choose both the number of characters per line and the number of lines per page. You can also choose the pitch of both characters and lines.

   - **Text Snaps To Character Grid** Disables the pitch settings, and lets you choose the number of characters per line and the lines per page.

4. Click the Apply To arrow, choose the option that specifies the portion of the document to which you want to apply the grid settings, and then click OK.

If you changed the text direction on the Document Grid tab for the whole document, Word automatically updates any existing content after you click OK. If you retained the original text direction for pages ahead of the insertion point and applied the This Point Forward setting, Word applies the grid effects for existing and new content after the insertion point. If necessary, Word begins a new page to separate content with different formats.

Displaying the Drawing Grid

You can display the drawing grid on your page to help you align objects and text, regardless of your language settings. To toggle the display of gridlines, click the View tab and then click Gridlines in the Show/Hide group.

If your setup supports East Asian languages, you can click the Drawing Grid button on the Document Grid tab in the Page Setup dialog box to access drawing grid settings. Figure 8-10 shows the Drawing Grid dialog box.

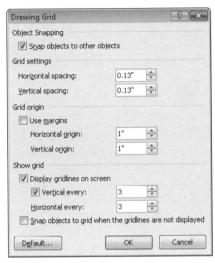

Figure 8-10 You can customize the display of the drawing grid by modifying settings in the Drawing Grid dialog box.

You can see the drawing grid only when you're working in Print Layout view.

Adding and Controlling Line Numbers

If you're working on a document that requires line numbering, such as a legal document or formal literature piece, line numbers can serve as useful references. Line numbers appear in the margin next to each line in a document. They enable quick references to specific lines in a document.

To add line numbers, you can select an option from Line Numbers on the Page Layout tab or choose settings from the Line Numbers dialog box, which can be accessed from the Layout tab in the Page Setup dialog box. Figure 8-11 shows both the Line Numbers options and the Line Numbers dialog box. Using these tools, you can choose whether to number the lines of an entire document continuously, restart numbering on each page, restart numbering in each section, or stop numbering for specific paragraphs. In addition, you can use the Page Setup dialog box to apply numbering to selected parts of a document in the same way you control margins and other page setup options.

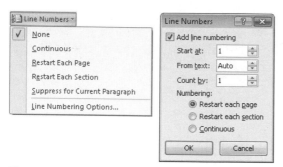

Figure 8-11 The Line Numbers feature enables you to add and control line numbering for a section, selected text, or the entire document.

To use the Line Numbers command on the Page Layout tab to control line numbering, follow these steps.

1. Position your insertion point in the document or section in which you want to add line numbers.

2. On the Page Layout tab, click the Line Numbers button, and then choose an option.

To use the Line Numbers dialog box (accessible from the Layout tab in the Page Layout dialog box) to control line numbering, follow these steps.

1. Click anywhere in a document you want to number, or click in a section you want to number.

2. On the Page Layout tab, click Line Numbers, and then click Line Numbering Options, or click the Page Setup Dialog Box Launcher in the Page Setup group on the Page Layout tab.

3. In the Page Setup dialog box, click the Layout tab if necessary.

4. On the Layout tab, click Line Numbers. The Line Numbers dialog box appears, as shown in Figure 8-11.

5. Select the Add Line Numbering check box. In the Start At box, type the number with which you want numbering to begin.

6. In the From Text box, specify number placement by using the up or down arrows, by typing a number (by default, the From Text spacing is measured in inches), or accept Auto (the default setting).

7. In the Count By box, enter a value to specify which lines should be accompanied by numbers. For instance, if you want to show a number next to every other line, you would enter **2** in the Count By box. To display a number next to each line, retain the default Count By setting of **1**.

8. In the Numbering section, click Restart Each Page if you want each page to be individually numbered, click Restart Each Section if you want the numbering to begin again with each subsequent section, or click Continuous if you want to number each line consecutively throughout the document.

9. Click OK to close the Line Numbers dialog box and return to the Page Setup dialog box. Click OK to close the Page Setup dialog box.

Making Room for Line Numbers

If you've created heading styles that extend all the way to the left margin of your page, you might find them truncated when you add line numbering. You can fix this by displaying the Line Numbers dialog box and changing the From Text setting. By default, From Text is set to Auto, but by decreasing the amount of space between numbering and text, you can usually make room for both line numbering and headings.

Outlining Documents for Clarity and Structure

Whenever you're tackling anything big, it helps to start with the end in mind. When it comes to creating long or complex documents, your outline is the foundation on which everything else is built. The outline represents the major ideas in your document and gives you a clear roadmap to follow as you're capturing the thoughts you want to share with others. It also helps you organize your presentation into manageable pieces that others can navigate, review, and respond to.

In this chapter, you'll learn all about the outlining capabilities of Microsoft Office Word 2007. Whether you love outlining and want to make the best use of all available tools or you're only creating the blasted thing because your supervisor asked for it, you'll find the tools easy to understand and use. With practice and a few tips and techniques, you might find yourself actually enjoying it.

Outlining Enhancements in Word 2007

The biggest change in Office Word 2007 is also the one that will make creating, modifying, and managing your outlines much easier. Word 2007 brings all the tools you need to outline your document together in one convenient place: the Outlining tab. To display the tools, click the View tab and click Outline in the Document Views group.

The Outline Tools group on the Outlining tab provides you with all the tools you need to create and set the various levels of your outline quickly. Just point and click the set the level of display you want to show in your outline; turn formatting on and off; and tweak the outline to your heart's content (see Figure 9-1).

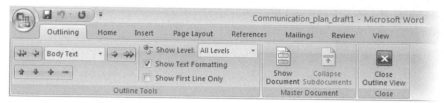

Figure 9-1 The Outlining tab on the Ribbon includes all the tools you need for working with multilevel outlines in Word 2007.

Creative Outlining with Word 2007

Although many of us learned about outlines for the first time in elementary school, working with outlines in the daily business world doesn't have to conform to any rigid rules that may be floating around in the back of your head. The idea of an outline is just to get your ideas down in a way that gives you a structure for your document and helps you ensure you're covering the major points you want to include in your document. If you find yourself stuck in the planning stage of your document, try some of these techniques to get the ideas flowing.

- **The process outline** Does your document lend itself to a series of steps? For example, if you're writing an article about managing an international project, plan out what you want to say as a series of steps. Perhaps the first thing you do in managing a global initiative is to determine the scope of the project. That's step 1. Next you take a look at the resources you have available. There's your second heading. Third, who are the members of your team? Continue until you have completed the process and then review your major steps. Your outline headings can evolve directly from those steps you've identified.

- **The question outline** You can also use a series of questions to help you identify the important sections of your outline. Basic questions might include these: What is this document about? (This would be your "Overview" or "Introduction" section.) Who is this document for? What is the mission of our company? Who are our department managers? Where is our facility? What types of services and products do we offer? Who are our customers? How have we improved since last year? What's new and exciting about us? What will we focus on next year?

  Each of these questions gives you a different vantage point from which to consider the content for your document. Put yourself in your readers' shoes. What will they want to see? What do they want to know about you? Questions can help you make sure you are providing the information that will best connect with the readers of your document.

- **The big-to-small outline** Another way to approach a writing task is to move from the big picture to the individual point of view. This works well in documents that you hope will influence others—for example, sales documents, annual reports, grant proposals, or fundraising materials. Your document starts with the big picture—the statement of a problem, concern, or desire that is common to most of us—and then moves toward the specific (how your company or organization uniquely meets the need you established in the big picture). For example, suppose that you are writing an annual report for Coral Reef Divers, a (fictional) nonprofit organization with a mission of preserving and protecting the remaining natural coral reef in the world. In the big perspective, you would talk about the environmental threats to the coral reef and the important role the coral reef serves in balancing the ecosystem. Then you could zoom in to talk about the specific factors your organization identifies as most important and finally, fully explore the services and options your organization provides as a response.

Eleven Reasons to Outline Your Next Complex Document

Even if you're a stream-of-consciousness writer, you'll find some benefit in outlining your long or complex documents. Once you create an outline in Office Word 2007, you've got something to start with—something you can use to build your document, edit it, and organize (or reorganize) it. And with that outline, you can even move seamlessly to and from a table of contents that's linked to the work in progress.

If you do not usually use outlining (and you're not alone), consider these reasons for outlining long documents in Word.

1. **You're more likely to meet your goals.** If your job involves writing grant proposals, producing product evaluations, writing annual reports, or composing print publications, you know that your document must reach a particular goal. You need to know where you're going, why you're going there, and the people you're trying to take with you. When you first type the document headings in Word, you're defining the steps that will take you to the goal of your document. Your headings reflect the major categories of information your audience will want to know. As you create the outline, you can make sure you're covering all the topics that you need to reach your goal.

2. **You can create an organized, thoughtful document.** Your outline will list not only the large categories but also smaller subtopics within each category. The multilevel capabilities Word outlines offer (up to nine levels) enable you to organize your thoughts to the smallest detail.

3. **The headings remind you where you're going.** Once you have an outline that you're happy with, you're free to write the document as your muse strikes. If you tend to write as inspiration leads, you can simply go with the flow and let the words fly—in the appropriate sections, of course. (If you change your mind, you can always move the sections later if you choose.) If you're more of a left-brain, analytical writer, you can craft your sentences within the structured topics, making sure you've got the requisite topic sentence, supporting sentences, and closing or transition sentence.

4. **You can easily reorganize your document at any time.** Word gives you the means to move parts of your document easily, even after your long document is filled with text. You can collapse topics to their headings and move them around

as you like. And of course, Undo always reverses your most recent action if you decide it was a bad move.

5. **You can expand and collapse topics.** The expand and collapse features of Word's outline enable you to change what you're viewing in the document. A fully expanded outline will show everything entered thus far—so all the text you've written, subheadings you've added, and notes you've inserted will be visible in a fully expanded outline view. If you want to limit the display to only headings and subheadings, you can collapse the outline to show only those items. This enables you to check to make sure that your organization is logical, that you've covered everything you want to cover, and that you have your topics in the right order.

6. **You can divide long documents into subdocuments or merge subdocuments into one long one.** The Master Document feature of Word enables you to divide long documents into smaller chunks so you can work with them more easily. When you pull the document back together, all the pieces can be merged into one coherent whole. Using the outlining feature enables you to see at a glance the most logical places for divisions.

7. **You can see what doesn't fit.** Outlining also gives you a way to see what *doesn't* work in your document. If there's a topic that really needs to be a separate document, or a heading that is begging for a rewrite, it will stand out. Of course, you can edit, move, and enter text in Outline view, so making those changes is a simple matter.

8. **You can easily change heading levels.** The outlining feature of Word comes with its own Ribbon full of commands, giving you the means to promote or demote headings and text. If you want to change a level 1 heading to a level 2 heading, for example, you can do so with the click of a button. This also works for text you want to raise to a heading or headings you want to drop to body text.

9. **You can work seamlessly with the table of contents.** If you've created a table of contents (TOC) for your document, you can update it on the fly and move directly to it to make changes, if needed. This saves you the hassle—and potential error—of creating a document with a separate TOC that might not be updated when the document is.

10. **You can easily divide up your document by section when you're working with a team.** If your company or organization is like many, producing the annual report is a big deal. Many people—from a variety of departments—may be involved in the creation, editing, design, and review of the document. When you work from an outline, you can easily assign specific sections to people in various departments—the finance manager gets to write the financial narrative, the operations manager drafts the section about the building expansion—you get the idea. Then you can put the document back together and use the outline to organize the document just the way you want it before you begin the final review stage.

11. **You can print your outline for handouts, reviews, or talking points.** Word gives you the option of printing only the outline of your document, which is a nice feature when you want to show others key points in a document or presentation but don't want them reading along word for word. Whether you do this in the review stage, as part of a collaborative effort, or to condense your finished document to a printable outline, you can display and print only the headings you want your readers to see.

Viewing a Document in Outline View

Being able to view the outline of your document is helpful whether you're starting a document from scratch or you're working with an existing file with text and headings already entered and formatted. You can display Outline view in several different ways: by clicking the View tab and choosing Outline in the Document Views group, by pressing Ctrl+Alt+O, or by clicking Outline in the View tools in the lower-right corner of the Word window.

Outline

If you've entered headings in your document and formatted them with one of heading styles (Heading 1, Heading 2, or Heading 3) provided by Word, they'll appear as headings in Outline view, as shown in Figure 9-2. The basic text styles applied to your document will be reflected in the outline, but all paragraph formatting (indents, before and after spacing, and line spacing) is suppressed. When you return to Print Layout or Web Layout view, the paragraph formatting will be visible again.

TROUBLESHOOTING

Headings don't show up in Outline view.

When you switch to Outline view, why don't any of your headings appear? If you didn't use the built-in heading styles Word offers—Heading 1, Heading 2, or Heading 3—Word won't automatically recognize the headings as outline levels. To correct the problem, click the headings in the outline one by one, click the Outline Level arrow in the Outline Tools group, and choose the heading level you want in the list. If you want to change all the headings at once, select all your headings (press and hold Ctrl while you click to the left of the headings you want to select) and then click the Outline Level arrow and choose the level you want to apply to the headings.

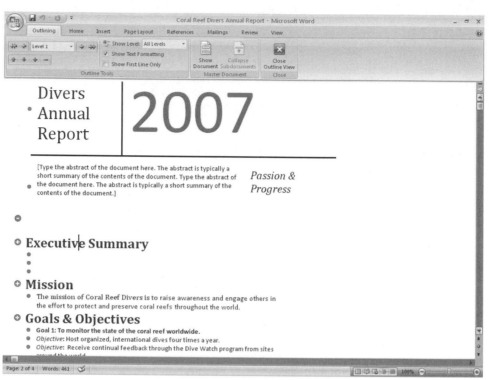

Figure 9-2 Outline view makes use of the headings styles you've applied in your document. Paragraph text also appears by default when you first display the outline.

Several different types of symbols appear in Outline view, as shown in Table 9-1. They provide clues as to what action to take while working in an outline.

Table 9-1 Outline Symbols

Symbol	Description
⊕	If double-clicked, alternately displays and hides subordinate headings and text paragraphs
⊖	Indicates that there are no subordinate headings or text paragraphs
⊕ **Goals & Objectives**	Shows that the topic includes body text or subheadings
● Goal 1: To monitor the state of the coral ● *Objective*: Host organized, international ● *Objective*: Receive continual feedback tl around the world. ● *Objective*: Stay up-to-date on the latest	Applied to lowest-level outline entry, indicating that it's formatted as body text

Exploring the Outlining Tools

When you display your document in Outline view, the Outlining tools appear automatically on the Ribbon. The Outlining tab provides two different groups: Outline Tools and Master Document. The Outline Tools group includes everything you need to work with the various levels in your outline and tailor the display of the outline to show only what you want to see (see Figure 9-3). The Master Document group offers two tools that will come in handy when you create and work with subdocuments. Table 9-2 lists and describes the Outlining tools.

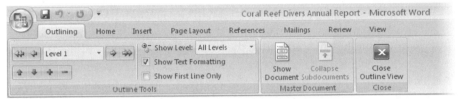

Figure 9-3 The Outlining tab on the Ribbon includes all the tools you need to apply, change, and view outline levels in your document.

Table 9-2 Outlining Tools

Tool	Name	Description
⇞	Promote To Heading 1	Raises the outline level of the selection to the highest outline level, Heading 1
⇦	Promote	Raises the outline level of the selection by one level
Level 1 ▾	Outline Level	Enables you to view and change the outline level of the selection
⇨	Demote	Lowers the outline level of the selection by one level
⇴	Demote To Body Text	Lowers the outline level of the selection to the lowest outline level, body text
⬆	Move Up	Moves the selection up one level in the outline
⬇	Move Down	Moves the selection down one level in the outline
✚	Expand	Expands the outline heading to show subheadings and text
▬	Collapse	Reduces the selection to top-level headings, hiding subordinate headings and text

Chapter 9

Creating a New Outline

Creating a new outline in Word is simple. If you're just starting a document, simply click the Outline button in the View tools in the lower-right corner of the Word window. Follow these steps to start the new outline.

1. Type the text for your heading. The heading is automatically formatted in the Heading 1 style.

2. Press Enter. The insertion point moves to the next line in the outline.

3. To create a sublevel, click Demote on the Outlining tab or press Tab. Word indents the insertion point and changes the first outline symbol (–) to a plus (+) symbol, indicating that the heading now has a subordinate entry. Type the text for that entry.

4. Press Enter to move to the next line in your outline. By default, Word creates the next heading at the same level as the heading you last entered. If you want to create another sublevel, click Demote or press Tab.

5. To raise an entry one heading level, click the Promote button or press Shift+Tab. If you want to move all the way out to the left margin and create a Heading 1 outline level when you have created multiple sublevels, click the Promote To Heading 1 button.

6. Continue typing entries until your outline is completed. Figure 9-4 shows a sample outline with multiple outline levels.

It's true that you must have your headings formatted in the styles Word will recognize—Heading 1, Heading 2, or Heading 3—for them to act and appear properly in the Outline window, but you can create styles you like for those headings. You can use the Styles gallery to change the formatting choices for those styles and save the changes in the current document. You can also have Word automatically make the changes to all similar heading styles in your document.

> **Note**
>
> In some instances, you might want to use the Tab key not to demote a heading level in your outline but to actually insert a Tab character between words. When you want to insert an actual tab in your outline, press Ctrl+Tab instead of simply pressing the Tab key.

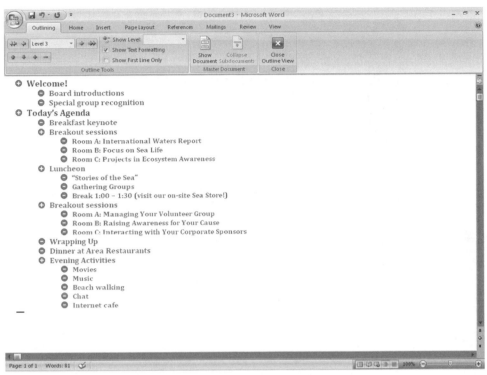

Figure 9-4 Outlining is a simple matter of identifying key topics in your document, naming them, and ordering them the way you want.

Choosing Outline Display

When you are working in Word's Outline view, you can customize the display so you see only the heading levels you want to work with. For example, you might want to see only the first-level heads in your outline so that you can make sure that all your most important topics are covered. Or perhaps you want to see every level, to check the completeness of the subtopics. You can easily move back and forth between various outline displays by using the buttons on the Outlining tab on the Ribbon.

Displaying Different Levels of Text

To limit the display of your outline to only Heading 1 levels, for example, click the Show Level arrow to display the list of levels. Click Level 1 to display only the first level, as shown in Figure 9-5.

Figure 9-5 In the Show Level list, control the levels displayed in Outline view by choosing what you want to see.

INSIDE OUT Copy Document Headings Without All the Text

Being able to collapse the outline display to headings only gives you a quick look at the overall organization of your document. If only you could copy and paste only the headings of your outline as well. Unfortunately, when you highlight the entire outline, copy it, and paste it into another document, the whole thing—headings and subordinate text—goes along for the ride. One workaround is to create a table of contents to the appropriate level and then convert the TOC to regular text. You can then copy the headings and paste them into a document.

Note

There are other methods of changing which heading levels appear: You can click the Expand or Collapse button on the Outlining tab, or you can double-click the Plus (+) symbol to the left of a heading to display subordinate items.

Showing the First Line of Text

When you want to see the paragraph text you've entered, you can have Word display only the first line of text so that you can see what the content of the paragraph is without displaying the entire paragraph. Why might you want to display only the first line of text?

- To check the order in which you discuss topics

- To decide whether to move text to a different part of the document

- To review the primary points you've covered under subheadings

When all levels in your outline are displayed, you can reduce the outline to only the first line of text by clicking the Show First Line Only check box in the Outline Tools group. The display changes to show the first text lines, as Figure 9-6 shows. To display full paragraphs again, click the check box a second time to clear it.

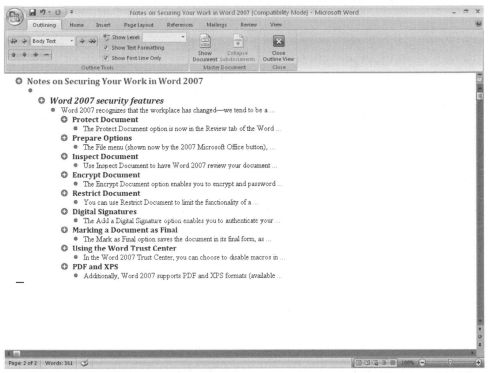

Figure 9-6 Displaying only the first line of a paragraph lets you see the general subject of your text so that you can make informed choices about reordering topics.

Removing and Showing Formatting

Another quick change you might want to make is to suppress the display of formatting in your outline. As you know, when you change to Outline view, the headings are shown with whatever character formatting they're assigned in the other Word views. When you're working in the outline, however, you might find formatting differences distracting while you consider the content and organization of your topics.

To hide the formatting in your outline, click the Show Text Formatting check box in the Outline Tools group on the Outlining tab. This control actually functions as a toggle, meaning that the first click hides the formatting and the second displays it again. Figure 9-7 shows you what a simple outline looks like when all formatting has been suppressed.

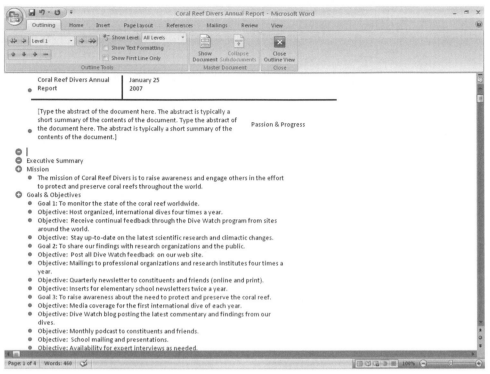

Figure 9-7 When you want to focus on the thoughts in your outline, you might want to hide the formatting.

Working with Headings in Outline View

Whether you create an outline from scratch or use the outline created as part of your existing document, you'll invariably want to change some headings and insert and delete others. Headings are easy to work with in Outline view—with a simple click of a tool, you can change heading levels, move headings in the outline, and even demote the heading to body text, if you like.

Adding a Heading

When you want to insert a heading in an existing outline, in Outline view, find the heading you want the new heading to follow. Then simply place the insertion point after that heading and press Enter. If you want the heading to be at the same level as the heading preceding it, simply type the new heading. If you want to promote or demote the heading level, click the appropriate button before typing your text.

Applying Outline Levels

You can choose the outline level for your heading by using the Outline Level list on the Outlining tab. Simply click in the heading to which you want to apply the outline level and then click the Outline Level arrow to display the list, as shown in Figure 9-8. Click your choice, and the format is applied to the heading.

Figure 9-8 If you know which outline level you want to assign to the new heading, choose it directly from the Outline Level list.

Promoting and Demoting Headings

Once you have text in your outline, you can easily change outline levels, moving a heading from level 1 to level 2, for example, or from body text up to level 3. Put simply, promoting a heading takes it one level higher in the outline, and demoting a heading moves it one level down in the outline.

Each time you click the Demote button, Word moves the heading one level down the outline level scheme. Outline view shows the change by indenting the heading and changing the formatting. Conversely, the Promote button raises the heading level of the selected text until you reach Heading 1, which is the highest outline level available.

When you want to demote and promote in larger increments, moving a heading all the way to the topmost level, for example, or changing a heading to body text, use the Promote To Heading 1 or Demote To Body Text buttons.

When might you want to promote or demote text? You could be working on a report, for example, and realize that a topic you've placed at a Heading 2 level is really part of another topic. You can first change the heading level to reflect the level the heading should be to fit in the outline where you want it to go, and then you can move the selection to that point. You can also drag and drop the selection where you want it to appear in the outline; you may need to adjust the heading level depending on where you drop the section.

Displaying Outline and Print Layout View at the Same Time

You can easily view your document in both Outline view and Print Layout view at the same time. Just drag the split bar (located at the top of the vertical scroll bar) down the screen to open another window displaying the current document.

—— Split bar

To change that area to another view, click in it to give it focus and then select the view you want (for example, Outline view). Figure 9-9 shows how the document appears when you are viewing a document in both Print Layout and Outline view.

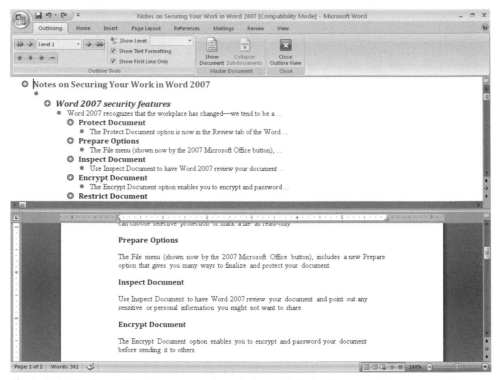

Figure 9-9 Use the split bar to open another window and display the current document using different views.

Changing Your Outline

Once you have all the heading levels the way you want them, you might decide that you want to move some of your outline topics around. That's one of the biggest benefits of using Outline view—you can easily see which topics fit and which don't, or which topics would work better somewhere else.

Expanding and Collapsing the Outline

The symbols in the Outline window give you clues about what, if anything, is subordinate to the level displayed in the outline. You can use these symbols (introduced in Table 9-1) to alternately display and hide sections and subsections in your document.

You'll find two easy methods for expanding and collapsing the topics in your outline. You can double-click the plus sign to the left of the heading you want to expand. Or, if you prefer, you can simply make sure the heading is selected and then click Expand.

Collapse works the same way—simply click in the heading of the topic you want to hide. Then double-click the plus sign or click Collapse on the Outlining tab.

Moving Outline Topics

Another benefit to Outline view is that you can move entire topics easily. Whether you choose to use the Outlining tools, cut and paste text using the Clipboard, or drag what you've selected from place to place, you can easily move portions of your document around as needed.

Moving Topics Up and Down

When you want to move part of an outline to an earlier point in your document or closer to the end, you can use two of the Outlining tools—Move Up and Move Down—to do the trick. Start by selecting the entire part you want to move and then click Move Up to move the selection up one heading. If you want to move it more than one level up, click Move Up as many times as needed to position the selection in the right place.

Use Move Down the same way: Select the part of your outline you want to move and then click Move Down on the Outlining tab. If you want to move the selection more than one level farther down, keep clicking Move Down.

If you want to move only a heading—not an entire topic—simply click in the heading before choosing Move Up or Move Down. Word moves only the selected heading and leaves any subordinate headings and text in place.

Cutting and Pasting Parts of the Outline

You can also cut and paste parts of your documents in Outline view. This is helpful when you know you want to move a topic, but you're not exactly sure where you want to put it. You can cut and paste part of an outline by following these steps.

1. Select the portion of the outline you want to move.

2. Click the Home tab and click Cut in the Clipboard group. (Alternatively, you can press Ctrl+X if you prefer.) The selected portion is removed from the outline to the Office Clipboard.

3. Scroll through the outline until you find the place where you'd like to paste your selection. Click to place the insertion point there.

4. Click Paste in the Clipboard group on the Home tab (or use Ctrl+V). The selection is pasted at the new location.

Forget What's on the Clipboard?

The Clipboard keeps track of everything you copy, cut, or paste while you're working in a specific application. When you are moving sections around in your document, you can easily lose track of what you've clipped out of your file. To view the Clipboard, click the Home tab and click the Dialog Box Launcher in the Clipboard group.

— Dialog Box Launcher

When you click the Clipboard Dialog Box Launcher, the Clipboard appears, displaying everything you've placed on the Clipboard recently (the Clipboard holds a total of 24 items). To work with the items on the Clipboard, click the item you want to use and select the command you want from the displayed menu.

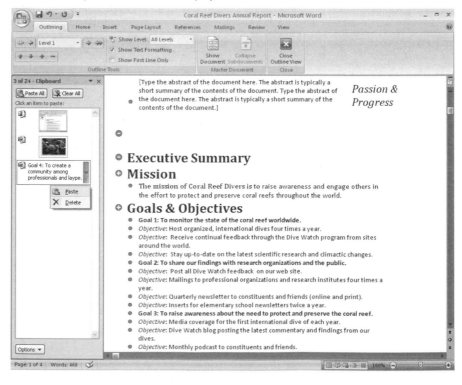

Dragging to a New Location

If the part of your outline you want to move is within dragging distance of the new location (meaning that you can highlight and drag the section to that point easily), you can simply highlight it and drag it to the new position. As you drag, the pointer changes, showing a small box beneath the arrow. A horizontal line moves from line to line, tracking the point at which the selection will be inserted when you release the mouse button.

You may want to display only high-level headings before you move part of your outline. This enables you to see more of your outline on the screen, and you'll have a shorter distance to drag what you're moving. Even if text is not displayed, subordinate headings and body text will be moved with the heading.

Printing Your Outline

At various stages throughout the process of viewing, editing, arranging, reorganizing, and formatting the headings in your outline, you might want to print a copy to see how things are shaping up. Printing is the same basic process, whether you're printing a long document or a simple outline. Here are the steps.

1. Switch to Outline view and then display your outline.

2. Display only those headings you want to print by using the Collapse and Expand buttons and selecting the outline levels you want to see.

3. Click the Microsoft Office Button and point to Print. Then click Print to display the Print dialog box, select your options, and click OK to print as usual. The outline is printed as displayed on the screen.

TROUBLESHOOTING

I have too many page breaks in my printed outline.

Suppose that you've finished working on the outline for the Coral Reef Divers report, and the development team is waiting to see what you've come up with. You've gone back over it several times to make sure you have all the sections organized properly and the outline levels set correctly. Everything looks good.

But when you print the outline, there are big gaps in the center of the pages. In the file, the text looks fine—what's the problem? Chances are the blank spots are due to Word's treatment of manual page breaks. If you've inserted manual page breaks in your document, you'll need to remove them before printing the outline; otherwise, the blank spots will prevail.

To remove the manual page breaks, click the Home tab and click the Show/Hide tool in the Paragraph group to display all the formatting marks in your outline. Then move to each page break symbol, double-click it, and press Delete. Save your document and print again. The unwanted breaks should be gone.

Using the Document Map vs. Using Outline View

If you've used previous versions of Word, you may already be familiar with the concept of the Document Map. The Document Map shown in Figure 9-10 creates a listing of headings in your document and displays them in a pane along the left side of the document. The headings are linked to the document so that you can click any topic to move easily to that part of the document. To display the Document Map, click the View tab and then click the Document Map check box in the Show/Hide group.

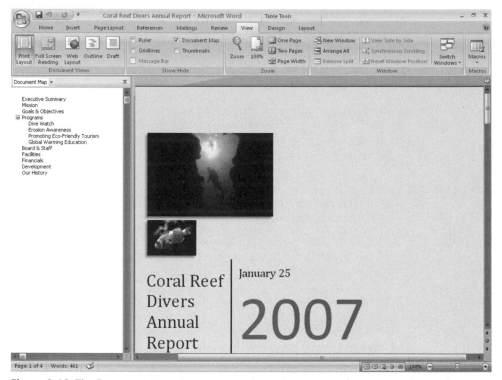

Figure 9-10 The Document Map gives you a quick way to view your document outline and navigate among sections of your document.

The great thing about the Document Map is that you can view your document in two ways at once—in the outline listed in the Document Map pane and in Print Layout view—and you can easily move to the topic you want to see by clicking the heading in the left pane of the work area.

Why have a Document Map *and* an outlining feature? First, the Document Map is a handy tool when you want to do things like check the wording of a topic, make sure the text you've added fits the heading, and see at a glance that you've covered all the topics you intended to cover. But when you want to change the heading levels of text, reorganize parts, or affect the table of contents in any way, you need to use Word 2007's Outlining feature. For major structuring changes, text reorganizations, heading modifications, and more, you'll want to work in Outline view. For simple, lay-of-the-land operations, the Document Map will give you a clear picture of your document in a form that you can access and navigate quickly, but for all other outline-related tasks, you'll find what you need in Outline view.

When you work in Microsoft Office Word 2007, you probably take for granted how the program can seamlessly flow text from margin to margin and page to page. On occasion, however, you might want to use Office Word 2007 to venture beyond basic word processing and into the realm of desktop publishing. For example, instead of filling a page with text, you might want to position and format blocks of text precisely within your document, or you might want to customize the overall look of your document by applying a uniform color scheme. Although Word 2007 doesn't offer all the features included in a desktop publishing application such as Microsoft Office Publisher 2007, it does include a nice collection of desktop publishing tools that can serve most of your everyday desktop publishing needs.

Specifically, the desktop publishing capabilities in Word 2007 let you control text layout by using text boxes, shapes formatted to serve as text containers, and frames. Furthermore, you can add backgrounds or watermarks to online and printed documents. In the first portion of this chapter, you'll learn how to use these common desktop publishing tools to create professional and imaginative document layouts.

After you learn about the desktop publishing features of Word 2007, you'll find several sections about borders and shading, two of the formatting features you can use to draw attention to elements in your documents. You might use these features, for example, to add a border to a table or create a shaded sidebar to differentiate a short feature from a main article in a newsletter.

Layout and Design Fundamentals

When you publish information, you need to focus on the words and pictures you use to convey your message. After all, your content is the whole point, and Word 2007 provides more tools than ever to aid you in adding and editing content. But interwoven into any document that you present to others is the need for a design that complements your message. Throughout any design project, you must keep in mind three fundamentals—alignment, balance, and whitespace (your ABWs!)—all of which relate to readability.

Two of the page layout components you use in Word 2007—backgrounds and text containers—add professional polish to documents when they're used properly, but they also offer easy avenues to design disaster. When working with backgrounds and text containers, think of giving your readers' eyes a rest. Just as you need space to physically walk around a room, your readers' eyes need space to move around a page. To make whitespace effective, you need to align document elements along expected paths and ensure that backgrounds don't create unnecessarily hard-to-read situations. Furthermore, while you think about the people who will be visiting your "room," also think about the purpose of your room (you don't want to end up with your bed in your bath!) If you're designing a document for a prestigious art gallery that has a lot of physical space, simulate that feel in your document by providing your readers with extra space. If you're designing a publication for an upcoming charity auction, you'll probably want to use less whitespace but tighten alignment to promote activity, action, and movement as you lead your audience through the information it needs.

To help illustrate on a very simple level, Figure 10-1 shows how making some basic layout choices to the informational page about Alien Ants shown on the left can greatly enhance the page's readability, as shown on the right. Though both pages use a simple background (white with a blue left edge) to simplify printing, breaking up the text and adding whitespace clearly makes the information more accessible while simultaneously communicating the open feeling of outer space along with a hint of a research lab.

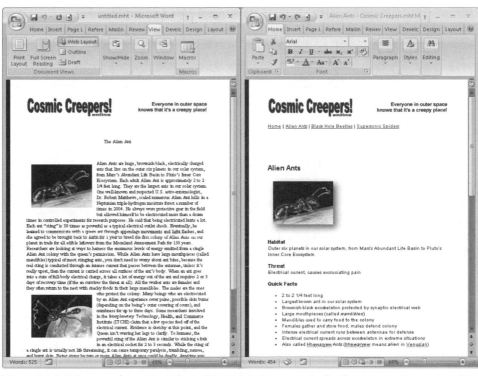

Figure 10-1 When you lay out text that will be printed or presented online, remember your audience will be reading your document! Guide them by aligning elements, adding whitespace, and avoiding overpowering backgrounds.

Using Backgrounds and Watermarks

One quick and often effective way to add information and visual impact to your documents is to add a background or watermark (or both) to online and printed documents. Backgrounds are generally used to create backdrops for Web pages, online documents, and e-mail messages, and they usually aren't the best choice for long documents or documents that will be printed in large quantities. In Word 2007, you can view backgrounds in all views except Draft view and Outline view.

If you want to create a more print-friendly background, you should consider using a watermark. A watermark is faded text or a pale picture that appears behind document text. Watermarks are often used to add visual appeal to a document or to identify a document's status, such as Draft or Confidential. You can see watermarks in Print Layout view, in Print Preview, or on printed documents. In this section of the chapter, you'll learn how to create, control, and delete backgrounds and watermarks on your Web pages and printed documents.

Creating Backgrounds and Watermarks

You can create custom backgrounds and watermarks for online pages (including Web pages and e-mail messages) as well as for printed documents. When you create a background for a document, you can use color gradients, patterns, pictures, solid colors, or textures that repeat, or *tile*, to fill the page. When you create a watermark, you add a light-colored picture (usually gray) or light-colored text that appears behind your document's contents. If you use text in a watermark, you can choose from built-in phrases or enter one of your own.

Adding Backgrounds to Online Pages

To add a color background to a page (such as a Web page, an online document, or an e-mail message), click the Page Layout tab, click Page Color, and then perform any of the following actions.

- Click a color on the color palette to add a background color.

> **Note**
>
> To preview background colors on a page, simply position your pointer over a color on the Page Color color palette. Word automatically changes the color of the background so you can view it without applying the change. To apply a color, click the color square.

- Choose More Colors to access additional colors (standard colors and those that you mix yourself) that you can apply to your background.

- Choose Fill Effects to access the Gradient, Texture, Pattern, and Picture tabs in the Fill Effects dialog box. Settings on these tabs enable you to create custom backgrounds.

After you choose a color or create a fill effect, Word applies the background to the document. You can see the background in all views except Draft and Outline views. By default, if you print the document, the background won't be printed. To print a document with its background displayed, you must configure settings in the Word Options dialog box before you print, as follows.

1. Click the Microsoft Office Button, Word Options, Display.

2. In the Printing Options section, select the Print Background Colors And Images check box, and then click OK.

> **Note**
>
> You can quickly check whether Word is configured to print background colors and images by viewing a document that contains background formatting in Print Preview.

> **Note**
>
> When you save a Web page with a background, Word saves background textures and gradients as JPG files and patterns as GIF files.

Adding Watermarks to Documents

To add a watermark to a document, display your document in Print Layout view and click the Page Layout tab. In the Page Background group, click Watermark. The Watermark gallery appears, as shown in Figure 10-2.

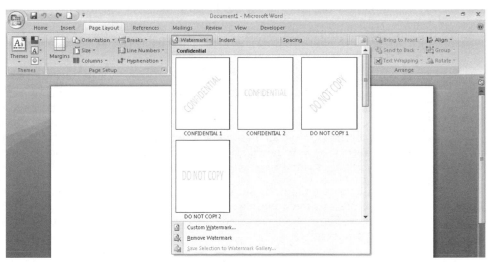

Figure 10-2 The Watermark gallery includes built-in watermarks such as Confidential, Draft, and Urgent.

You can also create a custom watermark using a picture or text by configuring the settings in the Printed Watermark dialog box. To open the Printed Watermark dialog box, click Custom Watermark near the bottom of the Watermark gallery. Figure 10-3 shows the Printed Watermark dialog box.

Figure 10-3 You can use the Printed Watermark dialog box to add picture and text watermarks to your documents.

You can insert a custom picture or text watermark by configuring the settings in the Printed Watermark dialog box, as described here.

- **Picture Watermark** To insert a picture watermark, click the Picture Watermark option and then click Select Picture to choose a picture for the watermark. You can use color or grayscale pictures for watermarks. The Scale option lets you specify a size for the watermark picture. In most cases, you should select the Washout check box (which is selected by default) so that the watermark doesn't interfere with your document's readability.

- **Text Watermark** To insert a text watermark, click the Text Watermark option and then type the text you want to use in the Text box or choose from text in the Text list. You can then select settings for the font, size, color, and layout for the watermark. You can display the watermark text diagonally or horizontally. In most cases, you should select the Semitransparent check box so that the watermark doesn't interfere with your document's readability.

After you have configured your picture or text watermark settings, click OK or click Apply to preview the watermark without closing the dialog box. If you like the results, click Close. Figure 10-4 shows a document (in Print Preview mode) that has a *Confidential* watermark.

Including Watermarks in Document Headers

Before Word 2002, many people created watermarks by adding objects (such as shapes) and images to document headers. You can continue to create watermarks in this manner in Word 2007. To do so, you manually paste or insert the watermark object or image into the document header. If you create watermarks this way, you can't use the Printed Watermark dialog box to configure the watermark's settings. The simplest way to create a watermark is by using the Printed Watermark dialog box, so you should use this dialog box to create watermarks whenever possible.

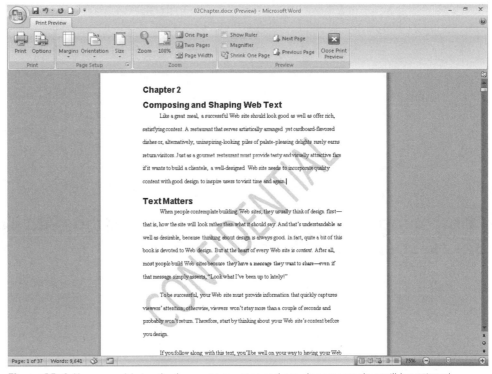

Figure 10-4 You can add standard or custom watermarks to documents that will be printed.

Changing and Removing Backgrounds and Watermarks

After you have added backgrounds and watermarks to online pages and documents that will be printed, you're free to change your mind at any time and change or remove them.

To change backgrounds or watermarks, use one of the following methods.

- **Change a background** Click the Page Layout tab, click Page Color, and then choose new background settings.

- **Change a watermark** Click the Page Layout tab, click Watermark, and then click a new thumbnail in the gallery or click Custom Watermark.

To remove backgrounds and watermarks, use one of these methods.

- **Remove a background** Click the Page Layout tab, click Page Color, and then choose No Color.

- **Remove a watermark** Click the Page Layout tab, click Watermark, and click Remove Watermark.

When you remove a background from a Web page, the page will be displayed using the default background color specified by the user's Web browser. Generally, the default background color is white or gray.

> **Note**
>
> If you created a watermark by inserting it in a document's header, you must open the header and manually delete or change the watermark. You can't use the Printed Watermark dialog box to modify and remove watermarks inserted into headers.

Controlling Text Placement and Formatting with Text Boxes, Shapes, and Frames

When you use Word 2007, you might occasionally find that you need to control text layout beyond setting margins, formatting paragraphs, and creating columns. At those times, you might benefit from entering your information into text containers: shapes that can contain text or *text boxes*. Text containers are free-floating objects (independent of the document's body text) that you can use to enclose information. You can then format these objects the same way you format drawings.

Generally, you'll use text boxes and shapes when you want to position several blocks of text on a page or continue the flow of a story from one area in your document to another. For example, you might be creating a newsletter in which a story starts on the cover page but concludes on another page later in the newsletter.

In addition to creating interesting page layouts and continuing a story from one text block to another (also referred to as *flowing text* in linked text boxes), you might also want to use text boxes to accomplish the following tasks.

- Format text blocks using drawing tools
- Rotate or flip text
- Change text orientation
- Align or distribute text blocks as a group

This section of the chapter describes how you can manipulate and control text using text containers—standard rectangular text boxes, built-in preformatted text boxes, and shapes formatted as text containers. Keep in mind that when you're working with text boxes and shapes, you must work in Print Layout view so that the text boxes and shapes appear on the screen as you work. Figure 10-5 shows a text box, a shape formatted to contain text, and a built-in text box in Print Layout view.

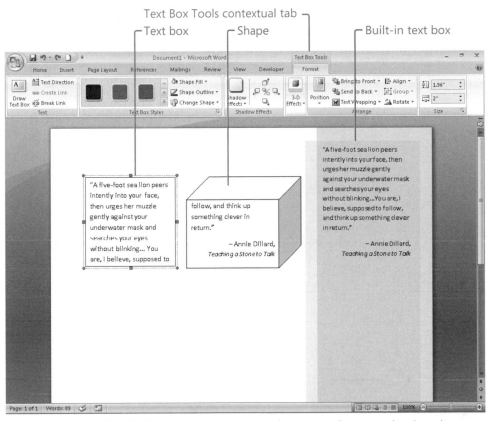

Figure 10-5 Regardless of whether you insert a standard square text box, a text box based on a shape, or a preformatted built-in text box, you can link text and format your text boxes using the Text Box Tools tab, which is displayed automatically when you work with text boxes.

As you can see in Figure 10-5, the active text box is surrounded by a frame-like border built from dashed lines and sizing handles. This border appears whenever you click a text box, and it serves a number of purposes, including enabling you to move and resize the text box and access text box properties.

Creating Text Boxes

Creating a text box is as easy as drawing a box or shape. You can create a text box by performing any of the following actions.

- Click the Insert tab, click Text Box in the Text group (or press Alt, N, X), and then click a built-in text box style.

- Click the Insert tab, click Text Box in the Text group (or press Alt, N, X), click Draw Text Box, and then drag the pointer in your document to draw a text box.

- Click an existing text box and then click Draw Text Box on the Text Box Tools tab.

- Click the Insert tab, click Shapes in the Illustrations group, select a shape, and add it to your document. Right-click the shape, and then choose Add Text from the shortcut menu.

> **Note**
>
> To add existing text to a text box, select the text, click the Insert tab, click Text Box, and click Draw Text Box. The selected text is automatically inserted into a standard text box.

By default, when you draw a text box or shape in Word 2007, a drawing canvas *does not* automatically open. This differs from previous versions of Word, which automatically placed text boxes on a drawing canvas. If you prefer, you can work with AutoShapes on a drawing canvas by configuring settings in the Word Options dialog box as follows.

1. Click the Microsoft Office Button, Word Options, Advanced.

2. In the Editing Options section, click the Automatically Create Drawing Canvas When Inserting AutoShapes check box.

3. Click OK.

After you close the Word Options dialog box, a drawing canvas will automatically be created when you insert a shape in your document.

Regardless of whether you work on or off the drawing canvas, you'll notice that the Text Box Tools tab opens automatically after you create a text box, as shown previously in Figure 10-5. This tab becomes available whenever a text box is selected.

As you create text boxes in your document, you can move and resize them in the same manner you move and resize drawing objects—by dragging them by their edges and sizing handles. To move a text box, point to the border to change the insertion point to four arrows, click anywhere on the border other than on a sizing handle, and then drag the text box. To resize a text box, drag the sizing handles (which appear as circles and squares in text box frames) to change the text box's width and height. Figure 10-5 shows a selected text box with its border and sizing handles.

Inserting Text into Text Boxes and Shapes

After you create text boxes or format shapes to hold text, you are ready to add text and formatting. You can insert text into containers in a few predictable ways, including the following.

- Drag information into a text box

- Select existing text, click Text Box on the Insert tab, and click Draw Text Box

- Click a text box and then click the Insert tab, click Object in the Text group, and then click Text From File to insert a file's contents into the text box

If you're planning to insert a longer story into a text box or a series of linked text boxes, you should consider typing and editing the story in a standard Word document before importing the information into the text box or text boxes (as described in the last item in the preceding bulleted list). That way, you can conduct most of your editing, formatting, and fine-tuning tasks in a standard document, which generally provides a larger viewing area than a text box or shape.

TROUBLESHOOTING

I can't find the Insert, File command.

In Word 2007, the location of the Insert, File command has changed. This command enables you to insert the contents of another file into your document. In Word 2007, to insert the contents of another document into a document or text box, follow these steps.

1. Click the Insert tab, click Object in the Text group, and then click Text From File.

2. In the Insert File dialog box, select the file you want to insert, and then click Insert.

Note

You can format text in text boxes in the same way you format document text. First click in the text box and then format the text using keyboard shortcuts, commands on the Ribbon, settings in the Font and Paragraph dialog boxes, styles, and so forth. You can even track changes to the text in a text box.

In addition to inserting text, you can insert graphics, tables, fields, and Content Controls into text boxes. Among the items that you cannot include in text boxes are the following.

- Citations
- Columns
- Comments
- Drop caps
- Endnotes
- Footnotes
- Index entries

Chapter 10

- Page and column breaks
- Tables of figures
- Tables of contents

To include these elements in a text container, you have to convert your text box into a floating frame, as described in the next section.

> **Note**
>
> A helpful feature of text containers is that when you run the spelling checker and grammar checker, Word also checks the information in text boxes and shapes.

Using Floating Frames for Comments, Footnotes, Tables, and Fields

Generally, your best bet when placing text into text containers is to use text boxes and shapes formatted to contain text because these objects are highly customizable. But if you need to insert text that includes comments, footnotes, endnotes, tables, or certain fields (such as tables of contents and index fields) in a text container, you have to use a *floating frame* instead of a text box because text boxes don't properly support these types of elements. A floating frame looks like a text box, it supports Word fields, but you can't format one as extensively as you can a text box.

You can easily convert an existing text box into a floating frame whenever necessary by following these steps.

1. If the text box you want to convert is on the drawing canvas, drag the text box off the canvas.

2. If the content of the text box is linked to another text box or text boxes, you must break the link(s). See "Linking Text Boxes to Flow Text from One Text Box to Another" on page 270 for more information about creating and breaking text box links.

3. Right-click the edge of the text box you want to convert and then choose Format Text Box from the shortcut menu (or Format AutoShape if the text box is a shape). Then click the Text Box tab in the Format Text Box dialog box or the Format AutoShape dialog box.

4. Click Convert To Frame. A message box appears, warning that you are about to change the text box to a frame and that some drawing formatting might be lost. Click OK.

After you convert a text box to a frame, the Text Box Tools tab will not be available.

Converting a Frame to a Text Box

You can't convert a frame element into a text box in the same way that you can covert a text box into a frame. Instead, you have to remove the frame and then create a text box. Though you can accomplish this in many ways, one of the easiest ways to move content out of a frame and into a text box is as follows.

1. Right-click the frame border and click Format Frame.

2. In the Frame dialog box, click Remove Frame. The frame will be deleted and its content will be selected on the screen by default.

3. With the content still selected, click Text Box in the Text group on the Insert tab, and then click Draw Text Box.

After you convert the frame to a text box, you might have to resize or adjust formatting. In addition, if you are working with a frame that includes a border, you might want to remove the border before you convert the frame to a text box; otherwise, you might end up with two borders to adjust.

Formatting Text Boxes and AutoShapes

By default, when you create a text box, it appears as a white (not transparent) box surrounded by thin (0.75 point) black lines. Fortunately, text boxes don't have to be limited to plain white rectangles strategically placed around your document. You can format text boxes and shapes designed to be text containers in the same manner that you format other drawing objects. For example, by using some of the formatting options on the Text Box Tools tab, you can apply fill and line colors by using the Shape Fill and Shape Outline tools, you can apply built-in Text Box Styles, and you can add a shadow and 3-D effects. To format text boxes and shapes using the Text Box Tools tab, select the text box or shape you want to format and then click the appropriate tool.

Note

To quickly make the Text Box Tools tab the active tab, double-click the edge of a text box or shape.

In addition to the formatting tools on the Text Box Tools tab, you can format text boxes using the Format Text Box (or Format AutoShape) dialog box. Namely, you can control the position of text inside text boxes and shapes, you can change a text box's shape, and you can have Word automatically resize a text box or a shape to accommodate the complete text of a story.

Controlling Text in Text Boxes and Shapes

You can change a text box's internal margin settings to control the distance between the text it contains and the text box or AutoShape's borders. Here are the steps you follow:

1. Click a text box or shape, rest the pointer on the frame until the insertion point appears as four arrows, right-click the frame, and then choose Format Text Box or Format AutoShape from the shortcut menu. The Format Text Box or Format AutoShape dialog box appears, depending on the type of text container you're formatting.

2. Click the Text Box tab, shown in Figure 10-6. The Text Box tab is the same in both the Format Text Box and Format AutoShape dialog boxes.

3. In the Internal Margin section, increase or decrease the left, right, top, and bottom margin measurements to control the distance between the text and the selected object's edges. Click OK to apply the settings.

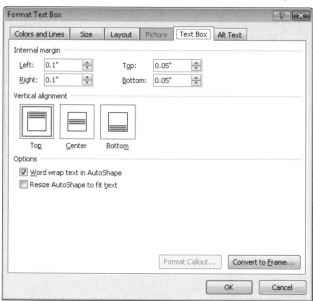

Figure 10-6 You can control the spacing around text in text boxes and AutoShapes by configuring the internal margin settings in the Text Box tab.

 In addition to controlling internal margins, you can change the orientation of text inside text boxes. To do so, select the text box and then click Text Direction in the Text group on the Text Box Tools tab. Continue to click the button to cycle through the available text direction options.

> **Note**
>
> When you change the text orientation in a linked text box, you change it in all linked text boxes in the story. In other words, you can't change the text direction in a single text box if it's part of a linked series of text boxes. For more information about linked text boxes, see "Linking Text Boxes to Flow Text from One Text Box to Another," on the next page.

Changing Text Box Shapes

The beauty of using AutoShapes is that you can change your mind about which shape you want to use at any time, even if the AutoShape is formatted as a text box. Changing the shape of a text box is similar to changing shapes that don't contain text. To do so, ensure that you're working in Print Layout view and then follow these steps.

1. Click the shape you want to modify. To select multiple shapes, press and hold Shift while clicking each.

2. On the Text Box Tools tab, in the Text Box Styles group, click Change Shape and then choose the shape you want from the gallery.

All the shapes you've selected take on the new shape, but they retain format settings such as color, internal margins, and so forth.

Resizing Text Boxes or AutoShapes Automatically to Show All Content

You can automatically resize a text box or a shape that contains text, graphics, and objects so that its dimensions change as necessary to display the content it contains. You can use this option only with nonlinked (stand-alone) text containers because linked text containers are designed to flow text to the next linked container if the content exceeds the current container's boundaries. To set up a stand-alone text container to resize automatically, follow these steps.

1. Right-click a text container's frame, choose Format Text Box or Format AutoShape, and then click the Text Box tab in the Format Text Box or Format AutoShape dialog box.

> **Note**
>
> After selecting a text container, you can also open the Format AutoShape or Format Text Box dialog box by using the Dialog Box Launcher in the Text Box Styles or Size groups on the Text Box Tools tab.

2. Select the Resize AutoShape To Fit Text check box and then click OK.

Chapter 10

The text container will automatically stretch or shrink to accommodate text and other content.

Linking Text Boxes to Flow Text from One Text Box to Another

If you've ever created a newsletter or a brochure, you know how tricky it can be to fill text areas and properly manage jumps from one page to another. In Word 2007, you can simplify these kinds of tasks by linking text boxes. When you link text boxes, any text that you insert into one text box will automatically flow into the next text box when the first text box cannot accommodate all the text. After you insert text into linked text boxes, you can edit the text to make your story longer or shorter, and Word will automatically reflow the text throughout the series of linked text boxes.

> **Note**
>
> The maximum number of links you can have in one document is 31, which means that you can have up to 32 linked text containers in one document.

When you want to link text boxes or shapes, you need to keep the following limitations in mind.

- Linked text boxes and AutoShapes must be contained in a single document (note that they cannot be in different subdocuments of a master document).

- No text box or AutoShape can already be linked to another series or story.

Before you flow text into a series of linked text boxes, you should be sure that you've made most of your changes to your text. Then draw the text boxes you want to link and into which you'll import your story. When your text is ready and your text boxes are drawn, follow these steps to link the text boxes and insert the text.

1. In Print Layout view, click the first text box or shape you want to insert text into and then click Create Link in the Text group on the Text Box Tools tab (or right-click the text box border and choose Create Text Box Link). The pointer changes to an upright pitcher.

2. Move the pointer to the text box you want to link to the first text box. When you move the upright pitcher pointer over the next text box, the pitcher tilts and turns into a pouring pitcher. Click the second text box to link it to the first text box.

3. To link a third text box to the others, click the text box you just linked to the first text box, click Create Link, and then click the third text box. You can create a chain of linked text boxes using this method.

> **Note**
>
> If you click Create Link and then decide that you don't want to link to another box, press Esc to cancel the linking process.

4. Once you have linked your text boxes, click in the first text box and insert text by typing, pasting, or inserting a file. Generally, the last approach is recommended because it enables you to insert prepared and edited text into your linked text boxes. For the steps you follow to insert text from a file, see "I can't find the Insert, File command" on page 265.

> **Note**
>
> If you have a complete story that's ready to flow into text boxes, you can insert the story into the text boxes while you link them. To do this, insert your story into the first text box and then link to the next text box as described in steps 1 and 2. When you use this approach, the text flows into the text boxes while you link them.

INSIDE OUT   Obtaining Word Count Statistics for Text Box Content

In Word 2007, you can include the text contained in text boxes in your document's word count statistic—this ability was not available in earlier versions of Word. Now text inside text boxes is included in word count statistics by default. To control whether to include text inside text boxes in the word count statistics, double-click Words on the status bar along the bottom of the Word 2007 window. The Word Count dialog box opens. Select or clear the Include Textboxes, Footnotes And Endnotes check box to count or exclude text inside of text boxes in your word count statistics.

Moving Between Linked Text Boxes

Next Text Box

Previous Text Box

After you link text boxes, you can easily jump from one text box to another. To do so, select a text box that's part of a linked series of text boxes. Right-click the text box's edge and then click Next Text Box to move to the next linked text box, or click Previous Text Box to move to the previous text box. You can also move to the next text box by positioning your insertion point at the end of the text in a filled text box and then pressing the Right Arrow key, or you can jump to the preceding text box by positioning your insertion point at the beginning of the text in a text box and then pressing the Left Arrow key.

> **Note**
>
> If you often need to move forward and back between linked text boxes, you might want to add the Next Text Box and Previous Text Box buttons to the Quick Access Toolbar. To learn how to customize the Quick Access Toolbar, see Chapter 2, "The 2007 Office System User Interface: What's Changed, What's the Same."

Copying or Moving Linked Text Boxes

You can copy or move a story (including text boxes and their contents) to another document or another location in the same document. If your story consists of multiple linked text boxes that aren't contained on a single drawing canvas, you will have to select all the linked text boxes in the story before you can copy the story and text boxes. If the story's linked text boxes are on a single drawing canvas, you can select and copy any text box in the series of linked text boxes to copy the entire story and the selected text box to another location. Or, you can select all the text boxes on the drawing canvas to copy the story and all the associated text boxes.

When you copy a text box (or a few linked text boxes but not an entire story) that's not on a drawing canvas, you copy only the selected text box or boxes, without the text box content. When you copy a single text box that is part of a complete story contained in text boxes on a single drawing canvas, you copy the entire story along with the selected text box. This means that when you paste the text box, you will probably need to resize it to see the entire story, or you will need to add text boxes and link them to the newly inserted text box.

If you want to copy a complete story along with all the text boxes containing the story, you can do so by selecting all the text boxes before copying them, as described here.

1. In Print Layout view, select a text box in the story by clicking the text box's frame.

> **Note**
>
> You must select a text box by its frame if you want to copy the text box. If you click inside the text box and then press Ctrl+C, Word won't copy anything. If you want to copy multiple text boxes, press Shift as you click each frame to select the text boxes.

2. Press Shift and then click the text boxes you want to copy or move—if all the text boxes appear either on or off a single drawing canvas, you'll copy the text boxes' contents as well as the text box containers.

3. Click Copy or Cut in the Clipboard group on the Home tab (or press Ctrl+C or Ctrl+X, or right-click a selected text box border and then choose Copy or Cut from the shortcut menu).

4. Click where you want to reposition the text boxes and then click Paste in the Clipboard group on the Home tab (or press Ctrl+V, or right-click and then click Paste).

To copy or move content that appears within a text box without copying or moving the text box, select just the text or content in the same way that you select standard text and content and then copy or move it in the same way you normally copy or move content in Word documents. To select and copy all the text in a linked story, click in the story, press Ctrl+A, and either copy and paste or drag the text to the new location. You can select all the text in a story by using Ctrl+A regardless of whether the story's text boxes are on a drawing canvas.

Breaking Text Box Links

You can break links between text boxes just as easily as you create them. When you break a link, you remove only the link between the selected text box and the text box that follows it in the series—you don't remove all the links in a linked series. Essentially, when you break a link, you divide a story into two series of linked text boxes, or segments. By default, the first series of linked text boxes contains the story, and linked text boxes in the second series are empty.

To break a link between text boxes, follow these steps.

1. In Print Layout view, click the border of the text box from which you want the text to stop flowing.

2. On the Text Box Tools tab, click Break Link (or right-click the text box border and then choose Break Forward Link).

At this point, text will stop flowing from the text box you selected. Text boxes that were included later in the linked series will be empty. If the text doesn't fit in the first series of linked text boxes after you break a link, you can create and link additional text boxes or enlarge existing text boxes to provide enough room to display the text.

> **Note**
> You can remove a text box from a linked series of text boxes without deleting any parts of your story. To do so, simply right-click the text box's border and then choose Cut from the shortcut menu. When you cut a linked text box, Word 2007 adjusts the story and flows the text into the next text box.

Deleting Linked Text Boxes Without Losing Text

To delete a text box, you simply select a text box and press Delete, or right-click the text box border and choose Cut. Performing this action on a nonlinked text box deletes both the text box and its contents. In contrast, when you delete a text box that's part of a linked series of text boxes, the text from the deleted text box automatically flows into the remaining linked text boxes. If the remaining text boxes aren't large enough to

Chapter 10

display a story in its entirety, you can resize the text boxes, create additional text boxes, or edit your story to fit. Keep in mind that Word doesn't notify you when text overflows the final text box's boundaries, so you should always be extra diligent about checking the flow of stories and making sure that no text is hidden.

> **Note**
>
> To avoid deleting an entire story when you delete a stand-alone, nonlinked text box, click in the text box, press Ctrl+A to select the story, and then either drag or copy the selected story into your document before you delete the text box.

Switching Between Text Boxes and Frames

The overall premise of both text boxes and frames is the same—to contain and offset information. The seemingly minor differences between text boxes and frames, however, can be significant in some cases. Text boxes, for example, provide greater formatting opportunities and text box linking capabilities. Frames, on the other hand, enable you to include endnotes, cross-references, comments, index markers, citations, and other fields—but you cannot link frames. Therefore, depending on your content needs, you might find that you need to change a text box into a frame or vice versa.

TROUBLESHOOTING

I want to link text boxes, but the Text Box Tools tab is missing.

In Word, you can link text boxes but not frames. After you convert a text box to a frame, you will no longer have access to the Text Box Tools tab when you click in the frame. To quickly tell if a container you are working with is a text box or frame, click the element's border. If the element is a text box, the selected border looks like this:

If you click the border of a frame, the selection looks like this:

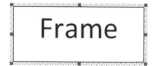

You can convert text boxes to frames and frames to text boxes as described in "Using Floating Frames for Comments, Footnotes, Tables, and Fields" on page 266. Keep in mind that whenever you make the switch, you must review your changes carefully to avoid inadvertently hiding text or removing design elements.

Configuring Word 2007 Layout Options

In addition to readily available page layout and component layout options, Word 2007 provides a large collection of option settings in the Word Options dialog box. In relation to layout options, if you can't find an option you are looking for on a tab, menu, or gallery, consider visiting the Layout Options list included in the Word Options dialog box. To access the Layout Options list, click the Microsoft Office Button, Word Options, Advanced. Then, scroll to the bottom of the Advanced screen and expand the Layout Options item. You'll find a list of options similar to the one shown in Figure 10-7. Scan through the options to see if any settings might meet your current or future needs. Note that none of the Layout Options check boxes are selected by default.

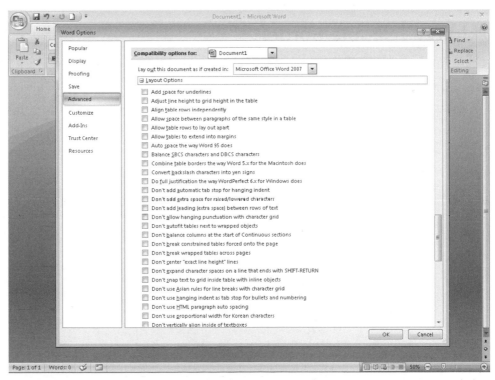

Figure 10-7 Word 2007 includes a long list of Layout Options that you can use on an as-needed basis. Reviewing the list helps you become aware of capabilities you might need now or in the future.

Commanding Attention with Borders and Shading

One of the major enhancements in Word 2007 is the addition of many professional and easy-to-use design features that make creating attractive documents simple. Sometimes producing a basic document on a clean white page is the best approach for communicating a message as clearly as possible. But at other times, you might want to shine a spotlight on a particular passage of text, a table, or an object on your page. You might create a border around a table, or use a shaded sidebar for a section of text that accompanies an article. You might add a border around a document's table of contents so that readers can refer to it easily. Borders and shading can add a special look to important elements and to help them stand out.

Adding a Simple Border

An easy way to add a plain border to an item in your document is to select the item and then use the Border button in the Paragraph group on the Home tab. In the Paragraph group, click the arrow to the right of the Border button, and a set of border options is displayed, as shown in Figure 10-8. Click Outside Borders to enclose the selected item in a border (or choose another border option if you prefer); the border option you select becomes the option shown on the face of the button, so you can apply this border style to another item by simply clicking the button.

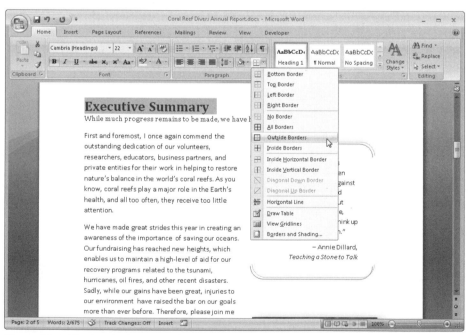

Figure 10-8 The Border button in the Paragraph group lets you apply a variety of border styles.

Note

Keep in mind that the Border button is a toggle button. This means that with a click of the button, you can add borders if they aren't present or remove borders if they are present.

INSIDE OUT   Clear Borders Quickly with No Border

Although you can use the toggle effect of the Border button to remove border lines, sometimes you'll want to clear existing borders before you apply new settings. To clear existing borders, highlight the item you want to modify, click No Border in the Border button's list, and then, while the item is still selected, click the border style you want to use.

Creating Enhanced Borders

A simple one-line border may do the trick when you are interested only in a box that sets items off from surrounding text. If you want to use a border as a design element on your page, you can use the Borders And Shading dialog box, shown in Figure 10-9, to tailor the selections to create a more sophisticated effect. The Borders And Shading dialog box gives you the option of choosing from a variety of looks for your border (including 3-D and shadow effects). You can also change the style, color, and width of a border's lines, or create a partial border—a border along the top and bottom, for example—by selecting the line segments you want to include.

To create a customized border, place the insertion point where you want the border to start or select the element you want to apply a border to. For example, if you want to add a border to a paragraph that lists your corporate Web site and contact information, select that paragraph. You can then open the Borders And Shading dialog box in one of these ways:

- On the Home tab, in the Paragraph group, click the arrow beside the Border button and then click Borders And Shading.

- Click the Page Layout tab. In the Page Background group, click Page Borders, and then click the Borders tab in the Borders And Shading dialog box.

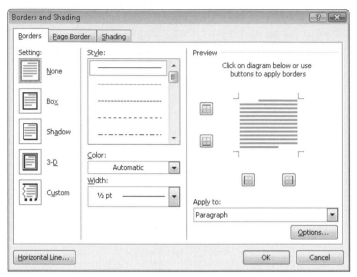

Figure 10-9 The Borders And Shading dialog box enables you to specify border types and border placement as well as line styles, colors, and widths.

Word offers some basic border settings that you can use, although you can create an almost unlimited number of combinations by adjusting the style, color, width, line, and shading settings. The Borders And Shading dialog box provides three tabs: Borders, Page Border, and Shading. Here's a quick overview of important border and shading options included on these tabs.

- The Borders tab (shown in Figure 10-9) contains options you can use to set the border style, color, and width. The Borders tab also has options for partial borders (for example, you can use the Preview area to indicate which edges of the selected item you want to assign a border to.

- The Page Border tab includes the same options you'll find on the Border tab, with one addition: The Art list at the bottom of the center section enables you to add special border art to the pages in your document (see Figure 10-10).

- The Shading tab enables you to put a background color or pattern behind selected text.

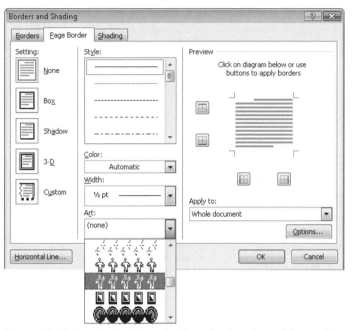

Figure 10-10 Use the Art list on the Page Border tab to add a special art border to your page.

Choosing Border Options

The Setting option is the first major choice you'll probably make when you use the Borders And Shading dialog box. This option controls the overall look of the border itself. The Setting options depend on whether you're adding a border to a table or to standard text. If you're working with standard text (a paragraph or a heading, for example), you can choose from the following border setting options:

- **None** Shows no border around selected text and objects; this is the default

- **Box** Encloses the selection in a simple line box

- **Shadow** Outlines the selection with a box and adds a drop shadow below and to the right of the selection

- **3-D** Creates a three-dimensional effect for the border, making it appear to "stand out" from the page

- **Custom** Enables you to configure the Preview area so you can choose and customize the line segments you want to include in your border

Chapter 10

If you're working with a table or selected table cells, the Borders tab appears as it's shown in Figure 10-11. You can choose among the following border setting options:

- **None** Shows no border around the table or selected cells

- **Box** Encloses the table or selected cells in a simple box

- **All** Outlines the entire table or selected cells, including borders between cells; this is the default border setting for a table or table cells.

- **Grid** Outlines a table or selected cells with a heavier exterior border and lighter interior borders

- **Custom** Enables you to configure the Preview area so that you can choose and customize the line segments you want to include in your border

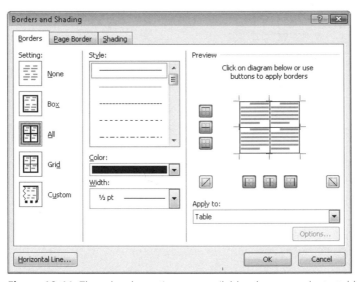

Figure 10-11 These border options are available when you select a table or a group of table cells.

> **Note**
> You can mix and match border types to achieve the effect you want. For example, you can add borders to part of a table and hide borders in other parts to create the appearance of underlined text when creating "fill-in-the-blanks" type forms. You can further combine border options, such as color and line widths, to make borders visually appealing.

To apply one of the Setting options shown in the Borders And Shading dialog box, select text or table cells or click in the paragraph, table, image, or other element that you want to format. Then display the Borders And Shading dialog box and click a Setting selection on the Borders tab. If you don't want to make any additional customizations to the border, you can simply click OK to return to your document. The border will be added to the current text, table, or selected object. If the cursor was positioned in a new blank paragraph before you displayed the Borders And Shading dialog box, the border will appear around the insertion point and will expand as you type. The border will surround paragraphs you add, images, tables, and other elements. To end the expansion of the border, either click outside the formatted area or press Enter at the end of the formatted area, and then use the Border button to format the new blank paragraph marker with the No Border setting.

> **Note**
>
> If you add a border and decide you really don't like it, you can do away with it immediately by clicking Undo on the Quick Access Toolbar at the top of the Word window or by pressing Ctrl+Z. You can also use the Border button in the Paragraph group on the Home tab and apply No Border to clear the border lines.

Selecting Line Styles for Borders

Word 2007 provides 24 line styles that you can use to create border effects. From simple, straight lines to dotted, double, and triple lines, you can create a variety of looks by changing line styles. Figure 10-12 shows a few examples of borders created with different line styles.

Chapter 10

> Coral Reef Divers went through an extensive financial review during our strategic planning program during the summer of 2006. We found that due to climactic conditions, volunteer availability, and the nature of the projects we've undertaken in under-represented areas, our operating expenses are fairly evenly divided among our international sites. As would be expected, our site operating costs are highest in the U.S., where our worldwide administrative offices are housed.

> Each international office includes one full-time paid staff member, one part-time paid staff member, and at least three volunteers (who are recognized throughout the year in various ways). At the present time, we pay rent for facilities in only three countries; the rest of our sites are donated by partnering NGOs, benefactors, or universities.

> "The colors of the sea are only the indirect signs of the presence or absence of conditions needed to support the surface life; other zones, invisible to the eye, are the ones that largely determine where marine creatures may live." --Rachel Carson,
> *The Sea Around Us*

Figure 10-12 The line style you choose has a dramatic effect on the overall look of a border.

To choose a line style for a border, display the Borders And Shading dialog box and select a line style in the Style list on the Borders tab. The Preview section shows the effect of your choices. Set any other border choices you want and then click OK. The document is updated with your changes.

TROUBLESHOOTING

There's not enough contrast in my double line.

If you create a double line and can't see enough contrast between lines of different weights, you can play around with the line widths to get a better contrast. Start by clicking in or selecting the area with the border. Then display the Borders And Shading dialog box by using the Border button and clicking Borders And Shading at the bottom of the list of border styles. In the Width list, choose a new line width setting and then, in the dialog box's Preview section, click the line you want to change.

Choosing a Border Color

When you first start adding lines and borders to your publication, Word uses the Automatic color by default (which will be black if you are using the standard Windows color scheme). But you have many other colors at your disposal. To specify border colors, follow these steps.

1. Click in or select the elements you want to format with border colors. If the content already has a border and you only want to color the lines, you can retain the current border and apply a color.

2. Click the Home tab. In the Paragraph group, click the arrow beside the Border button and then click Borders And Shading.

3. On the Borders tab of the Borders And Shading dialog box, select a Setting option and line style if you're creating a new border. If you're working with an existing border, you can make any changes that you want.

4. Open the Color list to display the color palette, as shown in Figure 10-13.

5. Select the color you want to use, or, if you don't see the color you were hoping for, click More Colors. The Colors dialog box appears, which you can use to find or mix the color you want.

If you're creating a new border, the color setting will be reflected in the Preview area immediately. If you're adjusting the color setting for an existing border, you need to click each line in the Preview area to apply the color setting. In this way, you can control the line color for each border line.

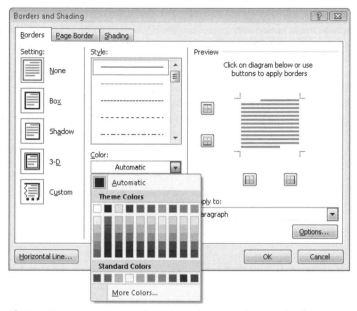

Figure 10-13 You can use the color palette to select a color for lines and shading.

Chapter 10

> **Note**
>
> The color palette is divided into two sections. The Theme Colors section provides colors from the document theme and the Standard Colors section offers primary colors. Clicking More Colors displays the Colors dialog box so that you can choose from a wide range of colors or create your own custom color. Any color that you select other than those offered in the Theme Colors section will not be swapped if the document theme colors change.
>
> When you need to match colors, choosing accurate border colors can become an especially important issue. For times like these, you should modify or create a new document theme. This will enable you to you create the custom colors once and they can be made available to any document. For more on customizing document themes, see the Word 2007 online help.

INSIDE OUT   Choosing the Best Colors for Borders

You can simplify the task of selecting colors that work well together by using one of the predesigned Word Themes as you create your document. When you use a Word Theme, the colors displayed in the Theme Colors section of the color palette help you choose colors that are already used consistently in the document color scheme. Otherwise, the trick to selecting effective colors for a document's text, images, table borders, lines, shading, and other components is to work with a color scheme that consists of three or four main colors that complement the document's design and provide appropriate contrast. After you identify a color scheme, you can play with the colors a little to add interest. For instance, if headings are dark blue, you might consider using the same blue or a slightly lighter shade of the same blue for borders and lines. In addition, document design often benefits from a consistent use of color across the board for similar design elements. For instance, in a magazine or newsletter, all sidebars might be placed in a green box while quotations appear in yellow boxes. That way, when readers see green, they know they're about to read a sidebar. When they see yellow, they recognize that they're reading a quotation. Color used wisely can greatly increase the readability and visual appeal of a publication.

Controlling Border Width

When you create a simple border, the default line width is ½ point, which is a simple, thin line. If you want to create a more dramatic effect—whether you leave the line black or use color—you can change the width of the line. To change the line width, display the Borders And Shading dialog box, click the Width arrow, and then select the width you want. Available point sizes range between ¼ point and 6 points.

Note

You can use line widths to create a special effect for partial borders. For example, to add a wide line above and below content, select the area you want to enclose between the lines, display the Borders And Shading dialog box, and then click the Custom Setting option. Select a line style, click the Width arrow, and choose a larger point size, such as 3 points. In the Preview section, click the top horizontal edge of the preview page. A line is added to the top border. Next, click the bottom horizontal edge of the preview page, and then click OK. Word adds the thick line border above and below the selected area.

Creating Partial Borders

Not every border you apply to a paragraph, a table, or an object needs lines that completely enclose it. You might want to add two lines, at the top and right side of a paragraph, for example, to help set it apart from an article that appears beside it. You might use only a top and bottom rule to contain your table of contents. Or you might use a single line to set off a quotation from the main text in a report or to mark the start of a new section.

Creating a partial border is a simple matter. You use the Custom Setting option and the Preview area of the Borders And Shading dialog box to accomplish it. Here are the steps.

1. Click in a table or paragraph or select the information or object you want to apply a border to.

2. On the Home tab, in the Paragraph group, click the arrow beside the Border button, and then click Borders And Shading.

3. On the Borders tab of the Borders And Shading dialog box, click the Custom Setting option.

4. Specify the border's line style, color, and width.

5. In the Preview area, click each edge of the preview page where you want border lines to appear, or click the button that corresponds to the edge or edges that should have a border line. Table 10-1 describes the available Preview buttons.

Table 10-1 Border Preview Buttons

Button	Description
	Adds a line along the top border
	Adds a line along the bottom border
	Adds a line along the left border
	Adds a line along the right border

Chapter 10

Using a Page Border

Many of the techniques you use to add a border to selected text, a table, or an object in a document can be used to add borders to pages as well. Figure 10-14 shows a document with a page border. You can create standard page borders or use an art border. This section shows you how.

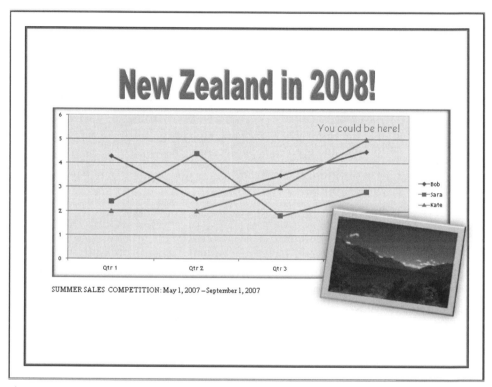

Figure 10-14 By default, page border settings are applied to all pages in the current document.

Creating a Page Border

When you add a page border, you use the Page Border tab of the Borders And Shading dialog box. The main difference between the Borders tab and the Page Border tab is the addition of the Art list (which is covered in the next section of this chapter). On the Page Border tab, after you select settings for your border, the border will be applied to an entire page, section, or document. Here's the process.

1. Click in a page or a section that will have a border.

2. On the Page Layout tab, in the Page Backgrounds group, click the Page Borders button.

3. On the Page Border tab, click a page border setting (None, Box, Shadow, 3-D, or Custom).

4. Select a line style from the Style list.

5. Select a color in the Color list, if you want to apply a color.

6. Click the Width arrow and then choose the line width you want. The style, color, and width settings are reflected in the Preview area.

7. If you want, use the Preview image to indicate which edges of the page you want to apply the border to.

8. In the Apply To list, specify where to apply the border. Available options are Whole Document, This Section, This Section–First Page Only, and This Section–All Except First Page. By default, Whole Document is selected in the Apply To list, and the border is added to all the pages in the current document.

9. Click OK to close the dialog box and apply the page border settings to the document.

INSIDE OUT   Changing the Border Only on the First Page

When you add a page border, Word applies the border to all the pages in your document by default. What if you want to skip the border on the first page or apply the border only to the first page of a section? You can do either of these things easily by using the Apply To setting on the Page Border tab in the Borders And Shading dialog box. To suppress the display of the border for the first page, click the Page Border tab in the Borders And Shading dialog box, click the Apply To arrow, and then select This Section–All Except First Page. To apply the border to the first page only, choose This Section–First Page Only in the Apply To list on the Page Border tab.

Adding an Artistic Border

The art page border feature, known in earlier versions of Microsoft Office as BorderArt, enables you to add an artistic touch to entire pages in your document. Special graphics are placed in patterns—either in black and white or in color—and used as borders for a page, group of pages, or selected sides of pages. To apply an artistic page border, follow these steps.

1. Click in the document to which you want to add the border.

2. On the Page Layout tab, in the Page Backgrounds group, click the Page Borders button.

Chapter 10

3. On the Page Border tab, click the Art arrow and then scroll through and select a decorative border. The Preview section displays your choice, as shown in Figure 10-15. To control which borders will contain the image, click the borders of the page in the Preview area to add and remove the border.

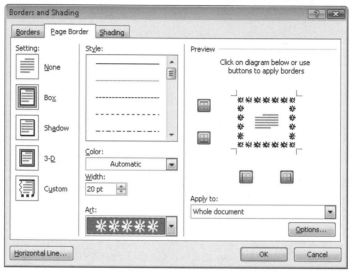

Figure 10-15 You can select from a number of art borders provided in Word.

4. In the Apply To list, choose which pages should include the border. You can select from Whole Document, This Section, This Section–First Page Only, or This Section–All Except First Page.

5. Click OK. The border is added to the document according to the settings you configured in the Borders And Shading dialog box.

Artistic borders can be colorful and vibrant—but they can also be a bit much for some professional documents. For that reason, you should use art borders sparingly and with discretion, determining their appropriateness on a case-by-case basis.

Adding Borders to Document Sections and Paragraphs

Whether you're interested in applying borders to a single word, paragraph, image, section, or page, you can do it easily by using the Apply To list in the Borders And Shading dialog box. The tab you choose at the top of the dialog box—Borders or Page Border—depends on the element you want to enclose in a border.

- If you want to create a border around a section in your document, click the Page Border tab. In the Apply To list, you'll find what you need to specify section bordering options.

- If you want to add a border around a paragraph, text, tables, images, selected table cells, or other elements in your document, click the Borders tab. The Apply To options on that tab will give you choices specific to the item you chose.

Bordering Sections

You might want to create a border for a document section when you have specific information you want to highlight or when you want to set a section apart from the flow of the text. To create a section border, start by placing the insertion point in the section you want to surround with a border. Display the Borders And Shading dialog box and then click the Page Border tab. Next configure the border effects—including the border setting option and line style, color, and width—and then click the Apply To arrow and select the option you need. Depending on the border you're creating (these options are not available for every type of border), you might see the following options.

- **Whole Document** Adds a border to every page in your document.

- **This Section** Adds a border only to the pages between the previous section break and the next section break. If the document doesn't contain any section breaks, the border is applied to every page in the document.

- **This Section—First Page Only** Finds the first page of the current section and adds a border only to that page. If you're working in a document without sections, the first page of your document will contain the border.

- **This Section—All Except First Page** Adds a border to all pages in the current section except the first page of the section. If you're working in a document without section breaks, all pages in the document will have a border except the first page.

To apply a border to a section, simply select the appropriate option from the Apply To list and then click OK. The border is added to the section as you specified. If you want to see how the border looks for the entire section, click the Microsoft Office Button, point to Print, and then click Print Preview. By clicking the Two Pages button in the Zoom group on the Print Preview tab, you can see the effect of your border selection on more than one page in your document. Click Close Print Preview on the Print Preview tab to return to the document window.

INSIDE OUT   Using Border Settings to Add Blank Lines

Here's a great way to add horizontal lines for write-in spaces in your documents. Press Enter to insert a number of blank lines in your document in the area where you want to create horizontal lines. Then select the blank lines, click the Border button's arrow, and then click the Inside Horizontal Border option. Evenly spaced lines are added automatically, extending from the left to the right margin.

Chapter 10

Adjusting Border Spacing

Word makes a few assumptions about the way borders appear in documents. By default, Word uses a small margin in borders applied to a paragraph and a larger margin in borders for sections and pages. When you add a border to a paragraph, Word adds a 1-point margin to the top and bottom and a 4-point margin along the left and right edges of the border. When you add a page or section border, Word adds 24-point margins measured from the edge of the page all the way around.

To set options that enable you to adjust spacing between borders and the content they enclose, display the Borders And Shading dialog box by clicking the arrow beside the Border button (in the Paragraph group on the Home tab) and then clicking Borders And Shading. Click the Borders tab if you're changing the options for a paragraph border, or click the Page Border tab if you're working with a page border for a document or document section.

Click Options in the Borders And Shading dialog box. If the Borders tab is displayed when you click Options, the Border And Shading Options dialog box appears as shown in Figure 10-16. If the Page Borders tab is selected, you will see the dialog box shown in Figure 10-17.

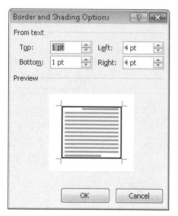

Figure 10-16 You control border margins and make choices about border alignment in the Border And Shading Options dialog box.

To make changes to the border margins, click in the box you want to change and type a new value, or use the up and down arrows to increase or decrease the value shown.

When you are working from the Borders tab, the Border And Shading Options dialog box allows you to configure only the space between the border and text. For page borders, Word automatically measures the margin from the edge of the page, but you can change the setting so that the measurement reflects spacing between text and the surrounding border. To make this change, click the Measure From arrow and choose Text.

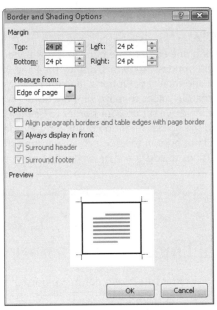

Figure 10-17 Click Options the Page Borders tab to display the options available for spacing the border of an entire page.

Other options in the Border And Shading Options dialog box are available if you're working with a page or section border. By default, Word includes any headers and footers inside the bordered area, and also by default, Word enables the Always Display In Front check box, which causes the border to be in front of any text or graphic objects that might overlap it. If you have other borders or tables within the bordered section, the Align Paragraph Borders And Table Edges With Page Border check box will also be available to you. If you want Word to align all these borders, select this check box.

After you've finished choosing border options, click OK to close the dialog box and then click OK a second time to return to your document.

> **Note**
>
> If you select a table before you display the Borders And Shading dialog box, your options in the Apply To list will show Text, Paragraph, Cell, and Table.

TROUBLESHOOTING

My border isn't printing correctly.

If your page border doesn't print along one edge of the page or is positioned too close to an edge, check the border's margin options. To do this, display the Page Border tab of the Borders And Shading dialog box and then click Options. In many cases, you can correct this problem by increasing the margin values to make sure the border is not placed outside your printer's printing range. If you've set up your border to be measured from Text, the space between the text and the border might be pushing the border into the nonprintable area. (Most printers will not print in the 0.5-inch area around the perimeter of the page.) Increase the margin settings to add space between the border and the text area.

Inserting Graphical Horizontal Lines

In some situations, you'll want only a divider line, not a complete border, to set off sections or special elements in a document. For example, if you're creating a report, you might want to mark the end of one section and the beginning of the next by adding a horizontal line. In those cases, you can use the Inside Horizontal Border option in the Border list to insert only a top or bottom partial border, or you can insert a graphical horizontal line. Applying the Inside Horizontal Border setting and creating partial borders are discussed earlier in this chapter, in "Creating Partial Borders" on page 285. The particulars of working with graphical horizontal lines—lines that are images—are covered in the next couple of sections.

Adding a Graphical Horizontal Line

Word provides a collection of graphical horizontal lines that you can insert in documents. To add a graphical horizontal line to a document, follow these steps.

1. Place the insertion point where you want to add the line.

2. Display the Borders And Shading dialog box and select the Borders or Page Border tab.

3. Click the Horizontal Line button in the lower-left corner of the dialog box to display the Horizontal Line dialog box, shown in Figure 10-18.

4. Scroll through the selections and click a line style to add the line.

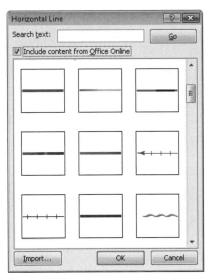

Figure 10-18 The Horizontal Line dialog box displays predesigned graphical lines that you can insert in your document.

After you place a horizontal line in a document, you can select, copy, paste, resize, move, and color it as you would other graphical items. Furthermore, you can insert additional instances of the line by choosing the Horizontal Line option from the Border button's menu.

Formatting a Graphical Horizontal Line

When you insert a graphical horizontal line by using the Horizontal Line dialog box, you're not committed to using the image as is. You can adjust several of the line's properties, including its width, height, and color. Specifically, you can perform either of the following actions.

- **Resize and position a line manually** To resize and position a graphical line manually, click the line and then drag the line's selection handles to resize it, or drag the selected line to move the image.

- **Adjust a graphical line's properties** To change a graphical line's width, height, color, alignment, brightness, and contrast, as well as to crop some graphical lines, use the Format Horizontal Line dialog box (shown in Figure 10-19). To open the Format Horizontal Line dialog box, right-click a graphical line and then choose Format Horizontal Line (or simply double-click the line).

Chapter 10

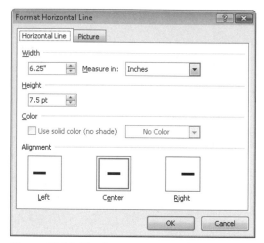

Figure 10-19 The Format Horizontal Line dialog box enables you to customize a graphical line's appearance and placement by configuring the line's settings.

Importing a Custom Line

If you create your own graphical lines in Word or another program (such as Microsoft Paint or Microsoft Office PowerPoint 2007), you can add the customized line files to your Horizontal Line gallery. To add a custom line to your Horizontal Line gallery so that it's available in the Horizontal Line dialog box, follow these steps.

1. In the graphics program you're using to create the line, save the file in a common graphics file format such as JPG, BMP, TIF, or WMF.

2. In Word, display the Borders And Shading dialog box.

3. On the Borders or Page Border tab, click Horizontal Line.

4. In the Horizontal Line dialog box, click Import to open the Add Clips To Organizer dialog box.

5. Navigate to the file you want to use, click it, and then click Add. The line is added to the gallery and remains selected.

6. Click OK to add the clip to your document. The Horizontal Line dialog box closes, and the line is placed at the insertion point in your document.

Adding Borders to Pictures

The process involved in adding borders to pictures takes you down a slightly different path. Instead of using the Borders And Shading dialog box, which is available when you're working with text sections, paragraphs, or entire pages, you can use the Picture Border tool (and let Live Preview show you the results of your choice) or add a border to a picture by changing the formatting settings for that picture in your document. Here's how it's done.

Using the Picture Border Tool

When you double-click a picture you've added to a document, the Ribbon displays the Picture Tools Format tab. On this tab, you can use the Picture Border tool in the Picture Styles group to select a line weight, line style, and color for a picture's border. When you click the Picture Border tool, you'll see the color palette and menu options shown in Figure 10-20.

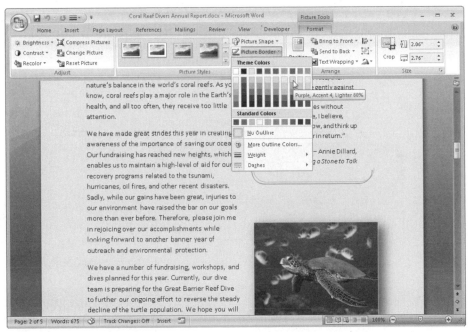

Figure 10-20 Use the Picture Border tool to add a border to pictures in your document. As you scroll over choices for line width, line style, and color, Live Preview displays your choices in the document.

When you use the Picture Border tool, you might not be able to choose all the options you need at one time. In other words, when you select a line weight for the picture border, the Picture Border menu closes. You have to click Picture Border again to open the menu and select a line style or border color. The benefits of Live Preview and the availability of the Theme Colors section in the color palette make up for the need to open the menu more than once to apply all the border attributes you might need.

Adding a Picture Border by Formatting the Picture

The other approach to applying a border to a picture is to use the Format Picture dialog box. Here are the steps you follow:

1. Right-click the picture to which you want to add the border, and then click Format Picture.

2. Drag the Format Picture dialog box to a position on the screen where you can also see the picture you're working with.

   As you change settings, the picture in your document is updated instantly, so you can see whether you want to keep those changes or try something else before closing the Format Picture dialog box. To undo a change you've made, click Ctrl+Z or click the Undo button on the Quick Access Toolbar.

3. Click the Line Color option in the navigation pane on the left. The default setting is No Line. When you choose either Solid Line or Gradient Line, additional options appear in the dialog box (see Figure 10-21). Select the options that let you create the border you want to add.

4. Click the Line Style option to choose the width, type, and style of the line used to create the border.

5. Click Close to return to your document.

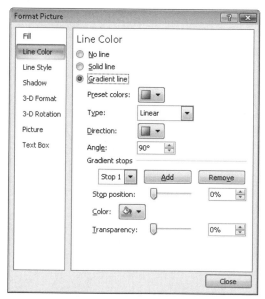

Figure 10-21 Use settings in the Format Picture dialog box to add a border to a picture.

Adding Table Borders

Word includes a whole set of border options if you're working with tables. The tools are easy to use—and fun to apply. This section provides the basic steps for adding borders and shades to your tables.

As you know, Word includes a great gallery of Table Quick Styles that you can apply to your tables. It may be that those formats apply all the borders you'll ever need. But if you want to add to a table style's effect by adding an outside border, or if you want to change the borders used in the style, knowing how to customize your table borders will come in handy.

One way to apply borders to your table is to right-click the table and choose Borders And Shading from the shortcut menu. In the Borders And Shading dialog box, you can choose the border setting, style, color, and width as you learned earlier in this chapter. If you want to experiment with custom lines and mix and match line styles in your table border, you can also work with the tools on the Table Tools Design tab. Here's how to do it.

1. Select the table element to which you want to apply the border. You might select the whole table or a column, row, or selection of cells. To select a specific cell, simply click it to position the pointer in that location.

2. Click the Table Tools Design tab, and then click the Line Style arrow in the Draw Borders group to choose the line style you want for the border. (See Figure 10-22).

3. Click the Line Weight arrow to choose the weight (or thickness) you want for the border.

4. Click the Borders arrow in the Table Styles group to display the list of Border options you saw earlier in this chapter. Click your selection to apply the border to the selected table elements.

> **Note**
>
> If you really like the border style you created for a table you've been working with, you can save the style and reuse it. Click the More button in the Table Styles gallery (available when the Table Tools Design tab is selected) and choose New Table Style from the bottom of the gallery. Enter a name for the new style and click OK to save it.

Chapter 10

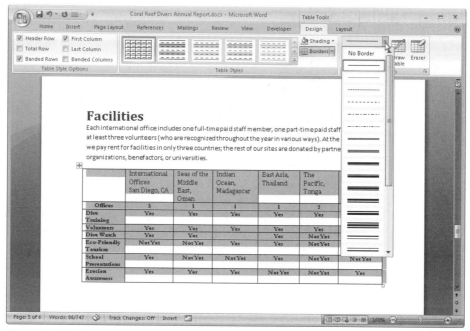

Figure 10-22 Choose the line style and weight before you add a border to table elements.

Applying Shading Behind Content

Sometimes you may want more than a border to make an element in your document really stand out. Adding shading can help call attention to passages of text that you want to highlight. You might add a shade, for example, to highlight a special quotation, to draw the reader's eye to an important summary, or as a way to make items pop out on the page. When you add shading to text, you can control properties such as the color, transparency, and pattern that are used to create the shaded effect.

Applying Shades to Tables and Paragraphs

Word includes many ready-made table styles that include many shading possibilities. You can use one of the preset table styles by selecting the table and then choosing the style you like from the Table Styles gallery on the Table Tools Design tab. When you want to apply custom shading to text, paragraphs, table cells, tables, or headings, you can use the Shading tab in the Borders And Shading dialog box or choose the Shading button in the Paragraph group on the Home tab (when you've selected text) or the Shading button on the Table Tools Design tab (when you have selected a table).

To apply shading effects, follow these steps.

1. Select the item you want to shade.

2. On the Home tab, in the Paragraph group, click the arrow beside the Border button and then click Borders And Shading.

3. Click the Shading tab. The Shading tab contains various options you can use to add and modify shades, as shown in Figure 10-23.

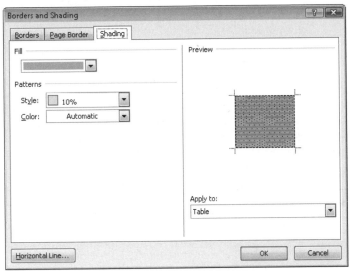

Figure 10-23 Adding shading can be as simple as selecting the information you want to appear on a shaded background and then choosing a fill color on the Shading tab.

> **Note**
>
> The borders and shading features of Word work independently, which means that if you add shading without adding a border, the item will appear with only the shade behind it—no outer border will be added automatically. To add a border to a shaded item, select it and then display the Borders And Shading dialog box. Choose border settings on the Borders tab and then click OK to apply the border to the shaded selection.

4. In the Fill section, click the color you want to apply. If you don't see the color you want, you can click More Colors to open the Colors dialog box and choose from another selection.

5. In the Patterns section, click the Style arrow to display your choices for the density or pattern of the color you select. (Keep in mind that applying a pattern to text can make the text very difficult to read.) Choose a lower percentage for a lighter shade. The Preview area shows the effect of each selection.

6. Click OK to apply the shading settings.

To remove shading, select the shaded content and then perform either of the following actions.

- Highlight the shaded area, click the Shading arrow in the Paragraph group on the Home tab, and then click No Color.

- Display the Borders And Shading dialog box, click the Shading tab, and choose No Color in the Fill area. In the Patterns area, select Clear from the Style list.

Shading Considerations

Remember that a little shading goes a long way. Applied thoughtfully and with your readers' needs in mind, shading can be effective in calling attention to certain elements and helping special design objects stand out on the page (especially in a complex document). But overusing shading or using the wrong mix of colors and patterns can make your document or Web page harder for people to read, which means they'll turn the page or click away from your site—and you'll lose your audience.

To use shading effectively, consider the following guidelines.

- **Use shading on a need-to-use basis** Don't sprinkle shades all the way through your document at random. Give a shade a reason, such as, "Every time we mention a new board member we'll provide a brief biography in a shaded sidebar."

- **Choose intensities carefully** A shade that looks light on the screen might be much darker in print. Always look at your document online and in print form whenever possible, even for online content. You never know when a reader will decide to print an online page for later reference.

- **Test your contrasts** When you add a colored shade behind text, be sure to increase the contrast between the color of the shade and the color of the text. If you choose a dark blue background, black text won't show up clearly. If you choose a dark background, select light (white or yellow) text. If you're in doubt about your color choices, use the Theme Colors section of the color palette to apply your color based on the element you are formatting, such as text or background, and let the document theme handle the contrasts for you.

- **Do test prints on a printer that produces comparable output** If you're printing colored shades, be sure to print a test page on a color printer.

- **If you're creating a Web page, use Web-safe colors for your shades** Most Web browsers today can support the standard colors used in the Windows palette. If you choose customized colors, however, some browsers might not display the color accurately. Test the display of the page with different browsers to check the colors you've selected. To see a listing of Web-safe colors and their RGB values, visit *www.creationguide.com/colorchart.html*.

A s you probably know, many finished documents (including this book!) reflect the efforts of a group of people who worked together to create a polished product. For example, a single document might first be written by an author and then modified by an editor, commented on by a technical reviewer, and inspected and approved by a project manager. Such team collaboration can be simplified tremendously by using the markup tools available in Microsoft Office Word 2007.

Benefits of an Organized Revision Process

Revising documents can be a messy and confusing business—sometimes, it can even get downright frustrating when ideas and well-formed language are lost forever amidst the web of modifications made by reviewers. Fortunately, with the revision tools provided by Office Word 2007, the revision process doesn't need to be painful—in fact, the process can be an enjoyable, educational endeavor when approached properly.

Over the years, the revision tools included in Word have been carving out a name for themselves in businesses, educational institutions, and personal arenas. Using markup tools, coworkers can collaborate on publications without losing ideas along the way, educators can require students to track and show changes while a class works through the process of writing a paper, and you can keep an eye on personal document changes, such as changes to legal agreements or contracts in negotiation. Of course, like all tools, the effectiveness of markup and revision tools stems from knowing how to use them.

In Word, numerous people can review the same document and incorporate changes and comments with those made by other people. After participants add their comments to a document, others in the group can insert their responses into the document as well. Throughout the process, Word dutifully tracks and color-codes everyone's comments and changes, as long as you configure the markup features properly. To help streamline the configuration and use of markup tools, Word 2007 now conveniently groups proofing, commenting, tracking, comparing, and document protection tools on the Review tab on the Ribbon. This chapter covers these markup features and reviewing options so that you can maximize your revision efforts when you work with various versions and renditions of documents, either on your own or with others.

Familiarizing Yourself with Markup Tools

Although you can track changes for your own purposes, the true strength of revision tools becomes clear when you collaborate with others. When you collaborate on a document, you can use Word to track and merge people's changes and comments, highlight information to draw attention to selected text and graphics, store versions of documents throughout the development process, and add ink and voice comments. Specifically, Word provides the following reviewing and markup tools.

- **Comments** Enable you to annotate a document with suggestions and questions without actually changing the document. In Word 2007, you can add text, ink, and voice comments to documents. Comments are identified by comment markers in the text, which can be either parentheses linked to balloons or parentheses accompanied by the commenter's initials, as described in "Adding and Managing Comments Effectively" on page 307.

- **Highlight tool** Enables you to draw attention to particular information (including a letter, word, phrase, sentence, paragraph, or graphic) by adding a color background to the information, as described in "Using the Highlight Tool" on page 304.

- **Ink support for Tablet PCs** Enables you to draw and write on documents directly by using a stylus or other drawing device.

- **Protect Document options** Enable you to restrict formatting and editing capabilities for reviewers, as mentioned in "Allowing Reviewers to Use Only the Comments Feature" on page 311.

- **Track Changes feature** Records editing changes, including deletions, insertions, and formatting changes made to a document. Word can track and color-code changes from multiple reviewers, and the changes can later be evaluated and accepted or rejected on a case-by-case or global basis. For more information about the Track Changes feature, see "Tracking Changes" on page 323.

- **Voice comment** Enables you to insert voice comments into a document.

You'll find that many key collaboration features can be accessed from the Review tab, shown in Figure 11-1.

Figure 11-1 The Review tab provides tools you can use to work with comments, tracked changes, proofing, document comparison, and document protection tools.

As you can see in Figure 11-1, the Review tab is an expanded, easier-to-use version of the Reviewing toolbar included in Microsoft Office Word 2003. The Highlight button (a fixture on the Home tab) can also be accessed on the new Mini toolbar. You can customize the Quick Access Toolbar to show the Ink Comment and Insert Voice commands if you want to use those tools. Table 11-1 describes the main markup features found on the Review tab.

For more information about customizing the Quick Access Toolbar, see "Customizing the Quick Access Toolbar," on page 32.

Table 11-1 Markup Features on the Review Tab

Button	Name	Description
New Comment	New Comment	Inserts a new comment
Delete ▾	Delete Comment	Deletes a selected comment; deletes only the comments shown on the screen (when a particular reviewer's or set of reviewers' comments are displayed or hidden); or deletes all comments at once
Previous	Previous Comment	Jumps to the previous comment in the current document relative to the insertion point
Next	Next Comment	Jumps to the next comment in the current document relative to the insertion point
Track Changes ▾	Track Changes	Controls whether the Track Changes feature is turned off or on, and provides access to tracking options and access to user name settings
Balloons ▾	Balloons	Controls whether revisions are shown in balloons; whether all revisions are shown inline (no balloons are shown); or whether only comments and formatting are shown in balloons
Final Showing Markup ▾	Display For Review	Controls how Word displays changes and comments in the current document; available options are Final Showing Markup, Final, Original Showing Markup, and Original
Show Markup ▾	Show Markup	Displays a menu that enables you to show or hide comments, ink annotations, insertions and deletions, and formatting. You can also use this button to show or hide comments and changes from specific reviewers and to control whether the markup area is displayed with a highlight or not.

Chapter 11

Button	Name	Description
Reviewing Pane	Reviewing Pane	Shows or hides the Reviewing pane, which displays the complete text of tracked changes and comments. The pane can be displayed along the left side of the window or the bottom of the window.
Accept	Accept Change	Accepts a selected tracked change in the document and moves to the next; accepts a change without moving to the next change; accepts all changes shown (when selected reviewer revisions are shown or hidden); or accepts all changes in the document
Reject	Reject Change	Rejects a change (which returns the text to its original state) and moves to the next change; rejects a change without moving to the next change; rejects all changes shown (when selected reviewer revisions are shown or hidden); or rejects all changes in the document
Previous	Previous	Jumps to the previous tracked change in the current document relative to the insertion point
Next	Next	Jumps to the next tracked change in the current document relative to the insertion point

Now that you've had a quick introduction to the main markup tools, you are ready to look at the finer details. This chapter starts with the simplest feature often associated with marking up documents—the Highlight tool.

Using the Highlight Tool

As in previous versions of Word, the Highlight tool is available for use in Word 2007, and its functionality remains the same. The Highlight tool in Word 2007 is included in the Font group on the Home tab and is also readily accessible on the Mini toolbar. This change streamlines the tool's availability and avoids unnecessary repetition of the button in the interface, which was the case in earlier versions of Word.

The main idea behind highlighting is to call attention to important or questionable text in documents. Highlighting parts of a document works best when the document is viewed online, although you can use highlighting in printed documents if necessary. When you use the Highlight tool, the main tasks you'll perform are adding, removing, finding, and replacing highlighting. The next few sections briefly describe these procedures.

Highlighting Information

Text Highlight

You can apply highlighting to a single block of selected text or graphics, or you can apply highlighting to a series of text areas or graphics. To apply a single instance of highlighting to information, select the information and then click the Text Highlight button on the Mini toolbar or in the Font group on the Home tab. To apply highlighting to multiple blocks of information, click the Highlight tool, select the text or graphic you want to highlight, and then select the next item in the document you want to highlight. The Highlight tool continues to highlight information as you select it. To turn off highlighting, click the Text Highlight button again, or press Esc.

You can change the highlight color by clicking the arrow next to the Text Highlight button on the Home tab or the Mini toolbar and choosing a color from the palette. The color you choose becomes the default highlight color for future highlighting (until you select a different color). Choosing a different color does not affect the color of highlighting you've already applied to the document.

> ### Note
>
> Be sure to choose a light highlight color if you're going to print your document with highlighted content, especially if the document will be printed in monochrome (including grayscale) or on a dot-matrix printer. If more than one person is going to be adding highlighting to a document, consider assigning highlight colors to each person or agree to standardize highlight colors to indicate a particular issue (for example, reviewers might use turquoise highlighting to specify that a page reference needs to be completed, bright green highlighting to draw attention to repeated information, and so forth).

INSIDE OUT   Considering Browsers When Highlighting

If you save highlighted text as part of a Web page, Word stores the highlighting information as part of the Web page's cascading style sheet (CSS). This information will be interpreted and displayed properly in Internet Explorer 3 and Netscape Navigator 4 and later versions, but earlier versions of those browsers (and other less widely used browsers) might not display the highlighting properly. If you're not sure which browsers viewers will use to display your Web page, you should consider using another method to draw attention to the text For example, you could use a font color, create a graphic of the highlighted text, or build a table and color the text's table cell to simulate a highlighted paragraph.

Removing Highlighting from Documents

You can remove the highlighting in a document when you no longer need to draw attention to the highlighted text or graphics. To remove highlighting, follow these steps.

1. Select the information you want to remove highlighting from, or press Ctrl+A to select the entire document.

2. Click the arrow next to the Text Highlight button and then choose No Color.

After you choose No Color, all instances of highlighting are removed from the selected text.

> **Note**
>
> You can display or hide highlighting (but not the text itself) on the screen and in a printed document without permanently removing the highlighting. To do so, click the Microsoft Office Button, Word Options, Display. In the Page Display Options section, clear the Show Highlighter Marks check box (the option is selected by default) and then click OK.

Finding Highlighted Items

If you want to jump from highlighted item to highlighted item, you can do so by using the Find And Replace dialog box. To find instances of highlighted text, follow these steps.

1. Click Find in the Editing group on the Home tab, or press Ctrl+F.

2. Click More to expand the Find tab.

3. Click Format, and then choose Highlight.

4. Click Find Next to jump to the next occurrence of highlighted text.

After Word finishes searching through the entire document, a dialog box appears that states that Word has finished searching the document. Click OK to complete the procedure.

> **Note**
>
> To clear the Highlight criteria from the Find What text box on the Find tab, click No Formatting in the Find And Replace dialog box.

Reformatting Highlighted Items with Another Highlight Color

You can change a single instance of a highlight color in a document, as well as change all instances of highlighting in a document to the same color. To change a single instance of a highlight color, choose another highlight color and then select the highlighted text.

To change the color of multiple instances of highlighting, you can use the Find And Replace dialog box. Using this technique, you can replace all existing highlighting (regardless of original highlight color) with a different color, as follows.

1. Click the Text Highlight Color arrow and select the color you want to assign to all highlighting.

2. Click Replace in the Editing group on the Home tab, or press Ctrl+H. The Find And Replace dialog box opens.

3. If necessary, click More to expand the Replace tab.

4. Make sure that no text appears in the Find What and Replace With boxes, position your insertion point in the Find What box, and then click Format and choose Highlight. The word *Highlight* should appear next to the Format label below the Find What box.

5. Click in the Replace With box and choose Format, Highlight.

6. Click Replace All, and then click OK in the message box that tells you how many replacements were made.

7. Click Close to close the Find And Replace dialog box.

In addition to replacing all highlighted text with a different color, you can use the preceding procedure to replace selected instances of highlighting with a new color. To do so, click Find Next instead of Replace All in step 6. You can then replace instances of highlighting with a new color on a case-by-case basis.

Adding and Managing Comments Effectively

Comments enable people who collaborate on documents to ask questions, provide suggestions, insert notes, and generally annotate a document's contents without inserting revisions or questions into the body of the document. When you work with a document that contains comments, you can display the comments in the Reviewing pane while viewing the document in any view, or in balloons if you're working in Print Layout, Full Screen Reading, or Web Layout view. You can display the Reviewing pane in Print Layout, Web Layout, Outline, and Draft views. If you have the Reviewing pane open and switch to the Full Screen Reading view, the Reviewing pane closes and comments are shown in balloons.

Chapter 11

When balloons display information, they appear next to your document's contents in either the left or right margin. Figure 11-2 shows a sample document in Print Layout view, with comment balloons along the right and the Reviewing pane along the left.

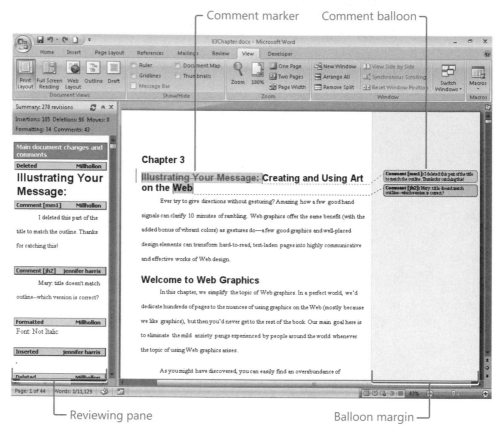

Figure 11-2 You can display color-coded comments in comment balloons or in the Reviewing pane. In both views, each comment includes the initials of the person who created the comment and a numeric identifier.

In addition to comment balloons, Word 2007 implements a number of visual cues when displaying comments. For example, notice in Figure 11-2 that in both the balloon and the Reviewing pane (in the shaded comment bar) the word *Comment* identifies the information as a comment. (You can also show insertions, deletions, and formatting changes in balloons and the Reviewing pane, as described in "Tracking Changes" on page 323.) Balloons and the comment bars in the Reviewing pane can be color-coded to associate them with particular users, and each comment bar in the Reviewing pane displays the user name of the person who inserted the comment. In addition, comments display the initials of the person who created the comment, and comments are automatically numbered throughout the document. The content associated with comments is shaded in the document to help link commented areas to corresponding comments. The shading of each instance of commented content matches the corresponding comment's balloon color, which simplifies identifying who created which comments. The combination of user initials, comment numbering, and color-coded content shading makes identifying and referring to comments quite easy.

Configuring Reviewers' User Names

Before you start inserting comments and tracked changes, you need to tell Word how to identify the marks you create. In other words, you need to configure your user name in Word. In fact, each person collaborating on the document must properly configure his or her user name to maximize the reviewing features. To set your user name information, you simply configure the Word Options settings. Word 2007 speeds up the process of accessing the settings by providing a link on the Review tab, as described here.

1. Click the Review tab, click the Track Changes arrow, and then click Change User Name. The Popular category in the Word Options dialog box is displayed. The user name settings are located in the Personalize Your Copy Of Microsoft Office section.

2. In the User Name box, type the name you want to use to identify your comments and then enter your initials in the Initials box, as shown in Figure 11-3.

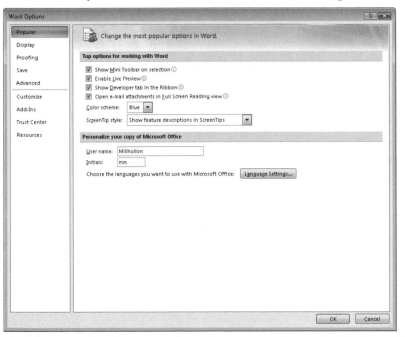

Figure 11-3 Word uses the user name and initials entered in the Word Options dialog box to identify comments in documents.

Keep in mind that the information you enter in the Word Options dialog box is used by all the 2007 Microsoft Office system programs. Any changes you make to these settings in Word will affect documents in other Microsoft Office system programs as well.

Fortunately, this is not as dire as it sounds. For example, if you're temporarily using someone else's computer to review a document, you can change the user name in the Word Options dialog box without affecting existing documents. Then, when you have finished working with the document on that computer, you can return to the Word Options dialog box to restore the original user information.

Configuring Colors Associated with Reviewers

By default, Word displays the comments and tracked changes for each reviewer of a document in a different color. If you prefer all comments and tracked changes to be displayed in a single color, you can change the default setting by clicking the Review tab, clicking the Track Changes arrow, and then clicking Change Tracking Options. The Track Changes Options dialog is shown in Figure 11-4.

Figure 11-4 By default, comments, insertions, deletions, and formatting changes are displayed in a different color for each reviewer.

Using the Track Changes Options dialog box, you can specify a color for all comments, insertions, deletions, and formatting changes. By default, By Author is selected for Insertions, Deletions, and Comments, which means that Word automatically assigns a different color to each person who inserts comments or tracked changes. Keep in mind that this setting doesn't always color-code each person's changes with the same color every time. Instead, the By Author option simply guarantees that every person's marks will appear in a distinct color—each person's color will most likely change each time someone reopens the document. For more information about configuring other options in the Track Changes Options dialog box, see "Adjusting the Appearance of Tracked Changes" on page 323.

If you're viewing a document in which comments for a number of reviewers have been color coded, you can quickly see which color is assigned to each reviewer. To do so, click Show Markup on the Review tab and then click Reviewers. You'll see a list of the reviewers' names accompanied by color-coded check boxes, as shown in Figure 11-5. (Of course, you can't see the color-coding in this book, but you can get an idea of how the color-coding system works.) In addition to seeing reviewer color assignments, you can use the list of reviewers to specify whose comments and tracked changes are displayed in the current document by selecting or clearing the check boxes next to a reviewer's name. When you clear a check box while in Print Layout, Full Screen Reading, or Web Layout view, that reviewer's comment and tracked changes balloons are hidden, and text inserted by the reviewer appears as regular body text. To display a reviewer's comments and changes again, just click the reviewer's check box.

Figure 11-5 You can use the Reviewers menu to quickly see the colors currently assigned to reviewers and to control whose comments and changes are displayed in the current document.

INSIDE OUT   **Optimizing a Document's Readability When Some Reviewers' Marks Are Hidden**

When you turn off the display of a reviewer's tracked changes, the text deleted by the reviewer appears as though it has been restored and text inserted by the reviewer appears as regular text. As you can imagine, this can result in some strange mixtures of restored and added text. If some text looks particularly confusing, display all reviewers' marks before you enter additional (and possibly unnecessary) revisions.

Allowing Reviewers to Use Only the Comments Feature

In addition to color-coding reviewers' comments, you can control who can add comments to a document during the review phases of a project. To do this, use the Editing Restrictions setting in the Restrict Formatting And Editing task pane, shown in Figure 11-6. Using the Editing Restrictions feature, you can ensure that the only modifications reviewers can make to your document are to add comments.

Chapter 11

Figure 11-6 The Restrict Formatting And Editing task pane enables you to limit reviewers' actions to only certain types of changes, such as inserting comments.

To set up editing restrictions, follow these steps.

1. Click Protect Document on the Review tab.

2. In the Restrict Formatting And Editing task pane, click the Allow Only This Type Of Editing In The Document check box and choose Comments in the list below the check box option.

3. Click More Users to specify any groups or users who are exceptions to the editing restriction.

4. Click Yes, Start Enforcing Protection. The Start Enforcing Protection dialog box opens.

5. If you want, type and confirm a password in the password boxes and click OK. If you specify a password, reviewers will have to enter the password before they can enter comments.

If you choose not to assign a password in step 5, reviewers will be restricted to inserting only comments by default. But if reviewers click the Stop Protection button in the Restrict Formatting And Editing task pane, they'll be able to unlock the document and edit your document freely. In other words, this document protection plan is really more of a deterrent than a fail-safe protection, but many times a deterrent is all you really need.

TROUBLESHOOTING

I forgot the document protection password.

If you forget the password for a protected document, you can recover the document by circumventing the password protection. To do so, select the entire document (by pressing Ctrl+A), copy the document (by pressing Ctrl+C), and paste the document (by pressing Ctrl+V) into a new, blank document. This process creates a new document based on the existing document.

Fortunately, when you copy and paste a document that contains tracked changes and comments, the newly created document retains all the reviewers' marks and color-coded settings. In contrast, when you copy and paste text that contains tracked changes in Word 2000 and earlier versions, the changes are accepted in the newly copied version of the text regardless of whether you're ready to accept the changes.

Inserting Standard Comments

After you configure your user name information, specify how to color-code reviewers' comments, and set any reviewer limitations, you are ready to insert comments into documents. Inserting a comment is a straightforward process. You can insert your comment at the insertion point, or you can select content that you want to associate with your comment. If you insert a comment at the insertion point, Word indicates the presence of your comment in the text by shading the nearest word and enclosing it in parentheses. (See Figure 11-2 for an example.) If you select content to be associated with a comment, Word marks the selected content in the same way, by shading the content and enclosing it in parentheses.

To insert a comment, follow these steps.

1. Position the insertion point where you want to insert a comment, or select the content you want to associate with your comment.

2. Click New Comment on the Review tab or press Ctrl+Alt+M.

    If you're working in Print Layout, Full Screen Reading, or Web Layout view, an empty balloon opens by default when you insert a comment. If you're working in Outline or Draft view, the Reviewing pane opens.

Note

By default, comment balloons are turned on in Print Layout, Full Screen Reading, and Web Layout views. If balloons are hidden, you can type comments in the Reviewing pane when you're working in any view.

3. Type the comment you want to make in the comment balloon or the Reviewing pane and then click outside the balloon or Reviewing pane to complete the comment.

Note

After you enter a comment in a balloon, you can press Esc to return the insertion point to the main body of the document.

If you want to change a comment after you create it, you can do so by clicking inside the comment balloon or Reviewing pane and then editing the text just as you edit standard text. If a comment is long and its contents aren't entirely displayed in a balloon, click the ellipses in the balloon to open the Reviewing pane. You can then modify the comment in the Reviewing pane. If the Reviewing pane isn't open or the ellipses aren't visible, click Reviewing Pane on the Review tab to open it. To close the Reviewing pane, click Reviewing Pane on the Review tab or press Alt+Shift+C.

INSIDE OUT Editing Text in the Reviewing Pane

As in Word 2002 and Word 2003, in Word 2007 you can't select text in the Reviewing pane and then press Backspace to delete it. Therefore, to delete text while working in the Reviewing pane, you need to either select the text and use the Delete key, or position your cursor at the text you want to delete and then use the Backspace or Delete key to delete the comment's text one character at a time. You can press Ctrl+Backspace or Ctrl+Delete to delete entire words at a time.

Inserting Voice and Handwritten Comments

If you are using a Tablet PC, you can include *voice comments* and *handwritten comments* with documents. Basically, voice comments are sound objects added to comment balloons. Before you can add a voice comment, you need to add the Insert Voice button to the Quick Access Toolbar. See Chapter 2, "The 2007 Office System User Interface: What's Changed, What's the Same," to learn how to customize the Quick Access Toolbar. To create ink comments, simply click the New Comment button on the Review tab and write your comment in the comment bubble.

Configuring Comment Balloon and Reviewing Pane Options

When you work with comment balloons (and track change balloons, as discussed in "Tracking Changes" on page 323), you can control a variety of balloon options. Specifically, you can format balloon and Reviewing pane label text (the text displayed on Reviewing pane bars above each comment or tracked change), specify when balloons will be displayed, adjust balloon width and placement, and specify whether lines should connect balloons to text.

Changing the Styles of Balloon and Reviewing Pane Text and Labels

You can modify the font styles of balloon and Reviewing pane text and labels (including the word *Comment* and user names) in the same manner you modify other styles in Word documents—by using the Styles task pane. To modify the Balloon Text style, which controls the balloon labels (such as Comment, Inserted, Deleted, and Formatted), and to change the Comment Text style (the text typed by reviewers), follow these steps.

1. Click the Styles Dialog Box Launcher on the Home tab (or press Ctrl+Alt+Shift+S) to open the Styles task pane.

2. In the Styles pane, click the Manage Styles button.

3. In the Manage Styles dialog box, select Alphabetical in the Sort Order list, select Balloon Text in the list of styles, and then click Modify.

4. In the Modify Style dialog box, select any options you want. Choose whether you want to make the changes to the current document only or add the formatting to the document's template (either Normal.dotm or another attached template), and then click OK.

5. In the Manage Styles dialog box, select Comment Text and click Modify.

6. In the Modify Style dialog box, select any options you want. Choose whether you want to make the changes to the current document only or add the formatting to the document's template, and then click OK twice to close both dialog boxes.

You can also modify comment text by selecting the text or label in an existing comment in the Reviewing pane or balloon, applying format settings, and then updating the style to match the selected text.

When you modify the Comment Text style, you change the appearance of the text only (not the labels) in the comment balloons and comment entries in the Reviewing pane (you do not modify the text displayed in tracked-change balloons or tracked-change Reviewing pane entries, as discussed in "Tracking Changes" on page 323.

Chapter 11

Showing and Hiding Balloons

If you prefer to work with the Reviewing pane and not balloons, you can turn off balloons. Or if you prefer, you can use balloons only to show comments and formatting changes. To control balloon display in Print Layout, Full Screen Reading, and Web Layout views, you can configure the Use Balloons option in the Track Changes Options dialog box, or you can use the Balloons tool on the Review tab, as follows.

1. On the Review tab, click Balloons.

2. On the Balloon menu, specify a balloon setting by choosing one of the following options.

- **Show Revisions In Balloons** Shows all changes in balloons (equivalent of Always in the Track Changes Options dialog box).

- **Show All Revisions Inline** Turns off balloons (equivalent of Never in the Track Changes Options dialog box).

- **Show Only Comments And Formatting In Balloons** Shows comments and formatting changes in balloons and shows inserted and deleted text inline (equivalent of Only For Comments/Formatting in the Track Changes Options dialog box).

Regardless of whether you hide or show balloons, comments will be displayed as ScreenTips when you position your mouse pointer over a comment marker.

> **Note**
>
> You can specify whether the lines used to connect balloons to text are displayed or hidden by selecting or clearing the Show Lines Connecting To Text check box in the Track Changes Options dialog box. When you clear the Show Lines Connecting To Text check box, balloons are displayed in the margin without a connector line when they aren't selected. When you select a comment, the comment is displayed with a solid line that connects the balloon to the comment marker in the text.

Adjusting Balloon Size and Location for Online Viewing

If you are new to balloons, you might find that they take some getting used to, even if you've used comments and tracking tools in the Reviewing pane. To help you customize balloons to suit your working style, Microsoft provides a couple of options you can use to control the width and position of balloons when you choose to view them. In fact, you can control balloon width and location for online viewing as well as for printing purposes. This section addresses configuring the online presentation of balloons. For more information about configuring balloons for printing, see "Printing Comments" on page 321.

To set the balloon width and specify whether balloons are displayed in the right or left margin, you must configure the Track Changes Options dialog box as follows.

1. Click the Track Changes arrow on the Review tab and then click Change Tracking Options.

2. In the Track Changes Options dialog box, make sure that the Use Balloons (Print And Web Layout) list box is set to Always or to Only For Comments/Formatting.

3. Click the Measure In arrow and select whether you want to measure balloons in inches or as a percentage of the page. For more information about the Inches and Percent options, see "Sizing Balloons—Inches vs. Percentage" below.

4. In the Preferred Width box, enter a percentage or measurement (in inches) for the width of the balloons.

5. In the Margin box, choose the Left or Right option to specify on which side of the document window you want balloons to appear.

6. Click OK to apply the balloon settings.

Unfortunately, you can't preview how your balloon settings will be displayed. The best approach when configuring balloons is to try a few settings and see which setting works best for you on your monitor.

INSIDE OUT   Sizing Balloons—Inches vs. Percentage

When you size balloons, Word configures them without compromising the document's content area. This is accomplished by expanding the view of your document (not by reducing the document's content area). To clarify, let's look at the two sizing options: Inches and Percent.

When you use the Inches setting, you provide a set size in which your balloons will appear in your document's margin. For example, if you specify 2 inches, your page's view will expand so that balloons will be displayed within an area that's 2 inches wide, starting from the document's margin.

Similarly, if you size balloons using the Percent option, the balloons will be displayed as a percentage of the page's size without compromising the document's content area. For example, if you specify balloons to be 100 percent, the balloons will be sized equal to 100 percent of the page, and the width of your view will be expanded accordingly (doubled, in this case).

You can easily see how balloons will be displayed relative to the current document by saving a setting (using Inches or Percent) and then viewing your document in Print Preview.

Chapter 11

Reviewing Comments

Let's say your document has made its rounds, and now it's up to you to review the comments reviewers have inserted into the document. You can review comments only, or you can review comments while you review tracked changes. In this section, we'll look at the process of reviewing comments only. (For more information about reviewing tracked changes, see "Tracking Changes" on page 323.) To review only comments in any view, you must first hide tracked changes. Then, follow these steps.

1. On the Review tab, make sure that either Final Showing Markup or Original Showing Markup is selected in the Display For Review list.

2. Click Show Markup on the Review tab and make sure that only the Comments option is selected on the menu. To accomplish this, you'll probably have to clear the check marks for Ink, Insertions And Deletions, and Formatting.

> **Note**
>
> The Markup Area Highlight option on the Show Markup menu controls whether the balloon area appears shaded. By default, Markup Area Highlight is selected, and the balloon area appears light gray.

After you complete these steps, comments and comment markers will be the only markup features visible in the current document. At this point, you can review the comments manually by scrolling through your document or the Reviewing pane, or you can jump from comment to comment by clicking the Next and Previous buttons in the Comments group on the Review tab. Depending on the current view, you can review comments as follows.

- **Draft view** Comments are displayed in the Reviewing pane. The Reviewing pane will open automatically when you click Previous or Next in the Comments group on the Review tab.

- **Full Screen Reading view without balloons** Comment markers are shown, but the Reviewing pane is not displayed. You can view the comment by positioning your cursor over the comment marker and reading the ScreenTip.

- **Outline view** Comments can be viewed as a ScreenTip or in the Reviewing pane. When you click Previous or Next in the Comments group on the Review tab, the Reviewing pane opens (if it isn't open already), and the view changes to Draft view automatically.

- **Print Layout, Full Screen Reading, or Web Layout view with balloons** The active comment balloon is indicated by a dark outline, darker shading, and solid connector line. Clicking Previous and Next moves from balloon to balloon. Note that in Full Screen Reading view, you can view comments but you cannot use the Previous and Next buttons; instead, press Ctrl+Down Arrow to proceed forward from balloon to balloon through a document or press Alt+Up Arrow or Alt+Down Arrow to move up or down among balloons on a single page. (The keyboard commands also work in Print Layout and Web Layout views.)

- **Print Layout or Web Layout view without balloons** Comments can be viewed in the Reviewing pane. If the Reviewing pane isn't open when you click Previous or Next, Word opens it automatically and highlights the previous or next comment.

> **Note**
>
> You can also browse from comment to comment by using the Select Browse Object feature (press Ctrl+Alt+Home) or the Go To tab in the Find And Replace dialog box (press Ctrl+G). On the Go To tab, you can select Comment in the Go To What list and then choose to view all reviewers' comments or a selected reviewer's comments by selecting Any Reviewer or a specific name in the Enter Reviewer's Name list.

When you view comments in balloons, you might notice that some comments have an ellipsis in the lower-right corner. This symbol indicates that the entire comment text doesn't fit in the balloon. To view the remainder of the comment, click the ellipsis to open the Reviewing pane, which will contain the entire contents of the comment.

Naturally, as you read through comments, you might want to respond to them. You can do so in the following ways.

- Type directly in a comment, in which case your response won't be color-coded according to your user name.

- Click in the comment you want to respond to and then click New Comment on the Review tab or press Ctrl+Alt+M. A new comment balloon is inserted directly below the comment you're responding to, or a blank entry opens in the Reviewing pane with the format Comment[initials##R##] in the header. The first number is the number of the comment, and the R## indicates that the comment is a response to the comment number indicated. To add your response, simply enter your comment.

> **Note**
>
> To quickly see when a comment was inserted and who created it, you can hover the mouse pointer over the comment balloon. When you do this, a ScreenTip displays the comment's creation date and time as well as the user name of the person who created the comment. If you're working in the Reviewing pane, each Reviewing pane bar displays the user name and insertion date and time automatically.

Deleting Comments

Generally, comments serve a temporary purpose—reviewers insert comments, someone addresses the comments, and then the comments are removed before the document's final publication (either online or in print). If you work with comments, you need to know how to delete them so that you won't unintentionally include them in your final publication. As you might expect, you can delete comments in several ways. Namely, you can delete a single comment, delete comments from a specific reviewer (or reviewers), or delete all comments, using the following techniques.

- **Delete a single comment.** Right-click a comment balloon and then click Delete Comment on the shortcut menu. Or select a comment balloon and then click Delete in the Comments group on the Review tab.

- **Delete comments from a specific reviewer.** First clear the check boxes for all reviewers by clicking Show Markup on the Review tab and choosing Reviewers, All Reviewers. Now display only the comments you want to delete by clicking Show Markup, clicking Reviewers, and then selecting the check box next to the reviewer's name whose comments you want to delete. (You can repeat this process to select additional reviewers as well.) To delete the displayed comments, click the Delete arrow in the Comments group on the Review tab and then click Delete All Comments Shown.

- **Delete all comments in the document.** Make sure that all reviewers' comments are displayed. (This is the default setting, but if all reviewers' comments aren't displayed, click Show Markup on the Review tab and choose Reviewers, All Reviewers.) Click the Delete arrow in the Comments group on the Review tab and then click Delete All Comments In Document.

Comments, Revisions, and the Document Inspector

You can remove all comments and revisions by using the Document Inspector. To do so, click the Microsoft Office Button, Prepare, Inspect Document. Be sure that the Comments, Revisions, Versions, And Annotations check box is selected. Then click Inspect. If the Document Inspector finds any leftover comments or revisions, you can click Remove All to accept all revision marks and delete all comments.

Keep in mind that when you use the Remove All option in the Document Inspector to delete all revisions and comments, you cannot use the Undo command to retrieve the revisions and comments. If you suddenly realize you do not want to remove the revisions and comments after you click Remove All, your only recourse is to close the document without saving changes.

For more information about using the Document Inspector, see Chapter 3, "Managing Security and Privacy in the 2007 Office System."

Keep in mind that when you delete all comments at once by choosing the Delete All Comments In Document option, you delete all comments in the document, regardless of whether they are displayed on the screen.

> **Note**
>
> You can also delete comments one at a time in the Reviewing pane. To do so, right-click a comment in the Reviewing pane and choose Delete Comment on the shortcut menu, or click in a comment and click Delete on the Review tab.

Printing Comments

As previously mentioned, you can control how comments are displayed on the screen as well as in print. "Configuring Comment Balloon and Reviewing Pane Options" on page 334 addresses how to control the display of comments in balloons and in the Reviewing pane. This section discusses the ways you can print comments. When you print a document containing comments (and tracked changes, for that matter), you can configure print settings in two areas: the Track Changes Options dialog box and the Print dialog box. Let's look first at the Track Changes Options dialog box.

In the Balloons section of the Track Changes Options dialog box (click the Track Changes arrow on the Review tab and then click Change Tracking Options to open the dialog box), you can specify how Word should adjust paper orientation to accommodate balloons. You can select any of the following settings in the Paper Orientation list.

- **Auto** Specifies that Word can determine the best orientation for your document, based on your margin settings and balloon width settings.

- **Preserve** Prints the document with the orientation specified in the Page Setup dialog box. This is the default setting.

- **Force Landscape** Prints balloons and the document in landscape format to allow the most room for the display of balloons.

After you choose how you want Word to handle page orientation issues when you print documents with comment balloons, you're ready to configure the Print dialog box.

In the Print dialog box (click the Microsoft Office Button, Print), you can specify whether to print the document showing markup (the default setting when comments and tracked changes are displayed), or you can opt to print just a list of the markup changes made in a document. Most likely, if you want to print a document's changes, you'll want to print the document showing changes instead of printing a list of changes. When you print a list of changes, the list can become long and confusing.

The easiest way to print a document with its comments is to print the document with comment balloons in the margin and hide the other types of margin balloons (including balloons that show insertions, deletions, and formatting changes). To efficiently print comments in a document, follow these steps.

1. Display your document in Print Layout view.

2. On the Review tab, click the Balloons button and choose Show Only Comments And Formatting In Balloons.

3. If you want, click Show Markup and clear the check mark for Formatting so that only comment balloons are shown. You can also hide inline revision marks if you want.

4. Click the Microsoft Office Button, Print or press Ctrl+P to open the Print dialog box.

5. In the Print dialog box, make sure that the Print What box shows Document Showing Markup, and then click OK.

The document will be printed with comment balloons in the margin. Word will reduce the view of the page to accommodate printing balloons in the margins. This doesn't affect your document's layout parameters—it's just a temporary modification for printing purposes when you're printing balloons along with a document.

> **Note**
>
> When you print a document with markup, the Markup Area Highlight shading (the light gray shading behind balloons onscreen) is not printed.

Saving a Document with Comments as a Web Page

You can save a document that contains comments and other marked-up text as a Web page. When you do this, Word retains the comments and tracked changes in the text. To save a reviewed document as a Web page, click the Microsoft Office Button, Save As, Other Formats. In the Save As dialog box, select Web Page in the Save As Type box and then click Save.

Keep in mind that the online display of comments and tracked changes in your document depends on your browser. In Microsoft Internet Explorer 4 and later, comments appear as dynamic ScreenTips, as shown in Figure 11-7. Also, revised text appears in a color other than black with underlining and strikethrough formatting, similar to how you see markup changes in Word when a single color is selected to show markup. In browsers earlier than Internet Explorer 4, and in Netscape Navigator 4 and later, comments appear as footnotes beneath the main Web page instead of as dynamic ScreenTips.

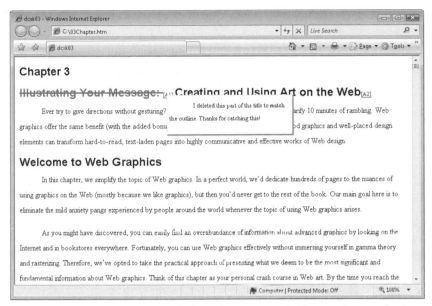

Figure 11-7 When you save a marked-up document as a Web page, Internet Explorer users can view comments in the form of dynamic ScreenTips by positioning the mouse pointer over a comment link.

Tracking Changes

Adding comments to documents is invaluable when reviewers need to annotate and query text, but you need another set of features when you want reviewers to conduct line-by-line edits to help smooth a document's text and layout. When your document is ready for detailed editing in a team setting, you'll want to turn to the Track Changes feature.

> **Note**
>
> If you've been using Word for a few versions now, you might still think of the Track Changes feature as the Revision Marks feature, which was the name of this feature in Word 95 and earlier.

When you turn on the Track Changes feature, Word can record the deletions, insertions, and formatting changes made by each reviewer who modifies the document. By default, Word displays each reviewer's changes in a different color so that you can easily identify the sources of changes within your document. When you work with a document that has been modified by reviewers, you can use the Display For Review list in the Tracking group on the Review tab to display the changed document in four views, as described here.

- **Final Showing Markup** The default display view. Displays the final document with deletions, comments, formatting changes, and moved content marked. Tracked changes are shown in balloons by default.

- **Final** Hides the tracked changes and shows how the document would appear if you accepted all the changes.

- **Original Showing Markup** Displays the original document and shows deletions, comments, formatting changes, and moved content.

- **Original** Hides the tracked changes and shows the original document so that you can see how the document would look if you rejected all changes.

Being able to display your document in these ways can help as you add, accept, and reject tracked changes. In addition, many configuration settings you use to control how comments are displayed (as discussed earlier in this chapter) also apply to tracked changes. In the sections discussing tracked changes that follow, you'll find references to topics covered in the comments sections in this chapter if the topic applies to both comments and tracked changes.

Before we get to the details of working with tracked changes, you should note that Word doesn't track some changes when you modify a document, including changes you make to the following.

- Background colors

- Embedded fonts

- Routing information

- Some types of mail merge information, such as whether a file is a main document or a data file

- Some table modifications

For the most part, you probably won't find that these limitations interfere with tasks involving tracked changes, but you should be aware of the exceptions, just in case. In addition, you will sometimes see a dialog box warning that an action—such as modifying a table—will not be marked as a change. In those cases, you have the option of clicking OK to proceed or Cancel to avoid making a change that won't be tracked.

Tracking Changes While You Edit

When you track changes in a document, you can opt to display or hide the tracking marks while you work. Generally, it's easier to hide tracked changes if you're editing and writing text and better to view tracking marks when you're reviewing a document's changes. When Word tracks changes, it automatically records insertions or deletions in balloons (depending on your view), which you can view in Print Layout, Full Screen Reading, or Web Layout view. Word marks tracked changes in a document as follows.

- **Added text** Appears in the reviewer's color with underlining.

- **Deleted text** Is displayed in the reviewer's color in a balloon. If the inline option is chosen, deleted text shows in the content area with a strikethrough line indicating the deletion.

- **Moved text** New in Word 2007, text moved within a document is automatically marked in green, with double-underlines marking the moved text. In addition, the balloons for moved text display a Go button in the lower-right corner that you can click to move from the original location to the new location and vice versa.

- **Text added and then deleted by the reviewer** Is displayed as if the text had never been added. (In other words, no marks appear in a document in places where a reviewer adds information and then deletes the added information.)

In addition to these actions, Word automatically inserts a vertical line, called a changed line, along the left margin to indicate that an editing or formatting change has been made. Finally, the Reviewing pane automatically generates a summary of changes, including the number of insertions, deletions, moves, formatting changes, comments, and a grand total.

Figure 11-8 shows a document in Final Showing Markup view, which displays inserted text in line; deleted, formatted, and moved text in balloons; and both parts associated with moved text in the Reviewing pane. Notice the changed line in the left margin, which specifies that the text to the right of the line has been modified in some way. For more information about configuring changed lines, see "Customizing the Appearance of Changed Lines" on page 329.

Also notice in Figure 11-8 the Track Changes: On indicator on the status bar at the bottom of the window. To add this indicator to your status bar, right-click the status bar and choose Track Changes on the Customize Status Bar menu. After you add the Track Changes indicator to your status bar, you can control whether the Track Changes feature is turned on or off simply by clicking Track Changes on the status bar.

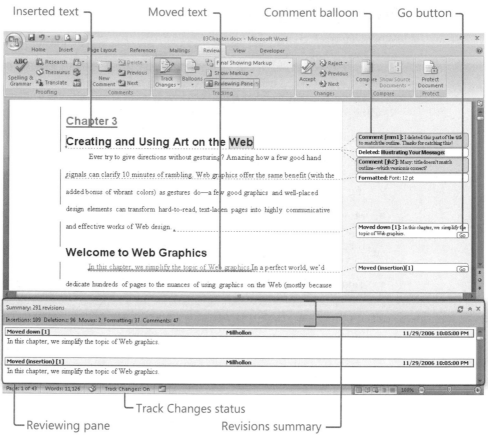

Figure 11-8 The Final Showing Markup view displays inserted text within the document and deletions, formatting changes, comments, and moved text in balloons in the margins. In addition, all changes are displayed in the Reviewing pane along with a summary of revisions.

You can track changes in a document by following these steps.

1. Open the document you want to edit, and then choose the view in which you want to edit the document: Print Layout, Web Layout, Outline, or Draft view.

2. Turn Track Changes on by using one of the following techniques (all of which are toggle commands, meaning that you can use the commands to turn Track Changes on or off).

- Click the top half of the Track Changes button (if you click the bottom half, you open the Track Changes menu).

- Press Ctrl+Shift+E.

- If you added Track Changes to your status bar, click Track Changes.

3. After Track Changes is on, make editorial changes, including inserting, deleting, moving, and reformatting the document's text and objects. Word tracks your changes, regardless of whether your view reflects the tracked changes as marked-up text.

As mentioned, you can record changes while displaying tracked changes on the screen, or you can hide the tracking marks while you work. In addition, you can always tell whether changes are being tracked by looking at the Track Changes button on the status bar, because the button indicates On or Off depending on your current working mode.

> **Note**
>
> You can control who can make tracked changes to your document by using the Restricted Formatting And Editing task pane, as described in "Allowing Reviewers to Use Only the Comments Feature" on page 311. To limit reviewers to making only tracked changes, click Protect Document on the Review tab. In the Restrict Formatting And Editing task pane, click the Allow Only This Type Of Editing In The Document check box, select Tracked Changes in the list, and click Yes, Start Enforcing Protection. Enter a password if you want to use one, reenter the password to confirm it, and click then OK. When tracked changes are protected, all changes are marked, and reviewers can't accept and reject changes made by other reviewers.

Adjusting the Appearance of Tracked Changes

Just as you can control the appearance of comments, you can control the appearance of tracked changes in your documents. A number of Track Changes options correspond to options available for comments, including the following.

- **Configuring user names** See "Configuring Reviewers' User Names" on page 309.

- **Configuring colors associated with reviewers** See "Configuring Colors Associated with Reviewers" on page 310.

- **Controlling balloon and Reviewing pane options** See "Configuring Comment Balloon and Reviewing Pane Options" on page 315.

In addition to these options, you can specify how inserted text and objects should be marked, how formatting changes should be identified, and how changed lines should appear in your document. These options are discussed in the next several sections.

> **Note**
>
> The settings you configure for displaying tracked changes are global and will apply to all documents you open in Word that include tracked changes.

Specifying How Insertions and Formatting Changes Are Displayed

You can change how Word identifies inserted and reformatted information when the Track Changes feature is turned on. You use the Track Changes Options dialog box (shown earlier in this chapter in Figure 11-4) to configure these settings, as follows:

1. Click the bottom half of the Track Changes button on the Review tab and then click Change Tracking Options.

2. In the Markup section of the dialog box, click the Insertions list and select how you'd like inserted text to be identified. You can choose to show insertions without any special formatting (in which case inserted text looks like regular, non-color-coded text and is indistinguishable from the original text). Or you can display inserted text in the reviewer's color only or in the reviewer's color and formatted as boldface, italic, underlined, double-underlined, or strikethrough. By default, inserted text appears in the reviewer's color with an underline.

3. Click the Deletions list and select how you'd like deleted text to be identified. You can display deleted text in the reviewer's color only or in the reviewer's color and formatted as boldface, italic, underlined, double-underlined, strikethrough, hidden, with a caret (^), with an octothorpe (#), or double-strikethrough. By default, deleted text appears in the reviewer's color as strikethrough text.

4. In the Formatting section, make sure the Track Formatting check box is selected if you want to track formatting changes. Then specify how formatting changes should be marked. The default setting is None, which means formatting changes aren't marked in the body of the text (although you can see the changes in a balloon). The Formatting options are the same as the Insertions options.

5. Use the Color boxes next to the tracking options to specify whether you want Word to assign author colors automatically. If you'd like, you can manually select a color to mark your changes, but you risk having your comments share a color with another reviewer if they also choose the same color. For clarity's sake, the By Author default setting is frequently used to show markup, comments, and formatting revisions in team projects.

> **Note**
> You cannot create custom colors for any of the settings in the Track Changes Options dialog box.

6. Click OK to save the settings.

Tracking Moved Text and Inline Shapes

New to Word 2007, you can track moved text and inline shapes. When you copy and paste or select and drag a complete sentence, paragraph, group of paragraphs, or an inline shape, Word marks the revision as *moved* content instead of *deleted* and *inserted* content. By showing text as moved, users can quickly see when information has been relocated as opposed to simply deleted or added.

By default, Word marks moved text in green, with a double strikethrough in the original location and a double underline in its new location. To control the Track Moves settings, open the Track Changes Options dialog box, select the Track Moves check box to toggle the feature on or off, and then select settings in the Moved From, Moved To, and Color lists if you want to use settings other than the defaults.

Showing Revisions in Tables

In Word 2007, you can now track many changes made to tables. Often when you make revisions to tables in earlier versions of Word, you receive a dialog box warning that your changes will not be marked. You will still see this message box on occasion in Word 2007—such as when you use the Eraser tool to remove a line in the table or the Draw Table tool to add a line—but many table changes can now be tracked and highlighted.

Unlike earlier versions of the program, Word 2007 can highlight table cells that are inserted, deleted, merged, or split during the revision process. By default, Word highlights each type of change using a different color. You can choose custom colors, if you prefer, including using the By Author option. To access the table revision settings, click the bottom half of the Track Changes button on the Review tab, click Change Tracking Options on the menu, and then configure the color options in the Table Cell Highlighting section of the Track Changes Options dialog box.

Customizing the Appearance of Changed Lines

Regardless of your selections for displaying and marking inserted, deleted, moved, and reformatted information, you can still use changed lines to indicate in a general way where changes have occurred in a document. As shown in Figure 11-8, Word automatically inserts a black vertical line, called a *changed line*, in the margin next to text that contains tracked changes. You can specify where changed lines are displayed on the page (along the right, left, or outside borders) and the color in which they are displayed. By default, changed lines are set to Auto and are display as black lines. To configure how changed lines are displayed, follow these steps.

1. Click the bottom half of the Track Changes button on the Review tab and then click Change Tracking Options on the menu.

2. In the Markup section, in the Changed Lines list, specify whether you want changed lines to be displayed along the left, right, or outside border. You can select the (None) setting if you'd rather not display changed lines when you use the Track Changes feature.

3. To specify a color for changed lines, click the Color arrow next to the Changed Lines list and then select a color.

4. Click OK to save your settings.

After you configure the changed lines settings, all documents you open that contain tracked changes will use the newly configured settings. In addition, any currently opened documents that contain tracked changes will be reformatted automatically to reflect the new settings.

> **Note**
>
> In Draft view, all changed lines appear on the left, regardless of the setting you configure in the Markup section in the Track Changes Options dialog box. The changed lines color setting applies in all views.

Accepting and Rejecting Proposed Edits

After a document has made the rounds through reviewers, and you receive a file containing a number of tracked changes, you can begin to finalize the document by accepting or rejecting the changes. As you review edits, you can address each edit on a case-by-case basis (generally, this is the recommended practice), or you can accept multiple changes at once. In either case, you can reject and accept proposed changes by using the appropriate buttons on the Review tab or by right-clicking changes or balloons and choosing options on the shortcut menu. Figure 11-9 shows the shortcut menu you see when you right-click moved text—notice the new Follow Move option, which enables you to jump to the origin or destination of the moved text in relation to the text you right-clicked. (If you right-click deleted text, you'll see the same menu without the Follow Move option, and if you right-click inserted text, the Accept Deletion and Reject Deletion options change to Accept Insertion and Reject Insertion.) The next few sections describe ways you can incorporate edits.

Figure 11-9 You can right-click tracked changes to access options that enable you to resolve proposed changes, including the option to jump to the origin or destination of moved text.

Note

Before you start accepting and rejecting tracked changes, consider saving a version of the document with all the tracked changes and comments intact. That way, if you want to return to the marked-up version of the document, you'll have a copy on hand.

Addressing Tracked Changes One at a Time

The key to accessing the changes you want to review is to configure your view properly before you start navigating among changes and making editorial decisions. When you're ready to resolve tracked changes, you should configure the following settings.

- **Show document markup** Show your document in either Final Showing Markup or Original Showing Markup view. You can do so by choosing either view in the Tracking group on the Review tab.

- **Specify the type(s) of changes to display** Use the Show Markup menu on the Review tab to specify which types of changes you want to review. Available options are Comments, Ink, Insertions And Deletions, and Formatting. You can review any combination of the four types of document changes as well as toggle the light gray highlight shown behind the balloons next to your document.

- **Display selected user revisions and comments** Click Show Markup on the Review tab, and then click Reviewers to open the list of reviewers. You can then choose which reviewers' markup changes you want to resolve. You can resolve all changes at one time (by selecting the All Reviewers option), or you can select any combination of listed reviewers.

Note

Unfortunately, the Reviewers menu closes automatically after each change you make to the list. Therefore, if you want to view the revisions and comments of only a couple reviewers out of a long list, first clear the All Reviewers check box (instead of clearing each name's check box one at a time). Then, click the names of the people who made the changes you want to review. The goal is to configure the list with as few clicks as possible to avoid having to reopen the list repeatedly.

- **Specify how balloons should be displayed** Click Balloons on the Review tab and then choose to show revisions in balloons, all revisions inline, or only comments and formatting in balloons.

- **Show or hide the Reviewing pane** Decide whether you want the Reviewing pane to be open while you work as well as whether it should appear along the bottom or left side of your window. To control the Reviewing pane, click the Reviewing Pane arrow on the Review tab and choose either the vertical or horizontal position. If you click the button without choosing an orientation, Word opens the Reviewing pane in its previous position.

After you display the changes and tools you want to work with, you can move from tracked change to tracked change using the Next and Previous buttons on the Review tab (in the same manner you jump from comment to comment), you can view and click edits in the Reviewing pane, or you can scroll through the document and address edits in a less linear manner. Regardless of how you arrive at a tracked change, you can handle it in any of the following ways.

- Right-click a change (in the document body, in the Reviewing pane, or in a balloon) and choose to accept or reject the item by using the shortcut menu.

- Click in a change and then click the Accept or Reject button on the Review tab. Or click the Accept or Reject arrow to take action and move to the next revision.

- Select a range of text and click the Accept or Reject button on the Review tab (or right-click to open the shortcut menu). All tracked changes in the selected text will be handled simultaneously.

After you accept or reject a change, Word displays the text as standard text. If you change your mind about a change, you can undo your action by clicking Undo on the Quick Access Toolbar or pressing Ctrl+Z.

Accepting or Rejecting All Tracked Changes at Once

At times, you might want to accept or reject all changes in a document. For example, maybe you've gone through the document with a fine-tooth comb, reading and changing the document in Final view. When you're satisfied with the document, you want to simply accept all changes instead of resolving each change individually. You can do so by executing a single command.

To accept or reject all changes in a document, use the Accept All Changes In Document or Reject All Changes In Document command. To access these commands, click the Accept or Reject arrow on the Review tab and choose the appropriate command from the menu, as shown in Figure 11-10.

Figure 11-10 You can accept or reject all changes or changes by a particular reviewer by using the Accept and Reject menus, which are accessible from the Review tab.

In addition to accepting or rejecting all changes in a document, you can show a subset of reviewers' changes and accept or reject just those changes. To control which changes are displayed in your document, click Show Markup on the Review tab, choose Reviewers, and then select which reviewers' changes you want to display and resolve. After you configure your display, click the Accept or Reject arrow and then choose the Accept All Changes Shown or Reject All Changes Shown option.

> **Note**
>
> Between resolving tracked changes individually and accepting or rejecting all changes in one step lies the realm of accepting and rejecting edits contained in selected text. In other words, you can resolve editing issues on a piecemeal basis. To do so, select text—for example, you might want to select a paragraph or two that you've reviewed—and then click Accept or Reject on the Review tab to accept or reject the tracked changes contained in the selected text.

Printing Documents That Contain Revisions

You can create printed versions of marked-up documents that include revision marks and balloons. When you print a document with markup showing, by default Word chooses the zoom level and page orientation to best display your document's markup. In addition, you can print just a list of the markup in a document by selecting List Of Markup in the Print What box in the Print dialog box.

For more information about printing documents containing tracked changes, comments, and balloons, see "Printing Comments" on page 321.

To print a document showing markup, follow these steps.

1. Open your document and switch to Print Layout view.

2. Display the tracked changes in the manner you want them to be printed by using the Display For Review list on the Review tab. In addition, select which reviewers' comments you want to print by clicking the Review tab, clicking Reviewers, and

specifying which reviewers' revisions and comments should be displayed and subsequently printed.

3. Click the Microsoft Office Button, Print to open the Print dialog box, make sure that Document Showing Markup is selected in the Print What list, and then click OK to print the document.

> **Note**
>
> You can save a document containing tracked changes as a Web page and post the page online. For more information about saving a marked-up document as a Web page, see "Saving a Document with Comments as a Web Page" on page 322.

Comparing and Combining Documents

At times, you might want to expedite a reviewing process by sending reviewers separate copies of an original document. Then, when reviewers return the documents, you can combine the changes into one document. At other times, you might want to compare two versions of a document and just look at the differences between the two documents. In Word, you can perform both of these actions by using the Compare feature on the Review tab. This section of the chapter describes comparing and combining documents.

Comparing Two Versions of a Document (Legal Blackline)

When you compare two versions of the same document, you can see what changes have been made to the original document regardless of whether Track Changes was turned on when modifications were made. The differences are shown in the original document as tracked changes. To compare two versions of one document and view the differences, follow these steps.

1. Click Compare on the Review tab and then click Compare on the menu. The Compare Documents dialog box opens.

2. In the Original Document section, use the arrow and folder icon to navigate to and select the original document.

3. In the Revised Document section, use the arrow and folder icon to navigate to and select the revised document.

4. Click More to set comparison options and verify that New Document is selected in the Show Changes In section (you can also choose to show changes in the original or revised document), as shown here:

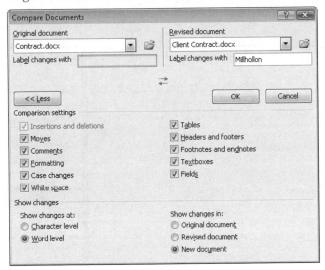

5. Click OK. The original and revised documents remain unaltered and a new document is created and shown automatically.

> **Note**
>
> If either (or both) of the documents being compared includes tracked changes, you'll see a message box stating that Word will compare the documents as if the tracked changes have been accepted. Click Yes to continue the comparison.

6. To view all three versions of the document at once, click Show Source Documents on the Review tab and choose Show Both. In this view, the original, revised, and compared documents are shown in your work area, as shown in Figure 11-11.

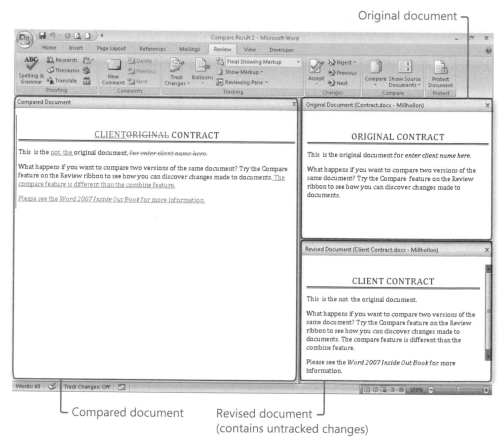

Figure 11-11 You can view the original, revised, and comparison results on the screen at the same time.

The new document displays the changed text in an unnamed document file. You'll need to save and name the file if you want to store it for future use.

Combining Revisions from Multiple Authors

You can combine revisions from multiple authors into one document to possibly streamline the review process. To do so, use the Combine option on the Compare menu, as follows.

1. Click Compare on the Review tab, and click Combine. The Combine Documents dialog box opens, which looks similar to the Compare Documents dialog box.

2. In the Original Document section, use the arrow and folder icon to navigate to and select the original document.

3. In the Revised Document section, use the arrow and folder icon to navigate to and select the revised document and then click OK.

Figure 11-12 shows a sample combination in which the original document (Combine Result 2, the result of a previous combination) is combined with a third revised document, resulting in the document labeled Combined Result 3.

> **Note**
>
> When you add a revised document to an existing combined document, the combined result file name appears in the drop-down lists so you can select it as part of the new combine process.

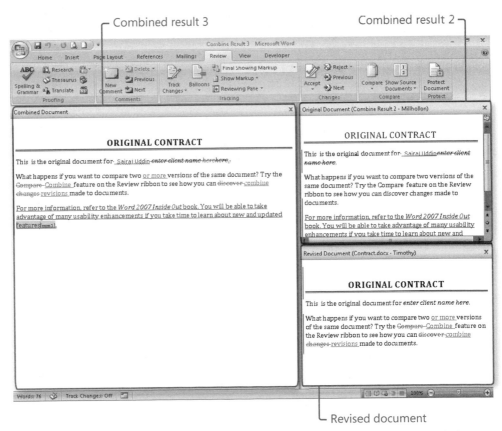

Figure 11-12 To combine more than two documents, simply combine your combined result document with another document containing changes. This figure shows the result of combining Combine Result 2 with a third revised document.

Note

At times, you might want to compare two documents side by side without merging them. In those cases, you should adjust your view without using the Compare or Combine features.

TROUBLESHOOTING

What happened to the File Versions feature?

In Word 2003, you could save versions of your document and store the information within the document file. Word 2007 does not offer the capability to save versions of your local documents. You can, however, view the version history of documents stored in a Document Library. To do so, open a file stored in a Document Library and then click the Microsoft Office Button, Server, View Version History, as shown here.

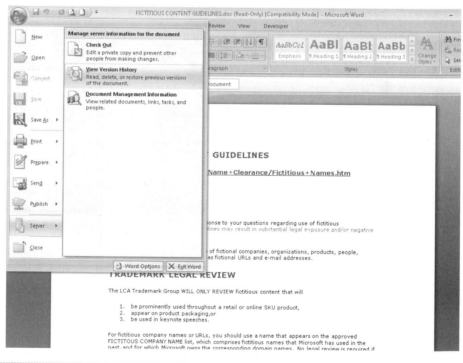

PART 4

Excel

Mark Dodge and Craig Stinson

In this chapter, we'll cover the basics, including moving around within the massive worksheet grid, entering and selecting data, and working with multiple worksheets and protecting their contents. You probably already know many of these techniques, but here we'll also present alternative methods. You might find a better, or faster, way to do something you do frequently. You'll find that Microsoft Office Excel 2007 offers a lot of alternatives.

In early versions of Microsoft Excel, worksheets, charts, and macro sheets were stored as separate documents. Since Microsoft Excel 5, however, all these types of data, and more, peacefully coexist in workbooks. You can keep as many worksheets containing as many different types of data as you want in a workbook, you can have more than one workbook open at the same time, and you can have more than one window open for the same workbook. The only limitations to these capabilities are those imposed by your computer's memory and system resources.

Moving Around Regions

You already know how to use scroll bars and the Page Up and Page Down keys. Office Excel 2007 offers many other ways to get around, including some unique tricks you'll find only in Excel 2007.

A *region* is a range of cell entries bounded by blank cells or column and row headings. In Figure 12-1, the range A3:E7 is a region, as are the ranges G3:H7, A9:E10, and G9:H10. (Strictly speaking, cell A1 is also a one-cell region because no adjoining cells contain entries.) For example, cell H10 is within a region, even though it's empty. The *active area* of the worksheet is the selection rectangle that encompasses all regions—that is, all the filled cells in the active worksheet—which in Figure 12-1 is A1:H10.

The techniques used to navigate regions are especially helpful if you typically work with large tables of data. Getting to the bottom row of a 500-row table is easier when you don't have to use the scroll bars. Read on to find out how.

Microsoft Office
Button

> **Note**
>
> The small square in the lower-right corner of the active cell is the *fill handle*. If the fill handle isn't visible on your screen, it means it isn't turned on. To turn it on, click the Microsoft Office Button, click Excel Options, click the Advanced category, and select the Enable Fill Handle And Cell Drag-And-Drop check box.

	A	B	C	D	E	F	G	H	I	J
	Regional Sales.xlsx									
1	Regional Sales									
2										
3	2008	Qtr 1	Qtr 2	Qtr 3	Qtr 4		Total	Average		
4	Region 1	1000	1050	1100	1150		4300	1075		
5	Region 2	1100	1150	1200	1250		4700	1175		
6	Region 3	1200	1250	1300	1350		5100	1275		
7	Region 4	1300	1350	1400	1450		5500	1375		
8										
9	Total	4600	4800	5000	5200		19600	4900		
10	Average	1150	1200	1250	1300		4900			
11										
12										
13										
14										
15										
16										

Figure 12-1 The four blocks of cells on this worksheet are separate regions.

Navigating Regions with the Keyboard

To move between the edges of regions, hold down the Ctrl key, and then press any of the arrow keys. For example, in Figure 12-1, cell A3 is the active cell; press Ctrl+Right Arrow to activate cell E3.

If a blank cell is active when you press Ctrl and an arrow key, Excel moves to the first filled cell in that direction or to the last available cell on the worksheet if it doesn't find any filled cells in that direction. In Figure 12-1, for example, if cell F3 is active when you press Ctrl+Right Arrow, the selection moves to cell G3; if Cell H3 is active, pressing Ctrl+Right Arrow activates cell XFD3—the last available cell in row A3. Just press Ctrl+Left Arrow to return to cell H3.

Navigating Regions with the Mouse

When you move the pointer over the edge of the active cell's border, the pointer changes from a plus sign to an arrow. With the arrow pointer visible, you can double-click any edge of the border to change the active cell to the cell on the edge of the current region in that direction—it is the same as pressing Ctrl and an arrow key in that direction. For example, if you double-click the bottom edge of the active cell in Figure 12-1, Excel selects cell A7.

The left side of the status bar displays the mode indicators in Table 12-1 when the corresponding keyboard mode is active.

Table 12-1 **Keyboard Modes**

Mode	Description
Extend Selection	Press F8 to turn on this mode, which you use to extend the current selection using the keyboard. (Make sure Scroll Lock is off.) This is the keyboard equivalent of selecting cells by dragging the mouse. Furthermore, unlike holding down the Shift key and pressing an arrow key, you can extend the range by pressing only one key at a time. Press F8 again to turn off Extend Selection mode.
Add To Selection	Press Shift+F8 to add more cells to the current selection using the keyboard. The cells need not be adjacent; after pressing Shift+F8, click any cell or drag through any range to add it to the selection. This is the keyboard equivalent of holding down Ctrl and selecting additional cells with the mouse.
Num Lock	Keeps your keypad in numeric entry mode. This is turned on by default, but its status is not usually displayed in the status bar. However, you can make it so by right-clicking the status bar anywhere and clicking Num Lock.
Fixed Decimal	To add a decimal point to the numeric entries in the current selection, click the Microsoft Office Button, click Excel Options, select the Advanced category, and select the Automatically Insert A Decimal Point check box in the Editing Options group. Excel places the decimal point in the location you specify in the Places box. For example, when you turn on Fixed Decimal mode, specify two decimal places, and type the number **12345** in a cell, the value 123.45 appears in the cell after you press Enter. Existing cell entries are not affected unless you edit them. To turn off Fixed Decimal mode, return to the Advanced category in the Excel Options dialog box, and clear the Automatically Insert A Decimal Point check box.
Caps Lock	Press the Caps Lock key to type text in capital letters. (This does not affect number and symbol keys.) To turn off Caps Lock mode, press the Caps Lock key again. The status of this mode does not usually display in the status bar, but you can make it so. Right-click the status bar anywhere, and click Caps Lock.
Scroll Lock	Press Scroll Lock to use the Page Up, Page Down, and arrow keys to move the viewed portion of the window without moving the active cell. When Scroll Lock mode is off, the active cell moves one page at a time when you press Page Up or Page Down and moves one cell at a time when you press one of the arrow keys. To turn off Scroll Lock mode, press the Scroll Lock key again.
End Mode	Press the End key, and then press an arrow key to move the selection to the edge of the region in that direction or to the last worksheet cell in that direction. This mode functions like holding down Ctrl and pressing an arrow key, except you need to press only one key at a time. To turn off End mode, press the End key again. End mode is also turned off after you press one of the arrow keys.
Overtype Mode	Click the formula bar or double-click a cell and press the Insert key to turn on Overtype mode (formerly known as Overwrite mode). Usually, new characters you type in the formula bar are inserted between existing characters. With Overtype mode turned on, the characters you type replace any existing characters to the right of the insertion point. Overtype mode turns off when you press Insert again or when you press Enter or one of the arrow keys to lock in the cell entry.

Navigating with Special Keys

Table 12-2 shows how you can use the Home and End keys alone and in conjunction with other keys to make selections and to move around a worksheet.

Table 12-2 Keyboard Shortcuts for Navigation

Press	To
Home	Move to the first cell in the current row.
Ctrl+Home	Move to cell A1.
Ctrl+End	Move to the last cell in the last column in the active area. For example, in Figure 12-1, pressing Ctrl+End selects cell H10.
End	Start End mode. Then press an arrow key to move around by cell region.
Scroll Lock+Home	Move to the first cell within the current window.
Scroll Lock+End	Move to the last cell within the current window.

Understanding Selection

Knowing how to select cells, rows, and columns in Excel is fundamental to using the program to its fullest potential. As you will see, there are many more ways to use selection techniques to isolate particular types of data, formats, objects, and even blank cells. Even though some of this information may seem basic, you'll probably encounter a few tips that will make your spreadsheet life a little easier:

- Before you can work with a cell or range, you must select it, and when you do, it becomes *active*.

- The reference of the active cell appears in the Name box at the left end of the formula bar.

- Only one cell can be active at a time, but you can select ranges of cells, and when you do, the active cell is in the upper-left corner of the selected range.

- Select all cells on a worksheet by clicking the Select All box located in the upper-left corner of your worksheet, where the column and row headings intersect.

For more about selection, read on.

Selecting with the Mouse

To select a range of cells, drag the mouse over the range. Alternatively, you can extend using two diagonal corners of the range you want to select. Click a cell at one corner of the range, and then press and hold the Shift key while clicking the cell diagonal to the first cell. For example, to extend the selection A1:B5 so it becomes A1:C10, hold down the Shift key, and click cell C10. When you need to select a large range, this technique is more efficient than dragging the mouse across the entire selection.

Zooming to Select Large Worksheet Areas

It's impossible to see an entire workbook on the screen. Knowing that, what do you do if you need to select a gigantic range of cells? You can drag the pointer past the window border and wait for the automatic scrolling to get you where you need to go, but this method can be frustrating if you have trouble managing the scrolling speed and keep overshooting the target.

A better method is to use the Zoom slider to get a bird's-eye view of the worksheet, as shown in Figure 12-2. Drag the Zoom slider at the bottom of the screen to the percentage you want. You can also click the Zoom percentage indicator adjacent to the slider to open the Zoom dialog box for more zooming options. The Zoom feature is limited to a range from 10 through 400 percent.

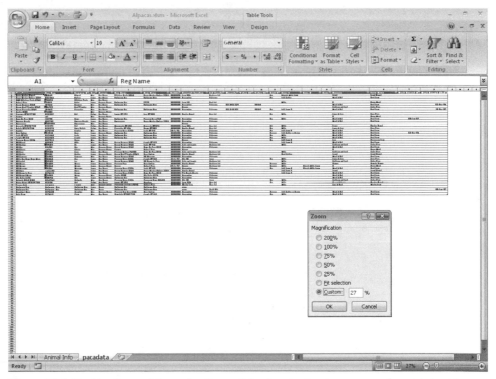

Figure 12-2 Use the Zoom slider or the Zoom dialog box to view large areas of a worksheet for easier selection.

Selecting Columns, Rows, and Multiple Areas

Multiple-area selections (also known as *nonadjacent* or *noncontiguous* selections) are selected cell ranges that do not encompass a single rectangular area, as shown in Figure 12-3. To select multiple-area ranges with the mouse, press the Ctrl key, and drag through each range you want to select. The first cell you click in the last range you select becomes the active cell. As you can see in Figure 12-3, cell G6 is the active cell.

Chapter 12

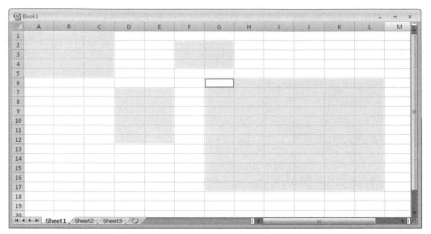

Figure 12-3 Hold down the Ctrl key and drag to select multiple-area ranges with the mouse.

To select an entire column or row, click the column or row heading. In other words, to select cells B1 through B1048576, click the heading for column B. The first visible cell in the column becomes the active cell, so if the first row visible on your screen is row 1048557, then cell B1048557 becomes active when you click the heading for column B, even though all the other cells in the column are selected. To select more than one adjacent column or row at a time, drag through the column or row headings, or click the heading at one end of the range, press Shift, and then click the heading at the other end. To select nonadjacent columns or rows, as shown in Figure 12-4, hold down Ctrl, and click each heading or drag through adjacent headings you want to select.

	A	B	C	D	E	F	G	H	I
1	Regional Sales								
2									
3	2008	Qtr 1	Qtr 2	Qtr 3	Qtr 4	Total	Average		
4	Region 1	1000	1050	1100	1150	4300	1075		
5	Region 2	1100	1150	1200	1250	4700	1175		
6	Region 3	1200	1250	1300	1350	5100	1275		
7	Region 4	1300	1350	1400	1450	5500	1375		
8	Total	4600	4800	5000	5200	19600	4900		
9	Average	1150	1200	1250	1300	4900			
10									
11									
12									
13									
14									
15									

Figure 12-4 Select entire columns and rows by clicking their headings, or hold down the Ctrl key while clicking to select nonadjacent rows and columns.

Use the following methods to select with the keyboard:

- To select an entire column with the keyboard, select any cell in the column, and press Ctrl+Spacebar.

- To select an entire row with the keyboard, select any cell in the row, and press Shift+Spacebar.

- To select several entire adjacent columns or rows with the keyboard, select any cell range that includes cells in each of the columns or rows, and then press Ctrl+Spacebar or Shift+Spacebar, respectively. For example, to select columns B, C, and D, select B4:D4 (or any range that includes cells in these three columns), and then press Ctrl+Spacebar.

- To select the entire worksheet with the keyboard, press Ctrl+Shift+Spacebar.

Selecting Regions

If you hold down the Shift key as you double-click the edge of an active cell's border, Excel selects all the cells from the current selection to the next edge of the region in that direction. The cell from which you start the selection process remains the active cell.

Using the Find & Select Commands

At the right end of the Home tab on the Ribbon, the Find & Select menu displays several helpful selection commands, as shown in Figure 12-5. In the middle of the menu are five commands that used to be buried in dialog boxes and have been promoted in Excel because of their widespread use: Formulas, Comments, Conditional Formatting, Constants, and Data Validation.

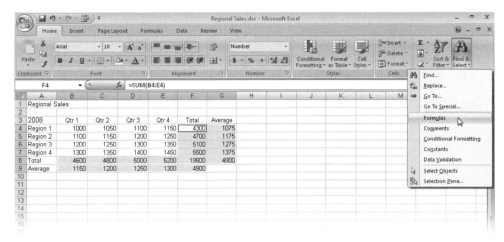

Figure 12-5 Use the Find & Select commands to zero in on specific items.

In Figure 12-5, we used the Formulas command to select all the formulas on the worksheet, which are highlighted by multiple selection rectangles. You can use these specialized selection commands for various purposes such as applying specific formatting to formulas and constants or auditing worksheets for errant conditional formatting or data validation cells.

The two Go To commands are also helpful for finding and selecting a variety of worksheet elements. To quickly move to and select a cell or a range of cells, click Go To (or press F5) to open the Go To dialog box; then type a cell reference, range reference, or defined range name in the Reference box, and press Enter. You can also use Go To to extend a selection. For example, to select A1:Z100, you can click A1, open the Go To dialog box, type **Z100**, and then press Shift+Enter.

For more information about defined range names and references, see "Naming Cells and Cell Ranges" on page 407 and "Using Cell References in Formulas" on page 394.

To move to another worksheet in the same workbook, open the Go To dialog box, and type the name of the worksheet, followed by an exclamation point and a cell name or reference. For example, to go to cell D5 on a worksheet called Sheet2, type **Sheet2!D5**. To move to another worksheet in another open workbook, open the Go To dialog box, and type the name of the workbook in brackets, followed by the name of the worksheet, an exclamation point, and a cell name or reference. For example, to go to cell D5 on a worksheet called Sheet2 in an open workbook called Sales.xlsx, type **[Sales.xlsx]Sheet2!D5**.

Excel keeps track of the last four locations from which you used the Go To command and lists them in the Go To dialog box. You can use this list to move among these locations in your worksheet. This is handy when you're working on a large worksheet or jumping around among multiple locations and worksheets in a workbook. Figure 12-6 shows the Go To dialog box displaying four previous locations.

Figure 12-6 The Go To and Go To Special dialog boxes are your selection transporters.

> **Note**
>
> In the Go To dialog box, Excel displays in the Reference box the cell or range from which you just moved. This way, you can easily move back and forth between two locations by pressing F5 and then Enter repeatedly.

Selecting with Go To Special

When you click the Special button in the Go To dialog box (or the Go To Special command on the Find & Select menu), the dialog box shown on the right of Figure 12-6 opens, presenting additional selection options. You can think of the Go To Special dialog box as "Select Special," because you can use it to quickly find and select cells that meet certain specifications.

After you specify one of the Go To Special options and click OK, Excel highlights the cell or cells that match the criteria. With a few exceptions, if you select a range of cells before you open the Go To Special dialog box, Excel searches only the selected range; if the current selection is a single cell or one or more graphic objects, Excel searches the entire active worksheet. The following are guidelines for using the Go To Special options:

- *Constants* refers to any cell containing static data such as numbers or text, but not formulas.

- *Current Region* is handy when you're working in a large, complex worksheet and need to select blocks of cells. (Recall that a *region* is defined as a rectangular block of cells bounded by blank rows, blank columns, or worksheet borders.)

- *Current Array* selects all the cells in an array if the selected cell is part of an array range.

- *Last Cell* selects the cell in the lower-right corner of the range that encompasses all the cells that contain data, comments, or formats. When you select Last Cell, Excel finds the last cell in the active area of the worksheet, not the lower-right corner of the current selection.

- *Visible Cells Only* excludes from the current selection any cells in hidden rows or columns.

- *Objects* selects all graphic objects in your worksheet, regardless of the current selection.

- *Conditional Formats* selects only those cells that have conditional formatting applied. Or you can click the Home tab, and click the Conditional Formatting command on the Find & Select menu.

- *Data Validation* using the All option selects all cells to which data validation has been applied; Data Validation using the Same option selects only cells with the same validation settings as the currently selected cell. You can also click the

Home tab, and click the Data Validation command on the Find & Select menu, which uses the All option.

Navigating Multiple Selections

Some of the Go To Special options—such as Formulas, Comments, Precedents, and Dependents—might cause Excel to select multiple nonadjacent cell ranges. After you make the selection, you might want to change the active cell without losing the multi-selection. Or you might want to type entries into multiple ranges you select so you don't have to reach for the mouse. Either way, you can move between selected cells. For example, the worksheet shown here has multiple ranges selected:

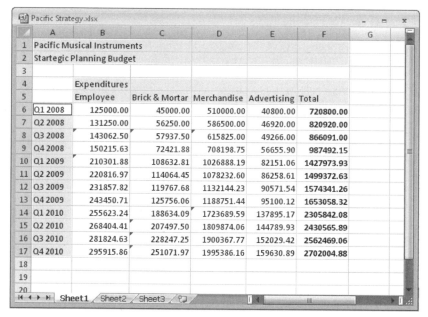

To move the active cell through these ranges without losing the selection, press Enter to move down or to the right one cell at a time; press Shift+Enter to move up or to the left one cell at a time. Or press Tab to move to the right or down; press Shift+Tab to move to the left or up. Pretty cool, eh? You might not think so until you have a lot of noncontiguous, noncolumnar data entry to do, but trust us. So, in the previous worksheet, if you press Enter until cell A17 is selected, the next time you press Enter the selection jumps to the beginning of the next selected region, in this case cell A1. Subsequently pressing Enter selects A2, then B1, then B2, and so on, until the end of the region—cell F2. Then the selection jumps to the next region, cell B4.

Selecting Precedents and Dependents

The Precedents and Dependents options in the Go To Special dialog box let you find cells that are used by a formula or to find cells on which a formula depends. To use the Precedents and Dependents options, first select the cell whose precedents or dependents you want to select. When searching for precedents or dependents, Excel always searches the entire worksheet. When you select the Precedents or Dependents option, Excel activates the Direct Only and All Levels options:

- Direct Only finds only those cells that directly refer to or that directly depend on the active cell.

- All Levels locates direct precedents and dependents plus those cells indirectly related to the active cell.

Depending on the task, you might find the built-in auditing features of Excel to be just the trick. On the Formulas tab on the Ribbon, the Formula Auditing group offers the Track Precedents and Track Dependents buttons. Rather than selecting all such cells like the Go To Special command, clicking these buttons draws arrows showing path and direction in relation to the selected cell.

Go To Special Keyboard Shortcuts

If you do a lot of "going to," you'll want to learn a few of these keyboard shortcuts, which will speed things up considerably:

- Press Ctrl+Shift+* to select the current region.
- Press Ctrl+/ to select the current array.
- Press Alt+; to select the visible cells only.
- Press Ctrl+[to select the direct precedents.
- Press Ctrl+Shift+{ to select all the precedents.
- Press Ctrl+] to select the direct dependents.
- Press Ctrl+Shift+} to select all the dependents.
- Press Ctrl+\ to select row differences.
- Press Ctrl+Shift+| to select column differences.

Selecting Row or Column Differences

The Row Differences and Column Differences options in the Go To Special dialog box compare the entries in a range of cells to spot potential inconsistencies. To use these debugging options, select the range before displaying the Go To Special dialog box. The position of the active cell in your selection determines which cells Excel uses to make its comparisons. When searching for row differences, Excel compares the cells in the selection with the cells in the same column as the active cell. When searching for column differences, Excel compares the cells in the selection with the cells in the same row as the active cell.

In addition to other variations, the Row Differences and Column Differences options look for differences in references and select those cells that don't conform to the comparison cell. They also verify that all the cells in the selected range contain the same type of entries. For example, if the comparison cell contains a SUM function, Excel flags any cells that contain a function, formula, or value other than SUM. If the comparison cell contains a constant text or numeric value, Excel flags any cells in the selected range that don't match the comparison value. The options, however, are not case-sensitive.

Techniques for Entering Data

Excel accepts two types of cell entries: constants and formulas. Constants fall into three main categories: numeric values, text values (also called *labels* or *strings*), and date/time values. Excel also recognizes two special types of constants called *logical values* and *error values*.

Making Entries in Cells and in the Formula Bar

To make an entry in a cell, just select the cell, and start typing. As you type, the entry appears both in the formula bar and in the active cell. The flashing vertical bar in the active cell is called the *insertion point*.

After you finish typing, you must "lock in" the entry to store it permanently in the cell by pressing Enter. Pressing Enter normally causes the active cell to move down one row. You can change this so that when you press Enter, either the active cell doesn't change or it moves to an adjacent cell in another direction. Click the Microsoft Office Button, click Excel Options, select the Advanced category, and either clear the After Pressing Enter, Move Selection check box or change the selection in the Direction drop-down list. You also lock in an entry when you move the selection to a different cell by pressing Tab, Shift+Tab, Shift+Enter, or an arrow key, among other methods, after you type the entry, as shown in Table 12-3.

Table 12-3 **Keyboard Shortcuts for Data Entry**

Press	To
Enter	Activate the cell below the active cell, or whatever direction you have selected for the After Pressing Enter, Move Selection check box in the Advanced category in the Excel Options dialog box.
Shift+Enter	Activate the cell above the active cell, or the opposite of the direction set for the After Pressing Enter, Move Selection check box in the Advanced category in the Excel Options dialog box.
Tab	Activate the cell one column to the right of the active cell.
Shift+Tab	Activate the cell one column to the left of the active cell.
Arrow Key	Activate the adjacent cell in the direction of the arrow key you press.

When you begin typing an entry, three buttons appear on the formula bar: Cancel, Enter, and Insert Function. When typing a formula where the entry begins with an equal sign (=), a plus sign (+), or a minus sign (−), a drop-down list of frequently used functions becomes available, as shown in Figure 12-7.

For more about editing formulas, see Chapter 13, "Building Formulas."

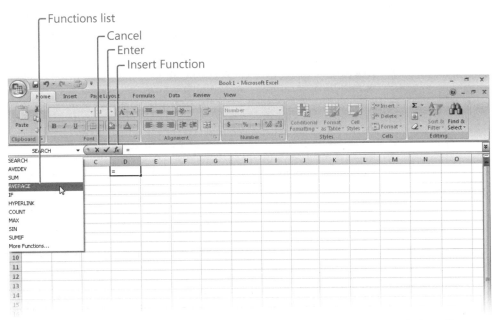

Figure 12-7 When you start entering a formula by typing an equal sign, the formula bar offers ways to help you finish it.

Chapter 12

Entering Simple Numeric and Text Values

An entry that includes only numerals 0 through 9 and certain special characters, such as + – E e ( ) . , $ % and /, is a numeric value. An entry that includes almost any other character is a text value. Table 12-4 lists some examples of numeric and text values.

Table 12-4 Examples of Numeric and Text Values

Numeric Values	Text Values
123	Sales
123.456	B-1
$1.98	Eleven
1%	123 Main Street
1.23E+12	No. 324

Using Special Characters

A number of characters have special effects in Excel. Here are some guidelines for using special characters:

- If you begin a numeric entry with a plus sign, Excel drops the plus sign.

- If you begin a numeric entry with a minus sign, Excel interprets the entry as a negative number and retains the sign.

- In a numeric entry, the characters E and e specify an exponent used in scientific notation. For example, Excel interprets 1E6 as 1,000,000 (1 times 10 to the sixth power), which is displayed in Excel as 1.00E+06. To enter a negative exponential number, type a minus sign before the exponent. For example, 1E–6 (1 times 10 to the negative sixth power) equals 0.000001 and is displayed in Excel as 1.00E–06.

- Excel interprets numeric constants enclosed in parentheses as negative numbers, which is a common accounting practice. For example, Excel interprets (100) as –100.

- You can use decimal points and commas as you normally would. When you type numbers that include commas as separators, however, the commas appear in the cell but not in the formula bar; this is the same as if you had applied one of the built-in Excel Number formats. For example, if you type **1,234.56**, the value 1234.56 appears in the formula bar.

- If you begin a numeric entry with a dollar sign ($), Excel assigns a Currency format to the cell. For example, if you type **$123456**, Excel displays $123,456 in the cell and 123456 in the formula bar. In this case, Excel adds the comma to the worksheet display because it's part of the Currency format.

- If you end a numeric entry with a percent sign (%), Excel assigns a Percentage format to the cell. For example, if you type **23%**, Excel displays 23% in the formula bar and assigns a Percentage format to the cell, which also displays 23%.

- If you use a slash (/) in a numeric entry and the string cannot be interpreted as a date, Excel interprets the number as a fraction. For example, if you type **11 5/8** (with a space between the number and the fraction), Excel assigns a Fraction format to the entry, meaning the formula bar displays 11.625 and the cell displays 11 5/8.

> **Note**
>
> To make sure Excel does not interpret a fraction as a date, precede the fraction with a zero and a space. For example, to prevent Excel from interpreting the fraction 1/2 as January 2, type **0 1/2**.

Understanding the Difference Between Displayed Values and Underlying Values

Although you can type 32,767 characters in a cell, a numeric cell entry can maintain precision to a maximum of only 15 digits. This means you can type numbers longer than 15 digits in a cell, but Excel converts any digits after the 15th to zeros. If you are working with figures greater than 999 trillion or decimals smaller than trillionths, perhaps you need to look into alternative solutions, such as a Cray supercomputer.

If you type a number that is too long to appear in a cell, Excel converts it to scientific notation in the cell, if you haven't applied any other formatting. Excel adjusts the precision of the scientific notation depending on the cell width. If you type a very large or very small number that is longer than the formula bar, Excel displays it in the formula bar using scientific notation. In Figure 12-8, we typed the same number in both cell A1 and cell B1; however, because cell B1 is wider, Excel displays more of the number but still displays it using scientific notation.

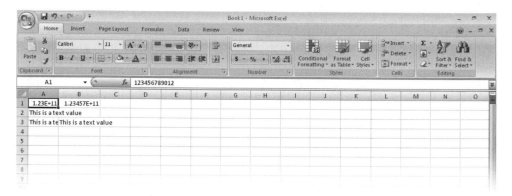

Figure 12-8 Because the number 123,456,789,012 is too long to fit in either cell A1 or cell B1, Excel displays it in scientific notation.

The values that appear in formatted cells are called *displayed values*; the values that are stored in cells and appear in the formula bar are called *underlying values*. The number of digits that appear in a cell—its displayed value—depends on the width of the column and any formatting you have applied to the cell. If you reduce the width of a column that contains a long entry, Excel might display a rounded-off version of the number, a string of number signs (#), or scientific notation, depending on the display format you're using.

Note

If you see a series of number signs (######) in a cell where you expect to see a number, increase the width of the cell to see the numbers again.

TROUBLESHOOTING

My formulas don't add numbers correctly.

Suppose, for example, you write a formula and Excel tells you that $2.23 plus $5.55 equals $7.79, when it should be $7.78. Investigate your underlying values. If you use currency formatting, numbers with more than three digits to the right of the decimal point are rounded to two decimal places. In this example, if the underlying vales are 2.234 and 5.552, the result is 7.786, which rounds to 7.79. You can either change the decimal places or select the Set Precision As Displayed check box (click the Microsoft Office Button, click Excel Options, click the Advanced category, and look in the When Calculating This Workbook area) to eliminate the problem. Be careful if you select Set Precision As Displayed, however, because it permanently changes all the underlying values in your worksheet to their displayed values.

Creating Long Text Values

If you type text that is too long for Excel to display in a single cell, Excel overlaps the adjacent cells, but the text remains stored in the original cell. If you then type text in a cell that is overlapped by another cell, the overlapping text appears truncated, as shown in cell B3 in Figure 12-8. But don't worry—it's still all there.

> **Note**
>
> The easiest way to eliminate overlapping text is to widen the column by double-clicking the column border in the heading. For example, in Figure 12-8, when you double-click the line between the A and the B in the column heading, the width of column A adjusts to accommodate the longest entry in the column.

Using Text Wrapping

If you have long text entries, text wrapping can make them easier to read. Text wrapping lets you type long strings of text that wrap onto two or more lines within the same cell rather than overlapping adjacent cells. Select the cells where you want to use wrapping, then click the Home tab on the Ribbon, and finally click the Wrap Text button, as shown in Figure 12-9. To accommodate the extra lines, Excel increases the height of the row.

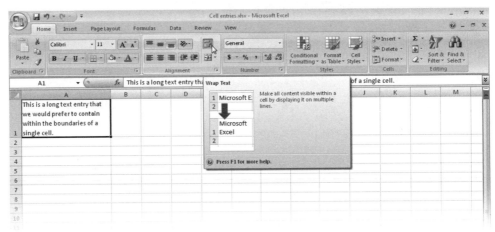

Figure 12-9 Click the Wrap Text button to force long text entries to wrap within a single cell.

Understanding Numeric Text Entries

Sometimes you might want to type special characters that Excel does not normally treat as plain text. For example, you might want +1 to appear in a cell. If you type **+1**, Excel interprets this as a numeric entry and drops the plus sign (as stated earlier). In addition, Excel normally ignores leading zeros in numbers, such as 01234. You can force Excel to accept special characters as text by using numeric text entries.

To enter a combination of text and numbers, such as G234, just type it. Because this entry includes a nonnumeric character, Excel interprets it as a text value. To create a text entry that consists entirely of numbers, you can precede the entry with a text-alignment prefix character, such as an apostrophe. You can also enter it as a formula by typing an equal sign and enclosing the entry with quotation marks. For example, to enter the number 01234 as text so the leading zero is displayed, type either **'01234** or **="01234"** in a cell. Whereas numeric entries are normally right-aligned, a numeric text entry is left-aligned in the cell just like regular text, as shown in Figure 12-10.

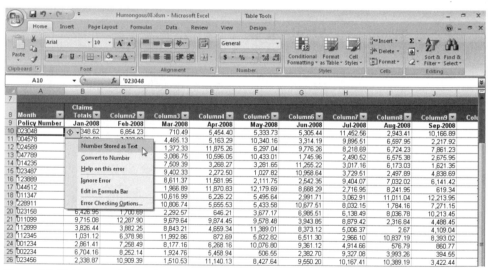

Figure 12-10 We typed the policy numbers in column A as text.

Text-alignment prefix characters, like formula components, appear in the formula bar but not in the cell. Table 12-5 lists all the text-alignment prefix characters.

Table 12-5 Text-Alignment Prefix Characters

Character	Action
' (apostrophe)	Left-aligns data in the cell
" (quotation mark)	Right-aligns data in the cell (see note)
^ (caret)	Centers data in the cell (see note)
\ (backslash)	Repeats characters across the cell (see note)

Only the apostrophe text-alignment prefix character always works with numeric or text entries. The caret, backslash, and quotation mark characters work only if, before typing them, you click the Microsoft Office Button, click Excel Options, select the Advanced category, and then scroll down to the Lotus Compatibility area and select the Transition Navigation Keys check box.

You'll find the Humongous08.xlsx file in the Sample Files section of the companion CD.

When you create a numeric entry that starts with an alignment prefix character, a small flag appears in the upper-left corner of the cell, indicating that the cell has a problem you might need to address. When you select the cell, an error-type smart tag appears to the right. Clicking this smart tag displays a menu of specific commands (refer to Figure 12-10). Because the apostrophe was intentional, you can click Ignore Error.

> **Note**
> If a range of cells shares the same problem, as in column A in Figure 12-10, you can select the entire cell range and use the smart tag action menu to resolve the problem in all the cells at the same time.

Entering Symbols

If you ever want to use characters in Excel that are not on your standard computer keyboard, you're in luck. Clicking the Insert tab on the Ribbon and then clicking the Symbol button gives you access to the complete character set for every installed font on your computer. Figure 12-11 shows the Symbol dialog box.

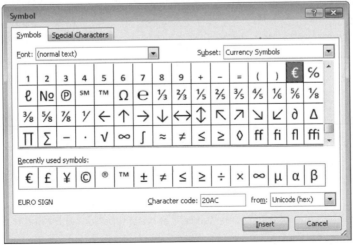

Figure 12-11 You can insert characters from the extended character sets of any installed font.

On the Symbols tab, select the font from the Font drop-down list; the entire character set appears. You can jump to specific areas in the character set using the Subset drop-down list, which also indicates the area of the character set you are viewing if you are using the scroll bar to browse through the available characters. The Character Code box displays the code of the selected character. You can also highlight a character in the display area by typing a character code number. You can select decimal or hexadecimal ASCII character encoding or Unicode using the From drop-down list. If you choose Unicode, you can select from a number of additional character subsets in the Subset drop-down list. The Special Characters tab in the Symbol dialog box gives you quick access to a number of commonly used characters, such as the em dash, the ellipsis, and the trademark and copyright symbols.

Making Entries in Ranges

To make a number of entries in a range of adjacent cells, first select those cells. Then press Enter, Shift+Enter, Tab, or Shift+Tab to move the active cell within the range. For example, to fill in a range of selected cells, select the range, and begin typing entries, as shown in Figure 12-12. Each time you press Enter, the active cell moves to the next cell in the range. The active cell never leaves the selected range until you specifically select another cell or range; in other words, when you reach the edge of the range and press Enter, the active cell jumps to the beginning of the next column or row. You can continue making entries this way until you fill the entire range. The advantage of this trick is that you don't need to take your hands off the keyboard to select cells with the mouse when making many entries at once.

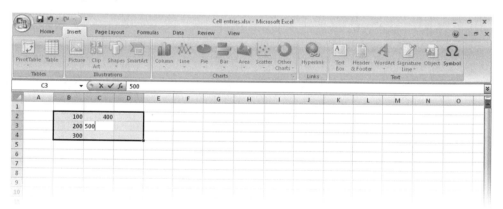

Figure 12-12 You can easily make entries in a range of cells by first selecting the entire range.

> **Note**
>
> To enter the same value in all selected cells at once, type your entry, and then press Ctrl+Enter.

Editing and Undoing Entries

You can correct simple errors as you type by pressing Backspace before you press Enter to lock in the cell entry, which erases the character to the left of the insertion point. However, to make changes to entries you have already locked in, you first need to enter Edit mode. (The mode indicator at the lower-left corner of the status bar has to change from Ready to Edit.) Use one of the following techniques to enter Edit mode:

- To edit a cell using the mouse, double-click the cell, and position the insertion point at the location of the error.

- To edit a cell using the keyboard, select the cell, and press F2. Use the arrow keys to position the insertion point in the cell.

By selecting several characters before you begin typing, you can replace several characters at once. To select several characters within a cell using the keyboard, enter Edit mode, place the insertion point just before or just after the characters you want to replace, and press Shift+Left Arrow or Shift+Right Arrow to extend your selection.

> **Note**
>
> If you don't want to take your hands off the keyboard to move from one end of a cell entry to the other, press Home or End while in Edit mode. To move through an entry one "word" at a time, press Ctrl+Left Arrow or Ctrl+Right Arrow.

If you need to erase the entire contents of the active cell, press Delete, or press Backspace and then Enter. Pressing Enter acts as a confirmation of the deletion. If you press Backspace accidentally, click the Cancel button or press Esc to restore the contents of the cell before pressing Enter. You can also erase the entire contents of a cell by selecting the cell and typing the new contents to replace the old. Excel erases the previous entry as soon as you begin typing. To revert to the original entry, press Esc before you press Enter.

Undo

Redo

To restore an entry after you press Delete or after you have locked in a new entry, click Edit, Undo; alternatively, press Ctrl+Z. The Undo command remembers the last 16 actions you performed. If you press Ctrl+Z repeatedly, each of the last 16 actions is undone, one after the other, in reverse order. You can also click the small arrow next to the Undo button to display a list of remembered actions. Drag the mouse to select one or more actions, as shown in Figure 12-13. After you release the mouse, all the selected actions are undone. The Redo button works the same way; you can quickly redo what you have just undone, if necessary.

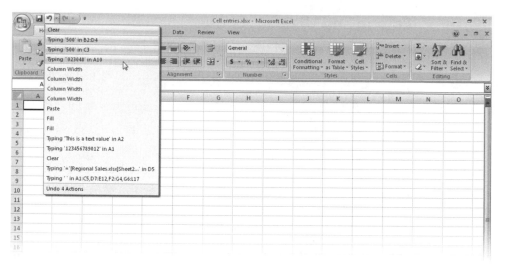

Figure 12-13 Click the small arrow next to the Undo button to select any number of the last 16 actions to undo at once.

Smart Tags

Smart tags give you instant access to commands and actions that are relevant to the current task. Many editing actions, such as copying and pasting cells, invoke a smart tag that appears adjacent to the last cell edited. If you click the tag, a smart tag action menu offers retroactive editing options:

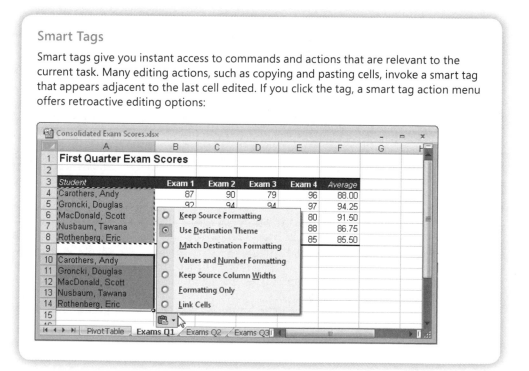

Managing Worksheets

You can have as many worksheets in a workbook as your computer's memory will allow (probably hundreds of worksheets, depending on how much data each contains); consequently, you don't need to try to fit everything onto one worksheet. The following sections present the features you can use to organize your worksheet world.

Inserting and Deleting Worksheets

To insert a new worksheet into an existing workbook, click the Insert Worksheet tab, which you can see in Figure 12-14 on the left. The new sheet tab appears to the right of the last worksheet in the workbook. You can also quickly insert worksheets by right-clicking any sheet tab to display the shortcut menu shown in Figure 12-14 on the right. Clicking Insert on this menu opens the Insert dialog box containing other items you can insert besides blank worksheets, including templates and Excel 4.0 macro sheets.

Figure 12-14 To insert a blank worksheet, click the Insert Worksheet tab, or right-click any sheet tab to display a worksheet-focused shortcut menu.

In addition to providing a convenient method for inserting, deleting, renaming, moving, and copying worksheets, this shortcut menu contains the Select All Sheets command. As its name indicates, you use this command to select all the worksheets in a workbook, which you will need to do to perform certain functions, such as copying or formatting, on all the worksheets at once. The View Code command on this shortcut menu launches the Visual Basic Editor, showing the Code window for the current worksheet.

> **Note**
>
> As you can see in the shortcut menu shown in Figure 12-14, the sheet tab shortcut menu also contains a Tab Color command. If you are a visually oriented person, you might find color-coding your worksheets to be as useful as changing the worksheet names.

You can also add multiple worksheets to a workbook at the same time. To do so, click a sheet tab, press Shift, and then click other sheet tabs to select a range of worksheets—the same number you want to insert—before clicking Insert Worksheet on the sheet tab shortcut menu. (Notice that Excel adds *[Group]* to the workbook title in the window title bar, indicating you have selected a group of worksheets for editing.) Excel inserts the same number of new worksheets as you selected and places them in front of the first worksheet in the selected range. Note that this does not copy the selected worksheets; it is just a way of telling Excel how many fresh, blank worksheets you want to insert at once.

You cannot undo the insertion of a new worksheet. If you do need to delete a worksheet, right-click its sheet tab, and click Delete. If you want to delete more than one worksheet, you can hold down Shift to select a range of worksheets, or you can hold down Ctrl and select nonadjacent worksheets, before you click Delete. Be careful! You cannot retrieve a worksheet after you have deleted it.

Naming and Renaming Worksheets

Notice that Excel numbers the new worksheets based on the number of worksheets in the workbook. If your workbook contains three worksheets, the first worksheet you insert is Sheet4, the next is Sheet5, and so on. If you grow weary of seeing Sheet1, Sheet2, and so on, in your workbooks, you can give your worksheets more imaginative and helpful names by double-clicking the tab and typing a new name.

You can use up to 31 characters in your worksheet names. Nevertheless, you should remember that the name you use determines the width of the corresponding sheet tab, as shown in Figure 12-15. Therefore, you might want to keep your worksheet names concise so you can see more than a couple of sheet tabs at a time.

Figure 12-15 Double-click the sheet tab to type a new name. You might want to keep it short.

Moving and Copying Worksheets

As you might expect, Excel provides an easy way to move a worksheet from one place to another in the same workbook. In fact, all you have to do is click a sheet tab to select it and then drag it to its new location. Figure 12-16 shows this process. When you drag a worksheet, a small worksheet icon appears, and a tiny arrow indicates where the worksheet will be inserted in the tab order.

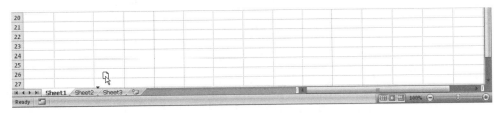

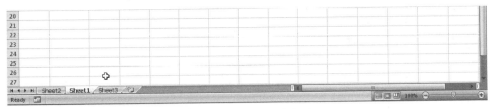

Figure 12-16 Click and drag sheet tabs to rearrange worksheets.

When you move worksheets, remember the following tips:

- If you want to move a worksheet to a location that isn't currently visible on your screen, drag past the visible tabs in either direction. The sheet tabs scroll in the direction you drag.

- You can move several worksheets at the same time. When you select several worksheets and drag, the pointer changes to look like a small stack of pages.

- You can copy worksheets using similar mouse techniques. First, select the worksheets you want to copy, and then hold down Ctrl while you drag the worksheets to the new location. When you copy a worksheet, an identical worksheet appears in the new location. Excel appends a number in parentheses to the copy's name to distinguish it from the original worksheet. For example, making a copy of Sheet1 results in a new worksheet named Sheet1 (2).

- You can move or copy nonadjacent worksheets at the same time by pressing Ctrl while you click to select the sheet tabs. Before dragging, release the Ctrl key to move the selected worksheets, or keep holding it down to create copies.

- You can click Move Or Copy on the sheet tab shortcut menu to handle similar worksheet management functions, including moving and copying worksheets between workbooks.

Chapter 12

Dragging Worksheets Between Workbooks

You can move and copy worksheets between workbooks by dragging. You use the same methods to move and copy that you use for worksheets in the same workbook. For example, with two workbooks arranged horizontally in the workspace, you can move a worksheet from one to the other by dragging it to the new location in the other workbook:

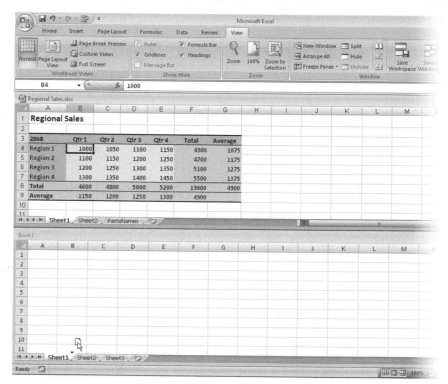

Note that you must arrange the two workbooks together on your screen to allow this to work. To do so, click the View tab on the Ribbon, then click the Arrange All button in the Window group, and finally select an arrangement option.

Viewing Worksheets

Excel provides a few helpful features you can use to change the way worksheets display. You can set up your workspace for specific tasks and then save the same view settings for the next time you need to perform the same task.

Splitting Worksheets into Panes

Worksheet panes let you view different areas of your worksheet simultaneously. You can split any worksheet in a workbook vertically, horizontally, or both vertically and horizontally, with synchronized scrolling capabilities. On the worksheet shown in Figure 12-17, columns B through M and rows 4 through 37 contain data. Column N and row 38 contain the totals. In Normal view, it's impossible to see the totals and the headings at the same time.

Horizontal split bar

	A	B	C	D	E	F
1	2008 Product Sales Projections					
3		Jan	Feb	Mar	Apr	May
4	Product 1	$7,317	$6,329	$2,110	$1,710	$2,984
5	Product 2	$2,814	$2,336	$9,199	$6,176	$2,842
6	Product 3	$2,875	$4,107	$5,528	$8,599	$9,769
7	Product 4	$4,365	$2,202	$5,607	$8,340	$5,832
8	Product 5	$9,451	$3,398	$3,472	$4,585	$3,453
9	Product 6	$7,810	$6,982	$7,018	$1,885	$4,336
10	Product 7	$9,976	$7,267	$5,006	$6,692	$8,388
11	Product 8	$2,536	$4,100	$6,328	$3,807	$7,850
12	Product 9	$3,104	$2,467	$5,349	$7,142	$9,305
13	Product 10	$5,442	$2,783	$1,642	$1,582	$2,456
14	Product 11	$7,816	$8,626	$6,938	$5,200	$8,197
15	Product 12	$2,786	$6,720	$4,754	$3,556	$2,535
16	Product 13	$7,363	$3,248	$7,295	$9,822	$2,076
17	Product 14	$9,917	$5,004	$6,873	$8,719	$8,399
18	Product 15	$6,593	$8,499	$1,404	$1,749	$5,999
19	Product 16	$2,036	$5,359	$8,656	$4,240	$2,690

Sheet1 / Sheet2 / **Sheet3**

Vertical Split bar

Figure 12-17 You can scroll to display the totals in column N or row 38, but you won't be able to see the headings.

You'll find the 2008 Projections.xlsx file in the Sample Files section of the companion CD.

It would be easier to navigate the worksheet in Figure 12-17 if it were split into panes. To do so, click the View tab on the Ribbon, and click Split; the window divides into both vertical and horizontal panes simultaneously, as shown in Figure 12-18. You can use the mouse to drag either split bar to where you need it. If you double-click either split bar icon (located in the scroll bars, as shown in Figure 12-17), you divide the window approximately in half. When you rest your pointer on a split bar, it changes to a double-headed arrow.

> **Note**
>
> Before clicking Window, Split or double-clicking one of the split bar icons, select a cell in the worksheet where you want the split to occur. This splits the worksheet immediately to the left or above the selected cell. If cell A1 is active, the split occurs in the center of the worksheet. In Figure 12-17, we selected cell B4 before choosing the Split command, which resulted in the split panes shown in Figure 12-18.

	A	B	C	D	E	F
1	2008 P	roduct Sales Projections				
3		Jan	Feb	Mar	Apr	May
4	Product 1	$7,317	$6,329	$2,110	$1,710	$2,984
5	Product 2	$2,814	$2,336	$9,199	$6,176	$2,842
6	Product 3	$2,875	$4,107	$5,528	$8,599	$9,769
7	Product 4	$4,365	$2,202	$5,607	$8,340	$5,832
8	Product 5	$9,451	$3,398	$3,472	$4,585	$3,453
9	Product 6	$7,810	$6,982	$7,018	$1,885	$4,336
10	Product 7	$9,976	$7,267	$5,006	$6,692	$8,388
11	Product 8	$2,536	$4,100	$6,328	$3,807	$7,850
12	Product 9	$3,104	$2,467	$5,349	$7,142	$9,305
13	Product 10	$5,442	$2,783	$1,642	$1,582	$2,456
14	Product 11	$7,816	$8,626	$6,938	$5,200	$8,197
15	Product 12	$2,786	$6,720	$4,754	$3,556	$2,535
16	Product 13	$7,363	$3,248	$7,295	$9,822	$2,076
17	Product 14	$9,917	$5,004	$6,873	$8,719	$8,399
18	Product 15	$6,593	$8,499	$1,404	$1,749	$5,999
19	Product 16	$2,036	$5,359	$8,656	$4,240	$2,690

Figure 12-18 With the window split, you can scroll each pane independently.

With the window split into four panes, as shown in Figure 12-18, four scroll bars are available (if not visible)—two for each direction. Now you can use the scroll bars to view columns A through N without losing sight of the product headings in column A. In addition, when you scroll vertically between rows 1 and 38, you'll always see the corresponding headings in row 3.

After a window is split, you can reposition the split bars by dragging. If you are ready to return your screen to its normal appearance, click the Split button again to remove all the split bars. You can also remove an individual split by double-clicking the split bar or by dragging the split bar to the top or right side of the window.

Freezing Panes

 After you've split a window into panes, you can freeze the left panes, the top panes, or both panes by clicking the View tab on the Ribbon, clicking Freeze Panes, and selecting the corresponding option, as shown in Figure 12-19. When you do so, you lock the data in the frozen panes into place. As you can see in Figure 12-19, the pane divider lines have changed from thick, three-dimensional lines to thin lines.

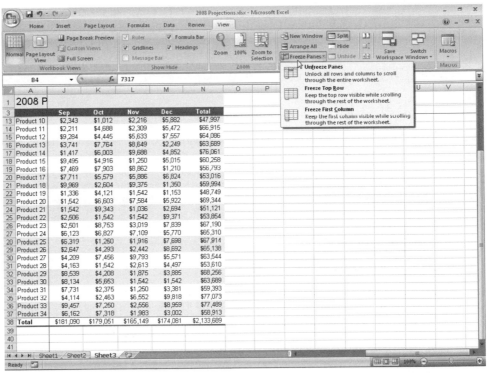

Figure 12-19 Freezing panes locks the top and/or left panes of a split window.

> **Note**
>
> You can split and freeze panes simultaneously at the selected cell by clicking Freeze Panes without first splitting the worksheet into panes. If you use this method, you will simultaneously unfreeze and remove the panes when you click Unfreeze Panes. (The command name changes when panes are frozen.)

Notice also that in Figure 12-18, the sheet tabs are invisible because the horizontal scroll bar for the lower-left pane is so small. After freezing the panes, as shown in Figure 12-19, the scroll bar returns to normal, and the sheet tabs reappear.

> **Note**
>
> To open another worksheet in the workbook if the sheet tabs are not visible, press Ctrl+Page Up to open the previous worksheet or Ctrl+Page Down to open the next worksheet.

After you freeze panes, scrolling within each pane works differently. You cannot scroll the upper-left panes in any direction. You can only scroll the columns (right and left) in the upper-right pane and only the rows (up and down) in the lower-left pane. You can scroll the lower-right pane in either direction.

INSIDE OUT   **Make Frozen Panes Easier to See**

Generally speaking, all the tasks you perform with panes work better when the windows are frozen. Unfortunately, it's harder to tell that the window is split when the panes are frozen because the thin frozen pane lines look just like cell borders. To make frozen panes easier to see, you can use a formatting clue you will always recognize. For example, select all the heading rows and columns, and fill them with a particular color.

Zooming Worksheets

As mentioned previously, you can use the Zoom control in the bottom-right corner of the screen or click the View tab on the Ribbon and use the two Zoom buttons to change the size of your worksheet display. Clicking a Zoom button displays a dialog box containing one enlargement option, three reduction options, and a Fit Selection option that determines the necessary reduction or enlargement needed to display the currently selected cells. Use the Custom box to specify any zoom percentage from 10 through 400 percent. The Zoom To Selection button enlarges or reduces the size of the worksheet to make all the selected cells visible on the screen. For example, clicking Zoom To Selection with a single cell selected zooms to the maximum 400 percent, centered on the selected cell (as much as possible) in an attempt to fill the screen with the selection.

> Note
>
> The Zoom command affects all the selected worksheets; therefore, if you group several worksheets, Excel will display all of them at the selected Zoom percentage.

For example, to view the entire worksheet shown in Figure 12-17, you can try different Zoom percentages until you get the results you want. Better still, select the entire active area of the worksheet, and click the Zoom To Selection button. Now the entire worksheet appears on the screen, as shown in Figure 12-20. Note that the Zoom percentage resulting from clicking Zoom To Selection is 85 percent, displayed next to the Zoom control at the bottom of the screen.

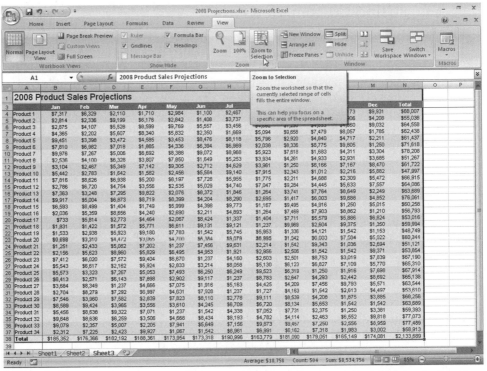

Figure 12-20 Click the Zoom To Selection button with the active area selected to view it all on the screen.

Of course, reading the numbers might be a problem at this size, but you can select other reduction or enlargement sizes for that purpose. While your worksheet is zoomed, you can still select cells, format them, and type formulas as you normally would. The Zoom option in effect when you save the worksheet is the displayed setting when you reopen the worksheet.

Note

The wheel on a mouse ordinarily scrolls the worksheet. You can also use the wheel to zoom. Simply hold down the Ctrl key, and rotate the wheel. If you want, you can make zooming the default behavior of the wheel. To do so, click the Microsoft Office Button, click Excel Options, select the Advanced category, and select the Zoom On Roll With IntelliMouse check box in the Editing Options area.

Using Custom Views

 Suppose you want your worksheet to have particular display and print settings for one purpose, such as editing, but different display and print settings for another purpose, such as an on-screen presentation. By clicking the Custom Views button on the View tab, you can assign names to specific view settings, which include column widths, row heights, display options, window size, position on the screen, pane settings, the cells that are selected at the time the view is created, and, optionally, the print and filter settings. You can then select your saved view settings whenever you need them, rather than manually changing the settings each time.

> **Note**
>
> Before you modify your view settings for a particular purpose, you should save the current view as a custom view, named Normal. This provides you with an easy way to return to the regular, unmodified view. Otherwise, you would have to retrace all your steps to return all the view settings to normal.

In the Custom Views dialog box, the Views list is empty until you click Add to save a custom view. Figure 12-21 shows the Custom Views dialog box with two views added, as well as the Add View dialog box you used to add them.

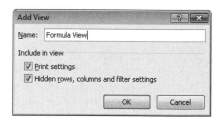

Figure 12-21 Click Add to name the current view and print settings in the Custom Views dialog box.

Protecting Worksheets

In addition to password protection for your files, Excel offers several features that you can use to protect your work—workbooks, workbook structures, individual cells, graphic objects, charts, scenarios, windows, and more—from access or modification by others. You can also choose to allow specific editing actions on protected worksheets.

By default, Excel *locks* (protects) all cells and charts, but the protection is unavailable until you click the Review tab on the Ribbon and click Protect Sheet to access the Protect Sheet dialog box, as shown in Figure 12-22. (You can also click the Format button on the Home tab and then click Protect Sheet.) The protection status you specify applies to the current worksheet only.

Figure 12-22 The Protect Sheet dialog box gives you pinpoint control over many common editing actions.

After protection is turned on, you cannot change a locked item. If you try to change a locked item, Excel displays an error message. As you can see in Figure 12-22, the Allow All Users Of This Worksheet To list contains a number of specific editorial actions you can allow on protected worksheets. In addition to the options visible in Figure 12-22, you can also allow users to sort, use Filter and PivotTable reports, and edit objects or scenarios.

Unlocking Individual Cells

If you click Protect Sheet without specifically unlocking individual cells, you'll lock every cell on the worksheet by default. Most of the time, however, you will not want to lock every cell. For example, you might want to protect the formulas and formatting but leave particular cells unlocked so you can type necessary data without unlocking the entire worksheet. Before you protect a worksheet, select the cells you want to keep unlocked, click Format on the Home tab, and click Lock Cell, as shown in Figure 12-23. Lock Cell is selected by default for all cells, so clicking it deselects it, unlocking the selected cells.

You can easily move between unprotected cells on a locked worksheet by pressing the Tab key.

One way to verify the locked status of a cell is to select it and look at the little padlock icon next to the Lock command. If the icon appears to be clicked already, it means that the selected cell is locked, which is the default state for all cells.

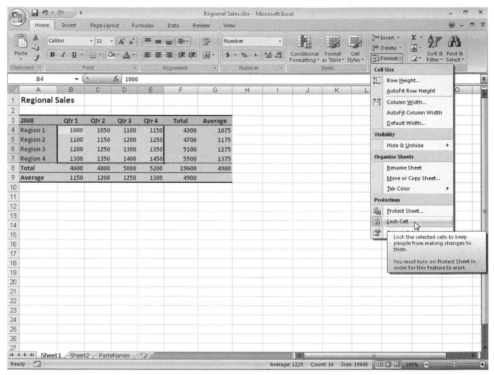

Figure 12-23 Click Format, Lock Cell to unlock specific cells for editing.

Note

Keep in mind that Excel does not provide any on-screen indication of the protection status for individual cells. To distinguish unlocked cells from the protected cells, you might consider applying a specific format, such as cell color or borders.

Protecting the Workbook

You can prevent the alteration of a workbook's structure and lock the position of the workbook window. To do so, click the Review tab on the Ribbon, and click Protect Workbook, Protect Structure And Windows to display the dialog box shown in Figure 12-24.

For more information, see "Protecting Workbooks" on page 390.

Figure 12-24 Use the Protect Structure And Windows dialog box to set the protection status for the entire workbook.

Allowing Password Access to Specific Cell Ranges

If you need to do more than protect workbooks or individual worksheets, use the Ribbon. Specifically, on the Review tab, in the Changes group, click Allow Users To Edit Ranges. Use the Allow Users To Edit Ranges dialog box, as shown in Figure 12-25, to provide editorial access to specific areas of a protected worksheet. You can even specify exactly who is allowed to do the editing.

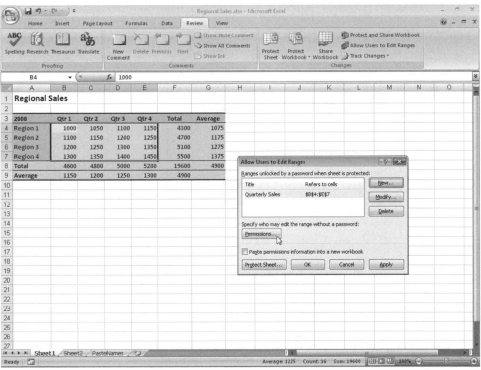

Figure 12-25 You can specify cells that can be edited, as well as the individuals who are allowed to edit them, by using the Allow Users To Edit Ranges dialog box.

When you click New in the Allow Users To Edit Ranges dialog box to add a cell range to the list, the New Range dialog box appears, as shown in Figure 12-26. Type a title for the range of cells you want to allow users to edit. Type a cell range or range name in the Refers To Cells box, or click in the box and drag through the range you want to specify.

Figure 12-26 Specify ranges you want to allow users to edit using the New Range dialog box.

Selecting the Paste Permissions Information Into A New Workbook check box is a handy way to keep track of who and what you've specified in the Permissions list. Note that you can click the Protect Sheet button for quick access to the Protect Sheet dialog box shown in Figure 12-22. You can click the Permissions button to specify individuals who are allowed to edit each range. When you do so, a dialog box like the one in Figure 12-27 appears.

Figure 12-27 Set permissions for individual users by clicking Permissions in the Allow Users To Edit Ranges dialog box.

The Permissions dialog box lists all the users who are authorized to edit the worksheet, as well as whether they will need to use a password to do so. For each item in the Group Or User Names list, you can specify password permissions in the box; click Allow or Deny to restrict editing without a password. This lets you, in effect, employ two levels of restriction, since you are restricting editing access to specified users anyway, and you can force even those users to type a password if you want to do so.

> **Note**
>
> You must specify a password in the New Range dialog box (shown in Figure 12-26) or in the identical Modify Range dialog box to turn on the permissions options that you set. If you don't specify a range password, anyone can edit the range.

You can add users and groups to the list in the Permissions dialog box by clicking Add and then clicking Advanced to display the full dialog box shown in Figure 12-28. Click Find Now to locate all the users and groups available to your system. However, if you are connected to a large network, this might take a long time, so you can use the Common Queries box to restrict your search. You can also use Object Types and Locations to restrict your search further. After you click Find Now, you can select items in the list at the bottom of the dialog box that you want to add. Press the Ctrl key to select multiple items. When you have located the users and groups you want to add, click OK.

Figure 12-28 Click Add in the Permissions dialog box to add to your list of authorized users.

> **Note**
> To add or change users on your computer, open User Accounts in Control Panel.

Remember, after all this, you still have to activate worksheet protection by clicking Protect Sheet on the Home tab or by clicking Protect Sheet in the Allow Users To Edit Ranges dialog box.

Hiding Cells and Worksheets

In a protected worksheet, if you applied the Hidden protection format to a cell that contains a formula, the formula remains hidden from view in the formula bar, even when you select that cell. To hide a selected cell or cells, click the Format button on the Home tab, and click Cells to display the Format Cells dialog box. Then click the Protection tab, and select the Hidden option. Formulas in hidden cells are still functional, of course; they are just hidden from view. In any case, the displayed result of the formula on the worksheet is still visible.

You can also hide rows and columns within a worksheet and even hide entire worksheets within a workbook. Any data or calculations in hidden rows, columns, or worksheets are still available through references; the cells or worksheets are hidden from view. To hide a worksheet, click the sheet tab of the worksheet you want to hide, and on the Home tab, click Format, Hide & Unhide, Hide Sheet, as shown in Figure 12-29. Unlike hiding cells, hiding rows, columns, or worksheets happens immediately. Afterward, you can click the corresponding Unhide command to restore the hidden item. However, if you hide a worksheet and then click Protect Workbook on the Review tab, the Unhide command is no longer available, which helps keep the hidden worksheet even better protected.

For more information about workbook protection, see "Hiding and Protecting Workbooks" on page 389.

Using Passwords

When you click Protect Sheet, Protect Workbook, or Protect And Share Workbook on the Review tab, you can assign a password that must be used to disable the protection. You can use unique passwords for each worksheet or workbook you protect.

> **CAUTION**
> Password protection in Excel is serious business. After you assign a password, you can't unprotect the worksheet or workbook without it. Don't forget your passwords! Remember, capitalization matters.

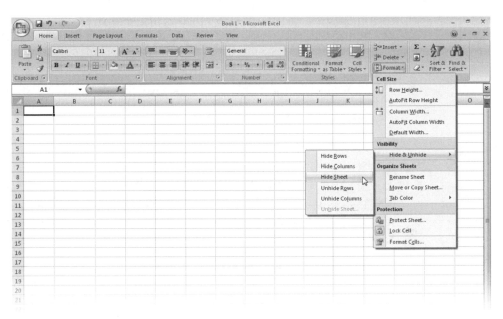

Figure 12-29 Use the Hide & Unhide commands to protect parts of your workbooks.

Managing Multiple Workbooks

This part of the chapter describes how to protect workbooks, how to use more than one workbook at a time, and how and why to split your view of a workbook into multiple windows. Generally when you start Microsoft Office Excel 2007, a blank workbook appears with the provisional title Book1. The only exceptions occur when you start Office Excel 2007 by opening an existing workbook or when you have one or more Excel files stored in the XLStart folder so that they open automatically.

If you start Excel with Book1 visible and then open an existing Excel file, Book1 disappears unless you have edited it. You can open as many workbooks as you like until your computer runs out of memory.

For more about working with multiple windows, see "Opening Multiple Windows for the Same Workbook" on page 385.

Navigating Between Open Workbooks

If you have more than one workbook open, you can activate a particular workbook in any of the following three ways:

- Click its window, if you can see it.

- If you have all your workbook windows maximized, you can shuffle through the open workbooks by pressing Ctrl+Tab to activate each workbook in the order you opened them. Press Shift+Ctrl+Tab to activate them in reverse order.

- On the View tab on the Ribbon, click a window name on the Switch Windows menu, which lists as many as nine open workbooks or, if you have more than nine, displays a More Workbooks command that presents a dialog box that lists all the open workbooks.

INSIDE OUT   Closing the Last Open Excel Window

Over the past few releases of Office, there has been some debate about the relative merits of the multiple document interface (MDI) and the single document interface (SDI). What are we talking about here? It's a difference in how documents are handled in the user interface. Users of previous versions of Excel have grown used to the MDI—where you can have multiple workbooks open but only one icon appears in the Windows system tray. Excel 2007 has switched to the SDI paradigm: Each open workbook creates a new icon in the system tray. A new workbook that appears when you first start Excel (or when you click the Microsoft Office Button and then click New) disappears when you open another workbook unless you have actually edited it. Then, when you click the Close button in the Excel title bar, Excel exits even though you may have thought you had another workbook open to prevent Excel from exiting.

The way to change this default SDI behavior is to click the Microsoft Office Button, click Excel Options, select the Advanced category, and in the Display group clear the Show All Windows In The Taskbar check box. If you still prefer the SDI approach, you can work around this issue by avoiding clicking the Close button and instead clicking the Microsoft Office Button, Close, which closes the active workbook but keeps the program open; by making sure you click the Close button in the workbook window instead of the Close button in the Excel window; or by developing the habit of typing a space character (or any character) in cell A1 as soon as you start Excel just to keep Book1 alive.

Arranging Workbook Windows

To make all open workbooks visible at the same time, click the View tab, and click Arrange All. Excel displays the Arrange Windows dialog box, shown in Figure 12-30, which also shows the workbooks arranged in the Tiled configuration with the screen divided into a patchwork of open documents. Figure 12-31 shows the same workbooks in the Horizontal configuration.

You'll find the 2008 Projections.xlsx, Humongous08.xlsm, and Pacific Sales.xlsm files in the Sample Files section of the companion CD.

If you select the Windows Of Active Workbook check box in the Arrange Windows dialog box, only the active workbook is affected by the configuration setting, and then only if more than one window is open for the active workbook. Excel arranges those windows according to the option you select under Arrange in the Arrange Windows dialog box. This is handy if you have several workbooks open but you have multiple windows open for one of them and you want only to arrange these windows without closing the other workbooks.

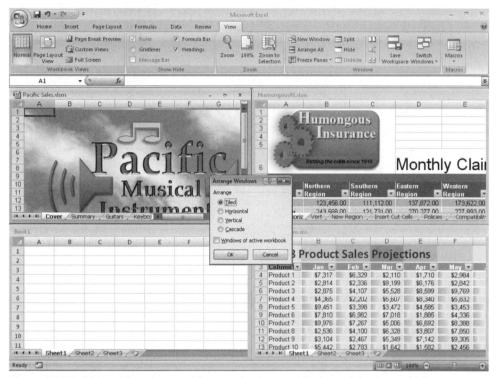

Figure 12-30 Clicking View, Arrange All opens the Arrange Windows dialog box, which gives you a choice of configurations.

For more information about working with multiple worksheets from one workbook, see "Opening Multiple Windows for the Same Workbook" on page 385.

> **Note**
>
> If you're working with several workbooks in a particular arrangement that is often useful, click the View tab, and click Save Workspace in the Window group. This preserves the current settings so you can re-create the window arrangement by opening one file.

Chapter 12

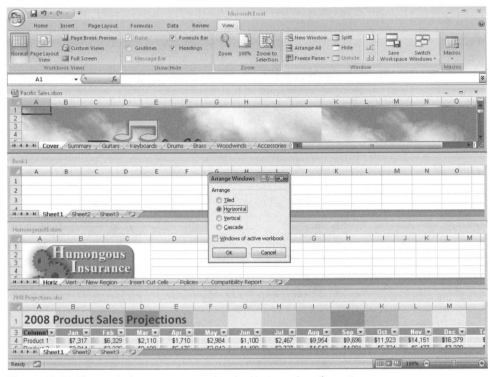

Figure 12-31 These windows are arranged in the Horizontal configuration.

Getting the Most Out of Your Screen

 You can maximize the workbook window if you need to see more of the active worksheet, but if that still isn't enough, you can click the Full Screen button on the View tab. When you do so, Excel removes the formula bar, status bar, Quick Access Toolbar, and Ribbon from your screen—everything except the maximized workbook—as shown in Figure 12-32.

To return the screen to its former configuration, press Esc.

The Full Screen button provides a convenient way to display the most information on the screen without changing the magnification of the data using the Zoom controls. For more information, see "Zooming Worksheets" on page 370.

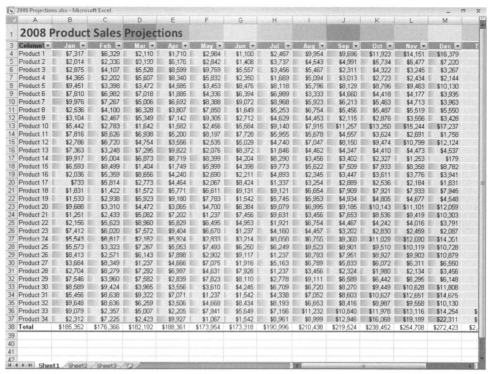

Figure 12-32 Clicking View, Full Screen hides the formula bar, status bar, Quick Access Toolbar, and Ribbon to maximize the screen space available for viewing your data.

> **Note**
>
> When you save a workbook, Excel also saves its characteristics, such as the window's size, position on the screen, and display settings. The next time you open the workbook, the window looks the same as it did the last time you saved it. When you open it, Excel even selects the same cells you selected when you saved the file.

Comparing Worksheets Side by Side

View Side By Side

The Arrange All button on the View tab is extremely helpful if you need to compare the contents of two similar workbooks, but another feature makes this task even easier. The View Side By Side button essentially packages the Horizontal window arrangement option with a couple of useful features to make comparison chores a lot easier. The View Side By Side button lives in the Window group on the View tab; it is the top button located to the left of the Save Workspace command, as shown in Figure 12-33.

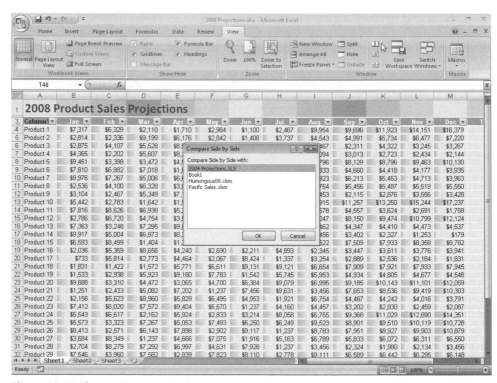

Figure 12-33 If more than two windows are open, select one in the Compare Side By Side dialog box.

Note

The Ribbon on your screen may look different from what you see in this book. The Ribbon display adjusts to the size of your screen, its resolution, and the size of the Excel window. For example, the six buttons in the middle of the Window group on the View tab may not display adjacent text labels if you have a smaller display or if Excel is not maximized.

You can click the View Side By Side button to arrange any two open windows, even if they are windows for the same workbook (as described in the next section). But unlike the Arrange button, View Side By Side performs its trick on no more or less than two windows. After you click the button, you will see a Compare Side By Side dialog box like the one shown in Figure 12-34 if you have more than two windows open. If so, select the window you want to compare, and click OK; this opens and arranges it along with the window that was active when you clicked View Side By Side. (The button name is a little bit misleading, because the windows are actually arranged horizontally—not really "side by side" but one above the other.)

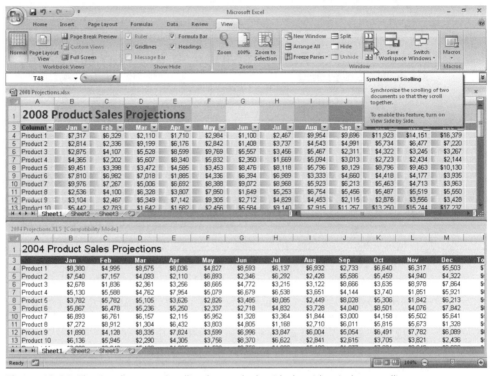

Figure 12-34 The Synchronous Scrolling button locks side-by-side window scrolling.

Synchronous
Scrolling

Reset Window
Position

After you activate "side-by-side mode," the two buttons below the View Side By Side button become active, as shown in Figure 12-34. The Synchronous Scrolling button locks the two windows together wherever they happen to be so when you scroll in any direction, the inactive window scrolls in an identical fashion. The Reset Window Position button puts the active window on top, which is handy. The window that is active when you click the View Side By Side button is the one that appears on top. If you want the other window on top, click the other window, and then click the Reset Window Position button to place it in the top position.

The View Side By Side button is a toggle—to turn off side-by-side mode and return to Normal view, click the View Side By Side button again.

Opening Multiple Windows for the Same Workbook

Suppose you've created a workbook like the one shown in Figure 12-35. You might want to monitor the cells on the summary worksheet while working on one of the other worksheets in the workbook. On the other hand, if you have a large worksheet, you

Chapter 12

might want to keep an eye on more than one area of the same worksheet at the same time. To perform either of these tasks, you can open a second window for the workbook by clicking New Window on the View tab.

	Month	Guitars	Keyboards	Drums	Band	Accessories	Total by Month
4	January	$7,835.31	$9,901.84	$15,292.36	$15,853.96	$8,441.21	$57,324.68
5	February	$6,118.82	$14,315.39	$11,196.22	$11,128.53	$10,113.58	$52,872.55
6	March	$7,986.38	$11,789.56	$8,264.24	$12,563.56	$4,032.54	$44,636.27
7	April	$7,241.70	$5,598.89	$6,732.80	$20,640.48	$9,862.34	$50,076.22
8	May	$10,244.89	$16,649.41	$8,669.96	$15,207.73	$8,556.62	$59,328.61
9	June	$9,492.45	$10,022.16	$14,219.95	$11,663.91	$7,475.17	$52,873.64
10	July	$6,376.39	$15,729.99	$12,884.35	$12,178.20	$7,201.69	$54,370.62
11	August	$12,944.92	$23,277.25	$8,833.54	$12,928.62	$5,761.74	$63,746.06
12	September	$9,217.92	$18,845.95	$11,392.41	$11,667.41	$6,483.13	$57,606.82
13	October	$4,375.62	$2,953.29	$8,180.50	$16,304.29	$8,183.63	$39,997.33
14	November	$10,130.28	$9,936.86	$9,585.57	$15,522.44	$8,598.60	$53,773.76
15	December	$13,467.24	$7,966.55	$12,713.94	$20,104.65	$4,703.73	$58,956.12
16	*Total by Product*	$105,431.92	$146,987.14	$127,965.84	$175,763.80	$89,413.98	$645,562.69

Pacific Musical Instruments — 2008 Sales Summary — Product

Figure 12-35 You can work on the summary worksheet while viewing supporting worksheets in the same workbook.

To view both windows on your screen, click View, Arrange All, and then select any of the Arrange options except Cascade. If you select the Cascade option, you'll be able to view only the top worksheet in the stack. If you select the Horizontal option, your screen looks similar to the one shown in Figure 12-36.

You might notice that Office Excel 2007 assigned the name Pacific Sales.xlsm:2 to the new workbook window. In addition, it changed the name of the original workbook window to Pacific Sales xlsm:1. Pacific Sales.xlsm:2 now becomes the active window, and as such, it's positioned on top, as indicated by the presence of scroll bars.

> **Note**
>
> Again, if other workbooks are open but you want to view only the windows on the active workbook, select the Windows Of Active Workbook check box in the Arrange Windows dialog box.

You can view any part of the workbook in any window associated with that workbook. In Figure 12-36, Pacific Sales.xlsm:2 originally displayed the summary worksheet when we first created it, because that was the active worksheet when we clicked the New Window button. Then we clicked the Brass tab in the new window, leaving the summary worksheet visible in Pacific Sales.xlsm:1.

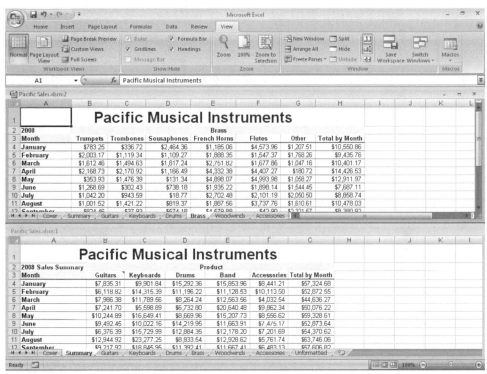

Figure 12-36 After clicking the New Window button to open a second window for the same workbook, select an Arrange option to fit both windows on the screen simultaneously.

Useful Inconsistencies of New Windows

When you create multiple windows of the same workbook, anything you do in one window happens in all windows—almost. New entries; formatting changes; inserted or deleted rows, columns, or worksheets; and just about any other editing changes are reflected in all windows. Display characteristics—or *views*—are not. This means you can zoom in or out and change anything in the Workbook Views and Zoom groups on the View tab as well as the Split and Freeze Panes commands. View adjustments affect only the active window. You can also click the Microsoft Office Button, click Excel Options, select the Advanced category, and then change the settings in the two Display Options sections: Display Options For This Workbook and Display Options For This Worksheet. You can apply these options differently to windows of the same workbook. Just select the name of window you want to change in the drop-down list, as shown in Figure 12-37.

Figure 12-38 shows a somewhat exaggerated example of worksheet auditing. In Pacific Sales.xlsm:1, formulas are displayed; the worksheet is zoomed in; and scroll bars, row and column headings, and gridlines are removed—all in an effort to review the formulas in the summary worksheet to make sure they refer to the proper cells. You can also use this technique to audit your worksheets.

Chapter 12

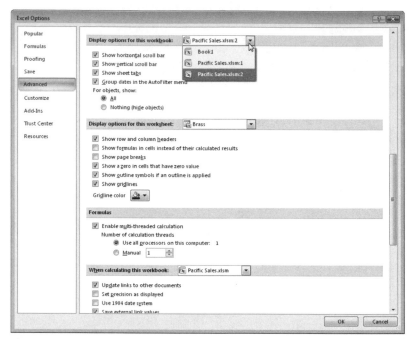

Figure 12-37 You can change the display characteristics of one window without affecting the other.

If you create a view like Pacific Sales.xlsm:1 in Figure 12-38 and want to be able to re-create it in the future, click the Custom Views button in the Workbook Views group on the View tab to save it. If you want to be able to re-create the entire workspace, including additional windows and their view settings, click the Save Workspace button in the Window group on the View tab.

For more information about custom views, see "Using Custom Views" on page 372. For more information about formulas, see Chapter 13, "Building Formulas."

INSIDE OUT   Close the Default Settings Window Last

When you have two windows open in the same workbook and then close one of them, the "number" of the open window isn't important, but the view settings are. In the example shown in Figure 12-38, if we finish our work and close Pacific Sales.xlsm:2, the modified view settings in Pacific Sales.xlsm:1 become the active view for the workbook. If we then save the workbook, we also save the modified view settings. Make sure you close the windows with view settings you don't want to keep before you close the one with the settings you want to use as the default—don't worry about the window number.

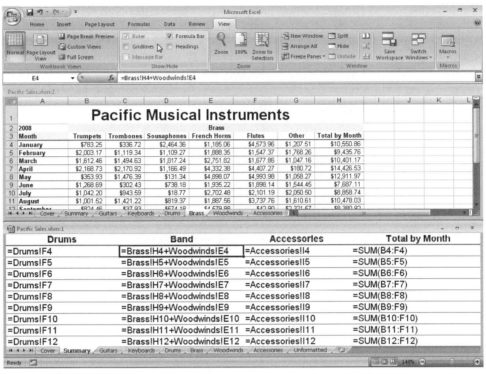

Figure 12-38 You can radically change view options in one window while maintaining a regular view of the same worksheet in another window.

Hiding and Protecting Workbooks

Sometimes you might want to keep certain information out of sight or protect it from inadvertent modification. You can conceal and protect your data by hiding windows, workbooks, or individual worksheets from view.

For information about protecting individual cells, see "Protecting Worksheets" on page 372.

Hiding Workbooks

At times, you might need to keep a workbook open so you can access the information it contains but not want it to be visible. When several open workbooks clutter your workspace, you can click the Hide button on the View tab to conceal some of them. Office Excel 2007 can still work with the information in the hidden workbooks, but they don't take up space on your screen, and their file names don't appear in the Switch Windows menu on the View tab.

Chapter 12

To hide a workbook, activate it, and click View, Hide. Excel removes the workbook from view, but the workbook remains open and available in the workspace. To bring the hidden workbook into view, click View, Unhide, and then select the name of the hidden workbook you want to redisplay. The Unhide command is available only when you have a workbook hidden. The Unhide dialog box, as shown in Figure 12-39, lists all the hidden workbooks.

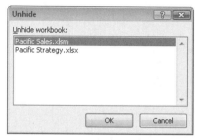

Figure 12-39 The Unhide dialog box lists all the workbooks you currently have hidden.

Clicking the Hide button conceals any open window. However, if you have multiple windows open for the same workbook, clicking the Hide button hides only the active window. The entire workbook isn't hidden. For more information, see "Opening Multiple Windows for the Same Workbook" on page 385.

TROUBLESHOOTING

Nothing happens when you try to open a workbook.

If, when you try to open a workbook, you don't see any error messages or dialog boxes but the workbook doesn't appear to open, the window was probably hidden when it was last saved. The workbook is actually open; you just can't see it.

If, in a previous Excel session, you clicked the Hide button on the View tab and then forgot about the hidden window when you exited Excel, you probably saw a message like "Do you want to save changes you made to Book1?" This would have been the hidden file—the change you made was the act of hiding it. The next time you open the file, it appears that nothing has happened, but if you look at the View tab, the Unhide button is active, which happens only when a hidden window is open in the workspace. Click the Unhide button, select the file name to make it visible once again, and then save it before exiting Excel.

Protecting Workbooks

Protecting a workbook not only prevents changes to the complement of worksheets contained in the workbook but can also prevent modifications to the way the workbook windows are displayed. To protect a workbook, click the Review tab, and click

Protect Workbook, Protect Structure And Windows to display the dialog box shown in Figure 12-40.

Figure 12-40 Clicking Review, Protect Workbook helps insulate your workbooks from inadvertent modification.

Selecting the Structure check box prevents any changes to the position, the name, and the hidden or unhidden status of the worksheets in the active workbook. When you select the Windows option, the workbook's windows cannot be closed, hidden, unhidden, resized, or moved—in fact, the Minimize, Maximize, and Close buttons disappear. This does not mean you cannot close the workbook; you can still click the Microsoft Office Button and then click Close. However, if you have more than one window open for the workbook, you cannot close any of them individually.

These settings take effect immediately. This command is a toggle—you can turn protection off by clicking Protect Workbook, Protect Structure And Windows again. If protection has been activated, a check mark appears next to the command on the Protect Workbook menu. If you specified a password in the Protect Structure And Windows dialog box, Excel prompts you to supply that password before it turns off the worksheet protection.

Encrypting Workbooks

Encrypt Document

You can provide another level of security for your workbooks by adding encryption. Encryption goes beyond simple password protection by digitally obscuring information to make it unreadable without the proper key to "decode" it. (Therefore, encrypted workbooks can be opened only by Excel 2007.) You apply encryption by clicking the Microsoft Office Button, Prepare, Encrypt Document. This displays a dialog box that prompts you for a password and then redisplays itself to confirm the password, as shown in Figure 12-41.

Figure 12-41 Applying a password to encrypt a workbook also turns on protection of the workbook structure.

After you click the Encrypt Document command, you'll need the password you provided to open the workbook again; the Protect Structure And Windows dialog box (refer to Figure 12-40) also uses this password to protect the workbook structure. Even if you turn off workbook protection, encryption is still active until you turn it off it by clicking the Encrypt Document command again and removing the password from the Encrypt Document dialog box.

Saving Workbooks or Windows as Hidden

Sometimes you might want to hide a particular workbook, perhaps even to prevent others from opening and viewing its sensitive contents in your absence. If so, you can save the workbook as hidden. A hidden workbook is not visible when it's opened. You can save a workbook as hidden by following these steps:

1. Close all open workbooks other than the one you want to hide, and then click View, Hide.

2. Exit Excel.

3. When a message appears asking whether you want to save changes to the workbook, click Yes.

The next time the workbook opens, its contents are hidden. To ensure that it cannot be unhidden by others, you might want to assign a password by clicking Review, Protect Workbook before hiding and saving the workbook.

Hiding Worksheets

If you want to hide a particular worksheet in a workbook, click the Home tab, and in the Cells group, click Format. In the menu that appears, click Hide & Unhide, and then click Hide Sheet. When you do so, the active worksheet no longer appears in the workbook. To unhide a hidden worksheet, click Unhide Sheet in the same menu, which becomes active after you have hidden a worksheet. The Unhide dialog box for worksheets is almost identical to the Unhide dialog box for workbooks shown in Figure 12-39. Select the worksheet you want to unhide, and then click OK.

Building Formulas

Formulas are the heart and soul of a spreadsheet, and Microsoft Office Excel 2007 offers a rich environment in which to build complex formulas. Armed with a few mathematical operators and rules for cell entry, you can turn a worksheet into a powerful calculator. In this chapter, we'll cover the basics, and then we'll look closer at using functions, defining names, building structured references, working with arrays, creating linking formulas, and constructing conditional tests.

Formula Fundamentals

All formulas in Excel begin with an equal sign. The equal sign tells Excel that the succeeding characters constitute a formula. If you omit the equal sign, Excel might interpret the entry as text.

To show how formulas work, we'll walk you through some rudimentary ones. Begin by selecting blank cell A10. Then type **=10+5**, and press Enter. The value 15 appears in cell A10. Now select cell A10, and the formula bar displays the formula you just typed. What appears in the cell is the displayed value; what appears in the formula bar is the underlying value, which in this case is a formula.

Understanding the Precedence of Operators

Operators are symbols that represent specific mathematical operations, including the plus sign (+), minus sign (−), division sign (/), and multiplication sign (*). When performing these operations in a formula, Excel follows certain rules of precedence:

- Excel processes expressions within parentheses first.

- Excel performs multiplication and division before addition and subtraction.

- Excel calculates consecutive operators with the same level of precedence from left to right.

Type some formulas to see how these rules apply. Select an empty cell, and type **=4+12/6**. Press Enter, and you see the value 6. Excel first divides 12 by 6 and then adds the result (2) to 4. If Excel used different precedence rules, the result would be different. For example, select another empty cell, and type **=(4+12)/6**. Press Enter, and you see the value 2.666667. This demonstrates how you can change the order of precedence using parentheses. The formulas in Table 13-1 contain the same values and operators, but note the different results because of the placement of parentheses.

Table 13-1 Placement of Parentheses

Formula	Result
=3*6+12/4–2	19
=(3*6)+12/(4–2)	24
=3*(6+12)/4–2	11.5
=(3*6+12)/4–2	5.5
=3*(6+12/(4–2))	36

If you do not include a closing parenthesis for each opening parenthesis in a formula, Excel displays the message "Microsoft Excel found an error in this formula" and provides a suggested solution. If the suggestion matches what you had in mind, simply press Enter, and Excel completes the formula for you.

When you type a closing parenthesis, Excel briefly displays the pair of parentheses in bold. This feature is handy when you are typing a long formula and are not sure which pairs of parentheses go together.

> **Note**
>
> If you are unsure of the order in which Excel will process a sequence of operators, use parentheses—even if the parentheses aren't necessary. Parentheses also make your formulas easier to read and interpret, which is helpful if you or someone else needs to change them later.

Using Cell References in Formulas

A cell reference identifies a cell or group of cells in a workbook. When you include cell references in a formula, the formula is said to be *linked* to the referenced cells. The resulting value of the formula depends on the values in the referenced cells and changes automatically when the values in the referenced cells change.

To see cell referencing at work, select cell A1, and type the formula **=10*2**. Now select cell A2, and type the formula **=A1**. The value in both cells is 20. If at any time you change the value in cell A1, the value in cell A2 changes also. Now select cell A3, and type **=A1+A2**. Excel returns the value 40. Cell references are especially helpful when you create complex formulas.

Entering Cell References by Clicking

You can save time and increase accuracy when you enter cell references in a formula by selecting them with your pointer. For example, to enter references to cells A9 and A10 in a formula in cell B10, do the following:

1. Select cell B10, and type an equal sign.

2. Click cell A9, and type a plus sign.

3. Click cell A10, and press Enter.

When you click each cell, a marquee surrounds the cell, and Excel inserts a reference to the cell in cell B10. After you finish entering a formula, be sure to press Enter. If you do not press Enter and then select another cell, Excel assumes you want to include the cell reference in the formula.

The active cell does not have to be visible in the current window for you to enter a value in that cell. You can scroll through the worksheet without changing the active cell and click cells in remote areas of your worksheet, in other worksheets, or in other work-books, as you build a formula. The formula bar displays the contents of the active cell, no matter which area of the worksheet is currently visible.

> **Note**
> If you scroll through your worksheet and the active cell is no longer visible, you can redisplay it by pressing Ctrl+Backspace. You can return to the upper-left corner of the worksheet by pressing Ctrl+Home.

Understanding Relative, Absolute, and Mixed References

Relative references—the type we've used so far in the sample formulas—refer to cells by their position in relation to the cell that contains the formula, such as "the cell two rows above this cell." *Absolute references* refer to cells by their fixed position in the worksheet, such as "the cell located at the intersection of column A and row 2." A *mixed reference* contains a relative reference and an absolute reference, such as "the cell located in column A and two rows above this cell." Absolute and mixed references are important when you begin copying formulas from one location to another in your worksheet. When you copy and paste, relative references adjust automatically, while absolute refer-ences do not. For information about copying cell references, see "How Copying Affects Cell References" on page 398.

A relative reference to cell A1, for example, looks like this: =A1. An absolute reference to cell A1 looks like this: =$A$1. You can combine relative and absolute references to cell A1 to create these mixed references: =$A1 or =A$1.

If the dollar sign precedes only the letter (A, for example), the column coordinate is absolute, and the row is relative. If the dollar sign precedes only the number (1, for example), the column coordinate is relative, and the row is absolute.

While entering or editing a formula, press F4 to change reference types quickly. The following steps show how:

1. Select cell A1, and type **=B1+B2** (but do not press Enter).

2. Press F4 to change the reference nearest to the flashing cursor to absolute. The formula becomes =B1+$B$2.

3. Press F4 again to change the reference to mixed (relative column coordinate and absolute row coordinate). The formula becomes =B1+B$2.

4. Press F4 again to reverse the mixed reference (absolute column coordinate and relative row coordinate). The formula becomes =B1+$B2.

5. Press F4 again to return to the original relative reference.

When you use this technique to change reference types, activate the formula bar by clicking it, and then you can either click in the cell reference you want to change before pressing F4 or drag to select one or more cell references in the formula and change all the selected references at the same time.

Creating References to Other Worksheets in the Same Workbook

You can refer to cells in other worksheets within the same workbook just as easily as you refer to cells in the same worksheet. For example, to enter a reference to cell A9 in Sheet2 into cell B10 in Sheet1, do this:

1. Select cell B10 in Sheet1, and type an equal sign.

2. Click the Sheet2 tab.

3. Click cell A9, and then press Enter.

After you press Enter, Sheet1 becomes active. Select cell B10, and you will see that it contains the formula =Sheet2!A9.

The worksheet portion of the reference is separated from the cell portion by an exclamation point. Note also that the cell reference is relative, which is the default when you select cells to create references to other worksheets.

Creating References to Worksheets in Other Workbooks

You can refer to cells in worksheets in separate workbooks in the same way you refer to cells in other worksheets within the same workbook. These references are called *external references*. For example, to enter a reference to Book2 in Book1, follow these steps:

Microsoft Office
Button

1. Create a new workbook—Book2—by clicking the Microsoft Office Button, clicking New, selecting Blank Workbook, and clicking OK.

2. Click the View tab, click Arrange All, select the Vertical option, and click OK.

3. Select cell A1 in Sheet1 of Book1, and type an equal sign.

4. Click anywhere in the Book2 window to make the workbook active.

5. Click the Sheet2 tab at the bottom of the Book2 window.

6. Click cell A2. Before pressing Enter to lock in the formula, your screen should look similar to Figure 13-1.

7. Press Enter to lock in the reference.

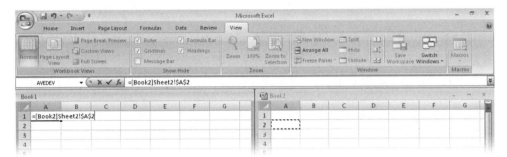

Figure 13-1 Enter external references easily by clicking the cell to which you want to refer.

Understanding Row-Column Reference Style

In the regular A1 reference style, rows are numbered, and columns are designated by letters. In R1C1 reference style, both rows and columns are numbered. The cell reference R1C1 means row 1, column 1; therefore, R1C1 and A1 refer to the same cell. Although R1C1 reference style isn't widely used anymore, it was the standard in some "classic" spreadsheet programs, such as Microsoft Multiplan.

To turn on the R1C1 reference style, click the Microsoft Office Button, click Excel Options, select the Formulas category, select the R1C1 Reference Style check box, and then click OK. The column headers change from letters to numbers, and the cell references in all your formulas automatically change to R1C1 format. For example, cell M10 becomes R10C13, and cell XFD1048576, the last cell in your worksheet, becomes R1048576C16384.

In R1C1 notation, a relative cell reference displays in terms of its relationship to the cell that contains the formula rather than by its actual coordinates. This can be helpful when you are more interested in the relative position of a cell than in its absolute position. For example, suppose you want to enter in cell R10C2 (B10) a formula that adds cells R1C1 (A1) and R1C2 (B1). After selecting cell R10C2, type an equal sign, select cell R1C1, type a plus sign, select cell R1C2, and then press Enter. When you select cell R10C2, the formula =R[–9]C[–1]+R[–9]C appears in the formula bar. Negative row and column numbers indicate that the referenced cell is above or to the left of the formula cell; positive numbers indicate that the referenced cell is below or to the right of the formula cell. The brackets indicate relative references. This formula reads, "Add the cell nine rows up and one column to the left to the cell nine rows up in the same column."

A relative reference to another cell must include brackets. Otherwise, Excel assumes you're using absolute references. For example, if we select the entire formula we created in the previous paragraph in the formula bar and press F4, the formula changes to =R1C1+R1C2 using absolute references.

How Copying Affects Cell References

One of the handiest benefits of using references is the capability to copy and paste formulas. But you need to understand what happens to your references after you paste so you can create formulas with references that operate the way you want them to operate.

Copying Relative References   When you copy a cell containing a formula with relative cell references, Excel changes the references automatically, relative to the position of the cell where you paste the formula. Referring to Figure 13-2, suppose you type the formula **=AVERAGE(B4:E4)** in cell F4. This formula averages the values in the four-cell range that begins four columns to the left of cell F4.

F4		fx	=AVERAGE(B4:E4)											
	A	B	C	D	E	F	G	H	I	J	K	L	M	N
1	**First Quarter Exam Scores**													
2														
3	Student	Exam 1	Exam 2	Exam 3	Exam 4	Average								
4	Carothers, Andy	87	90	79	96	88.00								
5	Groncki, Douglas	92	94	94	97									
6	MacDonald, Scott	96	95	95	80									
7	Nusbaum, Tawana	85	87	87	88									
8	Rothenberg, Eric	81	88	88	85									
9														
10														

Figure 13-2 Cell F4 contains relative references to the cells to its left.

You'll find the Exams.xlsx file in the Sample Files section of the companion CD.

You want to repeat this calculation for the remaining rows as well. Instead of typing a new formula in each cell in column F, you select cell F4 and press Ctrl+C to copy it (or click the Copy button in the Clipboard group on the Home tab). Then you select cells F5:F8, click the arrow next to the Paste button on the Home tab, click Paste Special, and then select the Formulas And Number Formats option (to preserve the cell and border formatting). Figure 13-3 shows the results. Because the formula in cell F4 contains a relative reference, Excel adjusts the references in each copy of the formula. As a result, each copy of the formula calculates the average of the cells in the corresponding row. For example, cell F5 contains the formula =AVERAGE(B5:E5).

Copying Absolute References   If you want cell references to remain the same when you copy them, use absolute references. For example, in the worksheet on the left in Figure 13-4, cell B2 contains the hourly rate at which employees are to be paid, and cell C5 contains the relative reference formula =B2*B5. Suppose you want to copy the formula in C5 to the range C6:C8. The worksheet on the right in Figure 13-4 shows what happens if you copy the existing formula to this range: You get erroneous results. Although the formulas in cells C6:C8 should refer to cell B2, they don't. For example, cell C8 contains the incorrect formula =B5*B8.

F5	▼	f_x =AVERAGE(B5:E5)												
	A	B	C	D	E	F	G	H	I	J	K	L	M	N

First Quarter Exam Scores

	Student	Exam 1	Exam 2	Exam 3	Exam 4	Average
4	Carothers, Andy	87	90	79	96	88.00
5	Groncki, Douglas	92	94	94	97	94.25
6	MacDonald, Scott	96	95	95	80	91.50
7	Nusbaum, Tawana	85	87	87	88	86.75
8	Rothenberg, Eric	81	88	88	85	85.50

Figure 13-3 We copied the relative references from cell F4 to cells F5:F8.

C5	▼	f_x =B2*B5

	A	B	C	D
2	**Hourly Rate**	22.25		
		Hours	*Wages*	
4	*Name*	*Worked*	*Due*	
5	DeVoe, Michael	27	600.75	
6	Fakhouri, Fadi	32		
7	Ito, Shu	40		
8	Ortiz, David J.	29		

C8	▼	f_x =B5*B8

	A	B	C	D
2	**Hourly Rate**	22.25		
		Hours	*Wages*	
4	*Name*	*Worked*	*Due*	
5	DeVoe, Michael	27	600.75	
6	Fakhouri, Fadi	32	0.00	
7	Ito, Shu	40	#VALUE!	
8	Ortiz, David J.	29	783.00	

Figure 13-4 The formula in cell C5 contains relative references. We copied the relative formula in cell C5 to cells C6:C8, producing incorrect results.

You'll find the Wages.xlsx file in the Sample Files section of the companion CD.

Because the reference to cell B2 in the original formula is relative, it changes as you copy the formula to the other cells. To correctly apply the wage rate in cell B2 to all the calculations, you must change the reference to cell B2 to an absolute reference before you copy the formula.

To change the reference style, click the formula bar, click the reference to cell B2, and then press F4. The result is the following formula: =$B$2*B5.

When you copy this modified formula to cells C6:C8, Excel adjusts the second cell reference, but not the first, within each formula. In Figure 13-5, cell C8 now contains the correct formula: =$B$2*B8.

Copying Mixed References   You can use mixed references in your formulas to anchor a portion of a cell reference. (In a mixed reference, one portion is absolute, and the other is relative.) When you copy a mixed reference, Excel anchors the absolute portion and adjusts the relative portion to reflect the location of the cell to which you copied the formula.

To create a mixed reference, you can press the F4 key to cycle through the four combinations of absolute and relative references—for example, from B2 to $B$2 to B$2 to $B2.

C8			f_x	=$B$2*B8	
	A	B	C	D	
2	**Hourly Rate**	22.25			
4	*Name*	*Hours Worked*	*Wages Due*		
5	DeVoe, Michael	27	600.75		
6	Fakhouri, Fadi	32	712.00		
7	Ito, Shu	40	890.00		
8	Ortiz, David J.	29	645.25		
9					
10					

Figure 13-5 We created an absolute reference to cell B2 before copying the formula.

The loan payment table in Figure 13-6 uses mixed references (and an absolute reference). You need to enter only one formula in cell C6 and then copy it down and across to fill the table. Cell C6 contains the formula = –PMT($B6,$C$3,C$5) to calculate the annual payments on a $10,000 loan over a period of 15 years at an interest rate of 6 percent. We copied this formula to cells C6:F10 to calculate payments on three additional loan amounts using four additional interest rates.

C6				f_x	=-PMT($B6,$C$3,C$5)	
	A	B	C	D	E	F	G

1						
2		**Loan Payment Calculator**				
3	*Years:*	15				
4			**Loan Amount**			
5		*Rate:*	$ 10,000	$ 20,000	$ 30,000	$ 40,000
6		6.00%	1,030	2,059	3,089	4,119
7		6.50%	1,064	2,127	3,191	4,254
8		7.00%	1,098	2,196	3,294	4,392
9		7.50%	1,133	2,266	3,399	4,531
10		8.00%	1,168	2,337	3,505	4,673
11						
12						

Figure 13-6 This loan payment table uses formulas that contain mixed references.

You'll find the Loan.xlsx file in the Sample Files section of the companion CD.

The first cell reference, $B6, indicates we always want to refer to the values in column B but the row reference (Rate) can change. Similarly, the mixed reference, C$5, indicates we always want to refer to the values in row 5 but the column reference (Loan Amount) can change. For example, cell E8 contains the formula = –PMT($B8,$C$3,E$5). Without mixed references, we would have to edit the formulas manually in each of the cells in the range C6:F10.

TROUBLESHOOTING

Inserted cells are not included in formulas.

If you have a SUM formula at the bottom of a row of numbers and then insert new rows between the numbers and the formula, the range reference in the SUM function doesn't include the new cells. Unfortunately, you can't do much about this. This is an age-old worksheet problem, but Excel attempts to correct it for you automatically. Although the range reference in the SUM formula will not change when you insert the new rows, it will adjust as you type new values in the inserted cells. The only caveat is that you must enter the new values one at a time, starting with the cell directly below the column of numbers. If you begin entering values in the middle of a group of newly inserted rows or columns, the range reference remains unaffected. For more information about the SUM function, see "Using the SUM Function" on page 461.

Editing Formulas

You edit formulas the same way you edit text entries. To delete characters in a formula, drag through the characters in the cell or the formula bar, and press Backspace or Delete. To replace a character, highlight it, and type its replacement. To replace a reference, highlight it, and click the new cell you want the formula to use; Excel enters a relative reference automatically. You can also insert additional cell references in a formula. For example, to insert a reference to cell B1 in the formula =A1+A3, simply move the insertion point between A1 and the plus sign, and either type **+B1** or type a plus sign and click cell B1. The formula becomes –A1+B1+A3.

Understanding Reference Syntax

So far, we have used the default worksheet and workbook names for the examples in this book. When you save a workbook, you must give it a permanent name. If you create a formula first and then save the workbook with a new name, Excel adjusts the formula accordingly. For example, if you save Book2 as Sales.xlsx, Excel changes the remote reference formula =[Book2]Sheet2!$A$2 to =[Sales.xlsx]Sheet2!$A$2. And if you rename Sheet2 of Sales.xlsx to February, Excel changes the reference to =[Sales.xlsx]February!$A$2. If the referenced workbook is closed, Excel displays the full path to the folder where the workbook is stored in the reference, as shown in the example ='C:\Work\[Sales.xlsx]February'!$A$2.

In the preceding example, note that apostrophes surround the workbook and worksheet portion of the reference. Excel adds the apostrophes around the path when you close the workbook. If you type a new reference to a closed workbook, however, you must add the apostrophes yourself. To avoid typing errors, open the closed workbook, and click cells with your cursor to enter references so that Excel inserts them in the correct syntax for you.

Using Numeric Text in Formulas

The seemingly oxymoronic term *numeric text* refers to an entry that is not strictly numbers but includes both numbers and a few specific text characters. You can perform mathematical operations on numeric text values as long as the numeric string contains only the following characters:

```
0 1 2 3 4 5 6 7 8 9 . + - E e
```

In addition, you can use the / character in fractions. You can also use the following five number-formatting characters:

```
$ , % ( )
```

You must enclose numeric text strings in quotation marks. For example, if you type the formula **=$1234+$123**, Excel displays an error message stating that Excel found an error in the formula you typed. (The error message also offers to correct the error for you by removing the dollar signs.) But the formula ="$1234"+"$123" produces the result 1357 (ignoring the dollar signs). When Excel performs the addition, it automatically translates numeric text entries into numeric values.

About Text Values

The term *text values* refers to any entry that is neither a number nor a numeric text value (see the previous section); Excel treats the entry as text only. You can refer to and manipulate text values using formulas. For example, if cell A1 contains the text *First* and you type the formula **=A1** in cell A10, cell A10 displays First.

For more information about manipulating text with formulas, see "Understanding Text Functions" on page 466.

You can use the & (ampersand) operator to *concatenate*, or join, several text values. Extending the preceding example, if cell A2 contains the text *Quarter* and you type the formula **=A1&A2** in cell A3, then cell A3 displays *FirstQuarter*. To include a space between the two strings, change the formula to =A1&" "&A2. This formula uses two concatenation operators and a *literal string*, or *string constant* (a space enclosed in quotation marks).

You can use the & operator to concatenate strings of numeric values as well. For example, if cell A3 contains the numeric value 867 and cell A4 contains the numeric value 5309, the formula =A3&A4 produces the string 8675309. This string is left-aligned in the cell because it's considered a text value. (Remember, you can use numeric text values to perform any mathematical operation as long as the numeric string contains only the numeric characters listed at the top of this page.)

Finally, you can use the & operator to concatenate a text value and a numeric value. For example, if cell A1 contains the text *January* and cell A3 contains the numeric value 2009, the formula =A1&A3 produces the string January2009.

Practical Concatenation

Depending on the kind of work you do, the text manipulation prowess of Excel may turn out to be the most important skill you learn in this book. If you deal with a lot of mailing lists, for example, you probably use a word-processing application such as Microsoft Office Word 2007. But read on—you might find that Excel has the tools you've been wishing for, and it just might become your text manipulation application of choice.

Suppose you have a database of names in which the first and last names are stored in separate columns. This example shows you how to generate a list of full names:

	E3	▼		*fx*	=A3&", "&B3	
	A	B	C	D	E	F
1	**Last Name**	**First Name**		**Full Name**	**Last Name First**	
2	DeVoe	Michael		Michael DeVoe	DeVoe, Michael	
3	Fakhouri	Fadi		Fadi Fakhouri	Fakhouri, Fadi	
4	Groncki	Douglas		Douglas Groncki	Groncki, Douglas	
5	Johnson	Willis		Willis Johnson	Johnson, Willis	
6	Nusbaum	Tawana		Tawana Nusbaum	Nusbaum, Tawana	
7						
8						

We created the full names listed in columns D and E using formulas like the one visible in the formula bar. For example, the formula in cell D2 is =A2&" "&B2, which concatenates the contents of the cells in columns A and B and adds a space character in between. The formula in cell E2 (shown in the illustration) reverses the position of the first and last names and adds a comma before the space character.

Pretty soon, you'll be using the term *concatenate* in everyday conversation. Instead of the old "ducks in a row" metaphor, you'll be saying, "We must concatenate our ducks." Caution is advised.

You'll find the Concatenation.xlsx file in the Sample Files section of the companion CD.

Understanding Error Values

An *error value* is the result of a formula that Excel can't resolve. Table 13-2 describes the seven error values.

Table 13-2 **Error Values**

Error Value	Cause
#DIV/0!	You attempted to divide a number by zero. This error usually occurs when you create a formula with a divisor that refers to a blank cell.
#NAME?	You typed a name that doesn't exist in a formula. You might have mistyped the name or typed a deleted name. Excel also displays this error value if you do not enclose a text string in quotation marks.
#VALUE	You entered a mathematical formula that refers to a text entry.
#REF!	You deleted a range of cells whose references are included in a formula.
#N/A	No information is available for the calculation you want to perform. When building a model, you can type **#N/A** in a cell to show you are awaiting data. Any formulas that reference cells containing the #N/A value return #N/A.
#NUM!	You provided an invalid argument to a worksheet function. #NUM! can indicate also that the result of a formula is too large or too small to be represented in the worksheet.
#NULL!	You included a space between two ranges in a formula to indicate an intersection, but the ranges have no common cells.

Using Functions: A Preview

In simplest terms, a *function* is a predefined formula. Many Excel functions are short-hand versions of frequently used formulas. For example, compare the formula =A1+A 2+A3+A4+A5+A6+A7+A8+A9+A10 with the formula =SUM(A1:A10). The SUM function makes the formula a lot shorter, easier to read, and easier to create. Some Excel functions perform complex calculations. For example, using the PMT function, you can calculate the payment on a loan at a given interest rate and principal amount.

All functions consist of a function name followed by a set of *arguments* enclosed in parentheses. (In the preceding example, A1:A10 is the argument in the SUM function.) If you omit a closing parenthesis when you enter a function, Excel adds the parenthesis after you press Enter, as long as it's obvious where the parenthesis is supposed to go. (Relying on this feature can produce unpredictable results; for accuracy, always verify your parentheses.)

For more information about functions, see Chapter 14, "Using Functions."

Using the Sum Button

Sum

No surprise—the SUM function is used more often than any other function. To make this function more accessible, Excel includes the Sum button on the Home tab on the Ribbon, which inserts the SUM function into a cell. (This button has an alter ego with identical functionality on the Formulas tab on the Ribbon, where it is called the Auto-Sum button.)

> **Note**
>
> You can quickly enter a SUM function in the selected cell by pressing Alt+=.

To see how this works, do the following:

1. Enter a column of numbers, like we did in Figure 13-7.

2. Select the cell below the column of numbers, and click the Sum button in the Editing group on the Home tab. The button inserts the entire formula for you and suggests a range to sum.

3. If the suggested range is incorrect, simply drag through the correct range, and press Enter.

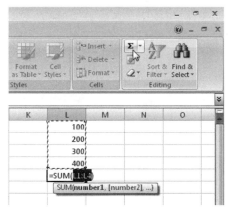 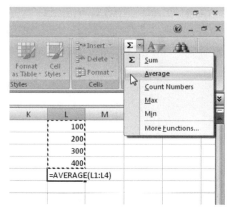

Figure 13-7 Use the Sum button to add a summary formula in a cell adjacent to columns or rows of numbers.

The Sum button includes a menu that appears when you click the arrow next to the button, as shown in Figure 13-7. You can enter the AVERAGE, COUNT, MAX, or MIN function almost as easily as you can enter the SUM function—all it takes is an extra click to select the function you want from the Sum menu. The More Functions command opens the Insert Function dialog box, where you can access any Excel function. If you select a contiguous cell range that is adjacent to rows or columns of numbers before clicking the Sum button, Excel enters SUM functions in each cell.

> **Note**
>
> Get a quick sum by selecting the cells you want to sum and then looking at the status bar, where Excel automatically displays the sum, the average, and the count (the total number of cells containing entries) of the selected range. Right-click the status bar to add more readouts for minimum, maximum, and numerical count..

For more information, see "Using the SUM Function" on page 461.

Inserting a Function

When you want to use a built-in function, click the Insert Function button on the Formulas tab on the Ribbon (or the little *fx* icon located on the formula bar). When you do so, the Insert Function dialog box shown in Figure 13-8 appears. For details about using the Insert Function dialog box, see "Inserting Functions" on page 458.

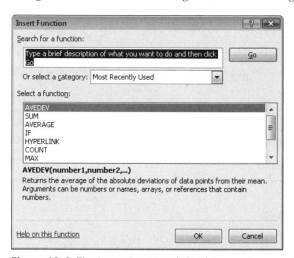

Figure 13-8 The Insert Function dialog box gives you access to all the built-in functions in Excel.

Using Formula AutoComplete

Excel 2007 makes it a little easier to create formulas with a new feature called *Formula AutoComplete*. Figure 13-9 illustrates what happens when you type an equal sign followed by the letter *S*—Excel lists all functions that begin with that letter. Formula

AutoComplete also provides lists of defined names and function arguments, as well as special codes and names used in structured references and Cube functions.

For more about defined names, see "Using Names in Formulas" on page 408; for more about structured references, see "Using Structured References" on page 420.

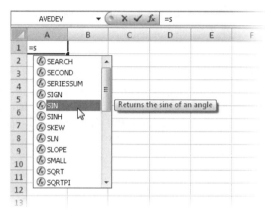

Figure 13-9 When you start to type a function, Excel lists all the functions that begin with that letter or letters.

You can just keep typing your formula, or you can click any of the items in the Auto-Complete list to see a pop-up description of what that function does. Scroll down the list to see more functions; to insert one of the functions into your formula, double-click it. You can type additional characters to narrow the list further. For example, typing **=si** in the example shown in Figure 13-9 would narrow the AutoComplete list to three functions: SIGN, SIN, and SINH. Formula AutoComplete also works within nested formulas. For example, if you started typing a formula such as **=SUM(SIN(A4),S** into a cell, the AutoComplete list would appear and readjust its contents for each letter you type in the formula.

Working with Formulas

We've covered most of the basics you need to know about how formulas and references work. In the following sections, we'll dig deeper, covering how to use defined names, intersections, structured references, and three-dimensional (3-D) formulas.

Naming Cells and Cell Ranges

If you find yourself repeatedly typing cryptic cell addresses, such as **Sheet3!A1:AJ51**, into formulas, we'll show you a better approach. You can assign a short, memorable name to any cell or range and then use that name instead of the cryptogram in formulas. Naming cells has no effect on either their displayed values or their underlying values—you are just assigning "nicknames" you can use when creating formulas.

After you define names in a worksheet, those names become available to any other worksheets in the workbook. A name defining a cell range in Sheet6, for example, is available for use in formulas in Sheet1, Sheet2, and so on, in the workbook. As a result, each workbook contains its own set of names. You can also define worksheet-level names that are available only on the worksheet in which they are defined.

For more information about worksheet-level names, see "Workbook-Wide vs. Worksheet-Only Names" on page 411.

Using Names in Formulas

When you use the name of a cell or a range in a formula, the result is the same as if you typed the cell or range address. For example, suppose you typed the formula **=A1+A2** in cell A3. If you assigned the name Mark to cell A1 and the name Vicki to cell A2, the formula =Mark+Vicki has the same result and is easier to read.

The easiest way to define a name follows:

1. Select a cell.

2. Click the Name box on the left end of the formula bar, as shown in Figure 13-10.

3. Type **TestName**, and then press Enter.

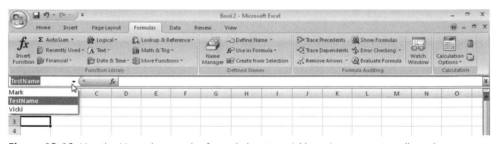

Figure 13-10 Use the Name box on the formula bar to quickly assign names to cells and ranges.

Keep the following basics in mind when using names in formulas:

-   The Name box usually displays the address of the selected cell. If you have named the selected cell or range, the name takes precedence over the address, and Excel displays it in the Name box.

-   When you define a name for a range of cells, the range name does not appear in the Name box unless you select the same range.

-   When you click the Name box and select a name, the cell selection switches to the named cells.

-   If you type a name in the Name box that you have already defined, Excel switches the selection instead of redefining the name.

- When you define a name, the stored definition is an absolute cell reference that includes the worksheet name. For example, when you define the name TestName for cell A3 in Sheet1, the actual name definition is recorded as Sheet1!$A$3.

> For more information about absolute references, see "Understanding Relative, Absolute, and Mixed References" on page 395.

Defining and Managing Names

Instead of coming up with new names for cells and ranges, you can simply use existing text labels to create names. Click the Define Name button on the Formulas tab on the Ribbon to display the New Name dialog box shown in Figure 13-11. In this example, we selected cells B4:E4 before clicking the Define Name button, and Excel correctly surmised that the label *Region 1* was the most likely name candidate for that range. If you are happy using the adjacent label as a name, just press Enter to define the name, or you can first add a note in the Comment box if you want to provide some helpful documentation.

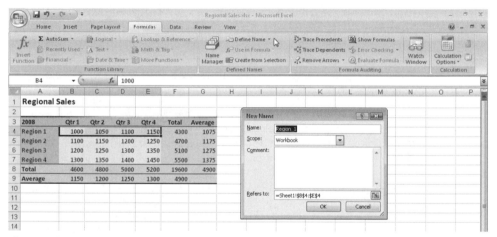

Figure 13-11 When you click Define Name on the Formulas tab, Excel suggests any label in an adjacent cell in the same row or column as a name.

You can, of course, define a name without first selecting a cell or range on the worksheet. For example, in the New Name dialog box, type **Test2** in the Name text box, and then type **=D20** in the Refers To text box. Click OK to add the name, which also closes the New Name dialog box. To see a list of the names you have defined, click the Name Manager button on the Formulas tab. The Name Manager dialog box appears, as shown in Figure 13-12.

The Name Manager dialog box lists all the names along with their values and locations. You'll see that the Refers To text box shows the definition of the name we just added, =Sheet1!D20. Excel adds the worksheet reference for you, but note that the cell reference stays relative, just as you typed it, while the Region_1 definition created by Excel uses absolute references (indicated by the dollar signs in the Refers To definition). Also note that if you do not enter an equal sign preceding the reference, Excel interprets the definition as text. For example, if you typed **D20** instead of **=D20**, the Refers To text box would display the text constant ="D20" as the definition of the name Test2.

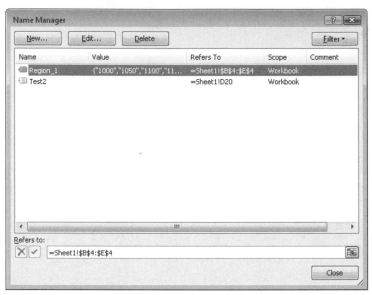

Figure 13-12 The Name Manager dialog box provides central control over all the names in a workbook.

When working with tables created using the new table features in Excel, some names are created automatically, and others are implied. If this sounds intriguing, see "Using Structured References" on page 420.

Editing Names

Although it is possible to edit name references directly using the Refers To text box in the Name Manager dialog box, it is preferable to click the Edit button at the top of the dialog box. Doing so opens the Edit Name dialog box, which is otherwise the same as the New Name dialog box shown in Figure 13-11. Although you can edit name references directly in the Name Manager dialog box, the Edit Name dialog box offers additional opportunities to change the name and to add a comment.

In the Edit Name dialog box, you can change cell references in the Refers To text box by typing or by directly selecting cells on the worksheet. When you click OK in the Edit Name dialog box, the Name Manager dialog box reappears, displaying the updated name definition. Clicking the New button in the Name Manager dialog box predictably displays the New Name dialog box; clicking the Delete button removes all selected names from the list in the Name Manager dialog box. Keep in mind that when you delete a name, any formula in the worksheet referring to that name returns the error value #NAME?.

Rules for Naming

The following rules apply when you name cells and ranges in Excel:

- You must begin all names with a letter, a backslash (\), or an underscore (_). You cannot use any other symbol.

- You cannot use spaces; Excel translates blank spaces in labels to underscores in defined names.

- You can't use names that resemble cell references (for example, AB$5 or R1C7).

- You can use single letters, with the exception of the letters *R* and *C* (uppercase and lowercase), as names.

- You can also use numbers, periods, and underscore characters.

A name can contain 255 characters. Excel does not distinguish between uppercase and lowercase characters in names. For example, if you create the name Tax and then create the name TAX in the same workbook, the second name overwrites the first.

Workbook-Wide vs. Worksheet-Only Names

Names in Excel usually function on a workbook-wide basis. That is, a name you define on any worksheet is available for use in formulas on any other worksheet. But you can also create names whose scope is limited to the worksheet level—that is, names that are available only on the worksheet in which you define them. You might want to do this if, for example, you have a number of worksheets doing similar jobs in the same workbook and you want to use the same names to accomplish similar tasks on each worksheet. To define a worksheet-only name, click the Scope drop-down list in the New Name dialog box, and select the name of the worksheet to which you want to limit the scope of the name.

TROUBLESHOOTING

My old worksheet-level names have changed.

In previous versions of Excel, you created worksheet-level names by preceding the name (not the cell reference) with the name of the worksheet, followed by an exclamation point. This no longer works in Excel 2007, and it's easier now anyway, using the Scope options in the New Name dialog box. If you have existing worksheet-level names in workbooks that you created using previous versions of Excel, they will still work after you import the workbooks into Excel 2007, but Excel modifies the name by removing the old designation that was part of the name (the worksheet name and exclamation point) and adds the Scope designation instead.

For example, to define TestSheetName as a worksheet-only name in Sheet1, select the range you want, click the Define Name button on the Formulas tab, type **TestSheet-Name** in the Name text box, and then select Sheet1 from the Scope drop-down list, as shown in Figure 13-13.

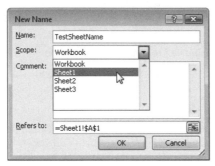

Figure 13-13 Use the Scope drop-down list to specify a worksheet to which you want to restrict a name's usage.

The following are some additional facts to keep in mind when working with worksheet-only and workbook-level names:

- Worksheet-only names do not appear in the Name box on the formula bar in worksheets other than the one in which you define them.

- When you select a cell or range to which you have assigned a worksheet-only name, the name appears in the Name box on the formula bar, but you have no way of knowing its scope. You can consider adding clues for your own benefit, such as including the word *Sheet* as part of all worksheet-only names when you define them.

- If a worksheet contains a duplicate workbook-level and worksheet-only name, the worksheet-level name takes precedence over the book-level name on the worksheet where it lives, rendering the workbook-level version of the name useless on that worksheet.

- You can use a worksheet-only name in formulas on other worksheets by adding the name of the worksheet followed by an exclamation point (no spaces) preceding the name in the formula. For example, you could type the formula **=Sheet1!TestSheetName** in a cell on Sheet3.

- You can't change the scope of an existing name.

Creating Names Semiautomatically

You can click the Create From Selection button on the Formulas tab on the Ribbon to name several adjacent cells or ranges at once, using row labels, column labels, or both. When you choose this command, Excel displays the Create Names From Selection dialog box shown in Figure 13-14.

Selecting Cells While a Dialog Box Is Open

The Refers To text boxes in the New Name and Name Manager dialog boxes (and many other text boxes in other dialog boxes) contain a *collapse dialog button*, which indicates that this is a text box from which you can navigate and select cells on the worksheet. For example, after you click the Refers To text box, you can click outside the dialog box to select any other worksheet tab, drag scroll bars, switch workbooks, or make another workbook active. In addition, if you click the collapse dialog button, sure enough, the dialog box collapses, letting you see more of the worksheet:

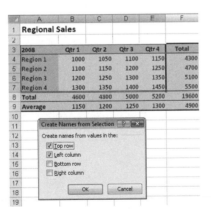

You can drag the collapsed dialog box around the screen using its title bar. When you finish, click the collapse dialog button again, and the dialog box returns to its original size.

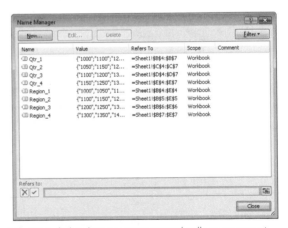

Figure 13-14 Use the Create Names From Selection dialog box to name several cells or ranges at once using labels.

Excel assumes that labels included in the selection are the names for each range. For example, Figure 13-14 shows that with A3:E7 selected, the Top Row and Left Column options in the Create Names dialog box are automatically selected, creating a set of names for each quarter and each product. Note that when using Create From Selection, you need to select the labels as well as the data. When you click the Name Manager button, you'll see the names you just created listed in the dialog box.

Naming Constants and Formulas

You can create names that are defined by constants and formulas instead of by cell references. You can use absolute and relative references, numbers, text, formulas, and functions as name definitions. For example, if you often use the value 8.3% to calculate sales tax, you can click the Define Name button, type the name **Tax** in the Name box, and then type **8.3%** (or **.083**) in the Refers To text box. Then you can use the name Tax in a formula, such as **=Price+(Price*Tax)**, to calculate the cost of items with 8.3 percent sales tax. Note that named constants and formulas do not appear in the Name box on the formula bar, but they do appear in the Name Manager dialog box.

You can also enter a formula in the Refers To text box. For example, you might define the name Price with a formula, such as =Sheet1!A1*190%. If you define this named formula while cell B1 is selected, you can then type **=Price** in cell B1, and the defined formula takes care of the calculation for you. Because the reference in the named formula is relative, you can then type **=Price** in any cell in your workbook to calculate a price using the value in the cell directly to the left. If you type a formula in the Refers To text box that refers to a cell or range in a worksheet, Excel updates the formula whenever the value in the cell changes.

Using Relative References in Named Formulas   When you are creating a named formula that contains relative references, such as =Sheet1!B22+1.2%, Excel interprets the position of the cells referenced in the Refers To text box as relative to the cell that is active when you define the name. Later, when you use such a name in a formula, the named formula uses whatever cell corresponds to the relative reference. For example, if cell B21 was the active cell when you defined the name Fees as =Sheet1!B22+1.2%, the name Fees always refers to the cell one row below the cell in which the formula is currently located.

Creating Three-Dimensional Names

You can create three-dimensional names, which use 3-D references as their definitions. For example, suppose you have a 13-worksheet workbook containing one identical worksheet for each month plus one summary sheet. You can define a 3-D name that you can use to summarize totals from each monthly worksheet. To do so, follow these steps:

1. Select cell B5 in Sheet1 (the summary sheet).

2. Click the Define Name button.

3. Type **Three_D** (or any name you choose) in the Name box, and type **=Sheet2:Sheet13!B5** in the Refers To text box.

4. Press Enter (or click OK).

Now you can use the name Three_D in formulas that contain any of the following functions: SUM, AVERAGE, AVERAGEA, COUNT, COUNTA, MIN, MINA, MAX, MAXA, PRODUCT, STDEV, STDEVA, STDEVP, STDEVPA, VAR, VARA, VARP, and VARPA. For example, the formula =MAX(Three_D) returns the largest value in the three-dimensional range named Three_D. Because you used relative references in step 3, the definition of the range Three_D changes as you select different cells in the worksheet. For example, if you select cell C3 and display the Name Manager dialog box, =Sheet2: Sheet13!C3 appears in the Refers To text box.

For more information on three-dimensional references, see "Creating Three-Dimensional Formulas" on page 419.

Using Names in Formulas

After you define one or more names in your worksheet, you can insert those names in formulas using one of several methods. First, if you know at least the first letter of the name you want to use, you can simply start typing to display the Formula AutoComplete drop-down list containing all the names beginning with that letter (along with any built-in functions that begin with that letter), as shown in Figure 13-15. To enter one of the names in your formula, double-click it.

AVEDEV		✗ ✓ ƒₓ	=SUM(R												
A	B	C	D	E	F	G	H	I	J	K	L	M	N	O	
1 Regional Sales															
2															
3 2008	Qtr 1	Qtr 2	Qtr 3	Qtr 4	Total	Average									
4 Region 1	1000	1050	1100	1150	4300	1075									
5 Region 2	1100	1150	1200	1250	4700	1175									
6 Region 3	1200	1250	1300	1350	5100	1275									
7 Region 4	1300	1350	1400	1450	=SUM(R										
8 Total	4600	4800	5000	5200	1	RADIANS									
9 Average	1150	1200	1250	1300		RAND									
10						RANDBETWEEN									
11						RANK									
12						RATE									
13						RECEIVED									
14						Region_1									
15						Region_2									
16						Region_3									
17						Region_4									
18						REPLACE									
						REPT									

Figure 13-15 Names you define appear in the Formula AutoComplete list when you type a formula.

For more information, see "Using Formula AutoComplete" on page 406.

You can also find a list of all the names relevant to the current worksheet when you click the Use In Formula button on the Formulas tab on the Ribbon, which you can click while in the process of entering a formula, as shown in Figure 13-16.

Clicking the Paste Names command at the bottom of the Use In Formula menu displays the Paste Name dialog box shown on the left in Figure 13-17 when you are editing a formula. If you click the command when you are not in Edit mode, a different version of the dialog box appears, as shown on the right in Figure 13-17. The difference is the Paste List button, which we'll discuss in the next section.

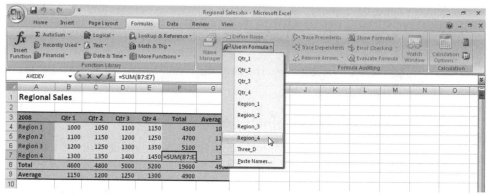

Figure 13-16 Click the Use In Formula button, and select a name to enter it into the selected cell.

Figure 13-17 The Paste Name dialog box changes, depending on whether you are editing within a cell.

Creating a List of Names

In large worksheet models, it's easy to accumulate a long list of defined names. To keep a record of all the names used, you can paste a list of defined names in your worksheet by clicking Paste List in the Paste Name dialog box, as shown in Figure 13-18. Excel pastes the list in your worksheet beginning at the active cell. Worksheet-only names appear in the list only when you click Paste List on the worksheet where they live. Paste List is really the only useful feature in the Paste Name dialog box, given the superior methods of using names described in the previous section.

> **Note**
>
> When Excel pastes the list of names, it overwrites any existing data without asking for permission first. If you inadvertently overwrite data, press Ctrl+Z to undo it.

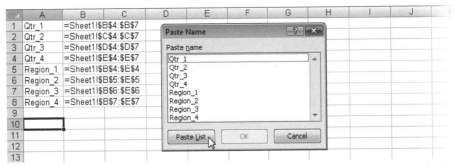

Figure 13-18 Click Paste List in the Paste Name dialog box to create a list of names and references starting at the active cell.

Replacing References with Names

You can replace cell references with their corresponding names all at once using the Apply Names command, which you access by clicking the arrow next to the Define Name button on the Formulas tab on the Ribbon. When you do so, Excel locates all cell and range references for which you have defined names and replaces them with the appropriate name. If you select a single cell before you click the Apply Names command, Excel applies names throughout the active worksheet; if you select a range of cells first, Excel applies names to only the selected cells.

Figure 13-19 shows the Apply Names dialog box, which lists all the cell and range names you have defined. Select each name you want to apply, and then click OK.

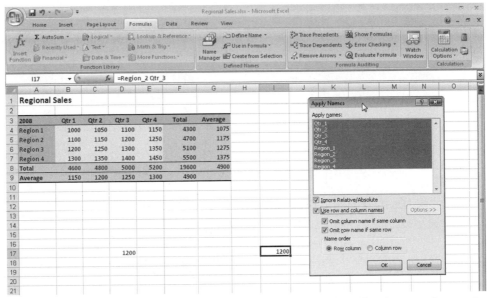

Figure 13-19 Use the Apply Names dialog box to substitute names for cell and range references in your formulas. Click Options to display all the options shown here.

Excel ordinarily does not apply the column or row name if either is superfluous. For example, Figure 13-19 shows a worksheet after we applied names using the default options in the Apply Names dialog box. Cell I17 is selected, and the formula bar shows it contains the formula =Region_2 Qtr_3, which before applying names contained the formula =D5. Because cell I17 isn't in the same row or column as any of the defined ranges, both the row and column names are included in the new formula. Cell D17 contained the same formula, =D5. But because D17 is in the same column as the referenced cell, only the row name is needed thanks to implicit intersection, resulting in the formula =Region_2.

If you prefer to see both the column and row names even when they are not necessary, clear the Omit Column Name If Same Column check box and the Omit Row Name If Same Row check box.

The Name Order options control the order in which row and column components appear. For example, if we applied names using the Column Row option, the formula in cell I17 in Figure 13-19 would become =Qtr_3 Region_2.

> For more information about implicit intersection, see "Getting Explicit About Intersections" below.

Select the Ignore Relative/Absolute check box to replace references with names regardless of the reference type. In general, leave this check box selected. Most name definitions use absolute references (the default when you define and create names), and most formulas use relative references (the default when you paste cell and range references in the formula bar). If you clear this check box, absolute, relative, and mixed references are replaced with name definitions only if the definitions use the same reference style.

The Use Row And Column Names check box is necessary if you want to apply names in intersection cases, as we have shown in the examples. If you define names for individual cells, however, you can clear the Use Row And Column Names check box to apply names to only specific cell references in formulas.

Using Go To with Names

Find & Select ▾

When you click the Find & Select button on the Home tab and click Go To (or press F5), any names you have defined appear in the Go To list, as shown in Figure 13-20. Select a name, and click OK to jump to the range to which the name refers. Note that names defined with constants or formulas do not appear in the Go To dialog box.

Getting Explicit About Intersections

In the worksheet in Figure 13-19, if you type the formula **=Qtr_l*4** in cell I4, Excel assumes you want to use only one value in the Qtr_1 range B4:B7—the one in the same row as the formula that contains the reference. This is called *implicit intersection.* Because the formula is in row 4, Excel uses the value in cell B4. If you type the same formula in cells I5, I6, and I7, each cell in that range contains the formula =Qtr_1*4, but at I5 the formula refers to cell B5, at I6 it refers to cell B6, and so on.

Figure 13-20 Use the Go To dialog box to select a cell or range name so you can move to that cell or range quickly.

Explicit intersection refers to a specific cell with the help of the intersection operator. The *intersection operator* is the space character that appears when you press the Spacebar. If you type the formula **=Qtr_1 Region_1** at any location on the same worksheet, Excel knows you want to refer to the value at the intersection of the range labeled Qtr 1 and the range labeled Region 1, which is cell B4.

Creating Three-Dimensional Formulas

You can use references to perform calculations on cells that span a range of worksheets in a workbook. These are called *3-D references.* Suppose you set up 12 worksheets in the same workbook—one for each month—with a year-to-date summary sheet on top. If all the monthly worksheets are laid out identically, you could use 3-D reference formulas to summarize the monthly data on the summary sheet. For example, the formula =SUM(Sheet2:Sheet13!B5) adds all the values in cell B5 on all the worksheets between and including Sheet2 and Sheet13.

You can also use 3-D names in formulas. For more information, see "Creating Three-Dimensional Names" on page 414.

To construct this three-dimensional formula, follow these steps:

1. In cell B5 of Sheet1, type **=SUM(**.

2. Click the Sheet2 tab, and select cell B5.

3. Click the right tab-scrolling button (located to the left of the worksheet tabs) until the Sheet13 tab is visible.

4. Hold down the Shift key, and click the Sheet13 tab. All the tabs from Sheet2 through Sheet13 change to white, indicating they are selected for inclusion in the reference you are constructing.

5. Select cell B5 in Sheet13.

6. Type a closing parenthesis, and then press Enter.

You can use the following functions with 3-D references: SUM, AVERAGE, AVERAGEA, COUNT, COUNTA, MIN, MINA, MAX, MAXA, PRODUCT, STDEV, STDEVA, STDEVP, STDEVPA, VAR, VARA, VARP, and VARPA.

Formula-Bar Formatting

You can enter spaces and line breaks in a formula to make it easier to read in the formula bar without affecting the calculation of the formula. To enter a line break, press Alt+Enter. Figure 13-21 shows a formula that contains line breaks. To see all of the formula in the formula bar, click the Expand Formula Bar button (the one with the chevron) at the right end of the formula bar.

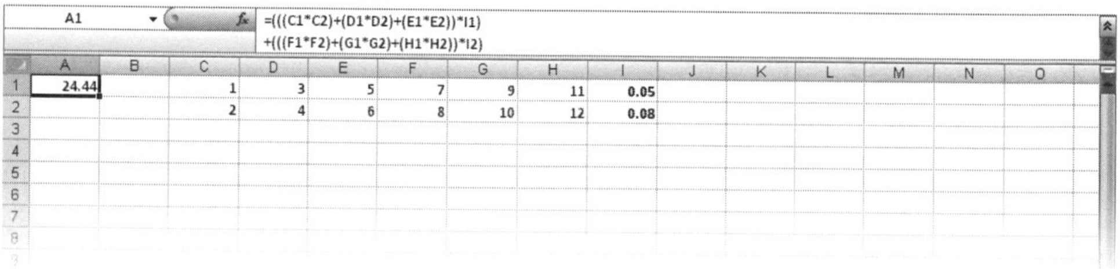

Figure 13-21 You can enter line breaks in a formula to make it more readable.

Using Structured References

Creating names to define cells and ranges makes complex formulas easier to create and easier to read, and *structured references* offer similar advantages, and much more, whenever you create formulas in tables or formulas that refer to data in tables. Structured references are dynamic; formulas that use them automatically adjust to any changes you make to the table.

Structured references rely on the structure imposed when you create a table using the Table button on the Insert tab on the Ribbon. Excel recognizes distinct areas of a table as separate components you can refer to using *specifiers* that are either predefined or derived from the table. Figure 13-22 shows a modified version of the Regional Sales worksheet that we converted to a table. We'll refer to this table as we discuss structured references.

When you refer to data in tables using formulas created by direct manipulation—that is, when you click or drag to insert cell or range references in formulas—Excel creates structured references automatically in most cases. (If a structured reference is not applicable, Excel inserts cell references instead.) Excel builds structured references using the table name and the column labels. (Excel automatically assigns a name to the table when you create one.) You can also type structured references using strict syntax guidelines that we'll explain later in this section.

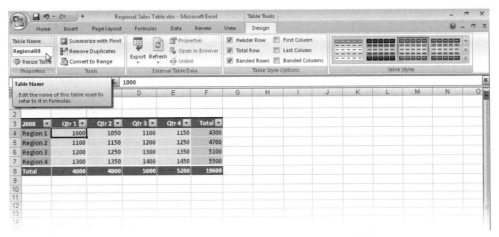

Figure 13-22 We created this table to illustrate the power of structured references.

> **Note**
>
> The capability to create structured references automatically using direct manipulation with the mouse is an option that is ordinarily turned on. To disable this feature, click the Microsoft Office Button, Excel Options, and then in the Formulas category, clear the cryptically titled Use Table Names In Formulas check box.

All Excel tables contain the following areas of interest, as far as structured references are concerned:

- **The table** Excel automatically applies a table name when you create a table, which appears in the Table Name text box in the Properties group on the Table Tools Design tab that appears when you select a table. Excel named our table Table3 in this example, but we changed it to Regional08 by typing in the Table Name text box, as shown in Figure 13-22. The table name actually refers to all the data in the table, excluding the header and total rows.

- **Individual columns of data** Excel uses your column headers in *column specifiers*, which refer to the data in each column, excluding the header and the total row. A *calculated column* is a column of formulas inside the table structure, such as F4:F7 in our example, which, again, does not include the header or total rows.

- **Special items** These are specific areas of a table, including the total row, the header row, and other areas specified by using *special item specifiers*—fixed codes that are used in structured references to zero in on specific cells or ranges in a table. We'll explain these later in this section.

No More Natural-Language Formulas

In previous versions of Excel, you could use adjacent labels instead of cell references when creating formulas, which was like using names without actually having to define them. This was called the *natural-language formulas* feature, but it was riddled with problems and has been replaced in Excel 2007 with structured references, which work much better. However, when you open a workbook created with a previous version of Excel containing natural-language formulas, the following, somewhat frightening, error message appears:

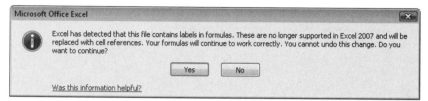

Despite the admonition that "Excel cannot undo this change," this mandatory conversion has little effect on your worksheets other than changing some of the underlying formulas. Excel correctly identifies the offending labels and replaces them for you with the correct cell references. If you still want your formulas to be more readable, you can then rebuild them using names or structured references.

Let's look at an example of a structured reference formula. Figure 13-23 shows a SUM formula that we created by first typing **=SUM(**, then clicking cell B4, then typing another comma, and finally clicking cell C4. Because the data we want to use resides within a table and our formula is positioned in one of the same rows, Excel automatically uses structured references when we use the cursor to select cells while building formulas.

H4			f_x =SUM(Regional08[[#This Row],[Qtr 1]],Regional08[[#This Row],[Qtr 2]])

Regional Sales Table

2008	Qtr 1	Qtr 2	Qtr 3	Qtr 4	Total		1st Half	2nd Half
Region 1	1000	1050	1100	1150	4300		2050	
Region 2	1100	1150	1200	1250	4700			
Region 3	1200	1250	1300	1350	5100			
Region 4	1300	1350	1400	1450	5500			
Total	4600	4800	5000	5200	19600			

Figure 13-23 We created the formula in cell H4 by dragging to select cells in the table.

The result shown in the formula bar appears to be much more complex than necessary because we could just type **=SUM(B4:C4)** to produce the same result in this worksheet. But the structured formula is still quite easy to create using the mouse, and it has the distinct advantage of being able to automatically accommodate even the most radical changes to the table, which ordinary formulas are not nearly as good at accommodating.

Let's examine a little more closely the structured reference contained within the parentheses of the SUM function shown in Figure 13-23. The entire reference string shown here is equivalent to the expression (B4,C4), which combines the cells on both sides of the comma. The portion of the reference string in bold represents a single, complete structured reference.

`Regional08[[#This Row],[Qtr 1]],Regional08[[#This Row],[Qtr 2]])`

Here's how the reference string breaks down:

- The first item, Regional08, is the table specifier, which is followed by an opening bracket. Just like parentheses in functions, brackets in structured references always come in pairs. The table name is a little bit like a function, in that it always includes a pair of brackets that enclose the rest of the reference components. This tells Excel that everything within the brackets applies to the Regional08 table.

- The second item, [#This Row], is one of the five special item specifiers and tells Excel that the following reference components apply only to those portions of the table that fall in the current row. (Obviously, this wouldn't work if the formula were located above or below the table.) This represents an application of implicit intersection (see "Getting Explicit About Intersections" on page 418).

- The third item, [Qtr 1], is a column specifier. In our example, this corresponds to the range B4:B7. However, because it follows the [#This Row] specifier, only those cells in the range that happen to be in the same row as the formula are included, or cell B4 in the example.

- The second reference follows the second comma in the string and is essentially the same as the first, specifying the other end of the range, or cell C4 in the example.

Understanding Structured Reference Syntax

Here are some of the general rules governing the creation of structured references:

- Table naming rules are the same as those of defined names. See "Naming Cells and Cell Ranges" on page 407.

- You must enclose all specifiers in matching brackets.

- To make structured references easier to read, you can add a single space character in any or all of the following locations:
  - After the first opening (left) bracket (but not in subsequent opening brackets)
  - Before the last closing (right) bracket (but not in subsequent closing brackets)
  - After a comma

- Column headers are always treated as text strings in structured references, even if the column header is a number.

- You cannot use formulas in brackets.

- You need to use double brackets in column header specifiers that contain one of the following special characters: tab, line feed, carriage return, comma, colon, period, opening bracket, closing bracket, pound sign, single quotation mark, double quotation mark, left brace, right brace, dollar sign, caret, ampersand, asterisk, plus sign, equal sign, minus sign, greater than symbol, less than symbol, and division sign; for example, Sales[[$Canadian]]. Space characters are permitted.

Using Operators with Column Specifiers

You can use three *reference operators* with column specifiers in structured references—a colon (:), which is the range operator; a comma (,), which is the union operator; and a space character ( ), which is the intersection operator.

For example, the following formula calculates the average combined sales for quarters 1 and 4 using a comma (the union operator) between the two structured references:

```
=AVERAGE(Regional08[Qtr 1],Regional08[Qtr 4])
```

The following formula calculates the average sales for quarters 2 and 3 by using colons (the range operator) to specify contiguous ranges of cells in each of the two structured references within the parentheses and by using a space character (the intersection operator) between the two structured references, which combines only the cells that overlap (Qtr 2 and Qtr 3):

```
=AVERAGE(Regional08[[Qtr 1]:[Qtr 3]] Regional08[[Qtr 2]:[Qtr 4]])
```

About the Special Item Specifiers

Excel provides five special codes you can use with your structured references that refer to specific parts of a table. You've already seen the special item specifier [#This Row] being used in previous examples. Here are all five special item specifiers:

- **[#This Row]** This specifier identifies cells at the intersection created in conjunction with column specifiers; you cannot use it with any of the other special item specifiers in this list.

- **[#Totals]** This refers to cells in the total row (if one exists) and otherwise returns a null value.

- **[#Headers]** This refers only to cells in the header row.

- **[#Data]** This refers only to cells in the data area between the header row and the total row.

- **[#All]** This refers to the entire table, including the header row and the total row.

Are Your References Qualified?

Two kinds of structured references exist: *qualified* and *unqualified*. Generally, you can use unqualified references in formulas that you construct within a table because the formulas are insulated from errors that may be introduced by inserting, deleting, or moving cells by virtue of the robust infrastructure of the table. When building formulas outside the protective structure of a table, it is advisable to use qualified references to protect against such errors. Here is an example of an unqualified reference that will work only within a table, followed by a qualified reference that produces the same result outside the table:

```
=[Qtr 1]/[Total]

=Regional08[[#This Row],[Qtr 1]]/Regional08[[#This Row],[Total]]
```

Using Formula AutoComplete with Structured References

As you enter your formulas, the Formula AutoComplete feature is there to help you along by displaying lists of applicable functions, defined names, and structured reference specifiers as you type. For example, Figure 13-24 shows a formula being constructed using a SUM function, along with an AutoComplete drop-down list displaying all the defined items that are available that begin with the opening bracket character (also called a *display trigger* in AutoComplete parlance) that you just typed in the formula. Notice that the list includes all the column specifiers for the example table, as well as all the special item specifiers, all of which begin with a bracket.

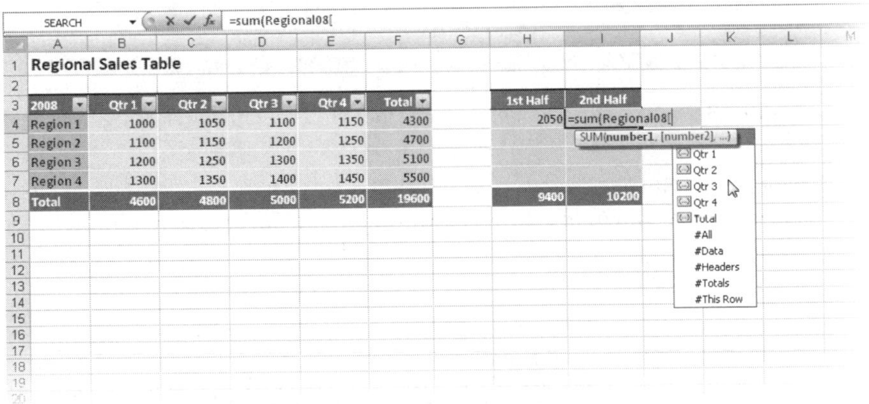

Figure 13-24 Structured reference specifiers automatically appear in the AutoComplete drop-down list if they are applicable when creating a formula.

To enter one of the items in the list in the formula, double-click it. The Formula Auto-Complete list will most likely open more than once as you type formulas, offering any and all options that begin with the entered letters or display triggers. For example, the AutoComplete list appeared after we typed **=S** with a list of all the items beginning with that letter and again after typing the **R** in Regional08.

For more information, see "Using Formula AutoComplete" on page 406.

Filling and Copying Structured References

As a rule, structured references do not adjust like relative cell references when you copy or fill them—the reference remains the same. The exceptions to this rule occur with column specifiers when you use the fill handle to copy fully qualified structured references outside the table structure. For example, in the worksheet shown in Figure 13-25, we dragged the fill handle to copy the % of Total formula in cell K4 to the right, and the column specifiers in the formulas adjusted accordingly.

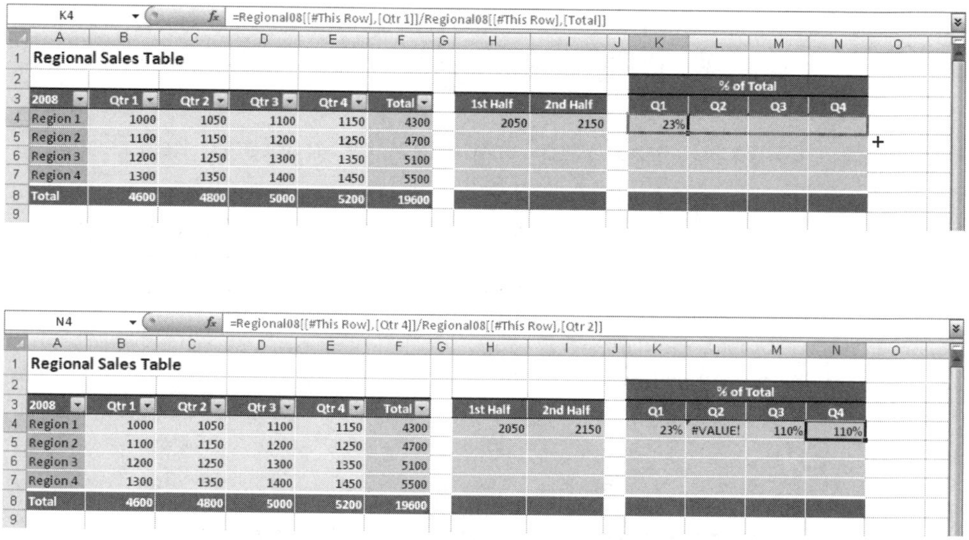

Figure 13-25 You can drag the fill handle to extend structured reference formulas into adjacent cells, but they behave a little bit differently than regular formulas.

The results illustrate some interesting structured reference behavior. Notice that the first formula shown in cell K4 divides the value in the Qtr 1 column by the value in the Total column. After we filled to the right, the resulting formula in cell N4 divides the value in the Qtr 4 column by the value in the Qtr 2 column. How did this happen?

As far as filling cells is concerned, tables act like little traps—you can check in, but you can't check out. The top formula shown in Figure 13-25 has two column specifiers: Qtr 1 and Total. When we filled to the right, the Qtr 1 reference extended the way we wanted, extending to Qtr 2, Qtr 3, and Qtr 4 in each cell to the right. However, the Total reference, instead of extending to the right (G4, H4, I4) like a regular series fill would, "wrapped" around the table (2008, Qtr 1 and Qtr 2), resulting in the formula displayed in cell N4 at the bottom of Figure 13-25. This is interesting behavior, and we're sure people will figure out ways to put it to good use.

What we need is a way to "lock" the Total column reference, but Excel doesn't offer any way to create "absolute" column specifiers like we can with cell references. We can substitute a cell reference for the entire Total reference, as shown in Figure 13-26. We used a mixed reference in this case, specifying the absolute column $F but letting the row number adjust so we could fill down as well.

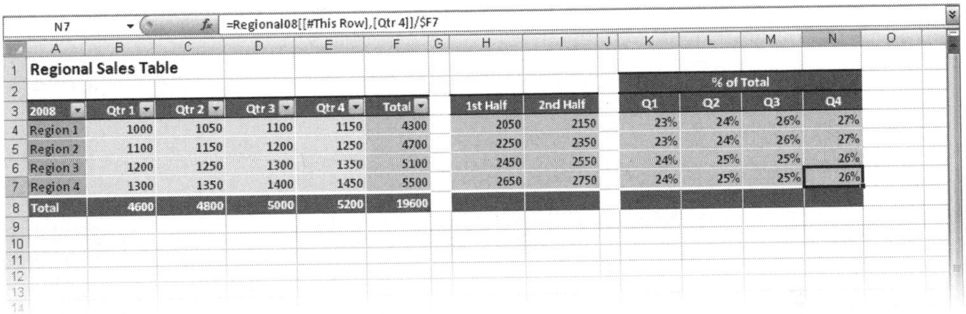

2008	Qtr 1	Qtr 2	Qtr 3	Qtr 4	Total	1st Half	2nd Half	Q1	Q2	Q3	Q4
Region 1	1000	1050	1100	1150	4300	2050	2150	23%	24%	26%	27%
Region 2	1100	1150	1200	1250	4700	2250	2350	23%	24%	26%	27%
Region 3	1200	1250	1300	1350	5100	2450	2550	24%	25%	25%	26%
Region 4	1300	1350	1400	1450	5500	2650	2750	24%	25%	25%	26%
Total	4600	4800	5000	5200	19600						

Figure 13-26 We replaced the second structured reference with an absolute cell reference to make filling these formulas work properly.

Note that if we were to select cell H4 in Figure 13-26 and drag the fill handle down, the formulas in each cell would not appear to adjust at all, and yet they would work perfectly. (The formula in cell H4 appears in Figure 13-23.) This is because explicit intersection, the built-in behavior of column specifiers, and the functionality of the [#This Row] specifier eliminate the need to adjust row references.

> **Note**
>
> When dragging the fill handle to the right in a cell containing a structured reference formula, pressing Ctrl prevents the column specifiers from adjusting as they usually would and instead copies the formula to the right without adjustment.

Worksheet Calculation

When you change the value in any of the cells to which a formula refers, Excel updates the displayed values of the formula as well. This updating process is called *recalculation*, and it affects only those cells containing references to cells that have changed. By default, Excel recalculates whenever you make changes to a cell. If a large number of cells must be recalculated, the word *Calculating* appears in the status bar, along with a percentage of progress meter if it's going to take a particularly long time. You can interrupt the recalculation process simply by doing something, such as using commands or making cell entries; Excel pauses and then resumes recalculation when you are finished.

> **Note**
>
> When you open an Excel 2007 workbook, Excel recalculates only those formulas that depend on cell values that have changed. However, because of changes in the way Excel 2007 recalculates, when you open a workbook that was created using a previous version of Excel (or saved in a previous Excel file format), Excel recalculates all the formulas in the workbook each time you open it. To avoid this, save it in the Excel 2007 (.xlsx or .xlsm) file format.

Recalculating Manually

To save time, particularly when you are making entries into a large workbook with many formulas, you can switch from automatic to manual recalculation; that is, Excel will recalculate only when you tell it to do so. To set manual recalculation, click the Calculation Options button on the Formulas tab on the Ribbon, and choose the Manual option. You can also click the Microsoft Office Button, Excel Options, and then select the Formulas category to display the additional options shown in Figure 13-27.

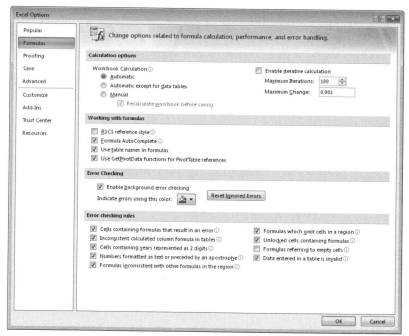

Figure 13-27 The Formulas category in the Excel Options dialog box controls worksheet calculation and iteration.

Here are a few facts to remember about calculation options:

- With worksheet recalculation set to manual, the status bar displays the word *Calculate* if you make a change; click it to initiate recalculation immediately.

- The Recalculate Workbook Before Saving check box helps make sure the most current values are stored on disk.

- To turn off automatic recalculation only for data tables, select the Automatic Except For Data Tables option.

Calculate Now

- To recalculate all open workbooks, click the Calculate Now button in the Calculation group on the Formulas tab on the Ribbon, or press F9.

Calculate Sheet

- To calculate only the active worksheet in a workbook, click the Calculate Sheet button in the Calculation group on the Formulas tab on the Ribbon, or press Shift+F9.

> ### Multithreaded Calculation
>
> If you have a computer with multiple processors or a hyperthreaded processor, Excel takes full advantage of the additional power by dividing the workload among available processors. Click the Microsoft Office Button, Excel Options, Advanced category, and look in the Formulas area. Excel automatically detects additional processors and displays the total number adjacent to the Use All Processors On This Computer option. The number of processors also appears in the status bar next to the word *Calculating*, if you have enough formulas to slow the calculation process enough for it to appear. If you want, you can turn this option off if you want to reserve some of your computer's processing bandwidth for other programs you need to run simultaneously.

Calculating Part of a Formula

You might want to see the result of just one part of a complex formula if, for example, you are tracking down a discrepancy. To change only part of a formula to a value, select the part you want to change, and press F9. You also can use this technique to change selected cell references in formulas to their values. Figure 13-28 shows an example.

If you're just verifying your figures, press the Esc key to discard the edited formula. Otherwise, if you press Enter, you replace the selected portion of the formula.

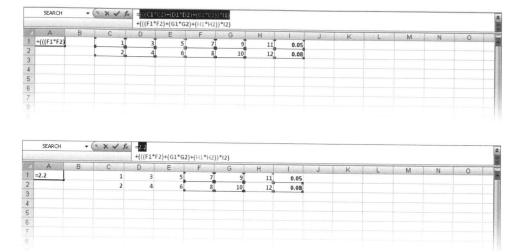

Figure 13-28 Select any part of a formula, and press F9 to convert it to its resulting value.

> **Note**
>
> You can also click the Evaluate Formula button on the Formulas tab to troubleshoot your workbook models.

Working with Circular References

A *circular reference* is a formula that depends on its own value. The most obvious type is a formula that contains a reference to the same cell in which it's entered. For example, if you type **=C1-A1** in cell A1, Excel displays the error message shown in Figure 13-29. After you click OK, Excel opens the Help dialog box, which displays a pertinent topic.

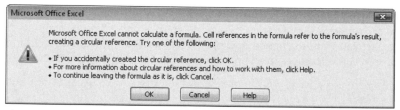

Figure 13-29 This error message appears when you attempt to enter a formula that contains a circular reference.

If a circular reference warning surprises you, this usually means you made an error in a formula. If the error isn't obvious, verify the cells that the formula refers to using the built-in formula-auditing features.

When a circular reference is present in the current worksheet, the status bar displays the text *Circular References* followed by the cell address, indicating the location of the circular reference on the current worksheet. If *Circular References* appears without a cell address, then the circular reference is located on another worksheet.

As you can see in Figure 13-30, when you click the arrow next to the Error Checking button on the Formulas tab and click Circular Reference, any circular references that exist on the current worksheet are listed on a menu that appears only if a circular reference is present. Click the reference listed on this menu to activate the offending cell.

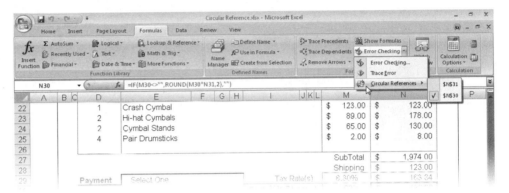

Figure 13-30 The Circular References menu appears if any circular references are present.

You can resolve many circular references. Some circular formulas are useful or even essential, such as the set of circular references shown in Figure 13-31. These formulas are circular because the formula in cell M30 depends on the value in M31, and the formula in M31 depends on the value in M30.

Figure 13-31 illustrates a useful circular reference scenario called *convergence*: The difference between results decreases with each iterative calculation. In the opposite process, called *divergence*, the difference between results increases with each calculation.

When Excel detects a circular reference, tracer arrows appear on the worksheet. To draw additional arrows to track down the source of an unintentional circular reference, select the offending cell, and then click Trace Precedents on the Formulas tab to draw tracer arrows to the next level of precedent cells, as shown in Figure 13-31.

You'll find the Circular Reference.xlsx file in the Sample Files section of the companion CD.

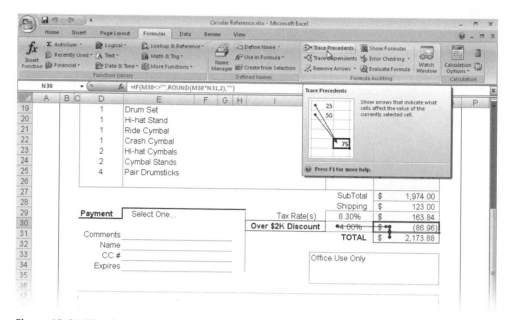

Figure 13-31 The discount formula in cell M29 is circular because it depends on the total, which in turn depends on the discount value in M29.

After you dismiss the error message shown in Figure 13-29, the formula will not resolve until you allow Excel to recalculate in controlled steps. To do so, click the Microsoft Office Button, Excel Options, Formulas category, and in the Calculation Options section, select the Enable Iterative Calculation check box. Excel recalculates all the cells in any open worksheets that contain a circular reference.

If necessary, the recalculation repeats the number of times specified in the Maximum Iterations box (100 is the default). Each time Excel recalculates the formulas, the results in the cells get closer to the correct values. If necessary, Excel continues until the difference between iterations is less than the number typed in the Maximum Change text box (0.001 is the default). Thus, using the default settings, Excel recalculates either a maximum of 100 times or until the values change less than 0.001 between iterations, whichever comes first.

If the word *Calculate* appears in the status bar after the iterations are finished, more iterations are possible. You can accept the current result, increase the number of iterations, or lower the Maximum Change threshold. Excel does not repeat the "Cannot Resolve Circular Reference" error message if it fails to resolve the reference. You must determine when the answer is close enough. Excel can perform iterations in seconds, but in complex circular situations, you might want to set the Calculation option to Manual; otherwise, Excel recalculates the circular references every time you make a cell entry.

The Solver add-in, a "what-if" analysis tool, offers more control and precision when working with complex iterative calculations.

Understanding the Precision of Numeric Values

Here are three interesting facts about numeric precision in Excel:

- Excel stores numbers with as much as 15-digit accuracy and converts any digits after the 15th to zeros.

- Excel drops any digits after the 15 in a decimal fraction.

- Excel uses scientific notation to display numbers that are too long for their cells.

TROUBLESHOOTING

Rounded values in my worksheet don't add up.

Your worksheet can appear erroneous if you use rounded values. For example, if you use cell formatting to display numbers in currency format with two decimal places, Excel displays the value 10.006 as the rounded value $10.01. If you add 10.006 and 10.006, the correct result is 20.012. If all of these numbers are formatted as currency, however, the worksheet displays the rounded values $10.01 and $10.01, and the rounded value of the result is $20.01. The result is correct, as far as rounding goes, but its appearance might be unacceptable for a particular purpose, such as a presentation or an audit.

You can correct this problem by changing the currency format, or you can click the Microsoft Office Button, Excel Options, Advanced category and in the section entitled When Calculating This Workbook, select the Set Precision As Displayed check box. However, you should select this check box only with extreme caution because it permanently changes the underlying values in your worksheet to their displayed values. For example, if a cell containing the value 10.006 is formatted as currency, selecting the Set Precision As Displayed check box permanently changes the value to 10.01.

Table 13-3 contains examples of how Excel treats integers and decimal fractions longer than 15 digits when they are typed in cells with the default column width of 8.43 characters.

Table 13-3 Examples of Numeric Precision

Typed Entry	Displayed Value	Stored Value
123456789012345678	1.23457E+17	123456789012345000
1.23456789012345678	1.234568	1.23456789012345
1234567890.12345678	1234567890	1234567890.12345
123456789012345.678	1.23457E+14	123456789012345

Excel can calculate positive values as large as 9.99E+307 and approximately as small as 1.00E−307. If a formula results in a value outside this range, Excel stores the number as text and assigns a #NUM! error value to the formula cell.

Using Arrays

Arrays are familiar concepts to computer programmers. Simply defined, an *array* is a collection of items. Excel is one of the few applications that facilitate array operations, in which items that comprise an array can be individually or collectively addressed in simple mathematical terms. Here is some basic array terminology you should know:

- An *array formula* acts on two or more sets of values, called *array arguments*, to return either a single result or multiple results.

- An *array range* is a block of cells that share a common array formula.

- An *array constant* is a specially organized list of constant values that you can use as arguments in array formulas.

Arrays perform calculations in a way unlike anything else. You can use them for worksheet security, alarm monitors, linear regression tables, and much more.

One-Dimensional Arrays

The easiest way to learn about arrays is to look at a few examples. For instance, you can calculate the averages shown in Figure 13-32 by entering a single array formula.

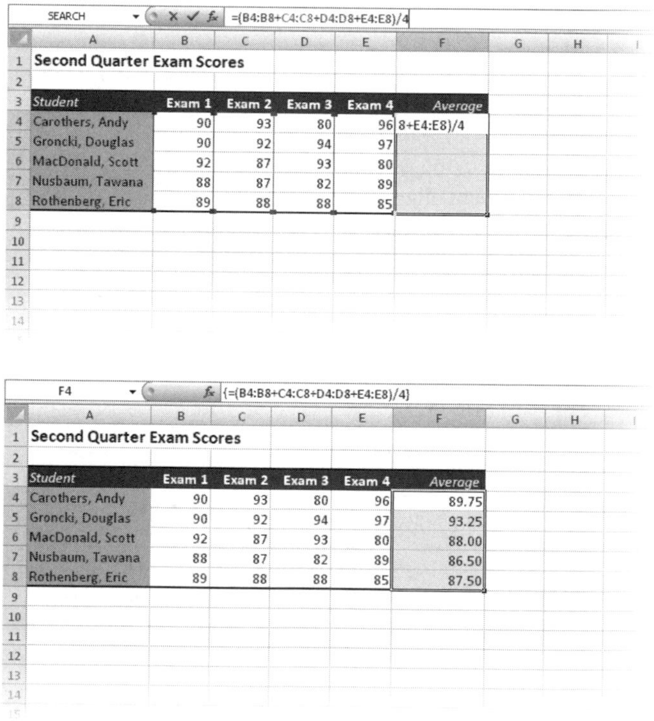

Figure 13-32 We entered a single array formula in the selected range F4:F8.

This particular example might be used to help protect the formulas from tampering because modifying individual formulas in cells that are part of an array is impossible. To enter this formula, do the following:

1. Select the range F4:F8.

2. Type the formula in the formula bar, as shown in Figure 13-32.

3. Press Ctrl+Shift+Enter.

The resulting single array formula exists in five cells at once. Although the array formula seems to be five separate formulas, you can't make changes to any one formula without selecting the entire formula—that is, the entire range F4:F8.

You can identify an array formula by looking at the formula bar. If the active cell contains an array formula, the entire formula, including the equal sign, is enclosed in braces—{ }—in the formula bar, as you can see in Figure 13-32.

Array Formula Rules

To enter an array formula, first select the cell or range that will contain the results. If the formula produces multiple results, you must select a range the same size and shape as the range or ranges on which you perform your calculations.

Follow these guidelines when entering and working with array formulas:

- Press Ctrl+Shift+Enter to lock in an array formula. Excel will then place a set of curly braces around the formula in the formula bar to indicate that it's an array formula. Don't type the braces; if you do, Excel interprets your entry as text.

- You can't edit, clear, or move individual cells in an array range, and you can't insert or delete cells. You must treat the cells in the array range as a single unit and edit them all at once.

- To edit an array, select the entire array, click the formula bar, and edit the formula. Then press Ctrl+Shift+Enter to lock in the formula.

- To clear an array, select the entire array, and press Delete.

- To select an entire array, click any cell in the array, and press Ctrl+/.

- To move an array range, you must select the entire array and either cut and paste the selection or drag the selection to a new location.

- You can't cut, clear, or edit part of an array, but you can assign different formats to individual cells in the array. You can also copy cells from an array range and paste them in another area of your worksheet.

Two-Dimensional Arrays

In the preceding example, the array formula resulted in a vertical, one-dimensional array. You also can create arrays that include two or more columns and rows, otherwise known as *two-dimensional arrays*. Figure 13-33 shows an example.

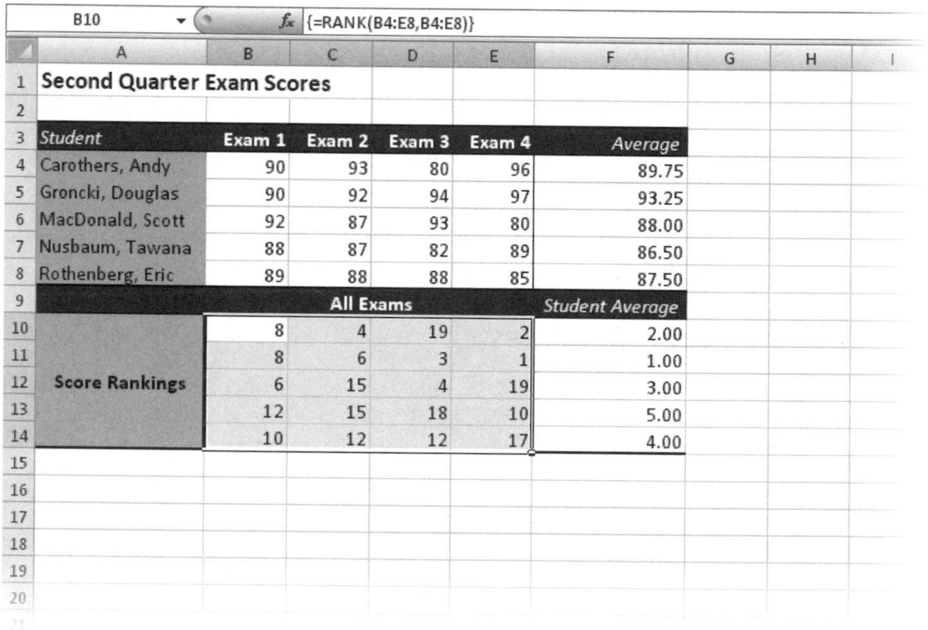

	A	B	C	D	E	F	G	H	I
	B10		▾	*fx*	{=RANK(B4:E8,B4:E8)}				
1	Second Quarter Exam Scores								
2									
3	*Student*	Exam 1	Exam 2	Exam 3	Exam 4	*Average*			
4	Carothers, Andy	90	93	80	96	89.75			
5	Groncki, Douglas	90	92	94	97	93.25			
6	MacDonald, Scott	92	87	93	80	88.00			
7	Nusbaum, Tawana	88	87	82	89	86.50			
8	Rothenberg, Eric	89	88	88	85	87.50			
9			All Exams			*Student Average*			
10		8	4	19	2	2.00			
11		8	6	3	1	1.00			
12	**Score Rankings**	6	15	4	19	3.00			
13		12	15	18	10	5.00			
14		10	12	12	17	4.00			
15									
16									
17									
18									
19									
20									
21									

Figure 13-33 We used a two-dimensional array formula in B10:E14 to compute the rank of each exam score. A similar one-dimensional array appears in F10:F14.

To enter a two-dimensional array, do the following:

1. Select a range to contain your array that is the same size and shape as the range you want to use.

2. Type your formula in the formula bar, and press Ctrl+Shift+Enter.

> **Note**
>
> Unfortunately, you can't create three-dimensional arrays across multiple worksheets in workbooks.

Single-Cell Array Formulas

You can perform calculations on a vast collection of values within a single cell by using an array formula that produces a single value as a result. For example, you can create a simple single-cell array formula to multiply the values in a range of cells by the values in an adjacent range, as shown in Figure 13-34.

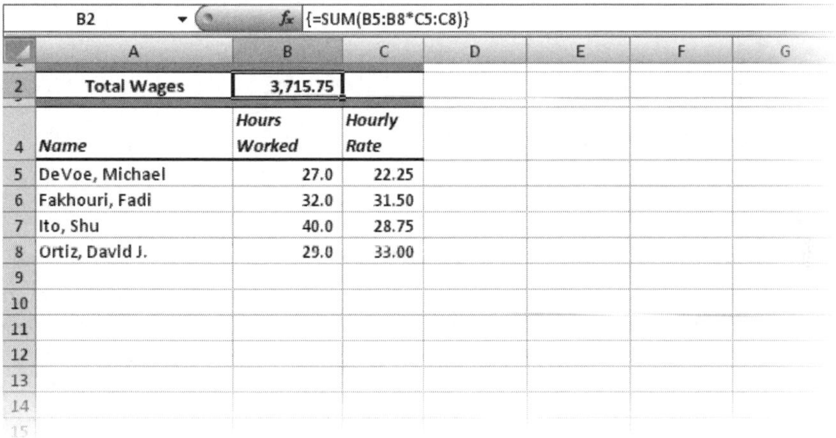

	B2			f_x {=SUM(B5:B8*C5:C8)}				
	A	B	C	D	E	F	G
2	Total Wages	3,715.75					
4	Name	Hours Worked	Hourly Rate				
5	DeVoe, Michael	27.0	22.25				
6	Fakhouri, Fadi	32.0	31.50				
7	Ito, Shu	40.0	28.75				
8	Ortiz, David J.	29.0	33.00				
9							
10							
11							
12							
13							
14							
15							

Figure 13-34 To calculate total wages paid, we used a single-cell array formula in B3 to multiply hours worked by wages due for each employee individually.

In the example shown in Figure 13-34, you must enter the formula as an array formula (by pressing Ctrl+Shift+Enter); entering it as a regular formula results in a #VALUE error. Our example shows a tiny worksheet, but an array formula like this can make fast work of giant tables.

Using Array Constants

An array constant is a specially organized list of values that you can use as arguments in your array formulas. Array constants can consist of numbers, text, or logical values. Although Excel adds braces for you when you enter array formulas, you must type braces around array constants and separate their elements with commas and semicolons. Commas indicate values in separate columns, and semicolons indicate values in separate rows. The formula in Figure 13-35, for example, performs nine computations in one cell.

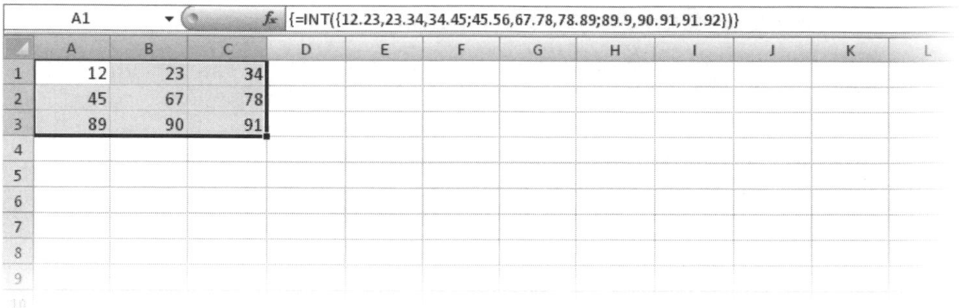

Figure 13-35 An array constant is the argument for this array formula.

A Single-Cell Array Formula Application

Suppose you want the total number of items in a table that satisfy two criteria. You want to know how many transactions of more than $1,000 occurred after a specified date. You could add a column to the table containing an IF function to find each transaction that satisfies these criteria and then total the results of that column. A simpler way to do this is to use a single array formula like this one: =SUM((A1:A100>39448)*(C1:C100>999)).

The 39448 in the formula is the serial date value for January 1, 2008. Enter the formula by pressing Ctrl+Shift+Enter. Each item in the first parenthetical expression evaluates to either a 1 (TRUE) or a 0 (FALSE), depending on the date; each item in the second parenthetical expression evaluates also to either a 1 or a 0, depending on whether its value is greater than 999. The formula then multiplies the 1s and 0s, and when both evaluate to TRUE, the resulting value is 1. The SUM function adds the 1s and gives you the total. You can add more criteria by adding more parenthetical elements to the formula; any expression that evaluates to FALSE (0) eliminates that transaction because anything multiplied by 0 is 0.

You could enhance this formula in several ways. For example, replace the serial date number with the DATEVALUE function so you can use "*1/1/2008*" as an argument instead of having to find the date value yourself. Even better, use cell references as arguments to each element so you can type variable criteria in cells rather than editing the formula.

To enter a formula using an array constant, follow these steps:

1. Select a range of cells the size you need to contain the result. In Figure 13-35, the argument to the INT function contains three groups (separated by semicolons) of three values (separated by commas), which produces a three-row, three-column range.

2. Enter an equal sign to begin the formula and, optionally, a function name and opening parenthesis.

3. Type the array argument enclosed in braces to indicate that the enclosed values make up an array constant. If you entered a function, type its closing parenthesis.

4. Press Ctrl+Shift+Enter. The resulting array formula contains two sets of curly braces—one set encloses the array constant, and the other encloses the entire array formula.

When entering array constants, remember that commas between array elements place those elements in separate columns, and semicolons between array elements place those elements in separate rows.

Understanding Array Expansion

When you use arrays as arguments in a formula, all your arrays should have the same dimensions. If the dimensions of your array arguments or array ranges do not match, Excel often expands the arguments for you. For example, to multiply all the values in cells A1:B5 by 10, you can use either of the following array formulas: { =A1:B5*10} or { ={ 1,2;3,4;5,6;7,8;9,10}*10}.

Note that neither of these two formulas are balanced; ten values are on the left side of the multiplication operator but only one is on the right. Excel expands the second argument to match the size and shape of the first. In the preceding example, the first formula is equivalent to { =A1:B5*{ 10,10;10,10;10,10;10,10;10,10} }, and the second is equivalent to { ={ 1,2;3,4;5,6;7,8;9,10}*{ 10,10;10,10;10,10;10,10;10,10} }.

When you work with two or more sets of multivalue arrays, each set must have the same number of rows as the argument with the greatest number of rows, and each must have the same number of columns as the argument with the greatest number of columns.

Linking Workbooks

Creating dynamic links between workbooks using external reference formulas provides a number of advantages. For example, you could break a large, complex company budget model into more manageable departmental models. Then you could link all the departmental workbooks (supporting workbooks) to a master budget workbook (a dependent workbook). In addition to creating more manageable and flexible models, linked workbooks can save recalculation time and memory.

The following sections discuss some special considerations to be aware of when working with workbooks linked by external reference formulas. For more information about external references, see "Creating References to Other Worksheets in the Same Workbook" on page 396 and "Creating References to Worksheets in Other Workbooks" on page 396.

Saving Linked Workbooks

When you create a set of linked workbooks, you should save the supporting workbooks before you save the dependent workbooks. For example, suppose you are modeling your company's 2008 budget in an unsaved workbook called Book1. When you save the workbook, you give it the name Budget.

Now suppose you have another active workbook in which you plan to enter actual (as opposed to budgeted) expenditures; you have already saved the workbook with the name Actual. This workbook contains links to your Budget workbook and, therefore, depends on the Budget workbook for some of its information. When you first created these links, the Budget workbook was identified as Book1.

If you save Book1 as Budget while the Actual workbook is still open, all references to Book1 in the Actual workbook change automatically to Budget. For example, if Actual contains the reference =[Book1]Sheet1!$A$1, the reference changes to ='[Budget.xlsx]Sheet1'!$A$1.

If you try to close the dependent Actual workbook before you save the supporting Book1 (Budget) workbook, however, you see the "Save Actual with references to unsaved documents?" warning. Click OK to save and close it. When you then save Book1 as Budget, Excel doesn't update the references to Book1 in the Actual workbook because it isn't open; the formulas continue to reference Book1. When you reopen Actual, Excel first displays a security warning, alerting you that automatic links are present. Click the Options button to display the dialog box shown in Figure 13-36, where you can select Enable This Content to allow linking formulas to function.

After you enable links, Excel then displays a message box that prompts you to update the linked information. If you click the Edit Links button, the dialog box shown in Figure 13-37 appears.

Excel is, of course, unable to find Book1. You need to click the Change Source button to locate the Actual workbook so Excel can reestablish the links.

Opening a Dependent Workbook

When you save a workbook that contains dependent formulas, Excel stores the most recent results of those formulas. If you open and edit the supporting workbook after closing the dependent workbook, the values of edited cells in the supporting workbook might be different. When you open the dependent workbook again, the workbook contains the old values of the external references in the dependent formulas, and Excel displays a security warning, alerting you that automatic links are present. Click the Options button to display the dialog box shown in Figure 13-36, where you can select Enable This Content to update the linked formulas. Excel then searches for the supporting workbook. If it finds the workbook, Excel reads the supporting values and updates the dependent formulas in the dependent workbook. Excel does not open the supporting workbook; it merely reads the appropriate values from it.

If Excel can't find the supporting workbook, it displays the alert "This workbook contains one or more links that cannot be updated." You can click Continue to open the workbook anyway, or you can click the Edit Links button to display the dialog box shown in Figure 13-37.

Linking Workbooks   **441**

Figure 13-36 Excel disables external links by default, requiring your intervention.

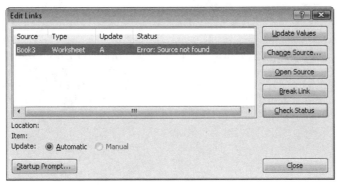

Figure 13-37 Use the Edit Links dialog box to manage all your external links.

Editing Links

You can open supporting workbooks, as well as specify different supporting workbooks, when you click the Edit Links button, located in the Connections group on the Data tab on the Ribbon. When you do so, a dialog box like the one shown in Figure 13-37. Here is some helpful information about using the Edit Links dialog box:

- An A in the Status column indicates a link that is updated automatically.

- An M in the Status column indicates a manual link that isn't updated until you click Update Values.

- Click Open Source to open the supporting workbook.

- Click Change Source to select a different supporting workbook.

- Click Break Link to convert all existing external references in formulas to their current values. You can't undo this action, so proceed with caution.

- Click Update Values to fetch the latest figures from the supporting workbook without having to open it.

- You can link objects and documents created in other applications, such as Word, to Excel worksheets and charts. When you do so, the Type column displays the application name and the object type.

Clicking the Startup Prompt button displays the Startup Prompt dialog box shown in Figure 13-38, which you can use to specify how links are handled whenever the workbook is opened.

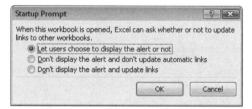

Figure 13-38 The Startup Prompt dialog box lets you customize the startup behavior of external links.

Ordinarily, Excel displays a security alert when you open a workbook containing linking formulas, which individual Excel users can choose to suppress on their computers. If you would prefer to suppress the security alert for the current workbook, you can do so by selecting either Don't Display The Alert And Don't Update Automatic Links or Don't Display The Alert And Update Links in the Startup Prompt dialog box.

> **Note**
>
> To change the default behavior of disabling automatic links, click the Microsoft Office Button, Excel Options, Advanced category, and then in the General section, clear the Ask To Update Automatic Links option.

Copying, Cutting, and Pasting in Linked Workbooks

You can use relative or absolute references to cells in other workbooks as you do in a single workbook. Relative and absolute references to cells in supporting workbooks respond to the Copy, Cut, and Paste commands and toolbar buttons in much the same way as references to cells in the same workbook do.

For example, suppose you type the formula **=[Form2.xlsx]Sheet1!F1** in cell A1 on Sheet1 of Form1 and then use Copy and Paste to copy this formula to cell B1. The formula in cell B1 becomes =[Form2.xlsx]Sheet1!G1. The original formula changes when you copy it to cell B1 because the reference to cell F1 is relative. However, if the formula in cell A1 of Form1 contained an absolute reference, such as =[Form2.xlsx]Sheet1!$F$1, the reference in the copied formula would not change.

Copying and Pasting Between Workbooks

When you copy a dependent formula from one workbook to another and that formula includes a relative reference to a third workbook, Excel adjusts the reference to reflect the new position of the formula. For example, suppose that cell A1 in Form1 contains the formula =[Form2.xlsx]Sheet1!A1. If you copy and paste that formula into cell B5 in Form3, the result is the formula =[Form2.xlsx]Sheet1!B5. Excel adjusts the formula to reflect its new relative position.

If you copy a formula that contains an absolute reference to another workbook, the formula remains the same. For example, suppose cell A1 in Form1 contains the formula =[Form2.xlsx]Sheet1!$A$1. If you copy and paste that formula into cell B5 in Form3, the resulting formula is the same.

Even if you copy a dependent formula to the workbook to which the formula refers, it's still a dependent formula. For example, if you copy the formula =[Form2.xlsx]Sheet1!$A$1 from cell A1 of Form1 to cell A3 on Sheet1 of Form2, the resulting formula is essentially the same, except that the book reference isn't necessary because the formula is in the same workbook. As a result, the formula becomes =Sheet1!$A$1.

Cutting and Pasting Between Workbooks

Excel does not adjust the relative references in a formula when you cut it from one workbook and paste it in another, as it does when you copy a formula. For example, suppose that cell A1 on Sheet1 of Form1 contains the formula =[Form2.xlsx]Sheet1!A1. If you cut that formula and paste it into cell B5 of Form3, the formula does not change.

When you cut and paste cells, Excel usually adjusts any references to those cells in the formulas of the workbook. Dependent formulas, however, do not follow the same rules. When you cut and paste a cell referred to by a dependent formula in a closed workbook, that formula isn't adjusted to reflect the change.

For example, suppose you create the formula =[Form2.xlsx]Sheet1!A10 in cell A1 in Form1. If you close Form1 and use Cut and Paste to move the entry to cell B10 of Form2, the formula in cell A1 of Form1 remains the same. You might expect the link to be broken because the worksheet containing the formula was closed when you modified the referenced cell. However, Excel manages to keep track of everything.

Creating Conditional Tests

A conditional test formula compares two numbers, functions, formulas, labels, or logical values. You can use conditional tests to flag values that fall outside a given threshold, for example. You can use simple mathematical and logical operators to construct logical formulas, or you can use an assortment of built-in functions. For information about using conditional test functions, see "Understanding Logical Functions" on page 471.

Each of the following formulas performs a rudimentary conditional test:

```
=A1>A2
=5-3<5*2
=AVERAGE(B1:B6)=SUM(6,7,8)
=C2="Female"
=COUNT(A1:A10)=COUNT(B1:B10)
=LEN(A1)=10
```

Every conditional test must include at least one logical operator, which defines the relationship between elements of the conditional test. For example, in the conditional test A1>A2, the greater than (>) logical operator compares the values in cells A1 and A2. Table 13-4 lists the six logical operators.

Table 13-4 Logical Operators

Operator	Definition
=	Equal to
>	Greater than
<	Less than
> =	Greater than or equal to
< =	Less than or equal to
< >	Not equal to

The result of a conditional test is either the logical value TRUE (1) or the logical value FALSE (0). For example, the conditional test =A1=10 returns TRUE if the value in A1 equals 10 or FALSE if A1 contains any other value.

Using the Conditional Sum and Lookup Wizards

Excel includes two useful tools called *wizards* that help you assemble frequently used yet confusing types of formulas. The Conditional Sum Wizard and the Lookup Wizard are provided as add-ins, which are special types of macros designed to integrate seamlessly into Excel. To see whether you have these wizards installed, look at the Formulas tab. If you see the Conditional Sum or Lookup buttons, as shown in Figure 13-39, then the respective wizards are installed.

Figure 13-39 The Conditional Sum and Lookup buttons live on the Formulas tab when installed.

If you don't see buttons for either add-in, click the Microsoft Office Button, Excel Options, and then click the Add-Ins category. In the Manage drop-down list at the bottom of the dialog box, select Excel Add-Ins, and then click the Go button to display the Add-Ins dialog box shown in Figure 13-40.

Figure 13-40 Use the Add-Ins dialog box to install additional tools.

In the Add-Ins dialog box, select the check boxes for both the Conditional Sum Wizard and the Lookup Wizard (and any others you want), and then click OK to install them. Excel will prompt you for permission to proceed—more than once, if you selected more than one add-in to install.

> **Note**
>
> The buttons you use to launch all but two of the Excel add-ins appear in the Solutions group on the Formulas tab; buttons for the Analysis Toolpak and the Solver add-in both appear in the Analysis group on the Data tab. For more information about the Analysis Toolpak, see Chapter 14, "Using Functions."

Chapter 13

Creating Conditional Sum Formulas

The Conditional Sum Wizard creates formulas using the SUM and IF functions. This wizard not only makes constructing these formulas easier and faster but also shows you how these formulas are constructed so you can build your own conditional formulas without the wizard.

For more information about the IF function, see "Understanding Logical Functions" on page 471.

To build a conditional formula, follow these steps:

1. Select the table or list containing the values you want to use, and click the Conditional Sum button on the Formulas tab to display the wizard page shown in Figure 13-41.

   If you click anywhere in the table before you start the wizard, Excel automatically selects the current region for you. If Excel selects the correct region, click Next. Otherwise, drag to select the range you want to use. Remember to include the row and column labels. After clicking Next, the page shown on the left in Figure 13-42 appears.

2. In the Column To Sum list, select the name of the column from which you want to extract totals.

   This is why you need to select the labels in Step 1 of the wizard. If the column labels do not appear in the list, click Back, and reselect the range.

 You'll find the Pacific Sales Transactions.xlsx file in the Sample Files section of the companion CD.

3. Still in Step 2 of the wizard, specify the condition to use when selecting the values you want to include in the total. In the Column list, select the name of the column containing the labels you want to conditionally check, select an operator in the Is list, and then select a value in the This Value list.

   The contents of the This Value list change depending on the column selected in the Column list. The This Value list displays only the unique values in the selected column, ignoring duplicates.

4. Click Add Condition.

   The criteria you specify are added to the list at the bottom of the page. You can add as many as seven conditions. If you change your mind about any condition, select the condition from the list, and click Remove Condition. When you have finished editing conditions, click Next.

5. In Step 3 of the wizard, either choose Copy Just The Formula To A Single Cell or choose Copy The Formula And Conditional Values.

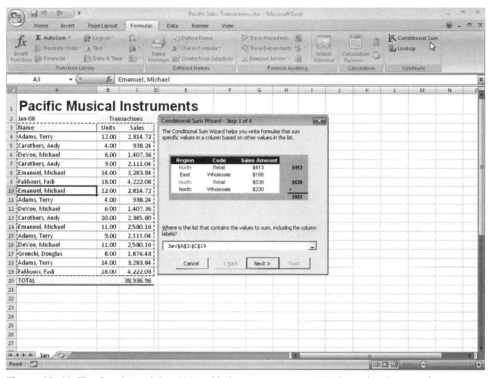

Figure 13-41 The Conditional Sum Wizard helps you construct SUM formulas that are choosy about what they include.

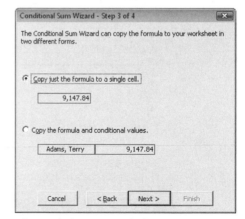

Figure 13-42 These wizard pages let you select the cells to include in your calculation.

6. Click Next, and then select the cell where you want to place the resulting formula. Or, if you chose the Copy The Formula And Conditional Values option in Step 3 of the wizard, the wizard adds an intervening step, letting you first select the cell where you want the conditional value to go.

7. Click Finish. Excel pastes the resulting formula (and the optional conditional value) in the worksheet in the locations specified.

You can add more conditional formulas, or if you already have a list of unique values you can use for comparison (such as salesperson names), you can copy the formula as needed (but only if you used the Copy The Formula And Conditional Values option in Step 3 of the wizard), as shown in Figure 13-43.

F4			f_x	{=SUM(IF($A$4:$A$19=E4,$C$4:$C$19,0))}					
	A	B	C	D	E	F	G	H	I	J
1	**Pacific Musical Instruments**								
2	Jan-08		Transactions						
3	Name	Units	Sales		Salesperson	Total Sales			
4	Adams, Terry	12.00	2,814.72		Adams, Terry	9,147.84			
5	Carothers, Andy	4.00	938.24		Carothers, Andy	5,394.88			
6	DeVoe, Michael	6.00	1,407.36		DeVoe, Michael	5,394.88			
7	Carothers, Andy	9.00	2,111.04		Emanuel, Michael	8,678.72			
8	Emanuel, Michael	14.00	3,283.84		Fakhouri, Fadi	8,444.16			
9	Fakhouri, Fadi	18.00	4,222.08		Groncki, Douglas	1,876.48			
10	Emanuel, Michael	12.00	2,814.72						
11	Adams, Terry	4.00	938.24						
12	DeVoe, Michael	6.00	1,407.36						
13	Carothers, Andy	10.00	2,345.60						
14	Emanuel, Michael	11.00	2,580.16						
15	Adams, Terry	9.00	2,111.04						
16	DeVoe, Michael	11.00	2,580.16						
17	Groncki, Douglas	8.00	1,876.48						
18	Adams, Terry	14.00	3,283.84						
19	Fakhouri, Fadi	18.00	4,222.08						
20	TOTAL		38,936.96						
21									
22									
23									
24									
25									
26									

Figure 13-43 We added a list of unique salesperson names (conditions) in column E and copied the conditional sum formula to cells F5:F9.

The resulting formula shown in the formula bar in Figure 13-43 is enclosed in braces, indicating an array formula. For more information about arrays, see "Using Arrays" on page 434.

INSIDE OUT   Watch Out for Spaces

The Conditional Sum Wizard isn't smart about space characters. For example, if a label in the column of criteria includes an invisible space character at the end of the text string, Excel excludes it from the total, even if all the instances are otherwise identical.

Creating Lookup Formulas

The Lookup Wizard creates formulas using the INDEX and MATCH functions. Like the Conditional Sum Wizard, it makes constructing lookup formulas easier and faster, and it also illustrates how these formulas are constructed so you can build them yourself later. For more information about the INDEX and MATCH functions, see "Understanding Lookup and Reference Functions" on page 476. To build a lookup formula, follow these steps:

1. Click the Lookup button on the Formulas tab to display the wizard page shown on the left in Figure 13-44.

 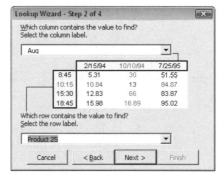

Figure 13-44 Specify the lookup range and the row and column you want to find using the first two steps of the Lookup Wizard.

Note

If the Lookup button does not appear on the Formulas tab, you need to install the add-in. See "Using the Conditional Sum and Lookup Wizards" on page 444.

2. Select the table or list containing the values you want to use. If you click anywhere in the table before you start the wizard, Excel automatically selects the current

region for you. If Excel selects the correct region, click Next; otherwise drag to select the range you want to use. Remember to include the row and column labels.

3. Click Next. The page shown on the right in Figure 13-44 appears.

4. Select the name of the column containing the value you want from the Select The Column Label drop-down list. (This is why you need to select the labels in Step 1 of the wizard.) If the labels don't appear in the list, click the Back button, and reselect the range.

5. Click Next, and then decide whether you want the lookup parameters as well as the result to be inserted in your worksheet, as shown in Figure 13-45. We recommend inserting the parameters (conditions), as we will show later. Select the Copy The Formula And Lookup Parameters option, and then click Next.

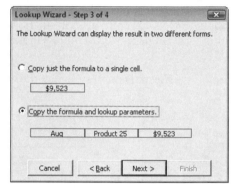

Figure 13-45 If you copy the formula to a single cell, the parameters are fixed; copying both the formula and the parameters lets you create a lookup table.

6. Select the cell where you want the resulting formula to be placed. If you chose the Copy The Formula And Lookup Parameters option in Step 3 of the wizard, the wizard adds two extra steps. If you did this, select the cell where you want the first parameter to go, click Next, and click a cell for the second parameter. Then click Next, and click the cell where you want the conditional formula to go.

7. Click Finish.

Figure 13-46 shows an example of how you can use the Lookup Wizard to build a lookup table.

As mentioned previously, when you select the Copy The Formula And Lookup Parameters option in Step 3 of the Lookup Wizard, Excels inserts the parameters in your worksheet; in our example, we specified cells P5 and Q5. The resulting lookup formula (in cell R5) refers to these inserted values using relative references. As you can see in the formula bar in Figure 13-46, the first arguments for the MATCH functions are relative references to our specified cells. Using relative references in this way, you can perform two tasks. First, you can type other valid parameters (Sept, Product 12, or both, for example) in the parameter cells (P5 and Q5), and the lookup formula finds the corresponding value at the new intersection. Second, because the parameter references are relative, you can copy the formula to additional cells and type additional parameters into cells in the same relative locations.

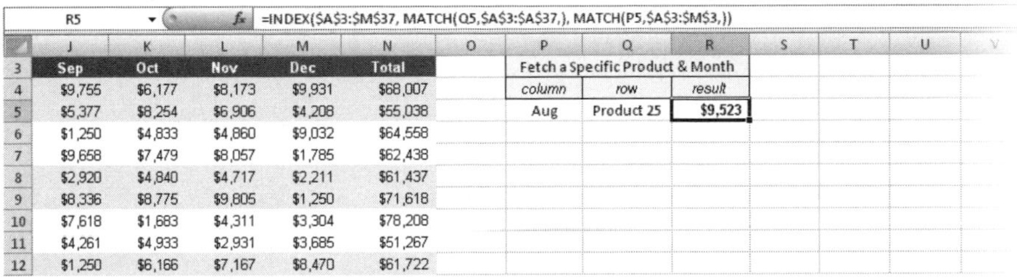

	J	K	L	M	N	O	P	Q	R	S	T	U	V
	R5		▾	*fx*	=INDEX($A$3:$M$37, MATCH(Q5,$A$3:$A$37,), MATCH(P5,$A$3:$M$3,))								
3	Sep	Oct	Nov	Dec	Total		Fetch a Specific Product & Month						
4	$9,755	$6,177	$8,173	$9,931	$68,007		column	row	result				
5	$5,377	$8,254	$6,906	$4,208	$55,038		Aug	Product 25	$9,523				
6	$1,250	$4,833	$4,860	$9,032	$64,558								
7	$9,658	$7,479	$8,057	$1,785	$62,438								
8	$2,920	$4,840	$4,717	$2,211	$61,437								
9	$8,336	$8,775	$9,805	$1,250	$71,618								
10	$7,618	$1,683	$4,311	$3,304	$78,208								
11	$4,261	$4,933	$2,931	$3,685	$51,267								
12	$1,250	$6,166	$7,167	$8,470	$61,722								

Figure 13-46 You can enter different months and product numbers to change the corresponding value in cell R5.

Worksheet *functions* are special tools that perform complex calculations quickly and easily. They work like the special keys on sophisticated calculators that compute square roots, logarithms, and statistical evaluations—except Microsoft Office Excel 2007 has hundreds of these special functions. Some functions, such as SIN and FACT, are the equivalent of lengthy mathematical formulas you would otherwise have to create by hand. Other functions, such as IF and VLOOKUP, can't be otherwise duplicated by formulas. When none of the built-in functions is quite what you need, you can create custom functions.

Starting with the section "Understanding Mathematical Functions" on page 461, this chapter describes some of the more useful functions Office Excel 2007 has to offer. To keep this book from threatening the structural integrity of your bookshelf, we've had to make some hard choices about which functions to highlight. Therefore, this chapter by no means represents a comprehensive reference. For complete information about all the built-in functions that Office Excel 2007 has to offer, you can use a number of on-screen tools, covered next in "Using the Built-In Function Reference in Excel."

Using the Built-In Function Reference in Excel

Fully describing each of the hundreds of worksheet functions would fill an entire book—or two, perhaps. To provide the greatest benefit, we had to decide which functions to focus on and which to mention only briefly. Admittedly, we tend to devote more ink to financial, information, and lookup functions than we do to engineering or trigonometric functions. We think this makes sense for the majority of our readers. If you need more information about functions that we do not cover in great detail, Excel offers several built-in resources:

Help

- **The online Help system** The Excel Help system includes a detailed description of each worksheet function. Just press F1 to display the Excel Help window, and then type a function name in the Search text box to find all the relevant Help topics. You can also click Function Reference in the Table Of Contents, where the functions are grouped into categories to help you find the one you need. For example, clicking the Logical category and then the Logical Functions topic displays the information shown in Figure 14-1.

Chapter 14

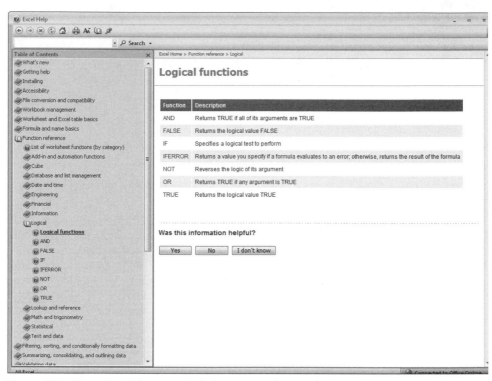

Figure 14-1 The online Help system includes a comprehensive function reference.

- **The Insert Function dialog box** You can use this dialog box, shown in Figure 14-2, to browse through the entire list of functions if you're not sure which function you need. To display the Insert Function dialog box, click the Insert Function button on the formula bar.

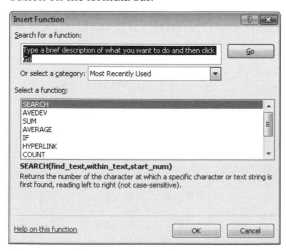

Figure 14-2 The Insert Function dialog box provides assistance with using functions.

- **The Function Arguments dialog box** This dialog box, shown in Figure 14-3, provides details about the function, and the required arguments appear as separate text boxes in the middle of the dialog box. Notice also the link to the relevant Help topic at the bottom of the dialog box. To display the Function Arguments dialog box, click the Insert Function button on the formula bar, select a function, and click OK. You can also click the Insert Function button while you are in the process of entering a formula *after* you type a valid function name and an open parenthesis to display the Function Arguments dialog box.

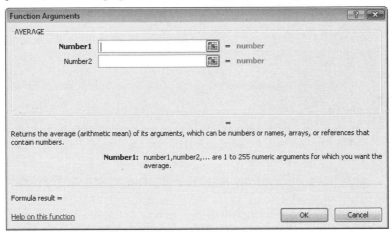

Figure 14-3 The Function Arguments dialog box provides assistance with entering function arguments.

> **Note**
>
> Drag the Function Arguments dialog box around the screen if you need to see the cells behind it. For maximum viewing, make the dialog box smaller by clicking one of the collapse dialog buttons on the right side of the argument boxes.

- **Function ScreenTips** These little pop-up descriptions that appear below selected formulas are useful if you are unsure about the syntax of a function as you type a formula; you can get help without even leaving the cell. After you type the required open parenthesis following any valid function name, the appropriate ScreenTip appears, as shown in Figure 14-4. The ScreenTip shows you the correct function syntax and any available alternate versions of the function (also shown in Figure 14-4). You can also click the function name in the ScreenTip to display the relevant topic from the online Help system. If you click an argument name in the ScreenTip, the corresponding section of the formula is highlighted for you, making it easy to identify each argument, as shown in Figure 14-4.

	J	K	L	M	N	O	P	Q	R	S	T	U	V	W
	AVEDEV		▼	× ✓ ƒx	=INDEX($A$3:$M$37, MATCH(Q5,$A$3:$A$37,), MATCH(P5,$A$3:$M$3,))									
3	**Sep**	**Oct**	**Nov**	**Dec**	**Total**		Fetch a Specific Product & Month							
4	$9,755	$6,177	$8,173	$9,931	$68,007		column	row	result					
5	$5,377	$8,254	$6,906	$4,208	$55,038		Aug	Product 25	=INDEX($A$3:$M$37, MATCH(Q5,$A$3:$A$37,), MATCH(P5,					
6	$1,250	$4,833	$4,860	$9,032	$64,558				$A$3:$M$3,))					
7	$9,658	$7,479	$8,057	$1,785	$62,438				INDEX(array, row_num, [column_num])					
8	$2,920	$4,840	$4,717	$2,211	$61,437				INDEX(reference, row_num, [column_num], [area_num])					
9	$8,336	$8,775	$9,805	$1,250	$71,618									
10	$7,618	$1,683	$4,311	$3,304	$78,208									
11	$4,261	$4,933	$2,931	$3,685	$51,267									
12	$1,250	$6,166	$7,167	$8,470	$61,722									
13	$2,343	$1,012	$2,216	$5,882	$47,997									
14	$2,211	$4,688	$2,309	$5,472	$66,915									
15	$9,284	$4,445	$5,633	$7,557	$64,086									

Figure 14-4 Click an argument name in the Function ScreenTip, which appears when you click an existing function, to highlight the corresponding argument in the cell.

Microsoft Office Button

> **Note**
>
> To turn off Function ScreenTips, click the Microsoft Office Button, click Excel Options, select the Advanced category, and then in the Display area, clear the Show Function ScreenTips check box.

- **Formula AutoComplete** As you type a formula, Excel provides pop-up lists that offer function names and defined names that match the letters you are typing in the formula. For example, if you type **=S** in a cell, Excel displays a scrolling list of all functions (and defined names, if any) that begin with the letter *S* that you can then double-click to insert into your formula.

For details, see "Using Formula AutoComplete" on page 406 and "Naming Cells and Cell Ranges" on page 407.

Exploring the Syntax of Functions

Worksheet functions have two parts: the name of the function and the arguments that follow. Function names—such as SUM and AVERAGE—describe the operation the function performs. Arguments specify the values or cells to be used by the function. For example, the function ROUND has the following syntax: =ROUND(*number, num_digits*), as in the formula =ROUND(M30,2). The M30 part is a cell reference entered as the *number* argument—the value to be rounded. The 2 part is the *num_digits* argument. The result of this function is a number (whatever the contents of cell M30 happens to be) rounded to two decimal places.

Parentheses surround function arguments. The opening parenthesis must appear immediately after the name of the function. If you add a space or some other character between the name and the opening parenthesis, the error value #NAME? appears in the cell.

> **Note**
>
> A few functions, such as PI, TRUE, and NOW, have no arguments. (You usually nest these functions in other formulas.) Even though they have no arguments, you must place an empty set of parentheses after them, as in =NOW( ).

When you use more than one argument in a function, you separate the arguments with commas. For example, the formula =PRODUCT(C1,C2,C5) tells Excel to multiply the numbers in cells C1, C2, and C5. Some functions, such as PRODUCT and SUM, take an unspecified number of arguments. You can use as many as 255 arguments in a function, as long as the total length of the formula does not exceed 8,192 characters. However, you can use a single argument, or a range that refers to any number of cells in your worksheet, as a formula. For example, the function =SUM(A1:A5,C2:C10,D3:D17) has only three arguments but actually totals the values in 29 cells. (The first argument, A1:A5, refers to the range of five cells from A1 through A5, and so on.) The referenced cells can, in turn, also contain formulas that refer to more cells or ranges.

Expressions as Arguments

You can use combinations of functions to create an expression that Excel evaluates to a single value and then interprets as an argument. For example, in the formula =SUM(SIN(A1*PI( )),2*COS(A2*PI( ))) the comma separates two complex expressions that Excel evaluates and uses as the arguments of the SUM function.

Types of Arguments

In the examples presented so far, all the arguments have been cell or range references. You can also use numbers, text, logical values, range names, arrays, and error values as arguments.

Numeric Values

The arguments to a function can be numeric. For example, the SUM function in the formula =SUM(327,209,176) adds the numbers 327, 209, and 176. Usually, however, you type the numbers you want to use in cells of a worksheet and then use references to those cells as arguments to your functions.

Text Values

You can also use text as an argument to a function. For example, in the formula =TEXT(NOW( ),"*mmm d, yyyy*") the second argument to the TEXT function, *mmm d, yyyy*, is a text argument specifically recognized by Excel. It specifies a pattern for converting the serial date value returned by NOW into a text string. Text arguments can be text strings enclosed in quotation marks or references to cells that contain text.

For more about text functions, see "Understanding Text Functions" on page 466.

Logical Values

The arguments to a few functions specify only that an option is either set or not set; you can use the logical values TRUE to set an option and FALSE to specify that the option isn't set. A logical expression returns the values TRUE or FALSE (which evaluate to 1 and 0, respectively) to the worksheet or the formula containing the expression. For example, the first argument of the IF function in the formula =IF(A1=TRUE,"Future ", "Past ")&"History" is a logical expression that uses the value in cell A1. If the value in A1 is TRUE (or 1), the expression A1=TRUE evaluates to TRUE, the IF function returns Future, and the formula returns the text Future History to the worksheet.

For more about logical functions, see "Understanding Logical Functions" on page 471.

Named References

You can use a defined name as an argument to a function. For example, if you click the Formulas tab on the Ribbon and use the Define Name button to assign the name Qtrly-Income to the range C3:C6, you can use the formula =SUM(QtrlyIncome) to total the numbers in cells C3, C4, C5, and C6.

For more about names, see "Naming Cells and Cell Ranges" on page 407.

Arrays

You can use an array as an argument in a function. Some functions, such as TREND and TRANSPOSE, require array arguments; other functions don't require array arguments but do accept them. Arrays can consist of numbers, text, or logical values.

For more about arrays, see "Using Arrays" on page 434.

Mixed Argument Types

You can mix argument types within a function. For example, the formula =AVERAGE(Group1,A3,5*3) uses a defined name (Group1), a cell reference (A3), and a numeric expression (5*3) to arrive at a single value. All three are acceptable.

Inserting Functions

The easiest way to locate and insert built-in functions is by clicking the Insert Function button. This button has two versions—one is the little *fx* button that appears on the formula bar, and the other is located in the Function Library group on the Formulas tab on the Ribbon. Either way, when you click Insert Function, the dialog box shown in Figure 14-2 appears. If you're not sure what function you need, type a description of what you are trying to do in the Search text box. For example, if you type **how many cells contain values** and then click the Go button, the Insert Function dialog box returns a list of recommended functions, similar to the list shown in Figure 14-5. As it turns out, the first function in the list of suggestions fills the bill. If you don't find the function you're look-ing for, try rewording your query.

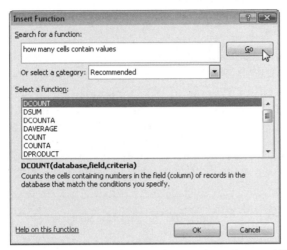

Figure 14-5 Ask a question in the Search text box, and Excel suggests some possible functions you can try.

You can also select a function category from the Or Select A Category drop-down list to display all the applicable functions available. Function categories include Financial, Date & Time, Lookup & Reference, Text, and more. The Recommended category keeps track of any functions returned as a result of using the Search text box.

When you select a function, the syntax and a brief description appear at the bottom of the dialog box. You can obtain help on a function selected in the Select A Function list by clicking the Help On This Function link at the bottom of the dialog box. When you select a function and click OK, Excel enters an equal sign to start a formula in the active cell, inserts the function name and a set of parentheses, and displays the Function Arguments dialog box, shown in Figure 14-3.

The Function Arguments dialog box contains one text box for each argument of the selected function. If the function accepts a variable number of arguments (such as SUM), the dialog box gets bigger as you type additional arguments. A description of the argument text box currently containing the insertion point appears near the bottom of the dialog box. To the right of each argument text box, a display area shows the current value of the argument. This display is handy when you are using references or defined names, because the value of each argument is calculated for you. The current value of the function (Formula Result) appears at the bottom of the dialog box.

Some functions, such as INDEX, have more than one form. When you select a function from the Insert Function dialog box that has more than one form, Excel presents the Select Arguments dialog box, shown in Figure 14-6, in which you select the form you want to use.

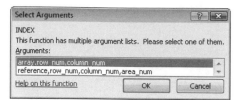

Figure 14-6 If a function has more than one form, the Select Arguments dialog box appears.

You can also use the Function Library group on the Formulas tab on the Ribbon to insert functions. Each of the categories listed in the Insert Function dialog box has a button or menu in the Function Library group. For example, clicking the More Functions button reveals a menu containing additional categories of functions, as shown in Figure 14-7. When you click one of the functions listed on any of these menus, Excel inserts the selected function in the formula bar, and the Function Arguments dialog box appears.

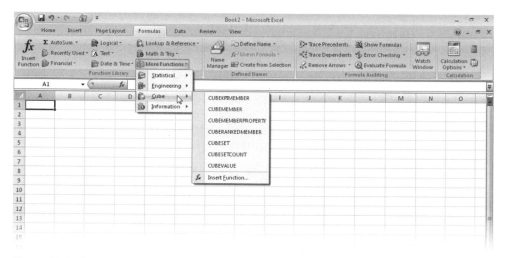

Figure 14-7 The Function Library group on the Formulas tab provides direct access to the built-in functions in Excel.

TROUBLESHOOTING

I get a #NAME? error.

You might get the #NAME? error for a few reasons, but one of the more common is typing the function name incorrectly. Here's a good habit to acquire if you type functions: Use lowercase letters. When you press Enter, Excel converts the name of the function to uppercase letters if you typed it correctly. If the letters don't change to uppercase, you probably typed the name of the function incorrectly. If you're not sure of the exact name or if you continue to get an error, perhaps it's time to consult Help or use the Insert Function dialog box.

Inserting References and Names

As with any other formula, you can insert cell references and defined names into your functions easily using the mouse. For example, to enter a function in cell C11 that averages the cells in the range C2:C10, select cell C11, type **=average(** and then select the range C2:C10. A marquee appears around the selected cells, and a reference to the selected range appears in the formula. Then type the closing parenthesis. If you define named ranges, constants, or formulas in your worksheets, you can insert them in your formulas. To do this, click the Formulas tab, click the Use In Formula button in the Defined Names group, and then select the name you want to use. When you click the name, it appears at the insertion point in the formula.

Understanding Mathematical Functions

Most of the work you do in Excel will probably involve at least a few mathematical functions. The most popular among these is the SUM function, but Excel is capable of calculating just about anything. In the next sections, we'll discuss some of the most used (and most useful) mathematical functions in Excel.

Using the SUM Function

The SUM function totals a series of numbers. It takes the form =SUM(number1, number2, . . .). The *number* arguments are a series of as many as 30 entries that can be numbers, formulas, ranges, or cell references that result in numbers. SUM ignores arguments that refer to text values, logical values, or blank cells.

> **Note**
> You can create powerful conditional SUM formulas using add-in tools. See "Using the Conditional Sum and Lookup Wizards" on page 444.

The Sum Button

Because SUM is such a commonly used function, Excel provides the Sum button on the Home tab on the Ribbon, as well as the AutoSum button on the Formulas tab. These buttons also include a menu of commonly used functions, including SUM. If you select a cell and click the Sum button, Excel creates a SUM formula and guesses which cells you want to total. To enter SUM formulas in a range of cells, select the cells before clicking Sum.

Automatic Range Expansion

Ever since the first spreadsheet program was created, one of the most common problems has been inserting cells at the bottom or to the right of a range that is already referenced in a formula. For example, suppose you type the formula **=SUM(A1:A4)** in cell A5 and then select row 5 and insert a new row. The new row is inserted above the selected row, thus pushing the SUM formula down to cell A6. It used to be that any numbers in the new inserted cell A5 were not included in the SUM formula. A few versions ago, Excel changed all that. Now you can insert cells at the bottom or to the right of a range referenced by a formula, and Excel adjusts the formulas for you—and this is key—*as soon as you type values in the new, inserted cells*. In other words, the SUM formula does not change unless and until you type a value in the inserted cell, now or later. This also works if, rather than inserting cells, you simply place the formula away from a column of numbers—in fact, it doesn't matter how many rows are between the formula and the values, as long as they are blank to start. (This does not work with formulas placed to the right of values that refer to columns.) If you type a value in the cell directly below the column of values that are referenced in the formula, the formula adjusts to accommodate it.

This works only immediately to the right or below a referenced range. Inserting cells at the top or to the left of a referenced range still involves editing the referencing formulas manually.

Using Selected Mathematical Functions

Math & Trig

Excel has 60 built-in math and trigonometry functions; the following sections brush only the surface, covering a few of the more useful or misunderstood functions. You can access them directly by clicking the Math & Trig button on the Formulas tab on the Ribbon.

The PRODUCT and SUMPRODUCT Functions

The PRODUCT function multiplies all its arguments and can take as many as 255 arguments that are text or logical values; the function ignores blank cells.

You can use the SUMPRODUCT function to multiply the value in each cell in one range by the corresponding cell in another range of equal size and then add the results. You can include up to 255 arrays as arguments, but each array must have the same dimensions. (Non-numeric entries are treated as zero.) For example, the following formulas are essentially the same:

```
=SUMPRODUCT(A1:A4, B1:B4)
{=SUM(A1:A4*B1:B4)}
```

The only difference between them is that you must enter the SUM formula as an array by pressing Ctrl+Shift+Enter.

For more information about arrays, see "Using Arrays" on page 434.

The MOD Function

The MOD function returns the remainder of a division operation (modulus). It takes the arguments (*number, divisor*). The result of the MOD function is the remainder produced when *number* is divided by *divisor*. For example, the function =MOD(9, 4) returns 1, the remainder that results from dividing 9 by 4.

Chapter 14

A MOD Example

Here's a practical use of the MOD function that you can ponder:

1. Select a range of cells such as A1:G12, click Conditional Formatting on the Home tab on the Ribbon, and then click New Rule.

2. Select the Use A Formula To Determine Which Cells To Format option in the Select A Rule Type list.

3. In the text box, type the formula **=MOD(ROW(), 2)=0**.

4. Click the Format button, and select a color on the Fill tab to create a format that applies the selected color to every other row. Note that if you select a single cell in an odd-numbered row before creating this formatting formula, nothing seems to happen, but if you copy or apply the format to other rows, you'll see the result. Click OK.

This formula identifies the current row number using the ROW function, divides it by 2, and if there is a remainder (indicating an odd-numbered row), returns FALSE because the formula also contains the conditional test =0. If MOD returns anything but 0 as a remainder, the condition tests FALSE. Therefore, Excel applies formatting only when the formula returns TRUE (in even-numbered rows).

The COMBIN Function

The COMBIN function determines the number of possible combinations, or groups, that can be taken from a pool of items. It takes the arguments (*number, number_chosen*), where *number* is the total number of items in the pool and *number_chosen* is the number of items you want to group in each combination. For example, to determine how many different 12-player football teams you can create from a pool of 17 players, type the formula **=COMBIN(17, 12)**. The result indicates that you could create 6,188 teams.

> **Try Your Luck**
>
> The COMBIN function can help you figure out just how slim a chance you have of getting the elusive ace-high straight flush in a game of five-card stud. You express the number of card combinations using the formula =COMBIN(52, 5), resulting in 2,598,960. That's not too bad when you consider the odds of winning the lottery. To figure that out, you need to know the number of possible combinations when choosing 6 numbers out of a total of 49. Type the formula **=COMBIN(49, 6)**, and the result is 13,983,816 possibilities. You'd better keep your day job either way.

The RAND and RANDBETWEEN Functions

The RAND function generates a random number between 0 and 1. It's one of the few Excel functions that doesn't take an argument, but you must still type a pair of parentheses after the function name. The result of a RAND function changes each time you recalculate your worksheet. This is called a *volatile* function. If you use automatic recalculation, the value of the RAND function changes each time you make a worksheet entry.

The RANDBETWEEN function provides more control than RAND. With RANDBETWEEN, you can specify a range of numbers within which to generate random integer values. The arguments (*bottom, top*) represent the smallest and largest integers that the function should use. The values for these arguments are inclusive. For example, the formula =RANDBETWEEN(123, 456) can return any integer from 123 up to and including 456.

Using the Rounding Functions

Excel includes several functions devoted to the seemingly narrow task of rounding numbers by a specified amount.

The ROUND, ROUNDDOWN, and ROUNDUP Functions

The ROUND function rounds a value to a specified number of decimal places, rounding digits less than 5 down and digits greater than or equal to 5 up. It takes the arguments (*number, num_digits*). If *num_digits* is a positive number, then *number* is rounded to the specified number of decimal points; if *num_digits* is negative, the function rounds to the left of the decimal point; if *num_digits* is 0, the function rounds to the nearest integer. For example, the formula =ROUND(123.4567, –2) returns 100, and the formula =ROUND(123.4567, 3) returns 123.457. The ROUNDDOWN and ROUNDUP functions take the same form as ROUND. As their names imply, they always round down or up, respectively.

Accounting
Number Format

> **Note**
>
> Don't confuse the rounding functions with rounded number formats, such as the one applied when you click the Accounting Number Format button on the Home tab on the Ribbon. When you format the contents of a cell to a specified number of decimal places, you change only the display of the number in the cell; you don't change the cell's value. When performing calculations, Excel always uses the underlying value, not the displayed value. Conversely, the rounding functions change the actual values of numbers.

The EVEN and ODD Functions

The EVEN function rounds a number up to the nearest even integer. The ODD function rounds a number up to the nearest odd integer. Negative numbers are correspondingly rounded down. For example, the formula =EVEN(22.4) returns 24, and the formula =ODD(–4) returns –5.

The FLOOR and CEILING Functions

The FLOOR function rounds a number down to its nearest given multiple, and the CEILING function rounds a number up to its nearest given multiple. These functions take the arguments (*number, multiple*). For example, the formula =FLOOR(23.4, 0.5) returns 23, and the formula =CEILING(5, 1.5) returns 6, the nearest multiple of 1.5.

> **Using the Flexible MROUND Function**
>
> Suppose you want to round a number to a multiple of something other than 10—for example, rounding numbers to sixteenths so that when formatted as fractions they never appear with a denominator larger than 16. The MROUND function rounds any number to a multiple you specify.
>
> The function takes the form =MROUND(number, multiple). For example, typing the formula =**MROUND(A1, .0625)** rounds the number displayed in cell A1 in increments of one-sixteenth. The function rounds up if the remainder after dividing *number* by *multiple* is at least half the value of *multiple*. If you want to apply this to an existing formula, just wrap the MROUND formula around it by replacing A1 (in the example) with your formula.

The INT Function

The INT function rounds numbers down to the nearest integer. For example, the formulas

```
=INT(100.01)
=INT(100.99999999)
```

both return the value 100, even though the number 100.99999999 is essentially equal to 101. When a number is negative, INT also rounds that number down to the next integer. If each of the numbers in the examples were negative, the resulting value would be –101.

The TRUNC Function

The TRUNC function truncates everything to the right of the decimal point in a number, regardless of its sign. It takes the arguments (*number*, *num_digits*). If *num_digits* isn't specified, it's set to 0. Otherwise, TRUNC truncates everything after the specified number of digits to the right of the decimal point. For example, the formula =TRUNC(13.978) returns the value 13; the formula =TRUNC(13.978, 1) returns the value 13.9.

AVERAGE vs. AVG

Some other spreadsheet programs use the AVG statistical function to compute averages. In some previous versions of Excel, typing the formula **=AVG(2, 4, 5, 8)** would result in a #NAME? error. Excel now accepts AVG, although when you type the function, an error dialog box appears, asking whether you want to change the function to AVERAGE. That's still kind of rude, but it works. Presumably, one reason why Excel doesn't just change AVG to AVERAGE for you is so you will learn to start using the correct function name.

When you use this function, Excel ignores cells containing text, logical values, or empty cells but includes cells containing a zero value. You can also choose the AVERAGEA function, which operates in the same way as AVERAGE except it includes text and logical values in the calculation.

Understanding Text Functions

 Text functions in Excel are some of the most useful word-processing and data-management tools you'll find anywhere—they perform tasks word-processing programs can't do. You'll find them conveniently listed for you when you click the Text button on the Formulas tab on the Ribbon.

 You can use the TRIM and CLEAN functions to remove extra spaces and nonprinting characters, which is great for cleaning up imported data—a task that ranges from difficult to impossible using search and replace. The UPPER, LOWER, and PROPER functions change the case of words, sentences, and paragraphs with no retyping. You might find yourself copying text from other documents into Excel just so you can apply these functions. After using text functions, select the cells containing the formulas, press Ctrl+C to copy, click the Paste button on the Home tab, and then click Paste Values to convert the formulas to their resulting (text) values. You can then copy the edited text into the original document.

In the following sections, we'll discuss the most useful Excel text functions.

Using Selected Text Functions

Text functions convert numeric entries, as well as *numeric text* entries, into text strings so you can manipulate the text strings themselves. Numeric text is a type of numeric entry that provides a few specific text characters in addition to numeric characters. For details, see "Using Numeric Text in Formulas" on page 402.

The TEXT Function

The TEXT function converts a number into a text string with a specified format. Its arguments are (*value, format_text*), where *value* represents any number, formula, or cell reference; and *format_text* is the format for displaying the resulting string. For example, the formula =TEXT(98/4, "0.00") returns the text string 24.50. You can use any Excel formatting symbol ($, #, 0, and so on) except the asterisk (*) to specify the format you want, but you can't use the General format.

The DOLLAR Function

Like the TEXT function, the DOLLAR function converts a number into a string. DOLLAR, however, formats the resulting string as currency with the number of decimal places you specify. The arguments (*number, decimals*) specify a number or reference and the number of decimal places you want. For example, the formula =DOLLAR(45.899, 2) returns the text string $45.90. Notice that Excel rounds the number when necessary.

If you omit *decimals*, Excel uses two decimal places. If you add a comma after the first argument but omit the second argument, Excel uses zero decimal places. If you use a negative number for *decimals*, Excel rounds to the left of the decimal point.

The LEN Function

The LEN function returns the number of characters in an entry. The single argument can be a number, a string enclosed in double quotation marks, or a reference to a cell. Trailing zeros are ignored. For example, the formula =LEN("Test") returns 4.

The LEN function returns the length of the displayed text or value, not the length of the underlying cell contents. For example, suppose cell A10 contains the formula =A1+A2+A3+A4+A5+A6+A7+A8 and its result is the value 25. The formula =LEN(A10) returns the value 2, which indicates the length of the resulting value 25. The cell referenced as the argument of the LEN function can contain another string function. For example, if cell A1 contains the function =REPT("-*", 75), which enters the two-character hyphen and asterisk string 75 times in a cell, the formula =LEN(A1) returns the value 150.

The ASCII Functions: CHAR and CODE

Every computer uses numeric codes to represent characters. The most prevalent system of numeric codes is ASCII, or American Standard Code for Information Interchange. ASCII uses a number from 0 to 127 (or in some systems, to 255) to represent each number, letter, and symbol.

The CHAR and CODE functions deal with these ASCII codes. The CHAR function returns the character that corresponds to an ASCII code number; the CODE function returns the ASCII code number for the first character of its argument. For example, the formula =CHAR(83) returns the text S. The formula =CODE("S") returns the ASCII code 83. If you type a literal character as the text argument, be sure to enclose the character in quotation marks; otherwise, Excel returns the #NAME? error value.

> Note
>
> If you use certain ASCII symbols often, you can use the ASCII code number with the CHAR function to create a symbol without using the Symbol button on the Insert tab on the Ribbon. For example, to create a registered trademark symbol (®) just type **=CHAR(174)**.

The Cleanup Functions: TRIM and CLEAN

Leading and trailing blank characters often prevent you from correctly sorting entries in a worksheet or a database. If you use string functions to manipulate text in your worksheet, extra spaces can prevent your formulas from working correctly. The TRIM function eliminates leading, trailing, and extra blank characters from a string, leaving only single spaces between words.

The CLEAN function is similar to TRIM, except it operates on only nonprintable characters, such as tabs and program-specific codes. CLEAN is especially useful if you import data from another program or operating system, because the translation process often introduces nonprintable characters that appear as symbols or boxes. You can use CLEAN to remove these characters from the data.

The EXACT Function

The EXACT function is a conditional function that determines whether two strings match exactly. The function ignores formatting, but it is case sensitive, so uppercase letters are considered different from lowercase letters. If both strings are identical, the function returns TRUE. Both arguments must be literal strings enclosed in quotation marks, references to cells that contain text, numeric values, or formulas that evaluate to numeric values. For example, if cell A5 and cell A6 on your worksheet both contain the text Totals, the formula =EXACT(A5, A6) returns TRUE.

For information about comparing strings, see "Creating Conditional Tests" on page 444.

The Case Functions: UPPER, LOWER, and PROPER

Three functions manipulate the case of characters in text strings. The UPPER and LOWER functions convert text strings to all uppercase or all lowercase letters. The PROPER function capitalizes the first letter in each word, capitalizes any other letters in the text string that do not follow another letter, and converts all other letters to lowercase. For example, if cell A1 contains the text *mark Dodge*, you can type the formula **=UPPER(A1)** to return MARK DODGE. Similarly, the formula =LOWER(A1) returns mark dodge, and **=PROPER(A1)** returns Mark Dodge.

Unexpected results can occur when the text contains punctuation, however. For example, if cell A1 contains the text *it wasn't bad*, the PROPER function converts it to It Wasn'T Bad.

Using the Substring Text Functions

The following functions locate and return portions of a text string or assemble larger strings from smaller ones: FIND, SEARCH, RIGHT, LEFT, MID, SUBSTITUTE, REPLACE, and CONCATENATE.

The FIND and SEARCH Functions

You use the FIND and SEARCH functions to locate the position of a substring within a string. Both functions return the position in the string of the character you specify. (Excel counts blank spaces and punctuation marks as characters.) These two functions work the same way, except FIND is case sensitive and SEARCH allows wildcards. Both functions take the same arguments: (*find_text, within_text, start_num*). The optional *start_num* argument is helpful when *within_text* contains more than one occurrence of *find_text*. If you omit *start_num*, Excel reports the first match it locates. For example, to locate the *p* in the string A Night At The Opera, you would type the formula **=FIND("p", "A Night At The Opera")**. The formula returns 17, because *p* is the 17th character in the string.

If you're not sure of the character sequence you're searching for, you can use the SEARCH function and include wildcards in your *find_text* string. Suppose you've used the names Smith and Smyth in your worksheet. To determine whether either name is in cell A1, type the formula **=SEARCH("Sm?th", A1)**. If cell A1 contains the text John Smith or John Smyth, the SEARCH function returns the value 6–the starting point of the string Sm?th.

If you're not sure of the number of characters, use the * wildcard. For example, to find the position of Allan or Alan within the text (if any) stored in cell A1, type the formula **=SEARCH("A*an", A1)**.

The RIGHT and LEFT Functions

The RIGHT function returns the rightmost series of characters from a specified string; the LEFT function returns the leftmost series of characters. These functions take the same arguments: (*text, num_chars*). The *num_chars* argument indicates the number of characters to extract from the *text* argument.

These functions count blank spaces in the *text* argument as characters; if *text* contains leading or trailing blank characters, you might want to use a TRIM function within the RIGHT or LEFT function to ensure the expected result. For example, suppose you type **This is a test** in cell A1 on your worksheet. The formula =RIGHT(A1, 4) returns the word *test*.

The MID Function

You can use the MID function to extract a series of characters from a text string. This function takes the arguments (*text, start_num, num_chars*). For example, if cell A1 contains the text This Is A Long Text Entry, you can type the formula **=MID(A1, 11, 9)** to extract the characters Long Text from the entry in cell A1.

The REPLACE and SUBSTITUTE Functions

The REPLACE and SUBSTITUTE functions substitute new text for old text. The REPLACE function replaces one string of characters with another string of characters and takes the arguments (*old_text, start_num, num_chars, new_text*). Suppose cell A1 contains the text Eric Miller, CEO. To replace the first four characters with the string Geof, type the formula **=REPLACE(A1, 1, 4, "Geof")**. The result is Geof Miller, CEO.

With the SUBSTITUTE function, you specify the text to replace. The function takes the arguments (*text, old_text, new_text, instance_num*). Suppose cell A1 contains the text Mandy and you want to place it in cell A2 but change it to Randy. Type **=SUBSTITUTE(A1, "M", "R")** in cell A2.

The *instance_num* argument optionally replaces only the specified occurrence of *old_text*. For example, if cell A1 contains the text *through the hoop*, the 4 in the formula =SUBSTITUTE(A1, "h", "l", 4) tells Excel to substitute an l for the fourth *h* found in cell A1. If you don't include *instance_num*, Excel changes all occurrences of *old_text* to *new_text*.

> **Note**
> You can create an array formula using the SUBSTITUTE function to count the number of occurrences of a text string in a range of cells. Use the formula =SUM(LEN(<range>)–LEN(SUBSTITUTE(<range>, "text", "")))/LEN("text") to count the number of times *text* appears in <range>. Type the formula, and press Ctrl+Shift+Enter.

The CONCATENATE Function

To assemble strings from up to 255 smaller strings or references, the CONCATENATE function is the function equivalent of the & character. For example, if cell B4 contains the text Pacific with a trailing space character, the formula =CONCATENATE(B4, "Musical Instruments") returns Pacific Musical Instruments.

TROUBLESHOOTING

Concatenated dates become serial numbers.

If you try to concatenate the contents of a cell formatted as a date, the result is probably not what you expect. Because a date in Excel is only a serial number, what you usually see is a formatted representation of the date. But when you concatenate the contents of a date-formatted cell, you get the unformatted version of the date. To avoid this problem, use the TEXT function to convert the serial number to a recognizable form. For example, suppose cell A1 contains the text *Today's Date is* and cell A2 contains the function =NOW() and is formatted to display the date in dd/mm/yyyy format. Nonetheless, the formula =CONCATENATE(A1, " ", A2) results in the value Today's Date is 39511 (or whatever the current date serial number happens to be). To remedy this problem, type the TEXT function as follows: **=CONCATENATE(A1, " ", TEXT(A2, "dd/mm/yyyy")).**

This version returns the value Today's Date is 03/04/2008 (or whatever today's date happens to be). Note that the formula includes a space character as a separate argument (" ") between the two cell reference arguments.

Understanding Logical Functions

 You use logical functions to test for specific conditions. These functions are often called *logical operators* in discussions of Boolean logic, which is named after George Boole, the British mathematician. You might have run across logical operators in *set theory*, used when teaching logical concepts in high school. You use logical operators to arrive at one of two conclusions: TRUE or FALSE. We'll discuss the most useful logical functions in the following sections. You can access the logical functions by clicking the Logical button on the Formulas tab on the Ribbon.

Using Selected Logical Functions

Excel has a rich set of logical functions. Most logical functions use conditional tests to determine whether a specified condition is TRUE or FALSE.

For more information about conditional tests, see "Creating Conditional Tests" on page 444.

Chapter 14

INSIDE OUT   Streamline Formulas Using the SUMIF Function

If you find yourself frequently using the IF function to perform conditional tests on individual rows or columns and then using the SUM function to total the results, the SUMIF function might make your work a little easier. With SUMIF, you can add specific values in a range, based on a criterion you supply. For example, you can type the formula **=SUMIF(C12:C27, "Yes", A12:A27)** to find the total of all numbers in A12:A27 in which the cell in the same row in column C contains the word Yes. This performs all the calculations you need in one cell and eliminates having to create a column of IF formulas.

The IF Function

The IF function returns values based on supplied conditional tests. It takes the arguments (*logical_test, value_if_true, value_if_false*). For example, the formula =IF(A6<22, 5, 10) returns 5 if the value in cell A6 is less than 22; otherwise, it returns 10. You can nest other functions within an IF function. For example, the formula =IF(SUM(A1:A10)>0, SUM(A1:A10), 0) returns the sum of A1 through A10 if the sum is greater than 0; otherwise, it returns 0.

You can also use text arguments to return nothing instead of zero if the result is false. For example, the formula =IF(SUM(A1:A10)>0, SUM(A1:A10), " ") returns a null string (" ") if the conditional test is false. The *logical_test* argument can also consist of text. For example, the formula =IF(A1="Test", 100, 200) returns the value 100 if cell A1 contains the string Test or returns 200 if it contains any other entry. The match between the two text entries must be exact except for case.

The AND, OR, and NOT Functions

Three additional functions help you develop compound conditional tests: AND, OR, and NOT. These functions work with the logical operators =, >, <, >=, <=, and <>. The AND and OR functions can each have as many as 255 logical arguments. The NOT function takes only one argument. Arguments can be conditional tests, arrays, or references to cells that contain logical values.

Suppose you want Excel to return the text Pass only if a student has an average score greater than 75 and fewer than five unexcused absences. In Figure 14-8, we typed the formula **=IF(OR(G4<5,F4>75), "Pass", "Fail")**. This fails the student in row 5 because of the five absences. If you use AND instead of OR in the formula shown in Figure 14-8, all students would pass.

H4	▼			*fx*	=IF(OR(G4<5,F4>75),"Pass","Fail")					

	A	B	C	D	E	F	G	H	I	J	K
1	**Math Exam Scores**										
2	Ms. Nagata										
3	*Student*	**Exam 1**	**Exam 2**	**Exam 3**	**Exam 4**	*Average*	*Absences*	*Pass/Fail*			
4	Carothers, Andy	87	90	79	96	88.00	2	Pass			
5	Groncki, Douglas	92	94	94	97	94.25	5	Fail			
6	MacDonald, Scott	96	95	95	80	91.50	0	Pass			
7	Nusbaum, Tawana	85	87	87	88	86.75	4	Pass			
8	Rothenberg, Eric	81	88	88	85	85.50	1	Pass			
9											
10											
11											
12											
13											
14											
15											

Figure 14-8 You can create complex conditional tests using the OR function.

You'll find the And Or Not.xlsx file in the Sample Files section of the companion CD.

The OR function returns the logical value TRUE if any one of the conditional tests is true; the AND function returns the logical value TRUE only if all the conditional tests are true.

Because the NOT function negates a condition, you usually use it with other functions. NOT instructs Excel to return the logical value TRUE if the argument is false or the logical value FALSE if the argument is true. For example, the formula =IF(NOT(A1=2), "Go", " ") tells Excel to return the text Go if the value of cell A1 is anything but 2.

Nested IF Functions

Sometimes you can't resolve a logical problem using only logical operators and the AND, OR, and NOT functions. In these cases, you can nest IF functions to create a hierarchy of tests. For example, the formula =IF(A1=100, "Always", IF(AND(A1>=80, A1<100), "Usually", IF(AND(A1>=60, A1<80), "Sometimes", "Who cares?"))) states, in plain language, the following: If the value is 100, return Always; if the value is from 80 through 99, return Usually; if the value is from 60 through 79, return Sometimes; or finally, if none of these conditions is true, return Who cares?. You can create formulas containing up to 64 levels of nested functions.

Other Uses for Conditional Functions

You can use all the conditional functions described in this section as stand-alone for-mulas. Although you usually use functions, such as AND, OR, NOT, ISERROR, ISNA, and ISREF, within an IF function, you can use formulas, such as =AND(A1>A2, A2<A3), also to perform simple conditional tests. This formula returns the logical value TRUE if

the value in A1 is greater than the value in A2 and the value in A2 is less than the value in A3. You might use this type of formula to assign TRUE and FALSE values to a range of numeric database cells and then use the TRUE and FALSE conditions as selection criteria for printing a specialized report.

Understanding Information Functions

More Functions

The information functions could be considered the internal monitoring system in Excel. Although they perform no specific calculations, you can use them to find out about elements of the Excel interface and then use that information elsewhere. We'll discuss the most useful of these functions in the following sections. You'll find these functions by clicking the More Functions button on the Formulas tab on the Ribbon and then clicking Information.

Using Selected Information Functions

With information functions, you can gather information about the contents of cells, their formatting, and the computing environment as well as perform conditional tests for the presence of specific types of values.

The TYPE and ERROR.TYPE Functions

The TYPE function determines whether a cell contains text, a number, a logical value, an array, or an error value. The result is a code for the type of entry in the referenced cell: 1 for a number (or a blank cell), 2 for text, 4 for a logical value (TRUE or FALSE), 16 for an error value, and 64 for an array. For example, if cell A1 contains the number 100, the formula =TYPE(A1) returns 1. If A1 contains the text Microsoft Excel, the formula returns 2.

Like the TYPE function, the ERROR.TYPE function detects the contents of a cell, except it detects different types of error values. The result is a code for the type of error value in the referenced cell: 1 for #NULL!, 2 for #DIV/0!, 3 for #VALUE!, 4 for #REF!, 5 for #NAME!, 6 for #NUM!, and 7 for #N/A. Any other value in the referenced cell returns the error value #N/A. For example, if cell A1 contains a formula that displays the error value #NAME!, the formula =ERROR.TYPE(A1) returns 5. If A1 contains the text Microsoft Excel, the formula returns #N/A.

The COUNTBLANK Function

The COUNTBLANK function counts the number of empty cells in the specified range, which is its only argument. This function is tricky because formulas that evaluate to null text strings, such as =" ", or to zero might seem empty, but they aren't and therefore won't be counted.

Using the IS Information Functions

You can use the ISBLANK, ISERR, ISERROR, ISEVEN, ISLOGICAL, ISNA, ISNON-TEXT, ISNUMBER, ISODD, ISREF, and ISTEXT functions to determine whether a referenced cell or range contains the corresponding type of value.

All the IS information functions take a single argument. For example, the ISBLANK function takes the form =ISBLANK(value). The *value* argument is a reference to a cell. If *value* refers to a blank cell, the function returns the logical value TRUE; otherwise, it returns FALSE.

TROUBLESHOOTING

My IS function returns unexpected results.

Although you can use a cell range (rather than a single cell) as the argument to any IS function, the result might not be what you expect. For example, you might think the ISBLANK function would return TRUE if the referenced range is empty or FALSE if the range contains any values. Instead, its behavior depends on where the range is in relation to the cell containing the formula. If the argument refers to a range that intersects the row or column containing the formula, ISBLANK uses implicit intersection to arrive at the result. In other words, the function looks at only one cell in the referenced range and only if it happens to be in the same row or column as the cell containing the function. The function ignores the rest of the range. If the range shares neither a row nor a column with the formula, however, the result is always FALSE. For more about intersection, see "Getting Explicit About Intersections" on page 418.

An ISERR Example

You can use ISERR to avoid getting error values as formula results. For example, suppose you want to call attention to cells containing a particular character string, such as 12A, resulting in the word Yes appearing in the cell containing the formula. If the string isn't found, you want the cell to remain empty. You can use the IF and FIND functions to perform this task, but if the value isn't found, you get a #VALUE! error rather than a blank cell.

To solve this problem, add an ISERR function to the formula. The FIND function returns the position at which a substring is found within a larger string. If the substring isn't there, FIND returns #VALUE!. The solution is to add an ISERR function, such as =IF(ISERR(FIND("12A", A1)), " ", "Yes"). Because you're not interested in the error, which is simply a by-product of the calculation, this traps the error, leaving only the results in which you are interested.

> **Note**
>
> When you type numeric values as text, such as **="21"**, the IS function, unlike other functions, does not recognize them as numbers. Therefore, the formula =ISNUMBER("21") returns FALSE.

Understanding Lookup and Reference Functions

Lookup &
Reference

Lookup and reference functions help you use your own worksheet tables as sources of information to be used elsewhere in formulas. You can use three primary functions to look up information stored in a list or a table or to manipulate references: LOOKUP, VLOOKUP, and HLOOKUP. Some powerful lookup and reference functions in addition to these three are available; we describe many of them in the following sections. You'll find a list of all these functions by clicking the Lookup & Reference button on the Formulas tab on the Ribbon.

Using Selected Lookup and Reference Functions

VLOOKUP and HLOOKUP are nearly identical functions that look up information stored in tables you have constructed. VLOOKUP and HLOOKUP operate in either vertical or horizontal orientation (respectively), but LOOKUP works either way.

When you look up information in a table, you usually use a row index and a column index to locate a particular cell. Excel derives the first index by finding the largest value in the first column or row that is less than or equal to a lookup value you supply and then uses a row number or column number argument as the other index. Make sure the table is sorted by the row or column containing the lookup values.

> **Creating Automated Lookup Formulas**
>
> You can create powerful lookup formulas using add-in tools. (The tools don't actually use any of the lookup functions.) For more information, see "Using the Conditional Sum and Lookup Wizards" on page 444.

These functions take the following forms:

```
=VLOOKUP(lookup_value, table_array, col_index_num, range_lookup)
=HLOOKUP(lookup_value, table_array, row_index_num, range_lookup)
```

Table 14-1 lists LOOKUP function arguments and their descriptions. The LOOKUP function takes two forms; the first is called the *vector form*, and the second is called the *array form*:

```
=LOOKUP(lookup_value, lookup_vector, result_vector)
=LOOKUP(lookup_value, array)
```

Table 14-1 LOOKUP Function Arguments

Argument	Description
lookup_value	The value, cell reference, or text (enclosed in quotation marks) that you want to find in a table or a range.
table_array	A cell range or name that defines the table in which to look.
row_index_num *col_index_num*	The row or column number of the table from which to select the result, counted relative to the table (not according to the actual row and column numbers).
range_lookup	A logical value that determines whether the function matches *lookup_value* exactly or approximately. Type **FALSE** to match *lookup_value* exactly. The default is TRUE, which finds the closest match.
lookup_vector	A one-row or one-column range that contains numbers, text, or logical values.
result_vector	A one-row or one-column range that must be the same size as *lookup_vector*.
array	A range containing numbers, text, or logical values to compare with *lookup_value*.

The difference between the lookup functions is the type of table each function uses: VLOOKUP works only with vertical tables (tables arranged in columns); HLOOKUP works only with horizontal tables (tables arranged in rows). You can use the *array form* of LOOKUP with either horizontal tables or vertical tables, and you can use the *vector form* with single rows or columns of data.

The array form of LOOKUP determines whether to search horizontally or vertically based on the shape of the table defined in the *array* argument. If the table has more columns than rows, LOOKUP searches the first row for *lookup_value*; if the table has more rows than columns, LOOKUP searches the first column for *lookup_value*. LOOKUP always returns the last value in the row or column containing the *lookup_value* argument; or you can specify a row or column number using VLOOKUP or HLOOKUP.

The VLOOKUP and HLOOKUP Functions

For the VLOOKUP and HLOOKUP functions, whether Excel considers a lookup table to be vertical or horizontal depends on where the comparison values (the first index) are located. If the values are in the leftmost column of the table, the table is vertical; if they are in the first row of the table, the table is horizontal. (In contrast, LOOKUP uses the shape of the table to determine whether to use the first row or column as the comparison values.) The comparison values can be numbers or text, but it is essential that they be sorted in ascending order. No comparison value should be used more than once in a table.

The *index_num* argument (sometimes called the *offset*) provides the second index and tells the lookup function which column or row of the table to look in for the function's result. The first column or row in the table has an index number of 1; therefore, the *index_num* argument must be greater than or equal to 1 and must never be greater than the number of rows or columns in the table. For example, if a vertical table is three columns wide, the index number can't be greater than 3. If any value does not meet these rules, the function returns an error value.

You can use the VLOOKUP function to retrieve information from the table in Figure 14-9.

C1		f_x =VLOOKUP(41,A3:C7,3)						
	A	B	C	D	E	F	G	H	I
1			14						
2									
3	10	17.98	5						
4	20	5.89	8						
5	30	5.59	11						
6	40	23.78	14						
7	50	6.79	17						
8									
9									
10									
11									
12									
13									
14									

Figure 14-9 You can use the VLOOKUP function to retrieve information from a vertical table like this one.

 You'll find the Lookup.xlsx file in the Sample Files section of the companion CD.

Remember that these lookup functions usually search for the greatest comparison value that is less than or equal to the lookup value, not for an exact match between the comparison values and the lookup value. If all the comparison values in the first row or column of the table range are greater than the lookup value, the function returns the #N/A error value. If all the comparison values are less than the lookup value, however, the function returns the value that corresponds to the last (largest) comparison value in the table, which might not be what you want. If you require an exact match, type **FALSE** as the *range_lookup* argument.

The worksheet in Figure 14-10 shows an example of a horizontal lookup table using the HLOOKUP function.

	A1	▼		f_x	=HLOOKUP(6,B2:E7,3)			
	A	B	C	D	E	F	G	H	I
1	101								
2		3	6	10	16				
3		5	100	99	1				
4		10	101	98	2				
5		25	105	95	3				
6		30	110	94	2				
7		35	125	90	1				
8									
9									
10									
11									
12									
13									

Figure 14-10 You can use the HLOOKUP function to retrieve information from a horizontal table like this one.

The LOOKUP Function

The LOOKUP function is similar to VLOOKUP and HLOOKUP and follows the same rules, but it is available in two forms, *vector* and *array*, whose arguments are described in Table 14-1.

Like HLOOKUP and VLOOKUP, the *vector form* of LOOKUP searches for the largest comparison value that isn't greater than the lookup value. It then selects the result from the corresponding position in the specified result range. The *lookup_vector* and *result_vector* arguments are often adjacent ranges, but they don't have to be when you use LOOKUP. They can be in separate areas of the worksheet, and one range can be horizontal and the other vertical. The only requirement is that they must have the same number of elements.

For example, consider the worksheet in Figure 14-11, where the ranges are not parallel. Both the *lookup_vector* argument, A1:A5, and the *result_vector* argument, D6:H6, have five elements. The *lookup_value* argument, 3, matches the entry in the third cell of the *lookup_vector* argument, making the result of the formula the entry in the third cell of the result range: 300.

The *array form* of LOOKUP is similar to VLOOKUP and HLOOKUP but works with either a horizontal table or a vertical table, using the dimensions of the table to figure out the location of the comparison values. If the table is taller than it is wide or the table is square, the function treats it as a vertical table and assumes that the comparison values are in the leftmost column. If the table is wider than it is tall, the function views the table as horizontal and assumes that the comparison values are in the first row of the table. The result is always in the last row or column of the specified table; you can't specify column or row numbers.

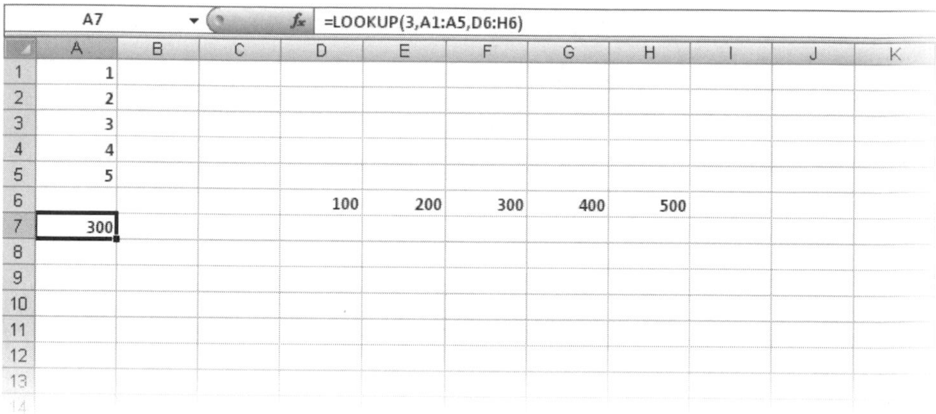

Figure 14-11 The vector form of the LOOKUP function can retrieve information from a nonparallel cell range.

Because HLOOKUP and VLOOKUP are more predictable and controllable, you'll generally find using them preferable to using LOOKUP.

The ADDRESS Function

The ADDRESS function provides a handy way to build a cell reference using numbers typed into the formula or using values in referenced cells. It takes the arguments (*row_num, column_num, abs_num, a1, sheet_text*). For example, the formula =ADDRESS(1, 1, 1, TRUE, "Data Sheet") results in the reference 'Data Sheet'!$A$1.

The CHOOSE Function

You use the CHOOSE function to retrieve an item from a list of values. The function takes the arguments (*index_num, value 1, value 2, . . .*) and can include up to 254 values. The *index_num* argument is the position in the list you want to return; it must be positive and can't exceed the number of elements in the list. The function returns the value of the element in the list that occupies the position indicated by *index_num*. For example, the function =CHOOSE(2, 6, 1, 8, 9, 3) returns the value 1, because 1 is the second item in the list. (The *index_num* value isn't counted as part of the list.) You can use individual cell references for the list, but you can't specify ranges. You might be tempted to create a function, such as =CHOOSE(A10, C1:C5), to take the place of the longer function in the preceding example. If you do, however, the result is a #VALUE! error value.

The MATCH Function

The MATCH function is closely related to the CHOOSE function. However, whereas CHOOSE returns the item that occupies the position in a list specified by the *index_num* argument, MATCH returns the position of the item in the list that most closely matches a lookup value.

> **Note**
>
> You can create powerful lookup formulas using add-in tools that use the MATCH and INDEX functions. See "Using the Conditional Sum and Lookup Wizards" on page 444.

This function takes the arguments (*lookup_value, lookup_array, match_type*), where *lookup_value* and the items in the *lookup_array* can be numeric values or text strings, and *match_type* defines the rules for the search, as shown in Table 14-2.

Table 14-2 MATCH Function Arguments

match_type	Description
1 (or omitted)	Finds the largest value in the specified range (which must be sorted in ascending order) that is less than or equal to *lookup_value*. If no items in the range meet these criteria, the function returns #N/A.
0	Finds the first value in the specified range (no sorting necessary) that is equal to *lookup_value*. If no items in the range match, the function returns #N/A.
–1	Finds the smallest value in the specified range (which must be sorted in descending order) that is greater than or equal to *lookup_value*. If no items in the range meet these criteria, the function returns #N/A.

When you use MATCH to locate text strings, you should specify a *match_type* argument of 0 (an exact match). You can then use the wildcards * and ? in the *lookup_value* argument.

The INDEX Function

The INDEX function has two forms: an array form, which returns a value, and a reference form, which returns a cell reference. The forms of these functions are as follows:

```
=INDEX(array, row_num, column_num)
=INDEX(reference, row_num, column_num, area_num)
```

The *array form* works only with an array argument; it returns the value of the result, not the cell reference. The result is the value at the position in *array* indicated by *row_num* and *column_num*. For example, the formula

```
=INDEX({10,20,30;40,50,60} , 1, 2)
```

returns the value 20, because 20 is the value in the cell in the second column and first row of the array.

> **Note**
>
> Each form of the INDEX function offers an advantageous feature. Using the reference form of the function, you can use multiple, nonadjacent areas of the worksheet as the *reference* lookup range. Using the array form of the function, you can get a range of cells, rather than a single cell, as a result.

The *reference form* returns a cell address instead of a value and is useful when you want to perform operations on a cell (such as changing the cell width), rather than on its value. This function can be confusing, however, because if an INDEX function is nested in another function, that function can use the value in the cell whose address is returned by INDEX. Furthermore, the reference form of INDEX doesn't display its result as an address; it displays the value(s) at that cell address. Remember that the result is an address, even if it doesn't look like one.

Here are a few guidelines to keep in mind when using the INDEX function:

- If you type **0** as the *row_num* or *column_num* argument, INDEX returns a reference for the entire row or column, respectively.

- The *reference* argument can be one or more ranges, which are called *areas*. Each area must be rectangular and can contain numbers, text, or formulas. If the areas are not adjacent, you must enclose the *reference* argument in parentheses.

- You need the *area_num* argument only if you include more than one area in *reference*. The *area_num* argument identifies the area to which the *row_num* and *column_num* arguments will be applied. The first area specified in *reference* is designated area 1, the second area 2, and so on.

Let's consider some examples to see how all this works. Figure 14-12 shows an example of an INDEX function. The formula in cell A1 uses the row coordinate in cell A2 and the column coordinate in cell A3 to return the contents of the cell in the third row and second column of the specified range.

The following example is a bit trickier: Using the same worksheet in Figure 14-12, the formula =INDEX(C3:E6, 0, 2) displays the #VALUE! error value because the *row_num* argument of 0 returns a reference to the entire column specified by the *column_num* argument of 2, or the range D3:D6. Excel can't display a range as the result. However, try nesting this formula in another function, as follows: =SUM(INDEX(C3:E6, 0, 2)). The result is 2600, the sum of the values in D3:D6. This illustrates the utility of obtaining a reference as a result.

Now we'll show how the INDEX function works with multiple ranges in the *reference* argument. (When you're using more than one range, you must enclose the argument in parentheses.) For example, in the formula =INDEX((A1:C5,D6:F10), 1, 1, 2), the *reference* range comprises two areas: A1:C5 and D6:F10. The *area_num* argument (2) tells INDEX to work on the second of these areas. This formula returns the address D6, which is the cell in the first column and first row of the range D6:F10. The displayed result is the value in that cell.

A1		▼		*fx*	=INDEX(C3:E6,A2,A3)					
	A	B	C	D	E	F	G	H	I	J
1	700									
2	3									
3	2		100	500	9000					
4			200	600	1100					
5			300	700	1200					
6			400	800	1300					
7										
8										
9										
10										
11										
12										
13										

Figure 14-12 Use the INDEX function to retrieve the address or value in a cell where information is located.

The INDIRECT Function

The INDIRECT function returns the contents of a cell using its reference. It takes the arguments (*ref_text, a1*), where *ref_text* is an A1-style or R1C1-style reference or a cell name. The *a1* argument is a logical value indicating which type of reference you're using. If *a1* is FALSE, Excel interprets *ref_text* as R1C1 format; if *a1* is TRUE or omitted, Excel interprets *ref_text* as A1 format. For example, if cell C6 on your worksheet contains the text value B3 and cell B3 contains the value 2.888, the formula =INDIRECT(C6) returns the value 2.888. If your worksheet is set to display R1C1-style references and cell R6C3 contains the text reference R3C2 and cell R3C2 contains the value 2.888, then the formula =INDIRECT(R6C3, FALSE) also returns the value 2.888.

For information about A1-style and R1C1-style references, see "Understanding Row-Column Reference Style" on page 397.

The ROW and COLUMN Functions

The result of the ROW and COLUMN functions is the row or column number, respectively, of the cell or range referred to by the function's single argument. For example, the formula =ROW(H5) returns the result 5. The formula =COLUMN(C5) returns the result 3 because column C is the third column on the worksheet.

If you omit the argument, the result is the row or column number of the cell that contains the function. If the argument is a range or a range name and you enter the function as an array by pressing Ctrl+Shift+Enter, the result of the function is an array that consists of the row or column numbers of each row or column in the range. For example, suppose you select cells B1:B10, type the formula **=ROW(A1:A10)**, and then press Ctrl+Shift+Enter to enter the formula in all cells in the range B1:B10. That range will contain the array result {1;2;3;4;5;6;7;8;9;10}, the row numbers of each cell in the argument.

The ROWS and COLUMNS Functions

The ROWS and COLUMNS functions return the number of rows or columns, respectively, referenced by the function's single argument in a reference or an array. The argument is an array constant, a range reference, or a range name. For example, the result of the formula =ROWS({100,200,300;1000,2000,3000}) is 2, because the array consists of two rows (separated by a semicolon). The formula =ROWS(A1:A10) returns 10, because the range A1:A10 contains ten rows. And the formula =COLUMNS(A1:C10) returns 3, because the range A1:C10 contains three columns.

The AREAS Function

You can use the AREAS function to determine the number of areas in a reference. *Areas* refer to individual cell or range references, not regions. The single argument to this function can be a cell reference, a range reference, or several range references. If you use several range references, you must enclose them in a set of parentheses so Excel doesn't misinterpret the commas that separate the ranges. (Although this function takes only one argument, Excel still interprets unenclosed commas as argument separators.) For example, suppose you assign the name Test to the group of ranges A1:C5,D6,E7:G10. The function =AREAS(Test) returns 3, the number of areas in the group.

The TRANSPOSE Function

The TRANSPOSE function changes the horizontal or vertical orientation of an array. It takes a single argument, *array*. If the argument refers to a vertically oriented range, the resulting array is horizontal. If the range is horizontal, the resulting array is vertical. The first row of a horizontal array becomes the first column of the vertical array result, and vice versa. You must type the TRANSPOSE function as an array formula in a range that has the same number of rows and columns as the *array* argument has columns and rows, respectively.

For quick and easy transposition, select the range you want to transpose, press Ctrl+C to copy the range, click the cell where you want the upper-left corner of the transposed range to begin, click the Paste button on the Home tab, and then click Transpose.

Analyzing Data with PivotTable Reports

A PivotTable report is a special kind of table that summarizes information from selected fields of a data source. The source can be a Microsoft Office Excel 2007 list, a relational database file, an Online Analytical Processing (OLAP) cube, or multiple *consolidation ranges* (multiple ranges containing similar data, which the PivotTable can assemble and summarize). When you create a PivotTable, you specify which fields you're interested in, how you want the table organized, and what kinds of calculations you want the table to perform. After you build the table, you can rearrange it to view your data from alternative perspectives. This ability to "pivot" the dimensions of your table—for example, to transpose column headings to row positions—gives the PivotTable its name and its analytical power.

Introducing PivotTables

PivotTables are linked to the data from which they're derived. If the PivotTable is based on external data (data stored outside Excel), you can choose to have it refreshed at regular time intervals, or you can refresh it whenever you want.

Figure 15-1 shows Books.xlsx, a list of sales figures for a small publishing firm. The list is organized by year, quarter, category, distribution channel, units sold, and sales receipts. The data spans a period of eight quarters (2005 and 2006). The firm publishes six categories of fiction (Mystery, Western, Romance, Sci Fi, Young Adult, and Children) and uses three distribution channels—domestic, international, and mail order. It's difficult to get useful summary information by looking at a list like this, even though the list itself is well organized.

 You'll find the Books.xlsx file in the Sample Files section of the companion CD.

Figure 15-1 It's difficult to see the bottom line in a flat list like this; turning the list into a PivotTable will help.

Figures 15-2 through 15-4 show several ways you can transform this flat table into PivotTables that show summary information at a glance.

The example on the left in Figure 15-2 breaks the data down first by category, second by distribution channel, and finally by year, with the total sales at each level displayed in column B. Looking at this table, you can see (among many other details) that the Children category generated domestic sales of $363,222, with more revenue in 2005 than in 2006.

In the example on the right in Figure 15-2, the per-category data is broken out first by year and then by distribution channel. The data is the same; only the perspective is different.

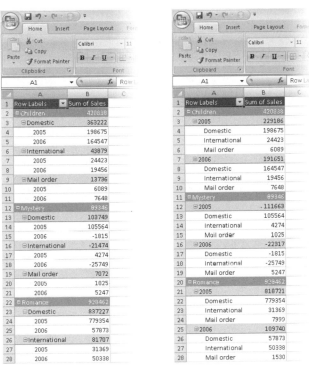

Figure 15-2 These two PivotTables provide summary views of the information in Figure 15-1.

Both the PivotTables shown in Figure 15-2 are single-axis tables. That is, we've generated a set of row labels (Children, Mystery, Romance, and so on) and set up outline entries below these labels. (And, by default, Office Excel 2007 displays outline controls beside all the headings, so we can collapse or expand the headings to suit our needs.)

Figure 15-3 shows a more elaborate PivotTable that uses two axes. Along the row axis, we have categories broken out by distribution channel. Along the column axis, we have years (2005 and 2006). And we added the quarterly detail (not included in the Figure 15-2 examples) so we can see how each category in each channel did each quarter of each year. With four *dimensions* (category, distribution channel, year, and quarter) and two axes (row and column), we have a lot of choices about how to arrange the furniture. Figure 15-3 shows only one of many possible permutations.

Chapter 15

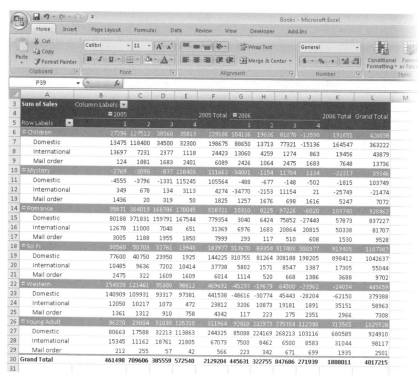

Figure 15-3 In this PivotTable, we've rearranged the data along two axes—rows and columns.

Figure 15-4 presents a different view. Now the distribution channels are arrayed by themselves along the column axis, while the row axis offers years broken out by quarters. The category, meanwhile, has been moved to what you might think of as a page axis. The data has been filtered to show the numbers for a single category, Mystery, but by using the filter control at the right edge of cell B2, we could switch the table to a different category (or combination of categories). Filtering the Category dimension by one category after another would be like flipping through a stack of index cards.

None of these tables required more than a few clicks to generate.

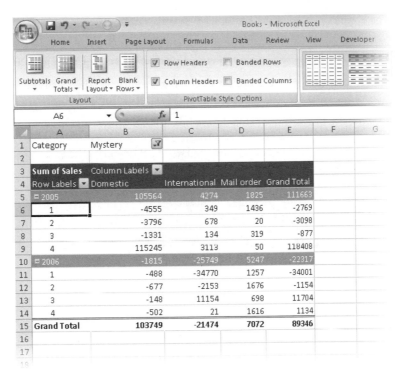

Figure 15-4 This PivotTable presents a "filtered" view, confining the report to a single category.

Creating a PivotTable

You can create a PivotTable from either an Excel range or an external data source. If you're working from an Excel range, your data should meet the criteria for a well-constructed list. That is, it should have column labels at the top (the headings will become field names in the PivotTable), each column should contain a particular kind of data item, and you should not have any blank rows within the range. If the range includes summary formulas (totals, subtotals, or averages, for example), you should omit them from the PivotTable; the PivotTable will perform its own summary calculations.

The source range on your Excel worksheet can be a table or an ordinary list. Starting from a table has the advantage of allowing for expansion. When you create a PivotTable from a table, Excel references your source data by its table name (either a default name, such as Table1, or the name you assign to the table). If you add rows to a table, the table name automatically adjusts to encompass the new data, and hence your PivotTable stays in sync with the expanded source data.

To create a PivotTable, select a single cell within the source data and do either of the following:

- Click the Insert tab, and then click PivotTable (in the Tables group).

- If your source data is a table and you're currently on the Design tab under Table Tools, click Summarize With PivotTable (in the Tools group).

Either way, the Create PivotTable dialog box appears. If your source data has a name (we've assigned the name BookSales to the source table in our example), that name appears in the Table/Range box. Otherwise, Excel discerns the extent of your source data and presents a range reference in that box:

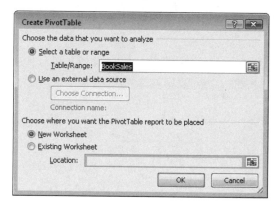

By default, your PivotTable arrives on a new worksheet, and that's generally a good arrangement. If you want it elsewhere, specify where in the Location box. After you click OK, Excel generates a blank table layout on the left side of the worksheet and displays the PivotTable Field List window on the right (see Figure 15-5). The PivotTable Field List window is docked at the right by default. You can make it wider or narrower by dragging the split bar on its left edge. You can also undock it or drag it across the worksheet and dock it on the left.

> **Note**
>
> If you want to work with only a subset of items in a field, you can filter the field before you add it to the table. If your data source is large, and particularly if the source is external, you can save some time by filtering in advance. (You can also filter fields after you have created the table, of course.) To filter a field before you add it to the table, select the field name in the PivotTable Field List window, and then click the arrow on the right. For more details, see "Filtering PivotTable Fields" on page 502.

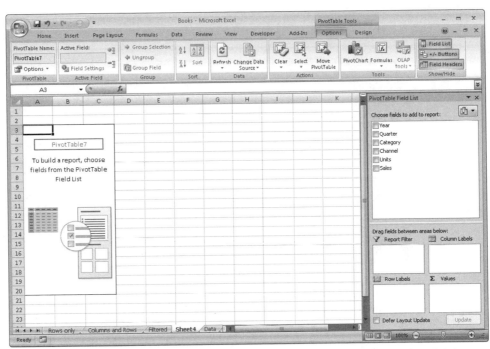

Figure 15-5 As you select the check boxes for fields in the PivotTable Field List window, Excel populates the table layout at the left side of the worksheet.

To put some fields and data on that blank layout, begin by selecting the check boxes for those fields in the Choose Fields To Add To Report area of the PivotTable Field List window. As you select fields, Excel positions them in the four boxes below. These four boxes represent the various components of the table. The Row Labels and Column Labels boxes hold the fields that will appear on the row and column axes. The Report Filter box holds the field (or fields) you want to use to filter the table (comparable to the Category field in Figure 15-4), and the Values box holds the field (or fields) you want to use for calculations—the data you're summarizing (your sales, for example).

Initially, Excel puts selected fields in default table locations that depend on their data types. Most likely you'll want some arrangement other than the one you get by default. That's not a problem, because you can move fields from one location to another easily; just drag them between the various boxes below the PivotTable Field List window. Let's look at an example.

To create the table shown in Figure 15-3, we want to put the Category and Channel fields in the Row Labels box, the Year and Quarter fields in the Column Labels box, and the Sales field in the Values box. When we select the check boxes for those fields, Excel drops the Category and Channel fields in the Row Labels box (because they are text fields) and the Sales field in the Values box (because it's a numeric field). These are all good guesses on the part of Excel—and, in fact, it's just what we want. In addition to putting field headings in the appropriate boxes, Excel begins creating our PivotTable—as Figure 15-6 shows.

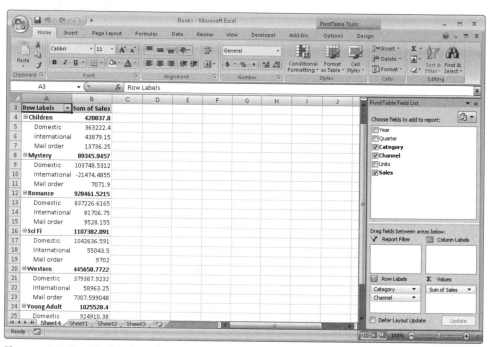

Figure 15-6 Excel builds the table, piece by piece, as you select fields.

So far, so good. The numeric formats aren't right, but we can fix that easily enough.

What remains is to put the Year and Quarter fields into the Column Labels box. Unfortunately, if we simply select their check boxes, Excel drops these fields in the Values box, because the fields are numbers and the program has a predilection for adding numbers. This (see Figure 15-7) is definitely not what we want.

The solution is simple: Select the check boxes for the Year and Quarter fields, and then drag the Sum of Quarter and Sum of Year headings from the Values box to the Column Labels box. (Alternatively, you can make sure your field headings go where you want them by dragging them directly from the Choose Fields To Add To Report box to the appropriate boxes below, disregarding the defaults.)

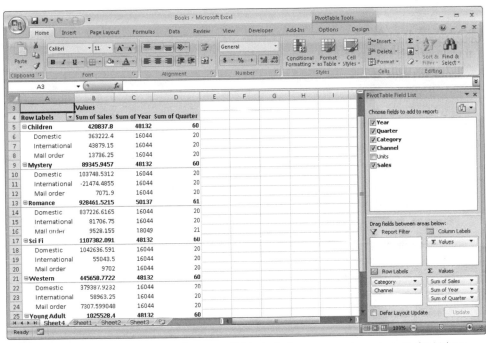

Figure 15-7 By default, Excel puts all numeric fields, including years and quarters, in the Values box. You can fix that by dragging field headings to the appropriate locations.

Rearranging PivotTable Fields

To pivot, or rearrange, a PivotTable, drag one or more field headings from one part of the PivotTable Field List window to another. For example, by using the mouse to change this configuration of the PivotTable Field List window:

to this one:

we can change the table from the form shown in Figure 15-3 to this:

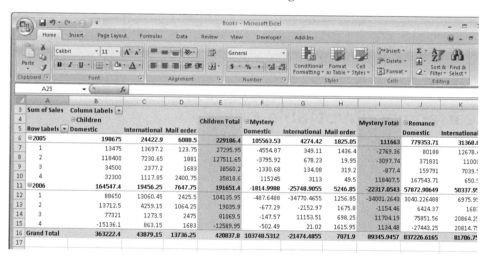

> ### Note
>
> If you don't see the PivotTable Field List window, select a cell in the PivotTable (it disappears when your selection is not within the table). If you still don't see it, click the Options tab under PivotTable Tools on the Ribbon, and then click Field List. This button is a handy way to toggle the field list in and out of view, letting you reduce distraction when you don't need to do any field rearrangement.

INSIDE OUT   Pivot Your Tables the Excel 2003 Way If You Prefer

Earlier versions of Excel let you move fields around by dragging them directly on the table, instead of requiring you to work with the PivotTable Field List window. If you prefer that way of working, right-click any cell in the PivotTable, and click PivotTable Options. In the PivotTable Options dialog box, click the Display tab. Then select the Classic Pivot-Table Layout (Enables Dragging Of Fields In The Grid) check box. Note, however, that this option also changes the appearance of your table from the compact, outline-style pre-sentation of Excel 2007 to the more space-consuming tabular style of earlier versions.

To rearrange fields within the same axis—for example to put Year before Quarter or Channel before Category in Figure 15-3, you can drag field headings from one place to another within the same area of the PivotTable Field List window. Often it's simpler to click the arrow to the right of the field heading you want to move. (For example, you might click the arrow to the right of Category in the Row Labels box.) The menu that appears includes easy-to-use positioning commands:

Refreshing a PivotTable

Because users often generate PivotTables from large volumes of data (and in many cases that data resides on external servers), Excel doesn't automatically update PivotTables when their source data changes. To refresh a PivotTable, right-click any cell within it, and click Refresh. Alternatively, under PivotTable Tools, click the Options tab, and then click Refresh in the Data group. Or, if you like keyboard shortcuts, press Alt+F5.

To ensure that your PivotTable is sorted whenever you open the file, click a cell within the table, click the Options tab under PivotTable Tools, and then click Options in the PivotTable group. In the PivotTable Options dialog box, click the Data tab. Then select the Refresh Data When Opening The File check box, and click OK.

Chapter 15

Changing the Numeric Format of PivotTable Data

As Figure 15-6 shows, Excel initially displays numeric PivotTable data in the General format, regardless of how it's formatted in your source range. To fix that, right-click a cell in the field you want to change, and then click Number Format.

Choosing Report Layout Options

PivotTables in Excel 2007, by default, use a more compact presentation style than earlier versions used. This default layout (called Compact) indents inner fields on the row axis beneath their outer fields, letting you see more information at a glance. If you prefer, you can select from two alternative layouts, called Outline and Tabular. To switch from one layout to another, select a cell within the table, click the Design tab under PivotTable Tools, click Report Layout (in the Layout group), and then click one of the displayed layouts (Show In Compact Form, Show In Outline Form, or Show In Tabular Form). Figure 15-8 compares the three layout options.

Note that the layout options affect the row axis only. For example, the outline form simply indents the distribution channels below each category of book.

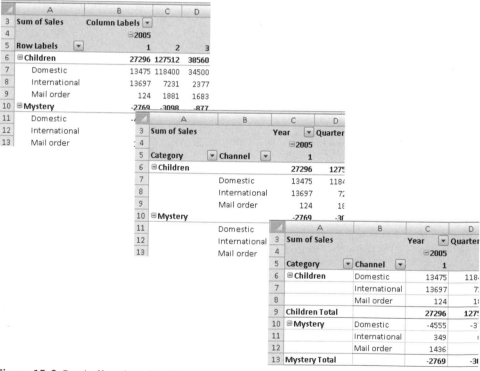

Figure 15-8 Excel offers three PivotTable layout options: Compact (left), Outline (center), and Tabular (right).

Formatting a PivotTable

The Design tab that appears on the Ribbon under PivotTable Tools when you select any part of a PivotTable includes a large selection of professionally designed PivotTable styles. These work just like—and, in fact, are similar to—the styles available with ordinary tables. By choosing from the PivotTable Styles gallery, you can ensure that your PivotTable looks good and uses colors consistent with the rest of your workbook. You can customize the built-in style choices by selecting or clearing the check boxes in the PivotTable Style Options group, and you can add your own designs by clicking New PivotTable Style at the bottom of the PivotTable Styles gallery. To display the PivotTable Styles gallery, click the More button at the bottom of the scroll bar. (This button is a small arrow with a line above it.)

Customizing the Display of Empty or Error Cells

Empty cells in a PivotTable are usually displayed as empty cells. If you prefer, you can have your PivotTable display something else—a text value such as NA, perhaps—in cells that would otherwise be empty. To do this, right-click any cell in the PivotTable, and click PivotTable Options. On the Layout & Format tab in the PivotTable Options dialog box, select the For Empty Cells Show check box, and in the text box type the text or value that you want to see.

If a worksheet formula references a cell containing an error value, that formula returns the same error value. This is usually true in PivotTables as well. Error values in your source data propagate themselves into the PivotTable. If you prefer, you can have error values generate blank cells or text values. To customize this aspect of PivotTable behavior, right-click any cell in the PivotTable, and click PivotTable Options. On the Layout & Format tab in the PivotTable Options dialog box, select the For Error Values Show check box. Then, in the text box, type what you want to see.

Merging and Centering Field Labels

When you have two or more fields stacked either on the column axis or on the row axis of a PivotTable, centering the outer labels over the inner ones can sometimes improve the table's readability. Just right-click a PivotTable cell, click PivotTable Options, and then select the Merge And Center Cells With Labels check box on the Layout & Format tab in the PivotTable Options dialog box. With this option, you can change this kind of presentation:

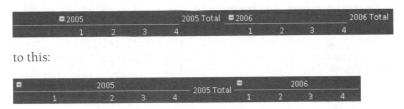

to this:

Hiding Outline Controls

You'll probably find outline controls useful in some contexts and not in others. They're great when you have large or complex PivotTables and you want to be able to switch quickly from a details view to an overview. But if you find they clutter the picture instead of enhancing it, you can banish them easily: Select a PivotTable cell, click the Options tab under PivotTable Tools, and then click the +/– Buttons in the Show/Hide group.

> **Note**
>
> With outline controls suppressed, you can still expand and collapse field headings. Select a heading in the field you're interested in, click the Options tab under PivotTable Tools on the Ribbon, and then click Expand Entire Field or Collapse Entire Field in the Active Field group.

Hiding *Row Labels* and *Column Labels*

The headings *Row Labels* and *Column Labels* that Excel displays near the upper-left corner of your PivotTable may prove distracting at times. You can suppress them by selecting a PivotTable cell, clicking the Options tab under PivotTable Tools, and then clicking Field Headers in the Show/Hide group. Note, however, that removing these labels also removes their associated filter controls—and you might want those controls from time to time (see "Filtering PivotTable Fields" on page 502). The Field Headers command is a toggle. Click it again to restore the headings—and the filter controls.

> **Note**
>
> You can change the name of a PivotTable field or an item within a field by selecting any occurrence of it and typing the name you want. When you change one occurrence, all occurrences in the table change.

Displaying Totals and Subtotals

By default, Excel generates grand totals for all outer fields in your PivotTable using the same summary function as the body of the table. In Figure 15-3, for example, row 30 displays grand totals for each quarter of each year, as well as for the years themselves. Column L, meanwhile, displays per-category totals by channel. The intersection of column L and row 30 displays the grandest of totals, the sum of all sales for the period covered by the table. Because the body of the table uses the SUM function, all these grand totals do as well.

To remove grand totals from a PivotTable, right-click any cell in the table, and click PivotTable Options. On the Totals & Filters tab in the PivotTable Options dialog box, clear the Show Grand Totals For Rows check box, the Show Grand Totals For Columns check box, or both check boxes.

Naturally, PivotTables are not restricted to calculating sums. For other calculation options, see "Changing PivotTable Calculations" on page 505.

Customizing Subtotals

By default, Excel creates subtotals for all but the innermost fields. For example, in Figure 15-3, cell B6 displays the sum of cells B7:B9 (the Children subtotal for Quarter 1 of 2005), cell C10 displays the sum of cells C11:C13 (the Mystery subtotal for Quarter 2 of 2005), and so on. Columns F and K display yearly subtotals. The innermost fields, Channel (for the row axis) and Quarter (for the column axis), do not have subtotals.

To find options affecting all subtotals, select a cell in the PivotTable, click the Design tab under PivotTable Tools, and then click Subtotals on the left edge of the Ribbon:

You can use this menu to turn subtotaling off altogether or to move row-axis subtotals from their default position above the detail items to a position below.

To customize subtotals for a particular field, right-click an item in the field, and then click Field Options. (Alternatively, select an item in the field, click the Options tab under PivotTable Tools, and then click Field Settings in the Active Field group.) Figure 15-9 shows the Field Settings dialog box for the Category field in our example PivotTable.

The Automatic option on the Subtotals & Filters tab in this dialog box means—as Automatic means throughout Excel—you're letting the program decide what to do. In other words, this option gets the default behavior. You can turn off subtotals for the selected field by selecting None. Selecting Custom lets you change the default subtotal calculation, such as from Sum to Average. And, as the text above the function list suggests, you're not limited to one function. You can select as many as you need by holding down Ctrl while you click. Figure 15-10 shows a PivotTable with four subtotaling calculations applied to the Category field. (Note that when you have multiple subtotals for a field, Excel moves them below the detail.)

Figure 15-9 In the Field Settings dialog box, you can override the default subtotaling behavior for a particular field.

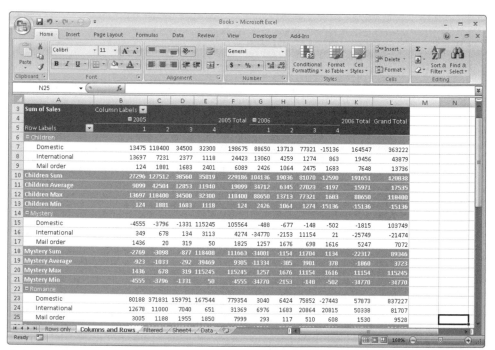

Figure 15-10 You can generate subtotals using more than one summary function; this table uses four for the Category field.

By using the Field Settings dialog box, you can also generate subtotals for innermost fields—subtotals that Excel usually does not display. Such inner subtotals appear at the bottom of the table (just above the grand total row) or at the right side of the table (just to the left of the grand total column). Figure 15-11 shows an example of inner-field subtotaling.

Sum of Sales	Column Labels ▼										
	2005				2005 Total	2006				2006 Total	Grand Total
Row Labels ▼	1	2	3	4		1	2	3	4		
Children											
Domestic	13475	118400	34500	32300	198675	88650	13713	77321	-15136	164547	363222
International	13697	7231	2377	1118	24423	13060	4259	1274	863	19456	43879
Mail order	124	1881	1683	2401	6089	2426	1064	2475	1683	7648	13736
Mystery											
Domestic	-4555	-3796	-1331	115245	105564	-488	-677	-148	-502	-1815	103749
International	349	678	134	3113	4274	-34770	-2153	11154	21	-25749	-21474
Mail order	1436	20	319	50	1825	1257	1676	698	1616	5247	7072
Romance											
Domestic	80188	371831	159791	167544	779354	3040	6424	75852	-27443	57873	837227
International	12678	11000	7040	651	31369	6976	1683	20864	20015	50339	81707
Mail order	3005	1188	1955	1850	7999	293	117	510	608	1530	9528
Sci Fi											
Domestic	77600	40750	23950	1925	144225	310755	81264	308188	198205	898412	1042637
International	10485	9636	7202	10414	37738	5802	1571	8547	1387	17305	55044
Mail order	2475	322	1609	1609	6014	1114	520	668	1386	3688	9702
Western											
Domestic	140909	109931	93317	97381	441538	-48616	-30774	45443	-28204	-62150	379388
International	12050	10217	1073	472	23812	3206	10873	19181	1891	35151	58963
Mail order	1361	1312	910	758	4342	117	223	275	2351	2966	7308
Young Adult											
Domestic	80663	17588	32213	113863	244325	85088	224169	268213	103116	680585	924910
International	15345	11162	18761	21805	67073	7500	8462	6500	8583	31044	98117
Mail order	212	255	57	42	566	223	342	671	699	1935	2501
Domestic Sum	388280	654704	342440	528257	1913681	438429	294118	774869	230035	1737452	3651132
International Sum	64605	49925	36587	37573	188689	1773	24094	67519	32560	177546	316235
Mail order Sum	8614	4978	6532	6710	26834	5429	3942	5298	8344	23013	49847
Grand Total	461498	709606	385559	572540	2129204	445631	322755	847686	271939	1888011	4017215

Figure 15-11 Subtotals for Channel, an inner field, appear in rows 30–32 of this table.

Sorting PivotTable Fields

You can sort a PivotTable field either by its own items (for example, alphabetizing the categories in Figure 15-11) or on the basis of values in the body of the table (for example, sorting categories in descending order of sales totals so the best-selling categories appear at the top). To sort a field, right-click any item in that field, and then click Sort. On the menu that appears, you can click Sort A To Z or Sort Z To A if you want to sort the field by its own items. If you want to sort the field by values in the body of the table, click More Sort Options. You'll see a dialog box similar to the one shown on the next page (with the name of the field you selected in the title of the dialog box).

To sort by values in the table body instead of by items in the selected field, open the Ascending or Descending list. The list will include the available value fields.

> **Note**
>
> To ensure that Excel retains your sort specification when you update your PivotTable, click More Options in the dialog box shown above. Then select Sort Automatically Every Time The Report Is Updated.

Filtering PivotTable Fields

Filtering a field lets you focus your table on a subset of items in that field. You can filter on the basis of the field's own content (only the Children and Young Adult categories, for example) or on the basis of values associated with the field (for example, the three categories with the best overall sales). You can apply filters either in the PivotTable Field List window or on the PivotTable. If you're working with a large external data source and you need only a subset of the data, you can save yourself some time by filtering in the PivotTable Field List window before you execute the query and create the table.

To filter in the PivotTable Field List window, select the heading for the field you want to filter, and then click the arrow to the right of the field heading. The dialog box that appears includes check boxes for each unique item in the selected field:

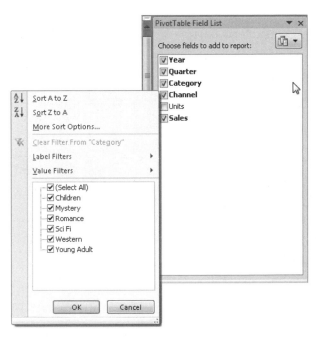

You can use the check boxes to select one or more particular items in your selected field. If your field is more complex than the example here, you might want to click Label Filters, in response to which Excel presents many additional filtering options:

The options that appear on this menu are tailored for the data type of the selected field. If your field holds dates instead of text, for example, you will see these options:

To filter a field on the basis of values associated with that field, click the arrow next to the field heading in the PivotTable Field List window, and then click Value Filters on the menu that appears. For example, to filter the PivotTable in Figure 15-3 so it shows only the three categories with the highest total sales, click the arrow beside Category, and then click Value Filters. In the Value Filters menu:

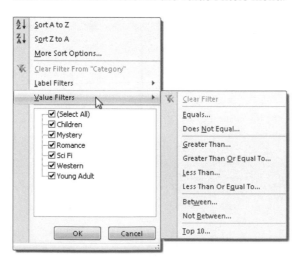

you would click Top 10, which would take you to the Top 10 Filter dialog box:

where you replace the 10 with a 3 and then click OK. Figure 15-12 shows the result.

Sum of Sales	Column Labels											
	⊟ 2005				2005 Total	⊟ 2006				2006 Total	Grand Total	
Row Labels	1	2	3	4		1	2	3	4			
⊟ Romance												
Domestic	80188	371831	159791	167544	779354	3040	6424	75852	-27443	57873	837227	
International	12678	11000	7040	651	31369	6976	1683	20864	20815	50338	81707	
Mail order	3005	1188	1955	1850	7999	293	117	510	608	1530	9528	
⊟ Sci Fi												
Domestic	77600	40750	23950	1925	144225	310755	81264	308188	198205	898412	1042637	
International	10485	9636	7202	10414	37738	5802	1571	8547	1387	17305	55044	
Mail order	2475	322	1609	1609	6014	1114	520	668	1386	3688	9702	
⊟ Young Adult												
Domestic	80663	17588	32213	113863	244325	85088	224169	268213	103116	680585	924910	
International	15345	11162	18761	21805	67073	7500	8462	6500	8583	31044	98117	
Mail order	212	255	57	42	566	223	342	671	699	1935	2501	
Grand Total	282651	463731	252576	319703	1318662	420790	324552	690013	307356	1742710	3061372	

Figure 15-12 We filtered the table to show only the three best-selling categories.

Note that when you apply a value filter to a field, Excel bases its calculations on the current grand total associated with that field. If we wanted to see the three top-selling categories for the year 2005 (in the example shown in Figure 15-3), we would need to filter the Year field as well as the Category field.

Changing PivotTable Calculations

By default, Excel populates the Values area of your PivotTable by applying the SUM function to any numeric field you put there or by applying the COUNT function to any nonnumeric field. But you can choose from many alternative forms of calculation, and you can add your own calculated fields to the table.

Using a Different Summary Function

To switch to a different summary function, right-click any cell in the Values area of your PivotTable, and then click Value Field Settings. (Alternatively, click the Options tab under PivotTable Tools, and then click Field Settings in the Active Field group.) Excel displays the Value Field Settings dialog box, shown in Figure 15-13. Select the function you want from the Summarize Value Field By list, and then click OK.

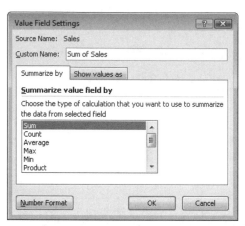

Figure 15-13 Using this dialog box, you can change the function applied to a field in the Values area of your PivotTable.

Excel fills in the Custom Name line in this dialog box according to your selection in the Summarize Value Field By list. If you switch from SUM to AVERAGE, for example, the Custom Name line changes to include the word *Average*. You can type whatever you like there, though.

Applying Multiple Summary Functions to the Same Field

You can apply as many summary functions as you want to a value field. To use a second or subsequent function with a field that's already in the Values area of your PivotTable, drag another copy of the field from the PivotTable Field List window into the Values box. Then select a Values area cell, return to the Value Field Settings dialog box, and select the function you want to use. The available functions are SUM, COUNT, AVERAGE, MAX, MIN, PRODUCT, COUNT NUMBERS, STDDEV, STDDEVP, VAR, and VARP.

Using Custom Calculations

In addition to the standard summary functions enumerated in the previous paragraph, Excel also offers a set of custom calculations. With these you can have each item in the Values area of your table report its value as a percentage of the total values in the same row or column, create running totals, or show each value as a percentage of some base value.

To apply a custom calculation, right-click a cell in the Values area, and then click Value Field Settings. Click the Show Values As tab in the Value Field Settings dialog box. Then select a calculation from the Show Values As list. Table 15-1 lists the available options.

When you select a calculation in the Show Values As list, the Base Field and Base Item boxes display choices that are relevant to your calculation. For example, as Figure 15-14 shows, if you select Difference From in our books example, the Base Field box displays Quarter, Category, Channel, and so on. If you select Quarter in this list, the Base

Item box presents the four quarters, along with the self-explanatory items (Previous) and (Next).

Table 15-1 Custom Calculation Options

Difference From	Displays data as a difference from a specified base field and base item
% Of	Displays data as a percentage of the value of a specified base field and base item
% Difference From	Displays data as a percentage difference from a specified base field and base item
Running Total In	Displays data as a running total
% Of Row	Displays each data item as a percentage of the total of the items in its row
% Of Total	Displays each data item as a percentage of the grand total of all items in its field
Index	Uses this formula: ((value in cell) * Grand Total of Grand Totals)) / ((Grand Row Total) * (Grand Column Total))

Figure 15-14 When you choose a calculation such as Difference From, the Base Field and Base Item boxes display relevant options.

Figure 15-15 and Figure 15-16 illustrate some ways you can modify default calculations and Values field names. The table in Figure 15-15 lists 2006–2007 performances at major opera houses around the world by theater, country, opera, composer, and performance date. The PivotTable in Figure 15-16 includes the Date field twice in the Values box. The default summary calculation for date data is Count, and that's fine because we want the number of performances and counting dates is a way to get that. But we used the Custom Name box in the Value Field Settings dialog box (refer to Figure 15-13) to change the name from Count of Date to No. of Performances. When we dragged the second instance of the Date field into the Values box, we used the Value Field Settings dialog box to make the field report the percentage of total. You could use similar techniques with other kinds of polling or survey applications.

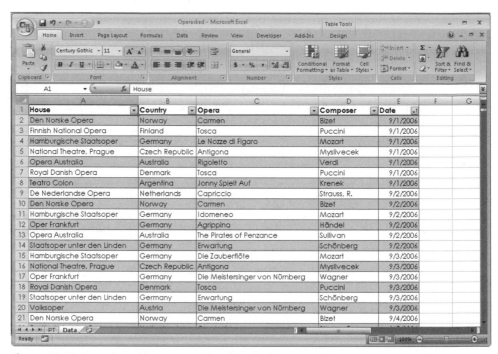

Figure 15-15 From this table, a PivotTable will apply the COUNT function to the Date field to count performances.

You'll find the OperaSked.xlsx file in the Sample Files section of the companion CD.

> **Note**
>
> If you filter a field, percentage-of-total calculations are based on the data that meets the filter criterion, not the unfiltered data set.

Using Calculated Fields and Items

In case custom calculations don't meet all your analytic needs, Excel lets you add calculated fields and calculated items to your PivotTables. A *calculated field* is a new field, derived from calculations performed on existing fields in your table. A *calculated item* is a new item in an existing field, derived from calculations performed on other items that are already in the field. After you create a custom field or item, Excel makes it available to your table, as though it were part of your data source.

Custom fields and items can apply arithmetic operations to any data already in your PivotTable (including data generated by other custom fields or items), but they cannot reference worksheet data outside the PivotTable.

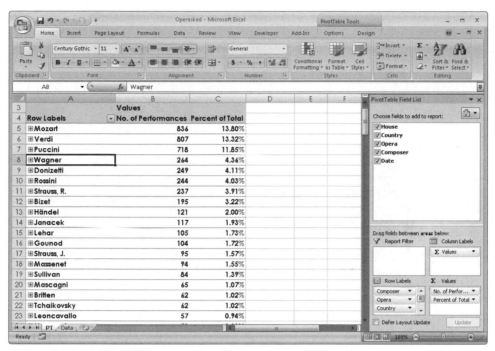

Figure 15-16 The PivotTable uses the Date field from Figure 15-15 twice—once to count perfor-mances, a second time to calculate percentage of total

Creating a Calculated Field

To create a calculated field, select any cell in the PivotTable. Then click the Options tab under PivotTable Tools, and click Formulas in the Tools group. On the Tools menu, click Calculated Field. Figure 15-17 shows the Insert Calculated Field dialog box.

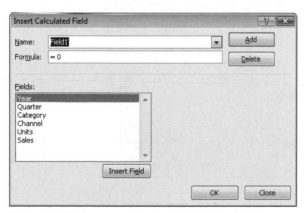

Figure 15-17 Create a calculated field in this dialog box.

Chapter 15

Type a name for your calculated field in the Name box. Then type a formula in the Formula box. To enter a field in the formula, select it from the Fields list, and click Insert Field. Figure 15-18 shows an example of a calculated field.

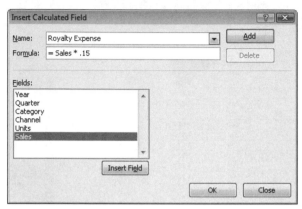

Figure 15-18 This calculated field multiples an existing field by a constant.

Excel adds a new calculated field to your PivotTable when you click either Add or OK. You can then work with the new field using the same techniques you use to work with existing fields.

Creating a Calculated Item

To create a calculated item for a field, select any existing item in the field or the field heading. Then click the Options tab under PivotTable Tools, and click Formulas in the Tools group. On the Formulas menu, click Calculated Item. Excel displays a dialog box comparable to the one in Figure 15-19.

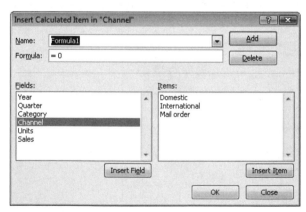

Figure 15-19 Use this dialog box to create a calculated item for a field.

To create a calculated item, type a unique name for the item in the Name box. Then enter a formula in the Formula box. You can select from the Fields and Items lists and click Insert Field and Insert Item to enter field and item names in the formula.

> **Note**
>
> You cannot create calculated items in fields that have custom subtotals.

Figure 15-20 shows an example of a calculated item. In this case the new item represents domestic sales divided by the sum of international and mail order sales.

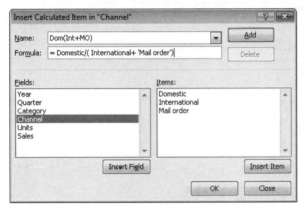

Figure 15-20 This calculated item will appear by default whenever you include the Channel field in the PivotTable.

Displaying a List of Calculated Fields and Items

To display a list of your calculated fields and items, along with their formulas, click the Options tab under PivotTable Tools, and then click Formulas in the Tools group. On the Formulas menu, click List Formulas. Excel displays the list on a new worksheet, as shown in Figure 15-21.

As the note in Figure 15-21 indicates, you need to be careful when a cell in your table is affected by more than one calculated field or item. In such cases, the value is set by the formula that's executed last. The Solve Order information in the list of calculated fields and items tells you which formula that is. If you need to change the solve order, select the worksheet that contains the PivotTable, click the Options tab under Pivot-Table Tools, and then click Formulas in the Tools group. On the Formulas menu, click Solve Order.

Chapter 15

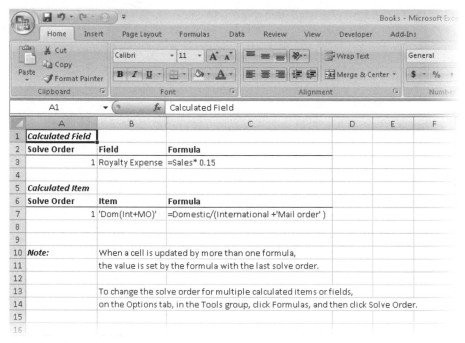

Figure 15-21 Excel lists calculated fields and items on a new worksheet.

Grouping and Ungrouping Data

PivotTables group inner field items under each outer field heading and, if requested, create subtotals for each group of inner field items. You might find it convenient to group items in additional ways—for example, to collect monthly items into quarterly groups or sets of numbers into larger numeric categories. Excel provides several options for grouping items.

Creating Ad Hoc Item Groupings

Suppose that after looking at Figure 15-3 you decide you'd like to see the domestic and international sales figures grouped into a category called Retail. To create this group, select the Domestic and International items anywhere in the table. Then click the Options tab under PivotTable Tools, and click Group Selection in the Group group. Excel creates a new heading called Group1:

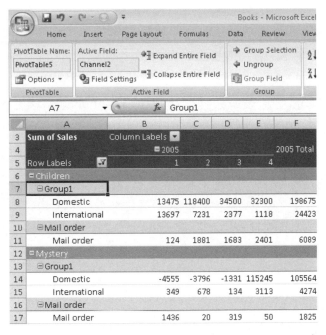

Now you can rename Group1 by simply typing over any instance of it.

Grouping Items in Date or Time Ranges

Figure 15-22 shows a PivotTable that summarizes daily transactions by payee. As you can see, the data in this table is extremely sparse. Most intersections between a day item and a payee item are blank.

You'll find the Transactions.xlsx file in the Sample Files section of the companion CD.

To make this kind of table more meaningful, you can group the date field. To do this, select an item in the field. Then click the Options tab under PivotTable Tools, and click Group Field. Excel responds by displaying the Grouping dialog box, shown in Figure 15-23.

Excel gives you a great deal of flexibility in the way your date and time fields are grouped. In the By list, you can choose any common time interval, from seconds to years, and if the standard intervals don't meet your needs, you can select an arbitrary number of days. You can also create two or more groupings at the same time (hold down Ctrl while you select); the results of grouping by both Quarter and Month are shown in Figure 15-24.

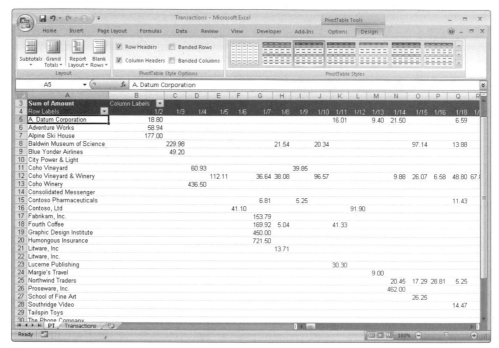

Figure 15-22 To make the data in this table more meaningful, you can group the date field.

Figure 15-23 Excel gives you lots of ways to group by date.

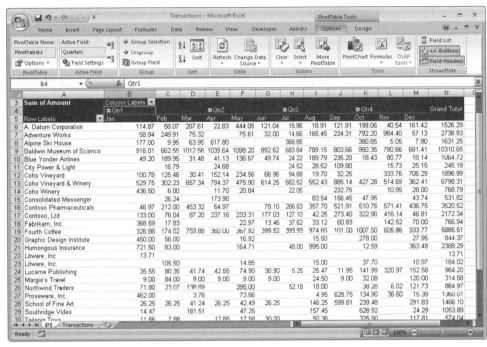

Figure 15-24 In this table, daily data is grouped by months and then by quarters.

Displaying the Details Behind a Data Value

If you double-click any PivotTable value that represents a summary calculation, Excel displays the details behind that calculation on a new worksheet. For example, in Figure 15-24, cell B13 informs us that we spent $529.75 at Coho Vineyard & Winery during the month of January. Double-clicking B13 reveals the details, as shown on the next page.

Chapter 15

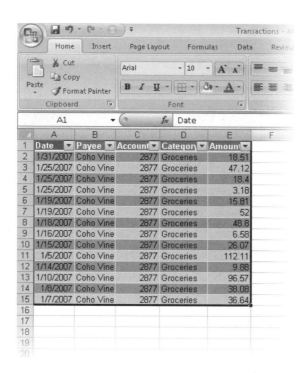

Creating PivotCharts

PivotCharts, like PivotTables, summarize tabular information and allow for easy transposition of fields and axes. They're a great way to study or present elements of your data set.

You can create a PivotChart directly from your source data by selecting a cell in the original data range, clicking the Insert tab, clicking the arrow beneath PivotTable in the Tables group, and then clicking PivotChart. After you specify or confirm your data source and indicate where you want the new PivotChart to reside (in a location either on the existing worksheet or on a new worksheet), Excel presents both a PivotTable layout and a blank chart canvas, along with a PivotChart Filter Pane (see Figure 15-25). Excel creates a PivotTable at the same time it creates a PivotChart—and hence you see a blank table layout. The PivotChart Filter Pane doesn't really add any capability that isn't available via the PivotTable Field List window, so you might want to close one or the other to make more room on the worksheet.

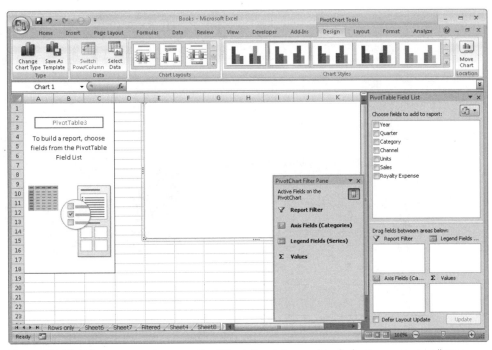

Figure 15-25 When you create a new PivotChart, Excel draws a blank chart canvas as well as a blank table layout. The program creates a PivotTable at the same time it creates the PivotChart.

Figure 15-26 shows a simple PivotChart created from this chapter's Books table. Because charts are generally most effective when applied to a modest amount of data, we've used the Report Filter box to restrict the presentation to a single category (Children), and we've filtered the Channel field to show international and mail order sales only. We've also tidied up a bit by closing the PivotTable Field List window and dragging the PivotChart Filter Pane to a less obtrusive position.

As you can see, when you select a PivotChart, Excel adds a new set of tabs on the Ribbon, under PivotChart Tools. With these tabs, you can manipulate and format your PivotChart the same way you would an ordinary chart.

A PivotChart and its associated PivotTable are inextricably linked. You can manipulate fields and axes in either, and the other stays in step.

Chapter 15

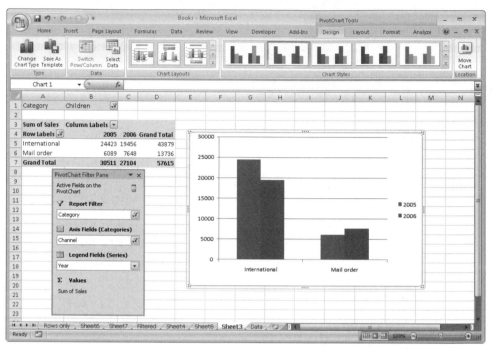

Figure 15-26 We've used a PivotChart to plot two distribution channels for one book category.

In Figures 15-25 and 15-26, we created a PivotChart directly from the source data. You can also create one from an existing PivotTable. Select any cell in the PivotTable, click the Options tab under PivotTable Tools, and then click PivotChart in the Tools group.

PART 5

PowerPoint

S. E. Slack

519

Introduction to PowerPoint 2007

A s with other programs in the 2007 Microsoft Office system, Microsoft Office PowerPoint 2007 has a new interface that makes it easy to complete even the most complicated tasks when creating a presentation. The point-and-click design places features at your fingertips, with a more visual and contextual experience that offers functions, tools, and commands in the order that most users commonly perform tasks. The tabbed navigational structure, Microsoft Office Button, and Quick Access Toolbar have replaced many menus of the past to help make Office PowerPoint 2007 more intuitive and logical to use.

In this chapter, you'll learn about what's new in PowerPoint 2007. You'll learn about how to customize the user interface to fit your needs; about where to find commonly used commands; and about features such as file formats, tables, themes, Master views, custom slide layouts, Slide Libraries, and program recovery features. Each of these capabilities makes creating dynamic presentations something anyone can do, regardless of previous PowerPoint experience.

Command Locations

The new Ribbon means you access the commands you used in PowerPoint 2003 differently in PowerPoint 2007. Since PowerPoint 2007 offers more than 1,000 commands, we won't cover all of them in this book; however, we will show you the most commonly used menus and toolbars in PowerPoint 2003 and compare them to their counterparts in PowerPoint 2007. Note that in PowerPoint 2007, you can often access a command in multiple ways; for example, you can access the Print command through the Microsoft Office Button and the Print Preview tab. Table 16-1 outlines the command locations that we have found the easiest to use. Remember that some contextual tabs will not become available until you click the previously listed command or option. If you're looking for a command that is not listed here, refer to PowerPoint 2007 Help.

For more information about the general features of the 2007 Office system user interface, see Chapter 2, "The 2007 Office System User Interface—What's Changed, What's the Same."

Table 16-1 Command Locations: PowerPoint 2003 and PowerPoint 2007

PowerPoint 2003 Menus and Commands	PowerPoint 2007 Location
File menu New, Open, Close, Save, Save As, Permission, Print, Exit	Microsoft Office Button.
Edit menu Undo, Redo	Quick Access Toolbar.
Edit menu Cut, Copy, Paste, Paste Special, Paste As Hyperlink, Duplicate, Office Clipboard	Home tab, Clipboard group.
Edit menu Find, Replace, Select All	Home tab, Editing group.
Edit menu Preserve Master, Rename Master	View tab, Slide Master, Edit Master group.
View menu Normal, Slide Sorter, Slide Show, Notes Page, Master Slide Master, Master Notes Master	View tab, Presentation Views group.
View menu Task Pane	Dialog Box Launchers within groups. For example, on the Home tab in the Font group, click the Dialog Box Launcher to open the Font dialog box.
View menu Toolbars, Formatting, Standard	Home tab.
View menu Toolbars, Drawing, WordArt	Drawing Tools tab, a contextual tab that appears when you insert a drawing object or WordArt.
View menu Toolbars, Tables And Borders	Table Tools tab, a contextual tab that appears when you insert a table.
View menu Ruler, Grids And Guides	View tab, Show/Hide group.
Insert menu New Slide, Duplicate Slide, Slides From Files, Title Slide, Slides From Outline	Home tab, Slides group.
Insert menu Picture, Diagram, Chart, Clip Art, From File	Insert tab, Illustrations group.
Insert menu WordArt, Text, Symbol, Date And Time, Header & Footer, Object	Insert tab, Text group.
Format menu Alignment options	Home tab, Paragraph group.

PowerPoint 2003 Menus and Commands	PowerPoint 2007 Location
Tools menu Spelling And Grammar, Research, Thesaurus, Language	Review tab, Proofing group.
Slide Show menu View Show	View tab, Presentation Views group.
Slide Show menu Set Up Show, Rehearse Timings, Record Narration, Hide Slide	Slide Show tab, Set Up group.
Slide Show menu Animation Settings, Custom Animation, Slide Transition	Animations tab, Animations group and Transition To This Slide group.

Customizing Office PowerPoint 2007

When you open PowerPoint 2007, you are automatically taken to the Home tab. This is one of seven tabs you will see initially—the others are Insert, Design, Animations, Slide Show, Review, and View, as shown in Figure 16-1. These tabs appear in the order they are most commonly used, but changing the interface for your personal style isn't hard; in fact, it's similar to changing the user interface in Microsoft Office Word 2007.

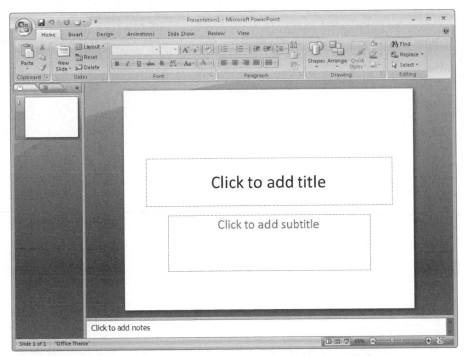

Figure 16-1 PowerPoint 2007 displays seven tabs on the Ribbon by default.

You can customize PowerPoint 2007 in a couple of ways: You can customize the Quick Access Toolbar to add or remove commands, and you customize the entire PowerPoint 2007 user interface and set other options to your liking by using the PowerPoint Options dialog box.

Customizing the Quick Access Toolbar

The Quick Access Toolbar is located above the Ribbon, although you can easily move it below the Ribbon by clicking the small arrow to its right and then clicking Show Below The Ribbon. The default commands included on the toolbar are Save As, Undo, and Redo or Repeat. (The last command toggles between Redo and Repeat depending on whether you've performed an action you can undo.) Most people, however, use additional commands just as often as these. For example, if you regularly use WordArt in your presentations, why use two clicks (Insert tab, WordArt) when you can just click the Quick Access Toolbar once?

Chapter 2 includes details for customizing Quick Access Toolbars throughout Office 2007.

Be judicious as you customize the Quick Access Toolbar in PowerPoint 2007—you can choose commands from more than 30 locations. The whole point of the toolbar is to make finding commands quick and easy. If you add dozens, you're defeating the toolbar's purpose.

Here are the steps you follow to customize the Quick Access Toolbar:

1. Right-click the Quick Access Toolbar, and then click Customize Quick Access Toolbar.

2. In the PowerPoint Options dialog box, you'll see the Customize page, as shown next.

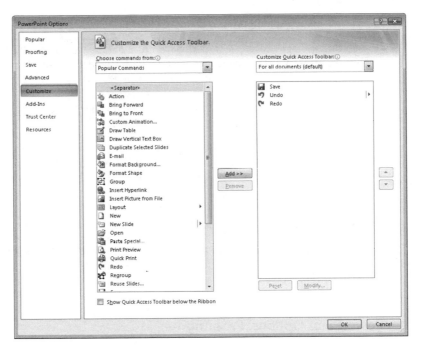

3. In the Choose Commands From list, select the tab or other location that contains the command you want to add.

4. In the list of commands, select the command you want to add, and then click Add.

5. To change the order of the commands on the Quick Access Toolbar, use the up and down arrows to the right of the command list.

CAUTION

When you click the Reset button near the bottom of the dialog box, be aware that PowerPoint 2007 resets the Quick Access Toolbar to the Microsoft defaults. If you want to remove a single item from the Quick Access Toolbar and you're in the Options dialog box, click the command you want to remove and then click the Remove button or double-click the item.

Chapter 16

Setting PowerPoint 2007 Options

To customize the look and feel of PowerPoint 2007, as well as set individual options within the program, you make changes through the Microsoft Office Button using the PowerPoint Options dialog box. Customization settings are organized in eight categories: Popular, Proofing, Save, Advanced, Customize, Add-Ins, Trust Center, and Resources. The "Customizing the Quick Access Toolbar" section on page 524 covers the Customize category; we'll cover the others in the following sections.

To access the following PowerPoint options, you must be in the PowerPoint Options dialog box. To open the PowerPoint Options dialog box, click the Microsoft Office Button, and then click PowerPoint Options. When the PowerPoint Options dialog box appears, click a category in the task pane on the left.

PowerPoint Options: Popular

You use the Popular category to modify the look and feel of PowerPoint 2007. Here you can change the color scheme, choose languages, turn on functions such as Mini toolbars, ScreenTips, Live Preview, and the Developer tab. You can also change your user name and initials with this option.

PowerPoint Options: Proofing

Use the Proofing category to choose how PowerPoint 2007 corrects and formats your text. AutoCorrect settings, spelling, and dictionary options are all included here. Be careful: The Proofing pane has two separate areas for spelling correction settings. You can change spelling correction options for all programs of the Microsoft Office system by selecting or clearing the check boxes below When Correcting Spelling In Microsoft Office Programs or just in PowerPoint 2007 by selecting or clearing the check boxes below When Correcting Spelling In PowerPoint. Pay attention when configuring these options if you want them to occur only in PowerPoint 2007.

PowerPoint Options: Save

The Save category lets you customize how—and how often—PowerPoint 2007 saves your documents. You'll find file format settings, AutoRecover settings, offline editing options, and embedded font information for file-sharing purposes here.

For more information about AutoRecover settings, see "Program Recovery" on page 543.

PowerPoint Options: Advanced

The Advanced category contains many of the more involved configuration settings, so take some time with this one. You can customize the way you edit, display, and print your presentations in this category, plus you can customize Web options. The Web Options dialog box offers you more than 50 choices for customizing your PowerPoint 2007 presentation for the Web.

PowerPoint Options: Add-Ins

You use the Add-Ins category to manage Component Object Model (COM) add-ins, PowerPoint 2007 add-ins, smart tags, and disabled items by active or inactive status. This category also lists template files referenced by currently open documents and add-ins automatically disabled because of incompatibility issues with PowerPoint 2007 or other programs in the Microsoft Office system.

PowerPoint Options: Trust Center

The Trust Center category is a new feature in PowerPoint 2007. With it, you can select privacy and security options for ActiveX controls, macro settings, and trusted publishers; however, we caution you against making changes here. Microsoft has determined these preset options to be the most secure settings for users. Changes to them can result in security and privacy risks for you.

For more information about security settings in the Trust Center, see Chapter 3, "Managing Security and Privacy in the 2007 Office System."

PowerPoint Options: Resources

Use the Resources category to contact Microsoft, perform diagnostics, obtain updates, and activate programs in the Microsoft Office system. You can also sign up for free online services.

File Formats

Chapter 16

PowerPoint 2007 uses the new Office XML format as its default file format, just like Microsoft Office Word 2007 and Microsoft Office Excel 2007. As a result, PowerPoint 2007 offers a new Save As default (which uses the file extension .pptx) when you save a document and also provides several other XML-related file format options for macros and templates. Chapter 32, "Office Open XML Essentials," provides an overview of XML itself, so we won't go into great detail about it here except to remind you of a few key features of the XML file format in PowerPoint 2007: data compression, improved file recovery, and integration.

For PowerPoint 2007, the compression aspect is important—many presentations contain graphics and other data that can make file sizes quite large. Using XML file formats to save a file means that the file size will be substantially reduced, improving your storage and bandwidth capabilities. The XML file format also segments your data so that if one part of your presentation becomes corrupted, recovery is easier—only that segmented part of the file might be irretrievable, not the entire presentation. And integration through XML means you can now create and use structured presentation templates that integrate XML content with other kinds of content—this makes linking to external data sources easier than before.

You can save your presentation in numerous ways, just like you always have. Choose the file format that is most appropriate for your audience and presentation. For example, if the majority of your audience uses the Microsoft Office system, saving your presentation in the new .pptx default should become your new standard. However, you should know that some formatting features can change or become lost when you open a PowerPoint 2007 presentation in earlier versions of PowerPoint or when you open a presentation created in an earlier version of PowerPoint in PowerPoint 2007. (See the "Data That Could Be Lost or Changed in PowerPoint 2007" sidebar on page 530.) Consider this if your audiences tend to use earlier versions of the Microsoft Office system, and save your presentation in the PowerPoint 97–2003 format (.ppt).

Here are the steps you follow to save a PowerPoint 2007 presentation in the XML file format:

1. Open the presentation you want to save.

2. Click the Microsoft Office Button.

3. Click Save As.

4. Name your file in the File Name box.

5. Click the arrow to the right of Save As Type, and then click PowerPoint Presentation (*.pptx), as shown here. (See Table 16-2 for additional XML file format options if .pptx is not the one you need.)

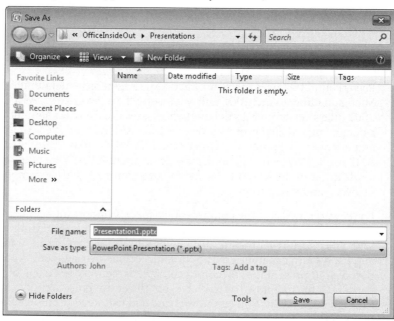

6. Click Save.

Table 16-2 **PowerPoint 2007 File Types and File Name Extensions**

Common File Types	File Name Extension
PowerPoint 97–2003 presentation	.ppt
PowerPoint 97–2003 template	.pot
PowerPoint 97–2003 slide show	.pps
PowerPoint 97–2003 add-in	.ppa
File Types Available with Add-Ins	**File Name Extension**
XML Paper Specification (XPS)	.xps
Portable Document Format (PDF)	.pdf
XML File Types	**File Name Extension**
PowerPoint 2007 presentation	.pptx
PowerPoint XML presentation	.xml
Macro-enabled presentation	.pptm
Template	.potx
Macro-enabled template	.potm
Macro-enabled add-in	.ppam
Slide show	.ppsx
Autonomous slide file	.sldx
Macro-enabled slide	.sldm
Office theme	.thmx

Opening a PowerPoint 2007 Presentation in PowerPoint 97–2003

If the presentation has not been saved in .ppt format, PowerPoint 97–2003 users who have downloaded and installed the Microsoft Office Compatibility Pack from Microsoft Office Online can open it; see *http://office.microsoft.com/en-us/downloads/default.aspx*. The updates and converters are free. Anyone who opens a PowerPoint 2007 presentation and has not yet downloaded the Compatibility Pack will be automatically presented with instructions for doing so.

Saving to PowerPoint 95 and Earlier File Formats

If you consistently work with people who use much older versions of PowerPoint, you'll have difficulties sharing PowerPoint 2007 files with them. Microsoft does not support saving PowerPoint 2007 files to PowerPoint 95 and earlier formats. One way to avoid these compatibility issues is to save your PowerPoint file in PDF or HTML format, because most people have used PDF or HTML.

Chapter 16

Data That Could Be Lost or Changed in PowerPoint 2007

PowerPoint 2007 doesn't support all the features of earlier versions of PowerPoint. If you save a file from an earlier version in a PowerPoint 2007 file, you will lose data associated with the following features:

- Presentation broadcast
- Microsoft Script Editor
- Publish and subscribe
- Send for review

In addition, the following features change when a user opens a PowerPoint 2007 presentation in an earlier version of PowerPoint:

- **Charts** These convert to Object Linking and Embedding (OLE) objects.
- **Shapes, pictures, objects, animations, two-dimensional (2-D) and three-dimensional (3-D) effects and text, gradient outlines, strikethroughs and double-strikethroughs on text, gradient, picture, and texture fills on text** These all convert to uneditable pictures.
- **Heading and body fonts** These convert to static formatting. If the file is reopened in PowerPoint 2007, these must be manually reformatted.
- **Custom slide layouts** These can be represented as multiple masters.
- **Drop shadows** These convert to hard shadows that can be edited.
- **Themes, theme colors, theme effects, and theme fonts** These convert to styles. Even though you can reopen the file again in PowerPoint 2007, these items cannot be automatically changed again using the original theme option.
- **Equations** These convert to pictures but, when reopened in PowerPoint 2007, become editable again.

About PDF and XPS File Formats

It might be advantageous for you to save your presentation in PDF or XPS file format. Both of these formats offer what are essentially *fixed layouts*—layouts that the user cannot change and that preserve the presentation's document formatting. It's also pretty easy to share these files, although both require that users have a viewer installed on their computers. PDF is the preferred format to use when sending your files for commercial printing production. The Windows Vista operating system and the 2007 Microsoft Office system have been created with XPS and PDF add-in capabilities.

Determining which one to use can be tricky—if your audience does not have Windows XP, Windows Vista, or Microsoft Windows Server 2003 with Microsoft Internet Explorer 6.0 or later, your users might be unable to view XPS documents. Many people, however, have become used to reading PDF documents and have already installed Adobe Acrobat Reader, which is a free download. Although you previously had to purchase Adobe software to create PDF documents, PowerPoint 2007 has a new capability that lets you create these documents instantly.

You can download the 2007 Microsoft Office Add-in: Microsoft Save As PDF or XPS from the Microsoft Office downloads site. (Go to *http://office.microsoft.com/en-us/downloads/CD101950461033.aspx* to obtain the add-in.)

To save your presentation in XPS file format, follow these steps:

1. Click the Microsoft Office Button.

2. Point to Save As, and then click PDF Or XPS.

3. In the Publish As PDF Or XPS dialog box that appears, click the arrow to the right of the Save As Type list, and then click XPS Document (*.xps).

4. Select the desired optimize option: Standard (Publishing Online And Printing) or Minimum Size (Publishing Online). Standard offers higher quality; Minimum Size offers a smaller file size.

5. Click Options to display the dialog box shown here. Use this dialog box to configure various options, such as publishing as slides or in handout format, publishing a single slide, and so on.

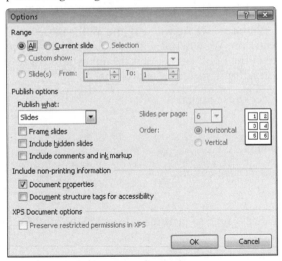

6. Click OK, and then click Publish.

To save your presentation in PDF file format, follow these steps:

1. Click the Microsoft Office Button.

2. Point to Save As, and then click PDF Or XPS.

3. In the Publish As PDF Or XPS dialog box that appears, click the arrow to the right of the Save As Type list, and then click PDF (*.pdf).

4. Select the desired Optimize option: Standard (Publishing Online And Printing) or Minimum Size (Publishing Online). Standard offers higher quality; Minimum Size offers a smaller file size.

5. Click Options to configure various options, such as publish as slides or in handout format, publish a single slide, and so on.

6. Click OK, and then click Publish.

Formatting

Formatting your presentation always requires some thought: Who is your audience? What kind of content do you have? How much time do you have to present it? Ultimately, your presentation format needs to quickly convey information in a way that attracts viewers and maintains their attention. A new feature in PowerPoint 2007 is Quick Style galleries—collections of formatting options shown in thumbnail view so you can make fast and easy choices when formatting your slides. Your slides change instantly with any theme changes, too, and give you a preview of how the new style will affect your presentation as you rest the pointer on a thumbnail. Quick Style galleries appear in a variety of locations; you'll recognize them easily as you use PowerPoint 2007. Figure 16-2 shows the Quick Style gallery for built-in theme effects.

The Home and Insert tabs are where you will find all the basic formatting items you need for your presentation. We will discuss more detailed formatting options in later chapters in this part of the book, but for now it's important to know that you can find the following formatting options on these two tabs.

The Home tab includes these options:

- Font choices

- Paragraph options

The Insert tab includes these options:

- Shapes

- Illustration choices (such as pictures, clip art, photo albums, SmartArt, and charts)

- Text options (such as text boxes, headers and footers, WordArt, dates and time, numbers, symbols, and objects)

- Movie and sound options

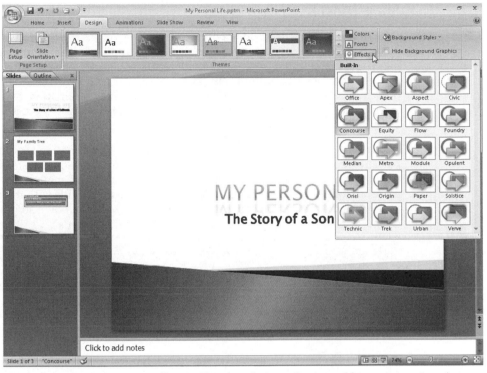

Figure 16-2 PowerPoint 2007 offers Quick Style galleries, collections of formatting options that make it quick and easy to format your presentation.

PowerPoint 2007 Views

One of the best features of PowerPoint, no matter which version you use, is the number of views you can use when developing a presentation. You can choose from four main views:

- **Normal** Four working areas in this view let you write content, rearrange slides, work on the current slide, and make notes.

- **Slide Sorter** This view shows you all your slides at once using a thumbnail format.

- **Notes Page** This view gives you a full-page format to use when creating notes.

- **Slide Show** This view lets you see your presentation the same way your audience will so you can verify the timing, effects, transitions, and other aspects of your presentation.

Slide Masters

One view that some users do not often use as effectively as they could is Slide Master view. With this view, you can create placeholders and layouts for your title and interior pages that are repeated from slide to slide, without you needing to define them again as you work on each page within your presentation. For example, if you want the date and presentation title to appear on every footer within your presentation, Slide Master view is the place to enter the information. After you enter this information, it will appear on every slide within the presentation, including newly added pages.

A *slide master* is basically part of a template that stores information for you through placeholders. Figure 16-3 shows an example. You can save a slide master as a single template file (.potx) and reuse it in different presentations, changing aspects to fit new presentations as needed. Each slide master can have a title slide with multiple layouts for the interior slides. You can use slide masters to create your own style and then add themes to them. (You'll learn about themes later in this chapter).

Figure 16-3 In Slide Master view, you can easily add recurring information to your slides, eliminating the need to enter the same information multiple times.

To add a slide master, follow these steps:

1. Click the View tab, and then click Slide Master in the Presentation Views group.

2. Click Insert Slide Master in the Edit Master group.

3. To remove placeholders from the slide master, click the placeholder border, and press Delete. If you want to keep all the placeholders, go to step 4.

4. To add placeholders, follow these steps:

   a. Select one of the thumbnail layouts in the task pane.

   b. Click the arrow next to Insert Placeholder in the Master Layout group on the Slide Master tab.

   c. Click a placeholder (Content, Text, Picture, Chart, Table, SmartArt, Media, Clip Art), and click on the slide where you want to add the placeholder.

   d. Repeat this process as often as necessary until you have added all the placeholders you want.

5. Click the Microsoft Office Button.

6. Click Save As.

7. Type a file name in the File Name box.

8. In the Save As Type list, select PowerPoint Template (*.potx).

9. Click Save.

Themes

By using the new theme options in PowerPoint 2007, you can easily ensure that your presentation has consistent colors, backgrounds, and fonts throughout the slides. The time you save when using a theme is precious, too—with a single click, you can change a presentation's background, text, graphics, charts, and tables.

PowerPoint 2007 opens with a blank slide unless you change the defaults. To establish a theme for your presentation, click the Design tab, and then click a theme in the Themes group. At the right of Themes group, you can use the scroll bar to display additional themes, as shown in Figure 16-4. You can also click the arrow below the scroll bar (the More button) to display all the options at once.

Colors, Fonts, and Effects appear to the far right of the Themes group. If you choose a particular theme style but don't care for the colors, for example, simply click the Colors command, and make a new choice. You can do the same for Fonts and Effects—a new selection automatically applies to the entire presentation theme. Next to the Themes group is the Background group. This is where you can further change the theme by applying a new background style and including or excluding background graphics.

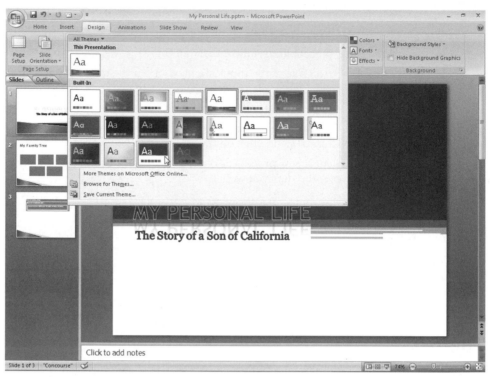

Figure 16-4 The new themes in PowerPoint 2007 give you the ability to change themes, fonts, colors, effects, and background styles with just a few clicks.

Theme Color Tips

Every theme offers four text and background colors, six accent colors, and two hyperlink colors. Clicking the Colors button on the Design tab in the Themes group shows you the current text and background colors. Click Create New Theme Colors at the bottom of the list to create your own set of colors.

Saving a Document Theme

You can save your own custom document theme at any time to change the colors, fonts, or line and fill effects of a document theme. Follow these steps:

1. Click the More button in the Themes group on the Design tab.

2. Click Save Current Theme.

3. Select the location, type a file name for the theme, and then click Save.

> **Note**
>
> Custom document themes are automatically saved to the Document Themes folder and added to the list of custom themes, unless you specify another location.

Tables

It's about time that the table feature in PowerPoint 2007 was updated! In fact, Microsoft has updated the feature throughout the Microsoft Office system to make using tables in Word 2007, Excel 2007, and PowerPoint 2007 much easier. In the following sections, we'll cover the most common aspects of using tables: adding a new one to your presentation, drawing your own table, copying a table from Word 2007 or Excel 2007, inserting a spreadsheet directly from Excel 2007, and applying and changing table styles.

Adding a New Table to Your Presentation

The most common way to add a table to your presentation is to use the standard options provided by PowerPoint 2007. You can easily make theme changes to a table created in this manner.

To add a table, follow these steps:

1. Click Table in the Tables group on the Insert tab. You will see the Insert Table drop-down box with rows and columns of cells.

2. Drag the pointer over the rows and columns of cells until you have the correct number of each for your table. As you do this, the header changes from "Insert Table" to "X x X Table," showing you how many rows and columns you have selected. Watch your slide, too. PowerPoint 2007 shows the table on your slide as you rest the pointer on the cells.

3. Click to add the table to your presentation.

Drawing a Table in Your Presentation

Sometimes, it's preferable to draw your own table rather than use the standard options provided by PowerPoint 2007. In that case, you simply need to use the Draw Table option. This option allows you to draw the borders of a table and then insert the columns and rows and add designs as you want. Although the automated table design option in PowerPoint 2007 is useful, sometimes building a table without any predetermined design can help you arrange the content you want to display in it more easily. Theme changes are easy to make when you draw your own table, too.

To draw a table, follow these steps:

1. Click Table in the Tables group on the Insert tab.

2. Click Draw Table. The pointer will change to a pencil when you rest it on the slide.

3. Define the boundaries of your table by clicking and then dragging the pencil diagonally to the size you want. Then click Draw Table in the Draw Borders group, and click within the table to draw row and column boundaries.

4. If you need to erase a line, click the Eraser tool in the Draw Borders group on the Design tab, under Table Tools. Then, click the line you want to erase.

5. When you have drawn the table to your satisfaction, type text in your cells.

Copying a Table from Word 2007 or Excel 2007

Often, a table exists in another program that makes a perfect visual reference for your PowerPoint 2007 presentation. You can copy the table to your presentation and then change the table to match your PowerPoint theme using the commands on the Design tab.

To copy a table from Word 2007 or Excel 2007, follow these steps:

1. In Word 2007 or Excel 2007, select the table you want to copy.

2. In Word 2007 or Excel 2007, click Copy in the Clipboard group on the Home tab.

3. In PowerPoint 2007, select the slide to which you want to copy the table.

4. In PowerPoint 2007, click Paste in the Clipboard group on the Home tab.

Inserting an Excel 2007 Spreadsheet

Inserting a blank Excel spreadsheet is advantageous because you can use the actual functionality of Excel in your presentation. The spreadsheet becomes an embedded object, however, so changes to your PowerPoint 2007 theme will not apply. Also, you cannot edit the spreadsheet with PowerPoint 2007 options. To insert a spreadsheet from Excel 2007, follow these steps:

1. In PowerPoint 2007, select the slide where you want to place the table.

2. Click the arrow below Table in the Tables group on the Insert tab.

3. Click Excel Spreadsheet.

4. An Excel spreadsheet appears on the slide. Add text by clicking a cell and typing the text.

A Word About Table Styles

In PowerPoint 2007, tables don't have to be boring and plain. Although the ability to add color and limited effects to tables has always been part of PowerPoint, it's now so easy to create a flashy table that you will likely have to restrain yourself from going overboard. When you add a table to a presentation, PowerPoint 2007 applies a style to it based on the overall presentation theme you have chosen. Change the theme, and your table changes as well (although the content won't change). Sometimes, however, you don't want a table to reflect the overall presentation theme. In that case, you will want to apply a table style.

Table styles are just combinations of formatting options you can select to change the look and feel of your table. You also have the option of changing a single cell or combination of cells by selecting shading, borders, and fonts. But let's talk about table styles specifically:

- Each style appears in a thumbnail view on the Design tab, under Table Tools, in the Table Styles group.

- You can apply or change a table style by double-clicking the table and making a selection from the Table Styles or Quick Styles group. (You can see previews of how the style will affect your table by simply resting the pointer on the style.)

- When you make a selection in either the Table Styles or Quick Styles group, the table will change instantly on your slide.

- You can remove styles by first clicking the Design tab, under Table Tools, and then clicking the More button in the Table Styles group. Finally, click Clear Table.

- Quick Style options include banded rows and columns, special formatting for the first or last columns in a table, a total row, and special formatting for the header row.

Chapter 16

Double Design Tabs?

When you double-click your table, you might notice that you now have two Design tabs on the Ribbon. The second Design contextual tab (which should be displayed after you double-click the table) is under Table Tools and is specifically for applying or changing table styles; the first Design tab is for making overall changes to presentation themes, backgrounds, and page setup.

Custom Slide Layouts

PowerPoint 2007 offers five built-in standard *layouts*—formats that contain place-holders for text, graphics, charts, and so on. A layout is essentially a slide master that PowerPoint 2007 has created for you; all you have to do is choose one you like and begin typing your information. However, these five standard layouts don't always meet the requirements for every presentation. In those cases, you'll want to create a custom layout. This was possible in earlier versions of PowerPoint, but PowerPoint 2007 offers a slightly different process.

> **Note**
>
> Adding a custom slide layout might seem at first glance to use the same steps as those involved in adding a slide master. The main difference—inserting a slide layout instead of a slide master—is critical, so it's important to keep the two processes separate in your mind. The insertion, but not removal, of placeholders is also a required step in custom layouts.

Creating a Custom Slide Layout

To create a custom slide layout, follow these steps:

1. Click Slide Master in the Presentation Views group on the View tab.

2. In the Navigation Pane on the left containing the slide thumbnails, click a location between slide masters where you want to add the new layout. Do not select a slide.

3. Go to the Slide Master tab, and click Insert Layout in the Edit Master group.

4. Now you need to add content to your slide. With your custom layout slide thumbnail highlighted, click the arrow below Insert Placeholder in the Master Layout group on the Slide Master tab.

5. Point to the placeholder you want, as shown next, and double-click it. To add another placeholder, repeat this step.

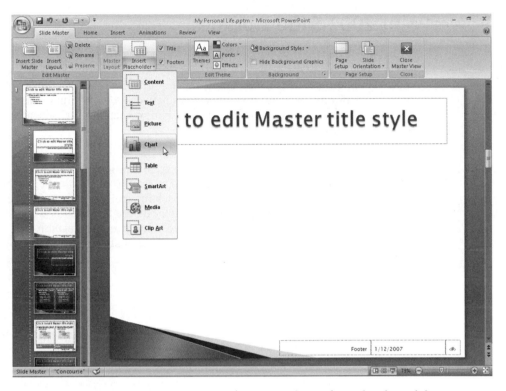

6. Arrange your placeholders the way you want them. If you decide to delete one, just click its border to select it, and press Delete.

7. Click the Microsoft Office Button, and click Save As.

8. Type a file name in the File Name box.

9. In the Save As Type list, click PowerPoint Template.

10. Click Save.

11. To return to your original document, click Close Master View on the Slide Master tab.

> **Note**
>
> Turn the title and footers on or off by selecting or clearing the check boxes next to those items in the Master Layout group on the Slide Master tab.

PowerPoint 2007 Slide Libraries

If you use PowerPoint, you know that sometimes reusing content from another PowerPoint presentation can save you a lot of time. PowerPoint 2007 works in conjunction with Microsoft Office SharePoint Server 2007, which lets people connect to documents, calendars, contacts, or tasks across a network. If your organization uses Office SharePoint Server 2007, you will be happy to know that you can take advantage of PowerPoint Slide Libraries.

Slide Libraries let users store slides in a central, shared location so that anyone on the network can share and reuse the information. Each time an existing slide changes in the library, SharePoint Server 2007 places a timestamp on it and checks the file out to the user—timestamping and checking it back in when the user is finished with the file. The library also has features to help you locate the latest version of a slide, as well as track and review changes to slides. A Slide Library must be established on Office SharePoint Server 2007 before any slides can be published to the library—your network administrator can do that for you.

> **Before Publishing to a Slide Library, Read This**
>
> PowerPoint 2007 automatically names each slide file with a unique identifier. Moving slides after publishing them means your slides will no longer appear in sequential order, which could affect you retrieving them later.

> **CAUTION**
>
> You must save your presentation to your hard disk before you can publish it to a Slide Library.

To publish slides to a Slide Library, follow these steps:

1. Click the Microsoft Office Button.

2. Point to Publish, and then click Publish Slides.

3. Select the slides you want to publish to the library in the Publish Slides dialog box. You can select all the slides by clicking the Select All button.

4. Type a name in the File Name box.

5. Type a description in the Description box.

6. Type or select the location of the Slide Library in the Publish To list.

7. Click Publish.

Program Recovery

Many PowerPoint users work with multiple PowerPoint files open at once, copying and pasting text, pulling in duplicate slides, or performing a variety of other tasks. Anyone who multitasks with several PowerPoint windows open knows that, occasionally, something goes wrong and the program stops responding. To avoid losing all your hard work when this happens, Microsoft has improved the ability of PowerPoint 2007 to save and recover the file you were working in, as well as to restore all your program windows to their status prior to the failure.

The AutoRecover option helps PowerPoint perform this feat. To turn on and adjust AutoRecover settings, follow these steps:

1. Click the Microsoft Office Button.

2. Click PowerPoint Options.

3. Click the Save category.

4. Verify that the Save AutoRecover Information Every X Minutes check box is selected.

5. In the Save AutoRecover Information Every box, type the number of minutes, or click the up and down arrows, to specify how often you want AutoRecover to preserve your document. Remember, if you do not manually save the file and instead rely only on AutoRecover, your file will be saved and restored only as often as you specify in this selection.

6 Click OK.

This chapter gave you an overview of how to begin using PowerPoint 2007 and how to customize it to meet your needs. Some features have changed from PowerPoint 2003, so this chapter also explored where you can now find commonly used commands and gave examples of the new steps for formatting content and creating tables.

New XML file formats are the key to the ability of PowerPoint 2007 to compress and recover documents. Office SharePoint Server 2007 offers PowerPoint 2007 users the ability to share and reuse presentations in Slide Libraries, while new features and tools, such as themes, Master views, and custom slide layouts, go a long way toward making PowerPoint 2007 an intuitive, useful way to share information.

In the other chapters in this part, you'll learn how to work with specific aspects of PowerPoint 2007 to create dynamic and effective presentations.

The use and placement of text within a Microsoft Office PowerPoint 2007 presentation are critical to ensuring that your audience understands your content. Too much text on a slide, and your audience gets lost; too little text, and the point isn't clear. As a result, learning how to use the text tools in Office PowerPoint 2007 is something that should be at the top of your to-do list.

In this chapter, you'll learn how to work with some of the basic text tools that Office PowerPoint 2007 provides. Specifically, you'll learn how you can use and manipulate text within PowerPoint 2007 presentations for maximum audience impact. You'll also learn about SmartArt text conversions, which can give your slides some flair. The addition of customized theme fonts and new or improved formatting and spelling tools can help you save time and produce professional results. And there is a text bonus: You can even write on slides easily and quickly in PowerPoint 2007.

Adding a Text Box to a Slide

The starting point for working with text is adding a text box to a slide. You can place text boxes anywhere on a slide, which means you can format the slide exactly as needed.

> **Note**
> You will find the most commonly used text tools on the Home tab on the Ribbon, but if you need to place a text box on a slide, go to the Insert tab instead. As always, you can add text to placeholders, shapes, and text boxes.

Here are the steps for adding a text box to a slide:

1. Go to the Insert tab.

2. Click Text Box in the Text group.

3. Rest your pointer at the location where you want to place the top-left corner of the text box on your slide, and drag the text box so it is the size you need.

After you have a slide with a text box in place, PowerPoint 2007 will move you intuitively to the Home tab with the Format contextual tab under Drawing Tools now available to you. Selecting the text box will make the commands in the Font and Paragraph groups on the Home tab active. Some features will be familiar to you from previous versions of PowerPoint—for instance, you can rotate or flip your text with the green rotation handle, you can start typing in the box when you see the blinking insertion point, and you can grab the sides or corners of the text box to resize it, as you can see in Figure 17-1.

Figure 17-1 Use the Insert tab to add a text box to a slide. You can format the text you add using commands in the Font and Paragraph groups, and you can resize and reposition the text box by using a handle.

Note

You can find all the commands you're used to using—related to font types and sizes, bold, italics, underline, color, and paragraph placement—in the Font and Paragraph groups on the Home tab on the Ribbon.

The Font group includes the following formatting options:

- **Font types** Dozens of font options let you change how the text looks. To make a headline look different from other text, for example, you can choose a completely different font for an instant effect.

- **Font size** You can change the size of the text as needed by highlighting the text and selecting a new size. This is helpful when text doesn't fit in a box that can't be enlarged or when you want to emphasize or deemphasize some of the content on the slide.

- **Font color** This formatting button changes the color of the text according to standard colors, preset theme colors, or custom options. Color is a great way to draw attention to selected text.

- **Bold, Italic, Underline, and Shadow** These buttons add the chosen formatting to the selected text. This is another good option for drawing attention to selected text.

- **Strikethrough** This button draws a line through the middle of the selected text. You typically use strikethrough during reviews of documents so that others can still see the original text.

- **Character spacing** This feature changes the space between text characters. It's a useful tool to use when trying to place a lot of text in a box instead of reducing the font to a size that can't be read well.

- **Change case** With this button, you can change all the selected text to uppercase, lowercase, or other capitalization choices. This is handy when you need to change large amounts of text for capitalization purposes.

- **Clear all formatting** This button clears all formatting from the selected text, leaving the text in a plain format. If you have applied several formats to your text, this option deletes all the formats at once and saves lots of time.

- **Decrease/increase font size** Instead of using the Font Size command, you can incrementally change the selected text to the next font size bigger or smaller with this option. This is a fast and easy way to make text fit in a box.

The Paragraph group includes the following options:

- **Alignment options** By clicking one of the four buttons here (left, right, center, and justified), you can quickly move large amounts of text to various locations within the text box.

- **Columns** Click this button to instantly convert a single-column text box into two, three, or more columns. Try this when you are working with small amounts of text instead of using bullets.

- **Line spacing** With this formatting option, you can reduce or enlarge space between lines. This can help you fit that last line of text onto a slide.

- **List levels** These buttons are particularly useful when you are working with bullets. With them, you can indent lines or remove indents from lines.

- **Bullet and Number** With these two options, you can create bulleted and numbered lists. Click the down arrow next to a button to see the many ways you can customize these two items.

- **Text direction** With this button, you can rotate text from horizontal to vertical and from right to left. Changing text direction on a headline can give your entire slide a modern, professional look.

- **Text alignment** Try the alignment options when you need to move your text up or down within a text box. You can place text at the top of the box, in the middle, or at the bottom. This can give you extra space on a slide, especially when working with multiple text boxes and images on a single slide.

- **SmartArt conversion** With this option, you can instantly change text to a preformatted graphic. It's a great way to draw attention to certain text, or you can use it to quickly spruce up a slide instead of adding images.

For more information about SmartArt, see "Adding Punch to Your Bulleted Lists" on page 553.

Finding and Replacing Words or Phrases

If you need to quickly find every occurrence of a certain word or phrase within your presentation or on even just one slide, you'll find the commands you need on the Home tab. By typing the word or phrase you want to find, you can have PowerPoint 2007 search the entire presentation and highlight every occurrence of the word or phrase it finds. You can easily quit the process by clicking the Close button whenever you want.

To find and replace words and phrases, follow these steps:

1. Click Find in the Editing group.

2. Type the text you're seeking in the Find What box.

3. Select the Match Case check box if you want an exact match between capitalized and lowercase letters, and select the Find Whole Words Only check box to ignore words that include only a portion of the text you're seeking.

4. Click Find Next.

To replace text, do this:

1. Click Replace in the Editing group.

2. Type the text you're seeking in the Find What box.

3. Select the Match Case check box if you want an exact match between capitalized and lowercase letters, and select the Find Whole Words Only check box if you want to ignore words that include only a portion of the text you're seeking.

4. Type the replacement text in the Replace With box.

5. Click Find Next to find the next occurrence of the word you're seeking.

6. Click Replace and then click Find Next if you want to replace the word and move to the next occurrence. Alternatively, click Replace All if you want PowerPoint 2007 to find and replace all occurrences of the word.

7. Click Close.

You can learn about the Mini toolbar in Chapter 2, "The 2007 Office System User Interface: What's Changed, What's the Same." In PowerPoint 2007, double-click a text box to display this toolbar. The formatting options are all ones you've seen before in PowerPoint—the Mini toolbar offers a combination of commands that are also included in the Font and Paragraph groups on the Home tab.

INSIDE OUT   Character Spacing

A cool tool that's easy to find and use in PowerPoint 2007 is the Character Spacing button. This lets you tighten or loosen text in a single word, sentence, or paragraph in order to make it fit perfectly in a text box. When you can't resize a text box on your slide and need to just squeeze in a few letters, for example, this is the button to use. Here's how to work with character spacing:

1. Highlight the text for which you want to change the spacing.

2. Click the Character Spacing button in the Font group on the Home tab. (The button displays AV with a double-headed arrow.)

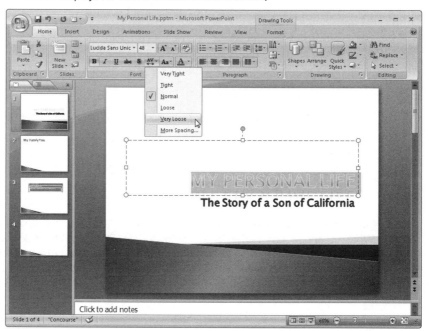

3. Click a spacing option, and you're done. You can also click More Spacing for customized choices. Click OK when you have customized character spacing to your satisfaction.

Creating and Saving Customized Theme Fonts

A handy new feature in PowerPoint 2007 lets you customize headers and body fonts together to create your own theme font. The next time you use a theme font (click Fonts in the Theme group on the Design tab, not on the Home tab), you can select the one you have created and apply it to your entire presentation with a single click. Here's how to create a theme font:

1. Click Fonts in the Themes group on the Design tab.

2. Click Create New Theme Fonts.

3. Select a heading font.

4. Select a body font.

5. Name the combination.

6. Click Save.

Formatting with WordArt

Standard formatting options, such as bold, italic, and underline, are all available on the Home tab. WordArt, however, is just as useful in formatting even though it is typically used sparingly in presentations.

WordArt Styles

You can find WordArt text effects in the Text group on the Insert tab. When you apply a WordArt text effect, PowerPoint 2007 displays the Format contextual tab under Drawing Tools. Using the Quick Style gallery in the WordArt Styles group, you can choose to apply WordArt to either selected text or all the text within a shape. New text features include character styles for additional text choices. You can also now add fills, lines, shadows, glow, kerning, and three-dimensional (3-D) effects to text. Plus, you can now choose from the following:

- All caps or small caps

- Strikethrough or double strikethrough

- Double or color underline

You can find information about SmartArt in "Adding Punch to Your Bulleted Lists" on page 553.

Adding WordArt Style to Text

Adding WordArt to your presentation is a fun way to add pizzazz to your text. The choices are numerous, especially because you can elect to make each letter in a word a separate WordArt style. The key to using WordArt successfully is to use moderation (one word or phrase); this will give you the maximum punch for the text involved.

Here's how to create WordArt for your text:

1. Select the text to which you want to add an effect.

2. Click the WordArt button in the Text group on the Insert tab, and select a WordArt style.

3. In the WordArt Styles group on the Format tab, under Drawing Tools, click the commands you want from the Text Fill, Text Outline, or Text Effects menu.

Don't fret if the style you like isn't in the color you want. You can easily adjust that by selecting the text and clicking a new color to fill the text on the Text Fill menu.

> **Note**
>
> The Text Fill menu has some other familiar options you might want to use; you can access the Picture, Gradient, and Texture commands all via this menu.

Also, you can outline the text quickly by using the new Text Outline menu. Take some time to explore this menu—it offers commands for changing the color, width, and style of the outline, which can help you draw attention to a word or phrase that your audience needs to remember.

WordArt text effects, which let you apply visual effects to individual letters along with words and phrases, now include the following:

- **Shadow** Choices include outer and inner shadows, with a Shadow Options command that lets you set the transparency, size, blur, angle, and distance of the shadow.

- **Reflection** Choices include several reflection variations, from faint to dark.

- **Glow** Glow variations let you outline your text in a colored glow using either theme colors or standard colors.

- **Bevel** Bevel choices range from convex to relaxed. Twelve choices are offered, with the option to choose additional 3-D settings that let you customize the bevel, depth, contour, and surface.

- **3-D Rotation** Choices are grouped in areas named Parallel, Perspective, and Oblique. You can also choose additional 3-D settings that you can customize for each. Note: Selecting the Keep Text Flat check box in the Format Text Effects dialog box essentially eliminates your 3-D effect.

- **Transform** This command lets you choose from an improved selection of warped and follow-path choices—drag the pink button on the text box, and the text will "follow" your movement when you select a Follow Path option. You can drag your text into circles if you desire using this option.

> ## Add the Same Effect to Text in Multiple Places
>
> Select the first piece of text, and then press and hold Ctrl while you select additional pieces of text. You can release the Ctrl key and then select the Text Fill, Text Outline, or Text Effects choices you want—PowerPoint 2007 applies those choices to each of your selected words, even if they are in different text boxes.

Adding Punch to Your Bulleted Lists

In most PowerPoint 2007 presentations, you'll see at least one slide with a bulleted list. Some presentations go overboard and include multiple slides with bulleted lists. Although these lists are easier for audiences to understand and follow at a glance, using several within one presentation can make a viewer's eyes glaze over. The next time you add a bulleted list to your presentation, consider converting the text to a SmartArt graphic. This gives your information a stronger visual impact, adds style, and cuts down on the appearance of repetitive slides for viewers, as you can see in Figure 17-2.

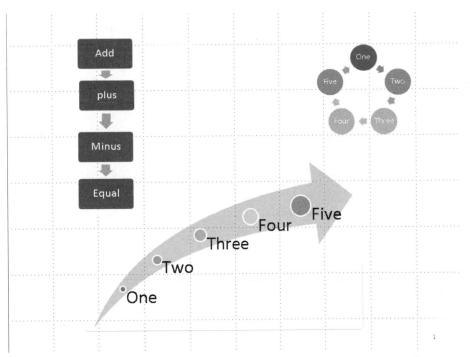

Figure 17-2 Instead of using repetitive bulleted lists on every slide, you can now easily convert your bulleted lists to graphics using the SmartArt conversion feature. A single click can take your bulleted lists from boring to eye-catching.

You can find the Convert To SmartArt command in the Paragraph group on the Home tab. Quick Style gallery choices let you easily convert bulleted lists to hierarchical, process, cycle, or relationship graphics. Your selected text is instantly placed into a graphic shape based on your Quick Style gallery choice; you can customize the shape by changing its color or adding a SmartArt style to it.

> **Note**
>
> When you initially choose a SmartArt graphic, PowerPoint 2007 explains when a particular graphic is typically used and with which levels of text it works best. This information will also sometimes appear when you select the graphic. Read this information carefully—it will help you choose the correct graphic to convey the biggest impact to your audience.

Follow these steps to convert bulleted text to a SmartArt graphic:

1. Click the bulleted text placeholder.

2. Click Convert To SmartArt in the Paragraph group on the Home tab.

3. Choose a layout from the gallery by clicking it. If you want more choices, click More SmartArt Graphics.

To change the colors in your SmartArt graphic, follow these steps:

1. Click to select the SmartArt graphic.

2. Click Change Colors in the SmartArt Styles group on the Design contextual tab, under SmartArt Tools.

3. Click the color that you want. Move your pointer from color scheme to color scheme to see how Live Preview lets you see the result of your color choice.

4. Don't like the colors that appear? Click Reset Graphic on the Design tab, under SmartArt Tools, and then repeat steps 1–3 until you are satisfied.

> **Note**
>
> When you select the graphic, the text pane will automatically appear next to the graphic. Simply type the text changes you want. The Mini toolbar will also appear if you double-click the text in your graphic, letting you make changes to the font size, type, and other characteristics.
>
> You can make the text pane appear by clicking the Close button and, alternatively, make it appear by clicking the double-arrow handle on the SmartArt graphic.

Working with the SmartArt Text Pane

The text pane, shown in the following illustration, displays your text in an outline or bulleted format that correlates directly to your SmartArt graphic. You open the text pane by clicking Text Pane in the Create Graphic group on the Design tab, under SmartArt Tools. Every graphic will map information differently, depending on the shape chosen. The shape you choose also determines whether sub-bullets appear as new shapes or as bullets within a single shape.

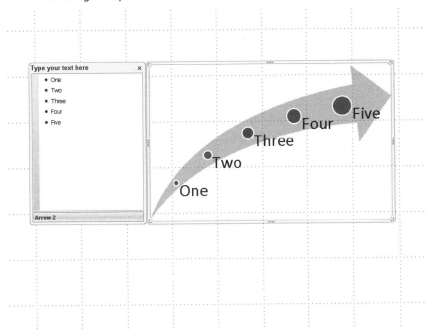

To create a new line of bulleted text in the text pane, press Enter, and then type the information on the new line.

To indent a line inside the text pane, follow these steps:

1. Select the line.

2. Click Demote in the Create Graphic group on the Design tab, under SmartArt Tools; alternatively, click Promote to negatively indent the line.

> **Note**
>
> After you have chosen a SmartArt layout for your bulleted list, you can change it simply by right-clicking the graphic. Click Change Layout, and the Choose A SmartArt Graphic dialog box appears. Make your changes as desired.

Writing on Slides During a Presentation

Another way to add text to your PowerPoint 2007 presentation is to use the pointer options as you present your slides. This is handy because often, when speaking to an audience, you want to make sure all eyes are pointed at the same spot on a slide. To circle items, underline words, draw arrows, or make similar marks in order to grab audience attention, you must be in Slide Show view. Then follow these steps:

1. Right-click the slide on which you want to write.

2. Click Pointer Options. Click Ballpoint Pen, Felt Tip Pen, or Highlighter.

3. To change the color of the pointer, click Ink Color, and change it to the color you like.

4. Drag the pointer to draw or write as needed.

5. To erase individual marks you have made, click Eraser under Pointer Options. Click the mark you want to erase. Be careful: This option erases all marks made by the pen until you lift the pen, so if you don't lift your pen from time to time, you could wind up erasing all marks on the slide with one click of the eraser.

6. To erase all marks on a slide, click Erase All Ink On Slide. This erases all marks you made, regardless of when they were made.

Using Headers and Footers

PowerPoint 2007 slides by default do not contain headers, just footers. You can certainly add headers to any slide by moving a footer to the header position. As you follow the steps in this section, it might be a little disconcerting to see the Header And Footer dialog box, shown in Figure 17-3, when in reality, you can add headers only to notes or handout pages through this dialog box. Just remember that the dialog box is referring to notes and handouts only, not slides, when references are made to headers.

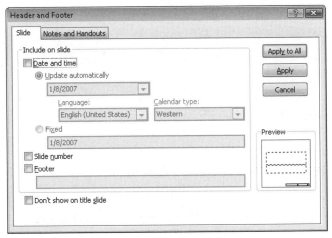

Figure 17-3 You add headers and footers via the Text group on the Insert tab. The Header And Footer dialog box offers choices for adding footers to slides or adding headers or footers to notes and handouts.

To add a footer to a slide, follow these steps:

1. Click Header & Footer in the Text group on the Insert tab.

2. In the Header And Footer dialog box that appears, click the Slide tab.

3. Select the check boxes for the items you want included on the slide:
   - **Date And Time** Select whether you want it updated automatically or prefer it fixed.
   - **Slide Number** This will default to the bottom-right position.
   - **Footer** This will default to the center position.

4. If you do not want the header or footer information to appear on the title slide, be sure to select that check box.

5. Click either Apply To All (for all slides) or Apply (for a single slide).

> **Note**
>
> Headers and footers will appear in the theme font selected for the presentation. Sometimes, these fonts are a bit elaborate, so it's a good idea to change them to an easy-to-read font such as Arial or Times New Roman and make them a 10-point font. These options won't distract viewers of your presentation.

Chapter 17

To add a header, footer, or both to notes or handouts, here are the steps to follow:

1. Click Header & Footer in the Text group on the Insert tab.

2. In the Header And Footer dialog box that appears, click the Notes And Handouts tab.

3. Select the check boxes for the items you want included on the notes or handouts:

   - **Date And Time** Select whether you want it updated automatically or prefer it fixed. This defaults to the upper-right corner.
   - **Header** This defaults to the upper-left corner.
   - **Page Number** This defaults to the bottom-right corner.
   - **Footer** This defaults to the bottom-left corner.

4. Click either Apply To All (for all slides) or Apply (for a single slide).

Working with Proofing Tools

Microsoft has improved the proofing tools across the 2007 Microsoft Office system. One item worth reviewing for PowerPoint 2007 is the contextual spelling option. If you have ever made a mistake such as "I will go their" and caught it only in front of an audience, then this will be a useful tool for you.

Basic typos are forgivable in most settings; misuse of grammar isn't. Contextual spelling helps find and fix this kind of error, letting you know the sentence should use "there" instead of "their." Because the Microsoft Office system clears the contextual spelling check box after installation if your system has less than 1 gigabyte (GB) of random access memory (RAM) available, you'll want to verify this feature works on your system. Figure 17-4 shows an example of the menu you see when you are proofing a presentation.

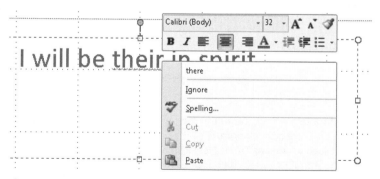

Figure 17-4 Using the contextual spelling proofing tool can help you avoid embarrassing mistakes during a presentation.

Slow Performance and Contextual Spelling

Using the contextual spelling option on systems with low memory can cause performance problems, specifically slow performance. If you notice your system not performing as quickly as usual, clear the Use Contextual Spelling check box in the PowerPoint Options dialog box, and see whether improvement occurs. If it does, consider adding memory so you can continue to use the spelling tool while keeping high performance.

To add contextual spelling and alerts to PowerPoint 2007, follow these steps:

1. Click the Microsoft Office Button, and then click PowerPoint Options.

2. Select the Proofing category.

3. Under When Correcting Spelling In PowerPoint, select the Use Contextual Spelling check box.

4. Be sure the Check Spelling As You Type check box is selected. If it isn't, the wavy red line that alerts you to a potential spelling error will not appear.

5. Click OK.

This chapter gave you an overview of how you can use and manipulate text within PowerPoint 2007 presentations for maximum audience impact. Several new options are available to you, such as SmartArt text conversions, which can give your slide show some flair. Customized theme fonts make it easy to personalize presentations according to your own style, and new or improved formatting and spelling tools help you save time and produce professional results. You can even write on slides easily and quickly in PowerPoint 2007.

Working with Objects, Diagrams, and Charts in PowerPoint 2007

In this chapter, you will learn how to work with objects, diagrams, and charts by using pictures, clip art, SmartArt graphics, sounds, movies, and animation. You have so many ways to add flair and substance to your presentation by using these items that you should spend some time trying the options available to you. After you see how easy it is to work with objects, diagrams, and charts, you'll want to add them to every presentation.

These types of additions to your presentation can add flair, but they should do more than that, too. When used to support the content on the slide properly, these items can reinforce the messages more effectively to your audience. Although using art and other items can be fun, consider carefully how the item is adding value to the slide. If it's just filling space, you probably don't need it. But if provides a visual image for the audience to remember your message, it's probably a good choice.

Here's an example: If you have text on a slide outlining the steps in a process, using a SmartArt layout that holds a different color for each step can help add punch to every step in the process. On the other hand, if you add a picture of a dog to the slide, the process steps aren't enhanced in any way. As you learn how to work with objects, diagrams, and charts in Microsoft Office PowerPoint 2007, consider the possibilities each item has in helping you get your message across to your audience.

Working with Pictures

Inserting pictures and clip art is pretty simple with Office PowerPoint 2007. In any presentation, you want these items to complement your text and drive home a point—not overpower the slide. Slide templates can help you determine a typical placement for these items, or you can resize them to work more effectively in your presentation.

Although you can always paste a picture into your presentation and then resize it by pulling the corners and sides, that's not the optimal way to insert a picture. Problems with pixelization can occur, and the picture might not be as crisp and clear as it could be when your audience views your presentation on their screens. Instead, save the picture to your hard drive in a location that's easy for you to find. Resize the picture externally into the exact size and shape you need.

To then insert a picture into your presentation, follow these steps:

1. With your presentation open to the slide where you want the picture placed, click the Insert tab.

2. In the Illustrations group, click Picture.

3. Find the picture you want by using the Insert Picture dialog box to locate the picture on your hard drive. When you have found it, select it.

4. Click Insert.

The picture will drop onto your slide. Now, notice that you have a new tab at the top of the PowerPoint 2007 window—the Format tab under Picture Tools, as shown in Figure 18-1. This tab makes you feel like you have been a graphic designer all your life—to customize the pictures in your presentation, you can choose from 28 picture styles and dozens of picture shapes, for example, and you can crop your pictures, add borders, or make other changes with a click or two of the mouse. We'll walk you through the groups on the Format tab so you clearly understand where various options are and how to use the most impressive ones.

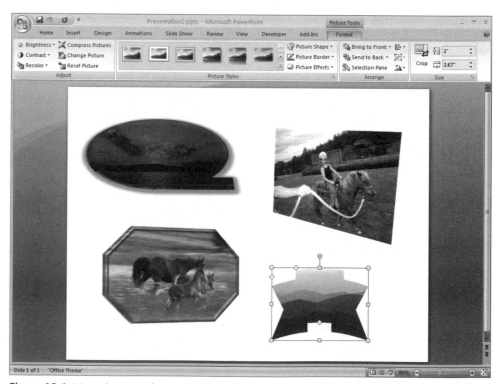

Figure 18-1 More than two dozen picture styles and dozens of picture shape, border, and effect choices under Picture Tools can help you use pictures effectively to grab audience attention.

Adjust Your Pictures

The Adjust group is where you will find six key tools to help ensure your picture retains good quality:

- **Brightness** Increase or decrease the brightness of the picture to give the picture a brightness (or not) that can improve clarity.

- **Contrast** Increase or decrease the contrast in the picture to make details stand out or fade away.

- **Recolor** Add style to your picture by recoloring it with selected color modes, by recoloring it with dark or light variations, or by turning the picture into a transparency.

- **Compress Pictures** Quickly compress the size of your picture in the presentation. This provides automatic compression when you save your picture and allows you to determine the compression size based on the target output (print, screen, or e-mail).

- **Change Picture** If you accidentally added the wrong picture, you can change it here without returning to the Insert tab.

- **Reset Picture** If you make changes to the picture and then decide you don't like them, this option instantly reverts the picture to its original shape and size.

Adding a Picture Style

The Picture Styles group is so much fun to play with! Select a picture in your presentation, and then rest your pointer on the various visual picture styles shown in this group. As you do, the picture will change to match the visual style on which your pointer is resting. Like a certain style? Click it, and voila! Your picture now appears in that style. For additional choices, click the More button to reveal a Quick Style gallery.

If you enjoyed that, you're going to really like this next one. Click Picture Shape in the Picture Styles group. The choices you find here allow you to change the shape of your picture while still retaining all its formatting. For example, if you want your picture to be shaped like an arrow, just click the arrow shape you prefer, and your picture will instantly change to that shape, "cutting" out the elements not needed for the shape. You can choose from more than 100 shapes, including the following:

- Rectangles

- Basic shapes, such as circles, ovals, and so on

- Block arrows

- Equation shapes

- Flowchart shapes

- Stars and banners

- Callouts

- Action buttons

Next, click Picture Border. This is where you can change the weight and type of line for your picture border (if you chose one) along with the color. These are self-explanatory to work with, so we'll move on to Picture Effects. This option is similar to the Text Effects option discussed in Chapter 17, "Working with Text." Here, you have preset options along with Shadow, Reflection, Glow, Soft Edges, and 3-D Rotation.

> **Note**
>
> You can place multiple picture effects on your shape—but if you do, remember that more is not always better! Something that might look cool to you might not be easy to see from the back of an auditorium, for instance. Play as much as you want, but use restraint when necessary.

Arrange Pictures

The Arrange group is where you'll find the commands that let you place a picture in front of or behind text, for example, or that let you rotate your picture to a different angle. Alignment options are in this group as well—explore Distribute Vertically or Distribute Horizontally, and watch how PowerPoint 2007 positions the picture for you on the slide. The real beauty of this group, however, resides in the Selection pane. Before you see how it works, be sure you have a slide open that has multiple shapes on it. The shapes can be anywhere; ideally at least one will be behind another.

Now, click the Selection Pane button. This reveals a Selection And Visibility pane on the right side of your screen, as shown in Figure 18-2. Every picture and other object on your slide—including text box shapes—will appear in this pane in the order the shape is located on the slide. Select a shape that is behind another, and click the blue up arrow button at the bottom of the pane to move the shape up. On your slide, the corresponding shape will now move in front of the shape it was hidden behind. You can continue to reorder shapes in this manner until you have them arranged to your satisfaction. Close the pane when you're finished.

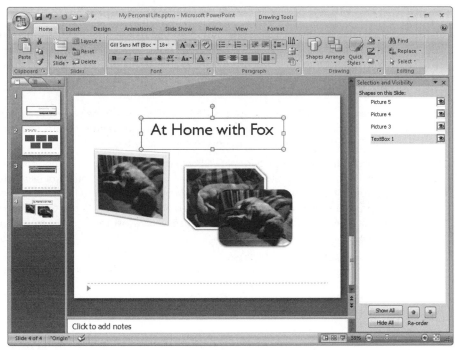

Figure 18-2 Use the Selection And Visibility pane to reorder pictures and objects on your slides.

Size

The final group on the Format tab is the Size group. You have four options to use:

- **Crop** Removes any unwanted portions of a picture.
- **Height** Changes the height of the shape.
- **Width** Changes the width of the shape.
- **Size And Position** The More arrow opens the Size And Position dialog box, which includes the option to display Web browser text as your picture loads when your presentation is accessed on the Web.

Sizing Photos

Resizing an image on a slide does not mean you have actually reduced the size of the image. In fact, the image will retain the same file size as when you inserted it. It's always smarter to resize your image using an external photo program and then insert it into your presentation—you will better control the size of the image along with your presentation.

When you resize the photo, use the JPEG or GIF format to help keep size reasonable while maintaining good quality. If you use a photo-imaging program, you can also work with TIF formats without sacrificing size and quality too much.

Although the new XML file format will help compress the presentation to some degree, do everything you can to keep your file size reasonable for your audience when you have photos in your presentation. Almost nothing is as annoying as receiving a large presentation on a dial-up connection! Remember: No image is far better than a bad image. If your picture is distracting to the audience, you've lost them on the true content of your slide.

Note

In PowerPoint 2007, you no longer have the option to download pictures directly from your scanner or camera. Instead, you need to download the pictures to your hard drive first and then insert them into your presentation.

Adding Clip Art

You can insert drawings, movies, sounds, and stock photography into your PowerPoint 2007 presentation. These items are typically stored in Clip Organizer, which places your clips into four collections:

- **My Collections** Clips you create and add to your own collection.

- **Office Collections** Clips offered in your 2007 Microsoft Office system.

- **Shared Collections** Clips that are typically available on shared file servers or common workstations. Your network administrator must create and export the collection for use.

- **Web Collections** Clips available through the Microsoft Office Online collection. These are available only when you have an active Internet connection.

To add clip art to your presentation, follow these steps:

1. Open your presentation to the slide where you want to add the clip art.

2. On the Insert tab, in the Illustrations group, click Clip Art.

3. Choose your clip art from the Clip Art pane on the right side of your screen. If you need more choices, click the Clip Art On Office Online link at the bottom of the pane.

4. Right-click the selected piece of art.

5. Click Insert.

Add Clips to Your Clip Organizer

When you open Clip Organizer for the first time, you can let it scan your computer for photos and other media files. It will organize the files it finds into separate collections, but it doesn't move or copy files. Instead, it leaves the files in their original locations and creates shortcuts to them so you can preview, open, or insert a file without digging through to its installed location. If you didn't allow Clip Organizer to search the first time you opened it, have no fear. Just follow these steps to automatically scan for clips:

1. In the Clip Art pane, click the Organize Clips link. It appears at the bottom of the pane.

2. In the Favorites – Microsoft Clip Organizer dialog box, click File.

3. Click Add Clips To Organizer.

4. Click Automatically. The Add Clips To Organizer dialog box opens.

5. If you want Clip Organizer to catalog clips in certain folders, click Options, and select or clear the check boxes for the folders you want. (It might take a few minutes for Clip Organizer to list the folders on your computer.) Click Catalog.

6. If you did not select specific folders, click OK. Clip Organizer will create collections for you and add keywords to your clips for easy searching.

Using SmartArt

In Chapter 17, you learned how to convert bulleted text to SmartArt. You can do more with SmartArt, however. The idea behind SmartArt is to allow you to create your own professional-looking graphics without a professional graphic designer. The graphics are simple to create, edit, and animate, which makes them easy to work with in your presentation. Plus, you can copy and paste SmartArt graphics created in PowerPoint 2007 into both Microsoft Office Excel 2007 and Microsoft Office Word 2007. You can also reuse SmartArt graphics from those programs in your presentation. Table 18-1 summarizes the SmartArt layout choices.

> **Note**
>
> You can work with seven types of graphics: List, Process, Cycle, Hierarchy, Relationship, Matrix, and Pyramid. Each type offers several layout options. If you switch layouts, PowerPoint 2007 places most of the text and other content, plus styles, colors, effects, and formatting, into the new format. Be careful, though: Some layouts contain a fixed number of shapes and cannot be changed to display more shapes. If this happens, find a new layout that will accommodate your content.

Table 18-1 **SmartArt Layout Choices**

If you want to...	Choose this layout...
Show a continual process	Cycle
Show a decision tree or create an organization chart	Hierarchy
Show nonsequential information	List
Show how parts relate to a whole	Matrix
Show process or timeline steps	Process
Show proportional relationships (largest component on top or bottom)	Pyramid
Illustrate connections	Relationship

Creating a SmartArt Graphic from Scratch

Creating a SmartArt graphic is a process that can take just seconds after you get the hang of it. Microsoft has done a good job with providing graphics that are professional, modern, and simple to use when creating SmartArt. Here are the steps you follow to create a SmartArt graphic from scratch:

1. On the Insert tab, in the Illustrations group, click SmartArt.

2. In the task pane on the left in the Choose A SmartArt Graphic dialog box, shown next, choose a layout type. Notice that the default is All.

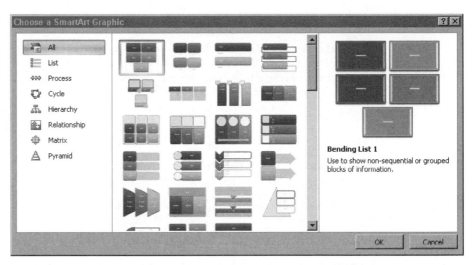

The middle task pane will display layout options based on your choice of layout type.

3. Click a layout option. Notice that the task pane on the right offers a detailed description of the layout option you have selected.

4. Click OK when you've decided on the layout.

5. Enter text as desired by typing it in the Type Your Text Here box or directly in the graphic.

6. When you have entered your content, click the slide anywhere outside the graphic.

TROUBLESHOOTING

I can't find the text pane for my SmartArt graphic.

Click the graphic, and then go to the Design tab under SmartArt Tools. (Note that you might see two Design tabs—be sure you have clicked the one under SmartArt Tools.) In the Create Graphic group, click Text Pane.

We explain how to change the colors and text in your SmartArt graphic in Chapter 17, but you might also want to apply a SmartArt style or add a picture to yours.

Adding a SmartArt Style to Your Graphic

SmartArt styles are a fast, easy way to change the look and feel of your SmartArt graphic. PowerPoint 2007 shows you the best match for your presentation based on its search of your presentation, but you can choose any style you want from the SmartArt Styles gallery. To add a SmartArt style to your graphic, follow these steps:

1. Select your graphic.

2. Under SmartArt Tools, go to the SmartArt Styles group on the Design tab.

3. Select one of the styles shown, or click the More button for the full SmartArt Styles gallery choices for that particular layout.

4. Click the style you want. Your graphic changes to reflect your choice.

Adding Pictures to a SmartArt Graphic

You can add pictures to fill any shape or use them as backgrounds for SmartArt graphics. Some shapes are even designed in a picture placeholder format because they work particularly well with pictures. It's important to consider the context of these pictures, however—always make sure your text is easily readable in front of the picture. If it competes in any way with the picture, you'll distract your audience.

To add a picture to fill a shape, follow these steps:

1. Select your graphic.

2. Select the shape to which you want to add the picture. (Select multiple shapes within a graphic by selecting the first shape and holding Ctrl while you select additional shapes.)

3. Go to the Format tab under SmartArt Tools. Click the arrow on the Shape Fill button.

4. Click Picture.

5. In the Insert Picture dialog box, select the picture you want to use.

6. Click Insert.

Here are the steps to add a picture as a background for a shape:

1. Right-click the SmartArt graphic on the outside border.

2. Click Format Object.

3. In the Format Shape dialog box, be sure the Fill category is selected in the task pane on the left. In the task pane on the right, select Picture Or Texture Fill.

4. Under Insert From, click the location of the picture you want to insert (File, Clipboard, or ClipArt).

5. If you want the picture to be transparent, tiled, stretched, offset, or rotated, make your choices now.

CAUTION

Be sure the Rotate With Shape check box is selected to avoid problems if you play around with the shape later.

6. Click Close.

Using Picture Placeholders in a Shape

In the SmartArt gallery, some layout options display a small square or circle on the corner of individual shapes within the layout. These small boxes, called *picture placeholders*, hold an icon of mountains and the sun, as shown in Figure 18-3.

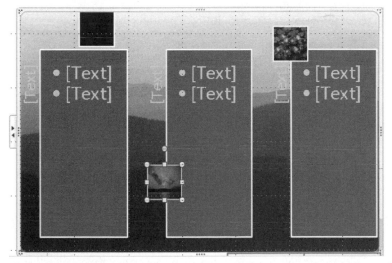

Figure 18-3 Picture placeholders let you use small pictures as visual additions for your text in certain SmartArt graphics. You can move them anywhere within the graphic.

Before you begin this next process, insert a SmartArt graphic that contains picture placeholders. Then follow these steps to work with a picture placeholder:

1. Click the picture placeholder icon in the center. This opens the Insert Picture dialog box.

2. Select the picture you want to use.

3. Click Open.

INSIDE OUT **Hiding Picture Placeholders**

Unfortunately, you cannot delete picture placeholders. You can, however, hide them. Just apply a fill to make them invisible to readers. If you are using a picture as a background, you might need to remove the background picture or move the picture placeholder to another location in the graphic where it's easier to match with the background picture.

Customizing Your SmartArt Graphic

Even though SmartArt graphics are designed to need little editing, sometimes it might be necessary to change them a bit to meet your needs. You can add or remove individual shapes, move shapes around, or even resize shapes. Resizing a shape works the same way as resizing a text box—grab a handle on the side or corner, and pull to the new size. Other changes require a little more effort but are still easy.

To add a shape to your graphic, follow these steps:

1. Select your graphic.

2. Select a shape within the graphic next to where you want the new shape to go.

3. Under SmartArt Tools, on the Design tab, go to the Create Graphic group. Click Add Shape.

4. Choose the new shape's placement by selecting Add Shape After, Before, Above, or Below. The shape will be placed in reference to the shape you have selected within the graphic.

> **Note**
>
> If you click the graphic shape representation *above* Add Shape, PowerPoint 2007 inserts a new shape into your shape without your input for placement.

To move a shape within your graphic, do this:

1. Select the shape within your graphic.

2. Drag it to the new location within the graphic. Notice that PowerPoint 2007 will not allow you to move it outside the graphic.

> **Note**
> To move a shape just a tiny bit, click the shape, hold Ctrl, and press the Up Arrow, Down Arrow, Right Arrow, or Left Arrow key. The shape will move one space over on the grid unless Snap Objects To Grid is turned off. In that case, it will move 1 pixel.

Adding Sounds

Adding sound to your presentation is something that most people do in one of two ways: too much or not at all. The trick with adding sound is to make sure it truly emphasizes a key point and is not simply being added for fun or shock value.

With PowerPoint 2007, you can embed only Windows Audio files (.wav) smaller than 100 kilobytes (KB) in a presentation. All other media file types—including larger .wav files—are linked. You can increase the .wav file size limit, but that will usually drastically increase the size of your file and is not recommended, especially when e-mailing presentations or using them over the Internet. Compatible sound file formats are as follows:

- Audio Interchange File Format (.aiff)
- AU Audio file (.au)
- Musical Instrument Digital Interface (.midi)
- MPEG Audio Layer 3 (.mp3)
- Windows Media Audio file (.wma)

The default sound option is usually to play a sound once, which is perfect for emphasizing a point. You can choose to keep a sound playing for the duration of your presentation or until you specifically stop it; go to the Custom Animation task pane to make these selections. (To open the Custom Animation task pane, on the Animations tab, in the Animations group, click Custom Animation.)

TROUBLESHOOTING

Is your sound or movie file not playing correctly?

If it isn't—even though it has a correct file name extension—the correct version of the *codec* (a compression method) might not be installed on your computer, or the file might not be encoded in a format recognizable to your media player. For example, sometimes people change extensions without realizing that this does not change the actual format of the file. You will need to download and install the correct version of the codec or use a different version of the file. Search the Internet for updated versions of the codec that are compatible with your media player and operating system.

To add sound to your presentation, use these steps:

1. Select the slide on which you want to place the sound.

2. On the Insert tab, go to the Media Clips group. Click the arrow on the Sound button. Clicking the arrow on the Sound button will provide you with a menu of options. If you click the icon *above* Sound, the Insert Sound dialog box appears.

3. Your options are Sound From File, Sound From Clip Organizer, Play CD Audio Track, and Record Sound. For purposes of this example, click Sound From Clip Organizer.

4. In the Clip Art task pane, click the sound you want to add.

5. A dialog box appears and asks you how you want to start the sound. Click Show Help to learn more about the Automatically and When Clicked options. Then click Automatically.

6. Test your sound by clicking the Slide Show button next to the Zoom slider at the bottom right of your screen.

   You can also preview a sound by double-clicking the sound icon on your slide or by going to the Options tab under Sound Tools and clicking Preview in the Play group.

TROUBLESHOOTING

Has your sound effect or movie disappeared?

PowerPoint 2007 creates a link to a sound or movie file's current location on your computer. If you move that sound or movie file, PowerPoint 2007 won't be able to find it, and you'll wonder where your sound effect or movie went. When you e-mail the presentation or use it from another computer, you must copy the linked files as well as the PowerPoint 2007 file into the same folder. One way to ensure your files are all together is to use the Package For CD feature—that copies your files to one location on a CD or in a folder and automatically updates sound and movie file links. The Package For CD feature is located on the Microsoft Office Button under Publish.

Including Movies

Adding movies to your presentation can add a professional touch. Most people use them to show demonstrations, but you can also use them to train others or show a speaker who could not attend an actual event. Movie files are always linked to your presentation, never embedded. The default is to show movies on just part of your slide, but you can change this default to show the movie in full-screen mode. Be careful with this option, though—it often results in blurry or distorted movies depending on the resolution involved.

Animated GIF files are sometimes referred to as movies, but technically they are not. As a result, not all movie options are available for GIF files, so keep that in mind if you run into trouble working with these files and using movie settings. For this section, information and instructions will refer to the following compatible movie file formats for PowerPoint 2007:

- Windows Media file (.asf)

- Windows Video file (.avi)

- Movie file (.mpg or .mpeg)

- Windows Media Video file (.wmv)

CAUTION

You cannot add Apple QuickTime movies (.mov) to PowerPoint 2007 presentations. Instead, you need to create a hyperlink to the .mov file or convert that file to a compatible file format that PowerPoint 2007 accepts.

Here's how to add a movie to your presentation:

1. In Normal view, select the slide where you want the movie added.

2. On the Insert tab, in the Media Clips group, click the arrow on the Movie button. Clicking the arrow on the Movie button will provide you with two options: Movie From File and Movie From Clip Organizer. Be careful: If you click the icon *above* Movie, the Insert Movie dialog box will open instead.

3. Click Movie From File or Movie From Clip Organizer. Your choice depends on the location of the movie you want to insert. Select the movie from the location you have chosen.

4. A dialog box appears and asks you to choose between launching the movie automatically or when clicked. Click your selection. PowerPoint 2007 adds the movie to the center of your slide.

If you want the movie to fill your entire screen when it plays, you need to make some minor adjustments. Here's how to play a movie in full-screen mode:

1. In Normal view, click the movie frame on your slide.

2. Go to the Options tab under Movie Tools.

3. In the Movie Options group, select the Play Full Screen check box.

4. Preview the movie to look for distortion or blurriness. If you have clicked the Automatically option, you can drag the movie frame completely off the slide into the gray area so that your audience never sees it (but still hears it).

> **Note**
>
> PowerPoint 2007 automatically generates a pause trigger effect when you insert a movie into your presentation. This means you must click the movie in order to start it when you show the slide. If you want your movie to start automatically when you show the slide, you must click Automatically when the dialog box prompt appears.

Playing with Animations

Animation is a great tool to help catch audience attention and add interest to your presentation. You can add custom animation to almost any item on a slide including placeholders, paragraphs, single bullets, and list items. You can animate your presentations in so many ways that we can't possibly cover them all in this book. Instead, we'll hit the highlights and then let you play on your own. As with other effects, keep animation to a minimum so your audience remains interested instead of being overwhelmed.

The key item to master when working with animation is the Custom Animation task pane, shown in Figure 18-4. This is where you control how and when you want an item to appear in your presentation—with this pane, you can see the type of effect, the order of multiple effects in relation to one another, and even a bit of the animation text, if there is any.

To display the Custom Animation task pane, follow these steps:

1. In Normal view, select the slide where you want to add the animation.

2. Go to the Animations tab, and click Custom Animation in the Animations group.

   The Custom Animation task pane will appear on the right side of your screen. Until you select an item for animation, the task pane options will be unavailable. When available, the initial options are as follows:

   - Add Effect
   - Remove
   - Start
   - Path
   - Speed

- Play
- Slide Show
- AutoPreview

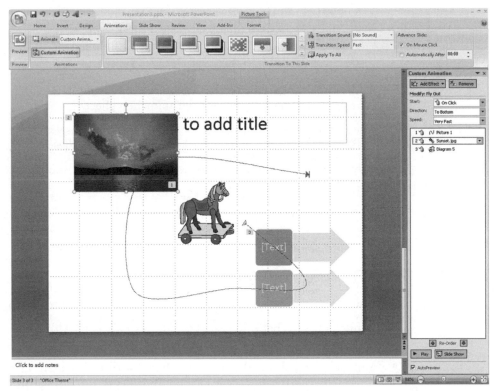

Figure 18-4 The Custom Animation task pane allows you to control how and when an item should appear in your presentation.

It's easy to add animation to an item by using the Custom Animation task pane. Here's how:

1. Select the item you want to animate.

2. In the Custom Animation task pane, the Add Effect button is now available. Click it.

3. Choose whether you want the animation to occur on its entrance or exit or whether you want the animation to emphasize a point during your presentation. You can also choose to make the item move in a motion around your slide. You make these choices by pointing to the option you want and then clicking an effect within that option.

Chapter 18

4. Under Modify: Custom Path, make selections as desired. The following are common custom effects; others will appear in relation to the effect you have chosen. For example, if you choose the spin effect, you might see options to modify the amount and speed of the spin.

- Start of animation (On Click, With Previous, After Previous).
- The path for the animation (Locked, Unlocked). Note: This option is also where you can edit points and reverse path directions.
- Speed (Very Slow to Very Fast).

5. By default, the AutoPreview check box is selected. This option lets you see your changes as you modify your selected animation effect.

Sometimes it's necessary to change the order of the animations you have created. You can do this in the Custom Animation task pane by following these steps:

1. In the Custom Animation task pane, select the item you want to move.

2. Drag it to the new location.

   A solid line will appear as you drag the item up and down. When the line is where you want the item, drop it there.

Animating SmartArt Graphics

When you animate SmartArt graphics, it's important to remember a few points:

- Connecting lines between shapes are always associated with the second shape. They will not animate individually.

- Animation will play in the order that shapes within a SmartArt graphic appear—you can reverse the order only for the entire object. If you want the animation to jump around, try creating multiple slides and graphics to create the effect you want.

- Diagrams created in earlier versions of PowerPoint and converted to SmartArt graphics might lose some animation settings or appear differently.

You can animate SmartArt graphics in various ways depending upon the layout involved. It's worth taking some time to play with a couple of different graphics to see how different levels and shapes react to different animation instructions. Here's how to animate a SmartArt object:

1. Click the SmartArt graphic.

2. Go to the Animations tab. In the Animations group, click the arrow to the right of Animate. There may be text in the box beside Animate that says "No Animation" or it might show other animation effect text.

3. Click an animation effect from the options provided in the displayed list.

Creating Charts and Diagrams

PowerPoint 2007 has 11 types of charts for you to choose from to help you display your data visually. Charts are a great tool in PowerPoint 2007 because they help the audience focus on key points visually, instead of trying to wrap their brains around lots of numbers in a sea of text. Each type of chart has a set of chart subtypes you can choose from—a Quick Style gallery appears in each chart type to help you quickly determine the chart you want. Figure 18-5 shows the Insert Chart dialog box.

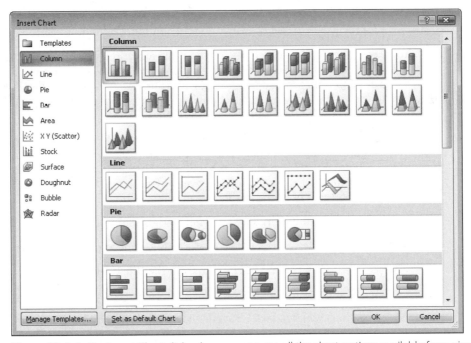

Figure 18-5 In the Insert Chart dialog box, you can see all the chart options available for a given chart type. It takes just two clicks to create a chart.

The 11 main chart types are as follows:

- **Column** Arranges data into columns with categories organized along the horizontal axis and values along the vertical axis

- **Line** Plots data into lines on a chart with categories organized on the horizontal axis and values along the vertical axis

- **Pie** Arranges data as a percentage of an entire pie

- **Bar** Uses bars to illustrate differences in individual pieces of data

- **Area** Draws attention to trends by arranging data into horizontal areas that show relationships of each part to the whole

- **XY** Arranges data in a scattered format on a chart

- **Stock** Arranges data in a specific order to illustrate fluctuations in stock prices and can also be used for scientific data

- **Surface** Shows the optimum combinations between two sets of numeric data

- **Doughnut** Is similar to a pie chart but can contain more than one data series

- **Bubble** Is similar to an XY chart but can compare sets of three values instead of two

- **Radar** Compares aggregate values of a number of data series

You can embed and insert charts into your presentation, as well as paste Excel 2007 charts or link to Excel 2007 charts. When you embed a chart, you can edit the data in Excel 2007, but the worksheet is saved with your PowerPoint 2007 file. If you copy or link to the chart, you must make changes to the actual worksheet—it is still a separate file and will not be saved with your PowerPoint 2007 file.

The advanced charting capabilities available with the Microsoft Office system will work only if you have installed Office Excel 2007. If you have not and you create a new chart in PowerPoint 2007, Microsoft Graph will open instead. The chart will appear along with a datasheet, where you must enter your own data. Other chart capabilities outlined in this chapter will not be available to you when using Microsoft Graph.

To create a chart in PowerPoint 2007, follow these steps:

1. In Normal view, select the slide where you want to place the chart.

2. Go to the Insert tab, and click Chart in the Illustrations group.

3. In the Insert Chart dialog box, click the chart type you want. Click OK.

4. The chart will be placed on your slide, and Excel 2007 will open a corresponding worksheet.

> **Note**
>
> Don't forget that you can always download diagram templates on Office Online. After all, why do all the work if the work is already done for you?

INSIDE OUT   **Using a Diagram from Microsoft Office 2003**

If you use a diagram in PowerPoint 2007 that was originally created in Excel 2003, Word 2003, or PowerPoint 2003 or earlier, you have the option to convert the diagram to an updated graphic. Double-click the diagram, and a dialog box will give you two options: convert the existing diagram to a SmartArt graphic or convert it to shapes. To keep the diagram as is, just click Cancel.

Saving a Chart Template

After you customize a chart, you can easily save and reuse it in the future by saving it as a chart template.

To save a chart as a chart template, follow these steps:

1. Click the chart you want to save as the template.

2. Under Chart Tools, go to the Design tab, and click Save As Template in the Type group.

3. In the Save Chart Template window, select the Charts folder in the Save In box.

4. In the File Name box, type the appropriate name for the chart.

5. Click Save.

The next time you want to use the chart, simply select the Templates folder in the Insert Chart dialog box, and then click your template to retrieve your chart.

Chart Formatting Options

It's easy to apply formatting to individual chart elements such as data markers, the chart area, the plot area, and the numbers and text in titles and labels to give your chart a little flair. (A *data marker* is a bar, area, dot, slice, or other symbol in a chart that represents a single data point or value that originates from a worksheet cell. Related data markers in a chart constitute a data series.) You can apply specific shape styles and WordArt styles, but you can also format the shapes and text of chart elements manually.

To format chart elements, follow these steps:

1. Click to select the chart element you want to format.

2. Under Chart Tools, click the Format tab, and in the Current Selection group, click the Chart Elements arrow.

Chapter 18

Chart Elements will display the name of a series, plot area, legend, or axis. Rest the pointer on the arrow in the box at the top of the Current Selection group, and the Chart Elements label text will appear.

3. Select the chart element you want to format.

4. Do one or more of the following:

- Click Format Selection, and in the formatting dialog box that appears make any changes you desire. Click Close.

- In the Shape Styles group on the Format tab under Chart Tools, make any desired changes to Visual Style, Shape Fill, Shape Outline, or Shape Effects for the chart.

- In the WordArt Styles group, make any desired changes to Text Style, Text Fill, Text Outline, or Text Effects.

Take a few minutes to experiment with this procedure. As you select different formats, you will see options change. It's a good idea to get used to all the different ways you can modify your chart so that when you're under a time constraint, you can easily find and select the options you want.

Collaborating and Sharing

In this chapter, you'll explore various methods for collaborating and sharing with Microsoft Office PowerPoint 2007. Improvements to both tasks make Office PowerPoint 2007 a highly useful tool for creating presentations in a team environment. From using templates in order to ensure a consistent format to working with Microsoft Windows SharePoint Services and Microsoft Office Groove 2007, you can work effectively with others in several ways.

In addition, this chapter covers protection and security measures that can help you ensure your presentation is safely managed after it leaves your hands. You will see how to make a presentation read-only, for example, as well as ways to handle reviews and approvals. As a final protection against sharing too much information by accident, the Document Inspector is a handy tool that helps you identify potential trouble spots. It can help you find and remove information such as comments, document properties, presentation notes, and other items you might not want your audience to see.

There's a lot to learn, so let's get started!

Using Templates

When you work with others, you are sometimes required to use a PowerPoint 2007 template, or you might want to require others to use a template. *Templates* are simply files that capture customizations made with slide masters, layouts, and themes. Using templates ensures that everyone's presentations in a certain department, for example, will all have the same look and feel because of the consistent format for all slides.

For more information about using slide masters, layouts, and themes, see Chapter 16, "Introduction to PowerPoint 2007."

You can typically change templates in any aspect you want, with all areas of the template flexible and adaptable to your needs. The beauty of a template is that the initial setup is done for you—all you have to do is modify the objects and text to suit your needs. Depending upon the template, items such as font and heading styles, background and color themes, placeholder locations and sizes, and slide masters might need modification. However, you can use many templates without modification of any kind.

> **Note**
>
> Every template has the file name extension .potx.

To create a template, follow these steps:

1. Begin by either using a default slide master or creating a new one. If you want to create a new one, do that before going to step 2.

For instructions for creating a slide master, see the "Slide Masters" section on page 534.

2. After you have the slide master you want to use, create a layout for the internal slide by using standard layouts or customizing your own.

3. Click the Microsoft Office Button, and click Save As. This will open the Save As dialog box, which is shown in Figure 19-1.

4. Type a name in the File Name box, or accept the one provided.

5. Click PowerPoint Template (*.potx) in the Save As Type list. You now see the Templates folder displayed in the Address bar.

6. Click Save.

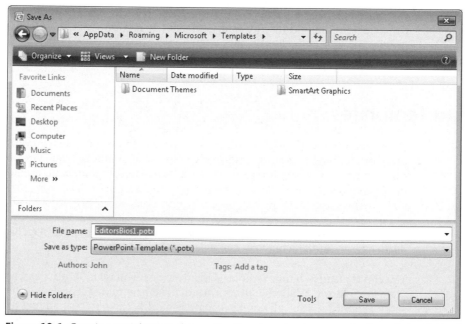

Figure 19-1 Creating templates to share with others is a simple process in PowerPoint 2007. Choosing the file name extension .potx and saving to your Templates folder will give you a presentation format that can be used over and over again.

Working with Windows SharePoint Services

We gave you an overview of Slide Libraries in Chapter 16. As a collaboration tool, Slide Libraries are great because you can make changes across multiple versions of a presentation—in effect, you can merge presentations easily and quickly. You do this through the use of linked presentations: As long as copies of a slide or presentation are linked within the Slide Library, changes to the original presentation are synchronized in designated copies. It works the opposite way, too—changes in copies of the original presentation will synchronize with the original presentation. Simply opening a linked presentation triggers PowerPoint 2007 to ask whether you want to check for slide updates.

> **Note**
> You might be tempted to click the Disable button when the Slide Update dialog box appears, but don't. When you're collaborating with others using a Slide Library, it's just good sense to do a quick check through the presentation to find out what has changed, if anything.

To check for changes on slides from a Slide Library, do the following:

1. Open a presentation with slides from a Slide Library.

2. A Check For Slide Updates dialog box appears (as shown in Figure 19-2). Click Check.

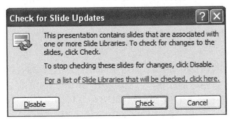

Figure 19-2 When working with Windows SharePoint Services technology, you should always check for updates to slides in presentations stored in a Slide Library.

3. Click OK if the There Are No Updated Slides At This Time, Click OK message appears. Otherwise, go to step 4.

4. If the Confirm Slide Update dialog box appears, compare the thumbnails to determine whether you want to replace your local slide with the new one from the library *or* whether you want to add the new one from the library to your presentation so you can compare them at full size.

5. To replace a slide, click Replace.

6. To add a slide for further comparison, click Append. The new slide will appear after the old one in your presentation.

Often, you will discover that a slide in the Slide Library is exactly what you need for a presentation. Rather than re-creating the slide, you can add the slide from the Slide Library directly into your presentation.

To add a slide from a Slide Library, do the following:

1. Open the presentation to which you want to add the slide.

2. On the Home tab, in the Slides group, click the arrow under New Slide.

3. Click Reuse Slides. The Reuse Slides pane will appear.

4. In the Reuse Slides pane, type the location of the Slide Library in the Insert Slide From box.

5. To find the correct Slide Library, click the horizontal arrow or Browse.

6. In the All Slides list, click the slide you want to add to your presentation.

7. Repeat steps 3–6 until you have added all the slides you want.

> **Note**
>
> To be notified when someone changes a slide in the Slide Library that you have already added to your presentation, take these steps when selecting the slide: At the bottom of the Reuse Slides pane, click the slide, and then select the Tell Me When This Slide Changes check box.

It's important to note that Microsoft Office SharePoint Server 2007 also has a versioning capability that allows you to track the history of all changes made to a slide in the Slide Library. Because that feature is really more a feature of Office SharePoint Server 2007, we won't go into detail here. If you are interested in learning more about it, ask your administrator for help.

> ### Working with Office Groove 2007
>
> When you run a PowerPoint 2007 presentation in Office Groove 2007, it opens in a presentation window separate from the Groove Workspace Explorer window. This window shows the presentation along with presentation controls, a membership pane, and a talk button for voice communications. You can scroll through the presentation, and members are taken to the slide you select.
>
> The person who initiates the presentation is the first presenter, but others can present if the first presenter invites them to present. Working with Groove 2007 is a great way to collaborate in real time with colleagues on a presentation—you can make changes instantly, and others can see them, which cuts down on review and approval time. For more information about working in Groove 2007, see Chapter 6, "Working as a Team in a Microsoft Office Groove Workspace," and Chapter 7, "Sharing and Communicating Using Microsoft Office Groove."

Reviewing, Approving, and Tracking Changes

Collaborating with others typically means your presentation will be shared with others during its development phase. And when others have a chance to work on your presentation, you're going to want a method for noting all the changes that are made. Obtaining reviews and approvals for your presentation is typically handled by attaching your presentation to an e-mail message and sending it to those you need input from. Reviewers then use the Comments feature to add, edit, or delete comments and show or hide revisions.

Each comment has the initials of the user who made it along with a number to identify the specific comment—these identifying characteristics make it easy to track who made a comment.

Adding Comments

Comments are simply notes that are added to an entire slide or to just a letter or word on a slide. After a comment has been added, reviewers can add new comments and even edit existing comments made by previous reviewers. It's important to remember that comments are simply that; they do not change any content in your presentation. Whether you agree or disagree with a comment, you will need to make the actual changes on the slide.

To add new comments to a slide, follow these steps:

1. Select the letter, word, or slide where you want to make the comment.

2. On the Review tab, in the Comments group, click New Comment.

3. In the comment box that appears on the slide, as shown next, make your comments.

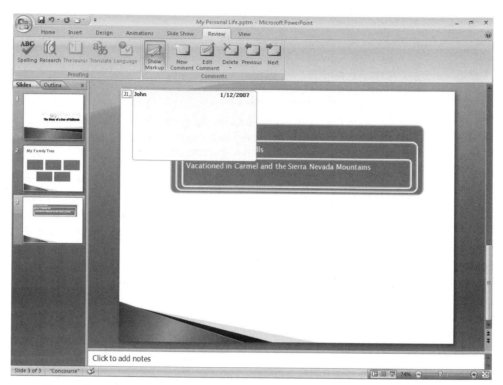

Notice that your name and the date appear in the comment box automatically. The Show Markup command will automatically be enabled when the comment box opens. If you do not want the comment box to appear automatically, click Show Markup to make it disappear.

4. When your comment is complete, click anywhere else on the slide to close the comment box.

Note

Comments will not appear during your slide show. However, if someone might read the presentation in another view, you should remove all comments from your slides before sharing the presentation with others. Comment boxes are distracting when viewing the presentation, and many people prefer to simply open a presentation and view it in Normal view—where your comments *will* appear. If you don't want to lose the comments forever, cut and paste them into the Notes pane for your slide, and pull that pane down low enough that readers won't be distracted by it.

Editing and Deleting Comments

Now that you have added a comment to your presentation, you can perform a couple of actions with it. You might need to edit a previous reviewer's comment (perhaps you need to respond to a reviewer's question, for example), or maybe you want to delete a comment.

> **Note**
>
> Edits to comments are not tracked in any way. You need to review and individually respond to or delete each comment in the presentation.

To edit a comment, do the following:

1. Click the comment box you want to open.
2. On the Review tab, click Edit Comment in the Comments group.
3. Type your new comments.
4. Click outside the box anywhere on the slide when you're done. This closes the comment box.

To delete a comment, follow these steps:

1. Click the comment box you want to open.
2. On the Review tab, click Delete in the Comments group.

You can move easily between comments by simply clicking the Previous and Next buttons in the Comments group on the Review tab.

> **Note**
>
> PowerPoint 2007 will automatically place comments in locations it sees as appropriate on your slide. If you prefer to have all your comments located in a certain area—for example, maybe you want them all located in the upper-right portion of a slide—you can simply click the thumbnail of the comment (where it lists your initials and comment number) and then drag it to the location you prefer.

Protecting Your Document

When you click the Microsoft Office Button, you see a command called Prepare. Click it, and you will see a variety of options available when you are preparing your presentation for distribution. In this section, you'll look at the Restrict Permission option. Unrestricted access is the PowerPoint 2007 default option. If you want to use the Do Not Distribute or Restrict Permission As option, you will need to use the Information Rights Management (IRM) service, which helps prevent your presentation from being forwarded, printed, or copied by unauthorized people.

> **Note**
>
> You must use IRM in conjunction with Microsoft Windows Server 2003; we explain IRM in more detail in Chapter 3, "Managing Security and Privacy in the 2007 Office System." IRM is not included in all versions of the Microsoft Office system, so you may or may not have access to it in your version of PowerPoint.

The first time you use select the Do Not Distribute or Restrict Permission As options, a Service Sign-Up dialog box appears and asks you to sign up for a trial service. If you accept, then you can take advantage of these options to protect your document. Every file that has restricted permission must have this license.

To restrict permission to content in files using IRM, follow these steps:

1. Be sure you have saved your document. Click the Microsoft Office Button, and point to Prepare.

2. In the menu that appears, point to Restrict Permission, and click Restrict Permission As or Do Not Distribute. (Both options work the same way.)

3. In the Select User dialog box, select, add, or remove user accounts.

4. Click OK.

5. In the Permission dialog box shown next, select the Restrict Permission To This Document check box.

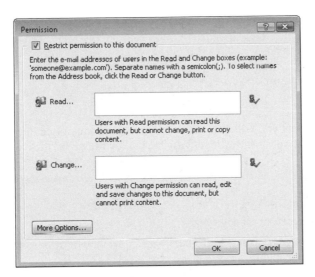

6. Add users to the Read or Change boxes, or both.

7. To provide additional authorizations for users, click More Options, and you'll see the dialog box shown here:

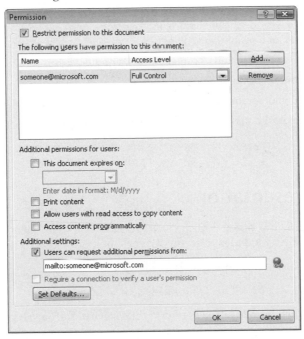

In this dialog box, you can set the following options:

- A file expiration date
- Print and copy options for users
- Programming access

8. Click OK.

Below the Ribbon, you will now see a Do Not Distribute notice that the file has been restricted. The creator of the document can click Change Permission to make changes.

What IRM Can—and Can't—Do

IRM can help prevent the following:

- Authorized recipients from forwarding, copying, modifying, printing, faxing, or pasting content
- The Print Screen feature from being used to copy restricted content
- Content from being used wherever it is sent
- Documents from being viewed after a file expiration date

IRM cannot prevent the following:

- Malicious programs such as Trojans, keystroke loggers, and spyware from erasing, stealing, or transmitting content
- The loss or corruption of content from computer viruses
- The hand-copying or retyping of content
- Digital photographs being taken of screens
- Copying of content by third-party screen-capture programs

Securing Your Presentation

When you use a PowerPoint 2007 presentation to convey confidential or sensitive information, it can be a good idea to secure the presentation with a password.

To set a password for your presentation, do the following:

1. Click the Microsoft Office Button, and click Save As.

2. Click Tools, located at the bottom-right corner of the Save As dialog box.

3. Click General Options to open the dialog box, shown next.

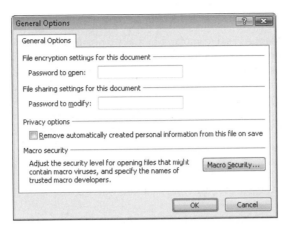

4. Type a password in the associated box for either the first or both of the following options:

    - **Password To Open** This choice allows readers to view the presentation but not make any changes to it.

    - **Password To Modify** This choice allows readers to both view and edit the presentation.

> **Note**
>
> To provide the best security for your presentation, require readers to use both passwords. Just make sure you use a different password for each option.

5. Click OK.

6. You should be prompted to retype your passwords for confirmation. Do this, and then click OK.

7. Click Save.

    You might be prompted to replace an existing presentation. Click Yes if this prompt occurs.

> **Note**
>
> Previous versions of PowerPoint allowed you to select Allow Fast Saves, which saved only those changes made since the last time you saved a document. This option is not available in PowerPoint 2007. Instead, PowerPoint 2007 scans your entire presentation every time you save it to help improve security.

Preventing Changes Using the Mark As Final Command

You can use the Mark As Final command to make a presentation read-only, but be careful—this command is *not* a security feature. When you mark a presentation as final, editing commands, proofing remarks, and typing are disabled for people viewing the document. The problem is that anyone can turn editing commands back on by simply turning off Mark As Final. In addition, a document marked as final in PowerPoint 2007 will not be read-only if it is opened in an earlier version of PowerPoint. This feature is useful only to help prevent readers from accidentally making changes.

To mark a document as final, follow these steps:

1. Click the Microsoft Office Button, and point to Prepare.

2. Click Mark as Final, as shown here, and then click OK:

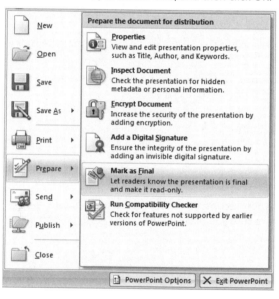

Using the Document Inspector

PowerPoint 2007 presentations are often shared outside organizations, which can create some privacy issues that most people don't usually consider. Hidden data that includes personal or sensitive information can be stored in a presentation, and it's easy to forget that the data is there—especially if you aren't aware that PowerPoint 2007 is recording it in the first place.

PowerPoint 2007 has a special feature that helps you locate this type of information: the Document Inspector. When you launch the Document Inspector, it will search your presentation for several types of information, including the following:

- **Comments and annotations** If this data is not removed, others can see the names of people who worked on your documents, comments from reviewers, and changes made to the document.

- **Document properties and personal information** Removing this information ensures others don't see the name of the person who most recently saved the document, when the document was created, or personal identifiers such as e-mail headers, send-for-review information, routing slips, printer paths, and file path information.

- **Invisible on-slide content** Although not easily seen by most, objects formatted as invisible for placeholder or other reasons can sometimes be discovered by others. Hidden text is another item that the Document Inspector can find for you.

- **Off-slide content** This identifies items that were dragged off the slide into the off-slide area, such as text boxes, clip art, tables, and graphics.

- **Presentation notes** It's easy to forget text placed in the Notes pane of a PowerPoint 2007 presentation because it doesn't appear on the screen. However, many notes are meant for private use; the Document Inspector helps you find them.

- **Custom XML data** You can find this identifying coding data and remove it with the Document Inspector.

It's your choice, of course, whether to remove the information the Document Inspector finds for you. To use the Document Inspector, follow these steps:

1. Click the Microsoft Office Button, and point to Prepare.

2. Click Inspect Document.

3. The Document Inspector dialog box will open, as shown on the next page.

Chapter 19

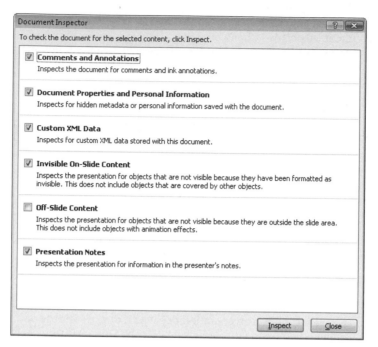

4. Select the information you want the Document Inspector to search for by selecting the corresponding check boxes.

5. Click Inspect.

   When the Document Inspector has completed its search, the dialog box shown next will appear with the inspection results. A Remove All button will appear to the right of items found—if you want to remove all the items, click the button. If you do not, you can always go into the document and remove individual items.

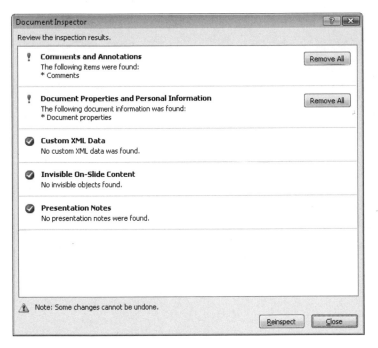

6. Click Close.

Working with External Data in PowerPoint 2007

When you create presentations in Microsoft Office PowerPoint 2007, you'll often have information in other applications that needs to be displayed in the presentation. Microsoft Office Excel spreadsheets are often used in business presentations, for example, and personal presentations often include multimedia items. No matter how you pull in data and objects, you must keep compatibility issues in mind before finalizing your presentation, as well as consider security and related issues.

In this chapter, you will learn what to watch for when working with earlier PowerPoint versions and how easy it is to work with Office Excel 2007 and Microsoft Office Access 2007 in Office PowerPoint 2007. We'll point out what to watch for when working with multimedia formats as well. Then this chapter will explore security issues and give you tips for blocking and unblocking external content, working with security alerts, and using trusted publishers. By the end of this chapter, you'll have a good understanding of how to use objects and data in PowerPoint 2007 while ensuring that your presentation is easy to view for your entire audience.

Working with Earlier Versions of PowerPoint

PowerPoint 2007 is a terrific tool, but it was not designed to work with every program in existence, including earlier versions of PowerPoint. PowerPoint 95 is a case in point: You cannot save a PowerPoint 2007 presentation in PowerPoint 95 or earlier file formats. Why? Well, for one thing, PowerPoint 95 is nearly obsolete in the world of presentations. Audiences today demand much more in visual presentations, and frankly, presentation creators demanded a tool that was easier to use. Great for its day, PowerPoint 95 is just not a tool for the twenty-first century.

You can, however, *open* a PowerPoint 2007 presentation in any earlier version of PowerPoint. You might need to install a Microsoft Office Compatibility Pack (download it from *www.microsoft.com*) to open it, and you will not be able to see all the features as they were designed in PowerPoint 2007. Pictures, for example, might not be editable, or charts might appear differently (see Table 20-1 for a comprehensive list). PowerPoint 2007 has a Compatibility Checker that looks for potential problems between it and earlier versions of the program. Use this checker when you are finished with a presentation and nearly ready to send it to readers. It generates a report (as shown in Figure 20-1) that gives you a summary of the potential compatibility issues and the number of times the issue appears in the presentation. The types of warnings shown are very specific—for example, "The table and any text in it cannot be edited when using earlier versions of PowerPoint."

Table 20-1 Changed Features When PowerPoint 2007 Presentation Is Opened in an Earlier Version of PowerPoint

PowerPoint 2007 Feature	Feature Change
Charts (except Microsoft Graph charts)	Charts are converted to OLE objects. These might look different if edited in an earlier version of PowerPoint and reopened in PowerPoint 2007.
Custom slide layouts	Might be represented as multiple masters.
Drop shadows	Soft outer shadows are converted to hard shadows that can be edited.
Heading and body fonts	Converted to static formatting.
Equations	Converted to pictures that can't be edited.
Shapes, pictures, objects, animations, and new effects	Typically converted to uneditable pictures.
SmartArt graphics	Converted to uneditable pictures.
Themes (including colors, effects, and fonts)	Converted to styles.

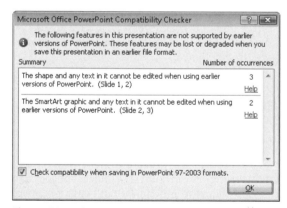

Figure 20-1 The Compatibility Checker in PowerPoint 2007 helps you identify potential problems for readers who will be opening the presentation in earlier versions of PowerPoint.

INSIDE OUT   Working with Version Compatibility Issues

If you are concerned about losing functionality permanently, the best way to work around compatibility issues is to save your presentation as a PowerPoint 2007 file, then save a second copy as a PowerPoint 97–2003 file. This lets you always make changes to the original presentation without worry.

To use the Compatibility Checker, follow these steps:

1. Click the Microsoft Office Button.

2. Click Prepare, and click Run Compatibility Checker.

3. When the Microsoft Office PowerPoint Compatibility Checker dialog box appears, review the items found, and determine whether you want to make any changes to your presentation.

4. If necessary, select Check Compatibility When Saving In PowerPoint 97–2003 Formats.

5. Click OK when your review is complete.

TROUBLESHOOTING

I don't understand the Compatability Checker warning message.

The Compatibility Checker has two types of messages. The most common warns that you will lose edit functionality when opening the file in earlier versions of PowerPoint but regain it when reopening the file in PowerPoint 2007. This warning will say "in earlier versions of PowerPoint" somewhere in the text.

The second warning type involves permanent loss of functionality, even when reopening the presentation in PowerPoint 2007. This type will *not* say "in earlier versions"—so the lack of that wording is your clue that functionality will be permanently lost.

If you have any doubt about what a particular Compatibility Checker warning means, you can look in Help for more details. Simply click the Compatibility Checker dialog box, and press F1.

You've learned a lot about what happens when you open a PowerPoint 2007 presentation in an earlier version of PowerPoint, but it's worth noting that you'll encounter some issues when you work the other way around—when you use PowerPoint 2007 to open a presentation created in an earlier version of the program. Four key features available in earlier versions of PowerPoint are not supported in PowerPoint 2007, which means they will not work when you open, say, a PowerPoint 2003 presentation in PowerPoint 2007:

- Presentation broadcast, which let you save earlier versions of PowerPoint in HTML format and run them on the Web

- Microsoft Script Editor, another Web-related feature that let you add text, edit HTML tags, and edit VBScript code

- Publish and subscribe, which let you save a file in HTML

- Send for review, which let you send presentations to others for feedback with Microsoft Office Outlook

> **Note**
>
> The send for review feature has basically been replaced by the Comments features, located in the Comments group on the Review tab.

Working with Excel 2007

In business, you use Excel 2007 to capture complex information and display it in spreadsheet format. In Chapter 18, "Working with Objects, Diagrams, and Charts in PowerPoint 2007," we showed you how to take this kind of information and turn it into a SmartArt graphic. But if you want to add or create an Excel spreadsheet and display it as is, it's pretty simple to do.

To add a new Excel 2007 table to PowerPoint 2007, you have two options: You can create a new one within PowerPoint 2007, as shown in Figure 20-2, or you can copy and paste an existing one from Excel 2007.

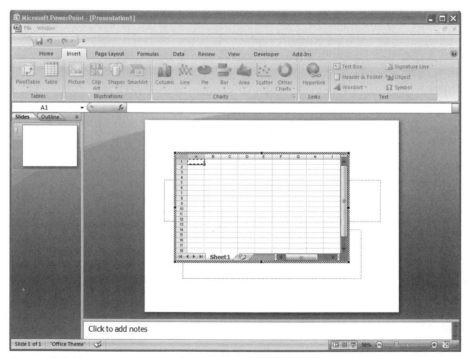

Figure 20-2 You can create a new Excel 2007 table within PowerPoint 2007 or paste in an existing one.

Create a New Excel 2007 Table in PowerPoint 2007

Creating a new Excel 2007 table within your PowerPoint 2007 presentation is simple. This is one of those clear integration points in the 2007 Microsoft Office system that make you realize you have the power of an office suite in your hands. To create a new Excel 2007 table in your presentation, follow these steps:

1. In PowerPoint 2007, select the slide where you want to add the table. On the Insert tab, in the Tables group, click Table.

2. Click Excel Spreadsheet.

3. Using the handles on the table, pull the table to the width and length you desire.

4. Begin typing your content in the cells.

Add an Existing Excel Table from Excel 2007

When you need to pull an existing Excel 2007 table into your presentation, it's another simple process. Just follow these steps:

1. In Excel 2007, click the upper-left cell of the table you want to copy. Drag to select the table or portions of the table.

2. In Excel 2007, on the Home tab, in the Clipboard group, click Copy.

3. In PowerPoint 2007, select the slide where you want to place the table. Click Paste in the Clipboard group on the Home tab.

TROUBLESHOOTING

My Excel table will copy as a picture only.

Sometimes when you try to copy and paste a table from Excel 2007 into PowerPoint 2007, you might see only the As A Picture or Copy As A Picture command in Excel. If you see this command but not Copy, you have clicked the Paste menu instead of the Copy command to the right of the Paste menu. Both are located in the Clipboard group, and it's easy to miss the Copy command because it's just a small icon.

Working with Access 2007

Using content from Office Access 2007 is rare, but occasionally you might want to do that. Tables will transfer reasonably well, but forms will sometimes not look anything like the original Access form. If you are simply trying to give a representation of the information in Access, it might be easier to do a screen capture of the item in question rather than copy the actual item.

Chapter 20

Add an Existing Table, Form, Report, or Other Object from Access 2007

Adding an existing Access item to your presentation is a quick process. Here's how to do it in the Datasheet view; some items can also be copied in other views:

1. In Access 2007, click the upper-left cell of the content you want to copy. Drag to select the content desired.

2. In Access 2007, go to the Clipboard group on the Home tab, and click Copy.

3. In PowerPoint 2007, select the slide where you want to place the table. Click Paste in the Clipboard group on the Home tab.

Use a Screen Capture to Copy Content from Access 2007

Sometimes things just don't drop into your presentation correctly, and that can occur with Access 2007 content, too. In that case, try using a screen capture to copy content from Access 2007 into your presentation. A screen capture takes a picture of the information displayed on your screen—just open Access 2007 to the screen you want to show in your presentation, and then follow these steps:

1. In Access 2007, select the item you want to copy.

2. Do one of the following:

   - To copy the entire active window, press Alt+Print Screen on your keyboard.
   - To copy the entire screen as it appears on your monitor, press Print Screen.

3. In PowerPoint 2007, select the slide where you want to place the screen capture. Press Ctrl+V.

TROUBLESHOOTING

The content I copied from Access 2007 is unreadable in PowerPoint 2007.

If you copy content from Access 2007 into PowerPoint 2007 and it appears unreadable, you need to resize the entire table to make the text visible. You can do this by grabbing the corner and side handles; it won't work if you try to resize from any other place on the table. If you just want to resize a column or row, you can—rest the pointer on the column or row line you want to change, and pull when the double lines and arrows appear. If resizing doesn't make the text readable, in PowerPoint 2007 look at your font size in the Fonts group on the Home tab. You might need to enlarge it.

Multimedia Formats

Even though we have already discussed importing objects and other media items in Chapter 18, we wanted to add a quick word here about working with multimedia formats. You might not be able to insert some items into your PowerPoint 2007 presentations, but you might be able to work around this and use them in your presentation anyway. Other multimedia formats simply won't work at all in PowerPoint 2007.

Apple QuickTime movies, for example, are actually Apple format, so it should be no surprise that they aren't going to work in PowerPoint 2007. To get around this, either create a hyperlink to the QuickTime movie or convert the QuickTime movie file to a Microsoft Windows video (.avi) file format or other compatible multimedia format that PowerPoint 2007 will let you insert.

Although you can't add a digital movie from a DVD to a PowerPoint 2007 presentation, third-party add-ins will let you play a video DVD during a presentation. Refer to *www.pfcmedia.com* if you're interested in trying an add-in for this purpose.

Blocking and Unblocking External Content

When you work with external content (content from the Internet or an intranet that is linked to a presentation), you should be careful with the source of the content. Hackers have developed what are called Web *beacons*—these send back, or "beacon," information from your computer to the server that hosts the actual external content. For example, maybe you have opened a presentation that contains images. As soon as you open the file, the image downloads and sends information about where the file is located to the original server that sent the presentation. Scary, isn't it? You didn't do anything except open the presentation. Other types of Web beacons that could be embedded in a PowerPoint 2007 presentation are linked media and data connections.

Linked media are typically media objects, such as a sound, linked to an external server. When a presentation is opened, the media object plays as part of the presentation. When it plays, it triggers the execution of code that runs a malicious script on your computer.

Data connections involve Excel 2007, which can impact you if you are using an Excel 2007 file with one of these connections. Simply opening the workbook involved triggers the execution of code that accesses databases by using stolen credentials.

You'll know when there is unethical external content in your presentation because when you open the file, the Message Bar will notify you that content has been blocked. Also on the Message Bar is the Options button, which lets you unblock the content in question. If you're positive the content is from a trustworthy source, it's best to move the file to a trusted location—usually a folder on your hard drive or on a network. After you place a file into the trusted location, you can open it from then on without further checks by the Trust Center security feature. See the next section for more details about the Trust Center.

Homographs and phishing schemes can invade your PowerPoint 2007 files. See the "Setting Up Security Alerts and Trusted Publishers" section on page 608 to learn more about the automatic security features of PowerPoint 2007. For more information about the security features of the Microsoft Office system, see Chapter 3, "Managing Security and Privacy in the 2007 Office System."

Using Trusted Locations

Trusted locations are established on a hard drive or a network. These locations essentially bypass the Trust Center security feature in PowerPoint 2007. For example, a document that contains macros might be considered a threat by the Trust Center. Moving the document to a trusted location lets you open the document without any changes to the macro settings.

If you are on a network, your administrator has probably created a trusted location for you. If not, you can use the trusted locations automatically created when you installed the Microsoft Office system. These are usually in Program Files/Microsoft Office/Templates or Office 12/Startup. You can also create and manage your own trusted location in PowerPoint 2007 using the Trust Center, which is shown in Figure 20-3.

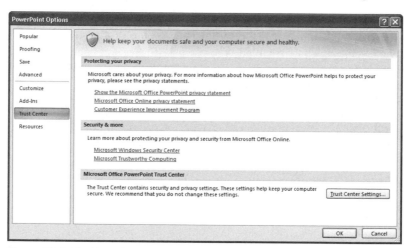

Figure 20-3 The Trust Center can protect your presentation from unethical external content.

Create a Trusted Location

When you don't want the Trust Center to verify the content when you open a file, you should create a trusted location for the file. Here's how to do that:

1. Open PowerPoint 2007.

2. Click the Microsoft Office Button, and click PowerPoint Options. Click Trust Center in the navigation pane on the left.

3. Under Microsoft Office PowerPoint Trust Center, click Trust Center Settings.

4. In the navigation pane on the left, click Trusted Locations. Then click Add New Location.

> **Note**
>
> Do *not* select your entire Documents or My Documents folder as a trusted location. Instead, create a subfolder within one of those folders, and make that your trusted location. Remember, you are trying to foil hackers, not help them!

5. Use Browse to select or create a folder location if necessary, as shown here. You can include subfolders if you like—to do so, select the Subfolders Of This Location Are Also Trusted check box.

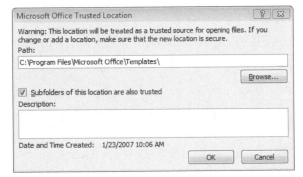

> **Note**
>
> If your security settings do not allow the remote or network path location you have entered to be designated as a trusted location, an error message will appear. Click OK and select a new location, or ask your administrator.

6. Type the purpose for the trusted location in the Description box.

7. Click OK.

Remove a Trusted Location

Sometimes it's necessary to remove a trusted location. For example, maybe the folder became corrupted, or maybe you have decided to place documents in a different location on the hard drive. Removing a trusted location is a simple process, as explained here:

1. Open PowerPoint 2007.

2. Click the Microsoft Office Button, and click PowerPoint Options. Click Trust Center in the navigation pane on the left.

3. Under Microsoft Office PowerPoint Trust Center, click Trust Center Settings.

4. In the navigation pane on the left, click Trusted Locations.

5. In the Trusted Locations Path pane, click the trusted location you want to remove.

6. Click Remove.

7. Click OK.

8. Click OK to close the PowerPoint Options dialog box.

Modify a Trusted Location

If you want to change the location of a trusted folder, follow these steps:

1. Open PowerPoint 2007.

2. Click the Microsoft Office Button, and click PowerPoint Options. Click Trust Center in the navigation pane on the left.

3. Under Microsoft Office PowerPoint Trust Center, click Trust Center Settings.

4. In the navigation pane on the left, click Trusted Locations.

5. In the Trusted Locations Path pane, click the trusted location you want to modify.

6. Click Modify.

7. In the Trusted Location dialog box, select the new location under Path by clicking Browse or by typing the new location.

8. Change the purpose details if necessary, and select or clear the Subfolders Of This Location Are Also Trusted check box.

9. Click OK.

10. Click OK to close the PowerPoint Options dialog box.

Setting Up Security Alerts and Trusted Publishers

Hackers are typically not stupid—they are actually some pretty intelligent people who are using their smarts for unsavory purposes. Examples include homograph and phishing attacks, which are Web-based fraud schemes that mimic well-known, trusted brands. *Phishing* uses spoofed messages disguised to look like the real thing (an e-mail message that contains Microsoft logos and links) but is really a trick to lure you into providing personal information. *Homographs* are words that have the same spelling as the real thing (Microsoft) but actually have a different meaning. For instance, you might see a link to *www.microsoft.com* that looks like it uses the English alphabet, but the *i* is actually a Cyrillic character from the Russian alphabet. Because you can't tell the difference, you could click the link and land on an untrustworthy Web site.

PowerPoint 2007 has an automatic default that warns you when it detects links to and files from suspicious Web sites. Do we recommend you turn off these security alerts? Of course not. You can do it in Trust Center Privacy Settings if you really want to, however. If the security alerts are annoying you because they routinely pop up involving files from someone you know has valid credentials, you might want to add this person to your trusted publishers list. A *trusted publisher* is a developer who creates macros, ActiveX controls, add-ins, or other application extensions *and* who meets all of the following criteria:

- The code project is signed by the developer with a digital signature.

- The digital signature is valid.

- The digital signature is current.

- The certificate associated with the digital signature was issued by a reputable certificate authority.

- The developer who signed the code project is a trusted publisher.

The criteria are critical—if you try to run published code that does not meet all of the criteria, the Trust Center will disable the code by default, and the Message Bar will still appear to notify you of a potentially unsafe publisher.

CAUTION

Be certain that you have had successful interactions with a developer before you add one to your trusted publishers list. You should add only trustworthy sources. If you receive a security alert dialog box for a developer, you will have the option of trusting all future documents from them. When a security alert dialog box appears for the publisher you want to add to your trusted publishers list, select Trust All Documents From This Publisher, and click OK.

Setting Up and Presenting a Slide Show

Now that you know how to do all kinds of cool things with Microsoft Office PowerPoint 2007, your final step will be actually pulling together a presentation with confidence and ease. Whether you have used Office PowerPoint 2007 before or not, it's always helpful to review the steps of setting up and presenting a slide show. After all, you're on display here as much as your presentation—you want everything to go smoothly and for every transition and click to take viewers exactly where you want them to go. In this chapter, we'll take you through the basic steps involved in creating slide shows, and we'll present more detailed information about using transitions effectively, using the new Presenter view, creating photo albums, and setting your printing options; we'll also throw in a few tips and tricks you might not know. Be sure to try some of the tips sprinkled throughout the chapter—and have fun delivering your presentation.

Learning the Basics

With any presentation, you need to have a set of slides prepared. Regardless of your presentation's content, certain items should be in any presentation to ensure that viewers can stay on track (if, for example, they are following the presentation during a webcast or phone conference) and to ensure that your presentation is copyrighted and even secured if necessary.

Keep Your Viewers on Track

Nothing is worse as a viewer of a PowerPoint presentation than to be momentarily distracted during a presentation on the phone or other remote arrangement and to lose the flow of the slides. Although we all want to assume our slides are so fascinating that no one could possibly turn away, it does happen. Help your readers with page numbers on every slide, along with clear headlines. Then, as you flip to a new slide, clearly state that you are on "page x," and state or paraphrase the page headline. Simple and effective, these two items will do more to keep your viewers on track than any other tip you will ever hear.

Copyright Your Work

Your presentation is your intellectual property—or your company's, if you have created the presentation for work. Why let anyone else get hold of your hard work and use it without crediting you?

A simple page at the end of your presentation, along with a copyright symbol on every slide, can help you establish copyright for your work. You can insert the symbol using these steps:

1. Open the slide where you want to place the copyright symbol (©), and click where you want to place the symbol.

2. On the Insert tab, in the Text group, click Symbol.

3. Select the copyright symbol in the Symbol dialog box, as shown here:

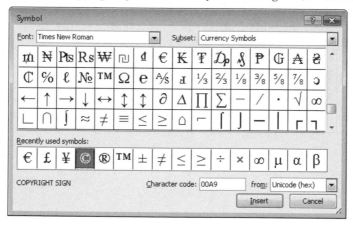

4. Click Insert.

5. Click Close.

> **Note**
>
> Some fonts may offer you a Subset list when the Symbol dialog box opens. You can use this list to choose from an expanded set of language characters and languages.

Secure Your Document When It's Complete

If you don't want your document changed, reused, or reappropriated, you need to properly secure it. We cover security features in the 2007 Microsoft Office system in depth in Chapter 3, "Managing Privacy and Security in the 2007 Office System," but, as a reminder, you can secure your presentation in two ways:

- You can set a password to open or modify (or both) a presentation.

- You can use Information Rights Management (IRM) features to restrict permissions for readers.

Make it part of your standard checklist to decide whether either of these security measures (or both) is required for every presentation you create.

In Chapter 19, "Collaborating and Sharing," you learned about the Document Inspector. Be sure to use this feature to find and remove hidden or personal information that may still be attached to your PowerPoint presentation.

CAUTION

Remember: The Mark As Final command does *not* secure your document. Anyone can simply turn off that command and change your document from read-only to an editable document. Use password-protection features instead to properly secure your presentation.

Verify Your Slide Show Before Delivery

Before you go public, you should rehearse your slide show to see how the presentation appears; ensure that there aren't any unsightly errors; and review timings, transitions, and special effects to verify they are all working properly. To start your slide show, follow these steps:

1. Open your presentation, and go to the Slide Show tab.

2. In the Start Slide Show group, click From Beginning. (You can also choose to start your show from the current slide you have selected in the navigation pane on the left.)

You'll want to take some time to rehearse the delivery of your presentation to be sure your timing is accurate and that you're comfortable with how the slides flow as you speak. To do that, follow these steps:

1. Open your presentation, and go to the Slide Show tab. Click Rehearse Timings in the Set Up group.

   A Rehearsal toolbar will appear, and PowerPoint 2007 will begin timing your presentation. This toolbar lets you advance to the next slide, pause, and repeat the slide as needed. It also shows you the timing for the individual slide as well as for the overall presentation.

2. After you set the timing on the last slide, a message box will appear with the total time for the presentation. If you want to keep the recorded slide timings, click Yes. If you do not, click No.

3. If you keep the slide timings, Slide Sorter view will appear and show you the presentation and the time.

> **Note**
>
> You might not always want to use slide timings with your presentation—some audiences may require a lengthier explanation on certain slides, for example. At the same time, you might not want to delete the timings completely. In that case, go to the Slide Show tab, and clear the Use Rehearsed Timings check box in the Set Up group. When you want to begin using them again, simply select the Use Rehearsed Timings check box.

Creating Custom Slide Shows

Custom shows are so useful, it's hard to know where to begin with all the benefits. Let's stick with the simple fact that a custom show lets you take one show—a single presentation—and adapt it quickly and easily for a variety of audiences. If you have ever cut and pasted slides from one presentation to use with a new audience, this feature will have immense appeal for you.

You can create a custom show in one of two ways: basic or hyperlinked. A *basic* custom show is a separate presentation that includes some slides from your original presentation. A *hyperlinked* custom show lets you create custom shows that link to the primary presentation.

Create a Basic Custom Show

Let's say you need to give a presentation to different groups in your organization. If your presentation has a total of 10 slides, you can create a custom show named Show 1 that includes just slides 2, 4, 6, and 8. A second custom show—Show 2—could contain slides 2, 3, 5, and 8. This method uses one presentation but lets you choose specific slides within that presentation depending upon your audience. It's one presentation with the same information for everyone, but you can choose which information to display to different audiences.

Here are the steps to create a basic custom show:

1. Open the presentation, and go to the Slide Show tab. Click Custom Slide Show in the Start Slide Show group.

2. Click Custom Shows.

3. In the Custom Shows dialog box, click New.

4. In the Define Custom Show dialog box, shown here, select the slides you want to show your first audience under Slides In Presentation.

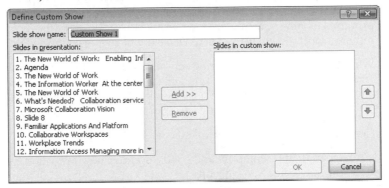

Use the Add and Remove buttons as needed to add more slides or remove slides as you build your custom slide show. Use the up and down arrows to move slides into a new sequence.

5. Name your show in the Slide Show Name box.

> **Note**
>
> To select multiple sequential slides, click the first slide, and then hold down Shift while you click the last slide that you want to select. To select multiple nonsequential slides, hold down Ctrl while you click each slide that you want to select.

6. Click OK. The Custom Shows dialog box will reappear. Click New again if you need to make another show, or click Edit, Remove, or Copy to make those changes instead.

7. When you have finished making custom shows and edits as needed, click Close.

You can highlight a show to preview and click Show if you want to see how it will appear to audiences.

> **Note**
>
> If you create a basic custom show from a presentation, you can always run the entire presentation in its original sequence.

Create a Hyperlinked Custom Show

But what if you want to create a primary presentation about your company's new president and then customize that presentation to help different departments understand how the president will work with them in particular? You can do that by creating a primary custom show that uses hyperlinks to let you move easily to Department A's presentation and then move easily to Department B's presentation later.

With this method, you can create completely different slides for each department within one presentation, but each department sees only the slides applicable to it. The advantage here is that you can have essentially one presentation with slides applicable to all audiences as well as "mini" customized presentations within it.

Here's how you create a hyperlinked custom show:

1. Open the presentation, and go to the Slide Show tab. Click Custom Slide Show in the Start Slide Show group.

2. Click Custom Shows.

3. In the Custom Shows dialog box, click New.

4. In the Define Custom Show dialog box, select the slides you want to show your first audience under Slides In Presentation.

   Use the Add and Remove buttons as needed to add more slides or remove slides as you build your custom slide show. Use the up and down arrows to move slides into a new sequence.

5. Name your show in the Slide Show Name box.

6. Click OK. The Custom Shows dialog box will reappear. Click New again if you need to make another show, or click Edit, Remove, or Copy to make those changes instead.

7. When you have finished making custom shows and edits as needed, click Close.

8. Select the text or object you want to use as your hyperlink. Go to the Links group on the Insert tab, and click Hyperlink.

9. In the Insert Hyperlink dialog box, shown next, select Place In This Document under Link To.

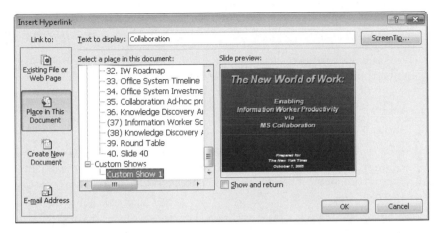

10. Under Select A Place In This Document, select the custom show you want to link to, and then select the Show And Return check box. Click OK.

Run a Custom Show

Now that you've created a custom show, you're going to want to show it to someone. Opening these shows is a slightly different process from opening a standard presentation. Just follow these steps:

1. Open the presentation, and go to the Slide Show tab. Click Custom Slide Show in the Start Slide Show group.

2. Click Custom Shows.

3. Select the custom show from the list provided. The show will automatically begin.

> **Note**
> Hyperlinked custom shows let you create a table of contents slide so you can navigate to different sections of your presentation quickly.

Adding Transitions

Think of slide transitions as the curtain opening and closing between scenes in a play—it helps the audience adjust quickly to the fact that a new slide or topic is appearing. Transitions are similar to animation effects in some ways; they are moving aspects of a slide with speed you can control and sound you can add.

With PowerPoint 2007, the transition possibilities are many. You can make a slide just fade away, or you can open a slide with stripes and bars or other shapes. Your transitions can go quickly or painstakingly slow, and you can even add sound to them. The Transition gallery makes it easy to choose a transition—just rest your pointer on a particular transition, and watch the transition play on your screen.

> **Note**
>
> You can apply dozens of different slide transitions, but from an audience perspective it's wise to stick with just one or two types throughout your presentation. Too many can become confusing for audiences—use transitions to support your content, not distract from it.

To add the same slide transition to all slides, do the following:

1. In Normal view, go to the navigation pane on the left, and select the Slides tab (if necessary). Click any slide thumbnail in the pane.

2. Go to the Animations tab, shown here, and click a transition style in the Transition To This Slide group.

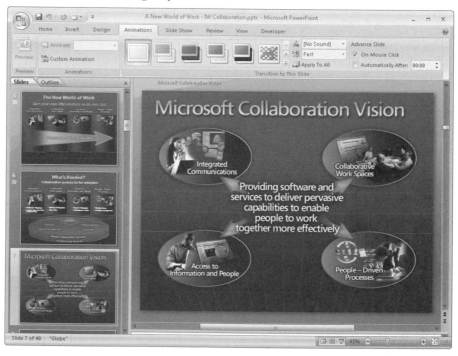

3. In the same group, click the arrow to the right of Transition Sound, and then click the sound you want to use.

4. In the same group, click the arrow to the right of Transition Speed, and then click the appropriate speed (Slow, Medium, or Fast).

5. In the same group, click Apply To All.

To add a different slide transition to each slide, follow these steps:

1. In Normal view, go to the navigation pane on the left, and select the Slides tab (if necessary). Click the slide thumbnail in the pane to which you want the transition applied.

2. Go to the Animations tab, and click a transition style in the Transition To This Slide group.

3. In the same group, click the arrow to the right of Transition Sound, and then click the sound you want to use.

4. In the same group, click the arrow to the right of Transition Speed, and then click the appropriate speed.

5. To make additional transitions for other slides, repeat steps 1 through 4.

Using Presenter View

A great new feature in PowerPoint 2007 is Presenter view, shown in Figure 21-1. This view gives you the ability to use two monitors during a presentation so that you can run other programs your audience won't see as the slide show runs. If you have ever presented slides and needed to refer to your speaker notes in the file or found yourself a little confused about what the next click or slide was going to bring, you will love Presenter view. This feature lets you do the following:

- You can use thumbnails to select slides out of sequence.

- You can preview text so you know exactly what will happen with your next click.

- You can see speaker notes in a large font size.

- You can black out screen content as needed and resume where you left off.

Chapter 21

Note

To use this view, you must have a computer that has a multiple-monitor capability, and that capability must be turned on. After you have verified both of these issues, turn on Presenter view, and start using it.

Figure 21-1 Presenter view in PowerPoint 2007 is a valuable tool.

To turn on multiple-monitor support in PowerPoint 2007, do the following:

1. Open the presentation.

2. On the Slide Show tab, go to the Monitors group, and select the Use Presenter View check box.

3. Click the arrow next to Show Presentation On, and then click a monitor for the presenter's monitor.

TROUBLESHOOTING

I can show Presenter view on and run the presentation from only one monitor.

If your computer does not detect multiple monitors, an error message will appear. Click Check if you want PowerPoint 2007 to perform an automated check for you. Otherwise, click Cancel, and switch to a computer that has the multiple-monitor capability.

After you have properly set up the monitors, you can deliver the presentation using Presenter view. Here are the steps:

1. Open the presentation.

2. Go to the Slide Show tab, and click Set Up Slide Show in the Set Up group.

3. In the Set Up Show dialog box, shown next, choose the options you want.

   - The Show Type options default to Presented By A Speaker or full-screen view.

- If you have narration or animations that you prefer not to use during the presentation, you can clear their check boxes under Show Options.

- The Show Options area also lets you change pen colors if you decide to write on slides during your presentation.

- Note that the Advance Slides default option is to use any timings you have established.

- Verify that the correct monitor is selected under Multiple Monitors and that the Show Presenter View check box is selected.

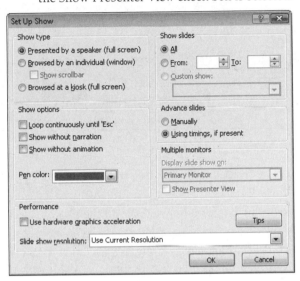

4. Click OK.

5. When you are ready to begin delivery, go to the View tab, and click Slide Show in the Presentation Views group.

Working with Photo Albums

Photo albums are still available in PowerPoint 2007 and are a fun, easy way to share a collection of images. You can add effects such as slide transitions, backgrounds, and themes as well as add captions, picture frames, and customized layouts. All you need before creating an album are digital images on your hard disk drive or on a disc. To create a photo album, follow these steps:

1. Open a new presentation.

2. On the Insert tab, in the Illustrations group, click the arrow under Photo Album.

3. Click New Photo Album. You'll see the Photo Album dialog box, as shown next.

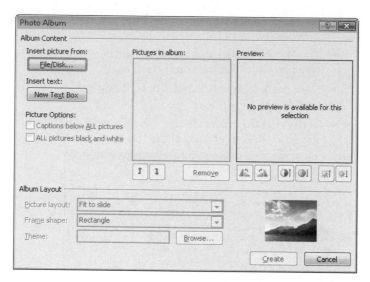

4. Click File/Disk under Insert Picture From.

5. In the Insert New Pictures dialog box, select the picture you want, and click Insert.

6. Continue selecting photos until you have all the photos selected that you want in your photo album.

7. Under Album Layout in the Photo Album dialog box, select the picture layout for each page in your album, and choose a shape for the frame. You can also apply a theme in this section.

8. Under Picture Options, you can select the check box to place captions below all pictures or to change all pictures to black and white. You cannot selectively add captions or black-and-white coloring here.

9. Use the arrows to change the placement of pictures.

10. Use the Rotate, Contrast, and Brightness buttons to rotate individual pictures or change their brightness or contrast.

11. Click Create.

CAUTION

Are you trying to add a picture with the From Scanner Or Camera option? Stop—it's not available in PowerPoint 2007. All digital images for use in PowerPoint 2007 must already be downloaded to your computer before you can insert them into a presentation.

When you're ready to change the pictures in your photo album, it's a very simple process. Just follow these steps:

1. Open the photo album presentation.

2. Go to the Insert tab, and click the arrow under Photo Album in the Illustrations group.

3. Click Edit Photo Album.

4. In the Edit Photo Album dialog box, make changes as desired (you can also add or remove photos here).

5. Click Update.

INSIDE OUT   Working with Captions in Your Photo Album

You can add captions to your pictures with the Edit Photo Album dialog box in the Picture Options section. If the Captions Below ALL Pictures check box isn't available, you need to specify a layout for the pictures in your photo album. Be sure Fit To Slide is not the layout you select—this options leaves no room for captions.

You can move the caption to another location on the slide by selecting the caption box and dragging it to the location you prefer. And if you don't like the font PowerPoint 2007 selected for your caption, just go to the Home tab, and change it by selecting the caption text and making changes using the commands in the Font group.

Publish Your Photo Album to the Web

When you have finalized your photo album, one easy way to share it with friends and family is to publish it to the Web. This option eliminates problems with e-mail inbox size limits or spam blockers—all you do is send a Uniform Resource Locator (URL) for others to visit. Here's how to publish a photo album to the Web:

1. Open the photo album you want to publish to the Web. Click the Microsoft Office Button, click Save As, and click PowerPoint 97–2003 Presentation.

2. Select the path or location for the Web page on a Web server in the Address bar.

3. Type a file name in the File Name box, or accept the suggested name.

4. In the Save As Type list, click Web Page. Note: This ensures that supporting files (such as pictures and sounds) are associated properly with your Web page.

5. Click Change Title, and type the title bar text in the Page Title box if you want something different displayed in browsers' title bars.

6. Click OK.

7. Click Publish. When the Publish As Web Page dialog box opens, set the following options:

   - Choose whether to publish the complete presentation or just certain slides.
   - Choose the desired browser support.
   - Verify your file name for accuracy.
   - Select the Open Published Web Page In Browser check box.

8. Click Publish.

> **Note**
>
> When you see the photo album displayed in the browser, note the URL. It might not always be what you expected!

Exploring Printing Options

You have several options for printing in PowerPoint 2007. You can print slides, handouts, notes, or outlines, and you can do it in color, black and white, or grayscale. The first step, then, is to decide what you want to print—some speakers may need notes and handouts, and others may need to print every slide for inclusion in a binder at, say, a large conference.

> **Note**
>
> After you have decided which print option to use, you should use Print Preview before actually printing anything. This preview step can save you some grief—it can help you spot graphics or text boxes that may be falling off a page, for example, or show you that the font in the print version is too small for easy reading.

When you're ready to use Print Preview, follow these steps:

1. Open the presentation, and click the Microsoft Office Button.

2. Rest your pointer on the arrow next to Print, and then click Print Preview.

3. If you need to change the headers and footers or the color setup, click Options in the Print group.

4. If you decide to change the print options, make changes in the Page Setup group under Print What.

5. Use the Zoom, Fit To Window, and Next/Previous Page commands as needed. When you are satisfied that the printing output will appear as desired, click Close Print Preview to return to the presentation and make additional edits to pages, or click Print to print directly from the Print Preview tab.

> **Note**
>
> The term *grayscale* describes a printing process where color images are printing in variations of gray tones between black and white. If you have a black-and-white printer and are printing color slides, this option is a good one. It will help readers see subtle differences offered by different colors and can make text easier to read.

Here are the steps for printing your presentation:

1. Open the presentation, and click the Microsoft Office Button.

2. Rest your pointer on the arrow next to Print, and then click Print.

3. In the Print dialog box, under Print Range, select the slides you want to print.

4. Under copies, select the number of copies needed.

5. Under Print What, select the print option desired (handouts, outline, notes, or slides).

> **Note**
>
> If you select handouts, you need to also tell PowerPoint how many slides per page are desired and whether you want them placed horizontally or vertically.

6. Make any other selections desired, such as the Scale To Fit Paper or Frame Slides check box.

7. Click OK. Your document will print.

You may have noticed as you walked through the Print options and Print Preview steps that there is a third printing choice called Quick Print. If you have already gone through your presentation and are confident that it needs no further changes, you can click this command. PowerPoint 2007 will automatically print the presentation for you without any prompts or options for changes. Be careful, though—this selection will default to the last options you selected in the Print dialog box. So, for example, if you last printed handouts and now want to print slides, you need to make that change on the Print Preview tab.

Note

You can go to Print Preview from the Print dialog box instead of going back through the Microsoft Office Button. Just click the Preview button in the bottom-left corner of the dialog box.

Slide Size and Orientation

Sometimes when you print a presentation, you need to make adjustments for inclusion in a binder or use with an overhead projector or some other format. If you need to change the orientation of your slides (switch between Portrait and Landscape), just go to the Design tab, and make the change in the Page Setup group by clicking Slide Orientation.

For other changes to your slide page setup, click the Page Setup button to display the Page Setup dialog box. This dialog box also lets you make changes to slide orientation, but it offers the Slides Sized For feature, too. You can manually change the slide width and height here and select predetermined options for slide sizing so you can easily set up your slides for different screen or paper sizes, as well as for overheads, banners, and custom sizes.

PART 6

Outlook

Jim Boyce, Beth Sheresh and Doug Sheresh

Introducing Outlook 2007

Microsoft Office Outlook 2007 sports a lot of new features that improve usability and add functionality. What's more, many of the familiar features in earlier versions have been revamped or fine-tuned in Office Outlook 2007. All of these changes come together to make Outlook 2007 an outstanding tool for communication, time and information management, and collaboration.

If you are an experienced Microsoft Outlook user, one of your first questions is no doubt, "What's new in Outlook 2007, and how do I find all of these new features?" That's what this chapter is all about. While we don't cover every little change or nuance of the new Outlook 2007 interface or new and improved features here, we offer a broad overview of the new features in Outlook 2007 to help you get up to speed quickly. We'll start with the most obvious—the user interface.

This chapter also provides an overview of the architecture in Outlook 2007 to help you learn not only how Outlook 2007 works but also how it stores data. Having that knowledge, particularly if you're charged with administering or supporting Outlook 2007 for other users, will help you use the application more effectively and address issues related to data storage and security, archiving, working offline, and moving data between installations.

This chapter explains the different options you have for connecting to e-mail servers through Outlook 2007 and the protocols—Post Office Protocol 3 (POP3) and Internet Message Access Protocol (IMAP), for example—that support those connections. In addition to learning about client support and the various platforms on which you can use Outlook 2007, you'll also learn about the options that are available for starting and using the program.

A New Interface

Certainly the most obvious difference in all of the 2007 Microsoft Office system applications is their new interfaces. Like the other Microsoft Office system applications,

Outlook 2007 sports a new interface. In some ways, however, the differences in Outlook 2007 are not as pronounced as they are in some of the other applications, such as Microsoft Office Word 2007. Outlook 2007 blends some new interface components with improvements to its existing components to achieve a new look and feel. Fortunately, you should be able to become comfortable with this new look and feel in a short time. Once you've made that transition, you'll come to really appreciate the new interface.

Let's take a look at the biggest difference from earlier versions—the Ribbon.

The Ribbon

Unlike some of the other 2007 Office release applications, the main Outlook 2007 window uses a familiar menu bar and toolbar combination to give you access to commands, options, and tools in Outlook 2007. The other applications, such as Office Word 2007, use a new feature called the Ribbon to give you quick access to commonly used features. Outlook 2007 does make use of the Ribbon, however, as you can see in Figure 22-1. The new message form is one of the many forms in Outlook 2007 that sports a Ribbon rather than the more familiar menu bar/toolbar combination.

Ribbon —

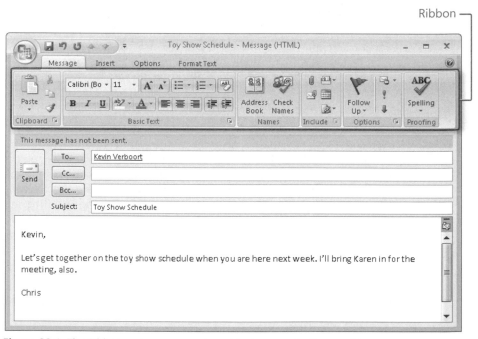

Figure 22-1 The Ribbon makes commands and features easily discoverable.

The Ribbon is something of a paradigm shift. Rather than provide a linear menu list of commands, the Ribbon divides features onto individual *tabs*, each of which comprises tools with related functions. For example, all of the tools that relate to inserting items into a new message are located together on the Insert tab of the new message form.

Each Ribbon tab is divided into *groups*, and each group organizes the features for a specific function. On the Message tab of the new message form, for example, the Basic Text group organizes the tools you use to format text in the message.

Is the new Ribbon design good or bad? After you spend the time to become familiar with it, you'll probably come to the conclusion that the Ribbon is an improvement over the "old" interface. The Ribbon helps expose some useful and powerful features that many people never used because they weren't aware they existed or they didn't take the time to dig through the menus to find them.

The Navigation Pane

The Navigation Pane was first introduced in Microsoft Outlook 2002 as part of Microsoft Office XP and took the place of the Outlook Bar. The Navigation Pane gives you quick access to all of your Outlook 2007 folders (Inbox, Calendar, and so on) and adapts depending on which folder you are using. For example, when you open the Calendar folder, the objects offered in the Navigation Pane change to reflect features available in the calendar, such as views.

The Outlook 2007 Navigation Pane looks at first blush to be much like the Navigation Pane in Outlook 2002 and Outlook 2003. The main difference in Outlook 2007 is the capability to show the Navigation Pane in a collapsed state, as shown in Figure 22-2.

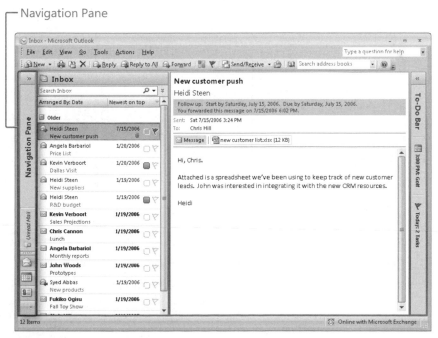

Figure 22-2 You can collapse, or autominimize, the Navigation Pane.

Essentially, the Navigation Pane, when collapsed, acts a little like the Microsoft Windows taskbar in autohide mode. The Navigation Pane sits at the left edge of the Outlook 2007 window as a narrow vertical toolbar. You can click items in the Navigation Pane to expand them for use. For example, click the Navigation Pane section to display the Favorite Folders and folder list or views for the current folder. After you click a folder in the list to select it, the pane is hidden again. Using the Navigation Pane in collapsed mode makes more space available for displaying the contents of a folder (such as your monthly calendar) while still keeping the Navigation Pane's features readily available.

The To-Do Bar

The To-Do Bar, shown in Figure 22-3, is another new feature in Outlook 2007 that brings together information from different Outlook 2007 sources and makes it readily available. It combines the Date Navigator, appointments for the day, and current tasks in one pane.

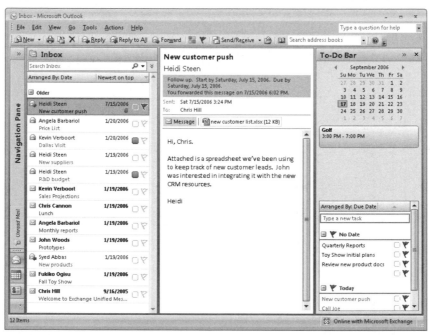

Figure 22-3 The To-Do Bar combines tasks, appointments, and the Date Navigator in one location.

As with the Navigation Pane, you can configure the To-Do Bar to automatically hide after you use it. In this mode, the To-Do Bar sits at the right edge of the Outlook 2007 window as a vertical toolbar. When you click the To-Do Bar, it expands to display its contents. You can then click a date to view its appointments in the Calendar window, work with tasks, and so on. When you click again in the main Outlook 2007 window, the To-Do Bar collapses back to a vertical toolbar.

Other Interface Changes

The Outlook 2007 interface is significantly changed in other ways in addition to the Ribbon, Navigation Pane, and To-Do Bar. For example, the Calendar window has been given a visual and functional overhaul. See "Calendar Changes" on the next page and "E-Mail Changes" on page 636 for details. Additional interface features are explored in other chapters where appropriate.

Instant Search

Outlook 2007 introduces its own Instant Search feature. For example, in the Inbox folder, you can click in the Search box and type a word or phrase, and Outlook 2007 quickly (but not quite instantly) displays the results of the search. You can work with the results of the search before the search is complete, so when you find the item you need, you can simply double-click it to open it—you don't have to wait for the search to complete.

Search is also improved in other ways in Outlook 2007. You can click the arrow next to the Search box to open the Query Builder, as shown in Figure 22-4, where you can specify additional search parameters to locate items. The contents of the Query Builder changes according to the folder in which you are working. For example, the search criteria in the Inbox pane is different from the criteria in the Calendar pane.

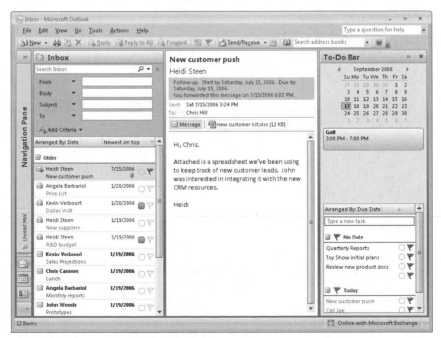

Figure 22-4 Use the Query Builder to perform advanced searches.

Calendar Changes

The Calendar folder has received some new interface changes and added features in Outlook 2007. For example, the calendar's appearance has been improved with additional color and visual elements. On the functional side, the calendar includes a Daily Task List pane at the bottom of the window, as shown in Figure 22-5. The Daily Task List shows the tasks that are due on the current date, such as tasks with that day as a due date or e-mail messages with a follow-up date of that day.

Figure 22-5 Use the Daily Task List in the Calendar folder to view your current tasks.

You can use the Daily Task List to open tasks and the other items it displays (such as messages), add new tasks, mark tasks as complete, assign tasks, print tasks, and perform other actions on the items. Tasks that you do not complete roll over to the next day, so they are not forgotten.

> **Note**
>
> The appearance of the Week view is another change in the Calendar folder. No longer a two-column, day-planner view, the Week view is more like the Work Week view in earlier versions.

Scheduling also sees improvement in Outlook 2007. When Outlook 2007 is used in concert with Microsoft Exchange Server 2007 for scheduling meetings, attendee schedules are automatically reviewed and a time is then proposed for the meeting. Naturally, you can select a different time if needed. Figure 22-6 shows the Meeting Assistant, which helps you choose a meeting time that works for the majority of attendees.

In addition, when you make a change to a meeting time, location, or agenda, the attendees receive an informational update rather than a request to accept the meeting changes.

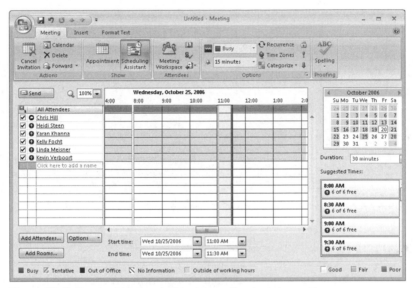

Figure 22-6 Use the Meeting Assistant to easily schedule meetings.

Another very useful improvement for scheduling in Outlook 2007 is calendar overlay. In earlier versions of Microsoft Outlook, you could open another Calendar folder in a new window to view the appointments in that calendar. As in Outlook 2003, Outlook 2007 will also let you view two calendars side by side. Even better, Outlook 2007 lets you overlay calendars to see a combined view, as shown in Figure 22-7. For example, assume that you keep your personal appointments separate from your business appointments. You can overlay the two calendars in Outlook 2007 for a complete, overall view.

Calendar overlay extends to Microsoft Windows SharePoint Services sites. You can view calendars stored on a SharePoint site and even overlay them with your own calendar, all right within Outlook 2007. For example, you could overlay your team calendar over your personal calendar to identify scheduling conflicts.

Chapter 22

Figure 22-7 Use calendar overlay to view multiple calendars in a combined view.

E-Mail Changes

Many people spend a majority of their time working in the mail folders in Outlook 2007. So Microsoft has improved mail features in Outlook 2007 in a number of ways, both visual and functional.

For example, Outlook 2007 now can automatically set up e-mail accounts for you based on a small amount of information you provide, such as your e-mail address and name. Outlook 2007 will attempt to determine the appropriate mail server and other settings based on that information, simplifying account setup. If Outlook 2007 is unable to set up the account, you can specify settings manually.

Here's a list of the most notable mail-related feature improvements in Outlook 2007:

- **Attachment Previewing** You can preview certain types of documents right in the Reading Pane without having to open the attachment or the message containing it. You simply click the item to preview it in the Reading Pane. Outlook 2007 supports previewing of Outlook 2007 items, images and text files, and documents created by Microsoft Office Word, PowerPoint, Excel, and Visio. This feature is extensible, enabling third-party developers to build preview capability for other attachment types.

- **Out Of Office Assistant** In earlier versions, Microsoft Outlook displayed a notification dialog box when you started Outlook with the Out Of Office Assistant turned on. In Outlook 2007, the notice appears on the status bar. A more important change to the Out Of Office Assistant is that you can now schedule the Out Of Office Assistant ahead of time, turning it on at the specified time. So a week or so before you will be out of the office, you can set it and forget it. The Out Of Office Assistant will turn on at the specified time all by itself and turn off at the set time, as well. In addition, you can specify different Out Of Office messages for recipients in your organization and those outside it. These last two features require Exchange Server 2007.

- **Unified Messaging** When Outlook 2007 is used with Exchange Server 2007, you can have your voice messages and faxes delivered to your Inbox along with your e-mail.

- **International Domain Names** Outlook 2007 supports internationalized domain names in e-mail messages, enabling people to specify addresses in their own languages in addition to English.

- **E-Mail Postmarks** Outlook 2007 stamps each message with a uniquely generated electronic postmark. This postmark serves two purposes. First, it helps reduce spamming by imposing a small processing load on the computer. This load is negligible when sending an average number of e-mail messages, but it imposes an unacceptable load on spammers trying to send messages to a large number of recipients. In addition, Outlook 2007 recognizes the postmark on messages that it receives, helping it to determine whether a message is not junk mail.

- **Junk Filter And Phishing Protection** Another improvement in Outlook 2007 is its enhanced junk filtering. Outlook 2007 also adds a phishing filter to help guard against phishing attacks in which official-looking but false messages attempt to direct you to malicious sites or obtain personal information such as credit card or banking information.

- **Managed Folders** This feature works in conjunction with Exchange Server 2007 to provide a means for archiving messages to meet legal requirements, such as Sarbanes-Oxley and HIPAA, and corporate policy requirements. Managed folders look and function like other message folders (such as the Inbox folder). However, the policies assigned to managed folders determine retention and other policy-based behavior. In addition, the user cannot move, rename, or delete managed folders. These restrictions ensure that the users cannot bypass retention policies.

Color Categories

You are no doubt familiar with categories in Outlook 2007. Categories in Outlook 2007 are like tags that you associate with Outlook 2007 items (such as messages, appointments, and tasks). In earlier versions of Microsoft Outlook, categories were defined using text only. You could choose from existing categories as well as create your own categories. You can organize Outlook 2007 items based on category—for example, grouping items in a folder based on their category assignments.

Outlook 2007 introduces color categories to make categories more visible and more useful, as shown in Figure 22 8. By associating a color with a category, you make it easier to quickly identify items that have a specific assigned category. This is particularly true when you are using a list view that is not grouped by category. For example, you might assign the Blue category to all e-mail messages from a certain sender. You can then identify at a glance when looking at the Inbox the messages from that sender.

Although Outlook 2007 shifts the category paradigm to a color-based model, you can still rely on your old text categories. The primary difference is that you can now also associate a color with those categories. For example, in earlier versions of Microsoft Outlook, you could create a category named Toy Show. Now, with Outlook 2007, you can also associate a color with that category, making its items easily identifiable.

> **Note**
>
> You can also assign a shortcut key to each category, enabling you to assign that category to items by simply pressing the shortcut key sequence.

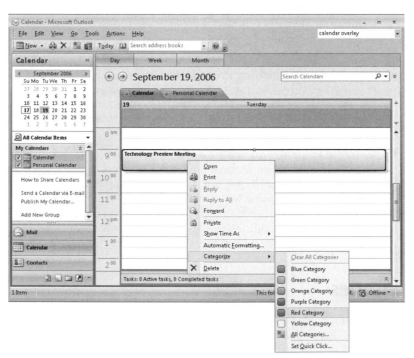

Figure 22-8 Outlook 2007 adds color to categories to make them more useful.

Collaboration and Sharing Improvements

Outlook 2007 adds several new features and improves on existing features to make collaboration and sharing even easier. SharePoint integration is a key new feature.

Integration with Office SharePoint Server

Outlook 2007 integrates with Microsoft Office SharePoint Server 2007 sites to enable you to interact with information stored on a SharePoint site. For example, you can connect shared calendars, document libraries, discussion lists, contacts, and tasks from a SharePoint site to Outlook 2007. SharePoint items show up in a folder named SharePoint Lists, which appears in the Navigation Pane along with your Outlook 2007 folders. You can then work with the items from the SharePoint site as if you were working on Outlook 2007 items. Changes that you make are updated on the SharePoint site.

> **Note**
> Outlook 2007 also integrates with Windows SharePoint Services versions 2 and 3.

The following list summarizes many of the key tasks that you can perform in Outlook 2007 with SharePoint items:

- **Connect a SharePoint library to Outlook 2007.** Connecting a SharePoint library to Outlook 2007 makes the library and its items available within Outlook 2007. You connect the library to Outlook 2007 from the SharePoint site.

- **Download a file from a SharePoint library to Outlook 2007.** You can download just a list of available files or the files themselves, or you can have Outlook 2007 download files in the background. The SharePoint site administrator can control how and whether files are downloaded to client systems.

- **Open a file from a SharePoint library using Outlook 2007.** You can navigate to a SharePoint library in the Navigation Pane, locate the file you want, and simply double-click the file to open it.

- **Edit a file from a SharePoint library using Outlook 2007.** You can modify a document from a SharePoint library offline from Outlook 2007 and save the changes to the library (assuming that you have sufficient permissions in the library).

- **Remove a SharePoint file from Outlook 2007.** You can remove one or more files from a SharePoint library list in Outlook 2007 without actually removing the documents from the SharePoint library. The document remains on the server but is removed from your cached list. This feature simplifies browsing libraries that contain a large number of items.

- **Remove a SharePoint library from Outlook 2007.** If you don't need to see a particular library anymore, you can easily remove it from Outlook 2007. Removing the library does not affect it on the server, but only removes it from the Navigation Pane in Outlook 2007.

- **Add a file to a SharePoint library by sending an e-mail message.** If the Share-Point document library is configured to accept documents by e-mail, you can add a document to a library simply by sending an e-mail message, with the document attached, to the library.

Shared Calendars

Outlook 2007 adds some great new features to make it possible to share your schedule with others and to view their schedules as well. For example, you can create a *calendar snapshot* that you can send in an e-mail message to others. The recipient can open the calendar in Outlook 2007 or in a Web browser.

Outlook 2007 also supports Internet Calendars, which are calendars stored on an Internet service and available for download and synchronization in Outlook 2007. You can create a calendar in Outlook 2007 and publish it to an Internet service or use other applications to create the calendar. If you subscribe to a calendar-sharing service, Outlook 2007 can query the service on a periodic basis to upload and download calendar changes. Microsoft offers Internet Calendar sharing through the Microsoft Office Online Web site.

> **Note**
> In addition to these calendar-sharing features, you can still save your calendar to a Web page, enabling you to publish your calendar to any Web server.

Shared Business Cards

You are probably familiar with contacts in Outlook 2007. In Outlook 2007, you can create electronic business cards complete with photos, logos, text, and other content. Outlook 2007 stores these business cards in the Contacts folder. You can share these business cards with others through e-mail and receive their cards as well.

Overview of Outlook 2007 Capabilities

Outlook 2007 provides a broad range of capabilities to help you manage your entire workday. In fact, a growing number of Microsoft Office system users work in Outlook more than 60 percent of the time. An understanding of the Outlook 2007 capabilities and features is important not only for using the Microsoft Office system effectively but also for managing your time and projects. The following sections will help you learn to use the features in Outlook 2007 to simplify your workday and enhance your productivity.

Messaging

One of the key features Outlook 2007 offers is messaging. You can use Outlook 2007 as a client to send and receive e-mail through a variety of services. Outlook 2007 offers integrated support for the e-mail services covered in the sections that follow.

> **Note**
>
> A *client application* is one that uses a service provided by another computer, typically a server.

Exchange Server

Outlook 2007 integrates tightly with Microsoft Exchange Server, which means that you can take advantage of workgroup scheduling, collaboration, instant messaging, and other features offered through Exchange Server that aren't available with other clients. For example, you can use any POP3 e-mail client, such as Microsoft Outlook 2007 Express or Microsoft Windows Mail (the Windows Vista incarnation of Outlook Express), to connect to a computer running Exchange Server (assuming that the Exchange Server administrator has configured the server to allow POP), but you're limited to e-mail only. Advanced workgroup and other special features—being able to recall a message before it is read, use public folders, view group schedules, and use managed folders for archiving and retention, for example—require Outlook 2007.

Internet E-Mail

Outlook 2007 provides full support for Internet e-mail servers, which means that you can use Outlook 2007 to send and receive e-mail through mail servers that support Internet-based standards, such as POP3 and IMAP. What's more, you can integrate Internet mail accounts with other accounts, such as an Exchange Server account, in order to send and receive messages through multiple servers. For example, you might maintain an account on Exchange Server for interoffice correspondence and use a local Internet service provider (ISP) or other Internet-based e-mail service for messages outside your network. Or perhaps you want to monitor your personal e-mail along with your work-related e-mail. In that situation, you would simply add your personal e-mail account to your Outlook 2007 profile and work with both simultaneously. You can then use rules and custom folders to help separate your messages.

For more information about messaging protocols such as POP3 and IMAP, see "Understanding Messaging Protocols" on page 654.

Chapter 22

HTTP-Based E-Mail

Outlook 2007 supports Hypertext Transfer Protocol (HTTP)–based e-mail services, such as Microsoft Hotmail. HTTP is the protocol used to request and transmit Web pages. This means that you can use Outlook 2007 to send and receive e-mail through Hotmail and other HTTP-based mail servers that would otherwise require you to use a Web browser to access your e-mail, as shown in Figure 22-9. In addition, you can download your messages to your local Inbox and process them offline, rather than remaining connected to your ISP while you process messages. Another advantage is that you can keep your messages as long as you want—most HTTP-based messaging services, including Hotmail, purge read messages after a given period of time. Plus, HTTP support in Outlook 2007 lets you keep all your e-mail in a single application. Currently, Outlook 2007 directly supports Hotmail. Check with your e-mail service to determine whether your mail server is Outlook 2007–compatible.

> **Note**
>
> You can use Outlook 2007 with your Hotmail account only if you have a paid Hotmail account, such as MSN Hotmail Plus or MSN Premium. You can't use Outlook 2007 to access a free Hotmail account.

Figure 22-9 HTTP-based mail servers such as Hotmail have traditionally required access through a Web browser.

Fax Send and Receive

Outlook 2007 includes a Fax Mail Transport provider, which allows you to send faxes from Outlook 2007 using a fax modem. In addition, third-party developers can provide Messaging Application Programming Interface (MAPI) integration with their fax applications, allowing you to use Outlook 2007 as the front end for those applications to send and receive faxes. Both Microsoft Windows 2000 and Microsoft Windows XP include built-in fax services that support sending and receiving faxes. The Fax Service in Windows 2000 also supports MAPI and Inbox integration with Outlook 2007 and is the only Microsoft-supplied fax service supported by Microsoft on the client side for Outlook 2007. The Windows 2000 Fax Service can deliver incoming faxes to an Outlook 2007 Inbox, as well as print them and deliver a copy to a file folder. The Windows XP Fax Service can deliver incoming faxes to a file folder or print them, but it does not support delivery to an Outlook 2007 Inbox.

Windows 2000 Fax Service is now the only fax support offered for Windows. Windows XP users need to purchase a third-party fax application

Extensible E-Mail Support

The Outlook 2007 design allows developers to support third-party e-mail services in Outlook 2007. Whatever your e-mail server type, Outlook 2007 provides a comprehensive set of tools for composing, receiving, and replying to messages. Outlook 2007 provides support for rich-text and HTML formatting, which allows you to create and receive messages that contain much more than just text, as shown in Figure 22-10. For example, you can send a Web page as a mail message or integrate sound, video, and graphics in mail messages. Outlook 2007 support for multiple address books, multiple e-mail accounts, and even multiple e-mail services makes it an excellent messaging client, even if you forgo the application's many other features and capabilities.

Chapter 22

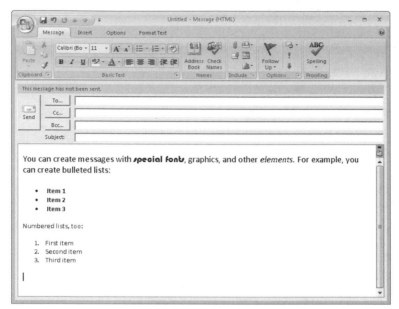

Figure 22-10 Use Outlook 2007 to create rich-text and multimedia messages.

Scheduling

Scheduling is another important feature in Outlook 2007. You can use Outlook 2007 to track both personal and work-related meetings and appointments, as shown in Figure 22-11, whether you are at home or in the office—a useful feature even on a stand-alone computer.

Where the Outlook 2007 scheduling capabilities really shine, however, is in group scheduling. When you use Outlook 2007 to set up meetings and appointments with others, you can view the schedules of your invitees, which makes it easy to find a time when everyone can attend. You can schedule both one-time and recurring appointments. All appointments and meetings can include a reminder with a lead time that you specify, and Outlook 2007 will notify you of the event at the specified time. You can process multiple reminders at one time, a useful feature if you've been out of the office for a while.

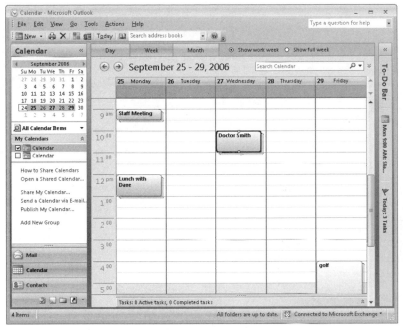

Figure 22-11 Track your personal and work schedules with Outlook 2007.

Organizing your schedule is also one of Outlook 2007's strong suits. You can use categories and types to categorize appointments, events, and meetings; to control the way they appear in Outlook 2007; and to perform automatic processing. Color labels allow you to identify quickly and visually different types of events on your calendar.

In addition to managing your own schedule, you can delegate control of the schedule to someone else, such as your assistant. The assistant can modify your schedule, request meetings, respond to meeting invitations, and otherwise act on your behalf regarding your calendar. Not only can others view your schedule to plan meetings and appointments (with the exception of items marked personal), but also you can publish your schedule to the Web to allow others to view it over an intranet or the Internet, as shown in Figure 22-12.

Chapter 22

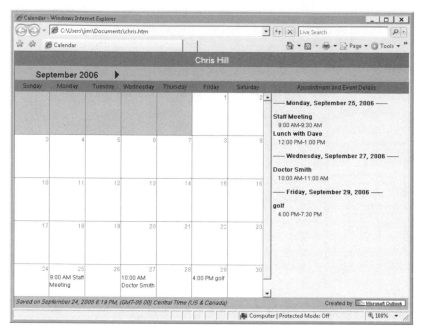

Figure 22-12 You can easily publish your schedule to the Web.

Contact Management

Being able to manage contact information—names, addresses, and phone numbers—is critical to other aspects of Outlook 2007, such as scheduling and messaging. Outlook 2007 makes it easy to manage contacts and offers flexibility in the type of information you maintain. In addition to basic information, you can also store a contact's fax number, cell phone number, pager number, Web page URL, and more, as shown in Figure 22-13. You can even include a picture for the contact.

In addition to using contact information to address e-mail messages, you can initiate phone calls using the contacts list, track calls to contacts in the journal, add notes for each contact, use the contacts list to create mail merge documents, and perform other tasks. The Contacts folder also provides a means for storing a contact's digital certificate, which you can use to exchange encrypted messages for security. Adding a contact's certificate is easy—when you receive a digitally signed message from the contact, Outlook 2007 adds the certificate to the contact's entry. You can also import a certificate from a file provided by the contact.

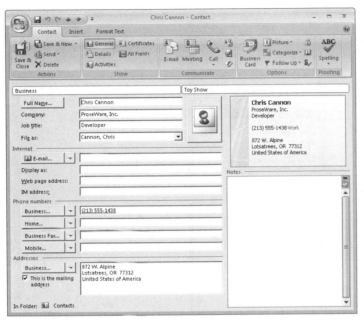

Figure 22-13 You can manage a wealth of information about each contact with Outlook 2007.

For details about digital signatures and encryption, see "Message Encryption" on page 662.

Task Management

Managing your workday usually includes keeping track of the tasks you need to perform and assigning tasks to others. Outlook 2007 makes it easy to manage your task list. You assign a due date, start date, priority, category, and other properties to each task, which makes it easier for you to manage those tasks, as shown in Figure 22-14. As with meetings and appointments, Outlook 2007 keeps you informed and on track by issuing reminders for each task. You control whether the reminder is used and the time and date it's generated, along with an optional, audible notification. You can designate a task as personal, preventing others from viewing the task in your schedule—just as you can with meetings and appointments. Tasks can be one-time or recurring events.

If you manage other people, Outlook 2007 makes it easy to assign tasks to other Outlook 2007 users. When you create a task, simply click Assign Task, and Outlook 2007 prompts you for the assignee's e-mail address. You can choose to keep a copy of the updated task in your own task list and receive a status report when the task is complete.

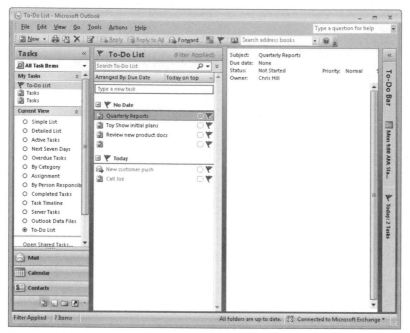

Figure 22-14 Use Outlook 2007 to manage tasks.

Tracking with the Outlook Journal

Keeping track of events is an important part of managing your workday, and the Outlook 2007 journal makes it simple. The Journal folder allows you to keep track of the contacts you make (phone calls, e-mail messages, and so on), meeting actions, task requests and responses, and other actions for selected contacts, as shown in Figure 22-15. You can also use the journal to track your work in other Microsoft Office system applications, giving you a way to track the time you spend on various documents and their associated projects. You can have Outlook 2007 add journal items automatically based on settings that you specify, and you can also add items manually to your journal.

When you view the journal, you can double-click a journal entry to either open the entry or open the items referred to by the entry, depending on how you have configured the journal. You can also configure the journal to automatically archive items in the default archive folder or in a folder you choose, or you can have Outlook 2007 regularly delete items from the journal, cleaning out items that are older than a specified length of time. Outlook 2007 can use group policies to control the retention of journal entries, allowing administrators to manage journaling and data retention consistently throughout an organization.

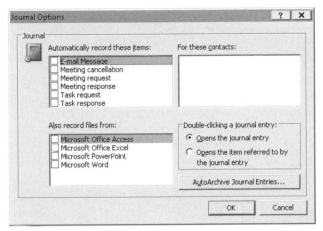

Figure 22-15 Configure your journal using the Outlook 2007 options.

Organizing Your Thoughts with Notes

With Outlook 2007, you can keep track of your thoughts and tasks by using the Notes folder. Each note can function as a stand-alone window, allowing you to view notes on your desktop outside Outlook 2007, as shown in Figure 22-16. Notes exist as individual message files, so you can copy or move them to other folders, including your desktop, or easily share them with others through network sharing or e-mail. You can also incorporate the contents of notes into other applications or other Outlook 2007 folders by using the Clipboard. For example, you might copy a note regarding a contact to that person's contact entry. As you can with other Outlook 2007 items, you can assign categories to notes to help you organize and view them.

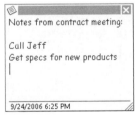

Figure 22-16 Use notes to keep track of miscellaneous information.

How Outlook Stores Data

If you work with Outlook 2007 primarily as a user, understanding how the program stores data helps you use it effectively to organize and manage your data on a daily basis, including storing and archiving Outlook 2007 items as needed. If you're charged with supporting other Outlook 2007 users, understanding how Outlook 2007 stores data allows you to help others create and manage their folders and ensure the security and integrity of their data. Finally, because data storage is the foundation of all of the Outlook 2007 features, understanding where and how the program stores data is critical if you're creating Outlook 2007–based applications—for example, a data entry form that uses Outlook 2007 as the mechanism for posting the data to a public folder.

You're probably familiar with folders (directories) in the file system. You use these folders to organize applications and documents. For example, the Program Files folder in the Microsoft Windows operating system is the default location for most applications that you install on the system, and the My Documents folder (called Documents in Windows Vista) serves as the default location for document files. You create these types of folders in Windows Explorer.

Outlook 2007 also uses folders to organize data, but these folders are different from your file system folders. Rather than existing individually on your system's hard disk, these folders exist within the Outlook 2007 file structure. You view and manage these folders within the Outlook 2007 interface, not in Windows Explorer. Think of Outlook 2007 folders as windows into your Outlook 2007 data rather than as individual elements that exist on disk. By default, Outlook 2007 includes several folders, as shown in Figure 22-17.

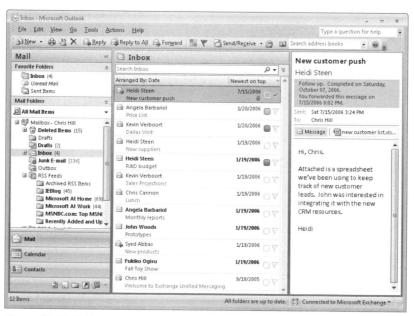

Figure 22-17 Folders organize your data in Outlook 2007.

Personal Folders—.pst Files

If your Outlook 2007 folders aren't stored as individual folders on your system's hard disk, where are they? The answer to that question depends on how you configure Outlook 2007. As in earlier versions of Microsoft Outlook, you can use a set of personal folders to store your Outlook 2007 data. Outlook 2007 uses the .pst extension for a set of personal folders, but you specify the file's name when you configure Outlook 2007. For example, you might use your name as the file name to help you easily identify the file. The default .pst file contains your Contacts, Calendar, Tasks, and other folders.

You can use multiple .pst files, adding additional personal folders to your Outlook 2007 configuration, as shown in Figure 22-18. For example, you might want to create another set of folders to separate your personal information from work-related data. You can add personal folders to your Outlook 2007 configuration simply by adding another .pst file to your profile.

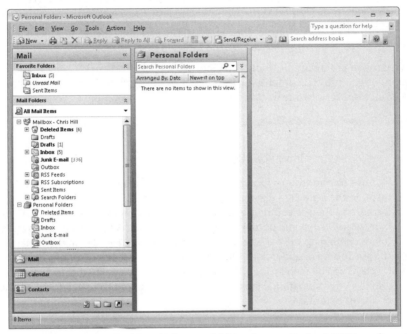

Figure 22-18 You can add multiple sets of folders to your Outlook 2007 configuration.

Options for Working Offline

If you use Outlook 2007 with Exchange Server and do not use local .pst files to store your data, you have two options for working with your mailbox data offline, and these methods differ only in the way synchronization occurs.

An .ost file allows you to work offline. The .ost file acts as an offline copy of your data store on the computer running Exchange Server. When you're working offline, changes you make to contacts, messages, and other Outlook 2007 items and folders occur in the offline store. When you go online again, Outlook 2007 synchronizes the changes between the offline store and your Exchange Server store when you perform a send/receive for the account. For example, if you've deleted messages from your offline store, Outlook 2007 deletes those same messages from your online store when you synchronize the folders. Any new messages in your Inbox on the server are added to your offline store. Synchronization is a two-way process, providing the most up-to-date copy of your data in both locations, ensuring that changes made in each are reflected in the other.

Outlook 2007 adds a new feature called Cached Exchange Mode. This mode works much the same as offline synchronization with an .ost file. In fact, Outlook 2007 uses an .ost file for Cached Exchange Mode. The main difference is that with Cached Exchange Mode, Outlook 2007 always works from the copy of your mailbox that is cached locally on your computer. Outlook 2007 then automatically handles synchronization between your offline cache mailbox and the mailbox stored on the server. With Cached Exchange Mode, you don't need to worry about synchronizing the two—Outlook 2007 detects when the server is available and updates your locally cached copy automatically.

When you create an Outlook 2007 storage file, Outlook 2007 defaults to a specific location for the file. The default location is the Local Settings\Application Data\Microsoft\Outlook folder of your user profile.

INSIDE OUT   Find Your Data Store

If you're having trouble locating your existing storage files, click File, Data File Management. In the Data Files dialog box, shown in Figure 22-19, select the file you want to locate, and then select the file location in the Filename column. If you can't see the entire path, drag the column border to expand the column. Alternatively, to go straight to the folder containing the file, select the file and click Open Folder. In the folder window, choose Tools, Folder Options. On the View tab of the Folder Options dialog box, select Display The Full Path In The Title Bar to view the fully qualified path to the file. You can also use your operating system's Find/Search command to search for all files with a .pst or an .ost extension.

If you use the same computer all the time, it's generally best to store your Outlook 2007 files on a local hard disk. In some situations, however, you will probably want to store them on a network share. For example, you might connect from different computers on the network and use a roaming profile to provide a consistent desktop and user interface regardless of your logon location. (A *roaming profile* allows your desktop configuration, documents, and other elements of your desktop environment to be duplicated wherever you log on.) In this situation, you (or the network administrator) would configure your profile to place your home folder on a network server that is available to you from all logon locations. Your Outlook 2007 files would then be stored on that network share, making them available to you on whichever computer you use to log on to the network. Placing your Outlook 2007 files on a server gives you the added potential benefit of incorporating your Outlook 2007 data files in the server's backup strategy.

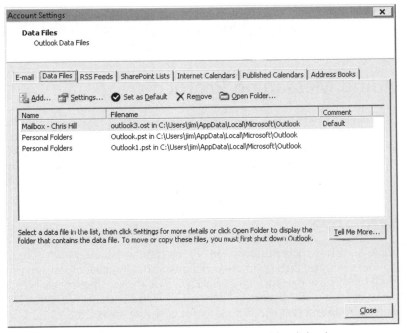

Figure 22-19 Locate your data files by using the Data Files dialog box.

TROUBLESHOOTING

You use a roaming profile and logon time is increasing.

If you use Outlook 2007 with Exchange Server, your best option is to use your Exchange Server mail store as the storage location for your data instead of using a .pst file. However, if you use a roaming profile, consider turning off Cached Exchange Mode or eliminating the use of an .ost file to reduce the excessive amount of traffic that would otherwise be required to transfer your mailbox data across the network. If you have a situation where you can't use Outlook 2007 to access your mailbox, you can turn to Outlook Web Access or Outlook Anywhere, which enable you to access your mailbox from a Web browser.

Sharing Storage Files

Outlook 2007 provides excellent functionality for sharing information with others. Toward that end, you can share your data using a couple of different methods. Exchange Server users can configure permissions for individual folders to allow specific users to connect to those folders and view the data contained in them. You can also delegate access to your folders to allow an assistant to manage items for you in the folders. For example, you might have your assistant manage your schedule but not your tasks. In that case, you would delegate access for the Calendar folder but not for the Tasks folder.

Understanding Messaging Protocols

A *messaging protocol* is a mechanism that messaging servers and applications use to transfer messages. Being able to use a specific e-mail service requires that your application support the same protocols the server uses. To configure Outlook 2007 as a messaging client, you need to understand the various protocols supported by Outlook 2007 and the types of servers that employ each type. The following sections provide an overview of these protocols.

SMTP/POP3

Simple Mail Transport Protocol (SMTP) is a standards-based protocol used for transferring messages and is the primary mechanism that Internet-based and intranet-based e-mail servers use to transfer messages. It's also the mechanism that Outlook 2007 uses to connect to a mail server to send messages for an Internet account. SMTP is the protocol used by an Internet e-mail account for outgoing messages.

SMTP operates by default on TCP port 25. When you configure an Internet-based e-mail account, the port on which the server is listening for SMTP determines the outgoing mail server setting. Unless your e-mail server uses a different port (unlikely), you can use the default port value of 25. If you want to use Outlook 2007 for an existing Internet mail account, confirm the SMTP server name and port settings with your ISP.

Post Office Protocol 3 (POP3) is a standards-based protocol that clients can use to retrieve messages from any mail server that supports POP3. This is the protocol that Outlook 2007 uses when retrieving messages from an Internet-based or intranet-based mail server that supports POP3 mailboxes. Nearly all ISP-based mail servers use POP3. Exchange Server also supports the use of POP3 for retrieving mail.

POP3 operates on TCP port 110 by default. Unless your server uses a nonstandard port configuration, you can leave the port setting as is when defining a POP3 mail account.

IMAP

Like POP3, Internet Message Access Protocol (IMAP) is a standards-based protocol that enables message transfer. However, IMAP offers some significant differences from POP3. For example, POP3 is primarily designed as an offline protocol, which means that you retrieve your messages from a server and download them to your local message store (such as your local Outlook 2007 folders). IMAP is designed primarily as an online protocol, which allows a remote user to manipulate messages and message folders on the server without downloading them. This is particularly helpful for users who need to access the same remote mailbox from multiple locations, such as home and work, using different computers. Because the messages remain on the server, IMAP eliminates the need for message synchronization.

INSIDE OUT   Keep POP3 Messages on the Server

IMAP by default leaves your messages on the server. If needed, you can configure a POP3 account in Outlook 2007 to leave a copy of messages on the server, allowing you to retrieve those messages later from another computer. IMAP offers other advantages over POP3. For example, with IMAP, you can search for messages on the server using a variety of message attributes, such as sender, message size, or message header. IMAP also offers better support for attachments because it can separate attachments from the header and text portion of a message. This is particularly useful with multipart Multipurpose Internet Mail Extensions (MIME) messages, allowing you to read a message without downloading the attachments so that you can decide which attachments you want to retrieve. With POP3, the entire message must be downloaded.

Security is another advantage of IMAP, because IMAP uses a challenge-response mechanism to authenticate the user for mailbox access. This prevents the user's password from being transmitted as clear text across the network, as it is with POP3.

IMAP support in Outlook 2007 allows you to use Outlook 2007 as a client to an IMAP-compliant e-mail server. Although IMAP provides for server-side storage and the ability to create additional mail folders on the server, it does not offer some of the same features as Exchange Server or even POP3. For example, you can't store contact, calendar, or other nonmessage folders on the server. Also, special folders such as Sent Items, Drafts, and Deleted Items can't be stored on the IMAP server. Even with these limitations, however, IMAP serves as a flexible protocol and surpasses POP3 in capability. Unless a competing standard appears in the future, it is possible that IMAP will eventually replace POP3. However, ISPs generally like POP3 because users' e-mail is moved to their own computers, freeing space on the mail server and reducing disk space management problems. For that reason alone, don't look for IMAP to replace POP3 in the near future.

For additional technical information about IMAP, go to *www.imap.org*.

MAPI

Messaging Application Programming Interface (MAPI) is a Microsoft-developed application programming interface (API) that facilitates communication between mail-enabled applications. MAPI support makes it possible for other applications to send and receive messages using Outlook 2007. For example, some third-party fax applications can place incoming faxes in your Inbox through MAPI. As another example, a third-party MAPI-aware application could read and write to your Outlook 2007 Address Book through MAPI calls. MAPI is not a message protocol, but understanding its function in Outlook 2007 helps you install, configure, and use MAPI-aware applications to integrate Outlook 2007.

Chapter 22

LDAP

Lightweight Directory Access Protocol (LDAP) was designed to serve with less overhead and fewer resource requirements than its precursor, Directory Access Protocol. LDAP is a standards-based protocol that allows clients to query data in a directory service over a TCP connection. For example, Windows 2000 uses LDAP as the primary means for querying the Active Directory directory service. Exchange Server supports LDAP queries, allowing clients to look up address information for subscribers on the server. Other directory services on the Internet employ LDAP to implement searches of their databases.

Like Outlook Express in Windows 2000 and Windows XP and Windows Mail in Windows Vista, Outlook 2007 allows you to add directory service accounts that use LDAP as their protocol to query directory services for e-mail addresses, phone numbers, and other information regarding subscribers.

NNTP

Network News Transfer Protocol (NNTP) is the standards-based protocol for server-to-server and client-to-server transfer of news messages, or the underlying protocol that makes possible public and private newsgroups. Outlook 2007 does not directly support the creation of accounts to access newsgroup servers but instead relies on Outlook Express or Windows Mail (depending on the operating system) as its default newsreader, as shown in Figure 22-20.

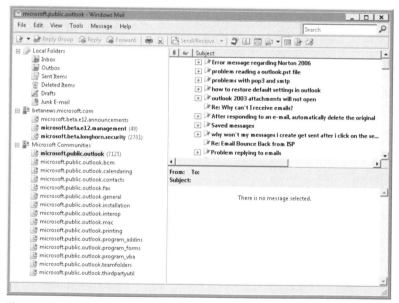

Figure 22-20 Outlook 2007 relies on Outlook Express or Windows Mail for reading and posting to public and private newsgroups.

> **Note**
>
> Microsoft Windows 2000 Server and Windows Server 2003 both include an NNTP service that lets a network administrator set up a news server to host newsgroups that can be accessed by local intranet or remote Internet users. Exchange Server allows the NNTP service to interface with other public or private news servers to pull newsgroups and messages via newsfeeds. Therefore, Windows 2000 Server and Windows Server 2003 by themselves let you set up your own newsgroup server to host your own newsgroups, and Exchange Server lets you host public Internet newsgroups.

Using Outlook 2007 Express or Windows Mail, you can download newsgroups, read messages, post messages, and perform other news-related tasks. Other third-party news applications offer extended capabilities.

HTML

HTML is the protocol used most commonly to define and transmit Web pages. Several e-mail services, including Hotmail, provide access to client mailboxes through Web pages and therefore make use of HTML as their message transfer protocol. You connect to the Web site and use the features and commands found there to view messages, send messages, and download attachments.

Outlook 2007 provides enhanced HTML support, which means that you can configure Outlook 2007 as a client for HTML-based mail services. As mentioned earlier in this chapter, Outlook 2007 includes built-in support for Hotmail. HTML support is purely a server-side issue, so HTML-based mail services other than Hotmail have to provide Outlook 2007 support on their own sites. Hotmail accomplishes this support programmatically by means of Active Server Pages (ASP).

INSIDE OUT   **Find Outlook 2007–Based Access in Hotmail**

The URL for Outlook 2007–based access in Hotmail is *http://services.msn.com/svcs/hotmail/httpmail.asp*. Outlook 2007 configures the URL automatically when you set up a Hotmail account in Outlook 2007, as shown in Figure 22-21. You can't browse to this URL through your Web browser to retrieve your e-mail, however.

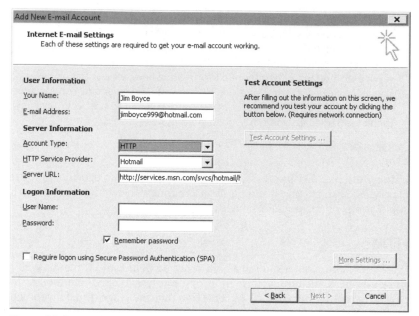

Figure 22-21 Outlook 2007 configures the URL automatically for Hotmail, but you must enter the URL manually for other HTTP-based e-mail services.

INSIDE OUT   Access Exchange Server 2003 with HTTP

Outlook 2007 can connect to an Exchange Server 2003 mailbox using HTTP as the protocol, expanding connection possibilities for users and decreasing firewall configuration and management headaches for administrators.

MIME

Multipurpose Internet Mail Extensions (MIME) is a standard specification for defining file formats used to exchange e-mail, files, and other documents across the Internet or an intranet. Each of the many MIME types defines the content type of the data contained in the attachment. MIME maps the content to a specific file type and extension, allowing the e-mail client to pass the MIME attachment to an external application for processing. For example, if you receive a message containing a WAV audio file, Outlook 2007 passes the file to the default WAV file player on your system.

S/MIME

Secure/Multipurpose Internet Mail Extensions (S/MIME) is a standard that allows e mail applications to send digitally signed and encrypted messages. S/MIME is therefore a mechanism through which Outlook 2007 permits you to include digital signatures with messages to ensure their authenticity and to encrypt messages to prevent unauthorized access to them.

For a detailed discussion of using Outlook 2007 to send digitally signed and encrypted messages, as well as other security-related issues such as virus protection and security zones, see Chapter 24, "Securing Your System, Messages, and Identity."

MHTML

MIME HTML (MHTML) represents MIME encapsulation of HTML documents. MHTML allows you to send and receive Web pages and other HTML-based documents and to embed images directly in the body of a message instead of attaching them to the message. See the preceding sections for an explanation of MIME.

iCalendar, vCalendar, and vCard

iCalendar, vCalendar, and vCard are Internet-based standards that provide a means for people to share calendar information and contact information across the Internet. The iCalendar standard allows calendar and scheduling applications to share free/busy information with other applications that support iCalendar. The vCalendar standard provides a mechanism for vCalendar-compliant applications to exchange meeting requests across the Internet. The vCard standard allows applications to share contact information as Internet vCards (electronic business cards). Outlook 2007 supports these standards to share information and interact with other messaging and scheduling applications across the Internet.

Security Provisions in Outlook

Outlook 2007 provides several features for ensuring the security of your data, messages, and identity. This section presents a brief overview of security features in Outlook 2007 to give you a basic understanding of the issues involved, with references to other locations in the book that offer more detailed information about these topics.

Protection Against Web Beacons

Many spammers (people who send unsolicited e-mail) use *Web beacons* to validate e-mail addresses. The spammers send HTML-based e-mail messages that contain links to external content on a Web site (the Web beacon), and when the recipient's e-mail client displays the remote content, the site validates the e-mail address. The spammer then knows that the address is a valid one and continues to send messages to it.

Chapter 22

Outlook 2007 blocks Web beacons, displaying a red X instead of the external image. You can selectively view blocked content on a per-message basis, or you can configure Outlook 2007 to view all content but control access to HTML content in other ways. You can also turn off Web beacon blocking, if you want, and control external HTML content in other ways.

See **Chapter 24 for an explanation of how to configure HTML message-handling options.**

Attachment and Virus Security

You probably are aware that a virus is malicious code that infects your system and typically causes some type of damage. The action caused by a virus can be as innocuous as displaying a message or as damaging as deleting data from your hard disk. One especially insidious form of virus, called a *worm*, spreads itself automatically, often by mailing itself to every contact in the infected system's address book. Because of the potential damage that can be caused by viruses and worms, it is critically important to guard against malicious code entering your system.

Outlook 2007 offers two levels of attachment security to guard against virus and worm infections: Level 1 and Level 2. Outlook 2007 automatically blocks Level 1 attachments, a category that includes almost 40 file types known to be potentially harmful to your system—for example, .exe and .vbs files. If you receive a Level 1 attachment, Outlook 2007 displays a paper clip icon beside the message but does not allow you to open or save the attachment. If you try to send a Level 1 attachment, Outlook 2007 displays a reminder that other Outlook 2007 users might not be able to receive the attachment and gives you the option of converting it to a different file type (such as a .zip file) before sending it.

If you receive a Level 2 attachment, Outlook 2007 allows you to save the attachment to disk but not open it directly. You can then process the file with your virus checker before opening it.

CAUTION

Your virus scanner is only as good as its definition file. New viruses crop up every day, so it's critical that you have an up-to-date virus definition file and put in place a strategy to ensure that your virus definitions are always current.

If you use Exchange Server to host your mailbox, the Exchange Server administrator can configure Level 1 and Level 2 attachments, adding or removing attachment types for each level. In addition, Outlook 2007 allows all users to control the security-level assignments for attachments.

Macro Viruses

Although viruses were once found almost exclusively in executable files, viruses embedded in documents containing macros have become very common, and Microsoft Office system documents are as subject to them as any other files. However, Outlook 2007 and other Microsoft Office system applications provide a means for you to guard against macro viruses. In Outlook 2007, you can select one of four options for macro security, as shown in Figure 22-22.

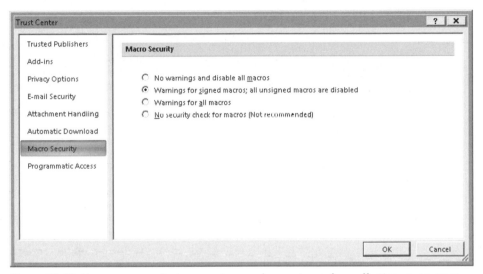

Figure 22-22 Use macro security to prevent macro-borne viruses from affecting your system.

Digital Signatures

Outlook 2007 allows you to add a certificate-based digital signature to a message to validate your identity to the message recipient. Because the signature is derived from a certificate that is issued to you and that you share with the recipient, the recipient can be guaranteed that the message originated with you, rather than with someone trying to impersonate your identity.

For information about how to obtain a certificate and use it to digitally sign your outgoing messages, see "Protecting Messages with Digital Signatures" on page 689.

In addition to signing your outgoing messages, you can also use secure message receipts that notify you that your message has been verified by the recipient's system. The lack of a return receipt indicates that the recipient's system did not validate your identity. In such a case, you can contact the recipient to make sure that he or she has a copy of your digital signature.

Chapter 22

> **Note**
>
> Although you can configure Outlook 2007 to send a digital signature to a recipient, there is no guarantee that the recipient will add the digital signature to his or her contacts list. Until the recipient adds the signature, digitally signed messages are not validated, and the recipient cannot read encrypted messages from you.

Message Encryption

Where the possibility of interception exists (whether someone intercepts your message before it reaches the intended recipient or someone else at the recipient's end tries to read the message), Outlook 2007 message encryption can help you keep prying eyes away from sensitive messages. This feature also relies on your digital signature to encrypt the message and to allow the recipient to decrypt and read the message. Someone who receives the message without first having the appropriate encryption key from your certificate installed on his or her system sees a garbled message.

Security Labels

The security labels feature in Outlook 2007 relies on security policies in Windows 2000 Server and Windows Server 2003 and is supported only on clients running Windows 2000, Windows Server 2003, or Windows XP. Security labels let you add additional security information, such as message sensitivity, to a message header. You can also use security labels to restrict which recipients can open, forward, or send a specific message. Security labels therefore provide a quick indicator of a message's sensitivity and provide control over the actions that others can take with a message.

Understanding Outlook Service Options

If you've been using a version of Outlook earlier than Microsoft Outlook 2002, you're probably familiar with the Outlook 2007 service options. Earlier versions of Outlook supported three service options: No Mail, Internet Mail Only (IMO), and Corporate/Workgroup (C/W). Outlook 2007, like Outlook 2002 and Outlook 2003, uses a *unified mode*. Outlook 2007 unified mode integrates mail services in Outlook 2007, which allows you to configure and use multiple services in a single profile. This means that you can use Exchange Server, POP3, IMAP, and Hotmail accounts all in one profile and at the same time.

Although Outlook 2007 makes a great e-mail client for a wide range of mail services, you might prefer to use only its contact management, scheduling, and other nonmessaging features and to use a different application (such as Outlook Express or Windows Mail) for your messaging needs. There is no downside to using Outlook 2007 in this configuration, although you should keep in mind that certain features, such as integrated scheduling, rely on the Outlook 2007 messaging features. If you need to take advantage of these features, you should use Outlook 2007 as your primary messaging application.

Options for Starting Outlook

Microsoft Office offers several options to control startup, either through command-line switches or other methods. You can choose to have Outlook 2007 open forms, turn off the Reading Pane (previously called the Preview pane), select a profile, and perform other tasks automatically when the program starts. The following sections describe some of the options you can specify.

Normal Startup

When you install Outlook 2007, Setup places a Microsoft Outlook 2007 icon on the Start menu. You can start Outlook 2007 normally by clicking the icon. You also can start Outlook 2007 by using the Programs menu (choose Start, All Programs, Microsoft Office, Microsoft Office Outlook 2007.)

If more than one profile exists, when Outlook 2007 is started normally, it prompts you for the profile to use, as shown in Figure 22-23. The profile contains your account settings and configures Outlook 2007 for your e-mail servers, directory services, data files, and other settings.

Figure 22-23 Outlook 2007 prompts you to choose a profile at startup.

You can use multiple profiles to maintain multiple identities in Outlook 2007. For example, you might use one profile for your work-related items and a second one for your personal items. To use an existing profile, simply select it in the drop-down list in the Choose Profile dialog box and then click OK. Click New to create a new profile. Click Options in the Choose Profile dialog box, shown in Figure 22-23, to display the option Set As Default Profile. Select this option to specify the selected profile as the default profile, which will appear in the drop-down list by default in subsequent Outlook 2007 sessions. For example, if you maintain separate personal and work profiles and your personal profile always appears in the drop-down list, select your work profile and then choose this option to make the work profile the default.

Safe Mode Startup

Safe mode is a startup mode available in Outlook 2007 and the other Microsoft Office system applications. Safe mode makes it possible for Microsoft Office system applications to automatically recover from specific errors during startup, such as a problem with an add-in or a corrupt registry setting. Safe mode allows Outlook 2007 to detect the problem and either correct it or bypass it by isolating the source.

When Outlook 2007 starts automatically in safe mode, you see a dialog box that displays the source of the problem and asks whether you want to continue to start the program, bypassing the problem source, or try to restart the program again. If you direct Outlook 2007 to continue starting, the problem items are disabled, and you can view them in the Disabled Items dialog box, as shown in Figure 22-24. To open this dialog box, choose Help and then click Disabled Items. To enable a disabled item, select the item and then click Enable.

Figure 22-24 Use the Disabled Items dialog box to review and enable items.

In certain situations, you might want to force Outlook 2007 into safe mode when it would otherwise start normally—for example, if you want to prevent add-ins or customized toolbars or command bars from loading. To start Outlook 2007 (or any other Microsoft Office system application) in safe mode, hold down the Ctrl key and start the program. Outlook 2007 detects the Ctrl key and asks whether you want to start Outlook 2007 in safe mode. Click Yes to start in safe mode or No to start normally.

If you start an application in safe mode, you cannot perform certain actions in the application. The following is a summary of these actions (not all of which apply to Outlook 2007):

- Templates can't be saved.

- The last used Web page is not loaded (Microsoft FrontPage).

- Customized toolbars and command bars are not opened. Customizations that you make in safe mode can't be changed.

- The AutoCorrect list isn't loaded, nor can changes you make to AutoCorrect in safe mode be saved.

- Recovered documents are not opened automatically.

- No smart tags are loaded, and new smart tags can't be saved.

- Command-line options other than /a and /n are ignored.

- You can't save files to the Alternate Startup Directory.

- You can't save preferences.

- Additional features and programs (such as add-ins) are not loaded automatically.

To start Outlook 2007 normally, simply shut down the program and start it again without pressing the Ctrl key.

Starting Outlook Automatically

If you're like most Microsoft Office system users, you work in Outlook 2007 a majority of the time. Because Outlook 2007 is such an important aspect of your workday, you probably want it to start automatically when you log on to your computer, saving you the trouble of starting it later. Although you have a few options for starting Outlook 2007 automatically, the best solution is to place a shortcut to Outlook 2007 in your Startup folder.

To start Outlook 2007 automatically when you start Windows, simply drag the Outlook icon from the Start menu or Quick Launch bar to the Startup folder in the Start menu.

Chapter 22

INSIDE OUT   Create a New Outlook 2007 Shortcut

If you don't have an Outlook 2007 icon on the desktop, you can use the Outlook 2007 executable to create a shortcut. Open Windows Explorer, and browse to the folder \Program Files\Microsoft Office\Office12. Create a shortcut to the executable Outlook. exe. Right-click the Outlook.exe file, and then choose Create Shortcut. Windows asks whether you want to create a shortcut on the desktop. Click Yes to create the shortcut.

INSIDE OUT **Change the Outlook 2007 Shortcut Properties**

If you want to change the way Outlook 2007 starts from the shortcut in your Startup folder (for example, you might want to add command switches), you need only change the shortcut's properties. For details, see "Changing the Outlook Shortcut" on the next page.

Adding Outlook to the Quick Launch Bar

The Quick Launch bar appears on the taskbar just to the right of the Start menu. Quick Launch, as its name implies, gives you a way to easily and quickly start applications—just click the application's icon. By default, the Quick Launch bar includes the Show Desktop icon as well as the Internet Explorer icon. Quick Launch offers easier application launching because you don't have to navigate the Start menu to start an application.

Note

If you don't see the Quick Launch bar, right-click the taskbar and verify that Lock The Taskbar is not selected on the shortcut menu. If it is, click Lock The Taskbar to deselect it. Then right-click the taskbar again, and click Toolbars, Quick Launch to add the Quick Launch bar to the taskbar.

Adding a shortcut to the Quick Launch bar is easy:

1. Minimize all windows so that you can see the desktop.

2. Using the right mouse button, drag the Microsoft Outlook icon to the Quick Launch area of the taskbar and then release it. If there is no Outlook shortcut on the desktop, right-drag the shortcut from the Start menu, instead.

3. Click Create Shortcut(s) Here.

Note

You can also left-drag the Microsoft Outlook icon to the Quick Launch bar. Windows informs you that you can't copy or move the item to that location and asks whether you want to create a shortcut instead. Click Yes to create the shortcut or No to cancel.

Changing the Outlook Shortcut

Let's assume that you've created a shortcut to Outlook 2007 on your Quick Launch bar or in another location so that you can start Outlook 2007 quickly. Why change the shortcut? By adding switches to the command that starts Outlook 2007, you can customize the way the application starts and functions for the current session. You can also control the Outlook 2007 startup window state (normal, minimized, maximized) through the shortcut's properties. For example, you might want Outlook 2007 to start automatically when you log on, but you want it to start minimized. In this situation, you would create a shortcut to Outlook 2007 in your Startup folder and then modify the shortcut so that Outlook 2007 starts minimized.

To change the properties for a shortcut, locate the shortcut, right-click its icon, and then choose Properties. You should see a Properties page similar to the one shown in Figure 22-25.

Figure 22-25 A typical Properties page for an Outlook 2007 shortcut.

The following list summarizes the options on the Shortcut tab of the Properties page:

> **Note**
>
> These options have slightly different names depending on which operating system your computer is running. Click Advanced on the Shortcut tab in Windows XP and Windows Vista to view additional settings.

- **Target Type** This read-only property specifies the type for the shortcut's target, which in the example shown in Figure 22-25 is Application.

- **Target Location** This read-only property specifies the directory location of the target executable.

- **Target** This property specifies the command to execute when the shortcut is executed. The default Outlook 2007 command is "C:\Program Files\Microsoft Office\Office12\Outlook.exe" /recycle. The path could vary if you have installed Microsoft Office in a different folder. The path to the executable must be enclosed in quotation marks, and any additional switches must be added to the right, outside the quotation marks. See "Startup Switches" on page 670 to learn about additional switches that you can use to start Outlook 2007.

- **Start In** This property specifies the startup directory for the application.

- **Shortcut Key** Use this property to assign a shortcut key to the shortcut, which allows you to start Outlook 2007 by pressing the key combination. Simply click in the Shortcut Key box, and then press the keystroke to assign it to the shortcut.

- **Run** Use this property to specify the startup window state for Outlook 2007. You can choose Normal Window, Minimized, or Maximized.

- **Comment** Use this property to specify an optional comment. The comment appears in the shortcut's ToolTip when you position the mouse pointer over the shortcut's icon. For example, if you use the Run As Different User option, you might include mention of that in the Comment box to help you distinguish this shortcut from another that launches Outlook 2007 in the default context.

- **Find Target/Open File Location** Click this button to open the folder containing the Outlook.exe executable file.

- **Change Icon** Click this button to change the icon assigned to the shortcut. By default, the icon comes from the Outlook.exe executable, which contains other icons you can assign to the shortcut. You also can use other .ico, .exe, and .dll files to assign icons. You'll find several additional icons in Moricons.dll and Shell32.dll, both located in the %systemroot%\System32 folder.

- **Advanced** Click this button to access the two following options for Windows XP. (These two options are directly available on the Shortcut tab for Windows 2000 users.)

  - **Run In Separate Memory Space** This option is selected by default and can't be changed for Outlook 2007. All 32-bit applications run in a separate memory space. This provides crash protection for other applications and for the operating system.

  - **Run With Different Credentials** Select this option to run Outlook 2007 in a different user context, which lets you start Outlook 2007 with a different user account from the one you used to log on to the computer. Windows prompts you for the user name and password when you execute the shortcut. This option is named Run As A Different User in Windows 2000.

Note

You also can use the RUNAS command from in the Command Prompt window to start an application in a different user context. For additional information, see the following section.

When you're satisfied with the shortcut's properties, click OK to close the Properties dialog box.

Using RUNAS to Change User Context

As explained in the preceding section, you can use the option Run As Different User in a shortcut's Properties page to run the target application in a different user context from the one you used to log on to the system. This option is applicable on systems running Windows 2000 or later.

You can also use the RUNAS command from the Command Prompt window in Windows 2000 or Windows XP to run a command—including Outlook 2007—in a different user context. The syntax for RUNAS is

```
RUNAS [/profile] [/env] [/netonly] / user:<UserName>program
```

The parameters for RUNAS can be summarized as follows:

- **/profile** Use this parameter to indicate the profile for the specified user if that profile needs to be loaded.

- **/env** Use the current user environment instead of the one specified by the user's profile.

- **/netonly** Use this parameter if the specified user credentials are for remote access only.

- **/user:<UserName>** Use this parameter to specify the user account under which you want the application to be run.

- **Program** This parameter specifies the application to execute.

Following is an example of the RUNAS command used to start Outlook 2007 in the Administrator context of the domain ADMIN. (Note that the command should be on one line on your screen.)

```
RUNAS /profile / user:admin\administrator
""C:\Program Files\Microsoft Office
\Office12\Outlook.exe" /recycle"
```

It might seem like a lot of trouble to type all that at the command prompt, and that's usually the case. Although you can use RUNAS from the Command Prompt window to run Outlook 2007 in a specific user context, it's generally more useful to use RUNAS in a batch file to start Outlook 2007 in a given, predetermined user context. For example, you might create a batch file containing the sample RUNAS syntax just noted and then create a shortcut to that batch file so that you can execute it easily without typing the command each time.

Startup Switches

Outlook 2007 supports a number of command-line switches that modify the way the program starts and functions. Although you can issue the Outlook.exe command with switches from a command prompt, it's generally more useful to specify switches through a shortcut, particularly if you want to use the same set of switches more than once. Table 22-1 lists the startup switches that you can use to modify the way Outlook 2007 starts and functions.

For an explanation of how to modify a shortcut to add command-line switches, see "Changing the Outlook Shortcut" on page 667.

Table 22-1 **Startup Switches and Their Uses**

Switch	Use
/a <filename>	Opens a message form with the attachment specified by <filename>
/c ipm.activity	Opens the journal entry form by itself
/c ipm.appointment	Opens the appointment form by itself
/c ipm.contact	Opens the contact form by itself
/c ipm.note	Opens the message form by itself
/c ipm.post	Opens the discussion form by itself
/c ipm.stickynote	Opens the note form by itself
/c ipm.task	Opens the task form by itself

Switch	Use
/c <class>	Creates an item using the message class specified by <class>
/CheckClient	Performs a check to see whether Outlook 2007 is the default application for e-mail, news, and contacts
/CleanFreeBusy	Regenerates free/busy schedule data
/CleanReminders	Regenerates reminders
/CleanSchedPlus	Deletes Schedule+ data from the server and enables free/busy data from the Outlook 2007 calendar to be used by Schedule+ users
/CleanViews	Restores the default Outlook 2007 views
/Folder	Hides the Outlook Bar and folder list if displayed in the previous session
/NoPreview	Hides the Preview pane and removes Preview Pane from the View menu
/Profiles	Displays the Choose Profile dialog box even if Always Use This Profile is selected in the profile options
/Profile <name>	Automatically uses the profile specified by <name>
/Recycle	Starts Outlook 2007 using an existing Outlook 2007 window if available
/ResetFolders	Restores missing folders in the default message store
/ResetOutlookBar	Rebuilds the Outlook Bar
/select <folder>	Displays the folder specified by <folder>

Choosing a Startup View

When you start Outlook 2007, it defaults to using the Inbox view, as shown in Figure 22-26, but you might prefer to use a different view or folder as the initial view. For example, if you use Outlook 2007 primarily for scheduling, you'll probably want Outlook 2007 to start in the Calendar folder. If you use Outlook 2007 mainly to manage contacts, you'll probably want it to start in the Contacts folder.

Chapter 22

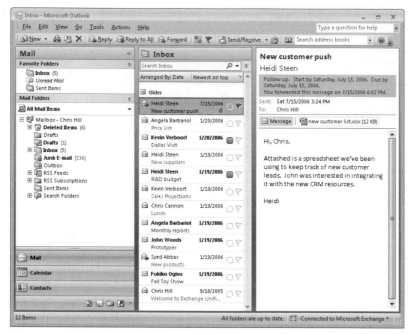

Figure 22-26 Inbox is the default view.

To specify the view that should appear when Outlook 2007 first starts, follow these steps:

1. Start Outlook 2007, and then choose Tools, Options.

2. Click the Other tab, and then click Advanced Options to display the Advanced Options dialog box, as shown Figure 22-27.

3. In the Startup In This Folder drop-down list, select the folder you want Outlook 2007 to open at startup.

4. Click OK, and then close the dialog box.

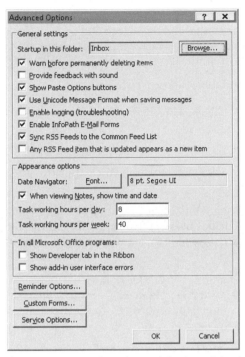

Figure 22-27 Use the Advanced Options dialog box to specify the Startup view.

If you switch Outlook 2007 to a different default folder and then want to restore Outlook Today as your default view, you can follow the preceding steps to restore Outlook Today as the default.

Simply select Outlook Today in the drop-down list or follow these steps with the Outlook Today window open:

1. Start Outlook 2007, and then open Outlook Today view.

2. Click Customize Outlook Today at the top of the Outlook Today window.

3. In the resulting pane, select When Starting Go Directly To Outlook Today, and then click Save Changes.

Creating Shortcuts to Start New Outlook Items

In some cases, you might want icons on the desktop or your Quick Launch bar that start new Outlook 2007 items. For example, perhaps you would like an icon that starts a new e-mail message and another icon that starts a new appointment item.

Sometimes you need to dash off a quick message, but you have to start Outlook 2007, wait for it to load, compose the message, and then close Outlook 2007 when you've finished. You can simplify the task of sending a new e-mail message by creating a shortcut to a mailto: item on the desktop or on the Quick Launch bar by following these steps:

1. Right-click the desktop, and then choose New, Shortcut.

2. In the Create Shortcut dialog box, type **mailto:** as the item to launch, and then click Next.

3. Type New Mail Message as the shortcut name, and then click Finish.

4. Drag the shortcut to the Quick Launch bar to make it quickly accessible without minimizing all applications.

When you double-click the shortcut, Outlook 2007 actually launches and prompts you for a profile unless a default profile has been set. However, only the new message form appears—the rest of Outlook 2007 stays hidden, running in the background.

You can use the Target property of an Outlook 2007 shortcut to create other types of Outlook 2007 items. Refer to "Changing the Outlook Shortcut" on page 667 to learn how to create an Outlook 2007 shortcut. See Table 22-1 for the switches that open specific Outlook 2007 forms. For example, the following two shortcuts start a new message and a new appointment, respectively:

```
"C:\Program Files\Microsoft Office\Office12\Outlook.exe" /c ipm.note
```

```
"C:\Program Files\Microsoft Office\Office12\Outlook.exe" /c ipm.appointment
```

> **Note**
>
> You can use the /a switch to open a new message form with an attachment. The following example starts a new message and attaches the file named Picture.jpg:
>
> ```
> "C:\Program Files\Microsoft Office\Office11\Outlook.exe" /a Picture.jpg
> ```

Finding and Organizing Messages

Without some means of organizing and filtering e-mail, most people would be inundated with messages, many of which are absolutely useless. Fortunately, the Microsoft Office Outlook 2007 junk e-mail filters can take care of most, if not all, of the useless messages. For the rest, you can use several Office Outlook 2007 features to help you organize messages, locate specific messages, and otherwise get control of your Inbox and other folders.

This chapter shows you how to customize your message folder views, which will help you organize your messages. You'll also learn about the Outlook 2007 search folders, which give you a great way to locate messages based on conditions that you specify and to organize messages without adding other folders to your mailbox. This chapter also explains how to use categories and custom views to organize your messages.

Finding and Organizing Messages with Search Folders

The Outlook 2007 search folders are an extremely useful feature for finding and organizing messages. A *search folder* isn't really a folder but rather a special view that functions much like a separate folder. In effect, a search folder is a saved search. You specify conditions for the folder, such as all messages from a specific sender or all messages received in the last day, and Outlook 2007 displays in that search folder view those messages that meet the specified conditions.

In a way, a search folder is like a rule that moves messages to a special folder. However, although the messages seem to exist in the search folder, they continue to reside in their respective folders. For example, a search folder might show all messages in the Inbox and Sent Items folders that were sent by Jim Boyce. Even though these messages appear in the Jim Boyce search folder (for example), they are actually still located in the Inbox and Sent Items folders.

Using Search Folders

It isn't difficult at all to use a search folder. The Folder List includes a Search Folders branch, as shown in Figure 23-1, that lists all of the search folder contents. Simply click a search folder in the Folder List to view the headers for the messages it contains.

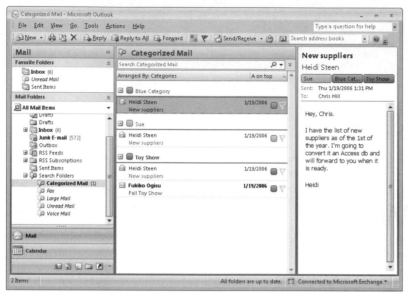

Figure 23-1 Search folders appear under their own branch in the Folder List. This folder shows all messages that are categorized.

Customizing Search Folders

Outlook 2007 includes five search folders by default, which you can use as is or customize to suit your needs:

- **Categorized Mail** This search folder shows all messages that have categories assigned to them.

- **Fax** If you are connected to a Microsoft Exchange Server 2007 mailbox with unified messaging enabled, this search folder will enable you to see all received faxes in your mailbox.

- **Large Mail** This search folder shows all messages that are 100 KB or larger.

- **Unread Mail** This search folder shows all messages that are unread.

- **Voice Mail** If you are connected to an Exchange Server 2007 mailbox with unified messaging enabled, this search folder shows all received voice-mail messages.

In addition, if you have migrated from Microsoft Office Outlook 2003, you might also have these search folders in your mailbox:

- **For Follow Up** This search folder shows all messages that are flagged for follow-up.

- **Important Mail** This search folder shows all messages that are marked as Important.

You can customize these existing search folders as well as those you create yourself. For example, you might increase the value in the Large Mail search folder from 100 KB to 200 KB if you frequently receive messages larger than 100 KB that you don't want included in the Large Mail search folder.

To customize an existing search folder, open the Folder List, right-click the folder, and then choose Customize This Search Folder to open the Customize dialog box, similar to the one shown in Figure 23-2.

Figure 23-2 Set the criteria or folders to include for a search folder in the Customize dialog box.

You can change the name of the search folder in the Name box in the Customize dialog box. To change the criteria for the search folder, click the Criteria button to display a dialog box that enables you to change your selection. The dialog box that appears depends on the criteria you used when you created the folder. For example, if you are modifying a search folder that locates messages from a specific sender, Outlook 2007 displays the Select Names dialog box so that you can specify a different person (or additional people).

> **Note**
>
> You can change the criteria of only two of the default search folders, the Large Mail and Categorized Mail folders. The criteria for the other three can't be changed. However, you can change the folders to be included in the search for all of the default search folders.

To change which folders are included in the search folder, click Browse in the Customize dialog box to open the Select Folder(s) dialog box. Select each folder that you want to include, or select the Personal Folders or Mailbox branch to include all folders in the mail store in the search. Select the Search Subfolders option to include in the search all subfolders for a selected folder. When you have finished selecting folders, click OK, and then click OK again to close the Customize dialog box.

Creating a New Search Folder

If the default search folders don't suit your needs, you can create your own search folder with the criteria and included subfolders that locate the messages you want. To create a search folder, right-click the Search Folders branch, and then choose New Search Folder to open the New Search Folder dialog box, shown in Figure 23-3.

Figure 23-3 Create a new search folder with the New Search Folder dialog box.

The New Search Folder dialog box provides several predefined search folders, and you can easily create a custom search folder by choosing one from the list. If the search folder you select requires specifying additional criteria, click the Choose button to open a dialog box in which you specify the criteria. Then, in the New Search Folder dialog box, select an account in the Search Mail In drop-down list to search that account.

> **Note**
>
> The Choose button appears in the New Search Folder dialog box only if the selected search folder requires additional configuration, such as the sender's name.

If the predefined search folders won't do the trick, scroll to the bottom of the Select A Search Folder list, select Create A Custom Search Folder, and then click Choose to open the Custom Search Folder dialog box to specify a custom criterion for the search folder, a search folder name, and subfolders to include.

Flagging and Monitoring Messages and Contacts

Outlook 2007 allows you to *flag* a message to draw your attention to the message and display an optional reminder when the follow-up action is due. The flag appears in the message header, as shown in Figure 23-4.

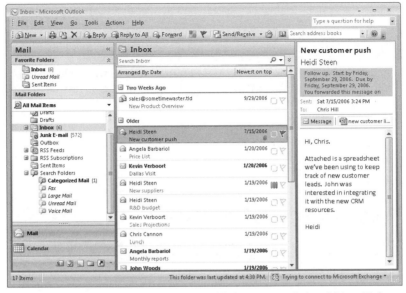

Figure 23-4 You can flag a message to highlight it or to include additional information.

Outlook 2003 offered six flag types, compared with just one in earlier versions. In Outlook 2007, colored flags are replaced by color categories, reducing follow-up flag colors to red and a few shades of pink. You can choose from one of five predefined flags or choose a custom flag. The predefined flags have date specifications of Today, Tomorrow, This Week, Next Week, and No Date. If you choose the custom flag option, you can specify any date you want. The predefined dates therefore give you a quick and easy way to assign a general follow-up date, while the custom option lets you specify a specific date.

Flagging Received and Previously Sent Messages

You can flag messages that you've received from others, as well as those you've sent. This capability gives you a way to flag and follow up messages from your end. You can flag messages in any message folder, including the Sent Items folder.

INSIDE OUT   Add Notes to Received Messages

You can use flags to add notes to messages you receive from others, giving yourself a quick reminder of pending tasks or other pertinent information. Outlook 2007 can generate a reminder for you concerning the flagged item. To set up Outlook 2007 to do so, right-click the message, choose Follow Up, Add Reminder, and then set a due date and time.

Follow these steps to flag a message you have received (or a message that resides in the Sent Items folder):

1. Locate the message you want to flag.

2. Right-click the message, choose Follow Up, and then select a follow-up period from the cascading menu (Today, Tomorrow, and so on), or to specify a custom date, choose Custom.

3. If you chose Custom, enter the follow-up action text in the Flag To field or select an existing action from the drop-down list, and then specify a start date and an end date.

4. Click OK.

Flagging Outgoing Messages

With Outlook 2007, you can flag outgoing messages for follow-up for yourself, the recipient, or both. So, the capability to flag an outgoing message lets you set a reminder on the message to follow up on the message yourself. For example, you might send an e-mail message to a coworker asking for information about a project. The follow-up flag could remind you in a week to follow up if you haven't had a response. You can also flag a message to generate a reminder on the recipient's computer.

Use the following steps to flag a message you send:

1. With the message form open prior to sending the message, on the Message tab on the Ribbon, in the Options Group, click Follow Up, and then click Add Reminder to open the Custom dialog box, shown in Figure 23-5.

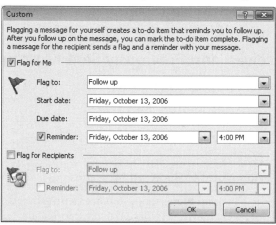

Figure 23-5 Select the flag text or type your own message in the Custom dialog box.

2. In the Flag To drop-down list, select the text you want to include with the flag, or type your own text in this box.

3. If you want to include a due date and a subsequent reminder, select the date in the Due Date drop-down list, which opens a calendar that you can use to select a

date. Alternatively, you can enter a date, day, time, or other information as text in the Due Date box.

4. Click OK, and then send the message as you normally would.

Follow these steps to flag a message for follow-up on the recipient's computer:

1. Open a new message form, and then click Follow Up in the Options group on the Message tab.

2. Choose Flag For Recipients to open the Custom dialog box.

3. Verify that the Flag For Recipients option is checked, and then select the follow-up action in the Flag To drop-down list.

4. Specify a reminder, and then click OK.

5. Complete the message, and then send it.

Viewing and Responding to Flagged Messages

A flag icon appears next to the message header for flagged messages in the message folder. If you have configured Outlook 2007 to display the Reading Pane, the flag text appears in the InfoBar. The flag icons also help you to identify flagged messages regardless of whether the Reading Pane is displayed. You can sort the view in the folder using the Flag column, listing all flagged messages together to make them easier to locate. To view the flag text when the Reading Pane is turned off, simply open the message. The flag text appears in the message form's InfoBar.

Outlook 2007 has no special mechanism for processing flagged messages other than the reminders previously discussed. You simply call, e-mail, or otherwise respond based on the flag message. To change the flag status, simply click the flag, or right-click a flagged message and then choose Flag Complete. To remove the flag from the message, right-click a flagged message, and then choose Clear Flag.

Flagging Contact Items

You can flag contact items as well as messages, marking them for follow-up or adding other notations to an item. For example, you might flag a contact item to remind yourself to call the person by a certain time or date or to send documents to the contact. A flag you add to a contact item shows up in all contacts views, but it isn't always readily apparent—for instance, the flag shows up as text in Address Cards and Detailed Address Cards views, as shown in Figure 23-6. In other views, Outlook 2007 uses a flag icon, as shown in Figure 23-7. As you can for messages, you can use one of the Outlook 2007 predefined flags to mark a contact item, or you can specify your own flag text.

Chapter 23

> **Note**
>
> The flag icon does not appear in Business Cards view. In some of the other views, you can use the Field Chooser to add the Follow Up Flag field to the view.

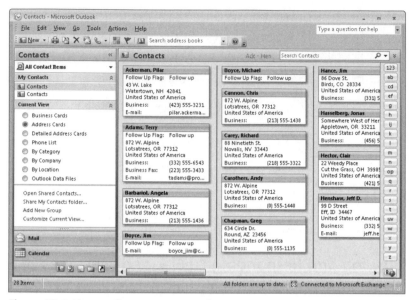

Figure 23-6 You can flag contacts as well as messages.

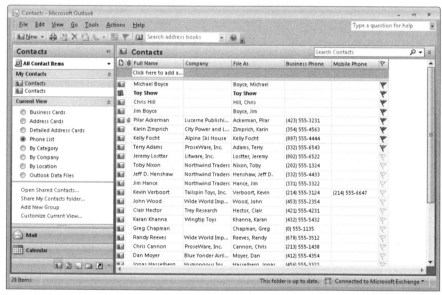

Figure 23-7 You can list items in the Contacts folder by flag.

Flagging a contact is easy—just right-click the contact, choose Follow Up, and then select a follow-up date. To assign a custom flag to a contact item, follow these steps:

1. Right-click the contact item, choose Follow Up, and then choose Custom.

2. In the Custom dialog box, select the flag type in the Flag To drop-down list, or type in your own text.

3. Specify the due date and time.

4. If desired, add a reminder, and then click OK.

Outlook 2007 uses the same icons for flagged contact items as it does for messages. A red flag icon indicates a pending action, and a check mark indicates a completed action. To change the flag status for a contact item, right-click the item, and then choose Mark Complete or Clear Flag.

Grouping Messages by Customizing the Folder View

To help you organize information, Outlook 2007 allows you to customize various message folder views. By default, Outlook 2007 displays only a small selection of columns for messages, including the From, Subject, Received, Size, Flag, Attachment, and Importance columns.

 For details on how to add and remove columns from a folder view to show more or less information about your messages, see "Working with the Standard Outlook Views" in "Working in and Configuring Outlook," one of the bonus chapters available on the companion CD.

You can easily sort messages using any of the column headers as your sort criterion. To view messages sorted alphabetically by sender, for example, click the column header of the From column. To sort messages by date received, click the column header of the Received column. Click the Attachment column header to view all messages with attachments.

In addition to managing your message view by controlling columns and sorting, you can *group* messages based on columns. Whereas sorting allows you to arrange messages in order using a single column as the sort criterion, grouping allows you to display the messages in groups based on one or more columns. For example, you might group messages based on sender, and then on date received, and finally on whether they have attachments. This method helps you locate messages more quickly than if you had to search through a message list sorted only by sender.

Grouping messages in a message folder is a relatively simple process:

1. In Outlook 2007, open the folder you want to organize.

2. Right-click the column header, and then choose Group By This Field if you want to group based only on the selected field. Choose Group By Box if you want to group based on multiple columns.

Filtering a View Using Categories

The addition of color categories in Outlook 2007 makes it very easy to identify specific messages or types of messages. For example, you might categorize messages you receive from specific people so that you can see at a glance that a message is from a particular person.

In some situations, you might want to customize a view so that you see only messages that have certain categories. For example, assume that you have categorized messages for two projects, each with a unique category. Now you want to view all messages from both projects. The easiest way to do that is to filter the view so that it shows only messages with those two categories assigned to them. You can do that using a custom view or a search folder.

Managing E-Mail Effectively

Before we offer tips on effective e-mail management, let's ask the question, "Why bother?" If you receive a large number of messages, the answer is probably staring you in the face—a chaotic Inbox full of messages. With a little bit of planning and effort, you can turn that Inbox into...well...an empty Inbox! When you leave the office at the end of the day with an empty Inbox, you'll be amazed at the sense of accomplishment you'll feel.

Here are some tips to help you get control of your mailbox:

- **Categorize, categorize, categorize.** Categorizing your messages offers several benefits. First, with the introduction of color categories in Outlook 2007, assigning categories to messages will help you quickly identify specific types of messages. Second, you'll be able to search for messages by category with filtered views, search folders, and the search features built into Outlook 2007. You can assign categories manually or assign them automatically with rules. Whatever the case, the more diligent you are in assigning categories, the more useful they will be for finding messages and organizing your mailbox.

- **Organize with folders.** Although you could simply leave all messages in the Inbox, moving messages into other folders will unclutter your Inbox and help you locate messages when you need them. There is no right or wrong way to structure your message folders—use whatever structure and number of folders suits the way you work. What is important is that you organize in a way that suits you.

- **Organize with rules.** Use rules to move messages into other folders, assign categories, and otherwise process messages when they arrive in your Inbox. Rules enable you to organize your messages automatically, potentially saving you an enormous amount of time.

- **Let search folders organize for you.** Search folders are an extremely useful feature in Outlook 2007. With a search folder, you can organize messages based on almost any criteria without actually moving the messages from their current locations. Search folders take very little effort to set up and offer you the benefit of being able to search your entire mailbox for messages that fit the search criteria. You can bring together in one virtual folder all messages in your mail store that fit the search criteria.

Microsoft Office Outlook 2007 includes features that can help protect your system from computer viruses and malicious programs, prevent others from using e-mail to impersonate you, and prevent the interception of sensitive messages. Some of these features—such as the ability to block specific types of attachments—were first introduced in Office Outlook 2002. Other security features—such as the ability to block external images in HTML-based messages—were introduced in Office Outlook 2003. This feature enables Outlook to block HTML messages sent by spammers to identify valid recipient addresses. These messaging security features are extended and enhanced in Office Outlook 2007.

This chapter begins with a look at the settings you can use to control HTML content. Because HTML messages can contain malicious scripts or even HTML code that can easily affect your system, the capability to handle these messages in Outlook 2007 is extremely important.

This chapter also discusses the use of both digital signatures and encryption. You can use a digital signature to authenticate your messages, proving to the recipient that a message indeed came from you, not from someone trying to impersonate you. Outlook 2007 enables you to encrypt outgoing messages to prevent them from being intercepted by unintended recipients; you can also read encrypted messages sent to you by others. In this chapter, you'll learn how to obtain and install certificates to send encrypted messages and how to share keys with others so that you can exchange encrypted messages.

Configuring HTML Message Handling

Spammers are always looking for new methods to identify valid e-mail addresses. Knowing that a given address actually reaches someone is one step in helping spammers maintain their lists. If a particular address doesn't generate a response in some way, it's more likely to be removed from the list.

One way spammers identify valid addresses is through the use of *Web beacons*. Spammers often send HTML messages that contain links to external content, such as pictures or sound clips. When you display the message, your mail program retrieves the remote data to display it, and the remote server then validates your address. These external elements are the Web beacons.

> **Note**
>
> Nonspammers also frequently include external content in messages to reduce the size of the message. So external content isn't a bad thing per se (depending on how it is used).

Since Outlook 2003, Outlook blocks external content from HTML messages by default, displaying a red X in the place of the missing content. The result is that these Web beacons no longer work because the external content is not accessed when the message is displayed. Messages that fit criteria for the Safe Recipients and Safe Senders lists are treated as exceptions—the external content for these messages is not blocked.

> **Note**
>
> You can rest the mouse pointer on a blocked image to view the descriptive alternate text (if any) for the image.

When you preview an image in the Reading Pane for which Outlook 2007 has blocked external content, Outlook 2007 displays a message in the InfoBar, indicating that the blocking occurred (see Figure 24-1). You can click the InfoBar and choose Download Pictures to view the external content. Outlook 2007 then downloads and displays the content in the Reading Pane. The same is true if you open a message; Outlook 2007 displays a warning message, telling you that the content was blocked (see Figure 24-2). You can click the warning message and choose Download Pictures to download and view the content. Outlook 2007's blocking of external content for messages in this way lets you take advantage of content blocking without using the Reading Pane.

If you edit, forward, or reply to a message containing blocked content (from an open message or a message displayed in the Reading Pane), Outlook 2007 displays a warning dialog box indicating that the external content will be downloaded if you continue. You can click OK to download the content and continue with the reply or forward, click No to tell Outlook 2007 to forward the content as text without downloading the content, or click Cancel to not open the message or download the content (see Figure 24-3). Thus, you can now reply to or forward a message without downloading the external content (which wasn't possible with previous versions of Outlook).

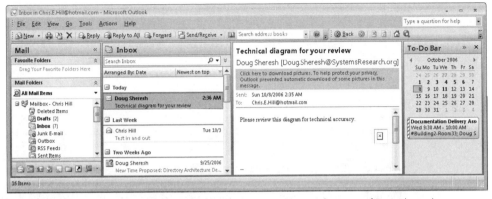

Figure 24-1 Click the InfoBar in the Reading Pane to view external content for a selected message.

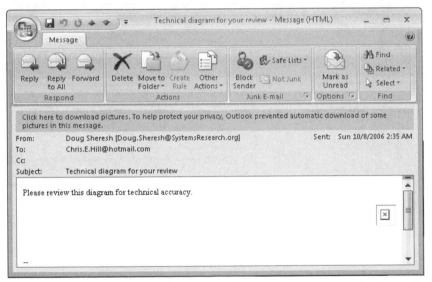

Figure 24-2 You can access blocked content when you open a message by clicking the InfoBar and selecting Download Pictures.

Figure 24-3 You can now forward or reply to a message with blocked content without downloading the content.

Outlook 2007 provides a few options to control the way content blocking works. To configure these options, choose Tools, Trust Center, and then click the Automatic Download page. Figure 24-4 shows the resulting Automatic Download settings page.

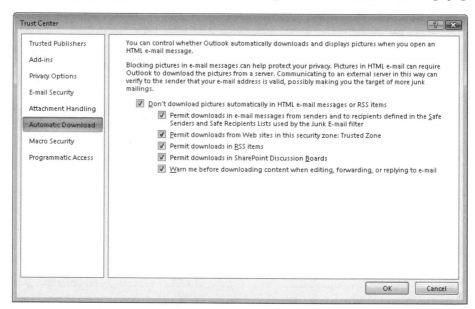

Figure 24-4 Configure content blocking with the Automatic Download settings page.

Configure content blocking using the following options:

- **Don't Download Pictures Automatically In HTML E-Mail Messages Or RSS Items** Select this check box to allow Outlook 2007 to block external picture content with the exception of messages that fit the Safe Senders and Safe Recipients lists. When selected, this check box enables the five check boxes below it to further refine content blocking.

- **Permit Downloads In E-Mail Messages From Senders And To Recipients Defined In The Safe Senders And Safe Recipients List Used By The Junk E-Mail Filter** Select this check box to allow Outlook to download content if the message is from a sender in your Safe Senders list or is addressed to a recipient in your Safe Recipients list.

- **Permit Downloads From Web Sites In This Security Zone: Trusted Zone** Select this check box to allow external content from sites in Microsoft Windows Security Center/Internet Explorer Trusted Sites zone.

- **Permit Downloads In RSS Items** Select this check box to allow external content included in RSS feeds.

- **Permit Downloads In SharePoint Discussion Boards** Select this check box to allow external content included in SharePoint Discussion Boards.

- **Warn Me Before Downloading Content When Editing, Forwarding, Or Replying To E-Mail** Select this check box to receive a warning about external content when you edit, reply to, or forward a message for which external content has been blocked.

To take advantage of the exceptions for external content, you must add the message's originating address to the Safe Senders list, add the recipient address to the Safe Recipients list, or add the remote domain to the Trusted Sites zone in Internet Options (in the Windows Security Center).

Protecting Messages with Digital Signatures

Outlook 2007 supports the use of *digital signatures* to sign messages and validate their authenticity. For example, you can digitally sign a sensitive message so that the recipient can know with relative certainty that the message came from you and that no one is impersonating you by using your e-mail address. This section of the chapter explains digital certificates and signatures and how to use them in Outlook 2007.

Understanding Digital Certificates and Signatures

A *digital certificate* is the mechanism that makes digital signatures possible. Depending on its assigned purpose, you can use a digital certificate for a variety of tasks, including the following:

- Verifying your identity as the sender of an e-mail message

- Encrypting data communications between computers—between a client and a server, for example

- Encrypting e-mail messages to prevent easy interception

- Signing drivers and executable files to authenticate their origin

A digital certificate binds the identity of the certificate's owner to a pair of keys, one public and one private. At a minimum, a certificate contains the following information:

- The owner's public key
- The owner's name or alias
- A certificate expiration date
- A certificate serial number
- The name of the certificate issuer
- The digital signature of the issuer

The certificate can also include other identifying information, such as the owner's e-mail address, postal address, country, or gender.

The two keys are the aspect of the certificate that enables authentication and encryption. The private key resides on your computer and is a large unique number. The certificate contains the public key, which you must give to recipients to whom you want to send authenticated or encrypted messages.

Think of it as having a "read content key" and a "create content key:" one key (the private key) lets you create encrypted content, and the other key (the public key) lets others read the content encrypted with the first key.

Outlook 2007 uses slightly different methods for authenticating messages with digital signatures and for encrypting messages, as you'll see later in the chapter. Before you begin either task, however, you must first obtain a certificate.

Obtaining a Digital Certificate

Digital certificates are issued by certificate authorities (CAs). In most cases, you obtain your e-mail certificate from a public CA such as VeriSign or Thawte. However, systems based on Windows servers running Certificate Services can function as CAs, providing certificates to clients who request them. Check with your system administrator to determine whether your enterprise includes a CA. If it doesn't, you need to obtain your certificate from a public CA, usually at a minimal cost. Certificates are typically good for one year and must be renewed at the end of that period.

If you need to obtain your certificate from a public CA, point your Web browser to the CA Web site, such as *www.verisign.com* or *www.thawte.com*. Follow the instructions provided by the site to obtain a certificate for signing and encrypting your e-mail (see Figure 24-5, for example). The certificate might not be issued immediately; instead, the CA might send you an e-mail message containing a URL that links to a page where you can retrieve the certificate. When you connect to that page, the CA installs the certificate on your system.

> **Note**
>
> Alternatively, in Tools, Trust Center, click E-Mail Security, and then click on Get A Digital ID to display a page from the Microsoft Web site that includes links to several certificate authorities. Select a vendor under Available Digital IDs (such as Verisign) and click the link to its Web site to obtain a certificate.

Figure 24-5 You can use the Web to request a digital certificate from a public CA.

If you're obtaining a certificate from a CA on your network, the method you use depends on whether the network includes an enterprise CA or a stand-alone CA.

If you're using Windows Vista as a domain client on a network with an enterprise CA, follow these steps to request a certificate:

1. Select the Windows button; in the Start Search box, type **MMC**. Click OK.

2. In the Microsoft Management Console (MMC), choose File, Add/Remove Snap-In.

3. In the Add Standalone Snap-In dialog box, select Certificates, and then click Add.

4. In the Certificates Snap-In dialog box, select My User Account, and then click Finish.

5. Click OK to return to the MMC.

6. Expand the Certificates–Current User branch.

7. Expand the Personal branch, right-click Certificates, and choose All Tasks, Request New Certificate. You can also right-click the Personal branch and choose All Tasks, Request New Certificate.

8. Follow the prompts provided by the Certificate Request Wizard and the enterprise CA to request your certificate. The certificate should install automatically.

To request a certificate from a stand-alone CA on your network (or if your computer is part of a workgroup), point your Web browser to *http://<server>/certsrv*, where <server> is the name or IP address of the CA. The CA provides a Web page with a form that you must fill out to request the certificate (see Figure 24-6). Follow the CA prompts to request and obtain the certificate. The site includes a link that you can click to install the certificate.

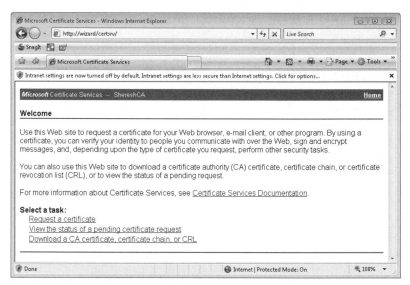

Figure 24-6 A Windows-based CA presents a Web form that you can use to request a certificate.

Copying a Certificate to Another Computer

You can copy your certificate from one computer to another, which means that you can use it on more than one system. The process is simple: you first export (back up) your certificate to a file, and then import the certificate into the other system. The following sections explain how to export and import certificates.

> **Note**
>
> As you use the Certificate Import Wizard and the Certificate Export Wizard (discussed in the following sections), you might discover that they don't precisely match the descriptions presented here. Their appearance and operation might vary slightly, depending on the operating system you're running and the version of Microsoft Internet Explorer you're using.

Backing Up Your Certificate

Whether you obtained your certificate from a public CA or from a CA on your network, you should back it up in case your system suffers a drive failure or if the certificate is lost or corrupted. You also should have a backup of the certificate so that you can export it to any other computers you use on a regular basis, such as a notebook computer or your home computer. In short, you need the certificate on every computer from which you plan to digitally sign or encrypt messages. To back up your certificate, you can use Outlook 2007, Internet Explorer, or the Certificates console (available in Microsoft Windows 2000, Microsoft Windows XP, and Windows Vista). Each method offers the same capabilities; you can use any one of the three.

Follow these steps to use Outlook 2007 to back up your certificate to a file:

1. In Outlook 2007, choose Tools, Trust Center, and then click the E-Mail Security page.

2. Click Import/Export to display the Import/Export Digital ID dialog box, shown in Figure 24-7.

3. Select the Export Your Digital ID To A File option. Click Select, choose the certificate to be exported, and click OK.

4. Click Browse and specify the path and file name for the certificate file.

5. Optionally, you can enter and confirm a password (using a password is a good idea because you are also exporting your private key).

6. If you plan to use the certificate on a system with Internet Explorer 4, select the Microsoft Internet Explorer 4.0 Compatible (Low-Security) check box. If you use Internet Explorer 5 or later, clear this check box.

7. If you want to remove this Digital ID from this computer, select the check box next to Delete Digital ID From System.

8. Click OK to export the file. The Exporting Your Private Exchange Key dialog box is displayed. Click OK to complete the export process.

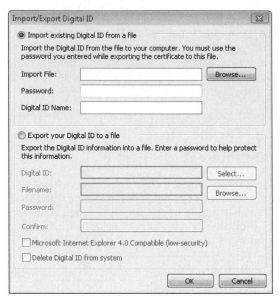

Figure 24-7 You can export certificates in the Import/Export Digital ID dialog box.

If you want to use either Internet Explorer or the Certificates console to back up a certificate, use the Certificate Export Wizard, as follows:

1. If you're using Internet Explorer, begin by choosing Tools, Internet Options. Click the Content tab, and then click Certificates. In the Certificates dialog box, shown in Figure 24-8, select the certificate you want to back up and click Export to start the wizard. If you're using the Certificates console, begin by opening the console and expanding Certificates–Current User/Personal/Certificates. Right-click the certificate to export, and then choose All Tasks, Export to start the wizard.

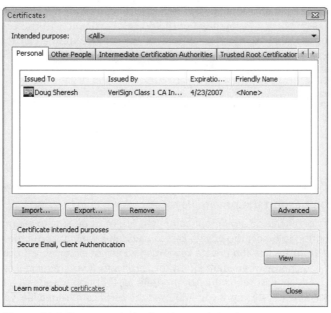

Figure 24-8 You can use the Certificates dialog box to export a certificate.

2. In the Certificate Export Wizard, click Next.

3. On the wizard page shown in Figure 24-9, select Yes, Export The Private Key; then click Next.

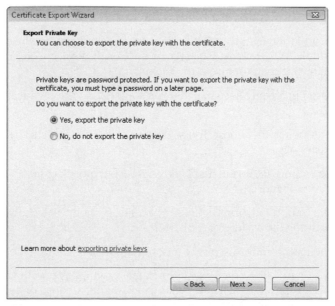

Figure 24-9 This wizard enables you to export the private key.

4. Select Personal Information Exchange; if other options are selected, clear them unless needed. (If you need to include all certificates in the certification path, remove the private key on export, or export all extended properties, and then select that option.) Click Next.

5. Specify and confirm a password to protect the private key and click Next.

6. Specify a path and file name for the certificate and click Next.

7. Review your selections and click Finish.

TROUBLESHOOTING

You can't export the private key.

To use a certificate on a different computer, you must be able to export the private key. If the option to export the private key is unavailable when you run the Certificate Export Wizard, it means that the private key is marked as not exportable. Exportability is an option you choose when you request the certificate. If you request a certificate through a local CA, you must select the Advanced Request option to request a certificate with an exportable private key. If you imported the certificate from a file, you might not have selected the option to make the private key exportable during the import. If you still have the original certificate file, you can import it again—this time selecting the option that will enable you to export the private key.

Installing Your Certificate from a Backup

You can install (or reinstall) a certificate from a backup copy of the certificate file by using Outlook 2007, Internet Explorer, or the Certificates console. You must import the certificate to your computer from the backup file.

The following procedure assumes that you're installing the certificate using Outlook 2007:

1. In Outlook 2007, choose Tools, Trust Center, and then click the E-Mail Security page.

2. Click Import/Export to display the Import/Export Digital ID dialog box, shown earlier in Figure 24-7.

3. In the Import Existing DigitalID From File section, click Browse to locate the file containing the backup of the certificate.

4. In the Password box, type the password associated with the certificate file.

5. In the Digital ID Name box, type a name by which you want the certificate to be shown. Typically, you'll enter your name, mailbox name, or e-mail address, but you can enter anything you want.

6. Click OK to import the certificate.

You can also import a certificate to your computer from a backup file using either Internet Explorer or the Certificates console, as explained here:

1. If you're using Internet Explorer, begin by choosing Tools, Internet Options. Click the Content tab, click Certificates, and then click Import to start the Certificate Import Wizard. If you're using the Certificates console, begin by opening the console. Right-click Certificates–Current User/Personal, and then click All Tasks, Import to start the wizard.

2. In the Certificate Import Wizard, click Next.

3. Browse and select the file to import, and then click Open. (If you don't see your certificate file, check the type of certificates shown in the Open dialog box by clicking the drop-down list to the right of the file name field.) After your certificate is selected in the File To Import dialog box, click Next.

4. If the certificate was stored with a password, you are prompted to enter the password. Provide the associated password and click Next.

5. Select the Automatically Select The Certificate Store Based On The Type Of Certificate option and click Next.

6. Click Finish.

Signing Messages

Now that you have a certificate on your system, you're ready to start digitally signing your outgoing messages so that recipients can verify your identity. When you send a digitally signed message, Outlook 2007 sends the original message and an encrypted copy of the message with your digital signature. The recipient's e-mail application compares the two versions of the message to determine whether they are the same. If they are, no one has tampered with the message. The digital signature also enables the recipient to verify that the message is from you.

> **Note**
> Because signing your e-mail requires Outlook 2007 to send two copies of the message (the unencrypted message and the encrypted copy), the signed e-mail message is larger.

Understanding S/MIME and Clear-Text Options

Secure/Multipurpose Internet Mail Extensions (S/MIME), an Internet standard, is the mechanism in Outlook 2007 that enables you to digitally sign and encrypt messages. The e-mail client handles the encryption and decryption required for both functions.

Users with e-mail clients that don't support S/MIME can't read digitally signed messages unless you send the message as clear text (unencrypted). Without S/MIME support, the recipient is also unable to verify the authenticity of the message or verify that the message hasn't been altered. Without S/MIME, then, digital signatures are relatively useless. However, Outlook 2007 does offer you the option of sending a digitally signed message as clear text to recipients who lack S/MIME support. If you need to send the same digitally signed message to multiple recipients—some of whom have S/MIME-capable e-mail clients and some of whom do not—digitally signing the message allows those with S/MIME support to authenticate it, and including the clear-text message allows the others to at least read it.

The following section explains how to send a digitally signed message, including how to send the message in clear text for those recipients who require it.

Adding Your Digital Signature

Follow these steps to digitally sign an outgoing message:

1. Compose the message in Outlook 2007.

2. On the Message tab in the Options group, click the Message Options Dialog Box Launcher (in the lower-right corner) to open the Message Options dialog box.

3. Click Security Settings to open the Security Properties dialog box, as shown in Figure 24-10.

Figure 24-10 You can add a digital signature using the Security Properties dialog box.

4. Select Add Digital Signature To This Message, and then select other check boxes as indicated here:

    - **Send This Message As Clear Text Signed** Select this check box to include a clear-text copy of the message for recipients who don't have S/MIME-capable e-mail applications. Clear this check box to prevent the message from being read by mail clients that don't support S/MIME.

- **Request S/MIME Receipt For This Message** Select this check box to request a secure receipt to verify that the recipient has validated your digital signature. When the message has been received and saved, and your signature is verified (even if the recipient doesn't read the message), you receive a return receipt. No receipt is sent if your signature is not verified.

5. If necessary, select security settings in the Security Setting drop-down list. (If you have not yet configured your security options, you can do so by clicking Change Settings.)

For details on security option configuration, see "Creating and Using Security Profiles" on the next page.

6. Click OK to add the digital signature to the message.

> Note
>
> If you send a lot of digitally signed messages, you'll want to configure your security options to include a digital signature by default; see the following section for details. In addition, you might want to add a button to the toolbar to let you quickly sign the message without using a dialog box.

For details about how to add such a button to the toolbar, see "You Need a Faster Way to Digitally Sign a Message" on page 703.

Setting Global Security Options

To save time, you can configure your security settings to apply globally to all messages, changing settings only as needed for certain messages. In Outlook 2007, choose Tools, Trust Center, and then click E-Mail Security. On the E-Mail Security page, shown in Figure 24-11, you can set security options using the following list as a guide.

- **Encrypt Contents And Attachments For Outgoing Messages** If most of the messages you send need to be encrypted, select this check box to encrypt all outgoing messages by default. You can override encryption for a specific message by changing the message's properties when you compose it. Clear this check box if the majority of your outgoing messages do not need to be encrypted.

For information about encryption, see "Encrypting Messages" on page 714.

- **Add Digital Signature To Outgoing Messages** If most of your messages need to be signed, select this check box to digitally sign all outgoing messages by default. Clear this check box if most of your messages do not need to be signed; you will be able to digitally sign specific messages as needed when you compose them.

- **Send Clear Text Signed Message When Sending Signed Messages** If you need to send digitally signed messages to recipients who do not have S/MIME capability, select this check box to send clear-text digitally signed messages by default. You can override this option for individual messages when you compose them. In most cases, you can clear this check box because most e-mail clients support S/MIME.

- **Request S/MIME Receipt For All S/MIME-Signed Messages** Select this check box to request a secure receipt for all S/MIME messages by default. You can override the setting for individual messages when you compose them. A secure receipt indicates that your message has been received and the signature verified. No receipt is returned if the signature is not verified.

- **Settings** Click Settings to configure more-advanced security settings and create additional security setting groups. For details, see the following section, "Creating and Using Security Profiles."

- **Publish To GAL** Click this button to publish your certificates to the Global Address List (GAL), making them available to other Exchange Server users in your organization who might need to send you encrypted messages. This is an alternative to sending the other users a copy of your certificate.

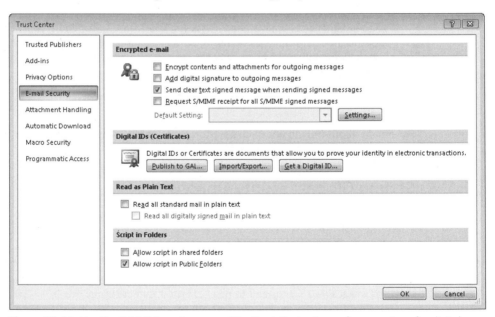

Figure 24-11 Use the E-Mail Security page of the Trust Center to configure options for digital signing and encryption.

Creating and Using Security Profiles

Although in most cases you need only one set of Outlook 2007 security settings, you can create and use multiple security profiles. For example, you might send most of your secure messages to other Exchange Server users and only occasionally send secure messages to Internet recipients. In that situation, you might maintain two sets of security settings: one that uses Exchange Server security and another that uses S/MIME, each with different certificates and hash algorithms (the method used to secure the data).

You can configure security profiles using the Change Security Settings dialog box, which you access through the Settings button on the E-Mail Security page of the Trust Center dialog box. One of your security profiles acts as the default, but you can select a different security profile any time it's needed.

Follow these steps to create and manage your security profiles:

1. In Outlook 2007, choose Tools, Trust Center, and then click the E-Mail Security page.

2. Click Settings to display the Change Security Settings dialog box, shown in Figure 24-12. Set the options described in the following section as needed. If you are creating a new set of settings, start by clicking New prior to changing settings because selecting New clears all other setting values.

   - **Security Settings Name** Specify the name for the security profile that should appear in the Default Setting drop-down list on the Security tab.

   - **Cryptographic Format** In this drop-down list, select the secure message format for your messages. The default is S/MIME, but you also can select Exchange Server Security. Use S/MIME if you're sending secure messages to Internet recipients. You can use either S/MIME or Exchange Server Security when sending secure messages to recipients on your Exchange Server.

   - **Default Security Setting For This Cryptographic Message Format** Select this check box to make the specified security settings the default settings for the message format you selected in the Cryptography Format drop-down list.

   - **Default Security Setting For All Cryptographic Messages** Select this check box to make the specified security settings the default settings for all secure messages for both S/MIME and Exchange Server security.

   - **Security Labels** Click to configure security labels, which display security information about a specific message and restrict which recipients can open, forward, or send that message. Security labels rely on security policies implemented in Windows 2000 or later.

   - **New** Click to create a new set of security settings.

   - **Delete** Click to delete the currently selected group of security settings.

   - **Password** Click to specify or change the password associated with the security settings.

   - **Signing Certificate** This read-only information indicates the certificate being used to digitally sign your outgoing messages. Click Choose if you want to choose a different certificate. Once you choose a signing certificate, all the fields in the Certificates and Algorithms are automatically populated.

Chapter 24

You assign the default signing and encryption certificates through Outlook 2007's global security settings; for information, see "Setting Global Security Options" on page 699.

- **Hash Algorithm** Use this drop-down list to change the hash algorithm used to encrypt messages. Hash algorithm options include MD5, SHA1, SHA256, SHA384, and SHA512. For more information on these hashing algorithms, see the following article: "The .Net Developers Guide Cryptography Overview" *(http://windowssdk.msdn.microsoft.com/en-us/library/92f9ye3s.aspx.)*

- **Encryption Certificate** This read-only information indicates the certificate being used to encrypt your outgoing messages. Click Choose if you want to specify a different certificate.

- **Encryption Algorithm** Use this drop-down list to change the encryption algorithm used to encrypt messages. The encryption algorithm is the mathematical method used to encrypt the data.

- **Send These Certificates With Signed Messages** Select this check box to include your certificate with outgoing messages. Doing so allows recipients to send encrypted messages to you.

Figure 24-12 Configure your security profiles in the Change Security Settings dialog box.

3. Click OK to close the Change Security Settings dialog box.

4. In the Default Setting drop-down list on the E-Mail Security page, select the security profile you want to use by default and then click OK.

INSIDE OUT   You Need a Faster Way to Digitally Sign a Message

If you don't send a lot of digitally signed messages, you might not mind the steps for getting to the Security Properties dialog box to sign a message you compose. However, if you frequently send digitally signed messages, but don't want to configure Outlook 2007 to sign all messages by default, all the clicking involved in signing the message can be onerous. To digitally sign your messages faster, consider adding a toolbar button that lets you toggle a digital signature with a single click by following these steps:

1. Open the Inbox folder in Outlook 2007.

2. Click New to display the message form for a new message.

3. In the message form, choose the Customize Quick Access Toolbar drop-down list (at the end of the Quick Access Toolbar) and click More Commands.

4. In the Choose Commands From drop-down list, select All Commands.

5. In the All Commands list, shown in Figure 24-13, select Digitally Sign Message and click Add, then OK to close the dialog box. The Digitally Sign Message icon will be added to the end of the Quick Access Toolbar. If you later want to switch security profiles, you can select the profile you want to use in the Default Setting drop-down list on the E-Mail Security page in the Trust Center dialog box.

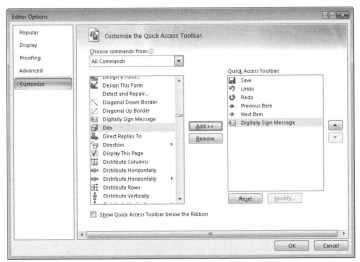

Figure 24-13 Use the Customize The Quick Access Toolbar to add the Digitally Sign Message command to the toolbar.

The Digitally Sign Message and Encrypt icons are also added to the Options group on the Message tab when you add a DigitalID to Outlook 2007. Click Close and then close the message form.

Now whenever you need to digitally sign or encrypt a message, you can click the appropriate button on the Quick Access Toolbar or in the Options group on the Ribbon when you compose the message. Outlook 2007 displays an outline around the button to indicate that the command has been selected, so you can tell at a glance whether the message will be signed, encrypted, or both.

Chapter 24

Reading Signed Messages

When you receive a digitally signed message, the Inbox displays a Secure Message icon in place of the standard envelope icon (see Figure 24-14) and shows a Signature button in the Reading Pane. The message form also includes a Signature button (see Figure 24-15). You can click the Signature button in either the Reading Pane or the form to display information about the certificate.

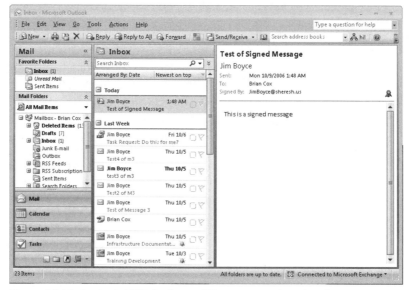

Figure 24-14 Outlook 2007 displays a different icon in the Inbox for secure messages.

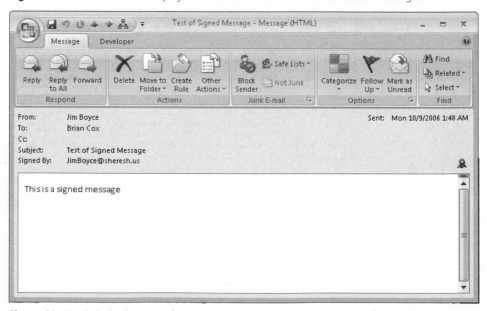

Figure 24-15 Click the Signature button on the message form to view certificate information.

Because Outlook 2007 supports S/MIME, you can view and read a digitally signed message without taking any special action. How Outlook 2007 treats the message, however, depends on the trust relationship of the associated certificate. If the certificate is not explicitly distrusted, Outlook 2007 displays the message in the Reading Pane. If the certificate is explicitly not trusted, you'll see only an error message in the Reading Pane header, as shown in Figure 24-16. When you open the message, you are alerted that there's a problem with the sender's certificate and the text of the message is not displayed. Outlook 2007 displays a dialog box that notes the error when you open the message (see Figure 24-17).

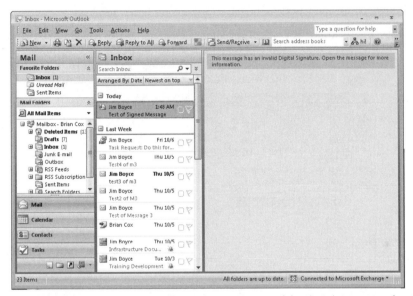

Figure 24-16 Outlook 2007 displays an error message if the digital signature of an incoming message is not trusted.

Figure 24-17 Outlook 2007 warns you when you open a message that has a certificate problem.

There is no danger in opening a message with an invalid certificate. However, you should verify that the message really came from the person listed as the sender and is not a forged message.

Changing Certificate Trust Relationships

To have Outlook 2007 authenticate a signed message and treat it as being from a trusted sender, you must add the certificate to your list of trusted certificates. An alternative is to configure Outlook 2007 to inherit trust for a certificate from the certificate's issuer. For example, assume that you have a CA in your enterprise. Instead of configuring each sender's certificate to be trusted explicitly, you can configure Outlook 2007 to inherit trust from the issuing CA—in other words, Outlook 2007 will implicitly trust all certificates issued by that CA.

Follow these steps to configure the trust relationship for a certificate:

1. In Outlook 2007, select the signed message. If the Reading Pane displays an error message, or if you aren't using the Reading Pane, open the message and click the Secure Message button to view the Message Security Properties dialog box (see Figure 24-18). Otherwise, click the Secure Message button in the Reading Pane.

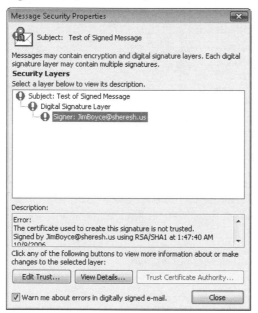

Figure 24-18 Use the Message Security Properties dialog box to view status and properties of the certificate.

2. Click Details, and in the Message Security Properties dialog box, click the Signer line, and then click Edit Trust to display the Trust tab of the View Certificate dialog box, as shown in Figure 24-19.

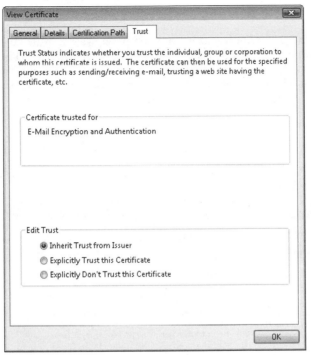

Figure 24-19 Use the Trust tab to configure the trust relationship for the certificate.

3. Select one of the following options:

- **Inherit Trust From Issuer** Select this option to inherit the trust relationship from the issuing CA. For detailed information, see the following section, "Configuring CA Trust."

- **Explicitly Trust This Certificate** Select this option to explicitly trust the certificate associated with the message if you are certain of the authenticity of the message and the validity of the sender's certificate.

- **Explicitly Don't Trust This Certificate** Select this option to explicitly distrust the certificate associated with the message. Any other messages that you receive with the same certificate will generate an error message in Outlook 2007 when you attempt to view them.

4. Click OK, click Close to close the Message Security Properties dialog box, and click Close again to close the Digital Signature dialog box.

For information on viewing a certificate's other properties and configuring Outlook 2007 to validate certificates, see "Viewing and Validating a Digital Signature" on page 711.

Configuring CA Trust

Although you might not realize it, your computer system by default includes certificates from several public CAs (typically VeriSign, Thawte, Equifax, GTE, or several others), which were installed when you installed your operating system. By default, Outlook 2007 and other applications trust certificates issued by those CAs without requiring you to obtain and install each CA's certificate.

The easiest way to view these certificates is through Internet Explorer:

1. In Internet Explorer, choose Tools, Internet Options and click the Content tab.

2. Click Certificates to open the Certificates dialog box (see Figure 24-20). Click the Trusted Root Certification Authorities tab, which contains a list of the certificates.

Figure 24-20 You can view a list of certificates in Internet Explorer's Certificates dialog box.

If you have a personal certificate issued by a specific CA, the issuer's certificate is installed on your computer. Messages you receive that are signed with certificates issued by the same CA inherit trust from the issuer without requiring the installation of any additional certificates. If you're working in a large enterprise with several CAs, however, you'll probably receive signed messages containing certificates issued by CAs other than the one that issued your certificate. Thus you might not have the issuing CA's certificate on your system, which prevents Outlook 2007 from trusting the certificate. In this case, you need to add that CA's certificate to your system.

If you need to connect to a Windows-based enterprise CA to obtain the CA's certificate and install it on your system, perform the following steps.

1. Point your Web browser to *http://<machine>/certsrv*, where <machine> is the name or IP address of the CA.

2. After the page loads, select Download A CA Certificate, Certificate Chain, Or CRL.

3. Select Download CA Certificate, and then choose to Open (at this point you could also Save it to your computer if you want to save the certificate file for later use).

4. Click Install Certificate to install the CA's certificate on your system. This will launch the Certificate Import Wizard. Click Next.

5. In the Certificate Store dialog box, select Automatically Select The Certificate Store Based Upon The Type Of Certificate. Click Next and then click Finish to add the CA certificate. You will be notified that the import was successful and will have to click OK twice to close the dialog boxes.

The procedure just outlined assumes that the CA administrator has not customized the certificate request pages for the CA. If the pages have been customized, the actual process you must follow could be slightly different from the one described here.

> **Note**
>
> If you prefer, you can download the CA certificate instead of installing it through the browser. Use this alternative when you need to install the CA certificate on more than one computer and must have the certificate as a file.

Configuring CA Trust for Multiple Computers

The process described in the preceding section is useful when configuring CA trust for a small number of computers, but it can be impractical with a large number of computers. In these situations, you can turn to group policy to configure CA trust in a wider area such as an organizational unit (OU), a domain, or an entire site.

You can create a certificate trust list (CTL), which is a signed list of root CA certificates that are considered trusted, and deploy that CTL through Group Policy. This solution requires that you be running the Active Directory directory service with Windows XP, and/or Windows Vista clients as domain members.

Follow these steps to create and deploy the CTL:

1. Log on to a domain controller and open the Active Directory Users And Computers console.

2. Create a new Group Policy Object (GPO) or edit an existing GPO at the necessary container in Active Directory, such as an OU.

3. In the Group Policy Editor, expand the branch User Configuration\Windows Settings\Security Settings\Public Key Policies\Enterprise Trust.

4. Right-click Enterprise Trust and choose New, Certificate Trust List to start the Certificate Trust List Wizard.

5. Click Next, and then specify a name and valid duration for the CTL (both optional), as shown in Figure 24-21. Select one or more purposes for the CTL in the Designate Purposes list (in this example, choose Secure Email), and then click Next.

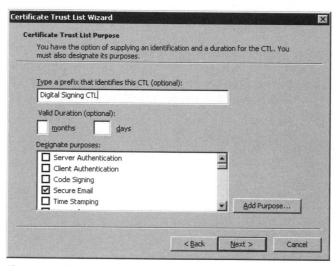

Figure 24-21 Select a purpose for the CTL and other properties, such as a friendly name for easy identification.

6. On the Certificates In The CTL page (see Figure 24-22), click Add From Store to add certificates to the list from the server's certificate store. Choose one or more certificates and click OK.

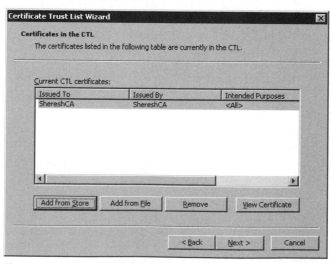

Figure 24-22 Add certificates to the CTL.

7. If the certificates are stored in an X.509 file, Microsoft Serialized Certificate Store, or PKCS #7 certificate file, click Add From File, select the file, and click Open.

8. Back on the Certificates In The CTL page, click Next. On the Signature Certificate page, select a certificate to sign the CTL. The certificate must be stored in the local computer certificate store instead of the user certificate store. Click Next after you select the certificate.

9. You can optionally choose the Add A Timestamp To The Data option and specify a timestamp service URL if one is available. Otherwise, click Next.

10. Optionally, enter a friendly name and description for the CTL to help identify it, click Next, and click Finish.

Viewing and Validating a Digital Signature

You can view the certificate associated with a signed message to obtain information about the issuer, the person to whom the certificate is issued, and other matters.

To do so, follow these steps:

1. Open the message and click the Signature button in either the Reading Pane or the message form; then click Details to display the Message Security Properties dialog box, which provides information about the certificate's validity in the Description box.

2. Click Signer in the list to view additional signature information in the Description box, such as when the message was signed (see Figure 24-23).

3. Click View Details to open the Signature dialog box, shown in Figure 24-24, which displays even more detail about the signature.

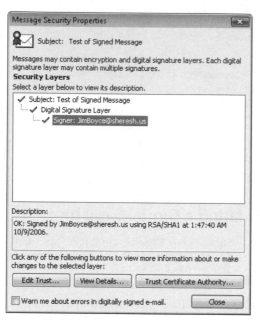

Figure 24-23 The Description box offers information about the validity of the certificate.

Figure 24-24 Use the Signature dialog box to view additional properties of the signature and to access the certificate.

4. On the General tab of the Signature dialog box, click View Certificate to display information about the certificate, including issuer, certification path, and trust mode.

5. Click OK, click Close to close the Message Security Properties dialog box, and click Close again to close the Digital Signature dialog box.

The CA uses a certificate revocation list (CRL) to indicate the validity of certificates. If you don't have a current CRL on your system, Outlook 2007 can treat the certificate as trusted, but can't validate the certificate and will indicate this when you view the signature.

You can locate the path to the CRL by examining the certificate's properties as follows:

1. Click the Signature button for the message, either in the Reading Pane or in the message form, and then click Details..

2. In the Message Security Properties dialog box, click Signer and then click View Details.

3. On the General tab of the Signature dialog box, click View Certificate and then click the Details tab (see Figure 24-25).

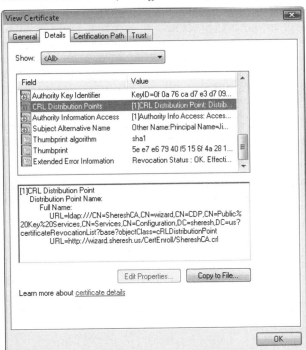

Figure 24-25 Use the Details tab to view the CRL path for the certificate.

4. Scroll through the list to find and select CRL Distribution Points.

5. Scroll through the list in the lower half of the dialog box to locate the URL for the CRL.

When you know the URL for the CRL, you can point your browser to the site to download and install the CRL. If a CA in your enterprise issued the certificate, you can obtain the CRL from the CA.

To obtain and install the CRL, follow these steps:

1. Point your browser to *http://<machine>/certsrv*, where <machine> is the name or IP address of the server.

2. Select the Retrieve The CA Certificate Or Certificate Revocation List option and click Next.

3. Click Download Latest Certificate Revocation List and save the file to disk.

4. After downloading the file, locate and right-click the file, and then choose Install CRL to install the current list.

Encrypting Messages

You can encrypt messages to prevent them from being read by unauthorized persons. It is, of course, true that with significant amounts of computing power and time any encryption scheme can probably be broken. However, the chances of someone investing those resources in your e-mail are pretty remote. So you can be assured that the e-mail encryption Outlook 2007 provides offers a relatively safe means of protecting sensitive messages against interception.

Before you can encrypt messages, you must have a certificate for that purpose installed on your computer. Typically, certificates issued for digital signing can also be used for encrypting e-mail messages.

For detailed information on obtaining a personal certificate from a commercial CA or from an enterprise or stand-alone CA on your network, see "Obtaining a Digital Certificate," on page 690.

Getting Ready for Encryption

After you've obtained a certificate and installed it on your system, encrypting messages is a simple task. Getting to that point, however, depends in part on whether you're sending messages to an Exchange Server recipient on your network or to an Internet recipient.

Swapping Certificates

Before you can send an encrypted message to an Internet recipient, you must have a copy of the recipient's public key certificate. To read the message, the recipient must have a copy of your public key certificate, which means you first need to swap public certificates.

> **Note**
>
> When you are sending encrypted messages to an Exchange Server recipient, you don't need to swap certificates. Exchange Server takes care of the problem for you.

The easiest way to swap certificates is to send a digitally signed message to the recipient and have the recipient send you a signed message in return, as outlined here:

1. In Outlook 2007, choose Tools, Trust Center, and then click the E-Mail Security page.

2. Click Settings to display the Change Security Settings dialog box.

3. Verify that you've selected S/MIME in the Cryptography Format drop-down list.

4. Select the Send These Certificates With Signed Messages option and click OK.

5. Click OK to close the Trust Center dialog box.

6. Compose the message and digitally sign it. Outlook 2007 will include the certificates with the message.

When you receive a signed message from someone with whom you're exchanging certificates, you must add the person to your Contacts folder to add the certificate by following these steps:

1. Open the message, right-click the sender's name, and then choose Add To Outlook Contacts. If the Reading Pane is displayed, you can right-click the sender's name in the pane and choose Add To Outlook Contacts.

2. Outlook 2007 displays the Contact tab of the contact form (see Figure 24-26). Fill in additional information for the contact as needed.

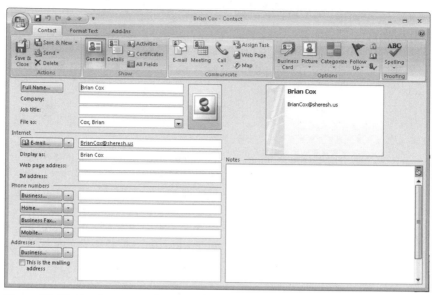

Figure 24-26 Use the contact form to add the sender's certificate to your system.

3. Click the Certificates button (in the Show group). You should see the sender's certificate listed (see Figure 24-27), and you can view the certificate's properties by selecting it and clicking Properties. If no certificate is listed, contact the sender and ask for another digitally signed message.

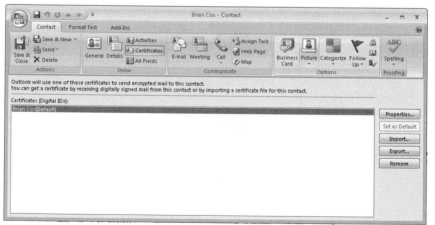

Figure 24-27 The Certificates button on the contact form displays the sender's certificate.

4. Click Save & Close to save the contact item and the certificate.

Obtaining a Recipient's Public Key from a Public CA

As an alternative to receiving a signed message with a certificate from another person, you might be able to obtain the person's certificate from the issuing CA. For example, if you know that the person has a certificate from VeriSign, you can download that individual's public key from the VeriSign Web site. Other public CAs offer similar services. To search for and download public keys from VeriSign (see Figure 24-28), connect to *https://digitalid.verisign.com/services/client/index.html*. Check the sites of other public CAs for similar links that enable you to download public keys from their servers.

The process for downloading a public key varies by CA. In general, however, you enter the person's e-mail address in a form to locate the certificate, and the form provides instructions for downloading the certificate. You should have no trouble obtaining the public key after you locate the certificate on the CA (there is a link to download the public key certificate from the CA to a file on your computer).

Save the public key to disk, and then follow these steps to install the key:

1. Open the Contacts folder in Outlook 2007.

2. Locate the contact for whom you downloaded the public key.

3. Open the contact item, and then click the Certificates button.

4. Click Import. Browse to and select the certificate file obtained from the CA and click Open.

5. Click Save & Close to save the contact changes.

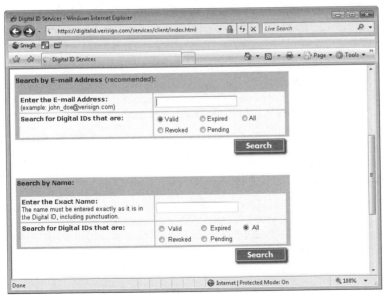

Figure 24-28 VeriSign, like other public CAs, provides a form you can use to search for and obtain public keys for certificate subscribers

Sending Encrypted Messages

When you have everything set up for sending and receiving encrypted messages, it's a simple matter to send one:

1. Open Outlook 2007 and compose the message.

2. In the message form, click the Encrypt icon in the Options group (on the Message tab).

Alternatively, do the following:

1. On the Message tab, click the Message Options Dialog Box Launcher in the Options group that displays the Message Options dialog box, and then click Security Settings.

2. Select Encrypt Message Contents And Attachments, and then click OK.

3. Click Close, and then send the message as you normally would.

4. If the message is protected by Exchange Server security, you can send it in one of three ways, depending on your system's security level:

   - If the security level is set to Medium (the default), Outlook 2007 displays a message informing you of your security setting. Click OK to send the message.

   - If the security level is set to Low, Outlook 2007 sends the message immediately, without any special action on your part.

   - If the security level is set to High, type your password to send the message.

> **Note**
>
> To make it easier to encrypt a message, you can add the Encrypt command to the Quick Access Toolbar in the message form. For details about the process involved in doing this, see "You Need a Faster Way to Digitally Sign a Message," on page 703.

Reading Encrypted Messages

When you receive an encrypted message, you can read it as you would read any other message, assuming that you have the sender's certificate. Double-click the message to open it. Note that Outlook 2007 uses an icon with a lock instead of the standard envelope icon to identify encrypted messages.

> **Note**
>
> You can't preview encrypted messages in the Reading Pane. Also, the ability to read encrypted messages requires an S/MIME-capable mail client. Keep this in mind when sending encrypted messages to other users who might not have Outlook 2007 or another S/MIME-capable client.
>
> You can verify and modify the trust for a certificate when you read a message signed by that certificate. For information on viewing and changing the trust for a certificate, see "Changing Certificate Trust Relationships" on page 706.

Importing Certificates from Outlook Express

If you have used Microsoft Windows Mail or Microsoft Outlook Express to send and receive secure messages, your Windows Mail Contacts (or Outlook Express address book) contains the public keys of the recipients. You can import those certificates to use in Outlook 2007 if they are not already included in the Contacts folder. Unfortunately, Windows Mail/Outlook Express doesn't export the certificates when you export its address book; instead, you must export the certificates one at a time.

Follow these steps to move certificates from Windows Mail or Outlook Express to Outlook 2007:

1. Open Windows Mail and select Tools, Windows Contacts (or, if using Outlook Express, choose Tools, Address Book).

2. In Windows Contacts (for Windows Mail) or the Address book (for Outlook Express), double-click the name of the person whose certificate you want to export.

3. Click the IDs tab in Windows Mail (or the Digital IDs tab in Outlook Express).

4. Select the certificate to export and click Export.

5. Save the certificate to a file. (Windows Mail and Outlook Express use the CER file extension.)

6. Open Outlook 2007, open the Contacts folder, and open the contact item for the person who owns the certificate you're importing.

7. Click the Certificates button, click Import, select the file created in step 5, and click Open.

8. Save and close the contact form.

Protecting Data with Information Rights Management

In response to market demands for a system with which companies can protect proprietary and sensitive information, Microsoft has developed an umbrella of technologies called Information Rights Management (IRM). Outlook 2007 incorporates IRM, enabling you to send messages that prevent the recipient from forwarding, copying from, or printing the message. The recipient can view the message, but the features for accomplishing these other tasks are unavailable.

> **Note**
>
> IRM is an extension for the Microsoft Office system applications of Windows Rights Management. For information on using IRM with other Office applications, see Chapter 3, "Managing Security and Privacy in the 2007 Office System."

There are two paths to implementing IRM with the Microsoft Office system. Microsoft offers an IRM service that, as of this writing, is free. This path requires that you have a Microsoft Passport to send or view IRM-protected messages. You must log in to the service with your Passport credentials to download a certificate, which Outlook 2007 uses to verify your identity and enable the IRM features. The second path is to install Microsoft Windows Server 2003 running the Rights Management Service (RMS) on Windows Server 2003. With this path, users authenticate on the server with NTLM or Passport authentication and download their IRM certificates.

The first path provides simplicity because it does not require that organizations deploy an RMS server. The second path provides more flexibility because the RMS administrator can configure company-specific IRM policies, which are then available to users. For example, you might create a policy template requiring that only users within the company domain can open all e-mail messages protected by the policy. You can create any number of templates to suit the company's data rights needs for the range of Microsoft Office system applications and document types.

Not everyone who receives an IRM-protected message will be running Outlook 2003 or Outlook 2007, so Microsoft has developed the Rights Management Add-On for Internet Explorer, which enables these users to view the messages in Internet Explorer. Without this add-on, recipients cannot view IRM-protected messages. With the add-on, recipients can view the messages, but the capability to forward, copy, or print the message is disabled, just as it is in Outlook 2007.

This chapter explains how to configure and use IRM in Outlook 2007 with the Microsoft IRM service. As of this writing, Windows Rights Management Services is available for Windows Server 2003 by download (currently as a Service Pack 2 release). Check *www.boyce.us* and *www.microsoft.com/windowsserver2003/technologies/rightsmgmt/ default.mspx* periodically for additional information on RMS as it becomes available.

Using Microsoft's IRM Service

To configure Outlook 2007 to use the IRM service and send IRM-protected messages, follow these steps:

1. Open Outlook 2007 and start a new message. With the message form open, choose Microsoft Office Button, Permission, Do Not Forward.

2. If you do not have the IRM add-on installed, Outlook 2007 displays the dialog box shown in Figure 24-29. Choose Yes, I Want To Sign Up For This Free Trial Service From Microsoft and click Next.

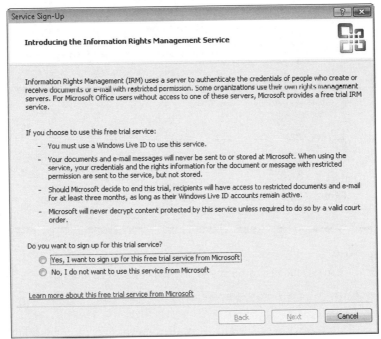

Figure 24-29 Choose Yes and click Next to start the enrollment process.

3. The wizard asks if you already have a Microsoft Passport. If so, choose Yes and click Next to open a sign-in dialog box and enter your Passport credentials. If not, choose No and click Next; then follow the prompts to obtain a Microsoft Passport.

4. After you obtain a Passport and click Next, Outlook 2007 displays the page shown in Figure 24-30. Choose Standard to obtain a certificate that you can use on your own computer. Choose Temporary if you need a certificate only for a limited time, such as when you are working from a public computer. Then click Next, Finish to complete the process.

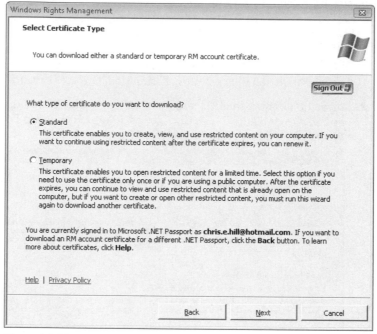

Figure 24-30 You can choose between a standard certificate and a temporary one.

> **Note**
> You can download a certificate for a given Passport 25 times or to 25 computers.

5. After the IRM certificate is installed on your computer, Outlook 2007 returns you to the message form. The InfoBar in the form displays a Do Not Forward message, as shown in Figure 24-31, indicating that the message is protected by IRM.

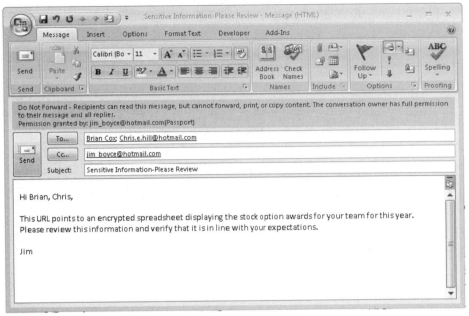

Figure 24-31 The InfoBar indicates when a message is protected by IRM.

6. Address the message and add the message body and attachments, if any, as you would for any other message. Then send the message.

Viewing IRM-Protected Messages

If you attempt to view an IRM-protected message without first obtaining a certificate, Outlook 2007 gives you the option of connecting to Microsoft's service to obtain one. After the certificate is installed, you can view the message, but Outlook 2007 indicates in the InfoBar (both Reading Pane and message form) that the message is restricted (see Figure 24-32). The commands for forwarding, copying, and printing the message are disabled.

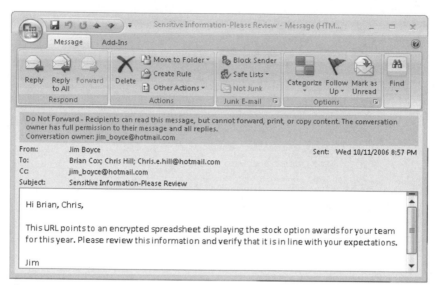

Figure 24-32 The InfoBar in the Reading Pane indicates that a message is restricted.

Working with Multiple Accounts

It's possible that you use more than one Microsoft Passport. If you have more than one Passport and need to choose between them when you send or view an IRM-protected message, open the message form for sending or viewing and choose Microsoft Office Button, Permission, Manage Credentials to open the Select User dialog box, as shown in Figure 24-33. Choose an account and click OK to use that account for the current message.

Figure 24-33 You can select from multiple accounts to restrict messages or view restricted messages.

If you have only one account configured on the computer and want to add another account, click Add to start the Service Sign-Up Wizard and download a certificate for another e-mail address and corresponding Microsoft Passport.

Collaboration with Outlook and Windows SharePoint Services

Windows SharePoint Services (version 3) is a collaboration tool used to build Web sites for team members to share data such as contacts and documents. One of the biggest advantages of Windows SharePoint Services, other than the fact that it allows team members to share information and collaborate easily, is that it fully integrates with the 2007 Microsoft Office system. Windows SharePoint Services allows you to share documents created with Microsoft Office system applications and even lets you share contacts stored in Microsoft Office Outlook 2007 with other team members.

Understanding Windows SharePoint Services Collaboration

Windows SharePoint Services V3 is a workgroup-class, Web-based portal product that can be used for collaboration, including document management for a team or workgroup within an organization. Each team requiring this collaboration functionality will typically have its own SharePoint site that team members can use to share documents, have threaded discussions, share lists of important information, and more.

Windows SharePoint Services is a Web-based tool, but it also provides integration with Microsoft Office system applications. Windows SharePoint Services provides a number of collaboration features, including the following:

- **Document sharing** Document sharing allows you to store documents on the SharePoint site, which can then be accessed by other team members. This is useful for sharing project-related documents, for example, or any other document that other team members might need access to. In addition to simple document storage, document sharing provides version control tools such as document check-in and checkout so that a document is not accidentally modified by more than one user at a time.

- **Picture libraries** Picture libraries are similar to document libraries in that they store pictures that can be shared among team members. This is basically a Web-based photo album.

- **Lists** Lists are formatted lists of information. The list format can vary based on the type of information being stored. A number of lists are predefined, such as Announcements, which are displayed on the main SharePoint Home page; Calendar, which can contain events relating to your team or project; Links, which stores Web links to pages that your team will find useful or interesting; and Tasks, which helps your team members keep track of work.

- **Discussion boards** Discussion boards allow team members to have threaded discussions on specific subjects. Discussion boards are useful to replace e-mail exchanges when more than two people are involved, as those involved can place comments and replies directly in the appropriate thread rather than exchanging a large number of e-mail messages.

- **Surveys** Surveys are simply a method of polling other team members for information.

As stated earlier, one of the key features of Windows SharePoint Services is its ability to integrate with Microsoft Office system applications. The features in Windows SharePoint Services that integrate with the Microsoft Office system include document sharing, which can be done from almost any Microsoft Office system application; lists, which can be synchronized with Microsoft Office Excel 2007 or Microsoft Office Access 2007 files; and Calendar lists, contacts, and alerts, which can be linked into Office Outlook 2007. In addition, Microsoft SharePoint Designer can be used to edit and customize Windows SharePoint Services pages. This chapter focuses mainly on the integration of SharePoint and Outlook 2007. SharePoint and Outlook 2007 have the tightest integration, as they are both collaboration tools, although each has a different focus.

Setting Up Alerts

Alerts (formerly called *subscriptions* in an earlier version of the software) are used when you want to be notified when content on the SharePoint site changes. Alerts are sent through e-mail. To set up an alert, follow these steps:

1. Locate the content for which you want to configure the alert. This can be virtually anything on the SharePoint site.

2. Click an item in a library. A menu appears, as shown in Figure 25-1. Select Alert Me to be alerted when that item is changed.

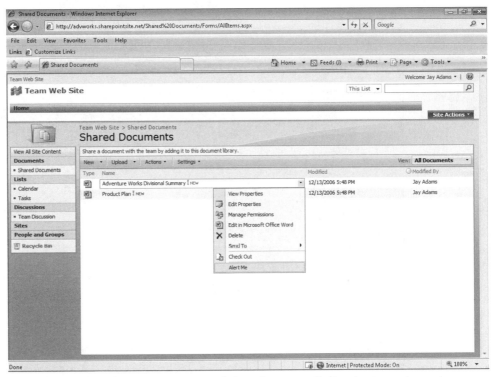

Figure 25-1 Select Alert Me to get an e-mail alert when a specific item has been changed.

3. The New Alert page, shown in Figure 25-2, displays the e-mail address to which alerts will be sent. On this page, select the types of changes you want to be alerted about. Some of the options shown in the figure are not available if you are configuring an alert for a specific item. You can be alerted about all changes; item additions, changes, or deletions; or updates to discussions involving the selected item or library.

4. Select the frequency for alerts from this item or library. The default setting sends an alert message every time the alert is triggered. You can also elect to receive only a daily or weekly summary of alerts. These options are useful if the item or library for which you are configuring the alert changes often.

5. Click OK, and the alert will be configured.

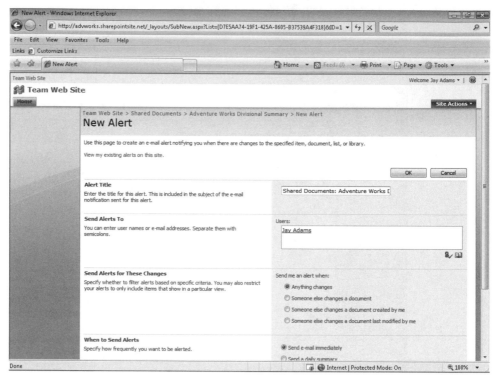

Figure 25-2 The New Alert page is used to configure the alert.

After you have created an alert, you will be notified each time the alert criteria set on the New Alert page are met. You can view a list of all of the alerts you have configured on the site by clicking View My Existing Alerts On This Site on the New Alert page. The My Alerts On This Site page, shown in Figure 25-3, shows all of the alerts you have configured on the site. You can delete an alert by selecting the check box next to the alert you want to delete and then clicking Delete Selected Alerts. It is also possible to add an alert for a list or document library (although not individual items) on the My Alerts On This Site page. Click Add Alert, select the library or list for the alert, and then click Next. Set the options on the New Alert page as described earlier in this section.

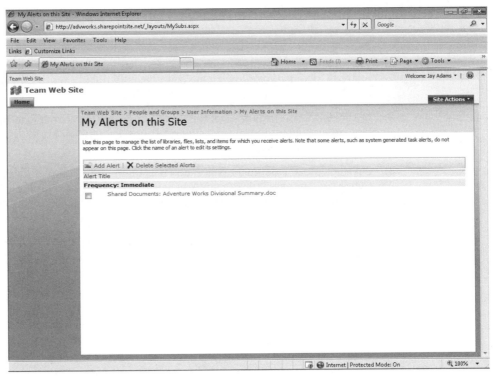

Figure 25-3 You can see all alerts you have configured on the site on the My Alerts On This Site page, which is accessible from the New Alert page.

Working with Shared Documents

Document sharing is simple with Windows SharePoint Services and can be done in one of two ways. If you have an existing Microsoft Office system document, it is an easy process to add the document to a document library in Windows SharePoint Services. If you don't already have a document created, you can create the document directly in the Windows SharePoint Services site. When you create a document in the Windows SharePoint Services site, the appropriate application opens automatically. When the document is saved, it is placed in the site automatically. In addition to creating and adding documents to the Windows SharePoint Services site, you can do a number of things with existing documents in Windows SharePoint Services: You can edit or remove existing documents, and you can use features such as document version history, checkout, and check-in to control versions.

Uploading a Document

To upload a document to a document library, follow these steps:

1. Locate and open the document library by clicking the library name (such as Shared Documents) on the Home page. Usually the library names appear under the Documents item on the Quick Launch bar.

2. In the document library, click the down arrow next to the Upload button. Click Upload Document to upload a single file, or click Upload Multiple Documents to upload several files at once.

3. On the Upload Document page, shown in Figure 25-4, click Browse, locate the file to upload, and then click Open. You can also click Upload Multiple Files to open a Microsoft Windows Explorer–style browser from which you can select multiple files to upload.

4. Existing files with the same name as the file or files being uploaded are not overwritten by default. If you want to overwrite any existing files, click the Overwrite Existing Files check box.

5. After you have specified or selected the files to upload, click OK. The documents are uploaded, and the Documents page appears.

You will now see the uploaded file listed in the document library.

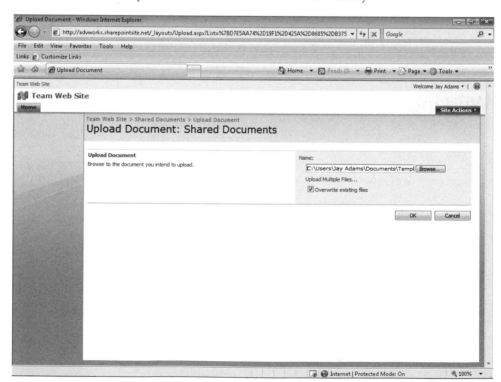

Figure 25-4 The Upload Document page is used to upload files to the document library.

Creating a Document from the Site

In addition to the preceding method of uploading an existing document to the document library, you can also create a new document directly from the document library site. The new document is created using the document template associated with the document library. By default, the Microsoft Office Word 2007 document template is associated with the Shared Documents library that is created when Windows SharePoint Services is installed. The Document Template setting is configured when a new document library is created, and you can set it for an existing library by clicking Settings on the document list and then clicking Document Library Settings. Click the Advanced Settings link, modify the Document Template setting, and then click OK.

To create a new document from your SharePoint site, follow these steps:

1. Open the document library in which you want to create the new document.

2. Click New, and then choose New Document, shown in Figure 25-5.

    The Microsoft Office system application associated with the document template specified for the selected document library is downloaded and opened in its native application, such as Microsoft Office Word 2007. Figure 25-5 shows how the SharePoint site communicates with Office Word 2007 to open up the default document template. Create and then save the new document to the document library.

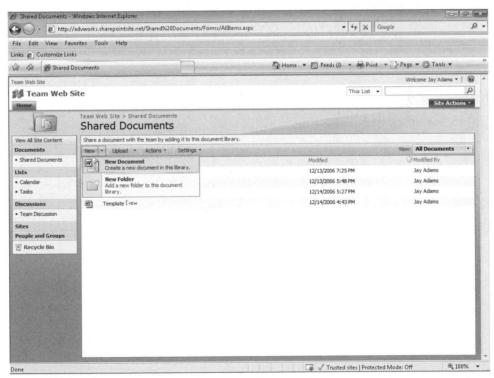

Figure 25-5 Click the New Document item on the New menu to create a new document from the SharePoint site.

Your newly created document will now be shown in the document library.

Working with Existing Documents and Version Control

Document options for each item in a document library are found in the item's drop-down menu. Position the mouse pointer over a document name, and a drop-down arrow appears. When you click the arrow, the Item drop-down menu appears. This menu was shown earlier in Figure 25-1. From this menu, you can edit the document (clicking the document name also has this effect); edit the document properties, which include the name and a descriptive title for the document; and delete the document from the library.

The key features in a shared document library are the version control features. In Windows SharePoint Services, these features include the ability to check a document in and out as well as view its version history. When you check out a document, other users can no longer edit the document until you return it to the document library by checking it in.

To check out a document, simply choose Check Out on the Item drop-down menu, as shown in Figure 25-6. Click OK when warned that you are about to check out the document. The icon in the Type column changes to display a green arrow to indicate that the document is checked out. After you specify that you want to check out the document, click the Item drop-down arrow again and click Edit In Microsoft Office Word (or whichever application name appears). The document is downloaded to your computer and displayed in the application for editing. Perform your edits. Click the Microsoft Office Button and then Save to have Word 2007 save the document to the SharePoint site.

INSIDE OUT   Force the Check-In of a Document

A user in the Administrator site group can force the checking in of a document even if another user has it checked out. This can be useful if a user checks out a document and forgets to check it back in and then leaves for the day, for example. An administrator can forcibly check the document back in so that other users can work with it. Changes made while the document was checked out might be lost in this case.

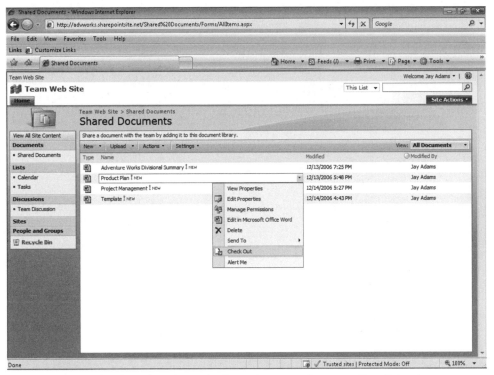

Figure 25-6 Use this drop-down list to check out documents from your SharePoint site.

When you have finished editing, you can close the document on your system and then return to the SharePoint site and check in the document. Checking a document back in to the document library is handled from the same drop-down menu as checking out. Click the Item drop-down arrow, and then click Check In. The Check In page shown in Figure 25-7 is displayed. Enter any comments for the version history, and then click OK. A message box appears, asking whether you want to continue. Click Yes. The document is then checked in.

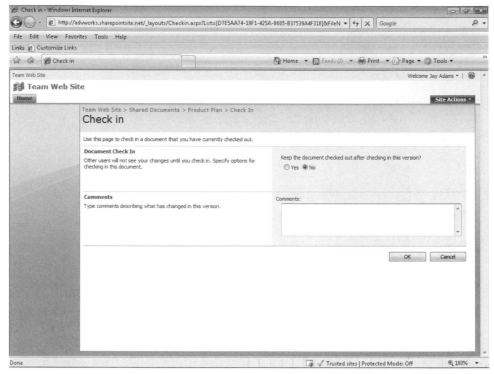

Figure 25-7 The Check In page is used to check in a document.

In the document library, choose Version History on the Item drop-down menu for a document. If version history is enabled for the document library, every time a document is checked in, it will appear in the version history, as shown in Figure 25-8. You can view each version of the document by hovering the mouse pointer over the date and time for a version and then clicking View. You also can restore a document by clicking the Restore option on this drop-down menu. You can delete old versions by clicking Delete Minor Versions.

INSIDE OUT   Enable Version History

Version history can be enabled from the Versions Saved page by clicking Site Actions and then clicking Site Settings on the right side of the screen. Under Site Administration, click Site Libraries And Lists, click Customize "Shared Documents," and then click Versioning Settings. Specify the level of version history to retain in the Document Version History area, and then click OK when you have finished.

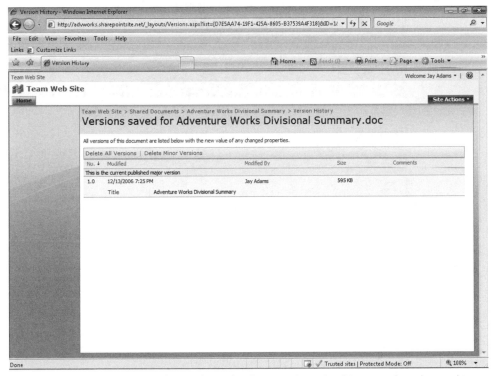

Figure 25-8 The Versions Saved page shows the document's version history and can be used to restore old versions of the document.

Working with Shared Contacts

Windows SharePoint Services 2.0 provides lists that can be used to share a variety of information. One of the defined list types is contacts, which is used to store contact information in a way similar to the Contacts folder in Outlook 2007. Shared contacts work only with Windows SharePoint Services 2.0, not with the latest version (Windows SharePoint Services V3).

Viewing Contacts on a Windows SharePoint Services Site

To view contacts on a Windows SharePoint Services 2.0 site, click Documents And Lists at the top of any Windows SharePoint Services 2.0 page. The contacts lists are in the Lists area of the page. By default, a list named Contacts is created when Windows SharePoint Services is installed; you might have more lists of contacts on your site. Click a contacts list name to view the list, as shown in Figure 25-9. From this list, you can add, edit, and delete contacts. An Item drop-down menu for contacts will be displayed if you hover the mouse pointer over the last name of a specific contact.

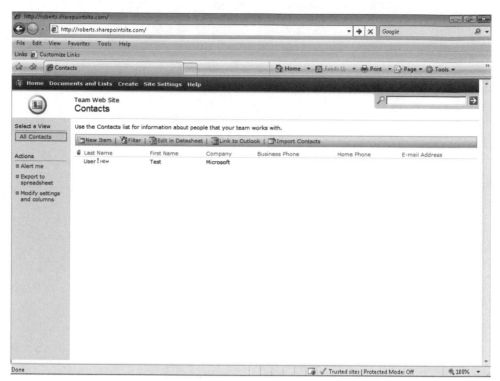

Figure 25-9 A contacts list shows the contact information in the familiar Windows SharePoint V3 layout.

Linking Windows SharePoint Services 2.0 Contacts Lists to Outlook

If you frequently use contacts in your Windows SharePoint Services team site, it might be a lot of effort to open the team site every time you need a contact. Windows SharePoint Services and Outlook 2007 provide a method of linking a contacts list from Windows SharePoint Services directly into Outlook 2007 so that the contacts in the Windows SharePoint Services site show up as a contacts folder in Outlook 2007. However, contacts lists linked from Windows SharePoint Services into Outlook 2007 cannot be edited; they can only be read. You must add, edit, or delete contacts in a linked folder directly in the SharePoint Services 2.0 site.

To link a contacts list in Windows SharePoint Services into Outlook 2007, open the contacts list, click Actions, and then click Connect To Outlook. Outlook 2007 will start if needed. Microsoft Internet Explorer displays a message asking whether it is OK to continue; click Yes. The message box shown in Figure 25-10 appears. This message box notifies you that a SharePoint site is attempting to link to Outlook 2007 and that the site is not trusted by default. Verify that the site URL in the message box is correct, and then click Yes.

> **Note**
>
> The message box notifying you that Windows SharePoint Services is attempting to link to Outlook 2007 appears so that rogue SharePoint sites cannot link into Outlook 2007 without your knowledge or permission.

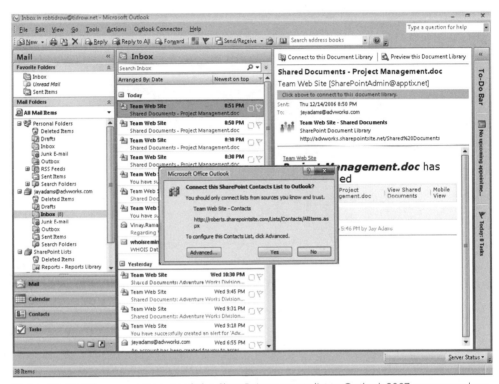

Figure 25-10 When you attempt to link a SharePoint contacts list to Outlook 2007, a message box appears, allowing you to verify that the SharePoint site is trusted before the link is created.

After you click Yes in this message box, the contacts list is linked into Outlook 2007, as shown in Figure 25-11. You now have two contacts folders in Outlook 2007, Contacts and Team Web Site–Contacts. You can open the new contacts folder linked from Windows SharePoint Services and view contacts, but you cannot add, edit, or delete contacts. (See "Copying Contacts from Outlook to Windows SharePoint Services 2.0" on page 740 for more information.)

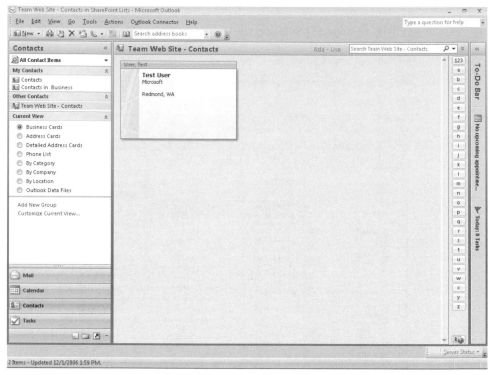

Figure 25-11 The new contacts folder linked from Windows SharePoint Services 2.0 is shown in Outlook 2007.

> **Note**
>
> The name in the Team Web Site—Contacts folder preceding the dash is the name of the SharePoint site, and the name following the dash is the name of the contacts list within the SharePoint site. If the name of the linked contacts list in Windows SharePoint Services were Project Contacts, for example, the linked folder in Outlook 2007 would be named Team Web Site—Project Contacts.

Copying Contacts from Windows SharePoint Services 2.0 to Outlook

Synchronizing contacts from Windows SharePoint Services 2.0 to Outlook 2007 is useful if you need access to an entire contacts list stored in a SharePoint site, but it is also possible to copy contacts from Windows SharePoint Services to Outlook 2007. This is useful if you need only a few contacts from Windows SharePoint Services in Outlook 2007 for use on a regular basis, or if you need the contacts stored in a single contacts folder in Outlook 2007. Note that if you edit the contact, your changes are not reflected in the Windows SharePoint Services contacts list, as the two copies of the contact are independent. See the next section to learn how to copy the contact back to Windows SharePoint Services.

The process for copying a contact from Windows SharePoint Services to Outlook 2007 is surprisingly simple. Windows SharePoint Services has the ability to export and import contacts to and from contacts lists on a SharePoint site in vCard (.vcf) format. To copy a contact from Windows SharePoint Services to Outlook 2007, follow these steps:

1. Open the contacts list in the SharePoint site from which you want to copy the contact.

2. Find the contact you want to copy, hover the mouse pointer over the contact's last name, click the drop-down arrow, and then click Export Contact.

3. You will typically see the Internet Explorer File Download dialog box, prompting you to open or save the file. Click Open.

4. The contact opens in Outlook 2007, as shown in Figure 25-12. Enter any additional information you want saved with the contact in the contact form, and then click Save And Close to save the contact in your Outlook 2007 Contacts folder.

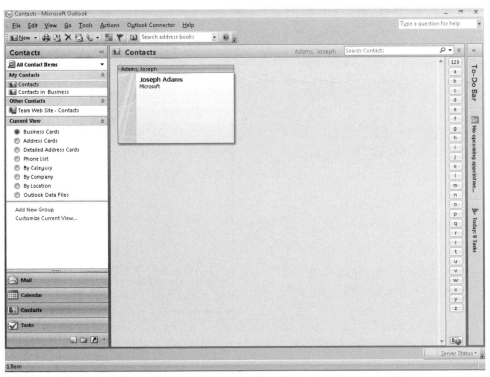

Figure 25-12 When you export a contact from the SharePoint site, the contact information opens in the Outlook 2007 contact form and you can save it to your Contacts folder.

Copying Contacts from Outlook to Windows SharePoint Services 2.0

The preceding two sections covered how to get your contacts from Windows SharePoint Services 2.0 into Outlook 2007, but the ability to move Outlook 2007 contacts into Windows SharePoint Services 2.0 is just as useful. If you are creating a Web site for your team, for example, and need to get a number of contacts from each team member's Contacts folder in Outlook 2007 into the Windows SharePoint Services contacts list, using the Import Contacts feature is much easier than adding each contact by hand. To copy contacts from Outlook 2007 to a SharePoint site, follow these steps:

1. In the SharePoint site, open the contacts list into which you want to import contacts.

2. Click Import Contacts.

3. In the Select Users To Import dialog box, shown in Figure 25-13, select the Outlook 2007 contacts folder containing the contact to import in the Show Names From The drop-down list. The Contacts folder is selected by default.

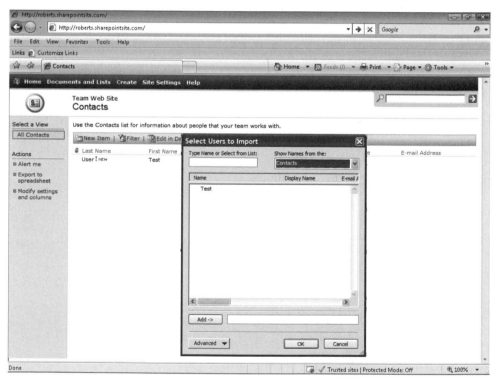

Figure 25-13 The Select Users To Import dialog box is used to select the contacts to import from Outlook 2007.

4. Select a contact in the list, click Add, and then click OK.

5. When the message box shown in Figure 25-14 is displayed, click Yes to allow access to the Outlook 2007 data. This message box warns you that someone is trying to access your data. If you will be adding more contacts from Outlook 2007, selecting the Allow Access For check box and specifying a time interval in the Select Users To Import dialog box prevents this message box from being displayed again for the length of time selected.

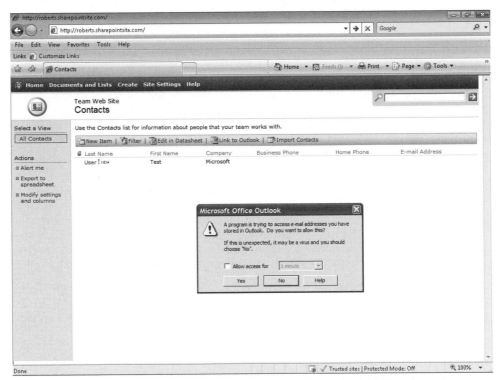

Figure 25-14 When someone tries to access your data stored in Outlook 2007, such as when importing contacts into Windows SharePoint Services, you are notified and can grant or deny access.

> **Note**
> Contacts stored in Outlook 2007 must have an associated e-mail address, or they will not appear in the Select Users To Import dialog box.

The contact will now be shown in the contacts list in the SharePoint site.

Linking a Team Calendar to Outlook

A SharePoint Calendar list in Windows SharePoint Services V3 can be linked to Outlook 2007. A Calendar list is used to maintain important events and is shared by the team members using the site. The Calendar list is created by default when Windows SharePoint Services is installed. Click Home and then click Calendar in the Lists area on the Quick Launch bar.

There are three ways to view events: Calendar view, All Events view, and Current Events view. These views are selected in the Calendar drop-down list. All Events view shows a listing of events, and Calendar view shows events in a traditional calendar format. The view you select has no effect on linking to Outlook 2007. When a Calendar list is linked to Outlook 2007, it is shown in the Outlook 2007 calendar format.

To link a Calendar list to Outlook 2007, follow these steps:

1. On the Quick Launch bar, click Calendar.

2. Click Actions, and then click Connect To Outlook.

3. A message box is displayed, warning you that a SharePoint folder is being added to Outlook 2007. (You might also get a message from Internet Explorer asking whether you want to continue. Click Yes, and then you'll see the message from Outlook 2007.) Click Yes to add the folder. This message box is similar to the one shown earlier in Figure 25-10, but instead of prompting you to connect a contacts list to Outlook 2007, you are prompted to connect a calendar to Outlook.

When the calendar is linked to Outlook 2007, it is displayed as shown in Figure 25-15. You can see the new calendar listed in the Navigation Pane on the left. Linked Calendar lists are read-only in Outlook 2007. To add, edit, or delete events, you must do so within the SharePoint site.

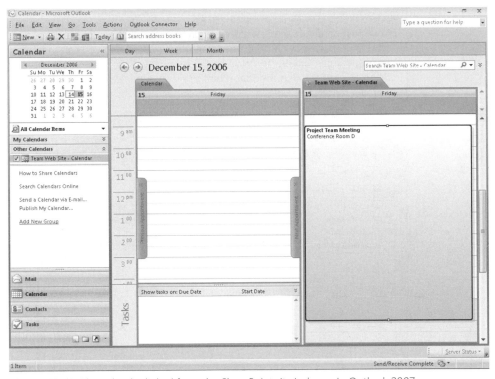

Figure 25-15 The calendar linked from the SharePoint site is shown in Outlook 2007.

Configuring Alerts in Outlook

We looked at alerts earlier in this chapter, in "Setting Up Alerts" on page 726. Whereas alerts in Windows SharePoint Services are sent through e-mail messages, Outlook 2007 includes integration that allows for the simple management of alert messages from a SharePoint site. The Outlook 2007 Manage Alerts tab in the Rules And Alerts dialog box provides links directly into the correct SharePoint site pages for alert management.

To manage SharePoint alerts from Outlook 2007, follow these steps:

1. Configure an alert for a resource on the SharePoint site. The alert notification will be sent to you through e-mail and will appear in your Inbox.

2. Ensure that a mail folder is open.

3. Choose Tools, Rules And Alerts. The Rules And Alerts dialog box appears.

4. Click the Manage Alerts tab, shown in Figure 25-16. Wait for Outlook 2007 to retrieve alert information from the SharePoint site.

> **Note**
>
> You must configure the first alert manually from the SharePoint site because when an alert is processed by Outlook 2007, the site is *trusted*, and you can then manage alerts from the Rules And Alerts dialog box. It is possible to manage alerts without first configuring an alert through the SharePoint site if an administrator adds the site as a trusted domain for alerts.

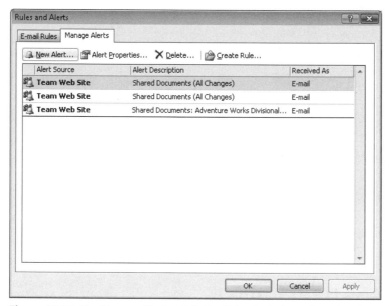

Figure 25-16 The Manage Alerts tab in the Rules And Alerts dialog box is used to manage SharePoint alerts directly from within Outlook 2007.

Adding Alerts from Outlook

You can now work with alerts directly within the client computer running Outlook 2007. To add a new alert, follow these steps:

1. Click New Alert on the Manage Alerts tab in the Rules And Alerts dialog box.

2. Expand Sources Currently Sending Me Alerts in the New Alert dialog box.

3. Select the SharePoint site in the list, as shown in Figure 25-17, and then click Open. You can also type the URL for the SharePoint site in the Web site Address box and then click Open.

Figure 25-17 Select the SharePoint site in which to create the new alert in the list in the New Alert dialog box.

4. The New Alert page in the SharePoint site opens automatically in a Web browser, as shown in Figure 25-18. Select the list or document library for which to set the alert, and then click Next.

5. Set the alert type and frequency as described in "Setting Up Alerts" on page 726.

6. Click OK to set the alert. You are then taken to the My Alerts On This Site page in the SharePoint site to review your alerts.

7. Switch to Outlook 2007.

8. Click the OK button to close the Rules And Alerts dialog box.

9. On the Tools menu, click Rules And Alerts.

10 Click the Manage Alerts tab in the Rules And Alerts dialog box. The new alert is shown on the Manage Alerts tab in the Rules And Alerts dialog box.

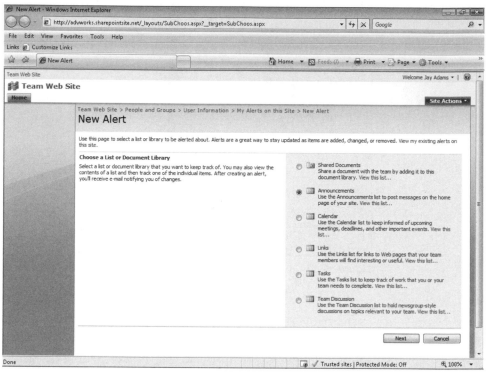

Figure 25-18 The New Alert page in the SharePoint site opens when you select the site from the list in the New Alert dialog box and click Open.

Editing and Deleting Alerts from Outlook

In addition to adding alerts directly from within Outlook 2007, you can edit existing alerts by following these steps:

1. Select the alert you want to edit on the Manage Alerts tab in the Rules And Alerts dialog box, and then click Alert Properties.

2. The Alert Properties dialog box opens, as shown in Figure 25-19. This dialog box shows the alert source as a clickable link to the home page of the SharePoint site and includes a link to the main alerts management page in the SharePoint site. Click Modify Alert to edit the alert.

3. The Edit Alert page in the SharePoint site opens in the Web browser. Make any changes you need on the Edit Alert page, and then click OK. You can also click Delete to remove the alert.

You can also remove alerts on the Manage Alerts tab by selecting the alert and then clicking Delete. You are prompted to verify the deletion, and the alert is removed when you click Yes.

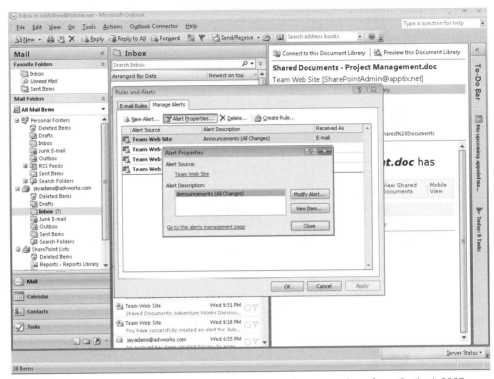

Figure 25-19 The Alert Properties dialog box is used to edit existing alerts from Outlook 2007.

Rules Based on Alerts

If you have a lot of alerts configured in a SharePoint site (or multiple sites), they can fill your mailbox quickly and distract from other messages. Outlook 2007 provides a simple way to create rules based on alerts. To configure a rule based on an alert, follow these steps:

1. Select the alert for which to configure a rule on the Manage Alerts tab in the Rules And Alerts dialog box.

2. Click Create Rule.

3. The Create Rule dialog opens, as shown in Figure 25-20. Specify what Outlook 2007 should do when it receives the selected alert. You can have Outlook 2007 display the alert in the New Item Alert window, play a sound, and move the message to a new folder.

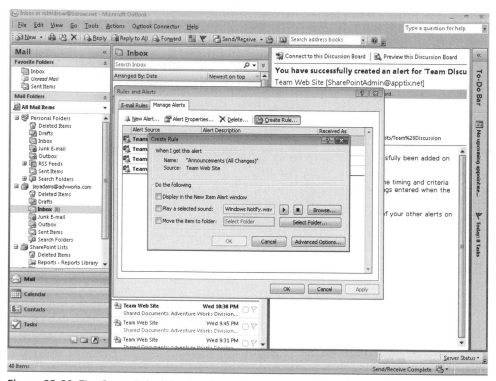

Figure 25-20 The Create Rule dialog box is used to create a rule based on an alert.

4. You can click Advanced Options to open the Rules Wizard and go into more detailed configuration for the rule. In most cases, this is not necessary for a basic alert.

5. Click OK to create the rule.

When the rule is created, the Success dialog box, shown in Figure 25-21, is displayed. You are notified that the rule is a client-side rule and given the option to run the rule against your mailbox immediately to find any messages that fit the rule criteria.

After you click OK in the Success dialog box, you can see the newly created rule by clicking the E-Mail Rules tab in the Rules And Alerts dialog box, which is already open.

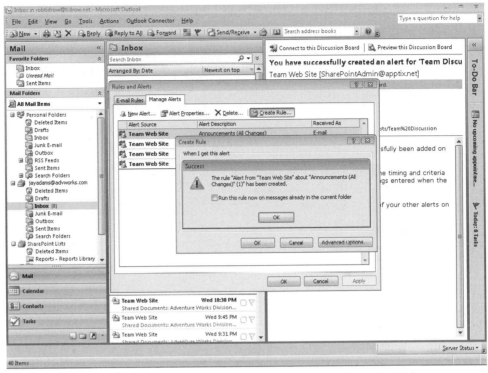

Figure 25-21 When the rule based on an alert is created, the Success dialog box is shown.

Using Outlook to Work with SharePoint Libraries and Files

In Outlook 2007, you can connect a SharePoint library to Outlook 2007. This makes the library and its items available within Outlook 2007 so that you don't have to use a Web browser to view and work with them—you can use Outlook 2007 instead. For example, you might want to have a list of current project documents that have been uploaded to your team's SharePoint site as you create e-mail messages to update your team members, support staff, and management.

By having the list of documents appear in Outlook 2007, you can quickly view the document name, its status, and other information without leaving Outlook 2007. Also, if you open a SharePoint document from within Outlook 2007, that file is stored locally on your hard drive while you view it. This makes the document open faster and reduces network traffic. If you make any edits to the document, you then check in the file to the SharePoint site. Files are stored on your hard drive in your personal folders (.pst) file.

Connecting a SharePoint Library to Outlook

To use Outlook 2007 to view and work with your SharePoint documents, you first connect a SharePoint library to Outlook 2007. This enables Windows SharePoint Services and Outlook 2007 to synchronize your files so that you can have them available for offline use in Outlook 2007.

To connect a library to Outlook 2007, follow these steps:

1. In a library, click the Actions menu. This menu contains a list of actions that you can perform in this library, as shown in Figure 25-22.

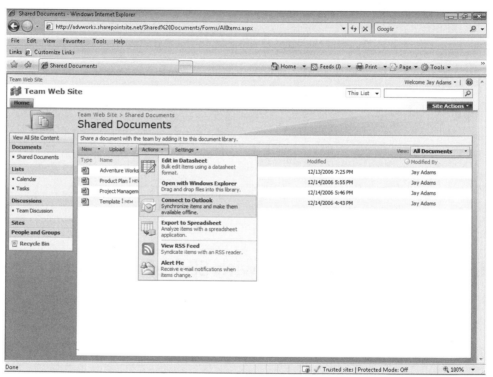

Figure 25-22 You can connect a SharePoint library to Outlook 2007 by using the Actions menu.

2. Click Connect To Outlook. A warning message might appear, telling you that you should connect lists only from sources you trust.

3. Click Yes. The Outlook Send/Receive Progress window appears as the library is connected. When finished, Outlook 2007 displays the library as a SharePoint list, as shown in Figure 25-23.

The libraries you connect to Outlook 2007 are in a folder named SharePoint Lists. The SharePoint Lists folder provides a view of file names, previews of documents, and links to download the files for viewing or editing.

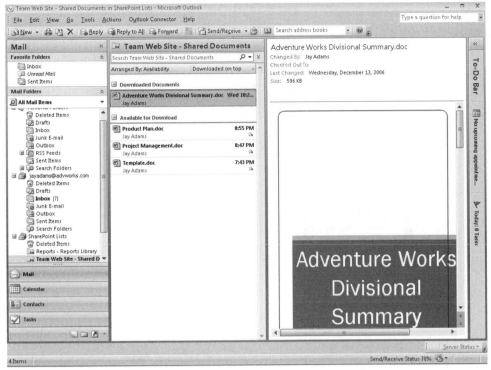

Figure 25-23 Outlook 2007 displays the connected library as a SharePoint Lists item.

Downloading Files from a SharePoint Library to Outlook

Sometimes when you connect a SharePoint library to Outlook 2007, the library is too large to download to your local hard drive. Instead, Outlook 2007 displays a group named Available For Download in the message list area, as shown in Figure 25-24. You can use this group to select individual files that you want to download to Outlook 2007. You can use the Ctrl key to select multiple files to download. Some files might include a button in the preview window labeled Download This Document. Click that button to download the file.

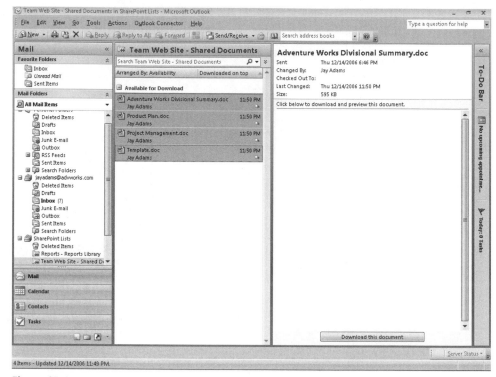

Figure 25-24 You can download files from a SharePoint site with Outlook 2007.

Opening Files from a SharePoint Site in Outlook

Once you have a SharePoint library connected to Outlook 2007, you can open files stored in that library from within Outlook 2007. Outlook 2007 enables you to view a number of different file formats, including the following:

- Microsoft Word documents
- Microsoft Excel worksheets
- Microsoft PowerPoint presentations
- Pictures

To open a SharePoint library file in Outlook 2007, browse to a folder in the SharePoint Lists folder in the Outlook 2007 Navigation Pane. Click a folder to display that folder's list of files in the messages list. Files are displayed here just like e-mail messages. Each file, however, includes information about that file, such as name, file format, last user to edit the file, checkout information, modification date and time, and size. Figure 25-25 shows the messages list pane resized to display all the file details for files listed in the Team Web Site–Shared Documents SharePoint list.

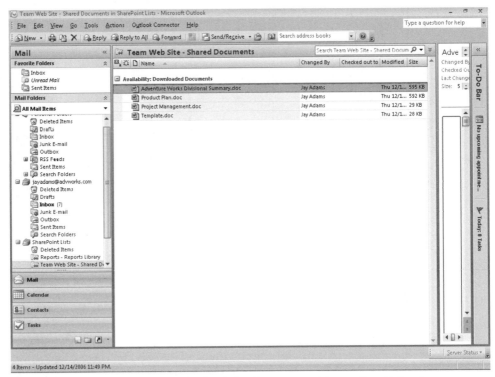

Figure 25-25 Outlook 2007 shows file details for files connected from a SharePoint site.

To open a file, you can click it to display the file in the Outlook 2007 Reading Pane. For example, Figure 25-26 shows a Microsoft Word file displayed in the Reading Pane.

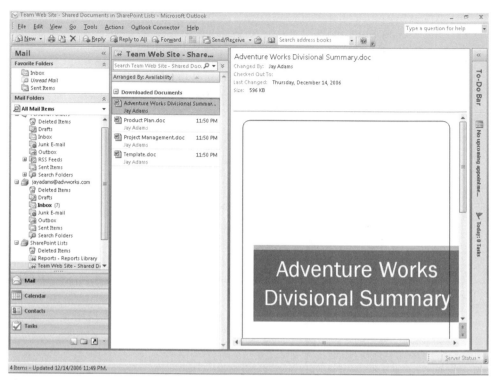

Figure 25-26 Outlook 2007 shows file details for files connected from a SharePoint site.

Editing Files from a SharePoint Site in Outlook

Not only can you open and view SharePoint files in Outlook 2007, you also can edit them. Before doing so, however, you should return to the SharePoint site and check out the document so that no one else can work on the document while you are working on it. (Outlook 2007 does not provide a way to check out the document locally.)

To edit the file, double-click it. Outlook 2007 displays a warning message about opening files from trustworthy sources only. Click Open to continue. The file opens in the default application for that file format (for example, an .xls file opens in Excel 2007, .ppt in PowerPoint 2007, and so on). For applications compatible with Windows SharePoint Services V3, a banner appears across the top of document telling you that the document is an offline server document and that you should save the file to the server later, as shown in Figure 25-27.

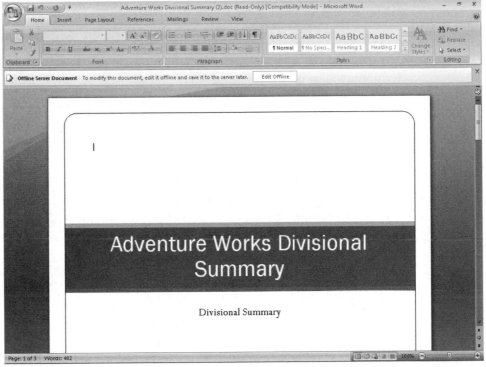

Figure 25-27 The Offline Server Document banner reminds you that the file you are editing needs to be updated to the server later.

Click the Edit Offline button. A message box appears, telling you that the document will be stored on your computer in the SharePoint Drafts folder. Click OK, and then edit the file. After you complete your edits, click the Microsoft Office Button and then click Save to save the file. Then click the Microsoft Office Button and click Close. If you are connected to your SharePoint site at this time, the Edit Offline dialog box appears. You can click the Update button to update the SharePoint site with your edited file. (You also can click Do Not Update Server to update the server later.)

When you click the Update button, the application (such as Word 2007) saves the changes to the SharePoint site.

If you chose not to update the files using the Update button, return to Outlook 2007, and then click the Send/Receive button when you are ready to update your files. Outlook 2007 synchronizes with the SharePoint site to save your changes in the online library.

Removing SharePoint Files in Outlook

You can remove one or more files from a SharePoint library list in Outlook 2007 without actually removing the documents from the SharePoint library. The document remains on the server, but it is removed from your cached list in Outlook 2007. This feature simplifies browsing libraries that contain a large number of items.

To remove files from a SharePoint library list that have been connected to Outlook, follow these steps:

1. In the Outlook 2007 Navigation Pane, select the library that contains the files you want to remove.

2. Click the file that you want to remove. To remove multiple files, press Ctrl as you click the files.

3. Right-click the file, and then choose Remove Offline Copy, as shown in Figure 25-28.

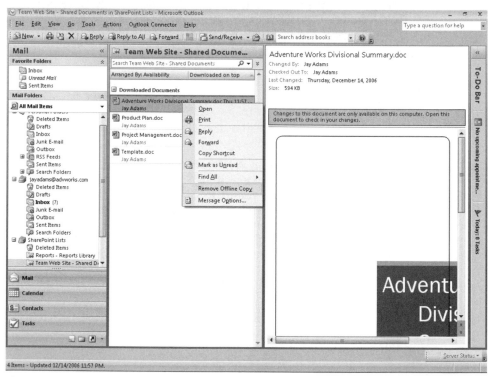

Figure 25-28 You can remove an offline file from Outlook 2007 but keep it in your SharePoint site.

When you remove a file from Outlook 2007, the Reading Pane removes the preview of the file and makes the file available for download. Outlook 2007 moves the file to the Available For Download group and adds a Download This Document button to the file.

Removing SharePoint Folders in Outlook

If you don't need a particular library anymore, you can easily remove it from Outlook 2007. Removing the library does not affect it on the SharePoint site but only removes it from the Navigation Pane in Outlook 2007. One thing to keep in mind, however, is that if you have not sent updates to the SharePoint site before you delete the folder, you will lose any edits you made to the offline files.

To remove a SharePoint folder, right-click it in the Navigation Pane. On the shortcut menu that appears, click Delete <NameOfLibrary>. The <NameOfLibrary> item is the name of the library you are removing. Click Yes.

Using E-Mail to Add a File to a SharePoint Library

If the SharePoint document library is configured to accept documents by e-mail, you can add a document to a library simply by sending an e-mail message, with the document attached, to the library. This is handy if you do not want to go through the process of opening your Web browser, connecting to your SharePoint site, locating a library, and uploading the file to it.

To use this feature, you need to know the e-mail address for the library you plan to send the file to. Some organizations include the e-mail address for libraries in their address book. If you have access to the library's settings, click the Settings button while viewing the library in your Web browser, and then click the library setting command (such as List Setting). Look in the List Information area for an E-Mail Address item. If your library is configured to receive files via e-mail, the address will appear here.

Others might include the e-mail address as part of the library's description—for example, placing the address beneath the title of the library so that users can see it while viewing the library in a Web browser. After you get the address, if your company does not already include the address in your Contacts folder or in the Outlook Address Book, add it your Contacts folder.

After you get the e-mail address, return to Outlook 2007, and then create your message. Attach the file that you want to send to the SharePoint site. Add the address of the library in the To box, and then click Send.

> **Note**
>
> Some organizations use SharePoint groups so that users can send an e-mail message and attachment to other members in a group. When you do this, the attached file is automatically added to the SharePoint site. If this is the case, type the address of the SharePoint group in the To box instead of the library address. The SharePoint group will already have the library address configured.

Exploring the New Look of Access 2007

Before you explore the many features of Microsoft Office Access 2007, it's worth spending a little time looking it over and "kicking the tires." Like a new model of a favorite car, this latest version of Access has major changes to the body (user interface) as well as a new engine under the hood (Access Data Engine). In this chapter and the next, we explore the changes to the user interface, show you how to navigate through Microsoft's new replacement for toolbars and menus called the Ribbon, and discuss the various components of an Access database and how they interact.

Opening Access for the First Time

The first time you open Office Access 2007, you are presented with two preliminary option screens. The first of these, the Privacy Options dialog box seen in Figure 26-1, lists three check boxes, which are selected by default. Note that you must have an active connection to the Internet to use these options. The Get Online Help check box, when selected, allows Access to search Microsoft Office Online's vast resources for content relevant to your search. Access downloads this information to your local computer for faster searching when you search for items in the Help section. Selecting this check box also means you will have the latest Help information at your disposal. The second check box, called Keep Your System Running, is a special tool you can download that interfaces with the 2007 Microsoft Office system. You can use this diagnostic tool to help identify problems with your Office installation. Although not required to run the 2007 Office release or Access 2007, this tool might assist you with locating the cause of any unforeseen system crashes.

The third check box in the Privacy Options dialog box, Make Office Better, allows you to sign up for Microsoft's Customer Experience Improvement Program. This utility tracks various statistics while you use Access 2007 and the 2007 Office release and sends that information to Microsoft. Note that this option does not send any personal information to Microsoft. By tracking how customers are using their products, Microsoft can improve its Office line of products for future releases. Click the Read Our Privacy Statement link in the lower-left corner to read Microsoft's privacy statement. After you make your selections or clear the check boxes you do not want, click the OK button to start using Access 2007.

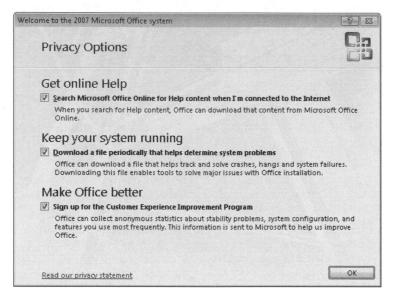

Figure 26-1 You can choose privacy options when you first launch Access 2007.

> **Note**
>
> The dialog box shown in Figure 26-1 is what we saw when opening Access 2007 for the first time using Microsoft Windows Vista. You might see a slightly different sequence of prompts if you install the 2007 Office release on Windows XP.

After selecting your options in the Privacy Options dialog box, you can always alter these settings later. For more information on changing these settings, see "Modifying Global Settings via the Access Options Dialog Box" on page 829.

> **CAUTION**
>
> If you are in a corporate network environment, you should check with your Information Technology department to determine whether your company has established guidelines before making selections in the Privacy Options dialog box.

Getting Started—A New Look for Access

If you are a seasoned developer with previous versions of Access, be prepared for quite a shock when you first open Access 2007. Microsoft has revamped the entire look and feel of Access as well as the other products in the 2007 Office release. To some degree, users of previous versions of Access will have a challenging task adjusting to all the changes the development team has incorporated into this version. If you are one of these users, you might even experience a short-term decrease in productivity as you become accustomed to where commands and tools are located on the new user interface element called the *Ribbon*. (See "Understanding the New Ribbon Feature" on page 783 for details about the Ribbon.) For first-time users of Access, Microsoft has spent a great deal of development effort trying to make the "Access experience" easier and more intuitive in this version. With a new Getting Started screen, a host of ready-to-use database applications available, and a context-driven, rich graphical Ribbon, users will have an easier and quicker time creating professional-looking database applications.

On first launching Access, you see a new Getting Started screen as shown in Figure 26-2. The Featured Online Templates section in the center of the screen displays database templates created by the Microsoft Access development team. These templates represent some of the more common uses for a database and are therefore presented to you first. On the left side of the screen you can find several different template categories grouped by subject. Click on one of these categories to change the display in the center of the screen to a list of templates in that category. The Local Templates category features database templates available on your local drive that were installed with Access. The From Microsoft Office Online category features database templates that you can download—but you must be connected to the Internet to see and download any templates in each of these categories. Microsoft is continually adding and modifying the selections available in the Microsoft Office Online categories, so the list you see might be different from that shown in Figure 26-2. If you have enabled your privacy options to have Access update these featured links, make sure to check these groups from time to time to see if a new template exists for your specific needs. For more information on Privacy Options, see "Understanding the Trust Center" on page 778.

Just above Featured Online Templates in the middle of the screen is a button labeled Blank Database. You use this button to start the process of creating a new empty database with no objects. See Chapter 27, "Creating Your Database and Tables," for details on how to create a new blank database.

The right task pane on the Getting Started screen displays a list of the Access databases you recently opened. To quickly open any of these databases, click on the file name in the list. Click More to see the Open dialog box where you can search for and open any database not in the list.

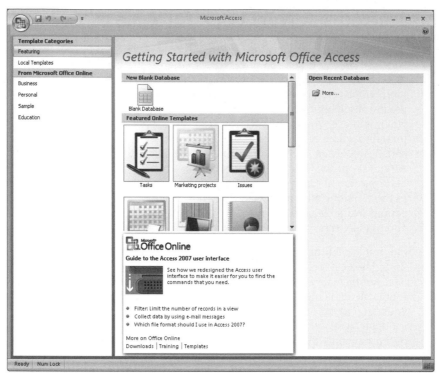

Figure 26-2 You can create a database from a template, create a new blank database, or search for a database file to open on the Getting Started screen in Access 2007.

At the bottom of the Getting Started screen, you see specific information related to Access 2007 such as articles, additional templates, and downloads available from Microsoft Office Online. The downloads can include tutorials, updates to your Help files, or white papers on advanced topics. Most of this content is aimed at showing you all the new features available in Access 2007 as well as pointing out online training materials that Microsoft has created. If you have enabled your privacy options to have Access update these featured links, this area of the Getting Started screen is automatically updated when new content becomes available. Updating the content occurs only if you have an active Internet connection established.

Opening an Existing Database

To showcase the new user interface (UI), let's take one of the template databases out for a test drive. Using the IssuesSample.accdb database on the companion CD, based on the Microsoft Issues template, we will highlight some specific areas of Access 2007. First, follow the instructions at the beginning of this book for installing the sample files on your hard drive. If necessary, start Access again to display the Getting Started screen shown in Figure 26-2. Click More under Open Recent Database in the right task pane to see the Open dialog box shown in Figure 26-3.

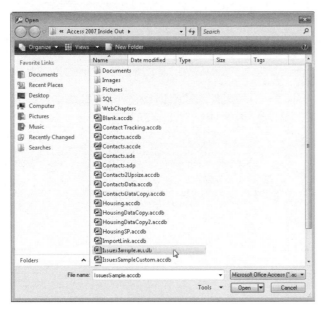

Figure 26-3 You can use the Open dialog box to find and open any existing database file.

In the Open dialog box, select the IssuesSample.accdb file from the folder in which you installed the sample databases, and then click Open. You can also double-click the file name to open the database. (If you haven't set options in Windows Explorer to show file name extensions for registered applications, you won't see the .accdb extension for your database files.) The Issues sample application will start, and you'll see the startup form for the Issues Sample database along with all the various database objects listed on the left side, as shown in Figure 26-4.

> **Note**
>
> If you installed the sample files for this book in the default location from the companion CD, you can find the files in the Microsoft Press\Office 2007 Inside Out folder on your C drive.

Figure 26-4 When you open the Issues Sample database, you can see the new user interface for Access 2007.

If you have used previous versions of Access, you immediately notice that Access 2007 has significant changes. We will discuss each of these user interface elements in greater detail in the following sections, but for now, here is a brief overview of the different elements. The upper-left corner of the screen contains a large button with the Microsoft Office logo on it. This button, called the Microsoft Office Button, replaces the File menu from previous editions of Access. Next to this button are a few smaller buttons on what is called the Quick Access Toolbar. This toolbar holds frequently used commands within Access 2007. Beneath the Quick Access Toolbar is a series of four tabs (Home, Create, External Data, and Database Tools) that contain many commands, options, and drop-down list boxes. These tabs are on what Microsoft refers to as the Ribbon and it replaces menu bars and toolbars from previous versions of Access. You will interact heavily with the Ribbon when developing and using Access 2007 databases because most of the commands you need are contained on it.

Beneath the Ribbon is a small message that says *Security Warning*. This Message Bar informs you if Access has disabled potentially harmful content in this database. See "Understanding Content Security" on page 776 to learn what this message means and what you can do to avoid it.

On the left side of the screen is the new Navigation Pane, which replaces the Database window from previous Access versions. In the Navigation Pane, you can find all the various database objects for this database (forms, tables, queries, and so on).

To the right of the Navigation Pane is where your database objects open. In Figure 26-4 you see that the Issue List form is open. All possible views of your database objects appear in this area. Just beneath the Navigation Pane and main object window is the status bar. The status bar displays text descriptions from field controls, various keyboard settings (Caps Lock, Num Lock, and Scroll Lock), and object view buttons.

Exploring the Microsoft Office Button

Microsoft Office
Button

The new Microsoft Office Button in Access 2007, shown in the upper-left corner of Figure 26-5, replaces the File menu from previous versions, and you can display its commands by clicking the Microsoft Office Button from the Getting Started screen or from within any database. Figure 26-5 shows you the available commands.

Figure 26-5 You can view many commands by clicking the Microsoft Office Button.

Using these commands you can do any of the following:

- **New** Create a new database file.

- **Open** Open any existing database file on your computer or network.

- **Save** Save design changes for the database object that is open and has the focus.

- **Save As** Save a copy of the current object, find add-ins to save the object with a different file format, or save a copy of the current database in 2007, 2002/2003, or 2000 Access format. When you click the Save As button, the default is to save a copy of the current open object that has the focus or the object that has the focus in the Navigation Pane. If you rest your mouse pointer on or click the arrow at the right, additional commands appear in a submenu to the right of the arrow. You can choose from these to save a copy of your entire database in any of the formats supported by Access 2007. Note that if you choose to save the entire database, Access closes the database you have open so that it can create the copy.

- **Print** Print the currently open object that has the focus or the object in the Navigation Pane that has the focus using the Print dialog box or the Quick Print feature, or use Print Preview to preview the printed appearance on screen. If you immediately click the Print button, Access opens the Print dialog box to print whatever object currently has the focus. Be careful here because the object that has the focus might not be the one currently on the screen. If the focus is on an object in the Navigation Pane, that object is printed instead of the object currently open. If you rest your mouse pointer on or click the arrow to the right of the Print button, a submenu presents two additional options called Quick Print and Print Preview. Quick Print immediately sends the selected database object to the printer whereas Print Preview lets you preview on your monitor what you are about to print. Here again, be careful about which object has the focus.

- **Manage** Compact and repair your database file, back up your database, or open the Database Properties dialog box to review and change properties specific to this database.

- **E-Mail** Export the currently open object that has the focus or the object in the Navigation Pane that has the focus in various formats and send to another person. Be careful here because the object that has the focus might not be the one currently on the screen. If the focus is on an object in the Navigation Pane, that object is exported instead of the object currently open. You can choose to export and send the object in the following formats: Excel, HTML, Rich Text Format, or as a Text File.

- **Publish** Publish the database to a document manager server or package your database as a CAB file and digitally sign it.

- **Close Database** Close the currently open database and return to the Getting Started screen.

You can also find these two buttons at the bottom of the menu:

- **Access Options** Opens the Access Options dialog box where you can choose and define many different settings and preferences for Access.

- **Exit Access** Closes the currently open database file as well as completely exits Access.

> **Note**
>
> For users of previous versions of Access, the Access Options dialog box is where you'll find many of the settings previously found in the Options dialog box that you opened from the Tools menu. For more information on the options available in this area, see "Modifying Global Settings via the Access Options Dialog Box" on page 829.

Chapter 26

Taking Advantage of the Quick Access Toolbar

Next to the Microsoft Office Button is the Quick Access Toolbar, shown in Figure 26-6. This special toolbar gives you "quick access" to some of the more common commands you will use in Access 2007, and you can customize this toolbar to include additional commands. Here are the default commands available on the Quick Access Toolbar:

- **Save** Saves any changes to the currently selected database object.

- **Undo** Undoes the last change you made to an object or a record.

- **Redo** Cancels the last Undo change you made to an object or a record.

At the right end of the Quick Access Toolbar is a small arrow. Click that arrow, and you'll see the Customize Quick Access Toolbar menu, as shown in Figure 26-6.

The top section of the menu displays common commands that you might want to add to the Quick Access Toolbar. Note that the three default commands—Save, Undo, and Redo—have check marks next to them. You can click any of these to clear the check mark and remove the command from the Quick Access Toolbar. You can click any of the other eight commands (New, Open, E-Mail, Quick Print, Print Preview, Spelling, Mode, and Refresh All) to add them to the right end of the Quick Access Toolbar. Near the bottom of this menu is More Commands, which allows you to fully customize what commands are available and how those commands appear on the Quick Access Toolbar. The Show Below The Ribbon option on the menu allows you to move the Quick Access Toolbar above or below the Ribbon depending on your preference. The last option on this menu, Minimize The Ribbon, causes Access to automatically collapse the Ribbon when it is not being used. When the focus is off the Ribbon, only the Ribbon tabs themselves appear when you click this command. Clicking any of the Ribbon tabs then causes Access to redisplay all the commands on top of any open objects. When you move the focus off any part of the Ribbon, it will again collapse to just the tabs.

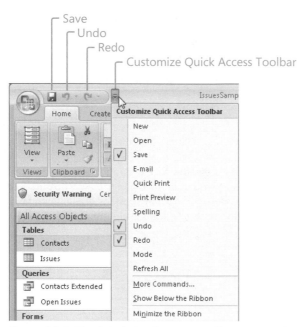

Figure 26-6 The default Quick Access Toolbar contains the Save, Undo, and Redo commands for the current object, and the command to customize the toolbar.

To customize the Quick Access Toolbar, click the arrow on the right end and click More Commands near the bottom of the menu. The Access Options dialog box with the Customize category selected appears, as shown in Figure 26-7.

On the left you can see a list of built-in Access commands that you can select to add to the Quick Access Toolbar. By default, the list shows commands from the Popular Commands category—commands that are used very frequently. You can change the list of commands by selecting a different category from the Choose Commands From list. The All Commands option displays the entire list of Access commands available in alphabetical order. Just below the list of available commands is a check box that you can select to show the Quick Access Toolbar below the Ribbon. Clear the check box to show the Quick Access Toolbar above the Ribbon.

The list on the right side of the screen by default displays what options are available on every Quick Access Toolbar for all your database files. If you add, remove, or modify the commands shown in the list on the right when you have chosen For All Documents (Default) in the Customize Quick Access Toolbar list, the changes are reflected in every database you open with Access 2007. To customize the Quick Access Toolbar for only the specific database you currently have open, click the arrow in the drop-down list and select the database file path for your current database from the list, as shown in Figure 26-8.

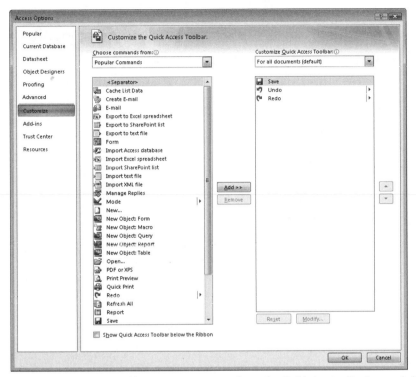

Figure 26-7 You can add or remove commands on the Quick Access Toolbar and change their sequence using the Customize category in the Access Options dialog box.

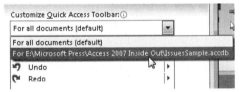

Figure 26-8 You can add or remove commands on the Quick Access Toolbar for the current database by selecting your database from the Customize Quick Access Toolbar list.

When you select the current database, the command list below it is now empty, awaiting the changes you request. Find a command in the list on the left, and then either double-click it or click the Add button in the middle of the screen to add this command to your custom Quick Access Toolbar, as shown in Figure 26-9. If you make a mistake and select the wrong command, select the command in the list on the right, and click the Remove button to eliminate it from your custom list.

Chapter 26

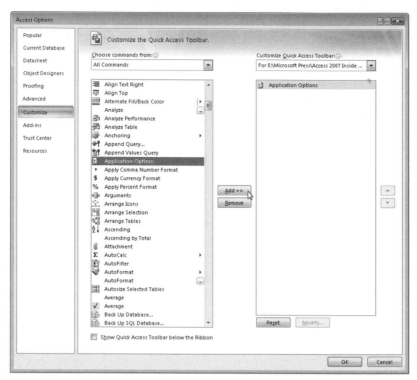

Figure 26-9 Add a command to the Quick Access Toolbar by selecting it in the list on the left and then clicking the Add button.

In addition to the built-in commands, you can also select any macros you have defined in this current database. To do this, select Macros in the Choose Commands From list on the left. A list of all your saved macro objects appears, and you can add these macros directly to your custom Quick Access Toolbar, as shown in Figure 26-10. We added one macro called mcrSample to this Issues Sample database to illustrate the next steps.

CAUTION

Do not add a macro to your Quick Access Toolbar when you have selected the option to customize the Quick Access Toolbar for all documents. Access displays an error if you try to click your custom macro command in a database that does not contain the macro you selected.

You can also assign custom button images to the macro objects you select. To do so, select one of your macros in the list on the right, and then click the Modify button to open the Modify Button dialog box shown in Figure 26-11. From here you can choose one of the predefined button images available and also change the display name for this option on your custom Quick Access Toolbar.

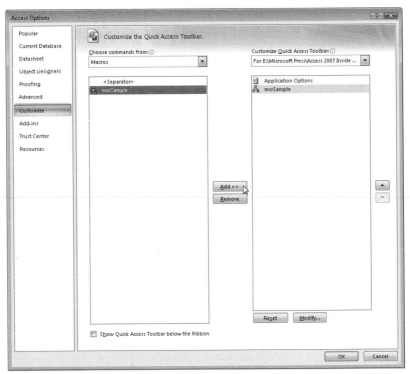

Figure 26-10 Add a saved macro object to the Quick Access Toolbar by selecting it in the list on the left and then clicking the Add button.

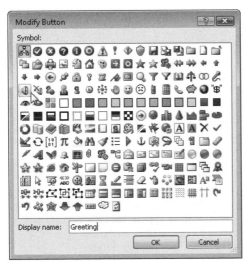

Figure 26-11 You can change the button face and the display name in the Modify Button dialog box.

After you have all the commands and macros you want on your custom Quick Access Toolbar, you might decide that you do not like the order in which they appear. Access 2007 allows you to easily modify this order using the Move Up and Move Down arrow buttons at the far right of the dialog box. (You can rest your mouse pointer on either button to see the button name.) Select a command you want to move in the list on the right and click the up arrow to move it up in the list as shown in Figure 26-12. Each successive click moves that command up one more place in the custom list. Likewise, the down arrow shifts the selected command down in the list. In Figure 26-12 you can see that we have moved the macro titled Greeting up above the Application Options command.

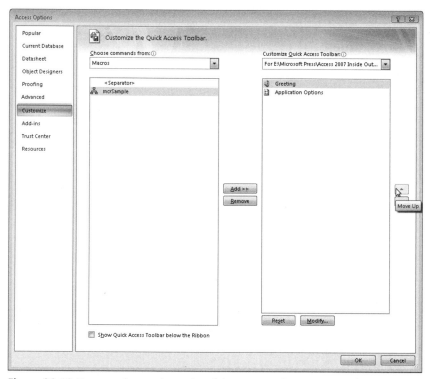

Figure 26-12 You can change the order of the commands on your Quick Access Toolbar by clicking the Move Up and Move Down arrow buttons.

From top to bottom in the list on the right, the commands appear in left-to-right order on the Quick Access Toolbar after the commands assigned to all databases. When you are completely satisfied with your revisions, click OK to save your changes. Observe that your custom Quick Access Toolbar now appears on the screen above or below the Ribbon depending on the choice you have selected. Figure 26-13 shows our completed changes to the Quick Access Toolbar for this specific database.

> **Note**
>
> You might have noticed the <Separator> option in the list on the left. Adding <Separator> to your custom Quick Access Toolbar places a small space below the command currently selected in the list on the right. You can add as many separators as you want to your custom Quick Access Toolbar to visually separate groups of commands.

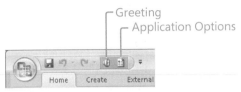

┌ Greeting
└ Application Options

Figure 26-13 Your two additional commands now appear on the Quick Access Toolbar for this database.

To remove an item from your custom Quick Access Toolbar, reopen the Access Options dialog box with the Customize category selected again by clicking the arrow on the Quick Access Toolbar and then clicking More Commands. To remove an item, select it in the list on the right and click the Remove button, and Access removes it from your list of commands. If you inadvertently remove a command that you wanted to keep, you can click the Cancel button in the lower-right corner to discard all changes. You can also find the command in the list on the left and add it back. Keep in mind that you can remove commands for all databases or for only the current database.

If you wish to restore the Quick Access Toolbar for all databases to the default set of commands, select For All Documents (Default) in the Customize Quick Access Toolbar list, and then click the Reset button. To remove all custom commands for the current database, select the database path in the Customize Quick Access Toolbar list and click Reset. Before removing any commands on the Quick Access Toolbar, Access displays a warning message shown in Figure 26-14. If you click Yes to this Reset Customizations message, Access resets the Quick Access Toolbar for this current database back to the defaults.

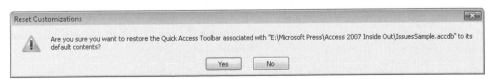

Figure 26-14 Access asks you to confirm resetting the Quick Access Toolbar back to the default commands.

INSIDE OUT   Adding a Command to the Quick Access Toolbar with Two Mouse Clicks

If you notice that you are using a command on the Ribbon quite often, Access 2007 provides a very quick and easy way to add this command to the Quick Access Toolbar. To add a command on the Ribbon to the Quick Access Toolbar, right-click the command and click Add To Quick Access Toolbar. This adds the command to the Quick Access Toolbar for all databases. Alternatively, you can quickly remove an item from your custom Quick Access Toolbar by right-clicking on the command and clicking Remove From Quick Access Toolbar.

Understanding Content Security

In response to growing threats from viruses and worms, Microsoft launched a security initiative in early 2002, called Trustworthy Computing, to focus on making all its products safer to use. In an e-mail sent to employees, Bill Gates summed up the seriousness of the initiative:

"In the past, we've made our software and services more compelling for users by adding new features and functionality, and by making our platform richly extensible. We've done a terrific job at that, but all those great features won't matter unless customers trust our software. So now, when we face a choice between adding features and resolving security issues, we need to choose security. Our products should emphasize security right out of the box, and we must constantly refine and improve that security as threats evolve."

Prior to Microsoft Access 2003, it was quite possible for a malicious person to send you a database file that contained code that could damage your system. As soon as you opened the database, the harmful code would run—perhaps even without your knowledge. Or the programmer could embed dangerous code in a query, form, or report, and your computer would be damaged as soon as you opened that object. In version 11 (Access 2003), you were presented with a series of confusing dialog boxes when you opened an unsigned database file if you had left your macro security level set to medium or high. After wading through the various dialog boxes, you could still be left with a database you were unable to open.

Access 2007 improves upon the security model by adding a new component to the Access interface called the *Trust Center*. This new security interface is far less confusing and intrusive than the Access 2003 macro security feature. With a security level set to high in Access 2003, you would not be able to open any database files because all Access databases could have some type of macros, VBA code, or calls to unsafe functions embedded in their structure. Any database with queries is considered unsafe by Access 2007 because those queries could contain expressions calling unsafe functions. In Access 2007, each database file opens without presenting you with a series of dialog boxes like in Access 2003. Depending on where your file is located on the local computer drive or network share, Access silently disables any malicious macros or VBA code without any intrusive dialog box messages.

> **Note**
>
> The sample databases included on the companion CD are not digitally signed, because they will become unsigned as soon as you change any of the queries or sample code. We designed all the sample applications to open successfully, but each displays a warning dialog box if the database is not trusted. If you have installed the database in an untrusted location, the application displays instructions in the warning dialog box that you can follow to enable the full application. See "Enabling Content by Defining Trusted Locations" on page 781 for information about defining trusted locations.

Temporarily Enabling a Database That Is Not Trusted

When you open an existing database or template, you might see a Security Warning message displayed in the Message Bar, just below the Quick Access Toolbar and Ribbon as shown in Figure 26-15. This message notifies you that Access has disabled certain features of the application because the file is not digitally signed or is located in a folder that has not been designated as trusted.

Message Bar

Figure 26-15 The Message Bar alerts you if Access has disabled certain content.

In order to ensure that any restricted code and macros function in this database, you must manually tell Access to enable this content by clicking the Options button on the Message Bar. This opens a dialog box, called Microsoft Office Security Options, as shown in Figure 26-16. This dialog box warns you that this file's content cannot be verified because a digital certificate was not found.

You can choose to have Access 2007 continue to block any harmful content by leaving the default option set to Help Protect Me From Unknown Content (Recommended). By having Access block any harmful content, you can be assured that no malicious code or macros can execute from this database. However, you also have to realize that because Access blocks all Visual Basic code and any macros containing a potentially harmful command, it is quite possible that this application will not run correctly if you continue to let Access disable potentially harmful functions and code. In order to have Access discontinue blocking potentially harmful content, you must select the Enable This Content option. After you select that option and click OK, Access closes the database and then reopens the file to enable all content. Access does not display the Message Bar after it reopens the file, and all functions, code, and macros are now allowed to run in this specific database.

Figure 26-16 You can enable blocked content from the Microsoft Office Security Options dialog box.

> **Note**
>
> When you enable content after opening an untrusted database, the database becomes trusted only for the current session. If you close the database and then attempt to reopen it, Access displays the warnings again on the Message Bar.

Understanding the Trust Center

You might have noticed in the lower-left corner of the Microsoft Office Security Options dialog box a link to the Trust Center. You can also open the Trust Center from the Access Options dialog box, which you can open by clicking the Microsoft Office Button discussed earlier. We will discuss the Access Options dialog box later in this chapter; see "Modifying Global Settings via the Access Options Dialog Box" on page 829.

Click Open The Trust Center in the Microsoft Office Security Options dialog box to view the advanced security settings. If the Message Bar is not currently available, click the Microsoft Office Button in the upper-left corner and then click Access Options. In the Access Options dialog box, click the Trust Center category on the left and then click the Trust Center Settings button. In the Trust Center dialog box, shown in Figure 26-17, you see six categories of security settings.

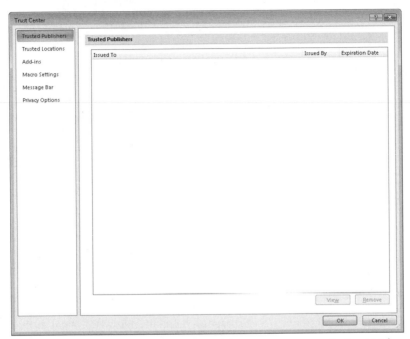

Figure 26-17 The Trust Center dialog box displays various categories in which you can select trust and privacy options.

Briefly, the categories are as follows:

- **Trusted Publishers.** Use to view and remove publishers you have designated as being trustworthy. When applications are digitally signed by one of these trusted publishers, Access does not disable any content within the database and the Message Bar does not display any warning. By default, digitally signed applications from Microsoft are trusted. You might see one or more additional trusted publishers if you have ever tried to download and run a signed application and have indicated to Windows that you trust the publisher and want to save the publisher's certificate.

- **Trusted Locations.** Use to designate specific folders and subfolders as trusted locations. Access considers any database files within this folder as trustworthy, and all content in these folders is enabled. In the Trusted Locations category, each designated trusted folder is listed with the file path, an optional description, and the date the entry was last modified. See "Enabling Content by Defining Trusted Locations" on the next page for details about using the options in this category.

- **Add-Ins.** Use to set specific restrictions on Access add-in files by selecting or clearing the three check boxes in this category. An add-in is a separate program or file that extends the capabilities of Access. You can create these separate files or programs by using Visual Basic for Applications (VBA) or another programming language such as C#. You can require that add-in files be signed by a trusted publisher before Access will load and run them. If you select the option to require that add-ins be signed, you can disable notifications for add-ins that are unsigned. For added security, you can disable all application add-in functionality.

- **Macro Settings.** Use to configure how Access handles macros in databases that are not in a trusted location. Four options are available with this feature, only one of which can be active at any given time. Table 26-1 discusses the purpose of each option.

Table 26-1 **Macro Settings**

Option	Purpose
Disable All Macros Without Notification	Access disables all harmful content, but does not notify you through the Message Bar.
Disable All Macros With Notification	Access disables all harmful content but notifies you through the Message Bar that it has disabled the content. This is the default option for new installations of Access. This is equivalent to the Medium macro security level option available in Access 2003.
Disable All Macros Except Digitally Signed Macros	Access allows only digitally signed macros (code in digitally signed databases). All other potentially harmful content is disabled. This is equivalent to the High macro security level option available in Access 2003.
Enable All Macros (not recommended, potentially dangerous code can run)	Access enables any and all potentially harmful content. In addition, Access does not notify you through the Message Bar. This is equivalent to the Low macro security option available in Access 2003.

- **Message Bar.** Use to configure Access either to show the Message Bar when content has been disabled or not to display the bar at all.

- **Privacy Options.** Use to enable or disable actions within Access regarding computing privacy, troubleshooting system problems, and scanning suspicious Web site links. The first check box under Privacy Options tells Access to scan Microsoft's online help site when you are connected to the Internet. If you clear this check box, Access scans only your local hard drive when you conduct a search in Help. The second check box, Update Featured Links From Microsoft Office Online, tells Access to display some current Microsoft Office Online featured links on the Getting Started screen. Selecting the third check box instructs Access to download and activate a special file from Microsoft's site that helps you troubleshoot Access and Office program installation and program errors. The fourth check box allows you to sign up for the Customer Experience Improvement Program. Microsoft uses this program to track statistics of the features you use the most frequently and gather information about your Microsoft Office system configuration. These statistics help determine changes in future program releases. The final check box under Privacy Options allows Access to automatically scan Office documents for possible links to and from suspicious Web sites. This last option is turned on by default to help safeguard your computer against documents containing harmful Web links.

Enabling Content by Defining Trusted Locations

You can permanently enable the content in a database that is not trusted by defining a folder on your hard drive or network that is trusted and then placing the database in that folder. Or, you can define the folder where the database is located as trusted. You define trusted locations in the Trust Center dialog box.

CAUTION

If you are in a corporate network environment, you should check with your Information Technology department to determine whether your company has established guidelines concerning enabling content on Access databases.

To define a trusted location, click the Microsoft Office Button and then click Access Options. In the Access Options dialog box, click the Trust Center category and then click the Trust Center Settings button. Access displays the Trust Center dialog box. Click the Trusted Locations category to see its options, as shown in Figure 26-18.

Click the Add New Location button. Access now displays the Microsoft Office Trusted Location dialog box shown in Figure 26-19.

Click the Browse button and locate the folder you want to designate as trusted. You can optionally designate any subfolders in that directory as trusted without having to designate each individual folder within the hierarchy. Enter an optional description you want for this folder, and click OK to save your changes. The new location you just specified now appears in the list of trusted locations. If you later decide to remove this folder as a trusted location, select that location, as shown in Figure 26-18, and then click the Remove button. Any Access databases in that folder are now treated as unsafe. Figure 26-18 also shows two check boxes at the bottom of the dialog box. The first check box allows you to define network locations as trusted locations. Microsoft recommends you not select this check box because you cannot control what files others might place in a network location. The second check box disables all Trusted Location settings and allows content only from trusted publishers.

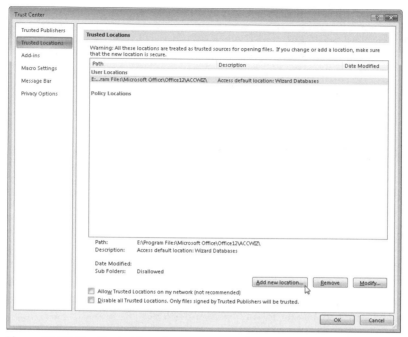

Figure 26-18 The Trusted Locations category in the Trust Center dialog box shows you locations that are currently trusted.

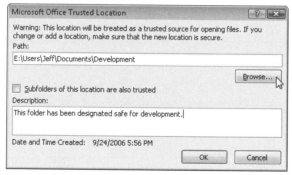

Figure 26-19 Creating a new trusted location from the Microsoft Office Trusted Location dialog box.

> **Note**
>
> To ensure that all the sample databases from the companion CD operate correctly, add the folder where you installed the files (the default location is the Microsoft Press\Office 2007 Inside Out folder on your C drive) to your Trusted Locations.

Understanding the New Ribbon Feature

One of the biggest changes to the new user interface in Access 2007 is the Ribbon, a replacement for the menu bars and toolbars that were in previous versions. The Ribbon, shown in Figure 26-20, is a strip that contains all the functionality of the older menu options (File, Edit, View, and so on) and the various toolbars, condensed into one common area in the application window. Microsoft's usability studies revealed that most users failed to discover many useful features that were previously buried several levels deep in the old menu structure. The Ribbon is a context-rich environment displaying all the program functions and commands, with large icons for key functions and smaller icons for less-used functions. Access displays a host of different controls on the Ribbon to help you build and edit your applications. Lists, command buttons, galleries, and Dialog Box Launchers are all on the Ribbon and offer a new rich user interface for Access 2007 and the other 2007 Microsoft Office system products.

Figure 26-20 The new Ribbon interface replaces menu bars and toolbars.

The Ribbon in Access 2007 consists of four main tabs—Home, Create, External Data, and Database Tools—that group together common tasks and contain a major subset of the program functions in Access. These main tabs are visible at all times when you are working in Access 2007 because they contain the most common tools you need when working with any database object. Other tabs, called *contextual tabs*, appear and disappear to the right of the Database Tools tab when you are working with specific database objects and in various views.

INSIDE OUT   Scrolling Through the Ribbon Tabs

If you click on one of the Ribbon tabs, you can then scroll through the other tabs using the scroll wheel on your mouse.

Each tab on the Ribbon has commands that are further organized into groups. The name of each group is listed at the bottom, and each group has various commands logically grouped by subject matter. To enhance the user experience and make things easier to find, Microsoft has labeled every command in the various groups. If you rest your mouse pointer on a specific command, Access displays a *ScreenTip* that contains the name of the command and a short description that explains what you can do with the command. Any time a command includes a small arrow, you can click the arrow to display options available for the command.

Home Tab

Let's first explore the Home tab shown in Figure 26-21.

Figure 26-21 The Home tab provides common commands for editing, filtering, and sorting data.

The Home tab has the following groups:

- **Views.** Most objects in an Access database have two or more ways to view them. When you have one of these objects open and it has the focus, you can use the View command in this group to easily switch to another view.

- **Clipboard.** You can use the commands in this group to manage data you move to and from the Clipboard.

- **Font.** You can change how Access displays text using the commands in this group.

- **Rich Text.** You can design fields in your database to contain data formatted in Rich Text. (See Chapter 27 for more details about data types.) You can use the commands in this group to format text in a Rich Text field.

- **Records.** Use the commands in this group to work with records, including deleting records and saving changes.

- **Sort & Filter.** You can use these commands to sort and filter your data.

- **Window.** Use the commands in this group to resize windows or select one of several windows you have open. Note that Access displays this group only when you have set your database to display Overlapping Windows rather than Tabbed Documents. For more details, see "Using the Single-Document vs. Multiple-Document Interface" on page 825.

- **Find.** The commands in this group allow you to search and replace data, go to a specific record, or select one or all records.

Create Tab

The Create tab, shown in Figure 26-22, contains commands that let you create new database objects. Each group on this particular tab arranges its specific functions by database object type.

Figure 26-22 The Create tab provides commands for creating all the various types of database objects.

The Create tab contains the following groups:

- **Tables.** Use the commands in this group to create new tables or link to a Microsoft Windows SharePoint Services list. You can learn more about Windows SharePoint Services in "Working with Windows SharePoint Services," one of the bonus chapters on the companion CD.

- **Forms.** You can create new forms using the commands in this group, including PivotChart and PivotTable forms.

- **Reports.** The commands in this group allow you to create new reports using available wizards or to start a new report design from scratch.

- **Other.** Use the commands in this group to create new queries or build macros or modules to automate your application.

External Data Tab

The External Data tab, shown in Figure 26-23, provides commands to import from or link to data in external sources or export data to external sources, including other Access databases or Windows SharePoint Services lists.

Figure 26-23 The External Data tab provides commands for working with external data sources.

This tab has the following groups:

- **Import.** The commands in the Import group let you link to data or import data or objects from other sources such as other Access databases, Microsoft Excel spreadsheets, Windows SharePoint Services lists, and many other data sources such as Microsoft SQL Server, dBase, Paradox, and Lotus 1-2-3.

- **Export.** You can use these commands to export objects to another Access database or to export data to Excel, a Windows SharePoint Services site, Microsoft Word, and more.

Chapter 26

- **Collect Data.** These two commands allow you to update data in your Access 2007 database from special e-mail options using Microsoft Office Outlook 2007.

- **SharePoint Lists.** Commands in this group allow you to migrate some or all of your data to a Windows SharePoint Services (version 3) site or synchronize offline data with an active Windows SharePoint Services site.

Database Tools Tab

The last tab that is always available on the Ribbon is the Database Tools tab, shown in Figure 26-24. The top part of Figure 26-24 shows the Database Tools tab when using an Access 2007 database (.accdb) and the bottom part shows the Database Tools tab when using Access 2000, 2002, or 2003 databases (.mdb).

Figure 26-24 The Database Tools tab gives you access to miscellaneous tools and wizards.

The Database Tools tab on the Ribbon includes the following groups:

- **Macro.** Commands in this group let you open the Visual Basic Editor, run a macro, or covert a macro either to a shortcut menu or to Visual Basic.

- **Show/Hide.** Commands in this group activate useful information windows. Use the Relationships command to view and edit your table relationships. (See Chapter 27 for details.) Click the Property Sheet command to open the Property Sheet dialog box that displays the properties of the object currently selected in the Navigation Pane. Click the Object Dependencies command to see which objects are dependent on the currently selected object. Select the Message Bar check box to reveal the Message Bar that displays any pending security alerts.

- **Analyze.** Use the commands in this group to print a report about your objects or run one of the two analysis wizards.

- **Move Data.** The two wizards available in this group allow you to either move some or all of your tables to SQL Server or move all your tables to a separate Access database and create links to the moved tables in the current database.

- **Database Tools.** You will see a different set of commands in this group depending on whether you have opened an Access 2000, 2002, or 2003 database (.mdb) or an Access 2007 database (.accdb). In both groups, you find commands to run the Linked Table Manager, the Switchboard Manager, make an execute-only version (.mde or .accde) of your database, or manage add-ins. In an .mdb file, you can find commands to encode/decode your database (encrypt it) and set a password that a user must know to run your database. In an .accdb file, you can find a command to create an encrypted version with a password.

- **Administer.** Access displays this group on the Database Tools tab only when you open an Access database file created in Access 2000, 2002, or 2003 (.mdb). The Users And Permissions command lets you edit and define users and object permissions in the legacy security system no longer supported in Access 2007 format (.accdb) database files. The Replication Options let you manage the legacy replication features no longer supported in Access 2007 format database files. For more information on these features, see *Running Microsoft Access 2000* (Microsoft Press, 1999) or *Microsoft Office Access 2003 Inside Out* (Microsoft Press, 2004).

Chapter 26

INSIDE OUT   Collapsing the Entire Ribbon

If you need some additional workspace within the Access window, you can collapse the entire Ribbon by double-clicking on any of the tabs. All the groups disappear from the screen, but the tabs are still available. You can also use the keyboard shortcut Ctrl+F1 to collapse the Ribbon. To see the Ribbon again, simply click on any tab to restore the Ribbon to its full height or press Ctrl+F1 again.

Understanding the New Navigation Pane

As part of the user interface overhaul in Office Access 2007, the development team introduced a new object navigation tool called the Navigation Pane. In previous versions of Access, you navigated among the various database objects through the Database window. Access grouped all database objects together by type and displayed various properties of each object alongside the object name depending on the view you chose.

Office Access 2007 replaces the Database window with the Navigation Pane shown in Figure 26-25. Unlike the Object bar in the old Database window that you could position anywhere in the Access workspace, the new Navigation Pane is a window that is permanently located on the left side of the screen. Any open database objects appear to the right of the Navigation Pane instead of covering it up. This means you still have easy access to the other objects in your database without having to shuffle open objects around the screen or continually minimize and restore object windows. In contrast to the Database window, the new Navigation Pane lets you view objects of different types at the same time. If the list of objects in a particular group is quite extensive, Access provides a scroll bar in each section so that you can access each object.

To follow along in the rest of this section, open the Issues Sample database (Issues-Sample.accdb) from the companion CD. Unless you have previously opened this database and changed the Navigation Pane, you should see the Navigation Pane on the left side of the screen, exactly like Figure 26-25.

Figure 26-25 The new Navigation Pane replaces the Database window from previous Access versions.

INSIDE OUT Quickly Jumping to a Specific Object in the Navigation Pane

Click an object in one of the groups in the Navigation Pane to select it and then press a letter key to quickly jump to any objects that begin with that letter in that particular group.

Shutter Bar Open/Close Button

You can easily expand or contract the width of the Navigation Pane by positioning your pointer over the right edge of the Navigation Pane and then clicking and dragging the edge in either direction to the width you want. Keep in mind that the farther you expand the width, the less screen area you have available to work with your database objects because all objects open to the right of the Navigation Pane. To maximize the amount of screen area available to work with open objects, you can completely collapse the Navigation Pane to the far left side of the application window by clicking the double-arrow button in the upper-right corner, called the Shutter Bar Open/Close Button. When you do this, the Navigation Pane appears as a thin bar on the left of your screen, as shown in Figure 26-26. After you have "shuttered" the Navigation Pane, the arrows on the button reverse direction and point to the right. Click the button again to reopen the Navigation Pane to its previous width. Access 2007 remembers the last width you set for the Navigation Pane. The next time you open an Access database, the width of the Navigation Pane will be the same as when you last had the database open. Pressing the F11 key alternately toggles the Navigation Pane between its collapsed and expanded view.

Chapter 26

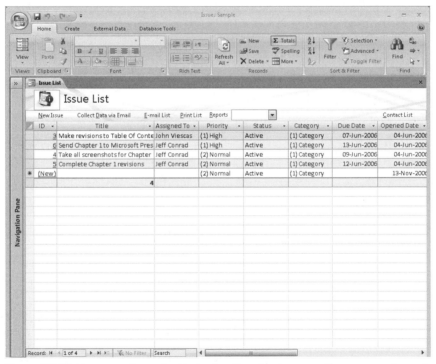

Figure 26-26 You can collapse the Navigation Pane to give yourself more room to work on open objects.

Exploring Navigation Pane Object Views

When you first open the IssuesSample.accdb sample database, the Navigation Pane shows you all the objects defined in the database grouped by object type and sorted by object name. You can verify this view by clicking the menu bar at the top of the Navigation Pane, as shown in Figure 26-27, which opens the Navigation Pane menu. Under Navigate To Category, you should see Object Type selected, and under Filter By Group, you should see All Access Objects selected. This is the view we selected in the database before saving it on the companion CD.

Figure 26-27 You can change the display in the Navigation Pane by selecting a different category or filter from the Navigation Pane menu.

This view closely matches the Database window in previous versions of Access where you could select tabs to view each object category, and each object type was sorted by object name. The objects in each of the six object types—Tables, Queries, Forms, Reports, Macros, and Modules—are grouped together. When the list of objects is longer than can be displayed within the height of the Navigation Pane, Access provides a scroll bar.

You can customize the Navigation Pane to display the object list in many different ways. Access 2007 provides a set of predefined categories for the Navigation Pane that you can access with a few mouse clicks. You can see these available categories by clicking the top of the Navigation Pane to open the menu, as shown previously in Figure 26-27.

Notice that this Issues Sample database lists six categories under Navigate To Category: Issues Navigation, Custom, Object Type, Tables And Related Views, Created Date, and Modified Date. The first category in the list, Issues Navigation, is a custom category specific to this database. We'll show you how to create and modify custom categories later in this section. Access always provides the other five categories in all databases to allow you to view objects in various predefined ways. We will discuss the Custom and Issues Navigation categories later in "Working with Custom Categories and Groups" on page 795.

INSIDE OUT Collapsing an Entire Group in the Navigation Pane

If you click the header of each object type where the double arrow is located, Access collapses that part of the Navigation Pane. For example, if you want to temporarily hide the tables, you can collapse that section by clicking the double arrow next to the word *Tables*. To bring the table list back to full view, simply click the double arrow that is now pointing downward, and the tables section expands to reveal all the table objects.

The Navigation Pane menu also provides commands under Filter By Group to allow you to filter the database object list. The filter commands available change depending on which Navigate To Category command you select. Notice in Figure 26-27 where Navigate To Category is set to Object Type that the Filter By Group section in the lower half of the Navigation Pane menu lists each of the object types that currently exist in your database. When you have the menu categorized by object type, you can further filter the list of objects by selecting one of the object types to see only objects of that type. Click one of the object types, Forms for instance, and Access hides all the other object types as shown in Figure 26-28. This feature is very useful if you want to view and work with only a particular type of database object. Click the All Access Objects filter command to again see all objects by object type.

By default, new blank databases created in the Access 2007 format display the object list in the Navigation Pane in a category called Tables And Related Views. You can switch the Issues Sample database to this category by opening the Navigation Pane menu that contains categories and filters, and then click the Tables And Related Views command as shown in Figure 26-29.

Figure 26-28 You can display only the Forms group of objects in Object Type view by applying a filter in the Navigation Pane menu.

Figure 26-29 The Tables And Related Views category on the Navigation Pane menu offers a different way to view your database objects.

After you click Tables And Related Views, the Navigation Pane should look similar to Figure 26-30. This particular view category groups the various database objects based on their relation to a common denominator—a table. As you can observe in Figure 26-30, each group of objects is the name of one of the tables. Note that in Figure 26-30 we collapsed the Ribbon in order to show you all the various database objects and groups. Within each group, you can see the table as the first item in the group followed by all objects that are dependent on the data from the table. So, Access lists all database objects dependent on the Issues data table together in the Issues group, and similarly, it lists all objects dependent on the Contacts table in the Contacts group. At first glance, you might be a bit confused as to the purpose of each object, but notice that the various types of objects each have their own unique icon to help you differentiate them. The Issues table, for example, is listed first with the icon for a table before the name and the word *Table* next to it. The remaining objects in the group are the various objects that are dependent on the Issues table in alphabetical order by name, and each object has an icon before the name that identifies the type of object.

Figure 26-30 The Tables And Related Views category in the Navigation Pane groups objects under a table.

Some objects appear in a category called Unrelated Objects, such as the macro called mcrSample and the module called basSampleSub in this Issues Sample database. Macros and modules contain code that you can reference from any object in your database. They always appear in the Unrelated Objects category of Tables And Related Views because Access does not search through the macro arguments and module code to see if any table references exist.

Chapter 26

INSIDE OUT   When to Use the Tables And Related Views Category

This particular view category can be quite useful if you are making some changes to a table and want to see what objects might be affected by the change. You can check each query, form, and report that is related to this table one at a time in this view to ensure that no functionality of the database is broken after you make a change to the underlying table.

Now that you have changed to Tables And Related Views, open the Navigation Pane menu again. Notice that the names of both data tables in this database are listed beneath Filter By Group as shown previously in Figure 26-29. Click Issues, and Access reduces the Navigation Pane to show only the objects related to the Issues table as shown in Figure 26-31. By filtering the Navigation Pane to one table, you have reduced the number of objects displayed and can focus your attention on only a small subset of database objects. You can open the Navigation Menu again and click All Tables to restore the complete list.

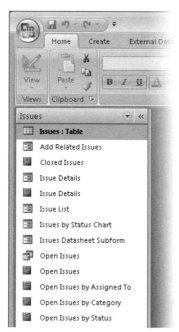

Figure 26-31 You can filter Tables And Related Views to show only the database objects dependent on one table.

Access provides two related types of object view categories on the Navigation Pane menu called Created Date and Modified Date, as shown in Figure 26-32. These categories list all the objects in descending order based on when you created or last modified the object. These views can be quite useful if you need to locate an object that you created or last modified on a specific date or within a range of dates. When you click either of these commands, Filter By Group on the Navigation Pane menu offers to filter by Today, Yesterday, one of the five days previous to that (listed by day name), Last Week, Two Weeks Ago, Three Weeks Ago, Last Month, Older, or All Dates.

Figure 26-32 The Created Date and Modified Date categories display objects in the order you created or last modified them.

> **Note**
>
> You will not see the same options listed in Figure 26-32 when you open your copy of Issues Sample because all the Modified dates will be older than three weeks. The only two options you will see are Older and All Dates.

Working with Custom Categories and Groups

We have not yet discussed the remaining two object categories available on the Navigation Pane menu of the Issues Sample database: Custom and Issues Navigation as shown in Figure 26-33. Whenever you create a new database, Access creates the Custom category that you can modify to suit your needs. Initially, the Custom category contains only one group, Unassigned Objects, containing all the objects defined in your database. As you'll learn later, you can change the name of the Custom category, create one or more custom groups, and assign objects to those groups.

When you create a new database using one of the many templates provided by Microsoft, nearly all these databases contain an additional predefined group designed to make it easier to run the sample application. We created the Issues Sample database using the Issues template, and the Issues Navigation category is predefined in that template. As with any custom category, you can create new groups, modify or delete existing groups, assign additional objects to the groups within the custom category, or delete the category and all its groups altogether.

Figure 26-33 Both Custom and Issues Navigation are custom categories available in the Issues Sample database.

To see an example of a finished custom category in this database, open the Navigation Pane menu and select Issues Navigation. The Navigation Pane changes to display the object list shown in Figure 26-34. This custom category contains three custom groups called Issues, Contacts, and Supporting Objects. There is actually a fourth group called Unassigned Objects, which you cannot see. In the following sections, you'll learn how to hide one or more groups.

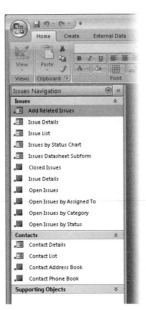

Figure 26-34 The Issues Navigation category displays a custom view of the various database objects.

In Figure 26-34, notice that each object icon has a small arrow in the lower-left corner. This arrow indicates that you are looking at a shortcut or pointer to the actual object. These shortcuts act similarly to shortcuts in Windows—if you open the shortcut, you're opening the underlying object to which the shortcut points. When you view custom categories and groups in the Navigation Pane, you are always looking at shortcuts to the objects. If you delete one of these shortcuts, you are only deleting the pointer to the object and not the object itself. We'll discuss more about working with these object shortcuts in "Hiding and Renaming Object Shortcuts" on page 811.

Exploring the Navigation Options Dialog Box

Now that you have seen how a completed custom view category looks in the Navigation Pane, you can create your own new category and groups within that category in this Issues Sample database for the Issues forms and reports and the Contacts forms and reports. If any database objects are currently open, close them so that they do not interfere with the following steps. First, let's create a custom category and then groups within that category to hold our designated database objects. To begin this process, right-click the menu bar at the top of the Navigation Pane and click Navigation Options on the shortcut menu, as shown in Figure 26-35.

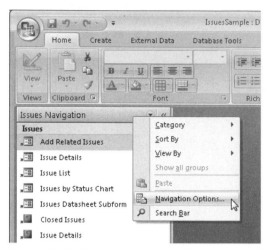

Figure 26-35 Right-click the top of the Navigation Pane and click Navigation Options to open the Navigation Options dialog box.

Access opens the Navigation Options dialog box as shown in Figure 26-36.

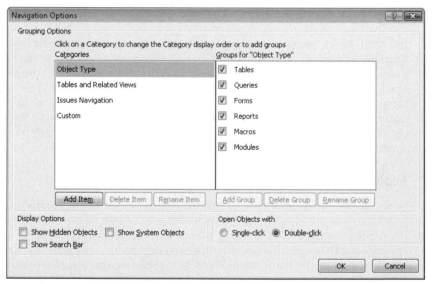

Figure 26-36 The Navigation Options dialog box lets you create and edit grouping and display options.

The Categories list under Grouping Options lists all the categories that have been defined in this database. In this list, you can see two built-in categories—Object Type and Tables And Related Views—that you cannot delete. The list also shows the Issues Navigation category that was defined in the template and the Custom category that Access defines in all new databases. When you select a different category in the list on the left, the list on the right displays the groups for that category. For example, click the Issues Navigation category on the left and notice that Access changes the list at the right to show the four groups defined in that category—Issues, Contacts, Supporting Objects, and Unassigned Objects, as shown in Figure 26-37.

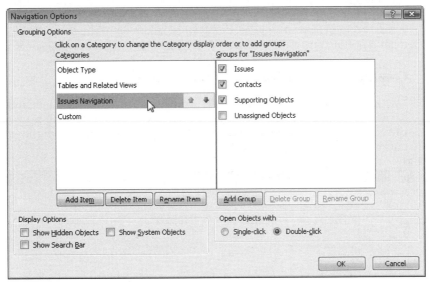

Figure 26-37 Four groups have been defined in the Issues Navigation category.

Next to each of the four groups for Issues Navigation is a check box. All but the last check box next to Unassigned Objects is selected. When you clear the check box next to any group on the right, Access does not display that group in the Navigation Pane. As you may recall, when you looked at the Issues Navigation category in the Navigation Pane, you could see only Issues, Contacts, and Supporting Objects. Because we cleared the check box next to Unassigned Objects in the Navigation Options dialog box, you are unable to view it in the Navigation Pane.

> Note
>
> The Tables And Related Views category by default includes one group for each table defined in the current database and one additional group called Unrelated Objects. The Object Type category includes one group for each of the six object types—tables, queries, forms, reports, macros, and modules.

In the lower-left corner of this dialog box, the Display Options section contains three check boxes—Show Hidden Objects, Show System Objects, and Show Search Bar. We'll discuss these options in detail in "Hiding and Renaming Object Shortcuts" on page 811 and "Searching for Database Objects" on page 820. The last section in the lower right of the Navigation Options dialog box is a new feature in Access 2007 called Open Objects With. When you select the Single-Click option, each object listed in the Navigation Pane acts like a hyperlink, so you need only one click to open the object. Double-Click, the default option, opens objects in the Navigation Pane with a double-click.

Creating and Modifying a Custom Category

To create your new navigation category, you could click the Add Item button. Or, because the unused Custom category already exists, you can use it to create your new category. Start by clicking Custom under Categories and then click the Rename Item button, as shown in Figure 26-38.

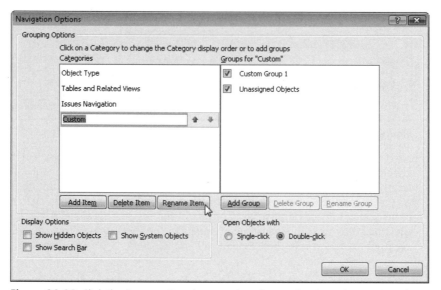

Figure 26-38   Click the Rename Item button when Custom is selected to rename that category.

After you click the Rename Item button, Access unlocks the Custom field in the Categories list so you can change the name. Delete the word Custom using the Backspace or Delete key and type **Issues Database Objects** for your new name as shown in Figure 26-39.

Under Groups For "Custom" for the Issues Database Objects category, you can see Custom Group 1 and Unassigned Objects, as shown in Figure 26-39. The Custom Group 1 group is an empty placeholder that Access defines in the Custom category in all new Access 2007 database files. By default, no objects are placed in this group for new databases. The Unassigned Objects group is also a built-in Access group for the Custom category. Access places all objects that are not assigned to any other groups in the Unassigned Objects group for display in the Navigation Pane.

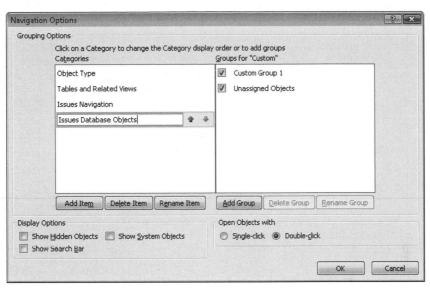

Figure 26-39 You can rename the Custom group by typing a new name in the field.

Creating and Modifying Groups in a Custom Category

Beneath the Groups list are three buttons: Add Group, Delete Group, and Rename Group. When you click Custom Group 1 in the list, you can see that all these buttons are available. The Add Group button creates another group under whichever group you have currently selected, the Delete Group button deletes the currently selected group, and the Rename Group button allows you to rename the current group. If you click the Unassigned Objects group, the Delete Group and Rename Group buttons appear dimmed. You cannot delete or rename this built-in group from any custom category.

For the Issues Database Objects category you need to create four groups. You can rename the Custom Group 1 group to a name of your choice, but you also need to create three additional groups. Let's start by renaming Custom Group 1 to Issues Forms. Click Custom Group 1 to select it and then click the Rename Group button. Access unlocks the name of this group so you can change it. Delete the word Custom Group 1 and type **Issues Forms** for your new name as shown in Figure 26-40.

You cannot change the name of the Unassigned Objects group, so you'll need to create additional groups. To create a new group, click the Add Group button. Access creates another group called Custom Group 1 below Issues Forms and unlocks it for you to enter a name as shown in Figure 26-41. Type **Issues Reports** for your new name and press Enter.

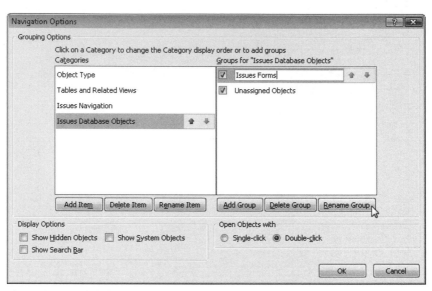

Figure 26-40 Click the Rename Group button when Custom Group 1 is selected to rename that group.

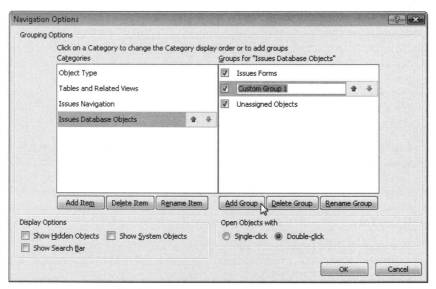

Figure 26-41 When you click the Add Group button, Access creates another Custom Group 1 group.

Follow the preceding steps to create two additional new groups for the Issues Database Objects category called Contact Forms and Contact Reports. In each case, start by clicking the Add Group button to have Access create another Custom Group 1. Type over that name and enter **Contact Forms** and **Contact Reports** for the two names. Your completed changes should now look like Figure 26-42 with your new custom category, four custom groups, and the Unassigned Objects group.

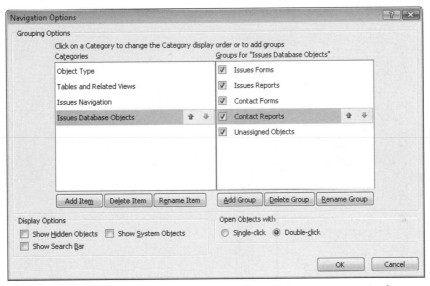

Figure 26-42 The completed Issues Database Objects category now contains five groups.

Next to whichever custom group is selected on the right are a Move Up arrow and a Move Down arrow that you can click to change the display order of the groups in this category. When you select this category from the Navigation Pane menu, Access displays the groups in the Navigation Pane based on the display order you set in the Navigation Options dialog box. In Figure 26-42, you can see arrow buttons next to the Issues Database Objects category and the Contact Reports group within that category. For now, keep the display order of the custom groups and categories as they are. Click OK to save your current changes.

INSIDE OUT   Understanding Display Order Rules for Categories and Groups

In the Categories list of the Navigation Options dialog box, you cannot change the display order of the Tables And Related Views and Object Type categories. All custom categories you create must appear below these two built-in categories.

The Unassigned Objects group in all custom groups you create can be displayed only at the bottom of the list of groups. You cannot place any custom groups below this built-in group. Similarly, the Unrelated Objects group within the Tables And Related Views category always appears at the bottom of the list.

To see how your changes appear in the Navigation Pane, click the top of the Navigation Pane to open the menu and select your new Issues Database Objects category, as shown in Figure 26-43.

Figure 26-43 After you select the new Issues Database Objects category, the Navigation Pane displays the custom groups you defined.

The Navigation Pane now displays each of your four custom group names along with the Unassigned Objects category as shown in Figure 26-44. Note that Access placed all your objects into the Unassigned Objects group and listed no database objects in any of the four custom groups. (In Figure 26-44 we collapsed the Ribbon to show you all the objects.)

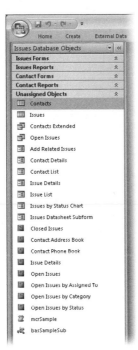

Figure 26-44 Access initially places all objects into the Unassigned Objects group after you create a custom category.

Creating Object Shortcuts in Custom Groups

Now that you have finished creating the category and group structure, it's time to move the objects into the groups you set up. You can move the forms that display or edit Issues into the new group called Issues Forms. To accomplish this task, hold down the Ctrl key and single-click each of the five forms that focus on Issues: Add Related Issues, Issue Details, Issue List, Issues by Status Chart, and Issues Datasheet Subform. This action causes Access to select all these objects. If you make a mistake by selecting an incorrect object, continue holding down the Ctrl key and single-click the incorrect object to unselect it. After you have selected all five form objects, right-click one of them and on the shortcut menu that appears click Add To Group and then Issues Forms to move the five selected form objects to that group, as shown in Figure 26-45.

Figure 26-45 You can move several objects to your custom group at the same time by selecting them and clicking Add To Group from the shortcut menu.

Access creates a shortcut to each of the five objects in the first group, as shown in Figure 26-46. Each of the icons now has a small arrow next to it to indicate that it is actually a shortcut to the respective database object and not the actual object itself, as we discussed earlier. If you delete a shortcut, you are deleting only the shortcut or pointer to the object and not the object itself.

Figure 26-46 After you move your objects to the first custom group, Access creates a shortcut to each object.

With the first set of objects assigned to a group, let's continue moving the other forms and reports. Hold down the Ctrl key and single-click on each of the following six reports: Closed Issues, Issue Details, Open Issues, Open Issues by Assigned To, Open Issues by Category, and Open Issues by Status. After you have selected these reports, right-click and click Add To Group. Click the group called Issue Reports and again note how Access creates a shortcut to each of these reports in our custom group as shown in Figure 26-47.

Figure 26-47 Group all your Issues reports together under Issues Reports by selecting them and clicking Add To Group from the shortcut menu.

INSIDE OUT Dragging and Dropping Objects into Custom Groups

You can also select objects you want to add to a custom group and drag and drop them into the group with your mouse. If you want a shortcut to appear in more than one group, add it to the first group, select it with your mouse, and while holding down the Ctrl key, drag and drop it into the second group. Holding down the Ctrl key tells Access you want to copy the shortcut, not move it. (Release the mouse button before releasing the Ctrl key to be sure the copy feature works correctly.)

Now repeat this process for the two contact forms called Contact Details and Contact List and move them to the group called Contact Forms. Similarly, move the two contact reports called Contact Address Book and Contact Phone Book to the group called Contact Reports. The Navigation Pane should now look like Figure 26-48.

Figure 26-48 All the form and report objects now have shortcuts in custom groups in the Navigation Pane.

Hiding Custom Groups in a Category

With the previous steps completed, you should now see only six objects in the Unassigned Objects group—a collection of data tables, queries, one macro, and one module. For now, assume that we do not want to have the users of this database application view these objects. We can hide this entire Unassigned Objects group of objects from the users by going back to the Navigation Options dialog box. Right-click the top of the Navigation Pane, and then click Navigation Options to open the Navigation Options dialog box again. In the Categories list, click the Issues Database Objects category to display our custom groups. Clear the Unassigned Objects check box to tell Access to hide this particular group when showing our custom Issues Database Objects view in the Navigation Pane as shown in Figure 26-49.

Click OK in the Navigation Options dialog box, and Access completely removes this group from view in the Navigation Pane. We are now left with a concise list of form and report objects separated into logical groups as shown in Figure 26-50.

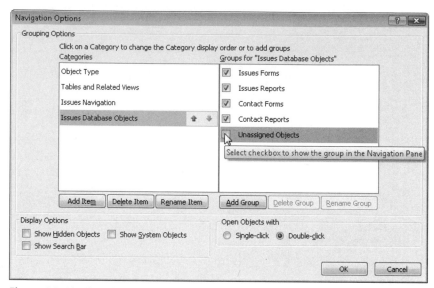

Figure 26-49 Clear the check box next to Unassigned Objects to hide this group in the Navigation Pane.

Figure 26-50 The completed changes to the Navigation Pane now display only form and report object shortcuts in four custom groups.

INSIDE OUT   **Hiding a Group Directly from the Navigation Pane**

You can also hide an entire group from view in the Navigation Pane by right-clicking that group and clicking Hide on the shortcut menu that appears.

Hiding and Renaming Object Shortcuts

We can further customize our list of objects by hiding object shortcuts directly in the Navigation Pane. For example, for illustration purposes right now, assume that you want to hide the data entry form called Issues Datasheet Subform from the current view. There are two methods for accomplishing this task, both of which you can access directly from the Navigation Pane. For the first method, right-click the Issues Datasheet Subform in the Navigation Pane and click Hide In This Group from the shortcut menu, as shown in Figure 26-51.

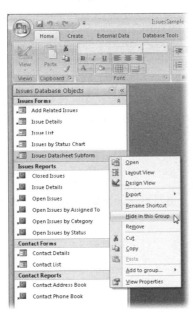

Figure 26-51 To hide an object in a specific group, right-click it and click Hide In This Group from the shortcut menu.

Access hides this object shortcut from view in the Navigation Pane but does not in any way delete or alter the existing form itself. Alternatively, you can right-click that object in the Navigation Pane and click View Properties from the shortcut menu, shown in Figure 26-51, to open the Properties dialog box for this object, as shown in Figure 26-52.

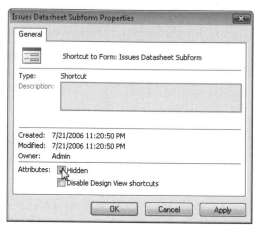

Figure 26-52 You can hide a database object or an object shortcut from view in the Navigation Pane by selecting the Hidden check box in the Properties dialog box.

The Properties dialog box displays the name of the object and whether this is a shortcut to an object. In the middle of the dialog box you can see any description inherited from the original object (which you can't modify), the date the object was created, the date the object was last modified, and the owner of the object. The Attributes section has two check boxes called Hidden and Disable Design View Shortcuts. In the Attributes section, select the Hidden check box and then click OK. In the Navigation Pane you will see the Issues Datasheet Subform disappear from view. Remember that you have hidden only the shortcut for this object and have not affected the actual form itself in any way.

You now know how to hide objects or object shortcuts from view in the Navigation Pane, but what if you want to rename the object shortcuts? Access 2007 allows you to easily rename the shortcuts to database objects without affecting the underlying names of the objects. To illustrate this procedure, let's rename one of the report object shortcuts. Right-click the Issue Details report and click Rename Shortcut from the shortcut menu as shown in Figure 26-53.

Figure 26-53 To rename an object shortcut in the Navigation Pane, right-click it and click Rename Shortcut.

Access sets the focus on this report in the Navigation Pane and unlocks the name of the shortcut. Enter a new name for this object, by typing **All Issue Details Report** and then pressing Enter, as shown in Figure 26-54. Access saves the new name of this report shortcut, but does not change the name of the actual report object to which the shortcut points.

The final custom Navigation Pane with all your modifications should now look like Figure 26-55. Behind the scenes, all the database objects are still present and unchanged, but you customized the display view for users of your database. You are now showing only a list of form and report shortcuts while other objects are hidden from view.

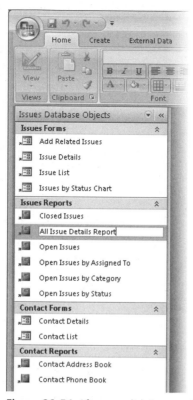

Figure 26-54 After you click Rename Shortcut, Access unlocks the object shortcut name so that you can change it.

Revealing Hidden Shortcuts

If you have followed along to this point, remember that you hid the form Issues Datasheet Subform from the current view in the Navigation Pane. To unhide this form, right-click the top of the Navigation Pane and click Navigation Options to open the Navigation Options dialog box. Select the Show Hidden Objects check box, as shown in Figure 26-56. Click OK to save this change and close the Navigation Options dialog box.

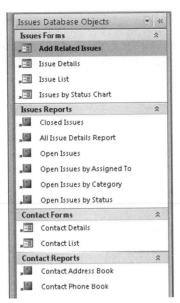

Figure 26-55 The customized Navigation Pane category and groups now display only form and report shortcuts.

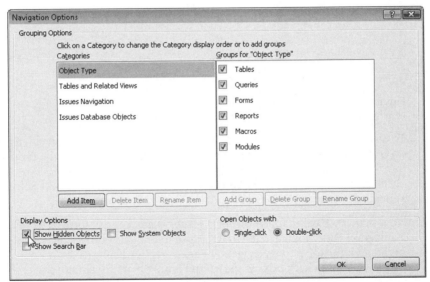

Figure 26-56 Selecting the Show Hidden Objects check box causes Access to display any hidden object shortcuts in the Navigation Pane.

When you return to the Navigation Pane, Access displays the shortcut to the form Issues Datasheet Subform in the Issues Forms group, as shown in Figure 26-57. If you look closely in Figure 26-57, you can see that Access displays the object dimmed

Chapter 26

compared to the other object shortcuts. This dimmed state is a visual cue that Access uses to indicate object shortcuts that are hidden. In Figure 26-57 you can also see that Access now shows the hidden group Unassigned Objects and all of the objects contained within it. All the objects in the Unassigned Objects group, along with the group name itself, also appear dimmed in the Navigation Pane.

Figure 26-57 Access displays any hidden shortcuts, objects, or groups in the Navigation Pane when you select the Show Hidden Objects check box.

To change the Hidden property of the form Issues Datasheet Subform, right-click that object in the Navigation Pane and click View Properties to open the Properties dialog box for this object, as shown in Figure 26-58. In the Attributes section, clear the Hidden check box and then click OK. You can see that the Issues Datasheet Subform no longer appears dimmed in the Navigation Pane.

Now that you have changed the form Issues Datasheet Subform to be visible in the Navigation Pane, you need to tell Access to hide the Unassigned Objects group again. Right-click the top of the Navigation Pane and click Navigation Options. Clear the Show Hidden Objects check box, as shown in Figure 26-59. Click OK to save this change and Access once again hides the Unassigned Objects group from view in the Navigation Pane.

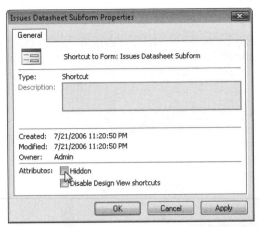

Figure 26-58 You can unhide a database object or an object shortcut from view in the Navigation Pane by clearing the Hidden check box in the Properties dialog box for the object or shortcut.

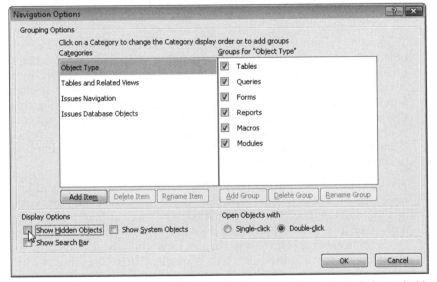

Figure 26-59 Clear the Show Hidden Objects check box to have Access hide any hidden object shortcuts, objects, or groups in the Navigation Pane.

On the companion CD, you can find a database file called IssueSampleCustom.accdb, which has all the changes from the steps we completed in the preceding sections. If you would like to compare your Issues Database Objects category and groups to our completed sample, open this file from the folder where you installed the sample files.

Sorting and Selecting Views in the Navigation Pane

By default, Access sorts the objects in the Navigation Pane by object type in ascending order. The Navigation Pane allows for several other types of object sorting. Right-click the menu at the top of the Navigation Pane and move the mouse pointer over Sort By as shown in Figure 26-60.

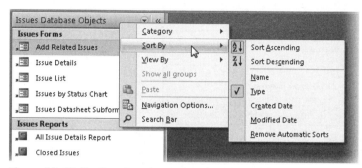

Figure 26-60 The Sort By submenu on the Navigation Pane menu allows for further Navigation Pane sorting.

The Sort By submenu has options to sort the Navigation Pane list by the name of the object, the object type, the created date, and the modified date. You can change the sort order from ascending to descending for any of these Sort By options by clicking Sort Ascending or Sort Descending at the top of the Sort By submenu. The last option on the Sort By submenu, Remove Automatic Sorts, lets you lay out your object list in any order you want within the Navigation Pane. With this option selected, you can click and drag your objects within their respective groups into any order, and Access will not re-sort them in alphabetical, type, created date, or modified date order after you have repositioned your objects in the list.

The View By submenu has three choices available—Details, Icon, and List—as shown in Figure 26-61. The Details view displays in the Navigation Pane the name of each object, its type, and the creation and modified dates, as well as places a large icon next to the name. The Icon view displays only the name of the object (or the shortcut name) next to a large icon of the object type. The List view similarly displays only the name of the object or shortcut, but the object icon is smaller than in the other two views.

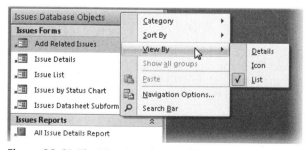

Figure 26-61 The View By submenu lists commands to view the Navigation Pane objects by Details, Icon, or List.

INSIDE OUT   Viewing Categories from the Navigation Pane Submenus

You can choose one of the view categories—either a custom category or one of the built-in categories—by right-clicking the Navigation Pane menu and selecting the Category submenu.

In Figure 26-62 you can see what the Navigation Pane looks like with the view set to Details. Notice that more information is displayed about each object, but you see fewer objects. To see the remaining objects you have to use the vertical scroll bar. If you changed your view to Details to test this, go back to the View By submenu and change the view back to List before continuing.

Figure 26-62 The Details view displays more information about each object in the Navigation Pane than Icon or List view.

Manually Sorting Objects in the Navigation Pane

So far we have seen how Access can sort the list of objects and object shortcuts in the Navigation Pane automatically for you. Access also allows you to manually sort the object lists so that you can further customize the display order. You must first tell

Access to stop automatically sorting your objects. Right-click the top of the Navigation Pane, click Sort By, and then click Remove Automatic Sorts as shown in Figure 26-63.

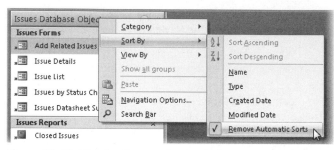

Figure 26-63 Click the Remove Automatic Sorts command to manually sort your object list in the Navigation Pane.

Now you can click and drag your objects and object shortcuts around into different positions in the Navigation Pane. For example, click and drag the Add Related Issues form shortcut in the Navigation Pane until you have your pointer between the Issue List and Issues by Status Chart forms. An I-beam pointer will appear while you drag to help you position the object, as shown in Figure 26-64. After you release the mouse, Access drops the form shortcut into the new position.

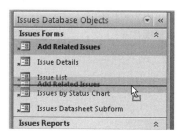

Figure 26-64 Click and drag your form shortcut into a new position within the Issues Forms category.

To have Access automatically sort the object list again, select any of the four available sort options above Remove Automatic Sorts from the Display Options menu.

Searching for Database Objects

In databases with a large number of database objects, locating a specific object can be difficult, so Access 2007 includes the Search Bar feature to make this task easier. By default, this feature is turned off, so you must turn it on through the Navigation Pane. You can enable this feature in one of two ways. For the first method, right-click the top of the Navigation Pane and then click Search Bar, as shown in Figure 26-65.

Alternatively, you can right-click the top of the Navigation Pane and then click Navigation Options from the shortcut menu to open the Navigation Options dialog box shown in Figure 26-66.

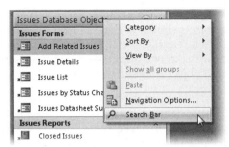

Figure 26-65 Click the Search Bar command on the Display Options menu to display the Search Bar.

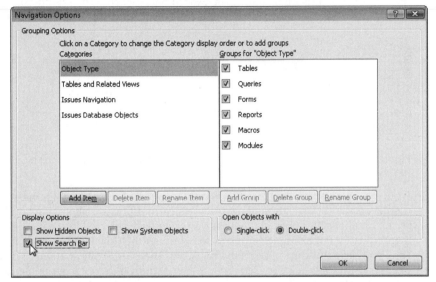

Figure 26-66 Select the Show Search Bar check box in the Navigation Options dialog box to display the Search Bar.

Select the Show Search Bar check box and then click OK. Access displays a Search Bar near the top of the Navigation Pane, as shown in Figure 26-67.

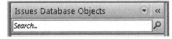

Figure 26-67 The Search Bar in the Navigation Pane helps you find specific database objects.

We think the Search Bar is misnamed. Rather than "search" for objects that match what you type in the search box, Access filters the list in the Navigation Pane. As you begin to type letters, Access filters the list of objects to those that contain the sequence of characters you enter anywhere in the name. For example, if you want to find an object whose name contains the word Address, type the word **address** in the Search Bar. As you enter each letter in the Search Bar, Access begins filtering the list of objects for any that contain the characters in your entered search string. With each successive letter you type, Access reduces the list of objects shown in the Navigation Pane because there are fewer objects that match your search criteria. Notice that as soon as you have typed the letters *add*, Access has reduced the list to two objects—Add Related Issues and Contact Address Book. The names of both objects contain the letters *add*.

After you finish typing the entire word *address* in the Search Bar, the Navigation Pane should like Figure 26-68. Access collapses any group headers if it does not find any objects (or object shortcuts if you're using a custom category) that meet your search criterion. In this case, Access located one object, Contact Address Book, with the word *address* in its name. To clear your search string if you need to perform another object search, either delete the existing text using the Backspace key or click the Clear Search String button on the right side of the Search Bar. Clearing the search box or clicking the Clear Search String button restores the Navigation Pane to show all displayable objects.

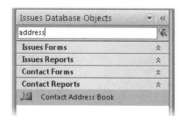

Figure 26-68 The Search Bar collapses any groups if it does not find any objects in that group that meet your search criterion.

Note that Access searches for objects only in categories and groups that are currently displayed in the Navigation Pane. If Access cannot find an object that you know exists in the database, it is possible that the view you have selected in the Navigation Pane is interfering. For example, suppose you conduct the preceding same search but this time you have only one group showing. Clear the Search Bar of any text by using the Backspace key or click the Clear Search String button. Now click the menu bar at the top of the Navigation Pane and select Issues Forms in the Filter By Group section of the Navigation Pane menu, as shown in Figure 26-69. The only group now displayed in the Navigation Pane is Issues Forms with four object shortcuts.

Enter the word **address** again in the Search Bar and notice that Access cannot locate any objects that meet your criterion. In Figure 26-70 you can see that Access shows an empty Navigation Pane because none of the four form object shortcuts in the Issues Forms groups have the word *address* in their name. This does not mean that no objects in the entire database have the word *address* in their name; it means only that Access could not locate any objects with that search criterion in the *current* view selected in the Navigation Pane.

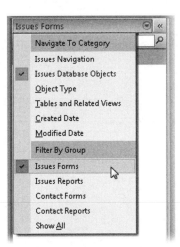

Figure 26-69 Select Issues Forms from the Navigation Pane menu to show only that group in the Navigation Pane.

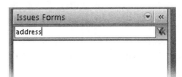

Figure 26-70 Access might not be able to find any objects that meet your criterion if your chosen display view is too restrictive.

If you know exactly the name of the object you want to find and the type of object as well, you can save some additional searching through object types you might not be interested in. For example, suppose you want to find a form that has the word *list* in its name. First open the Navigation Pane menu and click Object Type. Open the menu again and click Forms under Filter By Group to restrict the list of objects to display only forms, as shown in Figure 26-71.

INSIDE OUT   Using the Shortcut Menu to Display Only One Category

You can also right-click the Forms group header and click Show Only Forms so that only forms show in the Navigation Pane.

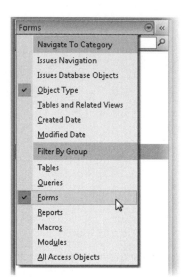

Figure 26-71 You can limit your search to form objects by selecting the Object Type category and Forms group from the Navigation Pane menu.

Type the word **list** in the Search Bar and Access searches through only data entry forms until it finds a match. In Figure 26-72, Access has found two forms that have the word *list* in their name—Contact List and Issue List.

Figure 26-72 After restricting the Navigation Pane to show only forms, text you enter in the Search Bar searches only in the Forms group.

INSIDE OUT   Maximizing Your Search to Include All Objects

If you need to search through all your database objects to find a specific named object, we recommend that you set the Navigation Pane menu category to one of the built-in categories such as Object Type or Tables And Related Views. Also check to see that all groups are visible in the Navigation Pane for that category to ensure that Access does not miss any objects when it conducts the search.

Using the Single-Document vs. Multiple-Document Interface

In previous versions of Access, all objects opened in their own window where you could edit, view, or print them. This type of interface, *multiple-document interface* (MDI for short), was the cornerstone for working with objects in Access. Office Access 2007 introduces a new interface model called *single-document interface* (SDI). In the SDI model, all objects open in a series of tabs along the top of the object window to the right of the Navigation Pane. In the older MDI model, switching between open objects usually meant constantly minimizing, resizing, and maximizing the various objects in order to work with them. In Figure 26-73 you can see two forms, one table, and one report open using MDI format. To switch among these objects you must move the objects around or minimize some of them, as shown near the bottom of the screen.

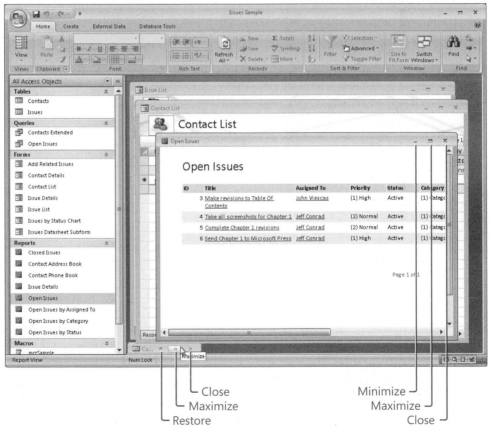

Figure 26-73 All open objects appear in their own separate window when using the multiple-document interface.

In the new SDI model, each open object appears on a tab to the right of the Navigation Pane. In Figure 26-74 you can see the same four objects open as before, but here each open object has its name listed at the top of a tab next to an icon for that particular type of database object. Switching among open objects is as simple as clicking on a different tab. The end result of this new interface is that you can easily see the names of all open objects and find the ones you need to work with much more quickly.

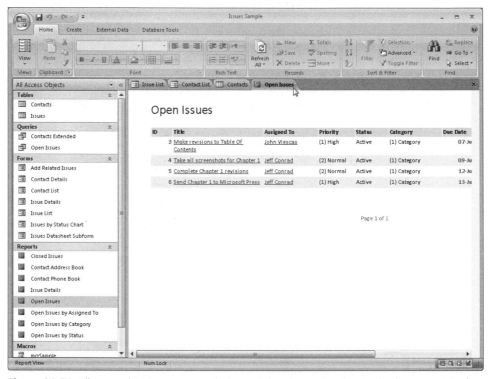

Figure 26-74 All open objects appear on their own tabs when using the single-document interface.

For new databases created in the Access 2007 format, Access uses the single-document interface by default, but for older databases in the MDB/MDE type format Access 2007 still opens those files in multiple-document interface mode. Access easily allows you to change the interface mode for any database through the Access Options dialog box. Click the Microsoft Office Button, and then click the Access Options button.

The Access Options dialog box opens and displays many options for customizing the look and feel of Access 2007. You can find an explanation of more of the various options in these categories in "Modifying Global Settings via the Access Options Dialog Box" on page 829. Click the Current Database category in the left pane to display a list of settings to tailor this current database. In Figure 26-75, note the section called Document Window Options in the Current Database category of the Access Options dialog box.

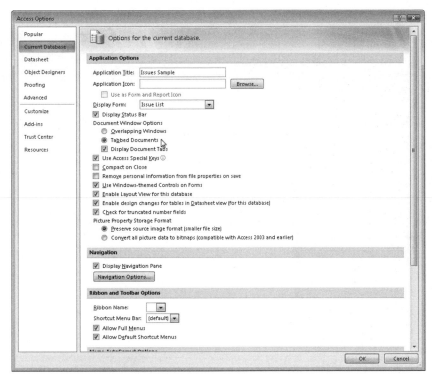

Figure 26-75 The Document Window Options section in the Current Database category of the Access Options dialog box controls the interface mode.

To work in multiple-document interface mode, select Overlapping Windows. For the single-document interface, with each object on its own tab, select Tabbed Documents. Under these two options is a check box called Display Document Tabs. You can select this check box only in conjunction with the Tabbed Documents option. When you select the Display Document Tabs check box, each object has a tab across the top of the object window with the object's name and an icon for the object type, as was shown in Figure 26-74. If you clear Display Document Tabs, you do not see any tabs for open objects nor do you see any Restore, Minimize, Maximize, or Close buttons for open objects.

In Figure 26-76 we have two forms, one table, and one report open, but you can see only the report because no object tabs are visible. Notice that you do not see any Restore, Minimize, Maximize, or Close buttons along the top of the object window, which means it is more difficult to switch among various open objects. It is possible, but awkward, to switch from one object to another by pressing Ctrl+F6.

After you make your selections in the Access Options dialog box, click OK to save your changes. Access applies these interface settings to this current database the next time you open the file. In order to see the interface change you need to close and reopen the database.

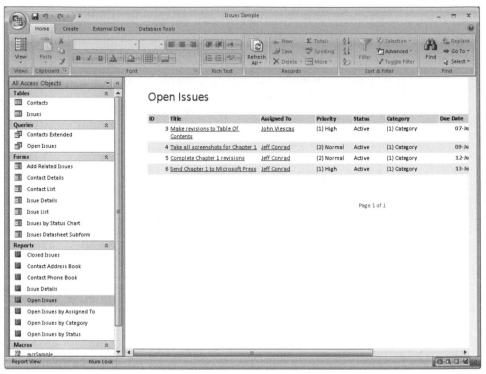

Figure 26-76 With Tabbed Documents selected and the Display Document Tabs check box cleared, no tabs for open objects appear at the top of the object window.

INSIDE OUT Why You Might Want to Use the Tabbed Documents Setting with No Tabs Visible

If you're creating an application for novice users, you might want to set up the application so that the user can work with only one object at a time. Presenting a single object minimizes the choices the user must make. However, you will have to be sure to include a method to allow the user to navigate to other objects, perhaps with command buttons that execute VBA code or macros to open and set the focus to other objects. You must carefully design such an application so the user never gets "trapped" in one object and unable to get to others.

Modifying Global Settings via the Access Options Dialog Box

In addition to all the various commands and options available on the Ribbon and in the Navigation Pane, Access 2007 has one central location for setting and modifying global options for all your Access database files or for only the database currently open. This location is the Access Options dialog box. To open the Access Options dialog box, click the Microsoft Office Button and then click Access Options, as shown in Figure 26-77.

Figure 26-77 Click the Microsoft Office Button and then click Access Options to open the Access Options dialog box.

The Access Options dialog box contains 10 categories in the left pane to organize the various options and settings. The first category, Popular, has settings that apply not only to Access 2007, but also to any other 2007 Microsoft Office system programs you might have installed. From here you can choose to display ScreenTips, select a color scheme for the application window, and enter a user name for use in all your 2007 Microsoft Office system applications. In the Creating Databases section, you can choose a default file format for new databases you create in Access 2007. By default, the file format is set to create all new databases in Access 2007 format. The Default Database Folder box displays the folder where Access saves all new database files unless you select a different folder when creating the database. Figure 26-78 shows the Popular category of the Access Options dialog box.

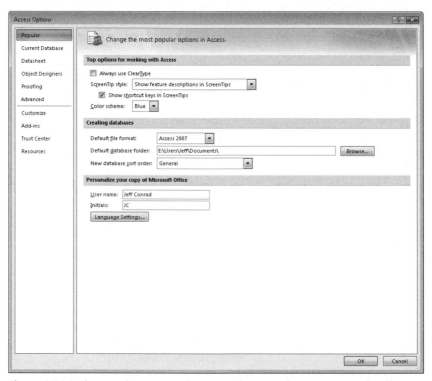

Figure 26-78 The Popular category has general settings for your Microsoft Office system applications.

The Current Database category, shown in Figure 26-79, has many settings that apply only to the database currently open. This category groups options into these sections: Application Options, Navigation, Ribbon And Toolbar Options, Name AutoCorrect Options, and Filter Lookup Options.

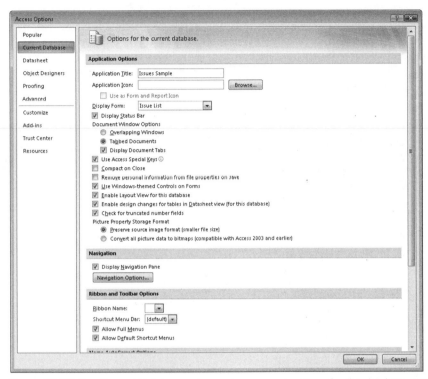

Figure 26-79 The Current Database category has general settings for the database currently open.

The Document Window Options section in this category was discussed previously in "Using the Single-Document vs. Multiple-Document Interface" on page 825. Use Windows-Themed Controls On Forms will be discussed in Chapter 29, "Building a Form.

The Datasheet category, shown in Figure 26-80, has settings that control the appearance of the datasheet views in your database. This category has options grouped in the following sections—Default Colors, Gridlines And Cell Effects, and Default Font—which allow you to modify the look of your datasheets with different colors, gridlines, and cell effects. You can also select a default font and size under Default Font. You'll learn more about applying these settings to datasheets in "Working in Query Datasheet View" on page 940 and in Chapter 29.

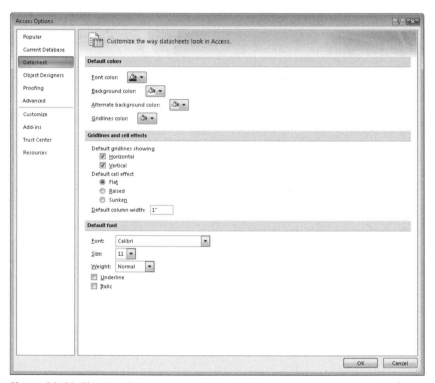

Figure 26-80 The Datasheet category has general settings to control the look of datasheets.

The Object Designers category, shown in Figure 26-81, includes settings for creating and modifying database objects in all databases. The Object Designers category is divided into four sections: Table Design, Query Design, Forms/Reports, and Error Checking. The Table Design section has settings for Default Field Type, Default Text Field Size, and Default Number Field Size. You'll learn more about the impact of these settings in Chapter 27. The Query Design section lets you select a default font and size for working in the query design grid. The Forms/Reports section has options that allow you to use the existing form and report templates or choose a custom template that you have created. The Error Checking section has several default options that Access looks for when checking for errors in your database file.

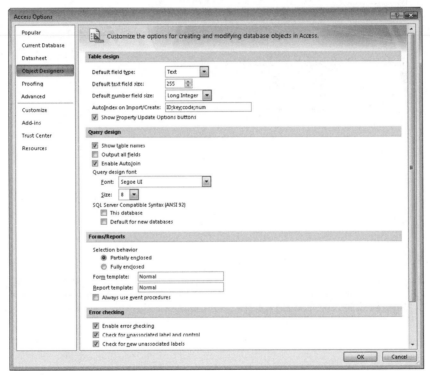

Figure 26-81 The Object Designers category has settings for working with database objects.

The Proofing category, shown in Figure 26-82, includes options for controlling the spelling and AutoCorrect features. You can click AutoCorrect Options to customize how Access helps you with common typing mistakes. You can also click Custom Dictionaries to select a custom dictionary to use when working with Access 2007 and the other 2007 Office release applications.

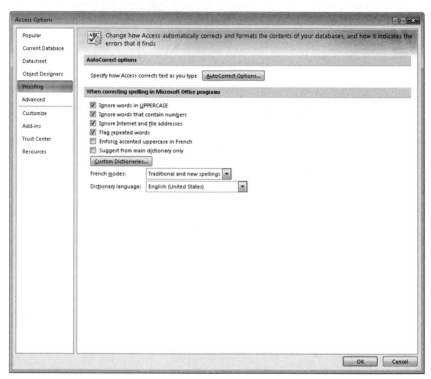

Figure 26-82 The Proofing category has settings for checking spelling and AutoCorrect.

The Advanced category, shown in Figure 26-83, contains a wide variety of settings for Access 2007. This category has options grouped in the following sections: Editing, Display, Printing, General, and Advanced. Each of the settings in this category applies to all database files you use in Access 2007.

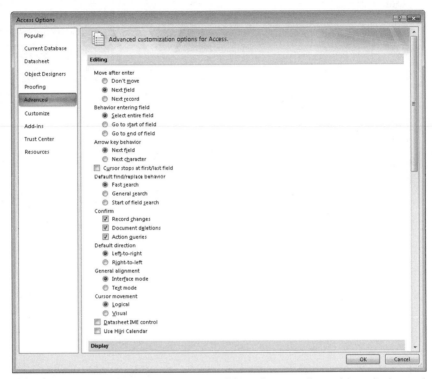

Figure 26-83 The Advanced category has options for controlling editing, display, and printing.

Chapter 26

The Customize category, shown in Figure 26-84, was discussed previously in "Taking Advantage of the Quick Access Toolbar" on page 769. This category is where you customize the Quick Access Toolbar. You can make modifications to the Quick Access Toolbar for this specific database only or to the Quick Access Toolbar for all Access databases.

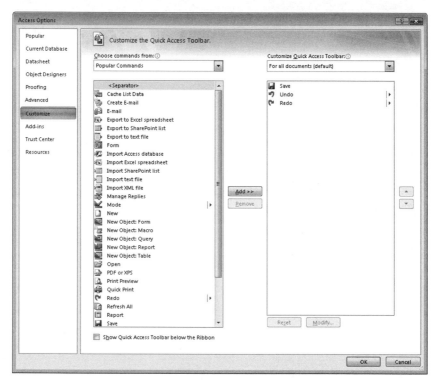

Figure 26-84 The Customize category allows you to customize the Quick Access Toolbar.

The Add-Ins category, shown in Figure 26-85, lists all the various Access add-ins that might be installed on your computer. You can manage COM add-ins and Access add-ins from this category, and each add-in has its various properties listed. COM add-ins extend the ability of Access and other Microsoft Office system applications with custom commands and specialized features. You can even disable certain add-ins to keep them from loading and functioning.

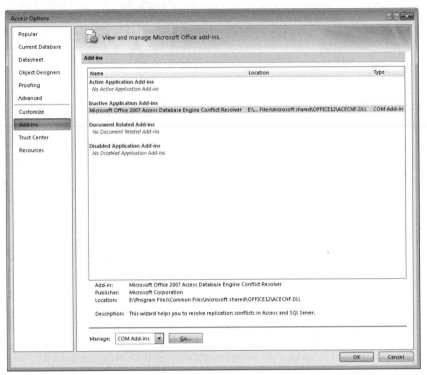

Figure 26-85 The Add-Ins category lists any installed Access add-ins and COM add-ins.

The Trust Center category, shown in Figure 26-86, is where you access all Trust Center options for handling security. As we discussed earlier in "Understanding Content Security" on page 776, you can open the Trust Center Settings dialog box that controls all aspects of macro security. This category also has links to online privacy and security information.

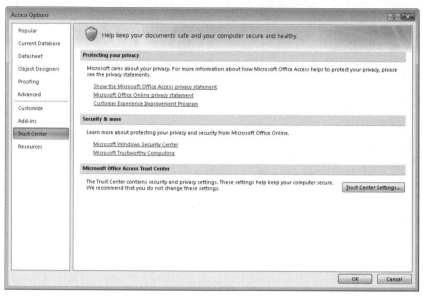

Figure 26-86 The Trust Center category has links to privacy and security information and the Trust Center Settings button to view more options.

The Resources category, shown in Figure 26-87, is the last category in the Access Options dialog box. This category has options grouped in the following sections: Get Updates, Run Microsoft Office Diagnostics, Contact Us, Activate Microsoft Office, Go To Microsoft Office Online, and About Microsoft Office Access 2007.

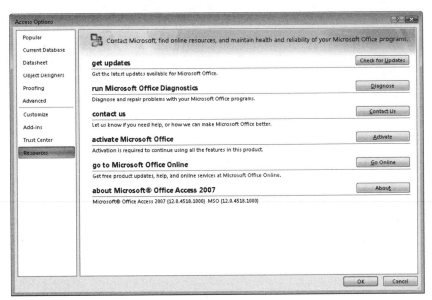

Figure 26-87 The Resources category has options for contacting Microsoft and utilities to repair problems with your 2007 Microsoft Office system applications.

Click Check For Updates to go to a Web site where you can run a program that verifies that you have the latest updates for your Microsoft Office system. Click Diagnose to run a procedure that verifies your Microsoft Office system installation and fixes most problems. Click Contact Us to go to a Web site where you can find links to support options, go to online support communities, or submit suggestions to improve the product or report a problem. Click Activate to verify that you have a valid installation of the Microsoft Office system and activate all features. Click Go Online to go to Microsoft Office Online to get updates and other services. Click About to open a dialog box that displays your current version and service pack level of Access and provides links to a system analyzer program and online technical support.

Creating Your Database and Tables

D efining tables in a Microsoft Office Access 2007 desktop database (.accdb file) is incredibly easy. This chapter shows you how it's done. You'll learn how to

- Create a new database application using a database template

- Create a new empty database for your own custom application

- Create a simple table by entering data directly in the table

- Get a jump start on defining custom tables by using table templates

- Define your own tables from scratch by using Design view

- Select the best data type for each field

- Define the primary key for your table

- Set validation rules for your fields and tables

- Tell Access 2007 what relationships to maintain between your tables

- Optimize data retrieval by adding indexes

- Set options that affect how you work in Design view

- Print a table definition

Note

All the screen images in this chapter were taken on a Microsoft Windows Vista system using the Blue color scheme.

INSIDE OUT   Take Time to Learn About Table Design

You could begin building a database in Access 2007 much as you might begin creating a simple single-sheet solution in a spreadsheet application such as Microsoft Excel—by simply organizing your data into rows and columns and then inserting formulas where you need calculations. If you've ever worked extensively with a database or a spreadsheet application, you already know that this unplanned approach works in only the most trivial situations. Solving real problems takes some planning; otherwise, you end up building your application over and over again. One of the beauties of a relational database system such as Access is that it's much easier to make midcourse corrections. However, it's well worth spending time up front designing the tasks you want to perform, the data structures you need to support those tasks, and the flow of tasks within your database application.

To teach you all you might need to know about table design would require another entire book. The good news is Access 2007 provides many examples for good table design in the templates available with the product and online. If you want to learn at least the fundamentals of table and application design, be sure to read Article 1, "Designing Your Database Application," that you can find on the companion CD.

Creating a New Database

When you first start Office Access 2007, you see the Getting Started screen, as shown in Figure 27-1. We explored the Getting Started screen in detail in Chapter 26, "Exploring the New Look of Access 2007." If you've previously opened other databases, you also see a most recently used list of up to nine database selections under Open Recent Database on the right.

Using a Database Template to Create a Database

Just for fun, let's explore the built-in database templates first. If you're a beginner, you can use the templates included with Access 2007 to create one of several common applications without needing to know anything about designing database software. You might find that one of these applications meets most of your needs right off the bat. As you learn more about Access 2007, you can build on and customize the basic application design and add new features.

Even if you're an experienced developer, you might find that the application templates save you lots of time in setting up the basic tables, queries, forms, and reports for your application. If the application you need to build is covered by one of the templates, the wizard that builds an application with one of the templates can take care of many of the simpler design tasks.

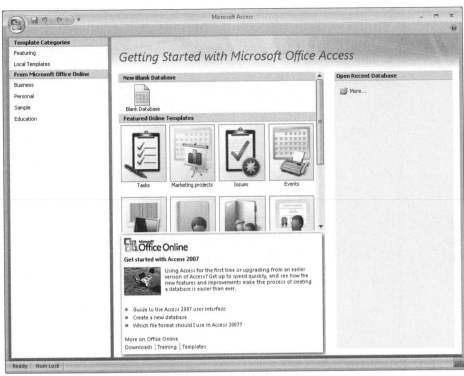

Figure 27-1 When you first start Access 2007, you see the Getting Started screen.

On the Getting Started screen, you can access the built-in local templates by clicking Local Templates under Template Categories on the left. You can also choose to download a template from Microsoft's Web site by clicking one of the options under From Microsoft Office Online. When you click one of the options under Template Categories or From Microsoft Office Online, the center section of the Getting Started screen changes to show graphics representing of each of the database templates available in that category. Click the Business category under Template Categories to see the list of business template options, as shown in Figure 27-2.

When you click on one of the template graphics in the center of the Getting Started screen, Access 2007 displays additional information about the purpose of the database in the right task pane. Click the Contacts template in the middle of the screen to see detailed information about the local Contacts database template, as shown in Figure 27-3. You can work with all templates from the Getting Started screen in the same way. This example will show you the steps that are needed to build a Contacts database.

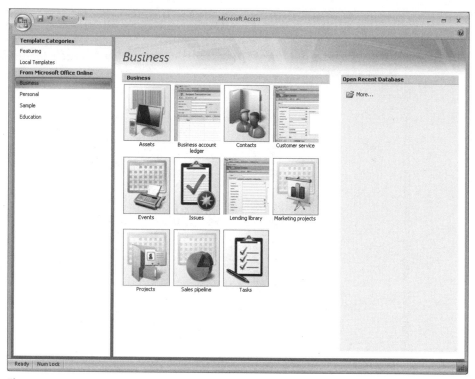

Figure 27-2 You access templates from Microsoft Office Online by selecting one of the categories to see a list of database templates for that category.

Browse

Access 2007 displays a larger graphic in the right task pane along with a brief description of the template's purpose. When you have selected an online template, Access 2007 also shows you the template size, the approximate download time, and the rating given this template by other users. Access 2007 suggests a name for your new database in the File Name text box and a location to save the file beneath the File Name text box. You can select the optional check box to instruct Access 2007 to link this new database to a Windows SharePoint Services site. For now, do not select this check box. You can modify the name of this database by typing in the File Name text box. If you want to change the suggested save location, click the Browse button to open the File New Database dialog box, as shown in Figure 27-4.

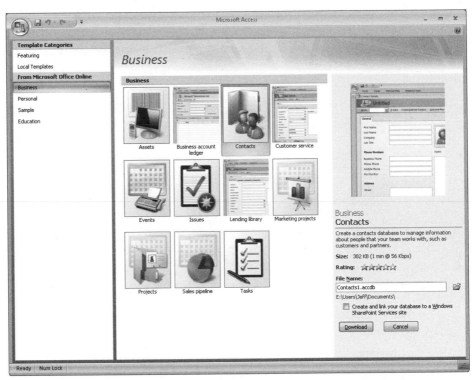

Figure 27-3 Choosing one of the database templates in the center of the screen shows you more information in the right task pane.

You can select the drive and folder you want by clicking the links on the left and browsing to your destination folder. After you select the specific folder to which you want to save this new database, click OK to return to the Getting Started screen. Your new folder location is shown beneath the File Name text box. If you decide at this point not to create the database, click the Cancel button to stop the process. Click the Download button when working with an online template or the Create button when working with a local template, and Access 2007 begins the process of creating this new database.

The first time you choose to download an online template, Access 2007 displays the Microsoft Office Genuine Advantage confirmation dialog box as shown in Figure 27-5. Each time you download a template, Access 2007 confirms that you have a valid and registered copy of the 2007 Microsoft Office system. If you do not want to see this dialog box again, select the Do Not Show This Message Again check box. Click Continue to proceed with the download and creation of your sample database.

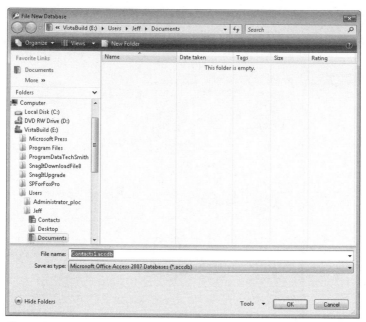

Figure 27-4 Use the File New Database dialog box to select a folder for saving the new database.

Figure 27-5 When you ask to download a template, Access verifies that you have a genuine copy of the 2007 Office release.

A progress bar appears on the screen informing you to please wait while Access 2007 creates the database. After a few seconds of preparation, Access opens the new Contacts database and displays the Contact List form, as shown in Figure 27-6. Close this new database for now by clicking the Microsoft Office Button and then clicking Close Database to return to the Getting Started screen.

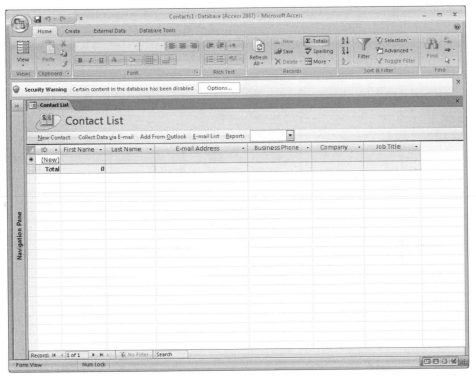

Figure 27-6 After you create the Contacts database from a template, Access opens the database and displays the Contact List form.

Creating a New Empty Database

To begin creating a new empty database when you start Access 2007, go to the New Blank Database section in the middle of the Getting Started screen (as shown in Figure 27-1) and click Blank Database. The right side of the Getting Started screen changes to display the Blank Database task pane, as shown in Figure 27-7.

You can click the Browse button to open the File New Database dialog box, shown previously in Figure 27-4, to select the drive and folder you want. In this example, we selected the Documents folder in Windows Vista for the current user. Next, type the name of your new database in the File Name text box—Access 2007 appends an .accdb extension to the file name for you. Access 2007 uses a file with an .accdb extension to store all your database objects, including tables, queries, forms, reports, macros, and modules. For this example, let's create a database with a table containing names and addresses—something you might use to track invitees to a wedding. Type **Kathy's Wedding List** in the File Name box and click the Create button to create your database.

Figure 27-7 From the Getting Started screen, click Blank Database in the center to open the Blank Database task pane on the right.

Access 2007 takes a few moments to create the system tables in which to store all the information about the tables, queries, forms, reports, macros, and modules that you might create. Access then displays the Navigation Pane for your new database and opens a new blank table in Datasheet view, shown in Figure 27-8.

When you open a database (unless the database includes special startup settings), Access 2007 selects the object you last chose in the Navigation Pane for that database. For example, if the last time you opened this database you worked on a table, Access highlights that object (a table) in the Navigation Pane. Access also remembers the view and filters you applied to the Navigation Pane. For example, if Tables And Related Views was the last selected view applied to the Navigation Pane, Access will remember this the next time you open the database.

Because this is a new database and no objects or special startup settings exist yet, you see a Navigation Pane with only one object defined. For new databases, Access, by default, creates a new table in Datasheet view called Table1 with an ID field already defined. However, Access has not saved this table, so if you do not make any changes to it, Access will not prompt you to save the table if you close it. The following sections show you various methods for creating a new table.

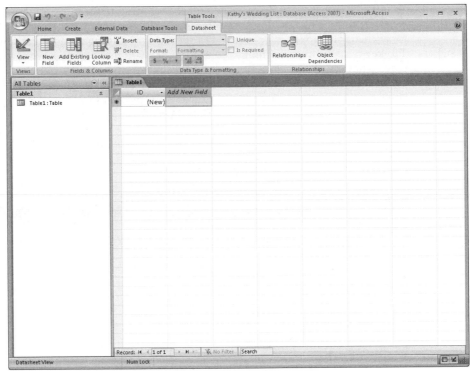

Figure 27-8 When you create a new blank database, Access 2007 opens a new table in Datasheet view for you.

Creating Your First Simple Table by Entering Data

If you've been following along to this point, you should still have your new Kathy's Wedding List database open with Table1 open in Datasheet view, as shown in Figure 27-8. (You can also follow these steps in any open database.) What you see is an empty datasheet, which looks quite similar to a spreadsheet. Access 2007 automatically created the first field, called ID, in the left column. Leave this field intact for now. In the second column Access has placed another field with the Add New Field heading. You can enter just about any type of data you want in this field—text, dates, numbers, or currency. But unlike a spreadsheet, you can't enter any calculated expressions in a datasheet. As you'll see later in the chapters about queries, you can easily display a calculated result using data from one or more tables by entering an expression in a query.

Because we're starting a list of wedding invitees, we'll need columns containing information such as title, last name, first name, middle initial, street address, city, state, postal code, number of guests invited, number of guests confirmed, gift received, and a gift acknowledged indicator. Be sure to enter the same type of data in a particular column for every row. For example, enter the city name in the seventh column (named Field6 by Access) for every row.

You can see some of the data entered for the wedding invitee list in Figure 27-9. When you start to type in a field in a row, Access 2007 displays a pencil icon on the row selector at the far left to indicate that you're adding or changing data in that row. Press the Tab key to move from column to column. When you move to another row, Access 2007 saves what you typed. If you make a mistake in a particular row or column, you can click the data you want to change and type over it or delete it. Notice that after you enter data in a column, Access 2007 guesses the most appropriate data type and displays it in the Data Type box on the Datasheet tab on the Ribbon.

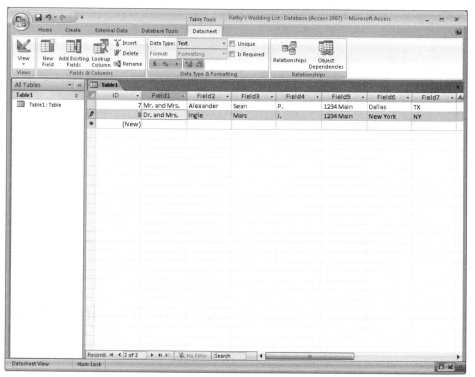

Figure 27-9 You can create the wedding invitee list table by entering data.

If you create a column of data that you don't want, click anywhere in the column and click Delete in the Fields & Columns group of the Datasheet contextual tab on the Ribbon. Click Yes when Access asks you to confirm the deletion. If you want to insert a blank column between two columns that already contain data, click anywhere in the column to the right of where you want to insert the new column and then click Insert in the Fields & Columns group of the Datasheet tab on the Ribbon. To move a column to a different location, click the field name at the top of the column to select the entire column, and then click again and drag the column to a new location. You can also click an unselected column and drag your mouse pointer through several adjacent columns to select them all. You can then move the columns as a group.

You probably noticed that Access 2007 named your columns Field1, Field2, and so forth—not very informative. You can enter a name for each column by double-clicking the column's field name. You can also click anywhere in the column and then click Rename in the Fields & Columns group on the Datasheet tab. In Figure 27-10, we have already renamed one of the columns and are in the process of renaming the second one.

ID		Title		Last Name	Field3		Field4		Field5	
	7	Mr. and Mrs.		Alexander	Sean		P.		1234 Main	
	8	Dr. and Mrs.		Ingle	Marc		J.		1234 Main	
*		(New)								

Figure 27-10 Double-click the column heading or click Rename in the Fields & Columns group on the Ribbon to rename a column in Datasheet view.

Save

After you enter several rows of data, it's a good idea to save your table. You can do this by clicking the Save button on the Quick Access Toolbar or by clicking the Microsoft Office Button and then Save. Access 2007 displays a Save As dialog box, as shown in Figure 27-11. Type an appropriate name for your table, and then click OK. If you deleted the ID field by mistake, Access 2007 displays a message box warning you that you have no primary key defined for this table and offers to build one for you. If you accept the offer, Access adds a field called ID and assigns it a special data type named AutoNumber that automatically generates a unique number for each new row you add. See "Understanding Field Data Types" on page 857 for details about AutoNumber. If one or more of the data columns you entered would make a good primary key, click No in the message box. In this case, Access 2007 should not display a message box, because it already generated the field called ID to serve as the primary key.

Figure 27-11 Access 2007 displays the Save As dialog box when you save a new table so that you can specify a table name.

Creating a Table Using a Table Template

If you look in the Wedding List sample database (WeddingList.accdb) included on the companion CD, you'll find it very simple, with one main table and a few supporting tables for data such as titles, cities, and groups. Most databases are usually quite a bit more complex. For example, the Housing Reservations sample database contains six

Chapter 27

main tables, and the Conrad Systems Contacts sample database contains more than a dozen tables. If you had to create every table "by hand," it could be quite a tedious process.

Fortunately, Access 2007 comes with table templates to help you build a few common tables. Let's move on to a more complex task—building tables like those you find in Conrad Systems Contacts. Click the Microsoft Office Button and then click New. This returns you to the Getting Started screen, ready to define a new blank database. For this exercise, create a new blank database and give it the name Contact Tracking.

To build a table using one of the table templates, close the table that Access 2007 created when you opened the database (Table1), click the Create tab on the Ribbon, and then click the Table Templates button in the Tables group. Access displays a list of five table templates—Contacts, Tasks, Issues, Events, and Assets, as shown in Figure 27-12. Microsoft uses the term *Quick Create* to refer to this one-click table creation feature.

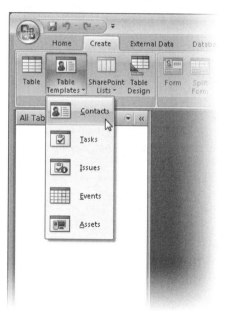

Figure 27-12 The five types of table templates help you create common types of tables.

The five table templates, which represent some of the more common types of table structures found in databases, are as follows:

- **Contacts** Use this table template when you need to track your personal or business contacts. Key fields in this template include the contact's company, job title, and phone numbers.

- **Tasks** Use this table template for keeping track of various tasks and projects needing completion. Key fields in this template include start and due dates for the task and percentage complete.

- **Issues** Use this table template for recording various personal or business issues. Some key fields in this template include the title of the issue and the issue status.

- **Events** Use this table template as a personal organizer of your appointments. This template includes fields for start and end times of the event, the event date, and even the location.

- **Assets** Use this table template for keeping track of your assets. Key fields in this template include the acquisition date, the original price of the asset, and the current price.

INSIDE OUT   What Happened to the Table Wizard?

The Table Wizard from previous versions of Access does not exist in Access 2007. Microsoft has replaced the Table Wizard with five table templates so that you can quickly build tables commonly found in most databases.

Click Contacts in the Table Templates list, and Access 2007 builds a complete table structure for a contacts table, as shown in Figure 27-13. Access creates a total of 18 fields to identify the data elements for this contacts table. Use the horizontal scroll bar or press Tab to see the field names to the right. This contacts table template includes fields such as Company, First Name, Last Name, E-mail Address, Job Title, and so on to identify a single subject—a contact. The Table Templates command also automatically defines a data type for each of these fields.

See Table 27-1 on page 858 for a full discussion of the various data types available within Access 2007.

INSIDE OUT   You Can Create and Modify Table Templates

Access 2007 uses special schema files coded in XML to define the properties for the five table templates. These five files have an .accfl extension and are located in the following folder in a default 2007 Office release installation: Program Files\Microsoft Office\Templates\1033\Access. If you choose to modify these template files, we recommend that you back up the original file to a safe location. You can open the .accfl files using Notepad or an XML reader. These XML view files are created using XML Schema Definition (XSD) language to describe the structure of the new table template tables. Access reads these files to determine the structure of the template files and then builds them following the instructions.

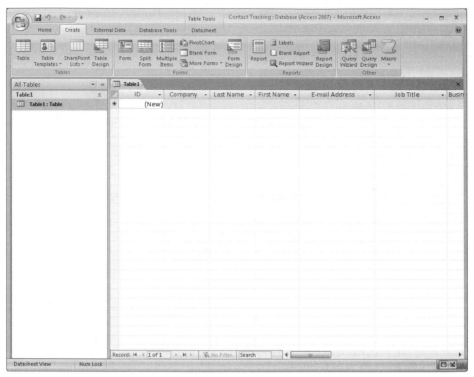

Figure 27-13 The Table Templates command builds a complete table with appropriate field types.

By default, Access 2007 assigned the name ID to the first field in this Contacts table. This field name is not very descriptive, so we will rename this field ContactID. There are several ways to rename a field using Access 2007, but for now we will focus on one of the easiest methods—renaming the field directly from Datasheet view. Double-click the heading of the ID field and then type **ContactID,** as shown in Figure 27-14. After you press Enter, Access immediately renames the field. Save this table now by clicking the Save button on the Quick Access Toolbar and name the table Contacts.

Figure 27-14 You can double-click a column heading in table Design view to change the name of the field.

You will further change this Contacts table later in this chapter so that it is more like the final tblContacts table in the Conrad Systems Contacts database. For now, close the Table window so that you can continue building other tables you need.

Creating a Table in Design View

You could continue to use table templates to build some of the other tables in the Contact Tracking database to mimic those in Conrad Systems Contacts. However, you'll find it very useful to learn the mechanics of building a table from scratch, so now is a good time to explore Design view and learn how to build tables without using table templates. The table templates, unlike the Table Wizard from previous versions of Access, offer only five choices for sample tables, and there is no way to pick and choose which fields to include or exclude. You can modify the template by changing the XML that defines it. By working in Design view, you'll see many additional features that you can use to customize the way your tables (and any queries, forms, or reports built on these tables) work when creating a table from scratch.

To begin creating a new table in Design view, click the Create tab on the Ribbon and then click the Table Design button in the Tables group. Access 2007 displays a blank Table window in Design view, as shown in Figure 27-15.

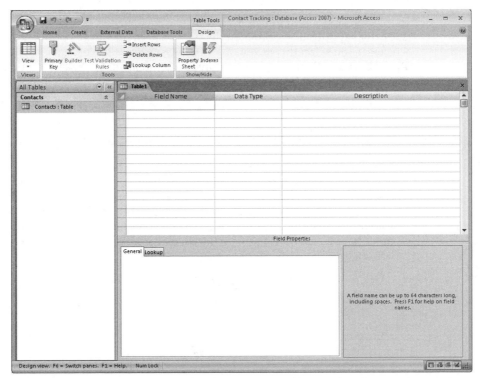

Figure 27-15 The Table Design command opens a new table in Design view.

In Design view, the upper part of the Table window displays columns in which you can enter the field names, the data type for each field, and a description of each field. After you select a data type for a field, Access 2007 allows you to set field properties in the lower-left section of the Table window. In the lower-right section of the Table window is a box in which Access displays information about fields or properties. The contents of this box change as you move from one location to another within the Table window.

For details about data type values, see "Understanding Field Data Types" on the next page.

Defining Fields

Now you're ready to begin defining the fields for the Companies table that mimics the one you can find in the Conrad Systems Contacts sample database (Contacts.accdb). Be sure the insertion point is in the first row of the Field Name column, and then type the name of the first field, **CompanyID**. Press Tab once to move to the Data Type column. A button with an arrow appears on the right side of the Data Type column. Here and elsewhere in Access 2007, this type of button signifies the presence of a list. Click the arrow or press Alt+Down Arrow to open the list of data type options, shown in Figure 27-16. In the Data Type column, you can either type a valid value or select from the values in the list. Select AutoNumber as the data type for CompanyID.

In the Description column for each field, you can enter a descriptive phrase. Access 2007 displays this description on the status bar (at the bottom of the Access window) whenever you select this field in a query in Datasheet view or in a form in Form view or Datasheet view. For example, enter **Unique Company ID** in the Description column for the CompanyID field.

INSIDE OUT   Why Setting the Description Property Is Important

Entering a Description property for every field in your table helps document your application. Because Access 2007 also displays the description on the status bar, paying careful attention to what you type in the Description field can later pay big dividends as a kind of mini-help for the users of your database. Also, because this data propagates automatically, you probably don't want to type something nonsensical or silly. Typing **I don't have a clue what this field does** is probably not a good idea—it will show up later on the status bar!

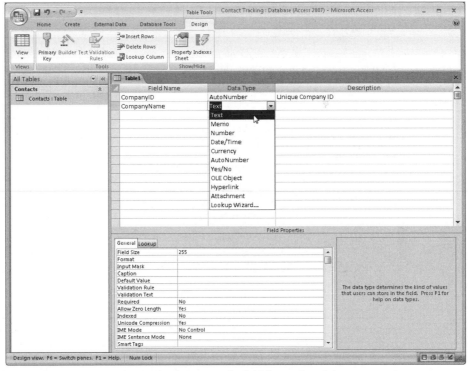

Figure 27-16 You can choose the data type of a field from a list of data type options.

Tab down to the next line, enter **CompanyName** as a field name, and then choose Text as the data type. After you select a data type, Access 2007 displays some property boxes in the Field Properties section in the lower part of the Table window. These boxes allow you to set *properties*—settings that determine how Access handles the field—and thereby customize a field. The properties Access displays depend on the data type you select; the properties appear with some default values in place, as shown in Figure 27-16.

For details about the values for each property, see "Setting Field Properties" on page 861.

Understanding Field Data Types

Access 2007 supports 10 types of data, each with a specific purpose. You can see the details about each data type in Table 27-1. Access also gives you an eleventh option, Lookup Wizard, to help you define the characteristics of foreign key fields that link to other tables.

Table 27-1 **Access Data Types**

Data Type	Usage	Size
Text	Alphanumeric data	Up to 255 characters
Memo	Alphanumeric data—sentences and paragraphs	Up to about 1 gigabyte (but controls to display a memo are limited to the first 64,000 characters)
Number	Numeric data	1, 2, 4, 8 or 16 bytes
Date/Time	Dates and times	8 bytes
Currency	Monetary data, stored with 4 decimal places of precision	8 bytes
AutoNumber	Unique value generated by Access for each new record	4 bytes (16 bytes for ReplicationID)
Yes/No	Boolean (true/false) data; Access stores the numeric value zero (0) for false, and minus one (–1) for true	1 bit
OLE Object	Pictures, graphs, or other ActiveX objects from another Windows-based application	Up to about 2 gigabytes
Hyperlink	A link "address" to a document or file on the World Wide Web, on an intranet, on a local area network (LAN), or on your local computer	Up to 8,192 characters (each part of a Hyperlink data type can contain up to 2,048 characters)
Attachment	You can attach files such as pictures, documents, spreadsheets, or charts; each Attachment field can contain an unlimited number of attachments per record, up to the storage limit of the size of a database file	Up to about 2 gigabytes
Lookup Wizard	The Lookup Wizard entry in the Data Type column in Design view is not actually a data type. When you choose this entry, a wizard starts to help you define either a simple or complex lookup field. A simple lookup field uses the contents of another table or a value list to validate the contents of a single value per row. A complex lookup field allows you to store multiple values of the same data type in each row.	Dependent on the data type of the lookup field

For each field in your table, select the data type that is best suited to how you will use that field's data. For character data, you should normally select the Text data type. You can control the maximum length of a Text field by using a field property, as explained later. Use the Memo data type only for long strings of text that might exceed 255 characters or that might contain formatting characters such as tabs or line endings (carriage returns).

Choosing Field Names

Office Access 2007 gives you lots of flexibility when it comes to naming your fields. A field name can be up to 64 characters long, can include any combination of letters, numbers, spaces, and special characters except a period (.), an exclamation point (!), an accent grave (`), and brackets ([ ]); however, the name cannot begin with a space and cannot include control characters (ANSI values 0 through 31). In general, you should give your fields meaningful names and should use the same name throughout for a field that occurs in more than one table. You should avoid using field names that might also match any name internal to Access or Visual Basic. For example, all objects have a Name property, so it's a good idea to qualify a field containing a name by calling it CustomerName or CompanyName. You should also avoid names that are the same as built-in functions, such as Date, Time, Now, or Space. See Access Help for a list of all the built-in function names.

Although you can use spaces anywhere within names in Access 2007, you should try to create field names and table names *without* embedded spaces. Many SQL databases to which Access can link (notably Oracle and Ingres) do not support spaces within names. Although SQL Server does allow spaces in names, you must enclose such names in brackets, or use quotes and execute a Set Quoted Identifier On command. If you ever want to move your application to a client/server environment and store your data in an SQL database such as Microsoft SQL Server or Oracle, you'll most likely have to change any names in your database tables that have an embedded space character. As you'll learn later in this book, table field names propagate into the queries, forms, and reports that you design using these tables. So any name you decide to change later in a table must also be changed in all your queries, forms, and reports. See "Setting Table Design Options" on page 891 for details about options to automatically propagate changes.

If you use reserved words or function names for field names, Access 2007 catches most of these and displays a warning message. This message warns you that the field name you chose, such as Name or Date, is a reserved word and you could encounter errors when referring to that field in other areas of the database application. Access still allows you to use this name if you choose, but take note of the problems it could cause. To avoid potential conflicts, we recommend you avoid using reserved words and built-in functions for field names.

When you select the Number data type, you should think carefully about what you enter as the Field Size property because this property choice will affect precision as well as length. (For example, integer numbers do not have decimals.) The Date/Time data type is useful for calendar or clock data and has the added benefit of allowing calculations in seconds, minutes, hours, days, months, or years. For example, you can find out the difference in days between two Date/Time values.

INSIDE OUT   Understanding What's Inside the Date/Time Data Type

Use the Date/Time data type to store any date, time, or date and time value. It's useful to know that Access 2007 stores the date as the integer portion of the Date/Time data type and the time as the fractional portion—the fraction of a day, measured from midnight, that the time represents, accurate to seconds. For example, 6:00:00 A.M. internally is 0.25. The day number is actually the number of days since December 30, 1899 (there will be a test on that later!) and can be a negative number for dates prior to that date. When two Date/Time fields contain only a date, you can subtract one from the other to find out how many days are between the two dates.

You should generally use the Currency data type for storing money values. Currency has the precision of integers, but with exactly four decimal places. When you need to store a precise fractional number that's not money, use the Number data type and choose Decimal for the Field Size property.

The AutoNumber data type is specifically designed for automatic generation of primary key values. Depending on the settings for the Field Size and New Values properties you choose for an AutoNumber field, you can have Access 2007 create a sequential or random long integer. You can include only one field using the AutoNumber data type in any table. If you define more than one AutoNumber field, Access displays an error message when you try to save the table.

Use the Yes/No data type to hold Boolean (true or false) values. This data type is particularly useful for flagging accounts paid or not paid or orders filled or not filled.

The OLE Object data type allows you to store complex data, such as pictures, graphs, or sounds, which can be edited or displayed through a dynamic link to another Windows-based application. For example, Access 2007 can store and allow you to edit a Microsoft Office Word document, a Microsoft Office Excel spreadsheet, a Microsoft Office PowerPoint presentation slide, a sound file (.wav), a video file (.avi), or pictures created using the Paint or Draw application.

The Hyperlink data type lets you store a simple or complex "link" to an external file or document. (Internally, Hyperlink is a memo data type with a special flag set to indicate that it is a link.) This link can contain a Uniform Resource Locator (URL) that points to a location on the World Wide Web or on a local intranet. It can also contain the Universal Naming Convention (UNC) name of a file on a server on your local area network (LAN) or on your local computer drives. The link can point to a file that is in Hypertext Markup Language (HTML) or in a format that is supported by an ActiveX application on your computer.

The Attachment data type, newly introduced in Access 2007, is very similar to the OLE Object data type in that you can use it to store complex data. However, unlike the OLE Object data type, you can now store *multiple* attachments in a single record. These files are stored in a binary field in a hidden system table. OLE objects usually result in database bloat because the files are not compressed, and Access also stores a bitmap thumbnail of the embedded file that can often be larger than the original file. For the Attachment data type, Access compresses each file, if it isn't already, and uses the original file rather than a generated thumbnail to minimize the amount of database bloat.

CAUTION

You can use the Attachment data type only with databases in the new .accdb file type. If you plan to create a database in the older .mdb format and have users with previous versions of Access use this database, you cannot define any fields as Attachment.

Setting Field Properties

You can customize the way Access 2007 stores and handles each field by setting specific properties. These properties vary according to the data type you choose. Table 27-2 lists all the possible properties that can appear on a field's General tab in a table's Design view, and the data types that are associated with each property.

Table 27-2 Field Properties on the General Tab

Property	Data Type	Options, Description
Field Size	Text	Text can be from 0 through 255 characters long, with a default length of 50 characters.
	Number	**Byte.** A single-byte integer containing values from 0 through 255.
		Integer. A 2-byte integer containing values from –32,768 through +32,767.
		Long Integer. A 4-byte integer containing values from –2,147,483,648 through +2,147,483,647.
		Single.[1] A 4-byte floating-point number containing values from -3.4×10^{38} through $+3.4 \times 10^{38}$ and up to seven significant digits.
		Double.[1] An 8-byte floating-point number containing values from -1.797×10^{308} through $+1.797 \times 10^{308}$ and up to 15 significant digits.
		Replication ID.[2] A 16-byte globally unique identifier (GUID).
		Decimal. A 12-byte integer with a defined decimal precision that can contain values from approximately -7.9228×10^{28} through $+7.9228 \times 10^{28}$. The default precision (number of decimal places) is 0 and the default scale is 18.
New Values	AutoNumber only	**Increment.** Values start at 1 and increment by 1 for each new row.
		Random. Access assigns a random long integer value to each new row.

Property	Data Type	Options, Description
Format	Text, Memo	You can specify a custom format that controls how Access displays the data. For details about custom formats, see the Access Help topic "Format Property—Text and Memo Data Types."
	Number (except Replication ID), Currency, Auto-Number	**General Number (default).** No commas or currency symbols; the number of decimal places shown depends on the precision of the data.
		Currency.[3] Currency symbol (from Regional And Language Options in Windows Control Panel) and two decimal places.
		Euro. Euro currency symbol (regardless of Control Panel settings) and two decimal places.
		Fixed. At least one digit and two decimal places.
		Standard. Two decimal places and separator commas.
		Percent. Moves displayed decimal point two places to the right and appends a percentage (%) symbol.
		Scientific. Scientific notation (for example, 1.05E+06 represents 1.05×10^6).
		You can specify a custom format that controls how Access displays the data. For details about custom formats, see the Access Help topic "Format Property—Number and Currency Types."
	Date/Time	**General Date (default).** Combines Short Date and Long Time formats (for example, 4/15/2007 5:30:10 PM).
		Long Date. Uses Long Date Style from Regional And Language Options in Control Panel (for example, Sunday, April 15, 2007).
		Medium Date. 15-Apr-2007.
		Short Date.[4] Uses Short Date Style from Regional And Language Options (for example, 4/15/2007).
		Long Time. Uses Time Style from Regional And Language Options (for example, 5:30:10 PM).
		Medium Time. 5:30 PM.
		Short Time. 17:30.
	Yes/No	**Yes/No (default).**
		True/False.
		On/Off.
		You can specify a custom format that controls how Access displays the data. For details about custom formats, see the Access Help topic "Format Property—Yes/No Data Type."

Property	Data Type	Options, Description
Precision	Number, Decimal	You can specify the maximum number of digits allowed. The default value is 18, and you can specify an integer value between 1 and 28.
Scale	Number, Decimal	You can specify the number of digits stored to the right of the decimal point. This value must be less than or equal to the value of the Precision property.
Decimal Places	Number (except Replication ID), Currency	You can specify the number of decimal places that Access displays. The default specification is Auto, which causes Access to display two decimal places for the Currency, Fixed, Standard, and Percent formats and the number of decimal places necessary to show the current precision of the numeric value for General Number format. You can also request a fixed display of decimal places ranging from 0 through 15.
Input Mask	Text, Number (except Replication ID), Date/Time, Currency	You can specify an editing mask that the user sees while entering data in the field. For example, you can have Access provide the delimiters in a date field such as __/__/__, or you can have Access format a U.S. phone number as (###) 000-0000. See "Defining Input Masks" on page 870 for details.
Caption	All	You can enter a more fully descriptive field name that Access displays in form labels and in report headings. (Tip: If you create field names with no embedded spaces, you can use the Caption property to specify a name that includes spaces for Access to use in labels and headers associated with this field in queries, forms, and reports.)
Default Value	Text, Memo, Date/Time, Hyperlink, Yes/No	You can specify a default value for the field that Access automatically uses for a new row if no other value is supplied. If you don't specify a Default Value property, the field will be Null if the user fails to supply a value. (See also the Required property.)
	Number, Currency	Access sets the property to 0. You can change the setting to a valid numeric value. You can also remove the setting, in which case the field will be Null if the user fails to supply a value. (See also the Required property.)
Validation Rule	All (except OLE Object, Replication ID, Attachment, and AutoNumber)	You can supply an expression that must be true whenever you enter or change data in this field. For example, <100 specifies that a number must be less than 100. You can also check for one of a series of values. For example, you can have Access check for a list of valid cities by specifying **"Chicago" Or "New York" Or "San Francisco"**. In addition, you can specify a complex expression that includes any of the built-in functions in Access. See "Defining Simple Field Validation Rules" on page 868 for details.

Chapter 27

Property	Data Type	Options, Description
Validation Text	All (except OLE Object, Replication ID, Attachment, and AutoNumber)	You can specify a custom message that Access displays whenever the data entered does not pass your validation rule.
Required	All (except AutoNumber)	If you don't want to allow a Null value in this field, set this property to Yes.
Allow Zero Length	Text, Memo, Hyperlink	You can set the field equal to a zero-length string ("") if you set this property to Yes. See the sidebar, "Nulls and Zero-Length Strings," on page 866 for more information.
Indexed	All except OLE Object and Attachment	You can ask that an index be built to speed access to data values. You can also require that the values in the indexed field always be unique for the entire table. See "Adding Indexes" on page 888 for details.
Unicode Compression	Text, Memo, Hyperlink	As of version 2000, Access stores character fields in an .mdb and .accdb file using a double-byte (Unicode) character set to support extended character sets in languages that require them. The Latin character set required by most Western European languages (such as English, Spanish, French, or German) requires only 1 byte per character. When you set Unicode Compression to Yes for character fields, Access stores compressible characters in 1 byte instead of 2, thus saving space in your database file. However, Access will not compress Memo or Hyperlink fields that will not compress to fewer than 4,096 bytes. The default for new tables is Yes in all countries where the standard language character set does not require 2 bytes to store all the characters.
IME Mode, IME Sentence Mode	Text, Memo, Hyperlink	On computers with an Asian version of Windows and appropriate Input Method Editor (IME) installed, these properties control conversion of characters in kanji, hiragana, katakana, and hangul character sets.

Property	Data Type	Options, Description
Smart Tags	All data types except Yes/No, OLE Object, Attachment, and Replication ID	Indicates the registered smart tag name and action that you want associated with this field. When the user views this field in a table datasheet, a query datasheet, or a form, Access displays a smart tag available indicator next to the field. The user can click on the indicator and select the smart tag action to perform.

[1] Single and Double field sizes use an internal storage format called floating point that can handle very large or very small numbers, but which is somewhat imprecise. If the number you need to store contains more than 7 significant digits for a Single or more than 15 significant digits for a Double, the number will be rounded. For example, if you try to save 10,234,567 in a Single, the actual value stored will be 10,234,570. Likewise, Access stores 10.234567 as 10.23457 in a Single. If you want absolute fractional precision, use Decimal field size or Currency data type instead.

[2] In general, you should use the Replication ID field size only in an Access 2003 format and earlier database that is managed by the Replication Manager.

[3] Note that Currency, Euro, Fixed, and Standard formats always display two decimal places regardless of the number of actual decimal places in the underlying data. Access rounds any number to two decimal places for display if the number contains more than two decimal places.

[4] To help alleviate problems with dates spanning the start of the century, we recommend that you select the Use Four-Digit Year Formatting check box in Access. Click the Microsoft Office Button, click Access Options, and then scroll to the General section in the Advanced category to find this option. You should also be sure that your Short Date Style in the Regional And Language Options dialog box uses a four-digit year. (This is the default in Windows XP and Windows Vista; you can double-check your settings by accessing Regional And Language Options within Control Panel.)

INSIDE OUT   Don't Specify a Validation Rule Without Validation Text

If you specify a validation rule but no validation text, Access 2007 generates an ugly and cryptic message that your users might not understand:

"One or more values are prohibited by the validation rule '*<your expression here>*' set for '*<table name.field name>*'. Enter a value that the expression for this field can accept."

Unless you like getting lots of support calls, we recommend that you always enter a custom validation text message whenever you specify a validation rule.

Chapter 27

Nulls and Zero-Length Strings

Relational databases support a special value in fields, called a *Null*, that indicates an unknown value. In contrast, you can set Text or Memo fields to a *zero-length string* to indicate that the value of a field is known but the field is empty.

Why is it important to differentiate Nulls (unknown values) from zero-length strings? Here's an example: Suppose you have a database that stores the results of a survey about automobile preferences. For questionnaires on which there is no response to a color-preference question, it is appropriate to store a Null. You don't want to match responses based on an unknown response, and you don't want to include the row in calculating totals or averages. On the other hand, some people might have responded "I don't care" for a color preference. In this case, you have a known "no preference" answer, and a zero-length string is appropriate. You can match all "I don't care" responses and include the responses in totals and averages.

Another example might be fax numbers in a customer database. If you store a Null, it means you don't know whether the customer has a fax number. If you store a zero-length string, you know the customer has no fax number. Access 2007 gives you the flexibility to deal with both types of "empty" values.

You can join tables on zero-length strings, and two zero-length strings will compare to be equal. However, for Text, Memo, and Hyperlink fields, you must set the Allow Zero Length property to Yes to allow users to enter zero-length strings. (Yes became the default in Microsoft Access 2002.) Otherwise, Access converts a zero-length or all-blank string to a Null before storing the value. If you also set the Required property of the Text field to Yes, Access stores a zero-length string if the user enters either "" (two double quotes with no space) or blanks in the field.

Nulls have special properties. A Null value cannot be equal to any other value, not even to another Null. This means you cannot join (link) two tables on Null values. Also, the question "Is A equal to B?" when A, B, or both A and B contain a Null, can never be answered "yes." The answer, literally, is "I don't know." Likewise, the answer to the question "Is A not equal to B?" is also "I don't know." Finally, Null values do not participate in aggregate calculations involving such functions as Sum or Avg. You can test a value to determine whether it is a Null by comparing it to the special NULL keyword or by using the IsNull built-in function.

Completing the Fields in the Companies Table

You now know enough about field data types and properties to finish designing the Companies table in this example. (You can also follow this example using the tblCompanies table from the Conrad Systems Contacts sample database.) Use the information listed in Table 27-3 to design the table shown in Figure 27-17.

Table 27-3 Field Definitions for the Companies Table

Field Name	Data Type	Description	Field Size
CompanyID	AutoNumber	Unique Company ID	
CompanyName	Text	Company Name	50
Department	Text	Department	50
Address	Text	Address	255
City	Text	City	50
County	Text	County	50
StateOrProvince	Text	State or Province	20
PostalCode	Text	Postal/Zip Code	10
PhoneNumber	Text	Phone Number	15
FaxNumber	Text	Fax Number	15
Website	Hyperlink	Website address	
ReferredBy	Number	Contact who referred this company	Long Integer

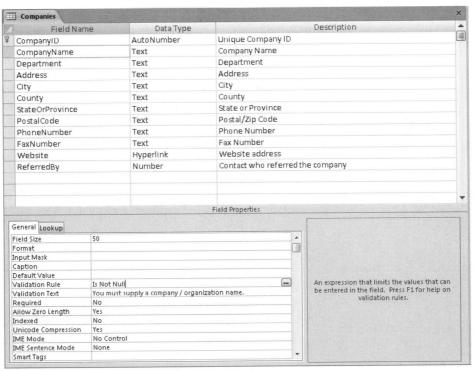

Figure 27-17 Your fields in the Companies table should look like this. You'll learn how to define validation rules in the next section.

Defining Simple Field Validation Rules

To define a simple check on the values that you allow in a field, enter an expression in the Validation Rule property box for the field. Access 2007 won't allow you to enter a field value that violates this rule. Access performs this validation for data entered in a Table window in Datasheet view, in an updateable query, or in a form. You can specify a more restrictive validation rule in a form, but you cannot override the rule defined for the field in the table by specifying a completely different rule in the form.

In general, a field validation expression consists of an operator and a comparison value. If you do not include an operator, Access assumes you want an "equals" (=) comparison. You can specify multiple comparisons separated by the Boolean operators OR and AND.

It is good practice to always enclose text string values in quotation marks. If one of your values is a text string containing blanks or special characters, you must enclose the entire string in quotation marks. For example, to limit the valid entries for a City field to the two largest cities in the state of California, enter **"Los Angeles" Or "San Diego"**. If you are comparing date values, you must enclose the date constants in pound sign (#) characters, as in #01/15/2007#.

You can use the comparison symbols to compare the value in the field to a value or values in your validation rule. Comparison symbols are summarized in Table 27-4. For example, you might want to ensure that a numeric value is always less than 1000. To do this, enter **<1000**. You can use one or more pairs of comparisons to ask Access to check that the value falls within certain ranges. For example, if you want to verify that a number is in the range of 50 through 100, enter either **>=50 And <=100** or **Between 50 And 100**. Another way to test for a match in a list of values is to use the IN comparison operator. For example, to test for states surrounding the U.S. capital, enter **In ("Virginia", "Maryland")**. If all you need to do is ensure that the user enters a value, you can use the special comparison phrase **Is Not Null**.

INSIDE OUT A Friendlier Way to Require a Field Value

When you set the Required property to Yes and the user fails to enter a value, Access 2007 displays an unfriendly message:

"The field '*<tablename.fieldname>*' cannot contain a Null value because the Required property for this field is set to True. Enter a value in this field."

We recommend that you use the Validation Rule property to require a value in the field and then use the Validation Text property to generate your own specific message.

Table 27-4 Comparison Symbols Used in Validation Rules

Operator	Meaning
NOT	Use before any comparison operator except IS NOT NULL to perform the converse test. For example, NOT > 5 is equivalent to <=5.
<	Less than
<=	Less than or equal to
>	Greater than
>=	Greater than or equal to
=	Equal to
<>	Not equal to
IN	Test for *equal to* any member in a list; comparison value must be a comma-separated list enclosed in parentheses
BETWEEN	Test for a range of values; comparison value must be two values (a low and a high value) separated by the AND operator
LIKE	Test a Text or Memo field to match a pattern string
IS NOT NULL	Requires the user to enter a value in the field

If you need to validate a Text, Memo, or Hyperlink field against a matching pattern (for example, a postal code or a phone number), you can use the LIKE comparison operator. You provide a text string as a comparison value that defines which characters are valid in which positions. Access understands a number of *wildcard characters*, which you can use to define positions that can contain any single character, zero or more characters, or any single number. These characters are shown in Table 27-5.

Table 27-5 LIKE Wildcard Characters

Character	Meaning
?	Any single character
*	Zero or more characters; use to define leading, trailing, or embedded strings that don't have to match any specific pattern characters
#	Any single digit

You can also specify that any particular position in the Text or Memo field can contain only characters from a list that you provide. You can specify a range of characters within a list by entering the low value character, a hyphen, and the high value character, as in [A-Z] or [3-7]. If you want to test a position for any characters *except* those in a list, start the list with an exclamation point (!). You must enclose all lists in brackets ([ ]). You can see examples of validation rules using LIKE here.

Validation Rule	Tests For
LIKE "#####" or	A U.S. 5-digit ZIP Code
LIKE "#####-####"	A U.S. 9-digit ZIP+ Code
LIKE "[A-Z]#[A-Z] #[A-Z]#"	A Canadian postal code
LIKE "###-##-####"	A U.S. Social Security Number
LIKE "Smith*"	A string that begins with *Smith*[1]
LIKE "*smith##*"	A string that contains *smith* followed by two numbers, anywhere in the string
LIKE "??00####"	An eight-character string that contains any first two characters followed by exactly two zeros and then any four digits
LIKE "[!0-9BMQ]*####"	A string that contains any character other than a number or the letter *B*, *M*, or *Q* in the first position and ends with exactly four digits

[1] Character string comparisons in Access are case-insensitive. So, smith, SMITH, and Smith are all equal.

Defining Input Masks

To assist you in entering formatted data, Access 2007 allows you to define an *input mask* for Text, Number (except Replication ID), Date/Time, and Currency data types. You can use an input mask to do something as simple as forcing all letters entered to be uppercase or as complex as adding parentheses and hyphens to phone numbers. You create an input mask by using the special mask definition characters shown in Table 27-6. You can also embed strings of characters that you want to display for formatting or store in the data field.

Table 27-6 Input Mask Definition Characters

Mask Character	Meaning
0	A single digit must be entered in this position.
9	A digit or a space can be entered in this position. If the user skips this position by moving the insertion point past the position without entering anything, Access stores nothing in this position.
#	A digit, a space, or a plus or minus sign can be entered in this position. If the user skips this position by moving the insertion point past the position without entering anything, Access stores a space.
L	A letter must be entered in this position.
?	A letter can be entered in this position. If the user skips this position by moving the insertion point past the position without entering anything, Access stores nothing.

Mask Character	Meaning
A	A letter or a digit must be entered in this position.
a	A letter or a digit can be entered in this position. If the user skips this position by moving the insertion point past the position without entering anything, Access stores nothing.
&	A character or a space must be entered in this position.
C	Any character or a space can be entered in this position. If the user skips this position by moving the insertion point past the position without entering anything, Access stores nothing.
.	Decimal placeholder (depends on the setting in the Regional And Language Options in Control Panel).
,	Thousands separator (depends on the setting in the Regional And Language Options in Control Panel).
: ; - /	Date and time separators (depend on the settings in the Regional And Language Options in Control Panel).
<	Converts to lowercase all characters that follow.
>	Converts to uppercase all characters that follow.
!	Causes the mask to fill from right to left when you define optional characters on the left end of the mask. You can place this character anywhere in the mask.
\	Causes the character immediately following to be displayed as a literal character rather than as a mask character.
"literal"	You can also enclose any literal string in double quotation marks rather than use the \ character repeatedly.

An input mask consists of three parts, separated by semicolons. The first part defines the mask string using mask definition characters and embedded literal data. The optional second part indicates whether you want the embedded literal characters stored in the field in the database. Set this second part to **0** to store the characters or to **1** to store only the data entered. The optional third part defines a single character that Access 2007 uses as a placeholder to indicate positions where data can be entered. The default placeholder character is an underscore (_).

Perhaps the best way to learn to use input masks is to take advantage of the Input Mask Wizard. In the Companies table of the Contact Tracking database, the PhoneNumber field could benefit from the use of an input mask. Click the PhoneNumber field in the upper part of the Table window in Design view, and then click in the Input Mask property box in the lower part of the window. You should see a small button with three dots on it (called the *Build* button) to the right of the property box.

Build

Click the Build button to start the Input Mask Wizard. If you haven't already saved the table, the wizard will insist that you do so. Save the table and name it Companies. When Access 2007 warns you that you have not defined a primary key and asks if you want to create a primary key now, click No. We'll define a primary key in the next section. On the first page, the wizard gives you a number of choices for standard input masks that it can generate for you. In this case, click the first one in the list—Phone Number, as shown in Figure 27-18. Note that you can type something in the Try It box below the Input Mask list to try out the mask.

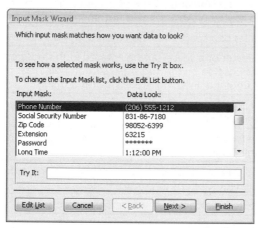

Figure 27-18 You can choose from several built-in input masks in the Input Mask Wizard.

Click the Next button to go to the next page. On this page, shown in Figure 27-19, you can see the mask name, the proposed mask string, a list from which you select the placeholder character, and another Try It box. The default underscore character (_) works well as a placeholder character for phone numbers.

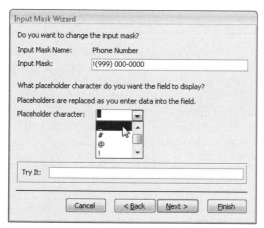

Figure 27-19 You can choose the placeholder character in the Input Mask Wizard.

Click Next to go to the next page, where you can choose whether you want the data stored without the formatting characters (the default) or stored with the parentheses, spaces, and hyphen separator. In Figure 27-20, we're indicating that we want the data stored with the formatting characters. Click Next to go to the final page, and then click the Finish button on that page to store the mask in the property setting. Figure 27-21 shows the resulting mask in the PhoneNumber field. You'll find this same mask handy for any text field that is meant to contain a U.S. phone number (such as the phone number fields in the Contacts table).

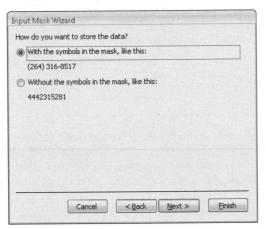

Figure 27-20 You can choose to store formatting characters.

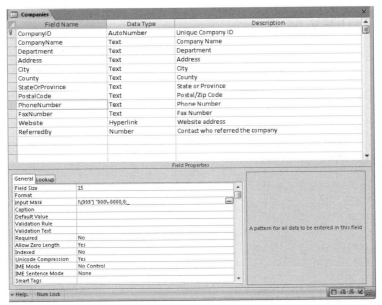

Figure 27-21 The wizard stores the input mask for PhoneNumber based on the criteria you selected.

> **Note**
>
> If you look closely in Figure 27-21, you can see a backslash before the area code and quotation marks around the second parenthesis. When you complete the Input Mask Wizard, Access initially does not display these extra characters. After you click off that field or save the table, Access adds the missing characters. The mask generated by the wizard is incorrect, but the table editor fixes it before saving.

CAUTION

> Although an input mask can be very useful to help guide the user to enter valid data, if you define an input mask incorrectly or do not consider all possible valid values, you can prevent the user from entering necessary data. For example, we just showed you how to build an input mask for a U.S. telephone number, but that mask would prevent someone from entering a European phone number correctly.

Defining a Primary Key

Every table in a relational database should have a primary key. Telling Access 2007 how to define the primary key is quite simple. Open the table in Design view and click the row selector to the left of the field you want to use as the primary key. If you need to select multiple fields for your primary key, hold down the Ctrl key and click the row selector of each additional field you need.

For details about designing primary keys for your tables, see Article 1, "Designing Your Database Application," on the companion CD.

After you select all the fields you want for the primary key, click the Primary Key button in the Tools group of the Design contextual tab on the Ribbon. Access 2007 displays a key symbol to the left of the selected field(s) to acknowledge your definition of the primary key. To eliminate all primary key designations, see "Adding Indexes" on page 888. When you've finished creating the Companies table for the Contact Tracking database, the primary key should be the CompanyID field, as shown in Figure 27-22.

Be sure to click the Save button on the Quick Access Toolbar to save this latest change to your table definition.

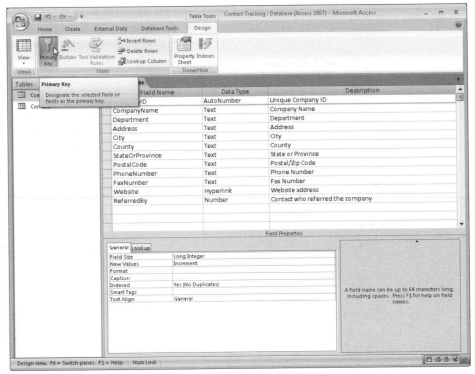

Figure 27-22 You can easily define the primary key for the Companies table by selecting the field in Design view and clicking the Primary Key button on the Ribbon.

Defining a Table Validation Rule

The last detail to define is any validation rules that you want Access 2007 to apply to any fields in the table. Although field validation rules get checked as you enter each new value, Access checks a table validation rule only when you save or add a row. Table validation rules are handy when the values in one field are dependent on what's stored in another field. You need to wait until the entire row is about to be saved before checking one field against another.

One of the tables in the Contact Tracking database—Products—needs a table validation rule. Define that table now using the specifications in Table 27-7. Be sure to define ProductID as the primary key and then save the table and name it Products.

Table 27-7 Field Definitions for the Products Table

Field Name	Data Type	Description	Field Size
ProductID	AutoNumber	Unique product identifier	
ProductName	Text	Product description	100
CategoryDescription	Text	Description of the category	50
UnitPrice	Currency	Price	
TrialVersion	Yes/No	Is this a trial version?	
TrialExpire	Number	If trial version, number of days before expiration	Long Integer

To define a table validation rule, be sure that the table is in Design view, and then click the Property Sheet button in the Show/Hide group of the Design contextual tab on the Ribbon, shown in Figure 27-23.

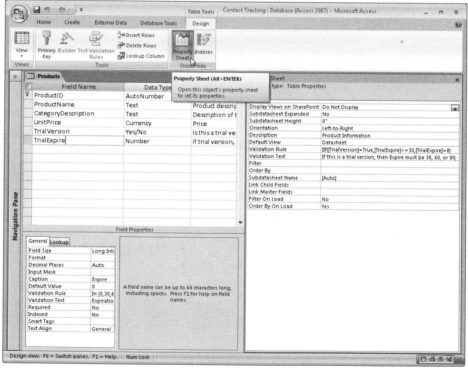

Figure 27-23 You can define a table validation rule in the property sheet for the table.

On the Validation Rule line in the table's property sheet, you can enter any valid comparison expression, or you can use one of the built-in functions to test your table's field values. In the Products table, we want to be sure that any trial version of the software expires in 30, 60, or 90 days. Zero is also a valid value if this particular product isn't a trial version. As you can see in Figure 27-23, we've already entered a *field* validation rule for TrialExpire on the General tab to make sure the TrialExpire value is always 0, 30, 60, or 90—In (0, 30, 60, 90). But how do we make sure that TrialExpire is zero if TrialVersion is False, or one of the other values if TrialVersion is True? For that, we need to define a *table-level* validation rule in the table's property sheet.

To refer to a field name, enclose the name in brackets ([ ]), as shown in Figure 27-23. You'll use this technique whenever you refer to the name of an object anywhere in an expression. In this case, we're using a special built-in function called *Immediate If* (or *IIF* for short) in the table validation rule to perform the test on the TrialExpire and TrialVersion fields. The IIF function can evaluate a test in the first argument and then return the evaluation of the second argument if the first argument is true or the evaluation of the third argument if the first argument is false. You must separate the arguments in a function call with commas. Note that we said *evaluation of the argument*—this means we can enter additional tests, even another IIF, in the second and third arguments.

In the Products table, you want to make sure that the TrialVersion and TrialExpire fields are in sync with each other. If this is not a trial version, the TrialExpire field value should be zero (indicating the product never expires), and if it is a trial version, TrialExpire must be set to some value greater than or equal to 30. The expression we used to accomplish this is as follows:

IIf([TrialVersion]=True,[TrialExpire]>=30,[TrialExpire]=0)

So, the first argument uses IIF to evaluate the expression **[TrialVersion] = True**—is the value in the field named TrialVersion True? If this is true (this is a trial version that must have a nonzero number of expiration days), IIF returns the evaluation of the second argument. If this is not a trial version, IIF evaluates the third argument. Now all we need to do is type the appropriate test based on the true or false result on TrialVersion. If this is a trial version, the TrialExpire field must be 30 or greater (we'll let the field validation rule make sure it's exactly 30, 60, or 90), so we need to test for that by entering **[TrialExpire] >= 30** in the second argument. If this is not a trial version, we need to make sure TrialExpire is zero by entering **[TrialExpire] = 0** in the third argument. Got it? If TrialVersion is True, then [TrialExpire] >= 30 must be true or the validation rule will fail. If TrialVersion is False, then [TrialExpire] = 0 must be true. As you might imagine, once you become more familiar with building expressions and with the available built-in functions, you can create very sophisticated table validation rules.

On the Validation Text line of the table's property sheet, enter the text that you want Access to display whenever the table validation rule is violated. You should be careful to word this message so that the user clearly understands what is wrong. If you enter a table validation rule and fail to specify validation text, Access displays the following message when the user enters invalid data: "One or more values are prohibited by the validation rule '< *your validation rule expression here* >' set for '*<table name>*'. Enter a value that the expression for this field can accept."

Not very pretty, is it? And you can imagine what the user will say about your IIF expression!

Understanding Other Table Properties

As you can see in Figure 27-23, Access 2007 provides several additional table properties that you can set in Design view. You can enter a description of the table in the Description property, and you'll see this description in the Navigation Pane if you ask for the Details view. For Default View, you can choose from Datasheet (the default), PivotTable, or PivotChart.

The Filter property lets you predefine criteria to limit the data displayed in the Datasheet view of this table. If you set Filter On Load to Yes, Access applies the filter you defined when you open the datasheet. You can use Order By to define one or more fields that define the default display sequence of rows in this table when in Datasheet view. If you don't define an Order By property, Access displays the rows in primary key sequence. You can set the Order By On Load property to Yes to request that Access always applies any Order By specification when opening the datasheet.

> **Note**
>
> If you apply a filter or specify a sorting sequence when you have the table open in Datasheet view, Access 2007 saves the filter in the Filter property and the sorting sequence in the Order By property. If you have Filter On Load or Order By On Load set to Yes, Access reapplies the previous filter or sort sequence criteria the next time you open the datasheet.

You can find five properties—Subdatasheet Name, Link Child Fields, Link Master Fields, Subdatasheet Height, and Subdatasheet Expanded—that are all related. Access 2000 introduced a feature that lets you see information from related tables when you view the datasheet of a table. For example, in the Contact Tracking database you have been building, you can set the Subdatasheet properties in the definition of Contacts to also show you related information from ContactEvents or ContactProducts. In the Housing Reservations sample database, you can see Departments and their Employees, or Employees and their Reservation Requests. Figure 27-24 shows you the Departments table in Housing.accdb open in Datasheet view. For this table, we defined a subdatasheet to show related employee information for each department.

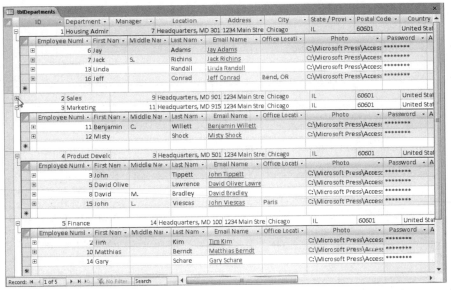

Figure 27-24 The datasheet for the tblDepartments table in the Housing Reservations sample database shows an expanded subdatasheet.

Notice the small plus and minus signs at the beginning of each department row. Click on a plus sign to expand the subdatasheet to show related employees. Click on the minus sign to shrink the subdatasheet and show only department information. Table 27-8 explains each of the Table Property settings that you can specify to attach a subdatasheet to a table.

INSIDE OUT   Don't Set Subdatasheet Properties in a Table

For a production application, it's a good idea to set Subdatasheet Name in all your tables to [None]. First, when Access 2007 opens your table, it must not only fetch the rows from the table but also fetch the rows defined in the subdatasheet. Adding a subdatasheet to a large table can negatively impact performance.

Also, any production application should not allow the user to see table or query datasheets because you cannot enforce complex business rules. Any data validation in a table or query datasheet depends entirely on the validation and referential integrity rules defined for your tables because you cannot define any Visual Basic code behind tables or queries.

Table 27-8 **Table Properties for Defining a Subdatasheet**

Property Name	Setting	Description
Subdatasheet Name	[Auto]	Creates a subdatasheet using the first table that has a many relationship defined with this table.
	[None]	Turns off the subdatasheet feature.
	Table.*name* or Query.*name*	Uses the selected table or query as the subdatasheet.
Link Child Fields	Name(s) of the foreign key fields(s) in the related table, separated by semicolons	Defines the fields in the subdatasheet table or query that match the primary key fields in this table. When you choose a table or query for the Subdatasheet Name property, Access uses an available relationship definition or matching field names and data types to automatically set this property for you. You can correct this setting if Access has guessed wrong.
Link Master Fields	Name(s) of the primary key field(s) in this table, separated by semicolons	Defines the primary key fields that Access uses to link to the subdatasheet table or query. When you choose a table or query for the Subdatasheet Name property, Access uses an available relationship definition or matching field names and data types to automatically set this property for you. You can correct this setting if Access has guessed wrong.
Subdatasheet Height	A measurement in inches	If you specify zero (the default), each subdatasheet expands to show all available rows when opened. When you specify a nonzero value, the subdatasheet window opens to the height you specify. If the height is insufficient to display all rows, a scroll bar appears to allow you to look at all the rows.
Subdatasheet Expanded	Yes or No	If you specify Yes, all subdatasheets appear expanded when you open the table datasheet. No is the default.

You can use the Orientation property to specify the reading sequence of the data in Datasheet view. The default in most versions of Access is Left-to-Right. In versions that support a language that is normally read right to left, the default is Right-to-Left. When you use Right-to-Left, field and table captions appear right-justified, the field order is right to left, and the tab sequence proceeds right to left.

The Display Views On SharePoint property by default is set to Follow Database Setting, which means links are created in the views list when this table is upsized to a Windows SharePoint Services site.

Defining Relationships

After you have defined two or more related tables, you should tell Access 2007 how the tables are related. You do this so that Access 2007 will be able to link all your tables when you need to use them in queries, forms, or reports.

Thus far in this chapter, you have seen how to build the main subject tables of the Contact Tracking database—Companies, Contacts, and Products. Before we define the relationships in this sample database, you need to create a couple of *linking* tables that define the many-to-many relationships between the Companies and Contacts tables and between the Products and Contacts tables. Table 27-9 shows you the fields you need for the Company Contacts table that forms the "glue" between the Companies and Contacts tables.

Table 27-9 Field Definitions for the Company Contacts Table

Field Name	Data Type	Description	Field Size
CompanyID	Number	Company/organization	Long Integer
ContactID	Number	Person within company	Long Integer
Position	Text	Person's position within the company	50
DefaultForContact	Yes/No	Is this the default company for this contact?	

Define the combination of CompanyID and ContactID as the primary key for this table by clicking the selection button next to CompanyID and then holding down the Ctrl key and clicking the button next to ContactID. Click the Primary Key button in the Tools group of the Design tab on the Ribbon to define the key and then save the table as CompanyContacts.

Table 27-10 shows you the fields you need to define the Contact Products table that creates the link between the Contacts and Products tables.

Table 27-10 Field Definitions for the Contact Products Table

Field Name	Data Type	Description	Field Size
CompanyID	Number	Company/organization	Long Integer
ContactID	Number	Related contact	Long Integer
ProductID	Number	Related product	Long Integer
DateSold	Date/Time	Date product sold	
SoldPrice	Currency	Price paid	

The primary key of the Contact Products table is the combination of CompanyID, ContactID, and ProductID. You can click on CompanyID to select it and then hold down the Shift key while you click on ProductID (if you defined the fields in sequence) to select all three fields. Click the Primary Key button in the Tools group of the Design tab on the Ribbon to define the key, and then save the table as ContactProducts.

You need one last table, the Contact Events Table, to define all the major tables you'll need for Contact Tracking. Table 27-11 shows the fields you need. The primary key for this table is the combination of ContactID and ContactDateTime. Note that we took advantage of the fact that a Date/Time data type in Access 2007 can store both a date and a time, so we don't need the two separate date and time fields. Save this last table as ContactEvents.

Table 27-11 Field Definitions for the Contact Events Table

Field Name	Data Type	Description	Field Size
ContactID	Number	Related contact	Long Integer
ContactDateTime	Date/Time	Date and time of the contact	
ContactNotes	Memo	Description of the contact	
ContactFollowUpDate	Date/Time	Follow-up date	

Now you're ready to start defining relationships. To define relationships, first close any Table windows that are open and then click the Relationships command in the Show/Hide group of the Database Tools tab on the Ribbon to open the Relationships window. If this is the first time you have defined relationships in this database, Access 2007 opens a blank Relationships window and opens the Show Table dialog box, shown in Figure 27-25.

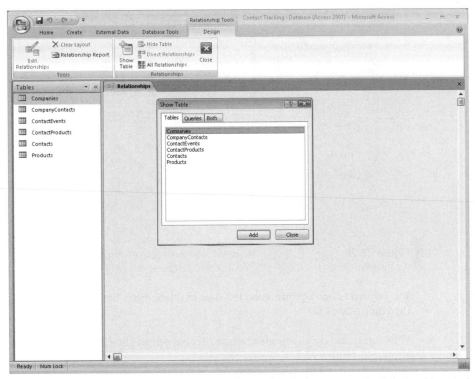

Figure 27-25 Access displays the Show Table dialog box when you open the Relationships window for the first time.

In the Show Table dialog box, select each table and click the Add button in turn. Click Close to dismiss the Show Table dialog box.

Defining Your First Relationship

A company can have several contacts, and any contact can belong to several companies or organizations. This means that companies have a many-to-many relationship with contacts. Defining a many-to-many relationship between two tables requires a linking table. Let's link the Companies and Contacts tables by defining the first half of the relationship—the one between Companies and the linking table, CompanyContacts. You can see that for the CompanyID primary key in the Companies table, there is a matching CompanyID foreign key in the CompanyContacts table. To create the relationship you need, click in the CompanyID field in the Companies table and drag it to the CompanyID field in the CompanyContacts table, as shown in Figure 27-26.

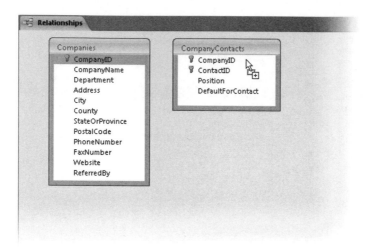

Figure 27-26 Drag the linking field from the "one" table (Companies) to the "many" table (CompanyContacts) to define the relationship between the tables.

> You can read about determining the type of relationship between two tables in Article 1 on the companion CD.

When you release the mouse button, Access opens the Edit Relationships dialog box, shown in Figure 27-27.

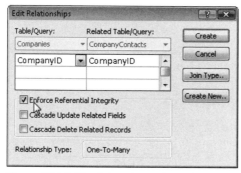

Figure 27-27 The Edit Relationships dialog box lets you specify the linking fields in two tables.

INSIDE OUT Creating Relationships from Scratch

You can also click the Edit Relationships command in the Tools group of the Design contextual tab on the Ribbon to create a new relationship, but you have to fill in the table and field names yourself. Dragging and dropping does some of this work for you.

You'll notice that Access 2007 has filled in the field names for you. If you need to define a multiple-field relationship between two tables, use the additional blank lines to define those fields. (We'll do that in just a second.) Because you probably don't want any rows created in CompanyContacts for a nonexistent company, select the Enforce Referential Integrity check box. When you do this, Access 2007 ensures that you can't add a row in the CompanyContacts table containing an invalid CompanyID. Also, Access won't let you delete any records from the Companies table if they have contacts still defined.

Note that after you select the Enforce Referential Integrity check box, Access 2007 makes two additional check boxes available: Cascade Update Related Fields and Cascade Delete Related Records. If you select the Cascade Delete Related Records check box, Access 2007 deletes child rows (the related rows in the *many* table of a one-to-many relationship) when you delete a parent row (the related row in the *one* table of a one-to-many relationship). For example, if you removed a company from the table Access 2007 would remove the related company contact rows. In this database design, the CompanyID field has the AutoNumber data type, so it cannot be changed once it is set. However, if you build a table with a primary key that is Text or Number (perhaps a ProductID field that could change at some point in the future), it might be a good idea to select the Cascade Update Related Fields check box. This option requests that Access automatically update any foreign key values in the *child* table (the *many* table in a one-to-many relationship) if you change a primary key value in a *parent* table (the *one* table in a one-to-many relationship).

You might have noticed that the Show Table dialog box, shown earlier in Figure 27-25, gives you the option to include queries as well as tables. Sometimes you might want to define relationships between tables and queries or between queries so that Access 2007 knows how to join them properly. You can also define what's known as an *outer join* by clicking the Join Type button in the Edit Relationships dialog box and selecting an option in the Join Properties dialog box. With an outer join, you can find out, for example, which companies have no contacts or which products haven't been sold.

INSIDE OUT   Avoid Defining a Relationship with an Outer Join

We recommend that you do not define an outer join relationship between two tables. Access 2007 automatically links two tables you include in a query design using the relationships you have defined. In the vast majority of cases, you will want to include only the matching rows from both tables. If you define the relationship as an outer join, you will have to change the link between the two tables every time you include them in a query.

We also do not recommend that you define relationships between queries or between a table and a query. If you have done a good job of naming your fields in your tables, the query designer will recognize the natural links and define the joins for you automatically. Defining extra relationships adds unnecessary overhead in your database application.

Click the Create button to finish your relationship definition. Access draws a line between the two tables to indicate the relationship. Notice that when you ask Access to enforce referential integrity, Access displays a 1 at the end of the relationship line, next to the *one* table, and an infinity symbol next to the *many* table. If you want to delete the relationship, click the line and press the Delete key.

You now know enough to define the additional one-to-many simple relationships that you need. Go ahead and define a relationship on ContactID between the Contacts and CompanyContacts tables to complete the other side of the many-to-many relationship between companies and contacts, a relationship on ContactID between the Contacts and ContactEvents tables, and a relationship on ProductID between the Products and ContactProducts tables. For each relationship, be sure to select the Enforce Referential Integrity check box.

Creating a Relationship on Multiple Fields

There's one last relationship you need to define in the Contact Tracking database between the CompanyContacts and ContactProducts tables. The relationship between these two tables requires multiple fields from each table. You can start by dragging the CompanyID field from the CompanyContacts table to the ContactProducts table. Access 2007 opens the Edit Relationships dialog box, shown in Figure 27-28.

Figure 27-28 Select multiple fields in the Edit Relationships dialog box to define a relationship between two tables using more than one field.

When you first see the Edit Relationships dialog box for the relationship you are defining between CompanyContacts and ContactProducts, Access 2007 shows you only the CompanyID field in the two lists. To complete the relationship definition on the combination of CompanyID and ContactID, you must click in the second line under both tables and select ContactID as the second field for both tables, as shown in Figure 27-28. Select the Enforce Referential Integrity check box as shown and click Create to define the compound relationship.

Figure 27-29 shows the Relationships window for all the main tables in your Contact Tracking database. Notice that there are two linking lines that define the relationship between CompanyContacts and ContactProducts.

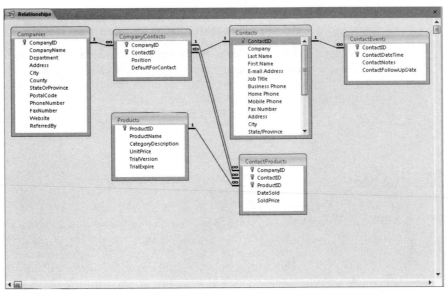

Figure 27-29 The Relationships window shows a graphical representation of all the main tables in your Contact Tracking database.

If you want to edit or change any relationship, double-click the line to open the Edit Relationships dialog box again. If you want to remove a relationship definition, click on the line linking two tables to select the relationship (the line appears highlighted) and press the Delete key. Access 2007 presents a warning dialog box in case you are asking it to delete a relationship in error.

Note that once you define a relationship, you can delete the table or query field lists from the Relationships window without affecting the relationships. To do this, click the table or query list header and press the Delete key. This can be particularly advantageous in large databases that have dozens of tables. You can also display only those tables that you're working with at the moment. To see the relationships defined for any particular table or query, include it in the Relationships window by using the Show Table dialog box, and then click the Direct Relationships button in the Relationships group of the Design contextual tab on the Ribbon. To redisplay all relationships, click the All Relationships button in the Relationships group.

When you close the Relationships window, Access 2007 asks whether you want to save your layout changes. Click Yes to save the relationships you've defined. That's all there is to it. Later, when you use multiple tables in a query in Chapter 28, "Creating and Working with Simple Queries," you'll see that Access 2007 builds the links between tables based on these relationships.

> ## INSIDE OUT **Additional Features in the Relationships Window**
>
> You can right-click any table in the Relationships window and then choose Table Design from the shortcut menu to open that table in Design view. You can also click Relationship Report in the Tools group of the Design contextual tab on the Ribbon to create a report that prints what you laid out in the window.

Adding Indexes

The more data you include in your tables, the more you need indexes to help Access 2007 search your data efficiently. An *index* is simply an internal table that contains two columns: the value in the field or fields being indexed and the physical location of each record in your table that contains that value. Access 2007 uses an index similarly to how you use the index in this book—you find the term you want and jump directly to the pages containing that term. You don't have to leaf through all the pages to find the information you want.

Let's assume that you often search your Contacts table by city. Without an index, when you ask Access 2007 to find all the contacts in the city of Chicago, Access has to search every record in your table. This search is fast if your table includes only a few contacts but very slow if the table contains thousands of contact records collected over many years. If you create an index on the City field, Access 2007 can use the index to find more rapidly the records for the contacts in the city you specify.

Single-Field Indexes

Most of the indexes you'll need to define will probably contain the values from only a single field. Access uses this type of index to help narrow the number of records it has to search whenever you provide search criteria on the field—for example, *City = Chicago* or *PostalCode = 60633*. If you have defined indexes for multiple fields and provided search criteria for more than one of the fields, Access uses the indexes together (using a technology called Rushmore from Microsoft FoxPro) to find the rows you want quickly. For example, if you have created one index on City and another on LastName, and you ask for *City = Bend* and *LastName = Conrad*, Access uses the entries in the City index that equal *Bend* and matches those with the entries in the LastName index that equal *Conrad*. The result is a small set of pointers to the records that match both criteria.

Creating an index on a single field in a table is easy. Open the Contacts table (which you created earlier using a table template) in Design view, and select the field for which you want an index—in this case, City. Click the Indexed property box in the lower part of the Table window, and then click the arrow to open the list of choices, as shown in Figure 27-30.

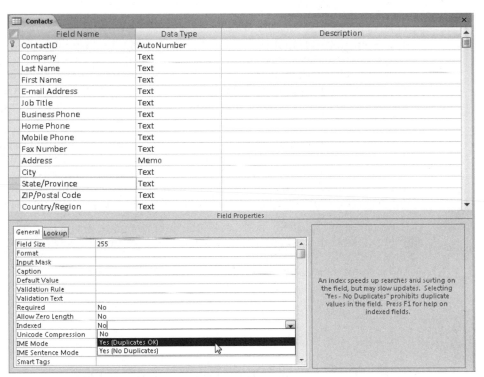

Figure 27-30 You can use the Indexed property box to set an index on a single field.

When you create a table from scratch (as you did earlier in this chapter for the Companies table), the default Indexed property setting for all fields except the primary key is No. If you use a table template to create a table (as you did for the Contacts table in this chapter), the template indexes fields that might benefit from an index. If you followed along earlier using a table template to build the Contacts table, you will find that the template built an index only for the ContactID and Zip/Postal Code fields. Any tables created using a table template could obviously benefit from some additional indexes.

If you want to set an index for a field, Access 2007 offers two possible Yes choices. In most cases, a given field will have multiple records with the same value—perhaps you have multiple contacts in a particular city or multiple products in the same product category. You should select Yes (Duplicates OK) to create an index for this type of field. By selecting Yes (No Duplicates) you can have Access 2007 enforce unique values in any field by creating an index that doesn't allow duplicates. Access 2007 always defines the primary key index with no duplicates because all primary key values must be unique.

> **Note**
>
> You cannot define an index using an OLE object or attachment field.

Multiple-Field Indexes

If you often provide multiple criteria in searches against large tables, you might want to consider creating a few multiple-field indexes. This helps Access 2007 narrow the search quickly without having to match values from two separate indexes. For example, suppose you often perform a search for contacts by last name and first name. If you create an index that includes both of these fields, Access can satisfy your query more rapidly.

To create a multiple-field index, you must open the Table window in Design view and open the Indexes window by clicking the Indexes button in the Show/Hide group of the Design contextual tab on the Ribbon. You can see the primary key index and the index that you defined on City in the previous section as well as the index defined by the table template (Zip/Postal Code). Each of these indexes comprises exactly one field.

To create a multiple-field index, move the insertion point to an empty row in the Indexes window and type a unique name. In this example, you want a multiple-field index using the Last Name and First Name fields, so *FullName* might be a reasonable index name. Select the Last Name field in the Field Name column of this row. To add the other field, skip down to the next row and select First Name without typing a new index name. When you're done, your Indexes window should look like the one shown in Figure 27-31.

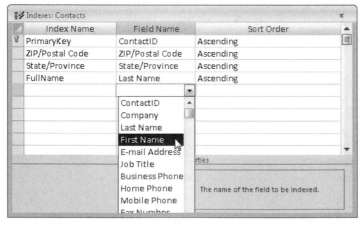

Figure 27-31 The FullName index includes the Last Name and First Name fields.

You can remove an existing single-field index by changing the Indexed property of a field to No. The only way to remove a multiple-field index is via the Indexes window. To remove a multiple-field index, select the rows (by holding down the Ctrl key as you click each row selector) that define the index and then press Delete. Access 2007 saves any index changes you make when you save the table definition.

Access 2007 can use a multiple-field index in a search even if you don't provide search values for all the fields, as long as you provide search criteria for consecutive fields starting with the first field. Therefore, with the FullName multiple-field index shown in Figure 27-31, you can search for last name or for last name and first name. There's one additional limitation on when Access can use multiple-field indexes: Only the last search criterion you supply can be an inequality, such as >, >=, <, or <=. In other words, Access can use the index shown in Figure 27-31 when you specify searches such as these:

Last Name = "Smith"
Last Name > "Franklin"
Last Name = "Buchanan" And First Name = "Steven"
Last Name = "Viescas" And First Name >= "Bobby"

But Access will not use the FullName index shown in Figure 27-31 if you ask for

Last Name > "Davolio" And First Name > "John"

because only the last field in the search (First Name) can be an inequality. Access also will not use this index if you ask for

First Name = "John"

because the first field of the multiple-field index (Last Name) is missing from the search criterion.

Setting Table Design Options

Now that you understand the basic mechanics of defining tables in your desktop database, it's useful to take a look at a few options you can set to customize how you work with tables in Design view. Close any open tables so that all you see is the Navigation Pane. Click the Microsoft Office Button and then click Access Options to see all the custom settings offered.

You can find the first options that affect table design in the Advanced category as shown in Figure 27-32. One option that we highly recommend you use is Use Four-Digit Year Formatting, found in the General section. When you enable four-digit year formatting, Access 2007 displays all year values in date/time formats with four digits instead of two. This is important because when you see a value (in two-digit medium date format) such as 15 MAR 12, you won't be able to easily tell whether this is March 15, 1912 or March 15, 2012. Although you can affect the display of some formats in your regional settings in Control Panel, you won't affect them all unless you set four-digit formatting in Access.

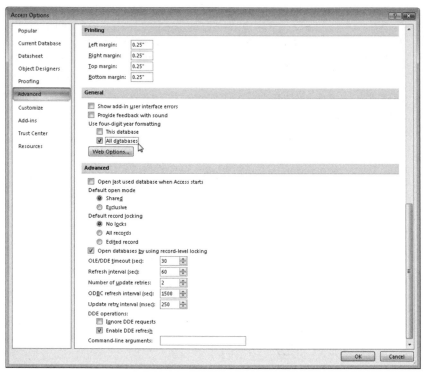

Figure 27-32 You can find settings that affect table design in the General section in the Advanced category of the Access Options dialog box.

As you can see in Figure 27-32, you have two options under Use Four-Digit Year Formatting in the General section. If you select the This Database check box, the setting creates a property in the database you currently have open and affects only that database. If you select the All Databases check box, the setting creates an entry in your Windows registry that affects all databases that you open on your computer.

In the Current Database category of the Access Options dialog box, you can configure an option that was introduced in Access 2000 called Name AutoCorrect that asks Access to track and correct field name references in queries, forms, and reports. If you select the Track Name AutoCorrect Info check box in the Name AutoCorrrect Options section, Access maintains a unique internal ID number for all field names. This allows you to use the Object Dependencies feature. It also allows you to select the next check box, Perform Name AutoCorrect, as shown in Figure 27-33.

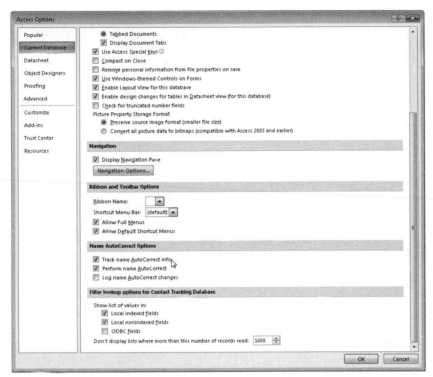

Figure 27-33 You can set Name AutoCorrect options in the Current Database category of the Access Options dialog box.

If you select the Perform Name AutoCorrect check box, when you change a field name in a table, Access 2007 automatically attempts to propagate the name change to other objects (queries, forms, and reports) that use the field. However, Track Name AutoCorrect Info requires some additional overhead in all your objects, so it's a good idea to carefully choose names as you design your tables so that you won't need to change them later. Finally, if you select the Log Name AutoCorrect Changes check box, Access 2007 logs all changes it makes in a table called AutoCorrect Log. You can open this table to verify the changes made by this feature. (Access doesn't create the table until it makes some changes.)

The next category that contains useful settings that affect table design is Object Designers. Click that category to see the settings shown in Figure 27-34.

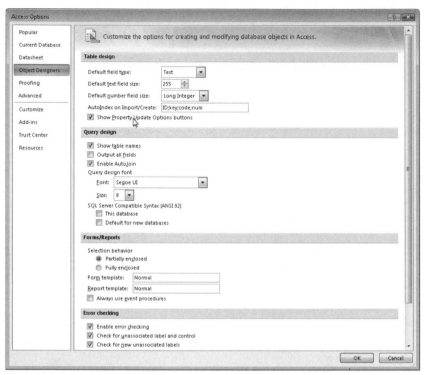

Figure 27-34 You can find settings that affect table design in the Object Designers category of the Access Options dialog box.

In the Table Design section, you can set the default field type and the default field size for Text and Number fields. The Default Field Type setting allows you to choose the default data type that Access 2007 selects when you type a new field name in table design and then tab to the Data Type column. When you select a data type of Text (either because it is the default data type or you select the Text data type in a new field), Access will automatically set the length you select in the Default Text Field Size box. When you select a data type of Number, Access sets the number size to your choice in the Default Number Field Size box of Byte, Integer, Long Integer, Single, Double, Decimal, or Replication ID. Use the AutoIndex On Import/Create box to define a list of field name prefixes or suffixes for which Access automatically sets the Index property to Yes (Duplicates OK). In the default list, for example, any field that you define with a name that begins or ends with *ID* will automatically have an index.

If you select the Show Property Update Options Buttons check box, a smart tag appears that offers to automatically update related properties in queries, forms, and reports when you change certain field properties in a table design.

You can find the last option that affects how your tables are stored (and, in fact, all objects in your database) in the Popular category, as shown in Figure 27-35. When you create a new database in Access 2007, you actually have a choice of three different file formats. These options also appear in the File New Database dialog box, but this setting in the Access Options dialog box controls which file format appears as the default. You should use the Access 2000 format if others with whom you might share this database are still using Access version 9 (2000), or you should use the 2002-2003 format if others sharing this database are still using Access version 10 (2002) or Access version 11 (2003). Selecting the Access 2007 format ensures maximum compatibility of what you build in Access with future versions of the product.

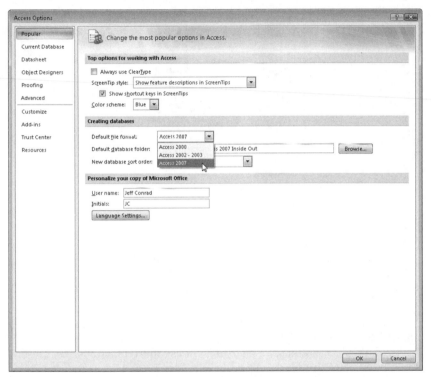

Figure 27-35 You can select your default database file format in the Creating Databases section of the Popular category in the Access Options dialog box.

Creating a Default Template for New Databases

Access 2007 introduces a new feature that allows you to create your own default database template for use with all new blank databases. Rather than set options for each new database after you create it, you can set your preferred options only one time and have those settings apply to each new database. To accomplish this, you first need to open a new blank database from the Getting Started screen. Click the Blank Database command on the Getting Started screen to display the Blank Database task pane on the right, as shown in Figure 27-36.

Figure 27-36 The Blank Database task pane appears on the right when you click the Blank Database command.

You must name this new database Blank in order for this procedure to work. Type **Blank** in the File Name text box, and then click the Browse button to open the File New Database dialog box. So that Access 2007 will use this template file for all new databases, you must place this file in a specific subfolder in the Microsoft Office folder. Navigate to the following folder on your system drive by clicking the folder icons in the left pane of the File New Database dialog box: \Program Files\Microsoft Office\Templates\1033\ Access, as shown in Figure 27-37. This file path assumes a default installation of the 2007 Microsoft Office system, so your exact file path might be different if you chose a custom installation and selected a different installation path.

Click OK in the File New Database dialog box to return to the Getting Started screen. If you followed the preceding instructions, the Blank Database task pane on the right should look like Figure 27-38. The File Name text box says Blank.accdb, and the path to the correct template location is displayed above the Create button.

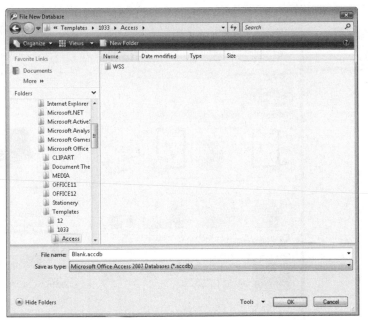

Figure 27-37 Save the Blank.accdb file in the correct subfolder in the Microsoft Office folder.

Chapter 27

CAUTION

If you are using Microsoft Windows Vista, you might not be able to save the Blank.accdb database into the needed template folder. Windows Vista uses User Account Control, which protects critical program folders. If your computer is connected to a domain, you get a prompt dialog box and then you can save to the correct folder. You might need to temporarily turn off User Account Control in order to save the database into the template folder. If you are in a corporate network environment, you should ask your system administrator for assistance with this procedure.

Click the Create button, and Access 2007 creates the new file and saves it in the appropriate template folder. By default, Access opens up a new blank table called Table1. You do not need this table, so close it and do not save it.

Now that you have an empty database with no objects, open the Access Options dialog box by clicking the Microsoft Office Button and then Access Options. Select all the options you want to set for any new databases in the various categories of the Access Options dialog box.

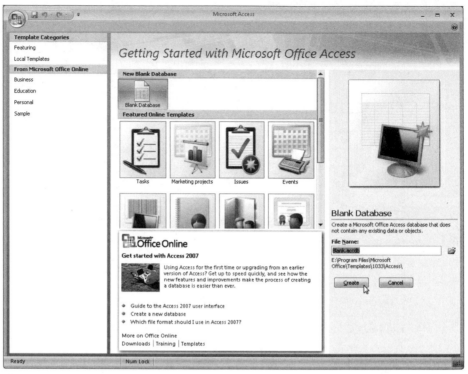

Figure 27-38 After you enter the correct name and select the correct location, you're ready to create your new database template.

 Included on the companion CD is a database called Blank.accdb that has the Access Options settings that we recommend for new databases. In the Current Database category, in the Name AutoCorrect Options section, we cleared the Track Name Auto-Correct Info check box. In the General section of the Advanced category, we selected the Use Four-Digit Year Formatting and This Database check boxes. We left all other options set to the defaults.

Note

You can also open the Visual Basic Editor (VBE) and select Options from the Tools menu to select options that apply to Visual Basic in all new databases. In the Blank.accdb sample database, we selected the Require Variable Declaration check box.

After you have defined all the settings you want, close the database and exit Access 2007. Each new blank database you create from the Getting Started screen will now include all the settings you selected for the Blank.accdb file. To make revisions to those settings, open the Blank.accdb file in the template folder and make whatever modifications are necessary. Figure 27-39 shows our Blank.accdb file in the appropriate template folder along with the other local database templates discussed at the beginning of this chapter.

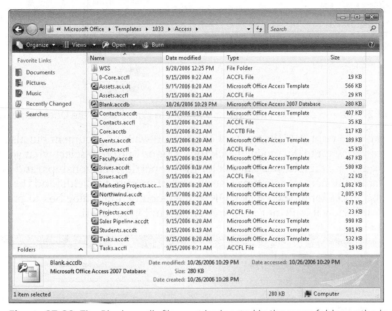

Figure 27-39 The Blank.accdb file must be located in the same folder as the local database templates.

Creating a custom blank database template saves you time by not having to continually set your personal Access options and VBE options each time you create a new database. In addition to this timesaver, you can also include specific code modules, forms, and any other database objects with new databases. If, for example, you have some common functions and procedures stored in standard code modules that you use in all your database files, you can include them in this Blank.accdb file. Instead of having to manually import these modules into all new databases, Access does all the work for you by including them in new databases.

Printing a Table Definition

After you create several tables, you might want to print out their definitions to provide a permanent paper record. You can do this by clicking Database Documenter in the Analyze group of the Database Tools tab on the Ribbon. Access 2007 displays several options in the Documenter dialog box, as shown in Figure 27-40.

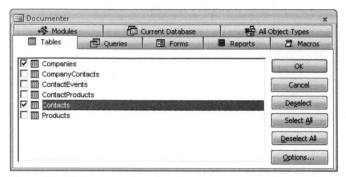

Figure 27-40 You can select the objects you want to document in the Documenter dialog box.

You can select not only the types of objects you want to document but also which objects you want to document. Click the Options button to select what you want reported. For example, you can ask for the properties, relationships, and permissions for a table; the names, data types, sizes, and properties for fields; and the names, fields, and properties for indexes. Click OK in the Documenter dialog box to produce the report and view it in Print Preview, as shown in Figure 27-41.

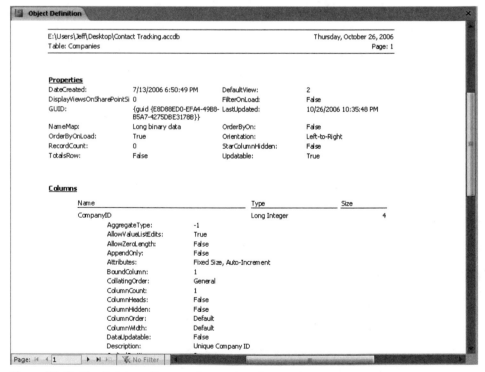

Figure 27-41 The Database Documenter previews its reports on your screen.

Database Limitations

As you design your database, you should keep in mind the following limitations:

- A table can have up to 255 fields.

- A table can have up to 32 indexes.

> **Note**
> Keep in mind that defining relationships with Referential Integrity turned on creates one additional index in each participating table that counts toward the 32-index limit per table.

- A multiple-field index can have up to 10 fields. The sum of the lengths of the fields cannot exceed 255 bytes.

- A row in a table, excluding memo fields and ActiveX objects, can be no longer than approximately 4 kilobytes.

- A memo field can store up to 1 gigabyte of characters, but you can't display a memo larger than 64 kilobytes in a form or a datasheet.

> **Note**
> Clearly, if you try to store a 1-gigabyte memo (which requires 2 gigabytes of storage because of double-byte character set support) or a 2-gigabyte ActiveX object in your database file, your file will be full with the data from one record.

- An ActiveX object can be up to 2 gigabytes in size.

- There is no limit on the number of records in a table, but an Access 2007 database cannot be larger than 2 gigabytes. If you have several large tables, you might need to define each one in a separate Access database and then attach them to the database that contains the forms, reports, macros, and modules for your applications.

Chapter 27

I n the last chapter, you learned how to create tables. Although you can certainly build forms and reports that get their data directly from your tables, most of the time you will want to sort or filter your data or display data from more than one table. For these tasks, you need queries.

When you define and run a *select query*, which selects information from the tables and queries in your database, Microsoft Office Access 2007 creates a *recordset* of the selected data. In most cases, you can work with a recordset in the same way that you work with a table: You can browse through it, select information from it, print it, and even update the data in it. But unlike a real table, a recordset doesn't actually exist in your database. Office Access 2007 creates a recordset from the data in the source tables of your query at the time you run the query.

As you learn to design forms and reports later in this book, you'll find that queries are the best way to focus on the specific data you need for the task at hand. You'll also find that queries are useful for providing choices for combo and list boxes, which make entering data in your database much easier.

Note

The examples in this chapter are based on the tables and data from the Conrad Systems Contacts sample database (Contacts.accdb), a backup copy of the data for the Contacts sample database (ContactsDataCopy.accdb), the Housing Reservations database (Housing.accdb), and the backup copy of the data for the Housing Reservations sample database (HousingDataCopy.accdb) on the companion CD included with this book. The query results you see from the sample queries you build in this chapter might not exactly match what you see in this book if you have reloaded the sample data using zfrmLoadData in either application or have changed any of the data in the tables.

Access 2007 provides two ways to begin creating a new query:

- Click the Query Wizard button in the Other group on the Create tab on the Ribbon. A dialog box appears that lets you select one of the four query wizards.

- Click the Query Design button in the Other group on the Create tab on the Ribbon to begin creating new query using the query designer.

To open an existing query in Design view, make sure you have queries showing in the Navigation Pane. To display all the queries in your database, click the bar at the top of the Navigation Pane and click Object Type under Navigate To Category and then click Queries under Filter By Group. You can open the query you want in Design view by selecting the query in the Navigation Pane and then pressing Ctrl+Enter. You can also right-click a query name in the Navigation Pane and click Design View on the shortcut menu. Figure 28-1 shows the list of queries for the Conrad Systems Contacts database. Please note that the figure shows you only some of the queries in the database. Use the scroll bar in the Navigation Pane to see the complete list of queries available in the Conrad Systems Contacts database.

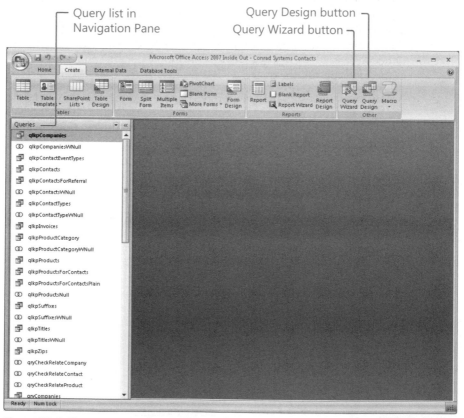

Figure 28-1 The Navigation Pane has been filtered to show all the queries in the Conrad Systems Contacts database.

Figure 28-2 shows a query that has been opened in Design view. The upper part of the Query window contains field lists, and the lower part contains the design grid.

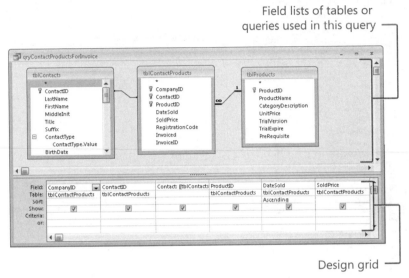

Figure 28-2 A query open in Design view shows the tables and field lists.

Selecting Data from a Single Table

One advantage of using queries is that they allow you to find data easily in multiple related tables. Queries are also useful, however, for sifting through the data in a single table. All the techniques you use for working with a single table apply equally to more complex multiple-table queries. This chapter covers the basics about building queries to select data from a single table.

The easiest way to start building a query on a single table is to click the Query Design button in the Other group on the Create tab (see Figure 28-1). Open the Conrad Systems Contacts database and then click the Query Design button. Access 2007 displays the Show Table dialog box on top of the query design grid as shown in Figure 28-3.

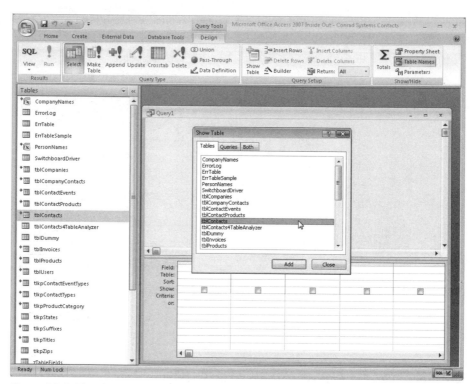

Figure 28-3 The Show Table dialog box allows you to select one or more tables or queries to build a new query.

Select tblContacts on the Tables tab of the Show Table dialog box and then click Add to place tblContacts in the upper part of the Query window. Click Close in the Show Table dialog box to view the window shown in Figure 28-4.

As mentioned earlier, the Query window in Design view has two main parts. In the upper part you find field lists with the fields for the tables or queries you chose for this query. The lower part of the window is the design grid, in which you do all the design work. Each column in the grid represents one field that you'll work with in this query. As you'll see later, a field can be a simple field from one of the tables or a calculated field based on several fields in the tables.

You use the first row of the design grid to select fields—the fields you want in the resulting recordset, the fields you want to sort by, and the fields you want to test for values. As you'll learn later, you can also generate custom field names (for display in the resulting recordset), and you can use complex expressions or calculations to generate a calculated field.

The second row shows you the name of the table from which you selected a field. If you don't see this row, you can display it by clicking Table Names in the Show/Hide group on the Design tab below Query Tools. This isn't too important when building a query on a single table, but you'll learn later that this row provides valuable information when building a query that fetches data from more than one table or query.

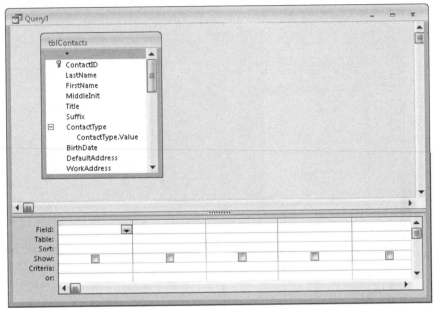

Figure 28-4 The Query window in Design view for a new query on tblContacts shows the table with its list of fields in the top part of the window.

In the Sort row, you can specify whether Access 2007 should sort the selected or calculated field in ascending or in descending order. In the Show row, you can use the check boxes to indicate the fields that will be included in the recordset. By default, Access 2007 includes all the fields you place in the design grid. Sometimes you'll want to include a field in the query to allow you to select the records you want (such as contacts born in a certain date range), but you won't need that field in the recordset. You can add that field to the design grid so that you can define criteria, but you should clear the Show check box beneath the field to exclude it from the recordset.

Finally, you can use the Criteria row and the row(s) labeled *Or* to enter the criteria you want to use as filters. After you understand how a query is put together, you'll find it easy to specify exactly the fields and records that you want.

Specifying Fields

The first step in building a query is to select the fields you want in the recordset. You can select the fields in several ways. Using the keyboard, you can tab to a column in the design grid and press Alt+Down Arrow to open the list of available fields. (To move to the design grid, press F6.) Use the Up Arrow and Down Arrow keys to highlight the field you want, and then press Enter to select the field.

Chapter 28

Another way to select a field is to drag it from one of the field lists in the upper part of the window to one of the columns in the design grid. In Figure 28-5, the LastName field is being dragged to the design grid. When you drag a field, the mouse pointer turns into a small rectangle.

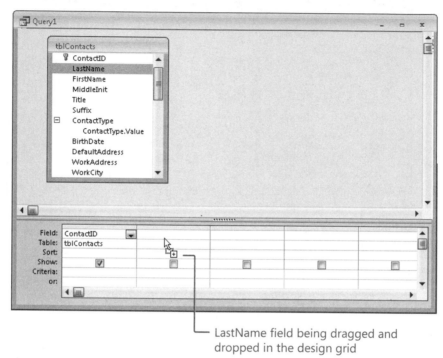

LastName field being dragged and
dropped in the design grid

Figure 28-5 You can drag a field from the table field list to a column in the design grid.

At the top of each field list in the upper part of the Query window (and also next to the first entry in the Field drop-down list in the design grid) is an asterisk (*) symbol. This symbol is shorthand for selecting "all fields in the table or the query" with one entry on the Field line. When you want to include all the fields in a table or a query, you don't have to define each one individually in the design grid unless you also want to define some sorting or selection criteria for specific fields. You can simply add the asterisk to the design grid to include all the fields from a list. Note that you can add individual fields to the grid in addition to the asterisk in order to define criteria for those fields, but you should clear the Show check box for the individual fields so that they don't appear twice in the recordset.

For this exercise, select ContactID, LastName, FirstName, WorkStateOrProvince, and BirthDate from the tblContacts table in the Conrad Systems Contacts database. You can select the fields one at a time by dragging and dropping them in the design grid. You can also double-click each field name, and Access will move it to the design grid into the next available slot. Finally, you can click on one field you want and then hold down the Ctrl key as you click on additional fields or hold down the Shift key to select a group of contiguous fields. Grab the last field you select and drag them all to the design grid. If you switch the Query window to Datasheet view at this point, you'll see all the records, containing only the fields you selected from the underlying table.

Setting Field Properties

In general, a field that is output by a query inherits the properties defined for that field in the table. You can define a different Description property (the information that is displayed on the status bar when you select that field in a Query window in Datasheet view), Format property (how the data is displayed), Decimal Places property (for numeric data other than integers), Input Mask property, Caption property (the column heading), and Smart Tags property.

For details about field properties, see Chapter 27, "Creating Your Database and Tables."

When you learn to define calculated fields later in this chapter, you'll see that it's a good idea to define the properties for these fields. If the field in the query is a foreign key linked to another table, you can also set the Lookup properties. Access propagates Lookup properties that you have defined in your table fields; however, you can use the properties on the Lookup tab in the query's Property Sheet pane to override them.

> ### Note
> The Access 2007 query designer lets you define Lookup properties for any text or numeric field (other than AutoNumber). The field doesn't have to be a defined foreign key to another table. You might find this useful when you want the user to pick from a restricted value list—such as *M* or *F* for a Gender field.

To set the properties of a field, click any row of that field's column in the design grid, and then click the Property Sheet button in the Show/Hide group of the Design contextual tab to display the property sheet, shown in Figure 28-6. Even though the fields in your query inherit their properties from the underlying table, you won't see those properties displayed here. For example, the BirthDate field in tblContacts has both its Description and Caption set to Birth Date and a Format set to mm/dd/yyyy. If you click in the BirthDate field in your query and open the property sheet, you will see that none of the properties show values. Use the property settings in the property sheet to override any inherited properties and to customize how a field looks when viewed *for this query*. Try entering new property settings for the BirthDate field, as shown in Figure 28-6.

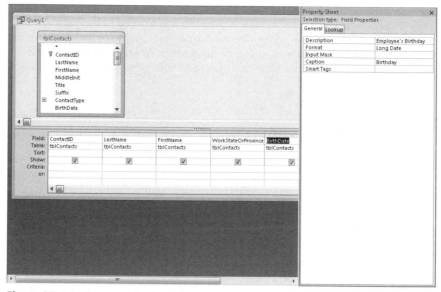

Figure 28-6 In the property sheet, you can set properties for the BirthDate field.

INSIDE OUT Switching Views to Check Field Properties

One of the quickest ways to see if a field in a query has the properties you want is to switch to Datasheet view. If the field isn't displayed the way you want, you can switch back to Design view and override the properties in the query.

If you make these changes and switch to Datasheet view, you'll see that the BirthDate column heading is now *Birthday*; that the date displays day name, month name, day number, and year; and that the text on the status bar matches the new description, as shown in Figure 28-7. (Grab the right edge of the Birthday header with your mouse and drag it right to open the column so that you can see all the date values.)

Field caption is changed ⌐

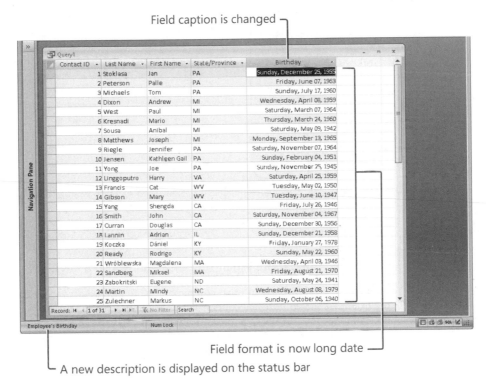

Field format is now long date ⌐

⌐ A new description is displayed on the status bar

Figure 28-7 The BirthDate field is now displayed with new property settings.

Entering Selection Criteria

The next step is to further refine the records you want by specifying criteria on one or more fields. The example shown in Figure 28-8 selects contacts working in the state of California.

Entering selection criteria in a query is similar to entering a validation rule for a field, which you learned about in Chapter 27. To look for a single value, simply type it in the Criteria row for the field you want to test. If the field you're testing is a text field and the value you're looking for has any blank spaces in it, you must enclose the value in quotation marks. Note that Access adds quotation marks for you around single text values. (In Figure 28-8, we typed **CA**, but Access replaced what we typed with "CA" after we pressed Enter.)

If you want to test for any of several values, enter the values in the Criteria row, separated by the word *Or*. For example, specifying *CA Or NC* searches for records for California or North Carolina. You can also test for any of several values by entering each value in a separate Criteria or Or row for the field you want to test. For example, you can enter *CA* in the Criteria row, *NC* in the next row (the first Or row), and so on— but you have to be careful if you're also specifying criteria in other fields, as explained in the section "AND vs. OR" on page 913.

Chapter 28

AND	True	False
True	True (Selected)	False (Rejected)
False	False (Rejected)	False (Rejected)

Figure 28-8 When you specify "CA" as the selection criterion in the design grid, Access returns only records with a WorkStateOrProvince equal to California.

INSIDE OUT   Be Careful When Your Criterion Is Also a Keyword

You should be careful when entering criteria that might also be an Access 2007 keyword. In the examples shown here, we could have chosen to use criteria for the two-character abbreviation for the state of Oregon (OR)—but *or*, as you can see in the examples, is also a keyword. In many cases, Access is smart enough to figure out what you mean from the context. You can enter

```
Or Or Ca
```

in the Criteria row under State, and Access assumes that the first *Or* is criteria (by placing quotation marks around the word for you) and the second *Or* is the Boolean operator keyword. If you want to be sure that Access interprets your criteria correctly, always place double quotation marks around criteria text. If you find that Access guessed wrong, you can always correct the entry before saving the query.

In the section "AND vs. OR," you'll see that you can also include a comparison operator in the Criteria row so that, for example, you can look for values less than (<), greater than or equal to (>=), or not equal to (<>) the value that you specify.

Working with Dates and Times in Criteria

Access 2007 stores dates and times as 8-byte decimal numbers. The value to the left of the decimal point represents the day (day zero is December 30, 1899), and the fractional part of the number stores the time as a fraction of a day, accurate to seconds. Fortunately, you don't have to worry about converting internal numbers to specify a test for a particular date value because Access 2007 handles date and time entries in several formats.

You must always surround date and time values with pound signs (#) to tell Access that you're entering a date or a time. To test for a specific date, use the date notation that is most comfortable for you. For example, *#April 15, 1962#*, *#4/15/62#*, and *#15-Apr-1962#* are all the same date if you chose English (United States) in the Regional And Language Options in Windows Control Panel. Similarly, *#5:30 PM#* and *#17:30#* both specify 5:30 in the evening.

INSIDE OUT   Understanding Date/Time Criteria

You must be careful when building criteria to test a range in a date/time field. Let's say you want to look at all records between two dates in the ContactEvents table, which has a date/time field—ContactDateTime—that holds the date *and* time of the contact. For all contact events in the month of January 2007, you might be tempted to put the following on the Criteria line under ContactDateTime.

```
>=#1/1/2007#  AND  <=#1/31/2007#
```

When you look at the results, you might wonder why no rows show up from January 31, 2007 even when you know that you made and recorded several calls on that day. The reason is simple. Remember, a date/time field contains an integer offset value for the date and a fraction for the time. Let's say you called someone at 9:55 A.M. on January 31, 2007. The internal value is actually 39,113.4132—January 31, 2007 is 39,113 days later than December 30, 1899 (the zero point), and .4132 is the fraction of a day that represents 9:55 A.M. When you say you want rows where ContactDateTime is less than or equal to January 31, 2007, you're comparing to the internal value 39,113—just the day value, which is midnight on that day. You won't find the 9:55 A.M. record because the value is greater than 39,113, or later in the day than midnight. To search successfully, you must enter

```
>=#1/1/2007#  AND  <#2/1/2007#
```

AND vs. OR

When you enter criteria for several fields, all the tests in a single Criteria row or Or row must be true for Access 2007 to include a record in the recordset. That is, Access 2007 performs a logical AND operation between multiple criteria in the same row. So if you enter *CA* in the Criteria row for StateOrProvince and *<#1 JAN 1972#* in the Criteria row for BirthDate, the record must be for the state of California *and* must be for someone born before 1972 to be selected. If you enter *CA Or NC* in the Criteria row for StateOrProvince and *>=#01/01/1946# AND <#1 JAN 1972#* in the Criteria row for BirthDate, the record must be for the state of California or North Carolina, *and* the person must have been born between 1946 and 1971.

Figure 28-9 shows the result of applying a logical AND operator between any two tests. As you can see, both tests must be true for the result of the AND to be true and for the record to be selected.

OR	True	False
True	True (Selected)	True (Selected)
False	True (Selected)	False (Rejected)

Figure 28-9 When you specify the logical AND operator between two tests, the result is true only if both tests are true.

When you specify multiple criteria for a field and separate the criteria by a logical OR operator, only one of the criteria must be true for Access 2007 to select the record. You can specify several OR criteria for a field, either by entering them all in a single Criteria cell separated by the logical OR operator, as shown earlier, or by entering each subsequent criterion in a separate Or row. When you use multiple Or rows, if the criteria *in any one of the Or rows* is true, Access 2007 selects the record. Figure 28-10 shows the result of applying a logical OR operation between any two tests. As you can see, only one of the tests must be true for the result of the OR to be true and for Access 2007 to select the record.

OR	True	False
True	True (Selected)	True (Selected)
False	True (Selected)	False (Rejected)

Figure 28-10 When you specify the logical OR operator between two tests, the result is true if either or both of the tests is true.

Let's look at a specific example. In Figure 28-11, you specify *CA* in the first Criteria row of the WorkStateOrProvince field and *>=#01/01/1946# AND <#1 JAN 1972#* in that same Criteria row for the BirthDate field. (By the way, when you type #1 JAN 1972# and press Enter, Access changes your entry to #1/1/1972#.) In the next row (the first Or row), you specify *NC* in the WorkStateOrProvince field. When you run this query, you get all the contacts from the state of California who were born between 1946 and 1971. You also get any records for the state of North Carolina regardless of the birth date.

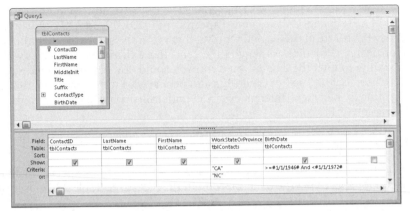

Figure 28-11 You can specify multiple AND and OR selection criteria in the design grid with additional OR lines.

In Figure 28-12, you can see the recordset (in Datasheet view) that results from running this query:

Contact ID	Last Name	First Name	State/Province	Birthday
15	Yang	Shengda	CA	Friday, July 26, 1946
16	Smith	John	CA	Saturday, November 04, 1967
17	Curran	Douglas	CA	Sunday, December 30, 1956
24	Martin	Mindy	NC	Wednesday, August 08, 1979
25	Zulechner	Markus	NC	Sunday, October 06, 1940
26	Villadsen	Peter	NC	Saturday, November 22, 1975
*	{New}			

Record: 14 ◄ 1 of 6 ► ►I ►❋ No Filter | Search |

Figure 28-12 The recordset of the query shown in Figure 28-11 shows only the records that match your criteria.

INSIDE OUT   Don't Get Confused by And and Or

It's a common mistake to get *Or* and *And* mixed up when typing compound criteria for a single field. You might think to yourself, "I want all the work contacts in the states of Washington *and* California," and then type **WA And CA** in the Criteria row for the WorkStateOrProvince field. When you do this, you're asking Access to find rows where *(WorkStateOrProvince = "WA") And (WorkStateOrProvince = "CA")*. Because a field in a record can't have more than one value at a time (can't contain both the values WA and CA in the same record), there won't be any records in the output. To look for all the rows for these two states, you need to ask Access to search for *(WorkStateOrProvince = "WA") Or (WorkStateOrProvince = "CA")*. In other words, type **WA Or CA** in the Criteria row under the WorkStateOrProvince field.

If you also want to limit rows from contacts in North Carolina to those who were born between 1946 and 1971, you must specify >=#01/01/1946# AND <#1/1/1972# again under BirthDate in the second Or row—that is, on the same row that filters for NC under WorkStateOrProvince. Although this seems like extra work, this gives you complete flexibility to filter the data as you want. You could, for example, include people who were born before 1969 in California and people who were born after 1970 in North Carolina by placing a different criterion under BirthDate in the two rows that filter WorkStateOrProvince.

Between, In, and Like

In addition to comparison operators, Access p rovides three special operators that are useful for specifying the data you want in the recordset. Table 28-1 describes these operators.

Table 28-1 Criteria Operators for Queries

Predicate	Description
Between	Useful for specifying a range of values. The clause *Between 10 And 20* is the same as specifying *>=10 And <=20*.
In	Useful for specifying a list of values separated by commas, any one of which can match the field being searched. The clause *In ("CA", "NC", "TN")* is the same as *"CA" Or "NC" Or "TN"*.
Like	Useful for searching for patterns in text fields. You can include special characters and ranges of values in the Like comparison string to define the character pattern you want. Use a question mark (?) to indicate any single character in that position. Use an asterisk (*) to indicate zero or more characters in that position. The pound-sign character (#) specifies a single numeric digit in that position. Include a range in brackets ([ ]) to test for a particular range of characters in a position, and use an exclamation point (!) to indicate exceptions. The range *[0-9]* tests for numbers, *[a-z]* tests for letters, and *[!0-9]* tests for any characters except *0* through *9*. For example, the clause *Like"?[a-k]d[0-9]*"* tests for any single character in the first position, any character from *a* through *k* in the second position, the letter *d* in the third position, any character from *0* through *9* in the fourth position, and any number of characters after that.

Suppose you want to find all contacts in the state of California or Pennsylvania who were born between 1955 and 1972 and whose first name begins with the letter *J*. Figure 28-13 shows how you would enter these criteria. Figure 28-14 shows the recordset of this query.

INSIDE OUT   Choosing the Correct Date/Time Criteria

If you're really sharp, you're probably looking at Figure 28-13 and wondering why we chose *Between #1/1/1955# And #12/31/1972#* instead of *>= #1/1/1955# And < #1/1/1973#* to cover the case where the BirthDate field might also include a time. In this case we know that the BirthDate field has an input mask that doesn't allow us to enter time values. So we know that using Between and the simple date values will work for this search.

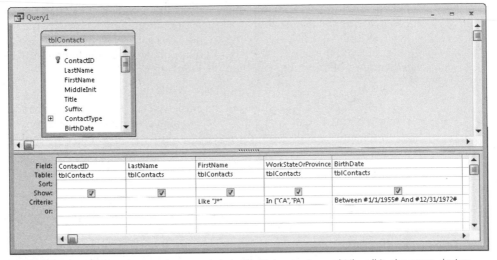

Figure 28-13 You can also restrict records by using Between, In, and Like all in the same design grid.

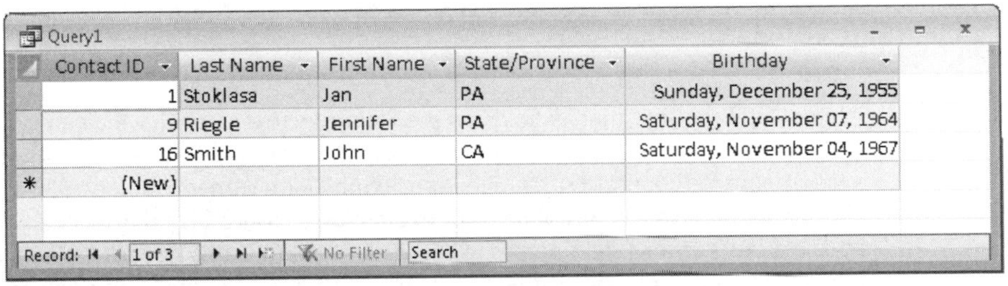

Figure 28-14 The recordset of the query shown in Figure 28-13 shows only the records that match your criteria.

For additional examples that use the Between, In, and Like comparison operators, see "Defining Simple Field Validation Rules" on page 858.

Using Expressions

You can use an expression to combine fields or to calculate a new value from fields in your table and make that expression a new field in the recordset. You can use any of the many built-in functions that Access 2007 provides as part of your expression. You *concatenate*, or combine, text fields by stringing them end-to-end, or you use arithmetic operators on fields in the underlying table to calculate a value. Let's switch to the HousingDataCopy.accdb database to build some examples.

Creating Text Expressions

One common use of expressions is to create a new text (string) field by concatenating fields containing text, string constants, or numeric data. You create a string constant by enclosing the text in double or single quotation marks. Use the ampersand character (&) between fields or strings to indicate that you want to concatenate them. For example, you might want to create an output field that concatenates the LastName field, a comma, a blank space, and then the FirstName field.

Try creating a query on the tblEmployees table in the HousingDataCopy.accdb database that shows a field containing the employee last name, a comma and a blank, first name, a blank, and middle name. You can also create a single field containing the city, a comma and a blank space, the state or province followed by one blank space, and the postal code. Your expressions should look like this:

```
LastName & ", " & FirstName & " " & MiddleName
City & ", " & StateOrProvince & " " & PostalCode
```

You can see the Query window in Design view for this example in Figure 28-15. We clicked in the Field row of the second column and then pressed Shift+F2 to open the Zoom window, where it is easier to enter the expression. Note that you can click the Font button to select a larger font that's easier to read. After you choose a font, Access 2007 uses it whenever you open the Zoom window again.

Chapter 28

> ### Note
>
> Access 2007 requires that all fields on the Field row in a query have a name. For single fields, Access uses the name of the field. When you enter an expression, Access generates a field name in the form *ExprN:*. See "Specifying Field Names" on page 933 for details about changing the names of fields or expressions. Notice also that Access automatically adds brackets around field names in expressions. It does this so that the field names in the SQL for the query are completely unambiguous. If this table had been designed with blanks in the field names, you would have to type the brackets yourself to ensure that the query designer interprets the names correctly.

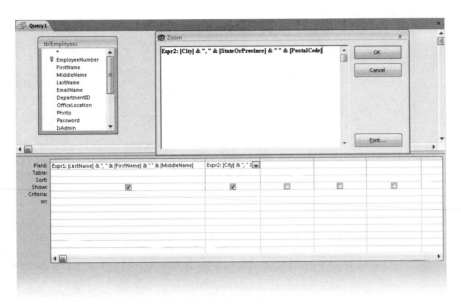

Figure 28-15 If you use the Zoom window to enter an expression, you can see more of the expression and select a different font.

When you look at the query result in Datasheet view, you should see something like that shown in Figure 28-16.

Expr1	Expr2
Koch, Reed	West Mansfield, OH 43358
Kim, Tim	Meredith, NH 03253
Tippett, John	Florence, AL 35630
DeGrasse, Kirk	Agua Dulce, CA 91350
Lawrence, David Oliver	Christiansburg, VA 24073
Adams, Jay	Ramona, SD 57054
Richins, Jack S.	Saint David, ME 04773
Bradley, David M.	Bayou La Batre, AL 36509
Eyink, Scott	Los Osos, CA 93402
Berndt, Matthias	Rockland, TX 75938
Willett, Benjamin C.	Austin, MO 64725
Shock, Misty	Newhall, CA 91381
Randall, Linda	Trail Creek, IN 46360
Schare, Gary	Rock Springs, AZ 85324
Viescas, John L.	,
Conrad, Jeff	,

Figure 28-16 Here is a query result with concatenated text fields.

Chapter 28

Try typing within the Expr1 field in Datasheet view. Because this display is a result of an expression (concatenation of strings), Access 2007 won't let you update the data in this column.

INSIDE OUT   Eliminating Extra Spaces When Concatenating Null Values

If you look very closely at Figure 28-16, you can see that we captured the image with the insertion point displayed at the end of the Expr1 field on the first row. Do you notice that there's an extra space after the first name? This happened because that person has no middle name, so what we're seeing is the extra blank we inserted after first name that is supposed to provide spacing between first name and middle name.

This isn't too much of a problem in this particular expression because you're not going to notice the extra blank displayed at the end of the name. But if you create the expression *First (blank) Middle (blank) Last* and if a record has no middle name, the extra blank will be noticeable.

When you use an ampersand, any Null field in the expression doesn't cause the entire expression to be Null. A little secret: You can also use the arithmetic plus sign (+) to concatenate strings. As you'll learn when you create arithmetic expressions, if a field in the expression is Null, the expression evaluates to Null. So, to solve the extra blank problem, you can create an expression to concatenate the parts of a name as follows:

```
FirstName & (" " + MiddleName) & " " & LastName
```

If MiddleName is a Null, the arithmetic expression inside the parentheses evaluates to Null, and the extra blank disappears!

Defining Arithmetic Expressions

In a reservations record (tblReservations in the Housing Reservations database), code in the form that confirms a reservation automatically calculates the correct TotalCharge value for the reservation before Access 2007 saves a changed row. If you strictly follow the rules for good relational table design (see Article 1, "Designing Your Database Application," on the companion CD), this isn't normally a good idea, but we designed it this way to demonstrate what you have to code to maintain the calculated value in your table. (Access 2007 won't automatically calculate the new value for you.) This technique also saves time later when calculating a total by month or total by facility in a report.

Table 28-2 shows the operators you can use in arithmetic expressions.

Table 28-2 **Operators Used in Arithmetic Expressions**

Operator	Description
+	Adds two numeric expressions.
−	Subtracts the second numeric expression from the first numeric expression.
*	Multiplies two numeric expressions.
/	Divides the first numeric expression by the second numeric expression.
\	Rounds both numeric expressions to integers and then divides the first integer by the second integer. The result is truncated to an integer.
^	Raises the first numeric expression to the power indicated by the second numeric expression.
Mod	Rounds both numeric expressions to integers, divides the first integer by the second integer, and returns only the remainder.

The expression to calculate the TotalCharge field is complex because it charges the lower weekly rate for portions of the stay that are full weeks and then adds the daily charge for extra days. Let's say you want to compare the straight daily rate with the discounted rate for longer stays. To begin, you need an expression that calculates the number of days. You can do this in a couple of different ways. First, you can use a handy built-in function called DateDiff to calculate the difference between two Date/Time values in seconds, minutes, hours, days, weeks, months, quarters, or years. In this case, you want the difference between the check-in date and the check-out date in days.

The syntax for calling DateDiff is as follows:

```
DateDiff(<interval>, <date1>, <date2>[, <firstdayofweek>])
```

The function calculates the difference between *<date1>* and *<date2>* using the interval you specify and returns a negative value if *<date1>* is greater than *<date2>*. You can supply a *<firstdayofweek>* value (the default is 1, Sunday) to affect how the function calculates the "ww" interval. Table 28-3 explains the values you can supply for *interval*.

> **Note**
>
> You can also use the settings you find in Table 28-3 for the *interval* argument in the DatePart function (which extracts part of a Date/Time value) and DateAdd function (which adds or subtracts a constant to a Date/Time value).

Table 28-3 **Interval Settings for DateDiff Function**

Setting	Description
"yyyy"	Calculates the difference in years. DateDiff subtracts the year portion of the first date from the year portion of the second date, so *DateDiff*("yyyy", #31 DEC 2006#, #01 JAN 2007#) returns 1.
"q"	Calculates the difference in quarters. If the two dates are in the same calendar quarter, the result is 0.
"m"	Calculates the difference in months. DateDiff subtracts the month portion of the first date from the month portion of the second date, so *DateDiff*("m", #31 DEC 2006#, #01 JAN 2007#) returns 1.
"y"	Calculates the difference in days. DateDiff handles this option the same as "d" below. (For other functions, this extracts the day of the year.)
"d"	Calculates the difference in days.
"w"	Calculates the difference in weeks based on the day of the week of *<date1>*. If, for example, the day of the week of the first date is a Tuesday, DateDiff counts the number of Tuesdays between the first date and the second date. For example, March 28, 2007 is a Wednesday, and April 2, 2007 is a Monday, so *DateDiff*("w", #28 MAR 2007#, #02 APR 2007#) returns 0.
"ww"	Calculates the difference in weeks. When the first day of the week is Sunday (the default), DateDiff counts the number of Sundays greater than the first date and less than or equal to the second date. For example, March 28, 2007 is a Wednesday, and April 7, 2007 is a Monday, so *DateDiff*("ww", #28 MAR 2007#, #02 APR 2007#) returns 1.
"h"	Calculates the difference in hours.
"n"	Calculates the difference in minutes.
"s"	Calculates the difference in seconds.

The second way to calculate the number of days is to simply subtract one date from the other. Remember that the integer portion of a Date/Time data type is number of days. If you're sure that the fields do not contain any time value, subtract the check-in date from the check-out date to find the number of days. Let's see how this works in the sample database.

Open the HousingDataCopy.accdb database if you have closed it and start a new query on tblReservations. Add EmployeeNumber, FacilityID, RoomNumber, CheckInDate, CheckOutDate, and TotalCharge to the query design grid. You need to enter your expression in a blank column on the Field row. You'll build your final expression in two parts so you can understand the logic involved. Using DateDiff, start the expression by entering

```
DateDiff("d", [CheckInDate], [CheckOutDate])
```

To calculate the number of days by subtracting, the expression is

```
[CheckOutDate] - [CheckInDate]
```

To calculate the amount owed at the daily rate, multiply either of the previous expressions by the DailyRate field. With DateDiff, the final expression is

```
DateDiff("d", [CheckInDate], [CheckOutDate]) * [DailyRate]
```

If you want to use subtraction, you must enter

```
([CheckOutDate] - [CheckInDate]) * [DailyRate]
```

You might be wondering why the second expression includes parentheses. When evaluating an arithmetic expression, Access evaluates certain operations before others, known as *operator precedence*. Table 28-4 shows you operator precedence for arithmetic operations. In an expression with no parentheses, Access performs the operations in the order listed in the table. When operations have the same precedence (for example, multiply and divide), Access performs the operations left to right.

Table 28-4 Arithmetic Operator Precedence

Access Evaluates Operators in the Following Order:	
1	Exponentiation (^)
2	Negation—a leading minus sign (–)
3	Multiplication and division (*, /)
4	Integer division (\)
5	Modulus (Mod)
6	Addition and subtraction (+, –)

Access evaluates expressions enclosed in parentheses first, starting with the innermost expressions. (You can enclose an expression in parentheses inside another expression in parentheses.) If you do not include the parentheses in the previous example, Access would first multiply CheckInDate times DailyRate (because multiplication and division occur before addition and subtraction) and then subtract that result from CheckOut-Date. That not only gives you the wrong answer but also results in an error because you cannot subtract a Double value (the result of multiplying a date/time times a currency) from a date/time value.

After you select the fields from the table and enter the expression to calculate the total based on the daily rate, your query design grid should look something like Figure 28-17.

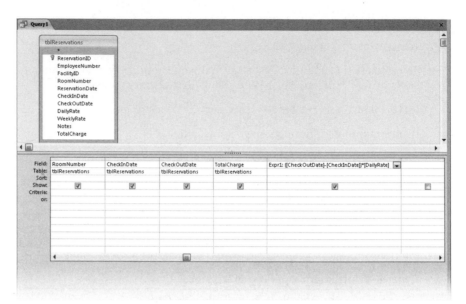

Figure 28-17 Use an expression to calculate the amount owed based on the daily rate.

When you switch to Datasheet view, you can see the calculated amount from your expression as shown in Figure 28-18.

Employee	Facility	Room	Check-In	Check-Out	Charge	Expr1
7	Main Campus Housing A	810	3/6/2007	3/18/2007	$455.00	480
7	Main Campus Housing B	111	3/24/2007	4/4/2007	$1,040.00	1100
5	North Satellite Housing D	305	3/20/2007	3/23/2007	$195.00	195
3	Main Campus Housing A	502	4/14/2007	5/1/2007	$1,420.00	1530
3	Main Campus Housing B	214	3/26/2007	3/28/2007	$100.00	100
10	Main Campus Housing A	902	4/1/2007	4/20/2007	$1,600.00	1710
1	South Campus Housing C	501	2/28/2007	3/13/2007	$1,200.00	1300
8	Main Campus Housing A	509	4/16/2007	4/29/2007	$620.00	650
2	Main Campus Housing B	504	4/20/2007	4/23/2007	$210.00	210
3	Main Campus Housing A	707	5/2/2007	5/15/2007	$680.00	715
5	Main Campus Housing B	301	3/25/2007	4/9/2007	$895.00	975
3	Main Campus Housing A	207	3/25/2007	4/5/2007	$570.00	605
8	Main Campus Housing A	111	4/4/2007	4/20/2007	$1,180.00	1280
7	Main Campus Housing A	708	4/27/2007	5/2/2007	$250.00	225
6	Main Campus Housing B	206	4/4/2007	4/15/2007	$830.00	880
7	South Campus Housing C	111	5/20/2007	5/27/2007	$255.00	280
4	South Campus Housing C	101	5/1/2007	5/22/2007	$1,920.00	2100
8	Main Campus Housing A	702	5/23/2007	5/28/2007	$450.00	450
5	Main Campus Housing B	610	5/23/2007	6/6/2007	$1,280.00	1400
5	Main Campus Housing A	309	5/5/2007	5/22/2007	$790.00	850
8	North Satellite Housing D	402	5/9/2007	5/20/2007	$830.00	880
8	South Campus Housing C	103	5/3/2007	5/8/2007	$350.00	350
12	Main Campus Housing B	414	6/11/2007	6/15/2007	$195.00	200
3	Main Campus Housing A	207	5/25/2007	5/29/2007	$220.00	220
5	South Campus Housing C	607	6/26/2007	6/28/2007	$110.00	110
5	Main Campus Housing B	303	6/30/2007	7/2/2007	$180.00	180

Record: 1 of 58

Figure 28-18 Access displays the results of your calculated expression in Datasheet view.

Note that not all the calculated amounts are larger than the amount already stored in the record. When the reservation is for six days or fewer, the daily rate applies, so your calculation should match the existing charge. You might want to display only the records where the new calculated amount is different than the amount already stored. For that, you can add another expression to calculate the difference and then select the row if the difference is not zero.

Switch back to Design view and enter a new expression to calculate the difference in an empty column. Your expression should look like this:

```
TotalCharge - (([CheckOutDate] - [CheckInDate]) * [DailyRate])
```

In the Criteria line under this new field, enter **<> 0**. Your query design should look like Figure 28-19, and the datasheet for the query now displays only the rows where the calculation result is different, as shown in Figure 28-20.

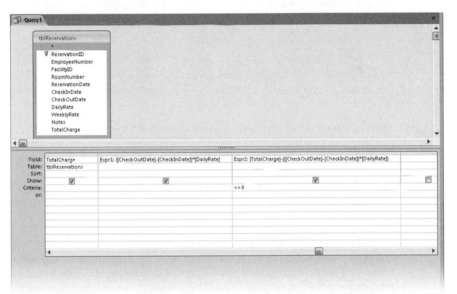

Figure 28-19 This expression and criterion finds the rows that are different.

Finding the rows that differ in this way has the added benefit of displaying the calculated difference. If you're only interested in finding the rows that differ but don't care about the amount of the difference, you don't need the second expression at all. You can find the rows you want by placing the expression <>[TotalCharge] in the Criteria line under the first expression you entered. This asks Access to compare the amount calculated at the straight daily rate with the value in the TotalCharge field stored in the record and display the row only when the two values are not equal.

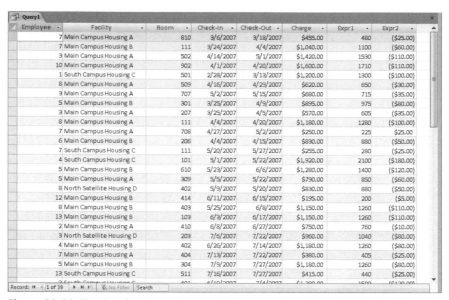

Figure 28-20 The datasheet now shows only the rows where the calculation is different than the stored value.

You might have inferred from the earlier discussion about entering criteria that you can use only constant values in the Criteria or Or lines. As you can see, you can also compare the value of one field or expression with another field or expression containing a reference to a field.

INSIDE OUT   Adding Parentheses to Expressions for Clarity

You might have noticed that we placed an extra set of parentheses around the original expression we built to calculate the amount at the daily rate before subtracting that amount from the stored value. If you study Table 28-4 carefully, you'll see that we really didn't have to do this because Access would perform the multiplication before doing the final subtract. However, we find it's a good practice to add parentheses to make the sequence of operations crystal clear—we don't always remember the order of precedence rules, and we don't want to have to go looking up the information in Help every time we build an expression. Adding the parentheses makes sure we get the results we want.

So far, you have built fairly simple expressions. When you want to create a more complex expression, sometimes the Expression Builder can be useful, as discussed in the next section.

Using the Expression Builder

For more complex expressions, Access 2007 provides a utility called the Expression Builder. Let's say you want to double-check the total amount owed for a reservation in the sample database. You have to work with several fields to do this—CheckInDate, CheckOutDate, DailyRate, and WeeklyRate. You need to calculate the number of weeks to charge at the WeeklyRate and then charge the remaining days at the DailyRate. To see how the Expression Builder works, start a new query on the tblReservations table. Click in an empty field in the design grid, and then click the Builder button in the Query Setup group of the Design contextual tab. Access opens the Expression Builder dialog box shown in Figure 28-21.

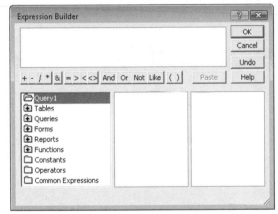

Figure 28-21 The Expression Builder dialog box helps you build simple and complex expressions.

In the upper part of the dialog box is a blank text box in which you can build an expression. You can type the expression yourself, but it's sometimes more accurate to find field names, operators, and function names in the three panes in the lower part of the dialog box and to use the various expression operator buttons just below the text box.

The expression you need to build, which we'll walk you through in detail in the next few pages, will ultimately look like this:

```
((DateDiff("d", [tblReservations]![CheckInDate], [tblReservations]![CheckOutDate])
\ 7) * [WeeklyRate]) + ((DateDiff("d", [tblReservations]![CheckInDate],
[tblReservations]![CheckOutDate]) Mod 7) * [DailyRate])
```

You can use the Expression Builder to help you correctly construct this expression. Start by double-clicking the Functions category in the left pane, then select Built-In Functions to see the list of function categories in the center pane, and the list of functions within the selected category in the right pane. Select the Date/Time category in the center pane to narrow down the choices. Here you can see the DateDiff function (that you used earlier) as well as several other built-in functions you can use.

Double-click the DateDiff function in the right pane to add it to the expression text box at the top of the Expression Builder. When you add a function to your expression in this way, the Expression Builder shows you the parameters required by the function. You can click any parameter to highlight it and type a value or select a value from one of the lists in the bottom panes. Click <<interval>> and overtype it with **"d"**. (See Table 28-3 for a list of all the possible interval settings.) You need to insert the CheckInDate field from tblReservations for <<date1>> and the CheckOutDate field for <<date2>>. Click <<date1>> to highlight it and double-click Tables in the left pane to open up the list of table names. Scroll down until you find tblReservations and select it to see the list of field names in the second pane. Double-click CheckInDate. Then click <<date2>>, and double-click CheckOutDate. You don't need the <<firstweekday>> or <<firstweek>> parameters, so click them and press the Delete key to remove them. (You can also remove the extra commas if you like.) The Expression Builder should now look like Figure 28-22.

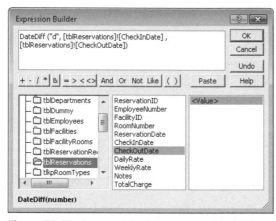

Figure 28-22 Create a calculation using table field names in the Expression Builder dialog box.

You'll notice that the Expression Builder pastes *[tblReservations]![CheckInDate]* into the expression area, not just *CheckInDate*. There are two good reasons for this. First, the Expression Builder doesn't know whether you might include other tables in this query and whether some of those tables might have field names that are identical to the ones you're selecting now. The way to avoid conflicts is to *fully qualify* the field names by preceding them with the table name. When working in queries, separate the table name from the field name with a period or an exclamation point. Second, you should enclose all names of objects in Access in brackets ([ ]). If you designed the name without any blank spaces, you can leave out the brackets, but it's always good practice to include them.

INSIDE OUT   Understanding Name Separators in SQL

In most cases you should separate the name of an object from the name of an object within that object (for example, a field within a table) with an exclamation point. When you build an expression in the Expression Builder, you'll find that the Expression Builder separates names using exclamation points. However, the standard for the SQL database query language uses a period between the name of a table and the name of a field within the table. To be most compatible with the SQL standard when constructing a query expression, use a period between a table name and a field name. Access accepts either an exclamation point or a period in query design.

Next, you need to divide by 7 to calculate the number of weeks. You're not interested in any fractional part of a week, so you need to use the integer divide operator (\). Note that there is no operator button for integer divide. The operator buttons are arranged horizontally below the expression text box. So, you can either type the operator or scroll down in the leftmost pane, select Operators to open that list, select Arithmetic in the second pane, and then double-click the integer divide operator (\) in the rightmost list to add it to your expression. Make sure the insertion point in the expression box is positioned after the integer divide operator and type the number **7**.

The next operation you need is to multiply the expression you have thus far by the WeeklyRate field from tblReservations. If you like, you can add left and right parentheses around the expression before adding the multiply operator and the field. Remember from Table 28-4 that multiplication and division are of equal precedence, so Access evaluates the division before the multiplication (left to right) even if you don't add the parentheses. But, as we noted earlier, we like to make the precedence of operations crystal clear, so we recommend that you add the parentheses. Press the Home key to go to the beginning of the expression, click the left parenthesis button, press the End key to go to the end, click the right parenthesis button, click the multiply operator (*) button, and finally select the WeeklyRate field from the tblReservations field list.

Note
WeekyRate and DailyRate are currency fields. DateDiff returns an integer, and the result of an integer divide (\) or a modulus (Mod) operation is an integer. Whenever you ask Access to evaluate an arithmetic expression, it returns a result that has a data type sufficiently complex to contain the result. As you might expect, multiplying an integer (a simple data type) with a currency field (a more complex data type) returns a currency field.

Chapter 28

You need to add this entire expression to the calculation for remaining days at the daily rate, so press Ctrl+Home again and add one more left parenthesis, press the Ctrl+End key, and click the right parenthesis button to complete this first part of the expression. Click the addition operator to add it to your expression. Rather than scan back and forth to add parentheses as we build the second part of the expression, click the left parenthesis button twice to start building the calculation for extra days. Add the DateDiff function again, click <<interval>>, and type **"d"**. Click <<date1>>, find Check-InDate in tblReservations again, and double-click it to add it to your expression. Click <<date2>> and double-click the CheckOutDate field. Remove <<firstweekday>> and <<firstweek>> from the function.

Now, you need to know how many days beyond full weeks are in the reservation. You might be tempted to divide by 7 again and try to extract the remainder, but there's a handy operator that returns only the remainder of a division for you—Mod. Scroll down in the left pane and select Operators. In the middle pane, select Arithmetic to see only the arithmetic operators in the right pane. Double-click Mod to add it to your expression after the parentheses.

We're almost done. Type the number **7** and click the right parenthesis button to close the Mod calculation. Click the multiply operator button, and then go back to tblReservations and double-click the DailyRate field. Click the right parenthesis button one last time to finish the expression. Verify that your completed expression exactly matches the one in Figure 28-23.

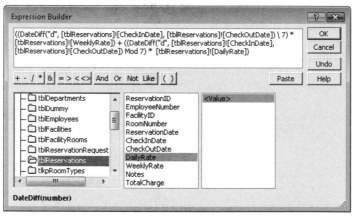

Figure 28-23 Your completed expression in the Expression Builder dialog box should match this figure.

Click OK to paste your result into the design grid. Go ahead and add ReservationID, FacilityID, RoomNumber, CheckInDate, CheckOutDate, and TotalCharge to your query grid. When you switch to Datasheet view, your result should look like Figure 28-24.

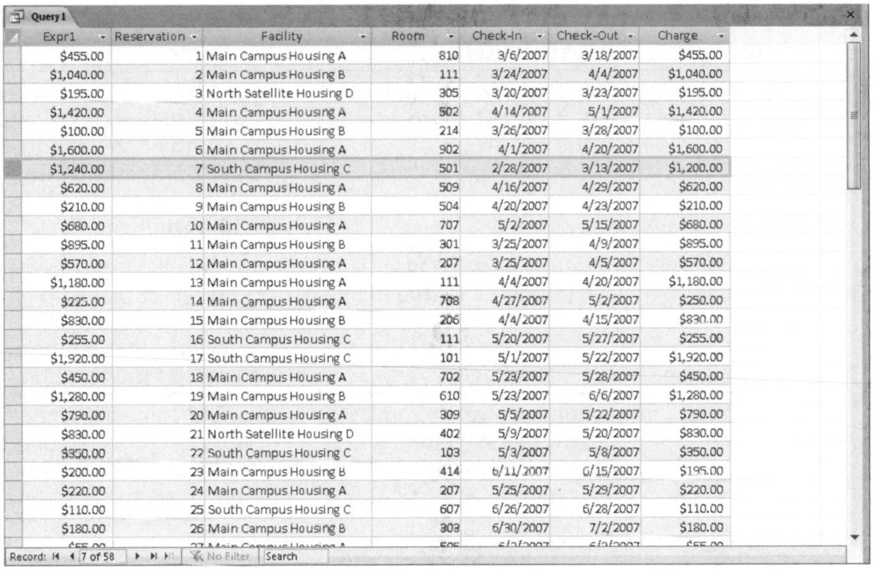

Figure 28-24 Switch to Datasheet view to see the result of your complex calculation expression.

Do you notice any stored values that don't match what you just calculated? (Hint: Look at the highlighted row.) If you haven't changed the sample data, you'll find several rows that we purposefully updated with invalid TotalCharge values. Here's a challenge: Go back to Design view and enter the criteria you need to display only the rows where your calculated charge doesn't match the TotalCharge stored in the table. You can find the solution saved as qxmplUnmatchedCharges in the HousingDataCopy.accdb sample database.

INSIDE OUT   Is the Builder Useful? You Decide

We personally never use the Expression Builder when we're creating applications in Access 2007. We find it more cumbersome than directly typing the expression we think we need and then trying it out. We included this discussion because some beginning developers might find that the Expression Builder helps them learn how to build correct expression and function call syntax.

We used the DateDiff function to solve this problem, but Access 2007 has several other useful functions to help you deal with date and time values. For example, you might want to see only a part of the date or time value in your query. You might also want to use these functions to help you filter the results in your query. Table 28-5 explains each date and time function and includes filter examples that use the ContactDateTime field in the tblContactEvents table in the Conrad Systems Contacts sample database.

Chapter 28

Table 28-5 **Date and Time Functions**

Function	Description	Example
Day(*date*)	Returns a value from 1 through 31 for the day of the month.	To select records with contact events that occurred after the 10th of any month, enter **Day([ContactDateTime])** in an empty column on the Field line and enter **>10** as the criterion for that field.
Month(*date*)	Returns a value from 1 through 12 for the month of the year.	To find all contact events that occurred in March (of any year), enter **Month([ContactDateTime])** in an empty column on the Field line and enter **3** as the criterion for that field.
Year(*date*)	Returns a value from 100 through 9999 for the year.	To find contact events that happened in 2007, enter **Year([ContactDateTime])** in an empty column on the Field line and enter **2007** as the criterion for that field.
Weekday(*date*)	As a default, returns a value from 1 (Sunday) through 7 (Saturday) for the day of the week.	To find contact events that occurred between Monday and Friday, enter **Weekday([ContactDateTime])** in an empty column on the Field line and enter **Between 2 And 6** as the criterion for that field.
Hour(*date*)	Returns a value from 0 through 23 for the hour of the day.	To find contact events that happened before noon, enter **Hour([ContactDateTime])** in an empty column on the Field line and enter **<12** as the criterion for that field.
DateAdd (*interval, amount, date*)	Adds an amount in the interval you specify to a date/time value.	To find contact events that occurred more than six months ago, enter **<DateAdd("m", −6, Date())** as the criterion under ContactDateTime. (See also the Date function below.)
DatePart (*interval, date*)	Returns a portion of the date or time, depending on the interval code you supply. Useful interval codes are "q" for quarter of the year (1 through 4) and "ww" for week of the year (1 through 53).	To find contact events in the second quarter, enter **DatePart("q", [ContactDateTime])** in an empty column on the Field line, and enter **2** as the criterion for that field.
Date()	Returns the current system date.	To select contact events that happened more than 30 days ago, enter **<(Date() − 30)** as the criterion under ContactDateTime.

Specifying Field Names

Every field must have a name. By default, the name of a simple field in a query is the name of the field from the source table. However, when you create a new field using an expression, the expression doesn't have a name unless you or Access assigns one. You have seen that when you create an expression in the Field row of the design grid, Access adds a prefix such as *Expr1* followed by a colon–that is the name that Access is assigning to your expression. Remember, the column heading for the field is, by default, the field name unless you specify a different caption property setting. As you know, you can assign or change a caption for a field in a query by using the field's property sheet.

Understanding Field Names and Captions

In the world of tables and queries, every field—even calculated ones—must have a name. When you create a field in a table, you give it a name. When you use a table in a query and include a field from the table in the query output, the name of the field output by the query is the same as the field name in the table. If you create a calculated field in a query, you must assign a name to that field. If you don't, Access assigns an ugly *ExprN* name for you. But you can override this and assign your own field name to expressions. You can also override the default field name for a simple field with another name. When you use a query in another query or a form or report, or you open a query as a record-set in Visual Basic, you use the field name to indicate which field you want to fetch from the query.

You can also define a Caption property for a field. When you do that, what you put in the caption becomes the external label for the field. You'll see the caption in column headings in Datasheet view. Later, when you begin to work with forms and reports, you'll find that the caption becomes the default label for the field. If you don't define a caption, Access shows you the field name instead.

You can change or assign field names that will appear in the recordset of a query. This feature is particularly useful when you've calculated a value in the query that you'll use in a form, a report, or another query. In the queries shown in Figures 28-15, 28-17, and 28-19, you calculated a value and Access assigned a temporary field name. You can replace this name with something more meaningful. For example, in the first query you might want to use something like FullName and CityStateZip. In the second query, RecalculatedCharge might be appropriate. To change a name generated by Access, replace *ExprN* with the name you want in the Field row in the query design grid. To assign a new name to a field, place the insertion point at the beginning of the field specification and insert the new name followed by a colon. Figure 28-25 shows the first query with the field names changed.

FullName	CityStateZip
Koch, Reed	West Mansfield, OH 43358
Kim, Tim	Meredith, NH 03253
Tippett, John	Florence, AL 35630
DeGrasse, Kirk	Agua Dulce, CA 91350
Lawrence, David Oliver	Christiansburg, VA 24073
Adams, Jay	Ramona, SD 57054
Richins, Jack S.	Saint David, ME 04773
Bradley, David M.	Bayou La Batre, AL 36509
Eyink, Scott	Los Osos, CA 93402
Berndt, Matthias	Rockland, TX 75938
Willett, Benjamin C.	Austin, MO 64725
Shock, Misty	Newhall, CA 91381
Randall, Linda	Trail Creek, IN 46360
Schare, Gary	Rock Springs, AZ 85324
Viescas, John L.	,
Conrad, Jeff	,

Figure 28-25 You can change the *Expr1* and *Expr2* field names shown in Figure 28-16 to display more meaningful field names.

Note that we could have made the column headings you see even more readable by also assigning a caption to these fields via the field's property sheet. We might have chosen something like Person Name for the first field and City-State-Zip for the second field. Keep in mind that setting the caption does not change the actual name of the field when you use the query in a form, a report, or Visual Basic code.

Sorting Data

Normally, Access 2007 displays the rows in your recordset in the order in which they're retrieved from the database. You can add sorting information to determine the sequence of the data in a query. Click in the Sort row for the field you want to sort on, click the arrow in this row, and then select Ascending or Descending from the list. In the example shown in Figure 28-26, the query results are to be sorted in descending order based on the calculated NewTotalCharge field. (Note that we have given the calculated field a field name.) The recordset will list the most expensive reservations first. The resulting Datasheet view is shown in Figure 28-27. You can find this query saved as qryXmplChargeCalcSorted in the HousingDataCopy.accdb sample database.

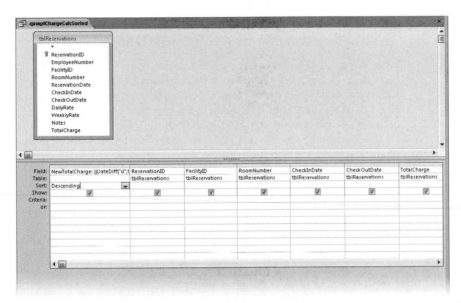

Figure 28-26 Access sorts the query results on the NewTotalCharge field in descending order.

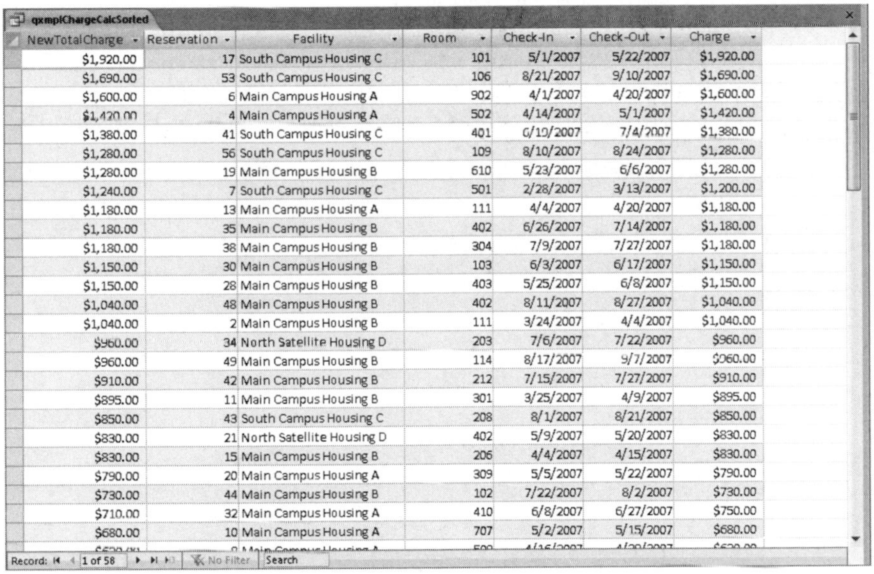

NewTotalCharge ▾	Reservation ▾	Facility ▾	Room ▾	Check-In ▾	Check-Out ▾	Charge ▾
$1,920.00	17	South Campus Housing C	101	5/1/2007	5/22/2007	$1,920.00
$1,690.00	53	South Campus Housing C	106	8/21/2007	9/10/2007	$1,690.00
$1,600.00	6	Main Campus Housing A	902	4/1/2007	4/20/2007	$1,600.00
$1,420.00	4	Main Campus Housing A	502	4/14/2007	5/1/2007	$1,420.00
$1,380.00	41	South Campus Housing C	401	6/10/2007	7/4/2007	$1,380.00
$1,280.00	56	South Campus Housing C	109	8/10/2007	8/24/2007	$1,280.00
$1,280.00	19	Main Campus Housing B	610	5/23/2007	6/6/2007	$1,280.00
$1,240.00	7	South Campus Housing C	501	2/28/2007	3/13/2007	$1,200.00
$1,180.00	13	Main Campus Housing A	111	4/4/2007	4/20/2007	$1,180.00
$1,180.00	35	Main Campus Housing B	402	6/26/2007	7/14/2007	$1,180.00
$1,180.00	38	Main Campus Housing B	304	7/9/2007	7/27/2007	$1,180.00
$1,150.00	30	Main Campus Housing B	103	6/3/2007	6/17/2007	$1,150.00
$1,150.00	28	Main Campus Housing B	403	5/25/2007	6/8/2007	$1,150.00
$1,040.00	48	Main Campus Housing B	402	8/11/2007	8/27/2007	$1,040.00
$1,040.00	2	Main Campus Housing B	111	3/24/2007	4/4/2007	$1,040.00
$960.00	34	North Satellite Housing D	203	7/6/2007	7/22/2007	$960.00
$960.00	49	Main Campus Housing B	114	8/17/2007	9/7/2007	$960.00
$910.00	42	Main Campus Housing B	212	7/15/2007	7/27/2007	$910.00
$895.00	11	Main Campus Housing B	301	3/25/2007	4/9/2007	$895.00
$850.00	43	South Campus Housing C	208	8/1/2007	8/21/2007	$850.00
$830.00	21	North Satellite Housing D	402	5/3/2007	5/20/2007	$830.00
$830.00	15	Main Campus Housing B	206	4/4/2007	4/15/2007	$830.00
$790.00	20	Main Campus Housing A	309	5/5/2007	5/22/2007	$790.00
$730.00	44	Main Campus Housing A	102	7/22/2007	8/2/2007	$730.00
$710.00	32	Main Campus Housing A	410	6/8/2007	6/27/2007	$750.00
$680.00	10	Main Campus Housing A	707	5/2/2007	5/15/2007	$680.00
	9	Main Campus Housing A	500	4/15/2007	4/20/2007	

Record: ◄ ◄ 1 of 58 ► ►► No Filter Search

Figure 28-27 Datasheet view shows the recordset of the query shown in Figure 28-25 sorted on the NewTotalCharge field.

INSIDE OUT   Why Specifying Sort Criteria Is Important

When Access 2007 solves a query, it tries to do it in the most efficient way. When you first construct and run a query, Access might return the records in the sequence you expect (for example, in primary key sequence of the table). However, if you want to be sure Access always returns rows in this order, you must specify sort criteria. As you later add and remove rows in your table, Access might decide that fetching rows in a different sequence might be faster, which, in the absence of sorting criteria, might result in a different row sequence than you intended.

You can also sort on multiple fields. Access honors your sorting criteria from left to right in the design grid. If, for example, you want to sort by FacilityID ascending and then by NewTotalCharge descending, you should include the FacilityID field to the left of the NewTotalCharge field. If the additional field you want to sort is already in the design grid but in the wrong location, click the column selector box (the tinted box above the field row) to select the entire column and then click the selector box again and drag the field to its new location. If you want the field that is out of position to still appear where you originally placed it, add the field to the design grid again in the correct sorting sequence, clear the Show check box (you don't want two copies of the field displayed), and set the Sort specification. Figure 28-28 shows the query shown in Figure 28-26 modified to sort first by FacilityID and then by NewTotal-Charge, but leave FacilityID displayed after ReservationID. We saved this query in the HousingDataCopy.accdb sample database as qxmplChargeCalcSortedTwo.

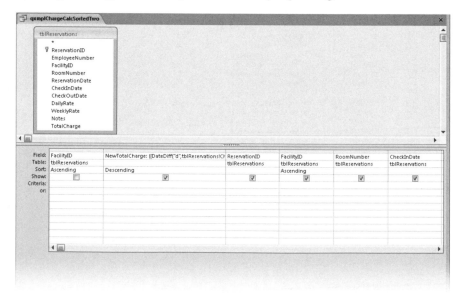

Figure 28-28 This example sorts on two fields while maintaining the original field sequence in the query output.

INSIDE OUT   **A Reminder: Why Lookup Properties Can Be Confusing**

If you open the datasheet of qxmplChargeCalcSortedTwo and scroll down in the record-set, you'll find the Facility column sorted Main Campus Housing A, Main Campus Housing B, South Campus Housing C, and North Satellite Housing D. Why does South appear before North if the values are supposed to be sorted in ascending order? The information you're seeing in the datasheet comes from the Lookup defined on the FacilityID column in tblReservations—you're seeing the related facility name from tblFacilities. However, the actual value of FacilityID is a number. You can click on the FacilityID column, open the field's property sheet, click the Lookup tab, and set the Display Control property to Text Box to see the actual number value. When you do this and look at the datasheet again, you'll see that the values are sorted correctly.

Testing Validation Rule Changes

You learned in Chapter 27 how to define both field and table validation rules. You can also change these rules even after you have data in your table. Access 2007 warns you if some of the data in your table doesn't satisfy the new rule, but it doesn't tell you which rows have problems.

Checking a New Field Validation Rule

The best way to find out if any rows will fail a new field validation rule is to write a query to test your data before you make the change. The trick is you must specify criteria that are the converse of your proposed rule change to find the rows that don't match. For example, if you are planning to set the Required property to Yes or specify a Validation Rule property of Is Not Null on a field (both tests mean the same thing), you want to look for rows containing a field that Is Null. If you want to limit the daily price of a room to <= 90, then you must look for values that are > 90 to find the rows that will fail. Another way to think about asking for the converse of a validation rule is to put the word *Not* in front of the rule. If the new rule is going to be <= 90, then Not <= 90 will find the bad rows.

Let's see what we need to do to test a proposed validation rule change to tblFacility-Rooms in the sample database. The daily room rate should not exceed $90.00, so the new rule in the DailyRate field will be <=90. To test for rooms that exceed this new limit, start a new query on tblFacilityRooms. Include the fields FacilityID, RoomNumber, RoomType, DailyRate, and WeeklyRate in the query's design grid. (You need at least FacilityID and RoomNumber—the primary key fields—to be able to identify which rows fail.) Under DailyRate, enter the converse of the new rule: either **>90** or **Not <=90**. Your query should look like Figure 28-29.

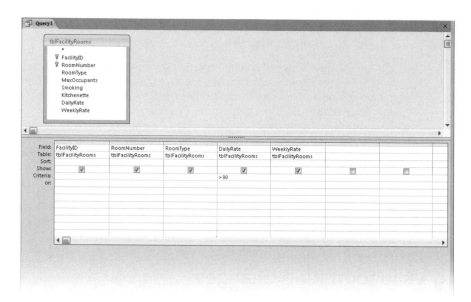

Figure 28-29 Create a new query to test a proposed new field validation rule.

If you run this query against the original data in the sample database, you'll find 26 rooms that are priced higher than the new proposed rule. As you'll learn in "Working in Query Datasheet View" on page 940, you can update these rows by typing a new value directly in the query datasheet.

Let's try something. Select one of the invalid values you found in the query datasheet and try to type the new maximum value of $90.00. If you try to save the row, you'll get an error message because there's a table validation rule that prevents you from setting a DailyRate value that when multiplied by 7 is more than the WeeklyRate value. It looks like you'll have to fix both values if you want to change your field validation rule.

Checking a New Table Validation Rule

Checking a proposed new field validation rule is simple. But what about making a change to a table validation rule? Typically, a table validation rule compares one field with another, so to check a new rule, you'll need more complex criteria in your query.

There's already a table validation rule in the tblFacilityRooms table in the HousingData-Copy.accdb sample database. The rule makes sure that the weekly rate is not more than 7 times the daily rate—it wouldn't be much of a discount if it were! Suppose you now want to be sure that the weekly rate reflects a true discount from the daily rate. Your proposed new rule might make sure that the weekly rate is no more than 6 times the daily rate—if an employee stays a full week, the last night is essentially free. Your new rule might look like the following:

```
([DailyRate]*6)>=[WeeklyRate]
```

So, you need to write a query that checks the current values in the WeeklyRate field to see if any will fail the new rule. Note that you could also create an expression to calculate DailyRate times 6 and compare that value with WeeklyRate. When the expression you want to test involves a calculation on one side of the comparison with a simple field value on the other side of the comparison, it's easier to compare the simple field with the expression. Remember, you need to create the converse of the expression to find rows that won't pass the new rule.

You can start with the query you built in the previous section or create a new query. You need at least the primary key fields from the table as well as the fields you need to perform the comparison. In this case, you need to compare the current value of WeeklyRate with the expression on DailyRate. Let's turn the expression around so that it's easier to see what you need to enter in the query grid. The expression looks like this:

```
[WeeklyRate]<=([DailyRate]*6)
```

To test the converse on the WeeklyRate field's Criteria row of your query, you need either

```
>([DailyRate]*6)
```

or

```
Not <=([DailyRate]*6)
```

Your test query should look like Figure 28-30.

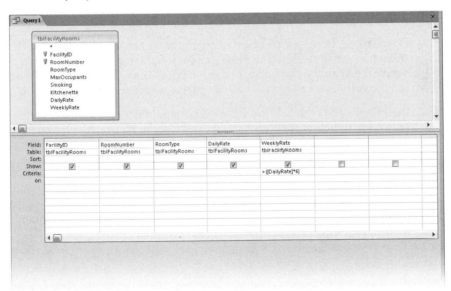

Figure 28-30 You can create a query to test a new table validation rule.

If you run this query, you'll find that nearly all the rows in the table fail the new test. When we loaded sample data into the table, we created weekly rates that are approximately 6.4 times the daily rate—so none of the rates pass the new test.

Working in Query Datasheet View

When you're developing an application, you might need to work in table or query Datasheet view to help you load sample data or to solve problems in the queries, forms, and reports you're creating. You might also decide to create certain forms in your application that display information in Datasheet view. Also, the techniques for updating and manipulating data in forms are very similar to doing so in datasheets—so you need to understand how datasheets work to be able to explain to your users how to use your application. If you're using Access 2007 as a personal database to analyze information, you might frequently work with information in Datasheet view. In either case, you should understand how to work with data editing, and the best way to learn how is to understand viewing and editing data in Datasheet view.

Before you get started with the remaining examples in this chapter, open Contacts-DataCopy.accdb from your sample files folder. In that database, you'll find a query named qryContactsDatasheet that we'll use in the remainder of this chapter. We defined this query to select key fields from tblContacts and display a subdatasheet from tblContactEvents.

Moving Around and Using Keyboard Shortcuts

Open the qryContactsDatasheet query in the ContactsDataCopy.accdb database. You should see a result similar to Figure 28-31. Displaying different records or fields is simple. You can use the horizontal scroll bar to scroll through a table's fields, or you can use the vertical scroll bar to scroll through a table's records.

In the lower-left corner of the table in Datasheet view, you can see a set of navigation buttons and the Record Number box, as shown in Figure 28-32. The Record Number box shows the *relative record number* of the current record (meaning the number of the selected record in relation to the current set of records, also called a recordset). You might not see the current record in the window if you've scrolled the display. The number to the right of the new record button shows the total number of records in the current recordset. If you've applied a filter against the table (see "Searching for and Filtering Data" on page 961), this number might be less than the total number of records in the table or query.

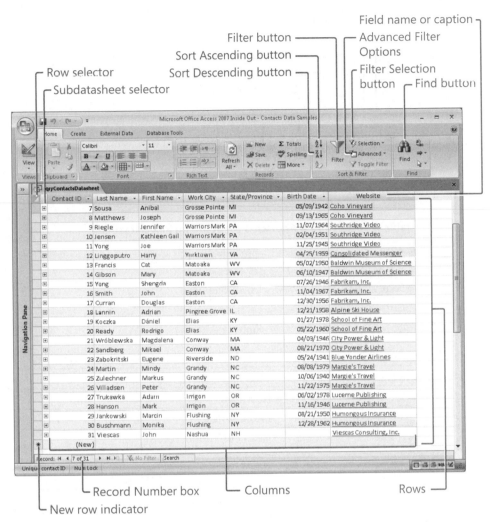

Figure 28-31 Open the Datasheet view of the qryContactsDatasheet query to begin learning about moving around and editing in a datasheet.

You can quickly move to the record you want by typing a value in the Record Number box and pressing Enter or by using the navigation buttons. You can also click the Go To command in the Find group on the Home tab on the Ribbon to move to the first, last, next, or previous record, or to move to a new, empty record. You can make any record current by clicking anywhere in its row; the number in the Record Number box will change to indicate the row you've selected.

You might find it easier to use the keyboard rather than the mouse to move around in a datasheet, especially if you're typing new data. Table 28-6 lists the keyboard shortcuts for scrolling in a datasheet. Table 28-7 lists the keyboard shortcuts for selecting data in a datasheet.

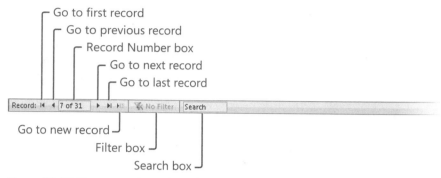

Figure 28-32 You can navigate through the datasheet records using the navigation buttons and Record Number box.

Table 28-6 Keyboard Shortcuts for Scrolling in a Datasheet

Keys	Scrolling Action
Page Up	Up one page
Page Down	Down one page
Ctrl+Page Up	Left one page
Ctrl+Page Down	Right one page

Table 28-7 Keyboard Shortcuts for Selecting Data in a Datasheet

Keys	Selecting Action
Tab	Next field
Shift+Tab	Previous field
Home	First field, current record
End	Last field, current record
Up Arrow	Current field, previous record
Down Arrow	Current field, next record
Ctrl+Up Arrow	Current field, first record
Ctrl+Down Arrow	Current field, last record
Ctrl+Home	First field, first record
Ctrl+End	Last field, last record
Alt+F5	Record Number box
Ctrl+Spacebar	The current column
Shift+Spacebar	The current record
F2	When in a field, toggles between selecting all data in the field and single-character edit mode

Working with Subdatasheets

Microsoft Access 2000 introduced a new feature that lets you display information from multiple related tables in a single datasheet. In the design we developed for the Conrad Systems Contacts sample database, contacts can have multiple contact events and contact products. In some cases, it might be useful to open a query on contacts and be able to see either related events or products in the same datasheet window.

You might have noticed the little plus-sign indicators in the datasheet for qryContacts-Datasheet in Figure 28-31. Click the plus sign next to the second row to open the Contact Events subdatasheet as shown in Figure 28-33.

Figure 28-33 Click the plus sign to view the contact event details for the second contact in a subdatasheet.

A subdatasheet doesn't appear automatically in a query, even if you've defined subdatasheet properties for your table as described in Chapter 27. We had to open the property sheet for the query in Design view and specify the subdatasheet you see. Figure 28-34 shows the properties we set. You can find more details about setting these properties in Chapter 27.

Chapter 28

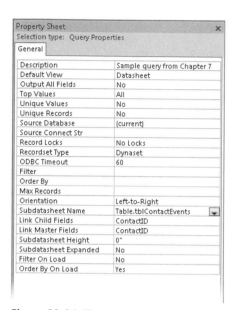

Figure 28-34 The property sheet for the qryContactsDatasheet query displays the subdatasheet properties.

You can click the plus sign next to each order row to see the contact event detail information for that contact. If you want to expand or collapse all the subdatasheets, click More in the Records group on the Home tab, click Subdatasheet, and then click the option you want as shown in Figure 28-35.

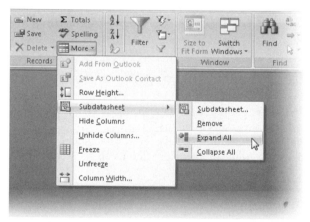

Figure 28-35 The Subdatasheet menu allows you to easily expand all subdatasheets, collapse all subdatasheets, or remove the currently displayed subdatasheet.

The information from the related tblContactEvents table is interesting, but what if you want to see the products the contact has purchased instead? To do this, while in Datasheet view, click More on the Home tab, click Subdatasheet, and then click Subdatasheet to see the dialog box shown in Figure 28-36.

Figure 28-36 You can choose a different table to display other related information in a subdatasheet from the Insert Subdatasheet dialog box.

We built a query in the sample database that displays the related company and product information for a contact. Click the Queries or Both tab and select qxmplCompanyContactProduct to define the new subdatasheet. Click OK to close the Insert Subdatasheet dialog box.

When you return to the qryContactsDatasheet window, click More on the Home tab, click Subdatasheet, and then click Expand All. You will now see information about each product ordered as shown in Figure 28-37. Note that you can also entirely remove a subdatasheet by clicking Remove on the menu shown in Figure 28-35. Close the query when you are finished.

In the next section, you'll learn more about editing data in Datasheet view. You can use these editing techniques with the main datasheet as well as with any expanded subdatasheet.

> **CAUTION**
>
> When you close qryContactsDatasheet after modifying the subdatasheet as explained in this section, Access will prompt you to ask if you want to save your changes. You should click No to retain the original subdatasheet on tblContactEvents that we defined so that the remaining examples in this chapter make sense.

Chapter 28

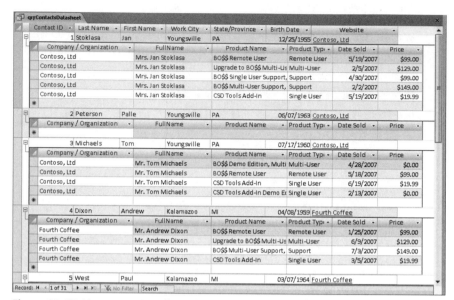

Figure 28-37 You can review all product information for a contact from the subdatasheet by expanding it.

Changing Data

Not only can you view and format data in a datasheet, you can also insert new records, change data, and delete records.

Understanding Record Indicators

You might have noticed as you moved around in the datasheet that icons occasionally appeared on the row selector at the far left of each row. (See Figure 28-31.) These *record indicators* and their meanings follow. Note also that Access 2007 highlights the current row.

 The pencil icon indicates that you are making or have made a change to one or more entries in this row. Access 2007 saves the changes when you move to another row. Before moving to a new row, you can press Esc once to undo the change to the current value, or press Esc twice to undo all changes in the row. If you're updating a database that is shared with other users through a network, Access locks this record when you save the change so that no one else can update it until you're finished. If someone else has the record locked, Access shows you a warning dialog box when you try to save the row. You can wait a few seconds and try to save again.

 The asterisk icon indicates a blank row at the end of the table that you can use to create a new record.

Adding a New Record

As you build your application, you might find it useful to place some data in your tables so that you can test the forms and reports that you design. You might also find it faster sometimes to add data directly to your tables by using Datasheet view rather than by opening a form. If your table is empty when you open the table or a query on the table in Datasheet view, Access 2007 shows a single blank highlighted row with dimmed rows beneath. If you have data in your table, Access shows a blank row beneath the last record as well as dimmed rows below the blank row. You can jump to the blank row to begin adding a new record either by clicking the Go To command on the Home tab and then clicking New Record, by clicking the New button in the Records group on the Home tab, or by pressing Ctrl+plus sign. Access places the insertion point in the first column when you start a new record. As soon as you begin typing, Access changes the record indicator to the pencil icon to show that updates are in progress. Press the Tab key to move to the next column.

If the data you enter in a column violates a field validation rule, Access 2007 notifies you as soon as you attempt to leave the column. You must provide a correct value before you can move to another column. Press Esc or click the Undo button on the Quick Access Toolbar to remove your changes in the current field.

Press Shift+Enter at any place in the record or press Tab in the last column in the record to commit your new record to the database. You can also click the Save command in the Records group on the Home tab. If the changes in your record violate the validation rule for the table, Access warns you when you try to save the record. You must correct the problem before you can save your changes. If you want to cancel the record, press Esc twice or click the Undo button on the Quick Access Toolbar until the button appears dimmed. (The first Undo removes the edit from the current field, and clicking Undo again removes any previous edit in other fields until you have removed them all.)

Access 2007 provides several keyboard shortcuts to assist you as you enter new data, as shown in Table 28-8.

Table 28-8 Keyboard Shortcuts for Entering Data in a Datasheet

Keys	Data Action
Ctrl+semicolon (;)	Enters the current date
Ctrl+colon (:)	Enters the current time
Ctrl+Alt+Spacebar	Enters the default value for the field
Ctrl+single quotation mark (') or Ctrl+double quotation mark (")	Enters the value from the same field in the previous record
Ctrl+Enter	Inserts a carriage return in a memo or text field
Ctrl+plus sign (+)	Moves to the new record row
Ctrl+minus sign (−)	Deletes the current record

INSIDE OUT Setting Keyboard Options

You can set options that affect how you move around in datasheets and forms. Click the Microsoft Office Button, click Access Options, and click the Advanced category to see the options shown here.

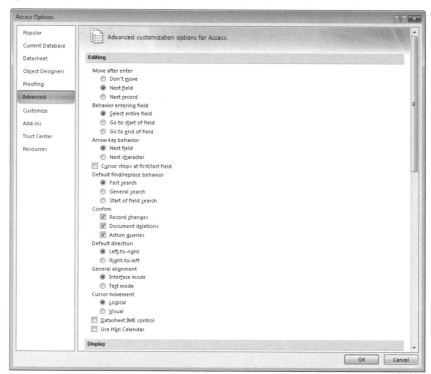

You can change the way the Enter key works by selecting an option under Move After Enter. Select Don't Move to stay in the current field when you press Enter. When you select Next Field (the default), pressing Enter moves you to the next field or the next row if you're on the last field. Select Next Record to save your changes and move to the next row when you press Enter.

You can change which part of the data of the field is selected when you move into a field by selecting an option under Behavior Entering Field. Choose Select Entire Field (the default), to highlight all data in the field. Select Go To Start Of Field to place an insertion point before the first character, and select Go To End Of Field to place the insertion point after the last character.

Under Arrow Key Behavior select Next Field (the default) if you want to move from field to field when you press the Right Arrow or Left Arrow key. Select Next Character to change to the insertion point and move one character at a time when you press the Right Arrow or Left Arrow key. You can select the Cursor Stops At First/Last Field check box if you don't want pressing the arrow keys to move you off the current row.

We personally prefer to set the Move After Enter option to Don't Move and the Arrow Key Behavior option to Next Character. We use the Tab key to move from field to field, and we don't want to accidentally save the record when we press Enter. We leave Behavior Entering Field at the default setting of Select Entire Field so that the entire text is selected, but setting Arrow Key Behavior to Next Character allows us to press the arrow keys to shift to single-character edit mode and move in the field.

Selecting and Changing Data

When you have data in a table, you can easily change the data by editing it in Datasheet view. You must select data before you can change it, and you can do this in several ways.

- In the cell containing the data you want to change, click just to the left of the first character you want to change (or to the right of the last character), and then drag the insertion point to select all the characters you want to change.

- Double-click any word in a cell to select the entire word.

- Click at the left edge of a cell in the grid (that is, where the mouse pointer turns into a large white cross). Access selects the entire contents of the cell.

Any data you type replaces the old, selected data. In Figure 28-38, we have moved to the left edge of the First Name field, and Access has shown us the white cross mentioned in the last bullet. We can click to select the entire contents of the field. In Figure 28-39, we have changed the value to Mike, but haven't yet saved the row. (You can see the pencil icon indicating that a change is pending.) Access also selects the entire entry if you tab to the cell in the datasheet grid (unless you have changed the keyboard options as noted earlier). If you want to change only part of the data (for example, to correct the spelling of a street name in an address field), you can shift to single-character mode by pressing F2 or by clicking the location at which you want to start your change. Use the Backspace key to erase characters to the left of the insertion point and use the Delete key to remove characters to the right of the insertion point. Hold down the Shift key and press the Right Arrow or Left Arrow key to select multiple characters to replace. You can press F2 again to select the entire cell. A useful keyboard shortcut for changing data is to press Ctrl+Alt+Spacebar to restore the data in the current field to the default value specified in the table definition.

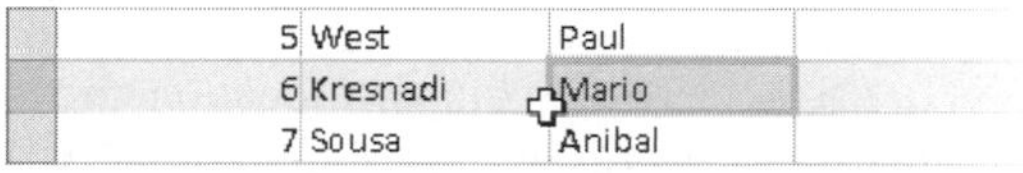

Figure 28-38 You can select the old data by clicking the left side of the column.

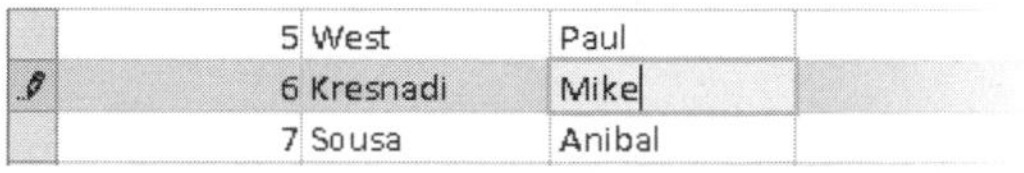

Figure 28-39 You can then replace the old data with new data by typing the new information.

Chapter 28

Replacing Data

What if you need to make the same change in more than one record? Access 2007 provides a way to do this quickly and easily. Select any cell in the column whose values you want to change (the first row if you want to start at the beginning of the table), and then click the Replace command in the Find group on the Home tab or press Ctrl+F to see the dialog box shown in Figure 28-40. Suppose, for example, that you suspect that the city name *Easton* is misspelled as *Eaton* in multiple rows. (All the city names are spelled correctly in the sample table.) To fix this using Replace, select the Work City field in any row of qryContactsDatasheet, click the Replace command, type **Eaton** in the Find What text box, and then type **Easton** in the Replace With text box, as shown in Figure 28-40. Click the Find Next button to search for the next occurrence of the text you've typed in the Find What text box. Click the Replace button to change data selectively, or click the Replace All button to change all the entries that match the Find What text. Note that you can select options to look in all fields or only the current field; to select an entry only if the Find What text matches the entire entry in the field; to search All, Up, or Down; to exactly match the case for text searches (because searches in Access are normally case-insensitive); and to search based on the formatted contents (most useful when updating date/time fields).

Figure 28-40 The Find And Replace dialog box allows you to quickly replace data in more than one record.

Copying and Pasting Data

You can copy or cut any selected data to the Clipboard and paste this data into another field or record. To copy data in a field, tab to the cell or click at the left edge of the cell in the datasheet grid to select the data within it. Click the Copy command in the Clipboard group on the Home tab or press Ctrl+C. To delete (cut) the data you have selected and place a copy on the Clipboard, click the Cut command in the Clipboard group on the Home tab or press Ctrl+X. To paste the data in another location, move the insertion point to the new location, optionally select the data you want to replace, and click the Paste command in the Clipboard group on the Home tab or press Ctrl+V. If the insertion point is at the paste location (you haven't selected any data in the field), Access inserts the Clipboard data.

INSIDE OUT   Using the Office Clipboard

If you select and copy to the Clipboard several items of text data, Access 2007 shows you the Office Clipboard task pane. Unlike the Windows Clipboard, this facility allows you to copy several separate items, and then select any one of them later to paste into other fields or documents. You might find this feature useful when you want to copy the contents of several fields from one record to another. You can, for example, copy a City field and then copy a State field while in one record and then later individually paste the values into another row. If you don't see the Office Clipboard, you can open it by clicking the Dialog Box Launcher button to the right of the word Clipboard in the Clipboard group of the Home tab. The Office Clipboard task pane will appear just to the left of the Navigation Pane.

To select an entire record to be copied or cut, click the row selector at the far left of the row. You can drag through the row selectors or press Shift+Up Arrow or Shift+Down Arrow to extend the selection to multiple rows. Click the Copy command or press Ctrl+C to copy the contents of multiple rows to the Clipboard. You can also click the Cut command or press Ctrl+X to delete the rows and copy them to the Clipboard.

You can open another table or query and paste the copied rows into that datasheet, or you can click Paste, then Paste Append in the Clipboard group on the Home tab to paste the rows at the end of the same datasheet. When you paste rows into another table, the rows you're adding must satisfy the validation rules of the receiving table, and the primary key values (if any) must be unique. If any validation fails, Access shows you an error message and cancels the paste. You cannot paste copies of entire records into the same table if the table has a primary key other than the AutoNumber data type. (You'll get a duplicate primary key value error if you try to do this.) When the primary key is AutoNumber, Access generates new primary key values for you.

The Cut command is handy for moving those records that you don't want in an active table to a backup table. You can have both tables open (or queries on both tables open) in Datasheet view at the same time. Simply cut the rows you want to move, switch to the backup table window, and paste the cut rows by using the Paste Append command.

When you paste one row, Access inserts the data and leaves your insertion point on the new record but doesn't save it. You can always click Undo on the Quick Access Toolbar to avoid saving the single pasted record. When you paste multiple rows, Access must save them all as a group before allowing you to edit further. Access asks you to confirm the paste operation. (See Figure 28-41.) Click Yes to proceed, or click No if you decide to cancel the operation.

Figure 28-41   This message box asks whether you want to proceed with a paste operation.

> **Note**
>
> You can't change the physical sequence of rows in a relational database by cutting rows from one location and pasting them in another location. Access always pastes new rows at the end of the current display. If you close the datasheet after pasting in new rows and then open it again, Access displays the rows in sequence by the primary key you defined. If you want to see rows in some other sequence, see "Sorting and Searching for Data" on page 957.

Deleting Rows

To delete one or more rows, select the rows using the row selectors and then press the Delete key. For details about selecting multiple rows, see the previous discussion on copying and pasting data. You can also use Ctrl+minus sign to delete the current or selected row. When you delete rows, Access 2007 gives you a chance to change your mind if you made a mistake. (See Figure 28-42.) Click Yes in the message box to delete the rows, or click No to cancel the deletion. Because this database has referential integrity rules defined between tblContacts and several other tables, you won't be able to delete contact records using qryContactsDatasheet. (Access shows you an error message telling you that related rows exist in other tables.) You would have to remove all related records from tblContactEvents, tblContactProducts, and tblCompanyContacts first.

> **CAUTION**
>
> After you click Yes in the confirmation message box, you cannot restore the deleted rows. You have to reenter them or copy them from a backup.

Figure 28-42   This message box appears when you delete rows.

Working with Hyperlinks

Microsoft Access 97 (also known as version 8.0) introduced the Hyperlink data type. The Hyperlink data type lets you store a simple or complex link to a file or document outside your database. This link pointer can contain a Uniform Resource Locator (URL) that points to a location on the World Wide Web or on a local intranet. It can also use a Universal Naming Convention (UNC) file name to point to a file on a server on your local area network (LAN) or on your local computer drives. The link might point to a file that is a Web page or in a format that is supported by an ActiveX application on your computer.

A Hyperlink data type is actually a memo field that can contain a virtually unlimited number of characters. The link itself can have up to four parts.

- An optional descriptor that Access displays in the field when you're not editing the link. The descriptor can start with any character other than a pound sign (#) and must have a pound sign as its ending delimiter. If you do not include the descriptor, you must start the link address with a pound sign.

- The link address expressed as either a URL (beginning with a recognized Internet protocol name such as http: or ftp:) or in UNC format (a file location expressed as \\server\share\path\file name). If you do not specify the optional descriptor field, Access displays the link address in the field. Terminate the link address with a pound sign (#).

- An optional subaddress that specifies a named location (such as a cell range in a Microsoft Excel spreadsheet or a bookmark in a Microsoft Word document) within the file. Separate the subaddress from the ScreenTip with a pound sign (#). If you entered no subaddress, you still must enter the pound sign delimiter if you want to define a ScreenTip.

- An optional ScreenTip that appears when you move your mouse pointer over the hyperlink.

For example, a hyperlink containing all four items might look like the following:

```
Viescas Download Page#http://www.viescas.com/Info/links.htm#Downloads
#Click to see the files you can download from Viescas.com
```

A hyperlink that contains a ScreenTip but no bookmark might look like this:

```
Viescas.com Books#http://www.viescas.com/Info/books.htm
##Click to see recommended books on Viescas.com
```

When you have a field defined using the Hyperlink data type, you work with it differently than with a standard text field. We included the Website field from tblContacts in the qryContactsDatasheet sample query (in ContactsDataCopy.accdb). Open the query and scroll to the right, if necessary, so that you can see the Website field, and place your mouse pointer over one of the fields that contains data, as shown in Figure 28-43.

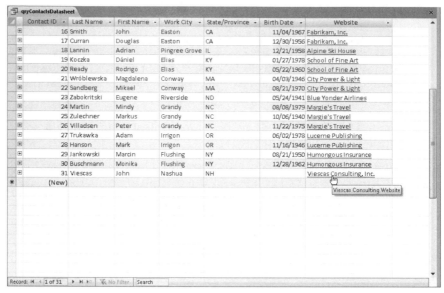

Figure 28-43 Place your mouse pointer over a hyperlink field in Datasheet view to show the hyperlink or the ScreenTip.

Activating a Hyperlink

Notice that the text in a hyperlink field is underlined and that the mouse pointer becomes a hand with a pointing finger when you move the pointer over the field. If you leave the pointer floating over the field for a moment, Access displays the ScreenTip. In the tblContacts table, the entries in the Website hyperlink field for some of the contacts contain pointers to Microsoft Web sites. When you click a link field, Access starts the application that supports the link and passes the link address and subaddress to the application. If the link starts with an Internet protocol, Access starts your Web browser. In the case of the links in the tblContacts table, all are links to pages on the Microsoft Web site. If you click one of them, your browser should start and display the related Web page, as shown in Figure 28-44.

Inserting a New Hyperlink

To insert a hyperlink in an empty hyperlink field, tab to the field or click in it with your mouse. If you're confident about the format of your link, you can type it, following the rules for the four parts noted earlier. If you're not sure, right-click inside the hyperlink field, select Hyperlink from the shortcut menu that appears, and then select Edit Hyperlink from the submenu to see the dialog box shown in Figure 28-45. This dialog box helps you correctly construct the four parts of the hyperlink.

The dialog box opens with Existing File Or Web Page selected in the Link To pane and Current Folder selected in the center pane, as shown in Figure 28-45. What you see in the list in the center pane depends on your current folder, the Web pages you've visited recently, and the files you've opened recently. You'll see a Look In list where you can navigate to any drive or folder on your system. You can also click the Browse The Web button (the button with a globe and a spyglass) to open your Web browser to find a Web site you want, or the Browse For File button (an open folder icon) to open the Link To File dialog box to find the file you want. Click Existing File Or Web Page and click the Recent Files option to see a list of files that you recently opened.

Figure 28-44 Here is the result of clicking a Web site link in the tblContacts table.

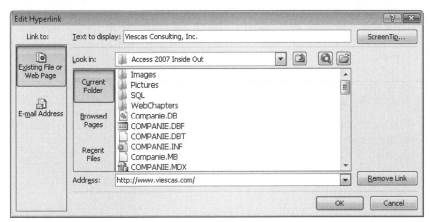

Figure 28-45 The dialog box used to insert a hyperlink shows you a list of files in the current folder.

We clicked the Browsed Pages option because we knew the hyperlink we wanted was a Web page that we had recently visited. You can enter the descriptor in the Text To Display box at the top. We clicked the ScreenTip button to open the Set Hyperlink Screen-Tip dialog box you see in Figure 28-46. You can type the document or Web site address directly into the Address box. (Yes, that's Jeff's real Web site address!)

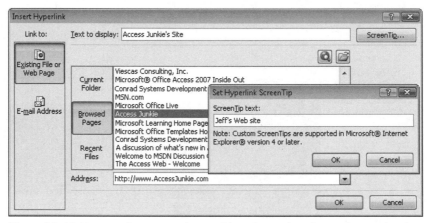

Figure 28-46 You can choose a Web site address from a list of recently visited Web sites.

The E-Mail Address button in the left pane lets you enter an e-mail address or choose from a list of recently used addresses. This generates a mailto: hyperlink that will invoke your e-mail program and start a new e-mail to the address you enter. You can also optionally specify a subject for the new e-mail by adding a question mark after the e-mail address and entering what you want to appear on the subject line.

Click OK to save your link in the field in the datasheet.

Editing an Existing Hyperlink

Getting into a hyperlink field to change the value of the link is a bit tricky. You can't simply click in a hyperlink field because that activates the link. What you can do is click in the field before the hyperlink and use the Tab key to move to the link field. Then press F2 to shift to character edit mode to edit the text string that defines the link. Figure 28-47 shows you a hyperlink field after following this procedure. You can use the arrow keys to move around in the text string to change one or more parts. In many cases, you might want to add an optional descriptor at the beginning of the link text, as shown in the figure.

The most comprehensive way to work with a hyperlink field is to right-click a link field to open a shortcut menu. Clicking Hyperlink on this menu displays a submenu with a number of options. You can edit the hyperlink (which opens the dialog box shown in Figure 28-45), open the link document, copy the link to the Clipboard, add the link to your list of favorites, change the text displayed in the field, or remove the hyperlink.

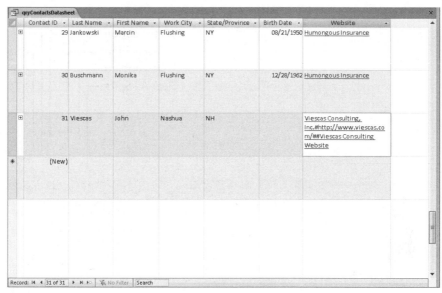

Figure 28-47 You can edit the text that defines a hyperlink directly in a datasheet.

Sorting and Searching for Data

When you open a table in Datasheet view, Access 2007 displays the rows sorted in sequence by the primary key you defined for the table. If you didn't define a primary key, you'll see the rows in the sequence in which you entered them in the table. If you want to see the rows in a different sequence or search for specific data, Access provides you with tools to do that. When you open a query in Datasheet view (such as the qryContactsDatasheet sample query we're using in this chapter), you'll see the rows in the order determined by sort specifications in the query. If you haven't specified sorting information, you'll see the data in the same sequence as you would if you opened the table or query in Datasheet view.

Sorting Data

Access 2007 provides several ways to sort data in Datasheet view. As you might have noticed, two handy Ribbon commands allow you to quickly sort the rows in a query or table datasheet in ascending or descending order. To see how this works, open the qryContactsDatasheet query, click anywhere in the Birth Date column, and click the Descending command in the Sort & Filter group on the Home tab. Access sorts the display to show you the rows ordered alphabetically by Birth Date, as shown in Figure 28-48.

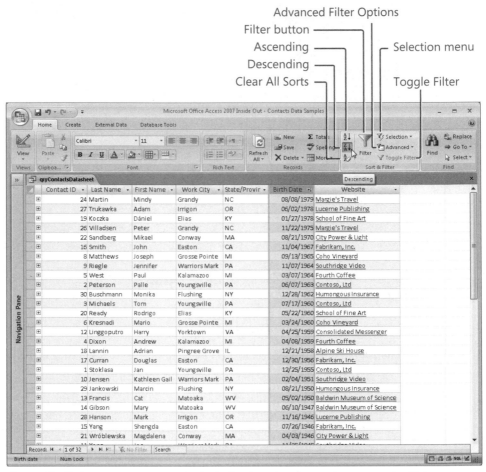

Figure 28-48 You can sort contacts by birth date by using the sort buttons on the Ribbon.

You can click the Ascending button to sort the rows in ascending order or click the Clear All Sorts button to return to the original data sequence. But before you change the sort or clear the sort, suppose you want to see contacts sorted by state or province ascending and then by birth date descending. You already have the data sorted by birth date, so click anywhere in the State/Province column and click the Ascending button to see the result you want as shown in Figure 28-49.

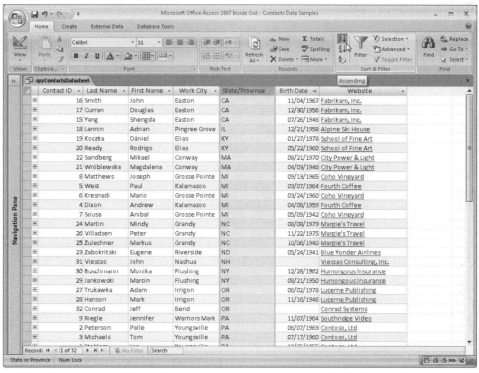

Figure 28-49 After applying the second sort, the records are now sorted by state or province ascending and then by birth date descending within state or province.

INSIDE OUT   Applying Multiple Sorts in Reverse Order

Notice that to sort by state or province and then birth date within state or province, you must first sort birth date and then sort state or province. We think that's backwards, but that's the way it works. If you had applied a sort on state or province first and then sorted birth date, you would have seen all the records in date order with any records having the same date subsequently sorted by state or province. If you want to sort on multiple fields, remember to apply the *innermost* sort first and then work your way outward.

Another way to sort more than one field is to use the Advanced Filter/Sort feature. Let's assume that you want to sort by State/Province, then by City within State/Province, and then by Last Name. Here's how to do it:

1. Click the Advanced button in the Sort & Filter group on the Home tab, and then click Advanced Filter/Sort. You'll see the Advanced Filter Design window (shown

Chapter 28

in Figure 28-50) with a list of fields in the qryContactsDatasheet query shown in the top part of the window.

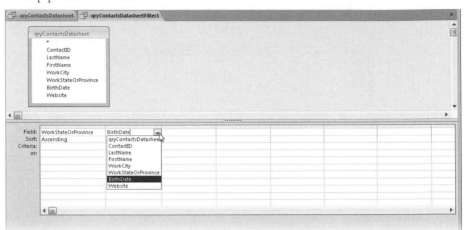

Figure 28-50 Select the fields you want to sort in the Advanced Filter Design window.

2. If you didn't click the Clear All Sorts button before opening this window, you should see the sorts you previously defined directly in Datasheet view on the WorkStateOrProvince and BirthDate fields. If so, click the bar above the BirthDate field to select it and then press the Delete key to remove the field.

3. Because you recently sorted by State/Province, the Advanced Filter Design window will show this field already added to the filter grid. If you skipped the sort step in Figure 28-48 or closed and reopened the datasheet without saving the sort, open the field list in the first column by clicking the arrow or by pressing Alt+Down Arrow on the keyboard. Select the WorkStateOrProvince field in the list. You can also place the WorkStateOrProvince field in the first column by finding WorkStateOrProvince in the list of fields in the top part of the window and dragging it into the Field row in the first column of the filter grid.

4. Click in the Sort row, immediately below the WorkStateOrProvince field, and select Ascending from the drop-down list.

5. Add the WorkCity and LastName fields to the next two columns, and select Ascending in the Sort row for both.

6. Click the Toggle Filter button in the Sort & Filter group of the Home tab on the Ribbon to see the result shown in Figure 28-51.

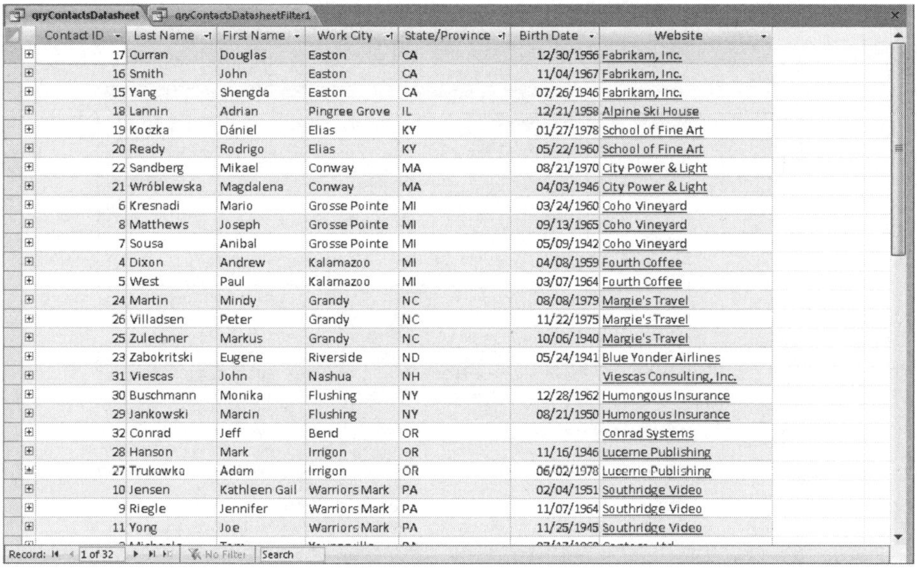

Contact ID	Last Name	First Name	Work City	State/Province	Birth Date	Website
17	Curran	Douglas	Easton	CA	12/30/1956	Fabrikam, Inc.
16	Smith	John	Easton	CA	11/04/1967	Fabrikam, Inc.
15	Yang	Shengda	Easton	CA	07/26/1946	Fabrikam, Inc.
18	Lannin	Adrian	Pingree Grove	IL	12/21/1958	Alpine Ski House
19	Koczka	Dániel	Elias	KY	01/27/1978	School of Fine Art
20	Ready	Rodrigo	Elias	KY	05/22/1960	School of Fine Art
22	Sandberg	Mikael	Conway	MA	08/21/1970	City Power & Light
21	Wróblewska	Magdalena	Conway	MA	04/03/1946	City Power & Light
6	Kresnadi	Mario	Grosse Pointe	MI	03/24/1960	Coho Vineyard
8	Matthews	Joseph	Grosse Pointe	MI	09/13/1965	Coho Vineyard
7	Sousa	Anibal	Grosse Pointe	MI	05/09/1942	Coho Vineyard
4	Dixon	Andrew	Kalamazoo	MI	04/08/1959	Fourth Coffee
5	West	Paul	Kalamazoo	MI	03/07/1964	Fourth Coffee
24	Martin	Mindy	Grandy	NC	08/08/1979	Margie's Travel
26	Villadsen	Peter	Grandy	NC	11/22/1975	Margie's Travel
25	Zulechner	Markus	Grandy	NC	10/06/1940	Margie's Travel
23	Zabokritski	Eugene	Riverside	ND	05/24/1941	Blue Yonder Airlines
31	Viescas	John	Nashua	NH		Viescas Consulting, Inc.
30	Buschmann	Monika	Flushing	NY	12/28/1962	Humongous Insurance
29	Jankowski	Marcin	Flushing	NY	08/21/1950	Humongous Insurance
32	Conrad	Jeff	Bend	OR		Conrad Systems
28	Hanson	Mark	Irrigon	OR	11/16/1946	Lucerne Publishing
27	Trukowko	Adam	Irrigon	OR	06/02/1978	Lucerne Publishing
10	Jensen	Kathleen Gail	Warriors Mark	PA	02/04/1951	Southridge Video
9	Riegle	Jennifer	Warriors Mark	PA	11/07/1964	Southridge Video
11	Yong	Joe	Warriors Mark	PA	11/25/1945	Southridge Video

Figure 28-51 After defining your sorts and clicking the Toggle Filter button, you can see the results of your sorting contact records by state or province, city, and then last name.

> **Note**
>
> If you compare Figure 28-49 with Figure 28-51, it looks like the records in Figure 28-49 were already sorted by city name within state. You might be tempted to leave out the sort on city in this exercise, but if you do that, you will not see the city names maintained in the same order. Remember, if you want data presented in a certain sequence, you must ask for it that way!

Close the qryContactsDatasheet window and click No when asked if you want to save design changes. We'll explore using the other options in the Sort & Filter group in the next sections.

Searching For and Filtering Data

If you want to look for data anywhere in your table, Access 2007 provides several powerful searching and filtering capabilities.

Using Find To begin this exercise, open the qryContactsDatasheet query in Datasheet view again. To perform a simple search on a single field, select that field, and then open the Find And Replace dialog box (shown in Figure 28-52) by clicking the Find command in the Find group on the Home tab or by pressing Ctrl+F.

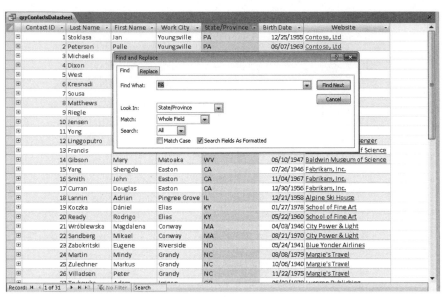

Figure 28-52 You can use the Find And Replace dialog box to search for data.

In the Find What text box, type the data that you want Access to find. You can include wildcard characters similar to those of the LIKE comparison operator. See "Defining Simple Field Validation Rules" on page 858 to perform a generic search. Use an asterisk (*) to indicate a string of unknown characters of any length (zero or more characters), and use a question mark (?) to indicate exactly one unknown character or a space. For example, *AB??DE* matches *Aberdeen* and *Tab idea* but not *Lab department*.

By default, Access searches the field that your insertion point was in before you opened the Find And Replace dialog box. To search the entire table, select the table or query name from the Look In list. By default, Access searches all records from the top of the recordset unless you change the Search list to search down or up from the current record position. Select the Match Case check box if you want to find text that exactly matches the uppercase and lowercase letters you typed. By default, Access is case-insensitive unless you select this check box.

The Search Fields As Formatted check box appears dimmed unless you select a field that has a format or input mask applied. You can select this check box if you need to search the data as it is displayed rather than as it is stored by Access. Although searching this way is slower, you probably should select this check box if you are searching a date/time field. For example, if you're searching a date field for dates in January, you can specify *-Jan-* if the field is formatted as Medium Date and you select the Search Fields As Formatted check box. You might also want to select this check box when searching a Yes/No field for Yes because any value except 0 is a valid indicator of Yes.

Click Find Next to start searching from the current record. Each time you click Find Next again, Access moves to the next value it finds, and loops to the top of the recordset to continue the search if you started in the middle. After you establish search criteria and you close the Find And Replace dialog box, you can press Shift+F4 to execute the search from the current record without having to open the dialog box again.

Filtering by Selection   If you want to see all the rows in your table that contain a value that matches one in a row in the datasheet grid, you can use the Selection command in the Sort & Filter group on the Home tab. Select a complete value in a field to see only rows that have data in that column that completely matches. Figure 28-53 shows the value PA selected in the State/Province column and the result after clicking the Selection button in the Sort & Filter group of the Home tab and clicking Equals "PA". If the filtering data you need is in several contiguous columns, click the first column, hold down the Shift key, and click the last column to select all the data; click the Selection button; and then click a filter option to see only rows that match the data in all the columns you selected.

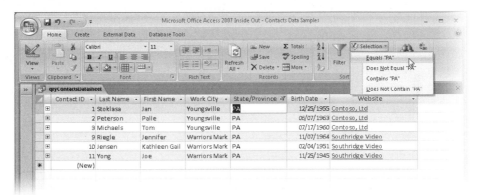

Figure 28-53 Here is the list of contacts in Pennsylvania, compiled using the Selection filter option.

Alternatively, if you want to see all the rows in your table that contain a part of a value that matches one in a row in the datasheet grid, you can select the characters that you want to match and use Selection. For example, to see all contacts that have the characters *ing* in their work city name, find a contact that has *ing* in the Work City field and select those characters. Click the Selection button in the Sort & Filter group of the Home tab, and then click Contains "ing". When the search is completed you should see only the three contacts who work in the cities named P*ing*ree Grove and Flush*ing*. To remove a filter, click the Toggle Filter button in the Sort & Filter group, or click Advanced in the Sort & Filter group and then click Clear All Filters.

> **Note**
>
> You can open any subdatasheet defined for the query and apply a filter there. If you apply a filter to a subdatasheet, you will filter all the subdatasheets that are open.

You can also add a filter to a filter. For example, if you want to see all contacts who live in Youngsville in Pennsylvania, find the value PA in the State/Province column, select it, click the Selection button in the Sort & Filter group of the Home tab, and then click Equals "PA". In the filtered list, find a row containing the word Youngsville in the Work City field, select the word, click the Selection button again, and click Equals "Youngsville". Access displays a small filter icon that looks like a funnel in the upper-right corner of each column that has a filter applied, as shown in Figure 28-54. If you rest your mouse on one of these column filter icons, Access displays a ScreenTip telling you what filter has been applied to that particular column. To remove all your filters, click the Toggle Filter button or click Advanced in the Sort & Filter group of the Home tab and click Clear All Filters.

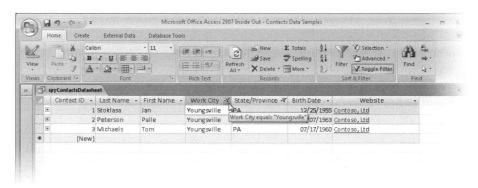

Figure 28-54 Access displays a ScreenTip on the filter icon in the column header to show you what filter is applied.

Using the Filter Window   To further assist you with filtering rows, Access 2007 provides a Filter window with predefined filter selections for various data types. Suppose you want to quickly filter the rows for contacts who have birthdays in the month of December. Click inside the Birth Date column in any row and then click the Filter button in the Sort & Filter group of the Home tab, and Access opens the Filter window for this field shown in Figure 28-55.

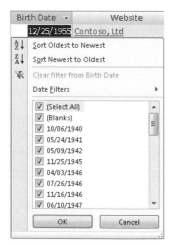

Figure 28-55 The Filter window for date/time fields displays filter criteria based on the dates entered in the field.

The Ascending and Descending buttons, discussed previously, are the first two options in the Filter window. (For a date/time field, Access shows you Sort Oldest To Newest and Sort Newest To Oldest. For a text field, Access shows you Sort A To Z and Sort Z To A, and for a numeric field, Access shows you Sort Smallest To Largest and Sort Largest to Smallest.) The third option, Clear Filter From Birth Date, removes all filters applied to the Birth Date field. The fourth option is Date Filters, which displays several submenus to the right that allow you to filter for specific date criteria. (For text fields, this option presents a list of text filters. For number fields, Access displays a list of the available numeric values.)

Beneath the Date Filters option is a list. The first two options in this list are the same for all data types. Select All selects all the options presented in the list. Blanks causes Access to search the field for any rows with no value entered—a Null value or an empty string. Beneath Select All and Blanks are every unique value entered into the Birth Date field for the current datasheet. If you select only one of these options, Access filters the rows that exactly match the value you choose.

In our example, to find all contacts who have a birthday in the month of December, click Date Filters, click All Dates In Period, and then you can filter the rows by an individual quarter or by a specific month. Click December and Access filters the rows to display only contacts who have birthdays in December, as shown in Figure 28-56.

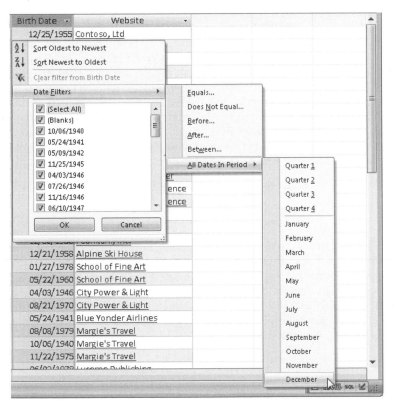

Figure 28-56 Date Filters presents built-in date filters for periods and months.

The result of this filter should return the four contacts who have birthdays in December as shown in Figure 28-57. Click the Toggle Filter button in the Sort & Filter group of the Home tab to remove the filter.

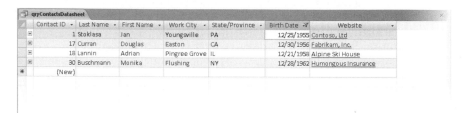

Figure 28-57 Four contacts in the table have birthdays in the month of December.

Using Filter By Form   Applying a filter using Selection is great for searching for rows that match *all* of several criteria (Last Name like "*son*" *and* State/Province equals "OR"), but what if you want to see rows that meet *any* of several criteria (Last Name like "*son" and State/Province equals "OR" or State/Province equals "PA")? You can use Filter By Form to easily build the criteria for this type of search.

When you click the Advanced button in the Sort & Filter group of the Home tab and click Filter By Form, Access 2007 shows you a Filter By Form example that looks like your datasheet but contains no data. If you have no filtering criteria previously defined, Access shows you the Look For tab and one Or tab at the bottom of the window. Move to each column in which you want to define criteria and either select a value from the drop-down list or type search criteria, as shown in Figure 28-58. Notice that each drop-down list shows you all the unique values available for each field, so it's easy to pick values to perform an exact comparison. You can also enter criteria, much the way that you did to create validation rules in Chapter 27. For example, you can enter *Like "*son*"* in the Last Name field to search for the letters *son* anywhere in the name. You can use criteria such as *>#01 JAN 1963#* in the Birth Date date/time field to find rows for contacts born after that date. You can enter multiple criteria on one line, but *all* the criteria you enter on a single line must be true for a particular row to be selected.

INSIDE OUT   Limiting the Returned Records

When your table or query returns tens of thousands of rows, fetching the values for each list in Filter By Form can take a long time. You can specify a limit by clicking the Microsoft Office Button and clicking Access Options. Select the Current Database category in the Access Options dialog box, and then scroll down to Filter Lookup Options For <name of your database>. In the Don't Display Lists Where More Than This Number Of Records Read option, you can specify a value for display lists to limit the number of discrete values returned. The default value is 1,000.

qryContactsDatasheet: Filter by Form
Contact ID
Last Name
First Name
Work City
State/Province
Birth Date
Website
Like "*son*"
"PA"
CA
IL
KY
MA
MI
NC
ND
NH
NY
OR
PA
VA
WV
Look for
Or
Or

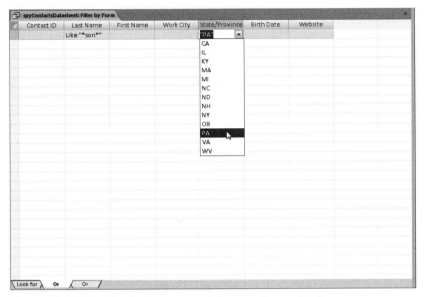

Figure 28-58 Use Filter By Form to search for one of several states.

If you want to see rows that contain any of several values in a particular column (for example, rows from several states), enter the first value in the appropriate column, and then click the Or tab at the bottom of the window to enter an additional criterion. In this example, "*OR*" was entered in the State/Province column on the Look For tab and "*PA*" on the first Or tab; you can see "PA" being selected for the first Or tab in Figure 28-58.

Each tab also specifies Like "*son*" for the last name. (As you define additional criteria, Access makes additional Or tabs available at the bottom of the window.) Figure 28-59 shows the result of applying these criteria when you click the Toggle Filter button in the Sort & Filter group of the Home tab.

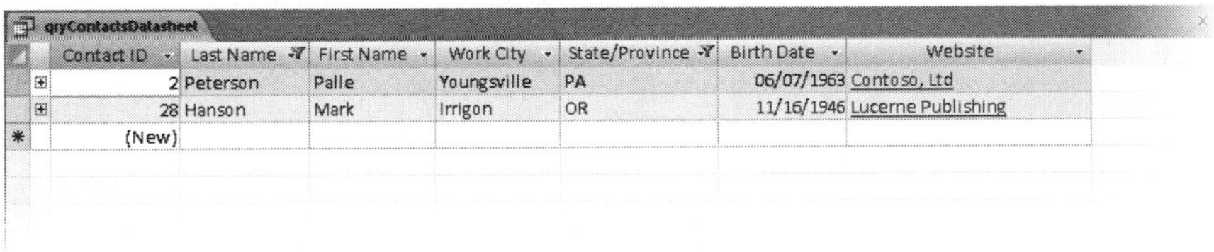

qryContactsDatasheet
Contact ID
Last Name
First Name
Work City
State/Province
Birth Date
Website
2 Peterson Palle Youngsville PA 06/07/1963 Contoso, Ltd
28 Hanson Mark Irrigon OR 11/16/1946 Lucerne Publishing
(New)

Figure 28-59 The contacts with names containing *son* in the states of OR and PA.

You can actually define very complex filtering criteria using expressions and the Or tabs in the Filter By Form window. If you look at the Filter By Form window, you can see that Access builds all your criteria in a design grid that looks similar to a Query window in Design view. In fact, filters and sorts use the query capabilities of Access to accomplish the result you want, so in Datasheet view you can use all the same filtering capabilities you'll find for queries.

INSIDE OUT

Saving and Reusing Your Filters

Access 2007 always remembers the last filtering and sorting criteria you defined for a datasheet. The next time you open the datasheet, click the Advanced button in the Sort & Filter group on the Home tab and click Filter By Form or Advanced to apply the last filter you created (as long as you replied Yes to the prompt to save formatting changes when you last closed the datasheet). If you want to save a particular filter/sort definition, click the Advanced button in the Sort & Filter group on the Home tab, click Save As Query, and give your filter a name. The next time you open the table, return to the Advanced button, and then click Load From Query to find the filter you previously saved.

Building a Form

From the perspective of daily use, forms are the most important objects you'll build in your Microsoft Office Access 2007 application because they're what users see and work with every time they run the application. This chapter shows you how to design and build forms in an Office Access 2007 desktop application. You'll learn how to work with a Form window in Design view to build a basic form based on a single table, and you'll learn how to use the Form Wizard to simplify the form-creation process. The last section of this chapter, "Simplifying Data Input with a Form," shows you how to use some of the special form controls to simplify data entry on your forms.

> **Note**
>
> The examples in this chapter are based on the forms, tables, and data in ContactsData-Copy.accdb on the companion CD included with this book. The results you see from the samples in this chapter might not exactly match what you see in this book if you have changed the sample data in the file. Also, all the screen images in this chapter were taken on a Microsoft Windows Vista system with the display theme set to Blue, and Use Windows-Themed Controls On Forms has been turned on in the sample databases. Your results might look different if you are using a different operating system or a different theme. We'll discuss the Use Windows-Themed Controls On Forms option later in this chapter.

Forms and Object-Oriented Programming

Access was not designed to be a full object-oriented programming environment, yet it has many characteristics found in object-oriented application development systems. Before you dive into building forms, it's useful to examine how Access implements objects and actions, particularly if you come from the world of procedural application development.

In classic procedural application development, the data you need for the application is distinct from the programs you write to work with the data and from the results produced by your programs. Each program works with the data independently and generally has little structural connection with other programs in the system. For example, an order entry program accepts input from a clerk and then writes the order to data files. Later, a billing program processes the orders and prints invoices. Another characteristic of procedural systems is that events must occur in a specific order and cannot be executed out of sequence. A procedural system has difficulty looking up supplier or price information while in the middle of processing an order.

In an object-oriented system, however, an object is defined as a subject that has *properties*, and you can invoke certain actions, or *methods*, to be performed on that subject. Objects can contain other objects. When an object incorporates another object, it inherits the attributes and properties of the other object and expands on the object's definition. In Access, queries define actions on tables, and the queries then become new logical tables known as *recordsets*. That is, a query doesn't actually contain any data, but you can work with the data fetched by the query as though it were a table. You can base a query on another query with the same effect. Queries inherit the integrity and formatting rules defined for the tables. Forms further define actions on tables or queries, and the fields you include in forms initially inherit the underlying properties, such as formatting and validation rules, of the fields in the source tables or queries. You can define different formatting or more restrictive rules, but you cannot override the rules defined for the tables.

Within an Access database, you can interrelate application objects and data. For example, you can set startup properties that prepare your application to run. As part of the application startup, you will usually open a switchboard form. The switchboard form might act on some of the data in the database, or it might offer controls that open other forms, print reports, or close the application.

Figure 29-1 shows the conceptual architecture of an Access form. In addition to operating on tables or queries in a database, forms can contain other forms, called *subforms*. These subforms can, in turn, define actions on other tables, queries, or forms. Events that occur in forms and subforms (such as changing the value of a field or moving to a new record) can trigger macro actions or Microsoft Visual Basic procedures. As you'll learn when you read about advanced form design, macro actions and Visual Basic procedures can be triggered in many ways. The most obvious way to trigger an action is by clicking a command button on a form. But you can also define macros or Visual Basic procedures that execute when an event occurs, such as clicking in a field, changing the data in a field, pressing a key, adding or deleting a row, or simply moving to a new row in the underlying table or query.

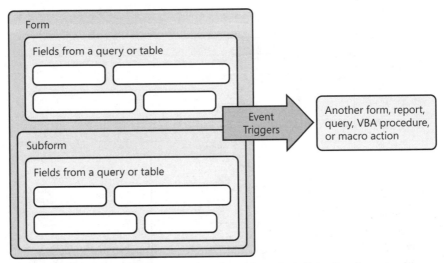

Figure 29-1 An Access form can contain other objects, including other forms, and you can set some of its properties to define procedures that respond to events.

Several of the more complex forms in the Conrad Systems Contacts and Housing Reservations sample databases are automated with Visual Basic. Figure 29-2 shows a few of the automated processes for the frmContacts form in the Conrad Systems Contacts database. For example, printing the contact currently displayed in the form is triggered by using a command button.

In addition to automating print options, code behind the frmContacts form automatically fills in the city and state when you enter a postal code and provides a graphical way to choose a date if you click the button next to a date. On the Events tab, when you enter a sale of a product to the contact, code automatically generates a product record.

Object-oriented systems are not restricted to a specific sequence of events. So a user entering a contact event in Access 2007 can open up a new form object in the Navigation Pane and start a search in a companies or products form window without having to first finalize or cancel work already in progress in frmContacts.

Clicking Print . . .

. . . opens the Contact Reports window.

Choosing a report option and clicking Print . . .

Typing a postal code automatically fills in the City and State fields.

Clicking a calendar icon opens a form to set the date graphically.

. . . opens the report.

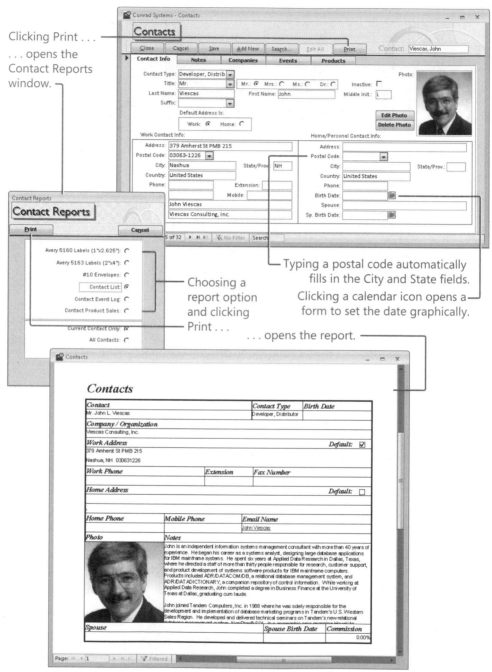

Figure 29-2 Some of the automated processes for the frmContacts form include opening a dialog box to choose a contacts report and automatically filling in the city and state when you enter a postal code.

Starting from Scratch—A Simple Input Form

To start, you'll create a simple form that accepts and displays data in the tblCompanies table in the Conrad Systems Contacts database. Later, you'll create a form for the tblProducts table in this same database by using the Form Wizard. To follow along in this section, open the ContactsDataCopy.accdb database.

Building a New Form with Design Tools

To begin building a new form that allows you to display and edit data from a table, you need to start with a blank Form window. You'll build this first form without the aid of the Form Wizard so that you'll understand the variety of components that go into form design. Click the Blank Form command in the Forms group on the Create tab. By default Access opens a blank Form window in Layout view with the field list displayed on the right, as shown in Figure 29-3.

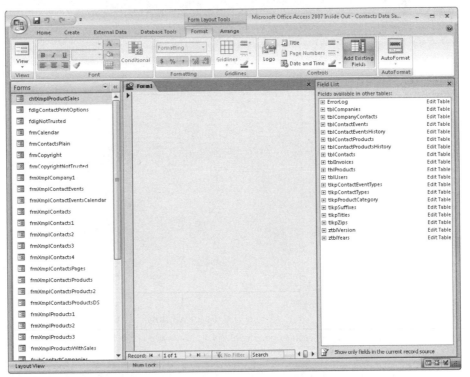

Figure 29-3 When you click the Blank Form command on the Ribbon, Access opens a new Form window in Layout view.

Access does not know at this point from which tables or queries you want to display and edit data. The field list on the right displays a list of each local or linked table. If you click the plus symbol next to the name of a table, Access expands the list and displays the name of every field in that table. You can click on a field name in the field list and drag and drop it onto your form. If you click the Edit Table hyperlink on the right side of the field list, Access opens that specific table in Design view.

When you ask Access to create a new blank form, Access initially displays the form in Layout view. To switch to Design view, click the arrow under the View button in the Views group and click Design View. Access switches the Form window to Design view and provides several design tools on the Design contextual tab under Form Design Tools on the Ribbon, as shown in Figure 29-4.

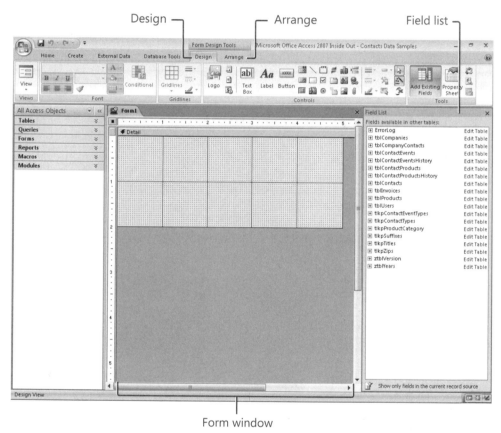

Figure 29-4 When you open a form in Design view you can use the form grid and tools to create your form elements.

Access starts with a form that has only a *Detail section*. The section has a grid on a background that is the color defined for 3-D objects in the Appearance Settings dialog box—usually a light gray or beige. You can click the edge of the Detail section and then drag the edge to make the section larger or smaller. (To see more of the grid you might also want to collapse the Navigation Pane on the left.) You can remove the grid dots from the Detail section by clicking the Show Grid command in the Show/Hide group on the Arrange tab under Form Design Tools. If you want to add a *Header section* or a *Footer section* to the form, click the Form Header/Footer command in the same Show/ Hide group.

Note

To set the color for 3-D objects, right-click on the desktop and then click Personalize. Click Windows Color And Appearance. In the Appearance Settings dialog box, click Advanced. In the Item list, click 3D Objects. Use the Color 1 list to set the color you want to use for 3-D objects.

The Detail section starts out at 5 inches (12.7 centimeters) wide by 2 inches (5.08 centimeters) high. The measurement gradations on the rulers are relative to the size and resolution of your screen. By default, Access sets the grid at 24 dots per inch horizontally and 24 dots per inch vertically. You can change the density of the grid dots by altering the Grid X and Grid Y properties in the form's property sheet. To replace the field list with the property sheet, click the Property Sheet command in the Tools group on the Design tab under Form Design Tools. You can find the Grid X and Grid Y properties near the bottom of the list on the Format tab of the property sheet when you have the form selected.

INSIDE OUT   Choosing a Form Width and Height

Although you can design a form that is up to 22 inches (55.87 centimeters) wide, and each form section can also be up to 22 inches high (a total of 66 inches if you include all three sections), you should design your forms to fit on your users' screens. We tend to design all our forms to comfortably fit on the lowest common screen resolution— 1024×768. A form to fit this size should be about 9.75 inches (24.8 centimeters) wide, and the sum of the heights of the sections should be about 5.6 inches (14.2 centimeters) to allow space for the Ribbon, status bar, and Windows taskbar. If your user has set a higher screen resolution, and your application is designed using overlapping windows, extra space will be available on the Access desktop to work with multiple form windows at a time. If you are using tabbed documents, extra space appears to the right and bottom of the form when the user opens it on a higher-resolution screen.

You can find a handy form, zsfrm1024x768, in several of the sample databases. When you're working in a higher resolution, you can open this form and overlay it on the form you're designing. If your form fits behind the sample form, your form should be displayed properly at the lowest common resolution.

The Grid X and Grid Y property settings determine the intervals per unit of measurement in the grid. You can enter a number from 1 (coarsest) through 64 (finest). You set the unit of measure (U.S. or metric) by default when you select a country on the Location tab in the Regional And Language Options dialog box. (You open this dialog box by first clicking Clock, Language, And Region in Control Panel and then clicking Regional And Language Options. If your Control Panel is set to Classic View, click Regional And Language Options.)

For example, if your unit of measurement is inches and you specify a Grid X setting of 10, Access divides the grid horizontally into 0.1-inch increments. When your measurement is in inches and you set the Grid X and Grid Y values to 24 or less, Access displays the grid dots on the grid. In centimeters, you can see the grid dots when you specify a setting of 9 or less. If you set a finer grid for either Grid X or Grid Y, Access won't display the grid dots but you can still use the grid to line up controls. Access always displays grid lines at 1-inch intervals (U.S.) or 1-centimeter intervals (metric), even when you set fine Grid X or Grid Y values.

Some Key Form Design Terms

As you begin to work in form design, you need to understand a few commonly used terms.

A form that displays data from your tables must have a record source. A *record source* can be the name of a table, the name of a query, or an SQL statement.

When a control can display information (text boxes, option groups, toggle buttons, option buttons, check boxes, combo boxes, list boxes, bound object frames, and many ActiveX controls), its *control source* defines the name of the field from the record source or the expression that provides the data to display. A control that has an expression as its control source is not updatable.

When a form has a record source, it is *bound* to the records in that record source—the form displays records from the record source and can potentially update the fields in the records. When a control is on a bound form and its control source is the name of a field in the record source, the control is *bound* to the field—the control displays (and perhaps allows you to edit) the data from the bound field in the current row of the record source. A control cannot be bound unless the form is also bound.

A form that has no record source is *unbound*. A control that has no control source is unbound.

Before proceeding further, you need to specify a record source for your new form. Although you can drag and drop fields from the field list and Access will figure out the appropriate record source for you, you have more control if you select a record source first. Click the All tab in the property sheet, click the arrow to the right of the Record Source property, and select the tblCompanies table from the list as shown in Figure 29-5.

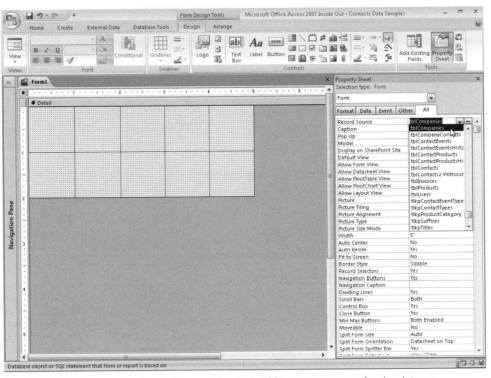

Figure 29-5 Select a record source to specify which table or query to use for the data on your form.

The following sections describe some of the tools you can use to design a form.

The Form Design Tools Contextual Ribbon Tabs

As you learned in Chapter 26, "Exploring the New Look of Access 2007," the Ribbon provides contextual tabs when Access displays objects in various views. When a form is in Design view, two contextual tabs appear—Design and Arrange under Form Design Tools. These contextual tabs, shown in Figure 29-6, are the "command center" of form design. These tabs provide all the essential tools and commands you need to design and modify your forms.

At the heart of these tabs is the Controls group found on the Design tab. This group contains buttons for all the types of controls you can use when you design a form. It also contains a button (named Insert ActiveX Control) that gives you access to all the ActiveX controls (for example, the calendar control that comes with Access) that you have installed on your system. To select a particular control to place on a form, click the control's button in the group. When you move the mouse pointer over the form, the mouse pointer turns into an icon that represents the control you selected. Position the mouse pointer where you want to place the control, and click the left mouse button to place the control on the form. If you want to size the control as you place it, drag the mouse pointer to make the control the size you want. (You can also size a control after you place it by dragging the sizing handles at its sides or corners.)

Figure 29-6 You can use the various commands on the two contextual tabs under Form Design Tools to create and edit your forms.

Top to bottom, left to right, the buttons in the Controls group are described in Table 29-1.

Table 29-1 Controls Group Buttons

Button	Description
Logo	**Logo.** Click this button to insert into a form a picture to be used as a logo displayed in an image control. (See the description of the image control later in this table.) When you click Logo, Access opens the Insert Picture dialog box where you can select the graphic or picture that you want to use as a logo. By default, Access places the logo in the form's Header section. If you have not revealed the form header and footer, the command adds those sections to your form before inserting the logo in the Header section.
	Title. Click this button to insert a new label control in a form's Header section to be used as a title for the form. (See the description of the label control later in this table.) If you have not revealed the form header and footer, the command adds those sections to your form before inserting the label control in the Header section.
	Insert Page Number. Click this button to open the Page Numbers dialog box where you can choose to insert page numbers in the Page Header or Page Footer section of the form in text box controls. (See the description of the text box control later in this table.) The Page Header and Page Footer sections appear only when you print the form.
	Date & Time. Click this button to open the Date And Time dialog box where you can choose to insert the date, the time, or both the date and time displayed in text box controls in the form's Header section. (See the description of the text box control later in this table.) You can choose different formats for both the date and time. If you have not revealed the form header and footer, the command adds those sections to your form before inserting the text box controls in the Header section.
ab| Text Box	**Text Box.** Click this button to create text box controls for displaying text, numbers, dates, times, and memo fields. You can bind a text box to one of the fields in an underlying table or query. If you let a text box that is bound to a field be updated, you can change the value in the field in the underlying table or query by entering a new value in the text box. You can also use a text box to display calculated values.

Button	Description
	Label. Click this button to create label controls that contain fixed text. By default, controls that can display data have a label control automatically attached. You can use this command to create stand-alone labels for headings and for instructions on your form.
	Button. Click this button to create a command button control that can activate a macro or a Visual Basic procedure. You can also specify a hyperlink address that Access opens when a user clicks the button.
	Combo Box. Click this button to create a combo box control that contains a list of potential values for the control and an editable text box. To create the list, you can enter values for the Row Source property of the combo box. You can also specify a table or a query as the source of the values in the list. Access displays the currently selected value in the text box. When you click the arrow to the right of the combo box, Access displays the values in the list. Select a new value in the list to reset the value in the control. If you bind the combo box to a field in the underlying table or query, you can change the value in the field by selecting a new value in the list. If you bind the combo box to a multi-value field, Access displays the list with check boxes to allow the user to select multiple values. You can bind multiple columns to the list, and you can hide one or more of the columns in the list by setting a column's width to 0. You can bind the actual value in the control to such a hidden column. When a multiple-column list is closed, Access displays the value in the first column whose width is greater than 0. Access displays all nonzero-width columns when you open the list.
	List Box. Click this button to create a list box control that contains a list of potential values for the control. To create the list, you can enter the values in the Row Source property of the list box. You can also specify a table or a query as the source of the values in the list. List boxes are always open, and Access highlights the currently selected value in the list box. You select a new value in the list to reset the value in the control. If you bind the list box to a field in the underlying table or query, you can change the value in the field by selecting a new value in the list. If you bind the list box to a multi-value field, Access displays the list with check boxes to allow the user to select multiple values. You can bind multiple columns to the list, and you can hide one or more of the columns in the list by setting a column's width to 0. You can bind the actual value in the control to such a hidden column. Access displays all nonzero-width columns that fit within the defined width of the control. If the list box control is unbound, you can allow the user to select multiple values in the list (also called a multiple-selection list box).
	Subform/Subreport. Click this button to embed another form in the current form. You can use the subform to show data from a table or a query that is related to the data in the main form. Access maintains the link between the two forms for you.
	Line. Click this button to add lines to a form to enhance its appearance.

Chapter 29

Button	Description
	Rectangle. Click this button to add filled or empty rectangles to a form to enhance its appearance.
	Bound Object Frame. Click this button to display and edit an OLE object field from the underlying data. Access can display most pictures and graphs directly on a form. For other objects, Access displays the icon for the application in which the object was created. For example, if the object is a sound object created in Windows Sound Recorder, you'll see a speaker icon on your form.
	Option Group. Click this button to create option group controls that contain one or more toggle buttons, option buttons, or check boxes. (See the descriptions of these controls later in this table.) You can assign a separate numeric value to each button or check box that you include in the group. When you have more than one button or check box in a group, you can select only one button or check box at a time, and the value assigned to that button or check box becomes the value for the option group. If you have incorrectly assigned the same value to more than one button or check box, all buttons or check boxes that have the same value appear highlighted when you click any of them. You can select one of the buttons or check boxes in the group as the default value for the group. If you bind the option group to a field in the underlying query or table, you can set a new value in the field by selecting a button or a check box in the group.
	Check Box. Click this button to create a check box control that holds an on/off, a true/false, or a yes/no value. When you select a check box, its value becomes –1 (to represent on, true, or yes), and a check mark appears in the box. Select the check box again, and its value becomes 0 (to represent off, false, or no), and the check mark disappears from the box. You can include a check box in an option group and assign the check box a unique numeric value. If you create a group with multiple controls, selecting a new check box clears any previously selected toggle button, option button, or check box in that group (unless other buttons or check boxes in the group also have the same value). If you bind the check box to a field in the underlying table or query, you can toggle the field's value by clicking the check box.
	Option Button. Click this button to create an option button control (sometimes called a radio button control) that holds an on/off, a true/false, or a yes/no value. When you select an option button, its value becomes –1 (to represent on, true, or yes), and a filled circle appears in the center of the button. Select the button again, and its value becomes 0 (to represent off, false, or no), and the filled circle disappears. You can include an option button in an option group and assign the button a unique numeric value. If you create a group with multiple controls, selecting a new option button clears any previously selected toggle button, option button, or check box in that group (unless other buttons or check boxes in the group also have the same value). If you bind the option button to a field in the underlying table or query, you can toggle the field's value by clicking the option button.

Button	Description
	Toggle Button. Click this button to create a toggle button control that holds an on/off, a true/false, or a yes/no value. When you click a toggle button, its value becomes –1 (to represent on, true, or yes), and the button appears pressed in. Click the button again, and its value becomes 0 (to represent off, false, or no). You can include a toggle button in an option group and assign the button a unique numeric value. If you create a group with multiple controls, selecting a new toggle button clears any previously selected toggle button, option button, or check box in that group (unless other buttons or check boxes in the group also have the same value). If you bind the toggle button to a field in the underlying table or query, you can toggle the field's value by clicking the toggle button.
	Tab Control. Click this button to create a series of tab pages on your form. Each page can contain a number of other controls to display information. The tab control works much like many of the option dialog boxes or property sheet windows in Access—when a user clicks a different tab, Access displays the controls contained on that tab.
	Insert Page. Click this button to add an additional tab page to your tab control. By default Access creates two pages for a new tab control object. Click on your tab control object on the design grid and then click the Insert Page command to add an additional tab page.
	Insert Chart. Click this button to add a chart on your form grid. Clicking this button and then placing the control on your form launches the Chart Wizard to walk you through the steps necessary to create a new chart.
	Unbound Object Frame. Click this button to add an object from another application that supports object linking and embedding. The object becomes part of your form, not part of the data from the underlying table or query. You can add pictures, sounds, charts, or slides to enhance your form. When the object is a chart, you can specify a query as the source of data for the chart, and you can link the chart display to the current record in the form by one or more field values.
	Image. Click this button to place a static picture on your form. You cannot edit the picture on the form, but Access stores it in a format that is very efficient for application speed and size. If you want to use a picture as the entire background of your form, you can set the form's Picture property.
	Insert Or Remove Page Break. Click this button to add a page break between the pages of a multiple-page form. (We think this tool is misnamed. To remove a page break, you must select the page break control and press the Delete key.)
	Insert Hyperlink. Click this button to add a hyperlink in a label control to your form design grid. This hyperlink can contain a Uniform Resource Locator (URL) that points to a location on the World Wide Web, on a local intranet, or on a local drive. It can also use a Universal Naming Convention (UNC) file name to point to a file on a server on your local area network (LAN) or on your local computer drives. The link might point to a file that is a Web page or even another object in your current database. Clicking this button opens the Insert Hyperlink dialog box.

Chapter 29

Button	Description
	Attachment. Click this button to insert an attachment control on the form design grid. You can bind this control to an attachment field in the underlying data. You can use this control, for example, to display a picture or to attach other files. In Form view this control presents the Manage Attachments dialog box where you can attach, delete, and view multiple attachment files stored in the underlying field.
	Line Thickness menu. Use this drop-down menu to change the selected line thickness. The available options are Hairline, 1pt, 2pt, 3pt, 4pt, 5pt, and 6pt.
	Line Type menu. Use this drop-down menu to change the selected line type. The available options are Transparent, Solid, Dashes, Short Dashes, Dots, Sparse Dots, Dash Dot, and Dash Dot Dot.
	Line Color menu. Use this drop-down menu to change the selected line color. You can choose from predefined color schemes or create a custom color from the Color Picker dialog box.
	Special Effect menu. Use this drop-down menu to change the look of the control to flat, raised, sunken, etched, shadowed, or chiseled.
	Set Control Defaults. Click this button if you want to change the default property settings for all new controls of a particular type. Select a control of that type, set the control's properties to the desired default values, and then click the Set Control Defaults command. The settings of the currently selected control become the default settings for any subsequent definitions of that type of control on your form.
	Select All. Click this button to select all the controls on the form design grid.
	Select. Click this button to select, size, move, and edit existing controls. This is the default command when you first open a form in Design view. This button becomes selected again after you have used one of the control commands to place a new control on your form.
	Use Control Wizards. Click this button to activate a control wizard. Click the button again to deactivate the wizard. When this button appears pressed in, a control wizard helps you enter control properties whenever you create a new option group, combo box, list box, or command button. The Combo Box and List Box Wizards also offer you an option to create Visual Basic code to move to a new record based on a selection the user makes in the combo or list box. The Command Button Wizard offers to generate Visual Basic code that performs various automated actions when the user clicks the button.
	Insert ActiveX Control. Click this button to open a dialog box showing all the ActiveX controls you have installed on your system. You can select one of the controls and then click OK to add the control to the form design grid. Not all ActiveX controls work with Access.

INSIDE OUT **Locking a Control Button**

When you click a button that is a form control, your mouse pointer reverts to the Select button after you place the selected control on your form. If you plan to create several controls using the same tool—for example, a series of check boxes in an option group—double-click the button for that control in the Controls group to "lock" it. You can unlock it by clicking any other button (including the Select button).

The Field List

Use the field list in conjunction with the Controls group to place bound controls (controls linked to fields in a table or a query) on your form. You can open the field list by clicking the Add Existing Fields button in the Tools group on the Design tab. If the form is bound to a table or query, Access displays the name of the underlying table or query along with all the fields available, as shown in Figure 29-7. Any tables that have relationships to the underlying table defined are displayed under Fields Available In Related Tables. The last section of the field list, Fields Available In Other Tables, lists the tables and fields from all other tables in this database. Click the Show Only Fields In The Current Record Source link to remove the bottom two sections of the field list. You can undock the field list by clicking the title bar and dragging it away from the right edge of the Form window. After you undock the field list, you can drag the edges of the window to resize it so that you can see any long field names. You can drag the title bar to move the window out of the way. When the list of available field names is too long to fit in the current size of the window, use the vertical scroll bar to move through the list.

To use the field list to place a bound control on a form, first click the button for the type of control you want in the Controls group. Then drag the field you want from the field list and drop it into position on the form. If you click the button for a control that's inappropriate for the data type of the field, Access selects the default control for the data type. For example, if you click anything but the Attachment button when placing an attachment field on a form, Access creates an attachment control for you anyway. If you try to drag any field after clicking the button for the subform/subreport, unbound object frame, line, rectangle, or page break control, Access creates a text box control or bound object frame control, as appropriate, instead. If you drag a field from the field list without clicking a control, Access uses either the display control you defined for the field in the table definition or a control appropriate for the field data type.

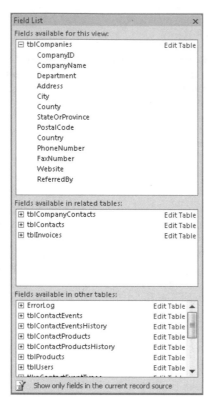

Figure 29-7 The field list shows the names of the fields in the bound table or query, any related tables, and fields from all other tables in the current database.

The Property Sheet

The form, each section of the form (header, detail, footer), and each control on the form have a list of properties associated with them, and you set these properties using a property sheet. Each control on a form, each section on a form, and the form itself are all *objects*. The kinds of properties you can specify vary depending on the object. To open the property sheet for an object, select the object and then click the Property Sheet button in the Tools group on the Design tab. Access opens a window similar to the one shown in Figure 29-8 on the right side of the Form window, replacing the field list. (You cannot have both the property sheet and the field list open at the same time.) If you have previously undocked either the field list or property sheet, the property sheet appears in the undocked window. If the property sheet is already open, you can view the properties specific to an object by clicking the object. You can also click the arrow under Selection Type and then select the object name from the list at the top of the property sheet.

Figure 29-8 You can view the properties of form controls and sections using the property sheet.

You can drag the title bar to move the property sheet around on your screen. You can also drag the edges of the window to resize it so that you can see more of the property settings. Because a form has more than 100 properties that you can set and because many controls have more than 70 properties, Access provides tabs at the top of the property sheet so that you can choose to display all properties (the default) or to display only format properties, data properties, event properties, or other properties. A form property sheet displaying only the data properties is shown in Figure 29-9.

When you click in a property box that provides a list of valid values, a small arrow appears on the right side of the property box. Click this arrow to see a list of the values for the property. For properties that can have a very long value setting, you can click the property and then press Shift+F2 to open the Zoom dialog box. The Zoom dialog box provides an expanded text box for entering or viewing a value.

Figure 29-9 If you click the Data tab on the form property sheet, Access displays only the data properties.

Build

In many cases, a window, dialog box, or wizard is available to help you create property settings for properties that can accept a complex expression, a query definition, or code (a macro or a Visual Basic procedure) to respond to an event. When such help is available for a property setting, Access displays a small button with an ellipsis next to the property box when you select the property; this is the Build button. If you click the Build button, Access responds with the appropriate window, dialog box, or wizard.

For example, suppose that you want to see the companies displayed in this form in ascending order by company name. The easiest way to accomplish this is to create a query that includes the fields from tblCompanies sorted on the CompanyName field, and then specify that query as the *Record Source* property for the form. To start, display the property sheet for the form, click the Data tab to display the form's data properties, click in the Record Source property box, and then click the Build button next to Record Source to start the Query Builder. Access asks whether you want to build a new query based on the table that is currently the source for this form. If you click Yes, Access opens a new Query window in Design view with the tblCompanies field list displayed in the upper part of the window and the property sheet open either in an undocked window or to the right, as shown in Figure 29-10.

> **Note**
>
> Unlike previous releases, after you open the property sheet in table, query, form, or report Design view, the window will be open for all objects in Design view until you close it. Likewise, if you close the property sheet in Design view, the window will be closed for all other objects in Design view until you reopen it.

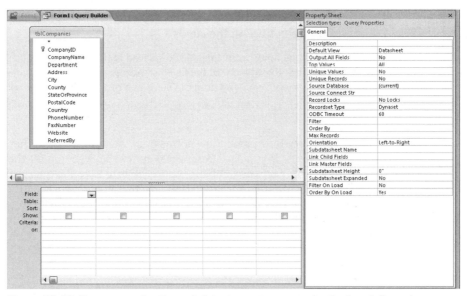

Figure 29-10 You can use the Query Builder to create a query for the form's Record Source property.

You'll need all the fields in the tblCompanies table for this form, so select them and drag them to the design grid. For the CompanyName field, specify Ascending as the sorting order. Close the property sheet for now by clicking the Close button on its title bar. Your Query Builder window should look like the window shown in Figure 29-11.

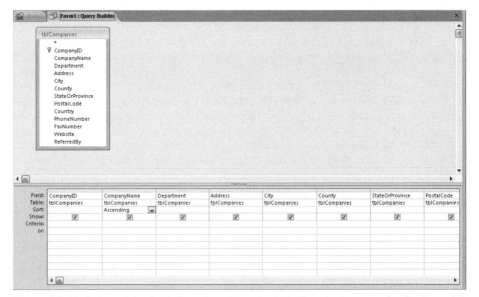

Figure 29-11 Select all the fields from the table to include them in the query for the Record Source property of the form.

INSIDE OUT **Selecting All the Fields**

To easily select all the fields from a field list displayed in the upper part of the Query window, double-click the title bar of the field list. Access highlights all the fields for you. Then simply click any of them and drag the fields as a group to the design grid.

If you close the Query Builder window at this point, Access asks whether you want to update the property. If you click Yes, Access stores the SQL text for the query in the Record Source property box. A better approach is to save the query and give it a name, such as qryCompaniesSortedByName. Do that now by clicking the Save As command in the Close group on the Design contextual tab under Query Tools, entering **qryCompaniesSortedByName** in the Save As dialog box, and then clicking OK. Now when you close the query, Access asks whether you want to save the query and update the property. Click Yes, and Access places the name of the query (rather than the SQL text) in the property sheet.

Building a Simple Input Form for the tblCompanies Table

Now let's create a simple input form for the tblCompanies table in the Conrad Systems Contacts database. If you've followed along to this point, you should have a blank form based on the qryCompaniesSortedByName query that you created using the Query Builder. If you haven't followed along, click the Blank Form command in the Forms group on the Create tab.

Click the arrow under View in the Views group on the Design tab and click Design View to switch from Layout view to Design view. You'll see the Form window in Design view and a set of design tools, as shown earlier in Figure 29-4. If necessary, open the property sheet by clicking the Property Sheet command in the Tools group of the Design tab under Form Design Tools. By default this new form is unbound, so click the Record Source property, click the arrow that appears next to the property box, and select tblCompanies from the list. Now the form is bound to the tblCompanies table, but we want to change the record source to a saved query based on the tblCompanies table. Select the Record Source property again, click the Build button, and follow the procedures discussed in the previous sections, whose results are shown in Figures 29-10 and 29-11; this will create the query you need and make it the source for the form.

In the blank form that now has the qryCompaniesSortedByName query as its record source, drag the bottom of the Detail section downward to make some room to work. All the fields in tblCompanies are defined to be displayed with a text box, so you don't need to click a button in the Controls group. If you'd like to practice, though, double-click the Text Box button in the Controls group before dragging fields from the field list. If the field list is not displayed, click the Add Existing Fields button in the Tools group on the Design tab. You can drag fields (for this exercise, all except the ReferredBy field) one at a time to the Detail section of the form, or you can click the first field (CompanyID), hold down the Shift key, and click the last field (Website) to select them all. After you drag and drop the fields, your form should now look something like the one shown in Figure 29-12. If you double-clicked the Text Box button to select it for multiple operations, click the Select button to unlock the selection.

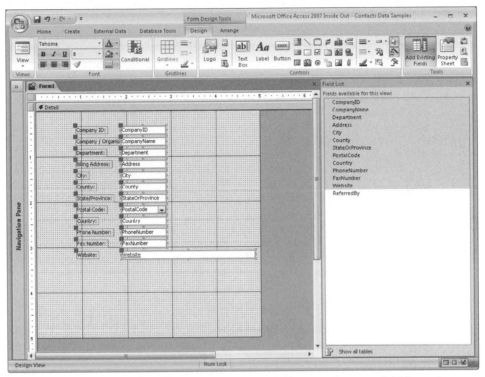

Figure 29-12 You can drag the fields from the qryCompaniesSortedByName field list to place these text box controls on the form design grid.

INSIDE OUT   Use the Shift or the Ctrl Key to Select Multiple Fields

A quick way to place several successive fields on a form is to click the first field you want in the field list, scroll down until you see the last field you want, and then hold down the Shift key while you click the last field. This procedure selects all the fields between the first and last fields you clicked. Holding down the Ctrl key and clicking several noncontiguous fields works, too. If you include a field in error, hold down the Ctrl key and click the selected field that you don't want. Click any of the selected fields and drag the fields as a group to the Detail section of the form. This has the added benefit of lining up all the controls in a vertical column.

When you position the field icon that you've dragged from the field list, the upper-left corner of the new text box will be at the position of the mouse pointer when you release the mouse button. Note that the default text box control has a label control automatically attached to display the bound field's Caption property (or the field name if the field does not have a caption), positioned 1 inch to the left of the text box. Also, in Design view, the label control displays its Caption property, and the text box control displays its Control Source property (the name of the field to which it is bound).

You should drop each text box about 1.25 inches (3 centimeters) from the left edge of the Detail section to leave room to the left of the text box for Access to place the control labels. If you don't leave room, the text boxes will overlap the labels. Even if you do leave room, if a caption is too long to fit in the 1-inch space between the default label and the default text box (for example, Company / Organization in Figure 29-12), the text box will overlap the label.

If you selected multiple fields in the field list and added them all with one drag-and-drop action, when you click the Property Sheet button immediately after adding the fields, the property sheet indicates that you have selected multiple controls. (In this example, we dragged all the selected fields to the Detail section at one time.) Whenever you select multiple controls on a form in Design view, Access displays the properties that are common to all the controls you selected. If you change a property in the property sheet while you have multiple controls selected, Access makes the change to all the selected controls.

Moving and Sizing Controls

By default, Access creates text boxes that are 1 inch wide (except for Hyperlink and Memo fields). For some of the fields, 1 inch is larger than necessary to display the field value—especially if you are using the default 8-point font size. For other fields, the text box isn't large enough. You probably also want to adjust the location of some of the controls.

To change a control's size or location, you usually have to select the control first. Be sure that you have clicked the Select button in the Controls group on the Design tab. Click the control you want to resize or move, and moving and sizing handles appear around the control. The handles are small boxes that appear at each corner of the control—except at the upper-left corner, where the larger handle indicates that you cannot use it for sizing. In Figure 29-12, handles appear around all the text boxes because they are all selected. To select just one control, click anywhere in the design area where there is no control; this changes the selection to the Detail section. Then click the control you want. If the control is wide enough or high enough, Access provides additional handles at the midpoints of the edges of the control.

To change the size of a control, you can use the sizing handles on the edges, in either of the lower corners, or in the upper-right corner of the control. When you place the mouse pointer over one of these sizing handles, the pointer turns into a double arrow, as shown in Figure 29-13. With the double-arrow pointer, drag the handle to resize the control. You can practice on the form by shortening the CompanyID text box so that it's 0.5 inch long. You need to stretch the company name, department, and address fields until they are each about 1.75 inches long. You might also want to reduce the state or province field to display two characters and decrease the Web site field to 1.75 inches.

Figure 29-13 You can drag a corner handle of a selected control to change the control's width or height or both.

To move a control that is not currently selected, click the control and drag it to a new location. After you click a control, you can move it by placing your mouse pointer anywhere between the handles along the edge of the control. When you do this, the mouse pointer turns into a pointer with a four arrow crosshair, as shown in Figure 29-14, and you can then drag the control to a new location. Access displays an outline of the control as you move the control to help you position it correctly. When a control has an attached label, moving either the control or the label in this way moves both of them.

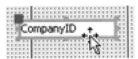

Figure 29-14 You can drag the edge of a selected control to move the control.

You can position a control and its attached label independently by dragging the larger handle in the upper-left corner of the control or label. When you position the mouse pointer over this handle, the pointer again turns into a pointer with a four arrow crosshair, as shown in Figure 29-15. Drag the control to a new location relative to its label.

Figure 29-15 You can drag the large handle of a selected control to move the control independently of its label.

You can delete a label from a control by selecting the label and pressing the Delete key. If you want to create a label that is independent of a control, you can click the Label button. If you inadvertently delete a label from a control and you've made other changes so that you can no longer undo the deletion, you can attach a new label by doing the following:

1. Click the Label button in the Controls group on the Design tab to create a new unattached label.

2. Select the label, and then click the Cut command in the Clipboard group on the Home tab to move the label to the Clipboard.

3. Select the control to which you want to attach the label, and then click the Paste command in the Clipboard group.

Chapter 29

The Font Group

The Font group on the Design tab under Form Design Tools, shown in Figure 29-16, provides a quick and easy way to alter the appearance of a control by allowing you to click buttons rather than set properties. Select the object you want to format and then click the appropriate button in the Font group. The Font group is also handy for setting background colors for sections of the form. Table 29-2 describes each of the buttons in this group.

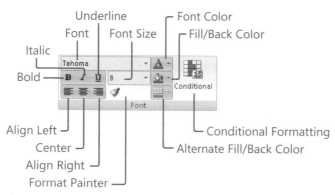

Figure 29-16 The Font group provides you with tools to change the appearance of form controls.

Table 29-2 Font Group Buttons

Button	Description
Font	Use to set the font for labels, text boxes, command buttons, toggle buttons, combo boxes, and list boxes.
Bold	Click to set font style to bold. Click again to remove bold.
Italic	Click to set font style to italic. Click again to remove italic.
Underline	Click to underline text. Click again to remove underline.
Font Size	Use to set font size.
Align Left	Click to left align text.
Center	Click to center text.
Align Right	Click to right align text.
Format Painter	Use to copy formatting from one control to another control.
Font Color	Use to set the font color of the control.
Fill/Back Color	Use to set the background color of the control or form area. You can also set the background color to transparent.
Alternate Fill/ Back Color	Use to set a background color for alternating rows for forms displayed in Datasheet, Split Form, or Continuous Form view.
Conditional Formatting	Use to define dynamic modification of the formatting of text boxes and combo boxes by testing the value in the control, by comparing values in one or more fields, or when the control has the focus.

INSIDE OUT   Using the Alignment Buttons

You can click only one of the alignment buttons—Align Left, Align Right, or Center—at a time. If you do not click a button, alignment is set to General—text data aligns left and numeric data aligns right. You can also set the Text Align property in the property sheet.

Depending on the object you select, some of the Font group options might not be available. For example, you can't set text color on an attachment or a bound object frame control. If you have the property sheet open and you scroll through it so that you can see the properties the Font group sets, you can watch the settings in the property sheet change as you click different options in the Font group.

Setting Border Color, Type, Line Thickness, and Special Effect

You can find a special set of commands at the right end of the Controls group on the Design tab below Form Design Tools to further customize the look of the controls on your form, as shown in Figure 29-17. Table 29-3 explains each of these buttons.

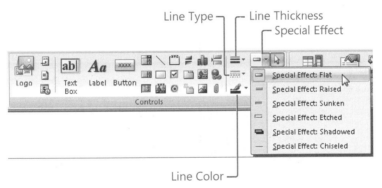

Figure 29-17 You can use commands in the Controls group on the Design tab to customize the borders of your controls.

Table 29-3 Border Formatting Commands for Controls

Button	Description
Line Thickness	When Special Effect is set to Flat (see below), use this command to set the border width from hairline to 6 points wide.
Line Type	You can make the border transparent or specify a border that is a solid line, dashes, short dashes, dots, sparse dots, dash dot, or dash dot dot.
Line Color	Use this command to set the border color of the control. You can also set the border color to transparent.
Special Effect	(Shown with list of options open.) You can set the look of the control to flat, raised, sunken, etched, shadowed, or chiseled.

Chapter 29

Depending on the object you select, some of the Controls group options might not be available. For example, you can't set the border color on a toggle button or command button because the color is always set to gray for this kind of control. If you have the property sheet open and you scroll through it so that you can see the properties these border commands set, you can watch the settings in the property sheet change as you click different options in the group.

Setting Text Box Properties

The next thing you might want to do is change some of the text box properties. Figure 29-18 shows some of the properties for the CompanyID text box control. Because the CompanyID field in the tblCompanies table is an AutoNumber field, which a user cannot change, you should change the properties of this control to prevent it from being selected on the form. Access provides two properties that you can set to control what the user can do. The *Enabled* property determines whether the control can receive the focus (the user can click in or tab to the control). The *Locked* property determines whether the user can enter data in the control. The defaults are Enabled Yes and Locked No.

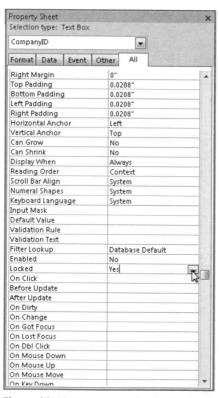

Figure 29-18 You can set the Enabled and Locked properties of the CompanyID text box control so that users cannot click into that control.

You can set the Enabled property of the control to No so that the user cannot click in or tab to the control. When you do this, Access prohibits access to the field but causes the control and its label to appear dimmed because the control is not locked. (When Access sees that a control is disabled but is still potentially updatable despite being bound to an AutoNumber, it causes the control to appear dimmed.) To display the control and its label normally, just set Locked to Yes.

If you specify a Format, Decimal Places, or Input Mask property setting when you define a field in a table, Access copies these settings to any text box that you bind to the field. Any data you enter using the form must conform to the field validation rule defined in the table; however, you can define a more restrictive rule for this form. Any new row inherits default values from the table unless you provide a different default value in the property sheet. The Status Bar Text property derives its value from the Description property setting you entered for the field in the table.

Setting Label Properties

You can also set separate properties for the labels attached to controls. Click the label for CompanyID to see the property sheet shown in Figure 29-19. Access copies the Caption property from the field in the underlying table to the Caption property in the associated control label. The default settings for the text box control on a form specify that all text boxes have labels and that the caption should have a trailing colon. When you added the CompanyID text box to the form, Access used the caption from the field's definition in the tblCompanies table (Company ID instead of the field name CompanyID), and added the trailing colon. Also, all controls on a form must have a name, so Access generated a name (Label0) that is the control type followed by an integer.

You also can correct the caption from inside a label by selecting the label, moving the mouse pointer inside the label until the pointer changes into an I-beam shape, and then clicking to set the insertion point inside the label text. You can delete unwanted characters, and you can type new characters. When you finish correcting a label caption, Access automatically adjusts the size of the control smaller or larger to adequately display the new name. You can change settings using the property sheet to adjust the size of a label, or you can also select the control and drag the control's handles to override the automatic resizing and manually adjust the size and alignment of the control.

Chapter 29

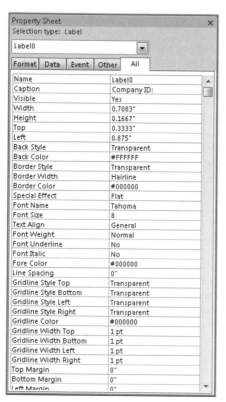

Figure 29-19 This is the property sheet for the CompanyID label control.

Setting Form Properties

You can display the form's properties in the property sheet (as shown in Figure 29-20) by clicking anywhere outside the Detail section of the form, by clicking the small square box in the upper-left corner of the Form window, or by selecting Form from the Selection Type combo box on the property sheet. On the Format tab in Figure 29-20, we set the caption to Companies / Organizations. This value will appear on the Form window's title bar in Form view or in Datasheet view.

Toward the bottom of the list of properties on the Format tab are the Grid X and Grid Y properties that control the density of dots on the grid as discussed earlier in this chapter. The defaults are 24 dots per inch across (Grid X) and 24 dots per inch down (Grid Y), if your measurements are in U.S. units. For metric measurements, the defaults are 5 dots per centimeter in both directions. Access also draws a shaded line on the grid every inch or centimeter to help you line up controls. If you decide to turn on the Snap To Grid command in the Control Layout group on the Arrange tab below Form Design Tools to help you line up controls on your form, you might want to change the density of the grid dots to give you greater control over where you place objects on the form.

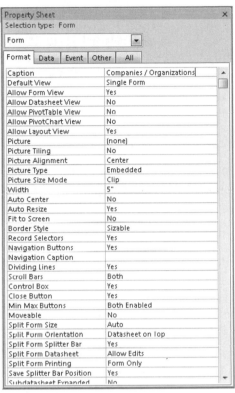

Figure 29-20 You can use the Caption property on the Format tab of the property sheet for the form to define a title for the form.

> **Note**
>
> You won't see the grid dots if you set either the Grid X or Grid Y property to more than 24 in U.S. measurements or more than 9 in metric measurements.

You can set the properties beginning with On Current on the Event tab of the property sheet to run macros or Visual Basic procedures. The events associated with these properties can trigger macro actions.

Customizing Colors and Checking Your Design Results

Let's explore some of the interesting effects you can design using colors. To make the fields on the form stand out, you can click in the Detail section and then set the background to dark gray using the Fill/Back Color button in the Font group on the Design tab. To make the labels stand out against this dark background, drag the mouse pointer around all the label controls or click the horizontal ruler directly above all the label controls, and then set the Fill/Back Color to white. If you haven't already moved and resized the labels, you can select all the labels and then widen them all to the left by clicking the left edge sizing handle of any of the labels and dragging left. This pulls the long Company / Organization caption over so that it doesn't overlap the Company-Name field. If you also want to make the Detail section fit snugly around the controls on your form, drag the edges of the Detail section inward.

INSIDE OUT   Using the Ruler to Select All Controls

To select all controls in a vertical area, click the horizontal ruler above the area containing the controls you want to select. Likewise, to select all controls in a horizontal area, click the vertical ruler.

When you finish working on this form in Design view, it might look something like the one shown in Figure 29-21.

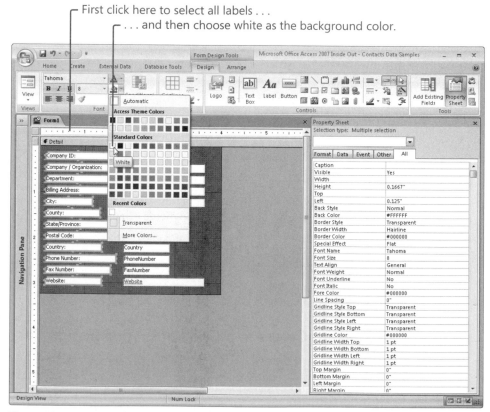

Figure 29-21 You can add contrast to the Companies / Organizations form by using the Fill/Back Color button.

Click the arrow below the View button in the Views group on the Ribbon and click Form View to see your form. It will look similar to the form shown in Figure 29-22. (You can find this form saved as frmXmplCompany1 in the sample database.) Note that the labels are all different sizes and the contrast might be too distracting. You could further refine the look of this form by making all the labels the same size and perhaps aligning the captions to the right. You could also make the label background transparent or the same color as the Detail section and change the font color to white.

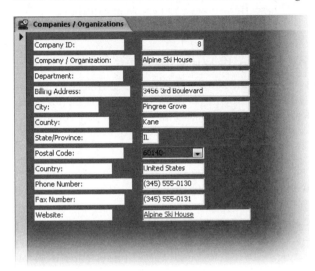

Figure 29-22 Switch to Form view to see how the Companies / Organizations form looks so far.

Click the Save button on the Quick Access Toolbar or click the Microsoft Office Button and then Save to save your new form design.

INSIDE OUT   Understanding the Allow Layout View Property

Access 2007 introduces a feature—Allow Layout view—to allow you to further modify the design of your forms even in a finished application. All new forms in Access have the Allow Layout View property set to Yes by default. This lets any user open the form in Layout view to make design changes. You should be sure to set this property to No in all forms before distributing a finished application to users. If you don't do this, users can make design changes to your forms, which is probably not a good idea in a production application.

Note that this property was called Allow Design Changes in Microsoft Access 2003. Setting this property to Yes in Access 2003 allowed the user to open the property sheet while in Form view and make changes to the form design by changing property settings. But Layout view in Access 2007 is much more powerful because the user can not only change properties but also move and add controls.

Working with Quick Create Commands and the Form Wizard

Now that you understand the basic mechanics of form design, you could continue to build all your forms from scratch in Design view. However, even the most experienced developers take advantage of the many wizards built into Access 2007 to get a jump-start on design tasks. This section shows you how to use quick create form commands and the Form Wizard to quickly build a custom form.

Creating a Form with the Quick Create Commands

Access 2007 introduces new quick create commands so that you can create new forms with one click on a Ribbon command. As you'll learn in this section, you can build forms designed in a variety of different views, so you can pick the style you need for the data-editing task at hand. You just walked through creating a form from scratch, so you should recall how much time it took to place all the fields on the form design grid, resize and move some of the controls, and change some of the form properties. The quick create commands can do a lot of the heavy work in designing a base form, which you can then modify to meet your specific needs.

Suppose you want to create a data entry form for the tblProducts table in the Conrad Systems Contacts database. Begin by opening the ContactsDataCopy.accdb database and click the top of the Navigation Pane to open the Navigation Pane menu. Click Object Type under Navigate To Category and Tables under Filter By Group to display a list of only the tables in this database. Select the tblProducts table in the Navigation Pane and then click the Form command in the Forms group on the Create tab. Access immediately creates a new single form based on the tblProducts table, including a control for every field in that table, and displays it in Layout view as shown in Figure 29-23.

As you can see, Access creates this form very quickly, and it looks professional. Switch to Design view for this form by clicking the arrow below the View button in the Views group on the Home tab and clicking Design View. Notice how Access creates a text box on the form for each field in the tblProducts table and an associated label for each text box with a caption, and aligns all the controls. Access also creates a bitmap picture logo and a label for the form's title in the Header section.

This form could still use some modification, such as entering a different form title and resizing some controls, but overall Access has completed a lot of the hard work of creating the form. Close this form, and do not save it.

Select the tblProducts table again in the Navigation Pane and then click the Split Form command in the Forms group on the Create tab. Access immediately creates a new split form containing every field in the tblProducts table and displays it in Layout view as shown in Figure 29-24.

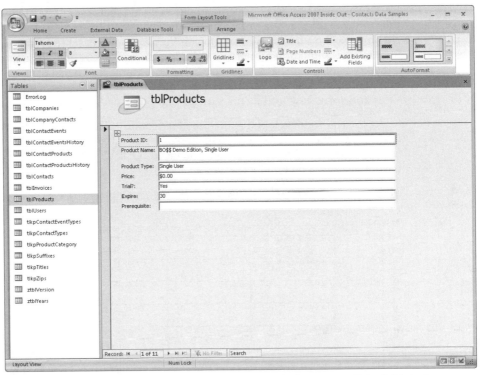

Figure 29-23 Access can save you time by creating a single form using all the fields in the selected table.

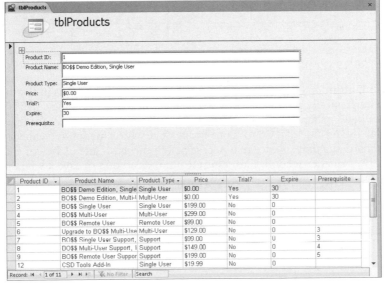

Figure 29-24 When you click the Split Form command, Access creates a new split form based on your table.

Here again Access creates controls and associated labels for all the fields in the tblProducts table. Switch to Design view by clicking the arrow in the Views group and clicking Design View. The form's Default View property is set to Split Form, and the Split Form Orientation property is set to Datasheet On Bottom. The top of the Form window displays the fields from the tblProducts table in Single Form view, and the bottom of the form displays all the records from the tblProducts table in Datasheet view. Close this form now, and do not save it when prompted.

Select the tblProducts table again in the Navigation Pane and then click the Multiple Items command in the Forms group on the Create tab. Access immediately creates a new continuous form based on all the fields in the tblProducts table and displays it in Layout view as shown in Figure 29-25.

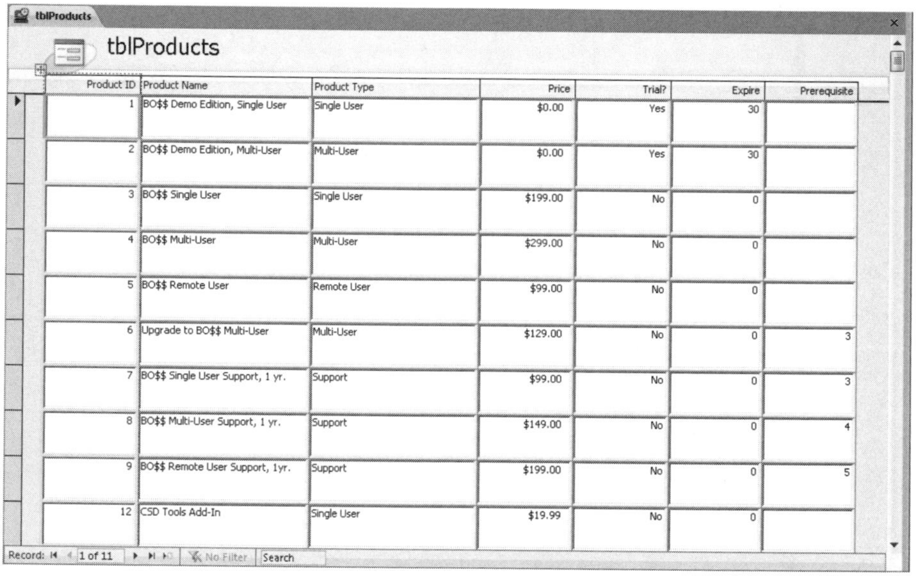

Figure 29-25 Use the Multiple Items command to create a continuous form.

In this continuous form, Access creates controls for all the fields in the tblProducts table horizontally across the Form window. Switch to Design view by clicking the arrow in the Views group and clicking Design View. The form's properties have been set to display the products in Continuous Form view, which means you can view more than one record at a time. Notice that Access places the associated label for each control in the form's Header section. Close this form now, and do not save it when prompted.

Select the tblProducts table again in the Navigation Pane, click the More Forms command in the Forms group on the Create tab, and then click the Datasheet command. Access immediately creates a new form in Datasheet view using all the fields in the tblProducts table and displays it as shown in Figure 29-26.

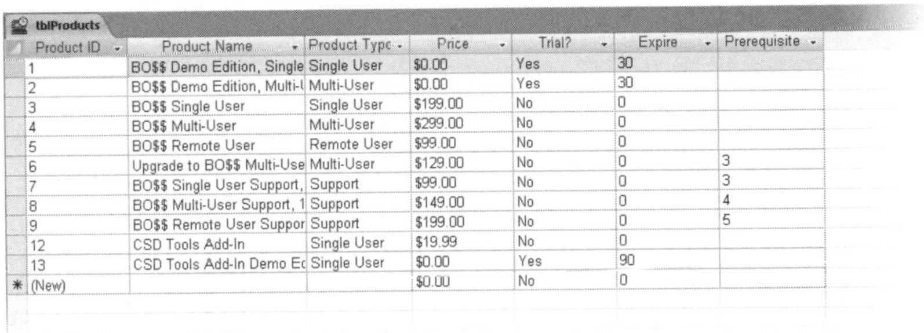

Product ID	Product Name	Product Type	Price	Trial?	Expire	Prerequisite
1	BO$$ Demo Edition, Single	Single User	$0.00	Yes	30	
2	BO$$ Demo Edition, Multi-U	Multi-User	$0.00	Yes	30	
3	BO$$ Single User	Single User	$199.00	No	0	
4	BO$$ Multi-User	Multi-User	$299.00	No	0	
5	BO$$ Remote User	Remote User	$99.00	No	0	
6	Upgrade to BO$$ Multi-Use	Multi-User	$129.00	No	0	3
7	BO$$ Single User Support,	Support	$99.00	No	0	3
8	BO$$ Multi-User Support, 1	Support	$149.00	No	0	4
9	BO$$ Remote User Suppor	Support	$199.00	No	0	5
12	CSD Tools Add-In	Single User	$19.99	No	0	
13	CSD Tools Add-In Demo Ed	Single User	$0.00	Yes	90	
* (New)			$0.00	No	0	

Figure 29-26 This datasheet form was created using the Datasheet command on the More Forms menu.

Switch to Design view by clicking the arrow in the Views group and clicking Design View. The form's properties have been set to display the products in Datasheet view, which means you can view more than one record at a time and all the records are stacked close together like a table datasheet. In datasheet forms, Access places a column header with the name that normally appears for an associated label for each control. Close this form now, and do not save it when prompted.

Access 2007 also has quick create commands for PivotChart and PivotTable views in the Forms group. You can use these commands to get a jump-start on creating PivotChart and PivotTable forms.

Creating the Basic Products Form with the Form Wizard

The quick create form commands are easy to use, but you have no flexibility on how Access initially creates the form. The Form Wizard is another tool you can use to quickly create forms in your database. Begin by opening the ContactsDataCopy.accdb database, and click the top of the Navigation Pane to display the Navigation Pane menu. Select Object Type under Navigate To Category and Tables under Filter By Group to display a list of only the tables in this database. Select the tblProducts table in the Navigation Pane, click the More Forms command in the Forms group on the Create tab, and then click the Form Wizard command. Access opens the first page of the Form Wizard, as shown in Figure 29-27.

You can select any field in the Available Fields list and click the single right arrow (>) button to copy that field to the Selected Fields list. You can also click the double right arrow (>>) button to copy all available fields to the Selected Fields list. If you copy a field in error, you can select the field in the Selected Fields list and click the single left arrow (<) button to remove the field from the list. You can remove all fields and start over by clicking the double left arrow (<<) button. For this example, click the double right arrow button to use all the fields in the tblProducts table in the new form.

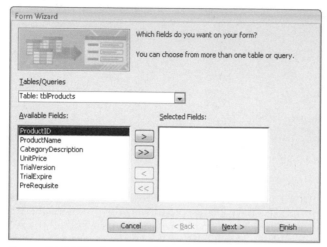

Figure 29-27 The first page of the Form Wizard displays fields you can select to include in your form.

You can select fields from one table or query and then change the data source name in the Tables/Queries combo box to select a different but related table or query. If you have defined the relationships between tables in your database, the Form Wizard can determine how the data from multiple sources is related and can offer to build either a simple form to display all the data or a more complex one that shows some of the data in the main part of the form with related data displayed in an embedded subform.

At any time, you can click the Finish button to go directly to the last step of the wizard. You can also click the Cancel button at any time to stop creating the form.

After you select all the fields from the tblProducts table, click Next. On the next page, the wizard gives you choices for the layout of your form. You can choose to display the controls on your form in columns, arrange the controls across the form in a tabular format (this creates a continuous form), create a form that opens in Datasheet view, or place the fields in a block "justified" view. For this example, select Columnar, and then click Next.

The wizard next displays a page on which you can select a style for your form, as shown in Figure 29-28. Note that if you choose to display the form in Datasheet view, the style won't apply to the datasheet but will appear if you shift from Datasheet view to Form view. The nice thing about this page is that the wizard shows you a sample of each selection on the left side of the page. You can look at each one and decide which you like best. In this example, the Solstice style is selected.

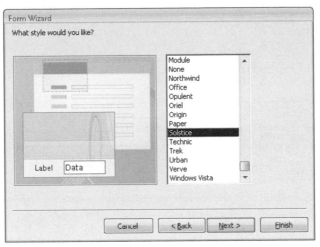

Figure 29-28 You can select a style for your form on the third page of the Form Wizard.

Note

When you select a style in the Form Wizard, the new style becomes the default for new forms you create using the wizard until you change the style setting again, either in the Form Wizard or with the AutoFormat commands.

Click Next to display the final page, where the Form Wizard asks for a title for your form. Type an appropriate title, such as **Products**. The wizard places this title in the Caption property of the form and also saves the form with this name. (If you already have a form named Products, Access appends a number to the end of the name to create a unique name.) Select the Open The Form To View Or Enter Information option, and then click the Finish button to go directly to Form view. Or you can select the Modify The Form's Design option, and then click Finish to open the new form in Design view. The finished form is shown in Form view in Figure 29-29.

Note

In the initial release of Access 2007, the Form Wizard failed to apply the background image specified for the style you select when you ask for a Columnar, Datasheet, or Justified form. Microsoft intends to fix this bug in the first service pack. If you do not see the background image, you can reapply the style to your form using AutoFormat. The figures that follow all show the background image applied.

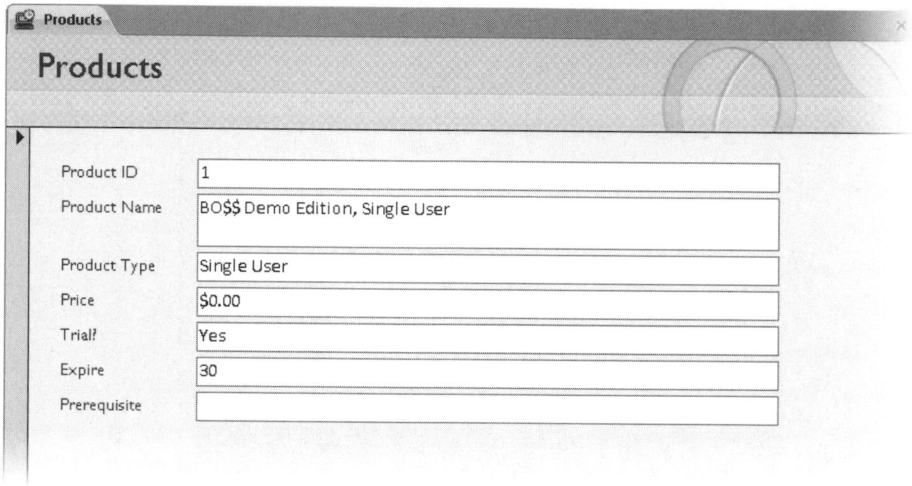

Figure 29-29 The Form Wizard creates a form in a columnar format using the Solstice style that is very similar to the form produced with the quick create commands.

Notice that the Solstice style uses labels sized alike with no ending colons on the captions. Also notice that all the fields in this style are left-aligned, regardless of data type.

If you're curious to see the tabular format, you can start a new form on the tblProducts table and use the Form Wizard again. Select all the fields on the first page of the Form Wizard, select Tabular for the layout, and set the style to Northwind. For a title, type **Products – Tabular**, and open the new form in Form view. It should look something like the form shown in Figure 29-30. Close this form when you finish looking at it.

Note

We modified the form you see in Figure 29-30 to preserve the default sunken effect for text box controls in the Northwind style. If you create this form on a Windows XP or Windows Vista system, choose Use Windows-Themed Controls On Forms in the Current Database category of the Access Options dialog box, and choose the default Windows XP theme in the Display Properties window in Windows XP, or choose the Windows Vista Basic color scheme in Appearance Settings in Windows Vista, the text boxes appear flat on your form.

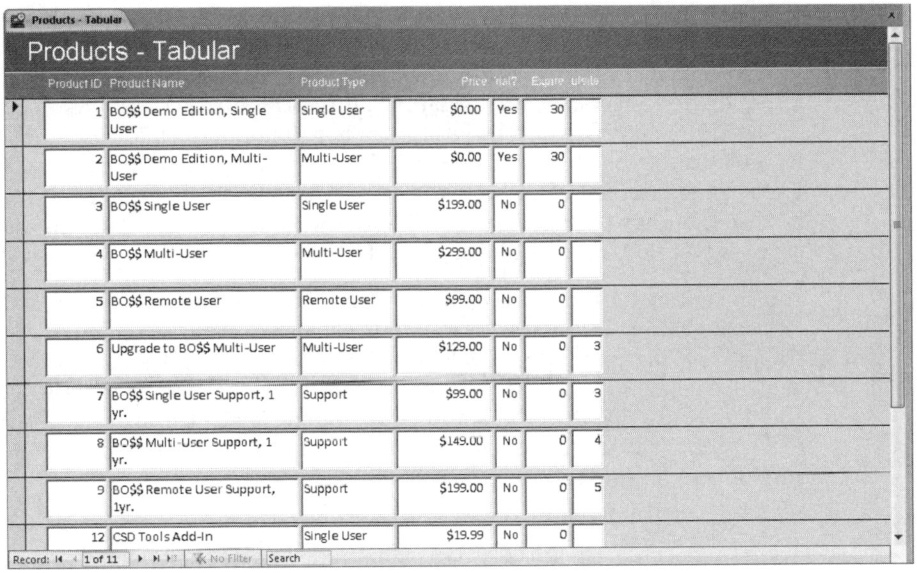

Figure 29-30 This Products form is in a tabular format using the Northwind style.

You can also investigate what a justified form looks like by going through the exercise again and selecting Justified for the layout on the second page in the Form Wizard. If you choose the Office style and name the form **Products – Justified** your result should look something like the one shown in Figure 29-31. Close this form when you finish looking at it.

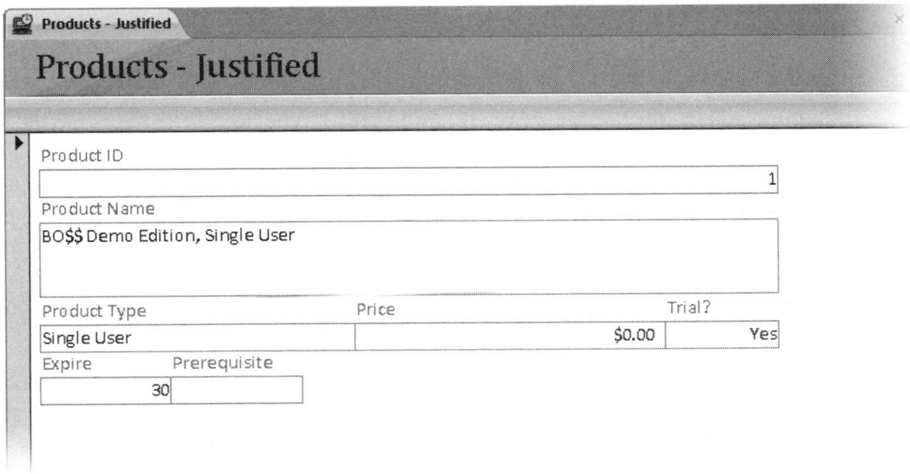

Figure 29-31 This is the Products form in a justified format using the Office style.

Modifying the Products Form

The Form Wizard took care of some of the work, but there's still a lot you can do to improve the appearance and usability of this form. And even though the Form Wizard adjusted the display control widths, they're still not perfect. Most of the text boxes are larger than they need to be. The Form Wizard created a two-line text box for product name when one should suffice. We personally prefer to see field labels right-aligned and bold so that they're easier to read. Finally, the ProductID field is an AutoNumber data type, so you should probably lock it and disable it so the user cannot type in the field.

You can either start with the columnar format form using the Solstice style (shown in Figure 29-29) or start a new form with the None style. (We decided to modify the Solstice style form from Figure 29-29 for the following examples.) Open the form in Design view. To help align controls, click outside the Detail section so that the form is selected and make sure that the Grid X and Grid Y properties in the form's property sheet are set to 24. (Leave the settings at Grid X = 5 and Grid Y = 5 if you're working in metric measurements.) Be sure the Show Grid command is selected in the Show/Hide group on the Arrange contextual tab.

Begin by selecting the ProductID text box and change the Enabled property to No and the Locked property to Yes as you learned to do earlier. We will leave the Special Effect property of this text box set to Flat to give your users a visual clue that they won't be able to type in the ProductID text box.

The Product ID field does not need to be as wide as it is, so click that control to select it and then click and drag the right edge of the text box control to the left. After the control is about 1 inch wide, release the mouse button and notice that Access resizes all the text box controls to the same width. The Form Wizard has applied a *control layout* so that all the controls will move and resize together. You can tell whether Access has applied a control layout to the controls by the small box with a crosshair inside just to the left of and slightly above the Product ID label, as shown in Figure 29-32.

To make individual size adjustments to the labels and text box controls, you need to highlight all the controls and turn off this control layout. Start by clicking the horizontal ruler just above the left edge of the label controls, and then drag in the ruler toward the right until the selection indicator touches all the labels and text box controls. (If you can't see the rulers, be sure that you have clicked the Ruler command in the Show/Hide group on the Arrange tab.) Release the mouse button to select all the controls and labels on the form grid, and then click the Remove button in the Control Layout group on the Arrange tab, as shown in Figure 29-32.

Control layout indicator

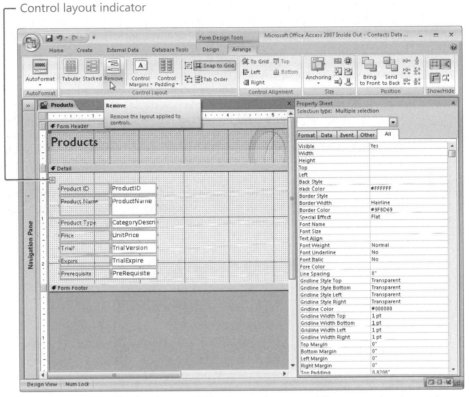

Figure 29-32 If you or Access has applied a control layout to the form controls, a box with a cross-hair appears next to the controls.

Now that you have removed any control layouts, you can continue making adjustments to the individual controls. The ProductName text box needs to be about 3 inches wide. You can set a specific width by clicking the control, opening the property sheet, clicking the Format tab, and typing **y** in the Width property (the fifth property down the list). The Form Wizard created a text box that is two lines high for ProductName, but it doesn't need to be bigger than one line. Select the control, and then grab the bottom sizing box in the middle of the control and drag it up to make the control smaller. Click the Size To Fit command in the Size group on the Arrange tab to resize the control to display one line. Click the Format tab in the property sheet and change the Scroll Bars property to None—the Form Wizard specified a vertical scroll bar in the two-line control that it designed. It doesn't make sense to show a scroll bar in a one-line control that is already wide enough to display all the data. Select the ProductName label, and then grab the bottom sizing box in the middle of the control and drag it up to make it the same height as the ProductName text box.

Now that you've made the ProductName text box and associated label smaller, you have extra space between it and the CategoryDescription text box. Select the Category-Description, UnitPrice, TrialVersion, TrialExpire, and PreRequisite text boxes and

Chapter 29

move them up close to the ProductName text box. Unless you turned off Snap To Grid in the Control Layout group on the Arrange tab, it should be easy to line up the controls in their new positions. As you move these four controls, their associated labels will stay aligned with the text boxes.

Next, fix all the labels. Click in the horizontal ruler above the column of labels to select them all. (Access selects the Products label in the form header during this procedure as well, so hold down the Shift key and click the label in the form header to clear it.) Click the Align Right and Bold buttons in the Font group on the Design contextual tab to change the appearance of the labels. Click the Products label in the form header and then click the Italic button in the Font group to add emphasis. Finally, click the Size To Fit command in the Size group on the Arrange tab to make the Product label shrink in size around the text. After you shrink the right margin of your form, move all the controls up closer to the form header and left side of the form grid, and shrink the bottom margin of the form, it should look similar to the one shown in Figure 29-33. Notice that none of the labels attached to the text boxes shows an ending colon. The Solstice style doesn't include them.

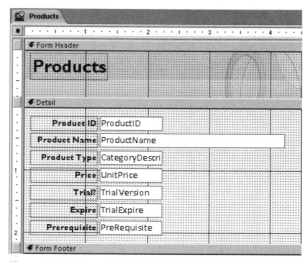

Figure 29-33 You can now see the modified Products form in Design view with the changes you applied.

Finally, switch to Form view and your form should look something like the one shown in Figure 29-34. The form now looks a bit more customized—and somewhat more like the frmProducts form in the Conrad Systems Contacts application. You can find this form saved as fxmplProducts1 in the sample database.

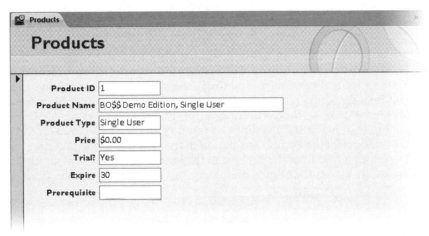

Figure 29-34 When you switch to Form view, you can see how the modified Products form looks at this point.

Simplifying Data Input with a Form

One drawback to working with a relational database is that often you have to deal with information stored in multiple tables. That's not a problem if you're using a query to link data, but working with multiple tables can be confusing if you're entering new data. Access 2007 provides some great ways to show information from related tables, thus making data input much simpler.

Taking Advantage of Combo Boxes and List Boxes

You can use a combo box or a list box to present a list of potential values for a control. To create the list, you can type the values in the Row Source property box of the control. You can also specify a table or a query as the source of the values in the list. Access 2007 displays the currently selected value in the text box portion of the combo box or as a highlighted selection in the list.

The CategoryDescription field in the tblProducts table is a simple Text data type. To help ensure data consistency, there's a separate lookup table that contains a list of predefined product types. There's also a referential-integrity rule that keeps you from entering anything other than a predefined type in the CategoryDescription field. However, you can type anything you like in the CategoryDescription text box (labeled *Product Type*) that the Form Wizard designed. Go ahead and type any random string of characters in the text box and then try to save the record. You should see an unfriendly technobabble message about "related record is required in 'tlkpProductCategory'."

You can help avoid this problem by providing a combo box to edit and display the CategoryDescription field instead. The combo box can display the list of valid values from the tlkpProductCategory lookup table to make it easy for your user to choose a valid value. The combo box can also limit what the user enters to only values in the list.

You can write Visual Basic code to detect when a user tries to enter something that's not in the list so that you can provide your own, more user-friendly, message.

To see how a combo box works, you can replace the CategoryDescription text box control with a combo box on the Products form. In Design view, select the CategoryDescription text box control and then press the Delete key to remove the text box control from the form (this also removes the related label control). Be sure the Use Control Wizards button is selected in the Controls group on the Design tab. Display the field list by clicking the Add Existing Fields button in the Tools group on the same Design tab. Next, click the Combo Box button in the Controls group and drag the CategoryDescription field from the field list to the form. The new control appears on the form, and Access starts the Combo Box Wizard, as shown in Figure 29-35, to help you out.

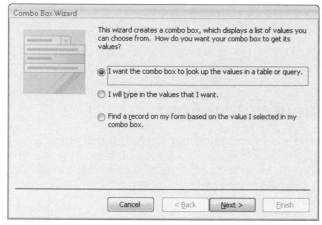

Figure 29-35 After you drop the CategoryDescription field onto the form grid, Access opens the first page of the Combo Box Wizard.

INSIDE OUT   Manually Changing a Text Box to a Combo Box

You can change a text box to a combo box by right-clicking on the text box control, clicking Change To on the shortcut menu, and then clicking Combo Box on the submenu. However, after you change a text box to a combo box in this way, you have to set the properties for the display list yourself.

Follow this procedure to build your combo box.

1. You want the combo box to display values from the tlkpProductCategory lookup table, so select the I Want The Combo Box To Look Up The Values In A Table Or Query option, and then click the Next button to go to the next page.

2. On the second page, the wizard displays a list of available tables in the database. Note that the wizard also provides an option to view queries or both tables and queries. Scroll down in the list and click Table: tlkpProductCategory to select that table, and click Next to go to the next page.

3. On the third page, the wizard shows you the single field in the table, CategoryDescription. Select that field and click the right arrow (>) to move it to the Selected Fields list. Click Next to go on.

4. The fourth page allows you to select up to four fields to sort either Ascending or Descending. Click the arrow to the right of the first field and then select the CategoryDescription field. The button next to the first box indicates *Ascending*, and you want to leave it that way. If you click the button, it changes to *Descending*, which is not what you want. (You can click the button again to set it back.) Click Next to go to the next page.

5. The wizard shows you the lookup values that your combo box will display as an embedded datasheet, as shown here. To size a column, click on the dividing line at the right edge of a column at the top, and drag the line. You can adjust the size of the column to be sure it displays all the available descriptions properly. Click Next to go on.

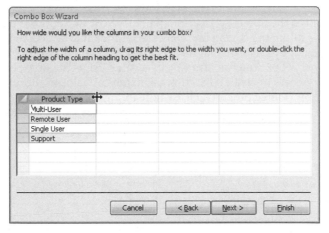

6. On the next page, the wizard asks whether you want to store the value from the combo box in a field from the table or query that you're updating with this form or simply save the value selected in an unbound control "for later use." Unbound controls are useful for storing calculated values or for providing a way for the user to enter parameter data for use by your macros or Visual Basic procedures. In this case, you want to update the CategoryDescription field, so be sure to select the Store That Value In This Field option and verify that CategoryDescription is selected in the list. Click Next to go to the last page of the wizard.

7. On the final page, shown here, the wizard suggests a caption that you probably want to correct. In this case, enter **Product Type** in the box. Click Finish, and you're all done.

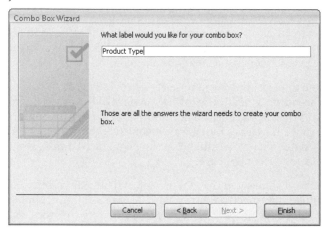

If you have the property sheet open, you can study the properties set by the Combo Box Wizard, as shown in Figure 29-36. The Control Source property shows that the combo box is bound to the CategoryDescription field. The Row Source Type property indicates that the data filling the combo box comes from the table or query entered in the Row Source property box. Notice that the wizard generated an SQL statement in the Row Source property box. You can also specify a value list as the Row Source property, or you can ask Access to create a list from the names of fields in the query or table specified in the Row Source property. Please note in Figure 29-36 that we show both the Data and the Format tabs so that you can see the properties we are discussing.

Figure 29-36 The Combo Box Wizard set these properties for the CategoryDescription field.

The Column Count property is set to 1 to indicate that one column should be created from the list. You have the option of asking Access to display column headings when the combo box is open, but you don't need that for this example, so leave the Column Heads property set to No. The wizard sets the Column Widths property based on the width you set in step 5. The next property on the Data tab, Bound Column, indicates that the first column (the only column in this case) is the one that sets the value of the combo box and, therefore, the value of the bound field in the table.

When you open the form in Form view, it should look like the one shown in Figure 29-37. You can see that the CategoryDescription combo box now shows the list of valid values from the lookup table. Notice also that the label the wizard attached looks more like the labels that the Form Wizard originally created. You can make this label look like the others by changing it to a bold font and right aligning it. (You can find this form saved as fxmplProducts2 in the sample database.)

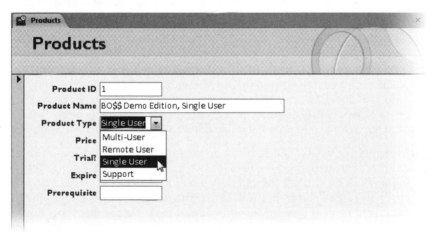

Figure 29-37 A combo box for the CategoryDescription field makes it much easier for the user to select a correct value.

INSIDE OUT   Having Access Select Closest Matches While Typing

If you want Access to select the closest matching entry when you type a few leading characters in a combo box, set the control's Auto Expand property to Yes.

Using Toggle Buttons, Check Boxes, and Option Buttons

If your table contains a field that has a yes/no, a true/false, or an on/off value, you can choose from three types of controls that graphically display and set the status of this type of field: toggle buttons, check boxes, and option buttons.

INSIDE OUT

Choosing Toggle Buttons and Check Boxes and Option Buttons—How to Decide?

Although you can certainly use any of these three controls to display an underlying Yes/No data type, you should try to use these controls in your application similarly to the way Windows uses them. Your users might be confused if you try to use them in a different way.

- Use a *toggle button* to display an option value. A toggle button works best to display an option that is on or off.

- Use a *check box* to display all simple yes/no or true/false values.

- Use an *option button* when the user needs to make a choice from several options. You should not use an option button to display simple yes/no or true/false values.

We personally never use a toggle button or an option button except inside an option group control.

The tblProducts table has a TrialVersion field that indicates whether the particular product is a free trial edition that expires in a specific number of days. As you can see in the original text box control created by the Form Wizard (see Figure 29-29), the word Yes or No appears depending on the value in the underlying field. This field might be more appealing and understandable if it were displayed in a check box control.

To change the TrialVersion control on the Products form, first delete the TrialVersion text box control. Display the field list by clicking the Add Existing Fields button in the Tools group. Next, click the Check Box button in the Controls group, and then drag the TrialVersion field from the field list onto the form in the open space you left on the form. Your form in Design view should now look like the one shown in Figure 29-38. Notice that the default check box also includes a label, but the label is positioned to the right of the control and does not include a colon. If you want to move the label, select it, and then use the large handle shown earlier in Figure 29-15 to move the label to the left of the check box. You should also change the font to bold to match the other labels.

After making final adjustments to the TrialVersion label, click the arrow under the Views button and click Form View to see the result. Your form should look like the one shown in Figure 29-39. One of the interesting side effects of using a special control to display data in a form is that the control properties carry over to Datasheet view. Switch to the Datasheet view of this form. The CategoryDescription field is displayed as a drop-down list on the datasheet and the TrialVersion field still looks like a check box. You might decide to design some forms to be used in Datasheet view, but you can customize the look of the datasheet by using controls other than text boxes while in Design view. By the way, this design sample is saved as fxmplProducts3 in the sample database.

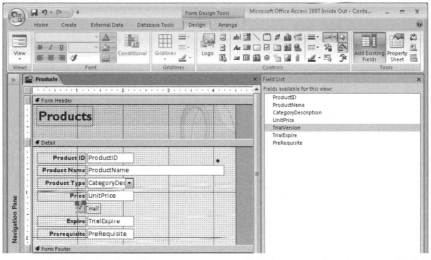

Figure 29-38 The Products form now contains a check box control to display the TrialVersion field.

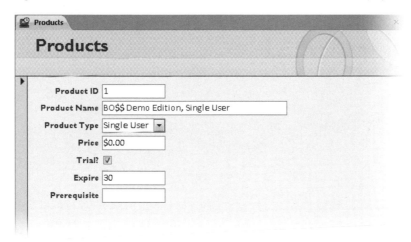

Figure 29-39 Your Products form now has both a combo box control and a check box control to simplify data entry.

Chapter 29

Constructing a Report

Constructing a report is very similar to building a form. In this chapter, you'll apply many of the techniques that you used in working with forms, and you'll learn about some of the unique features of reports. After a quick tour of the report design facilities, you'll build a simple report for the Conrad Systems Contacts database, and then you'll use the Report Wizard to create the same report. You'll see how to use the new Layout view to modify existing reports and create new ones. Finally, you'll see how to use the quick create Report command to create a report with one mouse click.

> **Note**
>
> The examples in this chapter are based on the reports, tables, and data in ContactsData-Copy.accdb on the companion CD included with this book. You can find similar reports in the Conrad Systems Contacts sample application, but all the reports in that sample file have custom Ribbons defined, so you won't see the four main Ribbon tabs when you open those reports. The results you see from the samples in this chapter might not exactly match what you see in this book if you have changed the sample data in the files. Also, all the screen images in this chapter were taken on a Microsoft Windows Vista system with the display theme set to Blue. Your results might look different if you are using a different operating system or a different theme.

Starting from Scratch—A Simple Report

In a contact tracking application, the user is going to want to take a look at recent events and perhaps work through a list of events that require follow-ups. Although the user could search for events in a form, the application should also provide a report that lists events by contact and shows the phone numbers the user needs. This report can be filtered by the application to print out only recent and upcoming events.

Most reports gather information from several tables, so you'll usually design a query that brings together data from related tables as the basis for the report. In this section, you'll build a relatively simple report to list contact events as you tour the report design facilities. The report you'll build uses the tblContacts, tblContactEvents, and tlkpContactEventTypes tables in the ContactsDataCopy.accdb sample database. The report groups contact event data by contact, prints a single line for each contact event, and calculates the number of contact events and the number of follow-ups for each contact.

Building the Report Query

To construct the underlying query for the report, you need to start with the tblContactEvents table. Click the Query Design button in the Other group on the Create tab. In the Show Table dialog box, select the tblContactEvents table, click the Add button to add it to the query design grid, and then add the tblContacts and the tlkpContactEventTypes tables as well. Click the Close button in the Show Table dialog box to dismiss it. You should see join lines between tblContacts and tblContactEvents on ContactID, and between tlkpContactEventTypes and tblContactEvents on ContactEventTypeID.

From the tblContacts table, add ContactID to the query design grid. The report needs to show the contact name, but it would be better to show the information concatenated in one field rather than separate title, first name, middle name, last name, and suffix fields. In the next column, enter this expression on the Field line:

```
Contact: ([tblContacts].[Title]+" ") & [tblContacts].[FirstName]
& " " & ([tblContacts].[MiddleInit]+". ") & [tblContacts].[LastName]
& (", "+[tblContacts].[Suffix])
```

Notice that the expression uses the plus sign concatenation operator to eliminate extra blanks when one of the fields contains a Null value—a technique you learned about in Chapter 28, "Creating and Working with Simple Queries."

The query also needs to include the contact's phone number, but the tblContacts table includes both a work and a home phone number. You can create an expression to examine the DefaultAddress field to decide which one to display. Microsoft Office Access 2007 provides a handy function, Choose, which accepts an integer value in its first argument and then uses that value to choose one of the other arguments. For example, if the first argument is 1, the function returns the second argument; if the first argument is 2, the function returns the third argument, and so on. The DefaultAddress field contains a 1 to indicate work address and a 2 to indicate home address. In the third field cell on the query design grid, enter the following:

```
Phone: Choose([tblContacts].[DefaultAddress], [tblContacts].[WorkPhone],
[tblContacts].[HomePhone])
```

To complete your query, include the ContactDateTime field from the tblContactEvents table and the ContactEventTypeDescription field from the tlkpContactEventTypes table. (ContactEventTypeID in tblContactEvents is a meaningless number.) Then include the ContactNotes, ContactFollowUp, and ContactFollowUpDate fields from the tblContactEvents table. Figure 30-1 shows the query you need for this first report. Click the Save button on the Quick Access Toolbar to save your new query. (You can find this query saved as qryRptContactEvents in the sample database.)

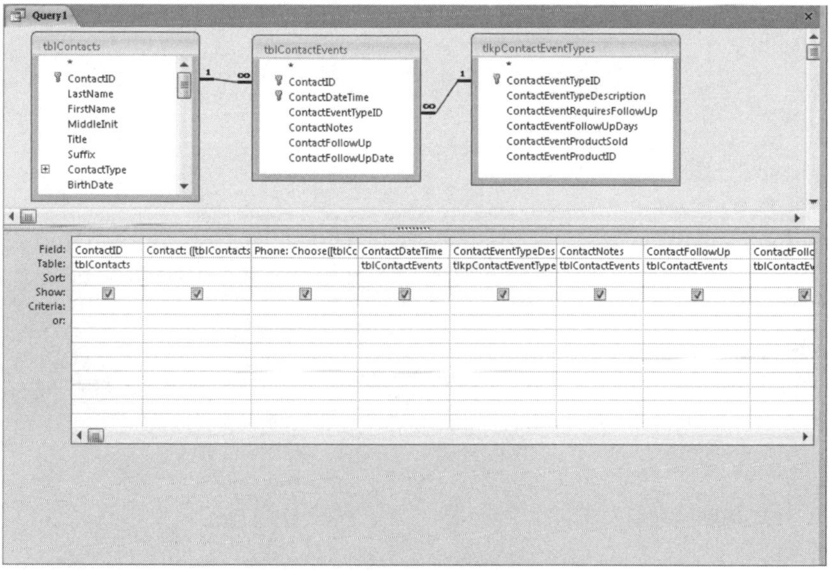

Figure 30-1 This query selects contact and contact event data for your report.

Note that although you're designing a report that will summarize the data, you are not building a totals query. If you used a totals query as the record source for the report, you would see only the summary in the report. One of the beauties of reports is that you can see the detail information and also ask the report to produce summaries. Also, you don't need to specify any sorting criteria here—you'll do that later in the report's Group, Sort, And Total pane.

Designing the Report

Now you're ready to start designing the report. Click the Report Design button in the Reports group on the Create tab to tell Office Access 2007 you want to begin creating a report in Design view, as shown in Figure 30-2.

The field list, the property sheet, and the Font and Controls groups on the Design contextual tab under Report Design Tools are similar to the features you used in building forms. See Chapter 29, "Building a Form," for detailed descriptions of their uses.

Access 2007 opens a new Report window in Design view, as shown in Figure 30-3. You can see the Report Design Tools collection of Ribbon tabs at the top of the Access window. The Report window is in the middle of the screen, and the property sheet is open to assist you in building your report. (If necessary, you can click the Property Sheet button in the Tools group on the Design tab to open this window.) To begin constructing your report you need to tell Access to use the qryRptContactEvents query as its record source. In the property sheet, select qryRptContactEvents (or the name of the query you just created) in the Record Source property, as shown in Figure 30-3.

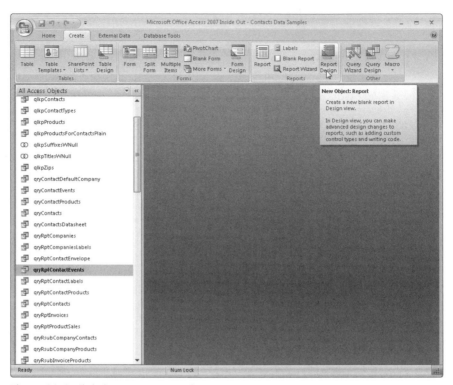

Figure 30-2 Click the Report Design button to start creating your report.

The blank report has Page Header and Page Footer sections and a Detail section between them, which is 5.25 inches (13.333 cm) high and 6.1694 inches (15.668 cm) wide. The rulers along the top and left edges of the Report window help you plan space on the printed page. If you want standard 1-inch side margins, the body of the report can be up to 6.5 inches wide on an 8.5-by-11-inch page. The available vertical space depends on how you design your headers and footers and how you define the top and bottom margins. As with forms, you can drag the edge of any report section to make the section larger or smaller. Note that the width of all sections is the same, so if you change the width of one section, Access 2007 changes the width of all other sections to match.

Within each section you see a grid that has 24 dots per inch horizontally and 24 dots per inch vertically, with a solid gray line displayed at 1-inch intervals. If you're working in centimeters, Access 2007 divides the grid into 5 dots per centimeter both vertically and horizontally. You can change these settings using the Grid X and Grid Y properties in the report's property sheet. (If the dots are not visible in your Report window, click the Grid command in the Show/Hide group on the Arrange contextual tab; if the Grid command is already selected and you still can't see the dots, try resetting the Grid X and Grid Y properties to lower numbers in the property sheet.)

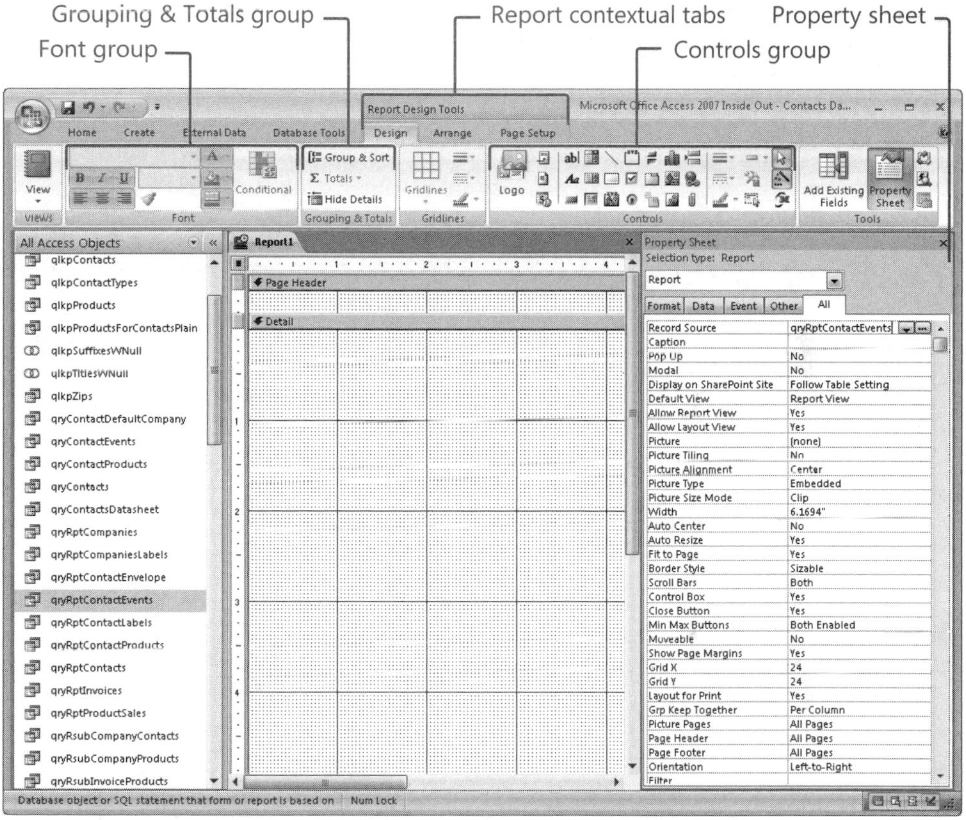

Figure 30-3 When you open a new Report window in Design view, Access displays all the tools you need to create the report.

The page header and page footer will print in your report at the top and bottom of each page. You can click the Page Header/Footer button in the Show/Hide group on the Arrange tab to add or remove the page header and page footer. You can also add a report header that prints once at the beginning of the report and a report footer that prints once at the end of the report. To add these sections to a report, click the Report Header/ Footer button in the same Show/Hide group. You'll learn how to add group headers and group footers in the next section.

Grouping Sorting, and Totaling Information

A key way in which reports differ from forms is that on reports you can group informa-tion for display using the Group, Sort, And Total pane. Click the Group & Sort button in the Grouping & Totals group on the Design tab (shown in Figure 30-3) to open the Group, Sort, And Total pane beneath the report design grid, as shown in Figure 30-4. (We collapsed the Navigation Pane in Figure 30-4.) In this pane you can define up to 10 fields or expressions that you will use to form groups in the report. The first item in the list determines the main group, and subsequent items define groups within groups.

Chapter 30

Because we have not yet defined any grouping or sorting in this report, the Group, Sort, And Total pane opens to a blank pane that allows you to click either Add A Group or Add A Sort.

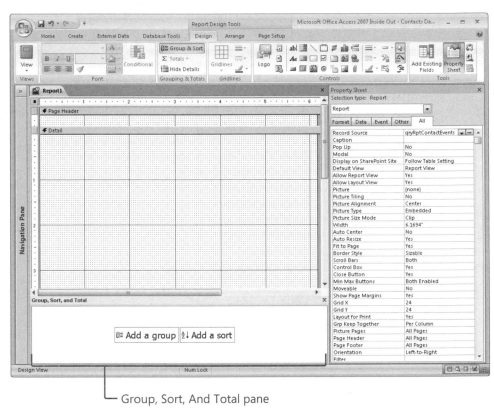

Figure 30-4 You can create groups and specify their sort order in the Group, Sort, And Total pane.

In the simple report you're creating for contact events, you need to group data by contact ID so that you can total the number of contact events as well as contact events that require follow-up for each contact. Click the Add A Group button in the Group, Sort, And Total pane. Access 2007 creates a new grouping specification and opens a list that contains all fields in the report's record source next to the Group On option, as shown in Figure 30-5. (We collapsed the Navigation Pane and closed the property sheet in Figure 30-5 so that you can see more of the Group, Sort, And Total pane.)

If you click away from the field list before selecting a field to define the group, Access 2007 closes the field list. Click the arrow on the Select Field box (or press Alt+Down Arrow while the focus is on the Select Field box) to open the list of fields from the underlying query or table. Select the ContactID field to place it in the Select Field box. You can also use the Select Field box to enter an expression based on any field in the underlying table or query. Open the field list again and click the Expression option below the list of fields, and Access opens the Expression Builder to help you create the expression. You let Access know you're entering an expression by first typing an equal sign (=) followed by your expression. We discussed the Expression Builder in Chapter 28.

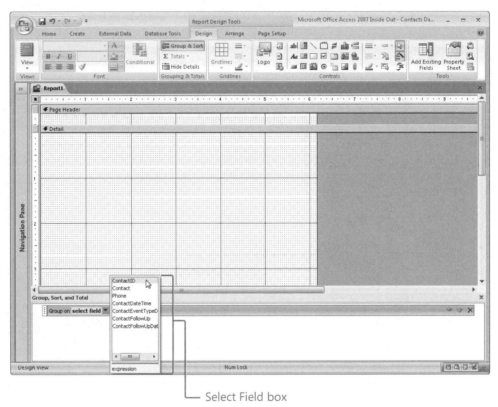

Select Field box

Figure 30-5 After you click Add A Group in the Group, Sort, And Total Pane, Access creates a new grouping specification and opens a field list to let you select the field that defines the group.

> **Note**
>
> When you define a grouping specification in a report, the report engine actually builds a totals query behind the scenes to perform the grouping. You cannot use Group By in a totals query on memo, OLE object, hyperlink, or attachment fields. For this reason, you cannot use Memo, OLE Object, Hyperlink, or Attachment data types in the Group, Sort, And Total pane.

After you select ContactID in the Select Field box, Access 2007 adds a new ContactID group header to the report grid beneath the Page Header group level, as shown in Figure 30-6. By default, Access sets the height of this new group level to ¼ inch. Access also displays the Add A Group and Add A Sort buttons beneath the first grouping specification so you can create additional grouping or sorting levels. To the right of Group On ContactID in the Group, Sort, And Total pane, Access now adds two new options—From Smallest To Largest and More.

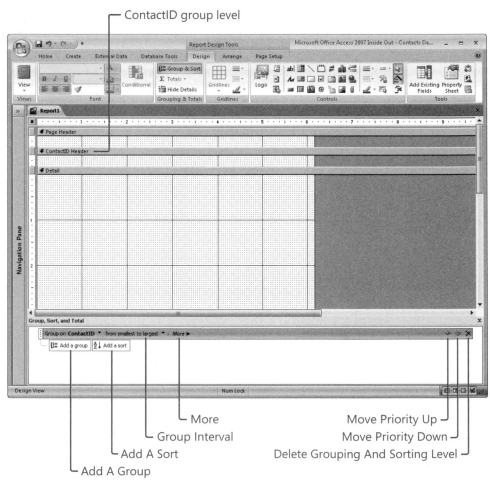

Figure 30-6 After you add a group in the Group, Sort, And Total pane, Access creates a new group level on the grid.

By default, Access 2007 sorts each field or expression in ascending order. You can change the sort order by selecting From Largest To Smallest from the list that appears when you click the arrow to the right of the second option (From Smallest To Largest in this example). In this case, you want to include the ContactID field so that you can form a group for each contact. Leave the sort order on From Smallest To Largest so that the report will sort the rows in ascending numerical order by the ContactID field. If you wanted to see the contacts in alphabetical order by last name, you would need to include the LastName field in your query (even if you didn't display it on the report), and group and sort on the LastName field. You could use the Contact expression that you included in the query, but then the report would sort the rows by title and first name.

> **Note**
>
> Access 2007 changes the choices in the second option in the grouping specification depending on the data type of the field or expression you specified in Group On. When the data type is Text, you'll see With A On Top and With Z On Top options. When the data type is Date/Time, you'll see From Oldest To Newest and From Newest To Oldest. If the data type is Yes/No, you'll see From Selected To Cleared and From Cleared To Selected. As you saw in our example, Access uses From Smallest To Largest and From Largest To Smallest for fields with a Numeric data type.

Click the More option in the ContactID grouping specification to see all the grouping and sorting options, as shown in Figure 30-7. Access now displays a total of eight grouping and sorting options. If you look at Figure 30-7, you can see that Access creates a sentence structure to help you understand how this grouping level will take shape. If you want to collapse the list of options, click Less at the end of the list.

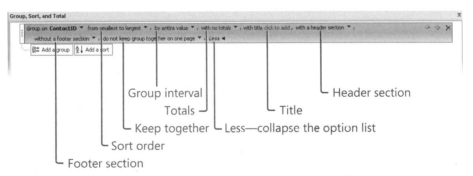

Figure 30-7 Click More to expand the list of grouping and sorting options.

The third option in the grouping specification (By Entire Value in our example) is called the group interval, which tells Access how to group the records. Click the arrow to the right of this option for a grouping based on the ContactID field, as shown in Figure 30-8. For AutoNumber, Number, and Currency data types, Access displays the following grouping options—By Entire Value, By 5s, By 10s, By 100s, By 1000s, and Custom, which lets you set your own interval. For Text data types, you can set the group interval to By Entire Value, By First Character, By First Two Characters, or Custom, which lets you set your own interval. For Date/Time data types, you can set the group interval to By Entire Value, By Day, By Week, By Month, By Quarter, By Year, or Custom, which lets you set your own interval. Leave the group interval set to By Entire Value for the ContactID group level.

Figure 30-8 The group interval displays different options based on the field's data type.

You use the fourth option in the grouping specification (which currently displays With No Totals in our example) to configure Access to list totals for a single field or for multiple fields. Click the arrow to the right of this option for a grouping based on the ContactID field, as shown in Figure 30-9. Select the field on which you want Access to calculate and display totals from the Total On list. In the Type box you can choose from several types of calculations based on the data type of the field you chose in the Total On box. Beneath the Type box are four check boxes for additional totaling options. Select the Show Grand Total check box to add a grand total for this field in the report's footer section. Select the Show Group Totals As % Of Grand Total check box if you want Access to calculate the percentage of the grand total for each group and place that percentage in the group header or footer. Select the Show In Group Header check box to place the total and optional percentage in the group's header section and the Show In Group Footer check box to place the total and optional percentage in the group's footer section. Leave the option for the Totals list set at With No Totals for the ContactID group level.

Figure 30-9 You can ask Access to calculate and display totals in the Totals list.

You use the fifth option in the grouping specification to define a title. You can choose to create a title that appears in a label control in the header section of the group. To create a title, click the blue Click To Add text. Access opens the Zoom dialog box, as shown in Figure 30-10, where you can enter a title. You can click Font to define the font, font style, size, and color of the title letters. After you enter a title, click OK, and Access creates a new label control in the group header section on the report grid. For the grouping based on the ContactID field, click Cancel to not enter a title at this time.

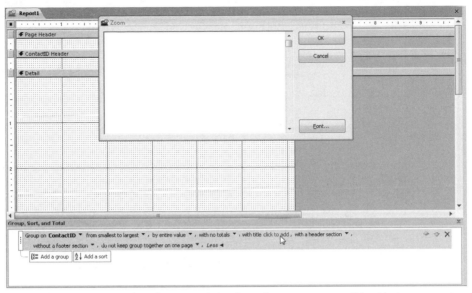

Figure 30-10 Access displays the Zoom dialog box when you want to add a title to a group header.

You use the sixth option in the grouping specification to display a header section for the specific group. Click the arrow to the right of this option and you can select either With A Header Section (the default selection) or Without A Header Section, as shown in Figure 30-11. When you select the option to include a header, Access creates the header section for the group for you. Conversely, Access removes the group header, and all controls in it, if you select the second option. If you have defined controls in the header section when you choose Without A Header, Access displays a confirmation dialog box explaining that you're deleting both the header and all its controls, and asks you to confirm the deletion. For the ContactID field in our example, leave the option set to the default—With A Header Section.

Figure 30-11 You can choose to have Access create a group header for you.

Similar to the header section option, you can use the seventh option to display a footer section for the grouping specification. Click the arrow to the right of this option and select either With A Footer Section or Without A Footer Section (the default selection), as shown in Figure 30-12. When you select the option to include a footer, Access creates the footer section for you. Conversely, Access removes the group footer, and all controls in it, if you select the second option. If you have defined controls in the footer section when you choose Without A Footer, Access displays a confirmation dialog box explaining that you're deleting both the footer and all its controls, and asks you to confirm the deletion. For the ContactID field you will need a place to put two calculated total fields (the count of contact events and the count of follow-ups). Click the arrow to the right of this option and select With A Footer Section.

Figure 30-12 Select the With A Footer Section option to include a footer section for the ContactID group on the report.

You use the last option in the grouping specification, as shown in Figure 30-13, to control how Access will lay out the report when you print it. Click the arrow to the right of this option, and you have three choices—Do Not Keep Group Together On One Page (the default), Keep Whole Group Together On One Page, and Keep Header And First Record Together On One Page.

The Do Not Keep Group Together On One Page option allows a section to flow across page boundaries. The Keep Whole Group Together On One Page option attempts to keep all lines within a section together on a page. If an entire group won't fit on the current page (and the current page isn't blank), Access moves to the top of the next page before starting to print the group, but the group still might overflow the end of the new page.

If you select Keep Header And First Record Together On One Page, Access does not print the header for the group at the bottom of the page if it cannot also print at least one detail record. For the Contact ID field, leave the option set to the default—Do Not Keep Group Together On One Page.

Figure 30-13 You can choose from among several options to control how the report will look when printed.

It would also be nice to see the contact events in descending date order for each contact (most recent or newest events first). To add the ContactDateTime field below ContactID, click the Add A Sort button and Access creates a new sort specification. Select Contact-DateTime in the Select Field box and change the sort order to From Newest To Oldest. Click More to display the rest of the options available to you for the sort specification. Leave the group interval set to By Entire Value, and leave the Totals option set to the default With No Totals. Do not add a title for this field and make sure to not include a group header or group footer. (If you add a header or footer, Access changes your specification from a sorting specification to a grouping specification.) Finally, keep the last option set to Do Not Keep Group Together On One Page. Your completed sorting specification for the ContactDateTime field should look like Figure 30-14.

Figure 30-14 Access will now sort the contact event records for your report in descending order.

You can change the priority of two or more grouping or sorting specifications by using the arrows on the right side of the Group, Sort, And Total pane. If you need to move a group up one level, select that group and then click the up arrow one time. Similarly, if you need to move a group down one level, select that group and then click the down arrow one time. Access repositions any group headers and footers for you during this process. To delete a group level, select it and then click Delete (the X) to the right of the up and down arrows. Close the Group, Sort, And Total pane now by clicking the Close button on its title bar or by clicking the Group & Sort button in the Grouping & Totals group on the Design tab.

INSIDE OUT   Understanding Who Controls the Sorting

You can specify sorting criteria in the query for a report, but after you set any criteria in the Group, Sort, And Total pane, the report overrides any sorting in the query. The best way to ensure that your report data sorts in the order you want is to always specify sorting criteria in the Group, Sort, And Total pane and not in the underlying query.

Completing the Report

Now you're ready to finish building a report based on the tblContactEvents table. Take the following steps to construct a report similar to the one shown in Figure 30-15. (You can find this report saved as rptXmplContactEvents1 in the sample database.)

1. Click the Title button in the Controls group on the Design tab to place a new label control in the Report Header section. By default, Access enters the name of the report, in this case Report1, in the label. Click inside this label and highlight or delete the existing characters, type **Contact Events**, and press Enter to change the label's caption. With the label control still selected, use the commands in the Font group on the Ribbon to change the font to Arial and the font color to Black. Next, click the Bold and Underline buttons in the Font group, and then click the Size To Fit command in the Size group on the Arrange tab to size the control to accommodate the new font adjustments. Access placed this title in a new section it created—the Report Header. Any control placed in the Report Header section gets printed only on the first page of the report. We want to see this label on every page, so select the label control and drag it down and drop it into the Page Header section. Now remove the Report Header section by clicking the Report Header/ Footer button in the Show/Hide group on the Arrange tab.

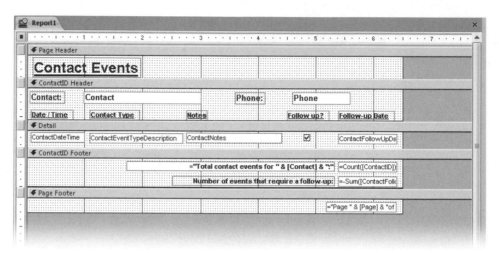

Figure 30-15 This is the completed Contact Events report that you will create in Design view.

2. Click the Add Existing Fields button in the Tools group on the Design tab to show the field list. If you see Fields Available In Related Tables and Fields Available In Other Tables, click Show Only Fields In The Current Record Source at the bottom of the field list to reduce the number of fields and tables you see. Drag the Contact field from the field list and drop it into the ContactID Header section. Use Arial 10-point bold for the label control and the text box control. Select the text box control and make it about 2 inches wide so that there's room to display all the characters in the contact name. Also drag and drop the Phone field into the header, and set the resulting text box control and the label control to Arial 10-point bold. Size all these controls to fit and line them up near the top of the section.

3. You'll need some column labels in the ContactID Header section. The easiest way to create them is to set up the text box control so that it has an attached label with no colon, set the defaults for the label control to the font you want, drag and drop the fields you need into the Detail section, and then cut the label controls from their respective text box controls and paste them into the header.

First, widen the design area of the report to about 6.5 inches and increase the height of the ContactID Header section to about 0.5 inch to give yourself some room to work. Next, to set the default properties for the text box and label controls, make sure the property sheet is open (click the Property Sheet button in the Tools group on the Design tab). Click the Text Box button in the Controls group on the Design tab. Select the All tab in the property sheet, scroll down, and check that the Auto Label property is set to Yes and that the Add Colon property is set to No. Also, set the Font Name property to Arial and the Font Size property to 8. Click the Label button in the Controls group, and set its font to Arial 8-point bold and underlined. (You set the font to bold by modifying the Font Weight property.)

Click the Add Existing Fields button in the Tools group to hide the property sheet and open the field list. Now drag the ContactDateTime, ContactEventType-Description, ContactNotes, ContactFollowUp, and ContactFollowUpDate fields from the field list and drop them into the Detail section one at a time.

Select the label for ContactDateTime, and then choose the Cut command in the Clipboard group on the Home tab (or press Ctrl+X) to separate the label from the control and move it to the Clipboard. Click the ContactID Header bar, and then click the Paste command in the Clipboard group (or press Ctrl+V) to paste the label in the upper-left corner of the ContactID Header section. Notice that you can now move the label independently in the ContactID Header section. (If you move the label before you separate it from its control, the control moves with it.) Separate the labels from the ContactEventTypeDescription, ContactNotes, ContactFollowUp, and ContactFollowUpDate controls one at a time, and move them to the ContactID Header section of the report.

> **Note**
>
> As you paste each label, you'll see warning smart tags appear that notify you that the labels aren't associated with any control. This is useful to know when you create labels in the Detail section. But in this case, this is what you want, so click the smart tag and select the Ignore Error option to turn off the warning for each label.

4. Line up the column labels in the ContactID Header section, placing the Date / Time label near the left margin, the Contact Type label about 1.1 inches from the left margin, the Notes label about 2.75 inches from the left margin, the Follow Up? label about 4.5 inches from the left margin, and the Follow-Up Date label about 5.4 inches from the left margin. You can set these distances in the Left property of each label's property sheet. Line up the tops of the labels by dragging a selection box around all five labels using the Select button in the Controls group on the Design tab and then clicking the Top command in the Control Alignment group on the Arrange tab.

5. You can enhance the appearance of the report by placing a line control across the bottom of the ContactID Header section. Click the Line button in the Controls group, and place a line in the ContactID Header section. To position this control at the bottom of the section, you need to find out the section's height. Click the ContactID Header bar to select the section, open the property sheet, and find the Height property. Next, select the line control, and set the following properties: Left 0, Width 6.5, and Height 0. Set the Top property equal to the Height of the section. (It's difficult to see this line in Figure 30-15, because it is hidden against the bottom of the section. You'll see it when you switch to Print Preview.)

6. You can make the text box control for ContactDateTime smaller (about 0.9 inch), and you need to make the ContactEventTypeDescription text box control about 1.6 inches wide. Set the Text Align property for the ContactDateTime and ContactFollowUpDate text box controls to Left. Access sized the text box for the ContactNotes field too wide because ContactNotes is a Memo data type. Select the ContactNotes and ContactEventTypeDescription text box controls together, and click the To Narrowest button in the Size group on the Arrange tab to make the ContactNotes text box the same width as the ContactEventTypeDescription text box.

7. Align the text box controls for ContactDateTime, ContactEventTypeDescription, ContactNotes, ContactFollowUp, and ContactFollowUpDate under their respective labels. You can align each one by placing each text box control to the right of the left edge of its label, selecting them both (hold down the Shift key while selecting each one), and then left aligning them by clicking the Left button in the Control Alignment group on the Arrange tab. Align the ContactFollowUp check box control visually under the center of its label. Select all the controls in the Detail section and top align them by clicking the Top button in the same group.

8. The height of the Detail section determines the spacing between lines in the report. You don't need much space between report lines, so make the Detail section smaller, until it's only slightly higher than the row of controls for displaying your data. (About 0.3 inch should suffice.)

9. Expand the height of the ContactID Footer section and then add a text box in this section under the ContactFollowUpDate text box control and delete its attached label. To calculate the number of events, click the text box control, and in the Control Source property in the property sheet, enter

   `=Count([ContactID])`

   It's a good idea to repeat the grouping information in the footer in case the detail lines span a page boundary. One way to do that is to add an expression in a text box. Add a second text box to the left of the first one (also delete its label) and stretch it to about 3.5 inches wide. Click the leftmost text box control to select it, and in the Control Source property in the property sheet, type

   `="Total contact events for " & [Contact] & ":"`

   Change the text box alignment to Right and change its font to Bold.

10. Add a second text box control in the ContactID Footer section under the first one. In the Control Source property in the property sheet, enter

    `= -Sum([ContactFollowUp])`

    Keep in mind that a True value in a yes/no field is the value −1. So, summing the values and then displaying the negative should give you a count of the contact events that require a follow-up. Click the attached label control and change the Caption property in the property sheet to

`Number of events that require a follow-up:`

Change Font Underline to No, right align the label, and size it to fit.

11. Add a line to the bottom of the ContactID Footer section to separate the end of the information about one contact from the next one. You can click the heading bar of the ContactID Footer to select the section and then look in the property sheet to find out the section's height, which should be about 0.5 inch. Select the line again, and in the property sheet set Left to 0, Top to the height of the section, Width to 6.5, Height to 0, and Border Width (the thickness of the line) to 2 pt.

12. Click the Insert Page Number button in the Controls group on the Design tab to open the Page Numbers dialog box shown here.

You want to display the current page number and the total number of pages on each page, so select the Page N Of M option under Format. The Page N option displays only the current page number. Next, to display these page numbers at the bottom of the report, select Bottom Of Page [Footer] under Position. The Top Of Page [Header] option places the control in the Page Header section of the report. In the Alignment list, select Right to display the page numbers on the right side of the page. The Left alignment option places the control that displays the page numbers on the left side of the report design grid, and the Center alignment option places the control in the center. The Inside alignment option places one control on the left side and one control on the right side of the report design grid. Access sets the Control Source property of these controls so that page numbers appear in the inside margin of pages in a bound book—odd page numbers appear on the left and even page numbers appear on the right. The Outside alignment option works just the opposite of Inside—even page numbers appear on the left and odd page numbers appear on the right.

Select the Show Number On First Page check box at the bottom of the dialog box to display the page numbers on all pages, including the first page. If you clear this check box, Access creates a control that will not show the page number on the first page. Click OK in the Page Numbers dialog box, and Access creates a new control in the Page Footer section.

13. Click the new text box control that you just created in the page footer, and look at the Control Source property in the property sheet. Access created the expression **="Page " & [Page] & " of " & [Pages]** in the Control Source property of the text box. [Page] is a report property that displays the current page number. [Pages] is a report property that displays the total number of pages in the report. Finally, change the Text Align property to Right for this new control.

After you finish, click the arrow below the View button in the Views group on the Ribbon and click Print Preview to see the result, shown in Figure 30-16. Notice in this figure that the detail lines are sorted in descending order by contact date/time. You'll recall from Figure 30-14 that the grouping and sorting specifications include a request to sort within group on ContactDateTime.

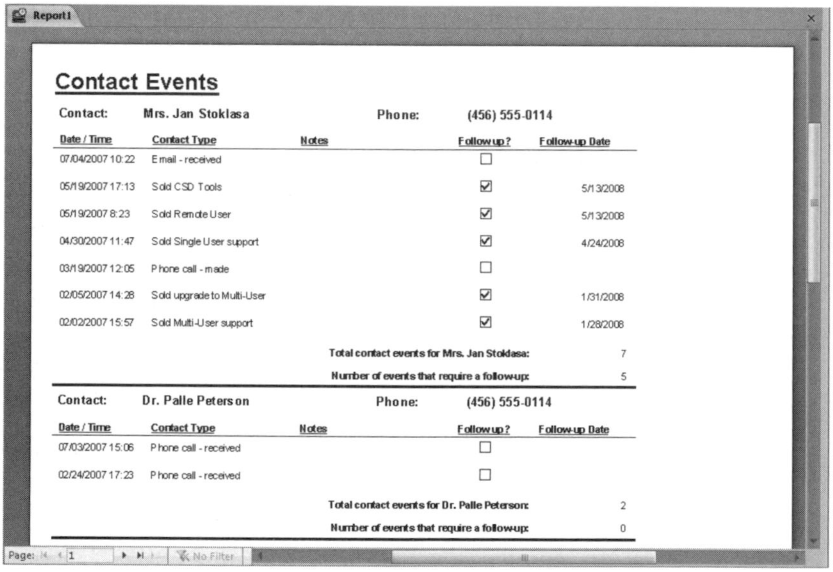

Figure 30-16 This is how your completed Contact Events report looks in Print Preview.

Now that you've seen how to create a report from scratch, you should have a good understanding of how to work with the individual design elements. In the remaining sections, we'll show you how to get a jump-start on your report design using the quick create Report command, the Report Wizard, and the new Layout view. You'll probably find that using one of these features is a good way to get a report started, and then you can use what you've learned thus far to fully customize your reports.

Using the Report Command

Access 2007 includes a new quick create Report command that makes it easy for you to quickly create quality reports. Similar to the quick create form commands, the Report command is a one-step process—you're not presented with any options or dialog boxes; Access simply creates a generic report with one click. You can use either a table or query as the base for the report. We'll create two quick reports to illustrate this process using the ContactsDataCopy.accdb sample database.

Open ContactsDataCopy.accdb, click the Navigation Pane menu, click Object Type under Navigate To Category, and then click Queries under Filter By Group to display a list of queries available in this database. The qryContacts query includes all the fields from the tblContacts table and sorts them by last name and then first name. Let's create a nice report of your contacts using this query. Scroll down to this query in the Navigation Pane, select it, and then click the Report command in the Reports group on the Create tab, as shown in Figure 30-17.

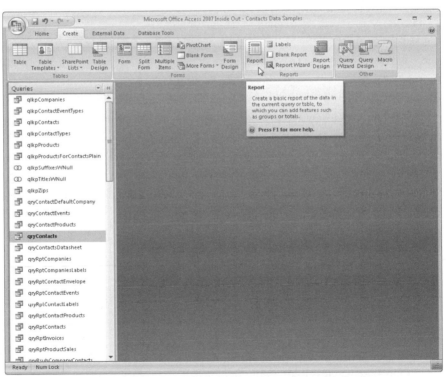

Figure 30-17 Click the Report command to let Access build a report using the qryContacts query.

After just a second or two, Access 2007 creates an entire report with all the fields in the query, complete with a logo, a title, the current date and time, a colored line beneath the column labels, and even a page count at the bottom of the pages, as shown

Chapter 30

in Figure 30-18. (You can best see the page count in Print Preview.) Access opens the report in Layout view so that you can begin the process of making modifications.

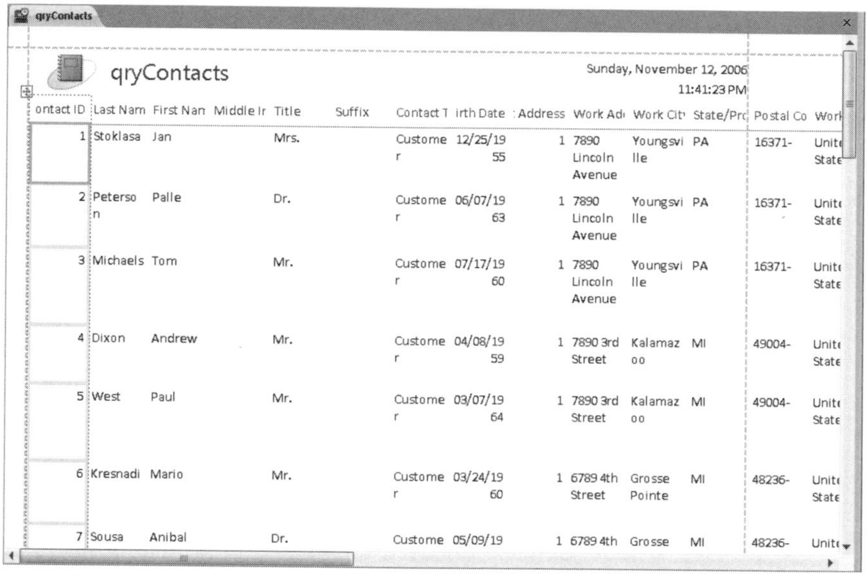

Figure 30-18 With one click, Access creates an entire formatted report for your convenience.

If you look closely at the report, you'll also see that there are significant problems with this layout. Access spread all the fields out in a tabular control layout. If you switch to Print Preview, you can see that this report would not be easy to read because the data in many columns wraps to multiple lines, and you have to scan across three pages to find all the data for each contact. If the number of contact records were even larger, the report would be extremely hard to follow. Access did much of the hard work for you in creating the report, but you still need to make many modifications in either Layout view or Design view to make the report readable. (We'll discuss Layout view in more detail later in this chapter.) Close this report now, and don't save it when prompted.

The qlkpProducts query includes all the fields from the tblProducts table and sorts them by product name. Select this query in the Navigation Pane and then click the Report command in the Reports group on the Create tab. Access 2007 creates another report very similar to the first one, as shown in Figure 30-19.

This query has only six fields, so Access was able to do a better job of laying out the fields horizontally. However, the Expire field and part of the Price field spill over onto a second page. Using the techniques you learned earlier in this chapter, it would probably take you less than a minute to resize some of the controls to fit everything onto one page and change the title. The rest of the report looks very usable as is. As you can see, the Report command can save you time over starting a report from scratch. Close the report, and don't save it when prompted.

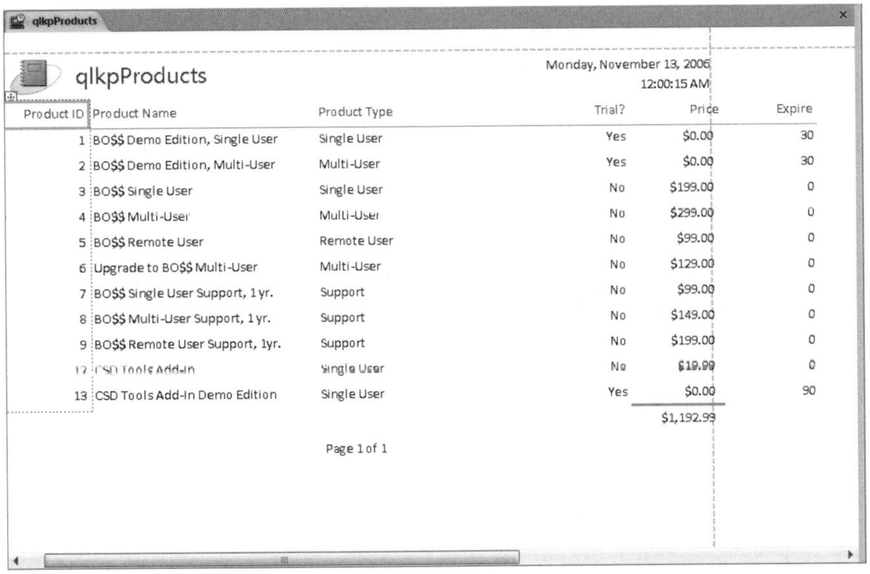
qlkpProducts

qlkpProducts

Monday, November 13, 2006
12:00:15 AM

Product ID	Product Name	Product Type	Trial?	Price	Expire
1	BO$$ Demo Edition, Single User	Single User	Yes	$0.00	30
2	BO$$ Demo Edition, Multi-User	Multi-User	Yes	$0.00	30
3	BO$$ Single User	Single User	No	$199.00	0
4	BO$$ Multi-User	Multi-User	No	$299.00	0
5	BO$$ Remote User	Remote User	No	$99.00	0
6	Upgrade to BO$$ Multi-User	Multi-User	No	$129.00	0
7	BO$$ Single User Support, 1 yr.	Support	No	$99.00	0
8	BO$$ Multi-User Support, 1 yr.	Support	No	$149.00	0
9	BO$$ Remote User Support, 1yr.	Support	No	$199.00	0
12	CSD Tools Add-In	Single User	No	$19.99	0
13	CSD Tools Add-In Demo Edition	Single User	Yes	$0.00	90
				$1,192.99	

Page 1 of 1

Figure 30-19 This report is easier to understand than the one created on a more complex query.

> **INSIDE OUT** **When to Use the Report Command**
>
> The Report command's strength is speed, not finesse. As the previous two examples demonstrate, this report option is not suited for all occasions. For complex queries or tables with quite a few fields, it might take you longer to clean up a report created with this one-click approach compared to starting from scratch. Although the Report command does create a simple total for the Price field, it does not create any groups or sorts, so you would have to manually add these. We find that the Report command is best suited for simple tables or queries that do not require a lot of complex report analysis.

Using the Report Wizard

The Report Wizard that Access 2007 provides to assist you in constructing reports is similar to the Form Wizard you used earlier to create forms. To practice using the Report Wizard, we'll build the Contact Events report again. Click the Navigation Pane menu, click Object Type under Navigate To Category, and then click Queries under Filter By Group. Select the qryRptContactEvents query in the Navigation Pane, and then click the Report Wizard button in the Reports group on the Create tab to open the Report Wizard.

Specifying Report Wizard Options

On the first page of the Report Wizard, shown in Figure 30-20, select the fields you want in your report. (If you have a table or query selected in the Navigation Pane and then click the Report Wizard button, Access automatically uses that object as the record source for the report.) You can select all available fields in the order in which they appear in the underlying query or table by clicking the double right arrow (>>) button. If you want to select only some of the fields or if you want to specify the order in which the fields appear in the report, select one field at a time in the Available Fields list and click the single right arrow (>) button to move the field to the Selected Fields list. If you make a mistake, you can select the field in the Selected Fields list and then click the single left arrow (<) button to move the field to the Available Fields list. Click the double left arrow (<<) button to remove all selected fields from the list on the right and start over.

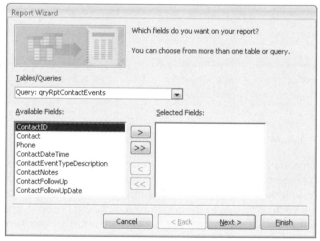

Figure 30-20 Select fields to include in the report on the first page of the Report Wizard.

To create the Contact Events report, you should select all the fields. Then, click the Next button to go to the next page.

INSIDE OUT   Selecting Fields from More Than One Table and/or Query

You can also select fields from one table or query and then change the table or query selection in the Tables/Queries list. The Report Wizard uses the relationships you defined in your database to build a new query that correctly links the tables or queries you specify. If the wizard can't determine the links between the data you select, it warns you and won't let you proceed unless you include data only from related tables.

The wizard examines your data and tries to determine whether there are any natural groups in the data. Because this query includes information from the tblContacts table that has a one-to-many relationship to information from the tblContactEvents table, the wizard assumes that you might want to group the information by contacts (the ContactID, Contact, and Phone fields), as shown in Figure 30-21. If you don't want any report groups or you want to set the grouping criteria yourself, select By tblContact-Events. In this case, the Report Wizard has guessed correctly, so click Next to go to the next step.

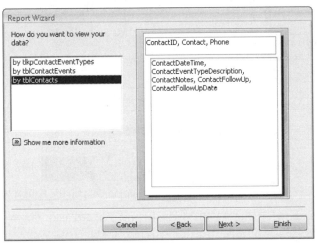

Figure 30-21 Make sure to verify the primary grouping criteria on the second page of the Report Wizard.

On the next page (shown in the background in Figure 30-22), the Report Wizard shows you the grouping already selected for ContactID and asks whether you want to add any grouping levels below that. (If you chose to set the criteria yourself—by choosing By tblContactEvents on the previous page—you will see a similar window with no first group selected.) You can select up to four grouping levels. The wizard doesn't allow you to enter an expression as a grouping value—something you can do when you build a report from scratch. If you want to use an expression as a grouping value in a report that you create with the Report Wizard, you have to include that expression in the underlying query. For this report, you could also group within each contact by the ContactDateTime field, so select that field and click the single right arrow to temporarily add it as a grouping level.

When you add grouping levels, the Report Wizard makes the Grouping Options button available for those levels. You can select the ContactDateTime By Month grouping level on the right side of this page and then click this button to see the Grouping Intervals dialog box, shown in Figure 30-22. For a text field, you can group by the entire field or by one to five of the leading characters in the field. For a date/time field, you can group by individual values or by year, quarter, month, week, day, hour, or minute. For a numeric field, you can group by individual values or in increments of 10, 50, 100, 500, 1,000, and so on, up to 500,000. As you can see, the Report Wizard has automatically assumed grouping by month when you added the ContactDateTime field as a grouping level. You don't need that grouping level in this sample, so cancel the Grouping Intervals dialog box, select ContactDateTime By Month on the right side of the page, and click the single left arrow to remove it. Then click Next.

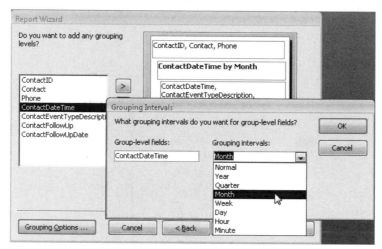

Figure 30-22 You can set grouping intervals on the grouping fields in the Report Wizard.

On the next page, shown in Figure 30-23, the Report Wizard asks you to specify any additional sorting criteria for the rows in the Detail section. (Access will sort the report at this point by the grouping level fields you specified on the previous page.) You can select up to four fields from your table or query by which to sort the data. By default, the sort order is ascending. Click the button to the right of the field selection list box to switch the order to descending. You can't enter expressions as you can in the Group, Sort, And Total pane. In this report, click the arrow to the right of the first box and select the ContactDateTime field. Click the button to the right once to switch it to Descending, as shown in the figure.

Click the Summary Options button to open the dialog box shown in Figure 30-24. Here you can ask the Report Wizard to display summary values in the group footers for any numeric fields the wizard finds in the Detail section. In this case, the Report Wizard sees that the ContactFollowUp field is the only one in the Detail section that is a number (a Yes/No data type). As you'll see later, the Report Wizard automatically generates a count of the rows, which explains why Count isn't offered as an option.

Select the Sum check box for this field. (You can add the minus sign after the wizard is done to get the correct count.) Note that you also have choices to calculate the average (Avg) of values over the group or to display the smallest (Min) or largest (Max) value. You can select multiple check boxes. You can also indicate that you don't want to see any detail lines by selecting the Summary Only option. (Sometimes you're interested in only the totals for the groups in a report, not all of the detail.) If you select the Calculate Percent Of Total For Sums check box, the Report Wizard will also display, for any field for which you have selected the Sum check box, an additional field that shows what percent of the grand total this sum represents. When you have the settings the way you want them, click OK to close the dialog box. Click Next in the Report Wizard to go on.

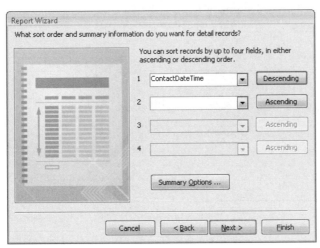

Figure 30-23 Select ContactDateTime on the fourth page of the Report Wizard to sort on that field.

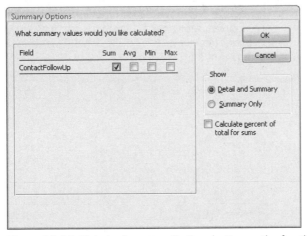

Figure 30-24 Click the Summary Options button on the fourth page of the Report Wizard to select additional summary options.

On the next page, shown in Figure 30-25, you can select a layout style and a page orientation for your report. When you select a layout option, the Report Wizard displays a preview on the left side of the page. In this case, the Outline layout option in Portrait orientation will come closest to the hand-built report you created earlier in this chapter. You should also select the check box for adjusting the field widths so that all the fields fit on one page.

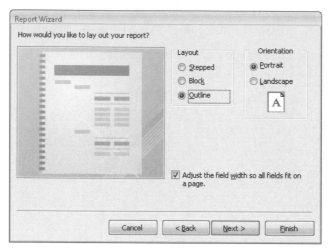

Figure 30-25 Choose a layout style and page orientation on this page of the Report Wizard.

Click Next to go to the next page of the Report Wizard. On this page you can select from 25 built-in report styles. If you defined your own custom report style using Auto-Format in Design view, you can also select your custom style. Some of the built-in styles are probably better suited for informal reports in a personal database. Other formats look more professional. Also, some styles include many color elements while others just a few. When you select a style option, the wizard displays a preview on the left side of the page. For this example, select the Access 2007 style. Click Next to go to the final page of the Report Wizard, shown in Figure 30-26.

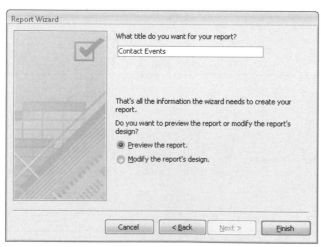

Figure 30-26 You can specify a report title on the last page of the Report Wizard.

Here, you can type a report title. Note that the wizard uses this title to create the report caption that is displayed in the title bar of the window when you open the report in Print Preview, the label that serves as the report header, and the report name. It's probably best to enter a title that's appropriate for the caption and label and not worry about the title being a suitable report name. If you're using a naming convention (such as prefixing all reports with *rpt* as we've done in the sample databases), it's easy to switch to the Navigation Pane after the wizard is done to rename your report. In this case, enter **Contact Events** as the title.

Viewing the Result

Select the Preview The Report option on the final page of the Report Wizard, and then click the Finish button to create the report and display the result in Print Preview, as shown in Figure 30-27. One of the first things you will notice is that Access has created alternating background colors for the detail lines to make it easier to see the data that goes with each record. This feature can be very useful if reports have a lot of information in the detail records and if the lines are packed close together.

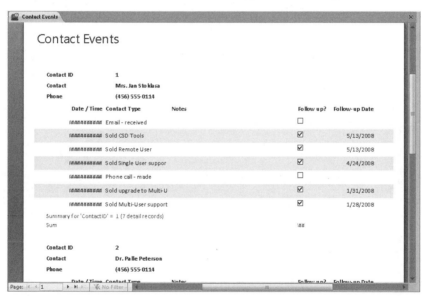

Figure 30-27 This is the first page of the Contact Events report created using the Report Wizard.

It's easy to use Design view or Layout view to modify minor items (such as adjusting the width and alignment of the ContactDateTime and ContactEventDescription fields and resizing the labels) to obtain a result nearly identical to the report you constructed earlier. You can see in Figure 30-27 that the ContactDateTime field displays # symbols for all the records. Access displays # symbols for date/time and numeric fields when it cannot display all the data in the control, but only when you select the Check For Truncated Number Fields check box under Application Options in the Current Database category of the Access Options dialog box. You also need to fix the expression in the text box that calculates the Sum of the ContactFollowUp field and change the format to display the number. (The Report Wizard set the format to Yes/No.) You should also change the Sum label associated with this calculation. We'll show you how to fix all these problems in the next section. You can find the Report Wizard's report at this point saved as rptXmplContactEvents2 in the sample database. As you might imagine, the Report Wizard can help you to get a head start on more complex report designs.

Modifying a Wizard-Created Report in Layout View

In the previous section you used the Report Wizard to create a report for contact events. Now you need to clean up this report so that it more closely resembles the Contact Events report you built from scratch earlier in this chapter. Using Layout view makes this process quick and easy. Right-click the Contact Events report in the Navigation Pane (or rptXmplContactEvents2) and click Layout View on the shortcut menu to open this report in Layout view, as shown in Figure 30-28.

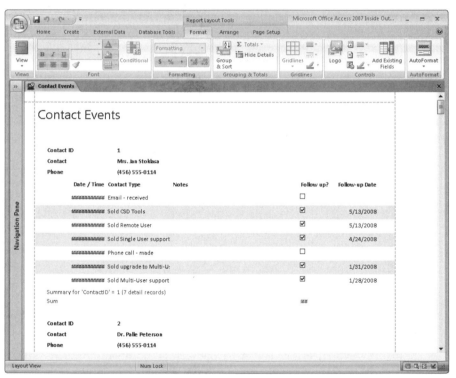

Figure 30-28 Open the Contact Events report in Layout view to begin making changes.

Access 2007 shows the Report Layout Tools collection of three contextual tabs—Format, Arrange, and Page Setup—on the Ribbon. The report design grid in Layout view looks less like a grid than a sheet of paper. You'll also notice that there are no page breaks in Layout view, and by default Access displays dashed lines along the edges of the report to denote the print margins.

You first need to make the ContactDateTime field wider to accommodate the data. In Layout view you can see live data, so making column adjustments like this is easy.

Click the ContactDateTime label in the first group (the label Date / Time), move your mouse pointer to the left edge of the highlighted control until it becomes a double-sided arrow, and then drag the control to the left until you can see the dates and times in the records, as shown in Figure 30-29. After you adjust the field width for the Date / Time label, click the Center button in the Font group on the Format tab to center the text in the label.

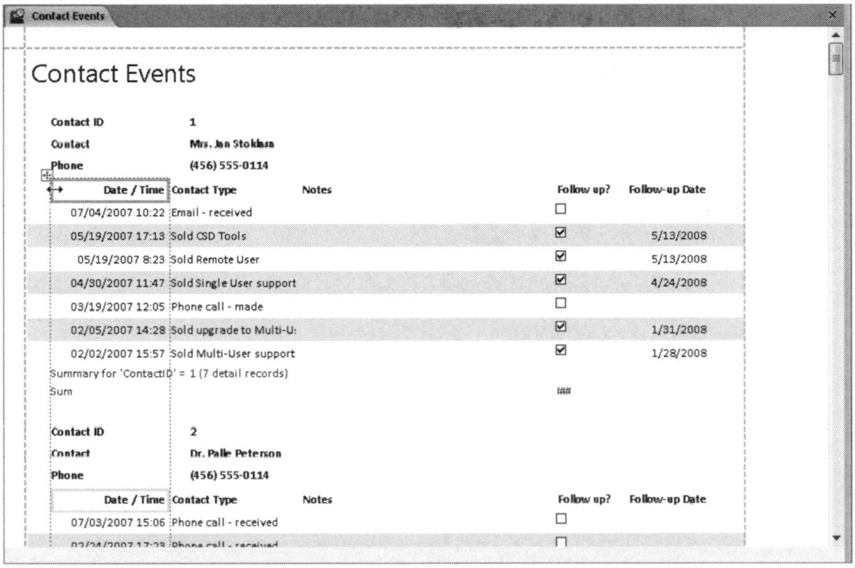

Figure 30-29 Drag the ContactDateTime label control to the left to resize the entire column.

The ContactEventTypeDescription field also needs to be wider because some of the data is being truncated. Click the ContactEventTypeDescription label in the first group (the label Contact Type), move your mouse pointer to the right edge of the highlighted control until it becomes a double-sided arrow, and then drag the control to the right until you can see all the various contact event descriptions in the records, as shown in Figure 30-30. After you make this adjustment, you can scroll down the records to see whether the increased width accommodates the data in each record. As you make the ContactEventTypeDescription field wider, Access pushes the remaining fields further to the right. If you look closely at Figure 30-30, you can see that the ContactFollowUpDate field now extends past the print margin. Without even having to switch to Print Preview, you know you have to make further field size adjustments in order to keep the data from spanning across pages.

The Notes field seems to be too wide, so let's shorten this field to make room for the other fields. Click the Notes field label and reduce the width by dragging the right edge to the left until the ContactFollowUpDate field is within the print margin.

The label for the number of events requiring follow-up displays only the word *Sum* at the moment. This label is certainly not very descriptive, so let's change it to something more meaningful. Double-click on the Sum label and type **Number of events that**

require a follow-up: directly over the word *Sum*. After you press Enter, Access automatically resizes the control to accommodate the new text, as shown in Figure 30-31.

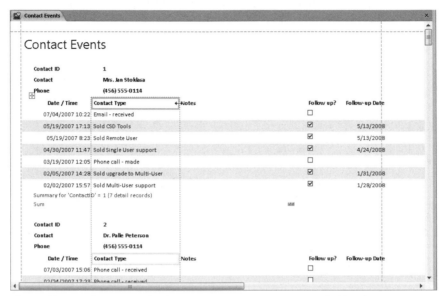

Figure 30-30 When you make the ContactEventTypeDescription field wider, Access moves the other columns to the right.

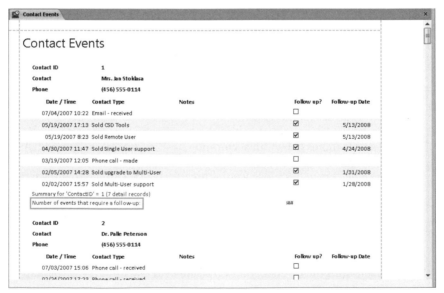

Figure 30-31 Access resizes the control for you in Layout view when you enter a new caption for a label.

You now need to move this label closer to the control that actually lists the sum of the follow-up check boxes. Because there are no controls between the label and the Sum control you have two choices—you can drag the right edge of the label to the Sum control (and right align the text) or you can move the label closer to the Sum control. Let's move this control closer instead of resizing it. Select the label control so that the edges are highlighted with a different color and then drag it closer to the Sum control, as shown in Figure 30-32. As you drag the control, Access displays an outline of the label's size dimensions so that you can easily judge how it will fit in its new position. Release the mouse to drop the label into place next to the Sum control.

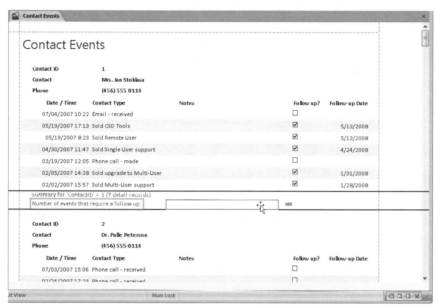

Figure 30-32 You can easily drag and drop controls into new positions using Layout view.

The Sum control in the Follow Up? column needs to be wider because it is displaying # symbols as was the ContactDateTime field. Resize this control by dragging its right edge. You can now see that Access displays only Yes or No values instead of an actual count. The Report Wizard in this case did not create an expression to correctly calculate the number of follow-ups. Select this control and click the Property Sheet command in the Tools group on the Arrange tab (or press the F4 key) to open the property sheet. Click the All tab on the property sheet and change the Control Source to

```
= -Sum([ContactFollowUp])
```

Move down to the Format property and select Standard from the list of formats to display a number in this control instead of Yes or No. Finally, move down to the Decimal Places property and choose 0 from the list of options to display only whole numbers in the field, as shown in Figure 30-33. Access now displays an integer value representing the number of follow-ups needed. Close the property sheet to see the entire report again.

Figure 30-33 Change the properties of the Sum Of ContactFollowUp control in order to display an integer instead of a Yes or No value.

The Report Wizard created alternating background colors for the detail records in this report. The color is light, so let's change that color to provide more contrast. Click the far left edge of the report next to one of the detail records, and Access highlights all the detail records, as shown in Figure 30-34.

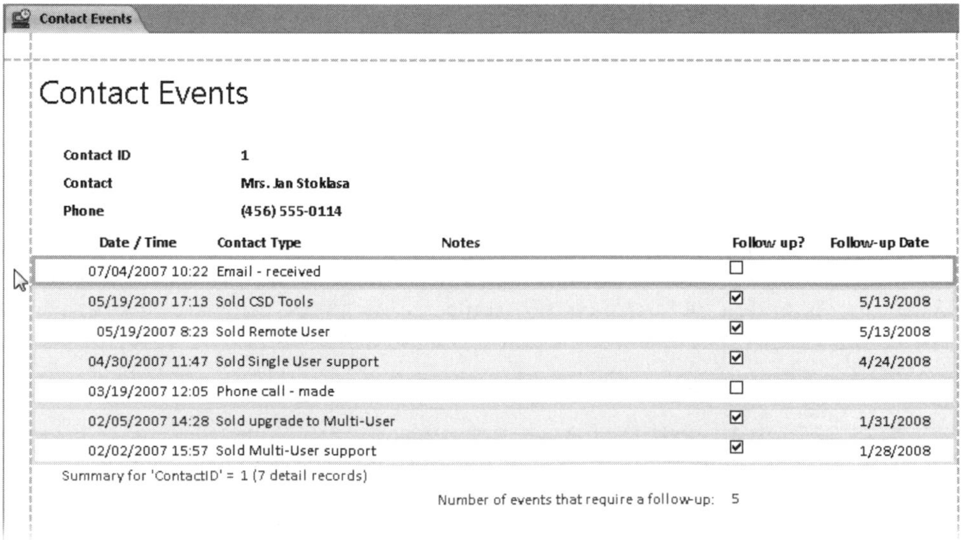

Figure 30-34 Click the left side of the report to highlight all the detail records.

Now click the arrow to the right of the Alternate Fill/Back Color button in the Font group on the Format tab to display a color palette. Select Medium Gray 1 to provide more contrast on the report, as shown in Figure 30-35.

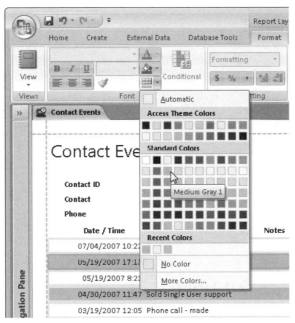

Figure 30-35 You can select an alternating background color to provide more contrast to your detail records.

Click the Save button on the Quick Access Toolbar to save the changes you made to this report. Switch to Print Preview to see how your completed report looks on paper, as shown in Figure 30-36. This report now looks very close to the Contact Events report you created from scratch earlier in the chapter. You can find this report saved as rptXmplContactEvents3 in the sample database. By using the Report Wizard to do all the heavy lifting and Layout view to make some quick changes, you can create a professional-looking report in a very short time.

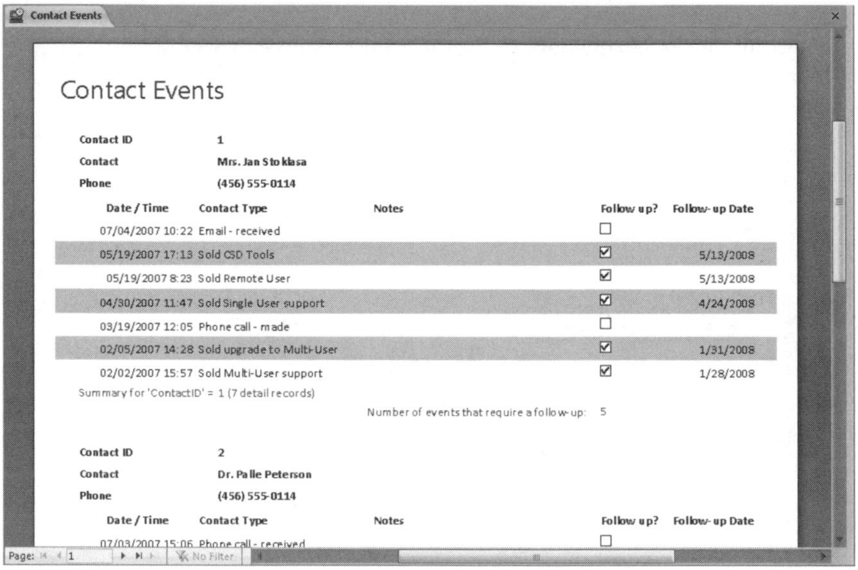

Figure 30-36 Your completed report now includes all the changes you made in Layout view.

Building a Report in Layout View

In this chapter you've learned how to create a report from scratch in Design view, to quickly build a simple report using the Report command, to create a report using the Report Wizard to get a jump-start on your work, and to use Layout view to modify an existing report. You've been creating a Contact Events report in the preceding sections, so we'll continue this example now using Layout view.

Starting with a Blank Report

If you want to follow along in this section, open the ContactsDataCopy.accdb database. Click the Blank Report button in the Reports group on the Create tab. Access 2007 opens a new blank report in Layout view with the field list displayed on the right, as shown in Figure 30-37.

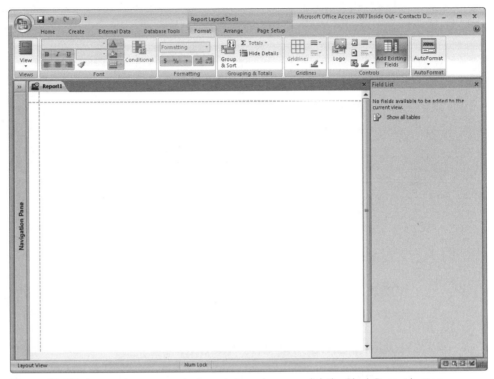

Figure 30-37 Access always opens in Layout view when you click the Blank Report button.

The report does not yet have a record source, so no fields are displayed in the field list. You can click Show All Tables in the field list to display a list of all tables in this database, but you want to use the saved qryRptContactEvents query that contains all the fields you need from several tables. Click the Property Sheet button in the Tools group on the Arrange tab, click the All tab, and select the qryRptContactEvents query for the Record Source property. Switch back to the field list by clicking the Add Existing Fields button in the Controls group on the Format tab, and then click Show Only Fields In The Current Record Source at the bottom of the field list to show only the eight fields in the query, as shown in Figure 30-38.

You should start this new report by entering a title, so click the Title button in the Controls group on the Format tab. Access places a label control in the upper-left corner of the report and enters the name of the report as Report1. Click inside this label, highlight the existing characters, and change the text to **Contact Events**. As you type the new characters, Access automatically resizes the label to accommodate the length of the new text. Press Enter to save the new title in the control.

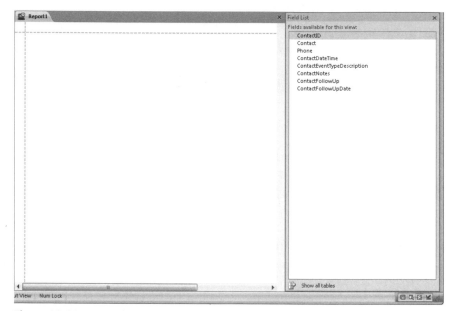

Figure 30-38 Assign the qryRptContactEvents query as the new report's record source.

Adding Grouping and Sorting

You need to set up the grouping and sorting options for the ContactID and Contact-DateTime fields as you did earlier in the chapter. Click the Group & Sort button in the Grouping & Totals group on the Format tab to open the Group, Sort, And Total pane. Click the Add A Group button and set the following options for ContactID, as shown in Figure 30-39:

```
Group On ContactID From Smallest To Largest, By Entire Value, With No Totals, With
Title Contact ID, With A Header Section, With A Footer Section, Do Not Keep Group
Together On One Page
```

As soon as you select ContactID in the Select Field box that opens when you click the arrow next to Group On, Access 2007 places a text box bound to ContactID and an associated label on the report. In Layout view, it's hard to see where the different report sections begin and end. When you create the ContactID group level, Access creates a header and footer for this group, but because you see live data in Layout view, the actual design layout can sometimes be hard to visualize. Right now it almost looks like the ContactID field is in the report's Detail section because you see all the records listed one right after another. Switch to Design view for a moment and take a quick look at what Access has created so far. In Figure 30-40, you can see that Access correctly placed the title label in the Report Header section instead of the Page Header section. The ContactID field and label are positioned in the new ContactID group level (as shown in the ContactID Header section). This is what you want, so switch back to Layout view to continue creating your report.

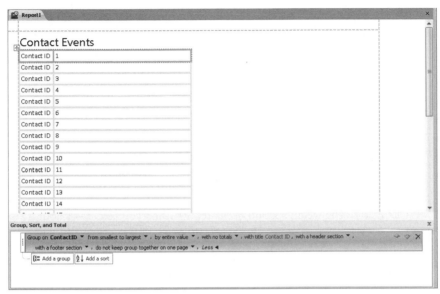

Figure 30-39 After you add ContactID as a group level, Access adds that field to the report grid.

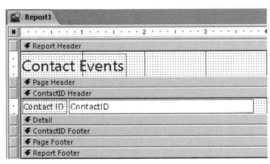

Figure 30-40 In Design view, you can see where Access has placed the various controls in the report sections.

You need to add a sort on the ContactDateTime field, so click the Add A Group button in the Group, Sort, And Total pane and set the following options for ContactDateTime:

```
Sort By ContactDateTime From Newest To Oldest, By Entire Value, With No Totals, With
Title Date / Time, Without A Header Section, Without A Footer Section, Do Not Keep
Group Together On One Page
```

INSIDE OUT

Save a Step by Choosing Add A Group Instead of Add A Sort

You could also click Add A Sort to define the sort on the ContactDateTime field, but Access 2007 won't add the field to the report layout. When you click Add A Group, Access builds a group header section and adds the ContactDateTime field. When you change the grouping specification to Without A Header Section, Access moves the ContactDateTime field into the Detail section for you. This saves having to find the field in the field list and add it yourself.

Just as before, Access places a new control and label on the report for you after you select the ContactDateTime field, as shown in Figure 30-41. In this case, Access places this field in the Detail section of the report when you select Without A Header Section. After you select Without A Header Section, you'll notice that With Title changes from Date / Time to Click To Add. Access moves the label and text box from the new Contact-DateTime Header section into the Detail section. The new label still shows Date / Time, but Access changes the specification to show Click To Add in the With Title column. You can now see the report beginning to take shape with two fields on the grid and the controls displaying live data. Close the Group, Sort, And Total pane now.

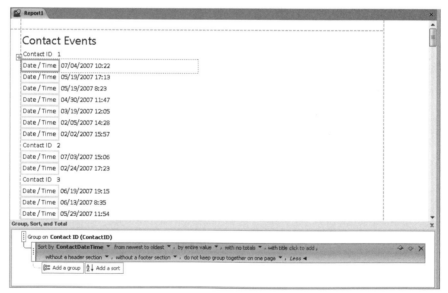

Figure 30-41 Access adds the ContactDateTime field to the Detail section below the ContactID field.

Now that you have all your grouping and sorting set up, you need to add the additional fields onto the report. If necessary, click the Add Existing Fields button in the Controls group on the Format tab to open the field list again. Click the Contact field in the field list, drag it onto the report, and drop it just below the Contact ID label and text box, as shown in Figure 30-42. When you have it correctly positioned, Access displays a horizontal I-bar below the Contact ID controls.

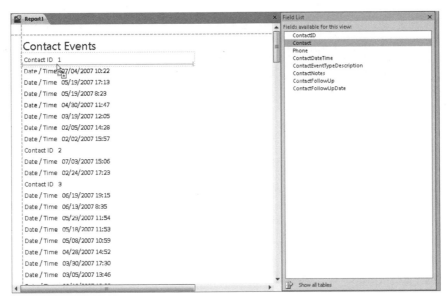

Figure 30-42 Drag the Contact field and drop it below the ContactID field.

Access places the Contact field right below the Contact ID label and text box controls and appears to push the Date / Time records down the page. Now that you have the Contact field in place, you really don't need the ContactID field at all. Earlier in the chapter when you built this report in Design view, you didn't include the ContactID field because the number itself is probably meaningless to whoever sees this report. The contact's name is more important, so let's delete the ContactID controls now. Click on either the ContactID label or text box and press Delete to remove these two controls from the grid. Alternatively, you can click the Delete button in the Records group on the Home tab. Your report should now look like Figure 30-43.

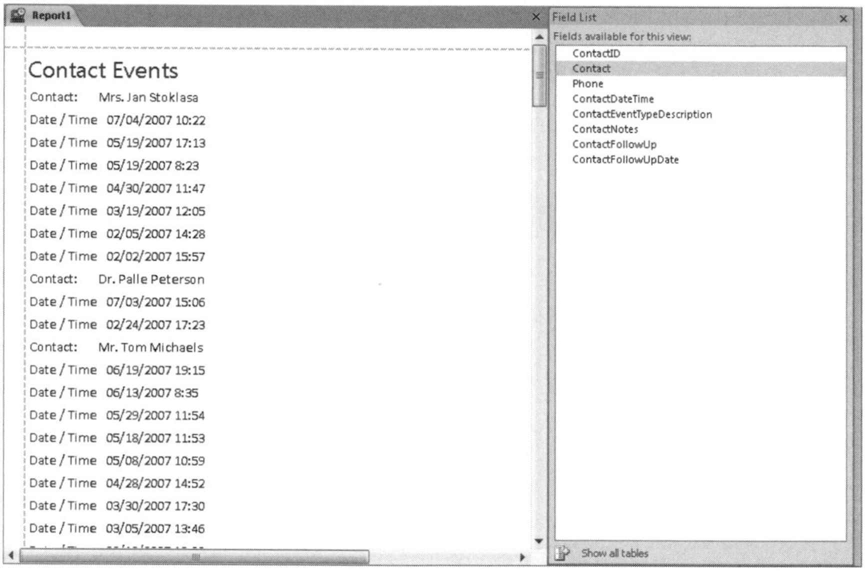

Figure 30-43 Access moves the other controls up after you delete the ContactID text box and label.

INSIDE OUT Why Delete the ContactID Controls?

It's true that you probably could have created the group header directly using the Contact field rather than ContactID to see a similar end result. However, for each contact, only the value in the ContactID field is guaranteed to be unique. (It's the primary key of the tblContacts table.) Although it's highly unlikely to find two contacts with the same name, it could happen, and you would end up with contact event data for multiple unique contact ID values grouped under one heading. Also, creating a group on a numeric value (ContactID) is slightly more efficient than creating a group on a text value (Contact).

Now let's add the Phone field to the report beneath the contact name. Click the Phone field in the field list, drag it onto the report, and drop it just below the label and text box controls for the first contact. As before, make sure the I-bar is right below the contact label and text box controls before releasing the mouse. Access places the Phone field in the ContactID Header section and lines up the control to match the Contact field. (You can switch to Design view if you'd like to see this.)

Working with Control Layouts

When you're designing a report in Layout view, Access 2007 automatically places any controls that you add to the report inside a *control layout*. Control layouts help you to align and position controls on reports and forms. You can think of a control layout as being similar to a table in Microsoft Word or a spreadsheet in Microsoft Excel. When you widen or narrow one control in a column, you change the width of any other controls in that column that are part of that control layout. Likewise, when you increase or decrease the height of a control, you're changing the height of all the controls on that row.

There are two kinds of control layouts in Access 2007— *stacked* and *tabular.* In a stacked control layout, Access "stacks" bound controls for different fields in a column and places all the labels down the left side. You can have multiple sets of stacked controls within a section. Any controls (including associated labels) in a stacked layout must all be in one section. In the report you've built thus far, Access has placed the contact and phone number controls in a stacked layout in the ContactID Header section. It has also placed the contact date/time controls in a stacked layout in the Detail section.

In a tabular control layout, Access places bound controls horizontally with labels along the top as column headings—much like rows on a spreadsheet. A tabular control layout can include controls in different sections of a report—for example, the labels can appear in a header section and the data controls in the Detail section. You'll learn later in this section how to convert the stacked layout for fields in the Detail section into a tabular layout.

INSIDE OUT   Is Layout View a Useful Way to Build Reports?

The answer depends on your level of expertise. As experienced developers, we find Layout view somewhat frustrating. It's not always obvious which section contains the controls for a field that we've just added to the report. Notice that we recommend you switch to Design view several times during the design process to verify where Access has placed controls. Also, Access automatically adds any field into a control layout, and you don't have much control over how it does this. Although control layouts can help you align controls in a pleasing way, they severely restrict how you place your controls and how you size them within a layout group. If you're an experienced developer, you might use Layout view to quickly place controls in a new report design, but then you'll probably switch to Design view to selectively remove control layouts so that you can finish customizing your design.

The text box controls for the Phone field and the Contact field are both too wide at this point. You can see this by clicking any of the controls for either field—Access draws a dotted line showing you the boundary of all the controls in the stacked layout group. Start by clicking the Phone field text box, move your mouse to the right edge until it becomes a double-sided arrow, and then click and drag the edge of the field to the left but make sure you don't shorten the field too much. Give yourself more room than you think you might need on the right side because as you resize the Phone field you'll notice that Access resizes the Contact field as well, and you need enough room in that field to display the names on one line. You can see this effect in Figure 30-44. (Note: The longest contact names are near the end of the list.) When you resize the Phone field, you resize the Contact field and vice versa, so if you shorten the Phone field too much, Access has to move some of the data in the Contact field down to a second line.

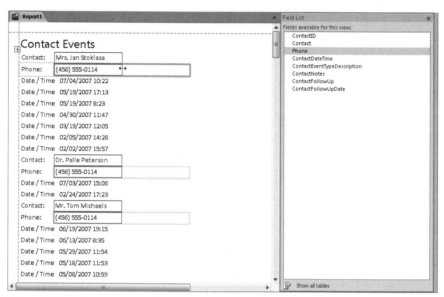

Figure 30-44 Access resizes the Contact and Phone fields together.

The only control in the Detail section of the report at the moment is the ContactDate-Time field. You'll eventually need to convert this stacked control layout to a tabular control layout, and you'll need some additional horizontal space. If you click the Con-tactDateTime text box, you'll see that it is far wider than it needs to be. Grab the right edge of the control and drag it to the left so that the text box is just wide enough to display all the data.

To see how this affects placing additional controls in the section, click ContactEvent-TypeDescription in the field list and drag it to the right edge of ContactDateTime. Access lets you place the horizontal I-bar either above or below the ContactDateTime field controls, but not to the right of the field, which is what you want to do. Go ahead and drop it below the first ContactDateTime control, as shown in Figure 30-45.

After you release the mouse, Access places the ContactEventTypeDescription field directly below the ContactDateTime field and sizes it to match the width of the Con-tactDateTime field, as shown in Figure 30-46. Because the width you chose for the ContactDateTime field won't allow the data in ContactEventTypeDescription to fit on one line for all records, Access expands the height on those records that have more characters.

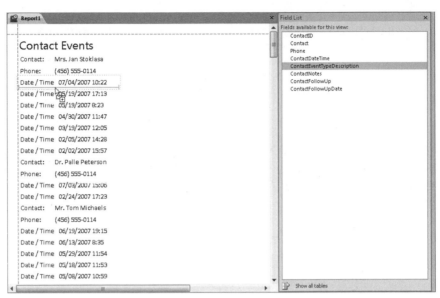

Figure 30-45 Drop the ContactEventTypeDescription field below the first ContactDateTime field.

Figure 30-46 Access places the ContactEventTypeDescription field into the stacked control layout with the ContactDateTime field.

If you added the remaining three fields—ContactNotes, ContactFollowUp, and Contact-FollowUpDate—to the report Detail section, Access would also stack these down the left edge on the report. You want to see these fields placed horizontally across the report, so you need to change the control layout in this section from stacked to tabular. Click the Date / Time label or text box, hold down the Shift key, and then click the Contact Type label or text box to select both controls. Click the Remove button in the Control Layout group on the Arrange tab to remove the control layout applied to this section, as shown in Figure 30-47.

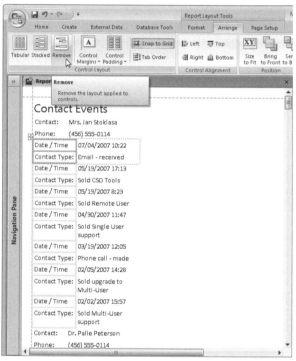

Figure 30-47 You can remove control layouts by clicking the Remove button on the Arrange tab.

Now that you have removed the control layout for the Detail section, these controls act independently—if you resize one control, the other will not resize. If you add new fields to the Detail section at this point, you might have some extra work in getting everything properly aligned. Because you want to see the other fields displayed horizontally, applying a tabular control layout to the Detail section will make placement and alignment of the new fields much simpler. Select the Date / Time and Contact Type labels or text boxes as you did previously, and then click the Tabular button in the Control Layout group on the Arrange tab, as shown in Figure 30-48.

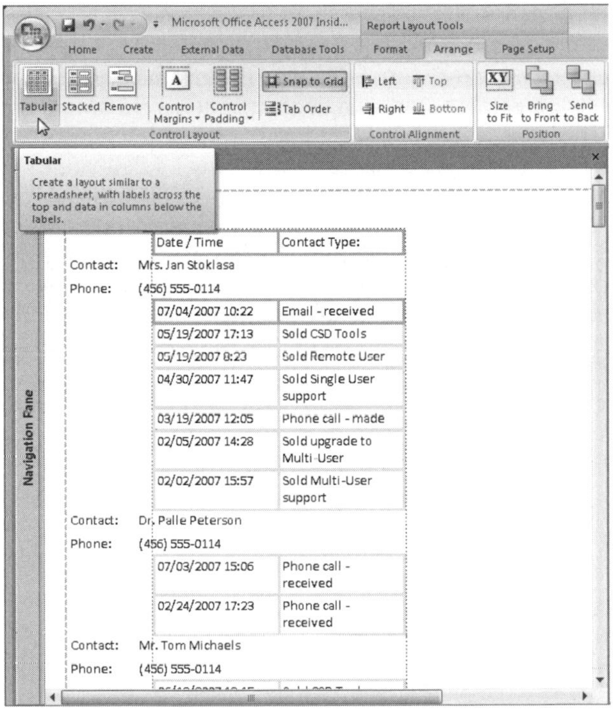

Figure 30-48 The tabular control layout arranges the controls with labels horizontally across the report.

INSIDE OUT   You Don't Have to Remove a Layout Before Converting It

Although we told you to select both controls in the Detail section and then click Remove, you don't actually have to do that. We added that step so that you could see the controls independent of the layout. When you want to convert a layout from stacked to tabular or vice versa, select the controls in the layout and then click the layout you want in order to directly convert it.

Access now places the labels and text box controls for the ContactDateTime and ContactEventTypeDescription fields in a tabular format. The two labels are placed horizontally across the report just below the report title. Access also moves the ContactEventTypeDescription text box to the right of the ContactDateTime text box control. (Access has actually placed the labels in the Page Header section—you can verify this by switching briefly to Design view.) During the switch to tabular format, Access also moves the labels and controls about one inch from the left side of the report. This layout is now closer to the report you built from scratch in Design view earlier in this chapter.

Because these two field controls are now next to each other instead of stacked, you can change the width of one of them without affecting the other. Let's move both the labels and text boxes back to the left margin of the report. Click the Date / Time label and increase the width by dragging its left edge to the print margin dotted line on the left side of the report. The Date / Time label is aligned with the left margin of the report, but now it's too wide, so decrease the width by dragging its right edge toward the left. As you resize the label, Access also resizes the ContactDateTime field control. Release the mouse when you can still see all the data in the ContactDateTime field control. Access moves the Contact Type label and the ContactEventTypeDescription field to the left after you reduce the width of the date/time controls. Now click the Contact Type label and expand the width to the right to allow extra room for the characters in the longest ContactEventTypeDescription field control. After you have expanded the width, Access reduces the height of the ContactEventTypeDescription field control to one line, as shown in Figure 30-49.

Figure 30-49 Expand the width of the ContactEventTypeDescription field so that the data fits on one line.

Now you're ready to add the three remaining fields to the report. Click ContactNotes in the field list and drag it to the right edge of the Contact Type label until you see a long vertical I-bar, as shown in Figure 30-50. The vertical I-bar indicates that the field is in the right position, so release the mouse. Access places a Notes label along the same line as the Date / Time and Contact Type labels and a Notes field next to the ContactDate-Time and ContactEventTypeDescription field controls in the Detail section, as shown in Figure 30-51.

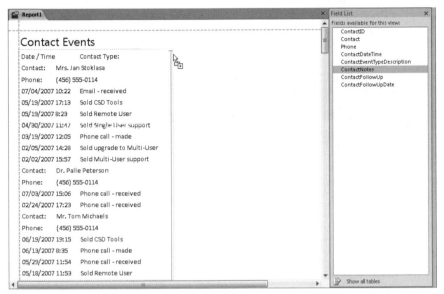

Figure 30-50 Use the vertical I-bar to help you position the ContactNotes field.

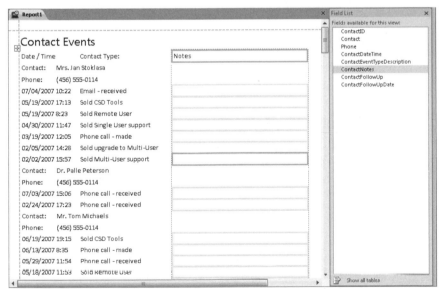

Figure 30-51 After you drop the ContactNotes field on the report, Access adds a label and text box control to the appropriate report sections.

The ContactNotes field is too wide at this point, so reduce its width by dragging its right edge toward the left side of the report. Now drag the ContactFollowUp field to the right of the Notes label using the same technique. After the ContactFollowUp field is in place, drag the last field, ContactFollowUpDate, into position to the right of the ContactFollowUp field. Close the field list so that you can see the whole report grid and the right print margin. Because these controls are in a tabular control layout, if you resize the width of one of them, the others move to the left or right accordingly. Make any small adjustments you need to the widths of the fields so that you can see all the data, but make sure the ContactFollowUpDate field does not extend past the right print margin. Your report at this point should look like Figure 30-52.

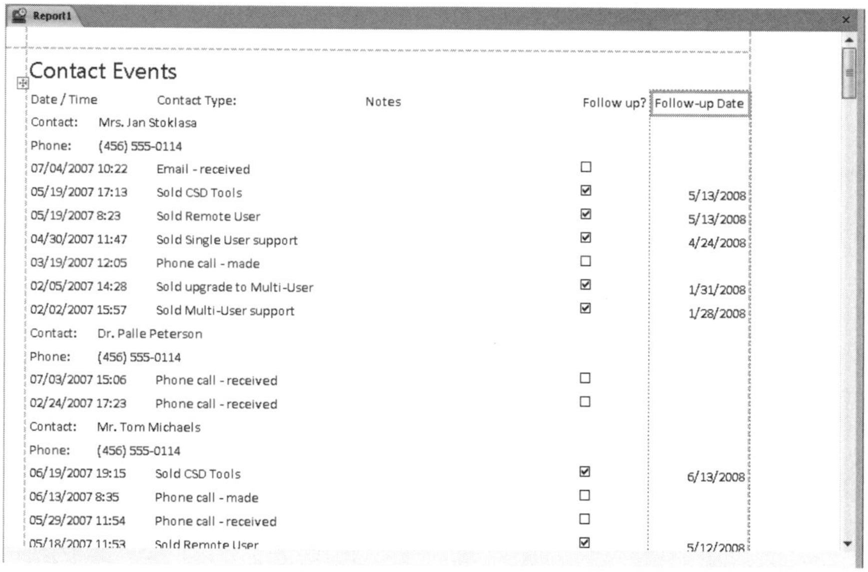

Figure 30-52 Your report is beginning to take shape with all the fields now in place.

Adding Totals to Records

All your fields are in place, so now you can add some controls for counting the events and follow-ups. You can add some of these elements to the report while in Layout view, but you'll still have to fine-tune the report using Design view, as you'll soon see. Start with adding a count of the follow-ups by right-clicking on the Follow Up? label and clicking Total Follow Up? and then Count Values, as shown in Figure 30-53.

Access places a new control in the ContactID Footer section in the same column as the ContactFollowUp field, as shown in Figure 30-54. Remember that when you created this report using the Report Wizard, you had to correct the Sum expression for the ContactFollowUp field to display a correct count of the number of contact events requiring a follow-up. (See page 1047.) In this case, Access correctly creates an expression to total the number of True values in the ContactFollowUp field. (The Count Records option, shown in Figure 30-53, would ask Access to calculate a simple count of the number of records in that group, which is not we want for this field.) To align the total with the check boxes, click the new control—where you see the number 5—and then click the Align Left button in the Font group on the Format tab.

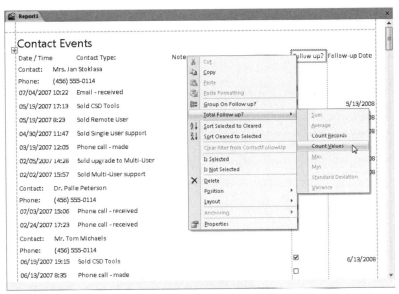

Figure 30-53 Click the Count Values command to create a control to total the follow-ups for each contact.

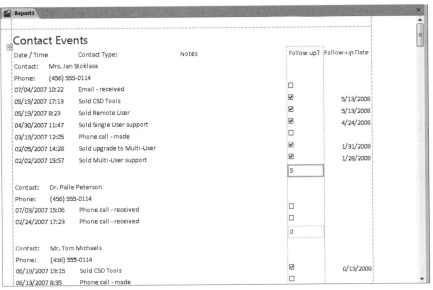

Figure 30-54 Access creates an expression to count the number of True values for the ContactFollowUp field.

You need to create a similar count of event records for each contact, so right-click the first ContactEventTypeDescription field (under the Phone field), and click Total Contact Type and then Count Values, as shown in Figure 30-55.

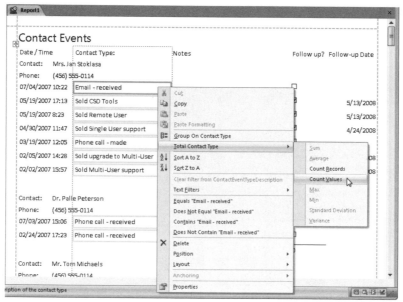

Figure 30-55 Click the Count Values option to create a control to total the event records.

Access places another new control in the ContactID Footer section in the same column as the ContactEventTypeDescription field, as shown in Figure 30-56. Access now displays a correct count of the number of events.

When the report is printed, it would be nice to have a page number at the bottom of the page. Click the Insert Page Number button in the Controls group on the Format tab to open the Page Numbers dialog box, discussed in "Completing the Report" on page 1031. Select the following options in the Page Numbers dialog box: Page N Of M, Bottom Of Page [Footer], Alignment set to Right, and Show Number On First Page. Click OK to close the Page Numbers dialog box.

> **Note**
>
> You won't immediately see a difference to the report in Layout view after you add a page count. If you scroll to the bottom of this report, you'll see the control says Page 1 Of 1. In Layout view, Access does not count the number of pages because it is not actually formatting the pages for printing. If you switch to Design view, you can see that Access placed the control on the right side of the report in the Page Footer section. If you switch to Print Preview, you can see the correct page numbers displayed on each page.

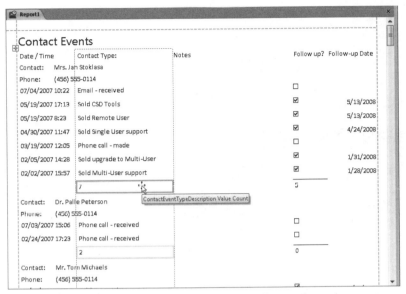

Figure 30-56 Access now correctly displays a total of events for each contact.

Applying an AutoFormat

Your report is functional right now, but with a little formatting you can make it look more professional and also easier to read. You could selectively add some color to certain controls to highlight specific areas, but here again you can let Access do most of the work. Access 2007 has 25 built-in AutoFormats to spice up your reports. You can easily click one of the AutoFormats to see what it would look like applied to your report. If you don't like it, click the Undo command on the Quick Access Toolbar and then try another one. To match the report you created previously using the Report Wizard, let's choose the Access 2007 AutoFormat style. Click the arrow under the AutoFormat button in the AutoFormat group on the Format tab to display the gallery of AutoFormats, and then click the Access 2007 style, as shown in Figure 30-57.

You see an instant change to several elements of your report. Access added some background color to all the labels going horizontally across the screen. The font size changed from 11 to 10 in some of the controls, and Access even added some alternating background color to the detail records, as shown in Figure 30-58.

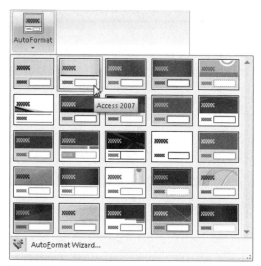

Figure 30-57 Select one of the AutoFormats to give your report a more professional look.

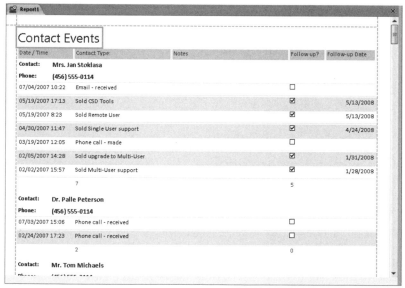

Figure 30-58 Access makes several visual changes to your report when you select an AutoFormat.

Save your report and then switch to Print Preview to see how your report will print on paper. The report still needs some fine-tuning to exactly match the reports you created earlier in this chapter. You need to add a label and a text box next to the two Sum controls in the ControlID Footer section to list the name of the contact and the descriptive text of follow-up information. You could also move the Title control into the Page Header section so that it appears on every page instead of only the first page. You can find this report (after we made these few changes) saved as rptXmplContactEvents4 in the sample database. As you can see, Layout view allows you to quickly create a professional-looking report in Access 2007.

You should now feel comfortable with constructing reports. In this chapter, you've seen that Access 2007 presents many tools and views to assist you in creating professional and functional reports. In most cases, you'll find that using a combination of these tools—Design view, Layout view, the Report command, and the Report Wizard—is the best way to create reports.

PART 8

Microsoft Office Programming Primer

Stephanie Krieger

I f you have any concerns about venturing into this chapter, take a deep breath and relax. You'll be perfectly comfortable here. This is the first thorough primer on Microsoft Visual Basic for Applications (VBA) written for advanced Microsoft Office users, and not for programmers.

I'm not a programmer, so I won't treat you like one. The fact is that you don't have to be a programmer to make effective use of VBA (or XML, as discussed in the next chapter). Yes, I use VBA and XML to develop solutions for clients, but that just means I'm taking advantage of all the tools that Microsoft Word, Microsoft Excel, and Microsoft PowerPoint have to offer for creating documents. If you can learn to format a table, create styles, or create fields in Word; to write formulas or generate charts in Excel; or to customize masters in PowerPoint, you can learn VBA.

After years of avoiding VBA because it seemed technical and scary, I fell head over heels one day after I had no choice but to venture into the Visual Basic Editor for a client. I discovered both how easy it is and how much you can do with VBA even with just a basic level of knowledge. But, the most important thing I discovered was how much of the VBA language I already knew just from being an advanced Microsoft Office user. Nearly all elements of VBA that are specific to each program are the names of features and tasks you already know from using the program. Keep in mind that VBA is just an additional way to work with, and expand the capabilities of, the programs you already know.

Outside of the program-specific features and task names, most VBA language and structure is virtually identical across Word, Excel, and PowerPoint. So, the majority of what you'll learn in this primer will apply to macros you may want to write in any of these programs. However, because I assume that this is your first introduction to writing VBA (or writing any programming language, for that matter), I use one program for most examples, to avoid the confusion of trying to cover too much too fast. Because Word is the primary document production program for Microsoft Office, most examples throughout this primer use Word VBA. Just keep in mind that, once you're comfortable with Word VBA, you can apply all of the basics you learn to VBA tasks in Excel and PowerPoint as well.

When and Why to Use VBA

One of my favorite examples of both when and why to use VBA if you're not a programmer came up one evening at dinner with a friend. She had been up until 3 A.M. the night before cleaning up tables for a report that was due that day. It was a Word document containing 50 tables copied from Excel that needed to be cleaned up and reformatted. The task took her, a power user, about six hours—which, at just over seven minutes per table, isn't bad.

But, she wanted to know if there was a quicker way for her to have gotten it done. She had created a few table styles and even recorded a macro for some of the formatting, but still had click into each table to apply them and then manually take care of any unique elements for each table.

In reply to her question, I asked if she knew any VBA, and she looked at me as if I had to be insane. But, then I told her that if she had known some basic VBA (just part of what you'll learn in this primer, by the way) she could have accounted for most of the differences between her tables in one macro and then formatted all of those tables at once. The task would have taken about six minutes instead of six hours. As you can imagine, learning VBA no longer seemed like a crazy idea.

Of course, this timesaving example is just one of several types of situations where you can benefit from VBA. You can often use a single line of code to save substantial time or even do things you can't do through the features in the user interface. Or, to take things further, you might also use VBA to create customizations or automation for your documents and templates, such as with custom dialog boxes that can help users complete form documents.

In general, the answer to the question of when to use VBA is the same as when to use any feature in the Microsoft Office programs—use it when it's the simplest solution for the task at hand. In the case of VBA, however, you may also be able to use it when there doesn't appear to be a solution for the task. VBA expands the capabilities of Word, Excel, and PowerPoint, so that you might find yourself with easy answers to tasks that you didn't even know were possible.

In the 2007 Microsoft Office system, however, it's important to ask yourself if VBA is still the simplest solution before you embark on a complex project. With the introduction of the Office Open XML Formats, you can do some things in the 2007 release more easily today with XML—such as automatically populating document content with data from other sources. Also, some functionality that would have required automation in the past can now be done with built-in features, such as using a Content Control to display a custom Building Block gallery when you need a selection of boilerplate text options that can't be deleted. However, VBA macros are still almost exclusively the way to go when you want to use automation to save time on repetitive or cumbersome tasks.

Introduction to the VBA Language and Code Structure

The easiest way to begin learning VBA is to record macros and then look at what you've recorded in the Visual Basic Editor. In the subsections that follow, we'll use this method to help you become acquainted with how to read VBA code.

> **Note**
>
> Macros can no longer be recorded in PowerPoint (which has always been the most limited of the three programs in terms of VBA capabilities), but you can still write VBA macros in PowerPoint. Macros can be recorded and written in Word and Excel.

So, what is a macro? A macro is simply a set of commands that can be executed together, similar to a paragraph style. However, where a style is a collection of settings that you can apply at once, a macro is a collection of actions.

Recording Macros

When you record a macro, literally every step you take is recorded, including moving your insertion point up or down or making a selection. Note that, while recording a macro, your insertion point can't be used as a selection tool. Use the arrows on your keyboard, along with the Shift key, to make selections as needed while recording a macro.

> **Note**
>
> Experienced users of VBA continue to find macro recording useful for learning how to accomplish new tasks in VBA. One thing we all run into at some point, however, is the fact that a handful of commands can't be recorded. For example, if you record a macro while adding items to the Quick Access Toolbar or the Quick Styles gallery, your steps won't be recorded. In some cases, a macro that can't be recorded means that you can't accomplish the task through VBA, but it doesn't always. You can do a great many things when writing VBA that can't be done by recording macros, such as applying a document Theme. Learn more about this later in this chapter, as well as how to get help for finding commands that can't be recorded.

 To begin recording a macro, on the Developer tab, in the Code group, click Record Macro. Or, on the status bar, click the Record Macro icon shown beside this paragraph.

Once you click Record Macro, the icon changes to a blue Stop Recording box. Click Stop Recording on either the Developer tab or the status bar when you've finished recording your macro.

Let's try one together, as an example. Say that you're starting a new, long presentation document. Each page of the document needs to begin with Headings 1, 2, and 3, consecutively, followed by a paragraph of body text. The first several pages of that document will each begin with the text *Company Overview–* in the Heading 1 paragraph, which will be followed after the em dash by different text on each page.

To save a bit of time, let's record a macro for setting up these pages.

Setting Up the Sample Document

Before recording the macro, I set up the document in the interest of using the simplest method for any task. I set Style For Following Paragraph for Headings 1, 2, and 3 to the style that follows each heading at the top of every page. I also added Page Break Before formatting to the Heading 1 style, so that my new pages are started automatically when I apply Heading 1. Even so, I can still save time on setting up these pages by using a macro.

If you'd like to save time on this document setup, you can find the file First Recording.docx that is included with the sample files on the book's CD. The document contains no text, just styles Heading 1 through Heading 3 customized as indicated in this sidebar.

With your insertion point at the top of the empty document, click Record Macro and then do the following.

1. In the Record Macro dialog box, type a name for your new macro. Macro names must start with a letter and can include letters, numbers, and the underscore character, but can't include spaces or most special characters.

   Notice in the Record Macro dialog box, shown here, that recorded macros are stored, by default, in the global template Normal.dotm.

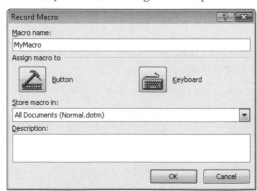

In the Save In drop-down list, you have the option to select any open document or template, including currently loaded global document templates (Building Block and Quick Style Set templates won't be available here). For now, leave the default Save In setting and click OK to begin recording.

2. Apply Heading 1 style to the active paragraph.

3. Type **Company Overview—** (To add the em dash, you can use the keyboard shortcut Ctrl+Alt+(keypad)-.)

4. Press Enter four times.

   Because Style For Following Paragraph has been set for the first three heading styles, these four hard returns add paragraphs with the styles Heading 2, Heading 3, and Body Text, consecutively, followed by an additional Body Text paragraph. That additional Body Text paragraph is where your insertion point will be when the macro starts to run again, so it will become Heading 1 style in the first step of the macro.

5. Click Stop Recording.

To run that macro, on the Developer tab, click Macros, select the macro you just recorded, and then click Run.

With this particular macro, you could run it each time you need to set up a page, or run it as many times as you'll need identical pages. Or, you could edit it to add functionality that enables it to do even more for you, such as automatically adding the number of pages you need. But, for the moment, let's just look at this macro as an example to demonstrate how to read VBA code.

How to Read VBA Code

To view the macro you just recorded, on the Developer tab, click Macros. Then, select your macro from the Macro Name list and click Edit. This will open the Visual Basic Editor with your macro open on screen. Your screen should look something like the following image.

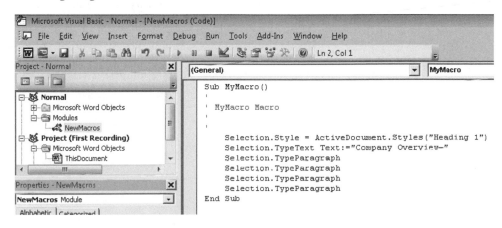

For now, focus on the macro itself—we'll look at the different elements of the Visual Basic Editor shortly.

- Sub stands for subroutine, which is basically just another term for macro. Every macro begins with **Sub** and ends with **End Sub**, as you see in the preceding example.

- The first few lines below **Sub** in the preceding example have an apostrophe at the beginning of the line. Those are comments. An apostrophe at the beginning of a line of VBA code means that there is no code to run on that line. When you record macros, VBA automatically adds some comment lines, one of which includes the name of the macro, as you see in the preceding image.

  You can delete any line that begins with an apostrophe without damaging the macro. Be sure, however, not to delete the apostrophe and leave other text on the line that you don't want to run as a VBA command. The apostrophe is what causes the line to be skipped when the macro runs.

- After the comment text, you see the commands that comprise the steps of this macro. If you tried this for yourself and you see more lines of code in your macro than in my sample, ask yourself if you took other steps. If, for example, you made a typo in the *Company Overview* text and went back to correct it, that could have been recorded as a collection of several steps. Remember that when a macro is recorded, every keystroke is recorded. So, each time you use a different arrow key to move your insertion point, for example, you'll get another line of code. Take a look again at the commands from the preceding macro.

```
Selection.Style = ActiveDocument.Styles("Heading 1")
Selection.TypeText Text:="Company Overview—"
Selection.TypeParagraph
Selection.TypeParagraph
Selection.TypeParagraph
Selection.TypeParagraph
```

Notice that this code doesn't include any unfamiliar terms, even if you've never seen a line of VBA code before. Selection, style, active document, type text, and type paragraph all refer to extremely basic Word tasks. The majority of program-specific terms in VBA will be similarly familiar, just from your experience with the program.

As you progress through this primer, you'll come to understand how to construct the lines of code you see above and how you can write your own macros that are even simpler than recorded macros for accomplishing the same tasks.

TROUBLESHOOTING

Why does my recorded macro have so many lines of code, when I only did one thing?

As mentioned earlier, when you record a macro, every keystroke is recorded. So, you often end up with much more code for a simple action than you would if you wrote the macro yourself.

In particular, if you use a dialog box to execute an action while recording a macro, you're likely to get far more code than you may expect. The reason for this is that, when you click OK to accept the settings in a dialog box, you're accepting all settings in that dialog box. VBA doesn't record your keystrokes while you're in most dialog boxes, so it must record every setting you accepted when you clicked OK.

For example, if one step in my macro was to bold a selected word, and I used the Bold icon in the Font group on the Home tab, the code for that command would look like this:

```
Selection.Font.Bold = wdToggle
```

If, on the other hand, I opened the Font dialog box to apply bold and then clicked OK to close the dialog box, the code for that command would include all of this:

```
With Selection.Font
.Name = "+Body"
.Size = 11
.Bold = True
.Italic = False
.Underline = wdUnderlineNone
.UnderlineColor = wdColorAutomatic
.StrikeThrough = False
.DoubleStrikeThrough = False
.Outline = False
.Emboss = False
.Shadow = False
.Hidden = False
.SmallCaps = False
.AllCaps = False
.Color = wdColorAutomatic
.Engrave = False
.Superscript = False
.Subscript = False
.Spacing = 0
.Scaling = 100
.Position = 0
.Kerning = 0
.Animation = wdAnimationNone
End With
```

Notice that what VBA did was record a setting for every option in the Font dialog box. This is because of the limitations related to recording macros with dialog box commands.

If you write a macro, or edit your recorded macro, you don't need to specify any setting unless you want the macro to execute that setting. In this example, if you were to delete everything between the lines that begin `With` and `End With`, except the `Bold` setting, you'd still get the result you need. (Learn about the `With...End With` syntax later in this primer, in "Grouping Statements" on page 1103.)

Statements, Procedures, Modules, and Projects

To begin to work in the Visual Basic Editor, one of the most important things to understand is how files work in VBA—that is, how macros are organized and stored. The following common items are the principal components you need to know.

- A *statement* is a single command or action in a macro—that is, it's a line of code. For example, `Selection.Font.Bold = wdToggle` is a statement. As you'll see in "Writing, Editing, and Sharing Simple Macros" on page 1085, when you think of VBA as a language, think of a statement as a sentence.

- A *procedure* is, essentially, another way of referring to a macro, although there are other types of procedures as well, such as *functions*. A function is a procedure that returns a result.

- A *module* is a collection of code. Think of a module as a code document. A module can contain several procedures. And, like documents, modules can be saved as files, copied, and shared.

- A *project* is the collection of all modules and related VBA objects in your document, template, or add-in. A project might have one or several modules, as well as other elements such as UserForms (dialog boxes).

Understanding and Using the Visual Basic Editor

Before you start working with VBA code, take a few minutes to settle in to your surroundings. To help you work more comfortably, the subsections that follow tell you a bit about each of the components of the Visual Basic Editor that are identified in the following diagram.

Project Explorer — Properties window   Procedure list

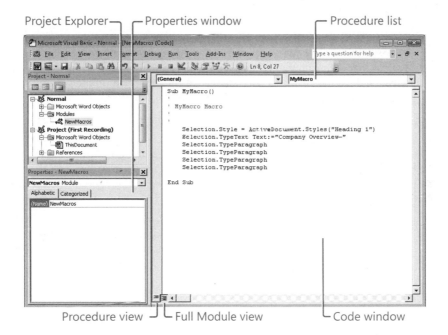

Procedure view — Full Module view   Code window

The Code Window

The Code window is where your procedures appear. This is where you type macros when writing code and where you find the macros you've recorded. Notice that the Procedure list is at the top right of the Code window. From this list, you can quickly move to any procedure in the active module.

Also notice the view options at the bottom of the screen. When you have several macros in a module, it can be helpful to view them one at a time. Full Module view is the default, but you can change this setting and many others through the Options dialog box, discussed in "Setting Up Your Workspace" on page 1085.

Project Explorer

Project Explorer is where you see the list of all VBA projects that are currently open or loaded. All open documents, as well as open or loaded document templates, appear here, whether or not they contain macros. You can collapse or expand a project to view the modules and objects that it contains.

> **Note**
>
> Documents appear in this list whether or not they're macro-enabled file formats. This is important to keep in mind because, if you add code to a document using an Open XML Format that ends with the letter *x*, you won't be able to save the document with its code. Save the document with the equivalent file format that ends in the letter *m* to enable your code to be saved along with the document or template.

- A project only has a Modules or Forms folder if it contains code modules or User-Forms. However, in Word and Excel, each project contains an Objects folder, such as the Microsoft Word Objects folder you see under each of the projects visible in the preceding image.

  In Word, the Objects folder contains a document object referred to as ThisDocument. In Excel, it contains both a ThisWorkbook object and a sheet object for each existing sheet in the workbook. Some types of code (such as a type of procedure known as a document-level event) are added directly in the Code window for the document object rather than in a module. However, you will often have projects that have no code added to the document objects. Learn more about using the document objects in "Introduction to Using Events" on page 1131.

The Properties Window

The Properties window shown in the preceding image doesn't look like much, but don't be fooled. For modules, the Properties window is generally used only to edit the module name. However, for some object types (such as UserForms), the Properties window becomes extremely important because it's populated with many settings that you can edit directly in that window, ranging from the height and width of a UserForm to the value to display on a form control (such as a text box or an option button).

To edit the name of a module in the Properties window, click into the name where it appears on either the Alphabetic or Categorized tabs, edit it as you would document text, and then press Enter to set it. Module naming rules are the same as macro naming rules—no spaces or special characters, and the name must begin with a letter.

> **Note**
>
> All names in VBA subscribe to a similar set of rules. Names must always start with a letter, and can't include spaces or most special characters. Most names are limited to 255 characters in length. However, module names can't exceed 31 characters, and macro names added in the Record Macro dialog box are limited to 80 characters.

Note that, when you record macros, they're always added to a module named NewMacros. You can rename that module if you like, but the next time you record a macro, a new module will be created with the name NewMacros.

Setting Up Your Workspace

You'll find many settings that can be customized in the Options dialog box, available on the Tools menu in the Visual Basic Editor. I don't recommend spending much time in this dialog box just yet, because you might not be familiar with many of the settings. But, it's good to know that it's there, because you will need it. I'll point out, throughout this primer, when settings can be customized in this dialog box.

Possible settings in the Options dialog box include default behavior for a number of programming actions (such as the way you're notified about errors in your code), the formatting for each type of text or notification you see in the Code window (such as comment text or errors), and the way the window itself is arranged.

In addition to settings in the Options dialog box, notice that you can drag to resize docked panes in the Visual Basic Editor window (such as the Project Explorer or Properties window), or close those you don't need. Use the View menu to access any windows you've closed. If you're unable to dock any window in the Visual Basic Editor, you can change the setting for that window on the Docking tab of the Options dialog box.

Writing, Editing, and Sharing Simple Macros

> **Note**
>
> All code samples shown throughout the headings in this section are available in procedures in a module named PrimerSamples.bas, that is included in the sample files on the book's CD. See "Saving and Sharing Macros" on page 1127 for help importing a module into your Visual Basic Editor.
>
> Most of the features you'll learn about in this section are programming basics. They're written here specifically for VBA. However, it might be useful to know, should you ever want to learn another programming language, that many of the concepts and terms used throughout this section are fairly standard across common programming languages.

One of the most important differences between macros you record and macros you write is that, when you record a macro, you need to select an object to act on it. But, when you write macros, you can usually identify items to act on instead of selecting them. That apparently simple difference gives you tremendous power and flexibility. For example, you can write a macro to act on all tables in your document automatically, rather than recording a macro that you run from each table.

The section you're beginning is the core of this primer. From creating a macro to read-ing and understanding essential VBA language constructs, the headings in this section progress in a logical order to help you learn in such a way that you can immediately put your knowledge into practice. I recommend reviewing the content under each heading and trying examples for yourself in the Visual Basic Editor. Be sure that you understand the content covered under each heading before progressing, and you'll be using VBA comfortably before you know it.

Creating Modules and Starting Procedures

To create a module, start by selecting the project (in Project Explorer) to which you want to add the module. Note that you can click any element contained in the project, such as the project name or the Modules folder (if one exists). Then, on the Insert menu, click Module.

> ### Note
> You can also insert a module from the Insert icon on the Standard toolbar. Notice that this icon defaults to what you last inserted (such as a module or a UserForm). Click the arrow beside the icon to select a different item from the available options, as you see here.
>
>

To rename the module, click into the name field in the Properties window, as men-tioned earlier. Type the new module name and then press Enter.

Once you have a module in which to create your macros, you can just click in the Code window and begin typing to create a macro. As you saw in the sample recorded macro, every macro begins with the term **Sub**, followed by the name of the macro, and then followed by a pair of parentheses. Those parentheses can be used to hold instructions for the macro or information about references in the macro, but it's rarely necessary to type anything between the parentheses for basic document production macros. Even if you type nothing between the parentheses, however, you must include the parentheses in this line.

Notice as well that every macro ends with the line **End Sub**. Many types of instructions you'll learn throughout this section are paired (such as **With** and **End With**, demon-strated in "Grouping Statements" on page 1103). When you type the first line of a macro (beginning with **Sub** and ending with the pair of parentheses) and then press Enter, VBA adds the **End Sub** line automatically. (If you prefer, you can omit the parentheses when you type the first line and VBA will add them as well.) But, with most paired terms, the end term isn't added for you. It's good practice to always type both ends of a paired structure at the same time, so that you don't forget to later. When macros become longer or more complex, finding the missing end portion of a paired structure can be a frustrating use of time.

So, to start a macro in your new module, type the following:

```
Sub MacroName()
End Sub
```

The statements that comprise your macro will go between these two lines.

> **Note**
>
> Throughout the next several headings in this section, code samples are provided that show only the relevant code for the particular topic. Remember that, to run that code in the Visual Basic Editor, it needs to appear within a procedure, so you need to add the surrounding **Sub** and **End Sub** statements discussed here.

Objects, Properties, and Methods

Just as the languages you speak are comprised of nouns, verbs, adjectives, and other parts of speech, VBA is comprised of objects, properties, and methods. Think of objects as nouns, properties as adjectives, and methods as verbs.

- An object is just that—it's a thing that can be acted on.

- A property is a characteristic of an object—something that describes the object, such as its size or style.

- A method is an action you can perform on an object. For example, **Save** and **Close** are both available methods for the **ActiveDocument** object.

The only difference between the sentence structure in a spoken language and in VBA is that, though you need a noun and a verb in any sentence, you need an object in every statement, but either a property or a method might be used to complete the statement. Let's take a look at a few examples.

- In the following statement, **ActiveDocument** is an object and **Save** is a method.

  ```
  ActiveDocument.Save
  ```

- In the following statement, **Selection** is the object (referring to the location of the insertion point—the actively selected content) and **Style** is a property of that selection. **Body Text**, in this case, is the setting for the indicated property.

  ```
  Selection.Style = "Body Text"
  ```

- Objects are often used as both objects and as properties of other objects, depending on where they're placed in a statement. In the following statement, **Tables(1)** refers to the first table in the active document. Though a table is an object, it's also used here as a property of the active document. **Style**, in this statement, is a property of the specified table.

```
ActiveDocument.Tables(1).Style = "Table Normal"
```

  Even though **Tables(1)** in this case is a property of **ActiveDocument**, it's still an object. Notice that the style being set is a property of the specified table.

  You typically don't need to think about whether an object is being used as an object or a property, similar to distinguishing whether an *-ing* verb (such as *creating*, *editing*, or *dancing*) is being used in a given sentence as a noun or a verb. What's important is to see that many objects, such as a table, require a higher-level object to make the reference specific enough for VBA to understand. For example, you can't write simply **Tables(1).Style** to indicate the style of the first table, because VBA needs to know what range you're referring to when you tell it to act on the first table. Otherwise, you might be referring to the first table in the document, the first table in the selection, or a number of other possible ranges. Just keep the distinction in mind that many objects can also be used as properties of other objects, because this will come in handy when you reach "Getting Help" on page 1127.

Looking at the preceding list of examples, you might be wondering how you're possibly supposed to memorize every possible object, property, and method name for each program in which you need to learn VBA. Well, relax. You hardly need to memorize anything at all when it comes to program-specific terms. When you understand the concept of using objects, properties, and methods to create statements, and you remember what you already know (the features of the program you're automating), you'll learn the names of the particular objects, properties, and methods the same way you learn vocabulary in a spoken language—simply by using it.

Object Models

The set of VBA vocabulary that's specific to a given program is known as the program's object model. The Visual Basic Editor in each program also contains a "dictionary" of sorts for that object model, known as the Object Browser. You can use the Object Browser (available from the View menu or by pressing F2) to search for the correct terminology to use for a given feature, or to see what properties or methods are available to a given object. For example, take a look at the range of results you get when you use the Object Browser in the Word Visual Basic Editor to search for the term *table*.

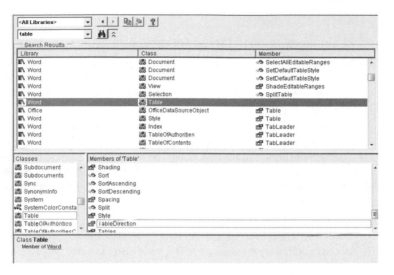

Notice in the preceding image that the selected item in the search results is the table object. The heading *Classes* refers to items in an object model that can have an available set of members—such as objects or modules. Properties and methods are members of a specified class. Notice the headings *Classes* and *Members Of 'Table'* in the bottom panes of the Object Browser.

> **Note**
>
> When searching for terms in the Object Browser, remember that terms don't get spaces between multiple words in VBA. Separate words in a single term are denoted by initial capital letters, such as the `ActiveDocument` object or the `PageSetup` property. Searching in the Object Browser isn't case-sensitive, but the Object Browser won't recognize multiple words as a single term. For example, searching for *page setup* in the Object Browser will return no results, but searching for *pagesetup* will return several.

In the following list, also notice the icons used in the Object Browser to denote objects, properties, methods, or library. These will also be seen while you're writing code, as explained under the next heading.

- Object
- Property
- Method
- Library (An object model is a type of library. For example, the results shown in the image of the Object Browser were members of the Word library, which is the same as saying the Word object model.)

TROUBLESHOOTING

Why do I get an error when I try to set some properties?

The key to this question is to remember that you sometimes need to use VBA statements to get information about the document as well as to apply settings or execute actions. Many properties are read-only, meaning that you can only use them to return information and not to apply a setting.

For example, `ActiveDocument.Name` is a read-only property to tell you the name of the active document. You can't set the name using this property, but that doesn't mean you can't name a document using VBA. Using this example, to change the name of the document, you'd use the `SaveAs` method (that is, `ActiveDocument.SaveAs`). With this method, it's possible to specify several settings for how you want the document saved, including its name.

To learn whether a property is read-only, select that property in the Object Browser. At the bottom of the Object Browser is a pane where you see the hierarchy for the selected item (what class and library it belongs to). This pane also indicates when a property is read-only, as you see in the example that follows.

```
Property Name As String
    read-only
    Default member of Word.Document
```

In the example shown here, Word is the library, and Document is the object to which the read-only property **Name** belongs. Learn more about ways to use read-only properties as this primer progresses.

Using Auto Lists

One of the main reasons you don't have to memorize the object model for the program you're automating is that the Visual Basic Editor often gives you the available options as you write. When you type an object, for example, followed by a period, you automatically see a list of properties and methods available to that object, as shown in the following image.

```
ActiveDocument.
    ActiveWritingStyle
    AddToFavorites
    Application
    ApplyDocumentTheme
    ApplyQuickStyleSet
    ApplyTheme
    AttachedTemplate
```

Notice the icons, shown earlier, that appear in this Auto List to indicate properties or methods. All the members of a given object (that is, all properties and methods available to that object) appear in the Auto List.

To scroll through an Auto List, you can use the up or down arrows as well as the Page Up and Page Down keys. You can also begin to type the item you need, if you know at least the first character, to move to that position in the Auto List. For example, if you type the letter *t* immediately after the period that follows **ActiveDocument**, the Auto List would move to the image you see here.

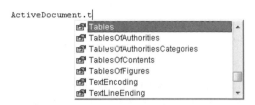

When you select the item you need in the Auto List, press the Tab key to add the item to your statement. (You can also press the spacebar instead of using the Tab key. However, doing so will add a space in your code after the selected item.) Note that, if you press Enter once an item is selected in an Auto List, you'll get an error unless the selected item was the last required term in the statement.

Variables

In addition to objects, properties, and methods, most macros use other types of terms as well, including variables and constants (the latter of which are discussed under the next heading in this section).

Variables are types of data used to represent objects, statements, or other elements required in your code. They're often used to save time and make code more efficient, such as by using a single term in place of a statement that you have to reference several times. They are also often used when you need to refer to any instance of a given object type, rather than specifying an instance of an object. Consider the following examples.

- If you need to refer to the full name (the **FullName** property includes the file path) of the active document in a few places within your macro, you might want to declare a variable to represent the full name of the document, as you see in the following statement.

  ```
  myName = ActiveDocument.FullName
  ```

  The name of the variable in this case is **myName**. Once you've typed this statement in your macro, you can use the term **myName** in place of **Active-Document.FullName** wherever you need to use the full name of the document.

- When you use loops (discussed later in this section) to execute a command for several instances of an object (such as if you want to apply the table style named Table Contemporary to even-numbered tables in the document), you might use a variable as a counter, to help you accomplish that.

  ```
  Dim myInt as Integer
  For myInt = 2 To ActiveDocument.Tables.Count
     ActiveDocument.Tables(myInt).Style = "Table Contemporary"
  Next
  ```

The preceding code uses a **For**…**Next** loop, explained in "Loops" on page 1106. However, notice how the variable **myInt** is used here.

- First, you declare the variable as an integer.

- Then, the start of the loop (the line that begins with the word **For**), tells the code to begin executing with the variable equal to the number 2 and run until the variable equals the number of tables in the document. Each time the loop executes, the number is automatically increased by 1.

- Next, notice that the variable is used to denote the table number in the statement that applies the style to the table.

Using variables in place of a complete statement, or as counters, are common, useful tools. Other uses of variables are demonstrated under applicable headings later in this chapter, including "Conditional Structures" (page 1111) as well as "Loops."

> **Note**
>
> For code that's easier to read, follow, and edit, use intuitive variable names. Variable names can't contain spaces and can't be a VBA term used for any other purpose (such as the name of an object, property, or method). Keeping those requirements in mind, make your variable names as short as possible, just to save yourself work.

Introducing Variable Data Types

As you saw in the preceding examples, variables can be used to represent different types of information, such as numbers, text strings, or objects. Several variable data types are available, and you can even create your own. However, to keep things simple as you begin using variables, following are commonly used variable data types.

Data Type	Possible Values
Boolean	True or False
Integer	An integer, ranging between –32,768 and 32,767
Long	A long integer, ranging between –2,147,483,648 and 2,147,483,647
Currency	A scaled integer, ranging from –922,337,203,685,477.5808 to 922,337,203,685,477.5807
String	A text string, such as a VBA statement (text strings are relatively unlimited—they can be up to approximately two billion characters in length)
Variant	A variant can be a number or a text string (if you don't specify the data type for a variable, it is a variant by default)

> **Note**
>
> For a complete list of data types supported in VBA and their definitions, search the topic "Data Type Summary" in Visual Basic Help, available from the menu bar in any Visual Basic Editor.

> **Note**
>
> You can also declare variables as specific types of objects (such as a table, a style, or a document). Variables declared as a specific object type are called *object variables*, and they offer additional benefits, discussed under the heading that follows. Note that this is *not* the same as the object *data type* that you'll see in complete lists of possible variable data types. The object *data type* was omitted from the preceding list because it's not recommended. On the other hand, *object variables* are an invaluable tool.

Declaring Variables

When you specify a variable type, which is called *declaring the variable*, you can save time and reduce errors. For more complex macros, declaring variables is also important because undeclared variables default to the variant data type, which uses more storage space than other data types, creating more work for the program running your macro.

Additionally, when you require that variables be declared in your modules, VBA lets you know while you're still working on your code if variables contain spelling errors that could cause an error when users run your macro. See "Running Macros and Compiling Projects" on page 1120 for more on this subject.

When you declare an object variable—that is, a variable declared as a specific type of object—VBA recognizes the object so that you get Auto Lists for completing statements that include the variable.

> **CAUTION!**
>
> When you declare a variable as a particular data type, you must use it as that data type. For example, if I declare `myInt` as a string, VBA won't understand if I use it in a statement as if it was a number (such as `For myInt = 2 to ActiveDocument.Tables.Count`, as demonstrated earlier). Variables you want to use as numbers must be declared with an appropriate numeric data type (see the preceding table for the possible values available to different numeric data types). Similarly, to use a variable as a text string, the information after the equal sign when you set the value of that variable must either be a VBA statement or a text string enclosed in quotation marks.

To declare a variable, use a **Dim** statement. For example:

```
Dim myInt as Integer
Dim myName as String
```

Once you type the word *as* in a **Dim** statement, you get an Auto List of available options to help you complete the statement, such as you see in the following image.

INSIDE OUT   Declare Multiple Variables in One Statement

You can declare multiple variables on the same line; just be sure that you specify a data type for each. For example, the statement that follows does *not* declare all three variables as strings.

```
Dim myName, myPath, myStyle as String
```

The preceding code will seem to work, and you'll not get any errors as a result, as long as **myStyle** is used as a string data type. That's because **myName** and **myPath** are declared as variants—no data type is specified for them. The correct statement to declare all three variables as strings would read as follows.

```
Dim myName as String, myPath as String, myStyle as String
```

To require variable declaration in a module, click in the very top of the module, type the words **Option Explicit**, and then press Enter. That statement is one of several you can place at the top of a module to apply to all procedures in your module. Notice that, when you press Enter after typing this statement, a line appears beneath it, just as a line automatically appears between macros. This section of the module is known as the General Declarations section.

Note

You can set the Visual Basic Editor to require variable declaration automatically whenever you create a new module, through the Options dialog box available on the Tools menu. On the Editor tab of that dialog box, select Require Variable Declaration.

Sharing Variables Throughout a Project

If you have multiple macros that need to refer to the same variables, you can declare them publicly for the entire project, so that you don't need to type out the declarations in each applicable macro.

To do this, type your variable declarations in the General Declarations section of any module in the project, and use the word **Public** instead of the word **Dim** to begin the statement. For example, the following statement makes **myName** a string variable, and **myIn** an integer variable, available to all procedures in the project.

```
Public myName as String, myIn as Integer
```

Note, however, that you must be in a procedure to assign a value to a variable. For example, you can declare **myIn** as an integer variable for use throughout the project, but the statement **myIn = 1** must appear inside a procedure. The way to use one set of variable values for multiple macros across all modules in your project is to put all value assignments for public variables in one macro, and then access that macro from any procedure where you need to use those values. To learn how to get that done, see "Running One Macro from Another" on page 1118.

> **Note**
>
> You can also use the General Declarations area at the top of a module to declare variables so that they're available to all macros in the same module, but not other modules. To do this, use **Private** or **Dim** instead of **Public** to start the variable declaration.

INSIDE OUT Never Write the Same Code Twice

One of the best pieces of advice I received when I first started learning VBA was that, if you have to type the same statement twice, ask yourself if there's a faster way. For example, consider the steps discussed in this section for declaring public variables to use the same set of declarations in all procedures throughout your project. Using grouping structures as well as loops (both discussed later in this section) are other ways to avoid doing the same work twice.

Keep in mind that writing efficient code isn't just about typing less. Just as in documents, the less work you do, the better your results will be every time—and the easier job you'll have when that content needs editing. What's more, efficient code also makes it easier for the program to run your macros, so you get macros that are easier to write, easier to edit, and easier to run.

TROUBLESHOOTING

What do I do when the variable type doesn't work?

If you don't know the variable type you need, can't find the variable type you think you need in the Auto List that appears in your `Dim` statement, or you get a "Type Mismatch" error, which means the variable type declared doesn't match the way you've used the variable, there is an easy way out.

Though it's not good practice to do this regularly, particularly in long or complex code, you can simply type `Dim <variable name>` and not specify it as a particular type. When you do this, VBA classifies the variable as a variant data type, so you won't get Auto Lists when using the variable in statements. But, even if you have `Option Explicit` set for the module, as I hope you do, you can declare a variable in this way and continue on. (Alternatively, to avoid other editors of the code thinking that you've accidentally omitted the data type, you can declare the variable as a variant.)

It's a bit of a sloppy workaround—what programmers refer to as a *hack*—but if you're writing simple macros just for your own use, there's really no harm in doing it occasionally, and it can save you time while you're still learning about variable types. Just try not to make it a habit.

Document Variables

In addition to the variables that you use in your macros, there is an object type named *Variable* in the Word object model. These are known as document variables, because you use them to store information in the document that's collected or created by your macros, rather than as a place to store data just while the macro is running—such as when you need the document to remember information from one use of a given macro to the next.

For example, in template automation projects I do for clients, I sometimes add document variables to store user preferences that are specific to the individual document, such as which of a selection of design choices the user wants for the active document. The document needs to store that information after the macro runs, so that the user's preferences are remembered the next time they use the design macros.

In Word, information of this sort can be stored using either a document variable or a custom document property (which you're most likely familiar with from the Document Properties dialog box). However, Excel and PowerPoint don't offer a document variable object, so custom document properties are the way to go for storing document-level data in your workbooks and presentations.

In addition to document-level data, there are several ways to store data on the application or system level—that is, so that data can be accessed by your macros for use by more than an individual document. One of the most common and easiest of these methods is storing data in the Windows registry.

As you can imagine, there are many uses for storing data in variables, document properties, or system-level resources such as the registry. To explore this topic, use the

Object Browser in your Visual Basic Editor to look up the **Variable** object, the property named **CustomDocumentProperties**, and the **GetSetting** and **SaveSetting** functions (these functions are used for storing information in the Windows registry).

Object Model Member Arguments

In addition to the variables that you can declare for use in your procedures, many items in the VBA object models include elements that use the same data types as variables to specify settings for that item. The elements, known as arguments (similar to arguments in an Excel formula), can be required or optional, and are most commonly seen for methods. Take a look at a few examples.

- When you use the **SaveAs** method of the **Document** object in a statement, you get the following options in the Quick Info ScreenTip that appears after you type the open parenthesis following **SaveAs**.

```
Documents(1).SaveAs (
```
```
SaveAs([FileName], [FileFormat], [LockComments], [Password], [AddToRecentFiles], [WritePassword],
[ReadOnlyRecommended], [EmbedTrueTypeFonts], [SaveNativePictureFormat], [SaveFormsData],
[SaveAsAOCELetter], [Encoding], [InsertLineBreaks], [AllowSubstitutions], [LineEnding], [AddBiDiMarks])
```

Most of the arguments shown in the preceding graphic are optional. Notice that optional arguments appear in the Quick Info inside brackets. Also notice that it's common for optional arguments not to specify a data type in the Quick Info.

- When you use the **Add** method for a **Table** object, you get the following arguments.

```
Documents(1).Tables.Add(
```
```
Add(Range As Range, NumRows As Long, NumColumns As Long, [DefaultTableBehavior],
[AutoFitBehavior]) As Table
```

The **Add** method is used for many objects in Word, Excel, and PowerPoint. It has different arguments, of course, for each, based on the type of object being added. For the **Table** object, the range argument (location where you want the new table to appear), number of rows, and number of columns are required. The range is an object variable (referring to the **Range** object), and the number of rows and columns both use the long data type (as noted in the Quick Info). Note that the optional AutoFit behavior setting is a variant data type, but it requires a value from an available set of constants. Learn about constants under the next heading in this section.

- The **HomeKey** method, shown in the following image, is used with the **Selection** object. It's the VBA equivalent of using the Home key on your keyboard.

```
Selection.HomeKey(
```
```
HomeKey([Unit], [Extend]) As Long
```

The two available arguments used here—both optional and both using the variant data type—determine how far your insertion point moves (Unit) and whether the selection is extended (equivalent of holding the Shift key when you press the Home key) or your insertion point is simply moved to the new location. Both of these arguments require selections from a set of available constants, discussed under the next heading in this section.

There are two ways to specify most arguments in statements such as those in the preceding list of examples. The first approach is to type the values for the arguments between parentheses immediately following the method (as you saw in the preceding images showing Quick Info ScreenTips for three sample methods). When you use that approach, type a comma after each value you add. You'll see that the active argument (the one for which you can add a value at your insertion point) is shown as bold in the ScreenTip. If you don't intend to include a value for each argument, type consecutive commas until the argument you want to specify is bolded. If you place an argument in the wrong position between parentheses, the method won't work correctly. Notice, however, that this approach can be confusing and difficult to read when you need to edit or troubleshoot a macro.

> **Note**
>
> Note that some types of arguments can be specified simply in quotation marks after the statement name.

Instead, for methods that take more than a single argument, specify each by typing the argument name, followed by a colon and an equal sign, followed by the value you want to assign. Separate each argument you specify with a single comma, and note that argument order doesn't matter when you use this approach. Take a look at the following two examples.

```
ActiveDocument.SaveAs FileName:="Sample.docx", WritePassword:="example"
Selection.HomeKey Unit:=wdStory, Extend:=wdExtend
```

Using the explicit approach shown here helps to keep your code easy to read, edit, and troubleshoot.

INSIDE OUT　　How Much Do You Really Need to Know About Arguments?

It's important to know the syntax for specifying arguments, but in most cases, you don't need to worry about the data type or whether the argument is required.

Of course, you typically see the data type for required arguments in the Quick Info. But, for optional arguments as well, you'll often know the type of information that needs to go there just from using the program. Because you're an experienced user of the program you're automating, you're likely to go looking for an argument that should be available for a given method (such as specifying a file type or setting a password for the file when you save a new document) more often than you'll need help to understand the ones you happen to find.

In the case of SaveAs, for example, not even the file name is a required argument because the Save As dialog box, as you've surely seen, always provides a default name. Word and PowerPoint either default to the first phrase in the document or, for blank documents, to the document or presentation number assigned when a new document was generated. In Excel, the Save As dialog box always defaults to the Book number assigned when the workbook was generated.

Always remember that one of the most important tools you have for working in VBA is your knowledge of the program you're automating. As an advanced user, VBA is likely to be easier for you to learn than it is for a professional developer who doesn't use the programs. Think of it this way—if you're already a pretty good skier, you're likely to learn how to snowboard much faster than someone who designs snowboards for a living but has never stepped foot on a mountain.

However, there will still be times when you'll need help determining what data type to use for an argument's value or knowing when an argument is required. You can find a description of each argument for most applicable object model members, along with its data type and whether it's optional or required, in the help topic for that item. Learn how to find the help you need easily in "Getting Help" on page 1127.

Constants

As mentioned under the preceding heading, many items in VBA require the use of another data type, known as a constant. Unlike variables that can change as needed, constants are used when a defined set of options exists for the feature. Most constants in VBA are either specific to the individual program object model or are available in VBA for any Microsoft Office program.

> **Note**
>
> It's possible to define your own constants in VBA as well. However, the discussion of constants in this chapter is limited to built-in constants, generally referred to as *intrinsic* constants.

Constants specific to the Word object model start with the letters *wd*; those specific to the Excel object model start with the letters *xl*; those specific to PowerPoint start with *pp*; and those for use across the Microsoft Office programs start with *mso*. There are also sets of constants that are specific to Visual Basic language and available to VBA in all of the Microsoft Office programs—these constants begin with the letters *vb*.

Because constants are defined members of an object model, you can search for them in the Object Browser. For the purposes of searching the Object Browser, note that a set of constants is considered a class and the constants within that set are the members of that class. Sets of available constants for a given argument are also usually easy to find through VBA help. Additionally, Auto Lists are available for many constant sets, particularly object and property constants. Take a look at a few examples.

- The **Type** property of the **Field** object is available as a set of constants, provided in an Auto List when you type a valid statement for using this property. The example shown here is the beginning of a conditional statement.

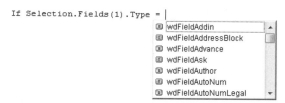

Learn about conditional statements in "Conditional Structures" on page 1111.

- Because different header or footer types are available in each section, the **Header** and **Footer** objects have a set of constants from which to select when you use those objects, as you see here.

- The first macro you saw in this primer recorded four consecutive statements for adding four paragraphs to the document. If you had written that macro instead, you could have used the constant **vbCr**, which is the VBA constant to indicate a carriage return. In that case, that first macro could have been written with the following code, in just two statements instead of six.

```
Selection.Style = ActiveDocument.Styles("Heading 1")
Selection.TypeText("Company Overview-" & vbCr & vbCr & vbCr & vbCr)
```

> **Note**
>
> The ampersand is used to combine the text and constant portions of the text string, just as you can do to combine text, functions, and cell references into a text string in Excel. Learn more about using operators in VBA in "Operators" on page 1113.

- Many arguments for different methods use the same sets of constants, which often are not available in Auto Lists, but are easy enough to find. For example, the **HomeKey** method shown earlier uses constants for both of its arguments. The Unit argument uses the **wdUnits** set of constants; the Extend argument uses the **wdMovementType** set of constants.

The easiest way to learn the constant set you need is to use the Type A Question For Help box in the Visual Basic Editor to look up the applicable method. This is because, in some cases, not all members of a constant set are available to all methods that use those constants. For example, **wdUnits** includes 16 constants, but only four of these are available when used with the **HomeKey** method. (The four available in this case are **wdLine** [the default if you don't specify the argument], **wdStory**, **wdRow**, and **wdColumn**—the last two of which apply only when your selection is in a table.) If you searched for the **HomeKey** method in VBA help, you'd see information about the available constants for both arguments. (Note that the heading later in this section that covers getting help shows you how to use the Object Browser and VBA help reference together to save time.)

Collection Objects

Objects for which there can be many of the object type within a given scope are available as both an object and a collection object. A collection is the entire collection of all of a given object type within the specified scope. This distinction is important because the object and its collection object can have very different members (that is, a very different set of available properties and methods). For example, compare the two statements that follow.

```
Documents(1).Tables.Count
Documents(1).Tables(1).AllowAutoFit = True
```

The first of the two preceding statements uses the **Tables** collection object. The second uses the **Table** object, specifying the first table in the collection. Both statements also use the **Document** object, specifying the first document in the **Documents** collection. (Note that the **Documents** collection in the Word object model refers to all currently open documents. The first document in the collection refers to the most recently opened document.)

The **Table** object has a very broad set of members, as you see in the following image. It's used whenever a single object is being referenced from the collection. Notice that only a fraction of this object's member list is visible in a single screen.

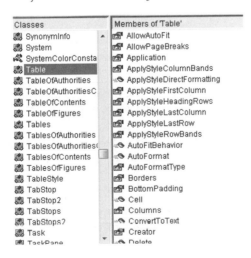

In contrast, the **Tables** collection object has very few members (shown in the following image), including only those items that can apply to the entire collection at once.

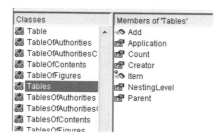

INSIDE OUT To Toggle or Not to Toggle

When you record some formatting options, such as applying bold or italic text formatting, you see the constant wdToggle set as the property's value. That's because, as you've likely noticed when using some types of font formatting, these settings toggle on and off—so you could, for example, apply a style that contains bold formatting to unbold text that was previously bolded.

However, when you write VBA macros, you can set toggle commands to absolute values where you need them, instead of using the wdToggle constant. To do that, instead of using wdToggle as the value, simply use either **True** or **False**.

Selection.Bold = True, for example, will result in bold text whether or not the selection was bolded before the macro ran.

TROUBLESHOOTING

I can't find properties or methods that should clearly be available to my object

If you look for a member of an object that you just know has to be there but it's not, the problem isn't a limitation in VBA, it's just syntax. And, more often than not, the **Range** object is the solution.

For example, if you want to act on all cells in a specific table, you might be looking for the following:

Documents(1).Tables(1).Cells…

However, when you get the Auto List after you type the C for the word *Cells*, you see that Cell is an option, but the Cells collection is not. Does this mean that VBA can't act on all cells in a table at once? Of course not. What VBA is looking for is the following.

Documents(1).Tables(1).Range.Cells…

The **Range** object is often used to specify that you're identifying the preceding object as the active scope of your statement. So, before you decide that you can't do what you need to do with a given object, try using range in your statement as you see in the preceding example, and see what options you get in the Auto List that follows that range.

The **Range** object is also an important one to know because it can give you added flexibility. People new to VBA often use the **Selection** object frequently because they don't know how to identify objects in the document without first selecting them, but that slows down your code and often limits what you can do. You can use the **Range** object to identify any element in your document—which lets you take action without having to first select the item in the document. So, it's less code for you to write and less code for the program to execute.

For example, the following statement identifies the page number on which the first table in the document ends, without having to first select that table.

```
ActiveDocument.Tables(1).Range.Information(wdActiveEndPageNumber)
```

Grouping Statements

Say that you're in a restaurant and you need three things from the waiter. If you ask for some ketchup, then ask for a glass of wine when the waiter drops off your ketchup, and then ask for a glass for your friend when the waiter returns with your wine, that's a lot of work for the waiter (not to mention that he might be tempted to sneeze in your soup).

Instead, if you say to the waiter, "I need some ketchup, please. I'd also like another glass of wine, and my friend will have one as well," you've given the waiter three tasks that he can execute together. That is, you've just grouped a set of statements (not to mention saving yourself from a possible cold).

Though VBA won't sneeze in your soup, macros do run more slowly when you force the program to execute several related tasks independently. Instead, grouping related statements together helps make your code more efficient (and saves you time writing code, because you'll be writing less).

Statements can be grouped using the **With…End With** structure, as you saw in the recorded macro example in the earlier Troubleshooting tip titled "Why does my recorded macro have so many lines of code…" You can use **With…End With** anywhere that two or more statements apply to the same object, or the same combination of objects, properties, and methods. For example, the very first macro looked at in this chapter contains six statements, all of which apply to the **Selection** object. So, if you had written that macro instead of recording it, you could have typed the following:

```
With Selection
    .Style = ActiveDocument.Styles("Heading 1")
    .TypeText "Company Overview-" & vbCr & vbCr & vbCr & vbCr
End With
```

Though you might not be saving much when the macro is just two lines long, imagine something a bit more lengthy. For example, say that you wanted to do several things to the first table in the document. Instead of starting each line with `ActiveDocument.Tables(1)`, you can group the statements using a `With…End With` structure, as follows.

```
With ActiveDocument.Tables(1)
    .Style = "Table Contemporary"
    .Range.Style = "Table text"
    .Columns(4).Shading.ForegroundPatternColor = wdColorLavender
    .Rows(1).Range.Style = "Table heading"
    .Rows(1).HeadingFormat = True
End With
```

In fact, you can take that grouping a step further. Notice that the first row of the table is referred to more than once. You can add a nested `With…End With` structure for those rows, as follows.

```
With ActiveDocument.Tables(1)
    .Style = "Table Contemporary"
    .Range.Style = "Table text"
    .Columns(4).Shading.ForegroundPatternColor = wdColorLavender
    With .Rows(1)
        .Range.Style = "Table heading"
        .HeadingFormat = True
    End With
End With
```

The thing to remember with grouping structures is that all items in the `With` statement must apply to all statements between `With` and `End With`, if the statement starts with a period (indicating that it uses the object referred to in the `With` statement). For example, you can do some things directly to the **Row** object that you can't do directly to the **Column** object, such as applying a style. In that case, you might want to first select the column for which you need to apply a paragraph style, as you see here.

```
With ActiveDocument.Tables(1)
    .Style = "Table Contemporary"
    .Range.Style = "Table text"
    With .Columns(4)
        .Shading.ForegroundPatternColor = wdColorLavender
        .Select
    End With
    Selection.Style = "Table Subheading"
    With .Rows(1)
        .Range.Style = "Table heading"
        .HeadingFormat = True
    End With
End With
```

In the preceding code, **Selection.Style** doesn't have to refer to the object in the **With** statement, because it isn't using that object.

CAUTION

As mentioned earlier in this chapter, remember that `With…End With` structures (as well as the code structures that follow under the next two headings) require a pair of statements. For ease of editing and to reduce errors, whenever you type the first part of the structure (the `With` statement in this case), type its paired closing statement (`End With`) as well, so that you don't forget to do so later.

TROUBLESHOOTING

How can I apply Theme fonts and colors with Word VBA?

In the preceding examples of grouping structures, you may have noticed that I used an intrinsic constant to apply a shading color. The set of constants you get when you apply colors in Word VBA code are from the standard Microsoft Office color palette that was available in earlier versions. These are not Theme colors.

However, if you find and try to use the `wdThemeColor…` constants, you'll find that they don't work as expected. (Note that in Excel VBA, the `xlThemeColor…` set of constants do work as expected.) So, how do you apply colors that will update if the document Theme changes?

If you record a macro in Word to apply a color from the Theme Colors palette, you'll see a numeric value in the resulting code that appears to represent the color you selected. That value actually represents the position you selected in the Theme Colors palette. So, using that value in your own macros will consistently apply the Theme color at that palette position.

For example, in the preceding grouping structure code sample, if you wanted to apply the Theme Color palette position for the Accent 1 color instead of the standard color lavender, the line of code to apply the color would read as follows.

```
.Shading.ForegroundPatternColor = -738131969
```

But, you don't have to take the time to discover the 60 values that comprise the 10 Theme colors in the palette and their variations. I've done it for you. Find a macro named ThemeColorReferenceTable in the file named Sample Macros.dotm that is included with the sample files on the book's CD. That macro (available from the SampleMacros module in the referenced file) will generate a new document with a table representing the Theme Colors palette. The color and associated value number for each position in the palette are applied to the table, so that you can save that table and use it as a reference tool whenever you need it.

Applying Theme fonts in Word VBA is much simpler. Wherever you would specify the font name, you simply specify that name as "+Headings" or "+Body" to apply the Theme heading or body font, rather than using the name of a specific font. For example, the first line of code that follows applies the font "Cambria." The second line applies the active Theme's heading font.

```
ActiveDocument.Paragraphs(1).Range.Font.Name = "Cambria"
ActiveDocument.Paragraphs(1).Range.Font.Name = "+Headings"
```

Loops

If I had to pick one feature of VBA that's the most useful on a daily basis for document production and document troubleshooting, it would be loops. Loops enable you to act on several instances of a given object within one macro. Fortunately, as much as loops can do for you, they're also extremely easy to use.

In this primer, we're going to look at variations on two of the most common types of loops, **For** loops and **Do** loops.

For Each...Next and For...Next Loops

A **For Each...Next** loop enables you to act on all instances of a given object within a specified range. For example, you might use this type of loop to format all tables in your document at once or to change the fill color of all text boxes in your document to a particular Theme color. Similarly, a **For...Next** loop enables you to specify a range of instances of the given object on which you want to act. For example, say that all tables in your document other than the first five need to have the same formatting. You can use a **For...Next** loop to specify that the formatting apply to only the tables you want.

To use a **For Each...Next** loop, start by declaring a variable of the object type upon which to act and then use that variable in your loop. Take a look at the code for the two examples given in the preceding paragraph.

- Apply the style Table Contemporary to all tables in your document.

```
Dim atb as Table
For Each atb in ActiveDocument.Tables
    atb.Style = "Table Contemporary"
Next atb
```

  The use of **atb** as the variable name for the table object is just a personal choice. As mentioned earlier in this chapter, you can use any name for a variable that meets VBA naming requirements (such as no spaces and a letter for the first character) and isn't the name of any member of an available object model.

- Remove any user-defined styles from the active document.

```
Dim ast as Style
For Each ast in ActiveDocument.Styles
    If ast.BuiltIn = False Then
        ast.Delete
    End If
Next ast
```

  Specifying the variable in the **Next** statement, as I do in both preceding examples, is optional. But, it's good practice to do this to avoid confusing the statements you need to keep or alter when you edit a macro, particularly when you use multiple loops in the same procedure.

To use a **For...Next** loop, start by declaring a numeric variable data type to use for counting the instances upon which you want to act. The code for the example given earlier—formatting all but the first five tables in the document—follows.

```
Dim myI as Integer
For myI = 6 to ActiveDocument.Tables.Count
    ActiveDocument.Tables(myI).Style = "Table Contemporary"
Next
```

Notice that I could have used a **With…End With** structure instead of retyping **Active-Document** each time I needed it. Of course, that would be more helpful if I was doing more than just applying a table style, as you see in the following example.

```
Dim myI as Integer
With ActiveDocument
    For myI = 6 to .Tables.Count
        With .Tables(myI)
            .Style = "Table Contemporary"
            .AutoFitBehavior (wdAutoFitWindow)
        End With
    Next myI
End With
```

In the preceding code, notice that I use the **For…Next** loop with nested **With…End With** structures to make this macro as efficient as possible to write, and as efficient as possible for Word to execute.

Do Loops

A Do loop, aside from being fun to say, can be another useful way of creating a loop for specified instances of an object. (Note that this type of loop is usually referred to as a **Do…Loop** structure, which helps to clarify the fact that, like **For…Next** loops or **With…End With** structures, a **Do…Loop** actually requires a pair of statements.)

Do…Loop structures can either be executed while a qualification is true or until a qualification becomes true. Similar to **For…Next** loops, **Do While…Loops** are usually used with a numeric variable. **Do Until…Loops** may be used with a numeric variable or until a given condition is true. Take a look at a couple of examples.

- Say that you're troubleshooting a document. Using Open And Repair, you find that a floating object is causing the unstable document behavior. But, you don't see any floating objects in the document (this would happen if floating objects were off the page or hidden behind opaque document elements because of the Behind Text wrapping style). Using a **Do…Loop**, you can delete all floating objects in the body of the document, as follows.

```
With ActiveDocument
    Do Until .Shapes.Count = 0
            .Shapes(1).Delete
    Loop
End With
```

In the preceding code, notice that **ActiveDocument.Shapes(1)** refers to the first shape in the document. I wouldn't use a **For…Next loop** in this case with a counter, because each time a shape is deleted, the shape object reference **.Shapes(myI)** would refer to a different object. Instead, if I continually delete the first shape until there are no more shapes, I don't need to be concerned with the way VBA counts the shapes in the document as their number is being reduced.

> **Note**
>
> In the case of deleting all shapes in a document, you may wonder why I didn't use a **For Each...Next** loop for this, since I want to act on all instances of shapes in the document. **For Each...Next** loops are an easy solution in most cases that require acting on all instances of an object type. However, there are two reasons why the **Do...Loop** was the better choice here. First, there's less code with a **Do...Loop** in this case because you don't need to declare the object variable before executing the loop. Second, there's an anomaly when you use a **For Each...Next** loop specifically to delete floating graphics (that is, members of the **Shapes** collection object) and one or more shapes may be left behind. Using the **Do...Loop** structure instead ensures that all shapes are deleted.

- The following code uses a **Do While...Loop** instead of a **For...Next** loop for formatting all tables with the Table Contemporary style and AutoFit To Window behavior.

```
Dim myI as Integer

myI = 6
With ActiveDocument
    Do While myI <=.Tables.Count
        With .Tables(myI)
            .Style = "Table Contemporary"
            .AutoFitBehavior (wdAutoFitWindow)
        End With
        myI = myI + 1
    Loop
End With
```

Notice in the preceding code that the integer variable was set to start counting at six, so the first five tables in the document would be ignored. The **Do While** statement says to execute the code in the loop while the integer value is less than or equal to the number of tables in the active document. Then, at the bottom of the commands that fall within the loop, I've added a counter for the integer variable to increase the number by one on each iteration of the loop.

In the first of the two preceding examples, a **Do...Loop** structure is a better choice than a **For...Next** loop (as explained in the text that follows that sample code). However, in the second of the preceding examples, a **For...Next** loop would have been the more efficient choice. Notice that, in the second example, if you use a **For...Next** loop, you don't need a separate statement for the counter—the **For** statement is a built-in counter.

So, how do you decide whether to use a **For...Next** loop or a **Do...Loop** structure? You just need to ask yourself a few simple questions, as follows.

> **Note**
>
> I wish I had conceived the questions that follow, but I can't take the credit. Many thanks to Beth Melton, this book's technical reviewer, for sharing her clear and concise approach to this topic (and others).

- Do you know the number of repetitions you need in the loop?

  As demonstrated by the preceding code samples in this section, if the answer is yes, use a **For...Next** loop. If the answer is no, use a **Do...Loop**.

- If using a **Do...**Loop structure, is the condition initially true?

  If the condition is initially true, you need a **Do While** statement to begin your loop. If, on the other hand, the loop needs to execute until the condition becomes true, start your loop with a **Do Until** statement.

There's one more variable to consider when deciding on the loop type you need. You can evaluate the condition specified in a **Do...Loop** structure either at the top of the loop (as shown in the earlier example of a **Do While...Loop** structure) or at the bottom of the loop (with a **Do...Loop Until** or **Do...Loop While** structure).

A top evaluation loop is structured as follows.

```
Do While <condition>
    <statements>
Loop
```

A bottom evaluation loop, on the other hand, looks like the following.

```
Do
    <statements>
Loop While <condition>
```

(Remember, in the preceding structures, to substitute **Until** for **While** if you need to execute the code *until* the condition becomes true.)

So, to determine whether you need a top or bottom evaluation loop, ask the following question: Must the code execute at least once?

If the code must run at least once for your macro to do what you need, use a bottom evaluation loop so that the condition isn't evaluated until after the first time the code runs. If the code doesn't have to run at least once, use a top evaluation loop so that the condition is evaluated before the first time the code runs. For example, in the sample **Do...Loop** structure shown earlier, in which case the loop is used to delete all shapes from the active document, a top evaluation loop is appropriate because the code doesn't need to run if the document contains no shapes from the outset.

The following diagram summarizes the decision process for selecting the best type of loop for your macro.

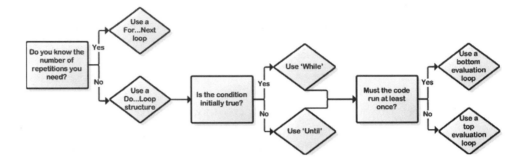

TROUBLESHOOTING

Using a loop to delete objects from a Word document leaves behind objects in the header and footer

If you press Ctrl+A to select the entire Word document and then press Ctrl+Shift+N to apply Normal paragraph style to everything selected, content in headers, footers, footnotes, endnotes, comments, or floating text boxes remains unaffected. This is because Select All really means selecting everything in the active Word story.

Similarly, when you work in VBA, some commands require that you execute them separately for each story in which you want to take action. For example, deleting all floating objects from the active document, as shown in this section of the primer, won't delete those objects in the header or footer stories. To do that, you need to access the particular story you need. To delete floating objects in the main header of section 1, for example, instead of `ActiveDocument.Shapes`, you would specify `ActiveDocument.Sections(1).Headers(wdHeaderFooterPrimary).Shapes`.

Keep in mind that you can nest multiple loops inside one another. For example, say that you want to apply a paragraph style to every header in the document. You need to loop through each header, in each section, which requires two loops, as follows.

```
Dim asc As Section
Dim hft As HeaderFooter
For Each asc In ActiveDocument.Sections
    For Each hft In asc.Headers
        hft.Range.Style = "Heading 1"
    Next hft
Next asc
```

Note that some actions require that you access the story in which you want to act before executing actions, rather than just identifying the story. Also, before you try to loop through all story ranges in a document, be sure that the type of object upon which you're acting is accessible to all story ranges, or you'll get an error. For example, floating objects aren't allowed in footnotes, endnotes, comments, or other floating objects, so including those ranges in your loop to delete shapes will throw an error.

Conditional Structures

As demonstrated with **For...Next** and **Do...Loop** structures, there are several ways to apply conditions to the commands you want to execute with VBA. Frequently, however, the condition you need may be something other than the instances of an object. Conditional structures in VBA, other than loops, are formed using the paired **If** and **End If** statements. Much like the IF function in Excel and the IF field in Word, **If...End If** structures in VBA are used for executing actions only when specified criteria are met. Take a look at the following examples.

- Say that you're creating automation to help format new business presentation documents. Your branding specifies that any presentation of longer than three pages should use landscape orientation. If the user clicks the button to use your formatting macro, you may want the macro to first check the length of the document and then set the orientation to landscape if the document exceeds three pages.

```
With ActiveDocument
   If .RangeInformation(wdActiveEndPageNumber) > 3 Then
      .PageSetup.Orientation = wdOrientLandscape
   End If
End With
```

- Say that you're applying a template to a document that uses only built-in Word styles, such as Body Text and Heading 1–9. Once you've reformatted the document content as needed, you may want to clean up the document styles to help ensure that the document continues to be formatted with the styles you want. The following code removes any styles from the document that are not built-in styles.

```
Dim ast As Style
For Each ast In ActiveDocument.Styles
   If ast.BuiltIn = False Then
         ast.Delete
   End If
Next ast
```

If...End If structures are often used with multiple conditions, such as when you want to set one value if the condition is true and another if it's false, as you see in the following example.

```
With ActiveDocument
  If .RangeInformation(wdActiveEndPageNumber) > 3 Then
     .PageSetup.Orientation = wdOrientLandscape
  Else
     .PageSetup.Orientation = wdOrientPortrait
  End If
End With
```

The preceding example adds an additional qualifier to the similar code shown earlier, so that if the document is three pages or shorter, your macro ensures that the document uses portrait orientation.

If statements can also include multiple conditions by including **ElseIf** statements. For example, say that you have many tables in your document with different layouts, but all financial tables have either four or six columns. Those financial tables with four columns should use the custom table style named Table Financial 4, those with six columns should use the style named Table Financial 6, and all other tables in the document should be formatted using Table Normal style.

```
Dim atb As Table
For Each atb In ActiveDocument.Tables
   With atb
        If .Columns.Count = 4 Then
              .Style = "Table Financial 4"
        ElseIf .Columns.Count = 6 Then
              .Style = "Table Financial 6"
        Else
              .Style = "Table Normal"
        End If
   End With
Next atb
```

Notice that both **If** and **ElseIf** statements require **Then** at the end of the line. Also notice that, regardless of the number of conditions in an **If** statement, **End If** is still required at the end of the complete structure.

Note

See "Trapping Individual Errors" on page 1126 for an example of another type of conditional structure known as **Select Case**. Though **If** structures are more common, **Select Case** can be an extremely efficient alternative and is definitely worth a look.

INSIDE OUT   The Value of Indenting Code

As you can see throughout the code samples in this chapter, code is indented to indicate statements within a group, loop, or condition. And, where multiple structures are nested, code is indented a bit further for each level of nesting.

Though VBA doesn't require indenting code, it's fairly standard practice to do so, because it makes the code and the logic of the macro's progression much easier to read.

For example, consider that when structures are nested, it's essential that the end state-ments of paired structures fall in the correct order. For example, if you nest an If...**End If** structure inside a For...**Next** loop, the **End If** statement needs to appear above **Next** (that is, if the **If** structure starts inside the loop, it has to end inside the loop). Indenting phrases can make it much easier to diagnose this type of hierarchy issue.

To indent a line of code, press the Tab key at the beginning of the line. Your indent will be kept when you press Enter. Backspace to remove the indent. Note that you can cus-tomize the indent width on the Editor tab of the Options dialog box. Tab Width is set to four characters by default.

To indent several lines of existing text, select those lines and then press Tab. Similar to behavior with outline numbered lists, using Tab and Shift+Tab with one or more para-graphs selected will demote or promote the text rather than deleting it. However, if only one statement is selected, you must be sure to select the entire statement or pressing a keystroke will replace the existing text.

Operators

VBA uses both symbols (such as &, <, >, =, +, -, /, *) and terms (such as And, Or) for operators, depending on the usage. In all cases, however, operators follow standard mathematical syntax rules. Take a look at a few examples.

- When I finish writing a chapter of this book, I need to copy all of the Heading 1 and Heading 2 paragraphs to update the table of contents. To do that, I make a copy of the document from which I delete any paragraphs that don't have those two styles applied.

```
Dim apr as Paragraph
For each apr in ActiveDocument.Paragraphs
   If apr.Style <> "Heading 1" And apr.Style <> "Heading 2" Then
         apr.Range.Delete
   End If
Next apr
```

Notice that the less than and greater than operators can be used together to mean "is not equal to."

- If, instead, I wanted to delete all paragraphs that match either of those criteria, I would have written the following code.

```
Dim apr as Paragraph
For each apr in ActiveDocument.Paragraphs
   If apr.Style = "Heading 1" Or apr.Style = "Heading 2" Then
         apr.Range.Delete
   End If
Next apr
```

- What if I wanted to delete all paragraphs that use Heading 1 or Heading 2 style, but only if they don't appear in a table?

```
Dim apr as Paragraph
For each apr in ActiveDocument.Paragraphs
   If (apr.Style = "Heading 1" Or apr.Style = "Heading 2") And _
   apr.Range.Information(wdWithinTable) = False Then
        apr.Range.Delete
   End If
Next apr
```

In the first line of the **If** structure, the space followed by an underscore at the end of the line is used to allow a single statement of code to break to a second line. Breaking the line is not required, but is used when the line of code is too wide to read in a single screen.

Notice in the preceding code that the conditions that use the logical operator **Or** are grouped in parentheses, with the **And** operator outside of the parentheses. Just as in a mathematical equation, that phrasing ensures that the condition within the parentheses is evaluated first.

As you've seen in examples throughout the primer to this point, an ampersand is used to combine arguments into a text string, and typical arithmetic operators can be used on numeric values as they are in Excel formulas, including +, - ,*, and /. The plus sign can be used in some cases to combine text strings, but when you want to mix different types of variables in a text string, the plus sign can cause a "Type Mismatch" error, because it tries to calculate a result rather than combine the strings. So, using the ampersand to combine arguments into a string is always a good practice.

Notice also throughout these examples that comparison operators can be used either individually or together, such as < to indicate "less than" or <= to mean "less than or equal to."

The operators mentioned in this section are likely to be all that you need, but this isn't an exhaustive list of every operator available in VBA. To learn about others, search for the topic Operator Summary in VBA help.

Message Boxes and Input Boxes

When creating macros for others to use, you're likely to need to either give the user information or have the user specify information. Use message boxes to share information and input boxes to collect it.

Message Boxes

A message box might just provide information, or it might require a response, such as Yes, No, Cancel, Abort, Retry, or Ignore.

The **MsgBox** command is one of several in VBA that can be used both as a statement and as a function. Use a **MsgBox** statement to provide information; use **MsgBox** as a function when you need a response from the user.

- To create a message box statement, type **MsgBox** with the string of text you want the user to see. For example, take a look at the following message box statement and the message box it produces when run in Word.

```
MsgBox "You're an unstoppable VBA genius!"
```

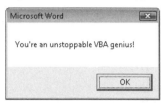

Even if your message box doesn't require a reply, however, you might want to get a bit more creative with it. The **MsgBox** command includes optional arguments that let you customize the title bar and add an information icon, such as in the following example.

```
MsgBox "You're an unstoppable VBA genius!",vbInformation,"My Message Box"
```

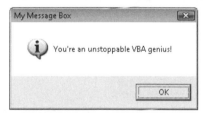

The intrinsic constant **vbInformation** is one of a set of options in the buttons argument that enables you to add both an icon (as you see here) and response buttons. The third argument customizes the title of the message box.

> **Note**
>
> Note that both message box and input box functions also include optional arguments for adding help files to those boxes. To learn about creating help files for use with your VBA automation, see the MSDN Library. MSDN (Microsoft Developer Network) offers a free library resource at *http://msdn.microsoft.com/library*, which provides a number of tools for those who want to continue learning about Microsoft Office programming capabilities.

- To use **MsgBox** as a function (that is, to require a response from the user), first declare an integer variable for your message box, so that you can use the response in the macro, as you see in the following example.

```
Dim myRes As Integer
myRes = Msgbox("Are you an unstoppable VBA genius?", vbQuestion _
+ vbYesNo, "My Message Box")
```

```
If myRes = vbYes Then
    Msgbox "I knew it!", vbExclamation, "My Message Box"
Else
    Msgbox "Hang in there.", vbCritical, "My Message Box"
End If
```

The first message box in the preceding code looks like this:

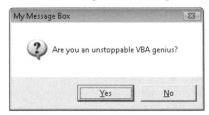

Depending upon your response, you then get one of the following two message boxes.

Notice the constant **vbYes** used to represent the response to the first message box. If you look up **vbYes** in the Object Browser, you find the set of constants that are available (shown in the following image) depending on the buttons you include in your message box.

Members of 'VbMsgBoxResult'
- vbAbort
- vbCancel
- vbIgnore
- vbNo
- vbOK
- vbRetry
- vbYes

Note

If you're thinking that you don't have to be a math whiz to know that a term comprised of several letters (such as **vbYes**) is not an integer, guess again. The seven constants that comprise the possible return values for a message box translate to the integers 1 through 7. So, you'll get the same result if you use the integer value instead of the constant. Use Quick Info to find the integer value you want. For example, if you have a macro that includes the constant **vbYes**, right-click in that constant and then click Quick Info to see its value.

Input Boxes

Input boxes are similar to messages boxes, except that they're always used as a function because they always require a response. Take a look at the following example.

```
Dim myInp As String
myInp = InputBox("How would you score on a basic VBA exam?", _
"My Input Box", "Perfect")
Msgbox myInp & " is pretty good!", vbExclamation, "My Input Box"
```

The input box from the previous example looks like this:

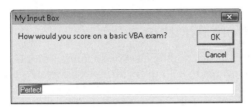

The text of the preceding message box is referred to as the prompt, the title bar text is the title argument (as in a message box) and the value you see in this image is the default value of "Perfect" specified in the third argument. Note that input boxes also include optional arguments for vertical and horizontal position on the screen (not shown here), if you don't want the box to automatically appear in the center of the screen.

Because the input box was declared as a string variable, notice that the response is used as part of a text string in a message box that looks like this:

If, instead, you need to use a response as a numeric value, declare the variable accordingly. In the following example, the input box asks for the number of columns to include in a new table being created by the macro. The variable defined as the input box reply is declared as an integer. (Notice that the input box in this case has only a prompt and a title bar—no default value is set, so the text box within the input box appears blank to the user.)

```
Dim myInp As Integer
myInp = InputBox("How many columns would you like?", "My Input Box")
With Selection
.Tables.Add Range:=.Range, NumRows:=5, NumColumns:=myInp
End With
```

> **Note**
>
> There is a possible problem, however, with the preceding code sample. If the response is not an integer (including if the user cancels the input box without adding a reply), the macro will end in an error. You can, however, add what's known as an *error handler* to correct for any error that may occur. Error handlers are an important part of writing macros effectively. Learn to work with basic error handlers later in this chapter, in "Creating Error Handlers" on page 1124. You'll find an example in that section of an error handler created specifically for the preceding macro.

Running One Macro from Another

When you create a solution, such as developing a set of document production macros for yourself or creating a set of macros to help users format a template, you're likely to have some of the same commands repeat in multiple macros. When those duplicated commands run to more than a few lines of code, it can be helpful to put the duplicated code into its own macro and run it as part of each of the macros that need it. That way, you don't have to write that code out in every macro where you need it.

Running one macro from another is also commonly done when several macros use the same variable definitions. For example, say that you declare the following public variables in the General Declarations section of the module.

```
Public myName as String, myComp as String, myIn as Integer
```

If several macros need to use the same values for that information, create a procedure just to store the values of those variables. That entire macro might look something like this:

```
Public Sub VarDefs()
myName = Application.UserName
myComp = ActiveDocument.BuiltinDocumentProperties("Company").Value
myIn = 1
End Sub
```

To then use these variable definitions in any macro in the project, just call the macro that includes the definitions. The statement to call a macro is just the word **Call** plus the macro name. If the macro exists in a different module from the macro where you're calling it, also specify the module name.

For example, to call the preceding macro from a macro in the same module, I would type the following statement.

```
Call VarDefs
```

If the macro from which I want to call **VarDefs** is in a different module, the statement would look like the following (assuming that **VarDefs** is in a module named **myMod**).

```
Call myMod.VarDefs
```

Note that, as long as the variables are declared as public, you don't actually have to specify Public in the Sub statement of the preceding macro to make the contents of that procedure available to other macros in the project. However, if you want to allow the contents of that procedure to be shared only by other macros in the same module (such as in cases where macros in a different module might need to share a different set of values for the same variables), use `Private Sub <procedurename>()` to start the macro. Keep in mind also that private procedures don't appear in the Macros dialog box available from the Developer tab, so identifying a procedure as private is also a good way to keep it hidden from the user.

CAUTION

When you call one macro from another for the purpose of using variable definitions, make sure the call to the source macro appears prior to where you use those variables in the destination macro.

Note

Your macros might share many types of variables in a given project. I've presented the preceding variable example to point out one place where the 2007 release may offer you a simpler solution than VBA, depending on your particular needs. For adding document property information to your documents and templates, you can use the built-in Document Property Quick Parts that have information already bound to Content Controls. For other types of information not available in the Document Property set of Quick Parts, see the next chapter of this book to learn how to bind Content Controls to your own custom XML data.

Setting Macros to Conditionally Stop Executing Commands

You can add a statement to end the macro under specified conditions or to exit just a part of the macro.

To end code execution entirely, just type **End** on its own line. For example, say that you want to stop a macro from running if no document is open. That code would look like this:

```
If Documents.Count = 0 Then
End
End If
```

To exit a loop when a condition is met, use an **Exit** statement specifically for the loop type, such as **Exit For** or **Exit Do.** Following is an example of an **Exit For** statement.

```
Dim ast as Style
For each ast in ActiveDocument.Styles
   If ast.NameLocal = "Sample" Then
      ast.Delete
      Exit For
   End If
Next
```

When you run one macro from another, you might also want to exit just the individual macro under certain conditions and not stop executing code altogether. For example, if you call one macro from another but only want to run the called macro under certain conditions, you can tell the code to exit that called macro with an **Exit Sub** statement, as you see in the following example.

```
If ActiveDocument.Tables.Count = 0 Then
Exit Sub
End if
```

Running Macros and Compiling Projects

You can run a macro directly from the Visual Basic Editor, or you can add it to the user interface to run it from the Quick Access Toolbar (or, in Word, from a keyboard shortcut).

Running Macros

To run a macro directly from the Visual Basic Editor (as I do frequently with on-the-fly document production macros), just click in the macro (anywhere between the **Sub** and **End Sub** lines will do) and then click the green Run Sub\User Form arrow icon on the Standard toolbar. This option is also available from the Run menu, or by pressing the F5 key.

To add a macro to the Quick Access Toolbar, click the arrow at the end of your Quick Access Toolbar and then click More Commands to open the Customization tab of the <Program> Options dialog box. Then, do the following.

1. In the Choose Commands From list, select Macros.

2. If you want to add the macro to the toolbar just for a specific document or template, select that document or template from the Customize Quick Access Toolbar list.

    To be available in this list, the document or template must use an Open XML Format and must be open at the time.

3. Select the macro to add from the list at the left and then click Add.

4. To customize the appearance of the macro on the Quick Access Toolbar, select it in the list on the right, and then click Modify. In the Modify Button dialog box, you can select a different icon and edit the way the name appears in the ScreenTip for that macro.

To add a macro to a keyboard shortcut in Word, open the Word Options dialog box to the Customize tab and then click the Customize button to open the Customize Keyboard dialog box. As you see in the following image, select Macros in the list on the left and then select the macro you want to assign to a shortcut on the right.

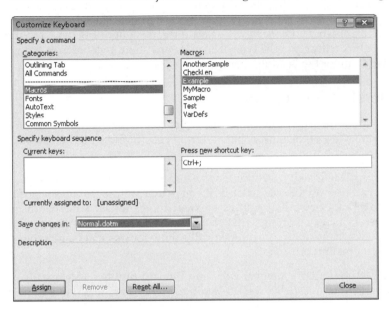

Press the keystroke combination you want to use—such as Ctrl+; shown in this example. A notice appears to let you know if the combination is already assigned. You can select it even if it's already assigned to another action, as long as you don't need the shortcut for that other action. Notice that you need to select the document or template in which to save the shortcut. Keyboard shortcuts can be saved in both Open XML Format and legacy format Word documents and templates.

Note

For many actions, you might want to run just one line of code at a time—such as to get information about your document or to execute a single action. In this case, you can run the code from the Immediate window in the Visual Basic Editor. This is an extremely handy option that you're likely to use regularly once you become accustomed to using VBA as a document production tool. Learn how to use the Immediate window later in this chapter.

Compiling Projects

As you're writing lengthy macros, or when you're ready to use your macros, compiling the project is an important step. Compilers are actually used to translate source code to executable code, which isn't strictly necessary for typical VBA macros. But, using the compiler in the Visual Basic Editor is an essential way to help ensure that your code works properly.

To compile a project, just select a module or click into a procedure in the project and then, on the Debug menu, click Compile <Project>. Depending on the size of the VBA project, compiling might be instantaneous or it might take a few moments. If VBA recognizes errors in your code, it will select the code containing the error and display a message box telling you the type of error. Learn about recognizing, fixing, and managing errors under the heading that follows.

Understanding Errors

Errors can occur when you compile a project or when you attempt to run a macro. Following are a few of the most common error types, along with their corresponding error numbers.

- "Type Mismatch" (error number 13) indicates that you're trying to act on an item in an unavailable way, such as if you define an integer variable for the response to an input box that requires a text string response. Note that the absence of this error doesn't guarantee that you've assigned the correct data type to your variable because VBA can automatically allow for incorrect data types under some circumstances.

- "Method or Data Member Not Found" (error number 461) usually indicates that you either misspelled a term or you referenced an item that doesn't exist.

- "Requested Member of the Collection Does Not Exist" (error number 5941) appears when you run a macro on a range that doesn't include the object you specified to act on. For example, this would occur if your macro includes the statement `ActiveDocument.Tables(3).Delete` and two or fewer tables are in the active document.

- "Object Required" (error 424) indicates that you need to specify an object upon which to act. This error might occur, for example, in a **For Each…Next** loop when you don't correctly define the collection of objects upon which you want to act. A similar error may appear as "Object Doesn't Support This Property or Method."

> **Note**
>
> Error numbers are provided in the preceding list because it is possible to correct for individual errors—that is, to write code that enables your macro to respond differently to different errors. When you do this, you need to identify the error by number, as discussed later in this section, in "Creating Error Handlers" on page 1124.

When an error occurs while you're compiling a project, the error statement is selected and a message box appears telling you the type of error and offering help. If you click the help option, an article explaining the error type is opened in most cases.

If an error occurs when you run a macro, a similar message box appears to indicate the error type, but it provides the options End, Debug, and Help. Just as with compile errors, the help option usually provides an article with more information on the error type. (Note also that clicking the help option doesn't close the error message for either compile or runtime errors.) Click End to dismiss a runtime error message if you're familiar with the error and know where to find it. Or, click Debug for guidance in correcting a runtime error.

When you click Debug, the statement that caused the error is highlighted. (Note that, by default, the statement is highlighted in yellow with a yellow arrow at the margin indicator bar, but you can customize this formatting in the Options dialog box.) This also puts the program into Break mode, which stops code from executing. When this occurs, "[break]" appears in the title bar after the project name. To exit Break mode, which removes the highlight from the error statement, click the Reset button on either the Standard toolbar or the Run menu. (Note that Break mode also restricts many actions in the application window. So, resolve the error and turn off Break mode before you return to working in the applicable program.)

If a compile error occurs at runtime (meaning that you didn't compile the code, but ran a macro that contains a compile error), the project goes into Break mode when you click OK to dismiss the error message. The title line of the macro that caused the error is highlighted and the error statement is selected.

Testing Your Macros and Debugging Errors

When you're not sure of the cause of an error, there are several ways to go about finding it efficiently. Some of these options can also be used when you want to see the results of just a portion of your code at a time, even if errors don't occur. A few of the easiest options for testing or debugging code are described in the following list.

- You can step into a macro to execute one line at a time and see the results as you go. To do this, click in the macro and then press F8 to start executing the macro one line at a time. Press F8 again each time you want to run the next statement.

  You can also click in a specific line in the macro and then press Ctrl+F8 to execute the macro up to the line where your insertion point appears.

- Use a breakpoint to run a macro using a traditional method (such as by pressing F5 from the Visual Basic Editor or running the macro from the Quick Access Toolbar) but execute statements only up to a specified line of code. To add a breakpoint, click the margin indicator bar to the left of the line of code. A circle appears on the window edge where you clicked, and the statement is shaded (in burgundy, by default), as you see in the following image.

  If you're not sure where to click, you can right-click in the statement instead, point to Toggle, and then click Breakpoint. To remove a breakpoint, just click the circle that appears to the left of the statement. (As with error notifications, you can customize the formatting of breakpoints in the Options dialog box.)

- You can comment out a block of code, so that it gets skipped when a macro runs. This is a great tool to use when you want to try running just part of your macro, especially if you have lines of code that aren't finished (which would otherwise throw an error when you run the macro). To do this, right-click the toolbar area and then click Edit to open the Edit toolbar. On that toolbar, you'll find Comment Block and Uncomment Block buttons as shown here, which add or remove an apostrophe from in front of each selected line of code.

Comment Block   Uncomment Block

Creating Error Handlers

When you write macros, particularly for others to use, it's a good idea to try to account for any errors you can control. You can account for many possible errors with conditional structures to protect the macro from conditions you know would cause an error. For example, if the macro acts on the active document, you can set the macro to end without taking any action if no documents are open, as shown in "Setting Macros to Conditionally Stop Executing Commands" on page 1119.

However, you might also want to set up error handlers to manage what the user sees if an unexpected error occurs. In some cases, you might even know that certain conditions could cause an error, but find it more efficient to add an error handler than to write code to account for every possibility.

The two most common types of error handlers are the statements `On Error Resume Next` and. `On Error GoTo ErrorHandler`. Let's look at those one at a time.

Use `On Error Resume Next` when a given instance of a loop, for example, might throw an error under certain conditions, but you'd still want the loop to continue running after it encounters an error. To do this, type `On Error Resume Next` on its own line early in the macro, before any code that could possibly throw the error for which you want the handler to correct. Then, if the possible error occurs, the user won't be notified—the code will just skip the instance it couldn't act on and continue on its merry way.

Use **On Error GoTo...** when you want to control what happens when an error occurs. For example, you might write an error handler that contains a message box telling the user that an error has occurred and what to do to correct it. Take a look at the following example.

```
Sub Sample()
On Error GoTo MyHandler
<code statements>
End
MyHandler:
MsgBox "Please place your insertion point in the table you want to copy before run-
ning this macro.", vbExclamation, "Please Try Again"
End Sub
```

Notice that this handler consists of an **On Error GoTo...** statement as well as another statement with the name of the handler followed by a colon (both in bold in the preceding sample). You can name the handler anything you like, within VBA naming conventions. Notice also the **End** statement that precedes the error handler, so that a macro that doesn't throw an error ends before the error handler is executed. If you call one macro from another, use **Exit Sub** in place of the **End** statement shown in the preceding example. The **End** statement ends all code execution. **Exit Sub** exits the active macro and returns to the macro from which it was called.

What this error handler indicates is that, if an error occurs, the code stops executing and moves to the line following **MyHandler:** to continue executing code from that point. In this case, the handler just displays a message box giving the user information on why they couldn't run the macro.

Note

A term followed by a colon is known as a Line Label. It's simply a way of naming a position in your code. If you weren't using an error handler, you could just type **GoTo SampleName** where you want the code to pick up at another position in the macro and then precede the new position with a line that reads **SampleName:**.

CAUTION !

If you add an error handler of any kind to your macro, be sure to comment that line out (add an apostrophe in front of the statement) when you test the macro. Otherwise, any errors might be ignored, causing you not to see the reason for an unexpected result. Also remember that an error handler can't account for code that comes before it. So, be sure to place an error handler before any code that might cause the error you want to address.

When deciding on how to handle errors for a particular macro, consider whether accounting for possible conditions or adding an error handler is the more effective way to go. For example, in the preceding code sample, if you just need the user to click in a table before running the macro, you might have added the following code at the beginning of the macro instead of an error handler.

```
If Selection.Information(wdWithinTable) = False Then
MsgBox "Please place your insertion point in the table you want to copy before run-
ning this macro.", vbExclamation, "Please Try Again"
End If
```

Trapping Individual Errors

As mentioned earlier in this chapter, you can identify different actions to take in an error handler based on the type of error. One way to do this is to use another type of conditional structure referred to as **Select Case**.

Similar to an **If…Else…End If** structure, the **Select Case…End Select** structure enables you to specify different actions based on conditions you identify. Select Case is not at all strictly for error handlers, but it's mentioned here because trapping individual errors offers a good example of using this type of structure.

While **If…End If** structures evaluate each **If**, **Else If**, or **Else** expression independently, you can use a **Select Case** structure when you want to compare several possible results to a single expression. Take a look at the following code, for example, that uses one of the input box macro examples from earlier in this chapter.

```
Dim myInp As Integer
ResumeInputBox:
On Error GoTo ErrorHandler
myInp = InputBox("How many columns would you like?", "My Input Box")
With Selection
    .Tables.Add Range:=.Range, NumRows:=5, NumColumns:=myInp
End With
End
ErrorHandler:
Select Case Err.Number
    Case 13
        MsgBox "Please enter a numeric value to continue.", vbInformation
        Resume ResumeInputBox
    Case Else
        Msgbox Err.Description
End Select
```

Similar to an **If…End If** structure, you can identify several cases with the **Select Case** structure and provide for all cases not specified with a **Case Else** statement. As with all paired structures, remember to add **End Select** at the end of the structure, or your code will return an error.

Getting Help

Of course, you can search for help using the Type A Question For Help box on the Visual Basic Editor menu bar. But, there are often faster ways to get to exactly what you need.

In the case of error messages, remember that the Help button in those message boxes takes you directly to a help article on that specific error message. If, however, you need information on an error message any time other than right when it occurs, search for the topic Trappable Errors—available from the Visual Basic Editor in Word, Excel, and PowerPoint. You can then use Ctrl+F for the find feature, to quickly locate the name or number of the particular error you need. The Trappable Errors article lists each error with a hyperlink to its article.

In the case of any object model member, right-click the name of the item where it appears in the code and then click Definition. This opens the Object Browser to the selected item—which might be enough information if you just need, for example, to see the available members of a selected object.

However, in the Object Browser, you can right-click any item and then click Help to open the help topic on that article. Note that some items, such as individual constants, might not have help articles—but articles are available for most members of the active object model.

Saving and Sharing Macros

You can export a module of code (as well as some other project elements, discussed later in this chapter), which is the equivalent of saving a copy of the file. To do this, right-click the module in the Project Explorer pane and then click Export. Choose a location and name the file, following file naming conventions. The file name doesn't need to match the module name. Notice also that VBA modules have the file extension .bas.

To import a module of code, such as the samples available on this book's CD (discussed in the next section), right-click the project in Project Explorer and then click Import. Browse to and select the .bas file you need, just as if you were opening a document.

> **CAUTION**
>
> If you export or import modules, remember that some modules refer to code outside of the module itself, such as when the project contains a UserForm (discussed in "Creating UserForms" on page 1134) or when one macro calls another from a different module in the project. Be sure that you're aware of the project components that need to work together, so that you export or make note of everything you'll need when you or someone else imports that content later.

Because you can share an entire VBA project by sharing the Word, Excel, or PowerPoint file in which the project is stored, exporting is more often used as backup. This is often a good idea, because if you lose a document or template, you of course lose any code it contained.

In particular, if you store a module of document production macros, for example, in Normal.dotm, exporting that module periodically for backup is an important safety measure, considering that you might solve some Word performance issues by deleting Normal.dotm and allowing Word to regenerate a new default template, in which case your macros would be lost.

Sharing Projects

To share an entire project, just compile the project, save the file, and share it as you would any file. Keep in mind, of course, that some networks block Microsoft Office files that contain macros—so you might want to either compress the file into a zip container (though, keep in mind that many networks search compressed files for prohibited file types) or arrange another method of safely sharing the project with others.

Some macro projects need to be saved as particular file types, such as for Excel and PowerPoint add-ins. Additionally, signing projects can help to avoid systems or programs blocking your macros.

You can also protect your code when sharing projects—such as when you want others to be able to use the macros, but not to be able to see or copy your source code. To do this, select the project in Project Explorer. Then, on the Tools menu, click <Project> Properties.

In this dialog box, you can rename the project (following VBA naming conventions), which does not affect the file name of the document, template, or add-in where the project resides. You can also click the Protection tab to require a password to view the code. You must enable the Lock Project For Viewing option and provide a password for this to work. When you do, double-clicking the project in Project Explorer will display a box where you can type the password. Without the correct password, the macros can still be run from the user interface, but their code can't be viewed.

> **Note**
> Password protection will start the next time the project is opened.

> **CAUTION**
> Be sure to keep a record of the name of the password you choose. Lost passwords might render your code permanently locked.

Using VBA to Save Time on Document Production and Troubleshooting

Once you understand the elements addressed in the preceding section of this chapter, you're ready to start using VBA. As mentioned earlier in this chapter, find a file named Sample Macros.dotm in the practice files you can find on this book's CD. That file contains two modules. One of those modules (named SampleMacros) includes a few of my favorite simple document production and troubleshooting macros. The other module (named AutomateUserForms) includes a couple of basic dialog boxes with related automation. (Note that dialog boxes are known in VBA as UserForms and are introduced later in this chapter.) Check out these macros and UserForms as examples, or use them as jumping off points for creating your own automation.

Before you go to it, however, there is one important tool in the Visual Basic Editor that can sometimes save you even more time than writing a macro. As mentioned earlier, when you just need to execute a single line of code, you don't need to write a macro at all—you just need the Immediate window.

Using the Immediate Window

To open the Immediate window in the Visual Basic Editor, press Ctrl+G. Note that this is not a toggle command. So, to close the Immediate window, click the X at the top-right corner of the window.

To execute a command in the Immediate window, type the command and then press Enter. Note that, because code executed from this window can only be one line long, you can press Enter from anywhere in the line, and it will not push text to a new line.

I use the Immediate window frequently for a few different purposes. Take a look at some examples.

- Use the Immediate window to get information about your document when troubleshooting problems, or to interact with your document in ways you can't from the user interface. For example, if Open And Repair tells you that a floating object is causing an error in the document, but you see no floating objects, you might want to go ahead and delete them all—as demonstrated in "Loops" on page 1106—or you might want to check first to see how many you're dealing with and then try to select them to know what they are before removing them.

  To ask a question in the Immediate window, start with a question mark. For example, to see how many shapes exist in the main document body, type the following.

  ```
  ?ActiveDocument.Shapes.Count
  ```

  When you press Enter from this line, you'll see the answer in the Immediate window. If any shapes exist, you might want to use the Immediate window to select one at a time and see what each is. To execute an action in the Immediate window, no leading character is necessary. Just type the statement and press Enter. In this case, type the following:

  ```
  ActiveDocument.Shapes(1).Select
  ```

Though you can only execute one line at a time in the Immediate window, you can type several lines if you need them, so that you don't have to keep retyping the same thing. You can't run individual lines of the same macro consecutively—the Immediate window doesn't work like running a procedure. Each time you execute a line, it's an entire procedure. So, things like loops or conditional statements that require more than one line can't be done here. But, you could leave the line **?ActiveDocument.Shapes.Count** and type **ActiveDocument.Shapes(1).Select** below it. You can continue to type lines as you need to in that window, placing your insertion point in the statement you want to execute before you press Enter.

> **Note**
>
> When you press Enter from the line **ActiveDocument.Shapes(1).Select**, the first floating object in the document is selected. But, because it might be off the page or hidden, you might not see it immediately. So, just remember what you already know. That is, VBA isn't a foreign program—it's an extension of the program you're using (Word, Excel, or PowerPoint).
>
> What does that mean? In this example, it means to use the methods you already know for getting to that object once you've used VBA to select it for you. For example, after telling VBA to select the shape, switch back to the document window (Alt+F11), press Ctrl+X to cut the selection from the document (if you're not able to see it), create a new document, and then paste (Ctrl+V) to see what the object is.

- You can use the Immediate window to execute tasks that aren't possible from the document window, as follows.

    - To reset the used range for the active worksheet (that is, the last used cell that is selected when you press Ctrl+End in a worksheet), use the following statement.

        `ActiveSheet.UsedRange`

    - To apply the setting to connect chart lines where empty cells exist in the data, you can use the Hidden And Empty Cells dialog box available from Select Data Source. However, if your chart is a combination chart that contains one or more series that aren't line series, that option is unavailable. In that case, use the Immediate window and type the following statement.

        `ActiveChart.DisplayBlanksAs = xlInterpolated`

- The Immediate window is also a good place to execute simple or repetitive actions that aren't available from the user interface. For example, say that you want to add a few hidden bookmarks to the document. Create hidden bookmarks by starting the bookmark name with an underscore, which can't be done from the Bookmark dialog box. Instead of writing a procedure that you have to run to add each bookmark after you select the range where you want the bookmark to appear, use the Immediate window to do this. Type the following statement.

```
Selection.Bookmarks.Add("_name")
```

In the above statement, substitute the name of your bookmark for *name*. Just place your insertion point where you want that bookmark to appear, then use Alt+F11 to switch back to the Visual Basic Editor and press Enter from this statement to add the hidden bookmark.

> **Note**
> Hidden bookmarks are often used in documents or templates as markers for where you want a macro to insert specified content (such as a user's reply in a dialog box).

- When you're not sure of the phrasing for an action that only requires a single statement, the Immediate window is a great way to test the code you think you need. You get the same Auto Lists and ScreenTips in the Immediate window that you get in a code module, so it's a good way to try out your syntax. Note, however, that the Immediate window is automatically cleared whenever you exit Word. So, if you want to reuse anything you figure out using the Immediate window, copy it into a module and save the module before ending your Word session.

Introduction to Using Events

> **Note**
> This and the remaining sections of this chapter are intended to provide a taste of some additional capabilities of VBA beyond the basic macro, for those who feel confident with the primer content to this point and would like to try something a bit more complex. These sections assume you've already mastered everything included in the primer to this point.

Events in VBA are procedures that run automatically when a specified event occurs. There are several types of events in VBA, such as those that occur with a specific document action (such as opening a document), an application-specific action (such as exiting the program), or an action taken in a dialog box (such as clicking a command button). In this section, the concept of events is introduced using document-level events.

The method shown here for adding document-level events to a project is available in Word and Excel. This is where we get to use the **ThisDocument** or **ThisWorkbook** object that you see attached to any project in the Project Explorer.

Most of the work to create the event is done for you using the drop-down lists at the top of the Code window. When you select Document (or Workbook in Excel) from the Object list at the top left of the window, as shown in the following image, the Procedure list at the top right of the window is populated with the available events.

Many more events are available in Excel than in Word, but the basics (such as open, save, close, and print) are available in both.

Document-level events can be simple or complex, just as any macro. At the simplest, say that you're working on an important, complex document with other document editors, and it's essential that all editors are aware of certain formatting requirements. The particular requirements involve table layout or other specifications that can't be controlled through document protection or any other built-in features. Adding a comment in the document would be fine, but this document keeps getting messed up, the deadline is looming, and so you want those formatting requirements to pop out at anyone who opens the document. Just create an event that displays a message box with your instructions, whenever the document is open.

To do this, take the following steps.

1. In the Word Visual Basic Editor, double-click the **ThisDocument** object and then select Document from the Object list.

   When you do this, a **Document_New** event is created for you because this is the default event type. If you don't want a **Document_New** event, you can delete it later.

2. To create a **Document_Open** event, select Open from the Procedure list.

   Notice that the **Sub** and **End Sub** statements are automatically created for you, along with the procedure name. Don't change the procedure name, because the name is what tells VBA this is a procedure to be run automatically under the specified circumstance.

3. Type the code for your macro. In this case, it's just a message box. Then, save and close the document.

The code for the event you just created would look something like this:

```
Sub Document_Open()
MsgBox "<text of your instructions>", vbCritical, "IMPORTANT!"
End Sub
```

Then, the next time that document is opened (and each subsequent time), a message box similar to the following image appears automatically.

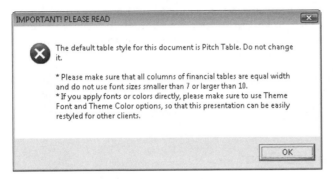

> **Note**
>
> To create line breaks and space between lines in a message box, as you see here, an easy option is to use the **vbCr** constant for adding a carriage return. Just place text portions of the string in quotation marks and separate each phrase with an ampersand. So, for example, to make a single line break, you would write **"<message text>" & vbCr & "<message text>"**. To create two consecutive line breaks (space between lines), you would put two **vbCr** constants, each between separate ampersands, between the text phrases in quotation marks (such as ...**" & vbCr & vbCr & "**...). Remember that constants, being VBA terms, are never surrounded by quotation marks, even when they appear as part of a text string.

Note that some document-level events require arguments between the parentheses in the **Sub** statement. When they do, those arguments are provided for you. For general macros of the type discussed in this primer, you don't need to be concerned at all with those declarations.

In Excel, notice that you can create document-level events for the workbook or for an individual sheet. To create an event procedure for a specific sheet, or just to view what events are available to worksheets, double-click a sheet object in Project Explorer instead of the **ThisWorkbook** object. When you select Worksheet from the Object list, you can see the available worksheet procedures in the Procedure list.

If you don't see an event you want in Word, you might be able to accomplish what you need using Word VBA to write procedures for controlling built-in Word commands. For example, Excel workbooks have an available event named BeforePrint, but Word documents do not. However, in Word, you can use VBA to control the built-in Word print command. For information on where you can learn how to use VBA to control built-in Word commands or to get information about application-level events, see "Next Steps for Working with Automation in Microsoft Office" on page 1141.

Creating UserForms (Dialog Boxes)

When you want to create automation to interact with the user in ways that a message box or input box can't do, create a dialog box (known in VBA as a UserForm). You can create a custom dialog box in VBA that looks very much like any built-in dialog box you see in Word, Excel, or PowerPoint.

If you've ever created form controls in a document or created and formatted AutoShapes on a PowerPoint slide, you already know most of what you need to know to create a custom dialog box. The following subsections walk you through steps to create and use a simple UserForm.

Designing a UserForm

To begin creating your dialog box, select the project (in Project Explorer) to which you want to add your dialog box. Then, on the Insert menu, click UserForm (or select User-Form from the Insert button on the Standard toolbar). When you do, an empty dialog box is created at a default size, as you see here.

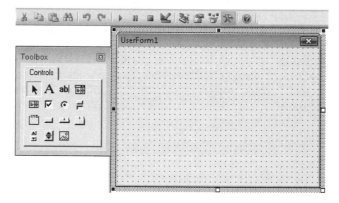

If the toolbox that you see in the preceding image doesn't appear automatically when the form is created, click the Toolbox icon that you see highlighted on the Standard toolbar in this image. The toolbox contains all of the controls you'll need for creating your form.

Before you start to add controls, take a look at the Properties window. You'll see a long list of available settings here (as you see in the following image), some of which you might want to customize immediately.

Following are some basic settings in this window that can be particularly helpful.

- Name—change the name of the dialog box, using VBA naming rules. This is the name that appears in the Project Explorer and that you'll use to refer to the dialog box in macros. It's common, though not required, to start UserForm names with the letters frm. For example, name this form **frmSample**.

- Caption—the caption is the text that appears in the title bar of the form. This can be any text string and is limited only by the width of the dialog box as to how much text can appear in the title bar.

- Height and Width—these settings control the size of the dialog box. You can also drag the handles on the form to resize it. However, using these options to set a precise size can come in handy for a few reasons, such as if you have a large dialog box that needs to fit within the user's window at low resolution.

- Left and Top—these settings control where the dialog box appears on the screen. If you set these measurements, remember to account for any users who might use a lower resolution setting for their screen.

Notice that you can also customize font, borders, and fill color for the form.

To add controls to the dialog box, in the Toolbox, click the control type you want and then either click or drag to create that control on the form, just as you would do with shapes on a PowerPoint slide. Point to each option in the Toolbox for a ScreenTip indicating the type of control.

In the steps that follow, we'll create the dialog box you see here.

To create this dialog box, we'll add the following controls.

- Two labels, containing the text To: and Re:.

- Two text boxes, one allowing for a single line of text in the To field, and the other allowing for text to wrap in the Re field.

- Two command buttons—one for OK and one for Cancel.

To create these controls, do the following.

1. Click the Label button in the Toolbox (the capital letter A), and then click the form, approximately where you want the label to appear. A label is similar to a text box in a document, so just click into it and replace the text with the text you want (To: for the first label).

CAUTION

Unlike many programs where you can edit graphic objects, such as text boxes, don't double-click on a UserForm to edit a control. If you do, you're likely to accidentally open the Code window for that UserForm and automatically add the default event for the control you double-clicked. Meanwhile, If this happens, just delete the structure for the unwanted event and then double-click the UserForm name in the Project Explorer to return to the form. Control events are discussed later in this section.

2. Select the label and then, in the Properties window, change its name to something easy to access in a macro. I named this first label labTo. To specify the accelerator keystroke, as you see in the preceding image, type **T** in the Accelerator field in the Properties window. Remember to press Enter to apply a value after typing in any field in this window.

3. To size the label to fit the text, with the label selected, click Format and then click Size To Fit. This will help you align the controls when you have them all on the form.

4. Ctrl+drag to duplicate the label and then set up the other two labels you need, using the same actions in steps 1–3.

5. Click the TextBox button in the Toolbox and then click the form. Just as you would with any shape, drag to size it as needed.

6. In the Properties window, name this text box. For ease of reference, I usually give text boxes the same name as their labels, but with a different prefix. So, for example, if I have a label named labTo, I would name the accompanying text box txtTo.

7. Press Ctrl+drag to duplicate the text box, then rename and resize as needed.

For the second (Re:) text box, notice that you need it to accept multiple lines. By default, a TextBox control only accepts a single line. To allow text to wrap to multiple lines, in the Properties window, set the MultiLine field to True. If you want to allow the user to add hard returns (by pressing Enter) in that field to start a new line, also change the EnterKeyBehavior field value to True.

8. Use the same procedure to create and name the two CommandButton controls.

Note that the text that appears on the command buttons (OK or Cancel) is typed as you would on a text box. Just click in the default text, then delete and replace it with the text you need. Also notice that the text in a label or on a command button is the text in the Caption field in the Properties window, so you can replace the text in that window if you prefer.

9. Notice that, on the Format menu, you have Align tools as well as Horizontal Spacing and Vertical Spacing options. Select controls as you would shapes on a slide and use these formatting tools to align the controls, as you see in the preceding sample.

It's worth noting that the Align options here work similarly to the way they work in Microsoft Visio and not as you may be familiar with from PowerPoint. That is, controls align to the first control you select. The dominant control has white handles when selected, so that you can easily identify the direction in which selected controls will align. (However, holding the Shift key while selecting constrains which controls you can select. If you hold the Ctrl key instead, you can select any controls on the form in any order, and the last object you select will be the dominant control.)

10. Right-click the form and then click Tab Order. In the Tab Order dialog box, move control names up or down as needed so that an applicable label appears immediately before its related text or combo box control, and so that the controls appear in the order in which you'd want to access them if you were tabbing through the dialog box. For the sample form, my completed Tab Order dialog box looks like the following.

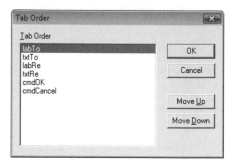

Note that, if a label doesn't precede its related field, using the accelerator key on the label won't access that field.

Once your controls are named and positioned, you're ready to add the automation you'll need to use this form.

Automating a UserForm

There are two parts to automating a dialog box, as follows.

- The code you add directly to the control, to manage its behavior in the dialog box.

- The code you write in a module to display the form and use it to interact with the user.

Depending on the types of controls that your dialog box includes, the code in your UserForm might get rather complex. For our sample dialog box, however, all we need is code to manage what happens when a command button is clicked. To do this, start by double-clicking the OK button.

When you double-click a control, the code for that control appears with a procedure created for you, using that control's default event Similar to document-level events (discussed earlier in this chapter), the name of the procedure connects it to a specific event. For command buttons, the default event is the one you'll usually want. For others, however, you might want to change the default event (for example, the default event for a check box is click, but you might need an event to occur when the value changes rather than when the box is clicked). As with document-level events, the available events in the Procedure list are those available to the type of control you're automating (the control selected in the Object list).

For the OK button, all you need to do is set it to hide the form. The macro that runs the form will continue to run after the form is hidden by the user. For the Cancel button, however, you'll want to unload the form and then end code execution (in two separate procedures), so that the macro doesn't continue to run.

You can refer to a UserForm as **Me** in code contained in that UserForm. Though you can also refer to the form by name, using **Me** is handy because you won't need to change the references if you change the form name. The code for the OK and Cancel buttons would look like this:

```
Private Sub cmdOK_Click()
Me.Hide
End Sub

Private Sub cmdCancel_Click()
Unload Me
End Sub
```

You can end code execution from the preceding event for the Cancel button. However, if you instead add a separate event—the **Terminate** event for the UserForm—you'll also account for the user clicking the close button in the title bar of the UserForm instead of using your Cancel command button. This additional event looks like the following.

```
Private Sub UserForm_Terminate()
    End
End Sub
```

To create this event, you can simply type it beneath the other events in the Code window for your UserForm. Or, select UserForm from the Objects list at the top of that Code window and then select Terminate from the Procedure list. Note that, when you select UserForm, its default event (Click) will be added to your code. You can simply delete that if you don't need it.

> **Note**
>
> To toggle between a UserForm and its code, right-click the form name in Project Explorer and then click View Code or View Object, as needed.

To automate the form in a procedure that you'll run from a module, set up anything you want to specify about how controls look when the dialog box is launched, then show the dialog box (using the **Show** method you see in the following sample) and then execute any commands you want for using the information the user adds in a dialog box. Take a look at one possible sample macro for automating the preceding dialog box.

```
Sub Fax()
   With frmSample
        .txtTo.Value = ""
        .txtRe.Value = ""
        .Show
        With ActiveDocument.Tables(1)
               .Cell(1, 2).Range.Text = frmSample.txtTo.Value
               .Cell(2, 2).Range.Text = frmSample.txtRe.Value
        End With
   End With
End Sub
```

Let's take a walk through this code.

- First, I set up a **With…End With** structure using my UserForm, which I named **frmSample**, as the object.

- Within that grouping structure, all controls that I added to the form are members of the **frmSample** object. So, when I start a new line inside that **With…End With** structure by typing a period, I get an Auto List that includes the control names I added to the form. In the preceding code, I set the values of the To and Re text boxes to nothing, so that the last value the user set wouldn't be accidentally left behind.

- The **Show** statement appears on a line by itself. This action displays the dialog box to the user.

  I added another **With…End With** structure here because typing **ActiveDocument.Tables(1)** is longer than typing **frmSample**, and I need to reference the first table in the document on each line where I'm placing the text the user adds to each text box in the dialog box into a specified table cell in the document. (Note that bookmarks, hidden bookmarks in particular, are another common method of identifying where in a document to place information collected in a dialog box.)

  Because **frmSample** and **ActiveDocument.Tables(1)** are completely separate objects, when my insertion point is inside the **ActiveDocument.Tables(1) With…End With** structure, notice that I can't use the **frmSample With…End With** structure that surrounds it. In a procedure this short, the second **With…End With** structure is used only to demonstrate placing one independent grouping structure within another—but where you have more dialog box controls, with more actions to take, doing this might save you some code.

To learn about adding and automating more complex controls on a dialog box (such as combo box or multipage controls) or to learn other options for automating your User-Forms (including what types of procedures you can do directly from the UserForm's code), see the additional resources recommended in the next section of this chapter.

Note

Because the macros provided in the preceding section reference UserForms, this code is not included in the sample file PrimerMacros.bas. Instead, find similar examples of basic UserForms and automation for those forms in the sample file Sample Macros.dotm, also referenced earlier.

Next Steps for Working with Automation in Microsoft Office

Once you've mastered the basics in this primer, you're likely to find more complex VBA to be quite easy. As mentioned earlier, Microsoft provides the MSDN Library, a free online resource, where you can find instructions and samples for quite a bit of VBA code.

Are you thinking, perhaps, that you might want to go even further? Now that you're writing macros, can VBA take you far enough, or does your work warrant a foray into professional development tools like Microsoft Visual Studio?

Tristan Davis, a program manager on the 2007 Office release product team and programmability guru, has this to say about how to set the goals that are right for you when it comes to automating Microsoft Office.

"There are three big steps I see in working programmatically with Office:

- First, people typically get into recording macros to automate their own common tasks, which ends up being a huge time saver when they find out they can do XYZ once and have it automatically repeated when they press a key combination. Relatively easy to do, but not a lot of power.

- Then, you can graduate to VBA. Usually, you want to change a macro you've recorded and somehow end up in the Visual Basic Editor to do it, ushering you into that new world. A lot more power once you figure it out, but more complex.

- Then, there's the big step up to the world of managed code: You're into Microsoft Visual Studio now using Visual Studio Tools for Office to do it. Another leap in available functionality, but now it's 'real' coding."

Tristan adds the graphs on the next page, to help you look at the cost/benefit of automating Microsoft Office from two perspectives.

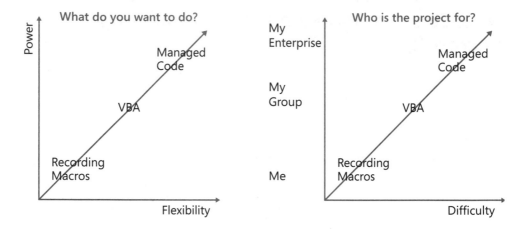

Before you go, however, the next chapter in this book provides a similar primer on the basics of using the Open XML Formats to edit documents, binding data to Content Controls in Word, and beginning to customize the Ribbon.

In my favorite novel, Alexandre Dumas' *The Count of Monte Cristo*, the imprisoned Abbe Faria wrote a book without access to paper or writing implements. A 19th century genius resourceful enough to turn MacGyver green with envy, the good Abbe fashioned a pen out of a fishbone, ink out of soot and wine, and 12 rolls of parchment from two shirts. Not bad for an old man who was locked away in a dungeon.

In previous versions of Microsoft Office, the idea of editing a document without first opening the program in which it's created is much like writing a book in a 19th century dungeon. Without the know-how of an Abbe Faria (or, in this case, a software engineer of equal talent), you're probably out of luck.

Well, thanks to the ingenuity of some talented software engineers, you no longer need to be a fictional genius (or hold an advanced computer science degree) to understand every bit of a document's structure well enough even to create one from scratch (if you're so inclined). Though you never have to know a thing about the XML behind your documents to use the 2007 Microsoft Office release programs, the benefits of getting to know the Office Open XML Formats can be great. Using the XML content for these new file formats, advanced Microsoft Office users can see and understand literally everything that goes into a 2007 release document.

The transparency of the new file formats can save time, add flexibility, improve integration with external content, and simplify essential tasks such as protecting the private content in your documents or troubleshooting document problems. But, my favorite thing about these new formats is just the fact that you don't have to be a programmer to reap many of the aforementioned benefits.

It's important to reinforce that this is not an introduction to the XML programming language, but to the Office Open XML Formats. That said, in this primer, you'll learn to understand the structure of an Office Open XML Format document and how to edit documents directly in their XML. You will also learn the basics of how to customize the Ribbon and how to create custom XML for binding data to document content.

Chapter Assumptions

As with the preceding Microsoft Visual Basic for Applications (VBA) primer, this chapter assumes not only that this may be the first time you've ever seen a line of programming code, but also that you're an advanced Microsoft Office user and comfortable with the features covered throughout this book.

Though this primer is written for Microsoft Office users and not for programmers, you might have noticed that I've already specified *advanced* users more than once. That's because incorrectly editing a document's XML can break a document faster than you can blink.

That statement isn't meant to scare you away. If you're an advanced user, learning to edit your documents' XML can be easy, and you can just as easily learn to quickly fix anything you may inadvertently break. Rather, I mention this primarily for the trainers or tech support professionals among you who might consider sending basic or intermediate users into a document's XML.

You'll gain tremendous power and flexibility by being able to edit a document's XML, but please don't consider it just another method for accomplishing document tasks—such as just one more option you'd teach in a Microsoft Word course for how to edit the definition of a paragraph style. This is an avenue for those with the skill to take document production and troubleshooting to a new level.

Consider this: If a document were a car, then the document's XML would be the tools of an auto mechanic. Before you can begin to understand what's going on under the hood, you need to know how to drive. That said, experienced drivers are going to have a great time with the tools in this chapter.

> **Note**
>
> As with the VBA primer in this book, much of what you'll learn in this chapter can be applied to any program that uses the Office Open XML Formats. However, because I assume that you're new to any use of XML, all examples in this chapter use Microsoft Office Word 2007 documents and tasks for consistency.

XML Basics for Reading Your Documents

XML is a language used to contain and describe data. In the case of Office Open XML, the data is your document content, and the description includes the settings required for that document to function in the applicable program as well as the settings you apply to the document.

Before you begin to explore a document's XML, the subsections that follow provide a bit of background and basics to help you prepare for the task.

Reading a Markup Language

XML is a markup language. Just as you mark up a document while reviewing it—with comments, corrections, or margin notes—a markup language marks up data with descriptive information about that data.

If you've ever looked at the HTML source code of a Web page, you already have some experience with the type of language you'll see throughout this primer. However, instead of paired formatting codes wrapped around text that you see in HTML (such as **text** to turn bold formatting on and then off), the Office Open XML Formats use paired codes nested in a hierarchy that compartmentalizes, organizes, and defines everything you need to know about your document.

The following example shows the word *text* along with its formatting definition. This word is part of a paragraph but is separated out in the source code (the markup) because it contains unique formatting. The bullets that follow the code sample explain in detail how to read this sample.

```
<w:r>
   <w:rPr>
       <w:b />
   </w:rPr>
   <w:t>text</w:t>
</w:r>
```

- The **w:** that begins each line indicates that this information is describing an Office Word 2007 document. You will see different prefixes in your Microsoft Office Excel 2007 and Microsoft Office PowerPoint 2007 documents. Also notice that each code is surrounded by angle brackets (<>).

- As with HTML source code, XML code used to describe content is usually paired, and the second of the pair (the end code) begins with a slash character.

- The section of code shown in the preceding sample is known as a *run*, noted by the **w:r** that introduces the first line of code. A run is a region of document content that contains similar properties.

  To complete the structure, the entire content of the paragraph to which the word *text* belongs is stored between the two ends of a higher-level paired code, not shown here, that indicates the start and end of the paragraph (**<w:p>** and **</w:p>**). The collection of paragraphs (and any other content) in the body of the document is in turn positioned within another paired code (**<w:body>** and **</w:body>**).

- The second and fourth lines in the sample comprise a paired code containing the formatting for the specified text. Notice that between those lines, the third line simply indicates that the specified text is bold **<w:b />**.

Because formatting information in Office Open XML is stored in a structure that defines where the formatting is to be applied, the specific formatting itself doesn't need a paired code. If the text for this sample were also italicized, for example, the code `<w:i />` would appear on its own line, also between the lines of the same paired code that contains the bold statement. Also notice that, because the bold (or italicized) statements stand on their own, they include a slash at the end of the single code to indicate that there is no end code for this statement. You'll see the slash at the end of other codes throughout this primer, wherever the item is not paired.

- The specified paragraph text appears on the fifth line, between a pair of codes (`<w:t>` and `</w:t>`) that indicate it's the text being described.

- The last line in the preceding example is the end code that indicates the end of the description for this specified text.

If the preceding example seems to be quite a lot of work for one word, don't lose heart. It's just an example of how you see Word formatting applied to text in the XML markup, used here to demonstrate how code in the Office Open XML Formats is spelled out. Though it also serves to demonstrate why working in the XML wouldn't be considered an equal alternative to the built-in program features for many document editing needs, that's not the reason for this example. Understanding how to read XML structure will help you work more easily when you begin to use a document's XML in ways that can simplify your work and expand the possibilities.

Don't worry about trying to memorize any specific codes used in the preceding example. The important thing to take away from this is the general concept of how the XML code is structured. Everything in XML is organized and spelled out, like driving directions that take no turn for granted. So, though the example given might seem like a lot of code for very little content, the fact that it's organized explicitly is the very thing that will make the tasks throughout this primer easy to understand even to those who are new to XML.

> **Note**
>
> If you look at the markup for one of your own documents, you may see code similar to the preceding example along with additional codes labeled `w:rsidR` and `rsidRPr`, each followed by a set of numbers. Those codes and their corresponding numbers are a result of the feature Store Random Number To Improve Combine Accuracy, which you can find on the Privacy Options tab of the Trust Center.
>
> Unless you intend to use the Combine feature (available from the Compare options on the Review tab) with a particular document, there's no benefit to enabling this option (but it is on by default). For the sake of simplicity, since these codes are not essential to your documents, they're not included in any XML samples throughout this chapter.

Understanding Key Terms

I'll introduce terms as they arise for each task, but there are a few terms that can be useful to note up front.

- The Office Open XML Formats are actually compressed folders containing a set of files that work together. ZIP technology (the .zip file extension) is the method used to compress the files into a single unit, and the set of files that comprise an Office Open XML Format document is referred to as the ZIP *package*.

- Each file within the package is referred to as a *document part*.

- When you read about XML, you often come across the word *schema*. An XML schema is a set of standards and rules that define a given XML structure. For example, multiple schemas are available for defining different components of Office Open XML, and you'll see reference to some of these in the document parts used for the tasks throughout this chapter. Anyone can freely use the schemas for the Office Open XML formats. Developers can also create their own custom schemas for custom document solutions. (Note, however, that creating schemas is an advanced XML skill that is beyond the scope of this chapter.)

 On the Resources tab of this book's CD, find the schema for customizing the user interface in the 2007 release programs that use the Office Open XML Formats. You can open this file, named customUI.xsd, in the Microsoft Windows utility program Notepad to view its content and give yourself an idea of the type of information contained in an XML schema.

XML Editing Options

Most professional developers use Microsoft Visual Studio for editing XML, but you certainly don't need to do that. You can use Notepad for the same purpose, or any of a wide range of programs from Microsoft Office SharePoint Designer 2007 to a number of freeware, shareware, and retail XML editors.

Many people who don't need a professional development platform for their work will use a freeware or shareware XML editor to see the XML hierarchy in a tree structure that's easy to read. When you edit XML in Notepad, it typically looks like running text with no manual line breaks.

For those who don't want to install another program for this purpose, you can use Microsoft Internet Explorer to view the XML in a hierarchical tree structure and easily find what you need, and then use Notepad to edit the XML. This is the approach I use for the examples throughout this primer.

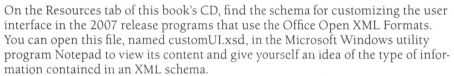

> **Note**
>
> Find a link to the download page for XML Notepad 2007, a free XML editing tool from Microsoft, on the Resources tab of this book's CD. XML Notepad provides both an editor and a viewer, along with features such as drag-and-drop editing and error checking. However, using the editor in XML Notepad requires some knowledge of XML language structure. So, for those who are seeing XML for the first time in this chapter, start with the Windows Notepad utility and consider moving up to XML Notepad once you get your bearings, if you find yourself yearning for a more structured editing environment.
>
> That said, even if you're not using XML Notepad 2007 regularly to edit your code, it can be a handy tool for understanding the structure of your code and troubleshooting syntax errors, as discussed later in this chapter. So, you might want to download it sooner than later.

When you open an XML file in Internet Explorer, you're likely to see a bar across the top of the screen indicating that active content was disabled. Right-click that bar and activate content to be able to expand and collapse sections of your code by using the minus signs you see beside each level of code that contains sublevels. For example, here's what the code shown earlier looks like when viewed in Internet Explorer.

```
- <w:r>
  - <w:rPr>
      <w:b />
    </w:rPr>
    <w:t>text</w:t>
  </w:r>
```

The same text in Notepad looks like this:

```
<w:r><w:rPr><w:b/></w:rPr><w:t>text</w:t></w:r>
```

TROUBLESHOOTING

> **The document won't open after I edit an XML file, but I know my code is correct.**
>
> Remember that a small syntax error (such as leaving off one of the angle brackets around a code) in one XML file within a document can cause that document to be unreadable. However, if you know that the code you typed is correct, there may be another reason that's just as easy to resolve.
>
> Some XML editors that display the XML code in an easily readable tree structure may add formatting marks (such as tabs or line breaks) when you add code to that XML structure. When this happens, these formatting marks can be interpreted as a syntax error (just like a missing bracket) and cause the document to which that XML file belongs to become unreadable in its native program.
>
> If you don't know how to recognize unwanted formatting marks in your XML editor or if the file won't open in your XML editor, see "Using XML Notepad and Word to Help Find Syntax Errors" on page 1163 for steps to help you locate the error.

Getting to Know the Office Open XML Formats

This section will show you how to access the ZIP package for an Office Open XML Format document and how to begin to make sense of what you find there. For the best results, I suggest that you take each subsection that follows step by step and be sure you understand and feel comfortable with the content before continuing onto the next.

Breaking into Your Document

Because each of your 2007 Office release Word, Excel, and PowerPoint documents is actually a ZIP package in disguise, you can just change the file extension to .zip to access all of the files in the package. There are a few ways to go about this.

CAUTION

If you have software installed that extracts files from a ZIP package, you might be able to look at the files in the ZIP package by using that extraction software, without first changing the file extension. However, you're unlikely to see the folder structure of the package when you do this, which is an essential part of the package integrity. Changing the extension takes just a second and enables you to view and manage your files in Windows Explorer, for familiar file access options.

- Append the .zip file extension to the existing file name. To do this in Windows Explorer, or on the Windows desktop, just click to select the file and then click again on the file name (this is slower than a double-click) to enter editing mode for the file name. For the same result, you can also press F2 once you select the file. Leave the existing file name and extension intact and just add .zip, so that you can open the package in Windows Explorer to see its content.

  When you change the file extension in Windows Explorer or from the Windows desktop, you'll see a warning that changing the file extension may make the file unusable. Just disregard this message and click Yes to confirm that you want to continue. (However, to protect your files, it's a good idea to save a copy of the document with its original file extension before appending the .zip extension or beginning to make changes in the XML.)

Note

Renaming the file to a .zip extension is easier to do if you are viewing file extensions. If you don't see the extension for your Office Open XML Format file (such as .docx), change your setting in Windows Explorer to view all file extensions. To do this in Windows Vista, in any Windows Explorer window, click the Organize button and then click Folder And Search Options. On the View tab, turn off the option Hide Extensions Of Known File Types and then click OK. To find the same option when working in Windows XP, in Windows Explorer, on the Tools menu, click Folder Options and then click View.

- You can save a copy of your file with the .zip extension, while it's open in its source program, to bypass the step of changing the extension later. In the Save As dialog box, type the entire file name followed by .zip inside quotation marks. The file is still saved in whatever format is listed (so you still need to choose a macro-free or macro-enabled file format, for example, as needed), just as if you saved it first and appended the .zip extension later. The only difference is that the file's ZIP package is immediately available to you without taking an additional step after you close the file. For example, to save a file named *sample.docx* as *sample.zip*, type **"sample.zip"** in the File Name box of the Save As dialog box.

INSIDE OUT That ZIP Package Is Still a Document

When you're editing the files in the ZIP package, you might not want to spend the time switching back and forth between the Office Open XML file extension (such as .docx) and the .zip extension. Well, you don't have to!

From the Open dialog box in Word, Excel, or PowerPoint, you can open documents that belong to the applicable program even when they're using the .zip file extension. To see your ZIP package file, just select All Files from the Files Of Type drop-down list beside the File Name box and then select and open the file as you would when using its original extension. There's nothing else to it. Word, Excel, and PowerPoint know that the Office Open XML Formats are ZIP packages and read the XML within those packages whether the file is saved using .zip or a file extension that belongs to the program.

Note that you can also open the ZIP package in the appropriate program through the Open With options available when you right-click the ZIP package on the Windows desktop or in Windows Explorer. If you do this, just be careful not to accidentally set the applicable program as the default for opening this file type, or you'll add an extra step for yourself every time you want to access the document parts in the ZIP package.

However, for ease of use as well as for sharing documents with Microsoft Office users of all experience levels, it's a good idea to make sure the file extension is changed back to its original state once you've finished editing the files in the ZIP package.

The Office Open XML File Structure

Once you change the file name to have the .zip extension, open the file in Windows Explorer. The example that follows walks you through the ZIP package of a simple Word document, originally saved with the .docx extension..

When you first view the ZIP package for a Word document in Windows Explorer, it will look something like the following.

Name	Type
_rels	File Folder
docProps	File Folder
word	File Folder
[Content_Types].xml	XML Document

Note that, at the top level of the ZIP package that you see in the preceding example, Excel and PowerPoint files look very similar except that the folder named **word** in the example is named **xl** or **ppt**, respectively, for the applicable program.

- The **docProps** folder is exactly what it sounds like—it contains the files for the document properties and application properties, ranging from author name to word count and software version.

- The **_rels** folder contains a file named *.rels*, which defines the top-level relationships between the folders in the package. Note that additional relationship files may exist, depending on the document content, for files within a specific folder of the package (explained later in this section).

  The relationship files are among the most important in the package because, without them, the various document parts in the package don't know how to work together.

- The file *[Content_Types].xml* also exists at the top level of every document's ZIP package. This file identifies the content types included in the document. For example, in a Word document, this list typically includes such things as the main document, the fonts, styles, Theme, document properties, and application properties. Files with additional content types, such as diagrams or other graphics, will have additional content types identified.

Exploring a bit further, when you open the folder named **word**, you see something similar to the following image.

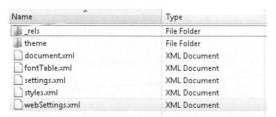

Name	Type
_rels	File Folder
theme	File Folder
document.xml	XML Document
fontTable.xml	XML Document
settings.xml	XML Document
styles.xml	XML Document
webSettings.xml	XML Document

- A new Word document contains XML files for the fonts, styles, settings (such as the saved zoom setting and default tab stops), and Web settings, whether or not formatting related to these items has been applied in the document. If headers, footers, footnotes, graphics, comments, or other content types have been added, each of them will have its own XML document part as well.

  In the ZIP packages for Excel and PowerPoint files, you'll see a similar organization, with XML document parts for file components (such as *styles.xml* in Excel or *tableStyles.xml* in PowerPoint). Additionally, the **xl** folder in an Excel ZIP package contains a **worksheets** folder by default, because there is a separate XML document part for each sheet in the workbook. The **ppt** folder in a PowerPoint ZIP package also contains folders named **slides**, **slideLayouts**, and **slideMasters**, by default.

- In addition to the XML document parts you see in the preceding image, notice the **theme** folder–which exists in the program-specific folder (**word**, **xl**, or **ppt**) for Word, Excel, and PowerPoint ZIP packages. The file contained in this **theme** folder contains all document Theme settings applied in the document. It is because of this file that you're able to share custom Themes by sharing documents, using the Browse For Themes feature at the bottom of each Themes gallery.

- The **_rels** folder inside the program-specific folder defines the relationships between the parts inside the program-specific folder. The relationship file contained in this **_rels** folder is called *document.xml.rels* for Word documents, *presentation.xml.rels* for PowerPoint documents, and *workbook.xml.rels* for Excel documents.

    Depending on the content in a given folder, its **_rels** folder might contain more than one file. For example, if a header exists in a Word document, the **word** folder contains a part named *header.xml,* and its **_rels** folder contains a file named *header.xml.rels.*

- Content in your document from other sources (such as embedded objects, media files, or macros) are either stored in their original format (as is the case for picture files) or as a binary file (.bin file extension). Because of this, you can save time on many tasks related to working with media files (such as pictures), as discussed in "Editing and Managing Documents Through XML" on page 1164.

- As mentioned at the beginning of this section, the ZIP package shown in the two preceding images is for a .docx file. Remember that the *x* at the end of the file extension indicates that it's a macro-free file format. If this were, instead, the package for a .docm file, you would also see a file named *vbaData.xml* and one named *vbaProject.bin.*

If you return to the top level of the ZIP package and then open the **docProps** folder, the following is what you'll see.

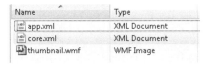

Name	Type
app.xml	XML Document
core.xml	XML Document
thumbnail.wmf	WMF Image

By default, this folder contains the files *app.xml* (for application properties such as word count and program version) and *core.xml* (for document properties such as the Document Properties summary information like author and subject). Additionally, if you use the options to save a preview picture or a thumbnail for your document, you see a thumbnail image file in the **docProps** folder. For Word and Excel, this will be a .wmf file and for PowerPoint it will be a .jpeg file.

> **Note**
>
> If you're running the 2007 Office release on Windows Vista, you'll find an option in the Save As dialog box in Word or Excel to save a thumbnail image of your document. In PowerPoint, or in all three programs when running Windows XP, you'll see the option Save Preview Picture in the Document Properties dialog box.

Taking a Closer Look at Key Document Parts

Let's take a look at the XML contained in a few of the essential document parts, to help accustom you to reading this file content.

The image you see below is the *[Content_Types].xml* file for the sample ZIP package shown under the preceding heading, as seen in Windows Explorer.

```xml
<?xml version="1.0" encoding="UTF-8" standalone="yes" ?>
- <Types xmlns="http://schemas.openxmlformats.org/package/2006/content-types">
    <Default Extension="wmf" ContentType="image/x-wmf" />
    <Default Extension="rels" ContentType="application/vnd.openxmlformats-
        package.relationships+xml" />
    <Default Extension="xml" ContentType="application/xml" />
    <Override PartName="/word/document.xml" ContentType="application/vnd.openxmlformats-
        officedocument.wordprocessingml.document.main+xml" />
    <Override PartName="/word/styles.xml" ContentType="application/vnd.openxmlformats-
        officedocument.wordprocessingml.styles+xml" />
    <Override PartName="/docProps/app.xml" ContentType="application/vnd.openxmlformats-
        officedocument.extended-properties+xml" />
    <Override PartName="/word/settings.xml" ContentType="application/vnd.openxmlformats-
        officedocument.wordprocessingml.settings+xml" />
    <Override PartName="/word/theme/theme1.xml"
        ContentType="application/vnd.openxmlformats-officedocument.theme+xml" />
    <Override PartName="/word/fontTable.xml" ContentType="application/vnd.openxmlformats-
        officedocument.wordprocessingml.fontTable+xml" />
    <Override PartName="/word/webSettings.xml" ContentType="application/vnd.openxmlformats-
        officedocument.wordprocessingml.webSettings+xml" />
    <Override PartName="/docProps/core.xml" ContentType="application/vnd.openxmlformats-
        package.core-properties+xml" />
</Types>
```

- The first line that you see in this or any XML file in an Office Open XML Format ZIP package will look very much like the first line in the preceding image. This line simply defines the type of XML structure being used.

- Notice that the second line, which begins **<Types...**, is the first half of a paired code for which the end code is at the bottom of this document. All other lines in this file are the definitions of the content types in this document.

  - On the second line, inside the **Types** code, you see **xmlns** followed by a URL. The reference **xmlns** refers to an XML *namespace*, which is a required component in several document parts. Technical though this term might sound, a namespace is nothing more than a way to uniquely identify a specified item. The reason for this is that there can be no ambiguous names in the ZIP package (that is, the same name can't be used to refer to more than one item). So, the namespace essentially attaches itself to the content it identifies to become part of that content's name.

It's standard to use a Web address as the namespace, but note that the file doesn't attempt to read any data from the specified address. In fact, if you try to access some of the URLs you see in the files of an Office Open XML ZIP package, you'll find that some are not even valid addresses. Typically, the address in a namespace identifies the location of the source schema or other definitions used to define the structure of the items assigned to that namespace, and the Web page associated with that address may actually contain those definitions. But, any URL can be used as a namespace—the address itself is actually irrelevant to the code.

- For the lines between the paired **Types** codes, notice that each defines one of the document parts you saw in the images of this sample ZIP package, under the preceding heading.

    - The first three lines in that group define the three file extensions included in this particular package, .rels (the relationship files), .wmf (the Windows metafile picture used for the document thumbnail), and .xml.

    - The remaining lines in that group, each named **Override PartName**, define the content type for each of the XML document parts that you saw in the **word** and **docProps** folders for this ZIP package. Take a look at just the first of the **Override PartName** lines, shown below. This one is for the main document content—the file *document.xml* that resides in the **word** folder.

        ```
        <Override PartName="/word/document.xml" ContentType="application/vnd.openxmlformats-
        officedocument.wordprocessingml.document.main+xml" />
        ```

Notice that the definition of the **Override PartName** that appears in quotation marks is actually the path to the specified file within the ZIP package. The content type definition that appears in quotation marks as the second half of that line of code is a reference to the content type definition defined in the applicable schema.

The following image shows you the content of the *.rels* file in the top-level **_rels** folder shown earlier for the sample ZIP package.

```
<?xml version="1.0" encoding="UTF-8" standalone="yes" ?>
- <Relationships xmlns="http://schemas.openxmlformats.org/package/2006/relationships">
    <Relationship Id="rId3"
      Type="http://schemas.openxmlformats.org/package/2006/relationships/metadata/core-
      properties" Target="docProps/core.xml" />
    <Relationship Id="rId2"
      Type="http://schemas.openxmlformats.org/package/2006/relationships/metadata/thumbnail"
      Target="docProps/thumbnail.wmf" />
    <Relationship Id="rId1"
      Type="http://schemas.openxmlformats.org/officeDocument/2006/relationships/officeDocument"
      Target="word/document.xml" />
    <Relationship Id="rId4"
      Type="http://schemas.openxmlformats.org/officeDocument/2006/relationships/extended-
      properties" Target="docProps/app.xml" />
  </Relationships>
```

> **Note**
>
> The *.rels* file should open without issue in Internet Explorer. But, if this doesn't work for you, append the .xml file extension to a copy of the *.rels* file, just for viewing purposes. Also note that, when in the ZIP package, files will only open in their default assigned program. To be able to open a document part in both Internet Explorer and Notepad, as needed, copy the file out of the ZIP package. Then, right-click the file and point to Open With to select the program you need.

- Notice that, although the content of the *.rels* file is very different from the content of the *[Content_Types].xml* file, the concept of the structure is the same. That is, the first line defines the XML standard being used, and the second line opens the paired code that stores the core file content and specifies a namespace for the content that appears between the lines of the paired code.

- Take a look at one of the relationship definitions from the *.rels* file—the one for the main *document.xml* document part. Notice that each relationship contains three parts—the **ID**, the **Type**, and the **Target**.

```
<Relationship Id="rId1"
   Type="http://schemas.openxmlformats.org/officeDocument/2006/relationships/officeDocument"
   Target="word/document.xml" />
```

  - An **ID** is typically named **rID#**. This structure is not required, however, so you might occasionally see relationships with different IDs.

  - The **Type** uses a type defined in the applicable schema, which appears as a Web address. As with an XML namespace, the document doesn't need to read data from that address. However, in this case, the **Type** is a specified element of the applicable schema and does need to be a content type recognized by the Office Open XML structure.

  - The **Target**, as you likely recognize, is the address within the package, where the referenced file appears. When you create a relationship yourself, it's essential that this be correct, because the relationship will do no good if it can't find the specified file.

Depending on the content in your files, you might run across defined relationships in your *.rels* files that aren't used to specify files in the ZIP package and therefore might take on a slightly different structure for the relationship target. For example, notice the following relationship from a *document.xml.rels* file for a document that contains a hyperlink to the Microsoft home page.

```
<Relationship Id="rId4"
   Type="http://schemas.openxmlformats.org/officeDocument/2006/relationships/hyperlink"
   Target="http://www.microsoft.com" TargetMode="External" />
```

Though the relationship ID and Type have the same structure as a relationship to a document part, notice that the target in this case is to an external hyperlink instead of a file in the package.

When you open a file in its originating program (Word, Excel, or PowerPoint), keep in mind that the *.rels* files are the first place the program looks to know how to put the pieces together for the purpose of opening that file.

Building a Basic Word Document from Scratch

The document shown in the preceding portions of this section is a simple Word document with all the defaults you get when you use Word to create a new document in the DOCX file format. Now, it's time to build a .docx file yourself, without using Word.

If you're thinking about skipping over the rest of this section because it sounds either too complicated or unnecessary for your needs, please wait. This exercise is important for three reasons.

1. You might be amazed at how easy this is to do. And, discovering the simplicity for yourself can help you master the tasks in this chapter that you want to learn.

2. You can find all the XML code you need for this section in a provided sample file (explained in a note that precedes the first part of the following exercise), if you prefer not to type out the XML for yourself.

3. This exercise is included early in the primer because doing a similar exercise when I was first learning about the Office Open XML Formats was the most helpful thing I did toward understanding the basics of how the parts in an Office Open XML ZIP package work and fit together.

That said, the exercise that follows walks you through creating a simple, essentials-only Word document. Though it's good practice for anyone creating Office Open XML Format documents through code to include all of the defaults that the source program (Word, Excel, or PowerPoint) includes when it creates a new document, only a few of those files are actually required for the source program (Word in our example) to be able to recognize and open the file. If you create a file that only contains the required bare basics, Word will recognize the missing pieces and add the document parts and relationships needed as you begin to use Word features in your document.

Every Office Open XML document requires *[Content_Types].xml* as well as a top-level **_rels** folder containing the *.rels* file. Each file also requires its program-specific folder with the main program-specific content file that goes in that folder (*document.xml* in a folder named **word**, in the case of a Word document). For a Word document, such as we're about to build, these are the only three files you must have in your ZIP package to create a .docx file that Word will recognize and open without an error. In Excel and PowerPoint, a few other files are required.

- An Excel .xlsx file also requires the **sheets** folder inside the **xl** folder, with an XML document part for at least one sheet. This is because an Excel workbook must contain at least one worksheet. Because of that **sheets** folder, the **xl** folder also needs its own **_rels** folder containing a workbook-level *.rels* file that defines the relationship between worksheets and workbook.

- A PowerPoint .pptx file also requires the **slideLayouts**, **slideMasters**, and **theme** folders (each of which contain required files), because a presentation must contain a Theme, at least one slide master, and at least one slide layout. These folders, all of which reside in the **ppt** folder, also require a **_rels** folder in that **ppt** folder to define the relationships between the presentation, slide master, and Theme. Note that the master and layout folders contain their own **_rels** folders, which is why there is no reference to the slide layouts in the presentation-level relationships file.

To create your first Word document from scratch, you'll need to create the files *[Content_Types].xml*, *.rels*, and *document.xml*, and place them in the correct folder structure. The steps that follow will walk you through getting this done.

> **Note**
>
> In the sample files that are included on this book's CD, find the Copy XML.txt file, which contains all of the code in this and subsequent sections of this chapter, that you can copy into the files you create in Notepad if you prefer not to type the XML yourself.

Create the Folder Structure

On your Windows desktop, or in any convenient location, create a folder named **First Document** (or any name you like; this name is for identification purposes in this exercise only). This folder will store the structure for your new .docx file. In that folder, create two subfolders, one named **_rels** and the other named **word**. It is essential that these two folders are correctly named. When you're done with this step, your folder structure should look like the following image.

Create the Main Document File

The main document file, *document.xml*, needs to reside in the **word** folder you just created. To create this file, do the following.

1. Open Notepad and save a new file as *document.xml*, inside the **word** folder you created. Be sure to type the .xml file extension as part of the file name, so that Notepad doesn't save the file in the .txt file format. (Notepad will save the file correctly when you type **document.xml** in the File Name box, even though the Save As Type list indicates a .txt file.)

2. In Notepad, add the following code to the *document.xml* file. This code is shown below first in Internet Explorer, so that you can see the organization of it, and then in Notepad, to see how it looks without the tree structure applied.

If you're typing this text from scratch, it's easier to copy from the version shown in the tree structure. If you do, note that you need a space between each XML namespace (*xmlns* definition) because those definitions all appear together inside the same code (the same pair of angle brackets). However, you don't need spaces between any codes that are enclosed in their own pair of angle brackets. Remember, however, that you can copy this code from the sample file Copy XML.txt, if you prefer.

```
<?xml version="1.0" encoding="UTF-8" standalone="yes" ?>
- <w:document xmlns:ve="http://schemas.openxmlformats.org/markup-compatibility/2006"
    xmlns:o="urn:schemas-microsoft-com:office:office"
    xmlns:r="http://schemas.openxmlformats.org/officeDocument/2006/relationships"
    xmlns:m="http://schemas.openxmlformats.org/officeDocument/2006/math"
    xmlns:v="urn:schemas-microsoft-com:vml"
    xmlns:wp="http://schemas.openxmlformats.org/drawingml/2006/wordprocessingDrawing"
    xmlns:w10="urn:schemas-microsoft-com:office:word"
    xmlns:w="http://schemas.openxmlformats.org/wordprocessingml/2006/main"
    xmlns:wne="http://schemas.microsoft.com/office/word/2006/wordml">
  - <w:body>
    - <w:p>
      - <w:r>
          <w:t>This is the first Word document I've created from scratch.</w:t>
        </w:r>
      </w:p>
    - <w:sectPr>
        <w:pgSz w:w="12240" w:h="15840" />
        <w:pgMar w:top="1440" w:right="1440" w:bottom="1440" w:left="1440" w:header="720"
          w:footer="720" w:gutter="0" />
        <w:cols w:space="720" />
        <w:docGrid w:linePitch="360" />
      </w:sectPr>
    </w:body>
  </w:document>
```

CAUTION

To accommodate the page layout for the book, code in the unstructured XML samples throughout this chapter may break to a new line in the middle of a term or use a hyphen to start a new line. When you view code in Notepad, it might appear to break in the middle of a word as well, but it won't use hyphens. Remember that all of the code between a single paired code (such as the <document> code shown here) is considered a single line and should not get manual line breaks when you type the code.

If you are typing this code yourself, double-check your syntax against the structured version of the same code that appears along with each unstructured sample. If copying the code instead of typing it, do so from the sample file named Copy XML.txt referenced earlier.

```
<?xml version="1.0" encoding="UTF-8" standalone="yes"?>

<w:document xmlns:ve="http://schemas.openxmlformats.org/markup-compatibil-
ity/2006" xmlns:o="urn:schemas-microsoft-com:office:office" xmlns:r="http://
schemas.openxmlformats.org/officeDocument/2006/relationships" xmlns:m="http://
schemas.openxmlformats.org/officeDocument/2006/math" xmlns:v="urn:schemas-mi-
crosoft-com:vml" xmlns:wp="http://schemas.openxmlformats.org/drawingml/2006/
wordprocessingDrawing" xmlns:w10="urn:schemas-microsoft-com:office:word"
xmlns:w="http://schemas.openxmlformats.org/wordprocessingml/2006/main" xmlns:
wne="http://schemas.microsoft.com/office/word/2006/wordml"><w:body><w:p><w:
r><w:t>This is the first Word document I've created from scratch.</w:t></w:
r></w:p><w:sectPr><w:pgSz w:w="12240" w:h="15840"/><w:pgMar w:top="1440" w:
right="1440" w:bottom="1440" w:left="1440" w:header="720" w:footer="720" w:
gutter="0"/><w:cols w:space="720"/><w:docGrid w:linePitch="360"/></w:sectPr></
w:body></w:document>
```

Once you're satisfied that your code is accurate, you can save and close this file. Notice that this code contains items you saw in the example from the preceding chapter section.

- The first line of code provides the XML version definition.

- The second line is the open code for the overall document content, where the namespaces are defined. Notice that a document file contains multiple name-spaces to cover different content types.

- The document content in this file is the single-line paragraph of text contained inside the paired **<body>** code.

- The last piece of content is the paired **<w:sectPr>** code, which you can see stores the basic section formatting (page setup) information. You can omit this information and the document will open in Word using default settings. Note that the formatting settings and values you see here are explained in the next section of this chapter.

Let's look at that document in one more format to help clarify the content. The image below shows the same *document.xml* file opened on the Tree View tab of the XML Notepad editor.

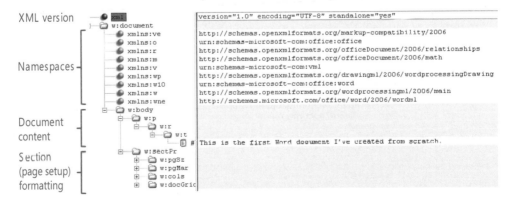

Create the Content_Types File

In Notepad, save a file named exactly *[Content_Types].xml* to the root of your **First Document** folder. As with the *document.xml* file, following are two versions of the code that you need to add to this file, first shown in Internet Explorer so that you can clearly see the tree structure, and next shown as run-of-text, similar to the way code appears in Notepad.

```
<?xml version="1.0" encoding="UTF-8" standalone="yes" ?>
- <Types xmlns="http://schemas.openxmlformats.org/package/2006/content-types">
    <Default Extension="rels" ContentType="application/vnd.openxmlformats-package.relationships+xml" />
    <Default Extension="xml" ContentType="application/xml" />
    <Override PartName="/word/document.xml" ContentType="application/vnd.openxmlformats-
      officedocument.wordprocessingml.document.main+xml" />
  </Types>
```

```
<?xml version="1.0" encoding="UTF-8" standalone="yes"?>
<Types xmlns="http://schemas.openxmlformats.org/package/2006/content-types"><Default
Extension="rels" ContentType="application/vnd.openxmlformats-package.
relationships+xml"/><Default Extension="xml" ContentType="application/xml"/><Override
PartName="/word/document.xml" ContentType="application/vnd.openxmlformats-officedocu-
ment.wordprocessingml.document.main+xml"/></Types>
```

As you see, this is a very simple file, containing the XML version statement at the top as well as the open code named **Types** that is the code in which all codes in the file are nested and where the namespace for the content types is defined. After that, you see the following.

- The only file extensions present in your basic Word document are .xml and .rels, so they are the only file extensions that require definition here.

- The only part name that requires definition as a content type is the main document (*document.xml*) because that is the only document part currently included, aside from the two structure-related files *[Content_Types].xml* and *.rels*.

Create the .rels File

The relationship file for this new document is the simplest of the three you need to create. In Notepad, create a new file and save it as *.rels*, inside the **_rels** subfolder you created within the **First Document** folder. Then, add the following content to that file (shown in both structured format and in Notepad run-of-text format).

```
<?xml version="1.0" encoding="UTF-8" standalone="yes" ?>
- <Relationships xmlns="http://schemas.openxmlformats.org/package/2006/relationships">
    <Relationship Id="rId1"
      Type="http://schemas.openxmlformats.org/officeDocument/2006/relationships/officeDocument"
      Target="word/document.xml" />
  </Relationships>
```

```
<?xml version="1.0" encoding="UTF-8" standalone="yes"?>
<Relationships xmlns="http://schemas.openxmlformats.org/package/2006/relationships">
<Relationship Id="rId1" Type="http://schemas.openxmlformats.org/officeDocument/2006/
relationships/officeDocument" Target="word/document.xml"/></Relationships>
```

In the preceding code, the XML version is defined (as it is in every .xml or .rels format file within the package); followed by the open code for the relationships content along with its namespace definition; followed by the single required relationship in this case, which is to the part named *document.xml*. See "The Office Open XML File Structure" on page 1150 for details on the three-part structure (ID, Type, and Target) of a relationship definition.

Compile and Open Your New Document

Once you save and close the **.rels** file, you can exit Notepad. You're now ready to put your ZIP package together and open the file in Word, using the following steps.

1. Open the **First Document** folder in Windows Explorer.

2. Select the file *[Content_Types.xml]* as well as the two subfolders (**_rels** and **word**).

3. Right-click, point to Send To, and then click Compressed (Zipped) Folder.

4. When the .zip folder is created, change the name (including the file extension) to **First document.docx**. Then, press Enter to set the new name and click Yes to confirm when you see the warning about changing file extensions.

Double-click to open your new Word document. It should open in Word without error. If it does not, see the Troubleshooting and Inside Out tips at the end of this section for help finding the problem.

Add More Content Types, Document Parts, and Relationships

Even though you didn't add all of the default content types and relationships that Word adds to a new document, all Word functionality is available to your new file. Make any edit (you can even type just a space if you like) and then save the file while it's open in Word. Then, close it, change the file extension to .zip, and take a look at what Word did to your files.

What you'll find is that Word added the default files it provides when it creates a new .docx file, and it added the necessary content type and relationship definitions to go along with them. Review the changes that Word made to your file. Once you're comfortable with the ZIP package content, you're ready to start working directly with the XML behind your Office Open XML documents.

TROUBLESHOOTING

How can I find the error when my ZIP package won't open in Word, Excel, or PowerPoint?

When an Office Open XML Format document won't open in Word, Excel, or PowerPoint, the problem can be as simple as a missing space, angle bracket, or another single character. But, when you have ZIP packages with multiple long files, how do you even begin to find the problem? Actually, in most cases you don't have to—Word, Excel, or PowerPoint will do it for you.

When you try to open the file and an error message appears, click the Details button on the error message. In most cases, the precise location of the error will be listed, and the error type might be included as well. Take a look at the following example.

In this example, I left the quotation mark off following one of the namespace definitions in the *document.xml* part. Notice that the detail here shows you the document part, the line within that part, and the location in that line where the error occurs. See the Inside Out tip that follows for more on interpreting the location references.

Note that, if you're using Internet Explorer to view and Notepad to edit your XML document parts, if there's an error in one of the parts, Internet Explorer will most likely be unable to open it in the tree structure. Because of this, if you use the error detail to lead you to the error location and try to correct it in Notepad, you can confirm that the error is corrected before returning the file to the ZIP package and changing the file extension back to its original state, just by trying to open it in Internet Explorer.

See the Inside Out tip that follows for some help on how to locate the error in your code without any wasted time or effort.

INSIDE OUT

Using XML Notepad and Word to Help Find Syntax Errors

Perhaps you tried to open a file in Word, as discussed in the preceding Troubleshooting tip, and got an error. Or, maybe you just created one of the XML parts for a new document, such as a *document.xml* file, and then tried to open it in Internet Explorer only to get a syntax error at that point.

The error message you see may indicate a line and position number, or it may indicate a line and column number. Note that column and position are not the same thing. Position is the easier of the two to identify, as it corresponds to characters.

One easy way to find the line and position number of the error is to try to open the file in XML Notepad, the free utility program mentioned earlier in this chapter (this is not the same as the Windows Notepad utility). So, if the Word error message tells you that the error occurred in the *document.xml* part, for example—or the error occurred in Internet Explorer when trying to open an individual XML part—you can try opening that document part in XML Notepad to instantly see the line and position number where the problem exists.

Keep in mind that everything within a paired code is considered a line of code. So, for example, in *document.xml*, line 2 refers to everything inside the paired <w:document...> code. Line 1 is the code that indicates the XML version. If then, for example, the XML Notepad error tells you that the error is located at line 2 and position 645, you're looking for character 645 in the second line of code. Copy that line of code (you can open it in Windows Notepad to do this) and paste it into a blank Word document. Then, open the Visual Basic Editor (Alt+F11), press Ctrl+G to open the Immediate window, and type the following code in that window. (You may want to turn off Word Wrap from the Format menu in Notepad before copying text to Word, to avoid copying unwanted formatting marks.)

```
ActiveDocument.Characters(645).Select
```

Substitute 645, of course, for the position of the error in your code. Press Enter from that line of code and then switch back to the document (Alt+F11), and you'll see the character causing the error selected on screen. No fuss, no muss, and no tearing your hair out because you can't find the error when you look at the amorphous blob of code that appears in Windows Notepad.

Editing and Managing Documents Through XML

Under each of the headings within this section, you'll find a different exercise for editing the document parts in the XML package. These exercises include editing text, formatting, and style definitions; replacing a picture; and removing comments from a document.

> **Note**
>
> The purpose of these exercises is to familiarize you with the structure and rules of a ZIP package and how to work with the XML syntax in the document parts to manage and troubleshoot documents. Some of the specific tasks in these exercises are not tasks that you would likely use the ZIP package for on a daily basis when working with individual documents (such as editing text or deleting comments from a document), because doing this in Word is faster and easier than doing it in the ZIP package for just one file.
>
> However, another benefit of being able to edit documents through the ZIP package is that developers can create automation to batch edit files without ever opening the source program. For example, a developer might create a program to remove comments from all files in a given folder. In that case, doing so through the ZIP package, without having to open the files in Word, greatly simplifies the automation.

Before You Begin Editing a Document Part

A couple of important points warrant noting before you begin editing Office Open XML Format ZIP packages.

- Most document measurements that appear in a document part for an Excel file will appear as the measurement you enter. For example, a 16-point font appears as the number 16; a one-inch margin appears as the number 1. Though this might seem like stating the obvious, I mention this because point size measurements do not appear as set in the document parts of a PowerPoint or Word ZIP package.

  - In Word, point size measurement for font sizes is doubled in the document part. So, for example, a 12-point font appears as the number 24. All other point size measurements are multiplied by 20 (that is, they use a unit of measure known as a *twip*, which is 1/20th of a point or 1/1440th of an inch). So, 12-point spacing after a paragraph appears as 240 in the *document.xml* part (if it's applied as direct formatting) or in the applicable custom style definition in *styles.xml*.

  - In PowerPoint, point size measurements are multiplied by 100. So, 12-point spacing after a paragraph or a 12-point font size applied to text would appear as the number 1200.

- Built-in, default style definitions are not stored in the XML for a Word document. Only the definitions for user-defined styles as well as any built-in styles that have been customized are accessible in *styles.xml*. Learn more about *styles.xml* in the Style editing exercise that follows later in this section.

Editing Text and Formatting

You can edit any document content or formatting directly in the ZIP package. In this sample exercise, we'll walk through editing text, adding text, changing the settings in a paragraph style, and adding direct formatting to specified text.

> **Note**
>
> To try the exercises in this section, you can either create your own sample document to work with or open one provided on this book's CD. To create your own sample file, create a new Word document containing one line of text, such as *This is my sample text*. Then, create a custom paragraph style but don't apply it to any text. To match the exercise in this section on editing styles, your custom style should include a 12-point Arial font, 12 points spacing after the paragraph, and the Theme Color Accent 1 for the font color. When you've finished this setup, save the file using the .docx format in a location where you can easily access it (such as the Windows desktop) and then close the file.
>
> To use the sample file provided, find the file Text editing.docx in the sample files included on this book's CD.

To edit the ZIP package, change the file extension for *Text editing.docx* (or your own sample file) from .docx to .zip. (Remember that you can do this by appending the .zip file extension if you like, rather than replacing the .docx extension, to save a bit of time when you're ready to change the file extension back to .docx.) Once you've opened the ZIP package, give the following exercises a try.

Edit Text and Settings in document.xml

To begin editing any document part, as mentioned at the start of this section, first copy it out of the ZIP package (for example, paste a copy on the Windows desktop). Do this with the *document.xml* file inside the **word** folder for your sample document, and then do the following.

1. Open *document.xml* in Internet Explorer. If you're using the sample document provided, the document content following the namespace definitions will look like the image that follows.

```
- <w:body>
  - <w:p>
    - <w:r>
        <w:t>This is my sample text.</w:t>
      </w:r>
    </w:p>
  - <w:sectPr>
      <w:pgSz w:w="12240" w:h="15840" />
      <w:pgMar w:top="1440" w:right="1440" w:bottom="1440" w:left="1440" w:header="720"
        w:footer="720" w:gutter="0" />
      <w:cols w:space="720" />
      <w:docGrid w:linePitch="360" />
    </w:sectPr>
  </w:body>
```

Notice the construction of the text. There is one paragraph of text, nested within the paired code **<w:p></w:p>**, followed by some document settings, including paper size and page margins. (If you're using your own file for this exercise and you see additional codes in *document.xml* labeled **rsidR** and **rsidPr**, see the note at the end of "Reading a Markup Language" on page 1145 for information about those codes and why they appear.)

> **Note**
>
> Most XML coding uses characters or abbreviations that are logical and easy to interpret by anyone who knows the program, such as **<w:p>** to refer to a Word paragraph, **pgSz** to refer to the size of the page, or **pgMar** to refer to page margins. In the comprehensive documentation for Office Open XML that you can learn more about in the last section of this chapter, you can find each and every one of these codes. However, you can see how, just using logic and what you know about the program, it's very easy to decipher an XML document part without having to memorize the XML language details.

2. Leave the document open in Internet Explorer, for easy reference, and open it in Notepad as well.

   You can save changes to the document in Notepad even while it's open in Internet Explorer, and you can then refresh the Internet Explorer page to view your saved changes.

3. Find the text *This is my sample text.* in Notepad, and then delete the word *sample*.

4. Copy the codes for that entire paragraph, starting with **<w:p>** and ending with **</w:p>**. Then, paste what you've copied immediately after the existing **</w:p>** code.

   You've just added a second paragraph to your document. You can now change the text that appears between the **<w:t>** and **</w:t>** codes that denote the paragraph text. I chose to have that new paragraph read *This is fun. I'm editing my Word document without opening Word.*

5. Change the left and right page margins to 0.75 inch each. Remember that you'll need to calculate the values in twips for *document.xml* to understand the values you add. Because there are 72 points to an inch, three-quarters of an inch is 54 points. To convert that number to twips so that *document.xml* understands it, multiply the number by 20. (Or, since a twip is 1/1440th of an inch, multiply 1440 by 0.75.) So, you'll enter **1080** as the left and the right margin values. Be sure to leave quotation marks and related codes intact when you change the numbers.

6. Save *document.xml* and then close Notepad. In Internet Explorer, refresh the page and check your changes.

   Following is what the body portion of document.xml looks like in my file after these changes.

```
- <w:body>
  - <w:p>
    - <w:r>
        <w:t>This is my text.</w:t>
      </w:r>
    </w:p>
  - <w:p>
    - <w:r>
        <w:t>This is fun. I'm editing my Word document without opening Word.</w:t>
      </w:r>
    </w:p>
  - <w:sectPr>
      <w:pgSz w:w="12240" w:h="15840" />
      <w:pgMar w:top="1440" w:right="1080" w:bottom="1440" w:left="1080" w:header="720"
        w:footer="720" w:gutter="0" />
      <w:cols w:space="720" />
      <w:docGrid w:linePitch="360" />
    </w:sectPr>
  </w:body>
</w:document>
```

7. When you're happy with your changes, copy *document.xml* back into the ZIP package, overwriting the existing *document.xml* file.

8. Open the document in Word.

   Because the next exercise also requires editing this ZIP package, save time by opening the .zip file in Word instead of changing the file extension back and forth. To do this, open Word and then press Ctrl+O for the Open file dialog box. Browse to the location of your ZIP package, change the file type list setting to All Files, and then select and open your ZIP package. As mentioned earlier, it will open like a regular Word document.

If you're happy with the changes and additions to your text, and the changes to your page margins, continue to the next exercise.

Add Formatting to Text in document.xml

In this exercise, you'll add some direct formatting to one paragraph in the sample document *Text editing.docx* and then add direct formatting to just part of the second paragraph. To do this, if you still have the copy of *document.xml* that you edited in the last exercise, continue using that file. If not, copy *document.xml* out of the ZIP package again. Then, do the following.

1. Open *document.xml* in both Internet Explorer (for reference) and Notepad (for editing).

2. Add direct formatting of bold and italics to the first paragraph in the document. To do this, in Notepad, take the following steps.

   Place your insertion point immediately before the **<w:t>** code for the first paragraph of text and then type the following code.

   ```
   <w:rPr><w:b /><w:i /></w:rPr>
   ```

   As you might recognize from the first code sample in this chapter, you've just added bold and italic formatting to the first paragraph in the document.

3. Save and close the file in Notepad. Then, return to the Internet Explorer window where *document.xml* is open, and refresh the page to check your changes. The paragraph you edited should look something like this:

   ```
   - <w:p>
    - <w:r>
     - <w:rPr>
        <w:b />
        <w:i />
       </w:rPr>
       <w:t>This is my text.</w:t>
      </w:r>
     </w:p>
   ```

4. When you're happy with your edits, copy *document.xml* back into the ZIP package, overwriting the version that exists. Then, in Word, press Ctrl+O for the Open file dialog box, and then select and open the ZIP package as you did in the previous exercise.

When you confirm that you completed the preceding steps correctly, the next exercise is to add direct formatting (a 14-point font in this example) to just part of the second paragraph in the document. Close the document when you're ready to continue, and then take the following steps.

1. Open *document.xml* in both Internet Explorer and Notepad. (Use the most recent copy of *document.xml* that you updated for the preceding exercise, if you still have it available. Otherwise, copy the file out of the ZIP package again.)

   If you're using *Text editing.docx* or a version of the same document that you created, the second paragraph contains the text *This is fun. I'm editing my Word document without opening Word.* The steps that follow will add a 14-point font size to just the first sentence in that paragraph.

2. Since you'll be adding formatting to just part of the paragraph, you first need to separate the parts of the paragraph that will have different formatting. To do this, take the following substeps.

First, place your insertion point between the two sentences of the second paragraph. (If you've been following along with the preceding exercises, your insertion point will be after the period that follows the text *This is fun.*) Type the following code between those two sentences, and then type a space (so that a space separates the new codes and the sentence they precede).

```
</w:t></w:r><w:r><w:t>
```

The first two codes in the preceding structure end the text and the text of the run and then end the run of code. The next two codes begin a new run of code, followed by a new text string. The space you added after the four new codes is the space that will appear between the two sentences of text in the document.

Inside the new **<w:t>** code (the last of the four codes you just typed), add a space after the letter *t* (and before the closing angle bracket), followed by **xml:space="preserve"**. That code should now look like the following.

```
<w:t xml:space="preserve">
```

This **"preserve"** statement tells the XML to preserve the space you added at the beginning of the second sentence, so that spacing between the separated sentences is retained. Following is the way the code for this paragraph should look at this point.

```
- <w:p>
  - <w:r>
      <w:t>This is fun.</w:t>
    </w:r>
  - <w:r>
      <w:t xml:space="preserve">I'm editing my Word document without opening
        Word.</w:t>
    </w:r>
  </w:p>
```

3. Now, it's time to add the 14-point font formatting to just the first sentence in the paragraph. In Notepad, place your insertion point immediately before the **<w:t>** code that precedes the first sentence in the second paragraph (the one for which you intend to add the formatting). Then type the following.

```
<w:rPr><w:sz w:val="28" /></w:rPr>
```

4. In Notepad, save and close the document. Then, in Internet Explorer, refresh the page to check your code. Code for the paragraph being edited should now look like this:

```
- <w:p>
  - <w:r>
    - <w:rPr>
        <w:sz w:val="28" />
      </w:rPr>
      <w:t>This is fun.</w:t>
    </w:r>
  - <w:r>
      <w:t xml:space="preserve">I'm editing my Word document without opening
        Word.</w:t>
    </w:r>
  </w:p>
```

Chapter 32

Notice that you used 28 to represent 14-point font size, as discussed earlier in this section. The paired **<w:rPr></w:rPr>** codes that you also used in the preceding exercise are the codes inside which you store any unique formatting for the specified text. As with the preceding exercise, you could add additional lines of code to represent other font formatting after **<w:sz w:val="28" />**, such as the bold or italic codes you used earlier.

When you're happy with the code you see in Internet Explorer, copy *document.xml* back into the ZIP package and once again, from Word, open the ZIP package file to check your results. If your results are successful, close the file and continue on to the next exercise.

Edit Custom Styles in styles.xml

This is the last exercise using the file *Text editing.docx*. In this exercise, you will edit a custom style that's saved in this document. To begin, copy the file *styles.xml* out of the **word** folder in the ZIP package for the sample file.

Open the file *styles.xml* in Internet Explorer. This is a long file that contains a list of every built-in style available to the document, other than those that are used by built-in features not used in the active document. The list includes the style visibility and priority settings that correspond to the settings on the Recommend tab of the Manage Styles dialog box. For example, the styles Header and Footer are used by the document header and footer. If you've not yet accessed the header and footer layer in the document, those styles won't appear in this *styles.xml* list.

However, only definitions of your own custom (user-defined) styles, or any built-in styles that have been customized, appear in *styles.xml* at all. The definitions of any built-in styles that are not customized do not appear anywhere in the ZIP package, because Word "knows" these settings, so it doesn't need to record them in the file's XML. If you see exceptions to this, they are most likely for styles new to Word 2007, because Word records these style definitions when the document is opened in an earlier version.

To begin this exercise, scroll to the bottom of *styles.xml* in Internet Explorer, where you'll see the custom style named MyStyle, which I created in the sample document. If you're using a similar sample document instead that you created by following the instructions at the start of this section, look for your own custom style name at the end of *styles.xml*. The code for the definition of MyStyle looks like this:

```
- <w:style w:type="paragraph" w:customStyle="1" w:styleId="MyStyle">
    <w:name w:val="MyStyle" />
    <w:basedOn w:val="Normal" />
    <w:qFormat />
  - <w:pPr>
      <w:spacing w:after="240" />
    </w:pPr>
  - <w:rPr>
      <w:rFonts w:ascii="Arial" w:hAnsi="Arial" />
      <w:color w:val="4F81BD" w:themeColor="accent1" />
      <w:sz w:val="24" />
    </w:rPr>
  </w:style>
```

Now, open *styles.xml* in Notepad. The following steps walk you through changing the paragraph spacing and the font included in this custom style.

1. Scroll to the bottom of the document and find the definition for the custom style that you just reviewed in Internet Explorer.

2. Notice that the paragraph spacing is set to 12 points after (which is written as the value 240 in the XML). Change this setting to 6 points after the paragraph by replacing 240 with 120. Then, add 6 points before the paragraph as well, by adding the following code immediately before or after the spacing after code.

   ```
   <w:spacing w:before="120"/>
   ```

3. Now, change the font. Notice that the font is listed twice, once in a code specifying ANSI text and one in a code specifying ASCII text. This is because Word styles can carry a separate font for those languages that don't use Latin text. To avoid having a separate setting added to your style (unless you deliberately want one), change the font in both of those settings from Arial to Times New Roman. Be sure to leave the quotation marks and all other code syntax intact. (Note that, if you have multiple editing languages enabled, you may see additional font definitions in your documents as well.) Then, save and close the file.

4. If you'd like to refresh the page in Internet Explorer to check your work, do so. Then, copy *styles.xml* back into the ZIP package, overwriting the existing version of the same file.

5. You're now done editing the ZIP package, so you can change the file extension back to .docx, and then double-click to open the file in Word. Check to confirm that the changes you made to the style look correct, either by checking the style definition in the Styles pane or by applying the style to an existing paragraph.

Congratulations! Now that you can edit text and formatting for your documents through the ZIP package, try two other exercises that follow for editing document content through the XML. These exercises include programmatically changing a picture in a Word document and removing the comments from a Word document.

Editing Pictures

> **Note**
>
> For the exercises titled "Editing Pictures" and "Removing a Document Part," use the files Content edit.docx and Fearless logo.png that you can find in the sample files included on this book's CD. The second of these is a logo image that you'll use in the first of the two exercises.
>
> If you prefer to create your own sample file, create a file that uses one picture in two places (such as in the body of the page and in a header) and add two comments to the document, using the Comments feature on the Review tab. For the picture, use a picture saved in the .png file format.

The sample file *Content edit.docx* is a simple starter document containing a few lines of text on two pages, as well as a placeholder picture for a logo on the front page and in the header of the second page (which is a new section). The file also includes two comments that will be used in the exercise that follows.

For this exercise, you'll use the ZIP package to replace the placeholder logo file. First, however, open the file *Content edit.docx* in Word, so that you can take note of the picture (the logo placeholder) that appears in both the second section header and in the body text of the first page. Notice that the picture has different sizing in the two positions and that it has a picture style applied where it appears on the first page of the document. Once you've noted this, close the file and then, in a Windows Explorer (or on the Windows desktop if that is where you've placed this file), change the file extension to .zip.

1. Open the ZIP package, and then open the **word** folder. Notice that this folder contains a **media** folder. The picture that appears in the document is stored in this folder.

2. Open the **media** folder. Notice that the picture is actually saved as a picture file. If you're using the sample files provided, the file name in the **media** folder is *image1.png*, as you see in the following image.

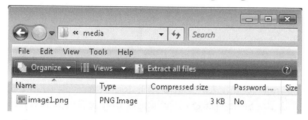

In fact, any pictures pasted or inserted into your document are saved as complete picture files in the media folder within the ZIP package, which is one of my favorite timesavers for using the ZIP packages in daily document production work. If you need to use a picture from an Office Open XML document in another document or another location, and you don't have the original picture file, simply copy the complete picture file out of the ZIP package and use or share it as needed.

3. To replace the placeholder image with the logo image, just rename the file *Fearless logo.png* to *image1.png*. Then, copy it into the ZIP package, replacing the existing *image1.png* in that package.

4. Open the file in Word.

   The placeholder logo has been replaced with the *Fearless logo.png* image in both locations, and all picture size, placement, and other formatting remains intact.

INSIDE OUT   Replace an Image File with a Different File Type

In the "Editing Pictures" exercise, you replaced one .png file with another just by changing the file name and copying the new picture. But, what if you need to replace a .png picture with a .bmp or a .jpg file, or you don't want to change the file name?

Changing the file name to match the existing image file allows you to replace the file without having to edit any relationships. However, you can replace the image file with another image of a different name and file type, as long as you edit the relationships and content types in the ZIP package accordingly.

To do this, open the **_rels** folder located in the **word** folder. In the case of the sample file, there are *.rels* files for both the document and the header. Copy both of these out of the ZIP package and then open each in Notepad. Find the reference to the file *image1.png* and change it to the name of your new image file, such as *Northwind.tif*. Then, copy the files back into the ZIP package, overwriting the existing files of the same names.

Note that the file *Northwind.tif* is available in the sample files on this book's CD, if you'd like to try this for yourself.

Next, copy *[Content_Types].xml* out of the ZIP package. and open that file in Notepad. Notice that there is a `Default Extension` definition near the top of the file for the .png format. You can either copy this entire definition string to add one for the .tif format, or (if there are no other .png images in your document) replace the two references to png in that string with tif, so that the string looks like the this:

```
<Default Extension="tif" ContentType="image/tif"/>
```

Save and close the file and copy it back into the ZIP package, overwriting the existing file of the same name. That's it. Just change the file extension back to .docx and open the file in Word to see your new image. If you've used *Northwind.tif*, the image will look exactly like *Fearless logo.png* in the preceding exercise, because these files use the same logo.

You know that the exercise in this sidebar worked, however, because the file wouldn't open and display the new image if you had not correctly revised the relationships and content type definitions.

Removing a Document Part

In this exercise, you'll remove all comments from the ZIP package. Doing this requires the following changes.

- Delete the *comments.xml* document part that resides in the **word** folder.
- Delete the relationship for the comments document part.
- Remove the comment placeholders from the *document.xml* file.

Take the following steps to do this.

1. Open the ZIP package for the sample file used in the preceding image exercise.

2. In the **word** folder, select and delete *comments.xml*.

3. In the **word** folder, open the **_rels** folder and copy the file *document.xml.rels* out of the ZIP package.

4. Open *document.xml.rels* in Notepad and delete the relationship to the comments part. Be sure to delete the entire relationship and nothing else. Though the relationship ID might vary if you're using a file other than the sample provided (indicated by the pound sign in the ID shown in the sample that follows), the content to delete should look like this.

```
<Relationship Id="rId#" Type="http://schemas.openxmlformats.org/officeDocu-
ment/2006/relationships/comments" Target="comments.xml"/>
```

5. Save and close the file. Then, copy the file back into the ZIP package, overwriting the existing file of the same name.

6. From the **word** folder, copy the file *document.xml* out of the ZIP package and then open that file in both Internet Explorer and Notepad.

7. In Internet Explorer, look for two comment references. Each one should look very much like the following image.

```
- <w:r>
  - <w:rPr>
      <w:rStyle w:val="CommentReference" />
      <w:rFonts w:asciiTheme="minorHAnsi" w:eastAsiaTheme="minorHAnsi"
        w:hAnsiTheme="minorHAnsi" w:cstheme="minorBidi" />
      <w:color w:val="auto" />
      <w:spacing w:val="0" />
      <w:kern w:val="0" />
    </w:rPr>
    <w:commentReference w:id="0" />
  </w:r>
```

Notice that the reference begins with the open code **<w:r>** (the reference to a run, or a portion of related content) and ends with the matching end code **</w:r>**. Most of the content between is similar to code you've worked with before. Notice that everything except the next-to-last line of this sample is information about formatting for the comment. The next-to-last line of the sample is the comment placeholder itself.

Just above the second comment reference, you'll see two lines of code that read **<w:commentRangeStart**... and **<w:commentRangeEnd**..., separated by a few other lines, as you see in the following image.

```
  <w:commentRangeStart w:id="1" />
- <w:r>
    <w:lastRenderedPageBreak />
    <w:t>My document text will start here.</w:t>
  </w:r>
  <w:commentRangeEnd w:id="1" />
```

These appear here because the second comment in this document was inserted with text selected, rather than being inserted at a blinking insertion point.

8. In Notepad, delete both complete comment references, including all lines of code shown in the first image in the preceding step, as well as the comment range start and end lines of code shown in the second image in the preceding step. Do *not* delete the lines between the comment range start and end statement, as those are part of the document text. Save and close the file when done, and then refresh the page in Internet Explorer to check your work.

9. Copy *document.xml* back into the ZIP package and change the file extension back to .docx. Open the file and you should see no sign of the two comments that previously existed.

> **Note**
>
> The content types file in a document containing comments includes a content type definition for comments. However, it's not necessary to delete a content type definition from this file when deleting a document part. As you noticed earlier in this chapter, when we first looked at the ZIP package content of a new, default Word file, several content types are included by default even if they're not used in the document. It's essential to remove the relationship for a deleted document part, but content types can remain without causing any problems.
>
> Also note that, if you didn't delete the comment placeholders from *document.xml*, the document still would have opened. The comment text would have been gone (you only need to delete the document part and its relationship to accomplish that), but the comment placeholders would remain.

Customizing the Ribbon

This is my favorite part of working with the new Office Open XML Formats. You can customize the Ribbon for any document or template in Word, Excel, or PowerPoint.

What's the catch? XML is the only way to get this done. Should that bother you? Not at all. If you successfully completed the preceding exercises and you feel comfortable with the basic components of an Office Open XML Format ZIP package, this is going to be a breeze.

For Excel and PowerPoint fans, the toolbar and menu customizations you can make from the Customize dialog box in earlier versions aren't stored in the document or template—you have to generate those from VBA if you want to share them with other computers. So, this new approach in the 2007 release provides more flexibility.

However, the Word devotees among you might be troubled by the fact that you can't customize the Ribbon from something like a Customize dialog box, because those customizations are saved in documents or templates in earlier versions. All I can say is this: Give XML a chance and you just might be delighted with the flexibility and simplicity of the new approach.

In this section, I'll take you through the required structure and basic syntax for customizing the user interface (referred to as the UI for the remainder of this section). Then, we'll walk through exercises to add a custom tab to the Ribbon and add a custom group to a built-in tab.

The Basic Components of Ribbon Customization

As with comments or images, or even the main document text, when you customize the UI for a document, template, or add-in, you need to add the appropriate relationship. However, there's not much more to it than that. UI customization requires the following components.

- A folder stored in the root of the ZIP package, named **customUI**.

- A document part inside the **customUI** folder named *customUI.xml*. (This is where the specific custom settings are stored.)

- A relationship for the customUI file in the top-level *.rels* file, located in the **_rels** folder in the root of the ZIP package. The syntax of that relationship is as follows (where **value** refers to a unique ID value, such as **"rID5"**):

```
<Relationship Type="http://schemas.microsoft.com/office/2006/relationships/ui/
extensibility" Target="/customUI/customUI.xml" Id="value" />
```

> **Note**
> You can change the order of the three elements included in a relationship definition without causing an error. For example, you might see the ID appear before the Type definition in some instances.

Adding a Ribbon Tab

When you add a custom tab to the Ribbon, you can choose to add that tab to the built-in Ribbon, or to use only your custom tabs. You specify the name for your custom tab and the name for each group on that tab, and then identify each item to be included. Custom tabs can contain built-in features, including custom Building Block galleries, and can also contain your own VBA macros.

The following image shows the content of a *customUI.xml* file that suppresses all built-in tabs and adds a custom tab named My Tab, with one custom group in which three built-in features are displayed, two of which have been given unique labels.

```
- <customUI xmlns="http://schemas.microsoft.com/office/2006/01/customui">
  - <ribbon startFromScratch="true">
    - <tabs>
      - <tab id="customTab" label="My Tab">
        - <group id="customGroup" label="My Sample Group">
            <button idMso="PasteSpecialDialog" visible="true" size="large" label="Choose a Paste
              Option" />
            <gallery idMso="TableInsertGallery" visible="true" size="large" label="Add Table" />
            <button idMso="FileSave" visible="true" size="large" />
          </group>
        </tab>
      </tabs>
    </ribbon>
  </customUI>
```

The resulting Ribbon for the preceding automation looks like this:

Note that, if you were to omit **startFromScratch** from the **<ribbon...** code, the custom tab would appear at the end of the Ribbon, following the built-in tabs. Notice a few things in particular about the preceding code.

- The hierarchy is very straightforward. The code referencing the Ribbon is the outermost code, inside that is the tabs collection, inside that is the individual tab, then the group, then within the group is each individual item you want to add to that group.

- The term **idMso** refers to a built-in item and the term **id** refers to a custom item.

- If you omit a label value from a built-in item, the built-in label is used. But, you can add a custom label to custom or built-in items.

> **Note**
>
> You can add custom images to buttons, just as you are able to do with toolbar and menu items in earlier versions. That is not done in the preceding sample code, but it is done in the second Ribbon customization exercise in this chapter, "Add a Group to a Built-In Ribbon Tab" on page 1180.

Chapter 32

After this code is added in *customUI.xml*, and that file is added to the **customUI** folder in the root of the ZIP package, all you need to do is add the relationship provided at the start of this section to the *.rels* file in the top-level **_rels** folder.

INSIDE OUT Watch Out for the Microsoft Office Button When Using *startFromScratch*

When you use the *startFromScratch* command referenced earlier in this section to replace the built-in Ribbon tabs with your custom tabs, don't forget about the Microsoft Office Button, which is a part of the Ribbon and can (for the most part) be customized as well.

When you start from scratch, the Microsoft Office Button still appears, but the only options that remain accessible by default through that button are New, Open, Save, Recent Documents, <Program> Options, and Exit. (To see an example of this, open the file Generate GUID.docm, available in the sample files included on this book's CD. This file is used for the data binding exercise later in this chapter.)

Ready to give it a try? The following exercise walks you through creating a custom tab for your document at the end of the built-in Ribbon in Word, with one custom group containing a selection of built-in commands.

Note

You don't need a sample file to execute this exercise. However, you can see a completed example of the exercise in the file named My tab.docx, in the sample files included on this book's CD.

1. In Word, create a new, blank document. Save your file to the Windows desktop as a .docx with a .zip file extension. As explained earlier in this chapter, in "Breaking into Your Document" on page 1149, type the entire file name (including extension) in quotation marks when in the Save As dialog box to save using the .zip file extension. Name the file First tab.zip and save it to your Windows desktop, for ease when following the remaining instructions. You can add content to the document if you like, but it's not necessary to do so. Close the file once it's saved.

2. On the Windows desktop, create a new folder named **customUI**. Note that this folder name is case sensitive, as are most XML commands.

3. Open Notepad and save a new file, named *customUI.xml*, into the **customUI** folder you just created.

4. In Notepad, add the following code to the file you just saved. This code matches the sample shown earlier in this section. (As with earlier exercises that require significant amounts of code, you can find this code in the sample file named Copy XML.txt, if you prefer to copy it rather than typing it yourself. For those who prefer to type it, see the image that follows showing the code structured as it appears in Internet Explorer, for ease of reference.)

```
<customUI xmlns="http://schemas.microsoft.com/office/2006/01/customui">
<ribbon><tabs><tab id="customTab" label="My Tab"><group id="customGroup"
label="My Sample Group"><button idMso="PasteSpecialDialog" visible="true"
size="large" label="Choose a Paste Option" /><gallery idMso="TableInsertGalle
ry" visible="true" size="large" label="Add Table" /> <button idMso="FileSave"
visible="true" size="large" /></group></tab></tabs></ribbon></customUI>
```

```
- <customUI xmlns="http://schemas.microsoft.com/office/2006/01/customui">
  - <ribbon>
    - <tabs>
      - <tab id="customTab" label="My Tab">
        - <group id="customGroup" label="My Sample Group">
            <button idMso="PasteSpecialDialog" visible="true" size="large" label="Choose a Paste
              Option" />
            <gallery idMso="TableInsertGallery" visible="true" size="large" label="Add Table" />
            <button idMso="FileSave" visible="true" size="large" />
          </group>
        </tab>
      </tabs>
    </ribbon>
  </customUI>
```

Once you add this code to *customUI.xml*, save and close the file. You might want to open the file in Internet Explorer to check your code against the preceding image.

5. Open *First tab.zip*. Drag the folder **customUI** and drop it into the root of the ZIP package, so that the top level of the ZIP package looks like the following image. (You can, of course, also cut or copy the folder and paste it into the ZIP package, instead of dragging it.)

Name	Type
_rels	File Folder
customUI	File Folder
docProps	File Folder
word	File Folder
[Content_Types].xml	XML Document

6. Open the **_rels** folder in the root of the ZIP package. Then, copy the *.rels* file out of the ZIP package.

7. Open *.rels* in Notepad and add the following code before the **</Relationships>** code. Be sure not to place this code in the middle of another relationship definition. (Note that # in the following code represents a number not already used for a relationship in this file.)

```
<Relationship Type="http://schemas.microsoft.com/office/2006/relationships/ui/
extensibility" Target="/customUI/customUI.xml" Id="rId#" />
```

Chapter 32

8. Save and close *.rels* and then copy it back into the ZIP package, overwriting the existing *.rels* file.

That's all there is to it. Time to open your file and check out the results.

To get comfortable with this code, I strongly recommend editing *customUI.xml* a few times with different settings. Try small buttons instead of large (just remove the `size="large"` reference to change the button size to small), add or remove a custom label for one of the commands, try adding a second group (just give the new group a unique name, such as `customGroup2`), or try using different commands. See the note that follows for help finding the correct syntax for the command you need.

> **Note**
>
> Find files that contain control IDs for every Word, Excel, and PowerPoint command in the sample files included on this book's CD. Control IDs refer to the `idMso` values in the preceding exercise.
>
> The files, named *WordRibbonControls.xlsx*, *ExcelRibbonControls.xlsx*, and *PowerPoint-RibbonControls.xlsx*, as well as the icon gallery workbook and *customUI* schema file (discussed in the next section) are available on the CD thanks to the 2007 release product team.

Add a Group to a Built-In Ribbon Tab

Adding a group to a built-in tab is an almost identical process to the preceding exercise. The difference is simply in how you reference the tab name. So, in the following exercise, you'll edit the *customUI.xml* file you created in that exercise to add your new custom group to the Home tab instead of a custom tab, and then specify the position on the Home tab where you want your new group to appear. And, because making this change requires just a minor edit to your existing *customUI.xml* file, we'll also customize the image for one of the buttons in this same exercise.

> **Note**
>
> In the file named Office2007IconGallery.xlsm, located in the sample files included on this this book's CD, you can find the idMso values for every available built-in button image. As with the control ID files mentioned earlier, this file was created by the 2007 release product team. Instructions for using this file are available directly in the file.

To begin, if you don't still have a copy (outside of the ZIP package) of the *customUI.xml* file you just created, copy this file out of the ZIP. Open the file in Notepad, and then do the following.

1. Find the code **<tab id=**... and edit that code to read as follows.

    ```
    <tab idMso="TabHome">
    ```

    Note that the label definition has been removed from this code. If you leave the label in the code when you change the tab id reference to the idMso reference to the Home tab, you'll rename the Home tab with the label value. (If you want to use a different built-in tab for this exercise, you can find the correct control ID for the tab names along with the control ID for feature names in the <Program>RibbonControls workbooks mentioned in the preceding section.)

2. Change the **<group**... code as follows.

    ```
    <group id="customGroup" label="My Sample Group" insertAfterMso = "GroupFont">
    ```

    All you've done here is add **insertAfterMso** and set its value to **"GroupFont"**. As you'll find in the WordRibbonControls workbook, **GroupFont** is the control ID for the built-in Font group that appears on the Home tab. The **insertAfter-Mso** setting specifies the position on the tab where you want your new group to appear. If you omit this setting, your group will appear at the end of the tab.

3. The last edit you'll make in this file is to add an idMso value for a custom image setting to appear in place of the built-in Paste Special image. To do this, edit the button code for the Paste Special dialog box to look like the following.

    ```
    <button idMso="PasteSpecialDialog" visible="true" size="large" imageMso = "Cre-
    ateReportFromWizard" label="Choose a Paste Option" />
    ```

    Notice that all you need to do here is add the **imageMso** statement with its value of **CreateReportFromWizard**. The **imageMso** IDs are available in the Office-2007IconGallery workbook mentioned earlier in this section. The icon I chose appears in Gallery 1 in that file, in the second column of the fourth row. You can choose any ID from any of those galleries provided in place of the one I selected. Just point to an icon in one of those galleries to find the correct syntax for referencing that icon.

4. When you've finished making changes, save and close the file and then copy it back into the ZIP package, overwriting the existing *customUI.xml* file. Change the file back to the .docx extension if you want to do so, and then open the file to see your new custom group added to the Home tab, following the Font group, as you see in the following image.

Chapter 32

Having fun yet? I certainly hope so. Now check out the next section of this chapter to learn how to bind Word Content Controls to custom XML data.

> **Note**
> Want the full skinny on customizing the UI? Find customUI.xsd (the schema for UI customization) on the Resources tab of this book's CD. Remember that you can open and review the text of .xsd format files in Notepad, where you can scan through all available syntax for UI customization.

TROUBLESHOOTING

My UI customization doesn't appear when I open the file in Word, Excel, or PowerPoint.

As shown earlier in this chapter, when you have a syntax or structural error in any document part in a ZIP package, the file might not open in the applicable program, but may instead display an error message. When you make errors in customUI syntax, this isn't always the case.

If your *customUI.xml* file contains an error, such as specifying a control ID that doesn't exist, the document or template will open without displaying any errors. However, the Ribbon customization you added won't appear.

When this happens, check the *customUI.xml* file for errors, such as referring to a gallery as a button or using an incorrect control ID. Remember also that most XML is case sensitive, so check for details such as the spelling and capitalization throughout your *customUI.xml* code.

Binding Data to Content Controls

The ability to bind external data to Content Controls in a Word document means that you can use XML to populate parts of a document with information that's stored in other sources. For example, use data binding to automatically populate the user's contact information in a typical business document or to populate fields in a boilerplate contract form. You can use any data source for this purpose that can be translated by XML—from data stored directly in the custom XML in the document's ZIP package, to data in a Microsoft Exchange Server directory or a Microsoft Windows SharePoint Services list.

In this section, we'll look at the required elements of a bound control and then I'll walk you through the process of binding Content Controls to a custom XML document part.

> **Note**
>
> Keep in mind that binding data is a two-way street. That is, when you have a Content Control bound to custom XML data, content added to that control in the document is added to your custom XML. One of the nicest benefits of this is that, for example, if you have the client's name as custom XML bound to several controls in your document, you can change the name in any one of those bound controls and all controls bound to the same data will automatically update.
>
> For a simple example of this, insert a couple of instances of the same Document Property Quick Part into your document and then edit the value in one of them. Then, for further examination, open the ZIP package for that document and check out its *document.xml* file to view the data binding code for those Quick Parts.

The Components of a Bound Content Control

There are a few more elements to data binding than you've encountered for previous tasks covered in this chapter. However, most of the components required here are similar to those you've already used, as follows.

- A folder stored in the root of the ZIP package, named **customXML**.

- Three elements inside the **customXML** folder, including the following.

    - One or more files containing the custom XML data (that is, the data to be bound to controls in the document). In the exercise that follows, this file is named *item1.xml*.

    - A file that defines the properties used (specifically, the referenced namespaces) for each custom XML file. In the exercise that follows, this file is named *itemProps1.xml*.

    - A **_rels** folder in which you'll create a relationship file for the custom XML. That relationship file in the following exercise is named *item1.xml.rels*.

- One Content Control in *document.xml* for each piece of custom XML data that you want to bind to a control.

- A relationship in the file *document.xml.rels* for the bound custom XML data.

The section that follows walks you through the process of binding two Content Controls to custom XML stored in the document's ZIP package. For working through the exercises that follow, you can use the file named *Data Binding.docx*, located in the sample files that are included on this book's CD. If you prefer to create your own file, you can base it on *Data Binding.docx*, which is simply a Word document containing two lines of text and two plain text Content Controls.

> **CAUTION**
>
> When binding data to Content Controls, use only plain text types of Content Controls, such as the Text , Drop-Down list, or Date Picker controls. Data binding doesn't support rich text content, such as tables and graphics, so attempting to bind data to a control that supports rich text leaves your document open to possible errors. (Remember that plain text controls do allow font and paragraph formatting, so you don't have to lose any formatting customization in the document when you want to bind controls to custom XML data.)

Binding a Control to Custom XML

To begin, save the file *Data Binding.docx* (mentioned on the preceding page), or your own comparable file, to the Windows desktop and change the file extension to .zip. Then, follow the steps under each of the subheadings that follow.

Create the Custom XML Files

1. On your Windows desktop, create a folder named exactly **customXML**. Then, inside that folder, create another folder named exactly **_rels**.

2. In Notepad, create a new file and save it in the root of your new **customXML** folder, as *item1.xml*. Add the following code to this new file and then save and close the file.

   ```
   <?xml version="1.0" encoding="UTF-8" standalone="yes"?><myinfo xmlns="http://
   www.arouet.net/AMOD/CustomXML.htm"><email>My e-mail address</email><motto>Add a
   favorite saying here.</motto></myinfo>
   ```

   For ease of reference, here's the way the preceding code looks in Internet Explorer.

   ```
      <?xml version="1.0" encoding="UTF-8" standalone="yes" ?>
    - <myinfo xmlns="http://www.arouet.net/AMOD/CustomXML.htm">
        <email>My e-mail address</email>
        <motto>Add a favorite saying here.</motto>
      </myinfo>
   ```

   Notice what's included in the preceding code. After defining the XML version, you identify a namespace for the set of fields you want to use as your custom XML items. The set of items in this sample is referred to as **myinfo**. The two fields included, which you'll map to Content Controls in this exercise, are **email** and **motto**. If you choose to do so, you can replace the placeholder text between the paired code with your own text for each of these fields.

3. In Notepad, create a new file and save it in the root of your new **customXML** folder, as *itemProps1.xml*. Add the following code to this new file and then save and close the file.

   ```
   <?xml version="1.0" encoding="UTF-8" standalone="no"?>
   ```

```
<ds:datastoreItem ds:itemTD="{462820BB-4D2B-41C2-812E-F3CA7850A5A9}" xmlns:
ds="http://schemas.openxmlformats.org/officedocument/2006/2/customXml"><ds:
schemaRefs><ds:schema Ref="http://www.arouet.net/AMOD/CustomXML.htm"/></ds:
schemaRefs></ds:datastoreItem>
```

For ease of reference, the following is the same code viewed in Internet Explorer.

```
<?xml version="1.0" encoding="UTF-8" standalone="no" ?>
- <ds:datastoreItem ds:itemID="{462820BB-4D2B-41C2-812E-F3CA7850A5A9}"
    xmlns:ds="http://schemas.openxmlformats.org/officedocument/2006/2/customXml">
  - <ds:schemaRefs>
      <ds:schema Ref="http://www.arouet.net/AMOD/CustomXML.htm" />
    </ds:schemaRefs>
  </ds:datastoreItem>
```

This code in this file provides information about the namespace used in the file where you store the custom XML items. Note that the data store item ID is used to identify the custom XML where you bind the data to controls in *document.xml*. The **datastoreItem** ID shown in the preceding code is what's referred to as a GUID (globally unique identifier). GUIDs are used in many places in programming to provide unique identification for a particular item being referenced in the code. For example, if you've ever explored the Windows registry, you've probably seen many GUIDs.

Note

Many professional development platforms, such as Visual Studio, provide tools for generating GUIDs. You can also find free tools on the Web for generating GUIDs. However, it takes just a fairly simple macro in VBA to get this done as well.

So, to save you some time when you need to generate your own GUIDs, I created a file named Generate GUID.docm, that you can find in the sample files included on this book's CD. When you open this file, enable macros and then click the single button available on the Ribbon.

As mentioned in the Inside Out tip on page 1178 about the `startFromScratch` UI customization command, you can also check out Generate GUID.docm to see an example of a `startFromScratch` Ribbon. The only tab available in that file is the one containing the GUID macro button. For those interested in the macro to generate GUIDs, you can also find that in the Visual Basic Editor once you open this file.

---

4. Once again, in Notepad, create a new file. This time, save the file into the **_rels** subfolder in the **customXML** folder you created, naming it *item1.xml.rels*. Add the following code to this new file and then save and close the file.

   ```
   <?xml version="1.0" encoding="UTF-8" standalone="yes"?>
   ```

   ```
   <Relationships xmlns="http://schemas.openxmlformats.org/package/2006/relations
   hips"><Relationship Id="rId1" Type="http://schemas.openxmlformats.org/officeD-
   ocument/2006/relationships/customXmlProps" Target="itemProps1.xml"/></Relation-
   ships>
   ```

Following, for ease of reference, is a look at this code in structured format, as shown in Internet Explorer.

```
<?xml version="1.0" encoding="UTF-8" standalone="yes" ?>
-<Relationships>
    <Relationship Id="rId1"
        Type="http://schemas.openxmlformats.org/officeDocument/2006/relationships/customXmlProps"
        Target="itemProps1.xml"/>
</Relationships>
```

Notice that this file simply creates a relationship to the custom XML properties file.

5. Open the ZIP package for the file *Data Binding.docx* (or your own similar file that you created for this exercise) and copy the entire **customXML** folder you created in the preceding steps into that ZIP package.

Once you've done this, it's time to bind that custom XML to controls in your document.

Binding Custom XML to Content Controls

To bind Content Controls to the custom XML you just created, you'll need to add just one statement in *document.xml* for each control that you want to bind, as well as one statement in the *document.xml.rels* file to create a relationship to the custom XML. To begin, copy both of these files out of the ZIP package.

> **Note**
>
> As you may recall from earlier exercises in this chapter, *document.xml* is located in the **word** folder in the ZIP package, and *document.xml.rels* is located in the **_rels** folder within the **word** folder.

Start by adding the data binding statements to *document.xml*. To do this, let's take a look at what the code looks like for the paragraph containing the first Content Control. That paragraph, including the control, looks like this when opened in Word:

My·e-mail·address·is:·Click·here·to·enter·text.¶

Following is the way that same paragraph looks in *document.xml*.

```
– <w:p>
  – <w:pPr>
      <w:pStyle w:val="BodyText" />
    </w:pPr>
  – <w:r>
      <w:t xml:space="preserve">My e-mail address is:</w:t>
    </w:r>
  – <w:sdt>
    – <w:sdtPr>
        <w:id w:val="29485172" />
      – <w:placeholder>
          <w:docPart w:val="DefaultPlaceholder_22610167" />
        </w:placeholder>
        <w:showingPlcHdr />
        <w:text />
      </w:sdtPr>
    – <w:sdtContent>
      – <w:r>
        – <w:rPr>
            <w:rStyle w:val="PlaceholderText" />
          </w:rPr>
          <w:t>Click here to enter text.</w:t>
        </w:r>
      </w:sdtContent>
    </w:sdt>
  </w:p>
– <w:p>
```

The code representing the Content Control in this paragraph begins with the line **<w:sdt>** in the preceding code. The data binding statement needs to be placed two lines beneath that, between **<w:stdPr>** and **<w:id...>**. Following is the statement to add to *document.xml* for binding the first control in the document to the **email** field from the custom XML file.

```
<w:dataBinding w:prefixMappings="xmlns:ns0='http://www.arouet.net/AMOD/CustomXML.
htm'" w:xpath="/ns0:myinfo[1]/ns0:email[1]" w:storeItemID="{462820BB-4D2B-41C2-812E-
F3CA7850A5A9}" />
```

For ease of reference, take a look at the same statement in Internet Explorer, shown with the immediately surrounding statements referenced earlier.

```
– <w:sdtPr>
    <w:dataBinding
      w:prefixMappings="xmlns:ns0='http://www.arouet.net/AMOD/CustomXML.htm'"
      w:xpath="/ns0:myinfo[1]/ns0:email[1]" w:storeItemID="{462820BB-4D2B-41C2-
      812E-F3CA7850A5A9}" />
    <w:id w:val="29485172" />
```

The **w:dataBinding** statement includes the following.

- **w:prefixMappings** is the namespace identified in *item1.xml*. Notice that this namespace is identified as **ns0**.

- **w:xpath** provides the path inside *item1.xml* where you can find the particular field being bound. In this case, the **email** field is within the group of fields named **myinfo**.

- **w:storeItemID** is the same GUID used in the *itemProp1.xml* file.

This statement will be identical, other than the **xpath**, for each control in this document that's mapped to the same data source. In fact, the only difference in the statement that you need to add to map the second control to the motto field is to change the word **email** to **motto** in the preceding statement, after you copy and paste that statement to the proper position for the Content Control that appears in the second paragraph.

Once you've finished adding these two statements to *document.xml*, save and close the file in Notepad. At this point, you might want to check the file in Internet Explorer to be sure you've added the code correctly. Remember that, if you made a structural error in adding the new XML, the code won't open in Internet Explorer.

Copy your updated *document.xml* file back into the ZIP package, overwriting the existing file of the same name. Once you do, the last step is just to add the relationship to the custom XML in *document.xml.rels*. Open that file in Notepad, and add the following relationship before the **</Relationships>** code.

```
<Relationship Id="rId#" Type="http://schemas.openxmlformats.org/officeDocument/2006/
relationships/customXml" Target="../customXML/item1.xml" />
```

CAUTION

As with previous relationship statement samples in this chapter, be sure to replace the pound sign in the preceding statement with a number that is not already used in *document.xml.rels*.

Save and close the document and then copy it back into the ZIP package, overwriting the existing file of the same name. That's it! You've bound your Content Controls to custom data. Open the file in Word to check out your results.

To try out your bound controls, modify the content inside the controls while the document is open in Word. Then, save and close the file, change the extension back to .zip, and view your changes in the custom XML.

Note

Want to save yourself the steps of writing out the code to bind your custom XML data to each control in the document? Tristan Davis, the Word 2007 Program Manager who has generously shared his knowledge and insights at the end of Chapter 31, turned me on to a tool that I highly recommend checking out. Matt Scott, a Software Design Engineer in Microsoft Research and former member of the Microsoft Office Word team, created the "Word 2007 Content Control Toolkit," which is free to download and available through a link you'll find on the Resources tab of this book's CD. Using this tool, which runs as a separate program outside of Word, you can simply drag a custom XML field and drop it on the control you want to bind to that data. It's a very cool timesaver and a good resource as well for helping you to understand how the data is mapped to the controls.

INSIDE OUT   Convert Control Types Between Plain Text and Rich Text

In the code shown in this section for the first paragraph in the *Data binding.docx* sample file, notice the `<w:text />` code that appears near the middle of the XML that represents the first Content Control. This text code is used to identify the control as a plain text control. If you were to insert a Rich Text control into a document and then view the XML, you'd see that this code (or anything like it) doesn't appear. In fact, this text code is the thing that separates rich text and plain text controls.

To turn any plain text control into a rich text control, all you need to do is delete the `<w:text />` code from the XML representing that control in *document.xml*. Similarly, if you want to bind data to controls in your document, but you've used the Rich Text control type, you can add the `<w:text />` code in the same position relative to those controls where they appear in *document.xml* to turn those controls into plain text controls, rather than spending extra time to replace the controls throughout your document.

Next Steps for Working with the Office Open XML Formats

The Office Open XML Formats have come about as the result of an enormous amount of work by an international committee of experts, working through a standards organization named Ecma International. Because this is an open standard, Ecma International makes the complete documentation of the language and standards related to these formats freely, publicly available.

The complete documentation is about 6,500 pages, broken into five core documents and several supporting documents, which are all available for download from Ecma International. For ease of reference, the final drafts of those documents (the most recent versions available as of press time for this book) are also available in PDF format on the Resources tab of this book's CD. Assuming, however, that you may not have the time or inclination to read several thousand pages on this subject, following is a brief summary of what you can expect to find in a few of these documents that I believe will be the most useful for those who want to go further with Office Open XML.

First, note that much of the content in these files is written for developers and assumes knowledge of XML. So, I definitely recommend getting comfortable with the content in this chapter before venturing too far into the standards documentation.

- *Office Open XML Part 1: Fundamentals* provides extensive technical detail for the structure of the ZIP packages and parts within them. However, it also provides one item in particular that might be of interest—an overview of the different types of Office Open XML used for documents from each of the applicable programs (such as WordprocessingML for Word or SpreadsheetML for Excel). Following the overview, the further you dive into this document, the more you'll find of the structural requirements for each type of Office Open XML.

- *Office Open XML Part 3: Primer* is an extensive primer, written for developers, on working with the features of the new formats. It provides quite a bit in the way of detailed examples and illustrations, and is a great place to go to continue learning once you have your bearings with the information provided in this chapter.

- *Office Open XML Part 4: Markup Language Reference* is a whopping 5,219 pages. It's a complete, detailed reference to the Office Open XML language, including the storage of custom XML data. As of the final draft, most of the first 32 pages of this PDF are tables of contents that break down the available terminology for use with documents from each program. I wouldn't recommend this resource to someone new to the Office Open XML Formats because its depth and breadth could easily be overwhelming. But, once you have the basics down, it's the ultimate reference tool if you decide to take your work with the XML formats to another level and, particularly, if you want to move toward projects in which you would create ZIP packages for complete documents through code.

Installing and Configuring the 2007 Office System

This appendix provides information about installing and configuring the 2007 Microsoft Office system. The appendix assumes you are installing Microsoft Office system applications on a computer running the Windows Vista operating system.

Installing the Microsoft Office System from the CD

To install the Microsoft Office system on your computer from the product CD, follow these steps:

1. Insert the CD into your computer's CD-ROM drive.

2. If AutoPlay is enabled on your computer, you'll see the AutoPlay dialog box. In the dialog box, click Run Setup.exe.

   Depending on the settings you have selected for User Access Control in Windows Vista, you might see a User Account Control dialog box notifying you that a program needs your permission to continue. Click Continue to initiate the Microsoft Office system setup program.

> **Note**
> If for some reason the setup program does not start or if AutoPlay is not enabled on your computer, you can run the Setup.exe program manually. Setup.exe is located in the root folder of the CD.

3. In the dialog box shown next, type the 25-character product key included on the CD package. If the product key you type is accepted, the Continue button is enabled. Click Continue to proceed to the next step in the installation. Select the I Accept The Terms Of This Agreement check box to accept the end-user license agreement, and then click Continue.

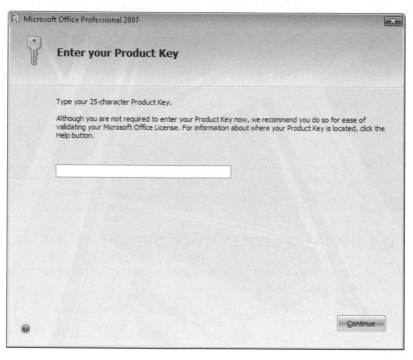

4. In the dialog box shown next, click Install Now to install the Microsoft Office system with its default configuration. Click Customize to specify a particular configuration for your Microsoft Office system setup.

> **Note**
>
> You might see other options in this dialog box if you are installing the Microsoft Office system on a computer on which a previous version of the Microsoft Office system is installed. For example, instead of the Install Now button, you'll see an Upgrade button. If you are upgrading from a previous version of the Microsoft Office system, you'll need to choose whether to remove or keep previous versions or to remove specific applications.

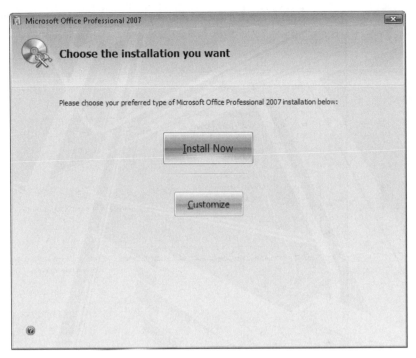

If you click Install Now, the setup program begins, and you'll see a progress bar as installation proceeds. When the installation is completed, you're given the option to visit Microsoft Office Online; otherwise, click Close.

If you click Customize, you'll see the dialog box shown next. The following information and the remaining steps in this section apply only if you click Customize.

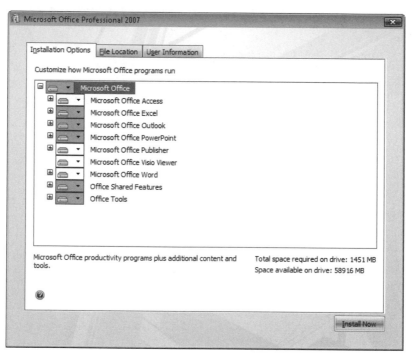

The Customize option lets you choose which Microsoft Office system applications you want to install, the folder to which you want to install the programs (by default, the programs are installed in Program Files\Microsoft Office), and user information that identifies you when you work with others on shared documents.

On the Installation Options tab, the Microsoft Office system applications appear beside an icon that indicates how the program will be installed and run. To change the settings for a particular program, click the arrow beside the icon, and choose one of the options shown here:

- **Run From My Computer** Installs the program on your hard disk. The program's additional features will not be installed (although you can install them later).

- **Run All From My Computer** Installs the program and its additional features to your hard disk.

- **Installed On First Use** Installs the program the first time you run it. Choosing this option might mean you need to insert the product CD to install the program.

- **Not Available** Indicates the program or one of its additional features is not available.

> **Note**
>
> A program icon with a white background indicates that a program and its additional features use the same installation method. A gray background means that the program and its additional features have a combination of installation methods. For example, you could run the program from your computer but install an additional feature when you first use it.

5. After you specify which programs and features you want to install and make any changes to the file location and user information settings using the options on their associated tabs, click Install Now.

> **Note**
>
> If you run the setup program without entering a product ID, you can run Microsoft Office system programs and use their full set of features for only a limited number of times. When you exceed that number, you will not be able to perform tasks such as creating and saving documents. You can activate your copy of the Microsoft Office system after you install it (which will require a valid product key) by opening one of the Microsoft Office system applications, clicking the Microsoft Office Button, and then clicking Options. In the Options dialog box for that program, click Resources. In the Resources category, click Activate.

Changing Your 2007 Office System Setup

After you have installed the Microsoft Office system (either the default installation or a custom configuration that you specified), you can run the setup program when you need to add or remove components, repair or reinstall applications and features in the event an application or feature becomes corrupted, or remove the Microsoft Office system from your computer.

Changing Your Setup from Control Panel

Here are the steps you follow to make changes to your initial Microsoft Office system setup from Windows Control Panel. (Again, these steps assume you have installed the Microsoft Office system on a computer running Windows Vista.)

1. On the Start menu, click Control Panel.

2. On the Control Panel home page, click Programs. On the Programs page, click Programs And Features. You'll see a page in Control Panel similar to the one shown here:

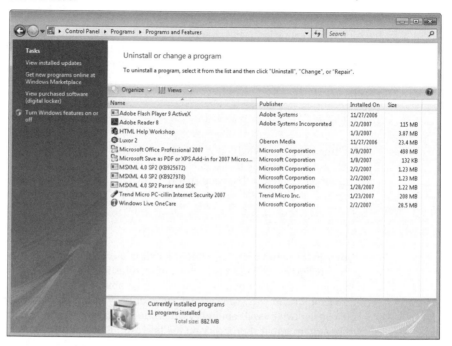

3. In the list of programs, click Microsoft Office Professional 2007 (or whichever edition of the Microsoft Office system you installed).

   - To remove the Microsoft Office system from your computer, click Uninstall, and then confirm your action in the message boxes that appear.

   - To add or remove programs and features or to repair the Microsoft Office system installation, click Change. You'll see the dialog box shown next.

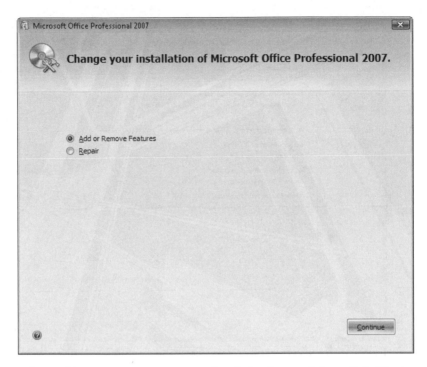

If you select Add Or Remove Features in this dialog box and then click Continue, you'll see the Installation Options tab in the dialog box shown in step 4 in "Installing the Microsoft Office System from the CD" on page 1192. Use this dialog box to select the program features you want to add or remove.

If you select Repair and then click Continue, the setup program reconfigures the installation of the Microsoft Office system to repair any defects it detects.

Changing Setup and Getting Updates from the Options Dialog Box

You can also make changes to your Microsoft Office system setup by using the Options dialog box for a specific application—say Microsoft Office Excel 2007. (The title bar on the Options dialog box will reflect the application you are using.) To open the Options dialog box, click the Microsoft Office Button, and then click (for example) Excel Options. Then click Resources. Figure 1 shows the Resources category in the Excel Options dialog box.

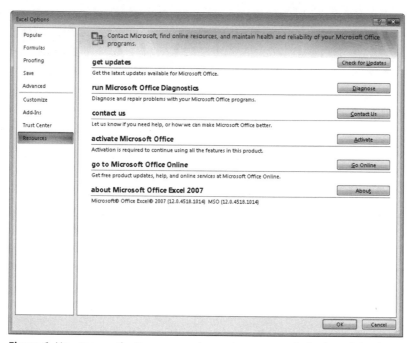

Figure 1 You can use the Resources category in a program's Options dialog box to get updates to the Microsoft Office system and to run Microsoft Office Diagnostics to help diagnose and repair problems with your Microsoft Office programs.

To check for product updates, click Check For Updates to open Windows Internet Explorer and connect to the Microsoft Update Web site. If this is the first time you have accessed the Microsoft Update Web site using your computer, select the I Accept The Terms Of Use check box, and then click Install to install Microsoft Update. If you see the User Account Control dialog box requesting permission to install Microsoft Update, click Continue. After Windows Vista checks for updates, you'll see a list of relevant updates that you can install, including updates for the Microsoft Office system.

Microsoft Office Diagnostics, shown in Figure 2, runs a series of tests that help determine why, for example, your computer is crashing. (You run Microsoft Office Diagnostics by opening the Options dialog box for a Microsoft Office application, clicking the Resources category, and then clicking the Diagnose button.) The Setup Diagnostic test looks for corrupt files or registry settings in your Microsoft Office system installation. (Corruption of this sort might be introduced by malicious viruses or by hardware errors or configurations.) This test can take 15 minutes or longer to run, so plan accordingly. Also, you can't run this test entirely unattended because you might need to insert your product CD, although this is not common. Microsoft Office Diagnostics can also review the information about crashes of the Microsoft Office system that have occurred recently on your computer. When you run this test, your computer connects to a server to look for any solutions that might be available for problems that caused these crashes.

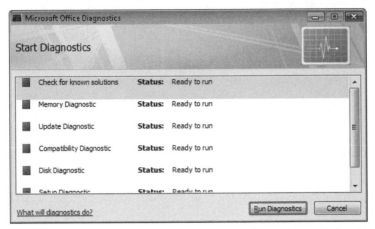

Figure 2 Microsoft Office Diagnostics runs a set of tests that can help solve problems with your installation of the Microsoft Office system.

The Disk Diagnostic test looks for evidence of problems with your hard disk, specifically looking for errors included in the Windows System event log and detected by the Self-Monitoring, Analysis, and Reporting Technology (SMART) feature of your hard disk. (SMART is a feature that some disk drive manufacturers provide to give users advance notice of potential hard disk failure.) The Memory Diagnostic test verifies the integrity of your computer's random access memory (RAM). The Compatibility Diagnostic test identifies conflicting versions of Microsoft Office Outlook that might be installed on your computer. (You cannot install two versions of Office Outlook on the same computer without causing instability.) The Update Diagnostic test verifies whether your computer is up-to-date with free service packs for the Microsoft Office system. This test is available only if you enable it, which you can do by setting the privacy option in the Trust Center that lets Microsoft periodically download a file that helps determine system problems. To enable the Update Diagnostic test, in the Options dialog box for a Microsoft Office system application, select the Trust Center category. Click the Trust Center Settings button, and then click Privacy Options. Under Privacy Options, select the Download A File Periodically That Helps Determine System Problems check box, and then click OK. Click OK again to close the Options dialog box. (You should wait approximately one week after selecting this option to provide time for your computer to download the file.)

For more information about setting privacy options, see Chapter 3, "Managing Security and Privacy in the 2007 Office System."

Appendix

Index to Troubleshooting Topics

Topic	Description	Page
PowerPoint	The content I copied from Access 2007 is unreadable in PowerPoint 2007.	604
PowerPoint	I can show Presenter view on and run the presentation from only one monitor.	620
Outlook	You use a roaming profile and logon time is increasing.	653
Outlook	You can't export the private key.	696
Programming Office	Why does my recorded macro have so many lines of code, when I only did one thing?	1081
Programming Office	Why do I get an error when I try to set some properties?	1090
Programming Office	What do I do when the variable type doesn't work?	1096
Programming Office	I can't find properties or methods that should clearly be available to my object.	1102
Programming Office	How can I apply Theme fonts and colors with Word VBA?	1105
Programming Office	Using a loop to delete objects from a Word document leaves behind objects in the header and footer.	1110
Programming Office	The document won't open after I edit an XML file, but I know my code is correct.	1148
Programming Office	How can I find the error when my ZIP package won't open in Word, Excel, or PowerPoint?	1162
Programming Office	My UI customization doesn't appear when I open the file in Word, Excel, or PowerPoint.	1182

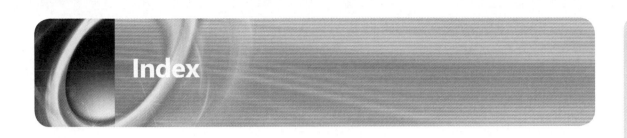

Index

Symbols and Numbers

& (ampersand)
  combining VBA text strings with, 1100, 1114
  concatenating text values with, 402–403
  consecutive line breaks in VBA, 1133
  input mask character, 871
  using with Null fields, 920

' (apostrophe, single quotation mark)
  adding in closed workbook reference, 401
  aligning Excel text with, 358, 359
  preceding VBA comment lines with, 1080

* (asterisk)
  multiplication operator, 393, 921, 923
  record indicator icon, 946
  wildcard character, 869

\ (backslash)
  displaying following character as literal, 871
  operator precedence of, 923
  repeating characters, 358, 359

[ ] (brackets)
  indicating relative cell reference with, 397–398
  placed around field names in expressions, 918
  use in structured reference syntax, 423–424

^ (caret)
  aligning Excel text with, 358, 359
  exponentiation and precedence order, 923
  used in arithmetic expressions, 921

: (colon)
  range operator in structured references, 424
  using with Line Labels, 1125

, (comma)
  separating arguments with, 424
  thousands separator, 871
  union operator in structured references, 424
  using in Excel, 354

. (decimal points)
  input mask placeholder, 871
  using in Excel, 354, 356

$ (dollar sign), 354

" (double quotation marks)
  enclosing strings with, 868, 871, 1093

  omitted around VBA constants, 1133
  specifying values for VBA arguments in, 1098

= (equal to) operator
  as comparative operator, 869
  as logical operator, 444
  starting formula with, 353

! (exclamation point), 871

/ (forward slash)
  division operator, 393, 921, 923
  fractions in Excel, 355

> (greater than) sign
  input mask character, 871
  as operator, 444, 869

>= (greater than or equal to) operator, 444, 869

< (less than) sign
  input mask character, 871
  less than operator, 444, 869

<= (less than or equal to) operator, 444, 869

– (minus) sign
  starting formula with, 353
  subtraction operator, 393, 921, 923

<> (not equal to) operator, 444, 869, 1113

(number sign)
  input mask character, 870
  single-digit wildcard character, 869
  truncated data indicated with multiple, 356

( ) (parentheses)
  added in functions automatically, 404
  including in expressions, 926
  negative constants in Excel, 354
  placement of, 394
  specifying values for VBA arguments in, 1098
  surrounding function arguments with, 456

% (percentage sign), 355

+ (plus sign)
  addition operator, 393, 921, 923
  concatenating strings with, 920
  expanding outlines, 244
  starting formula with, 353
  subdatasheet and data expansion with, 941, 943–946

X

About the Authors

Jim Boyce has been a freelance author and consultant for almost 20 years. He has authored and coauthored more than 50 books on computer operating systems, hardware, and applications. Jim is a former contributing editor for *Windows Magazine* and a frequent contributor to Microsoft.com, techrepublic.com, the Office Letter (*www.officeletter.com*), and other print and online publications.

Jeff Conrad has written and assisted with technical articles about Microsoft Access and created several Access add-ins that are provided freely to the Access community. He has been awarded Microsoft's Most Valuable Professional award for his continual involvement with the online Access community. Jeff is active in the Microsoft-sponsored Access public newsgroups and several other online forums where he is best known as the Access Junkie.

Mark Dodge started using spreadsheet programs in a corporate accounting office in 1985, began working in computer publishing in 1988, and has since written or edited more than two dozen books for Microsoft Press. Mark, an accomplished musician and award-winning photographer, lives with his wife on a beautiful island in Puget Sound, Washington.

Stephanie Krieger is a Microsoft Office System MVP and author of the book *Microsoft Office Document Designer*. A New York City–based consultant, she has helped many global companies develop enterprise solutions for Microsoft Office and taught numerous professionals and professional software trainers to build great documents by understanding the way that Microsoft Office programs "think."

Mary Millhollon, a certified expert-level Microsoft Office User Specialist in Word, is the owner of Bughouse Productions and a bona fide computer geek. Mary is a freelance writer, editor, Web designer, and Internet expert, working daily (and nightly) with desktop applications and online technologies. Her most recent publication is *Easy Web Page Creation* (Microsoft Press).

Katherine Murray is the author of many books on technology, with a special emphasis on Microsoft Office. Her most recent book, *First Look 2007 Microsoft Office System* (Microsoft Press, 2006) is available as a free download on the 2007 Microsoft Office download site. Katherine is the coauthor of *Microsoft Office Word 2007 Inside Out* and *MSN Spaces: Share Your Story*. She publishes a blog, called BlogOffice, that offers tips, updates, news, and resources related to a variety of Microsoft Office versions and events.

John Pierce is a freelance writer and editor. He worked as an editor and writer at Microsoft Corporation for nearly 12 years. He is the author of *Microsoft Office Access 2003 Inside Track* (with Paul Pardi) and the coauthor of *Microsoft Small Business Kit* and other books about Microsoft software.

Beth Sheresh (CNE) has more than 15 years of computer industry experience, including writing and editing technical books; network administration and consulting; and technical training design, development, and delivery. Beth's books include *Understanding Directory Services* (two editions) and *Microsoft Windows NT Server Administrators Bible–Option Pack Edition.* She also contributed chapters to *Microsoft Windows Server 2003 Inside Out.*

Doug Sheresh (MCSE) is an IT professional with over two decades of experience that encompasses network administration, consulting, technical support management, and managing technical writing projects. His expertise includes all aspects of technical training course development. He was the lead technical writer of the *Microsoft Windows 95 Resource Kit* and coauthor of *Understanding Directory Services, 2nd Edition* and *Microsoft Windows NT Server Administrators Bible–Option Pack Edition.*

Sally Slack is a writer and author with more than 16 years of experience in business and technical writing. She has also been an executive and business transformation communications consultant to IBM, Lenovo International, and State Farm Insurance, and she routinely writes for Microsoft, IBM, Sony, and other companies. She is a regular contributor to a variety of Microsoft Web sites, including Microsoft At Home and Work Essentials.

Craig Stinson, an industry journalist since 1981, was editor of *Softalk for the IBM Personal Computer,* one of the earliest machine-specific computer magazines. He is the author of more than 20 Microsoft Press books about Microsoft Windows and Excel. Craig lives with his wife and two children in Bloomington, Indiana.

John L. Viescas is the author of *Microsoft Office Access 2003 Inside Out* and the popular *Running Microsoft Access* books from Microsoft Press. He is president of Viescas Consulting, Inc., a respected provider of database application design and editorial consulting services. He has been recognized by Microsoft Product Support Services as a Most Valuable Professional (MVP) every year since 1993 for his contributions to the community of Access users.

What do you think of this book?

We want to hear from you!

Do you have a few minutes to participate in a brief online survey?

Microsoft is interested in hearing your feedback so we can continually improve our books and learning resources for you.

To participate in our survey, please visit:

www.microsoft.com/learning/booksurvey/

...and enter this book's ISBN-10 number (appears above barcode on back cover*).
As a thank-you to survey participants in the United States and Canada, each month we'll randomly select five respondents to win one of five $100 gift certificates from a leading online merchant. At the conclusion of the survey, you can enter the drawing by providing your e-mail address, which will be used for prize notification only.

Thanks in advance for your input. Your opinion counts!

* Where to find the ISBN-10 on back cover

ISBN-13: 000-0-0000-0000-0
ISBN-10: 0-0000-00000

00000

0 000000 000000

Example only. Each book has unique ISBN.

Microsoft
Press